THE CONSTITUTIONALIST

Notes on the First Amendment

GEORGE ANASTAPLO

SOUTHERN METHODIST UNIVERSITY PRESS
DALLAS, TEXAS

© 1971 : SOUTHERN METHODIST UNIVERSITY PRESS : DALLAS
Library of Congress Catalog Card Number 72-165793

To
MY CHILDREN
and to my Children's Children
with the Reminder that their revolutionary Forefathers
not only made the American, Greek, and Texas Wars of Independence
but thereafter instituted and maintained
new Governments of their own

CONTENTS

	PREFACE	ix
I.	"A JOURNAL OF PROCEEDINGS"	3
II.	"THE SUPREME LAW OF THE LAND"	11
III.	"CONGRESS SHALL MAKE NO LAW"	35
IV.	"ALL LEGISLATIVE POWERS HEREIN GRANTED"	53
V.	"ABRIDGING THE FREEDOM OF SPEECH"	93
VI.	"THE POWERS NOT DELEGATED TO THE UNITED STATES"	133
VII.	"A MORE PERFECT UNION"	171
VIII.	"THE BLESSINGS OF LIBERTY"	205
IX.	"WE DO ORDAIN AND ESTABLISH"	273

APPENDIXES

- A. STAGES IN THE FIRST CONGRESS OF THE FIRST AMENDMENT — 289
- B. *SCHENCK V. UNITED STATES*: CIRCULAR AND INDICTMENT — 294
- C. DUE PROCESS AND THE WORLD OF COMMERCE — 306
- D. CONSPIRACY AND THE JUDGE: A TRIAL IN CHICAGO — 312
- E. ACADEMIC FREEDOM AND ACADEMIC RESPONSIBILITY: *PRINCIPIIS OBSTA* — 324
- F. IN RE GEORGE ANASTAPLO (1950-61) — 331

NOTES — 419

INDEX — 809

PREFACE

"I HAVE a thousand things to offer in this Preface," observes Pierre Bayle in introducing his massive dictionary, "but as I cannot do it without running into an exorbitant length, which would discourage the Readers, I rather chuse to give my self some constraint, than offend their niceness. I shall therefore confine my self to five or six particulars." Such self-constraint is worthy of imitation by every author of a long book, especially so when the book is devoted as is mine to the study of constitutionalism, virtue, and freedom—and hence to the reign of moderation in human affairs. My five or six, if not seven, "particulars" follow.

This book is meant to be both instructive and entertaining, just as life itself (even in these troubled times) should and can be. It is a constitutional *commedia* which contains less than its title promises and yet more: less, in that it does not include a comprehensive review of cases on the First Amendment and in that it has relatively little *explicit* discussion of the religious liberty aspect of that amendment; more, in that it reaches far beyond the conventional discussions today of freedom of speech, the First Amendment, and the Constitution. Political discussion is quickly dated if it does not look past the crises which give rise to it—if it does not, that is, look to the principles of one's regime and even to the best possible regime ("that far country where there is neither aristocrat nor democrat").

The argument of this book is, I trust, sufficiently straightforward to require no extended introduction here. It is essentially a refinement of the argument developed between 1956 and 1964 for my doctoral dissertation at the University of Chicago, with special attention paid to how to read a constitution, particularly the thirty-three words of the forty-five-word First Amendment which are devoted to political freedom. It is an amendment—a declaration of our political faith as a united, self-governing people—in which "freedom of speech [and] of the press" is both literally and spiritually central. Critical to my argument is an examination of the position that should be taken today toward a Supreme Court case which has become in some respects rather quaint, *Schenck* v. *United States*: one finds in that 1919 case, to which Appendix B is devoted, the irresponsible "clear and present danger" and "falsely shouting fire in a theatre" language which has helped subvert our institutions for half a century.

The extensive notes, which (in their comments on the most trivial as well as on the most exalted things) both elaborate and qualify my original argument, were developed in large part between 1964 and 1970, and reflect the work in literature and in political philosophy, ancient and modern, I have been able to do since my training (in the classroom and in the courtroom) in legal and constitutional matters. The notes also cite various other writings of mine to which the reader is directed for expanded discussions of points which can only be touched upon in this book.

My career at the bar, *courte et bonne*, is documented in the final appendix to this volume, which has been prepared at the suggestion of the publisher. For me to have ignored (as much as I did ignore it in my dissertation) my bar admission litigation, which does bear somewhat on First Amendment and federalism problems in our time, might have seemed unduly humble; on the other hand, to have made much of it by exploiting it in the main body of this book

PREFACE   xi

might have seemed rather vain. An appendix provides a safe refuge in which to strike a mean between these two extremes, or at least in which to conceal an excess or deficiency. Lest too much be made by the reader of my difficulties at the bar since November 10, 1950, I appropriate the sentiment of the fifty-year-old Edmund Burke upon being repudiated by his Bristol constituency, "I have read the book of life for a long time, and I have read other books a little. Nothing has happened to me, but what has happened to men much better than me, and in times and in nations full as good as the age and the country that we live in."

However that may be, this entire book *is* quite personal, even autobiographical to a degree. The point of departure is that of a midwesterner, but a midwesterner whose odyssey has equipped and required him to learn something of the world which revolves around his Illinois. The circumstances of my permanent exclusion from the practice of law were such as to relieve me of both the security and the entanglements of a conventional academic career by limiting severely the employment available to me. One curious result of my disabilities is that I have been permitted and encouraged to explore as a teacher (and hence as a student), without any sustained concern for ordinary academic advancement, only the books written over the centuries by the most thoughtful men, something that most of my contemporaries have had neither the opportunity nor the incentive to do.

Acknowledgments are due both to the thousands of students in my courses at the University of Chicago, at the Clearing, at Rosary College, and at the University of Dallas who have accompanied me on my intellectual explorations, and to the handful of administrators who made these excursions possible: Maurice F. X. Donohue, formerly Dean of University College at the University of Chicago; Sister Candida Lund, formerly Chairman of the Political Science Department of Rosary College; Willmoore Kendall and Leo Paul S. deAlvarez, successive chairmen of the Politics and Literature Department of the University of Dallas; and Mertha Fulkerson, the remarkable woman who directed for so many years the summer program at the Clearing in Door County, Wisconsin. For the most timely refuge as a research associate provided me by the Industrial Relations Center of the University of Chicago, before I was hired as a teacher by Dean Donohue in 1957, I am grateful to Robert K.

Burns, Jeremiah J. German, Howard Johnson, Nicholas J. Melas, Edgar E. Swanson, Jr., and Richard T. Thornbury. (I continue to teach in the adult education program of the University of Chicago as well as in the Political Science and Philosophy Departments at Rosary College, with occasional seminars at the Clearing and at the University of Dallas.)

Acknowledgments are due as well to the readers of my doctoral dissertation (in whole or in part) whose many suggestions I have drawn upon in preparing this book. These readers (among whom are numbered the members of my dissertation committee at the University of Chicago) include Sara Prince Anastaplo, Laurence Berns, Mervin Block, Scott Buchanan, John Gormly, David Grene, Friedrich A. Hayek, Harry Kalven, Jr., Alexander Meiklejohn, C. Herman Pritchett, Cyril D. Robinson, Thomas S. Schrock, Malcolm P. Sharp, Edward Shils, Yves R. Simon, Richard M. Weaver, and Leo Strauss. The known diversity of opinion among them should make it evident that the readers whose assistance (along with the obvious influence of Hugo L. Black) I am privileged to acknowledge here cannot be held accountable for my conclusions.

Margaret L. Hartley, of Southern Methodist University Press, was most conscientious in preparing the manuscript for publication; Helen Margaret Anastaplo and her friend Winnifred Fallers, as well as George Malcolm Davidson Anastaplo, Sara Maria Anastaplo, and Theodora McShan Anastaplo, were generous in helping me with the manuscript and proofs, as were Joseph Cropsey and Philip B. Kurland at an earlier stage of these proceedings. (I have learned from Mrs. Hartley and her colleagues what the old and honorable traditions of responsible competence can mean in the world of publishing and how such traditions can contribute among us to the effectiveness—and hence to the genuine freedom—of serious expression.)

Acknowledgment is due, finally as well as first, to my parents, Theodore George Anastaplo (originally Anastasopoulos) and Margaret Syriopoulou Anastaplo, immigrants more than fifty years ago from an Arcadian village, who came to live in the city where I was born in 1925 (St. Louis) and in the Southern Illinois small town where I grew up (Carterville). They bequeathed me, among other things, the temperament and stamina which made it possible for me to endure, to profit from, and even to enjoy, both in this country and abroad, my instructive military, legal, and political adventures of the past quarter-century in the Air Force, in the courts, and in the market place.

It has been my fate and my privilege to find myself challenged again and again by dictatorial regimes. Thus, I found myself "expelled" from the Illinois bar in 1950, from Russia in 1960, and from Greece in 1970. What I am privileged to owe to the two-centuries-old American regime rooted in the Declaration of Independence need not be set down in detail here: the book which follows may be read as an extended acknowledgment of a considerable debt to my fundamentally good-natured country.

I do hope the discerning reader finds me entitled to say of this book what John Taylor of Caroline said of his own *Inquiry into the Principles of the Government of the United States*: "This essay does not aspire to the honor of proposing a new political system. It only endeavours to ascertain the principles of old ones. . . ."

GEORGE ANASTAPLO

Hyde Park
Chicago, Illinois
November 10, 1970

Congress shall make no law respecting an establishment of religion, or prohibiting the free exercise thereof; or abridging the freedom of speech, or of the press; or the right of the people peaceably to assemble, and to petition the Government for a redress of grievances.
—THE FIRST AMENDMENT

I. "A JOURNAL OF PROCEEDINGS"

PUBLIUS, in the first number of the *Federalist*, introduces his readers to the contents of the seven dozen essays which are to follow. He writes:

I propose, in a series of papers, to discuss the following interesting particulars:—The utility of the UNION to your political prosperity—The insufficiency of the present Confederation to preserve that Union—The necessity of a Government at least equally energetic with the one proposed, to the attainment of this object—The conformity of the proposed Constitution to the true principles of republican Government—Its analogy to your own state constitution—and lastly, The additional security, which its adoption will afford to the preservation of that species of Government, to liberty, and to property.

I propose, in this book, to initiate a study of the Constitution of the United States, particularly the freedom of speech and of the press provision of the First Amendment. Taking the *Federalist* as my model and adapting its principles and objective to my subject, I should like, "in [this book], to discuss the following interesting particulars":

I begin, in chapter 2, by presenting preliminary reflections on the nature of liberty and of constitutional government. The thesis of this book is stated here, and is then restated in the form of everyday examples. The role of the First Congress in the writing of the First Amendment is described (with Appendix A recording the stages or the drafts of the First Amendment in the First Congress). I then notice the assumptions usually relied upon in the course of constitutional interpretation, as well as the limitations and liabilities of such interpretation.

In chapter 3, after remarking the imperative character of the word "shall," I spell out that character by discussing both the effect of the removal of qualifications from various constitutional provisions where they are now found and the significance of the prohibitions where no qualification is found. The language of the First Amendment is compared with prohibitions less absolute in tone. I then examine qualifications that have been read by interpretation into the freedom of speech and of the press provision of the First Amendment, particularly Justice Holmes's influential "clear and present danger" test, conveniently (if perversely) summing up in a rewritten constitution the implications of such a mode of constitutional interpretation. The chapter closes with a recognition of the risks of absolute prohibitions upon "energetic" government and anticipates my discussion (in chapter 7) of our constitutional safeguards against such risks.

In chapter 4, after further development of these latter observations, I proceed to examine both the activities of Congress, in its lawmaking capacity, which are restrained by the First Amendment, and those activities of Congress which may not be directly affected by the restraint. I then examine the bearing of the First Amendment upon the activities of the Executive and the Judiciary as well as the constitutional relations between these two branches of government and the Congress. Suggestions are made, especially with American republicanism as the standard, about the safeguards there may be in the Constitution against the most serious state abuses with respect to freedom of speech and of the press and about what the people may do to freedom of speech consistent with our national dedication to constitutional self-government.

In chapter 5 I have recourse to authorities such as Blackstone, Cooley, and Dicey to define the English common law meaning of "liberty of the press" expressed in the "no-previous-restraint" rule. I assess American opinion (as distinguished from the common law) with respect to such matters, together with the legacy of suppression that some prefer to see as the dominant feature of American experience in the eighteenth century. A preliminary attempt is then made to state the freedom of speech principle upon which the Founding Fathers can be said to have acted with respect to constituted authority and to test that principle by the oft-heard pronouncement that no toleration should be permitted the intolerant. I examine the implications of the use of "abridging" in the First Amendment (particularly as that use bears on the problem of whether merely the common law standard of "liberty of the press" is preserved by the amendment) and then the principles and evidence which support my submission that the primary concern of "freedom of speech [and] of the press" in our Constitution is with political discussion by self-governing citizens (for which parliamentary "freedom of speech" is the historical prototype), not with the other kinds of communication which I describe. The chapter closes with a few rash speculations on the use in English of the words "liberty" and "freedom."

With chapter 6 I turn to a more direct study of the Constitution itself, particularly of the central question of whether Congress had even before adoption of the Bill of Rights any power to regulate speech and the press. There is first a discussion of the powers that may reside in the general government by virtue of a national common law, with special attention to the significance in this respect of the Sedition Act of 1798. This is followed by a discussion of the powers given Congress under the Constitution (such as those listed in Article I, section 8), of the general powers of Congress, of the problem of implied powers, and of the significance of the "necessary and proper" clause. The effect of the First Amendment, even if it should be understood that Congress never has had any power to regulate speech and the press, is noticed.

In chapter 7 I consider why the states are left relatively free to abridge freedom of speech and of the press under the constitutional system in which the First Amendment is found, and also the effect, in establishing a virtually unrestricted national freedom of speech, of this relative lack of restraint upon the states. I examine the role of states' rights, reinforced by the institution of slavery, in the emergence of freedom of speech and of the press as we know it, analyze the advantages and disadvantages of local control over alleged sedition, and indicate the role left to the general government in such matters. The transformation of the relation between states and nation after the Civil War, which was furthered by technological and economic developments and by the First World War, is then discussed, as I suggest that this resulted both in more restraint upon the states (through the Fourteenth Amendment) and in less restraint upon the general government (as seen in the invention of the "clear and present danger" test) than there had been before the transformation.

In chapter 8 I return to a more extensive examination of freedom of speech and of the press and, by reviewing the other great rights which are said by the English-speaking peoples to contribute to liberty and order, return also to an examination of the "true principles of republican Government" and of American constitutionalism. Each of the other great rights—the right to *habeas corpus,* to property, to trial by jury, to the ballot—is evaluated, with a suggestion of both its merits and its limitations. I consider the status of freedom of speech and of the press, both in its earliest form and in its distinctively American (even curiously aristocratic) development, and I indicate the ways in which this freedom may be protected. The abuses and dangers of freedom of speech and of the press are then discussed, with an extended illustration drawn from the nineteenth-century slavery controversy. A reminder follows of what freedom of speech can contribute to our "political prosperity," both in moderating public passions and in informing public servants. This, in turn, is followed by an introduction to the conditions and the education required for responsible freedom of speech and by an examination of the assumptions now made by intellectuals about the nature of truth. The reader is thus brought to the brink of political philosophy and to a reconsideration of the "species of Government" appropriate to the character of the American people.

Lastly, in chapter 9 I return, if only briefly, to critical problems discussed throughout the book, but as they may be seen by the philosophical as distinguished from the political man. I restate the virtues of freedom and of republican government, even as I recognize the inevitable limitations of that very political life which is necessary for the full development of the human being. The book then closes with what I trust is an appropriate reaffirmation of republican government in the United States today.

The constitutional interpretation examined in this book seemed, when I first formulated it a dozen years ago, far more "liberal" (as it now may seem, if only for a few years, somewhat more "conservative") than contemporary opinion and practice. "For my own part," said Pericles in his last recorded speech to the volatile Athenians, "I am the man I was and of the mind I was; but you are changed. . . ."

[*The American fishermen*] *have provided* [*a whaling code*] *which for terse comprehensiveness surpasses Justinian's Pandects and the By-Laws of the Chinese Society for the Suppression of Meddling with other People's Business. Yes; these laws might be engraven on a Queen Anne's farthing, or the barb of a harpoon, and worn round the neck, so small are they.*

I. A Fast-Fish belongs to the party fast to it.

II. A Loose-Fish is fair game for anybody who can soonest catch it.

But what plays the mischief with this masterly code is the admirable brevity of it, which necessitates a vast volume of commentaries to expound it.

First: What is a Fast-Fish? . . .

—MELVILLE, *Moby-Dick*

II. "THE SUPREME LAW OF THE LAND"

I

THIS INQUIRY is, as its subtitle suggests, an exploratory effort. The Constitutionalist—as may perhaps be true of anyone who takes political things seriously—is occasionally obliged to beg the question, to proceed as if there were more certainty and precision than there can be about such matters. If he knows what he is doing, he can serve his fellow citizens by fashioning a salutary lawyer's brief which tells "a likely story."¹

In telling such a story here, I return to several arguments again and again and develop them more and more. I am far more interested in having my reader agree with me about the questions and problems to be raised and about the general standards that may be invoked than about the solutions and interpretations I happen to offer. "We must not exhaust our subject," I hope to be entitled to say with Montesquieu, "so as to leave no work at all for the reader.

My business is not to make people read, but to make them think."

There are in this collection of arguments, questions, and suggestions—in this running debate that must be left essentially unresolved—materials for a comprehensive view of the Constitution and of the Bill of Rights, particularly as they bear on the problems of freedom of speech and of the press posed by the First Amendment.[2] We all sense that the rules laid down in this amendment, however interpreted, are vital to our form of government, both in what they permit citizens to contribute to the political life of the Republic and in the guidance they provide the public servant in the conduct of our affairs.

I am fortunate in being able to deal here with a political fact, "freedom of speech," which the American reader is privileged to know quite well: it is of the air which he breathes.[3] My task is that of explaining, and perhaps refining and thereby even strengthening, something which is inherent in our way of life.[4] Indeed, since it is so much a part of our life that we already know "in our bones" what it is,[5] I can postpone until chapter 5 my attempt to set forth in some detail what "freedom of speech" means to us.[6]

The aspect of liberty which dominates Anglo-American law is that which stresses the absence of interference with the person from without,[7] or at least the absence of arbitrary interference.[8] It has been said, on the other hand, that "License consists in doing what one lists; liberty consists in doing in the right manner the good only; and our knowledge of the good must come from a higher principle, from above."[9] This position is reflected in the Collect for Peace in the Book of Common Prayer: "O God, who art the author of peace and lover of concord, in knowledge of whom standeth our eternal life, whose service is perfect freedom. . . ."

Thus, for our purposes, the critical distinction is between two different kinds of ability or power: to do as one wishes, and to will or to do as one ought.[10] Cicero attempts to incorporate the former in the latter:

For what is liberty? The power to live as you wish. Who then lives as he wishes except one who follows the things that are right, who delights in his duty, who has a well-considered way of living thought out and provided for; he, who does not obey the laws because of fear but follows and respects them because he judges that to be most healthful; who says nothing, who does nothing, and who does not even think anything unless he does it voluntarily and freely; whose plans and courses of conduct all take their start from himself and likewise have their end in himself, there being no other thing that has more influence with him than his own will and judgment: to whom indeed Fortune, whose power is said to be supreme, herself submits—if, as the wise poet said, she is molded for each man by his manners? It thus happens to the wise man alone that he does nothing against his will, nothing with regret, nothing by compulsion.[11]

It is important, if we are to understand American constitutional law, to notice the extent to which we as a people place the emphasis upon "wish" rather than upon "ought." There is, of course, the expectation that properly formed citizens who are permitted to do as they wish are most apt to do as they ought and hence as is good for the community. Our style in these matters was caught in a comment by an American poet on why he liked his country:

We've got a good arrangement here. We're minding each other's business a certain amount and we're minding our own business a certain amount.
    Those fellows who started it did a good job. I say anything I damn please here.[12]

II

I know[13] of no other student of the Constitution today who would agree with me in all particulars of my interpretation of the First Amendment or even in the broad lines in which it is traced.[14] And yet, the position I set forth in these pages seems to me to interpret fairly and in the proper spirit the language of the Constitution and to take due account of the relevant historical and documentary evidence that I have been able to consider.

When I label this inquiry "exploratory," I do not mean to suggest that it should not be taken seriously. I believe the constitutional position explored and developed here to be a sensible one. Certainly, it offers a more reliable guide to what the law should be than the vacillations of the Supreme Court of the United States with respect to these matters since the First World War.[15] If it should be objected that I have concerned myself too much with the thought and attitudes of the men of the late eighteenth century, I would consider my attempt successful: those men were not only first, with the peculiar advantages of founders; they were also remarkably competent, with the result that their deliberations on enduring political problems are worthy of repeated reconsideration.

There happens to be very little that is essential to be gleaned from intensive researches into the background and writing of the First Amendment—very little that a thoughtful student cannot learn upon a careful inspection of the Constitution. Still, research is not without its uses, if only to assure the student that he can accept what seems to be evident in the document: it assures him that the historical evidence does not challenge, on any critical point, the "self-evident" meaning of the First Amendment with respect to "freedom of speech [and] of the press."[16]

It is the lawyer's way to dig up and into evidence, to examine "legislative history," to search for the "intentions" of framers of legal instruments. In this instance, I believe it can be shown, the lawyer's researches confirm the citizen's reflections, a conjunction particularly felicitous in a constitutional document.[17]

The significance of a constitution in a republican regime is suggested in the section on "The Importance of Adhering to Rules" with which Vice-President Thomas Jefferson prefaced the *Manual of Parliamentary Practice* that he prepared in 1800 for the Senate of the United States:

> Mr. Onslow, the ablest among the Speakers of the House of Commons, used to say, "It was a maxim he had often heard when he was a young man, from old and experienced members, that nothing tended more to throw power into the hands of administration and those who acted with the majority of the House of Commons, than a neglect of, or departure from, the rules of proceeding; that these forms, as instituted by our ancestors, operated as a check, and control, on the actions of the majority; and that they were, in many instances, a shelter and protection to the minority, against the attempts of power."
>
> So far the maxim is certainly true, and is founded in good sense, that as it is always in the power of the majority, by their numbers, to stop any improper measures proposed on the part of their opponents, the only weapons by which the minority can defend themselves against similar attempts from those in power, are the forms and rules of proceeding, which have been adopted as they were found necessary from time to time, and are become the law of the house; by a strict adherence to which, the weaker party can only be protected from those irregularities and abuses which these forms were intended to check, and which the wantonness of power is but too often apt to suggest to large and successful majorities. . . .

And whether these forms be in all cases the most rational or not, is really not of so great importance. It is much more material that there should be a rule to go by, than what that rule is; that there may be a uniformity of proceeding in business, not subject to the caprice of the Speaker, or captiousness of the members. It is very material that order, decency, and regularity be preserved in a dignified public body. . . .[18]

Some such position as that which I develop in this book seems to me the only means by which the constitutional law of freedom of speech can attain the regularity and decency that are useful for lawyers and citizens alike. I suggest as one virtue of my position that it makes reasonable allowance for the demands of both liberty and order. The deficiencies as well as the possibilities of human nature and of human society are anticipated.[19]

III

The conclusions of this study are submitted as an articulation of the principles implicit in the American Republic since its foundation almost two centuries ago. The argument that follows is an attempt to suggest, to the satisfaction of both citizen and lawyer, why this formulation warrants serious consideration. That argument may be summarized in this way:

The First Amendment to the Constitution prohibits Congress, in its law-making capacity, from cutting down in any way or for any reason freedom of speech and of the press. The extent of this freedom is to be measured not merely by the common law treatises and cases available on December 15, 1791—the date of the ratification of the First Amendment—but also by the general understanding and practice of the people of the United States who insisted upon, had written for them, and ratified (through their state legislatures) the First Amendment. An important indication of the extent of this freedom is to be seen in the teachings of the Declaration of Independence and in the events leading up to the Revolution.

Although the prohibition in the First Amendment is absolute —we see here a restraint upon Congress that is unqualified, among restraints that *are* qualified—the absolute prohibition does not relate to all forms of expression but only to that which the terms, "freedom of speech, or of the press" were then taken to encompass, political speech, speech having to do with the duties and concerns of self-governing citizens. Thus, for example, this constitutional provision is not primarily or directly concerned with what we now call artistic expression or with the problems of obscenity. Rather, the First Amendment acknowledges that the sovereign citizen has the right freely to discuss the public business, a privilege theretofore claimed only for members of legislative bodies.

Absolute as the constitutional prohibition may be with respect to Congress, it does not touch directly the great state power to affect freedom of speech and of the press. In fact, I shall argue, one condition for effective negation of congressional power over this subject (which negation is important for the political freedom of the American people) is that the states should retain some power to regulate political expression. It seems to me, however, that the general government has the duty to police or restrain the power of the states in this respect, a duty dictated by such commands in the Constitution of 1787 as that which provides that the "United States shall guarantee to every State in this Union a Republican Form of Government. . . ."[20]

IV

There are seven principal points critical to an understanding of the First Amendment, points which the citizen can grasp without legal training. These points can be illustrated by episodes drawn from everyday life and with respect to which the reasonable interpretation conforms to the legal mode of interpretation. The relevance of these points should be at once apparent to anyone familiar with recent discussions of the First Amendment.

One advantage of proceeding by the use of commonplace illustrations is that it permits us to begin to consider these problems of interpretation without immediately being caught up in the controversial features of any discussion of freedom of speech. Let us see, that is, how far common sense can take us.[21]

1. A father instructs his seven-year-old son:

While I am gone to the library, do not turn on the tap, except to get a drink of water; do not wake your mother, unless the telephone rings; do not strike any matches; and do not open the door, until you hear my voice.

Three of the restraints imposed upon the son are obviously qualified: circumstances may arise in which turning on the tap, waking the mother, or opening the door is permissible. It is evident that the father has thought of exceptions to his mandates and has expressed them. The fact that he has indicated exceptions in appropriate cases makes even more emphatic the absoluteness of the mandate respecting matches: it is clear that, so long as *this* father-son relation continues, there are to be no exceptions to the prohibition against striking matches in these circumstances.

Similarly, in the context of a constitution in which there are many qualified prohibitions upon the exercise of governmental power, the freedom of speech and press provision of the First Amendment stands out as an absolute prohibition. Whatever "freedom of speech, or of the press" includes, it is evident that it is extended absolute protection of some kind by the First Amendment. This point alone is sufficient to call into question the deliberate dilution by the Supreme Court of the constitutional prohibition, a dilution that is usually justified by reference to the "clear and present danger" test or to the obligation to "balance" one constitutional interest against another. But the Constitution has already done the balancing and provided safeguards against the dangers that our people is likely to encounter. Obviously, there must be some reason why the clear terms of the prohibition are evaded. To this we will return; but it is first necessary to notice that there *is* an evasion.

2. We modify our first illustration when we observe that there are older children in the family. We cannot simply assume that the older children are bound by the prohibitions directed against their younger brother. The instructions that have been left are clearly designed to govern the activity of the seven-year-old. We can infer from the instructions the considerations by which the other children should consider themselves bound: they should, for instance, be respectful of their mother's rest. But if they, in ordinary circumstances, are obliged to prepare meals for the household, they would be empowered to use the water more freely than the son and even to strike matches. There is implied an obligation, of course, to be careful not to set fire either to the house or to themselves.

Similarly, the prohibitions of the First Amendment are explicitly directed against Congress alone. The Judiciary and the Executive seem to be given more leeway. Thus, courts may be obliged on occasion, in order to be able to perform their own duties, to restrict what citizens may say. (We recall the traditional contempt power.) And we all know of the restraint that may legitimately be imposed by the President on the citizen in uniform. But however much more flexible in these matters the courts or the President may be, the general purpose of the prohibition against Congress should be respected by them to the extent that it is consistent with good government to do so. (It should be evident that the comments I am addressing to these illustrations are determined, in large part, by American circumstances, traditions, and constitutional controversies.)

3. My third illustration is more complicated. A new janitor is instructed by his employer about the temperature to be maintained in a building in which each of the apartments has its temperature control apparatus:

You are to leave apartment A alone. As for apartments B, C, and D, do not do anything to bring their temperatures below that outdoors.

Thus, it seems, the tenant in apartment A is to have complete control of his premises in *this* respect. Furthermore, the other three tenants are evidently the only ones permitted to reduce temperatures below outside temperatures in their respective apartments. The janitor, on the other hand, seems to have been left free to maintain or raise temperatures in apartments B, C, and D. Conceivably, a tenant's apartment temperature might adversely affect the entire building (for example, the water pipes may burst if the temperature is permitted to get too low), so that the raising of the temperature in each apartment might be necessary or desirable in the interest of all. But, for some reason, the tenant in apartment A is allowed complete control of *his* temperature. (Perhaps he is conducting delicate experiments or is always at home and can be relied upon not to allow extremes in temperatures.)

The wording of the employer's instructions suggests that the janitor has or would have had (but for the instructions) means for raising and lowering the temperature in all the apartments. What means does he have? Does he have authority to enter an apartment to adjust a tenant's controls? Or is there a central temperature control system in addition to the individual units or controls in each apartment? The instructions themselves do not provide an answer. Whatever means may be available, the janitor is left free to affect the temperature in apartments B, C, and D in some circumstances, but not the temperature in apartment A.

The wording of the instructions does imply that the janitor has or would otherwise have had the authority to do something. An examination of the premises would reveal whether there *is* an alternative central temperature control system. An examination of leases might be required to see if the janitor is authorized to enter the apartment for this purpose. Or do the employer's instructions authorize the janitor to enter apartments B, C, and D for this purpose, if there is no central system? What if the instructions to the janitor are circulated to the tenants along with or as part of their leases?

Similarly, in the First Amendment, Congress is restrained from doing anything *at all* about religious establishments; but Congress is pointedly left free to preserve or enlarge the "free exercise [of religion]," "freedom of speech," and "[freedom] of the press," perhaps even to supervise and adjust the extensive control the states have over speech, press, and the exercise of religion under the original Constitution. The problem remains, however, whether Congress has such power, either by grant elsewhere in the Constitution or only as one critical implication of the First Amendment.

4. My central illustration also draws upon the relation of landlord and tenant. This landlord, upon delivering the annual lease to his tenant, is obliged to assure him:

You shall continue to have at least the privileges that have been allowed heretofore.

Thus, it would seem that the tenant continues to be assured of the privileges he has had in previous years. But perhaps the tenant, although a layman, is aware that the lease prohibits the keeping of pets, the installation of a washing machine in the apartment, and the letting of rooms. Nevertheless, the tenant has, for years, kept a cat in the apartment, a washer in the bathroom, and a student in the extra bedroom. What defines "the privileges that have been allowed heretofore," especially in circumstances where the landlord had been obliged to give such an assurance in order to keep his tenant for another year—the terms of the lease or the previous practice with respect to *this* tenant? Whatever the landlord may later think —perhaps he may change his mind about whether he wants to keep this tenant, or decide that the tenant has now no choice but to stay with him because housing alternatives are no longer available for the tenant—may not the tenant reasonably anticipate that the privileges he is entitled to are not to be restricted to a lease printed years before, which he has not really studied or which may not be taken seriously by him and his fellow tenants?

Similarly, in the case of the First Amendment, "freedom of speech [and] of the press" undoubtedly meant much more to the American people, who insisted upon this guarantee being added to the Constitution—much more than mere reliance upon the reports about liberty of the press and about seditious libel by the authors of common law treatises and opinions, for the most part in England, a generation before. (The principal author, Judge William Blackstone, published his *Commentaries* in 1765-69.) The question remains, what *is* that "freedom of speech [and] of the press" which Congress may not curtail at all but which it may in some circumstances preserve or enlarge?

5. We now move out of doors. The players on the field agree on the rules. Four bases are to be arranged in a square of sixty-foot sides; no base runner may leave a base until the ball is released by the pitcher; a tenth player is to be placed anywhere in the outfield desired by the defensive team. It is obvious, without anyone saying so, that a "ball game" is planned. Certainly, it is not football or soccer or tennis—these are clearly ruled out even though these are all games in which a ball is important. But what if a baseball should be tossed into play? It would be a plausible suggestion: and if insisted upon, it could be defended and the baseball employed, troublesome (and even dangerous) as it might be to play at such close quarters with the harder ball. But to those who know anything about American sports, the rules laid down relate to softball: and a softball, for all its similarities to a baseball (especially when compared to a football, soccer ball, or tennis ball, to say nothing of a hockey puck or a badminton cock), is significantly different from it in this context.

Similarly, in the case of the First Amendment, it is plausible to suggest that all forms of "speech" or utterance are protected from any curtailment by Congress. The language does permit this suggestion. But one must think about the purpose of the rules laid down here and elsewhere in the Constitution, and consider the essentially political nature of the enterprise reflected in the technical terms, "freedom of speech [and] of the press." Thus, for example, utterances which are obscene may not raise First Amendment questions. This does not mean that Congress, assuming it does have the power to legislate at all with respect to such matters, may do as it wishes with obscenity or alleged obscenity: that is, such restraints as those imposed by ordinary due process standards would have to be taken into account—standards that are particularly troublesome to comply with in any attempt to define obscenity for criminal law purposes. Thus, it is not the protection of the First Amendment upon which defenders of alleged purveyors of obscenity should have to rely.

6. The occupant of a celebrated house is confronted by the demand of his neighbors that he not remodel the exterior of the house in which he lives. He promises that he will not, but only after having tried to explain that he does not own the house, that remodeling is not something he is empowered to do under the lease. Thus, it appears that the neighbors' concern was misdirected. However, is the promise simply worthless? It does set the neighbors somewhat at ease; it does assert, for the benefit of others who learn of the agreement (including the landlord), how intent the community is on preserving this exterior as it is. Perhaps, also, the promise should serve to guide the occupant in what he may do in exercising the powers he does have under the lease. Thus, the authority he may have to install an air conditioning unit or to provide his family a fire escape should not be so exercised as to affect significantly the appearance of the exterior.

Similarly, in the case of the First Amendment, the prohibition on Congress may be superfluous for the simple reason that the general government never had any authority to deal with speech or the press. This was an argument made by supporters of the Constitution during the ratification campaign to explain why a provision protecting liberty of the press was not needed. It still remains a question whether Congress has *any* power, even without the First Amendment, to abridge freedom of speech or of the press. But the First Amendment does indicate the importance attached to this freedom and can be expected to guide Congress in exercising the extensive powers it no doubt does have under the Constitution. Thus, it cannot be considered "necessary and proper" to abridge freedom of speech in order to accomplish a purpose or to exercise a power that *is* provided for Congress in the Constitution.

7. There is on a turbulent river a levee protecting an important city. This levee has been found adequate for many years. Then other levees are erected in the immediate area, particularly one of equal or even greater strength directly across the river from the original levee. (The total force of the river water, let us assume, remains constant.) The force concentrated on the original levee increases as outlets for expenditure of energy elsewhere along the river banks are blocked off. The problem of the engineer is that of determining whether that force can be contained at all points. The decision he must make, then, is whether particular areas are worthy of special protection, perhaps at the risk of flooding other areas. This does not mean that the areas in which flooding is to be permitted are to be left completely at the mercy of the river: construction on such land may make use of raised foundations, for instance, to minimize water damage; the crops planted may be selected with occasional flooding as a likelihood; in any event, rescue equipment should be available for exceptional flooding. In addition, such flooding may have to be curtailed by some means if it should lead to inundation from behind of an area elsewhere on the river that *is* intended to be protected by a levee.

Similarly, in the context of the American constitutional system, particular absolute prohibitions are possible only if other prohibitions are not simultaneously imposed. The complete protection of the First Amendment may be extended against the states only at the risk of reducing the extent of protection available against Congress. I believe it can be shown that it is far more important, for a variety of reasons, that Congress rather than the states be restrained. Yet, the pressure upon Congress to "do something" becomes very great if trouble spots in particular states cannot be taken care of in those states. In fact, I suggest in this book that the development of the "clear and present danger" test is intimately related to the extension against the states, by means of the Fourteenth Amendment, of the prohibitions of the First Amendment. This is, in short, an introduction to an argument on behalf of the salutary effects *among us* of federalism and of states' rights.

I do not suggest, however, that state power over speech and press is completely without restraint under the Constitution: I have already referred to the power in Congress to remove or modify state abridgments of freedom of speech or of the press. Furthermore, the general government is obliged to guarantee a republican form of government to each state, not only for the good of that state but for the benefit of the Union as well. Effective republican government implies that citizens should be permitted to discuss issues and candidates fully. In addition, there are due process standards, in the traditional sense, which limit what states may do in extending the criminal laws to speech and the press. (These standards, which may anticipate the Fourteenth Amendment, are equivalent to the raised foundations in my illustration.) In fact, for many purposes, an adequate criminal bar, with courts scrupulous about procedural standards, would provide substantial protection for freedom of speech and of the press. (The courts and bar, as well as Congress, are equivalent to the rescue teams referred to in the illustration.)

My seven illustrations have been designed to suggest how parts of the First Amendment and of the Constitution itself should be read so as to give full force to the entire instrument. I have suggested that the First Amendment prohibition against the abridgment of freedom of speech or of the press is absolute, that it is directed primarily against Congress, that it constitutes a precaution not only against undue assumption of power but also against a misuse of legitimate power, and that it may lose some of its effect if directed in its fullness against the states as well. Thus, we see provided in the First Amendment how Congress is to conduct itself with respect to freedom of speech and of the press.

V

In the most technical sense, the First Amendment was made by the states that ratified it—that is, by the states acting through their legislatures.[22] The first ten amendments, along with two others which failed of ratification, were proposed to the states by Congress on September 25, 1789, the day they passed the Senate, having previously passed the House of Representatives (where they originated). (*Annals*, I, pp. 433, 916[23]) Ratification was completed on December 15, 1791,[24] when the eleventh state (Virginia) approved those amendments, there being at that time fourteen states in the Union.[25]

Thus, the writing of the articles that were to become the first ten amendments was done during the first session of the First Congress. The Senate sat with closed doors at this time. Its records are confined for the most part to the entries in the Senate Journal of the motions and votes in that body. It is for this reason that one must rely on the much more extensive, but still incomplete, records of the House of Representatives for an *indication* not only of the discussion that accompanied the formulation of the amendments (much of which took place in committee), but also of the general understanding at that time both of the Constitution and of the accepted mode of constitutional interpretation. (There do not seem to be available any records of the debates in the state legislatures which ratified the amendments.) I have examined the records of the First Congress (1789-91) for whatever they may reveal about the thought of the Congress which wrote the First Amendment. It is to the debates in the House of Representatives that reference is so often made in the discussion that follows.[26]

It is not my purpose here to record the gloss on the First Amendment provided by the Supreme Court, but rather to aid the reader to approach directly and thereby perhaps better to understand the problems posed by the First Amendment. Several competent casebooks, law review articles, and treatises are available on current interpretations of the First Amendment by the Supreme Court and others.[27] No doubt, we must appreciate and usually conform to what the Supreme Court, at any particular moment, may have to say about this or any other constitutional problem. But we are not obliged to concede that the Supreme Court's interpretation is necessarily the correct one. Indeed, there is no reason to believe that the thoughtful student is not in just as good a position as any court to understand the First Amendment and to address himself to the problems raised by the national reliance upon "freedom of speech [and] of the press." Perhaps, indeed, the thoughtful citizen is in a better position than a court to do so, since he is neither bound as a judicial body may feel itself to be by precedents and dicta of earlier courts nor swayed by improper considerations that men in public life are sometimes not equipped or disposed to disregard.[28]

When we turn, therefore, to the records of the men of 1789, we do not satisfy a mere craving for history. Rather, we turn for instruction and suggestions to discussions which surpass in subtlety, precision, and relevance, notwithstanding dramatic changes in circumstances, much of the discussion we are apt to confront today. We thus join with the best of those who have gone before us in the search for an understanding both of the meaning and of the means of perpetuation of our political institutions.

If the citizen's understanding is properly grounded and his position adequately argued, legislatures and courts will eventually have to listen. For the Constitution is the ultimate touchstone, the courts have taught us, not what our public servants may happen to say about it.[29]

VI

Before we proceed further, let us consider certain problems in reading, or construing, the Constitution. There is no doubt that construction was anticipated, and relied upon, from the beginning. Thus, the Ninth Amendment attempts to limit what may be done through construction:

The enumeration in the Constitution, of certain rights, shall not be construed to deny or disparage others retained by the people.[30]

The Constitution cannot be depended on always to explain itself. But in construing it, the citizen must not proceed as if he can make of the Constitution simply what he wants to make of it—for that would be to proceed as if it did not exist.[31] Here, too, "ought" should govern "wish."

Not only does a constitution exist, but for the constitutional scholar, and this includes the thoughtful politician, the document takes on a meaning, life, and purpose of its own: it is regarded almost as a living body to be understood as a whole. Thus, John Laurance can "imagine some good effects were intended" by a particular provision of the Constitution. (*Annals*, I, p. 269) Such an assumption, which is implied in many of the debates of the First Congress, means that every part has a role, that there is nothing superfluous in the instrument.

A distinction may be made between what a constitution says and what its writers intended it to say. The former is thought to be the primary concern of citizens: James Madison can only speculate, with reference to a proposed constitutional amendment (respecting religious establishments), about the effects "he presumed the amendment was intended [to prevent]" (*Annals, I*, p. 730)— even though he was a leader of the congressional committee that had brought in the amendment. Fisher Ames stated in the House of Representatives the reliance to be placed on the Constitution as it came to view: "There were but few on this floor who were in [the Constitutional] Convention, and who could say what was the intention with which every clause was inserted. He was content to take it as he found it. . . ." (*Annals, I*, p. 909)

No doubt, many shared Madison's concern that a constitution should not incorporate "abstract propositions, of which the judgment may not be convinced." (*Annals, I*, p. 738) "Abstract propositions" do little more than express an opinion about something which may have any number of practical consequences. Such a proposition was introduced in the Senate to be added to the first set of amendments to the Constitution:

That there are certain natural rights, of which men, when they form a social compact, cannot deprive or divest their posterity; among which are the enjoyment of life and liberty, with the means of acquiring, possessing, and protecting property, and pursuing and obtaining happiness and safety.[32]

Still another proposition of this kind was introduced in the House (under Madison's sponsorship):

The powers delegated by this Constitution to the Government of the United States, shall be exercised as therein appropriated, so that the Legislative shall not exercise the powers vested in the Executive or Judicial; nor the Executive the powers vested in the Legislative or Judicial; nor the Judicial the powers vested in the Legislative or Executive. [*Annals, I*, pp. 760, 435-36]

That is, everyone would have been directed by this proposed amendment to take the Constitution at its word.[33] "Abstract propositions" must be distinguished, however, from "general principles";

for, as Elias Boudinot observed, "it was the duty of the House . . . to detail the general principles laid down in the Constitution, and reduce them to practice." (*Annals*, I, p. 271)

The use of abstractions, and even of general principles, arouses opposition in practical-minded men who are guided as much by the conclusions or practical effects of their reasoning as by its premises and its cogency. Thus, Thomas Tudor Tucker complains about a proposal that the preamble of an act be set down before the act itself is spelled out:

The principles mentioned in the [proposed] preamble, were of such extent as could not be determined; they might lead to consequences about which no member could form an opinion. He wished to know gentlemen's objects before he pledged himself. It was possible he might go with the mover, in agreeing to the result of his propositions; but he could not agree to fetter himself with restraints, or be led blindfolded, even to the truth itself. This mode of reasoning was like the Socratic; he could not discover what was to flow from affirming or denying. It was asking him, if he admitted this proposition and that; until he admitted so much, as to enable his adversary to draw from premises, which he had been allured to grant from their speciousness, conclusions he had never contemplated. He did not like the idea of making laws syllogistically. He hoped, therefore, the gentlemen would relinquish all idea of determining on the preamble, until the substantial proposition was agreed to. [*Annals*, I, pp. 838-39]

Ames's observation about the Constitutional Convention (quoted earlier in this section) had been anticipated by John Page:

The gentlemen tell us that these are the principles of the Constitution. I know not what were the intentions of its framers, but I see and judge of the work by my faculty of understanding; and nothing appears to convince me that the Constitution distributes the power in the manner gentlemen have said. [*Annals*, I, p. 580]

Differences of opinion result. Elbridge Gerry had a suggestion as to why such differences were inevitable. The Convention was in part responsible:

The [Constitution], it cannot be denied, is in many parts obscure; if Congress are to explain and declare what it shall be, they certainly will have it in their power to make it what they please. It has been a strong objection to the Constitution, that it was remarkably obscure; nay, some have gone so far as to assert that it was studiously obscure, that it might be applied to every purpose by Congress. [*Annals, I*, p. 503]

All parts of the Constitution, it has been said, must be taken as contributing something to the meaning of the whole. But the conclusion one reaches on certain issues might well depend on where one starts in the instrument: that is, one must ask whether there *is* a whole. The question debated at length in the First Congress of whether officers appointed by the President with the consent of the Senate can be removed at pleasure by the President may serve to illustrate this difficulty.[34] The President is empowered by the Constitution to require "the Opinion, in writing, of the principal Officer in each of the executive Departments, upon any Subject relating to the Duties of their respective Offices. . . ." Why should he be given power to do this if he also has the power to remove such officers at will (which means he can exert control over them in their activities, including the requirement from them of opinions in writing)? But if he is to be regarded as not possessing such removal power even with respect to heads of executive departments, why should judges be guaranteed their offices during good behavior? Thus Egbert Benson argued:

Now, the Constitution expressly declares, that the Judges, both of the Supreme and Inferior Courts, shall hold their offices during good behaviour. If it is declared, that they are to hold their offices by this particular tenure, it follows that the other officers of the Government should hold them only at pleasure. [*Annals, I*, p. 373]

If it is suggested that the critical question is not whether the President can remove such officers, but whether he can remove them without the consent of the Senate, then one must ask whether this restriction upon his control over subordinates is consistent with the obligation he has to see that the laws are faithfully executed. Still, this objection would apply as well to his inability to appoint without consent of the Senate, a restriction prescribed by the Constitution. But, it may be countered, that restriction (with respect to appointments) is explicitly ordained by the Constitution, implicitly leaving the President unfettered with respect to removals. Thus the argument proceeds, with different parts of the Constitution suggesting different conclusions.[35]

Is the Constitution treated as a unity when in fact it is not? Any strand followed through should lead to, or at least be consistent with, the meaning of the whole. But if it is not in fact a unity, diverse strands will lead to inconsistent meanings. Is unity to be secured then only by being clear about the overall purpose, in the light of which everything is to be interpreted? But what if there are several purposes—purposes which might appear to be in some ways conflicting? The Declaration of Independence refers to "Life, Liberty and the Pursuit of Happiness," without obviously establishing a priority.[36] The Preamble to the Constitution seems to do the same.

No one mind could control completely what went into the Constitution. But it is only when one mind takes a subject and molds it that there is even the opportunity for the kind of unity which sees chance eliminated and every part fitted into the whole. Not even the final draftsman of the Constitution could impose a unity upon it unless he had the power to change troublesome provisions. He might use ambiguity and thereby attempt to smooth over whatever conflicts remained, but that would not do more than establish an appearance of unity. The fact remains that one or two men of little consequence or comprehension could (in Convention) vote for or against a particular provision on grounds inconsistent with the tendency of the remainder of the instrument, thereby providing the margin of decision on close votes relating to critical issues. Such men may be moved by misapprehensions or by instructions from uninformed constituents that have little or nothing to do with the comprehensive scheme contemplated by the more astute members of the Convention.[37]

The quest for a unified interpretation is complicated by the fact that a constitution, unlike a play or a philosophical work, must be immediately applied to practical problems. Thus, theoretical formulations, which permit the philosophical writer to seek a unity on the highest level, may not be useful for this purpose. Was the mistake of the early American politicians to assume there had to be such consistency? But what alternative is there in expounding a constitution? Indeed, what alternative is there other than repeated recourse to the fundamental principles and issues which provide guidance for the resolution of the conflicts in allegiances implicit in practical affairs? Ames seemed to recognize the need for such recourse, even as he acknowledged the tentative nature of the conclusions that may be drawn:

> I take it to be admitted on all hands . . . that the power of removal from office, at pleasure, resides somewhere in the Government. . . . [Let gentlemen] revert to the principles, spirit, and tendency of the Constitution, and they will be compelled to acknowledge that there is the highest degree of probability that the power does vest in the President of the United States. I shall not undertake to say that the arguments are conclusive on this point. I do not suppose it is necessary that they should be so; for I believe nearly as good conclusions may be drawn from the refutations of an argument as from any other proof. [*Annals*, I, pp. 538-39]

One must revert, he advocated, "to the principles, spirit, and tendency of the Constitution." Critical to a proper understanding of that Constitution, Ames said elsewhere (*Annals*, I, p. 909), is the approach one must make to it "as an American, with an eye to that Constitution, the language of liberty in his mouth, and the love of it in his heart. . . ."

VII

A further caution is in order before we turn to the speech and press provision of the First Amendment, and this we are reminded of by Madison's almost casual interpretation of the religion provisions of the amendment. He "apprehended the meaning of the words to be, that Congress should not establish a religion, and enforce the legal observation of it by law, nor compel men to worship God in any manner contrary to their conscience." (*Annals*, I, p. 730) How much can "research" add to this? That is, in matters of this kind, especially matters drawing upon the political sense and aspirations of the community, may not one "overstudy" a provision of the Constitution, bringing to bear upon it a battery of scholarly apparatus simply inappropriate for the occasion?[38]

One result of an excessive concentration of scholarly equipment may be that the political or constitutional problem is mangled and the perspective distorted. A commentary on this danger is suggested by the graveyard scene of *Hamlet*. The Prince is examining a skull:

Hamlet. . . . Prithee, Horatio, tell me one thing.
Horatio. What's that, my lord?
Hamlet. Dost thou think Alexander looked o' this fashion i' the earth?

Horatio. E'en so.
Hamlet. And smelt so? pah!
[*Puts down the skull.*]
Horatio. E'en so, my lord.
Hamlet. To what base uses we may return, Horatio! Why may not imagination trace the noble dust of Alexander, till he find it stopping a bung-hole?
Horatio. 'Twere to consider too curiously, to consider so.
Hamlet. No, faith, not a jot; but to follow him thither with modesty enough, and likelihood to lead it: as thus: Alexander died, Alexander was buried, Alexander returneth into dust; the dust is earth; of earth we make loam; and why of that loam, whereto he was converted, might they not stop a beer-barrel?
    Imperial Caesar, dead and turn'd to clay,
    Might stop a hole to keep the wind away:
    O, that that earth, which kept the world in awe,
    Should patch a wall t' expel the winter's flaw!
But soft! but soft! aside: here comes the king.

The key to this passage for our purpose is Horatio's comment, "'Twere to consider too curiously, to consider so." We see reflected here Hamlet's constant problem, how he is to regard and act in a manner appropriate to the occasion by which he is confronted. Thus, he does not kill Claudius at prayers because he wants to attain, in this temporal realm, an effect through eternity as well: that is, he wants to send Claudius's soul to hell as well as deprive him of life on earth. Or, he insists upon allowing other-worldly influences (that is, his father's commands) to guide his actions in this world. Again and again, he fails to give each realm its due and only its due: he fails to do justice to things as they are. Similarly here: certainly, Alexander and Caesar can be translated into dust and barrel-stops: but when a man does that, when he allows his "imagination [to] trace" wildly, he fails to give due weight to the phenomena (in this case, political phenomena). One does not understand a king, a political man—perhaps not even the human being simply—if one insists upon doing what Hamlet does: "'Twere to consider too curiously, to consider so."

This Shakespeare suggests even in the way he has Hamlet close these speculations:

But soft! but soft! aside: here comes the king.

Prince Hamlet is not so abstracted that he is unable to see things properly at times. The king approaches: it is time for speculation to cease. He does not say, "Here comes a pile of dust," or "Here comes a future bung-hole stopper." No, it is a particular pile of dust, it is a king, something to be now considered in the manner in which men commonly consider political things.[39]

Let this serve as our prologue and warning as we turn to the First Amendment, to a consideration of American institutions and circumstances and what we can learn from them about both the human being and the citizen.

[A TRIBUNE:] It is a mind
That shall remain a poison where it is,
Not poison any further.
CORIOLANUS: Shall remain!
Hear you this Triton of the minnows? mark you
His absolute 'shall'?
—SHAKESPEARE, *Coriolanus*

III. "CONGRESS SHALL MAKE NO LAW"

I

"CONGRESS SHALL make no law . . . abridging the freedom of speech, or of the press. . . ." The prohibition imposed by this amendment is absolute in both its terms and its tone. It seems to say that certain legislation is strictly forbidden. It is important to settle this point first, because it affects (as we shall see) much that follows, including, perhaps, the very meaning of "freedom of speech, or of the press."

We must mark the imperative character of the word *shall*, as reflected in debates in the First Congress. James Jackson observed (referring to Article III, section 1 of the Constitution), "The word 'may' is not positive, and it remains with Congress to determine what inferior jurisdictions may be necessary, and what they will ordain and establish. . . ." (*Annals*, I, p. 802) William Smith, also referring to this judiciary article, explained,

The words, "shall be vested," have great energy; they are words of command; they leave no discretion to Congress to parcel out the Judicial powers of the Union to State judicatures, where a discretionary power is left to Congress by the Constitution; the word "may" is employed where a discretion is left; the word "shall" is the appropriate term; this distinction is cautiously observed. [*Annals*, I, p. 818][1]

II

The framers of the Constitution as well as of the first ten amendments made it clear where qualifications were intended upon restraints directed against the powers of government. Thus, in Article I, section 9 of the original Constitution, we find,

The Privilege of the Writ of Habeas Corpus shall not be suspended, unless when in Cases of Rebellion or Invasion the public Safety may require it.

No Capitation, or other direct, Tax shall be laid, unless in Proportion to the Census or Enumeration herein before directed to be taken.

No Money shall be drawn from the Treasury, but in Consequence of Appropriations made by Law. . . .

Consider, in each of these statements, the striking change if the qualification upon the restraint is removed:

The Privilege of the Writ of Habeas Corpus shall not be suspended.

No Capitation, or other direct, Tax shall be laid.

No Money shall be drawn from the Treasury.

Advocates of the first and second unqualified restraints upon government can be found in the records of the debates of the state ratifying conventions (in 1787-88). The third unqualified restraint (prohibiting drawing of money from the Treasury) would, of course, have made the new government virtually impossible to maintain. Both the advocates and the opponents of these unqualified restraints would have agreed that, so long as the Constitution governed, such language as this would have imposed absolute (that is, unavoidable) prohibitions upon the appropriate governmental power.[2]

Qualified restraints upon the government are to be found as well in the amendments to the Constitution:

No Soldier shall, in time of peace be quartered in any house, without the consent of the Owner, nor in time of war, but in a manner to be prescribed by law. [Amendment III]

The right of the people to be secure in their persons, houses, papers, and effects, against unreasonable searches and seizures, shall not be violated, and no Warrants shall issue, but upon probable cause, supported by Oath or affirmation, and particularly describing the place to be searched, and the persons or things to be seized. [Amendment IV]

. . . nor shall private property be taken for public use, without just compensation. [Amendment V]

Once again, consider the effect if the qualifications are removed from each of these amendments:

No Soldier shall be quartered in any house without the consent of the Owner.

No Warrants shall issue.

Private property shall not be taken for public use.

The importance of the qualification in the Third Amendment did not escape the members of the House of Representatives when the text of that amendment was debated. Thomas Sumter hoped that quartering never would be done without the consent of the owner, and moved to strike out the last part of the proposition. Roger Sherman replied that

> it was absolutely necessary that marching troops should have quarters, whether in time of peace or war, and that it ought not to be put in the power of an individual to obstruct the public service; if quarters were not to be obtained in public barracks, they must be procured elsewhere. [*Annals*, I, p. 752]

Gerry then attempted to insure that only "a civil magistrate" could order the quartering, according to law, when conditions required it. (*Annals*, I, p. 752) Thomas Hartley opposed this limitation, arguing that "those things ought to be entrusted to the Legislature; that cases might arise where the public safety would be endangered by putting it in the power of one person to keep a division of troops standing in the inclemency of the weather for many hours. . . ." (*Annals*, I, p. 752) It is evident throughout this debate that emergency conditions were being provided for: the rule that applies in time of peace may not suffice in time of war.

Qualified restraints upon Congress are to be found as well among the many suggested amendments to the Constitution that the First Congress considered but rejected. Thus, Aedanus Burke asked that Article I, section 4, be amended to read,

> Congress shall not alter, modify, or interfere in the times, places, or manner of holding elections of Senators, or Representatives, except when any State shall refuse or neglect, or be unable, by invasion or rebellion, to make such election. [*Annals, I*, p. 768][3]

In the Senate, we find such qualified restraints as this proposed unsuccessfully for adoption as amendments:

> That no commercial treaty shall be ratified without the concurrence of two-thirds of the whole number of the members of the Senate; and no treaty, ceding, contracting, restraining, or suspending the territorial rights or claims of the United States, or any of them, or their, or any of their rights or claims to fishing in the American seas, or navigating the American rivers, shall be ratified but in cases of the most urgent and extreme necessity.[4]

Thus we find provision made for "cases of the most urgent and extreme necessity" that may demand sacrifice of navigation and fishing rights.

These amendatory measures were under consideration at the same time as the First Amendment: the unqualified character of the restraint with respect to laws abridging freedom of speech and of the press in that amendment stands out sharply by contrast. Nothing is said in the First Amendment about such contingencies as "Rebellion or Invasion," "time of war," or "cases of the most urgent and extreme necessity."[5]

III

The significance of qualifications—and of their absence—is emphasized even more as one considers instances in which no qualification is included to temper the absoluteness of a restraint imposed upon Congress. Thus, we find in Article I, section 9 of the Constitution,

No Bill of Attainder or ex post facto Law shall be passed. . . .

No Tax or Duty shall be laid on Articles exported from any State. . . .

No Preference shall be given by any Regulation of Commerce or Revenue to the Ports of one State over those of another. . . .

No Title of Nobility shall be granted by the United States. . . .

Each of these restraints seems to be absolute: the only problem in some cases may be to determine what it is that is absolutely restrained. What *is* a bill of attainder or an *ex post facto* law? What is meant by "Tax or Duty"? Does "Title of Nobility" include all honors that might be given by a country? Thus, inevitably, problems remain—but they do not include the problem of deciding the constitutional attitude toward a recognized bill of attainder or an acknowledged title of nobility.

In the third provision, one question left open is that of definition, not that of the proper constitutional attitude when the appropriate definition or identification has been made. That provision does *not* read, "No Preference shall be given to the Ports of one State over those of another." Rather, we are told, Congress shall make no "Regulation of *Commerce or Revenue*" which prefers one state's ports to those of another. The provision does not say that one state's ports may not be preferred to those of another for *any* purpose: for there might arise circumstances—in time of war, for instance—when it would be necessary or convenient to prefer the ports of one state over those of another. But as for a preference which would result from a "Regulation of Commerce or Revenue," it is forbidden—and forbidden in absolute terms.

One may question whether all these restraints are wise, especially if the *ex post facto* provision should be taken to govern civil as well as criminal legislation.[6] But there can be no doubt that the restraints are absolute: no exceptions are to be permitted, whatever the dangers or evils that Congress might be led to expect as a result of its inability to act. Absolute as these restraints are, however, they are no more so than those found in the First Amendment.

If we turn again to the first ten amendments to the Constitution, we find additional restraints, applicable to Congress as well as to the Judiciary of the United States, that are absolute in character:

... nor shall any person be subject for the same offence to be twice put in jeopardy of life or limb; nor shall [he] be compelled in any criminal case to be a witness against himself.... [Amendment V]

In all criminal prosecutions, the accused shall enjoy the right to a speedy and public trial, by an impartial jury of the State and district wherein the crime shall have been committed, which district shall have been previously ascertained by law, and to be informed of the nature and cause of the accusation; to be confronted with the witnesses against him; to have compulsory process for obtaining witnesses in his favor, and to have the Assistance of Counsel for his defence. [Amendment VI]

In Suits at common law, where the value in controversy shall exceed twenty dollars, the right of trial by jury shall be preserved.... [Amendment VII]

Excessive bail shall not be required, nor excessive fines imposed, nor cruel and unusual punishments inflicted. [Amendment VIII]

There does remain for determination the meaning of such terms as "criminal case," "criminal prosecutions," "suits at common law," and "excessive," to say nothing of the elements of "trial by jury." But the Constitution is clear about what is to be done when it is determined that the situation *is* one of those provided for by these amendments. Thus, a person cannot be compelled, no matter what the circumstances or dangers of the community, to be "a witness against himself" in a criminal case; one cannot be deprived of a jury trial in the circumstances specified. There have been proposals made from time to time that some of the prohibitions laid down in these amendments should be modified. But it is generally recognized that these prohibitions are absolute so long as these amendments stand.

Unqualified restraints upon Congress are to be found as well among the suggested amendments to the Constitution that the First Congress considered but rejected. The discussion of the provision made for conscientious objectors in an early draft of the Second Amendment is instructive. That amendment at one stage concluded with the exception, "but no person religiously scrupulous shall be compelled to bear arms." (*Annals*, I, p. 749) Egbert Benson recognized the absolute character of this restraint and was moved to express reservations:

No man can claim this indulgence of right. It may be a religious persuasion, but it is no natural right, and therefore ought to be left to the discretion of the Government. If this stands part of the Constitution, it will be a question before the Judiciary on every regulation you make with respect to the organization of the militia, whether it comports with this declaration or not. It is extremely injudicious to intermix matters of doubt with fundamentals.

I have no reason to believe but the Legislature will always possess humanity enough to indulge this class of citizens in a matter they are so desirous of; but they ought to be left to their discretion. [*Annals*, I, p. 751]

Thus, special protection for conscientious objectors is not given the constitutional sanction that is provided for those who exercise freedom of speech or of the press. Rather, Congress is left with discretion in the former matter. Thomas Scott indicated one basis for different treatment, aside from what was implicit in Benson's reference to "natural right," when he argued,

There are many sects I know, who are religiously scrupulous in this respect; I do not mean to deprive them of any indulgence the law affords; my design is to guard against those who are of no religion. It has been urged that religion is on the decline; if so, the argument is more strong in my favor, for when the time comes that religions shall be discarded, the generality of persons will have recourse to these pretexts to get excused from bearing arms. [*Annals*, I, p. 767]

It is evident that Congress intended to retain control over this matter—it did not permit itself to be bound as it did with respect to freedom of speech and the press—even though it is likely that the members agreed with Daniel Carroll that "the rights of conscience are, in their nature, of peculiar delicacy, and will little bear the gentlest touch of governmental hand. . . ." (*Annals*, I, p. 730)

IV

Just how absolute *is* absolute? The first draft of the religion provision finally incorporated in what is now the First Amendment read,

The civil rights of none shall be abridged on account of religious belief or worship, nor shall any national religion be established, nor shall the full and equal rights of conscience be in any manner, or on any pretext, infringed. [*Annals*, I, p. 434]

What is added by the phrase, "in any manner, or on any pretext"? It should be noted that throughout the early drafts of the amendments there is a superfluity of language that is usually cut out by Congress in the course of its debates. Is this phrase superfluous? Or does the absence of such a phrase from the First Amendment connote there something less than an absolute restraint upon Congress?

The complications suggested by "superfluous" language may be seen in the Second Amendment as it now stands:

A well regulated Militia, being necessary to the security of a free State, the right of the people to keep and bear Arms, shall not be infringed.

Does the phrase, "being necessary to the security of a free State," imply a limitation upon what might otherwise have been an absolute or unqualified restraint? That is, may the right of the people to keep and bear arms be legitimately infringed when this would not contribute "to the security of a free State"? Does this phrase suggest, then, a purpose or reason which is to limit or qualify what is said about "the right of the people to keep and bear Arms"?

But if such a qualification may be "read into" this amendment, it can be read into all of them. For there are found in the Preamble to the Constitution[7] several purposes or objects of the Constitution which could be similarly taken to qualify the most absolute restraints upon government in that instrument, and even make much of the Constitution no more than advisory. Thus, it might be argued, "Congress shall make no law . . . abridging the freedom of speech, except when not to do so would make it difficult to form a more perfect Union, establish Justice, insure domestic Tranquillity, provide for the common defence, promote the general Welfare, or secure the Blessings of Liberty to ourselves and our Posterity."[8]

A phrase similar to the one we have been considering may be found in an early draft of the provision respecting freedom of the press: that right was referred to as "one of the great bulwarks of liberty." (*Annals*, I, p. 434) What if there should arise circumstances in which, rather than being a bulwark of liberty, freedom of the press is so used, or abused, as to become a threat to liberty? Would the reason of the enactment, presumably reflected in the descriptive phrase, take precedence over the form of the enactment? That is, may one temporarily ignore the absoluteness of such a restraint and consider instead whether liberty is indeed being protected by the exercise of the freedom of the press? Such questions as these seem to have been ruled out with respect to freedom of speech and of the press by the unconditional language of the First Amendment, at least to the extent that they are ruled out by such similarly unconditional provisions as that directing that a bill cannot become a law enacted by Congress without first being passed by both the House of Representatives and the Senate.

The absoluteness of the First Amendment is in contrast to the qualification found in some of the state constitutions at the time that amendment was written and ratified.[9] The Pennsylvania Constitution of 1790 was typical in this respect:

That the printing presses shall be free to every person who undertakes to examine the proceedings of the legislature or any branch of government: and no law shall ever be made to restrain the right thereof. The free communication of thoughts and opinions is one of the invaluable rights of man: and every citizen may freely speak, write, and print on any subject, *being responsible for the abuse of that liberty.*[10] [Italics added]

A qualification dependent on determinations of what constitutes an "abuse of that liberty" provides some scope for the exercise of discretion by public servants. The First Amendment, in its provisions respecting the freedom of speech and of the press, does not permit such discretion.[11] Nevertheless, an influential American writer on this subject said in 1920, "The express exception of 'abuse' was first made by Pennsylvania in 1790 . . . ; but since I regard such an exception as implied in the United States form, I have assumed in this book that there is no difference in legal effect."[12] Much of subsequent American constitutional adjudication on this subject has been led astray by just this assumption.[13]

Because of the unequivocal language of the First Amendment, I have not in this book assumed "such an exception as implied." Article I, section 10 of the Constitution exhibits the ability of the draftsmen of the constitutional period to indicate an exception where one was intended:

No State shall, without the consent of Congress, . . . engage in War, unless actually invaded, or in such imminent Danger as will not admit of delay.

V

There is no reason to suppose that the draftsmen of 1787 and of 1789 read any of these provisions, with respect to whether the restraint imposed upon government was unqualified, differently from the way we do. In response to the question, "May Congress ever . . . ?" they would probably have agreed with us as to which restraints should (because of their language) evoke the answer, "No, never."

This point has had to be labored, however, simply because twentieth century legislators, judges, and scholars have not respected the absolute restraints in the First Amendment as they respect the absolute restraints in other of the constitutional provisions that have been examined in this chapter. That is, the very men who respect the absoluteness of other parts of the Constitution scoff at "First Amendment absolutes."

A qualification has been read into the freedom of speech and of the press provisions of the First Amendment. This qualification has been most popularly stated by Justice Holmes:

We admit that in many places and in ordinary times the defendants in saying all that was said in the circular would have been within their constitutional rights. But the character of every act depends upon the circumstances in which it is done. . . . The question in every case is whether the words used are used in such circumstances and are of such a nature as to create a clear and present danger that they will bring about the substantive evils that Congress has a right to prevent. It is a question of proximity and degree. When a nation is at war many things that might be said in time of peace are such a hindrance to its effort that their utterance will not be endured so long as men fight and that no Court could regard them as protected by any constitutional right.[14]

We find here, in this 1919 opinion for the unanimous court in *Schenck v. United States*—an opinion in which the conviction of the defendants was upheld—the well-known "clear and present danger" language.[15] The critical sentence, at least in the light of my discussion thus far in this chapter, may well be, "When a nation is at war many things that might be said in time of peace are such a hindrance to its effort that their utterance will not be endured so long as men fight and that no Court could regard them as protected by any constitutional right." But, unlike the *habeas corpus* provision in Article I, section 9 of the Constitution and unlike the quartering of soldiers provision in the Third Amendment, the First Amendment does not distinguish between war and peace. Even the qualification with respect to the writ of *habeas corpus*, it should be noted, is not an automatic wartime exception, but rather one that is carefully drawn so as to be operative only in times of "Rebellion or Invasion," and even then only "when . . . the public Safety may require it."

The successors to Justice Holmes made even more permissive the qualifications he legitimated—and the improvident justice was powerless to restore the barriers he had overturned with his rhetorical flourish.[16] The inability of Justice Holmes to correct what he had done testifies to the prudence of an absolute restraint with respect to certain matters.[17] The extent to which the First Amendment restraint had been diluted is suggested by the language of Judge Learned Hand in his 1950 opinion in *Dennis* v. *United States* affirming the conviction of the first Communist Party leaders prosecuted under the Smith Act:[18] "In each case [courts] must ask whether the gravity of the 'evil,' discounted by its improbability, justifies such invasion of free speech as is necessary to avoid the danger."[19] The trial judge's instruction to the jury in *Dennis* had interpreted the statute (set forth in note 18 of this chapter) in this manner:

> . . . it is not the abstract doctrine of overthrowing or destroying organized government by unlawful means which is denounced by this law, but the teaching and advocacy of action for the accomplishment of that purpose, by language reasonably and ordinarily calculated to incite persons to such action. Accordingly, you cannot find the defendants or any of them guilty of the crime charged unless you are satisfied beyond a reasonable doubt that they conspired to organize a society, group and assembly of persons who teach and advocate the overthrow or destruction of the Government of the United States by force and violence and to advocate and teach the duty and necessity of overthrowing or destroying the Government of the United States by force and violence, with the intent that such teaching and advocacy be of a rule or principle of action and by language reasonably and ordinarily calculated to incite persons to such action, all with the intent to cause the overthrow or destruction of the Government of the United States by force and violence as speedily as circumstances would permit.[20]

This consideration—"as speedily as circumstances would permit"—eliminates whatever restraint on Congress Justice Holmes had hoped to retain in his "clear and present danger" test and whatever restraint Justice Brandeis had tried to restore in his 1927 reformulation of that test in *Whitney v. California*.[21] The trial judge's interpretation, which was sustained by both Judge Hand and the Supreme Court, virtually makes bad intention (or perhaps even bad character) criminal in these matters. For, the reader is asked to decide upon careful reading of the trial judge's charge, just what *action* on the part of defendants is required to establish criminality (in addition to some indication, evidently by means of speeches that have been made, of bad intention)?

Does not the devout Christian also take part in a "conspiracy" to overthrow by force and violence, with the aid of the awaited Messiah, all governments on earth, "as speedily as circumstances would permit"? The absurdity of this question is no doubt far more evident than its pertinency—but then, many (and probably all) of the sedition prosecutions in this century by the general government have been absurd. In any event, every student of this subject should study the circular (see Appendix B) which was the basis of the indictment in the *Schenck* case and with respect to which Justice Holmes invented the "clear and present danger" test, thereby supplying the decisive intellectual support for a half-century of First Amendment decisions. The *Schenck* circular is, indeed, "that famous text of which so many have talked, and which so few have read."[22]

It is significant that the courts often admit that the action of the general government, in applying particular laws of Congress, does abridge something which can be called "freedom of speech, or of the press." Another opinion in the *Dennis* case, "concurring in affirmance" by Justice Frankfurter (a writer with a reputation for precision), includes the typical admission: "The Smith Act and this conviction under it no doubt restrict the exercise of free speech and assembly. Does that, without more, dispose of the matter?"[23] Why not?[24] How should the justice have answered a similar question respecting a special act of Congress designed to "diminish during [his] Continuance in Office" the compensation he was to receive? The prohibition against such legislation with respect to compensation (in Article III, section 1 of the Constitution) is no more "absolute"[25] and no more important than the First Amendment prohibition against congressional legislation "restrict[ing] the exercise of free speech and assembly."[26]

Does not the exception developed by Justice Holmes and his successors tend to imply that the First Amendment merely cautions Congress that it should not prohibit or punish any speech which does not seem to reasonable men to require legislation?[27] Presumably, this caution might well be applied to all the legislative powers Congress might claim.[28] According to the view of those who thus sanction an abridgment of freedom of speech and of the press, the First Amendment would seem to say little more to Congress than, *Be legislators.*[29]

VI

Let me sum up what I have said, and anticipate much of the discussion that follows, by indulging in a little clarifying exaggeration.

The Constitution of the United States, if read as the courts and Congress have read the First Amendment, can be reduced (now that the Congress, President, and Judiciary have been established) to five simple provisions:

THE CONSTITUTION OF THE UNITED STATES

Article I: *The Congress of the United States shall make the laws.*

Article II: *The President of the United States shall execute the laws.*

Article III: *The Courts of the United States shall interpret the laws.*

Article IV: *The States should not get in the way.*

Bill of Rights: *Everybody should try to do his best and, when possible, behave himself.*

Would it be "to consider too curiously, to consider so?"[30]

VII

There may develop circumstances in which constitutional government must be temporarily sacrificed in order that it may be permanently saved. It is not inconceivable that there may again someday have to be recourse in America to emergency measures such as those which the Continental Congress was driven to when it gave General Washington dictatorial powers.[31] In such circumstances, our unwritten Constitution, incorporating the fundamental principles and aspirations of the American Republic,[32] may have to be looked to for guidance. Those would indeed be extreme, perhaps even catastrophic circumstances, circumstances which are impossible to predict and for which no adequate provision can be made in a written constitution but only in the character of a people. The most unexceptionable and even the most salutary part of a written constitution might, in some extreme circumstances, have to be suspended temporarily for the common good. In such emergencies, it would be folly to insist upon being bound by all constitutional limitations and directives.[33]

The effect of Justice Holmes's revision of the First Amendment, however, is to treat the Constitution during every emergency, or expectation of emergency, as if the most extreme emergency had developed. The result is that a far-reaching qualification has been, more than a century after the ratification of the Bill of Rights in 1791 and its political vindication in 1800, read into the First Amendment, a qualification the effect of which is (despite the relaxation of the 1960s) that there is in principle no substantial protection for freedom of speech to be drawn from the amendment.[34] When pressed far enough—as far as we have seen it go, even in time of peace, since the Second World War—Justice Holmes's doctrine means that no speech should be protected which is "not [to] be endured so long as men fight." Thus, when constitutional protection for unpopular discussion of vital public issues is most needed, the sovereign citizen body is told that it is not the time for talking.[35]

This revised constitutional doctrine tries to cope with the problem of dangerous talk. However narrowly "freedom of speech" is interpreted—provided it *is* conceded that it stands for *something*—there can surely arise circumstances in which the insulation of even that much from abridgment can threaten harm to the community. The "clear and present danger" test tends to conceal this problem by seeming to provide a solution to it. The test thereby serves to conceal the distinctive solutions provided in the overall constitutional scheme,[36] solutions which are more likely to be appreciated if one

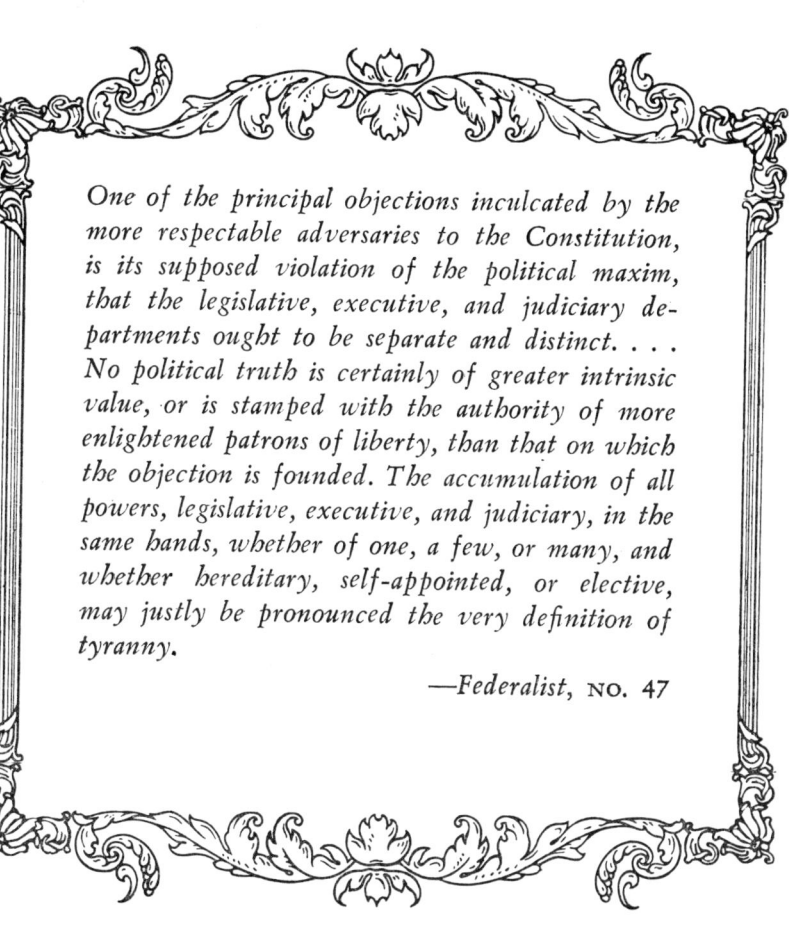

One of the principal objections inculcated by the more respectable adversaries to the Constitution, is its supposed violation of the political maxim, that the legislative, executive, and judiciary departments ought to be separate and distinct.... No political truth is certainly of greater intrinsic value, or is stamped with the authority of more enlightened patrons of liberty, than that on which the objection is founded. The accumulation of all powers, legislative, executive, and judiciary, in the same hands, whether of one, a few, or many, and whether hereditary, self-appointed, or elective, may justly be pronounced the very definition of tyranny.

—Federalist, NO. 47

accepts the absolute nature of the restraint upon Congress imposed by the First Amendment.

Those who deny or disparage the absoluteness of the restraint in the First Amendment usually labor under a misapprehension either as to what *is* thus protected or as to what activities of government are governed by the provision.[37] Thus they point to exceptions that any reasonable man is obliged to concede and thereby believe it to be demonstrated that the First Amendment cannot be accepted as it stands.[38]

Once the student appreciates the absoluteness of the restraint of the First Amendment, he is motivated[39] to consider properly two problems immediately suggested by the amendment, the problems I discuss in chapters 4 and 5: Against whom is this unqualified restraint directed? What is it that is absolutely protected in this way?

IV. "ALL LEGISLATIVE POWERS HEREIN GRANTED"

I

"CONGRESS SHALL make no law . . . abridging the freedom of speech, or of the press . . ." Simply stated, it seems to be Congress—or, perhaps, the government of the United States—in its lawmaking capacity which is restrained from abridging freedom of speech or of the press.

It is important to be clear about this. An absolute prohibition becomes feasible only when it is confined to its proper sphere and directed against the appropriate agent. In fact, an absolute prohibition that is not properly limited in its application tends to buckle under the strain of the necessities that governments encounter.[1]

There is, nevertheless, a natural tendency to extend as much as possible the application of a salutary restraint upon government from the sphere where it is most appropriate to all others in which abuses of power are anticipated. The danger is, however, that such indiscriminate extension will only dissipate the strength of the original restraint. To return to an earlier illustration, the effectiveness of a particular levee along a rampaging river is probably reduced by the erection of other levees in the neighborhood: the force concentrated on the original levee increases as avenues for expenditure of energy elsewhere along the river banks are blocked off.

The engineer who tries to protect too much may succeed only in protecting nothing adequately. If, as the courts often say, the Fourteenth Amendment extends fully against the states all the restraints on the government of the United States imposed by the First Amendment, there may be here an instance of "engineers" who, forgetting the nature of government and of men, tried to protect too much and perhaps sacrificed that which had once been securely protected.

Thus, I say with Madison that "I am inclined to think that *absolute* restrictions in cases that are doubtful, or where emergencies may overrule them, ought to be avoided."[2]

II

It seems, according to the First Amendment, that Congress in its lawmaking capacity is restrained from abridging freedom of speech or of the press. What activities of the government of the United States are subject to this control?

We are told in the opening provision of the Constitution that "All legislative Powers herein granted shall be vested in a Congress of the United States, which shall consist of a Senate and House of Representatives." This may seem to be qualified somewhat by the role given the President. As Alexander White observed, "The two Houses of Congress, with the qualified negative of the President, formed the legislative power of the United States. . . ." (*Annals, I,* p. 359) Madison made a more extended explanation:

The Legislative powers are vested in Congress, and are to be exercised by them uncontrolled by any other department, except the Constitution has qualified it otherwise. The Constitution has qualified the Legislative power, by authorizing the President to object to any act it may pass, requiring, in this case, two-thirds of both Houses to concur in making a law; but still the absolute Legislative power is vested in the Congress with this qualification alone. [*Annals, I,* p. 463]

Thus, if Congress is effectively restrained with respect to laws abridging freedom of speech or of the press, the lawmaking power of the government of the United States is thereby restrained.

The critical role assigned to Congress is indicated throughout the Constitution. The extent and concerns of the general government are marked out for the most part by the objects and powers allotted to Congress.[3] Thus, Madison speaks of "the Legislative power" as being not only "the most essential part of any free Government, but much the most extensive and essential in the Government of the United States." (*Annals*, I, p. 908) Ames immediately qualified Madison's observation by expressing the hope that

> it would never be considered, either within or without these walls, that the two Houses of Congress are the Government of the United States. He contemplated this Government as a Government of laws, and not of men. The makers of them could command nothing as to themselves; the Executive, with the Judges, were those who exercised the authority of the law. . . . [*Annals*, I, p. 909]

The emphasis is on law, which first must be made and under the authority of which the other departments of the government perform their proper roles.

It is apparent from the debates in the First Congress in the course of the framing of the Bill of Rights that it was thought the restraints then being defined would effectively control the government of the United States. Thus, Egbert Benson observed, "The committee who framed this report proceeded on the principle that these rights belonged to the people; they conceived them to be inherent; and all that they meant to provide against was their being infringed by the Government." (*Annals*, I, pp. 731-32) "Congress" and "the General Government," as the bodies being subjected to restraints, are often used interchangeably in the discussions.[4]

The use of "Congress" in the First Amendment, and only in that amendment, however, has given rise to the suggestion that the remainder, or almost all of the remainder, of the first ten amendments were intended to apply to the states as well as to the general government. The tenor of the discussion, as well as the form given to amendment proposals (both those accepted and those rejected), on the other hand, suggests to me a reluctance to impose any additional restraints upon the states. Only one amendment approved by the House of Representatives was clearly intended to restrain the states:

No State shall infringe the right of trial by Jury in criminal cases, nor the rights of conscience, nor the freedom of speech, or of the press.[5]

This proposed amendment was rejected by the Senate and hence was never submitted to the states for ratification. The most critical division in the First Congress on these matters was between two principal groups: one (the majority) opposed any amendments which cut into the legislative powers of the general government (especially with respect to commerce, revenue, war, and diplomacy); the other tried to impose such restrictions upon the general government even as they complained that the state governments had been too severely curtailed by the new Constitution.[6]

A decisive consideration here draws upon the preamble sent with what is now known as the Bill of Rights by Congress to the states which were to ratify the proposed amendments:

The Conventions of a number of the States having, at the time of their adopting the Constitution, expressed a desire, in order to prevent misconstruction or abuse of its powers, that further declaratory and restrictive clauses should be added; and as extending the grounds of public confidence in the Government, will best insure the beneficent ends of its institution. . . .[7]

The "powers" and "Government" referred to as objects of concern are obviously those determined by the Constitution. One need only consult the suggested amendments that were collected in the "Conventions of a number of the States" to substantiate this: they do not ask for restrictions upon the state governments. This preamble was written in the Senate, after the proposed limitation on the states with respect to trial by jury, freedom of speech and of the press, and the rights of conscience had there been eliminated from the list of amendments sent from the House.

There *are* limitations upon the states in the original Constitution (as in Article I, section 10), but most of these seem to be designed primarily to prevent the states from impeding the general government in the conduct of the affairs entrusted to its management.

The Bill of Rights, on the other hand, seems to be directed primarily, and probably exclusively, against the general government.[8]

III

What I mean by "legislation" and by "Congress in its lawmaking capacity" can be further defined by suggesting what activities of the general government are *not* included within the restraints of the First Amendment.

Congress as a deliberative body, or either house as a branch of the legislature, may not be directly affected by the restraint. Each house is authorized by Article I, section 5 of the Constitution to make its rules for conducting business. These rules can prescribe conduct in a house that legislation of the Congress probably cannot prescribe for the country at large: speakers can be silenced and topics of discussion can be strictly regulated; a member of the House of Representatives can be obliged "to confine himself to the point" of the subject before the House (*Annals*, I, p. 388); the House has rules of "Decorum and Debate" (*Annals*, I, pp. 99-100); the public can be forbidden to participate in the House's debates; petitions brought before the House may be required to be presented "in a decent manner." (*Annals*, I, p. 607)[9] We need not say that the First Amendment concerns itself with these matters:[10] these exercises of the rule-making power are *not* regulations which amount to laws abridging (or even affecting) the freedom of speech or of the press *of the country at large*.

Should the Congress or either house attempt by means of this rule-making power to have the effect in the country at large that a straightforward legislative enactment would have, the First Amendment restraints might then be applicable. It was recognized from the earliest days of the Republic, as reflected in the following comment by Madison, that an ordinarily legitimate exercise of power may sometimes conceal an effort to achieve an illegitimate object:

If the principle of proportioning the allowance to the quantum of services performed obtains, it will be found that the Judiciary will be as dependent on the Legislative authority, as if the Legislature was to declare what shall be their salary for the succeeding year; because, by abridging their services at every session, we could reduce them to such a degree, as to require a very trifling compensation indeed. . . . [*Annals*, I, pp. 648-49][11]

When we speak of "an illegitimate object" we may take our bearings from the First Amendment. Any legislative activity of the general government must conform, at least in its principal intended effects, to the standards and purposes of the First Amendment.[12] Nor can the rule-making power of the House or Senate be used by Congress as a substitute for legislative power. This restraint depends not merely upon the First Amendment but rather upon the general structure of the government and upon the resulting requirements for a duly established law. Here, as elsewhere, we are free and even obliged, in the words I associate with Chief Justice Marshall, to "strike through the mask."[13]

On its own floor, or in conducting its business as a legislative body, it seems that each house of Congress is left free to abridge what may be called freedom of speech. Complications arise, however, whenever there is a question whether the activity under scrutiny *is* directly related to the conduct of a legislative body. It seems to have been unquestioned since the First Congress that house debates could be held in secret.[14] Can anything other than holding closed sessions be done to insure that debates will not be "interfered with" (that is, discussed and criticized) by such outsiders as newspaper reporters and public commentators?[15]

James Jackson, in stating his opposition to *any* bill of rights, made an observation which suggests that he thought it arguable that Congress (and hence each house of Congress) had power to supervise what is written elsewhere about debates, a power which he was certain Congress would never exercise:

The gentleman endeavors to secure the liberty of the press; pray how is this in danger? There is no power given to Congress to regulate this subject as they can commerce, or peace, or war. Has any transaction taken place to make us suppose such an amendment necessary? An honorable gentleman, a member of this House, has been attacked in the public newspapers on account of sentiments delivered on this floor. Have Congress taken any notice of it? Have they ordered the writer before them, even for a breach of privilege, although the Constitution provides that a member shall not be questioned in any place for any speech or debate in the House? No; these things are offered to the public view, and held up to the inspection of the world. These are principles which will always prevail. I am not afraid, nor are other members, I believe, our conduct should meet the severest scrutiny. Where, then, is the necessity of taking measures to secure what neither is nor can be in danger? [*Annals*, I, pp. 442-43]

Although a constitutional provision (Article I, section 6) is cited as the source of the power which Congress may have to supervise what is written elsewhere about debates, is it not here assumed by Jackson that to exercise even such power in this way might constitute an invasion of the "liberty of the press"?[16]

Aedanus Burke, on a later occasion, defended a resolution which declared,

> That to misrepresent the debates of the House, whether it arises from incapacity, inattention, or partiality, has a mischievous tendency to infringe the freedom of debate, and that this House should no longer give sanction to it. [*Annals*, I, p. 917]

It was proposed in this resolution that the privilege be withdrawn from press reporters of sitting "at the very foot of the Speaker's chair, [which] gives a sanction and authenticity to [their] publications. . . ." (*Annals*, I, p. 917) Thus, "liberty of the press" seems here to have been balanced against "freedom of debate."[17] The difficulty placed in the way of full and frank debate by distorted reporting is suggested by Gerry:

> . . . the printers had it in their power, by misrepresentation, to make whom they pleased ridiculous in the eyes of the world, or to exalt those whose sentiments they favored. Viewing the publications in this point of light, they were matters of serious reflection; and, if they were conducted on principles of party, they might be one of the most dangerous engines in the hands of faction, and have a malignant and mischievous tendency upon the public voice of America. The debates of the British Parliament are not published, it is true; they never permit them to be taken down, they never give them the least sanction; because they know the serious consequences resulting from an improper use of such a liberty. But, notwithstanding all this, he was in favor of disseminating useful information, by a correct and impartial publication of the speeches. [*Annals*, I, p. 918]

Hartley, on the other hand, went so far as to suggest that he "contemplated the question as involving in it an attack upon the liberty of the press." (*Annals*, I, p. 919) But this resolution had already been withdrawn and no action was taken on the question. Perhaps the debate was sufficient to restrain the press. It seems to have been assumed, despite Hartley's objection, that the house did have the power, in the interest of "freedom of debate," to take *some* action against distorted accounts of its debates. It is in areas such as these that the distinction between making general laws and determining the rules of legislative proceedings becomes blurred.[18]

Similar problems arise with respect to other activities of Congress. Thus, the extent to which congressional resolutions were thought by some to be subject to the constitutional restraints applicable to legislation is suggested by the discussion of a proposed resolution to the effect that a joint committee of both houses be directed to wait upon the President to request that he recommend to the people a day of public thanksgiving and prayer, acknowledging God's favors, "especially by affording them an opportunity peaceably to establish a Constitution of government for their safety and happiness." (*Annals*, I, p. 914) Tucker's comment was that he

> thought the House had no business to interfere in a matter which did not concern them. Why should the President direct the people to do what, perhaps, they have no mind to do? They may not be inclined to return thanks for a Constitution until they have experienced that it promotes their safety and happiness. We do not yet know but they may have reason to be dissatisfied with the effects it has already produced; but whether this be so or not, it is a business with which Congress have nothing to do; it is a religious matter, and, as such, is proscribed to us. If a day of thanksgiving must take place, let it be done by the authority of the several States; they know best what reason their constituents have to be pleased with the establishment of this Constitution. [*Annals*, I, p. 915]

Thus it can be seen that Tucker, who was often found among that minority in the First Congress which was inclined to deplore and to attempt to limit the powers of the general government, was disposed to have even congressional resolutions subjected to the standards applied to legislation. Resolutions that are intended to have the effect of general laws should certainly have applied to them the restraints imposed by the Constitution on the lawmaking power of Congress.[19]

Much of what I have said here about Congress as a rule-making body—a body that regulates its own activities and controls the conditions for effective conduct of its business—can be said as well about Congress as an investigatory body. Congress, or either house of Congress, when it investigates—usually through a congressional committee—is not, in one sense, making laws. Rather, it may be deciding what legislation is needed.[20] A congressional committee is left free, so far as the First Amendment is concerned, to control what is said before it: witnesses are not permitted to speak as they wish and on whatever subject they choose; the committee can decide on the manner and extent of the testimony it will receive; the purpose of the committee, not that of the witnesses, determines procedures and agenda.[21]

Such an extensive power can no doubt be abused. When the subject being investigated is controversial enough, it is almost inevitable that it should be abused, whether it is an investigation of financiers in the 1930s, of Communists in the 1940s and 1950s, or of labor racketeers thereafter.[22] If congressional investigations are but the mask for legislation, the First Amendment should apply: Congress cannot abridge the freedom of speech of the community by adopting the policy of subjecting to punitive interrogation those who hold unpopular opinions. What Congress cannot do to the country at large by means of law, it should not be able to do without law.

It is not to the First Amendment, however, but to the Constitution as a whole that recourse should usually be had to correct or prevent the major abuses of Congress's power to investigate. There are two principal justifications for the power to investigate: that Congress must be left free to secure information which may serve as a basis for legislation, and (a related but subordinate point) that Congress must be able to determine how the laws already enacted are being enforced.[23] Or, put in Ames's terms, "a select committee [is] much better calculated to consider and arrange a complex business than [the entire House of Representatives]; he thought they were like the senses to the soul, and . . . could be made equally useful." (*Annals*, I, p. 663)

When the purpose of an investigation goes clearly beyond these "sensory" activities, the likelihood exists of usurpation on the part of Congress. The most critical usurpation, and the one most apt to result in abuses affecting the rights of individuals and the liberties of the community, is seen when Congress sets out to expose wrongdoers. The congressional committee sits, in this capacity, as "the Grand Jury of America" (a phrase occasionally used by its apologists). But Congress is a legislature; it cannot assume, except in the carefully defined impeachment contingency, the judicial role.²⁴ Congressmen are not able to approach individual cases with that disinterestedness and isolation from popular passion we expect from judges, especially judges who have been carefully chosen for appointment to lifetime posts. When the congressional committee sets out to expose and condemn, and even to some extent to punish, it is no longer "like the senses to the soul"; rather, it usurps the roles of the executive and judicial powers.

An application of the constitutional doctrine of "the separation of powers" should serve as a sufficient safeguard against most of the abuses of congressional committees that we have seen in recent decades. The simplest, and most effective, check upon such abuses—a check that would not significantly interfere with the power of Congress to perform its legislative function—would be for Congress (except in the most extraordinary cases) to deny its committees the power of subpoena and the power to compel testimony. Congress would still obtain all information that it otherwise gets—a refusal to testify is rarely informative—whether from financiers, Communists, or labor leaders, when it announces the general purposes of its investigation.²⁵

Thus, the abuses we have seen in congressional investigations can be substantially prevented by adherence to basic constitutional doctrine, not by an attempt to employ the First Amendment where it was not intended.²⁶ Related to the application of this constitutional doctrine is the requirement that the subject under investigation should be one with respect to which Congress *does* have the power to legislate. If the subject either has not been brought within the scope of congressional control or has been taken, in whole or in part, out of the hands of Congress, then an attempted investigation would be to no purpose and without foundation.²⁷ The First Amendment may be relevant here, at least to the extent that it leaves or takes jurisdiction over a subject, in whole or in part, out of the hands of Congress.

A more direct role for the First Amendment is implied in the argument that since legislation is needed to enforce the powers of an investigatory committee, this legislation should be evaluated in the light of the First Amendment, an evaluation that should take into account the subject matter of the particular investigation that is being conducted.²⁸ But, on the other hand, should we not say that the legislation which provides means of enforcing the prerogatives of investigatory committees is perfectly proper and that it is, so far as the First Amendment is concerned, only an accidental or incidental aspect of the application of that legislation that is offensive?[29] Thus, any legislation designed to support the investigatory power of Congress, if it is vulnerable, is likely to be so primarily because it assigns a judicial function to the legislature. One can also hope, of course, that the Congress can be brought to redevelop a sense of decorum and discretion with respect to such matters, rather than uncritically endorse and support those committees that are challenged and resisted by conscientious citizens.[30]

Congress can make no law—in fact, I have gone almost so far as to argue, can take no action (as legislature for the Union)—abridging the freedom of speech of the country at large, whatever it might do to provide that its own deliberations are conducted without outside interference. But can Congress (in exercising its freedom to speak) urge or request others to abridge freedom of speech? The First Congress resolved,

> That it be recommended to the Legislatures of the several States, to pass laws making it expressly the duty of the keepers of their jails, to receive, and safe keep therein, all prisoners commited under the authority of the United States. . . . [*Annals*, I, pp. 903-4]

A similar use of state institutions is indicated in Roger Sherman's suggestion that the states might be relied upon, by recourse to their respective modes of taxation, to collect for the general government the taxes laid by Congress. Thus, he notes, it would not be necessary "to adopt one uniform method of collecting direct taxes." (*Annals*, I, p. 777) Can a similar reliance be placed by Congress upon the power of the states to abridge, when necessary, freedom of speech? That is, cannot Congress exercise its collective "freedom of speech" to suggest to state legislatures how they might best exercise their powers over speech and the press? Perhaps this option in Congress helps make workable the federalism which is vital to American liberty. The exercise of such an option by Congress might not be subject to the prohibitions of the First Amendment.

There is one aspect of the lawmaking power of Congress that I have yet to consider for purposes of determining the extent to which the First Amendment limits what Congress may do. Does not the First Amendment, when it refers to "Congress," speak of Congress in its role as legislature for the government of the United States, that is, for the country at large? But there is also a role for Congress similar to that of the legislatures of the several states. For Congress is, in effect, the "state legislature" for that district incorporating the permanent seat of the general government or it is the "city council" for the capital city (which is coextensive with the federal district). The powers it has for this purpose may be more than, or at least in place of, those it has as legislature for the country at large. Should Congress as legislature for the federal district (as well as for American territories) be limited by the restraints that are imposed on Congress as the legislature for the Union?[31]

One of the acts of the First Congress provided

> that a district of territory, not exceeding ten miles square, to be located as hereafter directed, on the river Potomac . . . be, and the same is hereby, accepted for the permanent seat of Government of the United States: *Provided, nevertheless*, that the operation of the laws of the State within such district shall not be affected by this acceptance, until the time fixed for the removal of the Government thereto, and until Congress shall otherwise by law provide. [*Annals*, I, p. 2234]

The rationale of this provision was stated by Madison at a time when it appeared that the federal district would be located in Pennsylvania:

> . . . he wished, however, that the House would provide against one inconvenience, which was, to prevent the district in Pennsylvania, chosen by Congress, from being deprived for a time of the benefit of the laws. This, he apprehended, would be the case, unless Congress made provision for the operation of the laws of Pennsylvania, in the act by which they accepted of the cession of that State; for the State relinquished the right of legislation from the moment that Congress accepted of the district. [*Annals*, I, p. 926]

It is evident in Madison's statement that Congress's powers in the proposed federal district would not be limited to those ordinarily exercised by Congress in governing the country at large. (We shall return to this problem when I discuss in chapter 6 the limited power of Congress, even before the adoption of the First Amendment, with respect to speech and the press.)

I have suggested that "Congress" and "law" in the First Amendment should be taken with reference to the duties of the legislature of the general government as the legislature for the Union. I have also suggested several distinctions that a lawyer, who may be obliged to make all legitimate arguments on behalf of his client's cause, would be likely to disparage or at least ignore in his effort to advance that cause.[32] It is not to be expected that reliance on the august First Amendment will be foregone whenever it is possible to draw it into litigation. The only practicable way to avoid such disregard of distinctions is to be found not in the self-restraint of partisan lawyers but in the ability of "enlightened patrons of liberty" to set forth clearly and persuasively what is properly governed by various parts of the Constitution.

IV

The problem of freedom of speech in the United States today is, in large part, the problem of how the President influences his subordinates to behave. Executive innovations such as the federal loyalty programs have had a serious effect on freedom of speech.[33] The conditions permitted to develop since the programs were announced in 1947 helped make possible the sensational congressional investigations, the espionage scares, and the relentless Smith Act prosecutions we were subjected to. These conditions also permitted and induced frightened men in state governments to embark on uninformed campaigns against "subversives." (The promotion to high judicial office of men who had contributed to this devastation only made matters worse.) The national loyalty programs combined on a large scale, but with the ominous mystery of the Star Chamber, certain features both of the eighteenth-century prosecutions for seditious libel and of the "Palmer Raids" of January, 1920. A paralyzing state of intimidation threatened to settle down upon us.

Men truly bred to the law would almost instinctively have appreciated that much of what has been done in suppressing American Communists since the Second World War by the general government simply did not conform to traditional standards of legal propriety. One elementary constitutional principle has yet to be generally recognized even by critics of the loyalty programs: the Executive has no authority under the Constitution to make laws; all lawmaking power therein granted is clearly and deliberately vested in the Congress of the United States, and nowhere else.[34]

Congress has acquiesced in the usurpation which has seen the President establish, and maintain at great public expense, an elaborate government within the government, a government that makes "laws"[35] and holds "trials." I am reminded not only of the warning in *Federalist* No. 47 (seen in the epigraph to this chapter) but also of an episode that drew Judge Blackstone's scorn:

> It must be however remarked, that (particularly in [the later years of the administration of Henry VIII]) the royal prerogative was then strained to a very tyrannical and oppressive height; and, what was the worst circumstance, its encroachments were established by law, under the sanction of those pusillanimous parliaments, one of which, to its eternal disgrace, passed a statute, whereby it was enacted that the king's proclamations should have the force of acts of parliament; and others concurred in the creation of that amazing heap of wild and new-fangled treasons, which were slightly touched upon in a former chapter. Happily for the nation, this arbitrary reign was succeeded by the minority of an amiable prince; during the short sunshine of which, great part of these extravagant laws were repealed.[36]

It is to be hoped that any Congress which should reclaim the powers "justly belonging to it under the Constitution" would revive as well its sense of respect for the First Amendment of that Constitution.[37]

The President is not mentioned in the First Amendment, except as part of that "Government" to which petitions for redress of grievances may be addressed. But the President, with his duty to take care "that the Laws be faithfully executed," should be dependent on what Congress has done. And, if the Constitution is adhered to by Congress, none of the laws to be executed should be laws "respecting an establishment of religion, or prohibiting the free exercise thereof; or abridging the freedom of speech, or of the press. . . ." Whether the President is obliged not to execute a law which, in fact, abridges freedom of speech need not be a critical concern of this study.[38] Rather, it is but an instance (which can be vital for the nature of our community) of the general problem of the constitutional relation between Congress and the President.[39]

It is important, for a proper understanding of the American Constitution, not to underestimate the dominant role of Congress in the original conception. The Legislative Article is the first with which the reader is confronted.[40] What is said there determines, in great part, the scope of the Executive and Judiciary. This is reflected in the fact that, in the various state ratifying conventions, the discussion of the Constitution opened with an examination of Article I (the Legislative Article); and in most of them, of which a record survives, the bulk of the discussion (and sometimes all of it) is restricted to a close study of various sections of that first article.[41] A restriction then upon the exercise of power by Congress—unless it is so done as to place that power in the hands of another branch of government—is, in effect, a restriction upon the other branches of the general government as well.[42]

It is significant that none of the amendatory proposals suggested by Madison were to have been included in the Executive Article. This too suggests that the Executive was to be primarily limited to and by the obligation to see that the laws were faithfully executed. If Congress is effectively limited—if Congress's powers are adequately defined—then (it was thought) there is not much danger from the Executive, especially when there is an explicit provision for impeachment of the President and when such self-serving executive prerogatives as the power to grant titles of nobility have been suppressed. Indeed, Madison observed in the First Congress,

> In our Government it is, perhaps, less necessary to guard against the abuse in the Executive Department than any other; because it is not the stronger branch of the system, but the weaker. It therefore must be levelled against the Legislative, for it is the most powerful, and most likely to be abused, because it is under the least control. [*Annals*, I, p. 437][43]

The preeminence of Congress is seen also in Madison's emphasis upon legislative constructions of the Constitution:

> . . . I feel the importance of the question [of the removal power], and know that our decision will involve the decision of all similar cases. The decision that is at this time made, will become the permanent exposition of the Constitution; and on a permanent exposition of the Constitution will depend the genius and character of the whole Government. It will depend, perhaps, on this decision, whether the Government shall retain that equilibrium which the Constitution intended, or take a direction towards aristocracy or anarchy among the members of the Government. Hence, how carefully ought we to be to give a true direction to a power so critically circumstanced! [*Annals*, I, p. 495][44]

But the President does have other functions in addition to those defined by Congress or otherwise resulting from his exercise of "the executive Power" (Article II, section 1). He shall be commander in chief of the armed forces of the United States; he may, with the advice and consent of the Senate, make treaties; he shall from time to time give to Congress information of the state of the Union and recommend to its consideration such measures as he shall judge necessary and expedient. The power of the President as commander in chief of the armed forces seems, to some extent, independent of legislative enactments, even though Congress does have power to make certain rules for the armed forces and to provide for such forces.[45] The Third Amendment, regulating the quartering of troops, can be considered as addressing the President as well as Congress, inasmuch as he might have claimed a power as commander in chief, independent of Congress, to provide for housing troops under his command. Does the First Amendment, too, reach the activities of the President, particularly those of the commander in chief?

The right to speak freely suffers, in the armed forces, the fate of other rights the citizen usually exercises without restraint: the right to move about freely, to choose his occupation and associates, to dress as he pleases.[46] Serious burdens would be imposed on military leaders if soldiers continued to exercise while on duty all the rights of the citizen.[47] The commander in chief, and his subordinates, must be left free to regulate such incidents of life for the citizen in his military capacity as his residence, occupation, and dress.[48]

Restraints on these incidents are imposed either by the exercise of power inherent in the Executive (as commander in chief) under the Constitution or by virtue of authority granted by Congress in accordance with its power "To make Rules for the Government and Regulation of the land and naval Forces" (Article I, section 8). But, whether instituted by the Executive or by Congress, restraints among the military on expression do not seem to constitute an abridgment of "freedom of speech." This anticipates my discussion (in section 9 of chapter 5) of the kinds of expression and discussion encompassed by this First Amendment term. It suffices at this point simply to note that freedom of speech is not required for military life: citizens cannot be regarded as self-governing while they are actually performing their military duties.[49]

So far as the proper regulation of the armed forces is concerned, the omission from the First Amendment of any reference to the President may be seen as no more than an abundance of caution: a restraint upon the President probably would not have been taken in any event as affecting his control of the military.[50] There are, however, circumstances arising out of his roles both as the paramount executive officer of the Union and as commander in chief of the armed forces that might call for the execution of laws abridging freedom of speech, circumstances that alone might justify silence about any prohibition of the President's executing laws abridging freedom of speech.[51] Our concern, then, is not so much to see why the President is not mentioned in the First Amendment, but rather to indicate the extent to which the President *is* left free with respect to these matters. He is left free, that is, to the extent that he either exercises power not dependent on congressional legislation or executes laws that are enacted by an authority less fettered than Congress's.

There may be circumstances in which the President should apply or execute *state* laws abridging freedom of speech. Military forces might be required to put down rebellion in a state (upon request of that state) or to repel invasion of a state. If martial law is legitimately invoked,[52] there is no problem, for the provisions of the First Amendment probably would not apply. But there may be good reasons for enforcing, to the extent possible, the laws of the state. In such an emergency, state laws abridging freedom of speech (the legitimacy of which would not be affected by the First Amendment) might properly be employed or at least recognized by the President so long as he acts in the place of or on behalf of the state executive.[53]

There seems to be still another instance in which the President can so act constitutionally as to abridge freedom of speech. Once the writ of *habeas corpus* has been suspended by appropriate action, in the cases specified, the President is able, subject to later suit (or even, in extreme cases, impeachment) for false or improper arrest, to hold citizens for the commission of acts against which Congress could not constitutionally legislate.[54] Thus, the President (subject to limits set by Congress) can hold whomever he chooses to arrest in such circumstances. This could include those whose speaking or possibility of speaking he thought harmful to the country, even though that speech would be perfectly legal otherwise and would come well within the meaning of "freedom of speech" as it is ordinarily understood.[55]

The suspension of the writ of *habeas corpus* is one of the constitutional alternatives to the remedy that is offered by Justice Holmes's "clear and present danger" test. Such suspension is obviously a serious measure and not one to be undertaken lightly. I know of no instance of allegedly criminal political speech prosecuted this century in the federal courts that called for such drastic action, at least not in the country at large. But, the Constitution may be taken as saying, if our public servants will not declare the danger clear, serious, and present enough to call for the suspension of the writ of *habeas corpus,* then freedom of speech is to be left unimpaired, so far as the general government is concerned. If, however, a suspension is decreed, then the President may constitutionally take measures which would have the effect of a law abridging freedom of speech.[56]

Since the states, under both the original Constitution and the First Amendment, remain free to abridge freedom of speech and of the press, they are equipped to deal with any danger which is not so formidable as to require suspension of the writ of *habeas corpus*, but which is serious and immediate enough to move some men to have recourse to the "clear and present danger" test.[57] Should not the President (as well as Congress) advise the states of developments with respect to which the states might not otherwise take a national view, requesting that the states exercise their powers to abridge freedom of speech? Such a guide to state legislative action might on occasion be desirable. We see it today, for example, in presidential conferences on traffic laws, laws which are still regarded as largely within the primary jurisdiction of state governments.[58] The President is left free (as Congress may be when it acts by resolution) not to give orders but to offer *advice* on any subject to the governments of the states. This makes it more likely that the states will be moved to act in the national interest. (We shall return to this problem when I discuss in chapter 7 the advantages and disadvantages of leaving power in the states to abridge freedom of speech and of the press.)

The emphasis here upon state power suggests still another way in which the President may possibly act to abridge freedom of speech in a constitutional manner, and this is in collaboration with the Senate under the treaty power. Presumably, the President and Senate exercise in this manner the power the states could exercise separately if they each had the treaty power as sovereign states. It can be argued that this would include the power not only to agree (with other sovereigns) to abstain from making specified laws but also to undertake (at the request of other sovereigns) to make certain laws, even laws which abridge freedom of speech (when such speech affects relations with other countries and is the subject of negotiation). That is, when the President and Senate confront the treaty-making authority of other countries, all parties bring to the bargaining table the possibility of negotiating about all matters, internal and external, that affect relations between the countries. Otherwise, it would be argued, the treaty-making power is defective: the deficient agency is, to that extent, incomplete or impotent as a country among countries. It seems to be partly for this reason that the Senate is assigned a role in ratification of treaties, in order that the states may decide, through the Senate, whether they want to give up some of their power to control internal affairs. To the extent, that is, that a country is a member of the international community, its special local institutions (including freedom of speech) are vulnerable to international influences.[59] Need such treaties be implemented by legislation enacted by the Congress, or can they be self-executing? Once again we confront problems of constitutional limitations that are not peculiar to the First Amendment.[60]

Finally, to complete this survey of the ways in which the President may be left free to take action resulting, directly or indirectly, in an abridgment of freedom of speech, we must acknowledge that the President possesses the power and perhaps even the duty, as does the Congress or, for that matter, every citizen, to express approval—as an incident of *his* freedom of speech—of the exercise on occasion of that freedom which the people clearly have under the Constitution.

Perhaps, however, our duty today should be not to emphasize but rather to curb the powers and influence of the presidency.[61]

V

I should emphasize even more as I turn to the Judiciary what has already been said about the dominant role of Congress in the conduct of the affairs of the general government. The Executive, as we have seen, seems to have some powers under the Constitution in addition to those given it by Congress as well as those accruing to it as the executor of the laws made by Congress.[62] This is far less evidently the case with the Judiciary. So, to the extent Congress is restrained by the First Amendment, the Judiciary will likewise be largely restrained, at least to the extent that its primary concern is to interpret and apply the laws made by Congress.[63]

The ambiguous character of the relation between the Judiciary and Congress is suggested by Madison's original proposal for the placement within the body of the original Constitution of amendments relating to trials. (*Annals*, I, pp. 433-36) Some of the proposed amendments were to be inserted into Article I, section 9 (where restraints on Congress are collected):

No person shall be subject, except in cases of impeachment, to more than one punishment or one trial for the same offence; nor shall be compelled to be a witness against himself; nor be deprived of life, liberty, or property, without due process of law; nor be obliged to relinquish his property, where it may be necessary for public use, without a just compensation.

Excessive bail should not be required, nor excessive fines imposed, nor cruel and unusual punishments inflicted.

The rights of the people to be secured in their person, their houses, their papers, and their other property, from all unreasonable searches and seizures, shall not be violated by warrants issued without probable cause, supported by oath or affirmation, or not particularly describing the places to be searched, or the persons or things to be seized.

In all criminal prosecutions, the accused shall enjoy the right to a speedy and public trial, to be informed of the cause and nature of the accusation, to be confronted with his accusers, and the witnesses against him; to have a compulsory process for obtaining witnesses in his favor; and to have the assistance of counsel for his defence. [*Annals*, I, pp. 434-35]

All but the fourth of these proposed amendments remained designated for section 9 of Article I (the Legislative Article), so long as the amendments were intended for insertion into the original Constitution. The fourth, however, was shifted to section 2 of Article III (the Judicial Article), by the select committee which reviewed and revised Madison's original proposals. (*Annals*, I, p. 756) It there joined revised versions of amendments that Madison had originally proposed for Article III, section 2:

But no appeal to such court shall be allowed where the value in controversy shall not amount to ————dollars; nor shall any fact triable by jury, according to the course of common law, be otherwise re-examinable than may consist with the principles of common law.

[Replacing parts of the original Constitution:] The trial of all crimes (except in cases of impeachments, and cases arising in the land or naval forces, or the militia when on actual service, in time of war or public danger) shall be by an impartial jury of freeholders of the vicinage, with the requisite of unanimity for conviction, of the right of challenge, and other accustomed requisites; and in all crimes punishable with loss of life or member, presentment or indictment by a grand jury shall be an essential preliminary, provided that in cases of crimes committed within any county which may be in possession of an enemy, or in which a general insurrection may prevail, the trial may by law be authorized in some other county of the same State, as near as may be to the seat of the offence.[64]

In cases of crimes committed not within any county, the trial may by law be in such county as the laws shall have prescribed. In suits at common law, between man and man, the trial by jury, as one of the best securities to the rights of the people, ought to remain inviolate. [*Annals*, I, p. 435]

What is the principle of distribution here of the seven propositions between the First (Legislative) and Third (Judicial) Articles? The first three, and to some extent the fourth as well, seem to deal with court-related activities which are not conducted exclusively in the courtroom; in some respects, the Executive is involved, in others Congress (for example, by prescribing punishments). The final three, on the other hand, seem to deal with activities that are exclusively limited to what goes on in the courtroom (either in the trial court or on appeal): these are matters, it seems to be assumed, the courts would normally or otherwise deal with on their own but for constitutional limitations. (Similar considerations come to view as one works out the implicit principle of order in the Bill of Rights itself.)

Thus, a certain degree of independence, or autonomy, in the conduct by the Judiciary of its affairs is recognized. It is an independence that does not go so far as to insure the very existence of the Judiciary—for the power "to constitute Tribunals inferior to the Supreme Court" (and to determine the size, but not the existence, of the Supreme Court) rests in Congress (Article I, section 8).[65] The debates in the First Congress point up the dependent status of the Judiciary and suggest as well the extent of jurisdiction of the courts once they are established by congressional enactments.

Tucker observed that "the State courts were fully competent to the purposes for which [the proposed federal] courts were to be created, and that [federal courts] would be a burdensome and useless expense." (*Annals*, I, p. 783).[66] Smith described the contending positions as he argued for the creation of federal trial (or district) courts:

> ... some gentlemen are of opinion that the district court should be altogether confined to admiralty causes; while others deem it expedient that it should be entrusted with a more enlarged jurisdiction; and should, in addition to admiralty causes, take cognizance of all causes of seizure on land, all breaches of impost laws, of offences committed on the high seas, and causes in which foreigners or citizens of other States are parties. The committee are now to decide between these two opinions....
>
> It is very proper that a court in the United States should try offences against the United States. Every nation upon earth punishes by its own courts offences against its own laws. To seizures on land for breaches of the revenue laws, this power will not be censured; it would be *felo de se* to trust the collection of the revenue of the United States to the State judicatures.... [*Annals*, I, pp. 798-99][67]

The next stage of the debate saw further development of this argument. First, Theodore Sedgwick pointed out,

> ... we are so circumstanced that two distinct independent powers of judicial proceedings must exist; at least I do not see how we shall get rid of the difficulty, if it is one, until there shall be a change in the Constitution.
>
> I did not suppose it was a question at this day, whether this Government is to exercise all the powers of a Government or not ... yet what is the object of the present motion? Sir, it goes to divest the Government of one of its most essential branches; if this is destroyed, your Constitution is but the shadow of a Government. [*Annals*, I, p. 805]

Courts of the general government, he argued, are necessary for an effective administration or execution "of national laws and national treaties." It seems implied throughout that the general government needs a judiciary it can control. Ames argued,

> We see the difference between a treaty which independent nations make, and which cannot be enforced without war, and a law which is the will of the society.... A Government that may make but cannot enforce laws,

cannot last long, nor do much good. By the power, too, the people are gainers. The administration of justice is the very performance of the social bargain on the part of Government. [*Annals*, I, p. 806]

He went on to say,

> We live in a time of innovation; but until miracles shall have become more common than ordinary events, and surprise us less than the usual course of nature, he should think it a wonderful felicity of invention to propose the expedient of hiring out our judicial power, and employing courts not amenable to our laws, instead of instituting them ourselves as the Constitution requires. We might with as great propriety negotiate and assign over our legislative as our judicial power; and it would not be more strange to get the laws made for this body, than after their passage to get them interpreted and executed by those whom we do not appoint, and cannot control. [*Annals*, I, pp. 806-7]

The control by Congress of its courts can take several forms: the courts may be enlarged or contracted as may be their jurisdiction; rules of decision can be enacted which the courts are to apply; and, of course, there is the power of legislative impeachment of judges of such courts. It is evident that the subordinate and dependent role assigned to the courts, as is indicated here even in the language of those advocating the establishment of federal trial courts, makes the critical restraints with respect to free expression those placed upon Congress. In the ordinary course, a restraint upon Congress operates to control the Judiciary as well.[68]

But, it might be argued, to the extent that there is a national common law of crimes, which judges can determine independent of legislative enactments, the Judiciary might be said not to be restrained from enforcing or making more rigorous criminal sedition provisions of the common law, even if that common law should abridge freedom of speech.[69] On the other hand, Congress as the parallel legislature would have the power to control completely the common law. Presumably, then, the Judiciary cannot do anything that Congress could not undo or could not itself do. In fact, is not the common law court in these circumstances simply expressing the refined will of the community and thereby acting in the place of the legislature? If so, should not the Judiciary be bound as would be Congress? Thus, it can be argued that the First Amendment "repeals" or negates (in federal courts) so much of the common law of crimes as abridged freedom of speech or of the press. Certainly much of that common law had already been negated, as simply inappropriate for American conditions, both by its transportation to these shores[70] and, later on, by the American Revolution. Indeed, it can be further argued, the common law, as it stood in America at the time of the First Amendment, must be taken to incorporate to some extent (locally as well as nationally) the meaning of "freedom of speech, or of the press" found in the First Amendment.

The common law cannot conflict with statutes; neither the common law nor a statute can stand against the even more fundamental law of a constitution. This was recognized, for instance, by those who anticipated the effect of the religious-establishment provision (of what is now the First Amendment) on the conduct of cases in federal courts. Thus, Benjamin Huntington feared "that the words might be taken in such latitude as to be extremely hurtful to the cause of religion." (*Annals*, I, p. 730)[71] He went on to say that he understood the amendment

> to mean what had been expressed by the gentleman from Virginia [Madison];[72] but others might find it convenient to put another construction upon it. The ministers of their congregations to the Eastward were maintained by the contributions of those who belonged to their society; the expense of building meeting-houses was contributed in the same manner. These things were regulated by by-laws. If an action was brought before a Federal Court on any of these cases, the person who had neglected to perform his engagements could not be compelled to do it; for a support of ministers or building of places of worship might be construed into a religious establishment.
>
> By the charter of Rhode Island, no religion could be established by law; he could give a history of the effects of such a regulation; indeed the people were now enjoying the blessed fruits of it. He hoped, therefore, the amendment would be made in such a way as to secure the rights of conscience, and a free exercise of the rights of religion, but not to patronise those who professed no religion at all. [*Annals*, I, pp. 730-31]

Madison, in response,

> thought, if the word "national" was inserted before religion, it would satisfy the minds of honorable gentlemen. He believed that the people feared one sect might obtain a pre-eminence, or two combine together, and establish a religion to which they would compel others to conform. He thought

if the word "national" was introduced, it would point the amendment directly to the object it was intended to prevent. [*Annals*, I, p. 731][73]

Significant for our purposes here is the assumption made by Huntington which is not questioned but rather (it seems) recognized by Madison, that "if an action was brought before a Federal Court on any of these cases," the amendment might be successfully pleaded as a bar to the implementation of a statute construed as establishing a religion. Of course, this would be a state statute—but it is important to notice that it is assumed that the amendment would have an effect in a federal court. Whatever the effect if a statute of the general government were involved—for this would involve the problem of "judicial review" which I discuss in section 10 of chapter 8—it seems likely that an amendment, such as that relating to freedom of the press, could be effectively invoked to moderate the application of a provision of the common law in any proceeding. This analysis reinforces my suggestion that the First Amendment can be seen as negating so much of any national common law of crimes as may have abridged freedom of speech or of the press.

To what extent, on the other hand, are the courts left free to impose restrictions on speech and the press? The federal courts might, in some circumstances, have to apply or at least take cognizance of state acts abridging freedom of speech. The judiciary seems to be left free under the First Amendment to do so. Such application of state acts would, it is true, usually be in civil litigation; but even here cases could arise in which cognizance must be taken of the state criminal law.[74] Federal courts are left free, as well they might be, to regard as would a state court the existence and operation of local law. Otherwise, all state laws would eventually have to be refashioned in the image of acts of Congress and of constitutional provisions applying to the general government.

In addition, the federal judiciary might find itself in a position comparable to that in which I imagined the President, that of standing in the place of its counterpart within a state. This might come about either when the state government becomes, for some reason, unable or unfit to fulfill its proper function, or at a time or in a place where there is not yet or cannot be a state government (as in a territory or in what is now known as the District of Columbia). In either of these circumstances, the powers of a state, as distinguished from the general government, have to be exercised, and the federal judiciary is left free to do so.[75]

One further suggestion can be drawn from the restricted language of the absolute restraint of the First Amendment. The judiciary might, in some circumstances, have to restrain speech or writing that interferes with the effective operation of its processes in particular cases.[76] I refer here to the judicial contempt power recognized in section 17 of the Judiciary Act enacted by the First Congress in 1789:

> ... all the said courts of the United States shall have power to grant new trials, in cases where there has been a trial by jury, for reasons for which new trials have usually been granted in the courts of law; and shall have power to impose and administer all necessary oaths or affirmations, and to punish by fine or imprisonment, at the discretion of said courts, all contempts of authority in any cause or hearing before the same; and to make and establish all necessary rules for the orderly conducting business in the said courts, provided such rules are not repugnant to the laws of the United States. [*Annals*, I, p. 2189]

Evidently, there was no need to define or establish either "contempts of authority" or "the orderly conducting business": it seemed to have been assumed that these follow from the nature of judicial activity under the Constitution.

Any interference with the courts' ability to do that which they are supposed to do will be controlled, by fine or imprisonment if necessary. Presumably this would apply to interference that comes in the guise of an exercise of freedom of speech or of the press, no matter how narrow the First Amendment rights are taken to be.[77] Thus, the courts are left free to do what they have always done: no one can say what he wishes in court, no one connected with a case can say what he wishes outside the court while the case is pending, and no one unconnected with the case can try by means foreign to the judicial process to influence what goes on inside the courtroom in a particular case, whatever right he may have to criticize generally the courts or judges or even the results of a particular case after disposition is made of it.[78]

Congress, when it recognizes or decrees that such contempt power exists in courts, does not thereby make a law abridging freedom of speech. The critical limitation on courts is that they must conduct their business according to certain rules: thus, they must display impartiality by giving each party a fair chance to be heard, to present evidence, and to examine hostile witnesses. The protection to be guaranteed in court proceedings is not the freedom of speech found outside the courts but rather "due process of law." This due process of law can be considered freedom of speech and its rule of law adapted to the context and demands of judicial proceedings: it is an approach that is best calculated to bring out the truth about the matter at issue and to insure that justice will most likely prevail.[79]

We need not determine here the extent of the contempt power the Judiciary would have had independent of congressional allotment. It is unlikely that such power was thought to bear directly on the problem of freedom of speech. It was probably understood that courts must, in order to justify their action, relate what they are restraining to cases over which they have jurisdiction. A judge cannot make general rules about what may be said outside his court —but it is reasonable to insure that he shall be able to conduct properly a case over which he has, according to accepted standards, acquired jurisdiction.[80] There is no reason to believe that this judicial counterpart to freedom of speech, due process of law, is inadequate to contribute to the accomplishment in the courts of the objects which both freedom of speech and due process of law share.[81]

It should be noticed that courts are governed, by the Judiciary Act of 1789, in the rules they may make to insure orderly conduct of business. Such rules have to be "not repugnant to the laws of the United States."[82] This limitation suggests a further safeguard (in addition to the test of reasonableness) against unwarranted interference by a court, through contempt proceedings, with activities outside that court. Congress can correct court proceedings or rules which may have the effect of a general limitation upon freedom of speech. Thus, Congress possesses the power to "de-abridge"—that is, to enlarge—freedom of speech by correcting the courts when they go too far in the exercise of the power they do have to regulate their own affairs.[83]

Whatever scope the courts have on procedural matters, I have argued, they are as limited as is Congress with respect to the law that they either fashion or apply. Such law, whether statute or common, cannot abridge freedom of speech or of the press. It does not mean, however, that this freedom cannot coexist with the most severe restrictions upon utterances that might, if not restricted, interfere with the effective operation of the courts. Indeed, if (as I have suggested) the most extensive free speech presupposes the restriction of it to the appropriate domain, then an effective contempt power in the courts serves to support freedom of speech. Otherwise, uninhibited utterances would often undermine the efforts by learned and judicious men to establish justice, thereby endangering the social stability and public confidence that freedom of speech usually promotes and certainly requires.

It does no service to "freedom of speech" to try to appropriate for it more than is its due. Policy conspires with justice to encourage proper limitations.[84]

VI

The First Amendment does not explicitly govern what the states may do about speech or the press. State legislators are left somewhat more free than Congress to do what they think best about speech and the press in their local jurisdictions. The trust once reposed in the states is reflected even in the composition of the Congress, as explained by Page:

Some gentlemen contend that the Senate are a dangerous and aristocratic body; but I contend that they are a safe and salutary branch of the Government, representing the republican Legislatures of the individual States, and intended to preserve the sovereignty and independence of the State Governments, which they are more likely to do than the President, who is elected by the people at large. A popular President, influenced by the sentiments of his electors, may be induced to believe that it would be best for the general interest that those Governments were destroyed; but as long as we have that body independent of him, and secured in their authority, we may defy such impotent attempts; they will watch his conduct, and prevent the exercise of despotic power. But if they are weakened and stripped of their essential authority, they will become weak barriers against the strides of an uncontrolled power. [*Annals*, I, pp. 519-20]

We have seen that the First Congress did consider extending the restraints of what is now the First Amendment, except as to religious establishments, to the states as well. We have also seen that the Senate of the First Congress refused to agree to this proposal from the House (where it had been initiated by Madison). This had the effect, as I argue in chapter 7, of confirming the absolute nature of the prohibition of the First Amendment with respect to that which it does cover: if there should arise certain dangers, real or apparent, the states are left free to handle them. (Indeed, we can say, this may have been an unintended result of the rejection by the Senate of the proposed restraint against the states.[85]) It is within such a scheme that Tucker can make a valid distinction, with respect to religious matters, between what "is proscribed to [Congress]" and what is left to "the authority of the several States." (*Annals, I,* p. 915)[86]

The state governments are not without free speech restraints upon them, even aside from the Fourteenth Amendment.[87] It should be remembered that these are American legislatures, subject to control by American electorates and influenced, it is to be expected, by the American tradition of freedom. Furthermore, these legislatures (and their companion courts) are, in principle, as much influenced by their state constitutional guarantees with respect to speech and the press (whatever they may mean) as are the legislature and courts of the general government by guarantees in the national Constitution.[88] Finally, Congress may have some authority to supervise the exercise by the states of their powers to regulate speech and the press.

Such supervisory authority may be implied in the way the First Amendment is worded. Congress is told it must in no way concern itself with religious establishments; but it is prohibited only from laying restraints on the freedom of religion, speech, and the press. What is to be made of this difference in wording? The first draft of the religion provision—that is, Madison's original proposal—read (as we have seen),

The civil rights of none shall be abridged on account of religious belief or worship, nor shall any national religion be established, nor shall the full and equal rights of conscience be in any manner, or on any pretext, infringed. [*Annals, I,* p. 434]

The second version read,

No religion shall be established by law, nor shall the equal rights of conscience be infringed. [*Annals, I,* p. 729]

Another version, which furnished the model for the form we now have, was suggested and approved after concern was expressed lest the general government interfere with state religious arrangements:

Congress shall make no laws touching religion, or infringing the rights of conscience. [*Annals*, I, p. 731]

The final version changed "touching" to "respecting," which is probably not critical, and changed "religion" to "establishment of religion," which clearly is not so inclusive as the injunction against any congressional laws "touching religion." But Congress is not forbidden to make laws respecting "the rights of conscience [or the free exercise of religion]."

It would have been much simpler to have said throughout the First Amendment what is said there of the "establishment of religion":

Congress shall make no law respecting religion, the press, speech, or the right of assembly and petition.[89]

The differences in wording—the differences between what is said in the First Amendment about religious establishments (that is, "Hands off!") and what is said about freedom of religion, of speech, and of the press (that is, "No prohibitions or abridgments")—seem either to recognize and to preserve some preexisting power in Congress or to create thereby some power in Congress. This would be power, under either interpretation, to enlarge freedom of religion, freedom of speech, and freedom of the press—to enlarge them by protecting and encouraging these freedoms generally or by nullifying or diluting state restraints upon these freedoms.[90]

I turn first to the second possibility. How can a restraint upon Congress itself, with nothing more said, create any power in Congress? The answer to this question depends on the rules of interpretation to be used in reading a constitution (or, for that matter, any other legal document). An aspect of these rules is reflected in the language of one of the amendments proposed by Madison in the first list he submitted to the House of Representatives:

The exceptions here or elsewhere in the Constitution, made in favor of particular rights, shall not be so construed as to diminish the just importance of other rights retained by the people, or as to enlarge the powers delegated by the Constitution; but either as actual limitations of such powers, or as inserted merely for greater caution. [*Annals*, I, p. 435]

This proposition was considerably shortened to make what is now the Ninth Amendment:

The enumeration in the Constitution, of certain rights, shall not be construed to deny or disparage others retained by the people.

Part of the language—"either as actual limitations of such powers, or as inserted merely for greater caution"—is retained, in effect, in the statement prefixed to the amendments when they were sent to the states for ratification.[91] But another part, that which denies that the rights listed "enlarge the powers delegated by the Constitution," was dropped completely after Madison's first version. This provision would have applied to "exceptions" of particular rights anywhere in the Constitution. But do not some of the powers of the general government depend on the implicit grant that is made by virtue of incomplete prohibitions in the Constitution?[92] If the prohibition against enlargement of powers had been retained, it might have precluded such grants.

That is, a limited negative upon Congress's power may be taken to imply some power with respect to the subject dealt with, at least to the extent that the negative obviously falls short of being complete.[93] The explicit statement of a limitation ordinarily suggests that a power exists that has to be limited. An automobile driver wonders whether he is driving in the wrong direction on what may be a one-way street. There are no signs to be seen. But, upon coming to an intersection, he confronts a stop sign facing the direction from which he is coming. What does this restraint or prohibition imply about his "power" and "right" to have moved and to continue moving in the direction he is going?[94]

Does the First Amendment, then, grant to Congress power over speech and press (and even religion) to the extent that congressional power with respect to these matters is not suppressed by the amendment? What, on the other hand, is the significance of the preamble accompanying the Bill of Rights proposal sent by Congress to the states? It is there indicated that some of the prohibitions in the proposed Bill of Rights were declaratory. That is, they may be superfluous, designed merely to reassure the public. Are the provisions of the First Amendment among the declaratory ones?[95]

It suffices here to recall that a distinction *is* made in the First Amendment between religious establishments ("no law . . . respecting") and freedom of religion, speech, and the press ("no law . . . prohibiting . . . or abridging"). This is a distinction that must have had some purpose, in both the common-sense and the legal-sense view of things. I have suggested that such distinctions may create by implication the powers necessary to give them meaning. In this way, perhaps, there can be extracted from the First Amendment a congressional power to enlarge or protect (but not to abridge or prohibit) freedom of religion, of speech, and of the press, a power that could be used to supervise state action with respect to these matters.[96]

I return now to the first possibility mentioned at page 82—that the wording of the First Amendment recognizes and preserves some congressional power in the original Constitution with respect to freedom of religion, of speech, and of the press. What may there be in the original Constitution that gives Congress the power *to encourage* freedom of religion, of speech, and of the press, and thereby to supervise state action with respect to these freedoms? That is, what is there in the original Constitution that can reasonably be regarded by friends of freedom as a source of congressional power to moderate *state* governmental restraints upon the speech and press activities of citizens?[97]

There seem to be at least three passages in the original Constitution from which there might, without strained interpretation, be drawn some congressional power either to encourage freedom of speech and of the press or to supervise state regulation of these freedoms. These passages are in Article I, section 2, providing for the composition of the House of Representatives; in Article I, section 4, providing for the manner of election of the House of Representatives and of the Senate; and in Article IV, section 4, guaranteeing a republican form of government for the states.

The first sentence of Article I, section 2, reads:

The House of Representatives shall be composed of Members chosen every second Year by the People of the several States, and the Electors in each State shall have the Qualifications requisite for Electors of the most numerous Branch of the State Legislature.

May not the Congress have the power, perhaps even under this provision alone, to insure that the people do indeed choose the members of the House of Representatives (and, today, the members of the Senate as well)? A genuine choice by the people implies an adequate discussion of alternatives and of issues: that is, it implies freedom of speech and of the press, at least with respect to electoral issues. Would it not be unrealistic to confine this freedom to the period immediately preceding our biennial elections?[98]

Even more explicit is the first sentence in Article I, section 4, which provides,

> The Times, Places and Manner of holding Elections for Senators and Representatives, shall be prescribed in each State by the Legislature thereof; but the Congress may at any time by Law make or alter such Regulations, except as to the Place of chusing Senators.

Would the manner of holding elections, which the Congress can by law regulate, include the kind and amount of discussion that precedes the actual polling? State restrictions upon freedom of the press, for instance, might well constitute a critical interference with the best manner of holding elections and thus interfere with the right of the people to choose. The encouragement or protection of a free press within a state may be needed to make an election effectively the act of the people.

An exchange in the First Congress (to which I have already referred) illuminates the significance attached to the "Times, Places and Manner" provision of the Constitution. Indeed, the provision is fundamental to the constitutional scheme. Burke asked for an amendment that would have limited severely the power of Congress in this respect.[99] Ames insisted that Congress must retain ultimate power to regulate elections of its own members, lest it be hampered in its operations or threatened in its very existence by what may or may not happen in state legislatures. (*Annals*, I, p. 768) Gerry, in support of Burke's proposal, anticipated how Congress may abuse its power to regulate elections:

> [Congress may] abolish the mode of balloting; then every person must publicly announce his vote, and it would then frequently happen that he would be obliged to vote for a man or "the friend of a man," to whom he was under obligations. If the Government grows desirous of being arbi-

trary, elections will be ordered at remote places, where their friends alone will attend. [*Annals*, I, p. 769]

The friends of the original Constitution—that is, of a strong general government—saw Burke's proposed amendment (which was defeated, 23-28) as one that affected a vital power of the general government. They were willing to accept amendments denying any power in Congress to curtail freedom of speech, freedom of the press, and the right to trial by jury. But the Burke proposal would have made a radical change in the ultimate disposition of power as between the general government and the states, and this they did not propose to permit, even though several state ratifying conventions had asked for such a change. (*Annals*, I, pp. 769-70) The following passage reflects the sentiments of the friends of a strong general government:

Mr. Ames said that inadequate regulations were equally injurious as having none, and that such an amendment as was now proposed would alter the Constitution: it would vest the supreme authority in places where it was never contemplated.

Mr. Sherman observed that the Convention were very unanimous in passing this clause; that it was an important provision, and if it was resigned, it would tend to subvert the Government.

Mr. Madison was willing to make every amendment that was required by the States, which did not tend to destroy the principles and the efficacy of the Constitution; he conceived that the proposed amendment would have that tendency, he was therefore opposed to it. [*Annals*, I, p. 770]

Presumably, this "supreme authority" would include the prerogative, and perhaps the duty, in Congress to insure that the states do not so abridge freedom of speech and of the press as to subvert elections and thereby the general government.[100]

Our third provision, Article IV, section 4, reinforces the points already made about the implied power in Congress to protect freedom of speech and of the press from severe curtailment by the states. That provision reads,

The United States shall guarantee to every State in this Union a Republican Form of Government, and shall protect each of them against Invasion; and on Application of the Legislature, or of the Executive (when the Legislature cannot be convened) against domestic Violence.[101]

Here a duty is imposed upon the general government, not upon Congress alone.[102] A republican form of government was taken to refer primarily to a government chosen by the people (with the qualification often added, chosen for a regular and short term of office).[103] In addition, it seems to have been thought that virtually all citizens should be eligible for office.[104] Does not effective choice by the people imply, with respect to state government elections also, that the choice must not be simply perfunctory or nominal? A real choice must be offered the people—that is, an opposition must be given an opportunity to be heard, issues must be discussed or be open for discussion.[105] This, too, as I have suggested, may be implied by the Article I election provisions.[106] The guarantee in Article IV would reinforce the Article I provisions by governing state institutions as well as congressional elections.

Republican government may also require *some* degree of recognition of certain critical rights, among the foremost of which would be the general right to freedom of speech and of the press, independent of the bearing of this right upon the conduct of elections. Madison insisted that

> this House is bound by every motive of prudence, not to let the first session [of Congress] pass over without proposing to the State Legislatures, some things to be incorporated into the Constitution, that will render it as acceptable to the whole people of the United States, as it has been found acceptable to a majority of them. [*Annals*, I, p. 431]

He wanted the friends of the Constitution to promote a Bill of Rights incorporating "the great rights of mankind" and thereby prove "to those who were opposed to [the Constitution] that [its friends] were as sincerely devoted to liberty and a Republican Government [as its opponents]." (*Annals*, I, p. 432) Thus, republican government may imply, independent of electoral considerations, "the great rights of mankind."

It is from this perspective, then, that we can see how Congress can be said to have been given the power to supervise state regulations of speech or of the press, a congressional power that is recognized and preserved, if not created, by the First Amendment. Of the provisions I have discussed in this section, only the guarantee of a republican form of government to each state would directly impose the duty as well as the power on all branches of the general government, not on Congress alone, to supervise state regulations of speech and the press. Presumably, then, the federal courts (as part of the general government) are empowered to check significant departures in the states from republican institutions.[107] But, it should be noted, the right to freedom of speech (for example) would not be protected so unequivocally under this provision as it is by the First Amendment. Rather, freedom of speech would have to be revived in any particular instance only to the extent that it contributed (in those circumstances) to republican government. Thus, the courts could not intervene (on the authority of this provision) except to the extent that state restrictive measures effectively interfered with republican government. Such purposive considerations may affect also Congress's power under the electoral provisions of Article I.[108]

We have seen what safeguards may be developed from the original Constitution and the First Amendment against the most serious state abuses with respect to freedom of speech and of the press.[109] Nevertheless, the states were left relatively free under this dispensation to abridge these freedoms.[110] The wisdom of the decision to leave the states free of the unequivocal restraints of the First Amendment will be discussed in chapter 7 when I consider the effects both of the federalism of the Bill of Rights and of the modification of that federalism by the Fourteenth Amendment.

VII

The people are not restrained by the First Amendment from abridging freedom of speech. They can intimidate and even penalize socially and politically anyone whose opinions they do not like. They can to some extent act against the unpopular through state legislatures. They can and sometimes should do many things, or have many things done for them, that discourage the expression of certain opinions. This is inevitable in any free community.[111]

What the people cannot do is have the expression of such opinions penalized by any law of Congress: the people have agreed, in the solemn form of the First Amendment, not to resort to this expedient. But the First Amendment is itself subject to amendment: the people could repudiate their covenant of collective self-restraint and even substitute for it a constitutional provision severely, even permanently, abridging freedom of speech and of the press.[112]

This change, however, would not be merely a constitutional amendment, but rather a revolution, a change in the form of government. Indeed, the very notion of *a people* determining and constantly reviewing not only the conduct of government but the form of government itself implies freedom of speech and of the press. How else can they be a "people" who are able to deliberate and act in a manner appropriate to constitutional self-government? This is implied in the very fact that when the Constitution was brought forward to be ratified the people engaged in an extensive debate about its merits. Such debate is implied as well by the principles of the Declaration of Independence: for the people are both authorized and obliged continually to assess and, if necessary, to replace the form of government under which they live. Thus, the principles of the First Amendment may even be said to be inherent in the idea of a self-governing people. For this people to repudiate these principles would be to recognize themselves only as subjects, not at all as rulers.[113] These principles may also be regarded as reflecting, at least in the republican context, natural or inalienable rights.

Such principles require for their proper use and perpetuation a people alert to both their duties and their weaknesses. The opinions that the people have of themselves and of their constitution are vital to our form of government. Lincoln insisted again and again that

> in this age, and this country, public sentiment is everything. With it, nothing can fail; against it, nothing can succeed. Whoever molds public sentiment goes deeper than he who enacts statutes or pronounces judicial decisions. He makes possible the enforcement of them, else impossible.[114]

There is a danger, however, that public sentiment in such circumstances may come to cry out with the Athenians that "it was monstrous if the people were to be prevented [by the constitution] from doing whatever they wished."[115]

It is well for public servants too receptive to a sometimes turbulent and transitory public opinion[116] to be reminded of Sherman's salutary remarks in the First Congress:

> Gentlemen have had recourse to popular opinion in support of their arguments. Popular opinion is founded in justice, and the only way to know if the popular opinion is in favor of a measure, is to examine whether the measure is just and right in itself. I think whatever is proper and right, the people will judge of and comply with. [*Annals*, I, p. 316][117]

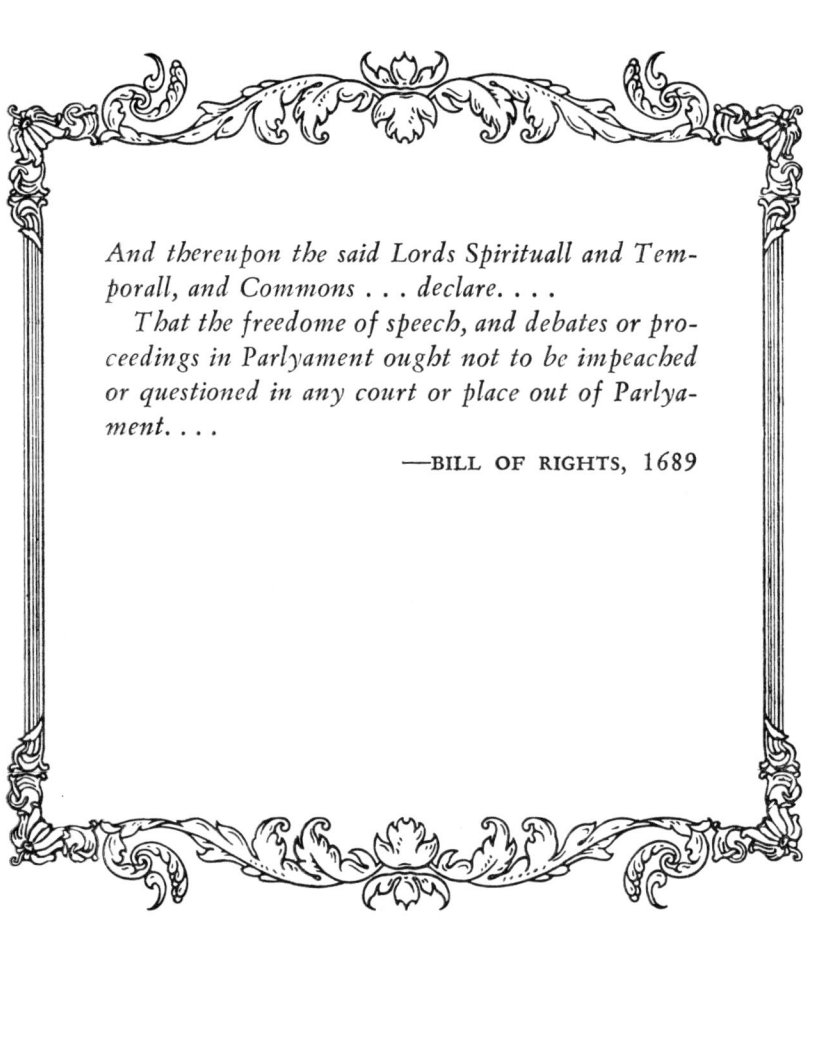

And thereupon the said Lords Spirituall and Temporall, and Commons . . . declare. . . .

That the freedome of speech, and debates or proceedings in Parlyament ought not to be impeached or questioned in any court or place out of Parlyament. . . .

—BILL OF RIGHTS, 1689

V. "ABRIDGING THE FREEDOM OF SPEECH"

I

WE HAVE SEEN that the prohibition in the First Amendment is absolute. We have also seen against whom this absolute prohibition is and is not directed. We must now see what it is that is protected in this way. It is for this inquiry that we turn to both legal and Anglo-American history to confirm our initial impression of the intended scope of the phrase, "freedom of speech, or of the press."[1]

We may well take our cue from Boudinot's observation in the First Congress, that "if we are to have the measures of the Parliament of Great Britain hung about our necks in all our public proceedings, and observations from their practice perpetually sounding in our ears, that practice ought to be defined and established." (*Annals, I,* p. 363)

II

We begin our determination of the probable meaning, in 1789-91, of "freedom of speech, or of the press" by looking first (as American legal scholars did from the time of Washington to that of Lincoln) into Judge Blackstone's treatise. (His authority remained great, despite the recognized unrepublican cast of his thought.[2]) The following passage concludes Blackstone's chapter on those public wrongs which constitute "Offences Against the Public Peace":

> In this and the other instances which we have lately considered, where blasphemous, immoral, treasonable, schismatical, seditious, or scandalous libels are punished by the English law, some with a greater, others with a less degree of severity; the liberty of the press, properly understood, is by no means infringed or violated. *The liberty of the press is indeed essential to the nature of a free state; but this consists in laying no previous restraints upon publications, and not in freedom from censure for criminal matter when published.* [Italics added] Every freeman has an undoubted right to lay what sentiments he pleases before the public; to forbid this, is to destroy the freedom of the press: but if he publishes what is improper, mischievous, or illegal, he must take the consequence of his own temerity. To subject the press to the restrictive power of a licenser, as was formerly done, both before and since the revolution,[3] is to subject all freedom of sentiment to the prejudices of one man, and make him the arbitrary and infallible judge of all controverted points in learning, religion and government. But to punish (as the law does at present) any dangerous or offensive writings, which, when published, shall on a fair and impartial trial be adjudged of a pernicious tendency, is necessary for the preservation of peace and good order, of government and religion, the only solid foundations of civil liberty. Thus the will of individuals is still left free; the abuse only of that free-will is the object of legal punishment. Neither is any restraint hereby laid upon freedom of thought or enquiry: liberty of private sentiment is still left; the disseminating, or making public, of bad sentiments, destructive of the ends of society, is the crime which society corrects. A man (says a fine writer on this subject) may be allowed to keep poisons in his closet, but not publicly vend them as cordials. And to this we may add, that the only plausible argument heretofore used for the restraining the just freedom of the press, "that it was necessary to prevent the daily abuse of it," will entirely lose its force, when it is shown (by a seasonable exertion of the laws) that the press cannot be abused to any bad purpose, without incurring a suitable punishment: whereas it never can be used to any good one, when under the control of an inspector. So true it will be found, that to censure the licentiousness, is to maintain the liberty of the press.[4]

"ABRIDGING THE FREEDOM OF SPEECH" 95

This passage presents in detail the common law with respect to liberty of the press as conceived by Blackstone in 1765. A passage from Judge Thomas M. Cooley (the nineteenth-century American scholar) sums up the common law and provides a point of departure for our discussion of Blackstone's position:

> It must be evident from these historical facts that liberty of the press, as now understood and enjoyed, is of very recent origin. (It is mentioned neither in the English Petition of Rights nor in the [English] Bill of Rights [of 1689]; of so little importance did it seem to those who were seeking to redress grievances in those days.) And commentators seem to be agreed in the opinion that the term itself means only that liberty of publication without the previous permission of the government, which was obtained by the abolition of the censorship. In a strict sense, Mr. Hallam says, it consists merely in exemption from a licenser. A similar view is expressed by De Lolme. "Liberty of the press," he says, "consists in this: that neither courts of justice, nor any other judges whatever, are authorized to take notice of writings *intended* for the press, but are confined to those which are actually printed." Blackstone also adopts the same opinion, and it has been followed by American commentators of standard authority as embodying correctly the idea incorporated in the constitutional law of the country by the provisions in the American Bill of Rights.[5]

After considering uses of the press and speech which may be penalized by criminal or civil suits, Cooley passed judgment upon the "no-previous-restraint" view of freedom of the press defined by Blackstone:

> But while we concede that liberty of speech and of the press does not imply complete exemption from responsibility for everything a citizen may say or publish, and complete immunity to ruin the reputation or business of others so far as falsehood and detraction may be able to accomplish that end, it is nevertheless believed that the mere exemption from previous restraints cannot be all that is secured by the constitutional provisions, *inasmuch as of words to be uttered orally there can be no previous censorship*, and the liberty of the press might be rendered a mockery and a delusion, and the phrase itself a byword, if, while every man was at liberty to publish what he pleased, the public authorities might nevertheless punish him for harmless publications. [Italics added]

Cooley disparaged the older rule as a "mere exemption from previous restraints."[6] I, on the other hand, am obliged to wonder what my predecessors from Milton to Blackstone saw in that rule to acclaim it the great right that they did.[7]

III

The English scholar Albert V. Dicey, writing a generation after Cooley, presented the rationale of the "no-previous-restraint" rule:[8]

"The liberty of the press," says Lord Mansfield, "consists in printing without any previous license, subject to the consequences of law." "The law of England," says Lord Ellenborough, "is a law of liberty, and consistently with this liberty we have not what is called an *imprimatur*; there is no such preliminary license necessary; but if a man publish a paper, he is exposed to the penal consequences, as he is in every other act, if it be illegal."

These dicta show us at once that the so-called liberty of the press is a mere application of the general principle, that no man is punishable except for a distinct breach of the law. This principle is radically inconsistent with any scheme of license or censorship by which a man is hindered from writing or printing anything which he thinks fit, and is hard to reconcile even with the right on the part of the Courts to restrain the circulation of a libel, until at any rate the publisher has been convicted of publishing it. It is also opposed in spirit to any regulation requiring from the publisher of an intended newspaper a preliminary deposit of a certain sum of money, for the sake either of ensuring that newspapers should be published only by solvent persons, or that if a newspaper should contain libels there shall be a certainty of obtaining damages from the proprietor. No sensible person will argue that to demand a deposit from the owner of a newspaper or to impose other limitations upon the right of publishing periodicals is of necessity inexpedient or unjust. All that is here insisted upon is, that such checks and preventive measures are inconsistent with the pervading principle of English law, that men are to be interfered with or punished, not because they may or will break the law, but only when they have committed some definite assignable legal offence. Hence, with one exception, which is a quaint survival from a different system, no such thing is known with us as a license to print, or a censorship either of the press or of political newspapers.[9] Neither the government nor any other authority has the right to seize or destroy the stock of a publisher because it consists of books, pamphlets, or papers which in the opinion of the government contain seditious or libellous matter. Indeed, it is questionable how far the Courts themselves will, even for the sake of protecting an individual from injury, prohibit the publication or republication of a libel, or restrain its sale until the matter has gone before a jury and it has been established by their verdict that the words complained of are libellous. Writers in the press are in short, like every other person, subject to the law of the realm, and nothing else. Neither the government nor the Courts have (speaking generally) any greater power to prevent or oversee the publication of a newspaper than the writing of a letter. Indeed, the simplest way of setting forth briefly the position of writers in the press is to say that they stand in substantially the same position as letter-writers. A man who scribbles blasphemy on a gate and a man who prints blasphemy in a paper or in a book commit exactly the same offence, and are dealt with in England on the same principles. Hence also writers in newspapers have, or had until very recently, no special privilege protecting them from liability. Look at the matter which way you will, the main feature of liberty of the press as understood in England is that the press (which means, of course, the writers in it) is subject only to the ordinary law of the land.

Thus, nothing is said, in this discussion of the liberty of the press, about any restraints upon the power of the legislature (except to the extent the legislature is restrained from establishing a system of censorship).[10] This liberty, then, consists not in any special immunity for the press—such as is seen in American constitutional provisions denying a power in the legislature to abridge freedom of the press—but rather in the insistence that the press is not subject to preventive surveillance or any other special liability. The ordinary law of the land—that is, the rule of law—is to apply with respect to the conduct of the press as it applies with respect to any other activity.[11]

This seemingly modest insistence that the press is not subject to special liability—that it is subject only to the rule of law as is any other activity—reflects the history of the art of printing. Printing was regarded in England "as merely a matter of state, and subject to the coercion of the crown."[12] The development or emergence of liberty of the press seems, thus, to have consisted in removing from the press the restraints of special government control.[13] The "liberty of the press" seems, in this sense, to be the *liberation* of the press from a rule other than that of law in the usual sense.[14]

Thus, according to this view of liberty of the press, the critical factor is an insistence on the rule of law, not an insistence on a restraint (as under the American rule) upon the power of the legislature to punish the abuses of the press (or, for that matter, upon its power to regulate any activity of the press). Just as Cooley had written of this English rule as a "*mere* exception from previous restraints," Dicey declared (as we have seen) "that the *so-called* liberty of the press is a *mere* application of the general principle, that no man is punishable except for a distinct breach of the law." (Italics added.)[15]

The rule of law may well insure much of the benefit that we have come to associate with American-style "freedom of the press" (which decrees a contraction of legislative power).[16] This rule of law, which is reflected in the central place given the writ of *habeas corpus* by lawyers, implies (in Anglo-American law) several recognized characteristics of due process. Due process of law requires that punishment follow only upon trial, that the law be clear and certain, that charges be specific, pertinent, and not vague, that trials be conducted by the judicial branch of the government. These elements of due process—indeed, the restraints and moderation imposed by judicial procedures (especially when administered by well-trained judges secure in lifetime posts)—are sufficient to protect against, or at least reduce, many of the threats to freedom of the press (or freedom of speech) that we confront from time to time.[17]

The rule of law, it should be noted, was implicit in the Constitution even before the addition of the Bill of Rights. It is implicit in the provisions governing *ex post facto* legislation, bills of attainder, and the writ of *habeas corpus*. Since there is nothing in the Constitution to suggest that Congress may regulate speech or the press for the country at large by other than ordinary legislative means,[18] the implication is that the rule of law controls any regulation with respect to them. These considerations would apply to the states as well, certainly to the extent that the *ex post facto* and bill of attainder provisions directed against the states imply the rule of law and to the extent that it is also implied by the republican form of government guarantee. Thus, freedom of speech and of the press is substantially protected against all American governments by the influence of a pervasive constitutionalism.[19]

Before proceeding to a discussion of the distinctively American addition to (or version of) "freedom of speech, or of the press," I return to another passage in Dicey in which he comments on one misunderstanding about English law:[20]

Both the revolutionists of France and the constitutionalists of Belgium borrowed their ideas about freedom of opinion and the liberty of the press from England, and most persons form such loose notions as to English law that the idea prevails in England itself that the right to the free expression of opinion, and especially that form of it which is known as the "liberty of the press," are fundamental doctrines of the law of England in the same sense in which they were part of the ephemeral [French] constitution of 1791 and still are embodied in the articles of the existing Belgian constitution; and, further, that our Courts recognize the right of every man to say and write what he pleases, especially on social, political, or religious topics, without fear of legal penalties. Yet this notion, justified though it be, to a certain extent, by the habits of modern English life, is essentially false, and conceals from students the real attitude of English law towards what is called "freedom of thought," and is more accurately described as the "right to the free expression of opinion." As every lawyer knows, the phrases "freedom of discussion" or "liberty of the press" are not to be found in any part of the statute-book nor among the maxims of the common law. As terms of art they are indeed quite unknown to our Courts. At no time has there in England been any proclamation of the right to liberty of thought or to freedom of speech. . . .

Any man may therefore say or write whatever he likes, subject to the risk of, it may be, severe punishment if he publishes any statement (either by word of mouth, in writing, or in print) which he is not legally entitled to make. Nor is the law of England specially favourable to free speech or to free writing in the rules which it maintains in theory and often enforces in fact as to the kind of statements which a man has a legal right to make. Above all, it recognizes in general no special privilege on behalf of the "press," if by the term we mean, in conformity with ordinary language, periodical literature and particularly the newspapers. In truth there is little in the statute-book which can be called a "press law." The law of the press as it exists here is merely part of the law of libel. . . .

We need not consider whether this is an adequate statement of English law today.[21] It is sufficient to see that this statement reinforces a view of the "liberty of the press" which "merely" insures that the press is to be subject to the rule of law, a view with an emphasis upon subsequent punishment rather than upon previous restraints.[22] This is essentially what Blackstone speaks of: his discussion of liberty of the press exhibits the concern that the press labor under no special liabilities, not that it enjoy any special privileges.

"Freedom of discussion" and "liberty of the press" are, "as terms of art," "quite unknown to our courts." What then do phrases such as "freedom of speech" and "freedom of the press" add to a system of law (unlike that which Dicey was describing) in which they *are* terms of art, in which they *are* accorded constitutional recognition and protection through "proclamation of the right," in which they *are* considered "fundamental doctrines of the law," and in which it *is* sometimes said that "every man [has the right] to say and write what he pleases, especially on social, political, or religious topics, without fear of legal penalties"? The elevation to constitutional status of "freedom of *speech*"—with respect to which there could never have been any rule of previous restraint for the people at large[23]—recognizes the development of something new in America.[24] It has something to do with the enthronement of the principle of self-government: the concern is more with public freedom than with private liberties.

IV

What effect, then, is to be given to the American constitutional provision which seems to remove from or prohibit to the legislature the exercise of certain powers that bear on the press and speech? The injunction that Congress shall make no law abridging freedom of the press is seen by some as merely ratifying the no-previous-restraint rule. But to interpret the First Amendment in this way neither explains the "freedom of speech" provision nor takes sufficient account of the distinctive character of American experience and expectations.

That Americans have been markedly distinguishable from even the English, especially in their attitude toward government and authority, has long been evident to observers here and abroad.[25] The pervasiveness of the American attitude is testified to by its appearance even among the military, a profession in which one would least expect to find it. Thus, Chester Wilmot (an Australian) reported, in his account of the Second World War in Europe,

Whatever professional respect the Americans had for Montgomery was tempered by personal suspicion, for his manner and methods aroused their traditional distrust of those who hold positions of great power. It was a matter not only of personality, but also of principle. The characteristic American resentment of authority, dating from the birth of the United States, has undoubtedly influenced command policy in their armed forces and has led to a considerable measure of independence and delegated responsibility at every level. "The American doctrine," says Eisenhower, "has always been to assign a Theater Commander a mission, provide him with a definite amount of force and then to interfere as little as possible with the execution of his plans." Extending this principle to the tactical sphere and objecting to the prescription of detailed geographical objectives, he writes: "A qualified commander should normally be assigned only a general mission, whether it be attack or defence, and then given the means to carry it out. In this way he is completely unfettered in achieving the general purpose of his superior."

Bradley carried this doctrine even farther, for he believed: "You don't even tell a corps or division commander how to do his job when you have an army. You assign a mission and it's up to the fellow to carry it out. Of course, if you are in a position to have a look and talk it over with the guy you may make suggestions, but he doesn't have to take them."[26]

In the British services, on the other hand, command is very much more rigid and centralised. Orders tend to be more detailed and their execution more closely supervised than is generally the case within the American forces. In his dispatch on the Normandy assault, Admiral Ramsay reported that the U.S. naval commanders serving under him thought his orders "extended to too much detail" and "had to exercise considerable restraint in submitting" to the degree of control which he imposed. On a higher level, Eisenhower says that he was shocked to find that "the British Chiefs of Staff in London maintained the closest kind of contact with their commanders in the field and insisted upon being constantly informed as to details . . . that in our service would only in exceptional circumstances go higher than a local army H.Q." He and many other Americans were disturbed by this practice, not least because they believed it resulted in military plans being influenced by political pressure applied from Downing Street through the Chiefs of Staff.[27]

The relative merits of these rival concepts of command need not concern us now, for what suits one nation may well be anathema to another. It is not surprising, however, that American generals found the British system irksome, especially as applied by Montgomery. To them his methods were the more objectionable because he was so clearly born to command and, even in his most tactful moments, he exercised his authority almost as a matter of right. . . .[28]

We have heard much of "conformity," of the deterioration in America of "individualism" in recent decades. But if, nevertheless, a foreign observer can say this of Americans and of the American military during the Second World War,[29] how much more "individualism," how much more of "the characteristic American resentment of authority" must there have been in 1789-91 when defiance of authority had so recently been successfully practiced against the most powerful nation on earth![30] One could say of this defiance, and of the habits it confirmed, what Ames said of the difficulty of suppressing smuggling: "The habit of smuggling pervades our country. We were taught it when it was considered rather as meritorious than criminal. . . ." (*Annals*, I, p. 299)

Similar habits had been formed of speaking freely about political matters. This is clearly evident in accounts of the American press during the period immediately preceding the Revolution, a press which enjoyed at that time virtually unlimited freedom to attack constituted authority.[31]

V

Nevertheless, the American experience of the eighteenth century has been portrayed by some scholars as leaving to the country little more than a legacy of suppression.

Repressive aspects of that experience had been brought to the attention of the First Congress by Smith:

In February, 1782, the [South Carolina] legislature met at Jacksonburg, and discriminated between friend and foe, between American and British subjects, by disposing of the estates of the latter, and banishing them. . . .

It has also been said that Carolina tendered an oath, to discover who were friends, and who were enemies. In March, 1778, the Legislature of South Carolina passed an act to oblige every free male inhabitant of that State, above sixteen years of age, to take an oath of allegiance to the State. As there were notoriously many persons then in the State who were inimical to its liberties, such a step was necessary to give a reasonable cause for obliging them to quit the country. [*Annals*, I, pp. 399, 402]

Arthur M. Schlesinger, even as he described the length to which freedom of the press was carried by the colonists in their struggle against Great Britain, reported that the patriots did not feel that American Tories were entitled to a like degree of freedom in opposition to the patriot cause.[32] Thus, the Tories suffered throughout this period from both official and unofficial action on the part of the patriots and their governments. It is evident that two quite divergent rules of conduct were invoked, one calling for unprecedented freedom of speech and of the press for critics of the British government, the other limiting severely the expression of sentiments by citizens who preferred to remain steadfast in their allegiance to the British Crown.

The extent of the suppression of Tory opinion during the Revolutionary period has been described by Leonard W. Levy. In his *Legacy of Suppression*[33] he provided a much more comprehensive account of such suppression than I can hope to set forth here, thereby relieving this discussion of the necessity of such a mournful account.

Issue must be taken, however, with Levy's interpretation of the period, an interpretation that he frankly describes as "revisionist." It is so revisionist that he is led to conclude that "freedom of the press" at the time the First Amendment was written meant no more than the Blackstonian prohibition of "previous restraints," leaving the common law of seditious libel unaffected.[34] (That which was then known as "seditious libel" we know as "agitation," "subversion," or "advocacy of the overthrow of the government by force."[35]

The fundamental difficulty with the Levy formulation, aside from the general problem of the significance of historical research in constitutional interpretation, arises from his failure to take due account of the change of regime in America. The intimate relation between freedom of the press, as we know it, and a republican regime was not appreciated by him, especially for a country with no substantial tradition of licensing.[36] Thus, the suggestive parallel of parliamentary free speech was not given its due.[37] And this failing, in turn, permitted him to minimize the problem I have noted of determining what the Blackstonian rule of no-previous-restraint can mean when not the press, but speech, is the subject under consideration.[38] Levy could see for himself, but did not credit eighteenth-century Americans with the insight, that "freedom of discussion and the law of libel were simply incompatible. . . ."[39]

But aside from these general considerations, the reader confronts difficulties in interpreting as Levy did the evidence that he accumulated. He mentioned, for instance, that there were very few prosecutions in the American colonies for seditious libel, since juries would not indict or convict, whereas there were hundreds of such trials during the seventeenth and eighteenth centuries in England.[40] Does not this difference reflect critical differences between the two countries in popular attitudes and in the effective law?[41] It is evident that the many instances Levy reported of reaffirmations in print of the Blackstonian formula were stimulated by public expression of much more liberal sentiments.[42]

It is because he failed to grasp the significance of evidence that he himself collected that Levy could not account for the sudden emergence of the Jeffersonian position with respect to freedom of speech and of the press. The Sedition Act of 1798 did incite men such as Jefferson and Madison to develop a position, but it is evident that much which had gone before, and much in the republican regime itself, called forth and reinforced the arguments that were used.[43] Many of these arguments were quite sophisticated; and they evidently fell on receptive ears, ears not so exclusively attuned as are those of some twentieth-century scholars to lawyers' repetitions of obsolete Blackstonian formulae on this subject.[44] The change was forecast in the Constitution itself by the remarkable restraint placed there upon the traditional far-ranging law of treason: if treason, that terrible crime for which many Englishmen had been executed, could be safely limited, what risk was there in denying the general government any power to deal with seditious libel?[45]

Levy did concede that those who were oppressed often asked for a general freedom of speech or of the press, but he pointed out that they conducted themselves otherwise when they were actually in power. He simply assumed that they did not "mean" what they said when out of power. Thus, the rebels asked for open discussion so long as the English controlled the courts.[46] But it should be understood that the First Amendment can be said to have been demanded not by those in power but, rather, by those out of power: these were citizens who were concerned lest political dissent be muzzled, on whatever pretext, by a strong central government.

Indeed, the problem of Levy's book is whether the legacy left by the men of 1776-1801, by the men of the Declaration of Independence, is really one essentially of suppression. Rather, the legacy that a more inspired interpretation of Levy's facts suggests is that left by a people groping for a dimly perceived standard of the freedom implicit in their institutions, a people who (after resisting the demands of tyranny) had had experience with repressive laws of their own that did not work and with a freedom that did work.[47] This legacy includes the rich rhetorical tradition that Levy unpolitically disparaged, as well as the acknowledged powerlessness of the general government to deal with seditious libel even before the First Amendment was added to the Constitution.[48]

The influence of the Declaration of Independence on the emergence of freedom of speech and of the press has not been generally recognized: the Declaration presupposes effective discussion by the people of the most important issues, even as to what should be the appropriate regime in changing circumstances. The extent to which this influenced the tenor of sentiments and distinguished the United States among the nations of the world is seen in the declaration made by the Federalist justice of the Supreme Court, James Wilson, in a 1790 lecture on law in Philadelphia (with President Washington in the audience):

> Surely I am justified in saying, that the principles of the constitutions and governments and laws of the United States, and the republics, of which they are formed, are materially different from the principles of the constitution and government and laws of England; for that is the only country, from the principles of whose constitution and government and laws, it will be contended, that the elements of a law education ought to be drawn. I presume to go further: the principles of our constitutions and governments and laws are materially *better* than the principles of the constitution and government and laws of England.
>
> Permit me to mention one great principle, the *vital* principle I may well call it, which diffuses animation and vigor through all the others. The principle I mean is this, that the supreme or sovereign power of the society resides in the citizens at large; and that, therefore, they always retain the right of abolishing, altering, or amending their constitution, at whatever time, and in whatever manner, they shall deem it expedient.
>
> By Sir William Blackstone, from whose Commentaries, a performance in many respects highly valuable, the elements of a foreign law education would probably be borrowed—by Sir William Blackstone, this great and fundamental principle is treated as a political chimera, existing only in the minds of some theorists; but, in practice, inconsistent with the dispensation of any government upon earth. . . .[49]

The rationale of free discussion, as we know it today, was partly anticipated three centuries ago in Milton's "Apology for Smectymnus":

> To defend libels, which is that whereof I am next accused, was far from my purpose. I had not so little share in good name, as to give another that advantage against myself. The sum of what I said was, that a more free permission of writing at some times might be profitable, in such a question especially wherein the magistrates are not fully resolved; and both sides have equal liberty to write, as now they have. Not as when the prelates bore sway, in whose time the books of some men were confuted, when they who should have answered were in close prison, denied the use of pen or paper. And the divine right of episcopacy was then valiantly asserted, when he who would have been respondent must have bethought himself withal how he could refute the Clink or the Gatehouse. If now therefore

they be pursued with bad words, who persecuted others with bad deeds, it is a way to lessen tumult rather than to increase it; whenas anger thus freely vented spends itself ere it break out into action, though Machiavel, whom he cites, or any other Machiavelian priest think the contrary.[50]

These sentiments are further developed on behalf of a confident, self-governing people for whom Jefferson wrote in 1779, "that it is time enough for the rightful purposes of civil government for its officers to interfere when principles break out into overt acts against peace and good order."[51]

This is the legacy that the American people, as one people, should be reminded of, whatever modifications might be required from state to state as circumstances change.[52]

VI

The American patriots permitted themselves almost unlimited scope in the expression of political opinions. John Adams evidently had no difficulty in justifying, in the Revolutionary period, what he was doing in defiance of legally constituted authority. He and his colleagues defended their principled defiance of the law in the name of "freedom of the press." How was the subsequent wartime suppression of the Tories justified by the patriots? That is, what did they take "freedom of the press" to mean?[53]

Anyone who is aware of the protection afforded to popular opinion by the institution of trial by jury would suspect that "freedom of the press" means more than the protection of opinions that happen to be popular at the time of trial. Otherwise, "freedom of the press" would add nothing substantial to the protection provided by "trial by jury." A fair-minded person, removed from the heat of a particular controversy, would have to concede that "freedom of the press" should include the protection of opinions of a nature similar to his own, similar in all relevant respects except for the fact of popularity. That is, it would have to include the protection of unpopular opinions contradicting the popular ones, opinions that cannot rely upon the protection of a jury trial. Judges in such circumstances would be obliged to dismiss an indictment or set aside a conviction by a jury if a right under the First Amendment would otherwise be infringed.[54]

This principle is in fact what the opposing sides can be said to have agreed upon, even if they would not explicitly recognize it in practice.[55] The patriots, in 1764-76 (that is, before they came to power in their respective states), did not rely, in justification of their position, simply on the fact that juries would not convict: they went farther than that by claiming that juries *should not* convict, that their attacks upon constituted authority were proper and legitimate and within the scope of "freedom of the press." They did not rely simply on any English common law notions of "liberty of the press," with its emphasis upon no-previous-restraint: they went much farther than that, claiming they had a right to make virtually any comment they wished to make about the conduct of government and about the activities of government officials.[56] If there was any qualification of this right, it was that the comment must be true, not that it had been made in good faith. But even this qualification may not have been accepted: they seem to have believed that the citizen was entitled to disseminate untruths if good government might thereby be advanced. And the more sophisticated among the patriots realized that untruths *were* deliberately disseminated on both sides in the great constitutional controversy of that period.

Thus, if the practice of the patriots, even in the days when ultimate British authority was still generally acknowledged, is any indication of what was generally thought about "liberty of the press," there was a significant departure in America from what English lawbooks might have said at that time or even from what judges in courts might have charged juries. It is particularly appropriate to rely in this manner upon popular understanding and general usage: after all, the demand for a Bill of Rights seems to have been largely popular in origin.[57]

But what is meant by saying, as I have, "This principle is in fact what the opposing sides can be said to have agreed upon"? It is true that each faction, when it had the advantage, attempted to suppress its opponents. Popular opinion, rather than legislative enactments, seems often to have been sufficient to curtail the expression of dissenting opinion. In some instances, this popular opinion would be supported by private violence or by threats of violence. No doubt there was some official suppression as well.

Yet each side, whenever threatened by either official or popular suppression, continued to regard itself as espousing views that should be protected, views that would not harm the community but would instead contribute to the common good. It then pleaded on principle for wider protection, and it would *then* have been willing to grant that its opponents should be permitted similar protection in like circumstances.[58] Although the dominant party was rarely disposed to be as tolerant as its opponents argued it should be, this does not invalidate the principle I have noticed, especially when it is granted that each of the two sides in the generation-long controversy was essentially decent.

Is it not in this sense, then, that all parties in America could be taken to have agreed implicitly upon the extent of protection desirable for the press? That the party dominant at any particular time might not have been able to live up to this "agreement" does not necessarily invalidate the reasonableness of the agreement, but merely testifies to the power of passion and self-interest, thereby emphasizing the need to establish more firmly in time of calm the agreements which are designed to serve the common good in times of turmoil.[59]

We should not take self-serving pronouncements lightly, especially if they should be obviously elevated: men are sometimes driven to recognize in adversity principles that they are too prone to ignore in periods of prosperity.[60] However one views this agreement, is there not merit to the suggestion that we can adopt as a safe guide to what "freedom of the press" means the standards invoked by the citizens who were to establish the Union, by the very men who founded the Republic for which the Constitution was written in 1787? If one cannot trust the actions as well as the pronouncements of these men for standards and guides with respect to this problem, whom can one trust? They felt themselves free, as responsible citizens and loyal subjects, to make the most devastating attacks on constituted authority, attacks that culminated in armed rebellion.

What legitimate recourse would they have said that the British government had to prevent such rebellion? The Declaration of Independence indicates the British government had had the legitimate recourse of redressing the grievances that had brought on the complaints and disorders. If these grievances had not been significant —if a government among a mature, alert, and experienced people had been doing justice—then it would have been highly unlikely that the attacks of a misguided minority would do any harm that was both permanent and severe.[61] The British government had the further recourse, as Dicey later said, of making it clear what would happen if rebellion did follow upon agitation and discussion.[62]

The British government—a respectable,[63] even though perhaps mistaken, judge in that controversy—thought that the cause of the patriots was *not* just. Certainly, this was a defensible position.[64] But the patriots were not willing to rely upon the judgment or opinion of constituted authority, even though it was an authority to which they and their fathers had long acknowledged allegiance. The principle they *acted* upon seemed to be that the American citizen should be left free to criticize his government, even in the most decisive manner, when he believes that that government acts improperly.[65]

This, then, seems to have been the principle the patriots, the Founding Fathers, can be said to have acted upon with respect to criticism of constituted authority.[66] The principle is not repudiated simply because they were not able to abide by it fully when they, in turn, became the constituted authority.[67] Immediate pressures deterred them; nor had they exercised sovereign power long enough to have learned, as citizens and government, to act with confidence. Indeed, their experience with themselves as rulers as well as subjects may have led many citizens to the opinion John Adams expressed in 1787: "It is weakness rather than wickedness which renders men unfit to be trusted with unlimited power."[68]

VII

It is sometimes said today that freedom should not be permitted those who, were they to gain power, would not in turn permit it to others.[69] (Of course, there is always the difficulty of being certain just how one *will* act upon assuming power.)[70]

This argument has a curious bearing on the experience of the Founding Fathers: they demanded and exercised before 1776 a degree of freedom which they were *not* immediately willing to grant, when they assumed power during the Revolutionary War, to the very men who had permitted them to act freely and effectively as British subjects enjoying English liberties.[71] (It was only after the war—only, that is, when the Loyalist was little more than an anachronism—that attempts at restitution and reform were made.)[72] Thus, on the basis of the qualification upon freedom that some argue for, freedom should not have been permitted the Founding Fathers before the Revolution.

But we know, it may be said, that however intolerant the patriots may have been once war started, their characters were such as to insure an eventual return to toleration and good government. Should, then, the most radical attacks upon constituted authority be permitted only to men of good character? Does this provide a practical guide for the conduct of the affairs of a vast republic? Both sides, in the course of the prerevolutionary controversy, *thought* some leaders among the opposition the worst of opportunists.[73] Can a test of character that men can rely upon in such circumstances—for it would be in the midst of passionate conflict that the test would have to be applied—be devised?[74] Is not a "good character" rule one that can be applied only by men entirely removed from the scene, scholars in universities, if not (even more removed) historians many years later? Practicable guides have to be provided for citizens and officials on the spot if a political community of a given character is to be preserved.[75]

Related to these considerations is the argument that the freedom to speak, to attack the government, should be least extensive (or even nonexistent) when the government is legitimate and good. This distinction is not found in any of the constitutional deliberations, however; and it is called into question by the fact that several state ratifying conventions called for constitutional provisions protecting freedom of the press. Thus, freedom of the press was not thought of with a view to bad governments only, but as critical to life under a good government as well, even the very Republic provided for by the Constitution.

We are again reminded of the extent to which the American Republic depended for its birth on an unlimited freedom of speech by the exuberant language of John Adams, commenting many years later on James Otis's famous speech of 1761 against the Writs of Assistance:

But Otis was a flame of fire; with a promptitude of classical allusions, a depth of research, a rapid summary of historical events and dates, a profusion of legal authorities, a prophetic glance of his eyes into futurity, and a rapid torrent of impetuous eloquence he hurried away all before him. American Independence was then and there born. The seeds of patriots and heroes, to defend the *Non sine Diis animosus infans*, to defend the vigorous youth, were then and there sown. Every man of an immense crowded audience appeared to me to go away as I did, ready to take arms against Writs of Assistance. Then and there was the first scene of the first act of opposition to the arbitrary claims of Great Britain. Then and there the child Independence was born. In fifteen years, i.e., in 1776, he grew up to manhood and declared himself free.[76]

Otis—"the great James Otis"[77]—is represented as "a flame of fire"; and, we are told, "Every man of an immense crowded audience appeared to me to go away as I did, ready to take arms against Writs of Assistance." These proud words may be usefully contrasted with the progeny of the "clear and present danger" test that we have had imposed upon us since the First World War.[78] Otis went unpunished for his incitement: no doubt, it would have been impossible to secure a jury that would either indict or convict.

It is of such materials and reflections, as well as those of Levy, that our understanding of "freedom of speech [and] of the press" must be formed.[79]

VIII

Three points remain for immediate consideration which bear on the question of whether the First Amendment was intended (as some say) primarily to do no more than to confirm the common law guarantee of "liberty of the press."[80]

1. One of the changes proposed and considered in the Senate, in the course of its review of the constitutional amendments submitted by the House, was that the speech and press provision should read,

The freedom of speech and of the press, in as ample a manner as hath at any time been secured by the common law, . . . shall not be infringed.[81]

This suggested change was rejected. If (as I have argued) the American ideas on this subject were far in advance of the English common law, then this provision should have been regarded as restrictive and could have been rejected on that ground alone.

2. A reliance upon the common law would have been complicated, in any event, by the fact that divergencies had developed in the common law of various states by the time the First Amendment was written.[82] Especially would this have been so with respect to speaking and publishing, activities that were essentially local in their

effects. The general understanding of "freedom of speech and of the press," on the other hand, would tend to ignore local circumstances and restrictions, particularly when the assurance sought was for the right to examine and discuss freely the activities and officers of the general government.[83]

3. What of the verb *abridging*: does it connote only the cutting down of previously defined legal rights, such as those that the common law establishes?[84] Although the word may be used in this sense,[85] it need not be limited to it, but may be used as well to refer to rights that do not have a technical legal basis and extent but rather can be said to be natural and even virtually unlimited.

Thus, there are instances in Blackstone in which *abridge* is clearly meant to refer to a standard drawn from nature or from natural right.[86] Nor is this usage restricted to Blackstone. It is consistent with usage prior to the writings of the First Amendment to employ *abridge* in circumstances where reference is made to the law of nature or to a standard of natural liberty to which man is entitled, of which he should not be deprived, but which is nevertheless rarely realized.[87]

This approach to what may be called "natural liberty" or "natural right" is reflected in the Ninth Amendment, where rights are recognized which exist independently of explicit enumeration. One such right, I have suggested, is that right of revolution of which freedom of speech may be considered a continuing, if partial and restrained, exercise. And this right of revolution *is* a natural right, not dependent on any positive law or explicit acknowledgment by constituted authority. Thus, "abridging" is not limited to a context in which previously defined legal rights are involved (of which the common law would have been the principal expression).

IX

In any event, it is not unreasonable to conclude, on the basis of the evidence examined of what was done and said prior to 1789-91, that "freedom of speech, or of the press" was very extensive, certainly in the popular understanding.

A comment by William W. Crosskey (who is not only a defender of the Sedition Act of 1798 but also the leading advocate today of an interpretation of the Constitution which assigns broad general powers to Congress) indicates how extensive "freedom of speech, or of the press" might have been in the popular understanding:

> As for the failure [of the First Amendment] to blot out all governmental power, state as well as national, respecting the subjects of "free speech," "free press," and "free assembly," this is by no means difficult to understand if the fact is borne in mind that Shays' Rebellion, in Massachusetts, and other similar disturbances, in certain of the other states, were not very far in the past when these amendments were drafted. For the still fresh memory of these events probably produced a desire for some governmental control over the three modes of agitating that had underlain them. In these circumstances, state power over these matters, subject to a negative control in Congress to prevent abuses by the states, was a natural compromise. . . .[88]

Is it not implied here by Crosskey that "freedom of speech, or of the press" was taken by Americans in 1789 as protecting even the kind of speech and press activity that led to Shays's Rebellion (as distinguished from rebellion itself)? This alone would suggest a much more extensive protection of speech and the press, understood in general usage to be provided against Congress by these words, than the common law offered.

But this extensive protection, as I have indicated, must be limited to its proper object: that is, a further refinement of what is meant by "freedom of speech, or of the press" is called for, in order that we may understand just what it was of which a virtually unlimited right of expression can be said to have been secured against the general government.[89]

I return to the passage from Blackstone quoted in section 2 of this chapter. The "fine writer" referred to by Blackstone seems to be Jonathan Swift. Gulliver reports the response by the king of Brobdingnag to Gulliver's account of the British:

> He laughed at my odd kind of arithmetic (as he was pleased to call it) in reckoning the numbers of our people by a computation drawn from the several sects among us in religion and politics. He said, he knew no reason, why those who entertain opinions prejudicial to the public, should be obliged to change, or should not be obliged to conceal them.[90] And, as it was tyranny in any government to require the first, so it was weakness not to enforce the second: for a man may be allowed to keep poisons in his closet, but not to vend them about for cordials.[91]

We see anticipated in this passage from Swift the coupling, in the First Amendment, of the subject of religion with that of speech and the press. There are, Swift had the king recognize, two principal subjects with respect to which the problem of suppression arises, "religion and politics." Thus, religious opinion (and expression) and political opinion (and expression) are central to this problem, not opinion and expression about every subject.[92]

The centrality of this combination, of religion and politics, was reflected in my quotation from Blackstone. Six kinds of libels are referred to there—"blasphemous, immoral, treasonable, schismatical, seditious, or scandalous"—two of which (the first and fourth) relate primarily to religious matters, two of which (the third and fifth) relate primarily to political matters, and two of which (the second and sixth) relate to both religious and political matters. Thus, improper utterances about political and religious matters, tending toward a breach of the peace, have to be guarded against.

In addition, Blackstone speaks of the danger of making one man "the arbitrary and infallible judge of all controverted points in learning, religion, and government." "Learning" here seems somewhat neutral;[93] the key terms are probably "religion" and "government": controversies about these matters, even with respect to learning, invite government supervision and interference. There is still another coupling of "religion" and "government" in Blackstone's argument that punishment for certain writings "is necessary for the preservation of peace and good order, of government and religion, the only solid foundations of civil liberty." (Presumably, the justification for such punishment would be removed, *even in Blackstone's view*, if it could be shown that "civil liberty" might be even better established and preserved, *as well as "peace and good order,"* in a community in which the most extensive freedom of expression is permitted. Would this not have been for him a significant lesson of American experience?[94])

Thus, in the Blackstonian passage dealing with "liberty of the press," the opinions that it is assumed would raise questions are those that deal with matters of religion and politics (or government), a pairing of topics that goes back to writers such as Milton and Swift and is caught up in the First Amendment.[95] Dicey also speaks, in one of the passages which I have reproduced, of "the right of every man to say and write what he pleases, especially on social, political, or religious topics, without fear of legal penalties."[96]

I submit, therefore, that it is primarily "political discussion" that is governed by that part of the First Amendment which protects "freedom of speech, or of the press."[97] This submission has been implicit throughout my discussion: that is, I have relied throughout on what the American reader already knows about the subject.[98] The political context, or at least orientation, of the speech-press-assembly-petition provision is indicated in Madison's description of an earlier draft:

> The right of freedom of speech is secured; the liberty of the press is expressly declared to be beyond the reach of the Government; the people may therefore publicly address their representatives, may privately advise them, or declare their sentiments by petition to the whole body; in all these ways, they may communicate their will. [*Annals*, I, p. 738]

Further indication of a political cast is seen in the fact that the nonreligious part of the amendment ends with the reference to petitioning the government for a redress of grievances. That is, political reform, growing out of complaints against the government, seems to be the principal object of this activity by the people.

Still another indication that it is political talk primarily that is protected by the First Amendment—the discussion that free men carry on as part of the duty to govern themselves, to investigate and decide on issues of a political nature, to choose public servants and to assess political measures—is given by the contexts and tenor of a multitude of eighteenth-century instances in which the terms "liberty [or freedom] of speech," and "liberty [or freedom] of the press" are used. In practically all instances contemporary with the writing of the First Amendment (many of which I quote in this volume[99]), in which the nature of the reference is clear, it is evident that a political context or character is assumed.[100]

Perhaps the most important indication of the political emphasis (as well as of the extent) of the First Amendment rights of "freedom of speech [and] of the press" is to be found in the parliamentary prototype of these rights,[101] that is, the "freedom of speech" or "freedome of debates" traditionally guaranteed to members of a legislature.[102] The justification for this immunity is that it encourages full and frank discussion of public business.[103] The distinctive emergence in the United States of "freedom of speech [and] of the press" reflects the extension of the public forum from the legislative halls to the country at large, an extension that is appropriate to a self-governing people.[104]

It is precisely because of the nature of our regime that the parliamentary privilege is so significant a precedent.[105] The extent and purpose of this privilege are suggested in the exchanges of 1621 between James I and the Commons. What Parliament had become late in the eighteenth century[106] can be said to have been inherent in that body almost two centuries before when it had had to struggle against powerful princes for the recognition of its most vital privilege. James I had written to the Speaker, December 3, 1621,

We have heard by divers reports, to our great grief, that our distance from the Houses of Parliament, caused by our indisposition of health, hath emboldened some fiery and popular spirits of some of the House of Commons to argue and debate publicly of matters far above their reach and capacity, tending to our high dishonour and breach of prerogative royal. These are therefore to command you to make known in our name unto the House, that none therein shall presume henceforth to meddle with anything concerning our government or deep matters of state, and namely, not to deal with our dearest son's match with the daughter of Spain, nor to touch the honour of that king or any other our friends and confederates: and also not to meddle with any men's particulars, which have their due motion in our ordinary courts of justice.[107]

In its Petition of December 9, the House responded,

... whereas your Majesty, by the general words of your letter, seemeth to restrain us from intermeddling with matters of government or particulars which have their motion in the courts of justice, the generality of which words, in the largeness of the extent thereof (as we hope beyond your Majesty's intention), might involve those things which are the proper subjects of parliamentary occasions and discourse: and whereas your Majesty doth seem to abridge us of the ancient liberty of parliament for freedom of speech,[108] jurisdiction and just censure of the House, and other proceedings there (wherein we trust in God we shall never transgress the bounds of loyal and dutiful subjects), a liberty which, we assure ourselves, so wise and so just a king will not infringe, the same being our ancient and undoubted right and an inheritance received from our ancestors, without which we cannot freely debate nor clearly discern of things in question before us, nor truly inform your Majesty; . . . we are therefore now again enforced, in all humbleness, to pray your Majesty to allow the same, and thereby to take away the doubts and scruples your Majesty's late letter to our Speaker hath wrought upon us . . .[109]

The king's answer was written the following day and included these sentiments:

. . . Now whereas, in the very beginning of this your apology, you tax us, in fair terms, of trusting uncertain reports and partial informations concerning your proceedings, we wish you to remember that we are an old and experienced king, needing no such lessons, being, in our conscience, freest of any king alive from hearing or trusting idle reports. . . .

In the body of your petition, you usurp upon our prerogative royal and meddle with things far above your reach, and then in the conclusion you protest the contrary; as if a robber would take a man's purse and then protest he meant not to rob him. . . . And touching your excuse of not determining anything concerning the match of our dearest son, but only to tell your opinion and lay it down at our feet, first we desire to know how you could have presumed to determine in that point without committing of high treason? . . .

And although we cannot allow of the style, calling it your ancient and undoubted right and inheritance, but could rather have wished that ye had said that your privileges were derived from the grace and permission of our ancestors and us (for most of them grow from precedents, which shows rather a toleration than inheritance), yet we are pleased to give you our royal assurance, that as long as you contain yourself within the limits of your duty, we will be as careful to maintain and preserve your lawful liberties and privileges, as ever any of our predecessors were, nay, as to preserve our own royal prerogative; so as your House shall only have need to beware to trench upon the prerogative of the crown; which would enforce us, or any just king, to retrench them of their privileges, that would pare his prerogative and flowers of the crown: but of this, we hope, there shall never be cause given.[110]

It was this royal challenge (with its imputation of high treason) that evoked, on December 18, 1621, the Great Protestation of the House of Commons, which included the declaration that

the arduous and urgent affairs concerning the king, state and defence of the realm, and of the church of England, and the maintenance and making of laws, and redress of mischiefs and grievances which daily happen within this realm, are proper subjects and matter of counsel and debate in parliament: and that in the handling and proceeding of those businesses every member of the House of Parliament hath and of right ought to have freedom of speech, to propound, treat, reason and bring to conclusion the same. . . .[111]

It is in this tradition that I offer the submission that the almost unlimited freedom of expression protected by the First Amendment against the general government relates primarily to the examination and discussion of public servants and of political matters by a self-governing people.[112]

The benefits to be derived from such freedom of debate are suggested by the surviving records of the Constitutional Convention and the First Congress.[113] These provide us standards against which our deliberations today, both in Congress and "out of doors," may be judged. That the public forum can never attain the competence reflected in these records is evident to anyone familiar with the divergent circumstances and the composition of these various bodies (that is, the Convention, the First Congress, and the public). But men are formed as much by the aspirations which they fail to fulfill as by the partial successes they settle for. The quality of such unfettered debate, at its best, is indicated in Madison's observation:

> . . . though I acknowledge that a majority ought to govern, yet they have no authority to deprive the minority of a Constitutional right; they have no authority to debar us the right of free debate. An important and interesting question being under consideration, we ought to have time allowed for its discussion. Facts have been stated on one side, and members ought to be indulged on the other with an opportunity of collecting and ascertaining other facts. We have a right to bring forward all the arguments which we think can, and ought to have an influence on the decision. It is unusual, on a partial discussion, even of questions of inferior magnitude, to decide in the course of a single day. How, then, can gentlemen reconcile their conduct of this day to the liberality they have hitherto shown? [*Annals*, I, p. 857][114]

The question considered in the House on that occasion related to the choice of the permanent site of the general government. The almost inevitably equivocal character of recourse to principles of this kind in political controversy is suggested by the fact that Madison's high-minded declaration here evidently concealed his desire to secure the postponement of a vote that threatened defeat of southern interests. Thus, Ames answered,

> ... when this subject came before the House the other day, when we solicited for delay, it was observed that the necessities of the Union required an immediate decision; that it would take up but little time. ... Now, when circumstances appear to be changed, when the calculation is made, when the House are ready to vote, gentlemen come forward and pretend that they want time. [*Annals, I*, p. 858]

But the intrusion or role of self-interest does not deny the validity of a recourse to principle; rather, the distortions induced by self-interest suggest that principle (not an absolute rule) is ultimately the only reliable recourse.[115]

The effect of self-interest, as well as of the character of the participants, is recognized in a comment by Scott in the course of the discussion of the location of the capital city of the general government:

> This he conceived to be a favorable moment to determine the great question that had agitated the minds of the people for several years. We might be assured, that at this time Congress possessed all their virtue and innocence; but it might be feared that would not be the case in future. Congress were now free from all factions, and as devoid as possible of the spirit of party and local views. [*Annals, I*, p. 788]

The end as well as the basis of the political community, and of that free public deliberation which characterizes republican government, is given expression by Madison in still another passage that some might, in the name of realism, unrealistically dismiss as simply self-serving:

> He hoped that all would concur in the great principle on which they ought to conduct and decide this business; an equal attention to the rights of the community. No Government, he said, not even the most despotic, could, beyond a certain point, violate that idea of justice and equal right which prevailed in the mind of the community. In Republican Governments, justice and equality form the basis of the system; and perhaps the structure can rest on no other that the wisdom of man can devise. In a Federal Republic, give me leave to say, it is even more necessary and proper, that a sacred regard should be paid to these considerations. ... [*Annals, I*, p. 861]

It is partly to insure that the claims to equality and justice of the entire community might be given proper consideration—to insure that such claims might be stated by those who have the greatest interest in seeing that they *are* stated and stated most effectively—that emphasis has been placed by us upon freedom of speech and of the press with respect to political matters.

X

I collect here, in order better to indicate just what is included within the protection of the First Amendment guarantee of "freedom of speech [and] of the press," some of the uses of words that are *not* included within my understanding of "political matters."[116] This catalog draws not only upon my understanding of the language we have been studying but, in addition, both upon indications contemporary with the enactment of the First Amendment and upon that account of freedom of speech which I have already sketched and which I develop at greater length in chapter 8.[117] It should at once be recognized that the use of words does not immunize activities otherwise criminal or otherwise harmful to the rights of another.

May treason, as defined in the Constitution, be committed by the use of words alone as well as by deeds?[118] Treason is clearly within the power of Congress to legislate against.[119] Setting aside for the moment problems of proof and those that arise from a misunderstanding of his purposes,[120] we may say that a citizen who commits treason is not engaged in the ordinary process of self-government. There is no reason, that is, for protecting constitutionally that kind of activity (however lenient Congress or the community may choose to be, in particular circumstances, in dealing with such conduct).

The same may be said of espionage, of the sabotage of military installations, or of the assassination of government officials, all of which crimes may be inaugurated or advanced by the use of words.[121] The general government, in the exercise of its defense powers, seems to have authority to deal with espionage and sabotage. In addition, certain kinds of fraud, which may rely primarily on words for their effectiveness, fall within the purview of Congress acting under its Commerce Clause powers. None of these cases raise free speech problems.[122]

The second general category in my catalog of utterances that do not qualify as political expression is less clearcut: obscenity. Let us assume, at least for the moment, power in Congress, aside from the use made of the overworked post office, to legislate on this subject.[123] Is there special protection under the First Amendment for expression that raises questions about obscenity? The problem has arisen in recent years in discussions of motion pictures, of so-called comic books, and of books ranging from D. H. Lawrence's *Lady Chatterley's Lover* down to the deliberately pornographic.[124]

This does not seem to me a First Amendment problem. Nor need the proper governmental attitude turn about a decision whether the publication in question *is* "obscene." There may be good reason for the appropriate government's restricting (in accordance with clearly defined criteria) the circulation of materials which may not be obscene but which may still have a harmful effect, particularly if their publication tends to legitimate (in the public mind, or for the unreflecting and ignorant) trash that *is* more directly objectionable and harmful.[125]

Although publishers may not be entitled, on the issue of obscenity (or on the related [if not identical] issue of undue portrayal of horror, violence, or crime), to the protection of the First Amendment, they are entitled to the rule of law which, I have argued, provides an extensive protection in itself. They and the community are also entitled to a careful consideration of just what obscenity consists in, what harmful effects may be expected from obscenity or from efforts to suppress it, and what the best means of proceeding are to secure what is desired without instituting either a general campaign of repression or a popular reaction against license which can interfere with free political expression as well.[126]

My suggestion here depends on the belief that however much an artist attempts to present problems basic to modern life, his discussion is not immediately political: it is usually not primarily related to problems of self-government, of discussing and deciding political issues.[127] Pleasure, rather than truth, is his principal objective as an artist.[128] It may be true that all serious art has a political bearing and effect—but to consider art as political expression would both ignore essential distinctions and deprive us of an intended and useful limitation.[129] A political argument does remain, however, and one that is protected by the First Amendment against suppression by the general government, and that is whether materials of this kind, or of any kind, should be suppressed. So long as *that* question can be raised and fully discussed, mistakes in suppressing obscenities (or anything else) can be corrected or endured.[130] We have seen, however, a reversal in emphasis: we live in an age when the utmost latitude has come to be permitted in "artistic" matters even as serious limitations have been placed from time to time upon political discussion.[131]

The deference to be paid to the needs of and the right to self-government could well justify the rule that, in cases of doubt, a particular publication is to be regarded as political and thus be entitled to the protection of the First Amendment. But this is easily determined *not* to be the case with most motion pictures, with almost all "comic books," and even with most of the books published every year. So far as the general government, or even any state government, is concerned, the property and liberty individuals have with respect to movies, comics, and most books is adequately protected, as I have indicated, by an insistence on the rule of law (with its prohibition of "no previous restraints").[132]

The third category in my catalog of the kinds of verbal expression that need *not* be covered by "freedom of speech [and] of the press" is that of private defamation. Although the government, and officers of the government as such, may be precluded by the First Amendment from prosecuting criminal actions for libel or slander, private individuals are not prevented by it from instituting civil suits.[133] The prohibitions of the First Amendment, as we have seen, are directed against the general government.[134]

I need do no more than mention here two categories which I have discussed earlier, that encompassing expressions which amount to contempt of court and that relating to what may be said by military personnel when subject to military discipline. Neither of these is ordinarily and directly protected by the First Amendment. A sixth category, however, is more ambiguous—that which relates to attacks "out of doors" upon proceedings and speakers in Congress. (This, too, has been discussed earlier.) How far may Congress go to insure that its debates shall not be interfered with or adversely affected by what is said outside Congress in the press and elsewhere? References to this problem in the First Congress are ambiguous: there is something here analogous to "contempt of court," especially when Congress is primarily concerned with preserving the integrity of its debates rather than with covert legislation.

For a possible seventh category in my catalog of forms of expression not necessarily covered by "freedom of speech [and] of the press," I return to the movies, along with which may be considered television and radio.[135] If a question of obscenity, or of other nonpolitical expression (such as the portrayal of crime and violence, or misrepresentation in advertisements), is raised, there need be no problem of the applicability of the First Amendment.[136] But what if these electronic media are used for political presentations? One difficulty presents itself, especially in the case of radio and to some extent even television: short of the use of jamming devices, a particular state would find it difficult to control or regulate locally what is told its citizens from other states. There would be, in effect, no authority anywhere to control the broadcast of political expressions if Congress should be precluded from interfering.[137]

There are, furthermore, limited air rights, limited access to television and radio audiences. And, an even more important consideration, these media are strikingly different from the press or speech: a much larger group can be immediately affected than could ever have been reached by a speech. It is, moreover, a group that is "assembled" and yet not seen or gauged by the speaker, by their fellow citizens, or by public servants. There is not even the safeguard we have when large audiences are reached by the press: printed material has to be read rather than, as with radio and television, passively absorbed.[138]

It is often said that radio and television are, as means of conveying political sentiments, essentially like the press. But should not a question be raised, in instances where technological development has been so marked as to change the very nature of the recipients' participation and of the "author's" influence, about the extent to which these forms of expression qualify as that "speech" and "press" referred to in the First Amendment? These are among the considerations that should be taken into account in weighing proposals for the regulation of political broadcasting. The spirit of the First Amendment, properly understood, should illuminate the legitimate regulation of these new media, just as it should guide our reflections about forms of expression besides those considered here.[139]

XI

I have attempted to justify my proposition that, if the freedom of speech and of the press claimed and exercised by the men who made the American Revolution and established the Constitution remains our standard, the freedom of Americans to engage in political discussion of the most radical kind cannot be impaired by Congress. Congress is absolutely precluded from interfering as a law-making body with this prerogative of the American people.

I have also attempted to justify the proposition that this right under the First Amendment is intimately related to the right and duty of self-government that Americans claim and exercise. The protection granted or acknowledged by the amendment is very extensive, covering absolutely (so far as Congress is concerned) as much as anyone may reasonably claim as political. The people, it may be said, are not to be kept by Congress from expressing whatever sentiments they wish about the way the general government is conducted, about their public servants, and even about the quality and value of existing institutions. Gerry was not expressing his opinion only when he observed that "in a republic every action ought to be accounted for. . . ." (*Annals*, I, p. 574), which means that every action may be examined.[140]

It is appropriate at this point to justify, by recourse to scholarly authority which reinforces my own account, the emphasis I have placed in this study upon the relation of freedom of speech to the fact of self-government under the Constitution. Once there is recourse to self-government—a shift to the establishment by the people of a constitution and government under the control of the people —there is a related shift in the view of what the people may legitimately say. Thus, William S. Holdsworth observed, "Stephen has pointed out that the view which the law takes of the offence of publishing seditious writings or uttering seditious words, will depend upon the view held as to the relation of rulers to their subjects." He quoted the following passage from Sir James F. Stephen's *History of the Criminal Law of England*:[141]

Two different views may be taken of the relation between rulers and their subjects. If the ruler is regarded as the superior of the subject, as being by the nature of his position presumably wise and good . . . it must necessarily follow that it is wrong to censure him openly, that even if he is mistaken his mistakes should be pointed out with the utmost respect, and that whether mistaken or not, no censure should be cast upon him likely or designed to diminish his authority. If, on the other hand, the ruler is regarded as the agent and servant, and the subject as the wise and good master, who is obliged to delegate his power to the so-called ruler . . . it is obvious that this sentiment must be reversed. Every member of the public who censures the ruler for the time being exercises in his own person the right which belongs to the whole of which he forms part. He is finding fault with a servant. . . . To those who hold this view fully, and carry it out to all its consequences, *there can be no such offence as sedition*.[142] There may indeed be breaches of the peace which may destroy or endanger life, limb or property, and there may be incitements to such offences. But no imaginable censure of the government, short of a censure which has an immediate tendency to produce such a breach of the peace, ought to be regarded as criminal. [Italics added]

And Holdsworth added, "The first of these two views was the accepted view in the seventeenth century. The second was gathering strength during the latter part of the eighteenth century, and is now the accepted view."[143]

The first of these views, that of the seventeenth century, is reflected in the Blackstonian "no-previous-restraint" version of "liberty of the press": the rulers are prevailed upon not to interfere with utterances until after they have been published; thereupon, authors of utterances with seditious tendencies may properly be punished. The second of the views that Stephen described—with its practical conclusion that "there can be no such offence as sedition"—is seen in the First Amendment, with its limitation upon the power of Congress and with its establishment as a "term of art" of the expression "freedom of speech, [and] of the press."[144]

These considerations are reinforced by a fact we have already noticed—that of the elevation of "freedom of speech," an activity that can be engaged in by the entire population, to the status theretofore held only by "liberty of the press." Until the establishment of the American Republic, "liberty of the press" had been emphasized when freedom of expression for the public at large *was* provided for. "Freedom of speech," which had theretofore been known only in discussions on the floor of a legislative body, can be said to have been expanded by the First Amendment to include the entire population: the real rulers were no longer to be found in parliament and among that minority of literate citizens with access to printing presses, but among the people at large.[145]

Stephen's analysis made a reservation in favor of suppression or punishment as criminal of those "breaches of the peace which may destroy or endanger life, limb or property, and . . . incitements to such offences." He spoke also of "an immediate tendency to produce . . . a breach of the peace." There can be no serious objection (except by the doctrinaire) to curtailing such incitements, to calling an immediate and temporary halt to imminently provocative activities. If a mistake is made by the authorities, provided the community keeps firmly in mind its general standards, the harm can be readily repaired. It is the long-run curtailment or suppression which is really harmful, which keeps the community from hearing and fully considering fundamental alternatives to the course of action pursued by the government. The sort of exception Stephen referred to (with respect to breaches of the peace) is analogous to the power of each house of Congress to control its proceedings, to insure that its business may be conducted in an orderly and expeditious manner.[146]

Such an "immediate" instance would no doubt be posed by the man who cries "Fire" in a theater.[147] But this is not an instance or problem that affects my analysis of the First Amendment: power exists to handle such breaches of the peace, such "imminent Danger," but it exists in the state governments, not in the general government. That is to say, the keeping of the peace is recognized, under the Constitution, as an essentially local concern; and it was at the local level (as we shall see in chapter 7) that the appropriate power was prudently left.

The passages I have quoted from Holdsworth and Stephen reinforce the good sense of Madison's observation that we "ought not to look for the meaning of terms used in the laws and Constitution of the United States, into the acceptation of them in other countries, whose situation and Government were different from that of United America." (*Annals*, I, p. 906)

XII

Several distinctions have been suggested in this chapter, in an attempt to ascertain the meaning of "freedom of speech [and] of the press" in the Constitution. These include the critical distinction between "political" and "nonpolitical" expressions.

Of course, there remain lines to be drawn. But in most cases in which Congress has power to act, there should not be much difficulty: by and large, it is easy to distinguish between a fraudulent claim for patent medicine sold in "interstate commerce" and dubious (but nevertheless privileged) claims made by men seeking votes or criticizing the government.[148] The analysis I have made and the rationale I have suggested with respect to the First Amendment do leave lines to be drawn, but lines markedly easier to locate than those which have been seen in the cases decided by the courts heretofore.[149]

In any event, there would be invalidated by my interpretation of the First Amendment most if not all of the convictions secured by the general government in this century against the political speech reported in cases from *Schenck* through *Dennis* and beyond. If seditious libel is recognized as clearly beyond the reach of Congress, there need not be as much concern as there should otherwise be about restrictions upon other forms of expression by Congress, whether the particular form of expression is condemned as "obscenity," "fraud," or "military insubordination." Since treason is carefully defined in the Constitution, the people, including dissenting citizens, remain *politically* free to criticize and correct any restrictive activities of the government which may get out of hand.

The courts, I have pointed out, admit that there does result from various acts of Congress an "abridgment" of freedom of speech,[150] but they justify this abridgment by falling back on the assumption that there are exceptions to the apparently absolute commands of the First Amendment. Should the absoluteness of these commands be respected and should exceptions such as the "clear and present danger" test (and a contemporary counterpart, the "balancing" test) be discarded, some would be tempted to conceal the admission of abridgment within the meaning of "freedom of speech" itself. I have suggested in this chapter that meaning of our First Amendment language which draws upon American experience as well as upon American political thought. In the chapters that follow, I shall examine the legitimate alternatives to the unconstitutional remedies which the courts and other public servants have devised in their confrontation of the inevitable problems created by the extensive freedom of speech and of the press guaranteed by the Constitution.

In order to present one useful interpretation of the First Amendment, I have tended to read the evidence a certain way. But it is more important, now that a position has been sketched and has been given what I trust is an adequate historical foundation, to acknowledge again the limitations of any constitutional argument. I do not suggest I have settled the meaning of the First Amendment. Indeed, I doubt that anyone can do that in such a study as this. But I do hope I have suggested to citizen and student alike the terms, manner, and direction of a more responsible course of constitutional interpretation than is usually employed among us.

XIII

As I close this analysis of the First Amendment and prepare for a discussion of the Constitution itself, a few speculations may be in order on the use in English of the words *liberty* and *freedom*.[151]

The typical eighteenth-century reference was to "liberty of the press" rather than to "freedom of the press." Were not those who made this choice of terms influenced by the emphasis in English law upon the *liberation* of the press from the "previous restraint" of licensing? "Freedom of speech," on the other hand, was much more likely to be used than "liberty of speech." This may reflect the traditional wording of the parliamentary privilege. Thus, the word associated with *speech* (that is, *freedom*) was selected when *speech* and *press* were coupled in the First Amendment and thereafter in other American constitutional documents. We are again reminded of the emergence in America of a self-governing people which now has the prerogatives of the once sovereign parliaments.

Americans today are much more apt to use *freedom* than *liberty*, when speaking of either speech or the press.[152] The example of the First Amendment may have influenced those who established this usage,[153] as may the bad name *liberty* got in some quarters because of the excesses of the French Revolution.[154] But, history or chance aside, *liberty* may have an inherent moral ambiguity that *freedom* does not have. That is, *freedom* can be said to imply an attitude of responsible or self-restrained liberty, a sense of liberty in which (as etymologists tell us) peace and love play a part, in which "ought" governs "wish."[155] Can the Constitution secure the *"Blessings* of Liberty" only to the extent that the inevitable *abuses* of liberty have been guarded against?

I am reminded of the distinction drawn by two writers sensitive to the nuances of the English language: " 'Liberty' and 'freedom' are not synonyms. . . . There is a challenging ring to 'liberty, a quiet assurance in 'freedom.' " It is this "quiet assurance" that I sense to be implicit in the Constitution, especially in its injunction that "Congress shall make no law . . . abridging the freedom of speech, or of the press; or the right of the people peaceably to assemble and to petition the Government for a redress of grievances."

But should not the "challenging ring" also remain available for the appropriate occasion?[156]

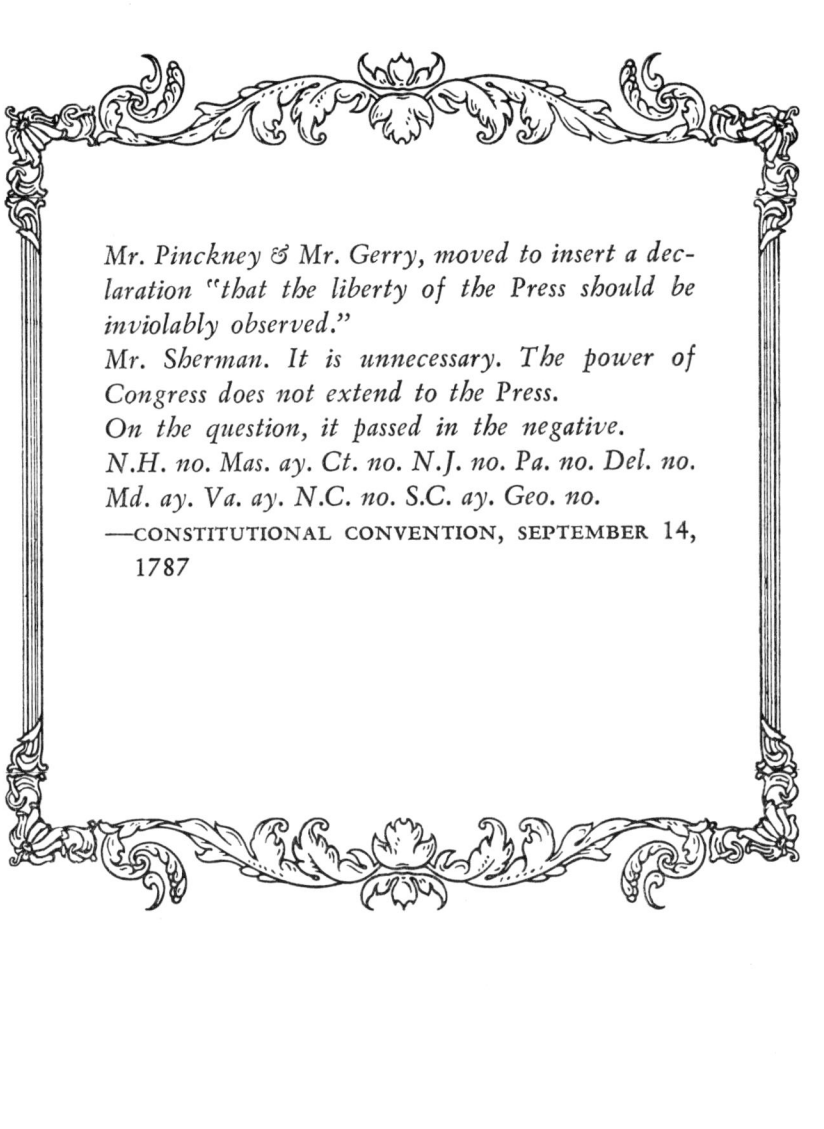

Mr. Pinckney & Mr. Gerry, moved to insert a declaration "that the liberty of the Press should be inviolably observed."
Mr. Sherman. It is unnecessary. The power of Congress does not extend to the Press.
On the question, it passed in the negative.
N.H. no. Mas. ay. Ct. no. N.J. no. Pa. no. Del. no. Md. ay. Va. ay. N.C. no. S.C. ay. Geo. no.
—CONSTITUTIONAL CONVENTION, SEPTEMBER 14, 1787

VI. "THE POWERS NOT DELEGATED TO THE UNITED STATES"

I

I TURN NOW to a more general consideration of the Constitution. My concern to this point has been primarily with the "liberty" guaranteed by the Bill of Rights; it will now be with the "order" that characterizes the Constitution. The fusion of these two elements is seen in what I have chosen to recognize as "freedom."

This freedom, or reasonable liberty, is the object of a Connecticut statute of 1728 bearing the title, "An Act to prevent Tumults and Disorders in Town-Meetings, Society Meetings, and Proprietor-Meetings":

> Whereas the Peace and good Order, of Town and Societies, do very much depend upon their Peaceable and Orderly Managing the Affairs of such Meetings; yet nevertheless, some designing Persons, of Ungoverned Tempers, are often Endeavouring, to Hinder or Defeat the Business of such Meetings, either by Tumultuous Noise, or by Opposing, Abusing or Inter-

rupting the Moderator of such Meeting in the Discharge of his Office. Which to Prevent:

Be it Enacted . . . That when any Town-Meeting, Society-Meeting, or Proprietor-Meeting, is Lawfully Assembled, if any Person or Persons whatsoever, in such Meeting, by Tumultuous Noise, Quarreling, or any Unlawful Action, shall disturb such Meeting, or hinder the Members thereof from proceeding Peaceably to the choice of their Moderator, or after the Moderator is chosen, shall Vilify or Abuse such Moderator, or Interrupt him in the discharge of his Office, or after he hath Commanded Silence, shall Speak in such Meeting, without his leave first had and obtained, (unless to ask reasonable Liberty for such Person to speak his Mind) such Person or Persons so Offending, in any of the Particulars above-mentioned, shall for every such Offence, pay a Fine of Five Shillings, in Current Money, to the Treasury of the Town, in which the Offence is Committed.

The act further provides,

That no such Meeting shall be Adjourn'd or Prorogu'd, but by the Voice of the Major part of the Members thereof, there present.

This latter proviso reminds us of the republican basis of American freedom.[1] We are reminded as well of Publius's observation in *Federalist* No. 71, "The republican principle demands that the deliberate sense of the community should govern the conduct of those to whom they intrust the management of their affairs. . . ."

II

During the ratification campaign of 1787-88, when the lack of a bill of rights was used by opponents of the Constitution as one ground of their attack upon the proposed instrument, the reply was made that such guarantees were not needed because Congress had no power in any event to legislate with respect to the matters that would be dealt with by a bill of rights. One finds in the next-to-last paper of the *Federalist*, for instance, Publius's development of this argument with respect to liberty of the press:

But a minute detail of particular rights is certainly far less applicable to a Constitution like that under consideration, which is merely intended to regulate the general political interests of the nation, than to a constitution which has the regulation of every species of personal and private concerns. . . .

I go further, and affirm that bills of rights, in the sense and to the extent in which they are contended for, are not only unnecessary in the proposed Constitution, but would even be dangerous. They would contain various exceptions to powers not granted; and, on this very account, would afford a colorable pretext to claim more than were granted. For why declare that things shall not be done which there is no power to do? *Why, for instance, should it be said that the liberty of the press shall not be restrained, when no power is given by which restrictions may be imposed?* I will not contend that such a provision would confer a regulating power; but it is evident that it would furnish, to men disposed to usurp, a plausible pretence for claiming that power. They might urge with a semblance of reason, that the Constitution ought not to be charged with the absurdity of providing against the abuse of an authority which was not given, and that the provision against restraining the liberty of the press afforded a clear implication, that a power to prescribe proper regulations concerning it was intended to be vested in the national government. This may serve as a specimen of the numerous handles which would be given to the doctrine of constructive powers, by the indulgence of an injudicious zeal for bills of rights.[2] [Italics added]

Arguments made in a political campaign have to be evaluated with special care. The writers of the Constitution would probably have included a bill of rights if they had foreseen the extent to which opponents of a strong central government would seize upon the omission of such a bill to attack the document. Faced with the necessity of winning immediate support for the instrument, without prior amendments, the supporters of the proposed Constitution insisted that a bill of rights was not needed because of the nature of the powers granted to Congress.[3] It is my contention in this chapter that this argument was used not only because it was convenient, but also because it was true. The same argument, as may be seen in the epigraph to this chapter, was made in the Constitutional Convention as well, at a time when something could have been done to remedy the omission of a bill of rights.

Just what are the powers of the general government, and particularly Congress, under the original Constitution, to regulate speech and the press? I shall discuss in this chapter the powers given to Congress under the Constitution, powers such as those listed in Article I, section 8; and the powers that may reside in the general government by virtue of a national common law. Proceeding first to consider this latter point, I must take note of the general opinion that there is no such national common law. An analysis of powers existing by virtue of such a common law would thus be generally regarded as unnecessary.[4] Is this general opinion correct?

III

Are there intended to be under the Constitution of the United States common law offenses against the nation? That is, are there under the Constitution criminal offenses which, although no statute of Congress has either established or defined them, may be recognized and prosecuted in the federal courts? Or, more precisely for our purpose here, are there any common law offenses relating to speech or the press which may be prosecuted in the federal courts? If there are common law offenses, Congress may legislate with respect to the matters thereby affected, if only to correct or guide judicial developments.[5]

In his monumental treatise Crosskey argued that there is, under the Constitution, a national common law, a common law not only with respect to disputes between private parties but with respect to crimes as well. For our purposes, his position on the common law, particularly as it bears upon freedom of the press, may be examined in the context of his discussion of the Sedition Act of 1798. I quote here his words on this subject, which are certainly as knowledgeable as any we are apt to find anyone using today in making the case for a national common law:

> . . . The Sedition Act [of 1798] had been a natural enough reaction to the extremely indecent campaign of public mendacity, by which, when the act was passed, the Jeffersonian party had long been seeking to undermine the Federalists in the public estimation and get their own candidates into office. These tactics, the Jeffersonians had begun, long before George Washington was out of office, much to that honest and honorable man's surprise and distress; and Jefferson, it is well known, actually took part in inspiring and directing much that then was being done, while he was still in Washington's cabinet. After John Adams took office, the Jeffersonian campaign of calumny became, however, even worse; and at last, in 1798, the Federalists determined that they must take action against it. This, they could very easily have done, according to the accepted ideas of the time, by prosecuting the Jeffersonian printers and speakers, for criminal libel, under the Common Law, as one of "the Laws of the United States." [Footnote omitted.] But under the Common Law, truth was not a defense in criminal prosecutions for libel; and because the Federalists were not attempting

to shut off fair comment on their acts, but only to end the campaign of calculated lying that had been organized against them, they were unwilling merely to resort to the Common Law. So, the much-abused Sedition Act was passed, providing that, in all trials in the national courts, for seditious utterances, proof of the truth of any utterance should be a complete defense; and as a further precaution, it was also enacted that the jury, in all such prosecutions, should be the judges both of the law and the facts of the case.

Except a stipulation in regard to punishments, the foregoing was the whole intent and tenor of the Sedition Act of 1798, so far as seditious utterances were concerned. It was, in fact, a liberalization of the Common Law, which, as we have seen repeatedly, was then regarded, as one of "the Laws of the United States." And when the act was attacked by the Jeffersonians, the Federalists said just this about their act, in their replies; and thus the status of the Common Law, as one of the laws of the nation, became injected into the controversy. . . .[6]

It was unfortunate, for the cause of those espousing a national common law, that the status of the common law should have been injected into *this* controversy. For, as I have already indicated, this was to expose one of the more vulnerable aspects of the common law to republican standards and to popular prejudices. A further passage from Crosskey is important here:

... The propaganda methods employed [by the Jeffersonians] in Connecticut under Granger and Edwards were of the same general character as those the party had earlier used, on a national scale, against George Washington and John Adams; and in the end, these methods produced, in Connecticut, an identical reaction from the party there in power. For, in May 1804, the Connecticut legislature enacted, in the exact words of the then extinct Sedition Act, that, in all libel prosecutions in the state's courts, truth should be a complete defense, and that the jury, in such prosecutions, should be the judges, both of the law and the facts of the case. The Jeffersonian printers were then put to proof of various of their reckless utterances; fined and bound over to keep the peace for the future, when they failed in such proof; and one printer, who refused to pay his fine with a view to making himself a martyr for the party's sake, was obligingly sent to jail.

According to Crosskey, "so far as seditious utterances were concerned," the Sedition Act of 1798 dealt with three points: it provided "that, in all trials in the national courts, for seditious utterances, proof of the truth . . . shall be a complete defense";[7] it enacted "that the jury in all such prosecutions, should be the judges both of the law and the facts of the case"; and it indicated "a stipulation in regard to punishments. . . ."[8]

The 1804 Connecticut statute Crosskey referred to provides almost in the exact terms of Congress's Sedition Act of 1798 for the first and second points. (These two points are to be found in section 3, and the third point in sections 2 and 4, of the Sedition Act.) The portion of the 1798 Sedition Act dealing with seditious utterances read as follows:

Sec. 2. And be it further enacted, That if any person shall write, print, utter, or publish, or shall cause or procure to be written, printed, uttered, or published, or shall knowingly and willingly assist or aid in writing, printing, uttering, or publishing, any false, scandalous and malicious, writing or writings against the Government of the United States, or either House of the Congress of the United States, or the President of the United States, with intent to defame the said Government, or either House of the said Congress, or the said President, or to bring them, or either of them, into contempt or disrepute; or to excite against them, or either or any of them, the hatred of the good people of the United States, or to stir up sedition within the United States; or to excite any unlawful combinations therein, for opposing or resisting any law of the United States, or any act of the President of the United States, done in pursuance of any such law, or of the powers in him vested by the Constitution of the United States, or to resist, oppose, or defeat any such law or act; or to aid, encourage, or abet, any hostile designs of any foreign nation against the United States, their people or Government, then such persons, being thereof convicted, before any court of the United States having jurisdiction thereof, shall be punished by a fine not exceeding two thousand dollars, and by imprisonment not exceeding two years.

Sec. 3. And be it further enacted, That if any person shall be prosecuted, *under this act*, for the writing or publishing any libel, *aforesaid*, it shall be lawful for the defendant, upon the trial of the cause, to give in evidence, in his defence, the truth of the matter contained in the publication charged as a libel. And the jury, who shall try the cause, shall have a right to determine the law and the fact, under the direction of the court, as in other cases.

Sec. 4. And be it further enacted, That this act shall continue and be in force until the third day of March, one thousand eight hundred and one, and no longer: Provided, That the expiration of the act shall not prevent or defeat a prosecution and punishment of any offence against the law, during the time it shall be in force.[9]

The 1804 Connecticut statute reproduces only section 3 of the 1798 Sedition Act, except for the four words I have italicized. These omissions point to an important difference in character between the 1798 and 1804 acts. The Connecticut 1804 truth-as-a-defense and jury-scope provisions stand alone: there is no doubt that they are intended to serve as a liberalization of pre-existing law.

That it *is* the common law being modified in Connecticut is indicated by the fact that (so far as I can discover) there is no statute anywhere in the 1808 Compiled Laws of Connecticut (or in the codes of earlier years) which this provision can be said to qualify.[10] That the 1804 provision is indeed a liberalization is suggested by the fact that it is added to the Declaration of Rights in the 1818 Connecticut Constitution (for which reason it is absent from the 1821 Connecticut Compiled Laws). This is further suggested by the title given to the Connecticut statute, "An Act to secure the Freedom of the Press." So long as the common law crime of seditious libel formally governed, as it seems to have done in Connecticut (that is, as an exercise of *state* power), this was indeed a liberalizing step.

If Congress in 1798 had done no more than the Connecticut legislature did in its 1804 statute, inferences might be more plausibly drawn about the existence of national common law crimes and about the intended effect of the 1798 provision. But sections 2 and 4 of the 1798 act point in another direction.[11] Section 4 provides for the automatic expiration of the act on March 3, 1801 (the last full day of President Adams's term). Of the more than ten dozen acts of the Fifth Congress, only a dozen (one of them the Alien Act of 1798) have automatic expiration dates.[12] The act to which the Sedition Act is an addition has no expiration date; nor does another act, enacted in the same session as the Sedition Act, which provides for the punishment of those communicating in an unauthorized manner with foreign states.[13] The impression is left that the Fifth Congress thought, for some reason, that the Sedition Act should not be placed on indefinite tenure. Certainly, there seems to have been the prudent tradition (which includes the Licensing Act of 1643 against which Milton wrote his *Areopagitica*), a tradition which we would do well to revive, of setting a definite time limit to acts of political repression.[14]

There are two other curious features about this expiration section. First, it is implied in Crosskey's analysis that upon the expiration of the act of 1798 the law would return to its harsher state under the common law. Thus, while in Connecticut a provision similar to section 3 was made permanent, by incorporation into the state constitution, the same (presumably liberalizing) provision in the 1798 Sedition Act is adopted only on a temporary basis. Second, the proviso in the expiration section (section 4) was not that there should be available the two *liberal* features of the act in the event of a prosecution for an offense committed during the life of the act; rather, the proviso expresses a concern lest the prosecution and punishment of "any offence against the law" should be defeated by the expiration of the act. The expiration portions of the dozen other acts listed in note 12 of this chapter do not have this kind of proviso.

Why, in Crosskey's view, should this saving provision in section 4 of the 1798 act have been necessary? Would not the offense continue (in his view) to be punishable at common law in the federal courts after the expiration of the act? The framers of the bill (if Crosskey is correct) should have been concerned, not that prosecutions may have been defeated by the expiration of the act, but rather lest prosecutions may have continued without the safeguards or advances provided by section 3 of the act. It is not here, however, that the emphasis is placed in section 4 of the act.[15]

Rather, the section 4 phrase, "any offence against the law," seems to point to the principal purpose and effect of the act of 1798: it defines and *establishes* certain crimes as crimes against the general government. As we have seen, Crosskey dismissed the remainder of the act relating to seditious utterances (especially section 2) as "a stipulation in regard to punishments." But it is manifestly more than that. True, the title of the act is couched in terms of "the punishment of certain crimes"—as are the titles of other acts of that period relating to crimes. But this is the form employed in the First Congress as well, even with respect to offenses dependent for their precise formulation on the existence of the United States under the Constitution.[16] Thus, it seems that the crime is being defined and established as such, not merely that an appropriate punishment is being prescribed. Crosskey tended to dismiss this, because he saw the act simply as an amelioration of an already existing national common law crime; but his emphasis upon section 3 ignored the import both of the words of section 4 and the evident intent of section 2. For section 2 marks out the crime—and it is an "offence against the law" which will be prosecuted. If the section had been merely "a stipulation in regard to punishments," it could simply have provided, "seditious libel shall be punished by. . . ."[17]

To sum up: The 1804 Connecticut statute did not require an equivalent to section 2 of the 1798 Sedition Act (which defined and established the crime); the United States Code, the act of 1798 seems to "say," did. Common law crimes existed in Connecticut, even as late as 1821.[18] The Sedition Act of 1798 does not, on its face, recognize any such common law crime in the country at large. Rather, it seems to establish the crime of seditious libel as committed against the interests of the general government.

At this point, I return to a note by Crosskey in which he reported John Marshall's views on the basis of the federal courts' "jurisdiction in cases of sedition":

. . . There is, in the Library of Congress, a letter of John Marshall's, dated November 27, 1800, to some unknown correspondent, which indicates, though not with complete clarity, Marshall's views at that date. He began by denying that the Common Law of England had been "adopted by the Constitution." The affirmative of this proposition, which, he pointed out, the opposition were affecting to combat, was one, he declared, that he had never heard any one maintain. As indicated in chapter xx, this issue was, in fact, a mere fraudulent pretense of the Jeffersonian party. "My own opinion," Marshall went on, "is that our ancestors brought with them the laws of England both statute and common law as existing at the settlement of each colony, so far as they were applicable to our situation. That on our revolution the preexisting law of each state remained so far as it was not chang[e]d either expressly or necessarily by the nature of the governments which we adopted. That on adopting the existing constitution of the United States the common and statute law of each state remained as before and that the principles of the common law of the state wou[l]d apply themselves to magistrates of the general as well as to magistrates of the particular government." It will be noted that Marshall does not say that "the principles of the [statute] law of the state wou[l]d apply themselves to magistrates of the general government." The only reason why the states' common law, as distinct from their statute law, could have been deemed so applicable was that their common law, unlike their statute law, was the *general* law of the country, applicable to everything of a state or national nature within it, when not displaced by a state or a national statute, as the case might be. "It was contended [by the Federalists]," Marshall concluded, "not that the common law gave the [national] courts jurisdiction in cases of sedition, but that the constitution gave it." What particular provision of "the constitution gave it," he did not say. In Aaron Burr's trial, in 1807, he spoke of the Common Law as "form[ing] the substratum of the laws of every state," and, at another point, as "forming the substratum of our [national] laws," as well. . . .[19]

We are left with the question implicit in Crosskey's discussion here. If there is no national common law, what particular provision of the Constitution gave the federal courts or, for that matter, the Congress jurisdiction in cases of sedition? Even the Sedition Act of 1798, as we have seen, does not clearly support a recognition of a national common law of crimes with respect to sedition.[20] If anything, in the light of Crosskey's discussion both of that act and of the 1804 Connecticut statute, the Sedition Act of 1798 stands as evidence against such recognition, to the extent that the opinion of the Fifth Congress is any evidence at all.

An awareness of the possibility of a national common law crime of seditious libel, with its implication of power in the judiciary to extend or otherwise modify this crime, would likely have led the friends of freedom of the press to include more than "Congress" as the explicit addressee of the First Amendment. Thus, the history of treason as judge-made, and judge-abused, was well known, and had led to the inclusion in the Judicial Article of the provision precisely limiting that crime. Instead, the advocates of a national common law crime of seditious libel seem to suggest, it was left to the Fifth Congress to do that which the First Amendment might well have done, restrain the power of the courts with respect to this common law crime, and thereby "ratify" the action to that effect of the jury in the famous 1735 trial of the printer John Peter Zenger.[21]

I have discussed Crosskey's minority opinion about what the Fifth Congress did. The common opinion today about what it did will be discussed in section 5 of this chapter.[22]

IV

It should be noted that the Fifth Congress which enacted the Sedition Act came ten years after the writing of the Constitution and its First Amendment. The Sedition Act was itself a party maneuver, in a time of political excitement both here and abroad, anticipating a repressive act the following year in England. Consequently, that Congress's view of the Constitution is suspect in this matter: similarly, today, we would not (in order to interpret disputed passages of the Constitution) consider ourselves bound by what an excited legislature did.[23]

The role then of President Adams merits consideration. The John Adams of the revolutionary period is pictured, in Schlesinger's book, as a "grim, tireless patriot" who held steadily to his purpose of stirring up the people against their rulers. Thomas Hutchinson, onetime royal governor of Massachusetts, described Adams as possessing the talent of "artfully and fallaciously insinuating into the minds of his readers a prejudice against the characters of all whom he attacked."[24] It is elsewhere indicated that Adams did not stop short of the use of exaggerations and deceptions. Indeed, as I have suggested in chapter 5, such conduct as he engaged in was subsequently condemned by the Sedition Act of 1798.

Despite his revolutionary period activity, Adams did as President ask for and execute the Sedition Act. Of course, he was then a quarter of a century older; and he was in power (defending a republican regime) rather than attacking those exercising monarchical (and allegedly tyrannical) power. But do not his own activities as President with respect to the Sedition Act testify to the prudence of his earlier desire to see power restrained? The restraints to be placed upon him do not depend on what he, as President, thought they should be: for the younger Adams would have argued that men in power are not in the best position to see clearly in such matters.[25] Consequently, if we are to defer at all to his theory of human nature and government, we must consider the possibility that the possession of power distorted his (and the Federalists') political judgment.

Thus, again and again, we find ourselves driven to a consideration of the nature and problems of government in general and of republican governments in particular.

V

How has the Sedition Act of 1798 come to be regarded through the past century and a half—and what bearing does this opinion have on our understanding of the powers of the general government, whether legislative or judicial, to regulate speech and the press?

If one relied simply on statutes, on the English case-law rendering of the comman law, and on treatises such as Blackstone's, one could well conclude that the 1791 meaning of "freedom of the press" is somewhat along the lines suggested by the Connecticut statute of 1804: that state act is seen, as its title indicates, as *securing* freedom of the press. But, it should be remembered, Connecticut ratified the Constitution very early in the ratification campaign. Indeed, Sherman of Connecticut urged the First Congress to proceed with business other than the amendments that Madison brought up again and again. He noted that his state had approved the Constitution "by a very great majority" without suggesting any amendments, adding that it would be "imprudent to neglect much more important concerns for this. The executive part of the Government wants organization; the business of the revenue is incomplete, to say nothing of the judiciary business." (*Annals*, I, p. 428) In fact, he questioned "if any alteration which can be now proposed would be an amendment, in the true sense of the word." (*Annals*, I, p. 428) It was left to White of Virginia to state what proved to be the more general attitude in the First Congress:

> . . . I think a majority of the people who have ratified the Constitution, did it under the expectation that Congress would, at some convenient time, examine its texture and point out where it was defective, in order that it might be judiciously amended. . . . I hope the subject may be considered with all convenient speed. I think it would tend to tranquilize the public mind. [*Annals*, I, p. 428]

It should also be noticed that the *Zenger* case had, a half century before, already established in the public mind the principles incorporated in the 1804 Connecticut statute, even though there was in Connecticut prior to 1804 no formal statutory or judicial reflection of this shift. It seems to me likely, that is, that the popular meaning of "freedom of the press" was far more liberal than the meaning lawyers had had occasion before 1791 to make explicit in judicial proceedings.[26]

One more set of distinctions is appropriate here in this attempt to assess popular reaction to the Sedition Act of 1798. First, many states recognized the continuing validity of the common law, perhaps even a common law of crimes; second, the powers of the state governments were much more extensive with respect to internal police and the concern to preserve domestic peace and public order; third, the general government occupied somewhat the position of the English government, against which the rights of the people were to be more zealously guarded than against the local governments over which the people had more direct and immediate control.[27] Once again, the popular understanding of what was expected, this time from the general government as contrasted to the state government, is important, particularly since the authoritative demand for the First Amendment restrictions upon Congress came from the state conventions ratifying the Constitution.

It should be noted that the dangers and disturbances arising from seditious activity had been handled by state governments before the United States Constitution and the courts provided therein were established. There was no reason to believe, or at least no general comment to the effect, that a change of primary supervisory responsibility with respect to speech or the press would be necessary under the new Constitution.[28] (The state of opinion with respect to commercial regulations, for example, was markedly different.) My impression is that the comment there was about speech and press regulation exhibited, instead, a concern lest the general government interfere with such matters, not that it should be empowered to deal with them.

VI

The significance in this matter of the popular understanding is pointed up by the markedly different attitudes, both at that time and to this day, with which Fox's Libel Act of 1792 and the Sedition Act of 1798 were and are usually regarded. The English act has been seen as a historic blow struck for freedom of the press; our Sedition Act, on the other hand, has been seen as a temporary step backward toward an age of repression.[29] But consider the terms of the much-praised Fox's Libel Act:

Whereas doubts have arisen whether on the trial of an indictment or information for the making or publishing any libel, where an issue or issues are joined between the King and the defendant or defendants, on the plea of not guilty pleaded, it be competent to the jury impanelled to try the same to give their verdict upon the whole matter in issue: Be it therefore declared and enacted by the King's most excellent Majesty, by and with the advice and consent of the lords spiritual and temporal, and commons, in this present Parliament assembled, and by the authority of the same, that on every such trial the jury sworn to try the issue may give a general verdict of guilty or not guilty upon the whole matter put in issue upon such indictment or information, and shall not be required or directed by the court or judge before whom such indictment or information shall be tried to find the defendant or defendants guilty merely on the proof of the publication by such defendant or defendants of the paper charged to be a libel, and of the sense ascribed to the same in such indictment or information.

II. Provided, always, that on every such trial the court or judge before whom such indictment or information shall be tried shall, according to their or his discretion, give their or his opinion and directions to the jury on the matter in issue between the King and the defendant or defendants, in like manner as in other criminal cases.

III. Provided also, that nothing herein contained shall extend or be construed to extend to prevent the jury from finding a special verdict, in their discretion, as in other criminal cases.

IV. Provided also, that in case the jury shall find the defendant or defendants guilty it shall be lawful for the said defendant or defendants to move in arrest of judgment, on such ground and in such manner as by law he or they might have done before the passing of this Act, any thing herein contained to the contrary notwithstanding.[30]

Fox's Libel Act provides only one of the two improvements later found in section 3 of the Sedition Act of 1798 (and in the 1804 Connecticut statute), the improvement with respect to the prerogatives of the jury in a trial for libel.[31] It was not until 1843 that evidence as to the truth of the alleged libel (the other improvement found in the American acts of 1798 and 1804) could be introduced by defendants in some English criminal libel prosecutions.[32] Thus, if any difference is to be remarked, the Sedition Act of 1798 was superior to Fox's Libel Act—*if* it is true that the 1798 act was simply relaxing the rigors of the common law theretofore recognized by federal courts.[33]

But the difference in popular attitudes toward these two acts is much more easily understood if the English setting is recognized as more repressive than the American. Thus, Fox's Libel Act should be seen as a distinct improvement in England, whereas the 1798 Sedition Act proved an affront to the American people, or at least (it is said) to a majority of the people, especially to those who believed that Congress had no power to legislate with respect to such matters. The 1798 act *has* been, as Crosskey said, "much-abused."[34]

Indeed, it is the 1804 Connecticut statute which is akin to Fox's Libel Act, constituting an amelioration of the common law of sedition in that state. Under the United States Constitution, the states were left free to abridge the freedom of the press: the 1804 statute, later incorporated in the 1818 Connecticut Constitution, placed a limitation upon the virtually unlimited power the Connecticut government had had in these matters.

Jeffersonian propaganda no doubt contributed to the bad name of the 1798 Sedition Act, as did the coupling of the Sedition Act with the even more repressive (but evidently unused) Alien Act of 1798.[35] But, as I have suggested, there was justification for the popular reaction against the Sedition Act.[36] And we are left with the problem that Crosskey (led by John Marshall) seemed to think must arise if national common law crimes (at least with respect to sedition) are not recognized. What particular provision of the Constitution otherwise gives the general government power to regulate the press with respect to sedition?

VII

My inquiry, which has been directed to the Sedition Act of 1798 but which applies as well to the sedition acts of the twentieth century, turns now to a consideration of the power given to the general government by the Constitution to regulate the press. This extended discussion and dismissal of the common law as the source of such power will no doubt have seemed to some merely "academic." But that discussion has been so extended because of the difficulty of otherwise finding in the Constitution the power that has come to be exercised in these matters.

The discussion, as it considered the common law, bore particularly on the problem of freedom of the press.[37] Much of the discussion in this chapter of the powers of Congress can be little more than a suggestion of the general problem of the powers defined and granted under the Constitution. To the extent that large constitutional questions, which bear on much more than the interpretation of the First Amendment, are involved here, these remarks must be left fragmentary and only suggestive.

Under the currently orthodox view of the powers of Congress, serious doubts must be entertained whether Congress has any power to deal with the matters addressed by sedition legislation. The question is usually ignored in discussions by courts and Congress today: they are concerned whether a "clear and present danger" exists, with scant attention paid to the problem of what power rests in Congress even if there should be a clear and present danger of something. Indeed, if the power exists in Congress, it would (if it is like most other powers of Congress) be available to be exercised whether or not there should be any danger. I return to Justice Holmes's notorious sentence in *Schenck* v. *United States*:

> The question in every case is whether the words used are used in such circumstances and are of such a nature as to create a clear and present danger that they will bring about the substantive evils that Congress has a right to prevent.

What *are* "the substantive evils that Congress has a right to prevent," a right presumably supported if not indicated by a grant of appropriate power to Congress by the Constitution? One may even wonder, in order to bring this problem to the fore, from what provision in the Constitution Congress draws power to interfere with any domestic activities urging people even to immediate armed rebellion against the government of the United States.

Sedgwick considered the general government to be "entrusted with the freedom and the very existence of the people. . . ." (*Annals, I*, p. 777) Such a government, he went on to say (speaking in opposition to a proposed amendment requiring Congress to wait upon state requisitions before resorting to direct taxation),

> . . . ought surely to possess, in a most ample degree, the means of supporting its own existence; and as we do not know what circumstances we may be in, or how necessary it may be for Congress to exercise this power, I should deem it a violation of the oath I have taken to support the Constitution were I now to vote for this amendment. [*Annals, I*, p. 777]

Others in the First Congress spoke of the *salus populi* as "the first object of republican Governments. . . ."[38] The problem remains, however, whether *concern* implies *power*. A satisfactory answer to the admittedly radical question I have asked as an aid to analysis— about the source of congressional power to prevent advocacy of immediate armed rebellion—would depend, in part, upon an understanding of the role of the states in our constitutional system. It would depend also on a rewording of the question (which may be central to this study) to read, What may the general government constitutionally do to avert armed rebellion?[39] This rewording implies, that is, that there are measures Congress can take, others (even though they might be more effective in particular circumstances) that it cannot take.[40]

In the course of debates in the First Congress relating to the implementation of the slave-trade provision in Article I, section 9 of the Constitution, Madison observed,

> It is a necessary duty of the General Government to protect every part of the empire against danger, as well internal as external. Every thing, therefore, which tends to increase this danger, though it may be a local affair, yet, if it involves national expense or safety, becomes of concern to every part of the Union, and is a proper subject for the consideration of those charged with the general administration of the Government. I hope, in making these observations, I shall not be understood to mean that a proper attention ought not to be paid to the local opinions and circumstances of any part of the United States, or that the particular representatives are not best able to judge of the sense of their immediate constituents. [*Annals, I,* p. 340]

Thus, there seems to be generated from "concern" "a proper subject for the consideration of those charged with the general administration of the Government." But when we consider the immediate proposal before the House, whether a tax should be placed until 1808 on the importation of slaves (up to the ten dollar limit permitted by the Constitution), we can appreciate that Madison's seemingly unlimited (and, I believe, for him uncharacteristic) view of the powers of Congress may be restricted by its context.[41] Tucker had argued earlier that "we have no right . . . to consider whether the importation of slaves is proper or not; the Constitution gives us no power on that point; it is left to the States to judge of that matter as they see fit." (*Annals, I,* p. 337) Madison's response was, in effect, that although the Constitution may not charge the general government with a direct concern with slavery, it does charge that government with the defense of the United States:

> . . . Every addition [South Carolina and Georgia] receive to their number

of slaves, tends to weaken and render them less capable of self-defence. In case of hostilities with foreign nations, they will be the means of inviting attack, instead of repelling invasion. [*Annals*, I, p. 340]

But, more precisely, the general government is charged with defense of the United States to the extent that that defense can be accomplished by the powers granted to that government. Thus, although the best defense might have been an immediate prohibition of all slave importation, and perhaps even the abolition of slavery itself, the government was empowered (before 1808) only to impose a ten-dollar import tax: the ends of the general government, that is, are both indicated and (particularly important in a compound republic such as ours) limited by the powers granted that government.[42]

The extent of these powers may be seen as broad or narrow, depending on the approach adopted toward the question of whether there are powers inherent in certain offices, powers that are granted in the very establishment of the office even without reference to particular powers. The negative was argued in the First Congress by Jackson (in the course of the removal power controversy):

It has been mentioned, that in all Governments the Executive Magistrate has the power of dismissing officers under him. This may hold good in Europe, where monarchs claim their powers *jure divino,* but it never can be admitted in America, under a Constitution delegating only enumerated powers. It requires more than a mere *ipse dixit* to demonstrate that any power is in its nature Executive, and consequently given to the President of the United States by the present Constitution. . . . [*Annals*, I, pp. 486-87][43]

The affirmative was suggested by Madison,

[The Constitution] declares that the Executive power shall be vested in a President of the United States. The association of the Senate with the President in exercising that particular function, is an exception to this general rule; and exceptions to general rules, I conceive, are ever to be taken strictly. [*Annals*, I, p. 496]

An attempt was made by Alexander White to bring together considerations of both recognized purposes and granted powers:

This is a Government constituted for particular purposes only; and the powers granted to carry it into effect are specifically enumerated, and disposed among the various branches. If those powers are insufficient, or if they are improperly distributed, it is not our fault, nor within our power to remedy. The people who bestowed them must grant further powers, organize those already granted in a more perfect manner, or suffer from the defect. We can neither enlarge nor modify them. [*Annals, I*, pp. 514-15]

The principal purposes of the government established under the Constitution, to the extent that those purposes are suggested by its powers, seem to be restricted to the four or five subjects specified by General Washington in a letter of September 17, 1787, prepared by the Convention, transmitting the Constitution to the Continental Congress:

The friends of our country have long seen and desired, that the power of making war, peace, and treaties, that of levying money and regulating commerce, and the correspondent executive and judicial authorities should be fully and effectually vested in the general government of the Union. . . .

The purposes set forth in the Preamble to the Constitution may be seen in this letter, or, that is, in the powers granted by the Constitution which are presumably summed up in the letter.[44]

Thus, to take an example, the general welfare (to which reference is made in the Preamble) is to be provided for or advanced to the extent and in the manner that the general welfare *can* be affected by legislation with respect to the four or five subjects referred to by Washington. These are the subjects to which Article I of the Constitution plainly addresses itself, as did the bulk of the discussion both in the federal convention and in the state ratifying conventions. Madison observed, for example, that the government could "promote the general welfare, by the re-establishment of public credit." (*Annals, I*, p. 346)

The Senate, in its reply to President Washington's speech before Congress of April 30, 1789, acknowledged that the general government should "strengthen the Union, conduce to the happiness, [and] secure and perpetuate the liberties of this great confederated Republic." (*Annals, I*, p. 32) Any general government, at least for Americans, would have to keep these ends in mind, no matter how powers were distributed. But the distribution and extent of such powers would be decisive in distinguishing one such government from another, thereby permitting citizens to understand what it is that *this* government provides and permits. An emphasis upon the powers set forth in the Constitution is seen again and again. Thus, Thomas Hartley observed

> that it had been asserted in the convention of Pennsylvania, by the friends of the Constitution, that all the rights and powers that were not given to the Government, were retained by the States and the people thereof. This was also his own opinion; but as four or five States had required to be secured in those rights by an express declaration in the Constitution, he was disposed to gratify them. . . . [*Annals*, I, p. 732]

But what "rights and powers" were given to the general government? And can the powers that *are* given be employed for any end? The Preamble speaks of "domestic Tranquility." Certainly, this is an objective to be taken into account in the exercise of certain powers:

> Mr. Scott thought the principles of the Union were the principles of equal justice and reciprocity. He conceived the question now before the House [the location of the federal city] as grand a link as any in the federal chain. The future tranquillity and well-being of the United States, he said, depended as much on this as on any other question that ever had or could come before Congress. [*Annals*, I, p. 788]

Other powers, such as the power to change the place of election of senators or to change the length of the President's term of office, cannot be assumed and exercised by the general government in order to promote domestic tranquillity, not because they could never contribute to that end, but simply because the exercise of these powers is not permitted by the Constitution.

VIII

But even the powers that are granted by the Constitution to the general government may be seen as powers granted to achieve certain ends. Can the revenue power,[45] for instance, be used to protect public morals or to encourage domestic manufactures, in addition to its use simply to raise money? Early in the First Congress, Madison urged his colleagues in the House quickly to enact a revenue bill in order to take advantage of the spring imports. The consideration of "a system of protecting duties" for encouraging domestic manufactures would require much more time, whereas there was a need for immediate tax legislation. (*Annals*, I, p. 110) And, he observed, "however much we may be disposed to promote domestic manufactures, we ought to pay some regard to the present policy of obtaining revenues." (*Annals*, I, p. 110) He did not express any doubts here—nor is it recorded that anyone else did so— that either the tax power or the commerce power could be used to promote manufactures.[46] Again and again, it was not the revenue alone that was considered in framing the bill governing import duties, but also whether the impost would encourage or discourage agriculture or industry or the carrying trade, some of which must have been considered altogether local in extent if not in effect. (*Annals*, I, pp. 149-50) Similarly, on a later occasion, Madison objected to a proposed impost, which would probably have discouraged importation of the affected item and thereby diminished revenue, that "there are no collateral good purposes to claim our attention in this case." (*Annals*, I, p. 169) A proposed duty on American ship tonnage was defended by Madison with the observation "that some small provision of this kind was necessary for the support of light-houses, hospitals for disabled seamen, and other establishments incident to commerce." (*Annals*, I, p. 176) Perhaps, then, the revenue power may be used in the manner I have described primarily because it is employed to supplement and support another power, that which permits the regulation of commerce.

Objections *were* made to some of the proposed revenues, but various of these objections were made in the course of discussions which conceded the power and perhaps even a duty in Congress to shape the commerce of the country. Thus, Laurance argued,

The gentleman [Madison] mentioned, that the commerce of Britain with this country was too great in proportion to that of other nations; but this is not a point for the Government to settle. I maintain, that the merchants of America are well able to understand and pursue their own interests, and the advantages which they obtain tend to the wealth and prosperity of the Union. [*Annals*, I, p. 184]

Laurance's further elaboration of these observations might well have been taken from Adam Smith. Madison was obliged to respond,

I am a friend to free commerce, and, at the same time, a friend to such regulations as are calculated to promote our own interests, and this on national principles. The great principle of interest is a leading one with me . . . I wish we were under less necessity than I find we are to shackle our commerce with duties, restrictions, and preferences . . . although interest will, in general, operate effectually to produce political good, yet there are causes in which certain factitious circumstances may divert it from its natural channel, or throw or retain it in an artificial one. [*Annals*, I, p. 185][47]

In any event, the act of the First Congress "for laying a duty on goods, wares, and merchandises, imported into the United States" opened with the preamble,

Whereas it is necessary for the support of Government, for the discharge of the debts of the United States, and the encouragement and protection of manufactures, that duties be laid on goods, wares, and merchandises, imported. . . . [*Annals*, I, p. 2129]

The power to lay duties is specifically granted by the Constitution: the use of that power to advance the three purposes set forth here (to support the government, to discharge debts, and to encourage manufactures) can be defended on the basis of a liberal reading of Article I, section 8. Even so, such use of the revenue power was to lead in the early years of the Republic to sectional quarrels that are reflected in the changes made in the opening clauses of Article I, section 8 by the constitutional convention of the Confederate States of America in 1861:[48]

The Congress shall have power—
1. To lay and collect taxes, duties, imposts, and excises, for revenue necessary to pay the debts, provide for the common defence, and carry on the Government of the Confederate States; but no bounties shall be granted from the treasury; nor shall any duties or taxes on importations from foreign nations be laid to promote or foster any branch of industry; and all duties, imposts, and excises shall be uniform throughout the Confederate States.
2. To borrow money on the credit of the Confederate States.
3. To regulate commerce with foreign nations, and among the several States, and with the Indian tribes; but neither this, nor any other clause contained in the Constitution, shall ever be construed to delegate the power to Congress to appropriate money to any internal improvement in-

tended to facilitate commerce, except for the purpose of furnishing lights, beacons and buoys, and other aids to navigation upon the coasts, and the improvements of harbors and the removing of obstructions in river navigation, in all which cases, such duties shall be laid on the navigation facilitated thereby, as may be necessary to pay the costs and expenses thereof.

Thus, divergencies in opinion concerning the revenue and commerce powers, especially concerning the extent of "commerce," were to furnish the occasion, if not the cause, for bitter sectional strife.[49] This is not to suggest, however, that powers properly belonging to Congress should not be exercised: for, as Ames pointed out, "We are sworn as much to exercise Constitutional authority, for the general good, as to refrain from assuming powers that are not given to us. We are as responsible for forbearing to act, as we are for acting." (*Annals*, I, p. 539)

Again, as to the revenue power and its proper use:[50] what if it should be used to advance an end not implied to the extent that the commerce power can be taken to imply the protection of manufactures? What, for instance, if it should be applied to the task of improving the morals of the people? Madison and Thomas Fitzsimmons seemed to agree, early in the First Congress, that the tax on ardent spirits should be made as high as possible, not only for the revenue that would be collected, but also in order that their consumption might be reduced, even though Fitzsimmons did say, ". . . lessening the consumption is not the object which the committee have in view; but surely, from the considerations I have mentioned, it is an article for us to draw all possible revenue from." (*Annals*, I, p. 126) Boudinot listed three objectives for a high import tax on ardent spirits: the raising of revenue, the discouragement of consumption, and the encouragement of domestic producers. (*Annals*, I, p. 127) Laurance acknowledged the moral case against ardent spirits, but advised his colleagues to consider the matter not as moralists but "as politicians" who must decide what is apt to raise the most revenue without encouraging smuggling. (*Annals*, I, p. 127)[51]

Nevertheless, it seemed generally agreed in the First Congress that it is legitimate, in fixing duties, to take into account considerations of the "morals of the people, commerce, or revenue" (*Annals*, I, p. 201)—and again, "the morality and health of . . . fellow-citizens" (*Annals*, I, p. 211)—even as it was recognized (through

Madison) that "the habits and prejudices of the community are not easily removed; the habit of using rum is so fixed, that it will perhaps take more than a century to change it to another object." (*Annals*, I, p. 204) Are such habits and prejudices, which relate to the morals of the community, a proper object of the general government? Doubts, which rested in part on his skepticism about what any government can do about such matters, were expressed by Ames in the course of his opposition to a proposed duty on molasses (from which rum was made):[52]

> ... I treat as idle the visionary notion of reforming the morals of the people by a duty on molasses. We are not to consider ourselves, while here, *as at church or school*, to listen to the harangues of speculative piety; we are to talk of the political interests committed to our charge. When we take up the subject of morality, let our system look towards that object, and not confound itself with revenue and protection of manufactures. If gentlemen conceive that a law will direct the taste of the people from spiritous to malt liquors, they must have more romantic notions of legislative influence than experience justifies. [*Annals*, I, pp. 222-23; italics added]

Later in the session, Jackson further developed Ames's theme: "Gentlemen talk of improving the morals of the people by taxation. For my part, I conceive revenue has nothing to do with the morals of the people. . . . All that I can contemplate is, drawing as much money as we can with equity. . . ." (*Annals*, I, p. 314) Morals, he conceded, were not irrelevant: legislators must consider what it is equitable to do. *They* must have morals adequate for this duty. But this government does not have the duty to preserve and advance morality, whether that of the people at large or of the legislators drawn from that people. A more explicit constitutional argument was employed when the proposal was made to levy a ten-dollar duty on the importation of slaves. We saw in the last section the constitutional argument, made by Tucker, against Congress's even considering whether the importation of slaves "is proper or not." (*Annals*, I, p. 337)[53]

It should be noted that nothing was said in the preamble to this 1789 revenue act about promoting or protecting the morals of the people.[54] Rather, objections had been raised to Congress's assuming responsibility for morality, objections that could have been reinforced by the reminder that the "sovereign states" had retained authority not only over most crimes but over the fields of education and religion as well.

Indeed, the critical question today for those concerned about the expanding power of the general government—which concern may be central to the problem of how vulnerable freedom of speech will be in the next century—is what influence that government is to be permitted to acquire and exert because of its financial resources. For example, extensive federal aid to education means, in principle and probably (eventually) in practice, that the general government would take over effective control of one of the critical duties clearly remaining to the states. An appreciation of the contributions of "states' rights" to American freedom should induce citizens to restrict the general government rigorously in this respect.[55]

IX

I have now discussed two different bases, which sometimes coincide, for governmental action under the Constitution: there are the powers which are explicitly granted by the Constitution and which Congress exercises as a matter of course and *as if* the very exercise of them were an end in itself; then there are the granted powers which are further determined, and perhaps even expanded, by purposes suggested elsewhere in the Constitution. In both cases, some power is given. The question is the extent to which such power may be applied: can it be used to advance an end other than the more narrow immediate one which is implied by the very power? What determines the limits of such extension?

These are general constitutional considerations not limited to our concern in this volume. Nevertheless, we must make a tentative judgment as we apply these considerations to the First Amendment. *Does* Congress have the power to regulate the press? Certainly, there is no explicit power to that effect. But what of the second basis to which I have just referred? One must look first at the four or five subjects of which Washington spoke[56] (as distinguished from the general purposes set forth in the Preamble to the Constitution): an activity not obviously falling within these subjects may be that of sedition, even sedition of the most radical or threatening kind.[57] That seems to have been left to the states to handle: and it is generally true that any sedition of which the United States might take cognizance is or can be considered sedition against a particular state and would thereby be subject to its jurisdiction. It is along these lines that Michael Jenifer Stone speculated:

I take it to be true that all the judicial powers not taken away by the Constitution from the States, remain to them, and I take them to be complete Republics, to have sovereign power, conformable to their nature; therefore, if the Constitution of the United States had not interfered in the subject, even of treason against the Union, the States, I apprehend, except in a few instances, could not [sic] have taken notice of it, because I do not know any kind of treason against the United States but is also treason against a particular State. If a man raises an army in the body of a State, unauthorized by the State, is it not rebellion against the State? Suppose it be done in this State [New York], and they tell you it is not the State of New York they mean to oppose, it is the General Government, pray is not this treason against the State of New York as a member of the Union? Is not a piracy committed against the United States committed against a particular State? If it had its sovereign authority unimpaired, would any gentleman contend that they had not power to try for piracy? I apprehend they would not. [*Annals*, I, p. 825]

Why then were piracy and treason associated, in the Constitution, with the general government? Because, one can answer, these offenses are closely related to the foreign and war policies of that government (just as counterfeiting, which is also provided for in the Constitution, is closely related to the national coining and commercial duties of the general government). But why cannot the same be said of sedition? Power to control sedition is not mentioned in the Constitution: to the extent that it is implied, it may be put outside the jurisdiction of the general government by the First Amendment. Nor is a sedition power intimately connected with a vital activity or concern of the general government:[58] the principal concern with which it *is* connected is that of domestic order, a concern which seems a duty primarily of the states,[59] so much so that the general government can be considered as obliged by Article IV, section 4 to act against "domestic Violence" only after the threatened state requests such protective action.[60] Thus, domestic matters relating to police and public order seem to be the concern primarily of the states.[61]

There remains, however, the problem of whether considerations relating to speech and the press can be taken into account in framing legislation (such as revenue laws), just as was done in the First Congress with respect to morality when imposts were placed on molasses.[62] Obviously, Congress—or congressmen—can take into account considerations concerning which they cannot legislate. Legislators have religious training which guides their thinking. It will have its influence upon them, but this is not to suggest that they can act to advance the cause of their religious sect. Or, rather, the Congress, as legislature, does not do this, whatever the incidental effect might be (for example, of a law prohibiting polygamy in American territories). And, as we have seen, even morality remained a secondary consideration in the First Congress.

Thus, the various considerations I have sketched tend to reinforce the contention of Publius and of Sherman (in the epigraph to this chapter) that, strictly speaking, there was no need for a guarantee of "liberty of the Press" simply because Congress had little if any power to deal with the press.[63] The advocates of radical amendment of the Constitution were confronted by a Congress intent upon leaving the Constitution as it was written by the convention. A review of the amendments proposed by various state governments and by members of Congress makes it clear that all of those cutting down the legislative power of the general government, especially with respect to the subjects to which the Constitution is primarily directed (war, peace, treaties, commerce, taxation), were ignored or discarded by Congress.[64] Even the Tenth Amendment appears, in this context, as merely declarative of a previously made allocation of powers. It is certain, the reader concludes upon examining the dozens of proposals that were rejected and comparing them to the dozen that were accepted, that Congress knew what it was doing in framing these amendments. It is no wonder, then, that Samuel Livermore should have acclaimed a proposed amendment requiring Congress to wait upon state requisitions before resorting to direct taxation as "of more importance than any yet obtained." Indeed, he could say of the amendments already agreed to, and which are now found in the Bill of Rights, that his constituents "would not value them more than a pinch of snuff; they went to secure rights never in danger." (*Annals*, I, pp. 774-75)

Should we not endorse, then, the conclusion anticipated in section 7 of this chapter, that under the orthodox view of the sources of congressional power, serious doubts must remain whether Congress had, under the original Constitution, any substantial power to regulate speech and the press?

X

My discussion in the three preceding sections seems to take care as well of the "necessary and proper" clause of the Constitution:

> The Congress shall have Power . . . To make all laws which shall be necessary and proper for carrying into Execution the foregoing Powers, and all other Powers vested by this Constitution in the Government of the United States or in any Department or Officer thereof. [Article I, section 8]

Of course, an uninhibited and unprincipled use of this clause could bring under congressional control practically every function of government, perhaps even to the virtual extinction of the state governments. But it was insisted throughout the ratification campaign by proponents of the Constitution—and the Constitution supports this insistence—that the "necessary and proper" clause must be taken to relate to subjects and purposes that Congress has. It does not create new functions or powers for Congress, but merely insures congressional power to do what is otherwise given to Congress to do.[65] What it is given to do is great, yet limited; certain matters are left almost entirely to the states.

It has always been recognized that the "necessary and proper" clause could be misused.[66] But even those on different sides of a debate on a particular measure (as, for instance, whether Congress has the power to designate a constitutional oath for state officials) could agree that the "necessary and proper" clause was keyed to, and limited by, explicit constitutional provisions.[67] Thus, Gerry said of this "sweeping clause, as it is frequently termed,"

> To this clause there seems to be no limitation, so far as it applies to the extension of the powers vested by the Constitution; but even this clause gives no legislative authority to Congress to carry into effect any power not expressly vested by the Constitution. [*Annals*, I, p. 266]

Laurance, who supported the proposed legislation of an oath of office,[68] responded:

> If the Constitution is the supreme law of the land, every part of it must

partake of this supremacy; consequently, every general declaration it contains is the supreme law. But then these general declarations cannot be carried into effect without particular regulations adapted to the circumstances. These particular regulations are to be made by Congress, who, by the Constitution, have the power to make all laws necessary or proper to carry the declarations of the Constitution into effect. The Constitution likewise declares that the members of the State Legislatures, and all officers, executive and judicial, shall take an oath to support the Constitution. This declaration is general, and it lies with the supreme Legislature to detail and regulate it. The law is to supply the necessary means of executing the principle laid down; for how can it be carried into effect in any other manner? [*Annals*, I, p. 269]

Similarly, Boudinot summed up with the observation that "it was the duty of the House, as had been well said by [Laurance], to detail the general principles laid down in the Constitution, and reduce them to practice." (*Annals*, I, p. 271)

One must fall back, then, on a determination of the "general principles" of the Constitution. The "necessary and proper" clause does not add anything essential to those principles, or to the extent of the power given to Congress. Even when it appears in another guise—for the "clear and present danger" and "balancing" tests are essentially twentieth-century versions of the "necessary and proper" clause, but versions which are *not* moored to "the general principles laid down in the Constitution"—the question remains, what are the powers and principal duties of the general government of the United States?

XI

In returning to this question, one must return also to the divergence between those favoring a broad, and those advancing a strict, interpretation of the Constitution. It was observed by Lee (*Annals*, I, p. 524): "This Government is invested with powers for enumerated purposes only, and cannot exercise any others whatever." (This may be a statement that both camps can endorse, for its significance depends on what "enumerated" means.) The strict-constructionists look upon the general government as a decisively limited government. Thus, White could argue (during the removal power controversy):

I differ also with my colleague [Madison] in the principle that he has laid down, that [the removal power] is in its nature an Executive power. The Constitution supposes power incident to Government, and arranges it into distinct branches, with or without checks; but it enumerates under each Department the powers it may exercise. The Legislature may exert its authority in passing laws relating to any of its particular powers. The Executive power is vested in the President; but the Executive powers so vested, are those enumerated in the Constitution. He may nominate, and, by and with the advice of the Senate, appoint all officers, because the Constitution gives this power, and not because the power is in its nature a power incident to his department. My ideas of the Legislative and Executive powers are precisely the same. The Legislature may do certain acts because the Constitution says they shall have the power to do them, and the Executive Magistrate is authorized to exercise powers because they are vested in him by the same instrument. It has given him the power of appointment under certain qualifications; the power of removal is incident to the power of appointment, and both [are] equally dependent upon the arrangement made in the Constitution; consequently, a dismission from office must be brought about by the same modification as the appointment. [*Annals*, I, pp. 466-67]

Another argument for this kind of insistence upon strict interpretation is seen in a comment by Stone:

It appears to me that the present Government originated in *necessity*, and it ought not to be carried further than *necessity* will justify.

I believe the scheme of the present Government was considered by those who framed it as dangerous to the liberties of America; if they had not considered it in this point of view, they would not have guarded it in the manner they have done. They supposed that it had a natural tendency to destroy the State Governments; or, on the other hand, they supposed that the State Governments had a tendency to abridge the powers of the General Government; therefore it was necessary to guard against either taking place. . . . [*Annals*, I, p. 809]

We have seen, in Tucker's response to the proposal that a joint committee of both houses be directed to wait upon the President to request that he recommend to the people a day of public thanksgiving and prayer, the extent to which such interpretation can be carried.[69] There the emphasis was upon the role of the states with respect to matters of religion; presumably, a similar argument could be made about the states with respect to the press, as well as about the lack of power in Congress to deal with such matters.

The arguments of the broad-constructionists, we have seen, are based in part on the assumption that there are powers that naturally belong to various branches of the government. Reinforcing this assumption is Madison's contention that "it was impossible to confine a Government to the exercise of express powers; there must necessarily be admitted powers by implication, unless the Constitution descended to recount every minutiae." (*Annals*, I, p. 761) The role of Congress in spelling out these minutiae is referred to by Hartley in a passage which returns us to the "necessary and proper" clause:

> But gentlemen say it is inconsistent with the Constitution to make this declaration [on the removal power of the President]; that, as the Constitution is silent, we ought not to be explicit. The Constitution has expressly pointed out several matters which we can do, and some which we cannot do; but in other matters it is silent, and leaves them to the discretion of the Legislature. If this is not the case, why was the last clause of the eighth section of the first article inserted? It gives power to Congress to make all laws necessary and proper to carry the Government into effect. [*Annals*, I, p. 481]

Both camps would probably agree with the proposition that it is evident from Article I of the Constitution, which is reflected in Washington's letter, that Congress is given the powers which are clearly national in nature, powers which were then thought of as either necessary or highly desirable to exercise on a national basis. This is obviously true about powers relating to international relations (war, peace, treaties). And, in the light of the Continental Congress's unsatisfactory experience with requisitions of funds and with state control of continental trade, this must have seemed to be true also about taxation and the regulation of commerce. Indeed, one can understand most of the restraints on the states found in section 10 of Article I as designed primarily to permit Congress to proceed effectively (and without undue state interference) in its adequately financed conduct of war, international relations, and commerce.[70] It is useful to remember Ames's declaration:

> I conceive, sir, that the present Constitution was dictated by commercial necessity more than any other cause. The want of an efficient Government to secure the manufacturing interests, and to advance our commerce, was long seen by men of judgment, and pointed out by patriots solicitous to promote our general welfare. [*Annals*, I, p. 221]

These considerations do not require that all other powers later thought to be better administered nationally than by the states should now be taken over by the general government. Rather, it must be said, the understanding and agreement implicit in the Constitution at the time it was ordained and established should be considered decisive in interpreting "that constitutional Compact which the People of America have made with each other."[71] But I do not rest on formal constitutionalism alone, important as that is: for, as I shall explain in the next chapter, there are good reasons for leaving certain powers to be exercised in an adequate and safe manner by the states, even though Congress could perhaps be more efficient in some respects.

XII

The First Amendment, I have suggested, was added to a Constitution under which "freedom of speech [and] of the press" was already largely protected from congressional abridgment simply because Congress had little if any power to regulate either speech or the press. Certainly the people were already exercising, as of right, various of the privileges protected by the First Amendment. Thus, petitions had already been submitted to the Congress; vigorous comment upon the proceedings of the legislature was common among citizens, as is evident in Madison's words quoted in section 13 of this chapter.

Nevertheless, Madison thought it desirable that these and the other rights incorporated in the Bill of Rights should be expressed in amendments to the Constitution. These are rights, he argued, "against which I believe no serious objection has been made by any class of our constituents." (*Annals*, I, p. 433) For there are (he had said) many citizens, "respectable for their talents and patriotism, and respectable for the jealousy they have for their liberty," who will be fearful until there are express constitutional guarantees of "the great rights of mankind." (*Annals*, I, p. 432) "It is a fortunate thing," he added, that

the objection to the Government has been made on the ground I stated; because it will be practicable, on that ground, to obviate the objection, so far as to satisfy the public mind that their liberties will be perpetual, and this without endangering any part of the Constitution, which is considered as essential to the existence of the Government by those who promoted its adoption. [*Annals*, I, p. 433]

His confidence that the proposed amendments did not endanger any part of the Constitution—did not cut into the powers granted the general government—reinforces my suggestion that there was not, in the original Constitution, any significant power to regulate speech and the press or, at least, to abridge the "freedom of speech, or of the press."

Indeed, Sherman was moved to argue that the proposed amendments were "a declaration of rights" in which the people were secure, "whether we declare them or not." (*Annals*, I, p. 715) But the First Amendment, even if only declaratory, is not without its uses. It may, as I suggested in section 6 of chapter 4, convey to or recognize in Congress some power to police and moderate state abridgments of freedom of speech and of the press.[72] No doubt, the amendment also calls attention to the status of freedom of speech and of the press under the Constitution.

Furthermore, to the extent that the First Amendment has a restrictive effect, it says that Congress cannot use the "necessary and proper" clause to extend powers it does have under the Constitution to the realms of speech and the press. Thus, Madison argued, in meeting objections to a bill of rights,

It is true, the powers of the General Government are circumscribed, they are directed to particular objects; but even if Government keeps within those limits, it has certain discretionary powers with respect to the means, which may admit of abuse to a certain extent, in the same manner as the powers of the State Governments under their constitutions may to an indefinite extent; because in the Constitution of the United States, there is [the necessary and proper clause which enables Congress] to fulfil every purpose for which the [General] Government was established. [*Annals*, I, p. 438]

And he went on to ask,

Now, may not laws be considered necessary and proper by Congress, (for it is for them to judge of the necessity and propriety to accomplish those special purposes which they may have in contemplation,) which laws in themselves are neither necessary nor proper; as well as improper laws could be enacted by the State Legislatures, for fulfilling the more extended objects of those Governments? I will state an instance, which I think in point, and proves that this might be the case. The General Government has a right to pass all laws which shall be necessary to collect its revenue; the means for enforcing the collection are within the direction of the Legislature: may not general warrants be considered necessary for this purpose, as well as for some purposes which it was supposed at the framing of their constitutions the State Governments had in view? If there was reason for restraining the State Governments from exercising this power, there is like reason for restraining the Federal Government. [*Annals, I*, p. 438]

Thus, what is now the Fourth Amendment should restrain such an application by the general government of the necessary and proper clause.[73] In a passage dealing with the language respecting religious establishments, Madison applied similar considerations to the First Amendment itself:

... Whether the words are necessary or not, he did not mean to say, but they had been required by some of the State Conventions, who seemed to entertain an opinion that under the clause of the Constitution, which gave power to Congress to make all laws necessary and proper to carry into execution the Constitution, and the laws made under it, enabled them to make laws of such a nature as might infringe the rights of conscience, and establish a national religion; to prevent these effects he presumed the amendment was intended, and he thought it as well expressed as the nature of the language would permit. [*Annals, I*, p. 730]

The revenue power, which Madison saw as possibly sanctioning the assumption of a power to issue the detested general warrants, could also be used to justify measures which would be equivalent, in either intent or effect, to the Stamp Act which had contributed to the outbreak of hostilities between Great Britain and her colonies. Certainly, the freedom of the press would thereby be threatened.[74] In addition, Congress has the undoubted power (in specified circumstances) to suppress domestic insurrections and to provide for the common defense. Such powers, as well as the more mundane power over copyrights,[75] might serve to cloak assaults upon the freedom of the press, especially when these powers are reinforced by the necessary and proper clause. The First Amendment stands as a barrier to such an application of the necessary and proper clause and of what I have suggested are today that clause's irresponsible substitutes, the "clear and present danger" and "balancing" tests.[76]

XIII

Not the least of the justifications for the Bill of Rights, including the First Amendment, was the desirability of taking account of "the degree of inquietude" that President Washington detected as resulting from its absence. (*Annals*, I, p. 28)[77] Thus, Madison urged prompt action upon constitutional amendments with the reminder,

> The applications for amendments come from a very respectable number of our constituents, and it is certainly proper for Congress to consider the subject, in order to quiet that anxiety which prevails in the public mind. Indeed, I think it would have been of advantage to the Government if it had been practicable to have made some propositions for amendments the first business we entered upon; it would have stifled the voice of complaint, and made friends of many who doubted the merits of the Constitution. [*Annals*, I, p. 427]

These sentiments are reflected in the preamble attached by the First Congress to the proposed amendments, where the Bill of Rights is offered "as extending the ground of public confidence in the Government," thereby "best insur[ing] the beneficent ends of its institution. . . ."

The respect bestowed upon the Bill of Rights, and especially upon the First Amendment, even by those who avoid a full application of the guarantees found therein, testifies to the role of these provisions not only as legal inhibitions but even more as constant reminders of the ways of free men. These guarantees provide venerable support for those who dare to teach lessons of restraint and humanity in times of harshness and abandon.[78]

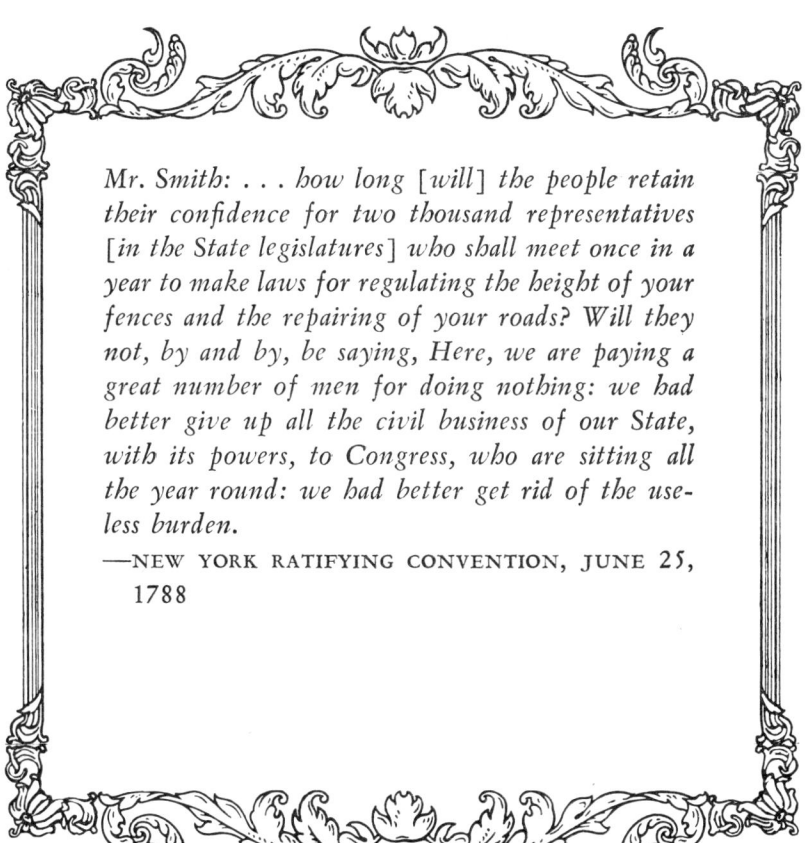

Mr. Smith: . . . *how long [will] the people retain their confidence for two thousand representatives [in the State legislatures] who shall meet once in a year to make laws for regulating the height of your fences and the repairing of your roads? Will they not, by and by, be saying, Here, we are paying a great number of men for doing nothing: we had better give up all the civil business of our State, with its powers, to Congress, who are sitting all the year round: we had better get rid of the useless burden.*
—NEW YORK RATIFYING CONVENTION, JUNE 25, 1788

VII. "A MORE PERFECT UNION"

I

IN FURTHER ELABORATION of the constitutional scheme within which the First Amendment makes sense, let us consider why the states, unlike the general government, are left relatively free to abridge freedom of speech and of the press.[1]

The wording of the First Amendment makes it clear that, no matter what is thought of the remainder of the Bill of Rights, this provision does not apply to the state governments. This is further indicated by the proposal for inclusion among the amendments to be added to the Constitution in the Bill of Rights of a provision (endorsed by the House of Representatives) limiting the states with respect to infringements of freedom of speech and of the press, freedom of religion, and trial by jury in criminal cases.

This proposal to restrain the states was rejected by the Senate despite Madison's description of it as "the most valuable amendment in the whole list." (*Annals*, I, p. 755) Indeed, he argued,

> If there were any reason to restrain the Government of the United States from infringing upon these essential rights, it was equally necessary that they should be secured against the State Governments. He thought that if they provided against the one, it was as necessary to provide against the other, and was satisfied that it would be equally grateful to the people. [*Annals*, I, p. 755][2]

Tucker had objected to this proposed amendment on the ground that although it was offered "as an amendment to the Constitution of the United States," "it goes only to the alteration of the constitutions of particular States." And, he continued, "It will be much better, I apprehend, to leave the State Governments to themselves, and not to interfere with them more than we already do; and that is thought by many to be rather too much." (*Annals*, I, p. 755) The emphasis, in the demand from the states for amendments, had been on measures curtailing the general government: it seemed suspicious, to those already apprehensive about the powers of the new general government, to include restraints upon the states among the amendments to be proposed. Even without such additional restraints upon the states, it was already thought by some, the states were going to wither away completely, or at least into nothing more than glorified election boards, under the Constitution.

The Senate had the duty to protect the power, dignity and rights of the states as state governments. Restraints on the general government, on behalf of either the states or the people, were acceptable; but restraints on the states on behalf of the people were not acceptable, however much the "tribunes of the people" (that is, the House of Representatives) might want them. In addition, one could point out, such state restraints as those proposed were, to the extent they were feasible and took account of local circumstances, adequately provided for in the state constitutions. There would be nothing to be gained by ruling out consideration of local circumstances, which would be one effect of having an impersonal and distant general government interfere in internal affairs. Besides, were not state governments the traditional guardians of the liberties of the people?

The proposed restraints upon state governments meant that there would have been a major area of social action (relating to the activities of speech and of the press as well as of religion) absolutely outside the control of any government in the United States. This would have been so, however narrowly "freedom of speech, or of the press" should be defined. And this would be unique in the original constitutional scheme of our compound republic: no other social activities are put completely outside legislative regulation.[3] Crosskey has reminded us that such disturbances as Shays's Rebellion suggested that state power to act, even to interfere with freedom of speech and of the press, is at times necessary, however carefully the general government was to be precluded from interference in these matters. In any event, it was so left by the Bill of Rights.

Perhaps, indeed, it is because the states were left free to deal with the inevitable abuses of free speech and a free press that an unlimited prohibition upon Congress came to be accepted as workable.[4] It can be suggested, therefore, that "self-interest" in the Senate made possible this condition for the development and consolidation of unparalleled free speech in an extensive republic.[5] That is, the senators, representing and protecting the interests of their states as governments, had preserved the power of the states to deal with speech and the press. The framers of the Constitution—or, at least, the authors of the *Federalist*—had argued that just such a salutary operation of self-interest was anticipated and provided for in our constitutional arrangement.

But whatever may be said about the significance of the American experience, I know of no one who did explicitly argue, in the constitutional period, that unlimited free speech, so far as the general government was concerned, was possible only if powers were left in the states to deal adequately with speech and the press, even to suppress freedom of speech or of the press.[6] But regardless of whether anyone else has ever made the point to the extent I do here, cannot it be maintained that "the Constitution makes this point," that this is what was "intended"? That is, the Constitution should be read in such a way as to explain what *is* there (even if only providentially) and why it has worked as it has.[7]

Nor is such reading of a constitution unrealistic in this case. For one would then be saying what can certainly be said, that freedom of speech can be effective, in First Amendment terms, and has been (or had been) effective, only because the states have been recognized as unhampered by such absolute restraints as are imposed upon Congress. Congress could responsibly keep its hands off and still be spared extreme demands "to do something" simply because it was apparent that the states were competent, equipped, and willing to deal with problems that Congress might otherwise, Constitution or no Constitution, have been compelled to deal with.

Thus, the exposition of what the Constitution "intends" is a constitutional, legitimate, and perhaps instructive way of making the point that the First Amendment did not at once become a dead letter simply because the states, for whatever reason, were permitted to retain some power to deal with speech and the press. (These are activities that it is hard for a legislature to ignore, activities that can be called "essential" for a government to police partly because it is so tempting [and sometimes necessary] for government to intervene and to regulate them.) It might well be, then, that the selfish act of the Senate—an act legitimately selfish, perhaps, in the sense that the Senate was supposed to look out this way for the interests of the states—"inadvertently" contributed to making the Bill of Rights, and particularly the First Amendment, workable and effective. Time was gained during which considerable national experience could be had with truly free speech, experience which would permit the repudiation of the tradition which had warned that liberty of this kind would inevitably lead to license and disorder.[8]

To recapitulate: The Founders did believe that liberty is possible in this country only if there is a proper balance in the powers allocated to the state and general governments. The Senate's constitutional function, then, is to insist upon protecting state sovereignty and power, even against demands that that power be sacrificed to what is declared to be a good cause. This function was performed (with the good effects and results I have suggested) when the Senate refused to accept the amendment limiting the states. We cannot claim, the Founders would concede, that all these particular effects were foreseen; but we did foresee and plan that such effects would result, and we left it to the working of self-interest to contribute to the achievement of desirable results.[9]

In any event, it was generally recognized at the time of the enactment of the First Amendment that the states were left free, so far as the Constitution of the United States governed, to do much to abridge freedom of speech and of the press.[10]

II

The role of the slavery controversy and its influence on the development and consolidation of freedom of speech in the country at large, along the lines set forth above, must not be underestimated.[11] If the general government did not have power to deal with slavery—and this proposition a considerable region of the country was prepared to maintain at all costs[12]—if *that* institution could be said to be primarily a state concern (despite its evident national and international effects), then it was plausible to maintain and agree that speech and the press were likewise free of the general government's control.[13]

Certainly, it now appears more plausible to argue—an argument confirmed by the outbreak of a civil war which resulted in part from an insistence on state as against national interests—that slavery should be subject to national regulation than to make such an argument about the regulation by Congress of speech and the press.[14] Southerners, furthermore, wanted to leave speech and the press outside the domain of the general government, because of the precedent congressional regulation of those activities could provide for slavery legislation by Congress. John Calhoun could discourage as unconstitutional proposed congressional legislation restraining the mailing of abolitionist material into the southern states lest that restraint be considered a precedent for legislation less friendly to slavery as well.[15]

We were reminded of this attitude in recent years when we saw southern congressmen, even those who are ordinarily hostile to labor unions, wary of labor legislation that could have provided precedents for interference by the general government with state regulation of segregation practices. Thus, southerners resisted attempts in 1959 to give the secretary of labor power to initiate suits to protect the rights of union members, lest this provide a model (as it has) for giving similar powers to the attorney general to act on behalf of citizens who claim infringements of their civil rights.

I have supported in this summary form a conclusion that is based on what is generally known about the role of slavery in American political development. This conclusion is that slavery contributed to the insistence on home rule—on states' rights—and this in turn contributed to congressional respect for freedom of speech and of the press. The insistence that the states should have almost exclusive concern with these problems prevailed and, for almost a century, the daring experiment was made: a great government proved able to survive and even prosper, notwithstanding the fact that it possessed no power to curtail or punish the most severe criticism of either its men or its measures. Indeed, Americans learned through this experiment that government became all the stronger for having given the citizen his head: the people were able to become convinced that they ruled themselves and to learn how to do so responsibly.[16] There had been, that is, an opportunity to put to the test the proposition advanced by Washington: ". . . The preservation of the sacred fire of liberty, and the destiny of the republican model of Government, are justly considered as deeply, perhaps as finally, staked, on the experiment entrusted to the hands of the American people." (*Annals*, *I*, p. 28)

III

It is particularly desirable, at a time when the role of state governments is depreciated and is left to be defended by men of dubious motives,[17] that we investigate further how states' rights contribute to freedom. Does not power have to be lodged somewhere to deal with both the real abuses, and, almost as important, the supposed abuses or dangers of freedom of speech and of the press? In fact, states' rights may serve for us as "the 'safety-valve' of the constitution."[18]

There *are* real abuses, particularly of a local or spontaneous nature, which will arise no matter how narrowly freedom of speech may be defined. Is it not simply doctrinaire to claim that there cannot result from unfettered speech immediate bad consequences that threaten and perhaps even seem to outweigh any possible long-run benefit?[19] I examine in chapter 8 the advantages that freedom offers. But abuses and dangers also exist. Their presence is recognized, for instance, in the need that courts have for power to protect their proceedings from certain kinds of criticism, even when such criticism is not only sincere but based on the truth. Speech that is the most unobjectionable in form, according to ordinary standards and practices, and that is delivered with the best of intentions, may, in some circumstances, produce irreparable or at least serious harm. If some police force is not empowered to deal with it, unconstitutional usurpation (in the interest of justice or of the public peace) is likely.

The ratification of such usurpation is seen in Justice Holmes's insistence in *Schenck* that no one has the right falsely to shout "Fire!" in a theater. Not only is the utterance described here not political—it is not a genuine free speech problem—but, even more important, it is an incident to be handled immediately and locally, not an incident illuminating Congress's power. Thus, Justice Holmes's illustration is most inappropriate: but this is what comes from having the same rule or standard for both a local area and the country at large. It is better to recognize appropriate distinctions and to provide for them. Otherwise, the responsible public servant is compelled to exercise authority not legally vested in him in order to continue the functions and meet the obligations of government. And, as John Vining pointed out, "being once accustomed to assume power, the habit is easily confirmed; so that shortly the aggregate of power assembles on the ground where you refused a just participation." (*Annals*, I, p. 570)

We have already seen the vital role played by the rule of law—and constitutionalism is the rule of law applied to the fundamental relations both among the departments of government and between public servants and the people[20]—as a substantial assurance of freedom of speech and of the press. Constitutional restraints that ignore abuses and dangers simply invite usurpation. We have been taught, Publius explains, "how unequal parchment provisions are to a struggle with public necessity."[21] When usurpation becomes habitual, with the disregard and disrespect for law on the part of both public servants and citizens that this implies, the orderly and restrained processes upon which freedom depends are undermined.[22] "Wise politicians will be cautious about fettering the government with restrictions that cannot be observed. . . ."[23]

IV

If it should be granted that power to deal with the abuses of speech and the press should be lodged somewhere, are there any reasons why the states should exercise this power rather than the general government? That is, can a rationale be provided for the original constitutional arrangement, for the formulation of the First Amendment as we have it? It should be noted that the "abuse" qualification in state constitutional provisions relating to freedom of speech and of the press—a qualification found in all but a few of the state constitutions—reflects the view that the states should be left free to deal with some activities of speech and the press.[24] That this view has prevailed throughout the history of the Republic is suggested by the fact that such qualifications have been included in the most recent as well as in the earliest state constitutions. Consider, for instance, the language of the West Virginia constitution of 1862:

No law abridging freedom of speech or of the press shall be passed; but the legislature may provide for the restraint and punishment of the publishing and vending of obscene books, papers, and pictures, and of libel and defamation of character, and for the recovery, in civil actions, by the aggrieved party, of suitable damages for such libel or defamation. Attempts to justify and uphold an armed invasion of the State, or an organized insurrection therein, during the continuance of such invasion or insurrection, by publicly speaking, writing, or printing, or by publishing or circulating such writing or printing, may be, by law, declared a misdemeanor, and punished accordingly.[25]

In prosecutions and civil suits for libel the truth may be given in evidence; and if it shall appear to the jury that the matter charged as libellous is true, and was published with good motives and for justifiable ends, the verdict shall be for the defendant.

These provisions may reflect the understanding that a simple affirmation of freedom of speech and of the press might by this time have raised a question about the state's power to do anything about the activities referred to in the qualifications (which include obscenity as well as the "justif[ication] and uphold[ing of] an armed invasion of the State, or an organized insurrection therein, *during the continuance of such invasion or insurrection*").[26]

However this may be, the advocate of good government replies, there remain two disadvantages to the constitutional arrangement left by the First Amendment: first, the exercise of the power over speech and the press by scores of states, rather than by one central government, is likely to be inefficient; second, and related to the first, the states do not have effective means for dealing with national problems even when they have come to appraise them with a view to the national interest. In rebuttal, the advocate of American freedom might answer as follows:

The disposition found in the Constitution of 1787 and essentially confirmed by the First Amendment permits variety in approaches to the regulation of speech and the press, a variety that may indeed be subversive when the one best way *is* known, but quite acceptable and even necessary when the policy arrived at is, as it is likely to be for us in these matters, the result of tentative opinions and transitory passions dependent on circumstances that vary from state to state. Our experience since the Second World War confirms what was known before, that mistakes here are most apt to result from misguided, even demagogic, political excitation. It is salutary if the opportunity remains for pockets of good sense and calm to exist, even in the most excited times: when repression is on a state-by-state basis, victimized individuals have asylums, *within their own country*, to which they can retire;[27] and the more reasonable elements in the most excitable states have plausible models elsewhere in the country to which they can direct attention in their efforts to correct and calm their fellow citizens.[28]

Huey Long had great influence in Louisiana—and yet, Americans elsewhere were not as much troubled as they would have been had he exercised such influence in Washington. He could be safely criticized outside Louisiana; and good men could leave that state just as opponents and victims of segregation are able to leave the South today. The ability of the country to live with and absorb gigantic aberrations in particular states is illustrated by the impact upon the country at large of the occasional hurricanes which have devastating effects on our coasts: the residents of the Midwest, for instance, are usually unaffected by such storms except perhaps for a few days of cloudy weather. Similarly, political repressions in distant states do not immediately disrupt life in more balanced communities.[29]

Furthermore—to continue this defense of American federalism—state power over speech and the press is not directly linked, as it would be in the general government, to responsibility for war and peace. Men entrusted with the national security easily lose sight of all other considerations. As Nietzsche observes, "How good bad music and bad reasons sound when one marches against an enemy."[30] In the states, however, legislators are relatively free of this kind of interference with a realistic appraisal of the dangers from which they set out to protect the community.

In addition, the limited resources of the states, when compared to the virtually unlimited borrowing power of the general government, tend to encourage self-restraint.[31] The general government thinks nothing, it seems, of establishing elaborate and hence expensive loyalty and security review programs for its employees—this is but a drop from the national bucket.[32] Although state legislatures may denounce subversives and prescribe loyalty oaths, it is quite another matter when substantial appropriations have to be provided to pursue these interests. The money put into a loyalty review program has to be taken from contending claimants, such as public school boards, mental health institutions, road commissions, and police agencies, each with lobbyists and legislative experts able to back up their demands on election day. This, too, encourages a more realistic appraisal by legislators of the dangers and requirements confronted by the community.

Related to the sense of financial responsibility imposed by "the facts of life" upon state governments is the duty that the states have to educate their citizens. Textbooks are selected (and hence shaped) by public officials. Does not this imply that the states should also be permitted (if anyone is) to regulate to some extent the most important part of education, the opinions and ideas that circulate among and shape the citizen body, young and old alike?[33] Should not this duty extend to both the moral and the political education of the people?[34] Thus, control over speech and the press would be but one aspect of the general power and duty of the state to supervise the education of its citizen body, a supervision that should be adjusted according to the circumstances and opportunities of the particular state. (Even so, the influences and effects of the "mass media" will be felt everywhere.)

Still another reason for lodging control over speech and the press in state governments is that they are less impersonal than the general government. A state government is much more like the small community, in the decisive sense that the alert citizen is much more likely to know, if not someone in the state legislature, at least someone who knows someone in the legislature.[35] It is one thing for a legislator in Washington to attempt to proscribe Communists or Nazis or whatever suits the fancy or the phobia of the moment, with the expectation that his proposed legislation will affect only bad men in some part of the country with which he is not too familiar. It is quite another for a state legislator to attack by such legislation, or by legislative investigations, people who may well be friends of friends. Self-interest alone would restrain him. He can more realistically appraise the danger and more easily learn whether there is really anything to get so concerned about. This may be one reason why the state legislatures, even though supposedly of a lower caliber than Congress, have had a less deleterious effect on freedom of speech and of the press since the Second World War.[36] It must be difficult, even for a rural legislator, to take seriously claims of a communist threat to his state—especially when neither he nor his fellow legislators (who, to get elected, manage to become quite familiar with their districts) have ever seen any dangerous Communists.[37]

It is significant that Senator Joseph R. McCarthy left the University of Wisconsin alone, even though it is one of the more "liberal" state universities. Instead, he badgered academic people at such schools as Harvard.[38] When the power to control speech and the press shifts to the general government, it means that the officials responsible for the exercise of this power are able to oppress citizens who have no direct influence on the election or appointment of such officials. Senator McCarthy would have done far less harm both to himself and to his country if he had been obliged to confine his attentions to citizens of his own state: it is likely he would have behaved himself better.[39]

I have suggested that the assignment of the regulation of speech and the press to the states permits adaptations to special local circumstances without committing the entire country to a single policy of laxity or repression. There may well be, from time to time, a section of the country in which immediate and drastic action may be needed to regulate speech and the press. In such circumstances, the local government is in the best position to learn what is needed at that moment, and thereupon to act. Such state governments remain subject to national influence: a free general government can always serve as an example for the states to follow. Many of the aberrations of state governments in recent years can be traced to the "leadership" of the general government, whereas the general government evidently ignored the examples of the calmer states.

Whatever arrangement is settled upon—so long as it *is* an institutional arrangement which does not presuppose an extraordinarily wise and powerful ruler who responds immediately to changing circumstances—there will be risks of some kind.[40] The traditional American constitutional arrangement does assume the risk that there might be repressive and unenlightened conduct by state governments. But this is a relatively minor risk, when compared to the bad effects we have experienced and can expect to recur whenever the powerful general government assumes the power to regulate speech and the press.[41]

V

It should again be acknowledged that much of what I have already said assumes, even if it does not depend upon, a skeptical attitude toward the federal sedition prosecutions and investigations we have seen in the twentieth century. It is hard to believe that the country would not have been at least as well off—if not much better off—without these governmental activities.[42] Even the courts that have upheld these prosecutions as constitutional have sometimes confessed doubts about both their necessity and their effectiveness and have on occasion recognized their harmfulness.

It is also hard to believe that the Communist Party leaders, who were sentenced to five years' imprisonment in 1949 and in a series of trials thereafter, did or said anything warranting such punishment. Should their ideas or activities be regarded as really dangerous to us, when we can survive the same arguments when made by a heavily armed Russia? Have the American Communist Party leaders ever reached or influenced as great an audience as did, in 1959, the foremost Communist in the world who, as the President's guest, repeatedly spoke from the most distinguished platforms in the country and before television cameras? And yet, we were then assured by the President that the American people could be expected to recognize and reject the guile of our Russian visitor.[43] It should have become difficult, after this officially sponsored exhibition,[44] to take seriously the claim of the government in the Smith Act cases. Indeed, one is tempted to wonder whether the Communist Party prosecutions are best understood as instruments of an unenlightened foreign policy.

It is appropriate to emphasize in this manner the ideas of the men prosecuted under the Smith Act: no acts of theirs were penalized but for the political speech that preceded or accompanied and thereby dramatized such acts.[45] The defendants were not charged simply with holding meetings, collecting dues, or training leaders. Rather, they were charged with such acts only insofar as they were colored or directed by or in the service of purposes defined and revealed in their proclaimed ideas.[46] No doubt, most of the leaders, when they were released, continued to hold the ideas which had earlier led to imprisonment—but there have been no second sedition prosecutions of any of the defendants in federal courts under the same statutory provision. Is there not still the same evidence as before that these men hold the ideas and posts they once held, have the same purposes they once had, try to live the life they had once lived, and thus commit again the "crimes" for which they had been imprisoned?

The provisions of the now discredited Sedition Act of 1798 dealt with a much more likely danger than does the Smith Act today. Certainly, the government could have been expected to be more unsure of itself then. In addition, the Smith Act, much more than did the Sedition Act, punishes an unpopular doctrine: one is penalized, fundamentally, for espousing (in concert) the wrong or forbidden ideas.

In any event, it is hard to believe that any risk represented by the defendants in any of the modern cases could not have been adequately handled by state prosecutions. (Congressional sedition legislation, it should be remembered, has been copied from "pioneering" state prototypes.) We also have the 1950-54 state sedition case of *Pennsylvania* v. *Nelson* to assure us that state governments can be as vigilant and harsh as the general government.[47] I have referred in section 9 of chapter 6 to the proposition that practically any crime against the United States could be a crime against a particular state as well, either against the state as a "sovereign power" or, at least, against the state as a member of the Union.[48] The disposition of states to do what they conceive to be their duty should not be underestimated.[49]

Our usual reliance upon the states is reflected in the fact that those governments have exclusive jurisdiction over most of the crimes committed in the United States, with the result that 90 percent of the prisoners in American jails are in state prisons. These include the crimes Americans normally consider worse than sedition (as distinguished from treason), such as murder, armed robbery, and rape.⁵⁰ The rationale of this assignment of jurisdiction has been stated by the director of the Federal Bureau of Investigation in response to the suggestion that there should be established an agency of the general government to take over responsibility for law enforcement from state and local police forces:

> The persons who endorse these grandiose schemes have lost sight of some very basic facts. America's compact network of state and local law enforcement agencies traditionally has been the nation's first line of defense against crime. Nothing could be more dangerous to our democratic ideals than the establishment of an all-powerful police agency on the federal scene. The truth of these words is clearly demonstrated in the experience of nations ruled by ruthless tyrants, both here in the western hemisphere and abroad.⁵¹

It seems that so public and so politically sensitive a crime as sedition should be even easier and more important for state governments to handle: in most cases, there is no problem in detecting the "crime" and ascertaining the "criminal."

Besides, the Congress and the President are left free, under the First Amendment, to counsel or request the states to take action. There are (as we have seen) precedents for such requests from the earliest days of the Republic to the most recent.⁵² If it should be decided that there is not available to the states enough effective power to deal with threats to national security,⁵³ or that the states refuse to exercise such power responsibly, an amendment of the Constitution can be considered.

The possibility remains, of course, that the refusal of some states to act may simply reflect that healthy skepticism Americans sometimes exhibit about alleged threats to their way of life. They are, after all, heirs to a venerable and remarkably successful experiment which has often been condemned and dismissed as unworkable.

VI

Where, under the original Constitution, was the general government left? Can it do nothing except advise the states, issue declarations deprecating certain developments and encouraging others, and perhaps investigate critical situations?⁵⁴ That *is* all, it should be remembered, it can do to prevent almost all the serious crimes that are usually said to affect the domestic tranquillity and good order of the community.⁵⁵ My thesis is that Congress, as distinguished from the states, has no more (and probably even less) authority under the Constitution to legislate with respect to sedition than it has to legislate with respect to murder or theft.

What are the "substantive evils" that may result from sedition "that Congress has a right to prevent"?⁵⁶ Congress *is* empowered and expected, under the Constitution, to do something about domestic insurrection, rebellion, the general breakdown of law and order. There are four steps that Congress can take to supplement the power of the states to deal with any speech or writing (which we can here call sedition) that could contribute to these substantive evils.⁵⁷

Congress can establish effective means for suppressing insurrection, should a seditious attempt be made, including the provision for adequate forces and for appropriate punishments. Thefts or murders, not properly suppressed in a state, can make rebellion more likely, but such a contingency does not give Congress power to legislate against murder or theft. Must not the same be said about the prospect of an unregulated outbreak of sedition in a state? As we saw in chapter 6, there is involved here not only the question of what Congress should want to accomplish, but in addition the question of the means constitutionally available for realizing the purposes Congress might legitimately have.⁵⁸

Congress can also make it clear to the country that the means for suppressing insurrection and enforcing the laws will be vigorously employed should rebellion be attempted. Thus, Congress can publicize deterrents against the commission of acts it does have power to deal with. (Congress and the state legislatures can do no more than this with most of the serious crimes over which they usually have jurisdiction.) Seditious speech, that is, may be outside the jurisdiction of Congress, even though one of the serious and even likely results of that speech may not be. Even with respect to treason, over which Congress has explicit jurisdiction given it in the Constitution, it seems doubtful that Congress can sanction prosecution or ordain punishment for conspiracies to commit treason before the commission of the overt acts required in Article III. Here, too, Congress must rely upon the promulgation of effective deterrents to citizens who have been properly trained.⁵⁹

If the usual constitutional methods do not work—if the rule

of law does not govern as in the usual circumstances (if, that is, a most extreme national emergency arises)— it is only prudent to notice that the rule of law can be to some extent set aside, but in a constitutional manner.[60] The privilege of the writ of *habeas corpus* can be suspended, if there is rebellion or invasion, permitting the President to detain legally those who constitute a grave risk because of what they say.[61] If, upon more mature reflection, the Congress deems the President's actions appropriate (or inappropriate) in the circumstances, he and his officers can be indemnified (or penalized) for their exercise of this power during the emergency.[62]

Perhaps the most effective step Congress can take to ward off domestic insurrection and rebellion is to remove the causes of dissatisfaction to the extent that it can do so by a wise exercise of the powers it does have. To the extent, for example, that Congress controls the prosperity of the community, it can control the economic influences that make for disaffection. Thus, Livermore said of Shays's Rebellion,

> ... Another burden ... was the rapidity of the course of prosecution in courts, by which debtors would be obliged very suddenly to pay their debts at a great disadvantage. Something like this occasioned the insurrection in the Commonwealth of Massachusetts. [*Annals*, I, p. 820]

In short, the advocate of good government can be assured that the most likely and frequent cause of sustained sedition *among us* is bad government.[63] Congress is left free and empowered so to conduct itself as to win the support of the American people. That is, the most political of crimes can be avoided or reduced to a minimum by the exercise of political common sense.[64] If the American people live under good government, they can be depended upon to protect their constitutional system against any who abuse freedom of speech and of the press. That, at least, is what we believe: this is what our experience can be said to have been.[65]

Justice Holmes spoke of "the substantive evils that Congress has a right to prevent." Does not the rule of law, as understood and established in the modern liberal state, create a presumption against the *prevention* of an evil in any particular case, as distinguished from what may be done by government either in developing the community or in dealing with evils already perpetrated? That is, whatever we may do in practice, there are few if any substantive evils that we knowingly concede the government under law has a right to prevent by imprisoning the man who might become an evildoer.[66] This fundamental principle of the rule of law, as we understand it, should be recognizable as having been implicit in the campaign mounted from Milton to Blackstone against "previous restraints."[67]

My objection is not that Justice Holmes begged the question when he invoked "a right to prevent." Rather, my objection is that he evidently did not realize he was begging the question, which means that he did not understand what he was saying and consequently could not anticipate properly the consequences of what he was doing. Justice Holmes and his disciples, I venture to suggest, have left in American law a deposit of facile thoughtlessness which runs deep and of which the "clear and present danger" test is merely a dramatic outcropping.

VII

I have argued that the national interest can be entrusted to the state governments in which we have left exclusive, or virtually exclusive, authority for control of what is known as sedition. That is, I have explained and defended the constitutional arrangement that was recognized to be in effect from the expiration in 1801 of the Sedition Act to the outbreak of the First World War.[68]

But, another advocate of free government may object, the issue has been misconceived throughout this chapter: the problem is not whether the states can be effective in dealing with harmful uses of freedom of speech and of the press, but whether they are responsible and restrained enough to be entrusted with such power. I touched upon this problem when I discussed in section 5 of this chapter the advantages of leaving all power to regulate speech and the press in the state governments. Still, the *Nelson* case, with the twenty-year punishment imposed by the Pennsylvania trial court upon a Communist Party leader convicted for a "Smith Act" type of offense, warns us how this state power may be abused.[69]

Even so, Nelson could have fled Pennsylvania without having to leave the United States.[70] Whether extradition would be likely in such circumstances would depend, in part, on how political crimes were regarded in the state to which he fled.[71] In any event, citizens throughout the country could express themselves freely against the laws and prosecutions of a particular state, and could do so in circumstances which would not be affected by the application of the sedition laws of the general government.

Though it is true that Nelson was sentenced to twenty years of imprisonment, dozens of men were sentenced in federal courts to five years of imprisonment for the same offense. The evidence accumulated in the federal courts in the course of these prosecutions was used in the Pennsylvania prosecution—indeed, the states would not ordinarily want to finance the preparation for cases in the way the general government has. (Such cases can be regarded as a kind of political luxury.) The federal court trials were conducted in practically every major city in the country, thereby arousing the public opinion which made antisedition activities in the states more likely.[72]

However harsh the *Nelson* case sentence may seem, the judgment and reliability of the states should not be made to stand or fall on that example alone.[73] We have permitted the states to make use of the death penalty, with relatively few restrictions, in cases involving murder, kidnapping, and rape. Although there *is* something special about regulation of speech and the press, it is not the severity of the penalty that is the key to a political analysis of the problem, but rather the effectiveness of the suppression that is attempted by means of prosecution. It should be noted that the states have not been as bad, or as pervasive in their effects, as the general government. Indeed, as I suggested in section 4 of chapter 4, the decisive measures taken by the general government since the Second World War may have been its extensive loyalty programs which were ratified and reinforced in their effects by the Smith Act prosecutions and by congressional investigations. Furthermore, whatever one may think of the *Nelson* case, it is not so severe as the case of *Rosenberg* v. *United States* with the death sentences that were not only pronounced in 1951 but, even more dreadful, carried out in 1953 against both parents of young children.[74] The *Rosenberg* case was, at least in part, a sedition case: the political opinions associated with the defendants affected both the judgment of and the sentence pronounced by the trial judge.[75]

Salutary as the Supreme Court action in the *Nelson* case may have been toward insuring justice to the defendant by ruling that state sedition statutes had been superseded by congressional legislation on the subject, that ruling must be considered questionable under the constitutional scheme I have sketched.[76] Indeed, if the theory of "supersession" is to be applied, as was done in the *Nelson* case, it is the state rather than the general government that should be able to claim primacy with respect to the crime of sedition, especially since it is doubtful (as we saw in chapter 6) that the general government has any constitutional power at all to deal with the offenses of which Nelson was accused and convicted.[77]

Certainly, the states may abuse whatever power remains to them to regulate speech and the press. But there are, under the old Constitution, some safeguards that make decency and restraint more likely. Congress, I have argued in section 6 of chapter 4, may intervene to insure genuinely free elections in a state. Traditional procedural standards in state trial courts can be insisted upon by the Supreme Court. These are explicitly required under the Fourteenth Amendment; but they seem to be implied as well in the original Constitution by the evident assumption throughout that the rule of law will be maintained in the states.[78] We recall Dicey's insistence that this rule of law is at the heart of the Englishman's conception of "liberty of the press."

Another protection against abuses by a state of its power to regulate speech and the press lies in the state constitutional provisions protecting freedom of speech and of the press. We should not ignore such prohibitions, even if they should be less comprehensive than their counterpart in the First Amendment.[79] We do rely on state constitutional provisions on many subjects, such as revenues, roads, schools, and terms of office of state officials. Nor do state supreme courts altogether disregard their state constitutional guarantees of freedom of speech and of the press. At the least, such guarantees provide a strong argument when citizens oppose, in the legislature or in the courts, the enactment or enforcement of a repressive law. Perhaps such provisions would be taken more seriously if state officials did not assume that a federal court will supervise and revise the measures that are politically easy for them to take or to permit. A lack of responsibility might well breed irresponsibility.[80]

We should remind ourselves as well that state enactments, both constitutional and statutory, may be tailored to the demands, requirements, and circumstances of a locality.[81] This variety may be salutary, especially wherever political immaturity and economic conditions create special problems. In addition, particular state enactments, both constitutional and statutory, can be amended as conditions or attitudes change much more easily than can the Constitution of the United States.

And yet there must remain, for the advocate of freedom who has become accustomed to hope for the supervision of state measures by the United States Supreme Court, the desire to find a basis for continuing such supervision under the Constitution.[82] This desire has found at least partial satisfaction in the use that has been made of the Fourteenth Amendment, especially the application against the states of substantive standards (not only to protect freedom of speech and of the press, but even more with respect to segregation and the taking of property). It should be noted at this point, however, that there was no reason to suppose in 1789 that state governments would be less respectful of the political liberties of the American citizens than the general government. In fact, it can be said that it was at the insistence of the states that the Bill of Rights was added to the Constitution. The states were even depended upon to check any activities of the general government which threatened the rights of the people. Thus, Madison predicted,

. . . the State Legislatures will jealously and closely watch the operations of this Government, and be able to resist with more effect every assumption of power, *than any other power on earth can do*; and the greatest opponents to a Federal Government admit the State Legislatures to be sure guardians of the people's liberty. [*Annals*, I, p. 439; italics added][83]

At one time, the states were considered at least as much dedicated to the rights of the people as the general government. But, some might counter—and this brings us to the problems discussed in the remainder of this chapter—the caliber of the state legislator and indeed of the states has declined since those heroic days.

VIII

I discussed in section 6 of chapter 4 the duty of the general government to assure each state a republican form of government. The Supreme Court has not made of this obligation what it should, with the result that it has had to look elsewhere to justify its intervention when state governments get seriously out of line.[84] In fact, little has been done with this provision since President Lincoln invoked it to justify action by the general government against rebellious states.[85] What the Supreme Court did in the *Nelson* case by reliance on a theory of "supersession" could have been better done, with more support in the Constitution, by indicating the presumptive invalidity for republican regimes today of state legislation directed against Communists.[86] This not only might have made the court less vulnerable to attack than it was on that occasion, but also would have contributed to the instruction of the American people concerning their form of government.

Before leaving the question of the alleged propensity of the state governments to abuse (more than would the general government) any power to regulate speech and the press,[87] I remind the reader that America was most highly acclaimed, both at home and abroad, as the land of reasonable liberty during that century when the states were recognized to have virtually unlimited power under the Constitution of the United States to regulate speech and the press while the general government was generally acknowledged to have almost none.

Also pertinent is the fact—not generally known even among students of constitutional law—that the *Nelson* case went to the Supreme Court of the United States after the Supreme Court of Pennsylvania had *reversed* the conviction in the trial court.[88] The Pennsylvania appellate court did rely primarily upon the "supersession" argument that the Supreme Court of the United States subsequently ratified. I suspect, however, that the state court would have found another and probably better reason (perhaps even in the Bill of Rights of that state) to justify its action, had the "supersession" argument not been available.

Is it too much to hope that since the state courts are also rooted in the American tradition, they can be induced, if given both the opportunity and the duty, to revive their former dedication to freedom under law?[89]

IX

I have suggested the role played by the slavery controversy in helping to solidify, and perhaps even to magnify, the place of the states in the American constitutional system. But this role of the states can be traced back still further, to the earliest days of the Republic.

The great constitutional feats of 1776-91 were accomplished by men who had been trained in colonial and state politics when local government was considerably more important than it is now. Those among the people with the greatest political souls aspire to the highest posts; they cannot take seriously, for long, the attractions of lesser offices. The ordinary citizen senses this hierarchy; he too realizes that municipal and state government positions, as we know them, have become merely stepping-stones to higher ones.[90]

It is difficult for us today to grasp what was once a commonplace, that state governments and state politics offered to ambitious men not only worthy, but even the highest, objects of their ambitions. We can no longer understand why Robert E. Lee saw his duty to Virginia as higher than and prior to any obligation to the United States.[91] The states could provide, so long as they continued to be taken seriously, invaluable training grounds for national affairs. And, so long as they were taken seriously, they could be— they would be, for that is how seriousness is indicated—entrusted with important tasks, tasks vital not only to the welfare of the state but also to the Union in which the states had been enrolled.[92]

Among the tasks entrusted to the state governments was one bearing on the subject of our discussion. The states, as has been shown, were left under the Constitution of 1787 and the First Amendment with powers far more extensive than those of Congress to regulate, and even to abridge, freedom of speech and of the press. The Civil War changed this, as it did so many other features of American life. The southern states tried to expand powers they already had. (I here interpret this development as a northerner.) This expansion would have destroyed the Union. The result of the war that followed, and of the postwar amendments to the Constitution, was not simply to preserve the Union but rather to begin a shift from a union to a nation.[93] The transformation of the United States into a world power confirmed and reinforced the shift that had set in with the Civil War.

X

Three aspects of the transformation that the Civil War brought to light are of particular interest to us here:

More and more power was assumed by, or was recognized to reside in, the general government. Thus, the jurisdiction and duties of Congress were seen to be much greater than before. (The expanding scope of the Commerce Clause illustrates this development.[94])

A subordinate role was assigned to the states; they became less "sovereign" than they had been before.[95] With this development there came a deterioration in the quality of the state governments, something that may have begun to happen to some extent in the North (and perhaps in the South as well) even before the war.

Related to this latter development was the extension against the states of the restraints and the safeguards of rights that had been imposed by the Constitution against the general government. This followed upon the unquestionably marked revision, brought about by the Civil War and ratified by the postwar amendments, of the power of a state to discriminate among its inhabitants according to race.[96]

The Fourteenth Amendment reflects both the second and the third of the three aspects of this transformation. This development reached its constitutional confirmation in this century with the 1925 United States Supreme Court decision in *Gitlow* v. *New York*.[97] Although the state prevailed on that occasion against a defendant charged with "the statutory crime of criminal anarchy," it was nevertheless held that First Amendment rights had been made applicable against state governments by the Fourteenth Amendment.[98] This was the culmination of a movement in public opinion which had been advanced by the Civil War crusade: the states were no better than the general government, the prevailing thought seems to have become, and so they should be subject to the same salutary restraints as the general government, restraints that protect the sacred rights of citizens.[99]

Thus, I do not suggest that the Fourteenth Amendment is alone responsible for the development illustrated by *Gitlow*. In fact, the amendment can itself be seen as one result and as an early manifestation of this development. The Civil War and the need to develop a large and powerful government which could and did overpower both "sovereign" states and the idea of state sovereignty made the Fourteenth Amendment possible. But that amendment was not only a result of this development; it also had the effect of contributing to it, extending the development through judicial proceedings, thereby providing Americans its necessary legitimation.

As the states were subordinated, it must have seemed anomalous to leave to them the duty of handling serious matters that some thought affected the very existence of the national community. Thus, the abuses of freedom of speech and of the press came to be regarded as a national problem, one that *the* government of Americans should deal with. Or, to approach the fact of state subordination from the perspective of the advocate of freedom, why should not the state governments, those secondary, reflecting luminaries, be subjected to the same restraints as *the* government, the one that gets things done, the government upon which the existence and welfare of the nation depend?

The rationale of a useful distinction between state and general government roles, with respect to the regulation of speech and the press, had long since been lost sight of, or perhaps had never been explicitly recognized.[100] The very success of the constitutional arrangement that had been established, whether by accident or design, may well have contributed to its undoing, for the arrangement had been such that men had been given an opportunity to learn that an extensive freedom of speech was possible under a powerful national government. The experiment had not only proved feasible; it had been acclaimed throughout the world as a great success. The Civil War confirmed the strength of a free government: Congress enacted no sedition law, even though rebellion threatened the life of the Union, intensified the divisions within the country, and moved a hostile army to the outskirts of the national capital. The states were relied upon, outside military zones, to police civilian abuses of freedom of speech and of the press.[101]

The conduct of Congress as well as the opinion of the public during the first century of the Republic seemed to give evidence of recognition that the states could be depended upon (except in the most extreme circumstances) to take care of both national and local interests and to exercise with prudence the power they had under the Constitution to regulate speech and the press. This recognition made possible the development of confident familiarity with the possibilities of national freedom of speech and of the press. But one of the conditions of this success—the assignment to the states of substantial powers in this field—had been lost sight of.

Even as freedom of speech was approaching the zenith of its

practical justification, one of the principal conditions for that ascent began to disappear: the states had been demoted in the constitutional system. Accompanying this development is the other that has been mentioned, the tendency to extend against the states the proven salutary restraints upon the general government.[102] Thus, the 1925 *Gitlow* case merely recorded a change in relationship between state and Union that had been seventy-five years in the making.[103] The states not only came to have applied against them the extensive restraints previously directed against the general government alone, but even more important (and perhaps earlier, thereby leading up to the application of these restraints), the states ceased to be thought of as responsible instruments capable of policing serious threats to the national community.[104]

XI

This decisive change in the relation between the state and the Union came after more than a century of experience with the old way. This had been a century in which the people, as both rulers and ruled, had tested the value and feasibility of such guarantees as freedom of speech. It had been demonstrated that the general government need not have power to curtail political speech in order either to protect itself or to provide for the general welfare. The general government, Americans had learned, was able to prosper without having this power within its own control. And this was an essentially new experience for modern governments and rulers. As it became accepted, and as people settled into their duties, the abuses of free speech may have become fewer, especially when officials relaxed and did not attempt those unnecessary suppressions which in turn create resentments and resistance which call for further (and perhaps, then, necessary) suppressions.

Thus, after more than a century of such experience, a general effective prohibition of all government action against speech and the press, by either the state or the general government, became more feasible than it would have been at the end of the eighteenth century. One effect of this experience was to repudiate whatever remained of the common law tradition of seditious libel in the states and to create, in the country at large, a comfortable reliance upon freedom of speech in everyday political affairs. Had the conditions prevailing in the nineteenth century continued, the extension against the states of the clear-cut and absolute prohibition that had been directed against Congress might have proved effective, at least for two or three generations.

But the United States became a world power: and with its growth in strength and prestige came a heightened awareness of dangers from abroad. Among these dangers were "foreign" doctrines that were said to threaten the tranquillity and even the very existence of the American nation.[105] A world war served to increase these fears and to provide the setting for the attempt to develop new measures to meet what seemed to be new problems. It was then felt that restraints should be applied to curb any agitation undermining national security. The states, however, were no longer the instruments they had once been thought to be.

There was, even before the First World War, a growing opinion that the states were not *responsible*. This opinion had a two-fold effect. It developed into the doctrine that eventually won acceptance in the *Gitlow* case: the states should be no more privileged than the general government to regulate speech and the press.[106] It also developed into the doctrine that the states could not be depended upon to control the abuses of freedom of speech and of the press. The critical point which these doctrines have in common is that the general government, not the states, should be for Americans the principal guide with respect to sedition.

More and more, the states were having applied to them the same standards as the general government:[107] they came to have applied to them the absolute restraints of the First Amendment. Certainly, they could not be trusted to handle dangers which the country faced. Instead, the general government must be relied upon. But the general government had long had facing it the evidently absolute restraints which were now being brought to bear against the states as well. Indeed, it began to appear that there no longer existed power anywhere to abridge freedom of speech or of the press. Thus, at a time when the need for such power seemed to be greater than ever before, constitutional relations had so changed as to eliminate altogether such effective power.

As the pressures mounted, there appeared a crack in the restraining surface, a surface stretched too tight against *any* abridgment of freedom of speech by *any* American government. The restraint upon *both* the general government and the states would be retained and extended; but that which was prohibited to government would have to be cut down. The "clear and present danger" test emerged. If the general government was to be responsible for policing abuses of freedom of speech and of the press, then something had to be done about the absolute restraint on the general government which had been carried over (by the First Amendment) from days of different federal relations. The "clear and present danger" test anticipated and permitted the explicit extension of the Bill of Rights to the states, preserved the form of the old restraint upon Congress, and in effect recognized in Congress a new power to regulate speech and the press.[108]

To sum up the argument presented in sections 10 and 11: we retain the notion that "freedom of speech" is a very extensive guarantee; we anticipate (and later explicitly establish) the position that the guarantee applies against the states as well as against the general government; and, as we make *these* concessions to the libertarian, we are driven to argue that some abridgments, by both the nation and the states, are permissible in certain circumstances—and the circumstances become less rare and even trivial as perils abroad mount. Thus, the "clear and present danger" test recognizes a genuine need—primarily related to local, almost spontaneous, disturbances—a need for which the means of legitimate satisfaction had been eliminated or thwarted by the depreciation of the states and, perhaps, by the terms of the Fourteenth Amendment. In any event, Americans have had their great free speech litigation in the twentieth century, not when the country first faced clear, present, and almost fatal dangers.

The effect of the current interpretation of the Fourteenth Amendment—for this is a shorthand way of referring to basic changes in federal relations—might be likened to the actions of well-meaning but unthinking friends of beauty who rip away the unattractive scaffolding that braces a noble structure. The condition of American freedom might well have been, and may continue to be, something we too easily dismiss as "states' rights."[109]

XII

My explanation of the emergence and significance of the "clear and present danger" test suggests one of the risks of constitutional changes in any well-established system. Changes were made in existing arrangements, arrangements that had produced effects which the changes inadvertently altered or eliminated.[110] In fact, such effects may not be appreciated until years later when further changes have to be made to compensate for their disappearance. This sequence may be reflected in the "clear and present danger" test, which seems to be a symptom—a reaction many years later—resulting from the disorder induced in the American constitutional system by the changes in federal relations reflected in the Fourteenth Amendment.[111]

The Fourteenth Amendment, to the extent that it is cause as well as effect, is an example of what can happen when a change is made which has far-reaching consequences—a change the proportions of which its proponents may never have foreseen, just as today we have yet to grasp its full significance. One must resort to basic constitutional principles to appreciate what has happened—and to anticipate what might happen in such cases. The antislavery authors of the Fourteenth Amendment acted for the sake of liberty as well as of equality; they did not seem to realize the extent to which our labyrinthian federalism contributed to that liberty, even while it permitted slavery.

But, the advocate of good government—or, some would say, of big government—might argue, since the total amount of repressive power remains the same (for the states and the general government may now be said to share in reduced portions that power over sedition which the states once had in full measure), American liberty is no more and no less threatened than heretofore. This would be so, the argument might continue, even if the *Nelson* case does mean that the general government is now the government primarily responsible for regulation of speech and the press. There are, however, as I have suggested, reasons why it is better to leave primary jurisdiction over such matters in the states rather than in the general government. One significant result of a shift such as that which has been taking place in recent decades may be that it removes the example of an extensive, relaxed, and successful freedom under the auspices of the general government from before the eyes of the people and their public servants in the several states.

There are serious problems that may be related to this shift from and depreciation of the state governments. But a solution to these problems does not lie in an abrupt return to the old arrangement.

One of the effects of the present arrangement, an effect which is one result of the shift since the Civil War, is the depreciation of the status of the state governments, the lowering of the level of state government personnel, the reduction of civic-mindedness seen in state governments and directed toward them by citizens. An abrupt shift back, even if politically feasible, would probably point up even more the inadequacy of such governments as they are now constituted and would thereupon provoke a reaction that would throw even more power to the general government.[112]

It should be recognized, moreover, that the states retain many of the powers they once had. The attitude with which citizens proceed may be decisive as to whether the states will exercise their powers efficiently and even as to whether they will continue to retain them. It should also be recognized that one valuable compensation for the downgrading of the states has been the increased importance of local private organizations with civic responsibilities.[113] Thus, the American capacity for local self-government continues to assert itself.[114]

Big government faces two problems: either the individuality (or just plain stubbornness) of the people asserts itself and inefficiency, if not anarchy, prevails, or general uniformity is imposed and initiative is suppressed for the sake of efficient administration. Eventually, the character and sense of duty of the citizen will be altered. Thus, the long-run effects of the constitutional changes I have been describing could be not only decisive but, perhaps, even irreversible. The reported incidence of citizen apathy, which is reinforced by the attractiveness to the common man of the material pleasures that prolonged prosperity furnishes, suggests how the American character will be changed.[115]

The obligation to fight a war in a clearly good cause, especially if accompanied by limited physical devastation in North America, might arrest current developments and even induce a temporary improvement of the American character. That is, the citizen has not yet become so self-centered and soft that such an obligation could not rally the best in him. But, of course, there is no assurance that devastation among us would be limited; nor would this remedy serve to insure long-run improvements.[116] A regime dominated by fear and hate, in which the community is shaken to its foundations and the normal rhythm of life is disrupted, provides no enduring substitute for one in which the character and aspirations of the citizen are shaped primarily by the community and not by influences essentially beyond its control.[117]

The remedies to be considered now should, I believe, be such as gradually return power to and demand more of the local community, however inefficient and awkward this might seem.[118] It would be helpful, in this respect, if the general government should once again be persuaded that it has no criminal jurisdiction over the political opinions and activities of the citizen.[119] It is not from such self-restraint that the Republic faces its principal threats, but rather from developments that make the citizen unfit to fulfill his civic duties or that convince him that his very survival depends on the surrender to the general government of authority over all vital activities of life. It is important for thoughtful Americans, at a time when the Republic is threatened by decay at home and by devastation from abroad, to reflect upon the challenges to the preservation of republican institutions examined in the writings of Thucydides and Plutarch, of Cicero and Shakespeare, and of Tacitus and Montesquieu.[120]

XIII

In an age when so much seems to be dependent on affairs abroad, on events so much out of our control, it is salutary that we should recall the attitude of a more confident and self-respecting generation. It was under the old dispensation, under the old Constitution, that the twenty-nine-year-old Lincoln could say,

> . . . At what point shall we expect the approach of danger? By what means shall we fortify against it? Shall we expect some transatlantic military giant to step the ocean and crush us at a blow? Never! All the armies of Europe, Asia, and Africa combined, with all the treasure of the earth (our own excepted) in their military chest, with a Bonaparte for a commander, could not by force take a drink from the Ohio or make a track on the Blue Ridge in a trial of a thousand years.
>
> At what point then is the approach of danger to be expected? I answer, If it ever reach us it must spring up amongst us; it cannot come from abroad. If destruction be our lot we must ourselves be its author and finisher. As a nation of freemen we must live through all time, or die by suicide.[121]

Every schoolboy today, aware of the developments of modern

science and technology,[122] can tell us what is wrong with this prophecy;[123] but only the prudent man among us knows what is right about it.[124]

After the excursion of the last two chapters into the labyrinth of American federalism, we now need to return to a more straightforward evaluation of freedom of speech and to several permanent questions, among them questions about the nature, purposes, and origins of our constitutional principles, written and unwritten—those constitutional principles which are fitting and proper for "a nation of freemen."

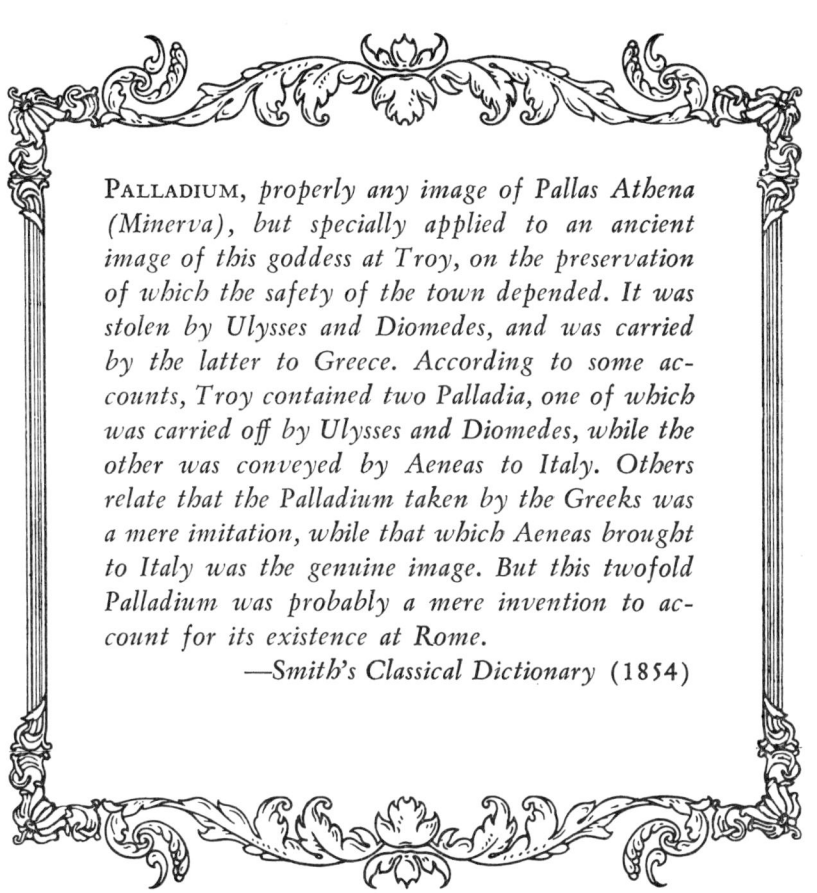

PALLADIUM, *properly any image of Pallas Athena (Minerva), but specially applied to an ancient image of this goddess at Troy, on the preservation of which the safety of the town depended. It was stolen by Ulysses and Diomedes, and was carried by the latter to Greece. According to some accounts, Troy contained two Palladia, one of which was carried off by Ulysses and Diomedes, while the other was conveyed by Aeneas to Italy. Others relate that the Palladium taken by the Greeks was a mere imitation, while that which Aeneas brought to Italy was the genuine image. But this twofold Palladium was probably a mere invention to account for its existence at Rome.*
—Smith's Classical Dictionary (1854)

VIII. "THE BLESSINGS OF LIBERTY"

I

IT IS NO MEAN ACHIEVEMENT when one learns to distinguish between the words of men and their deeds. This is a distinction which pays homage to the role of discourse and reason in human affairs.[1] It is a distinction that we often take for granted: it is well to be reminded of its significance. A biographer of Andrew Jackson was obliged to observe,

> There was an intensity and vigor about him which showed lack of training. His character had never been cultivated by the precepts and discipline of home, or by the discipline of a strict and close society, in which extravagances of behavior and excess of *amour propre* are promptly and severely restrained by harsh social penalties. There is, to be sure, a popular philosophy that home breeding and culture are of no importance. The fact, however, is not to be gainsaid that true honor, truthfulness, suppression of undue personal feeling, self-control, and courtesy are inculcated best, if not

exclusively, by the constant precept and example, in earliest childhood, of high-bred parents and relatives. There is nothing on earth which it costs more labor to produce than a high-bred man. It is also indisputable that home discipline and training ingrain into the character of men the most solid and valuable elements, and that, without such training, more civilization means better food and clothes rather than better men.

It is characteristic of barbarians to put their personality always at stake, and not to distinguish the man who disputes their notions from the man who violates their rights. It is possible, however, that the military virtues may flourish where moral and social training are lacking. Jackson was unfortunate in that the force of his will and the energy of his executive powers had never been disciplined, but the outbreak of the second war with England afforded him an arena on which his faults became virtues.[2]

Circumstances can arise when the use of words may violate the rights of another—but the ordinary use of words and the disputing of another's notions, even about the most important matters debated by a community, are not the same as deeds. It would seem, in any event, that "disput[ation] of notions" on political matters should enjoy a particularly high status in a civilized society. How high a status this right of political disputation—which falls within the American terms, "freedom of speech [and] of the press"—should be accorded is itself subject to dispute.

II

There are in the English-speaking world differences of opinion as to which of the rights claimed by and for the people is the highest, which provides the "greatest safeguard for liberty," which is "the palladium" of all the rights.[3] Five contenders for this distinction are the writ of *habeas corpus*, the right of trial by jury, freedom of speech and of the press, the right of suffrage, and the right of property. (I omit from detailed consideration here other rights which have been spoken highly of. Many of them may be considered as incorporated in one or more of the five I have listed.[4] These five are selected partly because of the attention they have been given through the years.)

How can these contending claims to primacy be reconciled? Each of these five rights can be shown to contribute, in some measure, not only to freedom but, when properly exercised, to justice and good order as well.[5] What, then, is distinctive about each of these rights? That is, what view of the highest good does each of them presuppose?

Before proceeding further, we must note that which is peculiarly American about all these rights when compared to the way in which the British regarded them. The difference is reflected in William Smith's description of the British Constitution:

> The Constitution of Britain is neither the *magna charta* of John, nor the *habeas corpus* act, nor all the charters put together; it is what the Parliament wills. It is true, there are rights granted to the subject that cannot be resumed; but the Constitution, or form of Government, may be altered by the authority of Parliament, whose power is absolute without control. [*Annals*, I, pp. 715-16]

The American Constitution, on the other hand, binds governments whose power is anything but "absolute without control."

III

Each of the rights for which primacy is claimed has had distinguished supporters. Trial by jury has behind it the authority of Magna Carta, where "it is more than once insisted on as the principal bulwark of our liberties."[6] *Habeas corpus*, on the other hand, is regarded by the legal-minded Blackstone (I, 135) as the most vital right:

> And by 31 Car. II. c. 2, commonly called the *habeas corpus* act, the methods of obtaining this writ are so plainly pointed out and enforced, that, so long as this statute remains unimpeached, no subject of England can be long detained in prison, except in those cases in which the law requires and justifies such detainer. . . .
>
> Of great importance to the public is the preservation of this personal liberty; for if once it were left in the power of any, the highest, magistrate to imprison arbitrarily whomever he or his officers thought proper, (as in France it is daily practised by the crown), there would soon be an end of all other rights and immunities.

The primacy of the right of suffrage is assumed in the *Federalist*, where it is seen (with the Constitution that is proposed) as a surer protection for all other rights and immunities of the people than a bill of rights and other "parchment guarantees."[7] It is in accordance with this sentiment, which reflects the importance of the electorate under the Constitution,[8] that it has been said that the most critical right to be secured to any minority is that of the ballot: when that right is guaranteed to a large minority, other rights follow in due course for that minority.[9]

The hold that the right of property has always had on the passions of men is evident in their everyday life. Much of their activity is governed by the attraction of property: indeed, our free enterprise system depends on this appetite.[10] There remains freedom of speech and of the press. Claims for its superior position are reflected in such evaluations of freedom of speech as that it is "the matrix, the indispensable condition, of nearly every other form of freedom."[11] Freedom of speech and of the press is the only one of the five that is not explicitly recognized (except in the form of the immunity guaranteed members of Congress) in the original Constitution.[12]

There has arisen in recent decades the doctrine of the "preferred position" of the rights protected under the First Amendment.[13] This doctrine has been used to explain and justify the disposition of the Supreme Court of the United States to read into the "due process" clause of the Fourteenth Amendment (so as to restrain the states) only a few of the rights protected against the general government instead of the entire array set forth in the Bill of Rights. No doubt this selection depends, at least in part, on current opinions about which are the most important rights of our people.

Is there any basis for the "preferred position" argument? It should be noted at once that the First Amendment is physically "first" in the list of amendments merely by virtue of chance developments. It was not intended by its framers to be first: two other proposed amendments, which were not ratified, preceded it in the list of proposed amendments sent by the Congress to the states for their approval.[14] Although no one would argue that the First Amendment is "preferred" because it happens to be in the first position, still the physical primacy ("In the beginning . . .") no doubt lends psychological support to the "preferred position" designation. (In political matters, appearances are important: this is the basis for the vital role of rhetoric in politics.)

The decisive argument advanced by those who propose for the rights of the First Amendment a preferred position among those found in the Bill of Rights draws upon the Constitution itself and the way of life, in its broadest political sense, that it incorporates.

Freedom of speech and of the press can be identified as the key elements in a people's efforts at self-government. To ask then about the status of freedom of speech among us is to ask (at least in modern times) about the nature of the regime.

Before I examine the status among us of freedom of speech, I believe it would be instructive to consider what is implied by each of the five rights I have set forth—or rather, what is implied by the claim to primacy made on behalf of each.[15] Each of these positions exhibits a different opinion about the regime—about, that is, the likely or the proper relation between the citizen or the people, on the one hand, and the government, on the other.[16]

IV

The insistence upon *habeas corpus* as preeminent is, at heart, an insistence upon the rule of law. This means, as we have seen in the passage taken from Blackstone's description of the Habeas Corpus Act, that "no subject . . . can be long detained in prison, except in those cases in which *the law requires and justifies* such detainer." It means, if "personal liberty" is to be preserved, that *arbitrary* power must be curbed: there must be rule according to law.[17] This, we have seen, is reflected in Dicey's reduction of the English "liberty of the press" to the proposition that the press, like any other activity, is subject to the rule of law.[18] The prohibitions upon bills of attainder and *ex post facto* legislation, which are directed in the Constitution against both the general and the state governments, may be regarded as attempts to define that "law" by which men should be ruled and for which they can be held responsible.

I suggest that the insistence upon *habeas corpus* implies much more than the availability of the writ designed to aid anyone detained by the civil authority: that is, a comprehensive system of law is implied. This is indicated in Smith's comments, in the course of a discussion of the impeachment power of Congress, about the value of legal procedures and traditions:

Gentlemen have found out that impeachment is a tedious process; I apprehend the person who is impeached will not think it a dilatory process, but such a one as is wisely inserted in the Constitution for the protection of his person and property. The delay of which gentlemen complain is the greatest bulwark of liberty. Our ancestors, who were tenacious of their privileges, guarded them in the best manner they could devise to prevent the inroads of despotism. As well may gentlemen complain of the tedious process in other criminal cases, by indictment of a grand jury and trial by a petit jury. I hope it is not contemplated (if it is, I hope never to see adopted in this country a summary process) to hurry on judgment without reflection. [*Annals*, I, pp. 470-71][19]

In still another passage, in the course of a discussion of the rules to be applied to the judiciary, Smith indicated another way in which legal institutions are utilized to assure citizens that arbitrary government has been guarded against:

The committee have been told that this multiplicity of courts, and of appeals, will distress the citizens; and the number of appeals in Great Britain has been alluded to. He had always heard, he said, that there was no country in the world where justice was better administered than in that country; to its excellent and impartial administration, the property, freedom, and civil rights of its citizens have been attributed. Were appeals too much restrained in this country, he questioned much whether a great clamor would not be raised against such a restriction. The citizens of a free country, when they lose their cause in one court, like to try their chance in another. This is a privilege they consider themselves justly entitled to; and if a litigious man harass his adversary by vexatious appeals, he is sufficiently punished by having the costs to pay. [*Annals*, I, p. 819]

Indeed, the rule of law implied by *habeas corpus* could well include that "due process of law" which, as Justice Holmes said, "embraces the fundamental conception of a fair trial, with opportunity to be heard."[20] The guarantee of the writ of *habeas corpus* can be taken to mean that due process of law will be permitted to continue unimpeded.[21]

One is moved to wonder whether there is something about the Anglo-American common law, with its ultimate reliance upon reason for the conduct of human affairs, that leads almost inevitably to constitutional law and even to republican government as we know it.[22] Everything has to be justified; everything is open to examination; everything has to appear consistent with reason."[23] But, the Englishman might say, the end result need not be republican government but simply the rule of law, whether under a republic or a monarchy. But does not monarchy mean, essentially, that there is no rule of law but rather rule of a man? That is, the monarchy that conforms to the rule of law is a severely limited monarchy. The alternative, then, seems to be constitutional government which, at least in our time, may have to be essentially republican.[24]

We are reminded of the reliance placed in the First Congress on an efficient system of government as the first great guarantee of the liberty of the people: constitutional government had to be firmly established. Despite attempts by some members to raise the subject of a bill of rights early in its first session, the First Congress postponed its consideration of this subject until the business of the House was well on its way, particularly with respect to taxation.

Even Gerry, who was anxious for fundamental amendments to the Constitution, could observe, "The people know we are employed in the organization of the Government, and cannot expect that we should forego this business for any other." (*Annals*, I, p. 445) Thus, Madison, although prompted by his Virginia constituency to urge early consideration of a bill of rights, was obliged to counsel his colleagues at one point:

... The great and material defects [of the government under the Articles of Confederation] are well known to have arisen from its inability to provide for the demands of justice and security of the Union. To supply those defects, we are bound to fulfill the public engagements; expectation is anxiously waiting the result of our deliberations; it cannot be satisfied without a sufficient revenue to accomplish its purposes. [*Annals*, I, p. 300]

The list of proposed amendments that was to make up our Bill of Rights was not agreed upon by the two houses of Congress until almost the final day of the first session. This reflects fairly the attitude of these men: all rights, even the most important for self-government, depend upon and are best protected by public order and confidence; responsible government must first be established before one can talk profitably, safely, and realistically of limitations and restraints. Perhaps, indeed, this rests on the assumption that community is prior to rights, that order is to be preferred to principled anarchy.[25]

Page expressed the doubts of some members of the First Congress about the desirability of efficient government when he said:

For my part, I shall ever prefer the security of my fellow-citizens, whether in or out of office, to a rigid observance of the rules of office; and an independent spirit in our officers, to a prompt servility. Energy of Government may be the destruction of liberty; it should not, therefore, be too much cherished in a free country. A spirit of independence should be cultivated; a sense of honor and virtue nourished with care; and though some irregularities might take place, they would be such as could not endanger public liberty. [*Annals*, I, p. 550]

And he added: "Need I repeat that this energy [of Government] is oftener employed against the liberty of a people, than in favor of it? The liberty and security of our fellow-citizens is our great object, and not the prompt execution of the laws." (*Annals*, I, p. 551) But no doubt the dominant sentiment in the First Congress, and among the Founding Fathers—and here I return to that rule of law which I have suggested is fundamental to the concept of *habeas corpus*—is that expressed two generations later by Senator Daniel Webster:

Liberty is the creature of law, essentially different from that authorized licentiousness that trespasses on right. It is a legal and a refined idea, the offspring of high civilization, which the savage never understood and never can understand. Liberty exists in proportion to wholesome restraint; the more restraint on others to keep off from us, the more liberty we have. It is an error to suppose that liberty consists in a paucity of laws. If one wants few laws, let him go to Turkey. The Turk enjoys that blessing. The working of our complex system, full of checks and restraints on legislative, executive, and judicial power, is favorable to liberty and justice. Those checks and restraints are so many safeguards set around individual rights and interests. That man is free who is protected from injury.[26]

Blackstone refers to the Habeas Corpus Act as "that second magna carta, and stable bulwark of our liberties." This is in the context of his discussion of how the Habeas Corpus Act reinforces the Magna Carta guarantee that no one will be deprived of liberty except according to the law of the land. Thus, this rule of law implies not only due process of law but, perhaps, to some extent, trial by jury—but trial by jury that is seen, in this context, as particularly effective and valuable as a means for determining the truth about an issue in controversy. The principal concern is that the law of the land be applicable in all cases.[27] It is assumed that liberty, justice and public order depend on the rule of law, on legality.[28] Perhaps, indeed, the writ of *habeas corpus* is (of all the rights we are dealing with) distinctively the lawyer's instrument, one that reflects both the achievement and the vulnerability of the legal mind which we see in Tocqueville's description:

Lawyers are attached to public order beyond every other consideration, and the best security of public order is authority. It must not be forgotten, also, that if they prize freedom much, they generally value legality still more: they are less afraid of tyranny than of arbitrary power; and, provided the legislature undertakes of itself to deprive men of their independence, they are not dissatisfied.[29]

V

The most pervasive, or at least the most evident, indication of the rule of law and of the restraint exercised by government is seen in the protection accorded to property. This right touches almost all members of the community, not only those who are politically minded.[30]

The constitutional significance of the rights of property has long been recognized. Milton asks, ". . . [W]hat stirs the Englishmen, as our wisest writers have observed, sooner to rebellion, than violent and heavy hands upon their goods and purses?"[31] The slogan, "No Taxation without Representation," attests to the continuation in America of the attitude that Milton reports.[32] The occasions for American resistance to British rule were instances in which property rights were treated in a manner that could be said to have put them at the mercy of unknown men across the seas, men who were responsible for the tax levies (including the Stamp Act), the trade regulations, and the port bills that had been imposed on the colonists from London.

This general attitude finds philosophical legitimation[33] in the writings of so respectable a figure as John Locke, who sees property rights and what we call civil liberties as intimately connected, so much so in fact that he can designate all rights (including those to life and liberty) as "property rights."[34] Perhaps even more influential is his legitimation as well of virtually unlimited acquisition and accumulation. The most radical challenges to his thesis, from critics such as Rousseau and Marx, have acknowledged the critical role of property in shaping society: they see property rights as questionable and propose to subjugate to considerations of the common good the gratification of private desires, thereby challenging an orientation toward acquisitiveness that goes back through Locke all the way to one of Marx's unsuspected masters, Machiavelli. (Another such master can be said to be St. Paul.)

The contemporary apostles of private property, those who regard as most critical for the American way of life the preservation of free enterprise, tend to view with suspicion, or at least with apathy, such rights as those to freedom of speech. They regard the effective exercise of those rights either as dependent on the existence of private property or as threats to property and hence to the common good.[35] They tend to favor the old, the ancestral, and the conventional, for these ratify and legitimate property. Even so, they are threatened by the emergence of the innovations that result from the imaginative and productive pursuit and use of the very property they cherish.

Free enterprise, with appropriate restraints on certain kinds of self-aggrandizement, does hold out extensive opportunities for individual self-assertion and development. The scope and amount of government power and influence are far less than would be the case if officials ran the economy. This means, as well, that there are economic refuges to which dissenters can repair against the onslaughts both of government and of an intolerant majority. Leon Trotsky wrote in 1937, "In a country where the sole employer is the State, opposition means death by slow starvation. The old principle, who does not work shall not eat, has been replaced by a new one: who does not obey shall not eat."[36] One should be reminded of Cephalus' appraisal of the value of wealth: wealth permits one to be virtuous.[37]

An eminent Cephalusian of the constitutional era, Noah Webster, went to the root of the matter: "In what then does *real* power consist? The answer is short and plain—in *property*. . . ."[38] He developed this answer with liberally italicized arguments:

. . . Thus the landed property in England will never be sufficiently distributed, to give the powers of government wholly into the hands of the people. But to assist the struggle for liberty, commerce has interposed, and in conjunction with manufacturers, thrown a vast weight of property into the democratic scale. Wherever we cast our eyes, we see this truth, that *property* is the basis of *power*; and this, being established as a cardinal point, directs us to the means of preserving our freedom. Make laws, irrevocable laws in every state, destroying and barring entailments; leave real estates to revolve from hand to hand, as time and accident may direct; and no family influence can be acquired and established for a series of generations —no man can obtain dominion over a large territory—the laborious and saving, who are generally the best citizens, will possess each his share of property and power, and thus the balance of wealth and power will continue where it is, in the *body of the people*.[39]

Webster then commented on the traditional opinion as to the basis of republican government:

Montesquieu supposed *virtue* to be the principle of a republic. He derived his notions of this form of government, from the astonishing firmness, courage and patriotism which distinguished the republics of Greece and Rome. But this *virtue* consisted in pride, contempt of strangers and a martial enthusiasm which sometimes displayed itself in defence of their country. These principles are never permanent—they decay with refinement, intercourse with other nations and increase of wealth. No wonder then that these republics declined, for they were not founded on fixed principles; and hence authors imagine that republics cannot be durable. None of the celebrated writers on government seem to have laid sufficient stress on a general possession of real property in fee-simple.

Indeed, he argued, "The system of the great Montesquieu will ever be erroneous, till the words *property or lands in fee simple* are substituted for *virtue,* throughout his *Spirit of Laws*." And he added,

Virtue, patriotism, or love of country, never was and never will be, till mens' natures are changed, a fixed, permanent principle and support of government. But in an agricultural country, a general possession of land in fee simple, may be rendered perpetual, and the inequalities introduced by commerce, are too fluctuating to endanger government. An equality of property, with a necessity of alienation, constantly operating to destroy combinations of powerful families, is the very *soul of a republic*—While this continues, the people will inevitably possess both *power* and *freedom*; when this is lost, power departs, liberty expires and a commonwealth will inevitably assume some other form.

Webster reviewed as well, and subordinated to the property arrangements, the other rights I am assessing in this chapter:

The English writers on law and government consider Magna Charta, trial by juries, the Habeas Corpus act, and the liberty of the press, as the bulwarks of freedom. All this is well. But in no government of consequence in Europe, is freedom established on its true and immoveable foundation. The property is too much accumulated, and the accumulations too well guarded, to admit the *true principle of republics*. But few centuries have elapsed, since the body of the people were vassals. To such men, the smallest extension of popular privileges, was deemed an invaluable blessing. Hence the enconiums upon trial by juries, and the articles just mentioned. But these people have never been able to mount to the source of *liberty, estates in fee,* or at least but partially; they are yet obliged to drink at the streams. Hence the English jealousy of certain rights, which are guaranteed by acts of parliament. But in America, and here alone, we have gone at once to the *fountain of liberty,* and raised the people to their true dignity. Let the lands be possessed by the people in fee-simple, let the fountain be kept pure, and the streams will be pure of course. Our jealousy of *trial by jury, the liberty of the press,* &c. is totally groundless. Such rights are inseparably connected with the *power* and *dignity* of the people, which rest on their *property.* They cannot be abridged. All *other* [free] nations have wrested *property* and *freedom* from *barons* and *tyrants;* we begin our empire with full possession of property and all its attending rights.

This emphasis on the primacy of property found sufficient support among Webster's contemporaries to lead some historians to regard the Constitution, and even the Revolution itself, as the product of a propertied class out to advance its own interests. Various provisions in the Constitution do reveal a concern for the protection of property: taxation is to be exacted on a per capita basis; the obligations of commerce are not to be impaired by the states; fugitive slaves are to be returned to their owners; property may not be taken without due process of law, and compensation must be made for any use of it for public purposes. Property rights, fully developed, are seen in the free enterprise economy that the United States has relied upon since its birth.

But economic activity is now such that even its immediate effects, and hence the related problems and solutions, tend to be national in scope.[40] Local management of such matters becomes increasingly unlikely.[41] Thus, an overriding concern for industrial prosperity induces our people toward a consolidated government, away from local self-government. This has been one important effect of the Northern victory in the Civil War, intensifying in this country a worldwide development.

Property, it can be said, encourages an independence of the will: with it, a man is more likely to be his own master. And if property holdings are to be retained or enlarged, prudence and self-restraint are required. Such considerations reinforce the argument for the right of property as the principal support of liberty. But it must also be understood that such an emphasis tends to recognize the primacy of certain[42] passions over reason, and indeed attempts to mobilize them for the common good.[43] It is a common good that is somehow to emerge from an enlightened pursuit of innumerable private goods.[44] But is not the emergence and even the determination of the common good essentially a matter of chance so long as property rights (that is, the appetites) are considered to be primary? The passions are blind: they may induce men to calculate, so as better to gratify them, but they do not encourage that reflection which permits men to distinguish among the passions and to see where happiness really resides.[45] The difficulty we indicate here is reflected in Socrates' insistence, in Plato's *Republic*, that the best men are to have no property of their own, that the city must be their property (and hence be the sole external object of their care).

A spokesman of the Soviet Union observed, in the course of a Chicago discussion, that Americans overrate "small privileges," such as making speeches in the street. "Which is more important," he asked, "making a speech on the public square or telling a factory boss he is wrong, and, if necessary, removing him?"[46] Such emphasis upon the economic aspect of life brings together the Communist and the capitalist—the disciples of Karl Marx and of Adam Smith—and reflects at least to this extent their agreement that the passions dictate to the reason.

VI

The insistence upon the right to trial by jury, particularly in criminal cases, may also be seen as concerned with the problem of legality, but in a different way from *habeas corpus*. The principal concern is not simply the rule of law, but rather that those against whom the law is to be applied should have an opportunity to control or moderate its effect. In fact, it could even be characterized as a means for protecting against too much legality.[47] This is reflected in Justice Holmes's observation:

> I confess that in my experience I have not found juries specially inspired for the discovery of truth. I have not noticed that they could see further into things or form a saner judgment than a sensible and well trained judge. I have not found them freer from prejudice than an ordinary judge would be. Indeed one reason why I believe in our practice of leaving questions of negligence to them is what is precisely one of their gravest defects from the point of view of their theoretical function: that they will introduce into their verdict a certain amount—a very large amount, so far as I have observed—of popular prejudice, and thus keep the administration of the law in accord with the wishes and feelings of the community.[48]

In a way, this is an insistence upon equality, an equality that insures home rule, but that is achieved or protected by an institution that provides a bulwark against a potentially oppressive government or against rules of law that are too far behind or too far ahead of the times.[49] Various elements of the traditional jury trial are preserved, including the right to be tried in the neighborhood where one is likely to be known (and, presumably, where one's cause is most likely to find sympathizers against the action of a distant government). Thus, James Jackson described the dangers of a judicial system which does not properly respect the defendant's residence:

An offender is dragged from his house, friends and connexions, to a distant spot, where he is deprived of every advantage of former character, of relations and acquaintance; the right of trial by a jury of the vicinage is done away, and perhaps he is carried to a place where popular clamor might for the moment decide against him; or, if allowed a trial by vicinage, or his neighbors, it is equally vexatious to drag him two or three hundred miles from his home, with evidences to try and give testimony at a distant place; every thing is to be dreaded from it. This, he observed, was contrary to our wonted customs, and we need but revert to the history of Britain, after the Conquest, to view what struggles that nation made against innovations of this nature. [*Annals*, I, p. 803]

It is no wonder that trial by jury should have been claimed in Magna Carta "by the barons, sword in hand, from King John." Americans were confirmed in their regard for this privilege by their experiences in the revolutionary period.[50] Thus, again and again, colonial administrators (for example, royal governors) refrained from prosecution of seditious newspaper publishers and editors, or were unsuccessful when they tried to prosecute, because of the resistance anticipated or encountered from the juries before which such prosecutions had to be brought.[51]

Even jurymen who were favorable to the Loyalist cause must have been deterred or at least influenced by the pressure brought upon them by the more ardent patriots among their fellow citizens.[52] An effort was made before the Revolution to avoid these difficulties by providing for the removal of certain cases to Great Britain for trial.[53]

Not only was conviction of a popular leader or editor unlikely before a local colonial jury, but even his indictment was most difficult to secure from a grand jury. In fact, royalists had to rely upon an information rather than an indictment in order to bring a matter to trial.[54] In such situations, adequate protection for a free press (and, if that were an issue, free speech as well) could be trial by jury.[55] As a practical matter, therefore, patriot editors were left unfettered throughout the colonies in the decade before the Revolutionary War broke out and continued in that condition during the war except in areas governed by British military forces.

The case for trial by jury in criminal cases seems to assume that liberty, justice, and public order depend on a power in the people to veto the application in their locality of the law of the land. A kind of defensive equality, resulting in a degree of home rule, is thereby assured. When the institution of trial by jury is criticized, it is often in the name of justice: local interests, prejudices, and customs outweigh the rule of law that is sought to be imposed from without or from above. Mark Twain's 1872 comment on this institution is illuminating, especially as it illustrates the tendency of trial by jury to promote local self-government or, if one wills, local anarchy:

Trial by jury is the palladium of our liberties. I do not know what a palladium is, having never seen a palladium, but it is a good thing, no doubt, at any rate. Not less than a hundred men have been murdered in Nevada—perhaps I would be within bounds if I said three hundred—and as far as I can learn, only two persons have suffered the death penalty there. However, four or five who had no money and no political influence have been punished by imprisonment—one languished in prison as much as eight months, I think. However, I do not desire to be extravagant—it may have been less.[56]

VII

In the right of suffrage, equality takes the offensive. There seems something almost magical about the act of a people voting and choosing their leaders, an act which Americans see enshrined in the reference by the Declaration of Independence to the "consent of the governed."[57] The magic, or the delusion, has become worldwide. Thus, we have seen in recent decades elections with one-party slates conducted in East Germany under both Nazi and Communist regimes.[58] The ritual of popular suffrage has become so potent that it cannot be dispensed with even when there is obviously neither free speech nor a choice among candidates (and hence no electorate).[59]

In America the popular sentiment that had expressed itself through the jury was raised to the point where it could form and direct the very government that had once been considered by some a threat to popular control.[60] As universal suffrage has become more important and effective, the efficacy and the efficiency of trial by jury in criminal cases have been increasingly questioned—except in those sections of the country where local sentiment and customs are in marked conflict with the national temper. Other former guarantees of the popular will have also been depreciated. Thus, whereas "the right of the people to bear arms" could once be regarded as "the best security of a free state" (*Annals*, I, p. 749), it has become virtually meaningless in modern constitutional law. Even that right which is affirmed so eloquently in the Declaration of Independence —the right of revolution against even a popular government which should become tyrannical—has come to be regarded in some quarters as subversive to the principle of popular sovereignty: the popular will should not be subject to examination. The right to property, which once seemed to offer citizens ultimate refuge from the demands of a government over which they had no control, has been left a subordinate role, especially as citizenship simply, and not propertied citizenship, qualifies one for participation in political life.[61]

The people that had once thought they needed against government the protection of trial by jury—as well as the right to bear arms and the right to be represented for purposes of taxation— became in due course the masters of government. Thus, Gerry can use "sovereignty of the Union" to refer to "the people"; an earlier age, only two decades before, would have tended to identify "sovereign" with "monarch." (*Annals*, I, p. 501)[62] The development of popular sovereignty as we now know it was implicit as well in such observations as that of Boudinot, who regarded "the freedom of election" as that "upon which alone the whole fabric [the Constitution] depends." (*Annals*, I, p. 639)[63] The emergence of popular sovereignty was perhaps implicit in the original Constitution. There was no containing it as new and less settled (and less tradition-bound) states were added to the Union. One of the provisions of the Judiciary Act of 1789 suggested, in its relaxed attitude toward forms, the tendency of the future:

... no summons, writ, declaration, return, process, judgment, or other proceedings in civil causes in any of the courts of the United States, shall be abated, arrested, quashed, or reversed, for any defect, or want of form, but the said courts respectively shall proceed and give judgment according to the right of the cause and matter in law shall appear unto them, without regarding any imperfections, defects, or want of form. . . . [*Annals*, I, pp. 2195-96]

Form, it seems, should give way to reason and justice. If reason is to be paramount, and if what is reasonable is to be determined by citizens who are recognized as political equals, then we must expect constitutional forms based on reservations about the capacity of the public either to fall into disuse (as happened with the electoral college) or to be deliberately changed (as happened with the election of senators by state legislatures).[64]

The original Constitution, however, did reflect the reservations about the popular will to which I have just referred. Thus, Lee pointed out,

The Senators are selected with peculiar care; they are the purified choice of the people, and the best men are likely to be preferred by such a choice; those who have shown the fullest proofs of their attachment to the public interest, and evinced to their countrymen their superior abilities. [*Annals*, I, p. 652]

White, on the other hand, challenged this view of the effect of the mode of selecting senators:

[In Rome] the Senators were considered as possessing some degree of divinity, and the rest of the people were not admitted to associate with them. Can it be supposed that the name of Senators will render those members superior to their fellow-citizens? [*Annals*, I, p. 654]

A similar difference of opinion was expressed in the course of the debate as to whether members of Congress should be constitutionally bound by instructions sent them by their constituencies. Stone, in opposing such instruction, argued,

I think [this] would change the Government entirely; instead of being a Government founded upon representation, it would be a democracy of singular properties. . . . In my opinion, [it] would bind [the representative] effectually, and I venture to assert, without diffidence, that any law passed by the Legislature would be of no force, if a majority of the members of this House were instructed to the contrary, provided the amendment became part of the Constitution. What would follow from this? Instead of looking in the code of laws passed by Congress, your Judiciary would have to collect and examine the instructions from the various parts of the Union. It follows very clearly from hence, that the Government would be altered from a representative one to a democracy, wherein all laws are made immediately by the voice of the people. [*Annals*, I, p. 739]

Page's comments on this issue may be particularly attractive to those who take public opinion polls seriously:

[The proposed instruction clause] was strictly compatible with the spirit and the nature of the Government; all power vests in the people of the United States; it is, therefore, a Government of the people, a democracy. If it were consistent with the peace and tranquillity of the inhabitants, every freeman would have a right to come and give his vote upon the law; but, inasmuch as this cannot be done by reason of the extent of territory, and some other causes, the people have agreed that their representatives shall exercise a part of their authority. To pretend to refuse them the power of instructing their agents, appears to me to deny them a right. [*Annals*, I, p. 744]

It had been left to Gerry to question Stone's terminology:

The gentleman from Maryland had said that the amendment would change the nature of the Government, and make it a democracy. Now he had always heard that it was a democracy; but perhaps he was misled, and the honorable gentleman was right in distinguishing it by some other appellation; perhaps an aristocracy was a term better adapted to it. [*Annals*, I, pp. 742-43]

"Aristocracy" implies that some men are or are thought to be, for one reason or another, better equipped than most to deal with the problems of the community. Hartley had already made an "aristocratic" argument against the proposed instruction clause:

When the passions of the people are excited, instructions have been resorted to and obtained to answer party purposes; and although the public opinion is generally respectable, yet at such moments it has been known to be often wrong; and happy is that Government composed of men of firmness and wisdom to discover and resist popular error. [*Annals*, I, p. 733]

Much of our political thought of the past two centuries has been based on the assumptions implicit in the following comment in the First Congress by Jackson:

> Can one man, however consummate his abilities, however unimpeachable his integrity, and however superior his wisdom, be supposed capable of understanding, combining, and managing interests so diversified as those of the people of America? . . .
> In a Republic, the laws should be founded upon the sense of the community; if every man's opinion could be obtained, it would be better; it is only in aristocracies, where the few are supposed to understand the general interests of the community better than the many. I hope I shall never live to see that doctrine established in this country. [*Annals, I*, pp. 724-25]

Thus, the emphasis upon the right of suffrage as the key right of the people may rest, fundamentally, on the premise that there is no significant distinction between "the few" and "the many," between those who understand "the general interests of the community" and those whose grasp of such interests is inferior. Liberty, justice, and public order, it is assumed, depend on equality simply: the votes to be counted are assumed to be cast by fellow citizens with underlying common interests.[65]

The problem remains, however, whether there is a real will of the people. Such a will would presuppose *a* people which knows what it should have. One is reminded of the insistence in Book II of Plato's *Republic* upon the fact that in almost all communities there are really two cities. This seems to be recognized as well in the oath prescribed by the First Congress for "justices of the Supreme Court and the district judges":

> I, A. B., do solemnly swear or affirm, that I will administer justice without respect to persons, and do equal right to the poor and to the rich, and that I will faithfully and impartially discharge and perform all the duties incumbent on me as_____, according to the best of my abilities and understanding, agreeably to the Constitution and laws of the United States. So help me God. [*Annals, I*, p. 2185]

It is recognized here, that is, that one of the perennial conflicts in a community is between rich and poor, that each has something to be said for it, and that the judge must, in order to do justice, give to each what is its due.[66] The distinction between rich and poor may reflect to some extent the distinction between those who are blessed with and those who are deprived of things even more important than money, things vital to one's ability to know and decide what is good.

Madison acknowledged both the rights and the limitations of "the people" when he said, "My idea of the sovereignty of the people is, that the people can change the Constitution if they please: but while the Constitution exists, they must conform to its dictates." (*Annals*, I, p. 739) Or, to put this sentiment in terms particularly appropriate to our subject here, we can repeat the words of Justice Jackson:

The very purpose of a Bill of Rights was to withdraw certain subjects from the vicissitudes of political controversy, to place them beyond the reach of majorities and officials and to establish them as legal principles to be applied by the courts. One's right to life, liberty, and property, to free speech, a free press, freedom of worship and assembly, and other fundamental rights may not be submitted to vote; they depend on the outcome of no elections.[67]

VIII

In the days when trial by jury, *habeas corpus*, the right of property, and the right of suffrage were each extolled as the most important safeguard for the rights and liberty of the people, freedom of speech and of the press did not generally have the exalted and independent status of the others.[68] Rather, it seems to have been regarded as an instrument in support of one or more of the other rights and of their respective ends. Thus, it has been seen as a means for making the suffrage effective,[69] or for opposing the oppression of rulers, or for informing the legislature of the sentiments of the people. In this sense, freedom of speech contributes to the self-government of equals—that is, to majority rule.[70]

Freedom of speech and of the press, as found in the First Amendment, was originally insisted upon as protection against a powerful and potentially arbitrary central government that was not, it was feared, ultimately subject to the will of the people. The general government, under the Constitution, occupies the place formerly assigned to the British Parliament in the colonial political world. It was likely, with this parallel and experience in mind, that those people who had doubts about the new government should insist upon the right to speak freely on political issues. This reinforces my conclusion (in chapter 5) that the extent of political speech permitted by Congress should be practically unlimited: extreme speech had been necessary before to defend rights, win independence, and establish a just regime; it remains available to preserve that regime and those rights from subversion.

A different approach seems to have been taken with respect to state governments, which the people knew from experience they controlled. A more direct restraint and mode of influence, in the form of the ballot, was known to be available there, with the result that the scope of permissible speech could be more limited with respect to state government activities. This meant, in effect, that it was understood that the sentiments of a minority, in the states, might be suppressed to some extent. "Freedom of speech," in these circumstances —whether determined by constitutions of the states or by the common law—could be more restrictive, less extensive, than in the country at large.

Had the general government been recognized from the very start as a truly popular institution, the potentially self-denying freedom of speech insisted upon by the people might have been explicitly limited: an "abuse" qualification, similar to that found in almost all state constitutions, might have been added; something more might have been said as well about giving power to Congress to deal with certain emergencies and dangers.[71] But the absolute prohibition upon Congress was proposed and ratified before the popular revolution was recognized. (Whether that revolution is taken to have occurred in 1800 or 1828 or, for that matter, in 1860 or 1865, does not matter for my immediate purposes.) The absoluteness of the terms of the First Amendment (which can be understood as following from our form of government) was something that might not have been insisted upon had the people possessed from the beginning an awareness of the political power they would have under the Constitution.

I am suggesting, that is, that freedom of speech and of the press was established in our heritage as a popular right, one designed to reinforce the protection the people have against potentially oppressive government. This right strengthened the bulwark provided by the right to trial by jury: with such trial, depending on jurors selected by lot from the citizens in a locality, no sedition prosecution of popular attacks upon the government is likely to be attempted; and if such a prosecution is attempted, assuming a grand jury can be found to indict, conviction is difficult, if not impossible, to secure. So long as freedom of speech could be seen, as it may have been seen at first, as protecting popular opinion against governmental repression, it deserved no special status of its own: trial by jury served this purpose even better than freedom of speech, for it extended such protection against government not only to speech but also to deeds reflecting popular attitudes.

It is as an instrument for enabling the public to make known to the government its sentiments, and thereby to influence if not control the government, that freedom of speech and of the press seems to be regarded in the Stephen-Holdsworth passage I have reproduced in section 11 of chapter 5. It was natural—some might even say, providential—that this freedom should be given special constitutional status, perhaps for the first time, by a people who have led the modern world toward popular self-government. It is a privilege of the people which permits them to apply the principle so aptly stated by Gerry, that "in a republic every action ought to be accounted for" (*Annals*, I, p. 574)—which means, in practical terms, that the people are free to examine public affairs and to demand explanations for whatever they believe should be better understood by them.

Presumably the people are equipped to judge because they can be depended upon to apply to their judgments about men in public life the experience and standards they have brought from private affairs. This seems to be implied in the reply of the Senate to President Washington:

We feel, sir, the force, and acknowledge the justness of the observation [made by Washington], that the foundation of our national policy should be laid in private morality. If individuals be not influenced by moral principles, it is in vain to look for public virtue; it is, therefore, the duty of legislators to enforce, both by precept and example, the utility, as well as the necessity, of a strict adherence to the rules of distributive justice. [*Annals*, I, p. 32]

Perhaps the compatibility, and even more the interdependence, of public virtue and private morality depended, in Washington's view, on "the Great Author of every public and private good." Compare the property-minded proposition that from private vices will somehow come public good.

IX

I have thus far in this chapter regarded "freedom of speech [and] of the press" (or perhaps, strictly speaking, "liberty of the press") as essentially a substitute for popular control of a government. And yet we now see freedom of speech continue to be exalted by some, at a time of effective popular rule, as itself the most important right of a people. How is this to be understood, since the opinion of the people, under a popular government buttressed by jury trials, does not need special protection?

The distinctive contribution today of freedom of speech and of the press is that it provides protection for minority opinion, even against the popular will. This protection becomes increasingly important as the majority realizes its power and finds institutional means for imposing its will. Indeed, in popular government, all "rights," except that of suffrage (and even that to some extent, particularly in the case of large minorities), protect *some* minority against the popular will.[72]

What is the minority protected by freedom of speech and of the press? It tends to be that minority of citizens who differ, either in talents or in political opinions, from the main body of the people, or who are capable of forming their opinions independently of the public.[73] Thus, the tendency of free speech in such circumstances—circumstances characterized by the rule of the public and of public opinion—is essentially aristocratic. It offers a sanctuary for the dissenter who is obliged to challenge popular dogmas and popular authority, even though it was first insisted upon by the popular party to protect itself against the "aristocrats" who had written the Constitution and who were expected to control the general government for generations.

Dicey's observation—that liberty of the press is, in England, not much more than the guarantee that the rule of law shall be applied to the press as it is to other activities subject to law—is relevant here. *Habeas corpus* (with its insistence upon the rule of law) and trial by jury (with its moderation of such rule when the law is not favorable to local opinions and customs) are the key rights in a system that is not popular, in which the people are seen as concerned with protecting themselves against oppression by the government. The more activities made to conform to the rule of law, the better; and if regulation of the press can be subjected to the general rule, the scope for arbitrary action is reduced even more. The ultimate objective of freedom of speech and of the press is, in such circumstances, to aid the people in securing to itself the political power of the community: that is, this right may not be as important to the people for this purpose once popular government is established. But the part it plays in helping the people to power and the acclaim given it in the process of doing so conspire to elevate it in traditional public esteem. It is sanctified thereby as a right even though the public might occasionally resent it: by the time it is thus sanctified, freedom of speech and of the press is part of "the old way"—and its enduring value is assumed.[74]

The distinctively American meaning of freedom of the press, when compared to the English tradition of regarding liberty of the press primarily as an extension of the rule of law to the regulation of the press, includes the stipulation that the power of the legislature is curtailed not only as to timing (which is critical to the English emphasis on "no previous restraints") but also with respect to the extent of legislative power over this subject. Even a great popular majority is limited in what it may do. What can justify this protection of minority expression if not the assumption that such protection will more likely result in the employment of reason and wisdom in public affairs? This belief is what makes freedom of speech in popular governments somewhat aristocratic in effect. Those who dissent from popular beliefs may be "half-baked" and dangerous; but they may also be thoughtful citizens who might not otherwise be able to contribute to the public good. The majority will have or will stimulate (and even cherish) half-baked or dangerous men, in any event; but, it can be argued, it is not likely to encounter thoughtful dissent without attempting to suppress it. The purpose of safeguarding the dissenter, it should be added, is not primarily to protect the wise man—for it is often in his interest to devote himself entirely to his private affairs—but rather to advance the interest of the community. Freedom of speech, then, not only provides the thoughtful man the opportunity to make a contribution to public affairs but also, by promising him immunity for what he says, may even be said to impose the duty upon him to make that contribution.

It is here, then, that the value for us of freedom of speech may be seen. The people, perhaps even more than their government, are, to some extent, forced to listen; their education, or at least their training, becomes possible, as reason and wisdom are given an opportunity to exert some influence on public affairs. The British seem to have achieved this result by having bred and bought an aristocracy with political power. Liberty of the press could there make sense as an insistence upon the rule of law: the recognized aristocrat needs no special privilege to speak freely.[75] A people with popular government, where there are no recognized spokesmen of merit, needs to rely upon an aristocratic right.[76] The more popular the government, the more likely it is that there will be hostility toward the man who rises above the city—unless he is invested with religious trappings or otherwise distinguished by fortune.

It is fortunate, therefore, that the American people should have had recourse, on the eve of the realization of their power in the country at large, to a statement of principles (in the Virginia Resolutions of 1798) which would henceforth bind them so long as their faith is good:

That the General Assembly [of Virginia] doth particularly protest against the palpable and alarming infractions of the Constitution, in the two late cases of the "alien and sedition acts," passed at the last session of Congress; [the second of] which acts exercises . . . a power not delegated by the Constitution, but on the contrary expressly and positively forbidden by one of the amendments thereto; a power which more than any other ought to produce universal alarm, because it is levelled against the right of freely examining public characters and measures, and of free communication among the people thereon, which has ever been justly deemed the only effectual guardian of every other right.[77]

X

These observations about the nature and purpose of freedom of speech and of the press affect our understanding of how that freedom is to be enforced or protected. Even from the earliest days of the Republic, some saw the Bill of Rights as a bulwark against popular tyranny, rather than as primarily that assurance for the people against powerful rulers I have described. Thus, Madison thought that constitutional restraints were advisable "against the community itself; or, in other words, against the majority in favor of the minority." (*Annals*, I, p. 437) He believed the greatest danger to liberty resided "in the body of the people, operating by the majority against the minority." The legislature was especially to be guarded against—that body (particularly in the House of Representatives) which from the beginning most directly reflected popular opinion. He went on to argue,

> It may be thought that all paper barriers against the power of the community are too weak to be worthy of attention. I am sensible they are not so strong as to satisfy gentlemen of every description who have seen and examined thoroughly the texture of such a defence; yet, as they have a tendency to impress some degree of respect for them, to establish the public opinion in their favor, and rouse the attention of the whole community, it may be one means to control the majority from those acts to which they might be otherwise inclined. [*Annals*, I, p. 437]

Thus, paper barriers are seen as a kind of noble rhetoric. But, one must wonder, what constitutional remedies are available when the government oversteps the bounds marked out by such barriers?

The most obvious remedy is one that is available to the majority: the offending government can be voted out of office. Presumably, this remedy is available also to the dissenter who is permitted to try to persuade the majority that the government action, although perhaps popular at the time of its adoption, was wrong. But it is unlikely that he would be successful in this attempt after he had failed in his effort to prevent the government action in the first instance (unless bad effects of that action had become evident). The only circumstances in which this recourse is likely to be effective are those in which the people have been impressed, in Madison's words, with "some degree of respect" for the constitutional barriers which have been transgressed.[78] It is doubtful whether this is the most practical recourse when freedom of speech has been effectively redefined by a popular government.[79] (That is, such evasions as the "clear and present danger" test and the "balancing" test have succeeded in compromising the respect of the people for the clear-cut rule the First Amendment had seemed to offer: the people are less likely to respect a judicially refined prohibition than a more unequivocal one. Enough of the "old way" remained for us to appeal to, with some success, after the Second World War. But if the old way is not revived in the minds as well as the hearts of men, the next appeal to public opinion in desperate circumstances is more liekly to be hopeless.[80])

Should not the threatened dissenter have recourse, in any event, to a tribunal not immediately under the control of the majority? It is probably true, as Justice Holmes said, "that legislatures are ultimate guardians of the liberties and welfare of the people in quite as great a degree as the courts."[81] Courts are unlikely to be able to uphold the liberties of a people if they are, *for a long period*, the only source of support for such liberties. But what of the "short-run"? It is evident that judges with lifetime tenure are somewhat more insulated from the effects of public opinion than are legislators or the President, and they work in surroundings and on problems that encourage the detachment expected of them.[82]

I can do little more than mention here the question that a minority, from generation to generation, preserves as a question against the weight of orthodox opinion:[83] do the federal courts, and particularly the Supreme Court of the United States, have the power to pass upon the constitutionality of acts of Congress?[84] It is generally known that the Constitution is silent on this issue: the Court exercises the power of judicial review by virtue of general public acquiescence with the language in *Marbury* v. *Madison*.[85]

The debates in the First Congress are inconclusive. The references to "paper barriers," such as that seen in the passage from Madison quoted earlier, suggest that there may have been no remedy in law for congressional disregard of prohibitions laid down in a bill of rights. The first Judiciary Act also seems to leave the question open. Thus, as Crosskey shows, section 25 of that act does not presuppose but is, at most, only consistent with judicial review of congressional legislation.[86] Indeed, one passage in the act points away from judicial review: ". . . all the said courts of the United States shall have power . . . to make and establish all necessary rules for the orderly conducting business in the said courts, provided such rules are not repugnant to the laws of the United States." (*Annals*, I, p. 2189) Repugnancy to the Constitution of the United States is not mentioned. Is this only because these rules would be made by judges who, it is assumed, would take the Constitution into account (just as the legislators would be making laws?)? Is each branch of the government assumed to take the Constitution into account, so much so that it is neither the duty nor the prerogative of any branch to revise (or nullify) the act of another branch?

Related to these observations is the claim Madison made, in the course of debate on the removal power of the President, on behalf of legislative construction of the Constitution:

> ... if it relates to a doubtful part of the Constitution, I suppose an exposition of the Constitution may come with as much propriety from the Legislature, as any other department of the Government. *If the power naturally belongs to the Government*, and the Constitution is undecided as to the body which is to exercise it, it is likely that it is submitted to the discretion of the Legislature, and the question will depend upon its own merits. [*Annals*, I, p. 461]

The words I have italicized suggest a distinction: legislative construction is as valid as judicial when the question is primarily that of what department (or, as we say, branch) of the general government is to exercise power which "naturally belongs to the Government."[87] Thus, the branches must adjust differences on such points among themselves.

But even with respect to cases limited to the proper allocation of power among branches of the government, dissents were expressed to Madison's position. Ames, who supported with Madison the inclusion of the removal-power provision, observed, "If we declare justly on this point, it will serve for a rule of conduct to the Executive Magistrate: if we declare improperly, the judiciary will revise our decision; so that at all events, I think we ought to make the declaration." (*Annals*, I, p. 477) Another supporter of this provision, Laurance, spoke in a similar vein:

> I take it ... that it is proper for the Legislature to speak their sense *upon those points on which the Constitution is silent*. I believe the judges will never decide that we are guilty of a breach of the Constitution, by declaring a Legislative opinion *in cases where the Constitution is silent*. If the laws shall be in violation of any part of the Constitution, the judges will not hesitate to decide against them.... [*Annals*, I, p. 486; italics added]

Opponents of this provision made even more of the distinctive power and role of the judiciary. Smith presented an argument based on the separation of powers:

Gentlemen have said that it is proper to give a legislative construction of the Constitution. I differ with them on this point. I think it an infringement of the powers of the judiciary. It is said, we ought not to blend the legislative, executive, or judiciary powers, further than is done by the Constitution; and yet the advocates for preserving each department pure and untouched by the others, call upon this House to exercise the powers of the judges in expounding the Constitution. . . . Sir, it is the duty of the Legislature to make laws; your judges are to expound them. [*Annals, I,* p. 470]

Gerry thereafter argued,

If the fact is, as we seem to suspect [by proposing a removal-power provision], that [the President and Senate] do not understand the Constitution, let it go before the proper tribunal; the judges are the Constitutional umpires on such questions. Why, let me ask gentlemen, shall we commit an infraction of the Constitution for fear the Senate or President should not comply with its directions? [*Annals, I,* p. 473]

But it is also on the basis of separation-of-powers considerations that the inclusion of a removal provision was supported. Thus, Baldwin regarded certain issues as inappropriate for disposition in judicial proceedings:

Gentlemen say it properly belongs to the Judiciary to decide this [removal-power] question. Be it so. It is their province to decide upon our laws; and if they find them to be unconstitutional, they will not hesitate to declare it so; and it seems to be a very difficult point to bring before them in any other way. Let gentlemen consider themselves in the tribunal of justice, called upon to decide this question on a mandamus. What a situation! almost too great for human nature to bear, they would feel great relief in having had the question decided by the representatives of the people. [*Annals, I,* p. 560]

Perhaps these issues should be viewed differently when the question is not so much either that of allocations of power among the branches of government or that of great issues which are essentially "political" (to employ the Supreme Court's term for the kind of problem that Baldwin referred to), but rather that of whether certain power *does* belong to the general government, especially when the rights of a citizen are urged against the legitimacy of such power. What can be said of judicial review in such circumstances, the circumstances most relevant in the context of a discussion of the applicability of the First Amendment? Consider this passage from Madison, in support of judicial review, as he attempted to meet the argument that bills of rights had not been found effectual in some states:

> It is true, there are a few particular States in which some of the most valuable articles have not, at one time or other, been violated; but it does not follow but they may have, to a certain degree, a salutary effect against the abuse of power. If they are incorporated into the Constitution, independent tribunals of justice will consider themselves in a peculiar manner the guardian of those rights; they will be an impenetrable bulwark against every assumption of power in the Legislative or the Executive; they will be naturally led to resist every encroachment upon rights expressly stipulated for in the Constitution by the declaration of rights. . . . [*Annals*, I, p. 439]

Benson indicated how the judiciary would conduct itself with respect to a particular proposed provision in the Bill of Rights: "If this [religious exemption for the militia] stands part of the Constitution, it will be a question before the Judiciary on every regulation you make with respect to the organization of the militia, whether it comports with this declaration or not." (*Annals*, I, p. 751) (A similar caution is implied in Stone's comment, quoted in section 7 of this chapter, in the course of the discussion in Congress of a proposed "instruction" amendment to the Constitution.)[88]

The case for and against judicial review must be left much as we found it. In support of it—or, rather, in support of the effort to make a case for it—is what Smith called "a just and venerable law maxim": "Wherever a man has a right, he has a remedy; if he suffers a wrong, he can have a redress. . . ." (*Annals*, I, p. 510)[89] The case against judicial review, on the other hand, is implied in a comment by Jackson in opposition to a bill of rights. He asked, with respect to New York, New Jersey, Virginia, South Carolina, and Georgia, "Those States have no bills of rights [in their constitutions], and is the liberty of the citizens less safe in those States, than in the other of the United States?" (*Annals*, I, p. 442) The character and vigilance of the people, he seems to have thought, rather than provisions of constitutions and courts, determine the nature of the regime.

But in any event, judicial review is with us. How it came to be as important as it now is suggests certain speculations. There seem to have been two principal "guardians of the people's liberty" under the original Constitution, the states and the House of Representatives. These collaborated in the effort which produced the Bill of Rights. President Washington, in his first address to the Congress (sitting in joint session), suggested that Congress take up consideration of amendments to the Constitution that would reflect "a reverence for the characteristic rights of freemen." (*Annals*, I, p. 29) The two houses responded separately to Washington's message: the House of Representatives acknowledged his suggestion about the protection of the rights of the people;[90] the Senate, in its reply to the message, ignored this suggestion altogether. It was in the House, as we have seen, that amendments were initiated; the Senate added nothing to the list received from the House: it contented itself with making changes, some of them critical for American federalism.

This sequence reflects an important aspect, to which I have referred, of the original constitutional design. The House of Representatives was to be the principal guardian, among the branches of the general government, of the rights of the people. The representatives are elected directly and frequently from the people; they presumably have the interests of the people most immediately in their view. The Senate, on the other hand, should be more concerned with the rights of the state govenments—the rights of the states as "sovereign" bodies. The amendment that provides for popular election of senators is a distortion of the design, increasing the direct power of the people. Thus, the states as states no longer have their interests so clearly provided for. Nor, as it has worked out, are the rights of the citizen now protected by the popularly elected Congress: to be more precise, the rights of the people have come to be seen primarily as the enforcement of the popular will rather than as the prerogatives and privileges of a citizen that should be maintained even in the face of majority demands.[91]

Thus, it has been the fate of one of the "guardians of the people's liberty" to have been transformed into the agent of the people's will. Madison had said of the other guardian, the state legislatures, that they would "jealously and closely watch every assumption of power" by the general government. (*Annals*, I, p. 439) To the extent that the states simply insist upon their power, to that extent they continue to serve this function.[92] But as the power of the general government has grown, it has become easier to implement the popular will throughout the nation and to disregard the rights of anyone who stands in the way of efficient implementation.

And yet, do we not find here the substitution that we have detected elsewhere? Another institution emerges, a new formula is devised, to right the balance that seems to be demanded by the American constitutional system and by the American character and tradition. The House of Representatives and the state legislatures withdraw as primary guardians of the people's liberty; the Supreme Court of the United States moves in, or is moved in, to assume this role:[93] judicial review grows into the role deserted by (or taken from) the states and the House of Representatives. Such review seems particularly appropriate for the protection of the rights to freedom of speech and of the press, rights which, to be meaningful in popular regimes, must promote intelligent opposition to majority opinion and actions. That the Supreme Court is strong enough and independent enough to maintain itself without informed support from us is doubtful—for it has never had the means of self-defense provided both the states (which can amend the Constitution and could at one time elect a chamber of the Congress) and the House of Representatives (which has effective control over the purse as well as an indispensable share in all other legislative powers). Especially is this doubtful if the Court should have to maintain itself for a long period against the popular will as expressed by Congress and the President. No doubt its vulnerability is reflected in the adjustments it does make to public opinion. As the bar's quality deteriorates even more than it has already, one can expect that the Supreme Court, which is drawn from and served by that bar, will reflect that deterioration and will exhibit less and less the dignity, the intelligence, and the character which win respect even from the ignorant.[94]

The Court, for all its limitations, may well have a braking effect on public opinion, giving the "better angels" of the American people an opportunity to assert themselves against the demands of momentary passions.[95] The vulnerability of the Court, as well as the abdication by the American bar of its duties, was hinted at in the tribute it was left to an English aristocrat to make before the American Bar Association at a time when that professional body had joined ignorant laymen in attacks upon the Court. Winston Churchill obliged the American bar to acknowledge its finer side with a toast at its A.B.A. London dinner in the summer of 1957: "The Supreme Court of the United States has often been the guardian and upholder of American liberty. Long may it continue to thrive!"[96]

XI

As a people, Americans exercise what Parliament and, under the Constitution, Congress are guaranteed for legislative purposes, the right to discuss the public business freely and without outside interference.[97] "Freedom of speech," as a right to be invoked outside the legislative body, seems to be a distinctively American development.[98] (When the issue of freedom of expression is raised in the English authorities, such as Blackstone, it is [as we have seen] primarily in terms of "liberty of the press."[99]) Thus, the American people are in effect brought into the legislative life of the community.[100]

"Liberty of the press" would to some extent also have this effect. But presses do cost money; they require special training on the part of both publishers and readers; and their use is less spontaneous than that of speech. The ascendancy of American republicanism seems to be reflected in the first place that is now given to freedom of speech.[101] The emergence of freedom of speech has helped obscure the significance of the no-previous-restraint rule that had been feasible and of importance only with respect to the press. It has also served to blur distinctions that might have been maintained between speaking and writing, since we are inclined to extend to freedom of the press the standards and rules that apply to freedom of speech.[102]

Indeed, partly because of the origins of "freedom of speech" in absolute guarantees to legislators and partly because of the role assumed by Americans as participants in self-government, our tendency seems to have been to permit citizens that unlimited freedom of expression found on the floor of Congress.[103] It should be remembered, however, that an effective exercise of such freedom in a legislative body depends, in part, upon the fact that that body can and does restrain itself. It can discipline, silence, and even expel members who abuse the privileges of the legislator.[104] Rules are devised which are designed to insure regular proceedings, thereby reducing the effects of surprises and momentary advantages. This design is reflected in Madison's response to a proposed reconsideration of a bill which he had unsuccessfully *supported* the day before:

> ... he was apprehensive that the proposed motion of reconsidering the bill, if successful, would be attended with dangerous consequences. He supposed the vote of yesterday amounted to a direct negative on the bill: of course it was lost, and could not be revived. He supposed that certain forms were necessary, in the passage of a bill, in order to prevent surprise, and he thought that this conduct would amount to a very summary proceeding. A full House might one day reject a bill, which a thin House might pass the subsequent morning. Considering all these circumstances, he was inclined to think the motion was out of order. [*Annals, I*, pp. 890-91]

Thus, members of Congress have been provided unlimited control of their own proceedings as well as the guarantee (in Article I, section 6 of the Constitution) that "for any Speech or Debate in either House [of Congress], they shall not be questioned *in any other place*." (Italics added) Is there anything comparable to this control in the American constitutional arrangement which serves as a salutary check upon the freedom that citizens have to discuss political affairs?

I have argued that Congress cannot discipline or silence citizens who abuse the freedom of political discussion. To some extent, on the other hand, the people can and do discipline one another, with social and other unofficial sanctions. The citizen realizes that there are things he should not say at certain times or in certain places—and that his neighbors will treat him better or worse accordingly. The politician, in particular, recognizes that his credit with the electorate usually depends on the care with which he seems to exercise his freedom to speak, not only abroad in the land but even on the floor of Congress.[105]

Furthermore, the people as states can restrain themselves in what they do in that national "parliament" (which public discussion and participation in self-government can be taken to be). Such restraint is permitted by the First Amendment: that is, the people, through the states, may (subject to supervision by the general government) restrain somewhat the speech used in the states, which means, in effect, the speech brought to bear on national issues and affairs. Our "freedom of debate," then, is not altogether unchecked, even though no "outside" interference (that is, by Congress) is permitted. But it may be that our problem from time to time is not that of too few but rather that of too many unofficial restraints upon respectable citizens, a situation that makes it difficult to have that "mature deliberation, ample discussion, and full information" needed to frame public measures properly. (*Annals*, I, p. 107) Thus, a people too apt to suppress dissent on serious issues should be reminded of the proposition stated by Tucker:

In order to preserve the peace and tranquility of the Union, it will become necessary that mutual deference and accommodation should take place [on important subjects]. And, in order that this may take place, it is proper that gentlemen deliver their sentiments with freedom and candor. [*Annals*, I, pp. 108-9]

No doubt, abuses by free-speaking citizens will have to be put up with.

XII

The abuses most likely to be seen are in the exercise of rights that are clearly recognized as protected. This emphasizes the duty of respectable citizens to choose with care the occasions when acknowledged rights are to be exercised.

An appropriate caution is reflected in a comment by Madison in the First Congress. It had been suggested by a member that the Rhode Island legislature be requested to call a state convention to consider ratifying the Constitution. The member asked that the House resolve itself into a committee of the whole to discuss this, a request that aroused the opposition of members who preferred not to intrude themselves into this delicate matter even to that extent but preferred rather to leave Rhode Island completely alone. Thus, Madison was obliged to say,

I believe, Mr. Speaker, there are cases in which it is prudent to avoid coming to a decision at all, and cases where it is desirable to evade debate; if there were not cases of this kind, it would be unnecessary to guard our discussions with the previous question. My idea on the subject now before the House is, that it would be improper in this body to expose themselves to have such a proposition rejected by the Legislature of the State of Rhode Island. It would likewise be improper to express a desire on an occasion where a free agency ought to be employed, which would carry with it all the force of a command. How far this is contemplated on the present occasion, I cannot tell; but I heartily wish that as little may be said about it as possible. I conceive this to be one of the cases to which the previous question is applicable; and, if the gentleman means to call the House to a direct decision on this motion, I shall step between, and interpose the previous question. [*Annals, I,* p. 423][106]

White, expressing a different attitude about such matters, replied (on another occasion) to an objection that a proposed discussion was on "a subject of considerable delicacy" with the declaration, "As to delicacy, I know of none, sir, that ought to be used while we are in pursuit of the public good. I speak, therefore, with candor what are my sentiments on this subject." (*Annals, I,* p. 633) (The subject on this later occasion related to the salaries appropriate for the President and the vice-president of the United States.)

Madison's position was stated, in a much more serious context, in the words of President Lincoln in 1862, "If there ever could be a proper time for mere catch arguments, that time surely is not now. In times like the present, men should utter nothing for which they would not willingly be responsible through time and in eternity."[107] These are not judgments that can be determined by rules of law. Rather, the traditions and good sense of a people and of their leaders must be relied upon. Critical to such good sense is the ability to recognize when one's rights should be foregone for the sake of a greater good than that which is implied in the immediate preservation or exercise of particular constitutional rights. That is, one is driven to consider and to respect the ends or purposes of freedom.

Perhaps the most important occasion on which this problem has been raised for Americans was that of the abolitionist agitation in the second quarter of the nineteenth century. An example in this connection is the behavior in the House of Representatives of the elderly John Quincy Adams (then a former President of the United States), when he (as a member of the House from Massachusetts) attempted to lay before that body the antislavery petitions supplied him for that purpose. It has been observed that Adams said more on freedom of speech in the course of this struggle than all the Supreme Court cases for the first one hundred years of this Republic.[108]

It has also been observed that Adams had "the instinct for the jugular."[109] That is, he had the capacity to discern and the will to attack the most vulnerable spot in the constitution of his opponents. The vulnerability of the South with respect to the institution of slavery was exposed in 1835 by Tocqueville:

I am obliged to confess that I do not regard the abolition of slavery as a means of warding off the struggle of the two races in the Southern states. The Negroes may long remain slaves without complaining; but if they are once raised to the level of freemen, they will soon revolt at being deprived of almost all their civil rights; and as they cannot become the equals of the whites, they will speedily show themselves as enemies. In the North everything facilitated the emancipation of the slaves, and slavery was abolished without rendering the free Negroes formidable, since their number was too small for them ever to claim their rights. But such is not the case in the South. The question of slavery was a commercial and manufacturing question for the slave-owners in the North; for those of the South it is a question of life and death. God forbid that I should seek to justify the principle of Negro slavery, as has been done by some American writers! I say only that all the countries which formerly adopted that execrable principle are not equally able to abandon it at the present time.

When I contemplate the condition of the South, I can discover only two modes of action for the white inhabitants of those States: namely, either to emancipate the Negroes and to intermingle with them, or, remaining isolated from them, to keep them in slavery as long as possible. All intermediate measures seem to me likely to terminate, and that shortly, in the most horrible of civil wars and perhaps in the extirpation of one or the other of the two races. Such is the view that the Americans of the South take of the question, and they act consistently with it. As they are determined not to mingle with the Negroes, they refuse to emancipate them.

Not that the inhabitants of the South regard slavery as necessary to the wealth of the planter; on this point many of them agree with their Northern countrymen, in freely admitting that slavery is prejudicial to their interests; but they are convinced that the removal of this evil would imperil their own existence.[110]

Such were the considerations that moved Lincoln to a charitable view of where responsibility lay for the curse of slavery. Adams, on the other hand—insofar as there is any indication in the *Diary* from which we can reconstruct his approach to such problems—was armed with a terrible righteousness.

The first *Diary* reference to petitions goes back to 1805, before Adams became President, while he was in the Senate:

Jan. 21—In Senate Dr. Logan presented the petition of certain Quakers, requesting the interference of Congress as far as they have power to check the slave trade. A question was made, whether the petition should be received, and very warmly debated for about three hours; when it was taken by yeas and nays—yeas nineteen, nays nine. [*Diary*, pp. 29-30][111]

His entries during that year included a comment upon the House of Representatives that came to be significant in the light of his own experience in the House thirty years later:

March 3 . . . Thus has terminated the second session of the Eighth Congress; the most remarkable transaction of which has been the trial of the impeachment against Samuel Chase [a justice of the Supreme Court of the United States]. This is a subject fruitful of reflections, but their place is not here. I shall only remark that this was a party prosecution, and has issued in the unexpected and total disappointment of those by whom it was brought forward. It has exhibited the Senate of the United States fulfilling the most important purpose of its institution, by putting a check upon the impetuous violence of the House of Representatives. It has proved that a sense of justice is yet strong enough to overpower the furies of faction; but it has, at the same time, shown the wisdom and necessity of that provision in the Constitution which requires the concurrence of two-thirds for conviction upon impeachment. [*Diary*, p. 35][112]

He added that "the essential characters which *ought* to belong to the Senate are *coolness* and *firmness*."

Fifteen years later (1820) Adams was to record as his "own deliberate opinion, that the more of pure moral principle is carried into the policy and conduct of a Government the wiser and more profound will that policy be." (*Diary*, p. 237) What "pure moral principle" consisted of will be seen in the controversy about the abolitionist petitions. His uncompromising attitude during that controversy is anticipated in his comments in an 1831 entry about Jefferson:

In the evening I read a few pages of Jefferson's correspondence. . . . Mr. Jefferson's love of liberty was sincere and ardent—not confined to himself, like that of most of his fellow slave-holders. He was above that execrable sophistry of the South Carolinian nullifiers, which would make of slavery the corner-stone to the temple of liberty. He saw the gross inconsistency between the principles of the Declaration of Independence and the fact of negro slavery, and he could not, or would not, prostitute the faculties of his mind to the vindication of that slavery which from his soul he abhorred. Mr. Jefferson had not the spirit of martyrdom. He would have introduced a flaming denunciation of slavery into the Declaration of Independence, but the discretion of his colleagues struck it out. He did insert a most eloquent and impassioned argument against it in his Notes upon Virginia; but on that very account the book was published almost against his will. [*Diary*, p. 412][113]

Unlike Jefferson, Adams did have "the spirit of martyrdom"— and this suggests both the attractiveness of the Massachusetts-man and the limitations of his political thought.

Adams, in his first term in the House of Representatives (he was, then, in 1832, sixty-four years old), recorded the procedure for handling petitions:

> Being Monday, the States were successively called for presentation of petitions; a most tedious operation in the practice, though to a reflecting mind a very striking exemplification of the magnificent grandeur of this nation and of the sublime principles upon which our Government is founded. The forms and proceedings of the House, this calling over of States for petitions, the colossal emblem of the union over the Speaker's chair, the historic Muse at the clock, the echoing pillars of the hall, the tripping Mercuries who bear the resolutions and amendments between the members and the chair, the calls of ayes and noes, with the different intonations of the answers from the different voices, the gobbling manner of the clerk in reading over the names, the tone of the Speaker in announcing the vote, and the varied shades of pleasure and pain in the countenances of the members on hearing it, would form a fine subject for a descriptive poem. [*Diary*, p. 430]

He recorded as well his first presentation of abolitionist petitions:

> Dec. 12 [1831] Attended the House of Representatives. . . . The petitions were called for by States, commencing with Maine and proceeding southward.[114] I presented fifteen petitions, signed numerously by citizens of Pennsylvania, praying for the abolition of slavery and the slave-trade in the District of Columbia. I moved that they should be referred to the Committee on the District of Columbia.
>
> The practice is for the member presenting the petition to move that the reading of it be dispensed with, and that it be referred to the appropriate, or to a select, committee; but I moved that one of the petitions presented by me should be read, they being all of the same tenor and very short. It was accordingly read. I made a very few remarks, chiefly to declare that I should not support that part of the petition which prayed for the abolition of slavery in the District of Columbia. . . . I was not more than five minutes upon my feet; but I was listened to with great attention. . . . [*Diary*, pp. 426-27]

His self-restraint at this stage is reflected in an entry of the month following:

Mr. Lewis is a member of the Society of Friends, and has taken much part for the last twenty years in the measures leading to the abolition of slavery. He came to have some conversation with me upon the subject of slavery in the District of Columbia. I asked him if he had seen the remarks that I made on presenting the petitions from Pennsylvania. He said he had—but wished to know my sentiments upon slavery. I told him I thought they did not materially differ from his own; I abhorred slavery, did not suffer it in my family, and felt proud of belonging to the only State in the Union which at the very first census of population in 1790 had returned in the column of slaves—none;[115] that in presenting the petition I had expressed the wish that the subject might not be discussed in the House, because I believed discussion would lead to ill will, to heart-burnings, to mutual hatred, where the first of wants was harmony; and without accomplishing anything else. [*Diary*, pp. 429-30]

This was in 1832.

Disharmony did develop in the years that followed, however. Adams wrote in 1835,

Aug. 11. There is a great fermentation upon this subject of slavery at this time in all parts of the Union. The emancipation of the slaves in the British West India Colonies; the Colonization Society here; the current of public opinion running everywhere stronger and stronger into democracy and popular supremacy contribute all to shake the fetters of servitude. The theory of the rights of man has taken deep root in the soil of civil society. It has allied itself with the feelings of humanity and the precepts of Christian benevolence. It has armed itself with the strength of organized associations. It has linked itself with religious doctrines and religious fervor. Antislavery associations are formed in this country and in England, and they are already cooperating in concerted agency together. They have raised funds to support and circulate inflammatory newspapers and pamphlets gratuitously, and they send multitudes of them into the Southern country, into the midst of the swarms of slaves. There is an Englishman by the name of Thompson, lately come over from England, who is travelling about the country, holding meetings and making eloquent inflammatory harangues, preaching the immediate abolition of slavery. The general disposition of the people here is averse to these movements, and Thompson has several times been routed by popular tumults. But in some place he meets favorable reception and makes converts. There has been recently an alarm of slave insurrection in the State of Mississippi, and several white persons have been hung by a summary process of what they call Lynch's law; that is, mob-law. . . . There are now calls [in the newspapers] at Boston for a town-meeting to put down the abolitionists; but the disease is deeper than can be healed by town-meeting resolutions.

Aug. 14. The accounts of the riots in Baltimore continue. In the State of Mississippi mobs are hanging up blacks suspected of insurgency, and whites suspected of abetting them. At Charleston, South Carolina, mobs of slaveholding gentlemen intercept the mails and take out from them all the inflammatory pamphlets circulated by the abolitionists, who, in their turn, are making every possible exertion to kindle the flame of insurrection among the slaves. We are in a state of profound peace and over-pampered with prosperity; yet the elements of exterminating war seem to be in vehement fermentation, and one can scarcely foresee to what it will lead. [*Diary*, pp. 462-63]

This account, from a friend of freedom and a vigorous opponent of slavery, suggests to me the conclusion that something ought to have been done to suppress the agitation and calm the people, North and South. It seems to have been assumed that the duty for moderating the conflict lay with state governments and with private citizens; Congress had no power with respect to such matters, at least short of the obligation to put down insurrections and preserve republican government in the states.

The most that the House of Representatives could do, it tried to do, by tabling the abolitionist petitions which it received. Such control Adams interpreted as an abridgment of his and his constituents' constitutional rights: when confronted by such a restraint, the high-spirited citizen is tempted to press for his rights at all costs. Thus began for Adams a struggle that was to last almost a decade, during which he was to record no more sentiments suggesting the need for moderating "the elements of exterminating war [which seem] to be in vehement fermentation." (Perhaps no solution short of the abolition of slavery could have permanently eliminated the conflict; but the foregoing of some rights by northerners and, one suspects, more respect by southerners for the rights as well as the sensibilities of others might well have kept men's minds clear.)

This struggle began with the new year (1836) upon Adams's presentation of a petition by 154 Massachusetts inhabitants "praying for the abolition of slavery and the slave-trade in the District of Columbia." (*Diary*, p. 464) Two weeks later, additional abolitionist petitions were presented by him. (*Diary*, p. 465) All such petitions were referred to a select committee of the House, which submitted its report to the House on May 18, 1836. This report declared, first, that Congress had no power to interfere with slavery in any state; second, that Congress ought not to interfere with slavery in the District of Columbia; and third, that since the agitation of the topic was disquieting, all petitions or papers relating to slavery "shall, without being either printed or referred, be laid upon the table, and that no further action whatever shall be had thereon." All three resolutions were passed over Adams's protest, the third by a vote of 117 to 68. And, the editor of the diary adds, "Such was the origin of the famous gag-rule." (*Diary*, pp. 465-66)[116]

Adams records that this committee report was immediately attacked in the House "with extreme violence, and a fiery debate arose, which continued until one o'clock, and then, by a suspension of the rules, for another half-hour." (*Diary*, p. 465) In the year that followed, Adams attempted to present other abolitionist petitions, including some purporting to come from slaves. This in turn led to an attempt on January 23, 1837, to censure him in the House of Representatives. (*Diary*, p. 476) He had occasion thereafter to record,

> April 19. . . . Upon this subject of anti-slavery my principles and my position make it necessary for me to be more circumspect in my conduct than belongs to my nature. I have, therefore, already committed indiscretions, of which all the political parties avail themselves to proscribe me in the public opinion. The most insignificant error of conduct in me at this time would be my irredeemable ruin in this world, and both the ruling political parties are watching with intense anxiety for some overt act by me to set the whole pack of their hireling presses upon me.
>
> It is also to be considered that at this time the most dangerous of all the subjects for public contention is the slavery question. . . . The exposure through which I passed at the late session of Congress was greater than I could have imagined possible; and, having escaped from that fiery furnace, it behooves me well to consider my ways before I put myself in the way of being cast into it again. [*Diary*, p. 479]

Nothing was said by Adams on this occasion about the desirability (acknowledged thirty years earlier) of "putting a check upon the impetuous violence of the House of Representatives." (*Diary*, p. 35) Rather, at the next session, he returned to the battle. Ordinary petitions were received by the House, but not those calling "for the abolition of slavery in the Territories; for refusing the admission of any new slave-holding State into the Union; and for the prohibition of the inter-State slave-trade." (*Diary*, p. 484) During September, 1837, Adams presented several dozen more such petitions, "reserv[ing] a considerable number for the winter session." (*Diary*, p. 484) He presented even more slavery petitions in December, all of which were tabled. One entry reflects the feeling of the time:

Dec. 20. Slade's motion of Monday, to refer a petition for the abolition of slavery and the slave-trade in the District of Columbia to a select committee, came up.

Polk, the Speaker, by some blunder had allowed Slade's motion for leave to address the House in support of the petition without putting the question of laying on the table. So Slade today got the floor, and in a speech of two hours on slavery, shook the very hall into convulsions. Wise, Legaré, Rhett, Dawson, Robertson, and the whole herd were in combustion. Polk stopped him half a dozen times, and was forced to let him go on. The slavers were at their wits' ends. At last one of them *objected* to his proceeding, on the pretence that he was discussing slavery in Virginia, and on this pretence, which was not true, Polk ordered him to take his seat. [*Diary*, pp. 490-91]

The following day a resolution was moved (and carried, 136 to 65), like that of an earlier session, "that no petitions relating to slavery or the trade in slaves in any State, district, or Territory of the United States shall be read, printed, committed, or in any manner acted upon by the House." (*Diary*, p. 491) Adams, when his name was called, responded, "I hold the resolution to be a violation of the Constitution, of the right of petition of my constituents, and of the people of the United States, and of my right to freedom of speech as a member of this House." (*Diary*, p. 491) He also recorded his exchange with a southerner on the floor of the House the following day:

... I bantered him upon his resolution, till he said that if the question ever came to the issue of war, the Southern people would march into New England and conquer it. I said I had no doubt they would if they could, and that it was what they were now struggling for with all their might. [*Diary*, p. 492]

Adams's entries continued to record the conflict: "Jan. 15 [1838].... There were a great multitude of abolition and anti-Texas petitions from all the free States; all laid on the table. I presented nearly fifty myself." (*Diary*, p. 493) The gag rule provoked further petitions, which poured in on Adams and his supporters:

Jan. 28. I received this day thirty-one petitions, and consumed the whole evening in assorting, filing, endorsing, and entering them on my list, without completing the work. With these petitions I receive many letters, which I have not time to answer. Most of them are so flattering, and expressed in terms of such deep sensibility, that I am in imminent danger of being led by them into presumption and puffed up with vanity. The abolition newspapers . . . contribute to generate and nourish this delusion, which the treacherous, furious, filthy, and threatening letters from the South on the same subject cannot sufficiently counteract. My duty to defend the free principles and institutions is clear; but the measures by which they are to be defended are involved in thick darkness. The path of right is narrow, and I have need of a perpetual control over passion. [*Diary*, p. 493]

The "control over passion" evidently did not require, in his view, that he not arouse the passion of others:

Feb. 14. . . . The call commenced with me, and I presented three hundred and fifty petitions. . . . There was one, praying that Congress would take measures to protect citizens of the North going to the South from danger to their lives. When the motion to lay that on the table was made, I said that "in another part of the Capitol it had been threatened that if a Northern abolitionist should go to North Carolina and utter a principle of the Declaration of Independence—" Here a loud cry of "Order! Order!" burst forth, in which the Speaker yelled among the loudest. I waited till it subsided, and then resumed, "that if they could catch him they would hang him." I said this so as to be distinctly heard throughout the hall; the renewed deafening shout of "Order! Order!" notwithstanding. The Speaker then said, "The gentleman from Massachusetts will take his seat"; which I did, and immediately rose again, and presented another petition. He did not dare to tell me that I could not proceed without permission of the House; and I proceeded. The threat to hang Northern abolitionists was uttered by Preston, of the Senate, within the last fortnight. [*Diary*, pp. 493-94]

The controversy raged through the year. On June 23, 1838, Adams was "peremptorily stopped by the Speaker" for his "disorderly words" on petitions. (*Diary*, p. 495) On December 14, he recorded his attempt to protest the treatment of additional petitions:

... When my name was called by the clerk, I rose and said, "Mr. Speaker, considering all the resolutions introduced by the gentleman from New Hampshire as—" The Speaker roared out, "The gentleman from Massachusetts must answer aye or no, and nothing else. Order!"

With a reinforced voice—"I refuse to answer because I consider all the proceedings of the House as unconstitutional." While in a firm and swelling voice I pronounced distinctly these words, the Speaker and about two-thirds of the House cried, "Order! Order!" till it became a perfect yell. I paused for a moment for it to cease, and then said, "A direct violation of the Constitution of the United States." While speaking these words with loud, distinct, and slow articulation, the bawl of "Order! Order!" resounded again from two-thirds of the House. The Speaker, with agonizing lungs, screamed, "I call upon the House to support me in the execution of my duty!" I then coolly resumed my seat. [*Diary*, p. 496]

Three years later—the tabling of abolitionist petitions had continued—Adams described himself in this manner:

March 29 [1841]. . . . The world, the flesh, and all the devils in hell are arrayed against any man who now in this North American Union shall dare to join the standard of Almighty God to put down the African slave-trade; and what can I, upon the verge of my seventy-fourth birthday, with a shaking hand, a darkening eye, a drowsy brain, and with all my faculties dropping from me one by one, as the teeth are dropping from my head—what can I do for the cause of God and man, for the program of human emancipation, for the suppression of the African slave-trade? Yet my conscience presses me on; let me but die upon the breach. [*Diary*, p. 519]

Adams's censure by the House was attempted again in early 1842 upon his presenting "a petition praying for the dissolution of the Union," a petition which he himself did not endorse. (*Diary*, p. 533) A bitter struggle followed, which Adams recorded thus:

Jan. 31. My occupations during the month have been confined entirely to the business of the House, and for the last ten days to the defence of myself against an extensive combination and conspiracy, in and out of Congress, to crush the liberties of the free people of this Union by disgracing me with a brand of censure and displacing me from the chair of the Committee on Foreign Affairs for my perseverance in presenting abolition petitions. I am in the midst of that fiery ordeal, and day and night are absorbed in the struggle to avert my ruin. God send me a good deliverance! [*Diary*, pp. 535-36]

Deliverance came on February 7, on a vote of 106 to 93 to table the censure motion. The end of the following year, however, found Adams in even greater agony:

Dec. 21 [1843]. In the House, the life-and-death struggle for the right of petition was resumed. The question of reception of the petition from Illinois was laid on the table—98 to 80—after a long and memorable debate. I then presented the resolves of the Massachusetts Legislature of the 23rd of March, 1843, proposing an amendment to the Constitution of the United States, making the representation of the people in the House proportioned to the numbers of free persons, and moved it should be read, printed, and referred to a select committee of nine. And now sprung up the most memorable debate ever entertained in the House. . . . [*Diary*, p. 561]

A northern legislature was challenging, in the resolves presented by Adams, the constitutional arrangement which permitted the southern states to count, for purposes of representation, three-fifths of their slaves. One can imagine the agitation of the southern members by observing Adams's: "The crisis now requires of me coolness, firmness, prudence, moderation, and fortitude beyond all former example. I came home in such a state of agitation that I could do nothing but pace my chamber." (*Diary*, p. 562) This petition was presented to a select committee, rather than tabled, but not before one of the southerners

called upon the reporters to take note of what he was about to say, asked the particular attention of the House, and declared once for all, and forever, that he renounced this WAR against Southern rights which had been for several years waged in the hall. He would vote for my motion to refer these resolves to a select committee, and hoped I should be chairman of it, that the whole committee should be of the same complexion, and that the whole mass of abolition petitions should be referred to the same committee, that we might make a report in our own way, and the House and the country might see what we were after. . . . [*Diary*, pp. 562-63]

The struggle continued, but with the majorities upholding the gag rule steadily declining. In 1842 the supporters of the rule had a margin of only four votes; in 1843, the margin was down to three. (*Diary*, p. 573) But then occurred what Adams considered a disaster:

"THE BLESSINGS OF LIBERTY"   251

Quincy, Nov. 8 [1844]. . . . James K. Polk of Tennessee is to be President of the United States for four years from the 4th of March, 1845. What the further events of this issue may be is not clear, but it will be the signal for my retirement from public life. It is the victory of the slavery element in the constitution of the United States. Providence, I trust, intends it for wise purposes and will direct it to good ends. [*Diary*, p. 572]

Within a month Adams was back in Washington in the House of Representatives, where the "good ends" he had prayed for were realized, apparently because "the slavery element" could (upon having elected a president) relax its vigilance:

Dec. 3 [1844]. . . . In pursuance of the notice I had given yesterday, I moved the following resolution: "Resolved, that the twenty-fifth standing rule for conducting business in this House, in the following words, 'No petition, memorial, resolution, or other paper praying the abolition of slavery in the District of Columbia or any State or Territory, or the slave trade between the States or Territories in which it now exists, shall be received by this House, or entertained in any way whatever,' be, and the same is, hereby rescinded." I called for the yeas and nays. Jacob Thompson of Mississippi, moved to lay the resolution on the table. I called for the yeas and nays on that motion. . . . The clerk called the roll, and the motion to lay on the table was rejected—81 to 104. The question was then put on the resolution; and it was carried—108 to 80. Blessed, forever blessed, be the name of God! [*Diary*, p. 573]

Adams's last significant diary entry related to the celebration of this victory:

March 13 [1845]. At the Patent Office, I applied to the Commissioner . . . for the ivory cane made from a single tooth, presented to me by Julius Pratt & Co. of Meriden, Conn., and which on the 23rd of April last I deposited in the Patent Office. There is in the top of the cane a golden eagle inlaid, bearing a scroll with the motto "Right of Petition Triumphant" engraved upon it. The donors requested of me that when the gag-rule should be rescinded I would cause the date to be added to this motto; which I promised to do, if the event should happen in my lifetime. . . . There is a gold ring immediately below the pommel of the cane, thus engraved:

TO JOHN QUINCY ADAMS
JUSTUM ET TENACEM PROPOSITI VIRUM

I crave pardon for the vanity of this memorial. [*Diary*, pp. 574-75][117]

One must wonder, however, whether the true memorial, not only to Adams but to all who contended with him (supporters and opponents alike) on constitutional principles regardless of costs, was not the Civil War of the next generation.[118] The reader sensitive to moral and political realities is prompted to wonder thus when he reflects on the problems that are ignored in Allan Nevins's editorial eulogy of this immoderately gallant former President of the United States:

> ... the most dramatic record of all is that of how, as an old man, he met the forces of slavery in the gate, fought the Southern advocates of the gag-rule from session to session, and, often beaten but never despairing, after a decade of unremitting conflict won an ever-memorable victory for the great Anglo-Saxon rights of free petition and of free speech.
> It was the happiest feature of Adams's public life that he lived to taste the full sweets of this victory over those whom in his acrid way he calls the slave-mongers, and to hear abolition petitions again referred to committees in the House. It was a happy fact also that he lived to make a tour of the West, in which he was able to see how warm a place his brave fight for freedom had won him in the hearts of the people of New York and Ohio.[119]

Many more such victories, the prudent man may observe, and constitutional government is undone.

This story suggests to me that the most serious abuses of freedom of speech and of the press among us are likely to occur in circumstances where there is no safeguard but the good sense and self-restraint of the best citizens, of men who know when and how to use delicacy while "in pursuit of the public good."[120] It is not enough to be right, in the strict constitutional sense. Rather, the good man should be concerned lest he deserve the rebuke that Cicero leveled against Cato—the rebuke with which Francis Bacon concluded his interpretation of the story of Cassandra:

> They say that Cassandra was beloved by Apollo; that she contrived by various artifices to elude his desires, and yet to keep his hopes alive until she had drawn from him the gift of divination; that she had no sooner obtained this, which had all along been her object, than she openly rejected his suit; whereupon he, not being permitted to recal the boon once rashly promised, yet burning with revenge, and not choosing to be the scorn of an artful woman, annexed to it this penalty,—that though she should always foretell true, yet nobody should believe her. Her prophecies therefore

had truth, but not credit: and so she found it ever after, even in regard to the destruction of her country; of which she had given many warnings, but could get nobody to listen to her or believe her.

This fable seems to have been devised in reproof of unreasonable and unprofitable liberty in giving advice and admonition. For they that are of a froward and rough disposition, and will not submit to learn of Apollo, the god of harmony, how to observe time and measure in affairs, flats and sharps (so to speak) in discourse, the differences between the learned and the vulgar ear, and the times when to speak and when to be silent; such persons, though they be wise and free, and their counsels sound and wholesome, yet with all their efforts to persuade they scarcely can do any good; on the contrary, they rather hasten the destruction of those upon whom they press their advice; and it is not till the evils they predicted have come to pass that they are celebrated as prophets and men of a far foresight. Of this we have an eminent example in Marcus Cato of Utica, by whom the ruin of his country and the usurpation that followed, by means first of the conjunction and then of the contention between Pompey and Caesar, was long before foreseen as from a watchtower, and foretold as by an oracle; yet all the while he did no good, but did harm rather, and brought the calamities of his country faster on; as was wisely observed and elegantly described by Marcus Cicero, when he said in a letter to a friend, *Cato means well: but he does hurt sometimes to the State; for he talks as if he were in the republic of Plato and not in the dregs of Romulus.*[121]

XIII

One need not be a defender of slavery to be able to appreciate the problems posed by the absolutely privileged exercise of free speech that I have just reviewed. Nor does my analysis depend on a determination of whether the Civil War was inevitable. Whether war would have come no matter what was said or done cannot now be demonstrated. But it does seem likely that men could, in the 1850s, have studied these matters with clearer heads than memories of the controversies of the 1830s and 1840s permitted. It should be recalled that at the very time when Adams was engaged in his "life-and-death struggle for the right of petition" in the House of Representatives, Lincoln was coauthor in the Illinois legislature of an 1837 protest which included the proposition, "They believe that the institution of slavery is founded on both injustice and bad policy, but that the promulgation of abolition doctrines tends rather to increase than abate its evils."[122] No one should speak of freedom of speech without acknowledging the possibility of abuses, without urging restraint in its use, and without exhibiting and thereby instructing others in that very exercise of restraint which is necessary if citizens are indeed to govern themselves.

But there is the obligation as well to remind one's fellow citizens by precept and example of the good that freedom of speech can do.[123] In this section and the one following I shall examine the case for freedom of speech, considering it first with the passions of men and then with man's reason primarily in view. My hope is to be able to say with Sidney, "Liberty produceth Vertue, Order and Stability."[124]

It is evident upon review of the abolitionist petitions controversy that the very attempt at suppression only made matters worse.[125] High-spirited men, especially those accustomed to freedom, do not take easily to the bridle.[126] Thus, Churchill can attribute "the pent-up anger and embitterment" encountered by Charles I in 1640 to the "eleven years of gag and muzzle" to which his ministers had subjected the opposition.[127]

It is apparent that some of the arguments for freedom of speech do not depend on a republican regime, but apply to any civilized regime. Frederick the Great could observe, "My people and I have come to an agreement which satisfies us both. They are to say what they please, and I am to do what I please." The prudent prince knows the value to him of an opportunity to discover public attitudes and grievances, to find out "which way the wind is blowing." Thus, Milton writes that

> Some princes, and great statists, have thought it a prime piece of necessary policy, to thrust themselves under disguise into a popular throng, to stand the night long under eaves of houses, and low windows, that they might hear every where the utterances of private breasts, and amongst them find out the precious gem of truth, as amongst the numberless pebbles of the shore; whereby they might be the abler to discover, and avoid, that deceitful and close-couched evil of flattery that ever attends them, and misleads them, and might skilfully know how to apply the several redresses to each malady of state, without trusting the disloyal information of parasites and sycophants. . . .[128]

Grievances that may be expressed can be ministered to before they become dangerous—whereas suppression of opinions can make matters worse, for it suppresses also the hope that something may be done about that which is complained of.[129] This is reflected in the remark by one of the authors of Attic comedy, that "freedom of speech is poverty's weapon; if one destroys this freedom he casts aside the shield of life."[130]

The people, it has been said, are customarily mild.[131] But an alert people, especially in a country accustomed to freedom, begins to suspect that "something is not right, when free discussion is feared by Government."[132] Men are inclined to believe, on the other hand, that anyone who is both respectful enough of the dignity of another and self-restrained enough to permit another to "have his say" is likely to behave decently toward that person's interests. That is, freedom can be said to respect "an ultimate sanctity of the individual as individual, unredeemed and unjustified."[133] Common sense dictates that no judgment upon any *modern* state should be made without an inquiry of the status there of freedom of speech and of the press.[134]

It has often been noticed that "Men living under Popular or Mix'd Governments, are more careful of the publick Good, than in absolute Monarchies."[135] John Adams observed that "people always bear the burden best, when they have, *or think they have*, some share in the direction."[136] Aristotle's distributive justice includes a concern with "a share of the Constitution."[137] Freedom of speech permits a people to believe that they have such a share, that they are participating in the government, that it is in a sense their own.[138] Rulers who destroy men's freedom sometimes try to retain its forms: "They cherish the illusion that they can combine the prerogatives of absolute power with the moral authority that comes from popular assent."[139] But it is not only moral authority that a properly defined freedom can bestow, but also a sense of fellow feeling which counters somewhat the sense of isolation within modern society.[140] In this way men can sustain and restrain one another. The prudent ruler knows that "the more we accomplish by opinion, the less we will have to do by law."[141] He also knows the happiness that men can enjoy in those rare periods when "we may think what we please, and express what we think."[142]

Several of these points are suggested in a passage from an address in 1792 by Thomas Erskine (in defense of Thomas Paine):

Nay, you will find, that in the exact proportion that knowledge and learning have been beat down and fettered, they have destroyed the governments which bound them. The Court of Star Chamber, the first restriction of the press of England, was erected, previous to all the great changes in the constitution. From that moment no man could legally write without an Imprimatur from the State; but truth and freedom found their way with greater force through secret channels; and the unhappy Charles, *unwarned by a free press*, was brought to an ignominious death. When men can freely communicate their thoughts and their sufferings, real or imaginary, their passions spend themselves in air, like gunpowder scattered upon the surface; but pent up by terrors, they work unseen, burst forth in a moment, and destroy every thing in their course. Let reason be opposed to reason, and argument to argument, and every good government will be safe.[143]

XIV

I have argued, as have others before me, that our republican institutions "can be best sustained by the diffusion of knowledge and the due encouragement of a universal, national spirit of inquiry and discussion of public events through the medium of the public press."[144] Freedom of discussion, I have suggested, is not only critical to the proper functioning of our institutions but is also the best means for the development, in our circumstances, of both public and private excellence.[145]

But it may be wondered whether the citizen, however much *he* may benefit from taking part in such discussion, has much to contribute to the complex problems that confront the general government. It is often said that citizens outside the government simply do not have the information that is required to make responsible judgments on critical issues, especially in foreign affairs.[146] There are, on the other hand, indications that the alert reader of the press has had a quite accurate notion of just what is going on, even in military affairs.[147] In fact, General Eisenhower warned us as he was about to leave the presidency that men in office may not be as free to face issues objectively and to make sound judgments as is an alert citizenry not subject to the influence that he feared from an immense military establishment and a large arms industry.[148] I suspect, furthermore, that the enduring issues that face the country require for their understanding, not classified information, but rather an understanding of the nature of man and of society.[149]

The restrictions on information that the alert, intelligent citizen faces would usually apply as well to the typical member of

Congress.[150] The congressman has before him each year more than sixteen thousand bills, of which fewer than four hundred may be enacted into law.[151] He depends on the opinions of his constituency for many of the decisions he must make. A large proportion of the population takes an active part in election campaigns and thereafter affects governmental decisions throughout the country. The diversity of circumstances of our people requires continual participation by citizens in discussion if those who have the authority are to be able to act responsibly.[152] This insures as well that everyone has at least the justice done him of having had his particular interest considered.[153]

It has been reported on good authority that the emergence of modern democracy has meant that the better men do not rise to the top, except perhaps in emergencies.[154] If it is the tendency of the modern regime to favor average citizens for political service, then it is just as well that public servants get as much help as they can from unfettered discussion.[155] Even the exceptional leader needs help in our complex, and yet somewhat delicately balanced, community. Chafee's reflections on the First World War period are appropriate here:

And I cannot fail to mention one other man [Woodrow Wilson], now dead, whom I never knew personally, but who was much in my thoughts during the months when I first wrote on freedom of speech. . . . [T]he material published since his death which I have used here only serves to place his participation in war-time suppression in a more unfavorable light than before. There are few sadder books than Ray Stannard Baker's two biographical volumes on *The War Years*. Woodrow Wilson, the man and the prophet, has turned into a series of fifteen-minute appointments. When war begins, all thinking stops. . . .[156]

Chafee also observed that he himself

was charged with excessive solicitude for the persons who were prosecuted and deported [during that war period]. This charge was most fairly expressed by my friend Arthur D. Hill: "The half-baked young men and women who suffered imprisonment for foolish talk were as inevitably victims of the war as the French children who were killed by German bombs, and their wrongs will seem to most of us to rank low in the scale of wartime suffering." There is some truth to this comment, but it seems to me unsound to regard the persons who are actually suppressed as the sole victims of suppression. In several pages in the present book I have pointed out that the imprisonment of "half-baked" agitators for "foolish talk" may often discourage wise men from publishing valuable criticism of governmental policies. Consequently, what might be well said is not said at all. Unfettered discussion of war aims in 1918 might have produced a better treaty, rallied liberals around President Wilson to carry the United States into the League of Nations, and saved English children from German bombs in 1941. Thus unremitting regard for the First Amendment benefits the nation even more than it protects the individuals who are prosecuted. The real value of freedom of speech is not to the minority that wants to talk, but to the majority that does not want to listen.[157]

The public servant caught up in a great crisis, particularly in time of war, is at that moment most apt to feel that he should not listen to others, especially to those of whose motives he cannot be certain. It is precisely then, Karl von Clausewitz writes, that the leader will be fortunate if the reports that reach him contradict each other, producing a sort of balance and themselves arousing criticism. It is much worse, he adds,

when chance does not render [the inexperienced leader] this service, but one report supports the other, confirms it, magnifies it, continually paints the picture in new colors, until necessity in urgent haste forces from us a decision which will soon be discovered to be folly, all these reports having been lies, exaggeration, errors, etc., etc. In a few words, most reports are false, and the timidity of men gives fresh force to lies and untruths. As a general rule, everyone is more inclined to believe the bad than the good. . . .[158]

President Truman was evidently one of those unexceptional men who had learned to appreciate what he could gain from the debates of others:

The discussion [about atomic energy policy] had been lively, and it was this kind of interchange of opinion that I liked to see at Cabinet meetings. This Cabinet meeting showed that honest men can honestly disagree, and a frank and open argument of this kind is the best form of free expression in which a President can get all points of view needed for him to make decisions. The decisions had to be mine to make.[159]

On the other hand, one of the truly momentous decisions of the Second World War—whether the atomic bomb was to be used in

Japan—was evidently made with very little significant discussion.[160] Another decision with grave domestic implications—the removal from the West Coast of all persons of Japanese descent—also suffered from this lack.[161] Abroad, the concentration camps in Germany and the labor camps in Russia were even more hidden from public view. (Are there measures now afoot that would not stand the light of publicity and the test of discussion but about which we will have grave doubts a generation hence?[162]) No doubt, the maintenance of open discussion of vital issues makes an occasional salutary government measure less effective than it would otherwise be. But is not the risk even greater if the people, both in and out of office, do not reason together about what the country is and what it should be doing?

"It is my duty to hear all," President Lincoln said, "but at last I must, within my sphere, judge what to do and what to forbear."[163] The teacher knows that he is often driven to bring out the best in himself when students really question and challenge him. Even so remarkable a man as Lincoln, the reader senses upon studying his speeches, emerged from the debates with Douglas with the formulation of his position clearly improved. And the people upon whom he had to depend in the great struggle that followed were thereby better prepared to do what was needed.

But for certain principles incorporated in our great constitutional documents, we would not be one people. And but for the role of the press among us, we would not be a people that can act. The reader who has lived where a good newspaper is read every day knows what this means to the life of the community.[164] But even ordinary newspapers serve functions that the government could not efficiently or safely handle as well. For example, the election returns we rely upon are those computed by the press; most of our information about the good and bad that men do all around us is to be found only in newspaper columns; even the disasters that strike our communities make no sense to us until the press puts the pieces together.[165] Such functions depend for their efficient performance upon a vital press—and, considering the nature (or, if one prefers, the prejudices) of the American intellectual, that must mean a free, a politically free, press. "We believe," declared one newspaper, "that one of the duties and opportunities of a great newspaper is to explore, with its own trusted staff and without prejudice, grave questions of national and international policy."[166] It is such a dedication on the part of the press, guided by men alert to their duties and aware of their deficiencies, that we must cherish.

But we must take care that we do not cherish only the useful. It is the civilized man and aristocrat in Churchill, not the citizen and the statesman, who is given the last word in a 1937 portrait of George Bernard Shaw:

If the truth must be told, our British island has not had much help in its troubles from Mr. Bernard Shaw. When nations are fighting for life, when the Palace in which the Jester dwells not uncomfortably, is itself assailed, and everyone from Prince to groom is fighting on the battlements, the Jester's jokes echo only through deserted halls, and his witticisms and commendations, distributed evenly between friend and foe, jar the ears of hurrying messengers, of mourning women and wounded men. The titter ill accords with the tocsin, or the motley with the bandages. But these trials are over; the island is safe, the world is quiet, and begins again to be free. Time for self-questioning returns; and wit and humour in their embroidered mantles take again their seats at a replenished board. The ruins are rebuilt; a few more harvests are gathered in. Fancy is liberated from her dungeon, and we can afford, thank God, to laugh again. Nay more, we can be proud of our famous Jester, and in regathered security rejoice that we laugh in common with many men in many lands, and thereby renew the genial and innocent comradeship and kinship of mankind. For when all is said and done, it was not the Jester's fault there was a war. Had we all stayed beguiled by his musings and his sallies, how much better off we should be! How many faces we should not have to miss! It is a source of pride to any nation to have nursed one of those recording sprites who can illuminate to the eye of remote posterity many aspects of the age in which we live. Saint, sage, and clown; venerable, profound, and irrepressible, Bernard Shaw receives, if not the salutes, at least the hand-clappings of a generation which honours him as another link in the humanities of peoples, and as the greatest living master of letters in the English-speaking world.[167]

XV

By and large, Americans exercise their freedom responsibly. We can still say of them what Madison said in 1789: "The citizens of America know that their individual interest is connected with the public." (*Annals*, I, p. 302) The reader need only reflect upon what he has seen in recent decades and compare alternatives not only in other centuries but in other countries as well. For we can also say of the American citizen today that which was said by Edward Gibbon of Belisarius—that his virtues were his own, his imperfections those of his time.

The most evident manifestation of a critical imperfection of our time is one that our governments have never even tried to correct. In fact, the repressive political legislation and administrative orders we have seen may only aggravate our condition. The manifestation I refer to is the coarsening of public discussion of all subjects. The newspapers, if they are not primarily responsible for this development, contribute to it. It has something to do with the emergence of a mass market in communications as well as with the rise of the standard of living and the tendency of affluence to drive sheltered and bored men to long for the "novel" and the "realistic."

The failure to appreciate this development is reflected in the great concern for obvious pornography expressed by the public press while the much more serious obscenities, seen in such displays as the routine desecrations referred to in note 124 of chapter 5, not only go unquestioned but are even accorded journalistic awards. Thus, for example, it has come to be expected of a good newspaper reporter that he must be callous and resourceful in obtaining access to and eliciting opinions from the shattered survivors of accidents and natural disasters. The public has come to expect such in-sights as part of its "right to know."

All this, I have suggested, is a result of popular culture, the culture of a peculiarly trained, or spoiled, public. Popular culture may well mean no culture—unless culture is taken in a sense that ignores all objective standards about developing human capacities.[168] Free speech, in a popular government, need not contribute to this debasing development: the purveyors of such "culture" do not need free speech protection—they merely give the public, the majority, what it thinks it wants. The suppression of freedom of speech—of the right to speak freely about political things—can even make matters worse: the Americans' reservoir of individuality and yearning for self-expression must then be emptied into other forms of expression. It may not be accidental that the great victories for unregulated literary expression have come in the century when political expression has been most severely penalized. The authors of the First Amendment might well wonder, should they trouble to gaze upon twentieth-century America, what the Communist Party leaders have been doing in jail and the authors of much of our more corrupting trash are doing out.[169]

Indeed, freedom of speech and of the press can contribute to an improvement of the situation I have described, for it contributes to the possibility of education in a popular regime, in that it permits the few to question the opinions and even the appetites of the many. The training of citizens remains the duty primarily of state governments.[170] It is appropriate, therefore, that whatever legitimate power remains to control speech and the press should be in the hands of the official educators of the people. It is to be hoped, of course, that responsible state action may emerge from the proper definition of function and from the general recognition of authority in the states.[171]

All this depends, in turn, upon the sense of duty—and hence, the education—of a few, either as individuals or as members of professions in a favored position to be properly trained and to exert influence out of proportion to their numbers. I have, on other occasions, suggested what the role of the American bar should be in this matter. It is difficult to overestimate the contribution that a free, learned, and responsible bar can make to republican constitutionalism.

But education itself rests upon a more fundamental consideration: what is true and false in political matters? This is a problem that is of special significance in democratic times, especially when the cherished equality of men is taken to support the proposition that that must be true which most men agree upon.

XVI

It has been the fate of the urbanely skeptical Justice Holmes to have allowed himself to become the dogmatist of the democratic faith with respect to the relation between truth and the opinions of the people. Thus, he declared in a dissenting opinion,

> Persecution for the expression of opinions seems to me perfectly logical. If you have no doubt of your premises or your power and want a certain result with all your heart you naturally express your wishes in law and sweep away all opposition. To allow opposition by speech seems to indicate that you think the speech impotent, as when a man says that he has squared the circle, or that you do not care wholeheartedly for the result, or that you doubt either your power or your premises. But when men

have realized that time has upset many fighting faiths, they may come to believe even more than they believe the very foundations of their own conduct that the ultimate good desired is better reached by free trade in ideas—that the best test of truth is the power of the thought to get itself accepted in the competition of the market, and that truth is the only ground upon which their wishes safely can be carried out. That at any rate is the theory of our Constitution. It is an experiment, as all life is an experiment. Every year if not every day we have to wager our salvation upon some prophecy based upon imperfect knowledge. . . .[172]

Had Justice Holmes limited himself to the statement of a prudential rule to the effect that the common good is most likely to be reached in this country by a "free trade in ideas" I would not be disposed to fault him.[173] But he seems to question the very idea of truth, even as he attributes to his observation the status of truth, but of a privileged truth which need not be one of those "fighting faiths" upset by time.[174] Indeed, he is here the intellectual stepfather of that far less learned, and consequently far more obviously rash, chief justice who proclaimed the absolute truth "that all concepts are relative."[175]

A more explicit recognition of prudential considerations in the establishment and conduct of a constitutional system is seen in the men of the First Congress. This is illustrated in a comment by Madison, who had previously described himself as an advocate both of "a very free system of commerce" (*Annals*, I, p. 111) and of the beneficial effects of interest in community affairs: "[A]lthough interest will, in general, operate effectually to produce political good, yet there are causes in which certain factitious circumstances may divert it from its natural channel, or throw or retain it in an artificial one." (*Annals*, I, p. 185) Thus, adjustments may have to be made in the normal operations of free trade in order that "political good" may be produced. And this implies, of course, that it can be known what the good is, what the demands, needs, and limitations of a community are.

The reliance upon men who know, and upon that which is knowable, is seen in Number 57 of the *Federalist*:

The aim of every political constitution is, or ought to be, first to obtain for rulers men who possess most wisdom to discern, and most virtue to pursue, the common good of the society; and in the next place, to take the most effectual precautions for keeping them virtuous whilst they continue to hold their public trust. The elective mode of obtaining rulers is the characteristic policy of republican government. The means relied on in this form of government for preventing their degeneracy are numerous and various. The most effectual one is such a limitation of the term of appointments as will maintain a proper responsibility to the people.

Once again we see that our bearings should be taken by "the common good of the society."[176]

Still another difficulty with Justice Holmes's "competition of the market" criterion lies in the fact that the market fluctuates: one day it is this, another day that, which is tested and accepted. But this is inevitable if there is nothing fixed or certain about "truth." Indeed, one must wonder why the "truth" or "good" of one day or of one market is to be preferred to that of any other. I turn again to the *Federalist*, this time to Number 63, for an indication of the older approach:

Thus far I have considered the circumstances which point out the necessity of a well-constructed Senate only as they relate to the representatives of the people. To a people as little blinded by prejudice or corrupted by flattery as those whom I address, I shall not scruple to add, that such an institution may be sometimes necessary as a defence to the people against their own temporary errors and delusions. As the cool and deliberate sense of the community ought, in all governments, and actually will, in all free governments, ultimately prevail over the views of its rulers; so there are particular moments in public affairs when the people, stimulated by some irregular passion, or some illicit advantage, or misled by the artful misrepresentations of interested men, may call for measures which they themselves will afterwards be the most ready to lament and condemn. In these critical moments, how salutary will be the interference of some temperate and respectable body of citizens, in order to check the misguided career, and to suspend the blow meditated by the people against themselves, until reason, justice, and truth can regain their authority over the public mind? What bitter anguish would not the people of Athens have often escaped if their government had contained so provident a safeguard against the tyranny of their own passions? Popular liberty might then have escaped the indelible reproach of decreeing to the same citizens the hemlock on one day and statues on the next.

Thus, it is well to determine, when evaluating the judgment of the market, what people that market is likely to be made up of and what their condition is likely to be.[177] That is to say, the role of the passions in deliberations, both communal and individual, must not be lost sight of.[178] Their distorting effect cannot be appreciated if there is no standard, unformed by chance passions, to which recourse might be had.

If the "market" should be limited to those best trained to pass on particular problems, that would constitute a qualification of Justice Holmes's popular formula. Men dedicated to the democratic creed are apt, however, to resent the suggestion that the superior training of some men should be deferred to.[179] Thus, in the First Congress, Page objected to a proposal which made it the duty of the secretary of the treasury to "digest and report plans for the improvement and management of the revenue, and the support of the public credit," observing that

> it might be well enough to enjoin upon him the duty of making out and preparing estimates; but to go any further would be a dangerous innovation upon the Constitutional privilege of this House; it would create an undue influence within these walls, because members might be led, by the deference commonly paid to men of abilities, who give an opinion in a case they have thoroughly studied, to support the minister's plan, even against their own judgment. Nor would the mischief stop here; it would establish a precedent which might be extended, until we admitted all the ministers of the Government on the floor, to explain and support the plans they have digested and reported: thus laying a foundation for an aristocracy or a detestable monarchy. [*Annals*, I, pp. 592-93]

Ames argued otherwise, raising questions about the inherent competence of a large assembly and, by implication, of the public at large (at least in the larger countries):

> ... The Secretary is presumed to have the best knowledge of the subject of finance of any member of the community.... It is, perhaps, a misfortune incident to public assemblies, that from their nature they are more incompetent to a complete investigation of accounts than a few individuals; perhaps in a Government so extended, and replete with variety in its mode of expenditure as this, the subject may be more perplexing than in countries of smaller extent and less variety of objects to guard. The science of accounts is at best but an abstruse and dry study; it is scarcely to be understood but by an unwearied assiduity for a long time; how then can a public body, elected annually, and in session for a few months, undertake the arduous task with a full prospect of success? If our plans are formed upon these incomplete investigations, we can expect little improvement; for I venture to say, that our knowledge will be far inferior to that of an individual, like the present officer. [*Annals*, I, pp. 595-96]

The response by Hartley to another speaker was intended as an answer to Ames as well:

> He thought the gentleman last up proved too much by his arguments; he proved that the House of Representatives was, in fact, unnecessary and useless; that one person could be a better judge of the means to improve and manage the revenue, and support the national credit, than the whole body of Congress. This kind of doctrine . . . is indelicate in a republic, and strikes at the root of all legislation founded upon the great Democratic principle of representation. It is true mistakes, and very injurious ones, have been made on the subject of finance by some State Legislatures; but I would rather submit to this evil, than, by my voice, establish tenets subversive of the liberties of my country. [*Annals*, I, p. 600]

And yet, we do repair to doctors and lawyers and watchmakers when confronted by disorders in our personal affairs and effects.

Related to these observations is the fact of the existence of "vulgar minds," whom Jackson described as "incapable of analyzing objects, accustomed to receive impressions without distinction, and to be determined rather by the opinions of others than by the result of their own examinations." (*Annals*, I, p. 830) And this in turn reveals the need for rhetoric, especially under a regime in which each mind, vulgar or refined, is said to be entitled to an equal voice.

My references to truth, vulgar minds,[180] the common good, passions and rhetoric—all of which are lost sight of if Justice Holmes's proposition is accepted as it stands—point to the need for traditional political philosophy, to the need for that study of men and communities which stands above, even as it takes account of, transitory and accidental political things.[181] It is only against the background of such study that prudential judgments can be expected.[182] It is in light provided by political philosophy that the underlying prudence of a sound constitutional arrangement can best be seen and that a constitution can be properly defended and, if need be, reformed.

We find, as we approach the end of our inquiry into the Constitution and its bearing on my reading of the First Amendment, that we have come to a new beginning. For we have yet to explore, to understand, and to evaluate the foundations and aspirations of our community. Thus, until we have learned what Americans do, should, and can want, our findings and suggestions must remain provisional.

XVII

I conclude my constitutional analysis with that new beginning. This beginning as well must be provisional, since it must (at least for the moment) take the American people and Constitution as they are rather than as they should be or even as they have been.

We have been concerned with definitions and constitutions, a concern that cannot be sufficient. One cannot ignore the complaints of a Lincoln against the evil done by men claiming exemptions under one or more of the safeguards of the Bill of Rights.[183] Indeed, it must be rare when an appeal to even well-established rights is not motivated or colored by factional, if not selfish, considerations, however much such rights are justified by invocations of the common good.

Still, an invocation of the common good does induce and permit us to shift the emphasis from the modern "rights of man" to the older "natural law" and the even older and more civic-minded "natural right," from an emphasis upon privileges to an emphasis upon duties. Thus, individual intelligence and action are called for, as well as individual example and self-sacrifice, if freedom is to be used responsibly.[184] The end of liberty, as Boudinot implied, may not be simply liberty:

A proper jealousy for the liberty of the people is commendable in those who are appointed and sworn to be its faithful guardians; but when this spirit is carried so far as to lose sight of its object, and instead of leading to avoid, urges on to the precipice of ruin, we ought to be careful how we receive its impressions. [*Annals*, I, p. 599]

Neither does a man seek and value freedom only to advance self-government and to make government productive of justice, but also to enhance the dignity and self-development of the human being. This sentiment found expression in Stone's exclamation:

We have expended our treasure, our blood, and our time, to very little purpose, if we do not think that liberty and safety exalt the human species. From the meanest to the highest rank in life, the propriety of conduct arises from the security and independence of situation. I will not pursue the argument further, than to observe, that from these principles it is, that there is more liberty and nobleness of soul in a common man in America, than in a Minister of State in Turkey . . . [*Annals*, I, pp. 568-69][185]

This exaltation comes, in part, through the realization that a man participates in ruling himself, that he has duties as well as privileges, and that the privileges are defined and defended by himself. The dignity of the citizen's activity is enlarged if he has the opportunity to explain himself, if (that is) he can do that which is distinctively human.[186] Thus, Stone justified rising to speak toward the end of a long debate:

> It is hardly to be expected . . . that any thing new can be offered at this stage of the debate; the committee will therefore believe that the motives for delivering our opinions do not arise so much from an expectation of being able to convince, as from a desire to assign the reasons upon which our vote is founded. [*Annals*, I, p. 563]

We are all too aware today, especially in an age when great social as well as suppressed psychic forces are thought to guide and even form our thoughts, that reasons are suspect, that there are such products of the human mind as "rationalizations." Nevertheless, we continue to be moved to believe that arguments can be taken seriously: the reasons men give may have always been the most important element in the decisions they make. This was recognized by even so great an advocate of the role of interest as Madison, in his acknowledgment that there *are* useful indications of which sentiments are to be taken seriously and which are not:

> As there is a great diversity of sentiment respecting the policy of the duty [on tonnage], I am very happy to find it is not prescribed by the geographical situation of our country. This evinces that it is merely difference of opinion, and not difference of interest. Gentlemen of the same State differ as much as gentlemen from the extremes of the continent. [*Annals*, I, p. 285]

This observation, too, must be taken into account in evaluating and guiding the exercise among us of freedom of speech and of the press.

Whatever the risks and limitations of freedom, it must be acknowledged that the character of the American people, as well as their traditions and laws, is such that freedom is what they do and will insist upon. They have, from their very founding, considered themselves "the freest people on the face of the earth."[187] The frontier experience and its legacy seem to have intensified and secured them in this attitude.[188]

No government which can endure, and which does not generally corrupt American aspirations, can proceed on any other assumption than that the freedom of the American citizen must be preserved.[189] Either the party challenging this freedom will be destroyed, as were the Federalists (probably the most talented and best educated political party we will ever have),[190] who made the mistake of failing to take seriously enough the emerging popular demand for liberty and who permitted themselves to be identified, partly because of the Alien and Sedition Acts, as the agents of aristocratic and even monarchic tendencies.[191] Or, and this is the more likely alternative in an age of material abundance, there will emerge an even greater emphasis on equality, an equality which produces a petty and pampered uniformity and, eventually, a denial of civic virtue.[192] Some form of liberty would remain, but it would be a form seeking release and fulfillment in essentially private activities, in what is now known as "self-expression."[193]

We would then have lost, in either case, the impressive spectacle[194] of a centuries-old community of freemen, confidently governing themselves as few other peoples have ever been able to do. The problem is how to preserve or, if need be, how to restore the virtue and character of the American people while continuing to recognize and nourish that which Milton spoke of when he referred to the "liberty of speaking, than which nothing is more sweet to man."[195]

BANQUO: *To me you speak not.*
If you can look into the seeds of time,
And say which grain will grow and which will not,
Speak then to me, who neither beg nor fear
Your favours nor your hate.
                     . . .
FIRST WITCH: *Lesser than Macbeth, and greater.*
SECOND WITCH: *Not so happy, yet much happier.*
THIRD WITCH: *Thou shalt get kings, though thou be none:*
So all hail, Macbeth and Banquo!
FIRST WITCH: *Banquo and Macbeth, all hail!*
MACBETH: *Stay, you imperfect speakers, tell me more.*

                        —SHAKESPEARE, *Macbeth*

IX. "WE DO ORDAIN AND ESTABLISH"

I

WE ARE A PEOPLE with a constant yearning for variety, for change. Our prosperity and our strength seem to have come as a result of change, of changes that have transformed the face of North America to a degree and at a rate unknown on any other continent. It is inevitable that change should still be regarded with favor among us.[1]

American openness to improvement reflects the rational element that pervades the community and its constitutions. One has, to mention an obvious contrast with the Old World, only to notice the division of most of our land into rectangular plots that represent much more the deliberate arrangement and much less the unreflective effects of history than is the case with the European countryside. One remembers also that men such as Washington and Lincoln served as surveyors in their youth.[2]

But some aspects of the yearning for variety are significantly different from what they were a century ago. To some degree, an astonishing material prosperity and its attendant advertising influences have cultivated variety for its own sake. To some degree, that is, the yearning results partly from our failure to appreciate what is solid, and even unchanging, in our way of life; for, one should say, the yearning in former times was with a view to some end, however dimly perceived.[3] Today, variety almost entirely for its own sake threatens to engulf us.[4]

The end of our way of life—the standards that are implied by it—is most authoritatively and explicitly set forth in the Declaration of Independence. These standards are reflected in the Constitution of the United States, and in our reliance as well on precedent and procedure for guidance and moderation in the conduct of our affairs. The ends of our regime are both restated and implicitly questioned most effectively in the Gettysburg Address. It is to these documents, and instruments such as these, that Americans must continually return for light on where they stand and where they should go.

The Constitution does not provide explicitly for the education of the American citizen: this duty has been left primarily to the states with their pre-Constitution powers. It seems to have been assumed that there would continue to develop and emerge among us the kind of man who had made the Revolution and thereafter the Constitution.[5] That is, it was believed educated men would arise as they had, and for the reasons they had, in the seventeenth and eighteenth centuries. That the perhaps inevitable democratization implicit in the Constitution, and in the political and economic circumstances which gave rise to that constitution, would modify the practice of centuries was evidently not foreseen. The role of educators has had to be undertaken not only by the institutions of the country, which are supported by the memory of great deeds, but perhaps even more by outstanding men who have not hesitated to use their great talents to teach Americans who they are and what they should do.[6]

This suggests the value to our community of the philosophical man interested in, if not engaged in, political matters. Indeed, it may be only in the liberal democratic society that such a man can flourish today as a human being and contribute as a citizen to the common good.⁷ But it is precisely the man of a philosophical disposition who is sometimes found questioning the tenets of the liberal society.

II

What *can* be said for freedom, and particularly for freedom of speech, which is generally taken not only as the principal form of freedom but also as the surest indication of its existence in a political community? That is, what *more* can be said here for the constitutional arrangement sketched out in this book?

The Greek language provides a suggestive summary of our problem. I begin with *parresia*, which is derived from two other words, *pas* and *resis*, the former meaning "every" or "everything," the latter, "a word," or "speech": the saying of everything. The saying of everything, *parresia*, came to be regarded in two ways: "liberty of speech," and, in a derogatory sense, "license of tongue." Thus, there are in the classical Greek the two connotations, with perhaps an emphasis upon the derogatory, that come down to our day.⁸ But, it should also be noted, the word has come to us through the Greek of the New Testament as well, where it is almost always regarded as praiseworthy, thereby contributing to the Christian influence upon our modern conception of freedom of speech.⁹

It has become fashionable—or at least more nearly fashionable than ever before in the United States—for thoughtful men to question the soundness of the American dedication to freedom of speech and, indeed, to freedom itself. The question is raised in the name of "virtue" and the "general welfare"; or it is reflected in considerable emphasis on law-abidingness in all circumstances.¹⁰ Freedom either is seen as entailing cumbersome restrictions that impede the ability of a government to act vigorously and intelligently in the national interest or is regarded as the cause of moral laxity, if not even of corruption, resulting from irresponsible permissiveness.

The United States, which is for the first time in its history clearly the most powerful country in the world, is seen as confronted with enemies that threaten its very existence in circumstances that require leadership and sacrifice of a high order. Perhaps this latter assessment is not unique: the country has confronted seemingly overwhelming threats before. But for the first time serious questions seem to be raised among us as to whether our republican government is equipped to conduct itself properly in such circumstances. These doubts seem to depend on conclusions about the quality both of our people and of the leaders who come to the fore (or, at least, of what those leaders can do in the face of a tradition of restraint upon governmental activity).

It might be said that these critics of the American way would like to enjoy the benefits of freedom without enduring its shortcomings.

III

There is deplored in republican government an inability to adjust to changing circumstances, an inability to mobilize immediately and forcefully the energies of the community. But one recalls a statement describing the events in the last week of July, 1914, when the tendency toward war among the still monarchical nations of Europe had gotten out of control: "All governments, including Russia's, and the great majority of their peoples, are peacefully inclined. But the direction has been lost and the stone has started rolling."[11]

Indeed, it should be argued that it is only in republican government that an essential flexibility is likely to be maintained: men of different temperaments and tendencies stand in the wings, so to speak, ready to move onstage when this or that particular type is needed. Other governments must make do (if legitimacy is to be preserved) with whatever their constitution has brought forth, no matter how circumstances change.[12]

The duty of the public-spirited man—the man who has the makings of leadership—is not to rule, but to be prepared to rule, when the opportunity presents itself for someone of his talents and disposition. The measure of his dedication is seen primarily in the care with which he has prepared himself for the appropriate occasion.[13]

In the exceptional case, this is the man who, striking out from the crowd, arrives at a reasoned determination of what his country needs and is capable of. He can distinguish the essential from the accidental or incidental—and he prepares himself for the critical problems of his country and of his age, problems that do not confront him for the first time during an election campaign or upon taking office but that have occupied his mind for years past. Indeed, if the community is fortunate, it has selected him primarily because it senses that he understands the critical problems better than any man among those who contend or are available for public office. He has thought through the problems, has considered them in such a way as to permit him to maintain a steady course even as circumstances shift and disasters strike.[14] And he knows that the secondary problems are worthy of no more than passing attention.[15]

Thus, republican government need not mean weak government: powerful offices are created under the Constitution—and the success of republican government depends, in part, on whether there are men capable of filling such offices. This, in turn, depends on the education that is available to men of the greatest talent and of the highest ambitions.

We have also the subordinate problem of whether such men *can* be recognized by an electorate that cannot (in the nature of things) be informed or trained to any high degree. The "personality" of the man must somehow assert itself.[16] This, it seems, is what television, if properly guided and supplemented by a responsible press, is particularly good at conveying (even though television *is* for most peoples, perhaps inevitably, a net loss): an electorate may get some impression of the kind of situation this or that man is naturally suited for—and whether a man can be trusted.[17]

To some extent also the choice of the right *kind* of man, as distinguished from this or that particular man, depends on the effectiveness of the work of the best man. Not only does he leave an impression of the kind of man he is—one who can be counted on for a certain kind of service—but even more important, he contributes, by his precepts and example, to the shaping of the opinion of the electorate about the kind of man who should be raised up and honored.

Indeed, it should be irrelevant for the best man, who shapes both the constitution and the people of his country, whether he ever occupies a constitutional office. Rather, he is one of whom can be said what Plutarch said of Philopoemen:

. . . He had a nature so truly formed for command that he could govern even the laws themselves for the public good; he did not need to wait for the formality of being elected into command by the governed, but employed their service, if occasion required at his own discretion; judging that he who understood their real interests was more truly their supreme magistrate, than he whom they had elected to the office. . . .[18]

A man of this caliber, if properly nurtured by his country and trained by his teachers, is willing and able to rule when circumstances require. He sees his public life as essentially a duty; his deepest pleasures and most serious concerns remain in the private realm.[19] Perhaps we should add that it is only if he appreciates properly the limits of public life and the attractions of the most exalted private life that he can be safely entrusted in tumultuous times with the highest duties and the greatest powers under the Constitution— if he appreciates, that is, the sentiments of an Edgar counseling his father about both the conditions and the end of human life:

> What, in ill thoughts again? Men must endure
> Their going hence, even as their coming hither;
> Ripeness is all. Come on.[20]

IV

This limitation on the satisfactions of the public life is not a feature of republican government alone but extends as well to the best regime.

The classic examination of the best regime is found in Plato's *Republic*. It is in Book VII of that work that we have the famous discussion of "the cave."

We begin our interpretation of the cave with the observation that Homer, who had been condemned by Socrates in Books II and III (and is to be reproached again in Book X) is somewhat rehabilitated in Book VII, and in a decisive respect. That is, Socrates quotes part of a saying by Achilles about preferring to live on earth as the serf of another. (516 D-E) The rest of this saying, we are required (and intended) to remember for ourselves, is to be found at the beginning of Book III: Achilles (Homer has reported) prefers life on earth as a serf to the role of ruler over the dead. (386 C) In Book III, such passages, and this one in particular, are forbidden: since they make men fearful of death, they are inappropriate in the training of good citizens. But in Book VII we find Socrates using this very passage in describing the reluctance of the liberated man to return to the cave: Socrates uses Homer, and the very passage that he had earlier condemned as subversive of civic virtue.

Of course, the two uses can be reconciled logically; but there remains an ambiguity, if only psychological, in that he used the same passage in two quite different ways.

Indeed, one is compelled to wonder whether one can accept without question anything that a serious writer presents on the surface of his work. This reservation is suggested long before Book VII of the *Republic*, but it should be emphasized for this particular setting. (One might also have wondered of course, how seriously Plato took the condemnation of Homer in Books II and III: he must have known as well as we do that the Homeric accounts had actually had the effect of inculcating in the young men of Greece a noble desire for the glory that is expected to attend heroism.) In any event, Plato (or more accurately, Socrates) reverses himself in his attitude toward a particular passage from Homer.[21]

The reader is put on notice to take care. We proceed to a consideration of the man liberated from his shackles and led up and out of the cave, the man who is thereafter reluctant to return to the cave. Later on (517 A) we learn of others who would kill anyone who might try to release them and lead them up. The earlier man was to some extent forced to make the ascent or, at least, to look at the bright light; but nothing is said of him trying to kill anyone. Thus, there is the implicit suggestion that the man actually liberated may be inherently more receptive to liberation than the homicidally minded prisoners referred to later. Then we note that the word "nature" is used in connection with the release of the earlier man. (515 C) That man, it may thereby be suggested, is better fitted to be released than most of the others.[22] It should also be noted that the other prisoners are not released; nor is an attempt even made to release them. Those who are in charge of releases seem to be aware of the natural possibilities and limitations of those shackled.

What city does *this* cave, *the* cave, represent then? It represents a city in which the philosopher does not rise spontaneously. Rather, the man of a philosophical disposition is led forth and trained, having been selected by the rulers to make the arduous ascent. In the ordinary city, we are told, the philosopher rises spontaneously— that is, without any deliberate effort on the part of the city to make him a philosopher.[23] Consequently, he is not obliged (as philosopher) to share in the labors of ruling. (520 B) But in the city of *this* cave, the element of spontaneity is missing; and an obligation exists. Consequently, we find the released man coming back, however reluctantly, to assume duties in the cave. Our suspicion grows that this cave is not simply any city, but the "best city" as well.[24]

Both cities exhibit features which reflect inevitable limitations of human nature. What then distinguishes the best from the ordinary city? In the best city—in the particular cave that we are shown—there are both shackled and unshackled. The unshackled must be the rulers, those who create and propagate the opinions which the people are to have.[25] Thus, the rulers—who else can they be but those who unshackle men of a fit nature, who have themselves made the ascent and have returned to serve out their obligations as rulers?—shape the opinions by which the shackled live. They are educators.

Perhaps it is only the legalistically disposed reader who would ask the further question: "Who shackled the prisoners?" Socrates speaks of shackles. This suggests an intelligent agent doing the shackling: these people could have been pictured as mired down in mud or otherwise caught by natural forces.[26] The first answer, of course, is that Socrates has shackled them—Socrates, who is the ruler of the community he has been creating in words. A more general answer is that such people are shackled by their rulers, by those who have made the ascent and return to rule.[27]

But, to return to an earlier question left unanswered, what distinguishes the best from the ordinary city? The ordinary city is in many ways similar to this cave. There may be shackling in the ordinary city; and people in the cave also live by opinion. But in the ordinary city, the people would shackle one another (and their "rulers") indiscriminately: the opinions would be promulgated by anyone who thinks it is in his interest to do so (or by those who think, but cannot know, they are acting for the common good). Perhaps those carrying the puppets would also be shackled, but in a different part of the cave, perhaps by longer chains: they would be deceived by their own illusions or by those of others.[28] In the best city, however, the rulers do not share the common illusions or, for that matter, any illusions. What they do is based on what they know to be for the good of all. The best city has this further advantage: the philosophic nature would be systematically recognized and developed.

It is apparent now why the philosopher has to be compelled, by being reminded of an implied contractual obligation, to return to rule in the city, in even the best city.[29] This is a worse life when a better is possible for him. (519 D) He must come back from an attractive private life to play games, to deal in sham and illusion. But he realizes that this is necessary, that most of the shackled would be harmed rather than helped by being exposed to the light, by "enlightenment." Perhaps the regulatory activities are to be left as much as possible to the shackled, to those prisoners most adept in the contests that the shackled hold, to those prisoners who take most seriously the lure and demands of worldly honor. (515 E) An adaptation of the saying quoted from Achilles may be appropriate here as well: the ruler of even the best city is like the ruler among the dead.

This, then, is the "beautiful" or "fair" city (527 C), the best city, that is created in the *Republic*. Clearly, Socrates does not present the cave as a pleasant or inviting place: it is dark and filled with error. But, Plato would have us understand, this is the result of the limitations placed upon social achievement by human nature and by the nature of things. This is what even the best city can look like when viewed from the highest perspective. The man who knows does not expect too much from political life.[30]

It should be an objective of the founders and perpetuators of republican institutions to nourish in the better men of action enough care for the community so that they will be willing to serve in its highest offices, when the occasion demands, but not so much that they feel deprived or unfulfilled and even desperate when they are not called by the electorate to undertake the burdens of office.[31]

V

But, it might be asked, is not the question confronting us, not whether the better men will care too much but, rather, whether they will care enough? Why should there be any dedication on their part to republican institutions or perhaps, indeed, to any political institutions?

Political institutions can be justified easily enough, if only by reminding even the philosophical-minded of the conditions for mere existence, as well as for civilized existence. The city is needed to produce the philosopher, who knows the city is not the last word.³² I have already referred in this chapter to some virtues of republican political institutions. One can add that the inherent flexibility of republican government means that the better men can exercise considerable influence even when they do not hold power, perhaps exercising under this dispensation the maximum of influence with the least trouble to themselves. The protection afforded the better men by the institution of freedom of speech—which would seem to be critical to the life of a form of government that depends on the popular choice of alternative men and programs—not only induces them to be bolder than they might otherwise be: it might even make it their duty to contribute, in the way they are best able, to the community that protects and sustains them.³³

A further obligation is suggested by considerations of the justice of republican government. The institution of free speech not only permits, and perhaps thereby obliges, the better man to speak on public issues. It also extends to the people at large an opportunity to express and protect themselves: it gives them by this means (reinforced by the ballot, but a ballot that makes sense only if there is truly free discussion beforehand) a share in the government—and thus makes it more likely that their particular interests will be given some consideration.³⁴ This sense of sharing, which is reinforced by participation in the economic goods of a prosperous community, may encourage restraint in political advocacy: one tends to be more tolerant (and protective) about one's own.

VI

One danger of much of the indiscriminate questioning of our constitutional institutions today—a questioning that may well place upon those institutions the sins of both commission and omission that might better be attributed to other aspects of modern life—is that the faith of the people in their form of government can be weakened.

Ours, it should be recalled again and again, is a government that provides an opportunity for the greatest participation by and interest of citizens in their political institutions. Not only is there the opportunity provided in national politics by both freedom of speech and the ballot, but there is also the effect of the federal arrangement: apprenticeships can be served on the local level for higher and higher offices; citizens can concern themselves with what is immediately affecting them; they can appraise potential national leaders while they campaign in precincts and serve in city, county, and state governments. The people learn to govern themselves, partly by instruction, partly by habituation.

This resource of local self-government should not be lightly surrendered. In the event of that worldwide nuclear war which sometimes seems inevitable, that people is most likely to survive on a civilized basis which is able on its own to organize and maintain itself in autonomous local communities once continental systems of production, direction, and communication have been shattered. The virtues of local self-government should not be lost sight of in the course of contemporary disparagement of the "magical omnipotence of 'State Rights.'"

VII

A salutary patriotism occasionally obliges us, at the risk of seeming naïve,[35] to overlook the limitations and problems of the American Republic while we sing its praises:

Millard Fillmore once observed to an English visitor, "Our people govern themselves, mostly, which does not leave much for the President to do." No doubt, the time when this was so must seem as obscure to some as the name of this president. And yet, do not the American people continue to govern themselves, mostly?

Is there not about this spectacle of a proud, self-governing and free people something not only attractive in its openness and freshness but even worthy of protection and honor from the best men? One is reminded of Rousseau's praise of Geneva and, perhaps better, of the implicit praise of democratic Athens even in Plato's majestic work—for was not a Socrates tolerated there for decades?[36]

The self-confidence of our people must rest, at least in part, on evident standards of right and wrong to which they can lend continued and dedicated support. Those who disparage the traditional standard of freedom of speech, for instance—that seemingly naïve and extensive freedom which the American sometimes characterizes as his right "to say what I damn please here"—undermine the regime at a vital point. The extent of American dedication in this respect is reflected even in the insistence on the part of those who would punish their heretical fellow citizens that it is really the actions (or prospective actions, that is "conspiracies"), not the ideas, of the victims that are to be penalized. But it happens that the prospective actions are anticipated primarily from the speeches —and the natural effect of such punishment is to discourage, if not to suppress, unpopular speech.

Such repression will sometimes deprive us of what we badly need to hear. In addition, the habit of repression can make this people brutal and harsh; or, if native good-naturedness does prevail, it can make us lose interest in politics and become simply materialistic and pleasure-seeking (which is another form of liberty). Our tradition of tolerance has promoted self-restraint on the part of governors and self-confidence, as well as self-restraint, on the part of the governed (who themselves are governors in turn). Freedom of speech in America somehow points to and supports civilized intercourse, and even civilization itself, among *this* people, an amalgamation of peoples which, but for its seemingly divisive discourse of one with another, is not otherwise a united people.

Besides, is there not something ignoble and petty, if not vulgar, in our official campaigns against allegedly subversive fellow citizens? What kind of man can support, let alone lead, such displays of fearfulness and, at times, vindictiveness as we have seen since the Second World War? Those who, in the name of freedom, propose to deny the privileges of free men to fellow citizens who might (if in power) deny freedom to others seem themselves to display not only ignorance of the source of our strength but even ingratitude toward the institutions that made them or, if not them, their fathers. One should prefer to see generosity and confidence, calmness and urbanity, not an unseemly recourse to political suppression. The strength and grace of a republic are reflected in the risks it is willing to run. Certainly one should "never expect to see a perfect work from imperfect man."[37]

Is it not evident that the only practical access to nobility for *this* people remains its dedication to freedom and to the manliness, disciplined self-confidence, humanity, pride, and even justice which can be said to be implied by that freedom? A vigorous defense of freedom seems to me the only cause which can have an enduring appeal for our young, especially when its defense is coupled, as it can be, with integrity of character. Those who dilute our ancient faith in freedom threaten the principal support of our regime. The swelling crusade for the justice of equality can have permanent worth only if our freedom, with its implications of excellence, can be preserved.

No doubt, there are among us abuses of freedom of speech. But why should our generation act as if it has been the first to discover them? The truly dangerous consequences of these abuses are anticipated in the Constitution, which reflects a deeper prudence than that policy which has recourse to periodic repression. The best safeguard against abuses is found in the good sense, the self-restraint, and even that "tone of impartial justice" of which a self-governing people is capable. It is found, that is, in the good government that has somehow resulted from our dedication to freedom and to freedom of speech. One can fully appreciate how well Americans govern themselves only if one compares the efforts made elsewhere to do at all what is done so well and even so casually here.[38]

American republicanism remains not only "the world's best hope" but also the noblest testimony that men have today of their faith in one another—in, that is, the ability of man to use his reason properly to secure for himself and his posterity the good things of this life. Timid men should be reassured that our republican experiment not only has worked, but has worked much better than eighteenth-century republicans had a right to hope for: it may well be the best which our political circumstances, nature, and traditional opinions will admit.

The republican of our day, however subject to continual reexamination his salutary opinions should be, is entitled to conclude, "We must not be afraid to be free."[39]

APPENDIXES

APPENDIX A. STAGES IN THE FIRST CONGRESS OF THE FIRST AMENDMENT

THREE COLLECTIONS should be mentioned here for the reader who should want to search out for himself the sources of the First Amendment: (1) Francis Newton Thorpe, *The Federal and State Constitutions, Colonial Charters, and Other Organic Laws of the States, Territories, and Colonies, Now or Heretofore Forming the United States of America* (Washington: Government Printing Office, 1909), includes (in seven volumes) all past as well as the 1909 versions of the instruments enumerated in its title; (2) Bennett B. Patterson, *The Forgotten Ninth Amendment* (Indianapolis: Bobbs-Merrill Company, 1955), includes in an appendix those portions of the *Annals of the First Congress* which bear on the writing and adoption of the proposed amendments now known as the Bill of Rights; (3) Edward Dumbauld, *The Bill of Rights and What It Means Today* (Norman: University of Oklahoma Press, 1957), includes in its appendixes a table for sources of provisions of the Bill of Rights, the English Bill of Rights of 1689, the Virginia Bill of Rights of 1776, the proposals for amendments made by the various states in the course of the ratification of the Constitution, and the stages of the Bill of Rights in the First Congress (1789).

It is sometimes instructive, in attempting to determine the meaning of an instrument, to reflect upon the stages through which it has been brought, what has been refined, and what has been deleted by its draftsmen. Several stages in the First Congress of the provision we now know as the First Amendment are set forth below. Four publications are drawn upon for this recapitulation: (1) *Annals of Congress (The Debates and Proceedings in the Congress of the United States)*, Vol. I (Washington: Gales and Seaton, 1834) (cited as *Annals, I*); (2) *History of Congress, Exhibiting a Classification of the Proceedings of the Senate and the House of Representatives, from March 4, 1789, to March 3, 1793* (Philadelphia: Lea & Blanchard, 1843) (cited as *History of Congress*); (3) *Journal of the House of Representatives of the United States* (New York: Francis Childs and John Swaine, 1789) (cited as *House Journal*); (4) *Journal of the First Session of the Senate of the United States of America* (New York: Thomas Greenleaf, 1789) (cited as *Senate Journal*).

The publications I have relied upon exhibit some minor discrepancies at various stages of the drafting. Indeed, the very delineation of "stages" depends, to some extent, on just where one chooses to draw lines, especially since two different developments (i.e., one with respect to religion, the other with respect to speech, press, assembly, and petition) were eventually merged into one provision. I do not include all variations considered in the First Congress, but only those which seem to be in the direct line of development of what is now the First Amendment (cf., e.g., p. 111, above; *History of Congress*, p. 161). A parallel (but eventually discarded) development with respect to limitations upon the states is included for its useful comparison to what became the First Amendment.

One can take one's bearings among the nine passages reproduced here by noticing that no. i is taken from Madison's original recommendations in the House of Representatives of June 8; no. ii is taken from the recommendations reported by the Select Committee in the House on July 28; no. vi is taken from the amendments passed by the House of Representatives on August 24; no. viii is taken from the amendments passed by the Senate on September 9; and no. ix is taken from the final version of the amendments agreed to after conference between the two houses and proposed by Congress on September 25, 1789, to the states for ratification. (In no. i and no. ii, the proposed amendments were to be inserted into the original Constitution as indicated. The "committee" referred to in no. ii is the House of Representatives sitting as a Committee of the Whole.)

The "third article" proposed to the states for ratification became what we know as the "First Amendment" upon the failure of the original "first article" and "second article" to be ratified. See chap. 2, n. 25, above.

i

Fourthly. That in article 1st, section 9, between clauses 3 and 4, be inserted these clauses, to wit: The civil rights of none shall be abridged on account of religious belief or worship, nor shall any national religion be established, nor shall the full and equal rights of conscience be in any manner, or on any pretext, infringed.

The people shall not be deprived or abridged of their right to speak, to write, or to publish their sentiments; and the freedom of the press, as one of the great bulwarks of liberty, shall be inviolable.

The people shall not be restrained from peaceably assembling and consulting for their common good; nor from applying to the Legislature by petitions, or remonstrances, for redress of their grievances. . . .

Fifthly. That in article 1st, section 10, between clauses 1 and 2, be inserted this clause, to wit: No State shall violate the equal rights of conscience, or the freedom of the press, or the trial by jury in criminal cases. [House of Representatives, June 8, 1789, *Annals*, I, pp. 434-35]

ii

The fourth proposition being under consideration, as follows:

Article 1. Section 9. Between paragraphs two and three insert "no religion shall be established by law, nor shall the equal rights of conscience be infringed." . . .

The next clause of the fourth proposition was taken into consideration, and was as follows: "The freedom of speech and of the press, and the right of the people peaceably to assemble and consult for their common good, and to apply to the Government for redress of grievances, shall not be infringed." . . .

The committee then proceeded to the fifth proposition:

Article 1. Section 10, between the first and second paragraph, insert "no State shall infringe the equal rights of conscience, nor the freedom of speech, or of the press, nor of the right of trial by jury in criminal cases." [House of Representatives, August 15 and 17, 1789, *Annals*, I, pp. 729, 731, 755]

iii

. . . Congress shall make no laws touching religion, or infringing the rights of conscience. [House of Representatives, August 15, 1789, *Annals*, I, p. 731]

iv

Congress shall make no law establishing religion, or to prevent the free exercise thereof, or to infringe the rights of conscience. [House of Representatives, August 20, 1789; *Annals*, I, p. 766]

v

No state shall infringe the right of trial by jury in criminal cases; nor the rights of conscience; nor the freedom of speech or of the press. [House of Representatives, August 21, 1789; *House Journal*, p. 108]

vi

Article the Third. Congress shall make no law establishing Religion, or prohibiting the free exercise thereof, nor shall the rights of conscience be infringed.

Article the Fourth. The freedom of speech and of the press, and the right of the people peaceably to assemble, and consult for their common good, and to apply to the government for redress of grievances, shall not be infringed.

Article the Fourteenth. No State shall infringe the right of trial by Jury in criminal cases, nor the rights of conscience, nor the freedom of speech, or of the press. [House of Representatives, August 24, 1789; *Senate Journal*, pp. 104, 105]

vii

The third article . . . Congress shall make no law establishing religion, or prohibiting the free exercise thereof.

The fourth article . . . That Congress shall make no law abridging the freedom of speech, or of the press, or the right of the people peaceably to assemble and consult for their common good, and to petition the government for a redress of grievances. [Senate, September 3-4, 1789; *History of Congress*, pp. 161-62]

viii

The third article . . . Congress shall make no law establishing articles of faith, or a mode of worship, or prohibiting the free exercise of religion, or abridging the freedom of speech, or the press, or the right of the people peaceably to assemble, and petition to the government for the redress of grievances. [Senate, September 9, 1789; *History of Congress*, p. 167]

ix

The Conventions of a number of the States having, at the time of their adopting the Constitution, expressed a desire, in order to prevent misconstruction or abuse of its powers, that further declaratory and restrictive clauses should be added; and as extending the ground of public confidence in the Government will best insure the beneficent ends of its institutions:

Resolved by the Senate and House of Representatives of the United

States of America in Congress assembled, two-thirds of both Houses concurring that the following articles be proposed to the Legislatures of the several States, as amendments to the Constitution of the United States, all or any of which Articles, when ratified by three fourths of the said Legislatures, to be valid, to all intents and purposes, as part of the said Constitution, viz:

Articles in addition to, and amendment of, the Constitution of the United States of America, proposed by Congress, and ratified by the Legislatures of the several States, pursuant to the fifth Article of the original Constitution. . . .

Article the Third. Congress shall make no law respecting an establishment of religion, or prohibiting the free exercise thereof; or abridging the freedom of speech, or of the press, or the right of the people peaceably to assemble, and to petition the Government for a redress of grievances.
[The First Congress, September 25, 1789; *History of Congress*, pp. 171-72]

APPENDIX B. *SCHENCK* v. *UNITED STATES:*
CIRCULAR AND INDICTMENT

JUSTICE HOLMES, in delivering on March 3, 1919, an opinion for the unanimous Supreme Court of the United States in *Schenck* v. *United States*, 249 U.S. 47, affirming the conviction of two defendants, observed (at 249 U.S. 48-49) that the first count of the indictment

charges a conspiracy to violate the Espionage Act of June 15, 1917, c. 30, § 3, 40 Stat. at L. 217, 219, by causing and attempting to cause insubordination, &c., in the military and naval forces of the United States, and to obstruct the recruiting and enlistment service of the United States, when the United States was at war with the German Empire; to-wit, that the defendants wilfully conspired to have printed and circulated to men who had been called and accepted for military service under the Act of May 18, 1917, a document set forth and alleged to be calculated to cause such insubordination and obstruction. The count alleges overt acts in pursuance of the conspiracy, ending in the distribution of the document set forth.

The document, a circular printed on two sides, was published in about

15,000 copies and partially distributed in August, 1917. Two defendants—the general secretary and recording secretary of the Socialist Party of Philadelphia—were convicted (after a two-day trial) December 20, 1917, in the District Court of the United States for the Eastern District of Pennsylvania. The four other defendants were acquitted (cf. chap. 3, n. 20, below). The two convicted defendants were recommended by the jury to the clemency of the court (cf. chap. 7, n. 77, below). Thus, the sentences, as recorded in the docket entry of the trial court, March 21, 1918, were,

Elizabeth Baer—imprisonment in Philadelphia County Prison for ninety days from this eleventh day of March, 1918, and fine of Five Hundred Dollars and costs of prosecution. Charles T. Schenck—imprisonment in Mercer County Jail, Trenton, N.J., for six months from this eleventh day of March, 1918, and pay costs of prosecution.

The *Brief for the United States* (filed January 2, 1919, in the Supreme Court of the United States) reproduced the principal section of the Espionage Act (of June 15, 1917) upon which the charges were based:

Sec. 3. Whoever, when the United States is at war, shall willfully make or convey false reports or false statements with intent to interfere with the operation or success of the military or naval forces of the United States or to promote the success of its enemies and whoever, when the United States is at war, shall willfully cause or attempt to cause insubordination, disloyalty, mutiny, or refusal of duty, in the military or naval forces of the United States, or shall willfully obstruct the recruiting or enlistment service of the United States, to the injury of the service or of the United States, shall be punished by a fine of not more than $10,000 or imprisonment for not more than twenty years, or both.

It should be noticed, in establishing the context of the *Schenck* case, that Woodrow Wilson was reelected President in November, 1916, by a slim margin, relying upon the slogan, "He kept us out of war." The United States entered the First World War on April 6, 1917, and enacted the Selective Draft Law on May 18, 1917. The war continued until November 11, 1918 (at which time it was driven underground for twenty years or so).

The *Brief for the United States* (which was signed by John Lord O'Brian, as "Special Assistant to the Attorney General for War Work") included, at page 13, the following characterizations of the two sides of the defendants' circular (the italics are the government's):

The unlawful purpose of the defendants is further clearly shown by the text of the circulars. The circular originally had one side printed. That was an attack upon the constitutionality of the draft law, full of bitter language against conscription, as "A conscript is little better than a convict," etc. It did contain an appeal for the repeal of the law. That was not sufficiently strong to satisfy the defendants' purpose. The executive committee resolved "that 15,000 leaflets be written to be printed on the *other side* of the leaflet now in use to be *mailed to men who have passed exemption boards*, also distribution." What was this "other side," which was to be specially mailed to drafted men? It was entitled "Assert Your Rights." It was a frank, bitter, passionate appeal for resistance to the Selective Service Law.

The defendants had said, at pages 14-15 of their *Brief* (filed December 12, 1918, in the Supreme Court; the italics are the defendants'):

Let us look, then, at the circular . . . , the distribution of which through the mails and otherwise was the basis of the prosecution in the case at bar. . . . The unconstitutionality and foolishness of conscription were asserted [in the circular] and people were called upon to assert their constitutional rights.
Both sides of the circular consist largely of quotations from and references to the Constitution. There was no attempt to hide the source of the circular. In fact, readers were urged to go to the Socialist Party Headquarters, 1326 Arch Street, Philadelphia, and *sign a petition to repeal the Conscription Act*. The worst that could be charged against the circular was that it said "A conscript is little better than a convict," and these, according to the Congressional Record, were the exact words used by Mr. Champ Clark in a speech in Congress.

The complete text on both sides of the circular in question is set forth in the pages that follow, as is thereafter the complete text of the indictment filed September 15, 1917. Obvious typographical errors in these documents have been corrected.

[THE CIRCULAR]
ASSERT YOUR RIGHTS!

Article 6, Section 2, of the Constitution of the United States says: "This Constitution shall be the *supreme law of the Land.*"

Article 1 (Amendment) says: "Congress shall make no law respecting an establishment of religion, or *prohibiting the free exercise thereof.*"

Article 9 (Amendment) says: "The enumeration in the Constitution of certain rights, shall not be construed to deny or disparage others retained by the people."

The Socialist Party says that any individual or officers of the law entrusted with the administration of conscription regulations, violate the provisions of the United States Constitution, the Supreme Law of the Land, when they refuse to recognize your right to assert your opposition to the draft.

If you are conscientiously opposed to war, if you believe in the commandment "thou shalt not kill," then that is your religion, and you shall not be prohibited from the free exercise thereof.

In exempting clergymen and members of the Society of Friends (popularly called Quakers) from active military service, the examination boards have discriminated against you.

If you do not assert and support your rights, you are helping to "deny or disparage rights" which it is the solemn duty of all citizens and residents of the United States to retain.

Here in this city of Philadelphia was signed the immortal Declaration of Independence. As a citizen of "the cradle of American Liberty" you are doubly charged with the duty of upholding the rights of the people.

Will you let cunning politicians and a mercenary capitalist press wrongly and untruthfully mould your thoughts? Do not forget your right to elect officials who are opposed to conscription.

In lending tacit or silent consent to the conscription law, in neglecting to assert your rights, you are (whether unknowingly or not) helping to condone and support a most infamous and insidious conspiracy to abridge and destroy the sacred and cherished rights of a free people. YOU ARE A CITIZEN, NOT A SUBJECT! You delegate your power to the officers of the law to be used for your good and welfare, not against you.

They are your servants. Not your masters. Their wages come from the expenses of government WHICH YOU PAY. Will you allow them to unjustly rule you? The fathers who fought and bled to establish a free and independent nation here in America were so opposed to the militarism of the old world from which they had escaped; so keenly alive to the dangers and hardships they had undergone in fleeing from political, religious and military oppression, that they handed down to us "certain rights which must be retained by the people."

They held the spirit of militarism in such abhorrence and hate, they were so apprehensive of the formation of a military machine that would insidiously and secretly advocate the invasion of other lands, that they limited the power of Congress over the militia in providing only for the calling forth of "the militia to execute laws of the Union, suppress insurrections and repel invasions." (See general powers of Congress, Article 1, Section 8, Paragraph 15.)

No power was delegated to send our citizens away to foreign shores to shoot up the people of other lands, no matter what may be their internal or international disputes.

THE PEOPLE OF THIS COUNTRY DID NOT VOTE IN FAVOR OF WAR. AT THE LAST ELECTION THEY VOTED AGAINST WAR.

To draw this country into the horrors of the present war in Europe, to force the youth of our land into the shambles and bloody trenches of war-crazy nations, would be a crime the magnitude of which defies description. Words could not express the condemnation such cold-blooded ruthlessness deserves.

Will you stand idly by and see the Moloch of Militarism reach forth across the sea and fasten its tentacles upon this continent? Are you willing to submit to the degradation of having the Constitution of the United States treated as a "mere scrap of paper?"

Do you know that patriotism means a love for your country and not hate for others?

Will you be led astray by a propaganda of jingoism masquerading under the guise of patriotism?

No specious or plausible pleas about a "war of democracy" can becloud the issue. Democracy cannot be shot into a nation. It must come spontaneously and purely from within.

Democracy must come through liberal education. Upholders of military ideas are unfit teachers.

To advocate the persecution of other peoples through the prosecution of war is an insult to every good and wholesome American tradition.

"These are the times that try men's souls."

"Eternal vigilance is the price of liberty."

You are responsible. You must do your share to maintain, support and uphold the rights of the people of this country.

IN THIS WORLD CRISIS WHERE DO YOU STAND? ARE YOU WITH THE FORCES OF LIBERTY AND LIGHT OR WAR AND DARKNESS?

(OVER)

LONG LIVE THE CONSTITUTION OF THE UNITED STATES
Wake Up, America! Your Liberties Are in Danger!

The 13th Amendment, Section 1, of the Constitution of the United States says: "Neither slavery nor involuntary servitude, except as a punishment for crime whereof the party shall have been duly convicted, shall exist within the United States, or any place subject to their jurisdiction."

The Constitution of the United States is one of the greatest bulwarks of political liberty. It was born after a long, stubborn battle between king-rule and democracy. (We see little or no difference between arbitrary power under the name of a king and under a few misnamed "representatives.") In this battle the people of the United States established the principle that freedom of the individual and personal liberty are the most sacred things in life. Without them we become slaves.

For this principle the fathers fought and died. The establishment of this principle they sealed with their own blood. Do you want to see this principle abolished? Do you want to see despotism substituted in its stead? Shall we prove degenerate sons of illustrious sires?

The Thirteenth Amendment to the Constitution of the United States, quoted above, embodies this sacred idea. The Socialist Party says that this idea is violated by the Conscription Act. When you conscript a man and compel him to go abroad to fight against his will, you violate the most sacred right of personal liberty, and substitute for it what Daniel Webster called "despotism in its worst form."

A conscript is little better than a convict. He is deprived of his liberty and of his right to think and act as a free man. A conscripted citizen is forced to surrender his right as a citizen and become a subject. He is forced into involuntary servitude. He is deprived of the protection given him by the Constitution of the United States. He is deprived of all freedom of conscience in being forced to kill against his will.

Are you one who is opposed to war, and were you misled by the venal capitalist newspapers, or intimidated or deceived by gang politicians and registrars into believing that you would not be allowed to register your objection to conscription? Do you know that many citizens of Philadelphia insisted on their right to answer the famous question twelve, and went on record with their honest opinion of opposition to war, notwithstanding the deceitful efforts of our rulers and the newspaper press to prevent them from doing so? Shall it be said that the citizens of Philadelphia, the cradle of American liberty, are so lost to a sense of right and justice that they will let such monstrous wrongs against humanity go unchallenged?

In a democratic country each man must have the right to say whether he is willing to join the army. Only in countries where uncontrolled power rules can a despot force his subjects to fight. Such a man or men have no place in a democratic republic. This is tyrannical power in its worst form. It gives control over the life and death of the individual to a few men. There is no man good enough to be given such power.

Conscription laws belong to a bygone age. Even the people of Germany, long suffering under the yoke of militarism, are beginning to demand the abolition of conscription. Do you think it has a place in the United States? Do you want to see unlimited power handed over to Wall Street's chosen few in America? If you do not, join the Socialist Party in its campaign for the repeal of the Conscription Act. Write to your congressman and tell him you want the law repealed. Do not submit to intimidation. You have a right to demand the repeal of any law. Exercise your rights of free speech, peaceful assemblage and petitioning the government for a redress of grievances. Come to the headquarters of the Socialist Party, 1326 Arch Street, and sign a petition to congress for the repeal of the Conscription Act. Help us wipe out this stain upon the Constitution!

HELP US RE-ESTABLISH DEMOCRACY IN AMERICA.
REMEMBER, "ETERNAL VIGILANCE IS THE PRICE OF LIBERTY."
DOWN WITH AUTOCRACY!
LONG LIVE THE CONSTITUTION OF THE UNITED STATES! LONG LIVE THE REPUBLIC!

Books on Socialism for Sale at
SOCIALIST PARTY BOOK STORE AND HEADQUARTERS
1326 ARCH ST. Phone, Filbert 3121

[THE INDICTMENT]

District Court of the United States, Eastern District of
Pennsylvania, June Sessions, 1917
No. 111.
UNITED STATES OF AMERICA
vs.
CHARLES T. SCHENCK, CHARLES SEHL, ELIZABETH BAER, JACOB H. ROOT
AND WILLIAM J. HIGGINS.
Indictment.
Filed Sept. 15, 1917.

Count 1.

The Grand Inquest of the United States of America, inquiring in and for the Eastern District of Pennsylvania, upon their respective oaths and affirmations, respectively do present, that heretofore, to wit, on August 13, 1917, at Philadelphia, in the Eastern District of Pennsylvania, and on divers dates thereafter, Charles T. Schenck, Charles Sehl, Elizabeth Baer, Jacob H. Root and William J. Higgins (hereinafter called the defendants) did knowingly, wilfully and unlawfully conspire together and with other persons to this Grand Inquest unknown, to violate certain provisions of Section 3 of Title I of an Act of Congress, approved June 15th, 1917, entitled "An Act to punish acts of interference with the foreign relations, the neutrality, and the foreign commerce of the United States, to punish espionage, and better to enforce the criminal laws of the United States and for other purposes," to wit: when the United States was at war did wilfully cause and attempt to cause insubordination, disloyalty, mutiny and refusal of duty in the military and naval forces of the United States and to obstruct the recruiting and enlistment service of the United States, to the injury of the United States, to wit: when the United States was at war with the German Empire, they did wilfully conspire to have printed and circulated copies of the following circular, to wit:

[Here follows the reproduction of both sides of the circular.]

to men who had been called and accepted for military service under the provisions of the Act of May 18, 1917, which said circular was calculated, when so distributed, to cause insubordination, disloyalty, mutiny and refusal of duty in the said military and naval forces of the United States and to obstruct the recruiting and enlistment service of the United States, to the injury of the United States.

And, thereafter, in order to effect the object of the said conspiracy:

1. On, to wit: August 13, 1917, at Philadelphia aforesaid, the said defendants, as members of the Executive Committee of the Socialist Party, did, at a meeting of the said Committee adopt a resolution of the following nature, to wit:

"M. and S. [Moved and Seconded] 15000 leaflets to be written to be printed on the other side of leaflet—now in use—to be mailed to men who have passed the exemption board, also distribution.

"M. and S. Secretary get bids on price of leaflets."

2. On, to wit: August 20, 1917, at Philadelphia aforesaid, at a further meeting of the said Executive Committee the said defendants did join in approving the minutes of the aforesaid meeting held August 13, 1917, wherein the resolution aforesaid was set forth as moved and seconded and did provide for the taking of certain action in furtherance of the aforesaid resolution, to wit:

"M. and S. That Comrade Schenck be authorized to spend $125. for sending leaflets through the mail. Carried."

3. On, to wit: August 16, 1917, at Philadelphia aforesaid, the said Charles J. Schenck, pursuant to the said resolution of August 13, 1917, did direct the printing of the circular aforesaid, and did direct the purchase of stamped envelopes for the purpose of distributing the said circulars through the mails;

4. On, to wit: August 18, 1917, and on divers dates thereafter, the said Charles J. Schenck, at Philadelphia aforesaid, did distribute and cause to be distributed the aforesaid circulars, together with stamped envelopes, to persons whose names are to this Grand Inquest unknown, entering on the premises at 1326 Arch Street, Philadelphia, which said premises constitute the headquarters of the Socialist Party in Philadelphia.

5. On, to wit: August 20, 1917, and on divers dates thereafter, the said

Charles J. Schenck, at Philadelphia aforesaid, did distribute and cause to be distributed the aforesaid circulars, together with stamped envelopes, to persons whose names are to this Grand Inquest unknown, entering on the premises of 1326 Arch Street, Philadelphia, which said premises constitute the headquarters of the Socialist Party in Philadelphia, and for the purpose of having the said circulars mailed to men who had been called and accepted for military service: contrary to the form of the Act of Congress in such case made and provided and against the peace and dignity of the United States of America.

Count 2.

And the Grand Inquest aforesaid, inquiring as aforesaid, upon their respective oaths and affirmations, as aforesaid, do further present that heretofore, to wit: on August 13, 1917, at Philadelphia, in the Eastern District of Pennsylvania, Charles T. Schenck, Charles Sehl, Elizabeth Baer, Jacob H. Root and William J. Higgins (hereinafter called the defendants) did knowingly, wilfully and unlawfully conspire to commit an offense against the United States: to wit: to use and attempt to use the mails and postal service of the United States for the transmission of matter declared to be nonmailable by Section 2 of Title XII of an Act of Congress, approved June 15, 1917, entitled "An act to punish acts of interference with the foreign relations, the neutrality, and the foreign commerce of the United States, to punish espionage, and better to enforce the criminal laws of the United States, and for other purposes," to wit: certain circulars which were in violation of Section 3 of Title I of said act, in that they were calculated to cause insubordination, disloyalty, mutiny and refusal of duty in the military and naval forces of the United States and to obstruct the recruiting and enlistment service of the United States, to the injury of the United States, and which said circulars were in effect, as follows, to wit:

[Here, again, follows the reproduction of both sides of the circular.]

And, thereafter, in order to effect the object of the said conspiracy:

1. On, to wit: August 13, 1917, at Philadelphia aforesaid, the said defendants, as members of the Executive Committee of the Socialist Party, did, at a meeting of the said committee, adopt a resolution of the following nature, to wit:

"M. and S. 15000 leaflets to be written to be printed on the other side of leaflet—now in use—to be mailed to men who have passed the exemption board, also distribution."

"M. and S. Secretary get bids on price of leaflets."

2. On, to wit: August 20, 1917, at Philadelphia aforesaid, at a further

meeting of the said executive committee the said defendants did join in approving the minutes of the aforesaid meeting held on August 13, 1917, wherein the resolution aforesaid was set forth as moved and seconded and did provide for the taking of certain action in furtherance of the aforesaid resolution, to wit:

"M. and S. that Comrade Schenck be authorized to spend $125 for sending leaflets through the mail. Carried."

3. On, to wit: August 16, 1917, at Philadelphia aforesaid, the said Charles T. Schenck, pursuant to the said resolution of August 13, 1917, did direct the printing of the circular aforesaid and did direct the purchase of stamped envelopes for the purpose of distributing the said circulars through the mails;

4. On, to wit: August 18, 1917, and on divers dates thereafter, the said Charles T. Schenck, at Philadelphia aforesaid, did distribute and cause to be distributed the aforesaid circulars, together with stamped envelopes, for the mailing of the said circulars to persons whose names are to this Grand Inquest unknown, entering on the premises at 1326 Arch Street, Philadelphia, which said premises constitute the headquarters of the Socialist Party in Philadelphia;

5. On, to wit: August 20, 1917, and on divers dates thereafter, did distribute and cause to be distributed the aforesaid circulars, together with stamped envelopes, to persons whose names are to this Grand Inquest unknown, entering on the premises of 1326 Arch Street, Philadelphia, which said premises constitute the headquarters of the Socialist Party in Philadelphia, for the purpose of having the said circulars mailed to men who had been called and accepted for military service:

Contrary to the form of the Act of Congress in such case made and provided and against the peace and dignity of the United States of America.

Count 3.

And the Grand Inquest aforesaid, inquiring as aforesaid, upon their oaths and affirmations as aforesaid, do further present that heretofore, to wit: on August 20, 1917, at Philadelphia aforesaid, the said Charles T. Schenck, Charles Sehl, Elizabeth Baer, Jacob H. Root and William J. Higgins (hereinafter called the defendants) did knowingly, wilfully and unlawfully use and attempt to use the mails and postal service of the United States for the transmission of mail matter declared to be nonmailable by Title XII of an Act of Congress, approved June 15, 1917, entitled "An Act to punish acts of interference with the foreign relations, the neutrality, and the foreign commerce of the United States, to punish espionage and better to enforce the criminal laws of the United States, and for other purposes," to wit: certain circulars of the following tenor, to wit:

[Here, again, follows the reproduction of both sides of the circular.]

in that the said defendants did wilfully authorize and direct the said Charles T. Schenck to have printed the aforesaid circulars and to expend the sum of $125, for sending said circulars through the mail to men passed by the exemption boards and which said circulars were non-mailable in that they were in violation of the provisions of Section 3, of Title I, of the aforesaid Act of June 15, 1917, in that said circulars were calculated to cause insubordination, disloyalty, mutiny and refusal of duty in the military and naval forces of the United States, and to obstruct the recruiting and enlistment service of the United States, to the injury of the United States: contrary to the form of the Act of Congress in such case made and provided and against the peace and dignity of the United States of America.

(Sgd.) FRANCIS FISHER KANE,
United States Attorney
Philadelphia, Pa., 4 September, A. D. 1917.

Justice Holmes's extended description, in his *Schenck* opinion, of the contents of both sides of defendants' circular is instructive. (Cf. chap. 3, nn. 22, 28, below.) He then went on to say for the court, at 249 U.S. 51-52:

... Of course the document [the circular] would not have been sent unless it had been intended to have some effect, and we do not see what effect it could be expected to have upon persons subject to the draft except to influence them to obstruct the carrying of it out. The defendants do not deny that the jury might find against them on this point.

But it is said, suppose that that was the tendency of the circular, it is protected by the First Amendment to the Constitution. Two of the strongest expressions are said to be quoted respectively from well-known public men. It well may be that the prohibition of laws abridging the freedom of speech is not confined to previous restraints, although to prevent them may have been the main purpose, as intimated in *Patterson* v. *Colorado*, 205 U.S. 454, 462 [1907]. We admit that in many places and in ordinary times the defendants in saying all that was said in the circular would have been within their constitutional rights. But the character of every act depends upon the circumstances in which it is done. *Aikens* v. *Wisconsin*, 195 U.S. 194, 205, 206. [1904] The most stringent protection of free speech would not protect a man in falsely shouting fire in a theatre and causing a panic. It does not even protect a man from an injunction against uttering words that may have all the effect of force. *Gompers* v. *Bucks Stove & Range Co.,* 221 U.S. 418, 439 [1911]. The question in every case is whether the words used are used in such circumstances and are of such a nature as to create a clear and present danger that they will bring about the substantive evils that Congress has a right to prevent. It is a question of proximity and degree. When a nation is at war many things that might be said in time of peace are such a hindrance to its effort that their utterance will not be endured so long as men fight and that no court could regard them as protected by any constitutional right. It seems to be admitted that if an actual obstruction of the recruiting service were proved, liability for words that produced that effect mght be enforced. The statute of 1917 in § 4 punishes conspiracies to obstruct as well as actual obstruction. If the act, (speaking, or circulating a paper,) its tendency and the intent with which it is done are the same, we perceive no ground for saying that success alone warrants making the act a crime. *Goldman* v. *United States,* 245 U.S. 474, 477 [1918]. Indeed that case might be said to dispose of the present contention if the precedent covers all *media concludendi.* But as the right to free speech was not referred to specially, we have thought fit to add a few words.

The Selective Draft Law (of May 18, 1917) had been upheld as constitutional on January 7, 1918. *Selective Draft Law Cases,* 245 U.S. 366 (1918).
Cf. *United States* v. *Spock,* 416 F.2d 165 (1969). Appended to these opinions, at 416 F.2d 192-93, is the *Spock* case defendants' "circular," "A Call to Resist Illegitimate Authority."

APPENDIX C. DUE PROCESS AND THE WORLD OF COMMERCE

I WAS ELECTED in 1964 to a three-year term on the nine-man Board of Directors of the ten-thousand-member Hyde Park Cooperative Society of Chicago, "running" on the following platform:

My family has enjoyed for more than a decade the facilities and services of the Co-op, regarding it as more than an ordinary commercial enterprise. I felt an obligation, as a member of the Society, to consent to stand as a candidate for the Board, when called upon by your nominating committee.
 I am sure that the other candidates are as qualified as I to serve. Indeed, most of the others probably know more than I about Co-op operations. I can, therefore, do no more than express my willingness to serve as a member of the Board if elected and, in that capacity, to exercise care, imagination and (I hope) intelligence in the conduct of the affairs of the Society.

Two of the four documents which follow were written by me as a member of the Board of Directors of the Society, the other two before and after this service on the Board. All four documents are reproduced in their entirety. The circumstances bearing on each document are evident therein.

The intimate relation between due process and freedom of speech is examined above in chapters 5 and 8. See also chap. 4, n. 33, below.

---

1. A Statement to the Membership of the Hyde Park Cooperative Society, June 10, 1966:

Everybody involved in the deliberations respecting the proposed boycott of Di Giorgio products agreed that the life of migrant farm workers in America is miserable, that decent men cannot help but be sympathetic to efforts to help them, that the National Farm Workers Association is conducting a strike in California against the Di Giorgio Corporation, that the company has offered to conduct an election among its employees, that the union has protested against conditions set by the company and has refused to agree to this election.

At this point unanimity ended, but it was precisely at this point that the duty of the Hyde Park Cooperative Society Board of Directors began. For the Board is obliged under the terms of the 1959 membership mandate, "to determine the legitimacy of the strike" before instructing the manager to remove struck goods from the shelves. The membership mandate implicitly recognizes that some strikes may be illegitimate, that some strikes are unfair and should not be supported by the Society. Presumably, the Board would want to consider legitimacy and fairness, mandate or no mandate, before acting against anyone involved in a controversy.

If the union's view of the facts is accepted, we have here a campaign of coercion and exploitation on the part of the company. If the company's view of the facts is accepted, we have here a campaign of intimidation and usurpation on the part of the union. The Board decided at its special meeting of June 2 that it did not have sufficient evidence to decide between the contending parties. (No dissent was recorded.) The Board also decided to accept my suggestion that announcements be posted by the products in question and that the claims of the union and the company be made available to consumers who would thereupon decide, presumably on the basis of what they know or believe they know about such matters, whether to buy these products. The Board at the same time initiated attempts to secure from relatively disinterested third parties as well as from the contending parties additional evidence bearing on this particular dispute. The good faith of the Board had been evident throughout.

The Board decided at its special meeting of June 8 to withdraw the company's goods from the shelves. (One dissent [my own] was recorded.) The only development of significance since the earlier decision was the vigorous campaign on behalf of the boycott [including their unilateral removal of goods from shelves] by a handful of well-intentioned members: the Board knew nothing essentially new about the merits of the controversy on June 8th that it did not know on June 2nd. It has been argued that we have under the mandate no discretion in such matters as this. It has also been argued that we cannot use standards of due process in arriving at our decisions in such matters. If these arguments are valid then we as a Board acting for the Society probably have no business judging and thereby coercing our suppliers with respect to matters not within our competence to judge properly.

I do believe we should do what we can to help migrant farm workers in this country. I have proposed actions by the Board, to be considered in the months ahead, that would go much further to help migrants than does the uninformed boycott of a particular supplier. I am prepared to support actions based on what we do know as citizens and consumers. When we intervene in a particular controversy, on the other hand, we are apt to find ourselves in the difficult, if not impossible, position of trying to adjudicate without the proper facilities between plausible contenders.

Everyone of us would want his own case in any controversy judged more objectively than the Board was equipped to judge on this occasion. It is easy and perhaps even natural to a partisan to brush general principles aside and to dismiss an advocacy of objectivity and due process as either naive or callous. But on this issue, too, the other side should be given its due.

My argument in this statement was not intended as a commentary on the propriety of a general boycott, such as with respect to all California grapes, which may or may not raise the problems discussed here. One of the actions I proposed to the Board of Directors as an alternative to an "uninformed boycott of a particular supplier" was that the Hyde Park Cooperative Society periodically donate from its substantial profits, to union organizers of migrant farm workers, whatever the board determined to be the difference between what Co-op customers pay for the products processed by migrant farm workers and what they would pay if migrant farm workers were paid what the board considered to be a decent wage. This proposal, which I continue to believe is constructive, has never been acted upon, so far as I know.

2. A Letter to the President of the Hyde Park Cooperative Society, October 31, 1966:

I hereby confirm my resignation from the Board of Directors of the Hyde Park Cooperative Society. I observed at the October 24th meeting of the Board that I would be obliged to resign if the lie detector tests for our employees approved on that occasion were carried out. I learned today that such tests began a few days ago.

I appreciate why the Board of Directors thought it necessary to take this step, and even why some of the employees who might be considered under suspicion would want to be "cleared" in this manner. I know how reluctant the Board was to approve this innovation and how concerned it was about the possible adverse effect on our insurance contracts of its refusal to so approve.

I still think, however, that the Board has lost its sense of proportion. The Co-op has for some time been losing much more each month in merchandise pilferage than the two thousand dollars in cash that has evidently been stolen since August and for the sake of which lie detectors are now being used. I realize that it is particularly disturbing to have to suspect misconduct by trusted employees. But we have long realized that some of the pilferage, which is inevitable in a store as large as ours, could be traced to employee misconduct. There is nothing in this new situation to require such potentially disruptive measures as the use of lie detectors.

The measure adopted does not seem to me consistent with the style of the Society. (Ours is a finer style, I should add, than that reflected in the rabble-rousing we saw employed so effectively against the Board at the Semi-Annual Membership Meeting of October 26th.) I recognize that there may be grave occasions on which lie detectors (and even more objectionable devices and methods) might legitimately be used. But this is not such an occasion. I cannot help but recall that decent and yet successful men managed their affairs, and protected themselves against theft as well as we are ever likely to do, before such dubious devices became available. No doubt, the other members of the Board know as well as I do the arguments against the use of lie detectors. These arguments are not met by going through the ritual of calling the cooperation requested of employees "voluntary."

I do hope it is not a mere difference of opinion that has moved me to resign. I have been able heretofore to accept other Board decisions to which I could not at all agree. Thus, I questioned the decision in June to remove a supplier's products from our shelves without (to my mind) an adequate showing to us of "the legitimacy of the strike"; I questioned the choice of location for the new furniture store, and even the preference of an imported furniture store to a first-rate bookstore for this community; I questioned the decision that there should be Sunday openings for the proposed furniture store.

But there is something about the character of the decision to use lie detectors on our own employees, supported as it is by the Board's insistence upon having to be "realistic" in operating the Co-op as a "business," that persuaded me that my greatest service to the Society at this time would be to disassociate myself in this way from what the Board is doing. There is nothing I can contribute as a Board member to the running of a successful business that others cannot provide at least as well as I during the remaining year of my term of office.

Should the lie detector use become the divisive issue among the membership that I warned against, I think it would be useful to both the Society and the Board to release in its entirety this explanation of my resignation. The Board of Directors as I know it is certainly better than the well-organized minority of vociferous, even professional, critics among the membership who will welcome this issue as still another excuse for self-righteous attacks upon the Board. Indeed, this letter of explanation would not be complete without the observation that I would have hesitated much longer before retiring from the post to which I was elected if I did not have such a high opinion of the business skills and dedication of the members of the Board.

The recourse to the use of lie detectors was approved at an executive meeting of the Board of Directors of the society. I chose to resign from the board partly because I could not at that time, because of the confidential nature of an executive meeting, disassociate myself from this decision publicly. Since then, however, the membership of the Board of Directors has changed completely and information about this episode is more generally available.

The lie detectors, as it turned out, did not disclose anything useful except that it is far easier for employers to be "principled" about another's employees (so far away as California) than about their own.

---

3. A letter to the editor, published in the *University of Chicago Maroon,* January 18, 1962:

Would not the cause of racial integration in the United States be nobly served by establishing around the University of Chicago a stable integrated community? And, considering the marked tendency generally in this city toward segregated communities (either Negro or white), must not special efforts be made to preserve Hyde Park as both Negro and white?

If the answers to these questions should be in the affirmative, the University's housing policy [of utilizing racial quotas in its rental properties] may not be as absurd, shocking or immoral as you have made it out to be. This is not to suggest that the [University] administration is best able to explain and defend its policy. Nor do I suggest that the University's policy should not be carefully examined periodically to reassure us that its objective remains just and its means decent.

See also chap. 4, n. 26, below.

4. A letter to the editor, published in the *Hyde Park Herald*, Chicago, Illinois, October 4, 1967:

> It is only natural that people with long memories should not want in any way to do business with Roy M. Cohn or any of the other accomplices of the late Senator Joseph R. McCarthy.
> The practical intent of this attitude is to deny Mr. Cohn an opportunity to engage in any business or profession which may be immediately dependent upon the public. Indeed, I understand that enough people have been of this persuasion to affect significantly Mr. Cohn's investment in the University National Bank [in Chicago's Hyde Park].
> It is characteristic of such a boycott that no suggestion need be made that Mr. Cohn continues to hold the political opinions he held more than a decade ago. Nor is there any serious attempt made to show that his political opinions (whatever they may now be) affect his competence or reliability as a vendor of the services he offers the public.
> We see in the campaign against Mr. Cohn the implicit disparagement of one critical safeguard against popular tyranny that was preserved even in the worst days of Sen. McCarthy, the recourse the politically-harassed citizen has had to the world of business. To carry our political vendettas into the realm of money-making reinforces the effects of government repression.
> Americans should be discouraged from establishing such precedents. We need to be reminded, instead, of the vital contribution to political and personal liberty that is made among us by the right to buy and sell freely and thereafter to keep and develop the property one has lawfully acquired. This right is a refuge to which any one of us may have to repair as times change. The realization that there is such a refuge makes our politics far less desperate than they would otherwise be.
> In short, we should restrain the natural but short-sighted desire "to get in our licks" when we can. We should, that is, resist the temptation to act as Mr. Cohn did in the days of his youth.

APPENDIX D. CONSPIRACY AND THE JUDGE: A TRIAL IN CHICAGO

I LOOKED IN, between September 1969 and February 1970, upon an average of two to three sessions a week in the Federal District Court of *U. S. v. Dellinger* (the so-called "Chicago Eight Conspiracy Trial"). One result of my attendance at the trial was an article in the *Chicago Sun-Times* of February 22, 1970 (sec. 2, p. 12). Since my article had to be fitted into the full page of the *Sun-Times* devoted to it, passages were cut out of it which I have restored in the reproduction below. (This has been reprinted in vol. 116 of the *Congressional Record* at p. E2420 [March 24, 1970].)

Five defendants were found guilty by a Chicago jury (on February 18, 1970) of having crossed state lines with the intention of inciting a riot during the August 1968 Democratic National Convention in Chicago. Each of the five convicted defendants was sentenced (on February 20) to five years imprisonment and fined five thousand dollars (as well as the costs of prosecution, which have been assessed as $41,748.60). Eight defendants and their lawyers in this federal trial were sentenced for contempt after having been pronounced guilty by Judge Julius J. Hoffman of courtroom behavior intended to disrupt the orderly administration of justice. One of the defendants (Bobby G. Seale) was sentenced for contempt on November 5, 1969, the other seven defendants and their two lawyers on February 14-15, 1970. The contempt sentences ranged from two months and eighteen days for defendant John R. Froines to four years and thirteen days for defense counsel William M. Kunstler. (The other trial lawyer for the defense was Leonard Weinglass; the other defendants were David Dellinger, Rennard Davis, Thomas Hayden, Abbott Hoffman, Jerry Rubin, and Lee Weiner.)

None of the participants in this prosecution conducted themselves as they should have. The government was the victim of its unbridled indignation, the defendants of their sentimental self-indulgence, and the judge (like Mayor Daley during August, 1968) of his injudicious vanity. But a fairminded critic of the defendants would have to recognize in them at least a perverse gallantry. Thus, there was in the Conspiracy Trial much that seemed a replay, in slow motion, of what happened in Chicago during Convention Week, with the same questionable behavior on the part of *all* the principal parties involved in both "confrontations." But in the final analysis, what was said by three English newspapermen in reporting on police behavior during Convention Week can be applied (with appropriate adjustments) to official behavior during the Conspiracy Trial as well:

Police violence is always sickening. But what distinguished the police action in Chicago from anything previously seen by members of our reporting team—whose collective experience covered riots in Paris, Belfast, Berlin, Calcutta, New York, Cleveland, and Detroit—was not simply its ferocity: it was the fact that the police went, quite literally, berserk.

(This quotation is from Lewis Chester, Godfrey Hodgson, and Bruce Page, *An American Melodrama: The Presidential Campaign of 1968* [New York: Viking Press, 1969], pp. 581-82.)

The lessons to be drawn from the colossal blunders of both Convention Week and the Conspiracy Trial include those indicated in the case study, "Chicago and Washington—A Tale of Two Cities," prepared by Joseph R. Sahid for the National Commission on the Causes and Prevention of Violence and published in the Commission's Staff Report, *Law and Order Reconsidered* (Washington: U. S. Government Printing Office, 1969), at pages 343, 351:

Two cities—Washington and Chicago—each recently experienced two major demonstrations. In Chicago, anti-war activities occurred on April 27, 1968, and at the Democratic National Convention in August [1968]. The March on the Pentagon in October 1968 and the counter-inaugural activities in January 1969 occupied Washington authorities. These demonstrations were organized by many of the same groups and attended by many of the same people. The Convention and the counter-inaugural activities involved about the same number of protestors and centered around major national events.

Yet the results of these events were markedly different. In Chicago, large-scale violence marred both activities. The violence in Washington, on the other hand, was minimal. The almost laboratory-like conditions afforded by the Democratic Convention and Inaugural protest activities prompted us to examine these two demonstrations in detail. We have concluded that the amount of violence that occurred during these demonstrations was directly related to the type of official response that greeted them. More specifically, repressive measures proved self-defeating: when officials decided to "get tough," chaos rather than order resulted. . . . Fruitful lessons can be learned from this comparison [of Chicago and Washington]. The encouragement of First Amendment rights, coordination and cooperation with protest leaders, education of the police and the larger community into viewing peaceful demonstrations as a matter of right, will usually lead, at least at this point in our nation's history, to obtaining the cooperation of the great majority of those who have gathered to protest.

We do not mean to suggest that mass protest gatherings are static—that tactics should be identical as time passes and issues and personalities change. The actions of the "Weathermen," an extremist fringe which engaged in offensive violence in Chicago in October, 1969, illustrate the danger in generalizations of any sort. Rather, the point is that in the area of mass demonstrations, where we all have so much to learn, it makes sense for those in authority to proceed cautiously, to avoid becoming rigid in outlook, and to employ force carefully.

The Anti-Riot Act of 1968, under which this case was brought, may be found in chap. 6, n. 75, below. My newspaper article on the case was reproduced as a paid advertisement by four downstate Illinois lawyers (Kevin Kelly, Craig Armstrong, Louis Olivero, and Leo Schwamberger) in the February 27, 1970, issue of the *Daily News-Tribune* (of LaSalle-Peru-Oglesby-Spring Valley, Illinois). They included, in their own preface to my article, such comments as these:

. . . We don't pretend, as did the President of the Illinois Bar Association, Mr. Henry Pitts, without having attended the many sessions of the trial, to pass judgment against the defendants or the defense lawyers, but we do say we understand the predicament and position of any defendant and any defense lawyer, to be forced to try a case before a hostile, vindictive, prejudiced judge. (In the federal courts, one is not entitled to a change of venue as a matter of right.) We do emphatically say that Mr. Anastaplo's point that there is a means of discipline and punishment for a litigant, for a lawyer, but practically speaking, no means of discipline for the trial judge, is well taken. . . . We do believe that there was some improper conduct by all the principals in the case. We do know the meaning of appearing before such judges, who thank God, are in the minority. We call attention to the underlying forces which were exemplified by the defendants, the active revulsion of millions of young people against a system that denied true democratic process in the selection of a presidential candidate in 1968. As the opposing candidate, President Nixon, an astute observer and politician, so clearly stated in the summer of 1968, McCarthy had the grass root support of the people but the party politicians wanted Humphrey and Humphrey would be nominated. . . . We understand the active protest and revulsion of the young people of this country against the continuous prosecution of the Viet Nam Conflict, the most futile and foolish war in history. . . . We understand the protest and revulsion of millions of young people against the deplorable deprivation of opportunity, educational, economic and cultural of about 15% of our population. . . . We call attention to our belief that the only conspiracy of which the defendants were, indeed, guilty, was a conspiracy to prevent the rape of democracy by Mayor Daley and the other willing servants of Establishment control, that is, by the vested interests of great wealth.

When four experienced and successful lawyers, in an Illinois farming area, are moved to adopt such opinions, it suggests that something may really be wrong with the country. When they feel free to publish such opinions, to pay for their promulgation, and to sign their names to them, it suggests what is right with the country.

My *Chicago Sun-Times* article of February 22, 1970, follows:

The verdict of the Conspiracy Trial jury was surprisingly discriminating. It not only completely exonerated two of the defendants, it also repudiated, with respect to all the defendants, the conspiracy charges of which so much had been made by the government. A conviction or acquittal on all counts of the indictment could have been explained away as merely the result of passion. But this particular verdict happens to ratify the impression of many courtroom observers of the trial, that there was no deliberate conspiracy among these defendants, that the most that could be charged to some of them was the making of irresponsible speeches on certain occasions during Convention Week.

Thus, the offenses for which this jury convicted five defendants—crossing state lines with the intent of inciting a riot—were not the offenses for which these defendants were really brought to trial as a group by the United States attorney. The offenses for which defendants were convicted were of the kind that are most efficiently disposed of in police court, after a trial of a few hours or (at most) a few days. The jury verdict, properly understood, shows up the federal government's case to have been an irresponsible attempt to vindicate in the federal courts the "police riot" with which our city government (exploiting our much-abused police) made such a mess of the crisis confronting it during Convention Week. This willingness by the federal government to allow its courts to be used for such political purpose has cost us dearly: it has undermined the trust of a significant part of our community, especially among the young, in the integrity of our judicial institutions; it has sustained unhealthy passions in other parts of our community against serious dissent.

It is now clear, not only from the verdict of the jury but even more from the evidence presented in this case by the government, that defendants John Froines, Bobby G. Seale and Lee Weiner should never have been included in the indictment on any count. It is also clear that a conscientious prosecutor should have moved to discharge at least these three defendants once his evidence and his conspiracy theory had been disclosed to be as flimsy as they were.

Without a conspiracy theory, there would have been no justification for bringing the eight defendants into court together. Without a conspiracy theory, there would have been a much shorter and far less expensive trial. Without a conspiracy theory, there would have been no circus atmosphere, no serious or sustained disruptive events, no spectacle of a defendant being bound and gagged for stubbornly (even if improperly) insisting on counsel of his choice. In short, there would not have been these disgraceful proceedings masquerading as a trial in federal court. The insistence of the government upon adhering to its disastrous conspiracy theory, without any substantial evidence to back it up, was not in the best tradition of responsible prosecution. It was simply asking for trouble—and it got it, something for which we the American people may have to pay for a long time to come.

It is now up to the appellate courts to review a rather questionable (and certainly mischievous) statute for its constitutionality and to assess whatever relevant evidence there is for its adequacy, especially since so many of the judge's rulings and attitudes left doubts about whether the defendants were permitted to make the case which they were entitled to make. One must wonder, furthermore, whether the discredited conspiracy approach, having opened the door as it did to considerable dubious evidence from the government, so confused matters as to make it virtually impossible for the jury to see what each defendant had done, which is (the way things turned out) what the jury should have considered.

It is now up to the informed public to decide what should be done hereafter about such prosecutions and indeed about such laws as that under which this misconceived prosecution was brought. One side effect of the prosecution is to confirm what has already been shown by several careful studies of Convention Week (including the government account, The Walker Report), that whatever mistakes were made by people such as the defendants, they were relatively insignificant compared to those made by the City of Chicago (against the advice, it should be noted, of the Department of Justice) in handling the demonstrations that any mature city inviting a national political convention should be prepared to expect.

As for the conduct in court of the defendants and their lawyers for which the judge has decreed prison sentences ranging from two months to four years, it is clear that some behavior in contempt of court was indulged in by both defendants and lawyers. But it is also clear that a number of the actions cited by this intelligent judge simply cannot survive examination, especially those which developed either with the acquiescence of the judge or from overzealous legal advocacy. It is up to the appellate courts to review the contempt citations, to consider whether they were entered in good time, whether the punishment was excessive, whether many of the instances cited were indeed contemptuous and whether they did disrupt the orderly administration of justice.

The fundamental problem, however, is not that of reassessing the judge's inventory of contemptuous actions—many should be dropped from his list and a few others could have been added to it—but rather that of assessing the context in which all this unfortunate conduct took place. There is considerable concern in this country about the threat to our judicial system of disruptive conduct in the courtroom. But we must consider what kind of defendants occasionally threaten such conduct, and in what circumstances. Such conduct (which is rare) is most likely to occur wherever defendants (because of their poverty or their status or their color) believe themselves unlikely to get "a fair shake" in court. Both the fears of widespread disruptive behavior and the measures which have been proposed for dealing with it are grossly exaggerated and are unbecoming for an America which should have learned by now how to use its great power responsibly and compassionately.

In considering the Chicago Conspiracy Trial, we citizens must do what the bar has refused to do in public, and that is to face up to the effect in this case of the judge himself. No fair-minded and informed community should discipline these lawyers and defendants without disciplining its judge as well. Judge Julius H. Hoffman's behavior in this case was consistently outrageous, almost always against the legitimate interests of the defendants. Much of the contemptuous conduct he alleges was provoked by him.

The defendants and their Eastern lawyers were confronted by a remarkably vindictive judge. The single greatest mistake the defendants made was not to realize in time that what this judge was doing to them had been done consistently over the years by him to other defendants as well, without regard to race, color or creed. It is common knowledge among the legal profession in Chicago, and can be confirmed by any survey of practicing lawyers, that this judge callously and systematically degrades and provokes the lawyers who happen to appear before him, unless they come from the office of the United States Attorney. Indeed, this is so well known that the government can be said to have had a duty to reconsider the explosive case it was bringing when it learned which judge was fated to try it: after all, our government has the recognized obligation to see that defendants receive a fair trial and to see that our legal institutions are not recklessly undermined.

Chicago lawyers who appear regularly in the federal courts have had to learn to bear up with Judge Hoffman's behavior. (Such judicial behavior should be distinguished, by the way, from the impartial strictness for which the late Judge John P. Barnes was justly celebrated.) Chicago lawyers have endured Judge Hoffman because they ordinarily have to bear up with him only a few days or, at worst, a few weeks at a time. In the Conspiracy Trial, however, defense counsel and their clients had to endure this judge for what must have seemed to them, as it did to courtroom observers, an eternity.

It is the duty of an informed bar to courageously interpose itself between a dictatorial judge and vulnerable counsel. Indeed, it was the duty of the local bar to have "blown the whistle" on Judge Hoffman many years ago, to have taken the steps necessary to restrain his unprofessional conduct. The unbecoming failure of the bar as well as of the press to make its opinion known about this kind of judge—an opinion which is, in Judge Hoffman's case, almost unanimously bitter among those who practice in the federal courts here—lends support to critics who would have us believe that this particular judge is essentially representative of what may be found in American courthouses today. It is the duty of all citizens, lawyers and laymen alike, to protect our country from the devastating effects of such judges. Too much depends on popular trust in our political institutions, especially among the underprivileged and the unfortunate, to permit that trust to be sacrificed to the atrocious behavior of obviously unfit public servants.

Two dangers confront us. One is that ten men might be required to serve prison sentences in circumstances where the government is at least as much to blame as they are for what happened both during Convention Week and in the course of their trial. The other danger is that further improper exercise of government power will provoke more resistance by offended citizens, which in turn can lead to even more repression in the name of "law and order." (Such improper exercise of government power was evident even in the way U.S. marshals were permitted to conduct themselves in the Federal Building throughout the Conspiracy Trial: they often seemed unable to distinguish between the way prison guards do treat convicts and the way public servants should treat citizens.)

It does not seem likely, despite what the defendants claim, that a paralyzing era of repression is about to begin in this country. But we should take care not to permit an imprudent government to go out of its way to prove the defendants right about this. That is, we should make sure that we have seen in the Chicago Conspiracy Trial the end of an era, an era in which public servants have been obliged to rediscover that it is a disservice to law and order to challenge high-spirited dissent (however irresponsible and disturbing it may be on occasion) with a self-righteous show of force rather than with intelligence and generosity and imagination.

The defendants (but not their lawyers) were in jail when I wrote and published this article, having been ordered there by the trial judge (on the contempt citations) immediately upon the case going to the jury on February 14, 1970. (This no doubt influenced the tone of my article.) They were kept there, on his absurd finding that they were "too dangerous" to be permitted out on bond pending appeal, until they were released on February 28 by an appellate court. (This "too dangerous" finding would not be modified by the trial judge even with respect to the two defendants who were acquitted by the jury on all charges on February 18. A long *Chicago Daily News* editorial, of February 17, 1970, "Is Contempt of Court Worse Than Murder?" concluded by questioning "the justice of giving a defense lawyer a harsher sentence [four years and thirteen days for contempt of court] than a culprit might receive for killing a man in the state of Illinois.")

A Solomonian disposition of this case would have been a directed verdict of acquittal for all the defendants by the trial judge on the substantive charges (including conspiracy), when the government rested its case December 5, 1969, with the imposition at that time of sentences for contempt for no more than three months for certain of the defendants. Of course, we will never know whether a judge capable of such restraint and discrimination would have had (even with this remarkably uninhibited squad of defendants) any serious and sustained contempts to contend with.

A much more serious "contempt" than that of any of the defendants was that of the government itself in choosing (largely for political purposes) to put together this ill-fated "conspiracy" and to "make a federal case of it." During the course of this months-long trial, another prominent "leader" of the "conspiracy," Sidney M. Peck (who had been named in the federal indictment as a coconspirator but not as a codefendant) was tried without a jury in a local state court with respect to actions related to the same August 1968 events. His trial lasted a couple of days. He was found guilty on February 5, 1970, of aggravated assault and resisting arrest, and was fined $500 in March, 1970.

There were no publicized disturbances in the course of the *Peck* trial. The defendant, upon being found guilty by Judge Felix M. Buoscio of less serious offenses than the state had originally charged, observed, "The judge made a courageous decision by calling attention to the fact that the force used to subdue me was not necessary." He described the judge as "really fair," adding, "I think that the decision in his own mind was an honest one." Thus, "dissenters" are not in principle unreceptive to fair-minded judges. A directed verdict by Judge Hoffman, along the lines I suggested, would have been an impressive contribution to the cause of law and order in both Chicago and the country at large, particularly for the sake of the young. Cf. "Verdict in New Haven," *Newsweek*, Sept. 14, 1970, p. 34.

An even more serious "contempt," also that of the government, is the prosecution of an undeclared and perhaps unconstitutional war, which arouses fierce sentiments easily exploited by both the outraged and the unscrupulous and which even the more hawkish adventurers among us are beginning to realize was a dreadful mistake. (See, e.g., *Congressional Record*, 116: S7894 [May 27, 1970]; ibid., 116: S9574 [June 23, 1970].) Is it not an encouraging sign with respect to the moral sensibilities of the country that the young resent and rebel against our remarkably ill-conceived and even callous Indochinese adventure?

The most distressing feature of the Chicago Conspiracy Trial (aside from the implications of the government's folly in bringing it in the first place) related to the public binding and gagging of a defendant (Bobby G. Seale). It would not have been difficult for a sensible judge to have devised several better ways to handle this defendant, ranging from allowing him to represent himself (as he requested almost from the very beginning of the trial) to the immediate severance of him (with a sentence for contempt) when it became evident that binding and gagging was "the only alternative." (See, on removing a disruptive defendant from the courtroom, *Illinois* v. *Allen*, 90 S.Ct. 1057, decided March 31, 1970.) What was really distressing was that the judge was *permitted* to bind and gag Seale, in the circumstances of this controversy, for several days running—that he was able to do this without being immediately stopped by responsible opinion in both Chicago and Washington, which should have told him (not necessarily in public) that "we cannot have *that*." Only if such effectively responsible opinion exists behind the scenes, so to speak, can the necessarily wide discretion of a republic's public servants be kept in check. This judge's vanity is such that a determined public opinion would have restrained him from conduct so destructive for both himself and the community. (A careful study of the transcript should reveal what was evident to some of us in court, that the defendant Seale was being "set up" for his final display of contempt on November 5, 1969, with the government improperly cooperating with the judge to provoke again Seale's intervention and thus to bring the contempt issue to a head, after he had been released from his bonds and gag and quietly settled down while the trial proceeded. A proper hearing on the contempt citations might have exposed this arrangement for all to see.) See chap. 4, n. 80, chap. 8, n. 52, below.

A draft-file-burning trial, with some dozen defendants (*U.S.* v. *Chase*), was conducted in Chicago in May-June 1970. My efforts to attend that trial with the credentials of a journalist, as I had the Conspiracy Trial (also in the federal court building), were frustrated by the United States marshal. Press accreditation technicalities were insisted upon by him (even though there was space available in the press, as distinguished from the always crowded spectator, section), which I unsuccessfully tried to comply with before the trial ended. Similar technicalities (which include weeks of processing of an application for a press card by the Chicago Police Department) had been waived with respect to me (and several others) by the same U.S. marshal during the Conspiracy Trial (on a "space available" basis)—but they were rigorously insisted upon (with respect to me), even though demand for press section space was markedly reduced, when the marshal recalled what I had had to say in my *Sun-Times* article about the conduct of his deputy marshals during the Conspiracy Trial. Thus, he pointedly reminded me of my article (that is, of my journalistic activity) even as he insisted upon the press accreditation technicalities, thereby once against exhibiting the petty "insolence of office" I had previously been obliged to call him on in print. One result of his vindictiveness was that I was not permitted an opportunity to confirm what others had suggested to me, that one reason the *Chase* trial (with even more defendants and lawyers than the Conspiracy Trial) was relatively orderly was that the trial judge was far more moderate than Judge Hoffman has ever been able to be. (Only one attorney was penalized for contempt at the conclusion of the *Chase* trial, drawing a fine of $500 on each of two citations.) See chap. 7, n. 76, below.

To speak, as some do, of the present situation in the United States as truly repressive of political dissent is to exhibit ignorance of what repression looks like. There is a world of difference between how dissenters are treated today and how they were treated in the 1950s. (None of the defendants or defense lawyers in *Dennis* v. *U.S.*, 341 U.S. 494 [1951], for instance, could command [as the Conspiracy Trial defendants and lawyers do] thousand-dollar lecture fees or publish "best sellers," even though Communist party leaders of that period were certainly more restrained in both word and deed than contemporary "radicals." The damage resulting from the *Dennis* decision was far more serious than that which is likely to result from the Conspiracy Trial after the appellate courts finish with it, even though that trial judge [Harold R. Medina] was far better than Judge Hoffman. [See, for a tribute to Judge Medina as a trial lawyer, William M. Kunstler, *The Case for Courage* (New York: William Morrow and Co., 1962), p. 312.])

Even more repressive than the America of either the 1950s or the 1970s is what I have encountered as a foreign correspondent the past four summers in Greece or as a tourist in July 1960 in Russia (from both of which I have been expelled at one time or another). (See the citations to reports on both my Russian and my Greek experiences in chap. 6, n. 1, below.) One way to make things far worse than they are in a country such as ours (where public opinion is so vital) is to insist that the worst has already come when it has not: such publicized misjudgments may encourage desperation on the part of potential victims, recklessness on the part of the authorities, and apathy or even fear and submissiveness on the part of the public.

The Chicago Conspiracy Trial seemed a curious mixture of a medieval witch trial (see George Bernard Shaw's *Saint Joan*) and something out of Gilbert and Sullivan. One can usefully consider, in reflecting upon the case and upon the underlying political problems it suggests, the following books and articles:

1) *Contempt* (with a preface by Ramsey Clark and an introduction by Harry Kalven, Jr.) (Chicago: Swallow Press, 1970). The most telling indictment of the judicial handling of the case is provided in the record of the contempt citations selected by the judge himself: that record is reproduced in full in this book.

2) Comments on the case by both participants and observers, including:

    a) James J. Kilpatrick, "Conservative's Verdict: 'Judge Hoffman Blundered Most,'" *Chicago Daily News*, February 20, 1970, p. 11;

    b) Bobby Seale, *Seize the Time* (New York: Random House, 1970), pp. 289-361;

    c) Tom Hayden, "The Trial," *Ramparts*, July 1970, p. 10;

    d) "[Michael] Harrington Blasts '7' Trial," *Chicago Sun-Times*, April 13, 1970, p. 28 ("All they can do by their actions is bring the right wing down hard against civil liberties. Civil liberties are precious rights. The defendants should not have played fast and loose with them.");

    e) The daily reports on the trial by James Singer and J. Anthony Lukas in the *Chicago Sun-Times* and the *New York Times*.

3) Norval Morris and Gordon Hawkins, *The Honest Politician's Guide to Crime Control* (Chicago: University of Chicago Press, 1970), pp. 203-

35 (on the exaggerated notion Americans have about criminal conspiracies, "the Mafia," etc.; the Conspiracy Trial defendants and their sympathizers also depend too much on a conspiracy theory in interpreting the government's folly).

4) The discussions of the Catiline Conspiracy found in the speeches of Cicero and the accounts of Sallust and Plutarch (for which Thucydides' account of Alcibiades is a good preparation).

5) The federal grand jury report, released May 15, 1970, on the Black Panther raid of December 4, 1969, by Chicago police (reprinted in the *Congressional Record* 116: E4860 [May 28, 1970]).

6) Joseph Cropsey, "Radicalism and Its Roots," *Public Policy*, 18 (1970): 301. (One limitation of our contemporary "radicals" is that they are, in their uninformed romanticism, not radical enough: they do not know what or where the roots are. One should begin to look, for modern sources, into Machiavelli's *Prince*, Bacon's *New Atlantis*, Hobbes's *Leviathan*, Rousseau's *Discourses*, and Kant's *Perpetual Peace*, as well as into the New Testament and Marx.)

7) George Anastaplo, "On Civil Disobedience: Thoreau and Socrates," *Southwest Review* 54 (1969): 203; "The Daring of Moderation: Student Power and *The Melian Dialogue*," *School Review* 78 (1968): 451. Discussion of various issues bearing upon an understanding of both the Chicago Conspiracy Trial and contemporary dissent may be found below in chap. 2, n. 12, chap. 3, nn. 14, 18, 20, 21, 22, chap. 4, nn. 78, 80, chap. 5, nn. 31, 91, 131, chap. 6, nn. 30, 38, 71, 75, chap. 7, nn. 30, 42, 45, 52, 59, 67, 69, 72, 74, 91, 116, 124, chap. 8, nn. 9, 18, 19, 27, 35, 36, 46, 52, 74, 78, 122, 135, 141, 143, 147, 149, 150, 162, 164, 169, 190, 193, chap. 9, nn. 1, 7. See, also, chap. 2, sec. 1, chap. 5, sec. 13, chap. 9, sec. 2, above, Appendix E, chap. 4, n. 116, chap. 5, nn. 57, 66, 78, 79, chap. 6, n. 1, chap. 7, nn. 73, 76, chap. 8, nn. 51, 56, 140, 178, chap. 9, nn. 11, 35, below; *Congressional Record* 116 (1970): E10520, E11057.

It should be noticed, before concluding this survey of the Chicago Conspiracy Trial, that there was (on the part of the government, the judge, and the defendants alike) much about this months-long encounter which was contrived, shallow, and hence tiresome. Cf. pp. 341-42, below. It should also be noticed—and this is attested to by the bickering in court between defense counsel and prosecutors and between the defendants and the judge as to who among them had really been closest personally to Martin Luther King and to Robert F. Kennedy—that this trial was, just as had been the 1968 Democratic National Convention, a "civil war" among American "liberals." See chap. 5, n. 71, chap. 8, n. 83, below. All that was proved by such "civil war" was that everyone embroiled in both the convention and the trial should have known better.

APPENDIX E. ACADEMIC FREEDOM AND ACADEMIC RESPONSIBILITY: *PRINCIPIIS OBSTA*

RESTRICTIONS UPON freedom of speech can be indirect, and even unintended, but nevertheless effective—perhaps (in some circumstances) even more effective than direct assaults, since those who would feel duty bound to resist explicit restraints may be lulled by concealed restrictions.

This is illustrated by a controversy at Rosary College during my tenure there as Chairman of the Political Science Department. I had occasion to develop my arguments on this subject in two documents which are reproduced below. These arguments touch upon problems of freedom of speech and of the press which are not limited to circumstances obtaining on the campus.

The first document was proposed by me as a statement to be adopted by the Rosary College community. In it I made an effort to concede something to each of the factions which had developed on campus in the course of the controversy we were engaged in. My proposal was introduced by a short memorandum which concluded, "I believe that the proposed declaration is a statement of principles and practices upon which we can all agree at this time. We may prevent thereby the intensification of a controversy which could seriously divide us for months and even years to come."

(The version of my proposal reproduced here includes modifications I made in the course of faculty discussions. I indicated a willingness to make, or to permit others to make, further modifications in my suggested text. I was during the 1969-1970 academic year also Lecturer in the Liberal Arts at the University of Chicago and [thanks to the ease of jet travel] Professor of Politics and Literature at the University of Dallas.)

---

1. A Proposed "Declaration on Behalf of Academic Statesmanship," Rosary College, March 9, 1970.

A controversy has arisen among us which is likely to be misunderstood both by some members of our academic community and by some of our friends off campus. We are obliged, therefore, to clarify this controversy, especially with respect to what should be expected hereafter in like circumstances.

We begin with the recognition of the good faith of all parties involved in this controversy, a controversy which has at least had the good effect of inducing us all to reexamine our general purposes and our practices.

Precisely what has happened during the past fortnight is itself subject to dispute and is not likely to be fully determined immediately. It suffices for our immediate purpose to notice how this matter has been reported in the press, as may be seen in an article in the *Chicago Tribune* of March 4, 1970, entitled, "Rosary Halts Kunstler Talk by High Bond":

> A speech by William M. Kunstler, Conspiracy Seven trial defense attorney, at Rosary College in River Forest on Sunday [March 8] has been cancelled, it was announced yesterday.
> Spokesmen for the college said that the three groups which were sponsoring the talk were unable to post a one-million-dollar bond to cover property damage that might result if Kunstler spoke.
> The College, in a letter delivered to the groups Monday [March 2], required the bond because of student riots that followed a talk by Kunstler in Santa Barbara, Cal., last week. The bond would have covered property damage to the College and the community.
> A spokesman for one of the committees said they were unable to post the bond. Other reasons for the cancellation, the spokesman said, will be disclosed after the groups meet tonight with . . . [the] president of the College.
> The three sponsoring groups were the Oak Park-River Forest Citizens Committee for Human Rights, the Student Government Association of Rosary College, and the campus affiliate of the National Students Association.

Whatever the facts may really have been on this and other campuses recently, we restrict ourselves on this occasion to the following observations and resolutions:

(1) The surety bond required (on advice of counsel) by the College was, in the words of its President's letter of March 2, to "cover any damages to person or property within a radius of five miles of Rosary College, such damage following from a speech or remarks made at the college by Mr. Kunstler . . . and/or anyone else speaking in connection with this particular program."

We understand that this requirement by an educational institution of a surety bond was an innovation prompted by a concern of the College administration for the possibly provocative effect of the scheduled speaker on his partisans. Since it has come to our attention that other schools have expressed an interest in this innovation, we conceive it our duty to comment upon our own experience with it.

We have not been able to learn that such a wide-ranging bond (which should be distinguished from the insurance Rosary College carries on its property) is commercially available at a premium that is not prohibitive. Since many of us believe that such a requirement (however it may have been regarded when a bond was first asked for) can no longer be considered realistic, the College should, in circumstances where the bond requirement might have been considered, address itself instead to the explicit question of whether the scheduled program should simply be postponed.

(2) We understand that it was not the intention of our College administration in this matter to bow to pressure or threats from off-campus critics of a scheduled speaker.

We rely too much in our educational enterprise upon the challenge and stimulus of visiting speakers to permit an effective veto with respect to our speakers by outsiders who threaten us in any way. We therefore take this opportunity to commend the President of the College for having insisted, despite attempts at intimidation by some off-campus critics, that the address by the Rev. Jesse Jackson [of Operation Breadbasket] scheduled on this campus for March 5 not be cancelled.

We expect and welcome the challenge that comes from the communities adjoining our campus when they express to us their concern and suggestions about the speakers we have here from time to time. We expect and welcome as well the willingness of the law enforcement agencies of those communities to protect this institution in the pursuit of its lawful affairs, especially against any minority which would unlawfully use violence either on campus or off.

(3) We believe that the President of the College should be shielded as much as possible from the many pressures that the prospect of a controver-

sial speaker or program can generate. The President is entitled to as much support as we can provide, including that support which the obligation to conform to established procedures affords an administrator attempting to deal with passionate demands for "immediate action."

Consequently, it is resolved that a Lecture Review Committee, representing the administration, faculty and students of this College, be immediately constituted in a manner to be designated by this body, which Committee alone will have the power to authorize the President to postpone a scheduled program on this campus, provided however that a postponement of a scheduled program (against the wishes of its sponsors) may be ordered on the President's authority alone when an anticipated danger to life or property is so serious and so imminent that it would be unreasonable to wait upon the convening of the Committee. When such emergency action has to be taken by the President, the Lecture Review Committee shall be convened as soon as possible thereafter, on the call of either the President or any member of the Committee, in order that the entire matter may be laid before the Committee for review, with a report on the matter to be made to the first regular meetings thereafter of the faculty and of the student government of this College.

(4) It is also resolved that the Lecture Review Committee reconsider during the current semester the standards and procedures relied upon in scheduling, postponing and cancelling campus programs. Its determinations, which should include a consideration of the problems that may be posed both by irresponsible or provocative speakers and by hostile or violent opponents of a scheduled speaker, shall be presented this semester to the administration, to the faculty and to the student body of the College for approval.

(5) It is further resolved, since it is believed by a significant number of us that the deliberations and decisions of this academic community with respect to these matters would be aided thereby, that there shall be extended either by the President of the College or by the Political Science Department of the College, within the next fortnight, separate invitations (accompanied by a copy of this Declaration and with the offer of appropriate honorariums) to Thomas A. Foran, United States Attorney for the Northern District of Illinois, and to William M. Kunstler, Defense Counsel in *United States* v. *Dellinger*, to discuss on separate occasions recent legal and political developments (particularly as they affect this and other campuses) with the administration, faculty and student body of the College as well as with those leaders of the neighboring River Forest and Oak Park communities selected for that purpose by the President and by the Lecture Review Committee.

(6) This Declaration is made in the name of this academic com-

munity by representatives, meeting in joint assembly, of the student body, faculty and administration of Rosary College.

(7) We call upon the Board of Trustees of Rosary College to endorse this Declaration and thereby to provide whatever additional support it can to our common effort to preserve among ourselves an informed, disciplined and useful freedom.

Although a few sentences and phrases in this proposal of March 9, 1970, came to be incorporated by the faculty in the series of divergent resolutions adopted during its twelve hours of meetings on this subject in March, the comprehensive proposal was not accepted nor was future recourse to a surety bond repudiated. (The relevant student organizations were prepared to accept my proposal.)

I should make it clear that I was never consulted in any capacity about the decision of the administration of the college to require a surety bond for Kunstler's appearance on campus. In fact, the first I knew of the surety-bond maneuver, or indeed of any official concern at all about Kunstler's prospective visit, was when the requirement of a bond was made public.

I *had* been informed by the President of the College a couple of weeks before the requirement of a surety bond was made public that Kunstler had just been invited to speak: no difficulty at all was indicated to me or anticipated at that time. I made the suggestion on that earlier occasion, as Chairman of the Political Science Department, that the United States Attorney be invited (as guest of the department) to speak the week after Kunstler from the same platform and on the same subject. Such an invitation was extended by the President shortly after I made this suggestion, but no public announcement relating thereto was made by the College. (I do not know the U.S. Attorney's response.)

Then there came the bank-burning at Santa Barbara, and thereafter rumblings from River Forest officials and residents, recourse to the surety-bond requirements, interminable faculty meetings, and several fruitless attempts on my part to discuss the matter privately with the by then much-harassed president of the college in order to work out a settlement of the controversy satisfactory to all concerned parties. I still believe this could have been done.

My announcement of March 25, 1970, relating to the department chairmanship merely ratified *de jure* what had been (in my opinion) exasperatingly *de facto* for several weeks. On the other hand, had I not understood myself to be a department chairman, I probably would not have considered myself obliged to concern myself as much as I did with this entire matter in faculty meetings: I rarely concern myself with campus politics, preferring to leave such concerns to those whose talents and inclinations equip them to enjoy them.

---

2. A STATEMENT TO THE ROSARY COLLEGE COMMUNITY, MARCH 25, 1970

I regret to announce (now that faculty deliberations about our "Kunstler affair" are concluded)
- (i) my resignation as Chairman of the Political Science Department of Rosary College,
- (ii) my postponement of the April series of four public lectures on the Chicago Conspiracy Trial which I had consented to give at this college, until such time as Mr. Kunstler has been extended another *bona fide* invitation to speak here.

I have discussed these decisions with the President of the College, who has authorized me to announce them immediately. Some of my reasons for these decisions follow.

The resignation of my chairmanship has been prompted by my obligation to disassociate myself in an instructive manner from the decisions of the administration (misled, in a moment of understandable panic, by incredibly bad advice) in dealing the past month with the scheduled Kunstler speech and thereafter with steadily growing faculty misgivings about the effective cancellation of that speech by the College. It is evident to me from the conscientious deliberations of the Academic Council about this matter that wide-ranging consultation among administrators, faculty and students at any time during the past month would have readily produced a dignified compromise acceptable to all of us. Unfortunately, vindication was preferred by administration partisans to reconciliation, despite my pleas that we let the past be and plan for the future.

The postponement of my lecture series reflects my opinion that it does not seem to me fair play that I should (in public lectures) express the serious criticisms I do have of the Conspiracy Trial defendants and their lawyers (including their speeches) from the very platform taken away from Mr. Kunstler three weeks ago. I believe this to be consistent with the condition I insisted upon in agreeing to an April debate on the Conspiracy Trial at the University of Chicago with the Assistant United States Attorney (Mr. Schultz)—the condition that I would not speak on that occasion if my opponent (the principal prosecuting attorney during the Trial) should be prevented by a hostile audience from having his say as well. It seems appropriate to announce the lecture series postponement now, rather than wait on further developments over Easter vacation with respect to any possible invitation to Mr. Kunstler, since publicity about the series would otherwise have to be sent out during the next few days.

I remain confident that the shabby controversy we have had to endure on this campus would have been avoided if certain of us had been consulted about or at least informed in advance of the intention of the College to insist upon "a surety bond [to be secured within forty-eight hours] in the amount of $1,000,000 [to] cover any damages to person or property within a radius of five miles of Rosary College, such damage following from a speech or remarks [to be] made at the College by Mr. Kunstler [on March 8]." This college community has yet to realize that the requirement of such a bond as that asked for on March 2 can only mean the cancellation of the speaker's appearance on a campus.

All my investigations show that a bond of the description demanded of Mr. Kunstler's student and off-campus sponsors (with whom I have never been in any way associated) simply is not available commercially: it is certainly not available immediately or at a premium which would not be obviously prohibitive. (This would be true whether the scheduled speaker be Mr. Kunstler or the Pope.) Other precautions (not excluding postponement) should be deliberately considered on those rare occasions when a speaker's appearance threatens life or property. I am confident that this community is so dedicated to free inquiry that it would be most reluctant to permit an obvious curtailment of a controversial speaker except in the most ominous circumstances.

The folly of our recourse to such delusions as a surety bond is that it conceals from us what we are really doing: "The voice is Jacob's voice, but the hands are the hands of Esau."

Arrangements were eventually made which permitted Mr. Kunstler to speak at Rosary College on May 16, 1970 (the next-to-last weekend of the academic year). The faculty had recommended on March 23 that the college auditorium be made available without charge to his original sponsors. The President of the College accepted this recommendation in April, thereby returning to the generous attitude the College had had over the years toward controversial speakers, an attitude I had been concerned to see preserved. There was, the second time around, no surety bond or any other such requirement. I have been reliably informed that the auditorium was packed to hear Kunstler and that there was absolutely no incident either on campus or within a radius of five miles thereof following upon his remarks. See App. F, sec. 9 (intro.), chap. 2, n. 7, chap. 3, n. 21, chap. 5, nn. 69, 93, chap. 7, n. 113, chap. 8, nn. 122, 177, below.

APPENDIX F. IN RE GEORGE ANASTAPLO (1950-61)

MUCH IS MADE in this book of the contributions of lawyers toward the maintenance among us of constitutional government. How one gets to be a lawyer—or is kept from becoming one—may therefore be in this context a relevant subject, particularly if it should suggest to us what a lawyer is or should be. It is, in any event, a subject on which I have been privileged to become something of an expert the past two decades as a result of my permanent exclusion from the practice of law.

My bar admission case is, I believe, instructive for illustrating the indirect restraints that threaten freedom of speech and for confirming the dependence of freedom of speech both upon due process of law and upon the vigilance of the respectable. It is most instructive as well for reminding us of the travesty of due process (of genuine law and order) that thoughtless lawyers and judges can resort to, even as they condemn their victims for refusing to promise (despite the Declaration of Independence) that they will in all possible circumstances abide by whatever "law" should happen to be imposed upon the country.

It was my defense of the revolutionary principles of the Declaration of Independence that most fiercely aroused the Illinois bar authorities against me a generation ago. It was difficult to make them recognize that the Declaration reminds us of the old-fashioned proposition that there are standards outside and above the agreements and teachings of men, government, and era, standards superior even to what "the people" might at any moment believe or choose. That is, the right of revolution implies an insistence upon the supremacy of man's reason in the conduct of human affairs. It is as a reminder of political truths, and indeed of the nature of man, that the Declaration of Independence remains our founding instrument: to defend it is, as Lincoln knew, to be patriotic in the deepest sense. (See Anastaplo, "The Declaration of Independence," *St. Louis U. L. J.*, 9 [1965]: 390. Compare the presumptuous disavowal with respect to the future as well as to the past required for many years [cf. chap. 8, n. 126, below] of the faculty of the University of California [in addition to the traditional constitutional oath]:

And I do further swear (or affirm) that I do not advocate, nor am I a member of any party or organization, political or otherwise, that now advocates the overthrow of the Government of the United States or of the State of California by force or violence or other unlawful means; that within the five years immediately preceding the taking of this oath (or affirmation) I have not been a member of any party or organization, political or otherwise, that advocated the overthrow of the Government of the United States or of the State of California by force or violence or other unlawful means except as follows: [If no affiliations, write in the words "No Exceptions"] and that during such time as I am a member or employee of the University of California I will not advocate nor become a member of any party or organization, political or otherwise, that advocates the overthrow of the Government of the United States or of the State of California by force or violence or other unlawful means.

It is decreed on this form, "No fee may be charged for administering this oath." But to be more concerned about the pocketbook than about the constitutional principles of academic personnel is indeed to "strain at a gnat, and swallow a camel." The Declaration of Independence was surrendered by respectable folk, without too much reluctance, to the Communist party—even though Marxists would be most reluctant to endorse the insistence of the Founding Fathers that *every* regime may properly be subjected to "the Right of the People to alter or to abolish" "any Form of Government [which] becomes destructive" of the ends of government.)

The tenor of the ungenerous, and even ruthless, times in which my case developed (since late 1950) is hinted at by the terms and tone of a memorandum distributed among the faculty of my law school on February

7, 1952. (See, e.g., chap. 7, n. 74, below.) This mimeographed memorandum, which I found in a University of Chicago Law School Library collection devoted to my case, was issued by Professors Walter J. Blum, Allison Dunham, Soia Mentschikoff, and Sheldon Tefft:

> We propose to ask the faculty to adopt the following statement by resolution at the faculty meeting on Monday, February 11. Your comments are invited.
> In the course of discussing the civil liberties aspects of interrogating applicants for admission to the bar about their views on Communism and about membership in the Communist Party, a number of students have requested an opinion about the legality of such a procedure.
> The faculty is of the opinion that a character and fitness committee, having the powers of the Illinois Committee, would be acting within its legal power in requesting an applicant to state his views on Communism and to reveal any affiliations with the Communist Party. The chances of successfully contesting the legal power of such a committee in this respect are so slight as to be not worth considering.
> If an applicant refuses to answer such inquiries, either because he questions the power of the committee or for any other reason, the committee would then be justified, as a matter of law, in refusing to certify his character and fitness.
> This suggests that a student who feels that he would not be willing to answer such inquiries would be well advised to consider now rather than later whether he can best serve his ideals by continuing his education in law.

There is no indication in the library collection of the action taken by the faculty on this proposal. But according to another memorandum in the collection, Professor Malcolm P. Sharp offered to the law school faculty on February 8, 1952, a substitute motion (see pp. 405-6, below):

> The faculty requests the Dean to appoint a committee of three to arrange for the selection of a representative student committee; and to confer with the student committee to consider steps that may be taken to obtain agreement by the Committee on Character and Fitness on a rational and known course of questioning of applicants for admission to the bar.

I have attempted, through the accounts collected below, to tell the story of what happened when I applied for admission to the Illinois bar in 1950 and in 1957, and to tell it in such a way as to make it apparent what was wrong, as well as what was right, with both me and the country at a time when so many of my fellow citizens were not altogether unwilling prisoners of the Cold War.

There are, of course, disagreeable features about any public contest regarding one's "character and fitness." One has to take great care not to make too much of oneself. Thus, even though I was advised by friendly lawyers to submit dozens, if not hundreds, of character references as well as to parade a number of witnesses before the committee, I could never bring myself to provide the committee more than what its rules required.

All the accounts reproduced in this appendix are, unless otherwise indicated, complete. Extensive bibliographies of additional materials are provided at pages 400-406, below. The following chronology should help the reader keep the adventure and its documents straight:

FIRST ROUND

Action	Date
Birth (in St. Louis, Mo.) of George Anastaplo	November 7, 1925
Original application of George Anastaplo for admission to the Illinois bar filed (in Chicago, Ill.) with the Committee on Character and Fitness for the First Appellate Court District of Illinois	October 26, 1950
Committee on Character and Fitness conducted hearings (in two sessions)	November, 1950- January, 1951
Committee on Character and Fitness refused (without any explanation) to issue a certificate of satisfactory character and fitness (Commissioner Stephen Love, dissenting)	June 5, 1951
Committee on Character and Fitness was required by the Supreme Court of Illinois to issue a report explaining its 1951 decision	April 19, 1954
Supreme Court of Illinois refused (unanimously) to reverse the Committee's ruling	September 23, 1954
Supreme Court of the United States refused to review the Illinois action (Justices Black and Douglas, dissenting)	February 28, 1955
Supreme Court of the United States denied both a petition for rehearing and a motion seeking the admission of George Anastaplo to its own bar	April 11, 1955

SECOND ROUND

Supreme Court of the United States announced its decisions in the bar admission cases of *Schware* v. *Board of Bar Examiners of New Mexico*, and *Konigsberg* v. *State Bar of California*	May 6, 1957
Petition for rehearing of his application for admission to the Illinois bar filed by George Anastaplo with the Committee on Character and Fitness	May 15, 1957
Committee on Character and Fitness refused to grant a rehearing (Commissioners Rothschild and Sawyier, dissenting)	July 2, 1957

IN RE GEORGE ANASTAPLO (1950-61) 335

Action	Date
Supreme Court of Illinois ordered the Committee on Character and Fitness to allow a petition for rehearing and to hear evidence relating thereto	September 17, 1957
Committee on Character and Fitness conducted hearings (in six sessions)	February-May, 1958
Committee on Character and Fitness again refused to issue a certification of satisfactory character and fitness (Commissioners Carey, Christianson, Hastings, Leighton, Rothschild, and Sawyier, dissenting)	April 9, 1959
Supreme Court of Illinois again refused to reverse the Committee's ruling (Justices Bristow, Davis, and Schaefer, dissenting)	November 19, 1959
Supreme Court of the United States agreed to review the Illinois action	May 2, 1960
George Anastaplo is expelled from Russia (during a camping tour of the Continent) for alleged "subversion of public order" (in one session)	July 28, 1960
Supreme Court of the United States heard oral argument in the bar admission cases	December 14, 1960
Supreme Court of the United States refused to reverse the Illinois action and also denied a motion seeking the admission of George Anastaplo to its own bar (Chief Justice Warren, Justices Black, Brennan, and Douglas, dissenting)	April 24, 1961
Supreme Court of the United States denied a petition for rehearing	October 9, 1961
George Anastaplo announced his retirement from "the practice of law"	October 13, 1961

1. THE COMMITTEE YIELDED TO TEMPTATION (NOVEMBER 10, 1950)

Malcolm Sharp (who had been my most valuable counsellor over the years) was asked by the *University of Chicago Maroon*, after the 1961 decision by the Supreme Court of the United States, "to write a brief summary of the events in the Anastaplo case." Professor Sharp's summary comment on the case appeared in the May 2, 1961, issue of the *Maroon*. (His academic references are all to the University of Chicago.)

MALCOLM SHARP'S SUMMARY, 1961

Mr. George Anastaplo, a distinguished alumnus of the College and the Law School, a veteran bomber navigator of the second world war, now a teacher in University College and a graduate student with the Committee on Social Thought, has been denied admission to the Bar of Illinois. Beginning during the sound and fury accompanying the Korean War, he has litigated his case for more than 10 years. By closely divided votes the authoritative bodies in Illinois have decided that he is lacking in moral character and fitness to practice law. By a five to four decision, the Supreme Court of the United States has just refused to interfere with their determination. The majority supported its decision by a reference to the Court's limited power to review state action.

In what does the lack of character and fitness appear? In November, 1950, in answer to a question, Mr. Anastaplo told a subcommittee of the Illinois Committee on Character and Fitness that he thought a Communist was not *per se* disqualified for admission to the Bar. This answer led Mr. Anastaplo, in response to further questions, to a defense of the "right" of revolution, which is a basic feature of Western constitutional law. It has been insisted upon by the Roman Catholic Church, elaborated by John Locke, expressed in the Declaration of Independence, strongly stated by Daniel Webster and Abraham Lincoln, among others, and now put into practice by Mr. Kennedy in aiding a rebellion against the Castro Government in Cuba. Apparently it is not a part of the basic dogma of the Communist Party, which is reported to believe in its own revolution and then no others.

Mr. Anastaplo's position seems to have put the subcommittee members into a frame of mind familiar to teachers who have faced students brighter than they. Teachers may with experience gain a certain amount of self-control in dealing with such situations. The Subcommittee, and later over the years the full Committee, yielded to temptation and badgered Mr. Anastaplo at endless length about the ancient conundrums connected with the right of revolution.

In the meantime the Subcommittee, at its first meeting, in its frustration over the right of revolution, asked Mr. Anastaplo whether he was a member of any Attorney General's list organization or of the Communist Party. Mr. Anastaplo declined to answer, as he later over the years declined to answer questions about his religious beliefs and about membership in a variety of organizations, including the Ku Klux Klan and the Democratic and Republican Parties.

In the final stages of the case, both the Committee and the Illinois Supreme Court recognized explicitly that there is not in the entire lengthy record any evidence of Mr. Anastaplo's membership in any organization whatever; or any evidence whatever unfavorable to his character or his fitness to practice law, unless what has thus far been referred to is such evidence. In the 10 years in which the case has attracted considerable attention in legal circles in Illinois, no one has suggested that Mr. Anastaplo is a Communist or a Communist Sympathizer, or even a Socialist or a New Dealer. Among the many strong statements in his behalf in the record is one from Professor Richard Weaver of our University. Among other things, Mr. Weaver says, "My own publications have often been attacked for their conservatism, but I must say that Mr. Anastaplo has shown a better and a more sympathetic understanding of the point of view expressed in them than the vast majority of students I meet. Everything I know about the applicant leaves me feeling that he is an unusually intelligent, balanced, and helpful American citizen."

A majority of representatives of the Illinois Bar appear to have defeated Mr. Anastaplo's attempt to gain admission to the Illinois Bar. The profession can take pride in a thoughtful dissent in the Committee, a clear and blistering dissent by Mr. Justice Bristow in the Illinois Supreme Court, and dissents in that Court by Mr. Justice Davis and Mr. Justice Schaefer. A considerable consolation for those of us who take Mr. Anastaplo's position seriously is the dissenting opinion of Mr. Justice Black, speaking for the Chief Justice, Mr. Justice Douglas, and Mr. Justice Brennan, in the Supreme Court of the United States. Mr. Anastaplo's case is perfectly stated and his arguments beautifully phrased. The result is a magnificent example of the interaction between the work of intelligent counsel, in this case Mr. Anastaplo acting on his own behalf, and a Judge of genius. . . .

Justice George W. Bristow's dissenting opinion, as well as that of Justices Charles H. Davis and Walter V. Schaefer (in the Supreme Court of Illinois), may be found at 18 Ill.2d 182, 163 N.E.2d 429, 439, 928 (1959-60). Justice Bristow's opinion was reprinted in *Lawyers Guild Rev.*, 19 (1959): 134. Justice Black's dissenting opinion may be found in section 6 of this appendix. The Committee dissenting report referred to by Professor Sharp is noted at page 347, below.

Other summaries of the events in the case are provided in various of the documents reproduced below.

2. I Thought You Were in Europe (November 5, 1955)

The conversation recorded below took place thirteen months after I had failed in the Supreme Court of Illinois (in 1954) to secure a reversal of the character committee's refusal (in 1951) to issue me the certification of my character and fitness required for admission to the Illinois bar (and seven months after I had failed [in 1955] to have the Illinois action reviewed in the Supreme Court of the United States).

A reconstruction of the conversation, reprinted here in its entirety, was prepared by me November 7 and 9, 1955, and is based on detailed notes I made on November 5, 1955, at 10:15 A.M. I swore to the accuracy of this reconstruction on February 28, 1958, before the character committee in the course of the rehearings conducted with respect to my application for admission to the bar. (See *In re George Anastaplo*, 366 U.S. 83 [1961], Transcript of Record, pp. 38-52, 63-68.) The chairman of the committee marked this document on the backs of its pages, without examining its contents, with the legend: "Exhibit A for Identification, Anastaplo Hearing 2/28/58."

The document was made available to the committee on my condition that it merely request it of me, after I suggested (upon disclosing the principal admission as well as the occupation, but not the name, of the Passenger) that the document cast doubt (through an authoritative source) upon the good faith of the official claim of the Illinois authorities (which had just been repeated by the committee and was to be repeated many times thereafter by both the committee and the Supreme Court of Illinois) that they were unable to pass judgment on my fitness for admission to the bar so long as I would not assure them I was not a member of the Communist party. (See section 3 of this appendix for the context of my offer of this document to the committee.)

The committee refused to run the risk of requesting the document, preferring to continue to ask me the questions about possible political affiliations which it knew that I would (on principle) refuse to answer. On the other hand, a submission of this document by me at that time, without a formal request from the committee, might have been exploited as an impropriety by the more hostile members of the committee. Several accounts (consistent with my reconstruction) have come back to me of the Passenger's having related this conversation on several occasions to his colleagues and others (in public as well as in private), thereby relieving me of any obligation I might have had not to release this fifteen-year-old document on my own authority.

The Supreme Court of Illinois opinion referred to in the conversation may be found at 3 Ill.2d 471, 121 N.E.2d 826 (1954). There are extensive quotations from that opinion, relevant to this conversation, in the Committee Report reproduced in section 4 of this appendix. (See, on the political importance of economic refuges among us, section 4 of Appendix C, above, p. 409, chap. 8, n. 36, below.)

The scene opens at the cab stand outside the Sherman Hotel in Chicago, Saturday, November 5, 1955, 10 A.M. (with a passenger taking the taxicab next in line):

Passenger. Can you take me to Jackson and State?
Taxi-Driver. Yes, sir.
Passenger. I know it is not very far.
Driver. But it is a little too far to walk.
Passenger. It sure is. Besides, I'm in a hurry.
Driver. It really is a beautiful day, isn't it?
Passenger. It's very nice—but we had a hard drive up here the other day.
Driver. Oh, yes? Where from?
Passenger. Peoria. Next time I'm going to come up by train.

Driver. That is a good idea this time of year. You never know what kind of weather you will run into. Do you live in Peoria?
Passenger. Yes. Are you familiar with the place?
Driver. I've been through there—and I have friends down there and have heard a lot about it. You are in business down there?
Passenger. Yes, I'm up here for a convention.
Driver. We have a lot of them in this town.
Passenger. I even had my picture in the *Tribune* this morning. My wife doesn't like it very much, however.
    [*Passes newspaper clipping forward to driver*]
Driver. Thank you. I'll look at it at the next stop-light.
Passenger. That's me in the upper right-hand corner.

> [*Newspaper photograph caption:*
> *Illinois Supreme Court justices at bar association dinner in Sherman Hotel last night. Left to right: Front—Justice Ray I. Klingbiel, East Moline; Chief Justice Harry B. Hershey, Taylorville; Justice Ralph L. Maxwell, Nashville. Rear—Justices George W. Bristow, Paris; Walter V. Schaefer, Chicago, and Joseph E. Daily, Peoria. Justice Charles H. Davis, Rockford, was not present. (Story on page 10, part 2)*]

Driver. Oh, yes: Justice Daily. I thought you looked familiar.
Passenger. Oh, you drive from the Sherman Hotel regularly?
Driver. No, sir, all over the city—I am only driving weekends while I work and go to school out at the University of Chicago.
Passenger. It's good you can do that.
Driver. But it's not because I had seen you around the hotel that I recognized you: you see, I argued a case before your court last spring.
Passenger. You didn't! Where?
Driver. At Springfield.
Passenger. But you're not admitted to the bar!?
Driver. That's the idea: I lost the case. And what's more, you wrote the opinion.
Passenger. [*Pause*] What case was that?
Driver. The Anastaplo case.
Passenger. *You* are not Anastaplo, are you?
Driver. I most certainly am!
Passenger. Well, isn't this something! [*Pause*] You applied for a new certificate?
Driver. No, sir, I applied for admission for the first time.

Passenger. I mean recently, for a new certificate of admission.
Driver. I've never been admitted.
Passenger. But you've asked them to take up your case again?
Driver. Oh, I wrote the Committee recently and wondered whether they might now certify me for admission in the light of what I had heard through friends about them not requiring any more answers from me.
Passenger. Why don't you just answer: you're not a Communist, are you?
Driver. That's not the point, sir.
Passenger. Well, why don't you answer?
Driver. It's not good for them to be encouraged to think they can ask such questions.
Passenger. I thought you were in Europe.
Driver. I was this summer, for a few months.
Passenger. You should answer and get admitted. *You're* not a Communist, are you.
Driver. But, Mr. Daily, that is not the point.
Passenger. No, it's not the point. But you should answer.
Driver. It's not a question of Communism.
Passenger. Well, you should answer anyway. No one ever thought you were a Communist.
Driver. What corner do you want off, Mr. Daily?
Passenger. Across State Street, over there, would be all right.
Driver. That'll be fifty-five cents, sir.
Passenger. [*Tosses a dollar bill forward*] We've discussed your case many times [*unclear here:* . . . with friends (?)]. [*Leaving the cab*]
Driver. You have some change, sir.
Passenger. It's all right. You'll be admitted some day.
Driver. I certainly hope so. Good day, sir.

Justice Daily led the four-man majority of the Illinois Supreme Court which affirmed, four years after our taxicab conversation, the committee report reprinted in section 4 of this appendix. 18 Ill.2d 182, 163 N.E.2d 429 (1959). (The Illinois court has seven members.)

It was always difficult (to the very end) for me to predict just what the Supreme Court of Illinois would do next with me. The votes in the Supreme Court of the United States, on the other hand, were at that time all too predictable: thus, the same members voted together on the two other bar-related cases decided the same day as mine. It did not seem to matter that the parties who "lost" along with me that day, Raphael Konigsberg (a bar admission case from California) and Albert M. Cohen (a disbarment case from New York), *were* represented by counsel, or that I was not: it was 5-4 all the way. (We did not realize, of course, that within a year or so there would be firmly established, even with respect to civil liberties, what came to be known as "the Warren Court.")

It had been the decision in the 1957 *Konigsberg* case that helped induce me to apply again for admission to the bar. That case was described in 1961, by Justice Harlan (who had dissented in 1957), in this fashion:

> ... In the first *Konigsberg* case this Court held that neither the somewhat weak but uncontradicted testimony, that [Konigsberg] had been a Communist Party member in 1941, nor his refusal to answer questions relating to Party membership, could rationally support any substantive adverse inferences as to [his] character qualifications, 353 U.S., at 266-274. ...
> [*Konigsberg* v. *State Bar*, 366 U.S. 36, 45-46 (1961)]

That is about the way it looked to me as well in 1957. There were, of course, evident loopholes in the 1957 majority opinion (written by Justice Black)—but Konigsberg *had* gotten a reversal (and what turned out to be an expensive "invitation" [for him as well as for me] to try and hence fail again). Konigsberg had first applied for admission to the California bar in 1953. (See pp. 355, 404, below. See, also, chap. 8, n. 88, below.)

The *Konigsberg* loopholes (having to do with the then yet-to-be-ascertained constitutional consequences of a formal warning to an applicant about the "obstructive" character of a refusal to answer questions), which Justice Black may have had to put into his opinion in order to get a majority in 1957, were magnified and exploited by Justice Harlan, as well as by the state bars, in 1959-61. Still, the uncertainty about the significance of the first *Konigsberg* decision did make my committee behave considerably better in 1957-59 than its predecessors had. (This may have also been in part due to the fact that they had gotten to know me as someone not without a plausible point to make.) The improved behavior (and much more restrained language) of the committee did not revive my legal career, but it did leave a much better record from which others (in the bar and out) can learn about the nature (and hence limitations as well as virtues) of our institutions. (One can learn as well from this record what "legal reasoning" is like: lawyers, and would-be lawyers, may be seen utilizing or trying to explain away judicial decrees, legal precedents, and the evidence.)

The differences between the contending parties may seem to the student a generation later trivial verbal differences. But something much more vital than that was at stake, and all the parties involved sensed it. One cannot begin to understand such encounters unless one notices and respects the obvious gulf between the parties: it is well to begin, that is, with the fact that the parties perceive themselves (not just for a moment but even after long exchanges) as fundamentally opposed in some decisive respect.

Thus, Professors Kalven and Steffen, in the 1960 *amicus curiae* brief they filed (as counsel for the American Civil Liberties Union) in the Supreme Court of the United States, insisted that the issues of the case "involve nothing less than a definition of the desired moral character of the American bar. . . ." Their brief concludes, "And we respectfully ask the Court to reverse the judgment below. In so doing, the Court will not only do justice in this case, but it will be vividly reaffirming for generations of applicants to come, the high place that candor, courage, and independence of mind have as attributes of that character and fitness which make the lawyer." (See pp. 333-34, above, pp. 360, 405-6, below.)

We can see in the next two sections of this appendix, on the other hand, how the character committee regarded the case.

3. Your Function Today is to Answer Questions, and Not to Ask Them (February 28, 1958)

A summary, with illustrative quotations, of one of my many appearances over a decade before the character committee might suggest to the reader how those proceedings were typically conducted. This summary is drawn from the Transcript of the Record (cited as R.) and from my Brief on the Merits, July 4, 1960, pp. 12-17, in the case brought to the Supreme Court of the United States in 1960. (The critical illustrative quotation from my initial hearing of November 10, 1950, may be found in n. 3 of Justice Black's opinion in section 6 of this appendix.)

My examination before the character committee (during the 1957-61 phase of the case) began on February 28, 1958, with a review and elaboration of various items on the standard applicant's questionnaire which I had been required to fill out, items relating to my education, military service, travel abroad, employment, legal studies, publications, and civic activities. This part of my examination lasted about forty-five minutes (R. 22).

The next stage (on the same afternoon) featured inquiries about organizations to which I might belong. (This was *before* any discussion, this time around, of the "right of revolution," the discussion which had led to the affiliations inquiries during the "first round" in 1950. See p. 379, below.) Commissioner Charles A. Bane had been assigned by the committee to conduct this part of the examination (R. 3, 22). I was asked by him about and denied membership in various veterans' organizations, alumni organizations, and civic organizations (R. 27). There then followed on the new record being made for this "second round" (which was the record officially reviewed in 1960-61 by the United States Supreme Court) the first question relating to possible membership in a "political organization" which I considered myself obliged to refuse to answer, the "foundation" for which question having been laid in this manner (R. 27-28):

> Commissioner Bane: Have you, since 1951 [when the committee had first refused to issue a certificate], become a member—let me ask you first of all, you are of Greek descent, Mr. Anastaplo?
> Mr. Anastaplo: That is true.
> Q. Your father and mother were both Greek?
> A. Greek descent, yes.
> Q. Since 1951, have you become a member of any nationality organization related to Greek Americans or the Greeks who were in this country?
> A. No, I have not.
> Q. Are you a member, for example, of Ahepa [a Greek-American fraternal organization]?
> A. No, sir.
> Q. Are you familiar with the list of organizations which have been designated by the Attorney General as subversive?
> A. I am familiar with the fact that some have been designated by the Attorney General, and I know of some that are on the list, but I am not familiar with the list itself.
> Q. Let me ask you, bearing in mind your Greek descent, whether you are a member of an organization which has been designated by the Attorney General as subversive, known as the American Council for a Democratic Greece?
> A. I have already answered a question about nationality groups. And I have answered other questions about groups—so long as they were—so long as I could in any way tell myself this was not a question involving political activity. Now, since you seem to want to put it in those terms, I simply have to call a halt to my answering that kind of question.

I was asked my grounds for refusing to answer "that kind of question." I recited objections based on the First and Fourteenth Amendments and on the *ex post facto* and bill of attainder clauses of the Constitution of the United States. I also noted that I did not believe that the term "activities," in the Supreme Court of Illinois order of September 17, 1957, which had decreed the rehearing, was intended (in the light of the litigation preceding the issuance of the order) to include political affiliations. (See p. 349, below; 18 Ill.2d 186; see, also, pp. 386, 391-92, below.) I then stated, in response to further questions, that I was under no coercion to take the position I did, that my position was not being taken because of any fear of perjury indictments if I answered one way or another, and that mine was not a position that relied upon the Fifth Amendment to the Constitution (R. 30-32). See pp. 354, 396, below. The examination continued (R. 32-34):

> Commissioner Bane: Let us proceed now, and let me ask you whether,

if I had not indicated to you that the American Council for a Democratic Greece is on the Attorney General's list, and if you had not known whether it was or not, would you have been willing to answer the question as to whether you were a member of that council?

Mr. Anastaplo: Probably, in the sense that I—

Q. Probably yes, you would have been willing to answer?

A. In the sense that I do not want to make it appear, and I would bend over backwards not to make it appear, that I am in any way obstructing the action of the committee, the function of the committee, or simply raising objections on technical points, or even not technical points, when they might not be altogether appropriate. Let me say this. One can argue that some of the other questions I answered were perhaps inappropriate. One can argue that. And if one wanted to be technical, perhaps one would have to argue it. But I simply want to lean over backwards to indicate that I would like to be as cooperative with this committee as possible. And since I am really ignorant—I have already told you—I am really ignorant of most of the names on that list, you could probably name a dozen of them right now, and I could not begin to tell whether they are on the list or not—I would probably cooperate to some extent in answering some of them, if I could in good conscience say to myself that I didn't know whether it was on the list. But if I know it's on the list, and I know that you are asking it off the list—I mean, this is all very vague perhaps to you—but if I know that somehow it has something to do with this kind of inquiry, the kind that I have been opposed to for seven years, then in good conscience I would have to refuse. You can take advantage of my ignorance if you like, but certainly it is ignorance, of what is on the list.

Q. Well, now, I am not taking advantage of your ignorance, as we have not done, because we have been frank with you—

A. That is true.

Q. —in indicating the organizations which are on the list. I now want to read the names or titles of certain other organizations which are on the list, according to the information that we have, and I want to ask you whether you have become a member of that organization since 1951, and in each case whether you are a member of it now.

A. May I ask first, why—does this committee care to say why they want to know?

Q. No, I want to ask the question, and then I want to get your answer.

A. May I ask another question if you don't want to answer that one?

Q. Mr. Anastaplo, you are being questioned, you are the applicant; you understand that?

A. But cannot—could not counsel ask the relevance of the inquiry that is being made?

Q. I don't believe that the committee is going to permit you to put on two hats, and be a witness one minute and—

A. Cannot I ask, then, the relevance of the inquiry?

Q. I will refer the matter to the chairman of our subcommittee, but it is my view that you are the witness and that your function today is to answer questions, and not to ask them.

As Commissioner Bane prepared to ask about my possible membership in various organizations designated by him as on "the Attorney General's list," I was permitted to object "that there has been no showing to me here, or by any other means, either of [the foundation for or relevance of] the question, or the validity of the list, or any showing that the list was devised for any purpose that relates to the purpose of this inquiry" (R. 34-35). Nevertheless, I was thereupon asked questions which I refused to answer about possible membership in the Abraham Lincoln School of Chicago, the Civil Rights Congress for Texas, the Council for Greek Americans, the Ku Klux Klan, the Silver Shirts of America, and the American Youth for Democracy, all of which were said to be organizations on the constantly changing "Attorney General's list," a list I myself had not even looked at for some years (R. 42-43). (See chap. 4, n. 35, chap. 5, n. 17, chap. 8, n. 126, below, on this list.)

To all these questions, as well as to the subsequent one about whether I was then or had ever been a member of the Communist party, I raised constitutional objections under the First and Fourteenth Amendments (R. 37-38). In addition, I offered evidence to the committee, "with respect to the Communist party question," that it had never been thought either by the committee or by the Supreme Court of Illinois that I was a Communist (R. 38-39). I pointed out that the evidence I was offering was not to be taken for *my* answer to this question but rather as casting doubt on the good faith and purpose of the inquiry the committee was then making about Communist party membership (R. 61, 64, 335-36). The committee, after a recess for deliberation in executive session, refused to ask me to submit this evidence. (R. 43-44. This evidence was the taxicab conversation recorded in section 2 of this appendix.) The substance of this proffered evidence was acknowledged in the fifth session of these hearings (on May 19, 1958) when the committee was obliged to concede (R. 234) (see, also, pp. 350, 366, 371-73, 396, 406, below):

. . . no one has stated [orally or in writing] to this Committee that you are or have ever been a Communist or a member of the Communist Party, or a member of the Ku Klux Klan, or a member of the organizations or any of the organizations listed as subversive by the Attorney General's list. . . .

I had in effect told the committee that I had not joined the American Council for a Democratic Greece, whatever that may have been, when I answered I had not become a member of "any nationality organization related to Greek Americans or the Greeks who were in this country." Why, then, was the question about the American Council for a Democratic Greece, as well as the others following it, pressed upon me by the committee? There is one simple answer: in order to put me on record as refusing to answer the question—not because the committee thought I might be a member of that organization and certainly not because the question was, or was thought by the committee to be, relevant to the inquiry it had been commissioned by the Supreme Court of Illinois to make. It did no credit to the Illinois bar that phony questions were deliberately conjured up, in the name of "character and fitness," to avoid the application of common sense and of what was then thought by the committee to be the prevailing law.

Such legalistic, and even disgraceful, exhibitions as that displayed here with respect to Greek-American organizations should suffice to put one on notice about the sincerity of the repeated complaint of the Illinois authorities that they simply could not pass judgment on my qualifications so long as I continued to "obstruct" their inquiry. See, e.g., pp. 358-60, below. It is instructive that a majority of the Supreme Court of the United States —especially the very members who had been touted by the uninformed as most "lawyerlike"—could fall for sophistry which simply disregarded the record made in the case under review. See p. 366, below. It was left to the dissenters among the committee, the Supreme Court of Illinois, and the Supreme Court of the United States (as well as among my law teachers and classmates) to pay the record in the case the respect due it.

4. BY REASON OF APPLICANT'S OWN RECALCITRANCE (APRIL 9, 1959)

The most competent opinion, by far, of the half-dozen written against me during a decade of litigation was the Report of the Committee on Character and Fitness issued on April 9, 1959. This report, written after twenty hours of hearings (in 1958) and almost a year of deliberation thereafter by the committee, discusses, and quotes from, the 1954 opinion of the Supreme Court of Illinois. The arguments of this report were to provide the basis for the subsequent majority opinions of the Supreme Court of Illinois (1959) and the Supreme Court of the United States (1961).

The 1959 majority report of the character committee was signed by Charles A. Bane, Richmond M. Corbett, Walter H. Moses, John M. O'Connor, Jr., Francis J. Seiter, Len Young Smith, Robert A. Sprecher, Edmund A. Stephan, D. Robert Thomas, Jerome S. Weiss, and Horace A. Young. (My original committee—that of 1950-51—refused to issue any explanation of its decision. Thus, I was matter-of-factly told on June 20, 1951, "The Committee does not make known the grounds on which its decisions are based." And on October 30, 1952, "The Committee has made no report on its actions nor an explanation of its decisions." A successor committee did issue a report in 1954, but only because, after I had submitted a brief and record to the Supreme Court of Illinois, the Court ordered that a report be prepared. I understand that the experience with my litigation contributed to long-needed improvements in the Rules of Procedure of the Illinois character committees. Cf. *In re Summers*, 325 U.S. 561 [1945]. It is now provided, for instance, "If upon such hearing the committee is not prepared to certify the applicant, it shall deliver a report of its findings and conclusions to the Board of Law Examiners and the Supreme Court, with a copy being furnished to the applicant." *Chicago Daily Law Bulletin*, March 31, 1967, pp. 2, 6. The 1950-51 committee—a monument to disrespect for due process of law, to say nothing of simple fairness—included John E. Baker, Jr., William P. Churchill, Stanford Clinton, Herbert C. DeYoung, Henry A. Gardner, Jr., John P. McGoorty, Jr., William A. McSwain, Stephen A. Mitchell, Paul O'Donnell, John E. Owens, Herbert C. Paschen, Don M. Peebles, Len Young Smith, Robert A. Sprecher, Arthur A. Sullivan, and Lionel G. Thorsness. They made the lone dissenter in 1951, Stephen Love, even more remarkable. It should be noted, as well, that *amicus curiae* briefs were filed on my behalf in both Springfield and Washington by the American Civil Liberties Union and by the National Lawyers Guild. The ACLU brief filed in 1954 in the Supreme Court of Illinois was signed by Leon M. Despres, Abner J. Mikva, Alexander L. Polikoff, and Bernard Weisberg; the Guild brief filed on that same occasion was signed by Pearl M. Hart, Jessica Davidson, and Robert J. Silberstein. The ACLU brief filed in 1960 in the Supreme Court of the United States was signed by Harry Kalven, Jr., and Roscoe T. Steffen [who had in 1959 filed a memorandum of their own on my behalf in the Supreme Court of Illinois as had Laurence Berns]. The Guild brief filed in 1960 in the Supreme Court of the United States was signed by David Scribner, Leonard B. Boudin, Ben Margolis, and William B. Murrish, as well as by Lorraine Binder, Louis Berry, David B. Finkel, and Charles Stewart. See pp. 236-37, above, chap. 2, nn. 5, 13, chap. 7, n. 74, below.)

The 1959 minority report was signed by James P. Carey, Jr., J. R. Christianson, James E. Hastings, George N. Leighton, Edward I. Rothschild, and Calvin P. Sawyier. This generous minority report is not reproduced here since it is superseded, as was the remarkable dissenting opinion of Justice Bristow in the Illinois Supreme Court, by the dissenting opinion of Justice Black in the Supreme Court of the United States. The minority report of the committee has been reprinted, along with its majority report, both in documents I filed in the Supreme Court of the United States and in *Lawyers Guild Review*, 19 (1959): 65. The minority discussed only the evidence; the majority dealt much more with the "law." (See Aristotle, *Rhetoric* 1375a25; Aquinas, *Treatise on Law*, Q. 90, A. 4.) It is indicative of how much the committee's (and the country's) concerns, standards, and approach were departures from American practice that all the cases cited by the majority were decided since 1943, with most of them products of the 1950s. Cf. *Cummings* v. *Missouri*, 4 Wall. [U.S.] 277 (1867); *Ex parte Garland*, 4 Wall. [U.S.] 333 (1867). See chap. 4, n. 35, below.

The 1959 majority report follows in its entirety, presenting as it does the strongest official statement against admitting me to the bar.

MAJORITY REPORT OF COMMITTEE ON CHARACTER AND FITNESS FOR THE FIRST APPELLATE COURT DISTRICT OF ILLINOIS, 1959

On June 5, 1951, the applicant, GEORGE ANASTAPLO, was notified by this Committee that on the basis of hearings conducted prior to that date he had failed to prove such qualifications as to character and general fitness as in the opinion of the Committee would justify his admission to the bar of Illinois.

The applicant appealed from this ruling to the Supreme Court of Illinois, seeking a reversal of this Committee's action. In proceedings entitled *In re Anastaplo*, 3 Ill.2d 471 (1954), the Supreme Court of this State denied applicant's petition. The applicant then appealed to the Supreme Court of the United States, which court, treating the appeal as a petition for writ of *certiorari*, denied *certiorari*, 348 U. S. 946.

In its opinion the Supreme Court of Illinois held, based upon *American Communications Association* v. *Douds*, 339 U. S. 382, 94 L. ed. 925, 70 S. Ct. 674 [1950], *Dennis* v. *U. S.*, 341 U. S. 494, 95 L. ed. 1137, 71 S. Ct. 857 [1951], and *Re Summers*, 325 U. S. 561, 89 L. ed. 1795, 65 S. Ct. 1307 [1945], that certain inquiries directed to applicant by this Committee concerning applicant's political affiliations and organizational memberships did not violate either the First or Fourteenth Amendment to the Constitution of the United States. (3 Ill. 2d at pp. 480-481 [1954].) In reaching this conclusion, our Supreme Court set forth the "established conspiratorial nature" of the Communist Party on the one hand and the position of great influence of attorneys in the community on the other, and its genuine doubt whether a Communist Party member could in good conscience take the oath required as a condition of admission to practice. (3 Ill.2d at p. 480.) From these premises it concluded:

Under any hypothesis, therefore, questions as to membership in the Communist Party or known subversive "front" organizations were relevant to the inquiry into petitioner's fitness for admission to the bar. His refusal to answer has prevented the committee from inquiring fully into his general fitness and good citizenship and justifies their refusal to issue a certificate. (3 Ill. 2d at p. 480.)

Finally, our Supreme Court held that an applicant—knowing that the right to practice law is conditioned upon proof of his good moral character, of his general fitness to practice law and of his good citizenship, and upon the taking of an oath to support the Illinois and Federal Constitutions—may not defeat "pertinent inquiry into his ability to fulfill such conditions by any claim of the right of free speech." (3 Ill. 2d at p. 482.) In this connection it analogized the principles applied in the field of public employment and held that the application for admission to the Bar constituted an agreement "to waive his constitutional right of free speech against relevant inquiry." (3 Ill. 2d at pp. 482-483.) The opinion concluded:

We conclude that the committee's inquiry into petitioner's membership in the Communist Party was relevant to a determination of his good citizenship and his ability to take the oath of lawyer in good conscience, and that petitioner's constitutional rights were not infringed upon by such action. On the present record the petition must be denied. (3 Ill. 2d at 483.)

On June 25, 1957, following the decisions of the Supreme Court of the United States in *Konigsberg* v. *State Bar of California*, 353 U. S. 252, 1 L. ed. 2d 810, 77 S. Ct. 722 [1957], *Schware* v. *Board of Bar Examiners of State of New Mexico*, 353 U. S. 232, 1 L. ed. 2d 796, 77 S. Ct. 752 [1957], and *Yates* v. *United States*, 354 U. S. 298, 1 L. ed. 2d 1356, 77 S. Ct. 1064 [1957], Anastaplo applied to this Committee by supplementary petition for rehearing of his application for admission to the Bar. On July 2, 1957, the Committee denied the application.

On September 17, 1957, the Supreme Court of Illinois entered the following order:

In 1951 the Committee on Character and Fitness for the First Appellate Court District denied the application of George Anastaplo for admission to the bar of Illinois. This Court affirmed the action of the Committee, (*In re Anastaplo*, 3 Ill. 2d 471.) and the Supreme Court of the United States denied certiorari. (348 U. S. 946.)

Subsequently the applicant filed with the Committee a petition for rehearing on the basis of certain decisions of the Supreme Court of the United States. The Committee denied this petition.

The principal question presented by the petition for rehearing concerns the significance of the applicant's views as to the overthrow of government by force in the light of *Konigsberg* v. *State Bar of California*, 353 U. S. 252 and *Yates* v. *U. S.*, 1 L. ed. 1356, 77 S. Ct. 1064. Additional questions presented concern the applicant's activities since his original application was denied, and his present reputation.

We are of the opinion that the Committee should have allowed the petition for rehearing and heard evidence on these matters, and the Committee is requested to do so, and to report the evidence and its conclusions.

On October 17, 1957, at the request of the Committee, acting pursuant to the Court's direction that he be granted a rehearing, applicant filed his responses to the customary questionnaire which the Committee requires be answered by all candidates for the Bar. In responding to the questionnaire, applicant, for the most part, supplied information to the Committee which supplemented the answers which were given to a previous questionnaire filed with the Committee on October 26, 1950. The Committee has also received the usual attorneys' affidavits and character affidavits from persons familiar with the applicant and has had communications from various individuals whose names were given as references by the applicant and who supplied information concerning Anastaplo's moral character and general fitness to practice as an attorney.

Thereafter, this Committee conducted hearings on February 28, 1958, March 21, 1958, April 7, 1958, April 23, 1958 and May 19, 1958. Applicant appeared personally and gave oral testimony which, including argument, aggregates 420 pages in the record. In addition, the applicant has submitted to the Committee various law review articles, newspaper reprints and other exhibits and has addressed several letter communications to the Committee which appear in the record. During the hearings the Committee repeatedly reminded applicant that he had the right to be represented by counsel and to call witnesses, but he has preferred to rest his case on his own testimony and advocacy. (R. 3, 55.)

Since applicant's original application was denied, he has been engaged principally in the academic life as an instructor and research assistant at the University of Chicago. From the character affidavits and reference letters which have been submitted to us, it would appear that the applicant is well regarded by his academic associates, by professors who had taught him in school and by members of the Bar who know him personally. We have not been supplied with any information by any third party which is derogatory to Anastaplo's character or general reputation. We have received no information from any outside source which would cast any doubt on applicant's loyalty or which would tend to connect him in any manner with any subversive group.

We have interrogated applicant at considerable length concerning his belief in the right to overthrow the government by force and violence. The applicant's views are perhaps best summed up in his own words which appear at p. 391 of the Record:

Almost everyone would agree there are times when a government should be overthrown by force. Ultimately, a citizen has to decide for himself when such a time comes—when the principles of the Declaration of Independence apply. The conscientious citizen reserves the right and duty to judge his government even as he takes the oath to support not that government but the Constitution. In fact, our Constitution can be said to have this right implicit in it, a right that protects the Constitution itself from subversion by a government that may be constitutional only in appearance. But, as I said when I first appeared before the full Committee on January 5, 1951, I do not think anyone would be justified at a time such as this, when the normal processes of government permit reasonable and peaceful change, to participate in action leading to the overthrow of government.

The right of revolution, as I understand it, is something that probably all the members of the Committee on Character and Fitness and of the Supreme Court of Illinois believe in. The Committee must realize that I would be no less reluctant than they to see this right of revolution exercised except in the most extreme circumstances. I trust that my position, and what I have contributed to its defence, indicate an abiding commitment to constitutional government.

In explaining his view the applicant relied on excerpts from the Declaration of Independence and Lincoln's inaugural address in 1861, and quotations from Thomas Aquinas and Daniel Webster. (R. 158-159, 160, 390.) The applicant in answer to specific questions stated that he believed that the decision as to violent overthrow is essentially an individual one, but that the person making the choice should take into account the gravity of the provocation, the chance of his efforts succeeding, the general harm that his action may produce in the community, and whether his view is shared by any appreciable number of people. (R. 161-162.) The following exchange at one of the hearings sheds further light on the applicant's views in this regard:

Q. It seems to me, the subjective versus the objective standard is quite important in connection with the questions we have been putting to you. If a group of Communists believe fervently, passionately, in the kind of system that is repugnant to us, if the standard is purely subjective, then they would have the right to overthrow the government as quickly as they could, would they not?
A. No, that is not simply the question, I mean—I do not assume that any fool who decides the Government should be overthrown has the right to do so. I am not saying any group of men, fools or not fools, simply because they decide to overthrow the Government, have a right to do so. I am saying only that under certain circumstances there is a right to overthrow governments.

Let me give you an example, a couple of examples, of recent date, of two unsuccessful revolutions which I think reflect the general American opinion, I won't say necessarily reflect mine, but the general American opinion. At the end of the war, toward the end of World War II, Hitler's generals made an attempt to overthrow him. You have all heard that. They were unsuccessful. Two years ago the Hungarians made an attempt to overthrow the government. They were unsuccessful. There is no doubt, I think, on the part of the general American population, that both of these attempts at revolution were legitimate in the sense that there was no principle about the right of revolution being violated here. The only problem that one would have, I suppose, in the general opinion would be in terms of the prudence, circumstances and consequences of the particular situations. (R. 166-167.)

The applicant has further stated to the Committee that he does not believe in the right to use force until peaceful means to redress an evil have been exhausted or appear futile. In relating his views with respect to overthrow to the political situation at the present time, applicant stated that he did not foresee any condition developing where revolution would be either desirable or valuable. (R. 170.)

A majority of the Committee has arrived at the conclusion that the views expressed by the applicant with respect to the right to overthrow the government by force or violence, while strongly libertarian and expressed with an intensity and fervor not necessarily shared by all good citizens, are not inconsistent with those held by many patriotic Americans both at the present time and throughout the course of this country's history and do not in and of themselves reveal any adherence to subversive doctrines. In view of this conclusion there is no need to consider in this connection either *Yates* v. *U. S.*, 354 U. S. 298 [1957], or *Konigsberg* v. *State Bar of California*, 353 U.S. 252 [1957]. However, the *Konigsberg* case is necessarily considered in respect to the Committee's authority to ask certain questions of applicant, *infra*, p. 355 [in this book].

Apart from applicant's views as to the overthrow of the Government by force, certain other views expressed by him in these proceedings bear upon his attitude toward established authority and orderly governmental procedures. The Committee regards these views as relevant to an inquiry into the character and fitness of an applicant for admission to the bar.

One such other matter was the applicant's refusal to deny that circumstances might exist under which he would resist by force Federal or State officials seeking to enforce judgments or decrees in proceedings against him personally which had become final after full review by the highest court having jurisdiction. (R. 174-178, 237-240.) In his language, "I would not care to say there might not be instances where resistance to an officer of the law executing such a mandate might not be improper." (R. 176.) If admitted to the Bar and advising a client, he testified that he would not advise the client to resist by force or other similar means a final judgment or decree against the client, because in his opinion it was his duty to advise the client only "with respect to the legal system as it exists." (R. 177.) "In so far as I am a lawyer, I can tell him what his rights are under the accepted law . . . under the Canons of Ethics I would be derelict in my duty if I presume to do much more than that." (R. 239.) He denied that he was arrogating to himself rights or privileges which he would deny to others as "citizens." (R. 239-240.) He testified that "If, however, he (the client) were thereupon to approach me on some other basis, not as an attorney, there may be other advice I would be willing to give him." (R. 240.) He saw no inconsistency between such an opinion and the taking of an oath loyally to support the Constitution of the State of Illinois and the Constitution of the United States "without any reservation whatsoever." (R. 238.)

These views raise a serious question whether the attitude expressed by applicant toward final court determinations binding upon him and toward attempts to enforce them in accordance with the law is consistent with the oath required of attorneys in Illinois. Upon admission, an attorney is an officer of the courts, and one who holds such views as the applicant's would fall within the condemnation expressed by the United States Supreme Court in the opinion signed by all the Justices in *Cooper* v. *Aaron*, 358 U. S. 1, 3 L. ed. 2d 5 [1958], and rendered on September 29, 1958:

No state legislator or executive or judicial officer can war against the Constitution without violating his undertaking to support it. (358 U. S. at p. 8.)

The further attitude expressed by applicant about advising others along the same subversive lines in his capacity as "citizen" as distinguished from his capacity as "attorney," also raises serious questions concerning his capacity to take the oath required of Illinois attorneys. Our Supreme Court in *In re Anastaplo*, 3 Ill. 2d 471, at p. 479 [1954], pointed out the importance of the fact in Bar application cases that attorneys hold positions of public trust which give them unique opportunities to impress their views and attitudes upon the public.

Perhaps the major issue presented to the Committee arose from the applicant's continued refusal to answer questions regarding possible Communist or other subversive affiliations. (R. 34, 35-37, 42-43, 46-47, 64, 65, 66, 94-97, 98-99, 105, 172-173, 336.) We felt justified in questioning applicant on such matters for the following reasons:

1. His refusal to respond to such questions in connection with his previous candidacy was undoubtedly the controlling reason why his application was denied by the Committee and was the pivotal point in the decision of the Supreme Court of Illinois affirming the Committee's action.

2. The Committee believes that its right to question the applicant on possible subversive affiliations has not been foreclosed by the *Konigsberg* decision. (*Konigsberg* v. *State Bar of California*, 353 U. S. 252 [1957].)

This view is clearly confirmed by the later decisions of the Supreme Court of the United States in *Lerner* v. *Casey*, 357 U. S. 468, 2 L. ed. 2d 1423, 78 S. Ct. 1311 [1958], and *Beilan* v. *Board of Education*, 357 U. S. 399, 2 L. ed. 2d 1414, 78 S. Ct. 1317 [1958], both of which expressly distinguished the *Konigsberg* case.

3. The Committee was convinced that the applicant's credibility in connection with his answers to questions pertaining to the right of overthrow and the enforceability of judicial decrees should be tested by questioning him about possible subversive beliefs and activities.

4. The Committee believed that the applicant's ability to take the oath in good faith as an attorney of this State could be seriously questioned if he were an active and disciplined member of the Communist Party, especially at this juncture of history. (R. 115-116.) The Committee repeatedly warned the applicant that questions regarding Communist affiliation were viewed as important by the Committee members and that his failure to respond to them could adversely affect his application for admission to the bar. (R. 37, 116-117.) The Committee further reminded applicant that Congress, the Supreme Court of the United States and various legislatures and courts had classified the Communist Party as something separate and distinct from other political parties, and that in several jurisdictions the Party had been branded as a criminal conspiracy. (R. 115-117.) The Committee further stated that it might view a doctrinaire adherence to Communist goals as one thing, but active membership in the Party as quite another, and pointed out that until the applicant gave a candid response to the Committee's questions it could not formulate any judgment on applicant's basic loyalty. (R. 132.)

5. The Committee was directed to report to the Court on the applicant's activities since his original application was denied. The principal way in which the Committee ascertains the activities in which a candidate has been engaged is by asking him questions.

Notwithstanding the foregoing, the applicant persistently refused to answer questions concerning Communist or other subversive affiliations. To explain his refusal he stated that such inquiries violated fundamental civil rights guaranteed to him by the First and Fourteenth Amendments to the Federal Constitution and by the Constitution of the State of Illinois. He did not rely upon any privilege against self-incrimination. He stated that his political beliefs were not a proper subject of inquiry by the Committee and bore no relevance to the question of his character and fitness.* He objected to any inquiry into such matters since the Committee, in his view,

---

* The applicant did not adopt this position at all stages of the hearing. He freely answered portions of the questionnaire dealing with constitutional doctrine and expatiated at length on his belief in violent overthrow.

had laid no foundation for such an inquiry and had no evidence before it which would justify what he considered an intrusion into his private beliefs; he did not consider that his views with respect to overthrow of the government or disobedience of judicial decrees furnished any basis for any such questions. (R. 139, 155-157, 173.)

The applicant relies heavily on the *Konigsberg* case to support his refusal to answer questions concerning possible subversive affiliations and activities. We read the *Konigsberg* case to hold that a committee performing functions similar to our own is not entitled to draw an inference of bad moral character merely from the applicant's refusal to answer questions concerning membership in the Communist Party if such refusal is based on a good-faith belief that the United States Constitution prohibited the type of inquiry which the Committee was making and if the reviewing court can "find nothing in the record which indicates that his position was not taken in good faith." (353 U. S. at p. 270.) The Court pointed out that the State Committee of Bar Examiners in California had at no point intimated to Konigsberg that he would be barred from the profession just because he refused to answer relevant inquiries or because he was obstructing the Committee. In the view of the Court the Committee's action was based principally upon inference which it drew from certain of applicant's past utterances, prior membership in the Communist Party and refusal to answer questions bearing upon present membership in the Party. (353 U. S. at p. 266.) The court held that considering the record as a whole such inferences were not permissible. The court expressly left open the question whether Konigsberg's constitutional objections to the Committee's questions were well founded and whether the Committee would be justified in insisting that its questions be answered. (353 U. S. at p. 270.)

The *Konigsberg* case is therefore not determinative in this proceeding. The United States Supreme Court in holding in that case that a committee like ours is not entitled to draw an inference of bad moral character merely from an applicant's refusal to answer questions concerning membership in the Communist Party, if such refusal is based upon a good faith belief that the United States Constitution prohibits the type of inquiry which the committee was making and if the Court could find nothing in the record to indicate bad faith on his part (353 U. S. 252, 270), did not hold that such a condition of a record affirmatively entitled an applicant to certification. Upon determination of the propriety of the questions and the lack of substance in the objections thereto the applicant would be entitled to another opportunity to answer, and if he persisted in his refusal to do so, the committee would not be acting inconsistently with *Konigsberg* in denying a certification.

Since the rehearing was granted herein, the United States Supreme

Court decided on June 21, 1958, the cases of *Lerner v. Casey*, 357 U. S. 468, 2 L. ed. 2d 1423, 78 S. Ct. 1311 [1958], and *Beilan v. Board of Education of Philadelphia*, 357 U. S. 399, 2 L. ed. 2d 1414, 78 S. Ct. 1317 [1958], in which the Court clearly determined the propriety of questions of the kind asked the applicant in these proceedings. We called applicant's attention to these two most recent decisions and offered to him the opportunity to change his testimony in any manner he saw fit in the light of them. (Committee letter to applicant dated September 16, 1958.) He declined. (Applicant's letter to the Committee dated September 23, 1958.) His continued refusal to answer, evidenced by his reply of September 23, 1958, deprives him on this record of any argument of similarity between his status and that of Konigsberg and of any benefits from the decision in the *Konigsberg* case.

In *Lerner v. Casey, supra*, petitioner, a subway conductor in the New York City Transit System, was discharged by his employer under the New York Security Risk Law on the ground that his refusal, based upon the privilege against self incrimination guaranteed by the Fifth Amendment, to answer a question of his employer as to his membership in the Communist Party, showed that he was of doubtful trust and reliability. Petitioner sued in the New York State Court for reinstatement, attacking his discharge on various grounds, including lack of due process. The New York Supreme Court dismissed the suit and the Appellate Division and Court of Appeals both affirmed. On certiorari the United States Supreme Court also affirmed. Justice Harlan for the majority said:

In other words, we read the court's opinion as meaning that a finding of doubtful trust and reliability could justifiably be based on appellant's lack of frankness, cf. *Garner v. Board of Public Works*, 341 U. S. 716 [1951]; *Beilan v. Board of Public Education, ante*, p. 399, decided today, just as if he had refused to give any other information about himself which might be relevant to his employment. It was this lack of candor which provided the evidence of appellant's doubtful trust and reliability which under the New York statutory scheme constituted him a security risk. The Court of Appeals went on to reason that had appellant refused, without more, to answer the question, the finding of "doubtful trust and reliability" would have undoubtedly been permissible, and that the basis for such a finding, in appellant's refusal to answer, was not destroyed by the claim of the Fifth Amendment privilege because the Commissioner was not required to accept that claim as an adequate explanation of the refusal.

Accepting as we do, these premises of the state court's opinion, we find no constitutional block to its decision sustaining appellant's dismissal from employment. . . .

Nor, as the Court of Appeals stressed, was the claim of possible self-incrimination made the basis for an inference that appellant was a Communist and therefore unreliable. Hence we are not faced here with the question whether party membership may rationally be inferred from a refusal to answer a question directed to present membership where the refusal rests on the belief that an answer might incriminate, cf. *Adamson* v. *California*, 332 U. S. 46 [1947], or with the question whether membership in the Communist Party which might be "innocent" can be relied upon as a ground for denial of state employment. Cf. *Wieman* v. *Updegraff*, [344 U. S. 183 (1952)]; *Konigsberg* v. *State Bar of California*, 353 U. S. 252 [1957]; *Schware* v. *Board of Bar Examiners*, 353 U. S. 232 [1957].

We think it scarcely debatable that had there been no claim of Fifth Amendment privilege, New York would have been constitutionally entitled to conclude from appellant's refusal to answer what must be conceded to have been a question relevant to the purposes of the statute and his employment, cf. *Garner* v. *Board of Public Works, supra*, that he was of doubtful trust and reliability. Such a conclusion is not "so strained as not to have a reasonable relation to the circumstances of life as we know them." *Tot* v. *United States*, 319 U. S. 463, 468 [1943]. This Court pointed out in *Garner* that a government employee can be required upon pain of dismissal to respond to inquiry probing into matters relevant to his employment, and that present membership in the Communist Party is such a matter. See also *Beilan* v. *Board of Public Education, supra*. Certainly it is not a controlling constitutional distinction that New York, rather than impose on employees, as in *Garner* and *Beilan*, an absolute duty to respond to permissible inquiry upon threat of dismissal for refusal, has in these proceedings held that an employee lacking in candor to his governmental employer evidences doubt as to his trust and reliability. Finally, unlike the situation involved in *Konigsberg* v. *State Bar of California, supra*, there is here no problem of inadequate notice as to the consequences of refusal to answer, for appellant was specifically notified that continued refusal might lead to his dismissal. (See 357 U. S. at pp. 476, 477-8.)

In *Beilan* v. *Board of Education of Philadelphia, supra*, petitioner, a public school teacher, was discharged by the local school board for "incompetency" under the Pennsylvania School Code, because of his refusal, continued after warning that failure to answer might lead to dismissal, to answer a question of his superintendent as to his membership in a Communist political association. On an administrative appeal, the superintendent sustained the local Board, but the County Court set aside the discharge. On appeal by the Board the Pennsylvania Supreme Court reversed and reinstated the discharge. On certiorari the United States Supreme Court affirmed. It held that due process was not violated by petitioner's discharge on the ground of "incompetency" evidenced by petitioner's refusal to answer the request of the superintendent for information as to the teacher's loyalty and as to his activities in certain subversive organizations, such refusal being based upon the Fifth Amendment and other constitutional objections.

Justice Burton said:

The only question before us is whether the Federal Constitution prohibits petitioner's discharge for statutory "incompetency" based on his refusal to answer the Superintendent's questions.

By engaging in teaching in the public schools, petitioner did not give up his right to freedom of belief, speech or association. He did, however, undertake obligations of frankness, candor and cooperation in answering inquiries made of him by his employing Board examining into his fitness to serve it as a public school teacher. . . .

The question asked of petitioner by his Superintendent was relevant to the issue of petitioner's fitness and suitability to serve as a teacher. . . . He made it clear that he would not answer any question of the same type as the one asked. Petitioner blocked from the beginning any inquiry into his Communist activities, however relevant to his present loyalty. The Board based its dismissal upon petitioner's refusal to answer any inquiry about his relevant activities—not upon those activities themselves. It took care to charge petitioner with incompetency, and not with disloyalty. It found him insubordinate and lacking in frankness and candor—it made no finding as to his loyalty. . . .

In the instant case, the Pennsylvania Supreme Court has held that "incompetency" includes petitioner's "deliberate and insubordinate refusal to answer the questions of his administrative superior in a vitally important matter pertaining to his fitness." 386 Pa., at 91, 125 A. 2d, at 331 [1956]. This interpretation is not inconsistent with the Federal Constitution. . . .

Our recent decisions in *Slochower* v. *Board of Education*, 350 U. S. 551 [1956], and *Konigsberg* v. *State Bar of California*, 353 U. S. 252 [1957], are distinguishable. . . .

In the *Konigsberg* case, *supra*, at 259-261, this Court stressed the fact that the action of the State was not based on the mere refusal to answer relevant questions—rather, it was based on inferences impermissibly drawn from the refusal. In the instant case, no inferences at all were drawn from petitioner's refusal to answer. The Pennsylvania Supreme Court merely equated refusal to answer the employing Board's relevant questions with statutory "incompetency." (357 U. S. at pp. 404-406, 408-409.)

In the instant case, as in *Lerner* and *Beilan*, and unlike the situation in *Konigsberg*, no problem exists as to inadequate notice of the consequences of a refusal to answer; the applicant was specifically notified both by the Illinois Supreme Court in its opinion in 3 Ill. 2d 471 [1954], and by this Committee on rehearing that his continued refusal to answer might lead to the denial of his application. (R. 37, 116-117.)

In the course of the rehearing proceedings, the Committee conducted no independent investigation into applicant's character, reputation or activities. The Committee has no personnel nor other resources for any such investigation. For this very practical reason, the Committee has traditionally asserted the view that it cannot be expected to carry the burden of establishing, by independent investigation, whether or not an applicant possesses the requisite character and fitness for admission to the bar. It is rather for the applicant to establish, on his own behalf, that he possesses the necessary qualifications and it is for the Committee to test, by hearings and inquiry of the applicant, the worth of the evidence which the applicant proffers.

Because the applicant has refused to answer questions, we are unable to report whether his activities since the denial of his original application have included membership, office holding or other activities in the various organizations listed on the Attorney General list of subversive organizations. We are also unable to report what his reputation is among the members of any organization with which he may be affiliated, since he has declined to inform us of his affiliations.

In the instant proceeding a majority of the Committee is of the opinion that applicant's petition for a license should be denied because he has failed to meet the burden which is on him of establishing his proper character and fitness. By refusing to answer questions deemed by the Committee to be relevant, he has thereby failed to establish that he has the necessary character and fitness and the Committee is therefore unable to certify him.

In this connection the Supreme Court in *In re Anastaplo*, 3 Ill. 2d 471, said (pp. 480, 483) [1954]:

It is our opinion, therefore, that a member of the Communist Party may, because of such membership, be unable truthfully and in good conscience to take the oath required as a condition for admission to practice, and we hold that it is relevant to inquire of an applicant as to his membership in that party. A negative answer to the question, if accepted as true, would end the inquiry on the point. If the truthfulness of a negative answer were doubted, further questions and information to test the veracity of the applicant would be proper. If an affirmative answer were received, further inquiry into the applicant's innocence or knowledge as to the subversive nature of the organization would be relevant. Under any hypothesis, therefore, questions as to membership in the Communist Party or known subversive "front" organizations were relevant to the inquiry into petitioner's fitness for admission to the bar. His refusal to answer has prevented the committee from inquiring fully into his general fitness and good citizenship and justifies their refusal to issue a certificate. . . .

We conclude that the committee's inquiry into petitioner's membership in the Communist Party was relevant to a determination of his good citizenship and his ability to take the oath of lawyer in good conscience, and that petitioner's constitutional rights were not infringed upon by such action. On the present record the petition must be denied.

A majority of the Committee continues to adhere to the views which were the basis of its decision on Anastaplo's prior application and which were expressed by the Supreme Court of Illinois in *In re Anastaplo*, 3 Ill. 2d 471 at 480-483 [1954], to the effect that it may properly interrogate an applicant as to membership in the Communist Party or in any other subversive group and that such inquiries are relevant to character and fitness. It believes that an applicant is not protected from such questions by any provisions of the State or Federal Constitutions. An applicant, of course, need not answer the question and cannot be punished for his refusal to respond. But his failure to reply, in our view, (i) obstructs the lawful processes of the Committee, (ii) prevents inquiry into subjects which bear intimately upon the issue of character and fitness, such as loyalty to our basic institutions, belief in representative government and *bona fides* of the attorney's oath and (iii) results in his failure to meet the burden of establishing that he possesses the good moral character and fitness to practice law, which are conditions to the granting of a license to practice law.

We draw no inference of disloyalty or subversion from applicant's continued refusal to answer questions concerning Communist or other subversive affiliations. We do, however, hold that there is a strong public interest in our being free to question applicants for admission to the bar on their adherence to our basic institutions and form of government and that such public interest in the character of its attorneys overrides an applicant's private interest in keeping such views to himself. By failing to respond to this higher public interest we hold that the applicant has obstructed the proper functions of the Committee. By reason of applicant's own recalcitrance he has failed to demonstrate the good moral character and general fitness to practice law necessary for admission to the Bar. We cannot certify the applicant as worthy of the trust and confidence of the public when we do not know that he is so worthy and when he has prevented us from finding out.

Certain members of the Committee (who are included within the majority who believe that applicant's petition for a license should be denied because he has failed to meet the burden which is on him of establishing his proper character and fitness) are of the further opinion that the record demonstrates affirmatively applicant's lack of the character and fitness necessary for admission to the Bar. They base their views upon (i) applicant's refusal, after the *Lerner* and *Beilan* decisions were called to his attention, to modify his refusal to answer the Committee's questions concerning Communist Party and other possible subversive affiliations and (ii) applicant's view that circumstances might exist under which he would not abide by, and might advise other citizens not to abide by, final decrees of a court of law and to resist by force their enforcement by appropriate legal process, when considered in connection with his views as to the overthrow of the government by force and violence.

It is the conclusion of the Committee that the application should be denied.

The Committee invoked a "higher public interest." It never seemed to appreciate the fact, however, that I was attempting to invoke (at my expense, not theirs!) an even higher public interest, not merely a "private interest in keeping [my] views to [my]self." Indeed, my views had been all too evident throughout these hearings (see the committee's lone footnote) as well as among all who knew of me in Illinois.

The Committee's dependence upon the *Beilan* and *Lerner* cases, in which there had been no extensive examination conducted by the state, ignored the implications of the fact that those were Fifth Amendment cases of "governmental employees." If lawyers *should* succeed in having themselves regarded as public employees, they would face the unattractive (and, for our Republic, even dangerous) prospect of having their income as well as their "loyalty" dictated by the government. (My letter of Sept. 23, 1958 analyzing *Beilan* and *Lerner* may be found at pp. 442-47 of the Transcript of Record I filed in the Supreme Court. See p. 392, below.)

The major reasons why the character committee ruled against me were omitted from this majority report. The first omitted reason was that evident in the exchange with Justice Daily recorded at p. 340, above, and hinted at by Professor Sharp (at p. 336, above): my refusal to submit to the demands of the pampered elders of the tribe. They were not used to being told publicly (even though some of them agreed privately) that a bar applicant's political affiliations were none of their business. (This is related to American "suspic[ion] of anything which smacks of 'holding back.' " See chap. 8, n. 74, pp. 372, 384-85, 396-97, below.)

The second omitted reason came out when one of the committee majority was provoked to admit, in justifying his vote to troubled friends, "Anastaplo always conducted himself before our committee as if he was better than us." (Cf. Aristotle, *Nicomachean Ethics* 1124b19.) This lawyer's complaint would be reinforced in the eyes of some by the letter I was moved to write in 1965 to a distinguished member of the Chicago bar who had been in 1959 another of the committee majority:

Our passing encounter at the [University of Chicago] Law School Alumni Dinner last night prompts me to send you the enclosed articles [I have written] and to observe that I have long considered your vote as the decisive one in the rejection by the character committee in 1959 of my application for admission to the bar. I say decisive since the newly-elected president of the bar association was able by his example to take with him, or at least reassure, other less eminent members of the committee in the course they were pursuing. And, as you may recall, a switch of only three votes would have given me the majority to which I was entitled.

I mention these observations not because of anything I want done about my career at this time—for I do consider myself retired from the practice of law—, but in order to remind you that both you and I know that you did not behave as you should have on that occasion.

Nor would I bother to extend to you the caution and counsel implied in these words if it did not seem to many of your fellow alumni that a distinguished career awaited you.

5. I'M SURE WE CAN RELY ON MR. ANASTAPLO (DECEMBER 14, 1960)

Laurence Berns, of St. John's College, Annapolis, Maryland, wrote to another professor on November 7, 1961 (and thereafter distributed in mimeographed form), the following account of my December 14, 1960, oral argument before the Supreme Court of the United States. (See, also, on the oral argument, *New York Times*, December 18, 1960, p. 40.)

LAURENCE BERNS'S LETTER REGARDING THE ORAL ARGUMENT IN 1960 BEFORE THE U.S. SUPREME COURT, 1961

George Anastaplo informs me that you are preparing a study of his bar admission case and would like to have some of my impressions of his oral argument before the Supreme Court of the United States. . . . A number of things about the oral argument stand out in my mind. First was Mr. Anastaplo's unhistrionic, lawyerlike approach. He began by talking about the Committee rules and how on any reasonable understanding of those rules he had fulfilled the requirements. I was somewhat fooled by the benevolent manner the Court displayed towards him. The only time there was any give and take was when Justice Frankfurter, during Mr. Anastaplo's discussion of the right to resist tyrannical or insane judicial decrees, got him to retract the words "so mistaken", arguing that being mistaken didn't seem to be heinous enough to justify revolution. Justice Clark smiled very benignly at Anastaplo throughout his presentation, but asked no questions. I was disturbed that Justice Whittaker and especially Justice Harlan were raising no questions or arguments. I had heard that Justice Harlan was a very good lawyer and therefore might be open to having his mind changed by a reasonable argument. His silence and expression led me to think that probably he had already made up his mind and wasn't even interested in hearing opposition arguments. His opinion, later, strengthened that impression. Also I felt that Mr. Anastaplo is more at home and at his best in give and take discussions, more so than he is at making set speeches. If the judges had let him know what they thought the problems with his position were, he would have been able to meet those problems directly. At first they might have held back in order not to rattle an inexperienced pleader. But is seemed pretty clear after the first half hour that he was not likely to get rattled.

My first surprise was upon hearing Assistant Attorney General [William C.] Wines speak [for the State of Illinois]. He was repeating exactly the same arguments (they were sophisms rather than arguments) that I thought had been demolished by Mr. Anastaplo's Reply Brief. Part of the surprise came from my realization that the Justices had apparently not read the briefs. I have been informed since that that is normal practice in the Supreme Court of the United States. The Justices were clearly very sharp and caught on to a number of the Attorney General's sophisms, but it took them ten or fifteen minutes to catch on to what they could have seen immediately had they read the briefs. For instance, Mr. Wines spoke about the clear warning that Illinois had given Mr. Anastaplo that a refusal to answer would act to exclude him. He went on for about ten minutes before Justice Stewart, I believe, asked him what the date of that warning was. It turned out to be the 1954 decision, the same decision which the very Court that issued the "warning" called into question by ordering the Character Committee to give Anastaplo a new hearing in 1957. Again, Mr. Anastaplo had emphasized the Committee rules. Mr. Wines minimized the importance of the Committee by stressing that the ultimate power of admission rests with the Illinois Supreme Court. Justice Black asked him whether the Court had ever refused to admit anyone who had been granted a certificate of entitlement by the Committee. Mr. Wines, it seemed to me, pretended to misunderstand the question repeatedly for about ten minutes again, by bringing up a few exceptional cases where the Court had admitted persons rejected by the Committee. He finally admitted that he knew of no cases of the sort the Justice was asking about. He brought up, as the Attorney General's brief did, those non-existent "very poorly written" essays which were supposed to have prompted the Committee to put political questions to Mr. Anastaplo. This, among other gross errors of fact, had been completely exposed in the Reply Brief. This time I wondered whether Mr. Wines had read the briefs, for being pushed as to where one could find those essays, if they existed, he finally turned to Mr. Anastaplo and said, "I'm sure we can rely on Mr. Anastaplo to tell us if they exist and where." In addition to relying on Mr. Anastaplo's character and fitness, he was also relying on the Justices' not having read the briefs. This was another one of those ludicrous incidents that made all talk of insufficient proof of good character look ridiculous. Mr. Anastaplo replied, and the statement was accepted, as a matter of course, both by the Court and by the opposition, that there were no such writings unless there was being referred to that one sentence on his application form which was quoted almost word for word from the Declaration of Independence. One got the suspicion that Mr. Wines, as representative of the Attorney General's office, may have been forced to defend a brief that he seemed too intelligent to have written.

The questioning of Mr. Wines was much more spirited, especially since Justice Frankfurter kept using Mr. Wines as a backboard to deflect his objections to Justice Black's questions. Once it had been clarified that according to the statute the Illinois Supreme Court was the ultimate admitting body, Justice Frankfurter seemed to think that enquiry into the significance of the Committee's role was out of order. Justice Black was obviously aware of these distinctions, but nevertheless insisted on learning how the law worked in practice, what the law is in effect. Since it would be absurd to think that the Illinois Supreme Court examines the merits of each application to its Bar, the relevance of the questions seemed obvious to me. Despite Justice Frankfurter's occasional displays of bad temper, I was impressed by the great dignity of the Court. The manly bearing of the Chief Justice contributed to this impression. His large size, handsomeness and apparent strength, combined with his kindly, pleasant and almost gentle manners, in addition to his quite plain diction, would seem to have the effect of putting those facing the Bench at their ease and at the same time impressing them with the dignity of the Court. I thought him a kind of living argument for democracy.

While everyone we spoke to, including opposition lawyers, were very laudatory about Mr. Anastaplo's presentation, he and I, though we felt (perhaps I should only speak for myself) he had done a good job, were a little disappointed. He had not, I think we felt, been at his best. On reflection, however, I felt that his choice of subjects and arguments—his lawyerlike emphasis on the Committee rules, the 1957 Illinois Supreme Court order, then the Declaration of Independence and the right to revolution and the report of Brown and Fassett ["Loyalty Tests for Admission to the Bar," *Univ. Chicago L. Rev.*, 20:65 (1959)] illustrating the corrupting effect of the unrestrained behaviour of the Committee—this, I thought, could scarcely have been improved upon.

He still had some fifteen minutes rebuttal time when the recess for lunch was called. I urged him strongly to make a fighting speech listing the errors of fact and fabrications of the opposition in order to make clear how the many concessions of the Committee and Courts had left the Attorney General with no substantial case. I particularly urged him to repeat "at least three times", what he had taken such pains to make clear in the record (even before the *Konigsberg* case supposedly settled the matter), what had been stated so clearly by Justice Bristow of the Supreme Court of Illinois, and what had been ignored in the Attorney General's brief and oral argument, namely, that he was not resting his case finally on a denial of the right of the Committee to ask its questions, but rather that his refusals to answer based, as had been generally conceded, on sincere and conscientious beliefs that such inquiries were unconstitutional and subversive of the public good, were not a sufficient basis for holding that he had failed to establish sufficient moral character for admission to the bar, especially in the light of his long, laborious and more than courteous cooperation with the Committee.

Instead of that he made a quite eloquent and high-minded speech, touching on the main points of the argument, the importance of the real issue, i.e., what kind of men we want our bar and nation to contain and encourage, how special pleading was completely out of order in this matter, how he did not want to be admitted on any other ground than what the law and sound public policy demand and finally his gratitude at having been allowed to appear before the Court. Although I thought a different kind of speech would have been more effective from the point of view of winning, I was glad he made the speech he did. He is quite capable of putting up a good fight, but evidently felt that attempting to gain sympathy by spelling out the rather shoddy tactics used against him would be somewhat unseemly in such august surroundings. He admitted that he might have done it differently if he had been fighting to win for someone else. This was the only occasion I know of where he admitted that he might have been at some disadvantage from handling his own case. By handling it himself he was making sure that it remained continually on a high plane.

A more serious (but far from conventional) criticism of my position than anything the committee or courts ever made, and one for which I have some sympathy, may be found in the thoughtful dialogue developed by Mr. Berns, "Two Old Conservatives Discuss the Anastaplo Case," *Cornell L. Rev.*, 54:920 (1969). (Compare the comments on my case by two other, and even more mature, conservatives, Willmoore Kendall, Book Review, *American Political Science Review*, 61:783 [1967]; Malcolm P. Sharp, "The Conservative Fellow Traveler," *Univ. Chicago L. Rev.* 30: 704 [1963]. See, also, *Univ. Chicago L. Rev.* 33:221 [1966].) But, it should be added, a character committee or court capable of making such criticism would have been sensible enough to recognize me as educable and hence safe, and perhaps even useful, to admit to the bar.)

6. He Took Too Much of the Responsibility of Preserving His Country's Freedom upon Himself (April 24, 1961)

The majority opinion in the Supreme Court of the United States was written by Justice Harlan. *In re Anastaplo*, 366 U.S. 82, 81 S.Ct. 978, 6 L.ed.2d 135 (April 24, 1961). This opinion has been summarized as follows in the syllabus prepared by the Reporter of Decisions, 366 U.S., at 82:

SYLLABUS OF THE OPINION OF THE MAJORITY OF THE COURT, 1961

A rule of the Supreme Court of Illinois provides that applicants shall be admitted by it to the practice of law after satisfactory examination by the Board of Examiners and certification of qualification by a Committee on Character and Fitness. In hearings before that Committee, petitioner refused to answer any questions pertaining to his membership in the Communist Party, not on the grounds of possible self-incrimination, but on the ground that such inquiries violated his freedom of speech and association. The Committee declined to certify him as qualified for admission to the Bar, solely on the ground that his refusals to answer such questions had obstructed the Committee's performance of its functions. The State Supreme Court denied him admission to practice. *Held*: Denial of petitioner's application for admission to the Bar on this ground did not violate his rights under the Fourteenth Amendment. Pp. 83-97.

(a) It is not constitutionally impermissible for a State to adopt a rule that an applicant will not be admitted to the practice of law if, and so long as, by refusing to answer material questions, he obstructs a bar examining committee in its proper functions of interrogating and cross-examining him upon his qualifications, *Konigsberg* v. *State Bar, ante*, p. 36. P. 88.

(b) Petitioner was not privileged under the Fourteenth Amendment to refuse to answer questions concerning membership in the Communist Party. *Konigsberg* v. *State Bar, supra*. P. 89.

(c) The fact that there was no independent evidence that petitioner had ever been a member of the Communist Party did not prevent the State, acting in good faith, from making this inquiry in an investigation of this kind. Pp. 89-90.

(d) During the hearings before the Committee, petitioner was given adequate warning as to the consequences of his refusal to answer the Committee's questions relating to membership in the Communist Party. Pp. 90-94.

(e) In the circumstances of this case, petitioner's exclusion from the Bar on the ground that he had obstructed the Committee in the performance of its duty was not arbitrary or discriminatory. Pp. 94-97.

Justice Harlan (pp. 356-57, above) concluded his opinion (366 U.S., at 97):

[O]ur function here is solely one of constitutional adjudication, not to pass judgment on what has been done as if we were another state court of review, still less to express any view upon the wisdom of the State's action. With appropriate regard for the limited range of our authority we cannot say that the State's denial of Anastaplo's application for admission to its bar offends the Federal Constitution. The judgment of the Illinois Supreme Court must therefore be affirmed.

Or, as Sharp observed [page 336, above], the majority opinion "supported its decision [affirming Illinois's action] by a reference to the Court's limited power to review state action." (See, with respect to this limitation, the motion discussed in section 9 of this appendix, below. Insofar as the majority opinion of the Supreme Court of the United States is distinctive, it is quoted from and dealt with in Justice Black's dissent and in my Petition for Rehearing [section 7 of this appendix].)

There is to be found in the *Anastaplo* case, 366 U.S. 82, 97, 81 S.Ct. 978, 987, 6 L.ed.2d 135, 145 (April 24, 1961) the following dissenting opinion by Justice Black (with whom Chief Justice Warren, Justice Douglas, and Justice Brennan concurred). (When Justice Black refers simply to "The majority," he is [unless otherwise indicated] referring to Justice Harlan's opinion for the majority of the Court.)

JUSTICE BLACK'S DISSENTING OPINION, 1961

The petitioner George Anastaplo has been denied the right to practice law in the State of Illinois for refusing to answer questions about his views and associations. I think this action by the State violated rights guaranteed to him by the First and Fourteenth Amendments. The reasons which lead me to this conclusion are largely the same as those expressed in my dissenting opinion in *Konigsberg* v. *State Bar of California*, the companion case decided today, *ante*, [366 U.S.] 56. But this case provides such a striking illustration of the destruction that can be inflicted upon individual liberty when this Court fails to enforce the First Amendment to the full extent of its express and unequivocal terms that I think it deserves separate treatment.

The controversy began in November 1950,[1] when Anastaplo, a student at the University of Chicago Law School, having two months previously successfully passed the Illinois Bar examination, appeared before the State's Committee on Character and Fitness for the usual interview preliminary to admission to the Bar. The personal history form required by state law had been filled out and filed with the Committee prior to his appearance and showed that Anastaplo was an unusually worthy applicant for admission. His early life had been spent in a small town in southern Illinois where his parents, who had immigrated to this country from Greece before his birth, still resided. After having received his precollege education in the public schools of his home town, he had discontinued his education, at the age of eighteen, and joined the Air Force during the middle of World War II—flying as a navigator in every major theater of the military operations of that war. Upon receiving an honorable discharge in 1947, he had come to Chicago and resumed his education, obtaining his undergraduate degree at the University of Chicago and entering immediately into the study of law at the University of Chicago Law School. His record throughout his life, both as a student and as a citizen, was unblemished.

The personal history form thus did not contain so much as one statement of *fact* about Anastaplo's past life or conduct that could have, in any way, cast doubt upon his fitness for admission to the Bar. It did, however, contain a statement of *opinion* which, in the minds of some of the members of the Committee at least, did cast such doubt and in that way served to touch off this controversy. This was a statement made by Anastaplo in response to the command of the personal history form: "State what you consider to be the principles underlying (a) the Constitution of the United States." Anastaplo's response to that command was as follows:

One principle consists of the doctrine of the separation of powers; thus, among the Executive, Legislative, and Judiciary are distributed various functions and powers in a manner designed to provide for a balance of power, thereby intending to prevent totally unrestrained action by any one branch of government. Another basic principle (and the most important) is that such government is constituted so as to secure certain inalienable rights, those rights to Life, Liberty and the Pursuit of Happiness (and elements of these rights are explicitly set forth in such parts of the Constitution as the Bill of Rights). *And, of course, whenever the particular government in power becomes destructive of these ends, it is the right of the people to alter or to abolish it and thereupon to establish a new government.* This is how I view the Constitution. (Emphasis supplied.)

When Anastaplo appeared before a two-man Subcommittee of the Committee on Character and Fitness, one of its members almost immediately engaged him in a discussion relating to the meaning of these italicized words which were substantially taken from that part of the Declaration of Independence set out below.[2] This discussion soon developed into an argument as Anastaplo stood by his statement and insisted that if a government gets bad enough, the people have a "right of revolution." It was at this juncture in the proceedings that the other member of the Subcommittee interrupted with the question: "Are you a member of any organization that is listed on the Attorney General's list, to your knowledge?" And this question was followed up a few moments later with the question: "Are you a member of the Communist Party?"[3] A colloquy then ensued between Anastaplo and the two members of the Subcommittee as to the legitimacy of the questions being asked, Anastaplo insisting that these questions were not reasonably related to the Committee's functions and that they violated his rights under the Constitution, and the members of the Subcommittee insisting that the questions were entirely legitimate.

The Subcommittee then refused to certify Anastaplo for admission to the Bar but, instead, set a further hearing on the matter before the full Committee. That next hearing, as well as all of the hearings that followed, have been little more than repetitions of the first. The rift between Anastaplo and the Committee has grown ever wider with each successive hearing. Anastaplo has steadfastly refused to answer any questions put by the Committee which inquired into his political associations or religious beliefs. A majority of the members of the Committee, faced with this refusal, has grown more and more insistent that it has the right to force him to answer any question it sees fit to ask. The result has been a series of hearings in which questions have been put to Anastaplo with regard to his "possible" association with scores of organizations, including the Ku Klux Klan, the Silver Shirts (an allegedly Fascist organization), every organization on the so-called Attorney General's list, the Democratic Party, the Republican Party, and the Communist Party. At one point in the proceedings, at least two of the members of the Committee insisted that he tell the Committee whether he believes in a Supreme Being and one of these members stated that, as far as his vote was concerned, a man's "belief in the Deity . . . has a substantial bearing upon his fitness to practice law."

It is true, as the majority points out, that the Committee did not expressly rest its refusal to certify Anastaplo for admission to the Bar either upon his views on the "right of revolution," as that "right" is defined in the Declaration of Independence, or upon his refusal to disclose his beliefs with regard to the existence of God,[4] or upon his refusals to disclose any of his political associations other than his "possible" association with the Communist Party. But it certainly cannot be denied that the other questions were asked and, since we should not presume that these members of the Committee did not want answers to their questions, it seems certain that Anastaplo's refusal to answer them must have had some influence upon the final outcome of the hearings. In any case, when the Committee did vote, 11-6, not to certify Anastaplo for admission, not one member who asked *any* question Anastaplo had refused to answer voted in his favor.

The reasons for Anastaplo's position have been stated by him time and again—first, to the Committee and, later, in the briefs and oral arguments he presented in his own behalf, both before this Court and before the Supreme Court of Illinois. From a legal standpoint, his position throughout has been that the First Amendment gave him a right not to disclose his political associations or his religious beliefs to the Committee. But his decision to refuse to disclose these associations and beliefs went much deeper than a bare reliance upon what he considered to be his legal rights. The record shows that his refusal to answer the Committee's question stemmed primarily from his belief that he had a duty, both to society and to the legal profession, not to submit to the demands of the Committee because he believed that the questions had been asked solely for the purpose of harassing him because he had expressed agreement with the assertion of the right of revolution against an evil government set out in the Declaration of Independence. His position was perhaps best stated before the Committee in his closing remarks at the final session [May 26, 1958]:

> It is time now to close. Differences between us remain. I leave to others the sometimes necessary but relatively easy task of praising Athens to Athenians. Besides, you should want no higher praise than what I have said about the contribution the bar can make to republican government. The bar deserves no higher praise until it makes that contribution. You should be grateful that I have not made a complete submission to you, even though I have cooperated as fully as good conscience permits. To the extent I have not submitted, to that extent have I contributed to the solution of one of the most pressing problems that you, as men devoted to character and fitness, must face. This is the problem of selecting the standards and methods the bar must employ if it is to help preserve and nourish that idealism, that vital interest in the problem of justice, that so often lies at the heart of the intelligent and sensitive law student's choice of career. This is an idealism which so many things about the bar, and even about bar admission practices, discourage and make unfashionable to defend or retain. The worthiest men live where the rewards of virtue are greatest.
>
> I leave with you men of Illinois the suggestion that you do yourselves and the bar the honor, as well as the service, of anticipating what I trust will be the judgment of our most thoughtful judges. I move therefore that you recommend to the Supreme Court of Illinois that I be admitted to the bar of this State. And I suggest that this recommendation be made retroactive to November 10, 1950 when a young Air Force veteran first was so foolish as to continue to serve his country by daring to defend against a committee on character and fitness the teaching of the Declaration of Independence on the right of revolution.

The reasons for the Committee's position are also clear. Its job, throughout these proceedings, has been to determine whether Anastaplo is possessed of the necessary good moral character to justify his admission to the Bar of Illinois. In that regard, the Committee has been given the benefit of voluminous affidavits from men of standing in their professions and in the community that Anastaplo is possessed of an unusually fine character. Dr. Alexander Meiklejohn, Professor of Philosophy Emeritus, at the University of Wisconsin, for example, described Anastaplo as "intellectually able, a hard, thorough student and moved by high devotion to the principles of freedom and justice." Professor Malcolm P. Sharp of the University of Chicago Law School stated: "No question has ever been raised about his honesty or his integrity, and his general conduct, characterized by friendliness, quiet independence, industry and courage, is reflected in his reputation." Professor Roscoe T. Steffen of the University of Chicago Law School said: "I know of no one who doubts his honesty and integrity." Yves R. Simon, Professor of Philosophy at the University of Chicago, said: "I consider Anastaplo as a young man of the most distinguished and lofty moral character. Everybody respects him and likes him." Angelo G. Geocaris, a practicing attorney in the City of Chicago, said of Anastaplo: "His personal code of ethics is unexcelled by any practicing attorney I have met in the state of Illinois." Robert J. Coughlan, Division Director of a research project at the University of Chicago, said: "His honesty and integrity are, in my opinion, beyond question. I would highly recommend him without the slightest reservation for any position involving the highest or most sacred trust. The applicant is a rare man among us today: he has an inviolable sense of Honor in the great traditions of Greek culture and thought. If admitted to the American Bar, he could do nothing that would not reflect glory on that institution."

These affidavits and many more like them were presented to the Committee. Most of the statements came from men who knew Anastaplo intimately on the University of Chicago campus where Anastaplo has remained throughout the proceedings here involved, working as a research assistant and as a lecturer in Liberal Arts and studying for an advanced degree in History and Social Sciences. Even at the present time, he is still there preparing his doctoral dissertation which, understandably enough, is tentatively entitled "The Historical and Philosophical Background of the First Amendment of the Constitution of the United States."

The record also shows that the Committee supplemented the information it had obtained about Anastaplo from these affidavits by conducting informal independent investigations into his character and reputation. It sent agents to Anastaplo's home town in southern Illinois and they questioned the people who knew him there. Similar inquiries were made among those who knew him in Chicago. But these intensive investigations apparently[5] failed to produce so much as one man in Chicago or in the whole State of Illinois who could say or would say, directly, indirectly or even by hearsay, one thing derogatory to the character, loyalty or reputation of George Anastaplo, and not one man could be found who would in any way link him with the Communist Party. This fact is particularly significant in view of the evidence in the record that the Committee had become acquainted with a person who apparently had been a member of a Communist Party cell on the University of Chicago campus and that this person was asked to and did identify for the Committee every member of the Party whom he knew.

In addition to the information it had obtained from the affidavits and from its independent investigations, the Committee had one more important source of information about Anastaplo's character. It had the opportunity to observe the manner in which he conducted himself during the many hours of hearings before it. That manner, as revealed by the record before us and undenied by any findings of the Committee to the contrary, left absolutely nothing to be desired. Faced with a barrage of sometimes highly provocative and totally irrelevant questions from men openly hostile to his position, Anastaplo invariably responded with all the dignity and restraint attributed to him in the affidavits of his friends. Moreover, it is not amiss to say that he conducted himself in precisely the same manner during the oral argument he presented before this Court.

Thus, it is against the background of a mountain of evidence so favorable to Anastaplo that the word "overwhelming" seems inadequate to describe it that the action of the Committee in refusing to certify Anastaplo as fit for admission to the Bar must be considered. The majority of the Committee rationalized its position on the ground that without answers to some of the questions it had asked, it could not conscientiously perform its duty of determining Anastaplo's character and fitness to be a lawyer. A minority of the Committee described this explanation as "pure sophistry." And it is simply impossible to read this record without agreeing with the minority. For, it is difficult to see what possible relevancy answers to the questions could have had in the minds of these members of the Committee after they had received such completely overwhelming proof beyond a reasonable doubt of Anastaplo's good character and staunch patriotism. I can think of no sound reason for further insistence upon these answers other than the very questionable, but very human, feeling that this young man should not be permitted to resist the Committee's demands without being compelled to suffer for it in some way.

It is intimated that the Committee's feeling of resentment might be assuaged and that Anastaplo might even be admitted to the Bar if he would only give in to the demands of the Committee and add the requested test oath to the already overwhelming proof he has submitted to establish his good character and patriotism. In this connection, the Court says: "We find nothing to suggest that he would not be admitted now if he decides to answer, assuming of course that no grounds justifying his exclusion from practice resulted. In short, petitioner holds the key to admission in his own hands." However well this familiar phrase may fit other cases, it does not fit this one. For the attitude of the Committee, as revealed by the transcript of its hearings, does not support a belief that Anastaplo can gain admission to the Illinois Bar merely by answering the Committee's questions, whatever answers he should give. Indeed, the Committee's own majority report discloses that Anastaplo's belief in the "right of revolution" was regarded as raising "a serious question" in the minds of a majority of the Committee with regard to his fitness to practice law and that "certain" members of that majority (how many, we cannot know) have already stated categorically that they will not vote to admit an applicant who expresses such views. Nor does the opinion of the Illinois Supreme Court indicate that Anastaplo "holds the key to admission in his own hands." Quite the contrary, that court's opinion evidences an almost insuperable reluctance to upset the findings of the Committee. Certainly, that opinion contains nothing that even vaguely resembles the sort of implicit promise that would justify the belief asserted by the majority here. And, finally, I see nothing in the majority opinion of this Court, nor in the majority opinions in the companion cases decided today, that would justify a belief that this Court would unlock the door that blocks his admission to the Illinois Bar if Anastaplo produced the "key" and the state authorities refused to use it.

The opinion of the majority already recognizes that there is not one scrap of evidence in the record before us "which could properly be considered as reflecting adversely upon his [Anastaplo's] character or reputation or on the sincerity of the beliefs he espoused before the Committee," and that the Committee had not received any " 'information from any outside source which would cast any doubt on applicant's loyalty or which would tend to connect him in any manner with any subversive group.' " The majority opinion even concedes that Anastaplo was correct in urging that the questions asked by the Committee impinged upon the freedoms of speech and association guaranteed by the First and Fourteenth Amendments. But, the opinion then goes on to hold that Anastaplo can nonetheless be excluded from the Bar pursuant to "the State's interest in having lawyers who are devoted to the law in its broadest sense. . . ."[6] I cannot regard that holding, as applied to a man like Anastaplo, as in any way justified. Consider it, for example, in the context of the following remarks of Anastaplo to the Committee—remarks the sincerity of which the majority does not deny:

I speak of a need to remind the bar of its traditions and to keep alive the spirit of dignified but determined advocacy and opposition. This is not only for the good of the bar, of course, but also because of what the bar means to American republican government. The bar when it exercises self-control is in a peculiar position to mediate between popular passions and informed and principled men, thereby upholding republican government. Unless there is this mediation, intelligent and responsible government is unlikely. The bar, furthermore, is in a peculiar position to apply to our daily lives the constitutional principles which nourish for this country its inner life. Unless there is this nourishment, a just and humane people is impossible. The bar is, in short, in a position to train and lead by precept and example the American people.[7]

These are not the words of a man who lacks devotion to "the law in its broadest sense."

The majority, apparently considering this fact irrelevant because the State might *possibly* have an interest in learning more about its Bar applicants, decides that Anastaplo can properly be denied admission to the Bar by purporting to "balance" the interest of the State of Illinois in "having lawyers who are devoted to the law in its broadest sense" against the interest of Anastaplo and the public in protecting the freedoms of the First Amendment, concluding, as it usually does when it engages in this process, that "on balance" the interest of Illinois must prevail.[8] If I had ever doubted that the "balancing test" comes close to being a doctrine of governmental absolutism—that to "balance" an interest in individual liberty means almost inevitably to destroy that liberty—those doubts would have been dissipated by this case. For this so-called "balancing test"—which, as applied to the First Amendment, means that the freedoms of speech, press, assembly, religion and petition can be repressed whenever there is a sufficient governmental interest in doing so—here proves pitifully and pathetically inadequate to cope with an invasion of individual liberty so plainly unjustified that even the majority apparently feels compelled expressly to disclaim "any view upon the wisdom of the State's action."

I, of course, wholeheartedly agree with the statement of the majority that this Court should not, merely on the ground that such action is unwise, interfere with governmental action that is within the constitutional powers of that government. But I am no less certain that this Court should not permit governmental action that plainly abridges constitutionally protected rights of the People merely because a majority believes that on "balance" it is better, or "wiser," to abridge those rights than to leave them free. The inherent vice of the "balancing test" is that it purports to do just that. In the context of its reliance upon the "balancing test," the Court's disclaimer of "any view upon the wisdom of the State's action" here thus seems to me to be wholly inconsistent with the only ground upon which it has decided this case.

Nor can the majority escape from this inconsistency on the ground that the "balancing test" deals only with the question of the importance of the existence of governmental power as a general matter without regard to the importance of its exercise in a particular case. For in *Barenblatt* v. *United States* the same majority made it clear that the "balancing test" is to be applied to the facts of each particular case: "Where First Amendment rights are asserted to bar governmental interrogation resolution of the issue always involves a balancing by the courts of the competing private and public interests at stake *in the particular circumstances shown.*"[9] (Emphasis supplied.) Thus the Court not only "balances" the respective values of two competing policies as a general matter, but also "balances" the wisdom of those policies in "the particular circumstances shown." Thus, the Court has reserved to itself the power to permit or deny abridgment of First Amendment freedoms according to its own view of whether repression or freedom is the wiser governmental policy under the circumstances of each case.

The effect of the Court's "balancing" here is that any State may now reject an applicant for admission to the Bar if he believes in the Declaration of Independence as strongly as Anastaplo and if he is willing to sacrifice his career and his means of livelihood in defense of the freedoms of the First Amendment. But the men who founded this country and wrote our Bill of Rights were strangers neither to a belief in the "right of revolution" nor to the urgency of the need to be free from the control of government with regard to political beliefs and associations. Thomas Jefferson was not disclaiming a belief in the "right of revolution" when he wrote the Declaration of Independence. And Patrick Henry was certainly not disclaiming such a belief when he declared in impassioned words that have come on down through the years: "Give me liberty or give me death." This country's freedom was won by men who, whether they believed in it or not, certainly practiced revolution in the Revolutionary War.

Since the beginning of history there have been governments that have engaged in practices against the people so bad, so cruel, so unjust and so destructive of the individual dignity of men and women that the "right of revolution" was all the people had left to free themselves. As simple illustrations, one government almost 2,000 years ago burned Christians upon fiery crosses and another government, during this very century, burned Jews in crematories. I venture the suggestion that there are countless multitudes in this country, and all over the world, who would join Anastaplo's belief in the right of the people to resist by force tyrannical governments like those.

In saying what I have, it is to be borne in mind that Anastaplo has not indicated, even remotely, a belief that this country is an oppressive one in which the "right of revolution" should be exercised.[10] Quite the contrary, the entire course of his life, as disclosed by the record, has been one of devotion and service to his country—first, in his willingness to defend its security at the risk of his own life in time of war and, later, in his willingness to defend its freedoms at the risk of his professional career in time of peace. The one and only time in which he has come into conflict with the Government is when he refused to answer the questions put to him by the Committee about his beliefs and associations. And I think the record clearly shows that conflict resulted, not from any fear on Anastaplo's part to divulge his own political activities, but from a sincere, and in my judgment correct, conviction that the preservation of this country's freedom depends upon adherence to our Bill of Rights. The very most that can fairly be said against Anastaplo's position in this entire matter is that he took too much of the responsibility of preserving that freedom upon himself.

This case illustrates to me the serious consequences to the Bar itself of not affording the full protections of the First Amendment to its applicants for admission. For this record shows that Anastaplo has many of the qualities that are needed in the American Bar.[11] It shows, not only that Anastaplo has followed a high moral, ethical and patriotic course in all of the activities of his life, but also that he combines these more common virtues with the uncommon virtue of courage to stand by his principles at any cost. It is such men as these who have most greatly honored the profession of the law—men like Malsherbes, who, at the cost of his own life and the lives of his family, sprang unafraid to the defense of Louis XVI against the fanatical leaders of the Revolutionary government of France[12]—men like Charles Evans Hughes, Sr., later Mr. Chief Justice Hughes, who stood up for the constitutional rights of socialists to be socialists and public officials despite the threats and clamorous protests of self-proclaimed superpatriots[13]—men like Charles Evans Hughes, Jr., and John W. Davis, who, while against everything for which the Communists stood, strongly advised the Congress in 1948 that it would be unconstitutional to pass the law then proposed to outlaw the Communist Party[14]—men like Lord Erskine, James Otis, Clarence Darrow, and the multitude of others who have dared to speak in defense of causes and clients without regard to personal danger to themselves. The legal profession will lose much of its nobility and its glory if it is not constantly replenished with lawyers like these. To force the Bar to become a group of thoroughly orthodox, timeserving, government-fearing individuals is to humiliate and degrade it.

But that is the present trend, not only in the legal profession but in almost every walk of life. Too many men are being driven to become government-fearing and time-serving because the Government is being permitted to strike out at those who are fearless enough to think as they please and say what they think.[15] This trend must be halted if we are to keep faith with the Founders of our Nation and pass on to future generations of Americans the great heritage of freedom which they sacrificed so much to leave to us. The choice is clear to me. If we are to pass on that great heritage of freedom, we must return to the original language of the Bill of Rights. We must not be afraid to be free.

[Justice Black's Footnotes]

1. As the majority points out, the record in the first series of hearings, which culminated in a denial of certiorari by this Court (348 U.S. 946 [1955]), is not a part of the record in this case but we take judicial notice of it. *National Fire Ins. Co. v. Thompson*, 281 U.S. 331, 336 [1930], and cases cited there.

2. "We hold these truths to be self-evident, that all Men are created equal, that they are endowed by their Creator with certain unalienable Rights, that among these are Life, Liberty, and the Pursuit of Happiness—That to secure these Rights, Governments are instituted among Men, deriving their just Powers from the Consent of the Governed, that whenever any Form of Government becomes destructive of these Ends, it is the Right of the People to alter or to abolish it, and to institute new Government, laying its Foundation on such Principles, and organizing its Powers in such Form, as to them shall seem most likely to effect their Safety and Happiness."

3. The following excerpt from the record of the first hearing indicates clearly the connection between Anastaplo's views on the "right of revolution" and the questions subsequently asked him about his "possible" political associations [Nov. 10, 1950]:

"Commissioner Mitchell: When you say 'believe in revolution,' you don't limit that revolution to an overthrow of a particular political party or a political government by means of an election process or other political means?

"Mr. Anastaplo: I mean actual use of force.

"Commissioner Mitchell: You mean to go as far as necessary?

"Mr. Anastaplo: As far as Washington did, for instance.

"Commissioner Mitchell: So that would it be fair to say that you believe the end result would justify any means that were used?

"Mr. Anastaplo: No, the means proportionate to the particular end in sight.

"Commissioner Mitchell: Well, is there any difference from your answer and my question?

"Mr. Anastaplo: Did you ask—

"Commissioner Mitchell: I asked you whether you thought that you believe that if a change, or overthrow of the government were justified, that any means could be used to accomplish that end.

"Mr. Anastaplo: Now, let's say in this positive concrete situation—I am not quite sure what it means in abstract.

"Commissioner Mitchell: I will ask you in detail. You believe that assuming the government should be overthrown, in your opinion, that you and others of like mind would be justified in raising a company of men with military equipment and proceed to take over the government of the United States, of the State of Illinois?

"By shaking your head do you mean yes?

"Mr. Anastaplo: If you get to the point where overthrow is necessary, then overthrow is justified. It just means that you overthrow the government by force.

"Commissioner Mitchell: And would that also include in your mind justification for putting a spy into the administrative department, one or another of the administrative departments of the United States or the government of the State of Illinois?

"Mr. Anastaplo: If you got to the point you think the government should be overthrown, I think that would be a legitimate means.

"Commissioner Mitchell: There isn't any difference in your mind in the propriety of using a gun or using a spy?

"Mr. Anastaplo: I think spies have been used in quite honorable causes.

"Commissioner Mitchell: Your answer is, you do think so?

"Mr. Anastaplo: Yes.

"Commissioner Baker: Let me ask you a question. Are you aware of the fact that the Department of Justice has a list of what are described as subversive organizations?

"Mr. Anastaplo: Yes.

"Commissioner Baker: Have you ever seen that list?

"Mr. Anastaplo: Yes.

"Commissioner Baker: Are you a member of any organization that is listed on the Attorney General's list, to your knowledge? (No answer.) Just to keep you from having to work so hard mentally on it, what organizations—give me all the organizations you are affiliated with or are a member of. (No answer.) That oughtn't to be too hard.

"Mr. Anastaplo: Do you believe that is a legitimate question?

"Commissioner Baker: Yes, I do. We are inquiring into not only your character, but your fitness, under Rule 58. We don't compel you to answer it. Are you a member of the Communist Party?"

4. As the majority points out, the Committee eventually did expressly disavow any right to insist upon an answer to this question. This came at the end of a long disagreement between Anastaplo and certain members of the Committee with respect to the vitality of an old Illinois decision which indicated that a belief in God might be necessary in order to take an oath to testify. The Committee's abandonment of the point came only after Anastaplo produced a more recent case disapproving the earlier decision. It is interesting to note that neither of the Committee members who had expressed such a strong interest in knowing whether Anastaplo believes in God voted in favor of his certification.

5. The record shows that although Anastaplo repeatedly requested that the Committee allow him to see any reports that resulted from these independent investigations, the Committee, without denying that such reports existed, refused to produce them.

6. *Konigsberg* v. *State Bar of California*, decided today, *ante*, [366 U.S.] 36, 52, which the majority here relies upon as also having settled the issue in this case.

7. These remarks were made by Anastaplo in his closing argument before the Committee. He also introduced evidence to the Committee that he had earlier expressed similar views in a book review published in 1954. See Anastaplo, Review: Drinker, Legal Ethics, 14 Law. Guild Rev. 144.

8. I think the majority has once again misapplied its own "balancing test," for the interests it purports to "balance" are no more at stake here than in *Konigsberg*. Moreover, it seems clear to me that Illinois, like California, is placing the burden of proof upon applicants for the Bar to prove they do not advocate the overthrow of the Government. Thus the decision here, like that in *Konigsberg*, is contrary to *Speiser* v. *Randall*, 357 U.S. 513 [1958].

9. 360 U.S. 109, 126. The majority in *Barenblatt* then proceeded to "balance" those interests on the basis of the particular record of that case. *Id.*, at 127-134.

10. Anastaplo's belief in the "right of revolution," as disclosed by this record, is no different from that expressed by Professor Chafee: "Most of us believe that our Constitution makes it possible to change all bad laws through political action. We ought to disagree vehemently with those who urge violent methods, and whenever necessary take energetic steps to prevent them from putting such methods into execution. This is a very different matter from holding that all discussion of the desirability of resorting to violence for political purposes should be ruthlessly stamped out. There is not one among us who would not join a revolution if the reason for it be made strong enough." Chafee, Free Speech in the United States 178 (Harvard University Press, 1942).

11. For a similar case, see *In re Summers*, 325 U.S. 561 [1945], in which a 5-4 majority of this Court upheld an informal order of the Illinois Supreme Court denying Bar admission to Clyde W. Summers on the ground that his religious beliefs were inconsistent with the Illinois Constitution.

12. At the time of his decision to volunteer his services in defense of Louis XVI, Malsherbes, a man of more than seventy, was apparently completely safe from the post-revolutionary blood bath which then enveloped France. For, although active in public life prior to the Revolution, he had always been a friend of the people and, in any case, he had largely passed out of the public mind with his retirement some years earlier. Within a year of his unsuccessful defense of the life of France's former king, however, he, together with his entire family, were convicted by a revolutionary tribunal on the vague charge of conspiracy against "the safety of the State and the unity of the Republic." Malsherbes was then taken to the guillotine where, after being forced to witness the beheading of the other members of his family, he paid with his life for his courage as a lawyer. This story has been interestingly told by John W. Davis. See Davis, The Lawyers of Louis XVI, in The Lawyer, April 1942, p. 5, at 6-13.

13. The story of Hughes' participation in the fight against the action of the New York Legislature in suspending five of its members in 1920 on the ground that they were socialists is told in John Lord O'Brian, Loyalty Tests and Guilt by Association, 61 Harv. L. Rev. 592, 593-594 [1948].

14. See *Barenblatt* v. *United States*, 360 U.S. 109, 147-148 [1959] (dissenting).

15. See, e.g., *Barsky* v. *Board of Regents*, 347 U.S. 442 [1954]; *Uphaus* v. *Wyman*, 360 U.S. 72 [1959]; *Barenblatt* v. *United States*, 360 U.S. 109 [1959]; *Uphaus* v. *Wyman*, 364 U.S. 388 [1960]; *Wilkinson* v. *United States*, 365 U.S. 399 [1961]; *Braden* v. *United States*, 365 U.S. 431 [1961]; *Konigsberg* v. *State Bar of California, supra*.

See Norman Redlich, "Justice Black at Eighty: The Common Sense of Freedom," *Nation*, March 21, 1966, pp. 322, 325-326. See, also, Irving Dilliard, *One Man's Stand for Freedom: Mr. Justice Black and the Bill of Rights* (New York: Alfred A. Knopf, 1963), p. 408.

Justice Black adopted, in describing how my controversy began before the character committee in 1950, the explanation offered by counsel for the state of Illinois. See p. 363, above; p. 384, below. My own recollection of the beginning is that recorded by Sharp in the second paragraph of his summary. See section 1 of this appendix. (Cf. the "second round" sequence described in section 3 of this appendix.) However that may be, the "trouble" really began (bringing the inquiry immediately to where Justice Black reports it in his note 3) when I gave the "wrong answer" on November 10, 1950, to the test question that was then being asked, on a hit-and-miss basis, of applicants appearing before the character committee for the routine ten-to-fifteen-minute appearance which was the final hurdle before admission to the bar: "Have you an opinion as to whether or not a member of the Communist Party would be eligible to take the oath of office of a lawyer in the State of Illinois, honestly, and be admitted as a lawyer?" But the opinion which really mattered, I soon learned, was that which I held about the Declaration of Independence. Justice Black *is* correct about that. See, e.g., pp. 331-32, above, pp. 396, 406, below.

After my case had become known among law school students in 1951, the test question employed by members of the Chicago committee to detect unwary, or imprudently spirited, applicants was, "What do you understand to be George Anastaplo's opinions and do you agree with them?" This sort of thing might seem to the uninitiated layman somewhat improper. But then, young applicants had been put on notice by too many distinguished law professors that anyone who "would not be willing to answer such inquiries would be well advised to consider [while still in law school,] rather than later, whether he can best serve his ideals by continuing his education in law." See p. 333, above; pp. 397, 405-6, below.

Irving Dilliard (who was, I believe, still a trustee of the University of Illinois at the time) concluded his January 1963 column in *Focus/Midwest* ("Tradition of Bigotry in the Illinois Bar"), in which he had discussed my case and that of a pacifist excluded from the practice of law in Illinois (*In re Clyde Summers*, 325 U.S. 561 [1945]), with the suggestion:

> Can it be that the deans of the major law schools of Illinois—those at Northwestern University, the University of Chicago and the University of Illinois—are content to allow the Illinois Bar to write still other Summers and Anastaplo cases into the record of Lincoln's state?
> Three or four Illinois law deans alone could get together to produce and issue a joint statement that would end this outrageous trespass on the great American Bill of Rights once and for all.
> Let the Illinois law deans—and their faculties—show leadership and they will find that Illinois lawyers by the hundreds will rally to their support. So will many lay men and women!

So far as I know, nothing came of Dilliard's appeal to the keepers of the bar's conscience. Instead, timidity and ambition prevailed, a curiously unseemly combination. See p. 401 (item 32), chap. 8, n. 28, below.

7. A Verona il Drappo Verde (June 19, 1961)

Petitions for rehearing rarely affect decisions announced by the Supreme Court of the United States. I expected from my own petition, therefore, nothing more than an opportunity to take my leave in an appropriate manner from the practice of law. The petition was filed June 19, 1961, and was denied by the Court on October 9, 1961, 366 U.S. 869 (1961).

The reference in my petition to the "Opinion of the Court" and to "this Court" are to the opinion of April 24, 1961, written by Justice Harlan for Justices Frankfurter, Clark, Whittaker, Stewart, and himself. (His opinion, which was then available only at 81 S.Ct. 978-87, is summarized at the beginning of section 6 of this appendix.) The "court below" refers to the Supreme Court of Illinois, and usually to the Nov. 19, 1959, majority opinion of that court. I refer several times to the order of the unanimous Supreme Court of Illinois (18 Ill.2d 186; Sept. 17, 1957), pursuant to which the rehearing was conducted. This order may be found at p. 349, above. I also refer to the majority report of the seventeen-member character committee (April 9, 1959), which may be found in section 4 of this appendix.

The dissenting opinion referred to and quoted from in my petition is, of course, Justice Black's. The other bar admission cases referred to in the petition are *Schware v. Board of Examiners of Nevada*, 353 U.S. 232 (1957), and *Konigsberg v. State Bar of California*, 353 U.S. 252 (1957), 366 U.S. 36 (1961). The *Schware* concurring opinion (referred to at the end of sec. ii of part 2 and thereafter) is by Justice Frankfurter. (Page references within my petition have been adjusted to this reprinting.)

IN THE
Supreme Court of the United States
October Term, 1960
No. 58
IN RE GEORGE ANASTAPLO, *Petitioner*
Petition for Rehearing

INTRODUCTION.

And let us not be weary in well doing: for in due season we shall reap, if we faint not.
—*Galatians*, vi, 9.

i.

It is highly probable that upon disposition of this Petition for Rehearing, petitioner will have practiced all the law he is ever going to. That is, he recognizes that this petition cannot reasonably be expected to affect a decision of this Court reached after long deliberation. Nevertheless, petitioner is obliged, if only to complete his effort, not to let pass unnoticed the errors in the Opinion of this Court.

Since no one would profit from a mere repetition of arguments developed in earlier briefs, this petition is directed primarily to a discussion of the novel problems raised by the Opinion of this Court. Petitioner will then have discharged the obligation to the profession and to the community that he assumed when this Court permitted him to appear as counsel *pro se*. That is, he will not only have stated his legal position but will also have recorded, among the papers he has filed in this Court, an adequate answer to the arguments that have been marshalled against him.

It must also be recorded that this entire controversy is itself but an image of a much more fundamental one which bears on the problem of the education and character of the citizen as well as of the lawyer. We must try to take seriously again the concern and conditions for virtue, nobility and the life most fitting for man.

Petitioner, exercising the prerogative of one retiring from a profession, would advise the new lawyer that he learn well not only the tools of his craft but also the texts that have come to us from the ancient world. It is in those texts that one may find the best models, both in word and in deed, for the conduct of oneself in public as well as in private affairs. It is there that the better natures are most likely to be exposed to the accents and majesty of human excellence.

ii.

But we must return one more time to our immediate problem. Perhaps it would be well at the outset to remind the reader that the question of membership in the Communist Party or in the Ku Klux Klan is not an issue in this case, but at most only the effect in a bar admission proceeding of a conscientious refusal to answer unusual inquiries about such membership when it is conceded that there is no allegation or evidence of membership, when the inquiries occur only in the context of badgering about philosophical and political views, particularly views about the right of revolution and the Declaration of Independence, and when petitioner's silence is couched in the form of a refusal to submit to something deemed by him to be in the nature of a test oath and to be improper, ungentlemanly and unconstitutional inquiry. One should be reminded also that it seems to be generally conceded that the evidence supporting petitioner's character and fitness, in the ordinary sense of these terms, is overwhelming and uncontroverted. Finally, the reader should be reminded that the only legitimate issue in this case is that of petitioner's qualifications for the practice of law, qualifications that rely for their effective application as much on the integrity and good sense of the legal profession as on the character and fitness of an applicant.

A leading member of petitioner's character committee, who was President of the Chicago Bar Association at the time he voted against petitioner's application, has collected seven "very difficult questions" which confronted him during his years with the committee. (Weiss, 45 Illinois Bar J. 821-822) He asks whether "a certificate of good moral character" can be granted to

(a) A boy with an excellent school record, an enlistee in the army, whose

family background were [sic] in all respects excellent except that investigation brought out the fact that he was a homosexual;
(b) A boy who had participated in a felony at an early age but whose subsequent acts indicate rehabilitation;
(c) An applicant who has wrongfully altered school records but who openly and candidly admits the error of his ways in later years;
(d) An applicant who refuses to answer what he considers questions pertaining to his personal beliefs;
(e) An applicant, the truth of whose statements are doubted, whose demeanor adds to those doubts, and in the course of the investigation refuses to take a lie test;
(f) An applicant who has served a jail term for an offense without making a defense in his own trial on a fallacious theory that to do so would be waiving his constitutional rights;
(g) An applicant formerly adjudged insane, then sane, and whose conduct before the Committee is completely irrational.

Is it not apparent that one of these cases is clearly *not* related to the usual problem of an applicant's moral fitness, to the problem of how he might conduct himself in critical situations requiring the use of a reasoned moral judgment by the lawyer? And is not this single exception the very one that alludes to petitioner's case, a case that developed out of petitioner's alleged political offenses?

Committees "on character and moral fitness" were neither intended nor designed to concern themselves with political offenses. They are so poorly prepared for this concern that they can only vacillate between the ridiculous and the dangerous when they abandon their proper function: they are ridiculous in their obvious inability to cope with any serious political threat to the bar or to the community; they are dangerous in their all-too-evident ability to cow the spirits and subvert the rights of applicants for admission to the bar. It is appropriate, in this connection, to remind ourselves of observations of Lord Cockburn in which he insists upon a distinction between the political and the non-political, a distinction that is sanctified by the experience and demands of "British freedom" (*Examination of the Trials for Sedition Which Have Hitherto Occurred in Scotland* (1888), I, 68):

It may be expedient to prosecute political delinquency, even to the death, but certainly not necessarily on account of the moral iniquity of the accused. Amidst conflicts of opinion, each half of the community is seditious in the sight of the other. When governments are unsettled, it has often been doubtful, with the purest characters, whether treason itself was not a duty. The English revolution made traitors *in law* of men of the highest personal honour; nor was it till things got solid, by the subsidence of the loose matter connected with that event, that personal integrity and political innocence became the same. To see no difference between political and other offenses is the sure mark of an excited or of a stupid head. . . .

1. THE RIGHT OF REVOLUTION: SEEING IS NOT BELIEVING.

i.

This Court has now held for the first time that it *is* consistent with eligibility for admission to the bar for an applicant to defend (as does petitioner) the right of revolution and the Declaration of Independence. 81 S. Ct., at 986. That this has been denied for a decade in Illinois—that petitioner's defense of the teachings of the Declaration of Independence has been one of his cardinal political offenses—is evident to any careful student of the record. Even the Attorney General of Illinois, in his brief as well as on oral argument, has gone so far as to claim that the inquiries by the character committee into petitioner's affiliations were prompted and justified by petitioner's quotation from the Declaration of Independence (R. 381-382) (Reply Brief, pp. 12-17). The sequence recorded in the transcript excerpt reproduced in Note 3 of the Dissenting Opinion reflects the hostile attitude throughout the years of the Illinois bar authorities when confronted by petitioner's opinions on the subject of rightful rebellion.

The Opinion of this Court can find, however, that "it is perfectly clear that the Illinois Bar Committee and Supreme Court [of Illinois] regarded petitioner's refusal to cooperate in the Committee's examination of him as the basic and only reason for a denial of certification." 81 S. Ct., at 986. This conclusion is reached in an Opinion which acknowledges, nevertheless, that "certain" members of the committee thought that petitioner's views "on the right to resist judicial decrees" "affirmatively demonstrated his disqualification for admission to the bar." *Ibid*. But, in Note 18, the Court rejects this admission by "certain" members with the explanation, "This of course could hardly be so in the context of the illustrations which Anastaplo gave of his views as to when a right to resist might arise."

The author of the Opinion of this Court thereby assures us that *he* would not have thought petitioner's views on this subject to raise doubts about his qualifications for the bar—but he imputes to these "certain members" more common sense and self-restraint than they exhibited during the hearings when he chooses to believe *they* could not have regarded unfavorably petitioner's views on this subject. It is a measure of the irrationality at work here that "certain members" *did* take a position that this Court cannot or does not want to believe these members, despite their explicit admission, could have taken. Yet, is it really unbelievable that such a position might have been taken by committee members who pressed petitioner about his religious beliefs and who behaved as several members are revealed by the record to have behaved? True, these members probably were not troubled by petitioner's "illustrations . . . of his views as to when a right to resist might arise"; but they did resent, and continue to resent, petitioner's reservation that *he* would have to rely upon *his own judgment* as to when constitutional government had been so subverted that the right of revolution might properly be exercised. Petitioner's reservation to himself of an independent judgment remains the critical difficulty with his eligibility: members of the committee have come to expect applicants for admission to *their* bar to be deferential to the point of servility. (See pages 397-99, below.)

Why not, in order to understand what petitioner has been confronted by for a decade and in order to appreciate the significance of the action taken against him—why not take these members at their word, especially when they went to the trouble, in the final paragraph of a committee report which was a year in preparation, to state clearly their position:

Certain members of the Committee (who are included within the majority who believe that applicant's petition for a license should be denied because he has failed to meet the burden which is on him of establishing his proper character and fitness) are of the further opinion that *the record demonstrates affirmatively applicant's lack of the character and fitness necessary for admission to the Bar.* They base their views upon . . . (ii) applicant's view that circumstances might exist under which he would not abide by, and might advise other citizens not to abide by, final decrees of a court of law and to resist by force their enforcement by appropriate legal process, *when considered in connection with his views as to the overthrow of the government by force and violence.* [R. 467. Emphasis supplied.]

How many are "certain members"? If there are as few as three—and at least five suggest themselves to the student of the record—then the majority of the committee is constitutionally tainted, even within the terms of the Opinion of this Court.

That is, the final vote of the committee was 11 to 6 against petitioner. If these three (or more) votes had shifted from the majority to the minority, the court below would have received from the committee a recommendation which would have "entitled [petitioner] to admission to the bar" (Rule 58, Sec. IX, Supreme Court of Illinois). (If these three (or more) commissioners had written a separate opinion, there would not have been the usual majority report for the court below simply to affirm.) But, it will be said, the more radical "certain members," even if they had not held as they did on the right of revolution offense, would still have voted against petitioner on the ground shared with the remainder of the majority. How can this be known? For all we know, the "certain members" of the majority took seriously the ground shared with the remainder of the majority (*i.e.*, the refusals of petitioner to answer any question about political affiliations) primarily because of petitioner's views on the right of revolution—primarily, that is, because of views that this Court now holds to be improper as a ground or even influence for exclusion from the bar.

Indeed, upon review of the record, one finds that for some members the right of revolution discussion is far more troublesome than petitioner's refusals to answer questions about political organizations to which he has been in no way linked by the committee. In fact, after petitioner had explained on request his views about the right of revolution, the chairman of the hearings raised again the question of affiliations:

Because I feel the question is relevant to the right of revolution category [prescribed by the Supreme Court of Illinois in the rehearing order set forth at 18 Ill. 2d 186], I am going to put a few specific questions to you again. Are you a member of the Communist Party? . . . Have you ever held office in the Communist Party? [R. 159-160. Emphasis supplied.]

The suspicion and hostility evoked to the last by petitioner's opinions are further reflected in the fact that his views on the right of revolution are condemned by "certain members" as *demonstrating affirmatively* applicant's lack of the character and fitness necessary for admission to the bar. (R. 467) Unbelievable? And yet true.

It should also be noted that it is likely that those of the majority who did not join in the candid final paragraph of the Committee Report were influenced by the attitude and arguments of those "certain members" of the majority who felt so strongly about petitioner's views on the right of revolution that they insisted on that final paragraph. Rational discussion and evaluation of a record can be hopelessly corrupted by the presence of such prejudice as is revealed in that final paragraph. This would be so whether these "certain members" constituted two commissioners or ten.

Finally, it should be noted that the position of the "certain members" is not attributed to them by conjecture or inference: rather, it is the position which they insisted upon including in the Committee Report with a view to expressing fully the basis of their critical votes and in the expectation of influencing (as they did) the decision of a closely-divided state supreme court. Is it consistent with sound judicial practice and lawyerlike analysis to disregard completely a ground that had been explicitly and deliberately set forth in this manner? Is not petitioner entitled to a review which at least begins with the acknowledged facts of *his* case?

ii.

This Court concludes Note 18 of its Opinion with the observation, "Nothing in the State Court's opinion remotely suggests its approbation of these views of 'certain' Committee members." Does it make any difference to this Court that there can be shown a suggestion of approbation, and much more than a suggestion, in the opinion of the court below? The court below does state, disregarding the terms of its own 1957 order (reprinted at 18 Ill. 2d 186) providing for the rehearing, that

the major issue presented to the committee arose from the applicant's continued refusal to answer questions regarding possible Communist or other subversive affiliations. [18 Ill. 2d, at 190]

But the court below also states, without subsequent qualification, that the Committee Report raises

a serious question whether the attitude expressed by Anastaplo toward final court determinations binding upon himself and toward attempts to enforce them conformably to the law is consistent with the oath required of attorneys in this State. An attorney is an officer of the courts. (*In re Day*, 181 Ill. 73.) In *Cooper* v. *Aaron*, 358 U. S. 1, 3 L. ed. 2d 5, the United States Supreme Court said, at page 8, "No state legislator or executive or judicial officer can war against the Constitution without violating his undertaking to support it."

The committee's report also suggests that Anastaplo's attitude with respect to advising others along the *same subversive* lines in his capacity as "citizen" in contradistinction to his capacity as "attorney" raises additional serious questions concerning his capacity to take the oath required of attorneys in this State. . . . [18 Ill. 2d, at 189-190. Emphasis supplied.]

Certainly, this is much more than a "remote" suggestion of approbation "of these views of 'certain' Committee members." In evaluating the record as a whole, including petitioner's refusals to answer questions about any political affiliations, what was the effect on the court below of its evident belief that petitioner's perfectly legitimate attitude (*i.e.*, opinions) ran along "subversive lines," that he was waging "war against the Constitution" and that his opinions raised "additional serious questions concerning his capacity to take the oath required of attorneys"? The court below does not conceal the fact that it was moved by these considerations, considerations that go back to petitioner's defense of the teachings of the Declaration of Independence.

In any event, the majority of the committee was made up (and, on this record, necessarily made up in order to constitute a majority) of "certain members" who were, by their own deliberate admission, strongly influenced by a consideration that this Court has now held to be clearly improper. 81 S. Ct., at 986. In addition to the "certain members" who found petitioner's views on "the right of revolution" evidence of bad character, the *entire* committee majority gave as one reason for insisting on the unanswered affiliations questions its conviction that the applicant's credibility in connection with his answers to questions pertaining to the right of overthrow and the enforceability of judicial decrees should be tested by questioning him about possible subversive beliefs and activities. [R. 458.]

Thus, the committee's adverse reaction to petitioner's views on the subject of revolution is admitted by the committee majority to have played a much greater role in petitioner's proceedings than this Court seems willing to let the committee or the court below admit.

iii.

At the very least, and for these reasons alone, the exclusion order should be reversed, with instructions to the Illinois bar authorities on remand that they reconsider the record already made in this case without giving *any* adverse effect to petitioner's allegedly "subversive" views on the right of revolution. The Opinion of April 24 seems consistent, in its declarations about the right of revolution aspect of the case, with such a reversal and remand. (That is, this Court has indicated that *if* adverse effect could be said to have been given to petitioner's views on revolution, the decision below should not be permitted to stand.)

But, as matters have been left by that Opinion, the Illinois bar authorities are not now required to reconsider their decision *and this record* to make certain that improper considerations were not brought to bear in exercising that "informed judgment as to whether the situation was an appropriate one for waiver of the Committee's continuing requirement . . . that [certain] questions must be answered." 81 S. Ct., at 986. Petitioner has been left only with the time-consuming and (for him) prohibitively expensive alternative of initiating still another rehearing and compiling still another record.

Nor is one encouraged to assume the risks and obligations of making a new record when one realizes that all of the present record subsequent to page 28, the point at which the first political affiliation question was left unanswered, has been dismissed as virtually immaterial. Indeed, one could say that *all* of the present rehearing was little more than a sham from the beginning since the court below ordered the rehearing after petitioner had explicitly and definitely stated in advance that he would not answer any questions about political affiliations (R. 484-489). (We return at pages 393-94 to the attempt by this Court to justify the manner in which the record has been dismissed.) Is it not fairer to make some use of the record we already have before setting out to build a new one?

Be that as it may, the passages that have been quoted from the majority opinions of the character committee and of the court below reveal the candid but improper attitude of the Illinois bar authorities toward petitioner's views on resisting court decrees, an attitude that it is reasonable to conclude influenced the reaction toward petitioner's refusals to answer certain questions. Petitioner has at last elicited the ruling that the Declaration of Independence, even as it applies to court decrees, may be defended by an applicant for admission to the bar. Why should not the Illinois bar authorities be required to exercise their "informed judgment" on the present record with this unprecedented ruling in mind, especially since only one vote in the court below and three votes in the character committee proved the margin of petitioner's exclusion? Only in this way will the ruling petitioner has earned after a decade of effort have any practical effect in *his* case. "The laborer is worthy of his hire."

It is respectfully requested, therefore, that the order below be reversed and that this case and record be remanded to the state supreme court "for further proceedings not inconsistent with the opinion of this Court."

2. THE BURDEN OF PROOF AND PETITIONER'S RECORD.

We attempt to show in the discussion that follows why the remand that has been requested could well include the ruling that petitioner has clearly established his character and fitness for the practice of law.

i.

One was obliged to believe, prior to the decision by this Court, that there *were* standards to be applied to state determinations of applicants' eligibility for admission to the bar. Yet, where is the alert bar applicant left by the Opinion of April 24th if not with the warning that there are no longer any constitutional standards in these matters to which state decisions must conform? It would be far fairer to the bar and applicants alike to announce that this Court simply does not review bar admission cases. This, at least, would have the advantage of lending support to the much-maligned cause of "states' rights." As it is now, however, this Court asserts its authority in these matters even as it abdicates the responsibility it has assumed.

Certainly, it is difficult to salvage any meaning at all from "burden of proof" if this record can be dismissed as not clearly establishing petitioner's eligibility for admission to the bar. There are more than 500 pages of record, drawing on committee sources that range over a decade; and yet (aside from the constitutionally-invalid references to petitioner's "subversive" views about the right of revolution) there is not alleged one item of adverse evidence in a record which has more than enough favorable and uncontroverted evidence to qualify a dozen applicants for admission to the bar.

What would this Court do in any other case, in which due process considerations were raised, if the ruling of the government body should be so patently in defiance of the clear and uncontradicted tendency of the evidence? Surely, prejudice and resentment on the part of the government body would be suspected—the very conclusion to which the Dissenting Opinion was driven upon reviewing the evidence in this record. 81 S.Ct., at 992. Is not petitioner entitled, in the terms of the *Schware* case, to a rational determination of his eligibility consistent with the long record that was carefully made in his case?

If there had been an automatic exclusion rule in Illinois (as distinguished from the "impossible" language we discuss at page 393), then one might, with some plausibility or at least with honest regret, say, "Yes, the evidence is uniformly, even overwhelmingly, favorable to petitioner's application for admission, but there happens to be a clear formal requirement that all unrepudiated questions asked by the committee must be answered before one can be admitted to the bar." But there has never been such a rule in Illinois; there is none today, except to the extent that the Opinion of this Court has now established it by inference.

No case, before April 24, 1961, announced an automatic exclusion rule; no statute or rule of court provides for it. Even the committee and the court below, by neglecting to mention (in their 1954, 1959, and 1960 opinions) certain unanswered questions (about the Ku Klux Klan, The Chicago Tribune, The Daily Worker, and the Republican and Democratic Parties), tacitly admitted there is no such rule. In fact, considering the irresponsibility of certain members of the committee, which is apparent in the record, there cannot be such a rule. Yet, the 1957 *Schware* and *Konigsberg* decisions, relying on which petitioner undertook to confront once again the Illinois bar admission authorities, seem to promise that there must be such a procedural or technical ground before a disregard of the weight of the evidence *can even begin to be justified*.

There are, in the Opinion of this Court, allusions to what are considered to be unrealistic allegations by petitioner of surprise that he should have been excluded from the bar because of his refusal to answer certain questions about political affiliations. 81 S.Ct., at 984; also, Note 16. But, as petitioner indicated as recently as his oral argument before this Court, he realized the probable consequences of standing by his position before the character committee. The surprise he *has* expressed is with respect to the belated attempt by the Attorney General of Illinois and by others to infer from the record, or from the history of cases in Illinois, a "warning" which amounts to or reflects something approaching an automatic exclusion rule in that State for refusal to answer *any* question later deemed to be "relevant."

The Illinois bar authorities—just as those in California—thought themselves obliged after 1957 to try to find or give such a warning. The California authorities (as is clear from the excerpts reproduced, at 81 S.Ct. 1005-1006, in the Opinion of this Court in the companion case) succeeded in doing so, but not without changing their rules and defying the spirit of this Court's mandate. The Illinois authorities, perhaps because they could not find a clear committee majority at any time during the four months of the hearing to support such an innovation, did not do so. They settled, instead, for no stronger than a "could and might" stipulation. (R. 103) Even this stipulation, as the record shows, was no more than the opinion of "one of the principal Committee members" (to use this Court's description of him, 81 S.Ct., at 984), a member who repeatedly insisted he could speak only for himself. (*E.g.*, R. 294-295, 297-298.)

The Opinion of this Court refers to the 1954 opinion of the court below as providing still another "warning" (81 S.Ct., at 985); but that opinion must be read in the light of the 1957 order of the same court overruling the character committee and providing for the current rehearing. It is laid down in this 1957 order that

the principal question presented by the petition for rehearing concerns the significance of applicant's views as to the overthrow of government by force . . . [18 Ill. 2d, at 186]

All references to the earlier unanswered questions about affiliations must be deemed to have been deliberately excluded from the 1957 order: petitioner and the committee were thereby put on notice that the affiliations questions which had loomed so large in the 1954 opinion were secondary if not altogether irrelevant. In effect, the 1954 opinion of the court below was tacitly repudiated by the 1957 order.

Even had this 1954 opinion not been repudiated, it would have survived as tainted by its adoption of the 1954 committee statement

that [although] the views and opinions expressed by petitioner on [the right of revolution] were not the basis for the denial of a certificate, . . . such views increased the importance of petitioner's refusals to answer and made more necessary a complete answer on the subject of membership in the Communist Party . . . [3 Ill. 2d, at 474.]

No applicant should be held to be "warned" by an opinion that clearly rests, in significant part, on a ground that is held by this Court to be improper, indeed even unthinkable and unbelievable.

The Opinion of this Court further states, in order to justify the disregard of the record made in this case,

Even as to one charged with crime due process does not demand that he be warned as to what specific sanction will be applied to him if he violates the law. It is enough that he know what sanctions "could and might" be visited on him. Anastaplo was entitled to no more. [81 S.Ct., at 985.]

But was not petitioner entitled to expect that the "law" laid down by the 1957 order of the court below would be determinative of the terms of the rehearing proceeding? Besides, is this really a question of the *range* of sanctions? One charged with crime *is* entitled to know what conduct is an occasion for any sanction that " 'could and might' be visited on him." Is not one also entitled to certainty about what is a requirement for admission to the bar, especially when a new-fashioned technical "requirement" is used to draw a curtain between this Court and the record compiled through many hours and months?

Had a clear warning, in the terms of the 1957 *Konigsberg* decision or reflecting even an *ad hoc* automatic exclusion rule, been given petitioner it would have made considerable difference in this case. Petitioner would have known as early as page 28 of the record that further discussion was for all practical purposes useless—and he could have conducted himself accordingly (*e.g.*, by requesting that the hearings be suspended and that the record be submitted to the court below for determination of this vital point). Such suspension of the hearings would also have served to keep out of the record the right of revolution exchanges which seriously prejudiced the case of petitioner in the minds of "certain members" and even of the entire committee majority. This step would have preserved unencumbered the affiliations issue for the state supreme court to consider in the light of its 1957 order of only a few months before.

The truth of the matter seems to be that the character committee did not give a clear warning because it did not know what its position *would* be. Furthermore, it was proceeding under recent directions from the Supreme Court of Illinois in which any reference to unanswered questions was markedly absent. (18 Ill. 2d, at 186) Even the member conducting the rehearing could admit at the final session (when asked by petitioner about the committee attitude toward the unanswered questions), "I don't know what stands out in other people's minds." (R. 294-295.) (The committee letter curiously relied upon in Note 15 of the Opinion of this Court is similarly non-committal, without even a reference to *any* unanswered questions. (R. 441)) In short, petitioner was permitted to proceed and depart with the understanding that the record as a whole would be evaluated with respect to his character and fitness in determining his application for admission to the practice of law.

ii.

An attempt *is* made by this Court to account for "the record as a whole." The Opinion of this Court explains that the long examination of petitioner, even after he had clearly stated he would not answer questions about political affiliations (R. 28, 484-490), indicated

> no more than that the Committee was attempting to exercise *an informed judgment* as to whether the situation was an appropriate one for waiver of the Committee's continuing requirement, earlier enforced after the first Anastaplo hearings, that such questions must be answered. [81 S.Ct., at 986. Emphasis supplied.]

(We have already reviewed this supposed "continuing requirement" as it was affected by the 1957 order of the court below and by what the committee could and could not say.) This Court attempts in this passage to justify the committee's prolongation of the hearings long after petitioner had failed to satisfy the "continuing requirement . . . that [certain] questions must be answered." This justification relies on an explanation that does not appear either in the report of the committee or in the opinion of the court below: there has been no suggestion heretofore that the Illinois bar authorities had been "attempting to exercise an informed judgment" as to whether they should waive their "continuing requirement."

In fact, the court below, in a passage quoted by this Court at 81 S.Ct. 982, repudiates any suggestion that such an "informed judgment" was being exercised: for Illinois insists that a determination that an applicant is eligible for admission to the bar "is *impossible* where [the applicant] refuses to state whether he is a member of a group dedicated [as the Communist Party is said to be] to the overthrow of the government of the United States by force and violence." (18 Ill. 2d, at 200-201. Emphasis supplied.) One does not deliberate or exercise any judgment at all about impossibilities. Aristotle, *N. Ethics*, III, iii.

Once again this Court, in order to lend constitutional plausibility to Illinois's action, implicitly vindicates petitioner's position by having to resort to the extreme of radically revising the rationale of the bar authorities. Petitioner is reduced to the expedient of addressing himself to this revised rationale for the first time in a petition for rehearing. One is tempted to say of this state of affairs what Athene was reduced to saying to usurping Zeus:

You may do this if you like, but we, the other gods, will not praise you for it. [*Iliad*, xxii, 180]

But let us, instead, address ourselves to the revised rationale. That is, let us assume, contrary to the express ruling of the court below that petitioner's refusals made his admission *impossible,* that an "informed judgment" was exercised as to whether to "waive" the "Committee's continuing requirement." Still, it must be asked, are there any limits to how an "informed judgment" might be exercised?

An "informed judgment" would seem to be even more circumscribed than "discretion": and yet we know that the exercise of discretion by courts cannot be unlimited, that it must respect in a reasonable manner the facts of a case. Must not the exercise of an "informed judgment" also be reasonable? Must it not, in petitioner's case, consider such factors as, how the unanswered questions arose in the first instance, what reasons petitioner gives for not answering such questions, whether there are responsible lawyers and judges who indorse petitioner's position, what the general weight of the evidence suggests about petitioner's qualifications for admission to the bar, how petitioner's attitude and conduct relate to the calling of a lawyer? But no factors of this or any other kind are referred to as taken into account by the committee in making the "informed judgment" now attributed to it.

The Opinion of this Court concludes with the observation that

our function here is solely one of constitutional adjudication, not to pass judgment on what has been done as if we were another state court of review, still less to express any view upon the wisdom of the State's action. [81 S.Ct., at 987]

Can one permit a judgment to pass muster as "informed" without considering at all its "wisdom"? What has become of "the dictates of reason" to which recourse was promised in the *Schware* concurring opinion? 353 U.S. 232, at 249 [1957].

iii.

We return then to the question, What *does* the record as a whole not only permit but require on the only issue of this case, the issue of petitioner's qualifications for admission to the bar? The Opinion of this Court does seem to express reservations about the wisdom of Illinois's action, even while it confirms the power of the State to act as it did. But does the action of the Illinois bar authorities have any "rational support in the evidence" of this record? (81 S.Ct., at 1000) Eleven members of a committee on character and fitness testify that petitioner has not satisfied them that "he possesses the good moral character and fitness to practice law." (R. 466) Presumably, they would, as character references for petitioner, be unable to answer the concluding questions on the standard confidential form used by the committee (R. 412),

> Do you consider applicant worthy of the highest trust and confidence? For example, would you recommend him as the guardian of a minor's estate?

Presumably, also, they pledge that they have applied in their assessment of petitioner the same standards that they have come to demand and expect of their colleagues at the bar, the very same standards which resulted in only 15 other rejections by this committee out of approximately 3000 applicants over a six-year period. (45 Illinois Bar J. 821)

Has petitioner demonstrated his qualifications for admission to the bar? If it can be honorably said, on a long record drawing upon ten years of examination and argument, that petitioner's qualifications have not been established, then he truly does not deserve ever to be admitted to the bar. For it must be conceded that his qualifications are as well established now as they ever can be—and it would be presumptuous toward this Court and toward the court below for petitioner to try again. If, on the other hand, his exclusion is condoned despite his evident qualifications, then something is seriously wrong with the American bar and perhaps even with America—and it would be unbecoming of petitioner, after he exhausts his legal remedies on the present record, to adopt on his own initiative the role of the perpetual suppliant.

In any event, we must all hope that the decision announced April 24th means more than that petitioner's career at the bar is at an end. We must all hope that it also means that Illinois will be able, eventually if not immediately, to provide itself a bar of the highest character and fitness, a bar which respects the precept restated by General Eisenhower earlier this month:

> Too much government planes off the peaks of excellence, hones down differences, dries up diversity, and leaves a bleak sameness.

3. THE KEY IN PETITIONER'S POCKET.

i.

It is observed by the opinion of this Court, 81 S.Ct., at 987, that

> we do not understand that Illinois' exclusionary requirement will continue to operate to exclude Anastaplo from the bar any longer than he continues in his refusal to answer. We find nothing to suggest that he would not be admitted now if he decides to answer, assuming of course that no grounds justifying his exclusion from practice resulted. In short, petitioner holds the key to admission in his own hands.

Let us assume, despite the explicit reservations of "certain members" about the Declaration of Independence teachings and despite the hostility manifested by various members toward a stubborn applicant who has defied them so long,—let us assume that petitioner can, if he would but answer in the negative the unanswered questions about affiliations with the Communist Party and the Ku Klux Klan, secure admission to the bar.

There is no doubt that petitioner *could* answer, without fear of legal sanctions, that he has never been a member of the Communist Party or of the Ku Klux Klan. There can be no doubt about this since it is evident from the record that everyone has long been aware that petitioner could have at any time safely given negative answers to such questions, either because they were truthful or because Illinois would not be able to impeach such answers if they were not truthful. (R. 174-180) In fact, the committee has acknowledged that it has

received no information from any outside source which would cast any doubt on applicant's loyalty or which would tend to connect him in any manner with any subversive group. [R. 453]

Suppose then that petitioner should now regard this prolonged litigation merely as a "test case" and proceed to answer in the negative all unanswered questions. What more would the committee know that it does not already know? That is, what of substance would be added to the record bearing on petitioner's character and fitness that has not been available to Illinois for ten years? It is obvious that only one more item could be added, the fact of petitioner's *submission*, a selfish and even unmanly submission to what he has considered for over a decade to be dangerous and uncalled for practices, practices which he knows to have been prompted in his case by a defense of the principles of the Declaration of Independence.

Whether or not petitioner is correct in his evaluation of these inquiries, it is generally conceded that he has long *believed* himself to be correct about a matter so vital to the bar and to the country that he has been willing to make serious sacrifices rather than acquiesce in such practices. Thus, if petitioner follows the advice implicit in the Opinion of this Court, the committee would gain the assurance of this single additional fact, the fact that petitioner had used a "key" against what he considers the best interests of the bar and of the country and that he had done so only to preserve his own career. Should this kind of behavior make him appear in a more favorable light before a tribunal of lawyers dedicated to the moral fitness of the bar?

It should also be noticed that unless the committee should already be convinced of petitioner's character and fitness, his decision to "go along" should be of no consequence: for the committee would not be any more or any less certain than it is now that petitioner is not a member of the Communist Party or of the Ku Klux Klan. Indeed, the situation is such now that the committee must take petitioner's word for it whether he is a "subversive" or "dangerous" man—unless, of course, the committee has already decided that petitioner's character is unreliable. Thus, either way, the key judgment has to be made on the basis of the evidence the committee already has, not on the basis of any denial of affiliations that petitioner can be induced to give. Were these factors taken into account by the committee in making the "informed judgment" now imputed to it or in arriving at its "good faith belief in the need for exploratory or testing questioning [about the affiliations] of the applicant" (81 S.Ct., at 983)?

In the light of such considerations, which include petitioner's reasons for the position he has taken, the "curtain" which petitioner is said to have drawn "upon the [committee's] investigation" is revealed as most transparent. (81 S.Ct., at 986) In fact, it is to such rationalizations as have been advanced to justify Illinois's action that Mr. Justice Holmes's strictures, quoted by this Court at 81 S.Ct. 1006, might better be applied,

> The provisions of the Constitution are not mathematical formulas having their essence in their form; they are organic living institutions transplanted from English soil. Their significance is vital, not formal. . . .

The flaw in the key analogy should now be apparent; it clearly raises self-interest above the public interest. Not infrequently, one who defends constitutional rights or important principles against attack has such a key on his person. (We have only to think of the Jehovah's Witness child and his power to avoid legal sanctions by simply rendering the required salute.) This is not the time for an old applicant to be bribed to learn new tricks.

ii.

It should be recorded that the Illinois bar authorities are up to their old tricks. The character committee sitting in Chicago has intensified, since April 24th, the bullying of young graduates which is so unbecoming to the bar, law schools and courts which permit it. (At least one affidavit describing current practices in fifteen proceedings can be supplied this Court.) Applicants are being asked whether they agree with the position of the majority of this Court in petitioner's case—with further questions as to political affiliations (including past and present membership in the Communist Party) ready to be directed to any applicant who is so unlearned as to withhold ready assent.

Thus, since the decision of this Court was announced, committee members have been reassured in their approach, an approach which remains contemptuous of the humiliation that sensitive but vulnerable youngsters endure when forced to submit to questions that they cannot help but regard as improper and demeaning. Evidently, the vindicated character commissioners do not choose to distinguish, as the Opinion of this Court attempts to do, between "wisdom" and "power": rather, they consider their "informed judgment" to have been inspected by the highest court in the land and to have been certified as conforming to "the dictates of reason."

Nor does it matter either to the committee or, it would seem, to any court, that bar applicants are coerced into the attitude recently expressed by a young man upon learning of the committee's resurgence:

I'll give any answer they want. They'll get no fight out of me after all I've been through to become a lawyer.

Whatever else the committee accomplishes is subject to debate; but that it has for years formed the young in this manner there can be no doubt. We are reminded of the report by Brown and Fassett, at 20 University of Chicago Law Review 501 (1953),

. . . The affair [of petitioner] made a considerable impression on his contemporaries at Chicago, one of whom wrote as follows: "Although I have never been a Communist nor a member of organizations on the Attorney-General's list, my attitudes are such that had I acted with complete sincerity, I would not have replied 'no sir' to the question I was asked [about membership in subversive organizations]. But, I decided in advance, as did most of my friends, to give the answers best fitted to secure admission to the Bar without difficulty.

On what can the committee rely to counteract the damage it does? Or is the hazing applicants receive preparatory to initiation into the profession designed to rid them of any lingering attachment they might have to courage, self-respect, and justice?

The merit of petitioner's resistance to such bullying is that it forces eventual consideration of the kind of bar and even the kind of citizen America wants. So long as he refuses to capitulate, that long will this question remain a serious one, even though its ultimate resolution will probably come at a time when it is no longer of any practical relevance to petitioner's legal and academic careers. Nevertheless, a bar worthy of its vital role in American republican government cannot emerge until it is recognized that there are principles and standards to which even a career at the bar may be deliberately sacrificed. Only when the bar is again made up, at least among its leaders, of men who accept this truth, only then can the profession be restored to the integrity and standing proper to it. Indeed, petitioner cannot hope, at a time when submission and self-interest are exalted above principle and civic virtue, to be more truly a lawyer than by reconciling himself to permanent exclusion from what he had once thought would be his profession.

Perhaps it is true that petitioner "took too much of the responsibility of preserving [his country's] freedom upon himself." 81 S.Ct., at 995. But he was young enough to hope that Americans who would not heed old precepts might yet learn from new examples.

CONCLUSION.

We have suggested that the exclusion order should be reversed, with instructions to the Illinois bar authorities on remand that they reconsider the record already made in this case without giving *any* adverse effect to petitioner's allegedly "subversive" views on the right of revolution and the Declaration of Independence. (Pages 384-89) This modification would seem to be consistent with the position actually taken by this Court in its Opinion.

Reasons have also been advanced for a reversal and remand that would be even more respectful of the record and of natural justice, a remand with the ruling that petitioner has clearly established his character and fitness for the practice of law. (Pages 389-95). That is, we suggest that the record in this case has still to be given its due.

It is only by an ungenerous disregard of the record as it developed, of the kind of challenges petitioner alone faced and of the manner in which he met them, that the action of the Illinois authorities has been upheld. The record—both before the committee and on appeal—that record of testimony and briefs remains as a guide to reforms that are needed in the education and character of the American bar.

Petitioner is satisfied he has acted as one ought. He is further satisfied that his action will continue to serve the best interests of the bar and of the country. The generous sentiments of the dissenting opinions elicited by his cause in Chicago, in Springfield, and in Washington keep alive hopes for the success of efforts to make the institutions and laws of our people a reflection of decency and perhaps even of nobility.

Petitioner leaves in the hands of the profession—lawyers, law teachers and judges alike—the career he might have had. He trusts he will be forgiven if he retains for himself only the immortal lines of another exile (*Inferno*, xv, 121-124),

Then he turned back, and seemed like one of those who run for the green cloth at Verona through the open fields; and of them seemed he who triumphs, not he who loses.

Respectfully submitted,
GEORGE ANASTAPLO, *Petitioner*
Counsel pro se

APPENDIX [TO THE PETITION FOR REHEARING]: BIBLIOGRAPHY

1.

Petitioner recognized several years ago that his chances of immediate success were small: "I am afraid I speak not to the generation of this Committee, but perhaps to my own generation and certainly to one that follows." (R. 363) He has, in order that he might be able to address properly those who follow, taken special pains with the briefs and record filed in the Supreme Court of the United States and with the 1958 Closing Argument before the Committee on Character and Fitness (from which the long quotations at 81 S.Ct. 990 and 993 [in Justice Black's dissenting opinion] are taken). Vital to petitioner's position has been his willingness to explain himself.

Petitioner has been obliged, in the course of this controversy, to discuss critical defects in the legal profession in the United States. On the other hand, the virtues of America are reflected in the fact that a student of law with remarkably few supporters has been able, for eleven years, to oppose the power of the state and to carry his cause to the highest judicial tribunal in the land. That he has been able to do this is itself worthy of note even by those who regret that the long encounter has not been given its natural completion by the Supreme Court of the United States. (All this is a tribute, as well, to the clarity of the Revised Rules of that Court.)

It is as an aid for the serious student of the continuing problems posed by the case that there are collected in this convenient place references to materials relating to petitioner's matter and to the position he has taken the past decade.

2.

There were two phases to this case, each culminating in action by the Supreme Court of the United States. The first, 1950-1955, was concluded by the denial of review, 348 U.S. 946, 349 U.S. 908 (1955); the second, 1957-1961, saw the action of Illinois upheld after certiorari was granted, [366 U.S. 82], 81 S.Ct. 978, 6 L. ed. 2d 135 (1961).

A substantial part of the record made during the first phase of the case is reproduced in 12 Lawyers Guild Rev. 163 (1952). The opinion of the Supreme Court of Illinois on that occasion is found at 3 Ill. 2d 471, 121 N.E. 2d 826 (1954). (The first report of the Committee on Character and Fitness (1954) has not been reprinted. It is described by petitioner at 19 Lawyers Guild Rev. 149 (1959) (R. 328).)

The record made during the second (*i.e.*, the current) phase of the case is printed in the Transcript of Record filed in the Supreme Court of the United States. (It is summarized at pages 12-57 of petitioner's Brief on the Merits (July 4, 1960).) Petitioner's Closing Argument before the Committee on Character and Fitness (R. 314; 1958) is reprinted at 19 Lawyers Guild Rev. 143 (1959). The second report of the Committee on Character and Fitness (R. 450; 1959) is reprinted at 19 Lawyers Guild Rev. 65 (1959). The opinion of the Supreme Court of Illinois on that occasion is found at 18 Ill. 2d 182, 163 N.E. 2d 429 (1959-1960). (The 1957 order of the Supreme Court of Illinois providing for the rehearing which forms the basis of the 1957-1961 litigation is set forth at 18 Ill. 2d 186, 163 N.E. 2d 431 (1959).)

The printed documents prepared by petitioner and filed in the Supreme Court of the United States include (1) Jurisdictional Statement, Jan. 11, 1955; (2) Petition for Rehearing, March 23, 1955; (3) Motion for Leave to File an Application for Admission to the Bar of the Supreme Court of the United States, March 23, 1955; (4) Petition for a

IN RE GEORGE ANASTAPLO (1950-61)   401

Writ of Certiorari, March 15, 1960 (granted, May 2, 1960); (5) Brief on the Merits, July 4, 1960; (6) Reply Brief, November 24, 1960 (in Note 21, the reference to Note 13 should be to Note 18); (7) Petition for Rehearing, June 19, 1961.

Petitioner attempted, both in 1955 and in 1960, to secure admission directly to the bar of the Supreme Court of the United States without prior admission to the bar of a State. It was hoped that in view of the special circumstances of this case, the Court might suspend the rule governing admission to its bar and make its own determination of the moral character, competence and experience that the regular mode of admission is designed to insure. The record made in Illinois and the manner in which petitioner conducted his case, both in his briefs and on oral argument, were thought to afford an adequate alternative basis for the requisite determination. It was hoped, that is, that the Court might thereby preserve for petitioner an aspect of his career even as it gave concrete evidence that it does not approve of "the wisdom of the State's action." Both attempts to secure direct admission failed. 349 U.S. 903 (1955); 81 S.Ct. 987, n20 (1961). See Brown, Loyalty and Security, p. 112, n41 (1958).

There were also filed in the Supreme Court of the United States (1) a "Brief [by the Attorney General of Illinois] for the State of Illinois, Respondents" (Nov. 4, 1960); (2) a brief amicus curiae by the Illinois Division of the American Civil Liberties Union (1960); (3) a brief amicus curiae by the National Lawyers Guild (1960).

3.

Comments and other materials bearing on petitioner's matter, prior to the decision of April 24, 1961, are set forth here in a more or less chronological order:

(1) The Carterville [Ill.] Herald, October 14 [or 21 or 28], 1950, p. 1; (2) 18 Univ. Chicago L. Rev. facing 421 (1951); (3) The University of Chicago Maroon, May 9, 1952, p. 2; (4) The New York Daily Compass, May 14, 1952, p. 7; (5) Expose, March 1953; (6) Expose, April 1953; (7) Brown and Fassett, 20 Univ. Chicago L. Rev. 480, 481-2, 501-2 (1953); (8) 13 Lawyers Guild Rev. 8 (1953); (9) Illinois A.C.L.U., The Brief, Feb. 1954, p. 3; (10) The Chicago Tribune, March 31, 1954, p. 2; (11) The Southern Illinoisan, March 31, 1954, p. 2; (12) The Carterville [Ill.] Herald, April 2, 1954; (13) United Press Dispatch, Springfield, Ill., May 12, 1954; (14) A.C.L.U., Civil Liberties, May 1954, p. 2; (15) 14 Lawyers Guild Rev. 38 (1954); (16) The Southern Illinoisan, Sept. 23, 1954; (17) The Chicago Daily News, Sept. 23, 1954, p. 14; (18) A.C.L.U. Letter, The Chicago Daily News, Oct. 11, 1954; (19) The Carterville [Ill.] Herald, Oct. 1, 1954, p. 2; (20) Illinois A.C.L.U., The Brief, Oct. 1954; (21) 12 New York Guild Lawyer, Oct. 1954, p. 2; (22) 36 Chicago Bar Record 67 (1954); (23) 43 Illinois Bar J. 226 (1954); (24) 26 Bar Examiner 96 (1955); (25) I. F. Stone's Weekly, March 7, 1955, p. 3; (26) The Marion [Ill.] Daily Republican-Leader, Dec. 26, 1956; (27) New York Guild Lawyer, April 1955, p. 4; (28) Note, 1955 Washington Univ. L. Q. 83 (1955); (29) Note, 2 U.C.L.A. L. Rev. 224 (1955); (30) Starrs, 18 Univ. Detroit L. J. 195, 216 (1955); (31) Note, 50 Northwestern Univ. L. Rev. 94 (1955); (32) Levi, Hearing before Subcommittee of Committee on Judiciary, U. S. Senate, 84th Cong., 1st Sess., "Recording of Jury Deliberations," Oct. 12, 1955, p. 30; (33) The Chicago Tribune, Sept. 18, 1957; (34) Cramton, 8 Univ. Chicago Law School Record (Special Supplement), p. 52, n235 (1958); (35) Ralph S. Brown, Jr., Loyalty and Security, pp. 111-112 (1958); (36) Anastaplo v. Radford, 14 Ill. 2d 520 (esp. 534) (1958) (a side effect); (37) C. Herman Pritchett, The American Constitution, pp. 465-466 (1959) (see, also, his forthcoming book); (38) 43 Minnesota L. Rev. 1025 (1959); (39) Weissman, 19 Lawyers Guild Rev. 126 (1959); (40) The Southern Illinoisan, Feb. 14, 1960; (41) Illinois A.C.L.U., The Brief, Feb. 1960, p. 7; (42) The Chicago Pnyx, March 15, 1960; (43) Note, 21 Ohio State Law J. 260 (1960); (44) Note, 31 Mississippi L. J. 303 (1960); (45) Trumbull, 42 Chicago Bar Record 57, 60 (1960); (46) The Chicago Daily News, Dec. 14, 1960, p. 5; (47) The Southern Illinoisan, Dec. 15, 1960, p. 2; (48) The New York Times, Dec. 18, 1960, p. 40; (49) 36 New York Univ. L. Rev. 184 (1961); (50) The Chicago Pnyx, Jan. 1, 1961; (51) The Chicago Sun-Times, Jan. 8, 1961, p. 59.

Special reference should be made to the comments by an early student of the case, Professor Malcolm P. Sharp of the University of Chicago Law School. (Petitioner is again privileged to acknowledge Mr. Sharp as his "most thoughtful and consequently most valuable supporter throughout all these years." R. 319; 19 Lawyers Guild Rev. 145 (1959).) Mr. Sharp's discussions of the case are found in (1) "A Comment," R. 475-484 (from Anastaplo, Some Rash Innovations and Speculations (1951)); (2) 20 Univ. Chicago L. Rev. 529, 541-544 (1953); (3) 16 Lawyers Guild Rev. 1, 2 (1956); (4) 17 Lawyers Guild Rev. 43 (1957); (5) The University of Chicago Maroon, Feb. 15, 1957, p. 9; (6) 28 Univ. Chicago L. Rev. 399 (1961); (7) The University of Chicago Maroon, May 2, 1961, p. 8 (cf. March 10, 1961, p. 5).

Professors Harry Kalven, Jr. and Roscoe T. Steffen, also of the University of Chicago Law School (authors of amici briefs submitted to the Supreme Court of Illinois (R. 498; 1959) and to the Supreme Court of the United States [for the American Civil Liberties Union] (1960)) have a discussion of the April 24th bar opinions of the Supreme Court of the United States scheduled to appear in a forthcoming issue of Law in Transition. Petitioner understands that it is likely that similar discussions by other scholars will appear soon in the Northwestern University Law Review, the University of Chicago Law Review, and the Louisiana Law Review. See, also, the newspaper accounts of and reactions to these opinions of the Court that are found in the April 25, 1961 issues of The Chicago Sun-Times (p. 5), The Chicago Tribune (p. 1), The New York Times (p. 28), The Philadelphia Inquirer (p. 7), The Washington Post (p. 1); and, The University of Chicago Maroon, April 28, 1961, pp. 3, 6 (cf. Feb. 3, 1961, p. 11).

4.

Fortunately, petitioner's literary activities during the past decade have not been restricted to bar admission problems. These activities include lectures delivered as part of his academic duties: (1) Some Reflections on the Hamlet of Shakespeare (1957); (2) Baseball: The American Political Game (1958); (3) Freedom, Justice and the Rule of Law —An Introduction to Due Process of Law (1959); (4) On Plato's Meno (1959); (5) The Declaration of Independence (1961); (6) The American Constitution (1961). (Several of these lectures are or will soon be available in mimeographed form.)

In addition, the following items by petitioner might be noted: (1) Letter, The Carterville [Ill.] Herald, April 27, 1951; (2) Review, Drinker, Legal Ethics, 14 Lawyers Guild Rev. 144 (1954); (3) Review, Blaustein and Porter, The American Lawyer, 14 Lawyers Guild Rev. 178 (1954); (4) Letter, The [London] Observer, Aug. 14, 1960 (see, also, The [London] Observer, editorial, Aug. 28, 1960); (5) Letter, The Carterville [Ill.] Herald, Aug. 25, 1960 (cf. The New York Times, July 29, 1960, 2:5, July 30, 1960, 5:7; The New York Herald-Tribune (Late City), July 29, 1960, 14:6).

In process: (1) Notes on the First Amendment [doctoral dissertation; see Sharp, Foreword, xvii, Alexander Meiklejohn, American Political Freedom (1960)]; (2) Madrid and Moscow [reflections on a six-month camping tour of Europe in 1960]; (3) Realism and the Practice of Law—A Lecture for Law Students.

An important aspect of petitioner's position before the Committee on Character and Fitness is summed up in his letter-to-the-editor printed in three Illinois newspapers (The Southern Illinoisan, April 9, 1961; The Chicago Pnyx, April 15, 1961; The Carterville Herald, May 4, 1961) (see, also, R. 416):

> The demands for congressional investigation of the John Birch Society imply that the American people are not able to look out for themselves. What necessary information can the Congress learn for us that the newspapers have not already discovered and published?
> A people that values its freedom should be reluctant to permit the government to do its thinking for it.

Comments and other materials bearing on this matter, subsequent to the decision of April 24, 1961, are set forth here (thereby supplementing the bibliography provided in the appendix to the petition for rehearing):

SUPPLEMENTARY BIBLIOGRAPHY, NOV. 10, 1970

1.

The differences in judicial opinion provoked by the bar admission cases were evident not only in the opinions of the Supreme Court of the United States but even in the courtroom when those opinions were announced on April 24, 1961. Thus, the *Washington Post* could report in an article headlined, "Court Deeply Divided on Controversial Cases: Justice Warren Chides Frankfurter for 'Lecture' on Decision in Murder" (April 25, 1961, p. 1):

> Chief Justice Earl Warren ripped into Justice Felix Frankfurter yesterday in the sharpest exchange of public remarks between Supreme Court Justices in years. The clash came as the Court ruled that states can bar lawyers from practicing if they refuse to answer questions about Communist Party membership and as it granted a fourth trial to Willie Lee Stewart, District of Columbia man convicted of murder.
>
> The first indication that tempers were frayed came after Justice John M. Harlan announced the Court's decision to affirm Illinois' refusal to license George Anastaplo to practice law. Justice Hugo L. Black, who led the dissenters in that 5-to-4 decision, said Anastaplo's troubles came because he "made the mistake of saying he believed fully in the Declaration of Independence." Anastaplo first got in trouble with the Illinois courts because he insisted he believes in a theoretical right of revolution.
>
> When Justice Black finished, Justice Harlan said, "It is clear from the opinion of the Illinois Supreme Court that he was denied admission not because he believes in the Declaration of Independence but because he refused to answer questions about his Communist Party membership." A few minutes later, Justice Black announced the Court's 5-to-4 decision to grant a new trial to Stewart who was convicted of a 1953 murder in the District of Columbia. . . .

Other comments by judges bearing upon or interpreting the bar admission cases, subsequent to the decision of April 24, 1961, are set forth here:

(1) *Scales* v. *U.S.* (Black, J., dissenting), 367 U.S. 203, 261 (1961); (2) *Lathrop* v. *Donohue* (Harlan, J., concurring), 367 U.S. 820, 849 (1961); ibid. (Black, dissenting), 367 U.S. 820, 874 (1961); (3) *Malloy* v. *Hogan*, 378 U.S. 1 (1964); (4) *Aptheker* v. *Secretary of State* (Clark, J., dissenting), 378 U.S. 500, 528 (1964); (5) *Baggett* v. *Bullitt* (Clark, J., dissenting), 377 U.S. 360, 384 (1964); (6) *City of El Paso* v. *Simmons* (Black, J., dissenting), 379 U.S. 497, 517 (1965); (7) *Hackin* v. *Lockwood*, 361 F.2d 499, 503 (1966); (8) *Hallinan* v. *Committee of Bar Examiners of State Bar of California*, 55 Cal. Rptr. 228, 421 P.2d 76 (1966); (9) *Time, Inc.* v. *Hill* (Black, J., concurring), 385 U.S. 374, 399 (1967); (10) *Spevack* v. *Klein*, 385 U.S. 511 (1967); ibid. (Harlan, dissenting), 385 U.S. 511, 528 (1967); (11) *Keyishian* v. *Board of Regents*, 233 F.S. 752, 753 (1964), 255 F.S. 981, 990, 991 (1966); ibid. (Clark, J., dissenting), 385 U.S. 589, 625 (1967); (12) *Johnson* v. *Avery*, 382 F.2d 353, 355 (1967); (13) *Goldberg* v. *Regents of University of California*, 57 Cal. Rptr. 463, 471 (1967); (14) *Vogel* v. *Los Angeles*, 64 Cal. Rptr. 409, 430, 434 P.2d 961, 982 (1967); (15) *Shoultz* v. *McNamara*, 282 F.S. 315, 320 (1968), *Clifford* v. *Shoultz*, 413 F.2d 868, 872 (1969); (16) *Law Students Civil Rights, etc.* v. *Wadmond*, 299 F.S. 117, 131, 146 (1969); (17) *In re Marvin*, 97 N.J. Sup. 62, 67, 234 A.2d 408, 411 (1967), *Application of Marvin*, 53 N.J. 147, 151, 249 A.2d 377, 379 (1969).

Several recent cases (particularly *Spevack*, *Aptheker*, and *Malloy*) have tended to undermine the 1961 rulings in *Konigsberg*, in *Anastaplo*, and in *Cohen* v. *Hurley*. See, also, *Gardner* v. *Broderick*, 392 U.S. 273, 277 (1968). There are currently three cases before the Supreme Court of the United States of applicants, or prospective applicants, for admission to the bar in Arizona, Ohio, and New York (*Baird* v. *State of Arizona*; *In the Matter of Stolar*; *Law Students Civil Rights, etc.* v. *Wadmond*). The really interesting question for me about these cases is not how the Court will decide them but whether it can thereafter persuade the state supreme courts and bar associations involved to comply with any decree the court might issue which should happen to be in any way favorable to the petitioners. It was to be expected that Raphael Konigsberg, who won 5-3 in 1957 and lost 5-4 in 1961, would continue to be denied admission to the California bar upon returning to Los Angeles from Washington. (I understand that he has attempted upon two occasions in recent years to secure admission in California, but without success.) But even Rudolph Schware, who won 8-0 in the Supreme Court of the United States in 1957, was never admitted to the New Mexico bar. He had to go elsewhere to become a lawyer. Are the bar authorities in Arizona, Ohio, and New York likely to be more respectful of the rule of law than those of California, Illinois, and New Mexico have been?

There is merit in Judge Motley's observation, in *Law Students Civil Rights* v. *Wadmond*, 299 F.S. 117, 146 (1969), when he says, after quoting from Justice Black's dissenting opinion in my case, "It is nothing short of a complete irony that lawyers who fought for and won constitutional protections for other professions are the last to receive protection for themselves."

2.

Non-judicial comments bearing on the bar admission cases, subsequent to the decision of April 24, 1961, are set forth here:

(1) Harry Kalven, Jr., and Roscoe Steffen, *Law in Transition* 21 (1961): 155; (2) *University of Chicago Maroon*, Oct. 26, 1961, p. 1; (3) *University of Chicago Maroon*, Nov. 2, 1961, p. 2; (4) Note, *A.B.A.J.* 47 (1961): 818-21; (5) Note, *Brooklyn L. Rev.* 28 (1961): 136; (6) Stanley A. Kaplan, *Chicago Bar Record* 43 (1961): 76, 82; (7) Note, *Harvard L. Rev.* 75 (1961): 129, 132; (8) Note, *Notre Dame Lawyer* 37 (1961): 246; (9) Otto Kirchheimer, *Political Justice* (Princeton: Princeton University Press, 1961), pp. 252-56; (10) Fred J. Cook, *St. Louis Post-Dispatch*, Feb. 21, 1962, p. 2B; (11) Cook, *Saga*, Mar. 1962, pp. 4, 18; May 1962, p. 12; June 1962, p. 13; (12) Irving Dilliard, *Chicago's American*, Apr. 4, 1962, p. 12; (13) Anastaplo, *Southern Illinoisan* (Carbondale, Ill.), Mar. 26, 1962, p. 4; (14) Mel Luna, *East St. Louis Sunday Journal*, Apr. 22, 1962, pp. 33-34; (15) Editorial, Lindsay-Schaub Newspapers (Illinois), May 17, 1962; (16) Irving Dilliard, *Focus/Midwest*, June 1962, p. 5; (17) William J. Martin, *Loyola Law Times* 2 (1962): 8; (18) Philip J. McGuire, *Illinois B. J.* 50 (1962): 446; (19) Note, *Iowa L. Rev.* 47 (1962): 507; (20) Note, *Vanderbilt L. Rev.* 15 (1962): 634; (21) Dilliard, *Washington U. L. Q.* 1962: 53, 60-63; (22) Annotation, *U.S. Supreme Court Reports* 6 L.ed. 2d 135, 1328, 1334-35 (1962); (23) C. Herman Pritchett, *American Constitutional Issues* (New York: McGraw-Hill, 1962), p. 296; (24) Dilliard, *Focus/Midwest*, Jan. 1963, p. 6; (25) Note, *Stanford L. Rev.* 15 (1963): 500; (26) Malcolm P. Sharp, *U. Chicago L. Rev.* 30 (1963): 704, 718-19; (27) Dilliard, *One Man's Stand for Freedom: Justice Black and the Bill of Rights* (New York: Alfred A. Knopf, 1963), p. 408; (28) Anastaplo, *U. Detroit L. J.* 42 (1964): 55, nn. 1, 2, 23, 26; (29) Charles A. Reich, *Yale L. J.* 73 (1964): 733, 763-64; (30) Anastaplo, *Carterville* (Ill.) *Herald*, Nov. 19, Dec. 3, Dec. 10, Dec. 17, Dec. 31, 1964; (31) Anastaplo, "Notes on the First Amendment" (University of Chicago, Ph.D. dissertation, 1964), pp. 308-10, 681, 699, 706, 715, 841; (32) Robert A. Sprecher, *A.B.A.J.* 51 (1965): 248, 251; (33) Carl M. Selinger and Rodric B. Schoen, *Natural Resources J.* 5 (1965): 299; (34) Anastaplo, *St. Louis U. L. J.* 9 (1965): 390, n. 20; (35) Norman Redlich, *Nation*, March 21, 1966, pp. 322, 325-26; (36) Sprecher, *Bar Examiner* 35 (1966): 33, 48, 54; (37) Kalven, *U. Chicago L. Rev.* 33 (1966): 194; (38) Abe Krash, *U. Chicago L. Rev.* 33 (1966): 205; (39) Vern Countryman and Ted Finman, *The Lawyer in Modern Society* (Boston: Little, Brown & Co., 1966), pp. 802-84; (40) Willmoore Kendall, *American Political Science Review* 61 (1967): 783; (41) Note, *North Carolina L. Rev.* 45 (1967): 1008; (42) Paul A. Freund et al., *Constitutional Law: Case and Other*

Problems (Boston: Little, Brown & Co., 1967), p. 2058; (43) *Columbia Survey of Human Rights* 1 (1968): 33; (44) Theodore J. Lowi, *Nation*, May 19, 1969, pp. 624, 627; (45) Laurence Berns, *Cornell L. Rev.* 54 (1969): 920; (46) Note, *Ill. B. J.* 57 (1969): 606; (47) Note, *Natural Resources J.* 9 (1969): 248; (48) Note, *Vanderbilt L. Rev.* 23 (1969): 131; (49) Moria C. Mackert, *Wis. L. Rev.* 1970: 471; (50) Note, *Yale L. J.* 78 (1969): 1352; (51) William F. Swindler, *Court and Constitution in the Twentieth Century* (Indianapolis: Bobbs-Merrill, 1970), pp. 199-202, 289, 465-66, 477; (52) William B. Lockhart, Yale Kamisar, and Jesse H. Choper, *Constitutional Law: Cases—Comments—Questions* (3d edition; St. Paul: West Publishing Co., 1970), pp. 805-6, 849-58, 978.

There may be found as well in the University of Chicago Law School Library a three-volume collection of materials on my case, for which I was asked to write in 1965 an introduction. I could not resist saying on that occasion,

> The following materials bearing on my character and fitness for admission to the Illinois bar are presented here in a more or less chronological order.
> The reader will notice that my statement of my position improved through the years. The reader should be reassured, especially if he is of a practical bent of mind, that I have never regretted the action I started in 1950. It cannot be denied, however, that inconveniences have resulted: it can be shown that I would have made (and no doubt spent) almost a quarter of a million dollars more during the last fifteen years than I did, had I been permitted to enter private practice; and it is evident that anyone with my law school and academic record and my publications, to say nothing of my talents, would be teaching somewhere in a good law school today (and perhaps even at the University of Chicago Law School) but for this bar admission controversy. But, on the other hand, I have been able to study and travel more than would have been likely if I had been permitted a conventional career.
> It must be difficult for the young reader in 1965 to appreciate how bad things were, or at least appeared to be, in 1950. Perhaps "we happy few" had something to do with giving our fellow-citizens the time they needed to come back to their senses and to recover their nerve.
> We, in any event, behaved ourselves.

3.

See, for passages in this book bearing on the bar admission cases, chap. 2, nn. 1, 17; chap. 3, nn. 4, 13, 20, 35; chap. 4, nn. 26, 107; chap. 5, nn. 135, 149; chap. 7, nn. 38, 72, 77, 81, 82, 86, 89; chap. 8, nn. 19, 36, 45, 88, 96, 164, below. See, also, pp. 236-37, Appendixes C, D, and E, above; chap. 2, n. 13; chap. 4, nn. 35, 84, 116; chap. 5, n. 64; chap. 6, n. 1 (see *Congressional Record* 116: E10520), n. 26; chap. 7, nn. 45, 70, 77, 87, 107; chap. 8, nn. 28, 78, 126, 190; chap. 9, nn. 5, 13, 14, 15, 29, 35, 39, below.

4.

See, on test oaths generally, Shakespeare, *King Lear*, act 1, sc. 1; Jane Austen, *Pride and Prejudice*, chap. 56; chap. 8, n. 126, below. See, also, the conscientious testimony on my behalf in January 1951 by Professor Wilber G. Katz, *Lawyers Guild Rev.* 12 (1952): 163, 175-76. It is a curious feature of test oaths that they often test more perceptively those who administer them or who acquiesce in their administration than they do the applicants who are required to undergo such testing. On the other hand, it can be said on behalf of the majority of my law school faculty, whose acquiescence permitted if it did not even encourage the bar committee in what it did, that many of them could plausibly assure themselves that I had only myself to blame for my difficulties. (But to whom should any of "my" achievements be credited?)

I conclude this supplementary bibliography with an early comment on my case which indicates some of my shortcomings as well as those of the bar authorities and (ultimately) of the law schools. It is from Walter Gellhorn, *Individual Freedom and Governmental Restraints* (Baton Rouge: Louisiana State University Press, 1956), pp. 136-37:

> ... Specifically, he would not say whether or not he was a Communist. His examiners, however, were not wholly without information on this point. ... Emerging from all the testimony [in 1950-51] is a picture of an opinionated, tenacious, and perhaps even over-scrupulous young man who would not hobble his ideas when they began to run ahead of his examiners' opinions. These qualities are not unprecedented among reputable lawyers, and sometimes they are not regarded as positive misfortunes. The examining committee in Anastaplo's case had no patience with them, nor did the Supreme Court of Illinois, which curtly said [in 1954] that it might attach to the "privilege" of practicing law whatever conditions the court might reasonably select—"and if an applicant does not choose to abide by such conditions he is free to retain his beliefs and go elsewhere."
>
> Anastaplo was probably wrong in insisting that revolution is a right. Of course it is true that Jefferson and Lincoln said the same thing. . . . In reality, nevertheless, the right to revolt comes into being only after a revolution has succeeded, at just about the same moment that its leaders receive garlands as the heroes of "the glorious revolution," instead of being beheaded as the treacherous instigators of a wretched plot. Still, Anastaplo's incomplete grasp of the realities did not wholly unfit him for a profession that has its full share of dreamers, quixotic and otherwise. One may doubt, too, whether the Illinois authorities were wise in resting their decision on an unanswered question when they possessed so much independent evidence that, in effect, provided the answer they sought.
>
> As a matter of fact, the admitting authorities ought to develop more concern about the questions they propound than about the answers they do not obtain. . . .

Of course, I cannot help wondering just what Jefferson and Lincoln *were* thinking of. *Is* it unrealistic to recognize that there are unsuccessful revolutionaries worthy of our respect and successful revolutionaries entitled to no more than our contempt? Does not this tell us something important about the principle of rightful rebellion? What, in short, *is* justice? See, e.g., chap. 7, n. 77, chap. 8, n. 124, below.

8. On the Other Hand, the Virtues of America (October 13, 1961)

I wrote on October 13, 1961, a farewell letter to the Chief Justice of the Supreme Court of Illinois (with a copy to the chairman of the Committee on Character and Fitness):

FAREWELL LETTER TO THE ILLINOIS SUPREME COURT, 1961

The Supreme Court of the United States denied on October 9th the Petition for Rehearing in my bar admission case.

I should like, now that that court has confirmed my exclusion from the bar, to thank the Illinois Supreme Court and its character committee for the time and effort devoted to this controversy the past decade. I wish to acknowledge also the generosity and thoughtfulness of those who have supported my application.

I have been obliged, in the course of this controversy, to discuss critical defects in the legal profession in the United States. On the other hand, the virtues of America are reflected in the fact that a student of law with remarkably few supporters has been able for so long to oppose the power of the state and to carry his cause to the highest judicial tribunal in the land. That he has been able to do this is itself worthy of note even by those who regret that the long encounter has not been given its natural completion by that tribunal.

I make these parting acknowledgments at this time since I do not anticipate any further attempt, on my own initiative, to secure admission to the bar of any state. As is evident from Mr. Justice Black's dissenting opinion, my qualifications are now as clearly recorded as they ever will be. An applicant's eligibility for the bar can have little more to be said for or against it after litigation which has been so extensive as to require his expenditure of more than five thousand dollars [in filing fees and printing costs alone]. Certainly, the surrender now, for my personal advancement, of the traditional American principles which I still believe to have been in the public interest to develop and defend would recommend me only to the unreflecting.

We must all hope that the decision confirmed this week means that Illinois will be able, eventually if not immediately, to provide itself a bar of the highest character and fitness. Should my position or temperament ever be recognized as useful to the administration of justice in this state, I trust the Illinois Supreme Court will not hesitate to call on me for any further contribution I might honorably make to constitutional government and the rule of law.

This is the way things have been ever since: I *have* made my case; renewed efforts in the courts would divert me from more important pursuits. Indeed, I may even be accused by some, despite the "chilling effect" my litigation has always had on my academic prospects, of having quit while I was still ahead.

Eight well-known Chicago lawyers did make an effort in 1966, on their own initiative, to secure my admission to the Illinois bar. This group, which was led by Calvin Sawyier (who had been a member of my character committee), included a judge and three law professors. (They were, in addition to Sawyier, Alex Elson, Elmer Gertz, Harry Kalven, Jr., Stanley A. Kaplan, Jewel Lafontant, Nathaniel L. Nathanson, and George L. Quilici.) Their petition, which was filed with the character committee on April 27, 1966, concluded (after extolling my virtues and neglecting my shortcomings) with the plea

that the Committee grant this Petition and determine that, in the exercise of its discretion, it will entertain a petition for rehearing by said applicant, George Anastaplo, and in connection therewith waive the right to ask him those questions which he has heretofore refused to answer.

The petition was denied by the committee on May 17, 1966. No dissents were announced.

Another effort was made (in early 1969) to "admit" me to the bar, evidently as an instructive prank by law students who must feel they know a lawyer when they hear of one (even though they might not know how to spell his name). The extralegal means employed by the pranksters are indicated by the following announcement in the *Illinois Bar Journal* 57 (1969): 606:

The application of George Anastaplao, University of Chicago, 1307 East 60th St., Chicago 60637, which was published in the January 1969 listings [of applications for membership in the Illinois State Bar Association, for which membership in the bar is a prerequisite], has been found to be a forgery. Such application has therefore been voided. This forgery was called to our attention by George Anastaplo, who is a Lecturer in the Liberal Arts at the University of Chicago and Chairman of the Political Science Department at Rosary College.

What will become of such students when they "grow up"? If one-tenth of the well-established lawyers who have told me at one time or another that they had followed my decade-long efforts with sympathy, admiration, and respect had expressed such sentiments publicly in the 1950s, the misguided men I had to contend with (who thought they were acting for an appreciative bar) would have capitulated. Cf. Shakespeare, *King Henry V*, act 4, sc. 3, ll. 16-67. Cf., also, chap. 7, n. 81, below.

9. EXTRAORDINARY SITUATIONS WARRANT EXTRAORDINARY REMEDIES (1950-61)

One concern I had throughout my bar admission litigation was to reconcile what Professor Kalven has been kind enough to call my "thoughtful theoretical argument for federalism in the free-speech area" with my efforts to have the Supreme Court of the United States correct my exclusion from a state bar. (See Harry Kalven, Jr., *The Negro and the First Amendment* [Chicago: University of Chicago Press, 1965], p. 219. My federalism argument does recognize "procedural due process" and other limitations upon the states, limitations which are made explicit in the Fourteenth Amendment and which may be implicit in such provisions of the Constitution of 1787 as that which guarantees to each state "a Republican Form of Government." But it recognizes as well the critical role "state sovereignty" has played in the success of constitutionalism in America. See, e.g., chap. 7, nn. 17, 35, 107, chap. 8, n. 83, below.)

I wanted, on the one hand, to make as strong a case as possible before the Supreme Court. (My academic prospects, for instance, would probably have been considerably improved by a favorable decision by the Court on *any* of my requests.) I wanted, on the other hand, to acknowledge the "states' rights" position I had been working out over the years in my research. It is partly for this reason that I would have preferred a "victory" in Springfield rather than in Washington. Another reason was that it was quite evident in those days that Illinois would have been somewhat reluctant to obey a mandate from Washington to admit anyone to its bar—and admission to the bar *was* what I had to aim at (for it had obviously become the key to other things I might want to do as well).

These were not idle concerns. The treatment by Nevada and California of the bar applicants in the 1957 *Schware* and *Konigsberg* cases reminds us that it is not only in the South that respectable lawyers and judges have managed to circumvent inconvenient decrees by federal courts —and all in the name of "character and fitness," a forerunner of "law and order." The effect of *exclusion* from the bar (as distinguished from what would have happened if I had never applied for admission) upon nonlegal, and especially academic, employment was quite pronounced. The following comment, in November 1961, by the dean of a good law school makes explicit what was evident (but rarely conceded so openly) in many contacts I have made since 1951 with universities, colleges, and law schools: "At the present time we have no vacancy, and even if we should have one soon, reality and candor force me to tell you that your appointment here would raise a storm of protest and produce discord that could not possibly be for the best interests of our School or for you." What can one say in such circumstances? I tried: "I am delighted by the candor of your letter of the 28th. Your opinion of the effect I would have upon your School is perverse but welcome flattery."

(I did happen, almost a decade later, to be the guest of an out-of-state university law school, for a lecture and seminars, at a time when serious disorders linked to the Vietnam war threatened the entire campus of that university. My role turned out to be one of moderating certain passions on campus, so much so that I could receive thereafter from the office of *that* law school dean the following report: "Our campus is still somewhat turbulent, and our law students are enjoying the experience of being involved in the issues and action. Perhaps your visit in some way prompted their constructive response to recent events." Cf. Appendix E, above.)

But let us return to the Supreme Court of the United States.

The reconciliation I devised in 1955 between what I, as a citizen, wanted and what I, as a student of American constitutionalism, had learned may be seen in what Professor Ralph Brown (of the Yale Law School) has called "an ingenious petition asking that Anastaplo be admitted directly to the bar of the Supreme Court [of the United States]." (See Ralph S. Brown, *Loyalty and Security* [New Haven: Yale University Press, 1958], p. 112.) There may have been something tongue-in-cheek about this proposal, as there was perhaps about much of what I did before the character committee and the courts—after all, it would have been rather unbecoming for me to regard my personal difficulties as the end of the world—but then, there was something tongue-in-cheek (but nevertheless usefully revealing) as well about the baby-slicing proposal devised by Solomon. (Besides, I always had, over the years, the task of offering bored commissioners and busy judges something to arouse and sustain their interest.) Even so, I consider this "ingenious petition" my distinctive contribution to the annals of Supreme Court practice: the motion does deserve a better fate than it has thus far enjoyed.

Extracts from various papers I filed over the years in the Supreme Court of the United States, as well as the entire motion itself (which I filed originally in 1955 and revived in 1960), should tell the story of this "extraordinary remedy" as it was presented to an unappreciative court. The motion was filed on March 23, 1955, at the same time as my petition for rehearing. I attempted in that petition to secure reversal by the Supreme Court of the United States of its determination (of February 28, 1955) not to review the 1954 decision by the Supreme Court of Illinois. I explained in this petition for rehearing (in a section helpfully entitled, "What Can Be Done?") what the accompanying "Motion . . . for Leave to File an Application for Admission to the Bar of the Supreme Court of the United States" was about.

Some repetition among the extracts set forth below is unavoidable if each is to be intelligible. The Jurisdictional Statement referred to below is my application for review by the Supreme Court of the United States, which was filed Jan. 11, 1955, and denied Feb. 28, 1955.

ANASTAPLO, PETITION FOR REHEARING, SUPREME COURT OF THE UNITED STATES, MARCH 23, 1955, PP. 8-10

4. What Can Be Done?

We should like to emphasize our earlier argument that the unwisdom of the action of the court below [the Supreme Court of Illinois] should also be considered by this Court as within its constitutional powers to evaluate and correct. (Jurisdictional Statement, pages 39-40) It is the purpose of this Petition, as a first step toward such correction, to secure a reversal of the decision [of February 28, 1955] dismissing this appeal.

We are proceeding at this time, furthermore—while the circumstances of the matter are fresh in this Court's mind—to submit independently of this Petition a motion designed to invoke additional action which this Court could take to correct, in part, the situation as it now stands. This is the Motion for Leave to File an Application for Admission to the Bar of the Supreme Court of the United States which appellant submits at the same time as this petition. . . .[10] The Motion is related to the Illinois decision (and this Petition) to the extent that that decision leaves appellant technically ineligible for admission to the bar of this Court, even though he may be fully equipped to serve in that capacity.[11] It would seem particularly appropriate to grant the requested leave in a situation where it might otherwise appear that this Court is not disturbed that a spirited and persistent defense of The Declaration of Independence has cut short a career at the bar.

[Notes for the 1955 Petition for Rehearing]

[Note 10.] The granting of such leave, it is suggested, would not only provide some protection for this Court against arbitrary selection by state courts of prospective applicants for the Bar of this Court, but would also serve, in effect, to protect some of appellant's rights. . . . In addition, the granting of such leave might tend to influence state courts and local bar associations for the better in these matters. Particularly would this action be appropriate, it is suggested, if the denial of review in this matter rested and continues to rest not on any judgment as to the merits of appellant's cause but rather on a self-limiting policy on the part of this Court with respect to federal-state relationships. Experimentation, we further suggest, should not be the exclusive province of the states in these matters.

In this way, furthermore, appellant can attempt to make a lawyer's contribution to the administration of justice. For if this Court does not reverse its decision dismissing his appeal, it seems that he will have no opportunity to make further contributions as an Illinois attorney, under present circumstances, unless the Illinois authorities should on their own motion see fit to call him to the bar as one obviously qualified to serve. Cf. Gale, "Myra Bradwell, The First Woman Lawyer," 39 A.B.A.J. at 1080 (1953).

[Note 11.] Problems relating to appellant's character and fitness to serve as a member of the Bar of this Court, as well as his competency and experience, are referred to in the Motion. These considerations do not depend, of course, on any determination of whether appellant is correct in the constitutional arguments he has made in this case. As indicated in the Motion, a brief as well as the statements of the necessary sponsors could accompany the Admission Application for which permission is sought in that Motion. In addition, that Motion and any other materials could be presented in whatever form this Court may consider appropriate.

MOTION BY GEORGE ANASTAPLO FOR LEAVE TO FILE AN APPLICATION FOR ADMISSION TO THE BAR OF THE SUPREME COURT OF THE UNITED STATES, MARCH 23, 1955; JULY 4, 1960

George Anastaplo respectfully moves for leave to file an application for admission to the Bar of the Supreme Court of the United States even though he cannot produce the required certificate from the presiding judge or clerk of the highest court of his State evidencing the fact that he has been for at least three years a member of the bar of that court. He is prepared, however, to provide this Court with materials relating to the purpose of the requirements set forth in Rule 5 and to indicate why such an alternative course of action should be permitted in his case.

Appellant has before this Court at this time litigation respecting his admission to the bar of the Supreme Court of Illinois. (. . . The term, "appellant," is taken from the pending matter so that terminology may be uniform throughout. . . .) Although this Motion is submitted independently of that litigation, reference is made to that litigation since there are connected with it circumstances fresh in this Court's mind which are related to the purposes of this Motion. Various materials that have been filed with this Court should indicate that appellant is fully qualified to serve as a member of the Bar of this Court. That is, whether or not he is deemed correct in the constitutional position he has taken, there is ample evidence (which he is prepared to supplement) as to his character and fitness to practice law. (No real doubt, aside from the effect of differences of opinion about certain theoretical matters, is expressed with respect to these qualifications even by the authorities who have denied him admission in Illinois.) Appellant is also prepared to hold himself open to whatever further examination this Court may wish to administer.

In addition to materials relating to character and fitness, this Court already has before it various indications of the competency and experience which the three-year requirement (Rule 5) is apparently designed to insure. Appellant has satisfactorily completed legal studies at a reputable law school (R. 6, 66) and has passed the written bar examination in Illinois

(R. 4). In addition, he has for several years now personally conducted protracted litigation and prepared all materials relating to that litigation, including the Jurisdictional Statement submitted to the Court earlier this term. These various documents, as well as the Record in this matter, should satisfy what is probably the purpose of the three-year requirement in this respect. Here, too, supplementary material could readily be made available.

This Motion is being made in the belief that extraordinary situations warrant extraordinary remedies, so much so that the rules of this Court should be waived accordingly whenever this Court can do justice without disappointing the reasonable expectations of any party. If, appellant's arguments notwithstanding, it has seemed to this Court that it should not directly intervene in the management by a state of its bar matters, no matter what this Court may think of the wisdom of the state action, this Motion is designed to provide an opportunity for this Court to protect to a limited extent the rights of a particular individual. Furthermore, it is believed that this Motion also suggests how this Court can act to protect itself to some extent against any arbitrary standards and conduct of the states which supply the members of the Bar of this Court. (Jurisdictional Statement, pp. 39-40)

Action of the kind requested by this Motion would seem particularly appropriate in a situation such as this where an individual who has been denied admission to a state bar under unprecedented circumstances has demonstrated his overall qualification for the practice of law.

[This Motion for Leave to File an Application for Admission to the Bar of the Supreme Court of the United States was denied (along with the Petition for Rehearing) by the Supreme Court of the United States on April 11, 1955. *In re Anastaplo*, 349 U.S. 903, 908 (1955). This motion was submitted again by me in 1960 along with my Brief on the Merits, the relevant excerpts from which follow.]

ANASTAPLO, BRIEF ON THE MERITS, SUPREME COURT OF THE UNITED STATES, JULY 4, 1960, PP. 6, 82-83, 90-91

Questions Presented for Review
... 8. Aside from the effect of other constitutional limitations upon state action, does this Court have the power to examine, for their wisdom as well as their reasonableness, the methods and standards employed in the state courts which supply the bar of this Court and to correct state action which excludes an applicant qualified to practice both in his State and before this Court. If such power exists, should this Court exercise it in this

instance to provide for the admission of petitioner to the Illinois bar or, at least, to the federal bar and the bar of this Court? . . .

II. *Freedom of Speech and the Free Exercise of Religion*[61]

Even more basic constitutional considerations than petitioner's due process arguments are objections that draw upon the First Amendment. That is to say, the States are said to be obliged not to abridge the rights of citizens to freedom of speech and to the free exercise of religion.[62] . . .

Conclusion

For the foregoing reasons, relating to both the common good and individual rights, it is requested that this Court provide for petitioner's admission to the Illinois bar, preferably with the status of an attorney retroactive to that morning in November of 1950 when this case unexpectedly began. In addition, petitioner again advances the suggestion that he be admitted directly and at this time to the bar of this Court, independently of the action Illinois might be induced to take. Such direct admission would insure one remedy that this Court can provide without having to depend on the sometimes reluctant cooperation of a state court.[76]

Thus, this Court is again offered the opportunity not only to endorse but even to extend the contribution that petitioner has attempted to make to a responsible and independent bar, and through the bar to his country.

[Notes for Brief on the Merits]

[Note 61.] The committee was obliged, after a grievous research blunder by one of its members, to rule out of its consideration petitioner's refusal to answer questions about religion. (R. 137-38, 185-94, 256). But anyone familiar with human nature must realize that petitioner won no support from men who were shown to be so obviously in error that their colleagues took the unprecedented step of repudiating their questions. (See Note 41, this Brief) Mr. Justice Bristow's comment [in the Supreme Court of Illinois] reflects the serious problem of religious freedom implicit here (Appendix, Pet. Writ. Cert., 58-59 [18 Ill.2d 182, 205-6]):

> This precise point, that refusal to answer may be indicative of good character, is evident in the record. Applicant courageously and properly refused to answer the unconstitutional religious inquiries. . . . This line of inquiry, persisted in since the very first session, and apparently based upon an 1856 decision, was later admitted by the committee to be improper and unconstitutional since 1870.
>
> The *per curiam* opinion [in the Supreme Court of Illinois] completely overlooked this portion of the record. I cannot follow that course, particularly since the record shows that applicant's refusal to answer these reli-

gious questions had so prejudiced the committee that one member stated that the refusal to answer had a "substantial bearing on his [applicant's] fitness to practice law." Such prejudice could hardly be wiped out by the statement of the chairman that these improper questions would not be taken into consideration.

[Note 62.] This doctrine can be traced back, through cases such as *West Virginia Board of Education* v. *Barnette*, 319 U.S. 624 [1943], and *Cantwell* v. *Connecticut*, 310 U.S. 296 [1940], to *Gitlow* v. *New York*, 268 U.S. 652 [1925]. Although petitioner has serious reservations about the policy of the Fourteenth Amendment as interpreted in the *Gitlow* case, he recognizes that some such limitation upon the States must be insisted upon so long as Congress does not acknowledge and exercise the power that seems to have been given it under the First Amendment to ameliorate or remove state abridgements of the freedom of speech. Similarly, this Court has an obligation (in petitioner's view) either to review for their wisdom as well as constitutionality restrictions upon entry into the state bars or to provide means by which qualified citizens might be admitted directly to the bar of this Court and to the federal bar without prior admission to the bar of any State. (See Note 76, this Brief.) Direct admission of petitioner to the bar of this Court is included in the request for relief set forth in the Conclusion to this Brief.

Petitioner discusses the problem of the proper relation between State and Union with respect to freedom of speech in a PhD dissertation which is nearing completion, *Notes on the First Amendment*. It is sufficient and appropriate for his purposes here, however, to accept the orthodox view on this problem. (It should be further noted that there is no doubt that the Constitution of Illinois guarantees the right to freedom of speech against any infringement by the State of Illinois. Art. II, Sec. 4. This prohibition alone would be sufficient to justify an applicant's condemnation as unconstitutional the committee's inquiries about political affiliations. See, also, Art. V, Sec. 25, Constitution of Illinois.)

[Note 76.] The rationale of direct admission is suggested in Note 62 of this Brief. We understand that disbarment by federal courts does not automatically flow from disbarment by state courts. Should not this Court insist in appropriate cases upon a like independence from the state courts' determinations with respect to bar admissions? Additional discussion of petitioner's proposal is to be found in the 1955 papers submitted by him to this Court (Jurisdictional Statement, 39-40; Petition for Rehearing, Notes 10, 11; Motion by George Anastaplo for Leave to File an Application for Admission to the Bar of the Supreme Court of the United States [denied, 349 U.S. 903, 908]). See, also, No. 8, Questions Presented for Review (this Brief).

Related to this proposal as well as to the review sought of the action by Illinois is petitioner's suggestion that this Court has the power and obligation to examine the methods employed in the state courts which supply the bar of this Court and to correct state action which excludes an applicant who is qualified to practice both in his State and before this Court. Such a power would seem to rest in the paramount judicial body in the United States and would be comparable to Congressional power to evaluate and correct State electoral requirements. Although the Congressional power is derived from an explicit constitutional provision, it provides a model for a Court that has never hesitated to enforce implied prohibitions against the burdening by States of federal instrumentalities. *McCullough* v. *Maryland*, 4 Wheat. 316 [1819]. Of course, the power of States to admit is not, "while this Court sits," the power to deprive this Court of counsel. But this state power, if not examined scrupulously both for unwisdom as well as unconstitutionality by this Court in situations where marked departures from usual and accepted practices are evident, is the power to affect adversely the quality of the bar of the Supreme Court of the United States as well as of the subordinate federal courts which are more limited in self-protection. The assertion of any latent power to examine state bar admission policies and practices would be particularly appropriate in an era when scholarly research and judicial action seem to be limiting the scope of previously accepted constitutional limitations upon government action. [This paragraph was adapted from a section on "Federal-State relations" in the Jurisdictional Statement I filed in the Supreme Court of the United States, January 11, 1955 (p. 39).]

The courts, bar associations, and law schools of the period we have been reviewing—the period during which the young of today were formed and against which they are rebelling (sometimes blindly)—were all too often dismally lacking in imagination, humor, generosity, and gallantry, to say nothing of legal craftsmanship. This is reflected by the sterility of the majority of the Supreme Court of the United States in disposing of my motion for admission to its bar when I revived it in 1960 (366 U.S., at 97 [1961]):

Apart from anything else, there is of course no room under our Rules for the suggestion made in petitioner's brief that he be admitted to the Bar of this Court, "independently of the action Illinois might be induced to take." See Rule 5, Revised Rules of this Court.

No doubt, Justice Harlan thought he was thereby making an argument.

His use of the word "Revised," however, should have reminded him that any rule that the Court makes it can surely unmake. After all, it has been written, "The Sabbath was made for man, and not man for the Sabbath." Or, as was observed of Justice Davis a century ago, "when he was sure justice required a decision in a particular way, he could always find a good reason for doing so." See chap. 7, n. 77, below. (See, for revisions and amendments of the Rules of the Supreme Court of the United States, "by order of the Court," 346 U.S. 943 [1954], 349 U.S. 973 [1955], 363 U.S. 859 [1960], 366 U.S. 979 [1961], 368 U.S. 803 [1961], 373 U.S. 955 [1963], and 388 U.S. 927 [1967].)

This, then, is an introduction to the story of my public service as a civilian and in defense of the Declaration of Independence. It can be no more than an introduction: the record and briefs permit the parties and courts to speak for themselves—and these are available to anyone interested in and perhaps more capable than I am of doing justice to all sides to our controversy. I believe it fitting and proper, as I prepare to bring this collection of accounts to a close, to return to Illinois—to the concluding remarks of a brief filed April 29, 1959, in the Supreme Court of Illinois, the brief in which I answered the committee report of April 9, 1959 (which is reprinted in section 4 of this appendix):

> It is my belief that this Court was misled by the Committee when it reviewed my matter in 1954. I show in my Closing Argument how this was done. I am gratified to acknowledge that we have this time a more temperate majority report—it is mistaken, confused and at times rather devious, but still it *is* more temperate than the 1954 Report [of the Committee]. And it is significant that we have this time an impressive minority report signed by one-third of the Committee.
>
> I am confident that these dissenting commissioners, four of whom had signed the 1954 Committee Report, will never have cause to regret the honorable position they have taken. I know that I stand with pride on the record that has been made the last two years. I hope this Court can see its way clear to uphold publicly those old-fashioned American principles that it has been my duty, pleasure and good fortune to support and defend.

The press recorded me as saying, when asked to comment upon the announcement from Washington of the Supreme Court's decision, "I'll just go ahead and mind my own business." *Chicago Tribune,* April 25, 1961, p. 1. But to mind his own business is, I have learned, difficult for a busybody to do: there is always someone else in need of "caution and counsel." Still, this does require and permit him to examine his own life in the process, which is truly his own business.

See, on the Declaration of Independence and rightful rebellion, pp.

89, 104-5, 108-9, 220, 331-32, 336, 350-53, 360, 362, 368, 375-79, 384-89, 391, 406, above; chap. 2, n. 1, chap. 3, n. 36, chap. 4, nn. 84, 112, chap. 5, nn. 36, 64, 65, chap. 6, nn. 1, 26, chap. 7, n. 120, chap. 8, nn. 7, 9, 10, 71, 98, chap. 9, nn. 3, 28, below. See, also, pp. 112, 274, 403, above.

NOTES

CHAPTER II

1. See Plato, *Timaeus* 29B-D (see, also, *Timaeus* 30B, 48C-D, 53D, 55D, 56A-B, 57D, 59C-D, 68B, 68D, 72D, 91A. Cf. Plato, *Critias* 106A-B, 121B-C; Shakespeare, *Coriolanus*, act 1, sc. 1, lines 82-83 ("a pretty tale"); Jean Jacques Rousseau, *The First and Second Discourses*, ed. Roger D. Masters (New York: St. Martin's Press, 1964), p. 103. Cf. Plato, *Republic* 414D-E; Aristotle, *Metaphysics* 1074b1-6. See chap. 4, n. 75, chap. 8, nn. 135, 169, 178, chap. 9, n. 27, below. See, also, chap. 6, n. 43, chap. 7, nn. 23, 24, below. Compare Exod. 1:17, 19-21 and Immanuel Kant, *Critique of Pure Reason* (New York: St. Martin's Press, 1965), p. 9, note a. Cf., also, Matt. 13:10-11.

The perspective from which this whole study may be viewed is that found in George Anastaplo, "Human Being and Citizen: A Beginning to the Study of Plato's *Apology of Socrates*," in Joseph Cropsey, ed., *Ancients and Moderns: Essays on the Tradition of Political Philosophy, in Honor of Leo Strauss* (New York: 1964), p. 16. In that article, at p. 34, l. 14, "committed" should read "dedicated" (I have come to see that "dedicated" is generally better than the more fashionable "committed" with its existential implications, just as "duty" is generally better than the bureaucratic "responsibility" and just as "country" or "*polis*" [city] or even "nation" is generally better than the soulless "state"); in n. 32, "to identify himself as 'No-Name' " should read, "to be nameless"; in n. 46, "And one's city, too, is usually the result of chance" should read, "And one's native city, too, is the result of chance." Throughout this article on the *Apology*, "demonic" should read "daemonic" (to suggest the generally obsolete but still useful sense of the word).

Also important for an understanding of the basis upon which my suggestions rest is my article, "The Declaration of Independence," *St. Louis U. L. J.* 9 (1965): 390. (At p. 395, l. 15, of that article, "refutes" should read "denies"; at p. 410, l. 24, "do" should read "pursue"; at p. 411, l. 4, "however" should be struck out; at p. 412, l. 13, a question mark should be added; and at p. 412, l. 28, "above" should be retained outside the quoted phrase.) There should be added to the conclusion of part 1, sec. 3 (at p. 398) the sentence, "It is as a reminder of absolutes, and indeed of the nature of man, that the Declaration of Independence remains our founding instrument." See chap. 8, sec. 16, above.

The tension evident in this study may be inevitable for anyone who tries to "live with" both the *Apology of Socrates* and the Declaration of Independence—for anyone, that is, who finds himself drawn to two public declarations which are, despite their superficial compatibility, radically divergent in their presuppositions and implications. Thus, an attempt is made herein to see American constitutional law and political thought from the perspective of our ancient teachers. See chap. 8, n. 181, chap. 9, n. 28, below; cf. chap. 9, n. 33, below.

A number of other articles and lectures (including the seventeen lectures appended to my doctoral dissertation) address the principles and problems of constitutional government. These pieces, as well as many of the notes in this book, attempt to assess through the eyes of the American constitutionalist the experiences and impressions of my generation's odyssey since the Second World War. One can get an idea here of what the last three decades have meant to some of us. (My dissertation, "Notes on the First Amendment" [University of Chicago, 1964] is available in multilith form in the principal law school libraries. See chap. 6, n. 1, below, for my publications on contemporary Greek affairs. One sees in Greece today how difficult it is to restore constitutional government and liberty once they have been subverted. Cf. pp. 450-51, below.)

What the lawyer (upon whom American constitutionalism seems to depend) should be like is suggested by a colleague's description of "a practicing attorney" in the Constitutional Convention of 1787 as

> a gentleman of superior abilities, [who] joins in a public debate with great art and eloquence. Having laid the foundations of a compleat classical education at Harvard College, he pursues every other study with ease. He is well acquainted with books and characters, and has an accommodating turn of mind, which enables him to gain the confidence of men and to understand them. [U.S., Congress, House, *Documents Illustrative of the Formation of the Union of American States*, 69th Cong., 1st sess., 1927, H. Doc. 398, p. 108; William Pierce describing Abraham Baldwin]

See chap. 2, n. 3, below, and Appendix F. See, also, Laurence Berns, "Two Old Conservatives Discuss the Anastaplo Case," *Cornell L. Rev.* 54 (July 1969): 920-26. Professor Theodore J. Lowi (in the *Nation*, 208:624, 627 [May 19, 1969]) said of *In re George Anastaplo*, 366 U.S. 88 (1961) (which had begun November 10, 1950):

> Exactly ten years after the Illinois Bar's first decision [in 1951], the now somewhat older young man conceded that his exclusion [from the bar] was permanent, took his loss of occupation, accepted his $5,000 personal costs in fighting the case, earned himself a Ph.D. and became a professor.

I appropriate for this study the "Notice on the Notes" which Rousseau provides for his Second Discourse (*The First and Second Discourse*, ed. Roger D. Masters [New York: St. Martin's Press, 1964], p. 98) (see, also, ibid., p. 284, n. 18):

> I have added some notes to this work, following my lazy custom of working in fits and starts. These notes sometimes stray so far from the subject that they are not good to read with the text. I have therefore relegated them to the end of the Discourse, in which I have tried my best to follow the straightest path. Those who have the courage to begin again will be able to amuse themselves the second

CHAPTER TWO, NOTES 2-3: PAGE 12   421

time in beating the bushes, and try to go through the notes. There will be little harm if others do not read them at all.

See Plato, *Republic* 432B-E. See, also, chap. 2, n. 31, below.

2. The First Amendment is reproduced as the epigraph for chapter 1 above. Comparable passages in several state constitutions are set forth at pp. 43, 178, above; and in chap. 3, nn. 9, 10, chap. 5, n. 128, below. See, also, chap. 3, n. 12, chap. 4, n. 88, chap. 5, n. 5, chap. 6, n. 26, chap. 8, n. 71, below.

See, on the religion provisions of the amendment, chap. 2, n. 38, below. See, also, lectures 6, 15, and 16, appended to my dissertation, as well as my Declaration of Independence article. Much of my discussion of the speech and press provisions applies to the religion provisions as well. Cf. chap. 4, n. 110, chap. 8, n. 4, below.

Many of the legal and constitutional questions to which this book is addressed were first suggested in the courses of three members of the faculty of the Law School of the University of Chicago in 1948-50: William W. Crosskey, Harry Kalven, Jr., and Malcolm P. Sharp. See Malcolm P. Sharp, "The Old Constitution," *U. Chicago L. Rev.* 20 (1953): 529, 536, n. 15; Sharp, Foreword, in Alexander Meiklejohn, *Political Freedom: The Constitutional Powers of the People* (New York: Harper & Bros., 1960); Harry Kalven, Jr., "The Law of Defamation and the First Amendment," in *Publishing and the Law*, Law School Conference on the Arts (Chicago, 1952); Kalven, *The Negro and the First Amendment* (Chicago: University of Chicago Press, 1966); William W. Crosskey, *Politics and the Constitution in the History of the United States* (Chicago: University of Chicago Press, 1953). I had heard, while still in the College of the University, the series of lectures by Alexander Meiklejohn which were later published as *Free Speech and Its Relation to Self-Government* (New York: Harper & Bros., 1948) and still later as *Political Freedom: The Constitutional Powers of the People*. See, for the influence of Leo Strauss on a generation of University of Chicago students of political philosophy, George Anastaplo, "For Leo Strauss: A Leave-taking," *University of Chicago Maroon*, Feb. 16, 1968, p. 7 (as corrected, Feb. 27, 1968, p. 4).

See, also, with respect to Sharp, p. 402, above, chap. 2, n. 14, below. Cf. pp. 333, 380, 405, 409, above.

3. "In a slightly conventional memorial oration upon Clay, Lincoln had said of him [in 1852] that 'he loved his country, partly because it was his own country, and mostly because it was a free country.' He might truly have said the like of himself." Lord Charnwood, *Abraham Lincoln* (Garden City, N.Y.: Garden City Publishing Co., 1917), pp. 122-23. (Lincoln has been, among eminent Americans, *the* Constitutionalist. "[C]onstitutional government is at stake," he said in 1862. "This is a fundamental idea going down about as deep as anything." *Complete Works*, ed. John G. Nicolay and John Hay [New York: Century Co., 1902], 2:235. See chap. 7, n. 124, chap. 8, n. 2, below.)

A generation earlier, Tocqueville had written:

> I know of no country in which there is so little independence of mind and real freedom of discussion as in America. In any constitutional state in Europe every sort of religious and political theory may be freely preached and disseminated; for there is no country in Europe so subdued by any single authority as not to protect the man who raises his voice in the cause of truth from the consequences of his hardihood. If he is unfortunate enough to live under an absolute government, the people are often on his side; if he inhabits a free country, he can, if necessary, find a shelter behind the throne. The aristocratic part of society supports him in some countries, and the democracy in others. But in a nation where democratic institutions exist, organized like those of the United States, there is but one authority, one element of strength and success, with nothing beyond it. [*Democracy in America* (New York: Random House, Vintage Books, 1954), 1:273-74]

See chap. 7, nn. 1, 81, chap. 8, n. 36, chap. 9, n. 1, below; also chap. 8, sec. 9, Appendix C, above, chap. 9, n. 26, below.

4. See Aristotle, *Nicomachean Ethics* 1095b5-14.

> But being cast in the role of teacher, I must try to play it. And in doing so, I recall that, when theories are debated, the teacher's duty is not to give authoritative answers, but rather to clarify questions by challenging their assumptions. He should seek not to end a discussion, but to start it, or to keep it going. [Meiklejohn, *Political Freedom*, pp. xii-xiii]

Cf. chap. 8, n. 70, below.

5. See Augustine, *Confessions* (New York: Simon & Schuster, Pocket Books, 1957), p. 224:

> For what is time? Who can readily and briefly explain this? Who can even in thought comprehend it, so as to utter a word about it? But what in discourse do we mention more familiarly and knowingly, than time? And, we understand, when we speak of it; we understand also, when we hear it spoken of by another. What then is time? If no one asks me, I know: if I wish to explain it to one that asketh, I know not. . . .

See, also, Plato, *Timaeus* 37E, 48B-C, 49B-C; Aristotle, *Physics* 193a5-10; *The Thirteen Books of Euclid's Elements*, ed. Thomas L. Heath (New York, 1956), 1:242-43; Moses Maimonides, *The Guide of the Perplexed* (Chicago: University of Chicago Press, 1963), pp. 196-97, 281-82. (See Plato, *Sophist* 243B, 260A, *Meno* 80B.)

Bones are one thing, however, and skin quite another: the New York Civil Liberties Union announced its willingness to take up the defense of tattooing (which had been banned in the city for health reasons) as an exercise in free speech and "artistic expression." *Chicago Sun-Times*, Mar. 20, 1966, p. 50. At times, this organization (chap. 5, n. 70, below) is to freedom of speech what the well-meaning but impulsive Chaerephon was to Socrates. See Plato, *Apology* 21A. Cf. "A Test Case for Old Glory," *Life*, Mar. 31, 1967, pp. 18-25, 65-66. See, also, chap. 8, nn. 135, 193, below. Cf. p. 347, above.

In any event, I suspect that only free men can profit from this book. See Aristotle, *Nicomachean Ethics* 1094b29-1095a11, 1103a14-b26, 1104b4-1105a15; chap. 8, n. 45, below. But, it should be noticed, not all who live in a free country are truly free; nor do all essentially free men live in free countries. Thus, it is said in the London *Observer*, Dec. 21, 1969, p. 17, of a book called *Portnoy's Complaint*, that it may be "a report on the slavery of freedom."

6. Unless otherwise indicated in the context, "freedom of speech" is used in this book to refer to both "freedom of speech" and "[freedom] of the press," as well as to "the right of the people peaceably to assemble, and to petition the Government for a redress of grievances." See chap. 8, n. 108, below. See, also, chap. 5, nn. 3, 139, below. (The First Amendment speaks of "*the* freedom of speech [and] of the press," whereas we tend to omit the article which I have italicized. Does the former usage place greater emphasis on freedom, whereas ours places greater emphasis on the phrase as a unit? Perhaps, also, the dropping of the article here [as well as from the Constitutional phrase, "the Congress"] suggests greater familiarity with and even casualness toward the institutions thus referred to. May the article have been used in "the freedom of speech" merely to conform, in the same amendment, to its necessary use [before and after] in "the free exercise [of religion]" and in "the right of the people peaceably to assemble"?)

We can take for our purposes, as an adequate provisional account of a "free press," that given (with examples) by a 1967 study of the Freedom of Information Center at the University of Missouri. A free press was defined in that study as "one in which newspapers, periodicals, news agencies, books, radio, and television have absolute independence and critical ability, except for minimal libel and obscenity laws. The press has no concentrated ownership, marginal economic units, or organized self-regulation." The study, which rated among seven categories 94 of the 115 independent nations of the world with a population of more than one million, listed sixteen countries in the highest category ("Free, high degree") : Australia, Belgium, Canada, Costa Rica, Denmark, Finland, Guatemala, the Netherlands, Norway, Peru, the Philippines, Sweden, Switzerland, United States, Uruguay, Venezuela. The second category ("Free, moderate controls") included (among others) England, France, West Germany, Ireland, Italy, and Japan. The third category ("Free, many controls") included (among others) China (Formosa), Greece (pre-coup), India, Mexico, and South Africa. Fourteen nations were listed in the most repressive category ("Controlled, high degree"): Albania, Algeria, Bulgaria, Chad, China (Mainland), Cuba, Czechoslovakia, Ethiopia, East Germany, North Korea, Poland, Rumania, Soviet Union, Upper Volta. A completely controlled press was defined as "one with no independence or critical ability. Under it, newspapers, periodicals, books, news agencies, radio and television are completely controlled directly or indirectly by government, self-regulatory bodies or concentrated ownership." *Chicago Tribune*, May 29, 1967, p. 10. (I have recorded here the ranking of various of the countries I refer to in this book. Greece since 1967 would have to be added to the most repressive category. North Vietnam belongs there as well, while South Vietnam seems significantly less repressive. See chap. 6, n. 1, chap. 8, n. 101, chap. 9, n. 34, below.)

The freest press in the world today may be, in one sense, the *Congressional Record*, reflecting as no other journal can divergent sectional prejudices and personal interests. A study of its contents, which eventually include most articles and documents of topical interest published (as well as speeches and interviews recorded) all over the country, provides one a useful indication of what one's fellow citizens are concerned about and moved by. (Its principal deficiency today is with respect to "radical" opinion of the "Left"—but even that finds its way in as "bad examples." See, e.g., the excerpts from Justice Douglas's *Points of Rebellion* reprinted by his critics: *Cong. Rec.* 116: H1029 [Feb. 18, 1970], H1806 [Mar. 16, 1970]. Cf. ibid., 116: H3127 [Apr. 15, 1970].) Thus, since the motion of only one member of Congress usually suffices to have something reprinted in the *Record*, one can sometimes get from it a better idea than from the national press and broadcast industry of what some of "the silent majority" may be feeling. (See, e.g., the attack by a Louisiana congressman on Martin Luther King, *Cong. Rec.* 116: H2636-7 [Apr. 2, 1970].) The freedom of *this* press is dependent, of course, upon the virtually unlimited parliamentary immunity enjoyed by members of Congress. (See, e.g., chap. 5, pp. 115-18, above, chap. 5, n. 37, below.) The *Record*, I should add, can be useful in American government courses, especially when used as a supplement to the *Federalist*, Tocqueville, Lincoln, Melville, or Mark Twain. (That is, the instructor should constantly keep in view the sentiment of Charles Swann, "The fault with our journalism is that it forces us to take an interest in some triviality or other every day, whereas only three or four books in a lifetime give us anything that is of real importance," Marcel Proust, *Remembrance of Things Past* [New York: Random House, 1934], 1:20. Independence, as well as triviality, may be encouraged by mere numbers: thus, there were in the United States, in 1969, 1,752 English-language daily newspapers, 7,249 radio stations, and 662 television stations. *1970 World Almanac* [New York: Newspaper Enterprise Association, 1969], pp. 351, 896. Cf. chap. 5, n. 53, below.)

As for "free speech": we can say, provisionally, that free speech means one can say what one thinks without thinking whether one should.

What "free press" and "free speech" *can* mean, in practice, is displayed in a "Protest Buttons" advertisement in the *Progressive*, Nov. 1967, p. 51: the questionable slogans available included, "War is good business, invest your son," "Where is Oswald now that we need him," and "Legalize private murder, why should the government have all the fun." See, on the freedom of advertising, the *New York Times* editorial, "Fur Christmas," Dec. 14, 1967, p. 46. See chap. 6, n. 23, chap. 7, n. 123, chap. 8, nn. 36, 135, below. See, also, chap. 5, n. 145, below.

See, in chap. 5, sec. 13, above, the distinction between "freedom" and "liberty."

7. "Liberty, or Freedom, signifieth, properly, the absence of opposition; by opposition, I mean external impediments of motion; and may be applied no less to irrational, and inanimate creatures, than to rational." Hobbes, *Leviathan*, chap. 21. (See, in the same chap-

ter, the consistency between "liberty" and "necessity." See, also, the end of chap. 26. Cf. Kant, *Critique of Pure Reason*, pp. 28, 409-15.)

> And words whereby we conceive nothing but the sound are those we call *absurd, insignificant,* and *nonsense*. And therefore if a man should talk to me of a *round quadrangle,* or *accidents of bread in cheese,* or of *a free subject, a free will,* or any *free* but free from being hindered by opposition, I should not say he were in an error but that his words were without meaning—that is to say, absurd. [Hobbes, *Leviathan*, chap. 5]

See the text at chap. 8, n. 172, below. "Hobbes is nearly the only writer who seems to me capable of using the word 'liberty' without talking nonsense." Sir James Fitzjames Stephen, *A History of the Criminal Law of England* (London: Macmillan & Co., 1883), 2:348n. See chap. 7, n. 5, below.

It was also Hobbes who observed that men "naturally love liberty and dominion over others. . . ." *Leviathan,* chap. 17. Starbuck says of Ahab: "Who's over him: he cries—aye, he would be a democrat to all above: look, how he lords it over all below!" Herman Melville, *Moby Dick,* chap. 38. Cf. Edwin Muir, *Latitudes* (New York: B. W. Huebsch, 1924), p. 290:

> The greatest danger to freedom lies not in the existence of men of despotic personality, but in that of men with no personality at all. These will gladly permit freedom to be abolished; they simply do not know what is happening, they are perfectly unconscious of any wrong. The dominating man at least knows within himself what the emotion of liberty is; and it is not entirely impossible to make him respond to the call of common liberty. But the others—Freedom and slavery are only names to them and will never be anything else.

See Aristotle, *Politics* 1267a3-18; Shakespeare, *Sonnet* 94. See, also, chap. 7, n. 77, below.

The problem of liberty is suggested in (and by the fact of) Martin Heidegger's 1933 Rectoral Address (under Nazi sponsorship), "The Self-Assertion of the German University." "The address contains Heidegger's supreme appeal to the will as the lever for shaping man's destiny in his universe and, in the case of science, for unlocking the essence of all things." Herbert Spiegelberg, *The Phenomenological Movement,* 2d ed. (The Hague: Nijhoff, 1965), 1:309. See, e.g., Heidegger, *Die Gelbstbehauptung der deutschen Universität* (the Rectoral Address) (Breslau: Wilh. Gottl. Korn, 1933 [?]), pp. 13-15 (in a provisional translation by Max Plaut):

> . . . Only an intellectual world guarantees the people its greatness. For it forces it to the point at which the continuous deciding between the will to greatness and the sufferance of decadence becomes the cadence for the march into its future history which our people has set out on. If we will this nature of science, then the faculty of the university must really advance into the outermost posts of danger of the continuous world uncertainty. . . . From the resoluteness of the German student body, to hold firm to German fate in its extremity, comes a will to the nature of the university. This will is a true will insofar as the German student body by means of the new student law places itself under the law of their nature and in the first place defines this nature. To give the law unto oneself is the highest freedom. The much-acclaimed "academic freedom" will be expelled from the German university; for this freedom was false because merely negating. It meant predominantly carelessness, frivolous intentions and inclinations, license to do or to leave undone. The concept of the freedom of the German student will now be restored to its truth. . . .

See, also, chap. 8, nn. 140, 193, below. Cf. chap. 8, nn. 124, 127, chap. 9, n. 19, below.

8. "A land [England], perhaps the only one in the universe, in which political or civil liberty is the very end and scope of the constitution [citing Montesquieu, *The Spirit of the Laws,* bk. 11, chap. 5]. This liberty, rightly understood, consists in the power of

doing whatever the laws permit; which is only to be effected by a general conformity of all orders and degrees to those equitable rules of action by which the meanest individual is protected from the insults and oppression of the greatest." William Blackstone, *Commentaries on the Laws of England*, 1:6. See the note to p. 126 of the American edition of 1859. See, also, Plato, *Epistles* 8.354D-355A.

9. Leo Strauss, *What Is Political Philosophy?* (Glencoe, Ill.: Free Press, 1959), p. 51. See, also, G. W. F. Hegel, *The Philosophy of History* (New York: Wiley Book Co., 1944), p. 38. One is reminded of Karl Marx's admonition, "Gentlemen! Do not allow yourselves to be deluded by the abstract word *freedom*." Karl Marx, *The Poverty of Philosophy* (Moscow: Foreign Languages Publishing House, 1960), p. 222. See, also, Montesquieu, *The Spirit of the Laws* (New York: Hafner Publishing Co., 1949), 11:2, 3; 12:1, 2, 3; Tocqueville, *Democracy in America*, 1:44-45.

10. Lord Byron wrote, in a letter of Mar. 10, 1824, from Messolonghi, Greece, "[T]his is a land of liberty, where most people do as they please, and few as they ought." *The Selected Letters of Lord Byron* (New York: Grosset & Dunlap, Universal Library, 1953), p. 268.

> What is liberty? Leisure. What is leisure? Liberty. If you can at any moment in the day say "I can do as I please for the next hour" then for that hour you are at liberty. If you say "I must now do such and such things during the next hour whether I like it or not" then you are not at liberty for that hour in spite of Magna Carta, the Declaration of Rights (or of Independence), and all the other political title-deeds of your so-called freedom. . . . Historians and journalists and political orators may assure you that the defeat of the Armada, the cutting off of King Charles's head, the substitution of Dutch William for Scottish James on the throne, the passing of the Married Women's Property Acts, and the conquest by the Suffragettes of Votes for Women, have set you free; and in moments of enthusiasm roused by these assurances you may sing fervently that Britons never never will be slaves. But though all these events may have done away with certain grievances from which you might be suffering if they had not occurred, they have added nothing to your leisure and therefore nothing to your liberty. The only Acts of Parliament that have really increased liberty: that is, added to the number of minutes in which a woman's time is her own, are the Factory Acts which reduced her hours of industrial labor, the Sunday Observance Acts which forbid commercial work on every seventh day, and the Bank Holiday Acts. [George Bernard Shaw, *The Intelligent Woman's Guide to Socialism and Capitalism* (New York: Brentano's, 1928), pp. 320-22]

Cf. chap. 8, n. 16, below. See Sidney and Beatrice Webb, *Soviet Communism: A New Civilisation*, 2d ed. (London: Longmans, Green & Co., n.d.), pp. 1033 ff. See, also, chap. 9, sec. 5, above. Cf. F. A. Hayek, *The Constitution of Liberty* (Chicago: University of Chicago Press, 1960), pp. 30-32, 428, n. 14. Cf. chap. 5, n. 49, below.

See Isaiah Berlin, "Two Concepts of Liberty," An Inaugural Lecture Delivered before the University of Oxford, Oct. 21, 1958 (Oxford, 1958); Leo Strauss, "Relativism," in Helmut Schoeck and James W. Wiggins, eds., *Relativism and the Study of Man* (Princeton: D. Van Nostrand Co., 1961), p. 135; Howard B. White, "Comment on Morgenthau's 'Dilemmas of Freedom,' " *American Political Science Review* 51 (1957): 724. See, also, chap. 8, n. 92, below.

Lincoln observed in 1864 that the "world has never had a good definition of the word liberty, and the American people, just now, are much in want of one." *Complete Works*, 2:513. (See ibid., 1:182.) Lord Acton has said that liberty is a term of two hundred definitions. Robert H. Jackson, *The Supreme Court in the American System of Government* (New York: Harper & Row, 1963), p. 76. The diversity of definitions is reflected in an observation by Soame Jenyns, a member of Parliament, who wrote in 1765 ("The Objections to the Taxation of Our American Colonies by the Legislature of Great Britain, Briefly Consider'd"),

> The liberty of an Englishman is a phrase of so various a signification, having

within these few years been used as a synonymous term for blasphemy, bawdy, treason, libels, strong beer, and cyder, that I shall not here presume to define its meaning; but I shall venture to assert what it cannot mean; that is, an exemption from taxes imposed by the authority of the Parliament of Great Britain. . . . [Samuel Eliot Morison, *Sources and Documents Illustrating the American Revolution, 1764-1788, and the Formation of the Federal Constitution* (London: Oxford University Press, 1962), p. 20]

See Plato, *Republic* 360E.

Perhaps it is appropriate that "liberty" should be so difficult to confine, that it should be so diverse and unbounded. (See the second sentence of Bacon's essay, "Of Truth.")

11. Cicero, *Paradoxa* 5.34.

Adaptations of this sentiment may be found in writers as diverse as John Wise (in *A Vindication of the Government of New England Churches* [1772]: "Therefore, as Plutarch says, those persons only who live in obedience to reason are worthy to be accounted free; they alone live as they will who have learned what they ought to will."), Ralph Waldo Emerson (in his essay, "Fate": "So far as a man thinks, he is free."), and Leo XIII (in *Libertas Praestantissimum* [On Human Liberty]: "But man is by nature rational. When, therefore, he acts according to reason, he acts of himself and according to his free will: and this is liberty."). See, also, chap. 5, n. 156, below, and in chap. 3, n. 1, below, the passage from Lessing's *Nathan the Wise*.

Hayek, on the other hand, would "put the reader on guard against [the] sophism that we are free only if we do what in some sense we ought to do." *Constitution of Liberty*, p. 16. (Related to this is Hayek's observation, ibid., p. 8, "I hope our generation may have learned that it has been perfectionism of one kind or another that has often destroyed whatever degree of decency societies have achieved.") Cf. Plato, *Republic* 431 B-C, 576 A-B; Xenophon, *Memorabilia* IV, 5.4, *Oeconomicus* I, 22-23.

See chap. 6, n. 43, chap. 7, n. 5, chap. 8, nn. 26, 37, chap. 9, nn. 3, 38, below. See, also, chap. 5, n. 94, chap. 7, n. 66, chap. 8, nn. 124, 127, below.

12. "Poet [Robert] Frost's Coffee Hour Gives Press Strong Taste of His Ideas," *Washington Post*, May 2, 1961, sec. B, p. 1. A more political, less "individualistic" version of Frost's sentiments may be seen in the comment by a veteran of Concord and Lexington to a historian interviewing him sixty-two years later: "Young man, what we meant in going for those red-coats, was this: we always had governed ourselves and we always meant to. They didn't mean we should." Charles Warren, *The Making of the Constitution* (Boston: Little, Brown & Co., 1937), p. 4. See chap. 5, n. 28, chap. 8, n. 193, chap. 9, n. 19, below.

Justice Black observed, in speaking for the Court in *Bridges v. California*, 314 U.S. 252, at 270-71 (1941),

> The assumption that respect for the judiciary can be won by shielding judges from published criticism wrongly appraises the character of American public opinion. For it is a prized American privilege to speak one's mind, although not always with perfect good taste, on all public institutions. And an enforced silence, however limited, solely in the name of preserving the dignity of the bench, would probably engender resentment, suspicion, and contempt much more than it would enhance respect.

(Is not the current rebellion of the young in part due to their "suspicion [of] and contempt [for]" the "enforced silence" of too many of their elders in the 1950s?) See Appendix D, above.

An emphasis on "wish" is reflected in chap. 8, sec. 13, above; on "ought," in chap. 8, sec. 14, above.

See, for a systematic analysis of "Liberty, of Freedom," *Research on Freedom: Report of Dialectical Discoveries and Constructions* (San Francisco: Institute for Philosophical Research, 1954), vol. 1. See, also, "Liberty," chap. 47 of *The Great Ideas, or Syntopicon* . . . (Chicago: William Benton, 1952) (with many references); Hayek, *Constitution of*

Liberty, pp. 11-21; Jacob Klein, "The Problem of Freedom," *The College* (St. John's College), Dec. 1969, p. 4; Yves R. Simon, *Freedom of Choice* (New York: Fordham University Press, 1969); chap. 7, n. 28, chap. 8, n. 169, below.

13. I have found over the years that many points I make in this book which I had thought were original with me have been anticipated since 1787 by other students of the Constitution. See chap. 7, n. 100, below.

The first public presentation of the principal arguments of this book was on October 19, 1959, at a luncheon meeting of the Chicago chapter of the National Lawyers Guild (Cyril D. Robinson, presiding). (See chap. 9, n. 9, below.) That audience liked what I had to say about freedom of speech but not what I had to say about states' rights. More "conservative" critics have liked what I had to say about states' rights.

I should add that the National Lawyers Guild was during the 1950s one of the few truly conservative and even gallant organizations in America: for it dared to dedicate itself to the defense of the Constitution and the Bill of Rights at a time when more respectable organizations, such as the American Bar Association, simply misbehaved. See, e.g., pp. 236-37, above.

14. Professor Malcolm P. Sharp (chap. 2, n. 2, above) and I have influenced each other over the years, and while we have not agreed at all times we have tended, in our views on leading points of constitutional law bearing on the First Amendment, to approach one another.

References to Sharp's position on various of the points discussed in this book may be found by consulting the bibliography cited in chap. 7, n. 74, below.

15. Congress has vacillated much less, consistently pursuing a more repressive policy than the Court, sometimes relying on the Court to bring legislative policy within constitutional limitations, at other times finding in the Court's opinions legitimation of that policy. (See, for the effects of Executive innovation on freedom of speech since the Second World War, chap. 4, sec. 4, below. See, also, chap. 8, n. 126, below; cf. chap. 2, n. 34, below.) See chap. 8, n. 88, below.

16. See, on "self-evident," Aquinas, *Summa Theologica, Treatise on Law*, Q. XCIV, A.2; see, also, my article, "The Declaration of Independence," *St. Louis U. L. J.* 9 (1955): 390, 398-99; Lincoln, *Complete Works*, 1:215-16.

See, on the perils of scholarship, my abridged comment on Leonard W. Levy's *Legacy of Suppression* in Book Review, *N.Y.U. L. Rev.* 39 (1964): 735. See, also, chap. 5, nn. 1, 34, 143, below.

I have learned from experience what others have tried to tell us about historical enterprises:

> But he that shall bind himself to make antiquity his rule, if he read but part, besides the difficulty of choice, his rule is deficient, and utterly unsatisfying; for there may be other writers of another mind, which he hath not seen; and if he undertake all, the length of man's life cannot extend to give him a full and requisite knowledge of what was done in antiquity. . . . [*The Prose Works of John Milton* (London: J. Johnson, 1806), 1:177-78]

See, also, chap. 2, n. 29, chap. 5, nn. 34, 141, chap. 6, n. 50, below. Cf. chap. 6, n. 6, below.

17. Gulliver complains that lawyers have

> a peculiar cant and jargon of their own, that no other mortal can understand, and wherein all their laws are written, which they take special care to multiply; whereby they have wholly confounded the very essence of truth and falsehood, of right and wrong; so that it will take thirty years to decide whether the field left me by my ancestors for six generations belongs to me, or to a stranger three hundred miles off. [Jonathan Swift, *Gulliver's Travels* (New York: Rinehart & Co., 1948), pp. 242-43]

See, on "my," chap. 8, n. 30, below.

Parts of my argument may be hard for nonlawyers to follow (e.g., chap. 6, secs. 2-3, above). Some lawyers, on the other hand, may find much of what I say either trivial or incomprehensible. (I had occasion to say, at p. 62 of the *Brief on the Merits* [of July 4, 1960] I prepared for my bar admission litigation in the Supreme Court of the United States [Appendix F, above],

> If, in his use of long footnotes, petitioner exhibits the failing of an academician, he must plead in justification the regret that he has never been permitted to become a lawyer. If, in his attacks upon the committee and in defense of himself, he is self-righteous and even tiresome, he must apologize for having become too much of a lawyer.)

18. *The Complete Jefferson*, ed. Saul K. Padover (New York: Duell, Sloan & Pearce, 1943), pp. 699-701. See, at pp. 714-17, "Order in Debate." See chap. 8, n. 64, below. Congressman Burt L. Talcott has said that the rules of the House of Representatives today

> most nearly guarantee the four objectives of a representative parliament; namely, one, the expeditious disposition of legislation; two, the right of the majority, even a slim majority, to work its will; three, the concomitant right of the minority, even a small minority, to be heard; and, four, the right of the citizens to know. [*Congressional Record*, 115: H6671 (July 31, 1969)]

See, on the implications of the rules of the Constitutional Convention of 1787, Paul Eidelberg, *The Philosophy of the American Constitution* (New York: Free Press, 1968), p. 32.

Walter Bagehot spoke of "the slow and steady forms necessary for good consideration" and of custom, "that fixed routine," as "the first check on tyranny." *The English Constitution*, World Classics (London: Oxford University Press, 1963), pp. 95, 230. (See chap. 9, n. 3, below.) "We are concerned solely with 'procedural regularity' which, as Mr. Justice Brandeis said in *Burdeau* v. *McDowell*, 256 U.S. 465, 477 (dissenting) [1921], has been 'a large factor' in the development of our liberty." Justice Douglas, in *Harris* v. *U.S.*, 382 U.S. 162, 167 (1965).

"A constitution is to a nation what self-control under established rules of conduct is to a man. The only time when it is of value is just the time when the temptation to violate it is strong, and that is the time when it contravenes temporary and party interests." William Graham Sumner, *Andrew Jackson*, American Statesmen (Boston: Houghton Mifflin Co., 1897), p. 98. See chap. 7, n. 107 (end), n. 124, below.

"A written constitution may safeguard to a great extent and for a long time the conscience of a minority, but not entirely and forever; for a written constitution is only a fundamental enactment that is difficult to alter." Patrick Devlin, *The Enforcement of Morals* (London: Oxford University Press, 1965), p. 89. Cf. chap. 7, n. 103, chap. 8, n. 67, below.

19. See, e.g., chap. 5, sec. 8; chap. 9, n. 39, below. See, also, chap. 7, n. 77, below. A useful introduction to the principal Anglo-American authors who are usually considered "libertarian" is available in Harry M. Clor's *Obscenity and Public Morality* (Chicago: University of Chicago Press, 1969), particularly chap. 3. See chap. 5, n. 1, below.

20. "A Republican Form of Government," as provided for in Article IV, sec. 4, of the Constitution of the United States, is discussed in chap. 4, sec. 6, chap. 7, sec. 8, chap. 9, sec. 3, above, and in chap. 4, n. 86, chap. 6, n. 40, chap. 7, n. 107, chap. 8, n. 13, below.

"General government" is used in this book to refer to what some call "federal government" and others "national government." Both "federal" and "national" reflect more partisan interpretations of the Constitution than does "general." See the lectures, "The American Constitution of 1787: Form and Matter" and "The Gettysburg Address: America's Political Religion," appended to my dissertation. See, also, Tocqueville, *Democracy in America*, 1:164.

The pedagogical use here of "general government" revives (if only in an epitaphial study) the usage in the First Congress and for almost a century thereafter. (See, e.g., Lincoln, *Complete Works*, 1:196, 559, 574, 593; cf. ibid, 2:6. See, also, Chief Justice Taney, in *Luther* v. *Borden*, 7 How. [U.S.] 1, 42 [1849].)

"Federal Courts," on the other hand, *was* used in the First Congress (see, e.g., the passage quoted in the text at chap. 4, n. 72, below): it is, furthermore, more convenient to use in this book than "courts of the general government."

I prefer "states' rights" to either "state's rights" (e.g., chap. 4, n. 101, below) or "state rights" (e.g., chap. 7, n. 95, below): reference is made by "states' rights" not only to the prerogatives of each of the states but also to whatever prerogatives the states may have collectively, independent of the general government (as, for example, with respect to amending the Constitution). In almost all cases (one exception may be found in chap. 8, n. 10, below), I use "state" to refer to one of the members of the Union. See chap. 2, n. 1, above. (Has the American usage of "state" as a member of the Union kept us from adopting the European usage and hence kept us from regarding our political community as soulless? We are much more likely to refer to that community as "country" or "nation.")

21. The illustrations that follow were published in slightly different form in my article, "Freedom of Speech and the First Amendment," *U. Detroit L. J.* 42 (1964): 55, 60-66. See chap. 4, n. 74, below.

22. The Constitution had been written in a remarkably short time by a Convention meeting behind closed doors in Philadelphia in 1787. It was adopted upon ratification by nine of the states, the remaining states being bound only as they ratified it.

In conformity to the resolution of the Constitutional Convention, and to the resolution of the Congress (constituted under the Articles of Confederation) of Sept. 28, 1787, "a Convention of Delegates chosen in each State by the people thereof" severally ratified the Constitution in the following order (the figures in brackets indicating the yeas and nays): (1) Delaware, Dec. 7, 1787 [30-0]; (2) Pennsylvania, Dec. 12, 1787 [46-23]; (3) New Jersey, Dec. 18, 1787 [30-0]; (4) Georgia, Jan. 2, 1788 [26-0]; (5) Connecticut, Jan. 9, 1788 [128-40]; (6) Massachusetts, Feb. 6, 1788 [187-168]; (7) Maryland, Apr. 28, 1788 [63-11]; (8) South Carolina, May 23, 1788 [149-73]; (9) New Hampshire, June 21, 1788 [57-46]; (10) Virginia, June 25, 1788 [89-79]; (11) New York, July 26, 1788 [30-27]; (12) North Carolina, Nov. 21, 1789 [184-77] (after having refused to ratify in 1788); (13) Rhode Island and Providence Plantations, May 29, 1790 [34-32]; (14) Vermont, Jan. 10, 1791 [105-4]. U.S., Congress, Senate, *The Constitution of the United States of America*, 87th Cong., 1st sess., 1951, Sen. Doc. 49, p. 24.

23. *Annals, I*, refers throughout this book to the records of the First Congress (of which considerable use is made here) found in *Annals of Congress. The Debates and Proceedings in the Congress of the United States: The First Congress, 1789-1791* (Washington: Gales & Seaton, 1834). (*Annals*, V, will refer to the *Annals . . . The Fifth Congress, 1797-1798* [published in 1851].) "Since the *Annals* were compiled several years after the Congressional debates from accounts contemporary with those proceedings, all speeches are reported in the third person." James Morton Smith, *Freedom's Fetters: The Alien and Sedition Laws and American Civil Liberties* (Ithaca: Cornell University Press, 1956), p. 38n. See, on the reliability of these records, Crosskey, *Politics and the Constitution*, pp. 702-3; Crosskey, "Mr. Chief Justice Marshall," in Allison Dunham and Philip B. Kurland, *Mr. Justice* (Chicago: University of Chicago Press, 1964), pp. 6, 27; Irving Brant, "The Madison Heritage," *N.Y.U. L. Rev.* 35 (1960): 882, 899-900.

The full names and the states of the members of the House of Representatives in the First Congress are set forth alphabetically in n. 26, below.

24. Chafee, apparently assuming that the ratifications of ten states sufficed, reported Nov. 3, 1791, as the date ratification of the Bill of Rights was completed. Zechariah Chafee, *Freedom of Speech* (Cambridge: Harvard University Press, 1920), p. 4.

The first ten amendments to the Constitution appear officially at 1 *U.S. Statutes* 97.

25. The first ten amendments to the Constitution (numbers 3 through 12 of the amendments proposed by Congress on Sept. 25, 1789) were ratified by the states in the following order: (1) New Jersey, Nov. 20, 1789; (2) Maryland, Dec. 19, 1789; (3)

North Carolina, Dec. 22, 1789; (4) South Carolina, Jan. 19, 1790; (5) New Hampshire, Jan. 25, 1790; (6) Delaware, Jan. 28, 1790; (7) New York, Feb. 27, 1790; (8) Pennsylvania, Mar. 10, 1790; (9) Rhode Island, June 7, 1790; (10) Vermont, Nov. 3, 1791; (11) Virginia, Dec. 15, 1791. U.S., Congress, Senate, *The Constitution of the United States of America*, 82d Cong., 2d sess., 1953, Sen. Doc. 170, p. 39.

Number 1 and Number 2 of the proposed amendments (see Appendix A, above) read:

> After the first enumeration, required by the first article of the Constitution, there shall be one Representative for every thirty thousand, until the number shall amount to one hundred; after which, the proportion shall be so regulated by Congress, that there shall be not less than one hundred Representatives, nor less than one Representative for every forty thousand persons, until the number of Representatives shall amount to two hundred, after which, the proportion shall be so regulated by Congress that there shall not be less than two hundred Representatives, nor more than one Representative for every fifty thousand persons.
>
> No law, varying the compensation for the services of the Senators and Representatives, shall take effect until an election of Representatives shall have intervened. [Bennett B. Patterson, *The Forgotten Ninth Amendment* (Indianapolis: Bobbs-Merrill, 1955), p. 89 (copied from the Appendix to the *Journal* of the United States Senate)]

(Patterson reprinted, ibid., pp. 100-212, that portion of the *Annals* of the First Congress relating to the first twelve amendments proposed to the Constitution of the United States.)

Number 1 of the proposed amendments was ratified by ten states (one short of the requisite number); number 2, by six states. *The Constitution of the United States*, 82d Cong., 2d sess., p. 39. No returns were made by the states of Connecticut, Georgia, and Massachusetts. William Hickey, *Constitution of the United States of America* (Baltimore: J. Murphy & Co., 1879), p. 36.

In another sense, the First Amendment was made (i.e., confirmed politically) by the presidential and congressional elections of 1800.

26. The full names and states of the members of the House of Representatives of the First Congress are here set forth alphabetically. (Last names only are usually used, in conjunction with citations to *Annals, I.* See chap. 2, n. 23, above.) *Abridgment of the Debates of Congress from 1789 to 1856* (New York: D. Appleton & Co., 1857), 1:20.

Fisher Ames (Mass.); John Baptista Ashe (N.C.); *Abraham Baldwin* (Ga.); *Egbert Benson* (N.Y.); Timothy Bloodworth (N.C.); Theodorick Bland (Va.); *Elias Boudinot* (N.J.); Benjamin Bourne (R.I.); John Brown (Va.); *Aedanus Burke* (S.C.); Lambert Cadwalader (N.J.); *Daniel Carroll* (Md.); George Clymer (Pa.); Isaac Coles (Va.); Benjamin Contee (Md.); *Thomas Fitzsimons* (Pa.); William Floyd (N.Y.); Abiel Foster (N.H.); George Gale (Md.); *Elbridge Gerry* (Mass.); Nicholas Gilman (N.H.); Benjamin Goodhue (Mass.); Samuel Griffin (Va.); Jonathan Grout (Mass.); *Thomas Hartley* (Pa.); John Hathorn (N.Y.); Daniel Heister (Pa.); *Benjamin Huntington* (Conn.); Daniel Huger (S.C.); *James Jackson* (Ga.); *John Laurance* (N.Y.); *Richard Bland Lee* (Va.); George Leonard (Mass.); *Samuel Livermore* (N.H.); *James Madison* (Va.); George Mathews (Ga.); Andrew Moore (Va.); Frederick Augustus Muhlenberg (Pa.); *John Page* (Va.); *Josiah Parker* (Va.); George Partridge (Mass.); James Schureman (N.J.); *Thomas Scott* (Pa.); *Theodore Sedgwick* (Mass.); Joshua Seney (Md.); John Sevier (N.C.); *Roger Sherman* (Conn.); Thomas Sinnickson (N.J.); *William Smith* (S.C.); William Smith (Md.); *Michael Jenifer Stone* (Md.); John Steele (N.C.); Jonathan Sturges (Conn.); *Thomas Sumter* (S.C.); Peter Sylvester (N.Y.); George Thatcher (Mass.); Jonathan Trumbull (Conn.); *Thomas Tudor Tucker* (S.C.); Jeremiah Van Rensselaer (N.Y.); *John Vining* (Del.); Jeremiah Wadsworth (Conn.); *Alexander White* (Va.); Hugh Williamson (N.C.); Henry Wynkoop (Pa.). (I have italicized here the names of the members of Congress quoted in this study. Madison spoke more than anyone else in the first session of the First Congress [124 times, compared to 60 times for Gerry and 55 times for Fitzsimons, the second and third most frequent speakers]. Irving Brant, *James Madison, Father of the Constitution, 1787-1800* [Indianapolis: Bobbs-Merrill, 1950], p. 246.)

27. I do cite and quote from judicial opinions, not as necessarily authoritative but to show either how certain arguments can be formulated or how my interpretation can be countered. (My principal use of Supreme Court opinions is in footnotes; my principal use of the *Annals* of the First Congress is in the text.)

The most comprehensive annotation of the Constitution is E. S. Corwin, N. J. Small, and L. S. Jayson, eds., *The Constitution of the United States of America: Analysis and Interpretation* (Washington: Government Printing Office, 1964). It was prepared by the Legislative Reference Service of the Library of Congress. Useful recent presentations of orthodox constitutional doctrines (the first prepared by a professor of law, the second by a political scientist) may be found in Arthur E. Sutherland, *Constitutionalism in America: Origin and Evolution of Its Fundamental Ideas* (New York: Blaisdell Publishing Co., 1965) and in C. Herman Pritchett, *The American Constitution* (New York: McGraw-Hill, 1968). Also useful, particularly for its review of Communist party legislation and litigation since the Second World War, is Milton R. Konvitz, *Expanding Liberties: Freedom's Gains in Postwar America* (New York: Viking Press, 1966). Thomas I. Emerson's useful guides to First Amendment litigation are cited in chap. 8, n. 81, below. See chap. 6, n. 50, below.

The quotation in the text from Montesquieu is from *Spirit of the Laws*, 21:20.

28. See Lincoln, *Complete Works*, 1:228:

> Judicial decisions are of greater or less authority as precedents according to circumstances. That this should be so, accords both with common sense and the customary understanding of the legal profession. If this important decision [*Dred Scott* v. *Sanford*, 19 How. 393 (1857)] had been made by the unanimous concurrence of the judges, and without any apparent partizan bias, and in accordance with legal public expectation and with the steady practice of the departments throughout our history, and had been in no part based on assumed historical facts which are not really true; or, if wanting in some of these, it had been before the court more than once, and had there been affirmed and reaffirmed through a course of years, it might be, perhaps would be, factious, nay, even revolutionary, not to acquiesce in it as a precedent. But when, as it is true, we find it wanting in all these claims to the public confidence, it is not resistance, it is not factious, it is not even disrespectful, to treat it as not having yet quite established a settled doctrine for the country.

See, also, ibid., 1:421, 2:5; cf. 1:368-69; chap. 3, n. 14, chap. 4, n. 44, and the text at chap. 8, n. 87, above. (Compare the remarkably different "circumstances" attending *Brown v. Board of Education*, 347 U.S. 483 [1954].)

See, on *Dred Scott*, Sutherland, *Constitutionalism in America*, pp. 385-400, 437-41. See, also, chap. 8, nn. 83, 109, below.

29. Chief Justice Marshall, even as he argued for the authority of a long-established interpretation of a constitutional provision, conceded that this need not be so where "the great principles of liberty [are] concerned." *McCulloch* v. *Maryland*, 4 Wheat. [U.S.] 316, 401 (1819). (*Federalist* No. 63 expects that "the House of Representatives, with the people on their side, will at all times be able to bring back the Constitution to its primitive form and principles [in the event of senatorial usurpation]." There may be, in the reference to "primitive form and principles" [perhaps through Locke, if not directly] a trace of Machiavelli.)

The influence of Protestantism, with its insistence upon recourse to the Scriptures, may be detected in our insistence upon the Constitution as the ultimate touchstone. See chap. 9, n. 9, below. This attitude is reflected in such passages from Milton as the following:

> Thus finally it appears, that those purer times were not such as they are cried up, and not to be followed without suspicion, doubt, and danger. The last point wherein the antiquary is to be dealt with at his own weapon, is, to make it manifest that the ancientest and best of the fathers have disclaimed all sufficiency in themselves that men should rely on, *and sent all comers to the scriptures, as all-sufficient.* . . . [W]ill not this holy man [Cyprian], with all the whole con-

sistory of saints and martyrs that lived of old, rise up and stop our mouths in judgment, when we shall go about to father our errours and opinions upon their authority? In the 73d Epist. he adds, "In vain do they oppose custom to us, if they be overcome by reason; as if custom were greater than truth, or that in spiritual things that were not to be followed, which is revealed for the better by the Holy Ghost." In the 74th, "Neither ought custom to hinder that truth should not prevail; for custom without truth is but agedness of errour." [Milton, *Prose Works*, 1:21-22; italics added]

See, also, ibid., 1:24-25, 61, 75, 177-78; chap. 2, n. 16, above, chap. 5, n. 34, below. Cf. Vatican II, *Constitution on Divine Revelation*, chap. 2, art. 10, chap. 6, arts. 24-25; also, chap. 2, n. 18, above; chap. 5, n. 50, chap. 8, nn. 170, 171, below.

30. Is not the principal unenumerated right referred to in the Ninth Amendment that which the people had recently exercised in establishing the independence of the United States, the right of revolution? (English royal charters sometimes "save[d] to the subjects all other rights and privileges before had, though not mentioned [t]herein.")

See, on the perils of a complete enumeration of rights, Blackstone, *Laws of England*, 1:164; *Political Thought of Woodrow Wilson*, ed. E. David Cronon (Indianapolis: Bobbs-Merrill, 1965), p. 504; also, Willmoore Kendall, "The Bill of Rights and American Freedom," in Frank S. Meyer, ed., *What Is Conservatism?* (New York: Holt, Rinehart & Winston, 1964), pp. 49-50. Cf. Joseph Story, *Commentaries on the Constitution of the United States* (2d ed.; Boston: Little, Brown & Co., 1851), chap. 44, sec. 1905.

Does the Ninth Amendment imply that the enumeration in the Constitution of certain powers for the general government may be construed to deny or disparage other powers for that government, except to the extent such powers are provided for by the Necessary and Proper Clause?

See, for citations to current discussions, James F. Kelley, "The Uncertain Renaissance of the Ninth Amendment," *U. Chicago L. Rev.* 33 (1966): 814. See, on the Necessary and Proper Clause, *Federalist*, pp. 144, 177-78, 191-93, 198-202; also, pp. 160-61, above. See, also, chap. 2, n. 38, chap. 4, n. 91, chap. 6, n. 63, below.

31. John Randolph said of certain constitutional doctrines (in 1824), "They go the whole length. If they prevail, there are no longer any Pyrenees—every bulwark and barrier of the Constitution is broken down; it is become a *tabula rasa*, a *carte blanche*, for every one to scribble on it what he pleases." Quoted in Russell Kirk, *Randolph of Roanoke* (Chicago: University of Chicago Press, 1951), p. 99. (If the Constitution is to be considered as "growing," my discussion can be seen as a suggestion as to what it should grow to. See chap. 8, n. 83, chap. 9, n. 3, below. Cf. chap. 5, n. 43, below [on "crystallization"].) See, also, chap. 6, n. 50, below. Cf. chap. 7, n. 3, below.

The Anglo-American lawyer is disciplined (confined as well as guided) in how he proceeds by centuries-old customs governing the reading of statutes:

And it was resolved . . . that for the sure and true interpretation of all statutes in general . . . four things are to be discerned and considered: 1st. What was the common law before the making of the Act. 2nd. What was the mischief and defect for which the common law did not provide. 3rd. What remedy the Parliament hath resolved and appointed to cure the disease of the commonwealth. And 4th, The true reason of the remedy; and then the office of all the judges is always to make such construction as shall suppress the mischief, and advance the remedy, and to suppress subtle inventions and evasions for continuance of the mischief, and *pro privato commodo*, and to add force and life to the cure and remedy, according to the true intent of the makers of the act, *pro bono publico*. [*Heydon's Case* (1584), 3 Co. Rep. at f 7 b]

"It is therefore a very proper rule of construction, that the whole is to be examined with a view to arriving at the true intention of each part, and this Sir Edward Coke regards as the most natural and genuine method of expounding a statute." Thomas Cooley, *Constitutional Limitations* . . . (8th ed.; Boston: Little, Brown & Co., 1927), 1:127 (citing

CHAPTER TWO, NOTES 32-33: PAGE 26   433

Co. Lit. 381a). See, also, Blackstone, *Laws of England*, 1:59-62; the text at chap. 2, n. 37, below, and chap. 7, n. 86, below. (Coke says [*Co. Lit.* 381a-b], "Here are three things worthy of observation concerning the construction of statutes. First, that it is the most naturall and genuine exposition of a statute to construe one part of the statute by another part of the same statute, for that best expresseth the meaning of the makers. . . . Secondly, the words of an act of parliament must bee taken in a lawfull and rightfull sense. . . . Thirdly, that construction must be taken of a statute in suppression of the mischiefe, and in advancement of the remedie. . . .")

It was said of John Marshall, in 1799, "[He] is too much disposed to govern the world according to rules of logic; he will read and expound the constitution as if it were a penal statute, and will sometimes be embarrassed with doubts of which his friends will not perceive the importance." Albert J. Beveridge, *The Life of John Marshall* (Boston: Houghton Mifflin Co., 1916), 2:437. (See *U.S.* v. *Wiltberger*, 5 Wheat. [U.S.] 76, 95-96 [1820].) Perhaps underlying our principles of interpretation is the approach indicated in "Rule 1" of Isaac Newton's "Rules of Reasoning in Philosophy":

> We are to admit no more causes of natural things than such as are both true and sufficient to explain their appearances. To this purpose the philosophers say that Nature does nothing in vain, and more is in vain when less will serve; for Nature is pleased with simplicity, and affects not the pomp of superfluous causes.
> [*Principia* (Berkeley: University of California Press, 1962), p. 398]

Lawyers and judges become accustomed, in many thousands of hours of drafting and interpreting routine legal documents, to a way of thinking about controlling documents that the nonlegal scholar, whose contact with legal materials is almost exclusively (and thus disproportionately) with Supreme Court opinions (and not even with the records that lead to such opinions), must find it very difficult to appreciate or to imitate. The serious student of American constitutional law should enlist himself in at least the first-year program of studies in a good law school. See Wilson, *Political Thought*, pp. 4-5; Sutherland, *Constitutionalism in America*, pp. 349-50. Cf. chap. 2, n. 17, above, and chap. 6, n. 26, below. See, also, Berns, "Two Old Conservatives Discuss the Anastaplo Case," *Cornell L. Q.* 54 (1969): 920, 925-26.

What do constitutional government and the rule of law require? (The likely alternative today is the lawlessness either of anarchy or [as is more likely] of tyranny.) The established way of talking about legal instruments has to be somewhat respected by the constitutionalist if the truth is to be learned (e.g., about the intentions of his predecessors) and if he is to be able to transmit to his successors what *he* thinks it good to transmit, thereby promoting stability even while permitting reform. (Of course, language is in large part conventional. But it is "most naturall and genuine" for men to have this as well as other conventions. See chap. 7, n. 77, chap. 8, n. 171, below.) Cf., on the other hand, the essential agreement on this point (on behalf of sophistry) between the "legal realist" and the "radical": chap. 7, n. 124, chap. 8, n. 28, below. On the other hand, may not contemporary "radicalism" be one natural (even public-spirited) reaction against the subversion of standards by respectable "realism"? Indeed, do not the teachings of the Declaration of Independence remain the best instrument available to us today in our efforts to establish or preserve a decent community despite the well-meaning assaults upon prudence by the "realist," "radical," and "reactionary" alike? See Appendix F, chap. 2, n. 1, above, chap. 4, n. 36, below. (Cf. Vice-President Agnew's "Know-Nothing" attack, presumably in the name of popular sovereignty, upon elitism. *Chicago Sun-Times*, Oct. 16, 1970, p. 42. See, for the "elitism" of the Founding Fathers, the remarks by Roger Sherman reproduced at p. 89, above. See, also, chap. 8, n. 135, below.)

See chap. 7, n. 86, below.

32. *History of Congress: Exhibiting a Classification of the Proceedings of the Senate and the House of Representatives, from March 4th, 1789, to March 3rd, 1793* (Philadelphia: Lea & Blanchard, 1843), p. 164 (hereafter cited as *History of Congress*).

33. Does not the mandate of the Tenth Amendment come down essentially to such

a directive as well? "The powers not delegated to the United States by the Constitution, nor prohibited by it to the States, are reserved to the States respectively, or to the people." See Story, *Commentaries on the Constitution*, chap. 44, sec. 1908.

See chap. 7, n. 79, below.

34. Madison had proposed "that there shall be established an Executive Department, to be denominated the Department of Foreign Affairs, at the head of which there shall be an officer, to be called the Secretary to the Department of Foreign Affairs, who shall be appointed by the President, by and with the advice and consent of the Senate; and to be removable by the President." *Annals*, I, pp. 370-71. Smith, however,

> moved to strike out the words "who shall be appointed by the President, by and with the advice and consent of the Senate." He conceived the words to be unnecessary; besides, it looked as if they were conferring power, which was not the case, for the Constitution had expressly given the power of appointment in the words there used. He also objected to the subsequent parts of this paragraph, because it declared the President alone to have the power of removal. . . . Mr. Smith said he had doubts whether the officer could be removed by the President. He apprehended he could only be removed by an impeachment before the Senate, and that, being once in office, he must remain there until convicted upon impeachment. [*Annals*, I, pp. 371-72]

Madison replied to Smith,

> What would be the consequence of such construction? It would in effect establish every officer of the government in the firm tenure of good behaviour; not the heads of Departments only, but all the inferior officers of those Departments, would hold their offices during good behaviour, and that to be judged by one branch of the Legislature only on the impeachment of the other. If the Constitution means this by its declarations to be the case, we must submit; but I should lament it as a fatal error interwoven in the system, and one that would ultimately prove its destruction. I think the inference would not arise from a fair construction of the words of that instrument. [*Annals*, I, p. 377]

(The resolution of the controversy by the First Congress may be seen in n. 35, below. Consider the significance for constitutional interpretation of the suspiciously convenient suggestion, in *Federalist*, p. 482, that the presidential power "to require, in writing, of the principal officer" is "a mere redundancy in the plan.")

There may have been implied in this removal power controversy the fundamental problem of whether there are powers inherent in the Congress, President, and courts of the United States, independent of specific grants in the Constitution. See chap. 6, n. 19, below.

" . . . [T]he intense opposition of the 'States' Rights' Minority to the decision [in the First Congress] in favor of the President's removal power—a power absolutely essential to his proper functioning—becomes easy to understand: it was a decision, *in principle*, in favor of a general national legislative authority, as well." Crosskey, *Politics and the Constitution*, p. 369; see, also, ibid., pp. 1033-35.

See, also, Brant, *James Madison*, pp. 258-61.

> The Constitution has left it doubtful whether the President is obliged to consult the Senate in the removal as well as in the appointment of Federal officers. *The Federalist* (No. 77) seems to establish the affirmative; but in 1789 Congress formally decided that as the President was responsible for his actions, he ought not to be forced to employ agents who had forfeited his esteem. See Kent's *Commentaries on American Law* (New York, 1826), Vol. I, p. 289. [Tocqueville, *Democracy in America*, 1:129, n. 15]

Cf. Story, *Commentaries on the Constitution*, chap. 37, secs. 1537-44.

The Supreme Court first passed on this issue (which had been involved, by the way, in President Andrew Johnson's impeachment [see Sutherland, *Constitutionalism in America*,

CHAPTER TWO, NOTES 35-37: PAGES 28-29   435

pp. 445-46]) in *Myers v. U.S.*, 272 U.S. 52 (1926) (sustaining the power of the President alone to remove purely executive officers). Justice Holmes concluded his one-page dissent on that occasion, "The duty of the President to see that the laws be executed is a duty that does not go beyond the laws or require him to achieve more than Congress sees fit to leave within his power." 272 U.S., at 177. Cf., with respect to inherent presidential powers, *Humphrey's Executor v. U.S.*, 295 U.S. 602 (1935); *Youngstown Sheet & Tube Co. v. Sawyer*, 343 U.S. 579 (1952).

See chap. 4, nn. 42, 60, below. See, also, chap. 2, n. 15, above, chap. 4, n. 75, below.

35. The act passed by the First Congress establishing the Department of Foreign Affairs may be found at *Annals*, I, pp. 2132-33:

> Be it enacted, &c., That there shall be an Executive Department, to be denominated the Department of Foreign Affairs; and that there shall be a principal officer therein, to be called the Secretary for the Department of Foreign Affairs, who shall perform and execute such duties as shall, from time to time, be enjoined on or intrusted to him by the President of the United States, agreeable to the Constitution, relative to correspondences, commissions, or instructions, to or with public ministers from foreign States or princes, or to memorials or other applications from foreign public Ministers, or other foreigners, or to such other matters respecting foreign affairs as the President of the United States shall assign to the said department. And furthermore, that the said principal officer shall conduct the business of the said department in such manner as the President of the United States shall, from time to time, order or instruct.
>
> Sec. 2. And be it further enacted, That there shall be in the said Department an inferior officer to be appointed by the said principal officer, and to be employed therein as he shall deem proper, and to be called the chief clerk in the Department of Foreign Affairs; and who, whenever the said principal officer shall be removed from office by the President of the United States, or in any other case of vacancy, shall, during such vacancy, have the charge and custody of all records, books, and papers appertaining to the said department. . . .

It is instructive to notice which objections to Madison's proposal (n. 34, above) were conceded, which were sidestepped, and which were indirectly repudiated.

See, for another illustration of the difficulty of reading the Constitution as a whole (this one bearing on the status of slavery in the Constitution), H. von Holst, *John C. Calhoun*, American Statesmen (Boston: Houghton Mifflin Co., 1892), pp. 127-28. See, also, Harry V. Jaffa, *Equality and Liberty* (New York: Oxford University Press, 1965), p. 172; cf. chap. 4, n. 56, below (on a possible conflict between the First Amendment and the *habeas corpus* provision).

See Aristotle, *Nicomachean Ethics* 1094b23.

36. But see my article, "The Declaration of Independence," which includes a discussion of the centrality of "Liberty" in that instrument. *St. Louis U. L. J.* 9, pp. 390, 406-8.

See Aristotle, *Nicomachean Ethics* 1095a31. See, also, chap. 2, n. 8, above, chap. 8, n. 3, below.

37. Thus, Madison can admit reservations about the merit of particular provisions in the Constitution. *Annals*, I, p. 582. Compare the observation of Lincoln, "It has been said, and I believe truly, that the Constitution is not altogether such as any one of its framers would have preferred. It was the joint work of all, and certainly the better that it was so." *Complete Works*, 2:390. See Aristotle, *Politics* 1281a11-1282b14; chap. 8, n. 153, below.

See, on the other hand, Crosskey, *Politics and the Constitution*, p. 674: " . . . The Constitution of the United States is, in other words, *not* an internally inconsistent document; it is internally consistent in a remarkable degree; an extraordinarily fine example of eighteenth-century legal craftsmanship, and a great credit to Gouverneur Morris and James Wilson, whose work it chiefly is." See, also, chap. 2, n. 31, above.

Compare Madison's description (in cipher) of the *Federalist*, in a letter to Jefferson of Aug. 10, 1788:

> I believe I never have yet mentioned to you that publication. It was undertaken last fall by Jay, Hamilton, and myself. The proposal came from the two former. The execution was thrown, by the sickness of Jay, mostly on the two others. Though carried on in concert, the writers are not mutually answerable for all the ideas of each other, there being seldom time for even a perusal of the pieces by any but the writer before they were wanted at the press, and sometimes hardly by the writer himself. [*The Writings of James Madison*, ed. Gaillard Hunt (New York: G. P. Putnam's Sons, 1904), p. 246]

The use of cipher reflects the exclusive, if not aristocratic character of Virginia politics.

Cf. chap. 8, n. 89, below. (Is not the assumption of unity in the Constitution essentially the same as that assumed for the New Testament and even for the Old and New Testaments together?)

38. The religion provision then read, "No religion shall be established by law, nor shall the equal rights of conscience be infringed." *Annals*, I, p. 729. See Appendix A, above.

Madison went on to say, in the speech quoted from in the text and in his next two speeches,

> Whether the words [of the religion provision] are necessary or not, he did not mean to say, but they had been required by some of the State Conventions, who seemed to entertain an opinion that under the clause of the Constitution, which gave power to Congress to make all laws necessary and proper to carry into execution the Constitution, and the laws made under it, enabled them to make laws of such a nature as might infringe the rights of conscience, and establish a national religion; to prevent these effects he presumed the amendment was intended, and he thought it as well expressed as the nature of the language would admit. . . . [He] thought, if the word "national" was inserted before religion, it would satisfy the minds of honorable gentlemen. He believed that the people feared one sect might obtain a pre-eminence, or two combine together, and establish a religion to which they would compel others to conform. . . . [He] observed that the words "no national religion shall be established by law," did not imply that the Government was a national one. . . . [*Annals*, I, pp. 730-31]

See, for their bearing on the religion provisions of the First Amendment, pp. 76-77, above, and chap. 2, n. 2, above; chap. 2, n. 39, chap. 4, nn. 72, 73, 110, 111, chap. 5, nn. 31, 51, 52, 55, 69, 91, 92, 96, 97, 100, 148, chap. 7, nn. 1, 34, 59, 68, 77, 115, 124, chap. 8, nn. 4, 36, 70, 135, chap. 9, nn. 1, 9, 20, 38, 39, below. See, also, among the lectures appended to my dissertation, "Church and States: The Beginnings of an Argument" and "Utopia or Tyranny: The Universal Declaration of Human Rights"; Sutherland, *Constitutionalism in America*, pp. 539-46.

The records of the convention that met in 1788 in North Carolina to consider and reject ratification of the Constitution are particularly useful with respect to the religion provisions. Jonathan Elliot, *Debates in the Several State Conventions on the Adoption of the Federal Constitution* (Philadelphia: J. B. Lippincott & Co., 1863), 4:1.

39. Laments such as Hamlet's may be seen elsewhere in Shakespeare. Thus we find in *King John* (act 5, sc. 7) an anticipation of Hamlet's mood by Prince Henry (immediately upon the death of the king): "What surety of the world, what hope, what stay, when this was now a king, and now is clay?" A variation upon this sentiment may be found in *Cymbeline* (act 4, sc. 2): "Thersites's body is as good as Ajax's, When neither are alive." (Consider, also, Juvenal's *Expende Hannibalem: quot libras in duce summo in duce summo invenies.* "Weigh the dust of Hannibal. How many pounds will you find in that great leader?" H. P. Jones, *Dictionary of Foreign Phrases and Classical Quotations* [Edinburgh: John Grant, 1963], p. 40.) Cf. chap. 7, n. 115, chap. 9, n. 31, below (on Alexander the Great). See Gen. 2:7.

One critical implication of Hamlet's imaginative tracing may be more evident in Diderot's dialogue, "Conversation between d'Alembert and Diderot" (1769):

CHAPTER TWO, NOTE 39: PAGE 32   437

> *Diderot* . . . Flesh can be made from marble, and marble from flesh. . . .
> *d'Alembert* . . . I don't quite see how a body can be made to pass from the state of inactive to that of active sensitiveness.
> *D.* . . . I'll tell you, since you want to be put to shame; it occurs every time you eat. . . .
> *d'A.* Whether it's true or false, I like this passage from marble into humus, from humus to the vegetable kingdom, from the vegetable to the animal kingdom, to flesh.
> *D.* . . . Here, in four words you have the general formula. Eat, digest, distil *in vasi licito, et fiat homo secundum artem* [in a suitable vessel, let a man be made by art]. And to expound before the Academy the process of the formation of a man or an animal, one need employ only material agents, the successive results of which would be an inert being, a feeling being, a thinking being, a being solving the problem of the precession of the equinoxes, a sublime being, a marvelous being, a being growing old, fading away, dying, dissolved and given back to the soil. [L. W. Beck, ed., *Eighteenth Century Philosophy* (New York: Free Press, 1966), pp. 172-75]

Thus, the problem is raised of the nature of the human soul. Does it, for instance, exist separate from the body? Hamlet's speculations could raise doubts not only about any concern in Hamlet for the disposition of Claudius's soul but even about the existence of the Ghost itself. Is there, that is, anything that rises above and survives the transitory clay into which "Imperial Caesar" is turned? See chap. 9, n. 38, below. (Shakespeare would have us notice that if Hamlet *had* killed Claudius "at prayers," Claudius would not have [according to the current orthodoxy] been spared from eternal damnation. When Hamlet does kill Claudius, what "becomes" of Claudius? Or of the others when they die, including Hamlet? Does Shakespeare care? Are *we* intended to care? [We do see that one's other-worthly effects are despite oneself.] Horatio, it should also be noticed, declares himself in Act 5, sc. 2, to be "more an antique Roman than a Dane"; and Hamlet *now* sees the death of even a suicide as producing "felicity." Cf. Act 5, sc. 2, ll. 50-51 ["not shriving time allowed"]. See chap. 8, nn. 107, 186, below.)

Practical men rebel at such "extremist" speculations and their paralyzing effects. (See, e.g., Callicles' rebuke of Socrates in Plato's *Gorgias*.) Is not an implication of the protest by Tucker against the "Socratic" "mode of reasoning" (*Annals, I*, p. 838) (in the passage reproduced in the text after n. 33, above) that there is not, for practical affairs, a whole? There *is* a sense in which the Socratic mode of reasoning (if not moderated publicly) threatens the illusions upon which practical life, and especially political activity, may rest. (See chap. 9, nn. 7, 27, 30, below.) This problem is touched upon in chap. 9, sec. 4, above (esp. in chap. 9, n. 24), with its discussion of the Cave in Plato's *Republic*: we are reminded that Hamlet, in the graveyard scene (act 5, sc. 1), leaps into the open grave. In both authors, that is, the "action" is taken below the surface: the underpinnings, the foundations, of things are exposed to light. See chap. 8, n. 34, chap. 9, n. 39, below. See, also, chap. 8, nn. 135, 169, below. The immoderate and hence impolitic character of the Socratic mode of reasoning is reflected in an observation by Samuel Johnson, "Questioning is not the mode of conversation among gentlemen." *Oxford Dictionary of Quotations* (London: Oxford University Press, 1959), p. 273. (Consider, also, Kant's characterization of skeptics as "a species of nomads." *Critique of Pure Reason*, p. 8. Cf. ibid., p. 395.) But see Plato, *Gorgias* 521D.

Moderation, on the other hand, is seen in Horatio's insistence upon addressing Hamlet as "my lord." Neither Hamlet's speculations nor their friendship induce Horatio to forget their political relation. (Horatio's respect for the world of affairs may be reflected in the fact that he, alone of the principal characters of the play, survives. [See, on the self-preserving prudence of Edgar in *King Lear*, p. 278, above, chap. 9, n. 20, below.] Consider, also, the "outcast" Ishmael of *Moby Dick*, who alone survives from the crew of the *Pequod* [an old "American" name] because he is physically, as well as spiritually, on the periphery of the Titanic challenge by Captain Ahab.) See, on Shakespeare's Faulconbridge, Horatio, and Prospero, Howard B. White, "Bastards and Usurpers: Shakespeare's

King John," in Cropsey, *Ancients and Moderns*, p. 174: "Had Horatio been in Hamlet's position, he certainly would have controlled the action that Hamlet did not control. That does not mean that either Faulconbridge or Horatio could have controlled the action that Prospero controlled." See, e.g., Horatio's "Be ruled. . . ." Act 1, sc. 4, l. 90.

I try in this study to restrict my playing of Hamlet to the subterranean region of footnotes: my text, on the other hand, examines not the underlying skull but rather the fleshed-out face of constitutional law. That is, the appearances of things are important and should be respected: indeed, the noble as well as the merely useful may depend on the apparent, on the surface of things. (See chap. 8, n. 2, below.) The rhetorical element in constitutional law cannot be disregarded, but neither should it be magnified unduly. See chap. 4, n. 13, chap. 5, n. 43, below. See, also, chap. 2, n. 31, above, chap. 8, nn. 28, 181, below. Cf. the imprudent *King* Hamlet's "angry parle."

In any event, the writer on politics and law should be prepared to distill the most exalted and permanent things from the most trivial and transitory. (See, e.g., Plato, *Gorgias* 491A-B, *Banquet* 221E-222A.) If he should be diligent, fortunate, and hence properly prepared, he may be entitled to say as did Littleton in the Epilogue to his *Institutes*:

> And know, my son, that I would not have thee beleeve, that all which I have said in these bookes is law, for I will not presume to take this upon me. . . . Notwithstanding albeit that certaine things which are moved and specified in the sayd bookes, are not altogether law, yet such things shall make thee more apt, and able to understand and apprehend the arguments and reasons of the law, &c. For by the arguments and reasons in the law, a man more sooner shall come to the certaintie and knowledge of the law.

See chap. 5, n. 141, below. (Coke begins his commentary on this passage of Littleton's by counseling us:

> Here observe the great modestie and mildnesse of our author, which is worthy of imitation. . . . And herein our author followed the example of Moses, who was a judge, and the first writer of law; for he was *mitissimus omnium hominum qui fuit in terris*, as the holy historie testifieth of him. [*Co. Lit.* 394b]

See Exod. 2:11-12, 32:19-28; Deut. 28:15-68. See, also, John 5:45-47; 7:19; Acts 7:22.) Or he may be inspired to say, in the mode of Proust's narrator (*Remembrance of Things Past*, 1:8):

> . . . so in that moment all the flowers in our garden and in M. Swann's park, and the water-lilies on the Vivonne and the good folk of the village and their little dwellings and the parish church, and the whole of Combray and of its surroundings, taking their proper shapes and growing solid, sprang into being, town and garden alike, from my cup of tea.

See chap. 5, n. 126, below.

Cf. Lucretius, *On the Nature of Things*, 1:921-50. But see chap. 9, n. 21, below.

CHAPTER III

1. Presidents have objected from time to time to congressional use of "shall" in legislation touching upon what they regard as presidential prerogatives.

Coriolanus develops further, in the passage following that found in the epigraph to this chapter, the significance of "shall." Shakespeare, *Coriolanus*, act 3, sc. 1, lines 89-112.

The dying Elizabeth is reported to have replied, to an insistence that she must go to bed, that the word "must" was not used to princes, adding the observation, "but you know I must die and that makes you presumptuous." John Buchan, *A Book of Escapes and Hurried Journeys* (Boston: Houghton Mifflin Co., 1923), p. 259. A similar story is told of Louis XV, who, "at the point of death, had been deeply vexed by the word *must* [*il faut*], clumsily used by his chief physician. . . ." Stendhal, *The Red and the Black*, trans. M. R. B. Shaw (Baltimore: Penguin Books, 1953), p. 332. See Montesquieu, *The Spirit of the Laws* (New York: Hafner Publishing Co., 1949), 12:10; also, *Federalist* No. 26 (where "shall not" is regarded as "prohibitory" and "ought not" as "cautionary"); William W. Crosskey, *Politics and the Constitution in the History of the United States* (Chicago: University of Chicago Press, 1953), pp. 550, 552.

Compare this exchange in Lessing's *Nathan the Wise* (act 1, sc. 3):

> *Nathan.* . . . I always thought that a dervish—the genuine kind of a dervish—would not let anything be made of himself.
> *Dervish.* By the Prophet! That I am not genuine may also well be true. However, when one *must* —
> *N.* Must! Dervish! A dervish *must*? No man must "must"—and a dervish should have to "must"? What then might he have to "must"?
> *D.* That which is requested of him in the right manner and what he perceives as good: that is what a dervish "must."
> *N.* By our God! Here you speak the truth. Let yourself be embraced, man. . . .

See the text at chap. 2, n. 11, above.

2. See, for Madison's use of "absolute" and "qualification," *Annals*, I, p. 463 (reproduced at the beginning of chap. 4, sec. 2, above). See, also, chap. 4, n. 44, below.

Federalist No. 85 speaks of "the absolute and universal exclusion of titles of nobility" by the Constitution. This cannot be said with respect to the First Amendment: there *is* an absolute prohibition (i.e., addressed to Congress), but it is not universal (i.e., the states are not governed by that amendment). But there are, with respect to titles of nobility, explicit prohibitions governing both the general government and the states.

3. The Article I, section 4, provision is reproduced in the text at p. 85, above. See, at the same place, Ames's objection to Burke's proposal.

4. *History of Congress*, pp. 165-66.

The Constitutionalist confronts on occasion the plea of "necessity," a plea that may be dangerous either to ignore or to respect: circumstances may be decisive, as well as the institutions devised for such circumstances (as is discussed in chap. 7 of this book).

Francis Bacon—that prophet of modernity who can serve as the patron saint of all of us whose standing with the bar is dubious—counsels in his essay, "Of Innovations," "It is good also not to try experiments in states, except the necessity be urgent, or the utility evident." Another great lawyer—and a more respectable one—observes, "The pretence for which arbitrary measures [in the reign of King James I] was no other than the tyrant's plea [citing Milton, *Paradise Lost*, 4:393], of the *necessity* of unlimited powers in works of evident utility to the public, 'the supreme reason above all reasons, which is the salvation of the king's lands and people.'" Blackstone, *Laws of England*, 3:74. Lincoln—still another great lawyer—was obliged to condition a military directive "upon tolerably clear necessity." *Complete Works*, ed. John G. Nicolay and John Hay (New York: Century Co., 1902), 2:179. See chap. 4, n. 56, below. Cf. chap. 3, n. 33, below.

Bacon's departure from the received teaching is evident in his essay, "Of Empire": "Neither is the opinion of some of the schoolmen to be received, 'that a war cannot justly be made but upon a precedent injury or provocation.' For there is no question but a just fear of an imminent danger, though there be no blow given, is a lawful cause of a war." What the Schoolmen were apprehensive of may be seen in another of Bacon's essays, "Of the True Greatness of Kingdoms and Estates":

> But it is so plain "that every man profiteth in that he most intendeth," that it needeth not to be stood upon. It is enough to point at it; that no nation which doth not directly profess arms, may look to have greatness fall into their mouths. . . . Incident to this point is, for a state to have those laws or customs which may reach forth unto them just occasions (as may be pretended) of war. For there is that justice imprinted in the nature of men, that they enter not upon

wars (whereof so many calamities do ensue) but upon some, at the least specious, grounds and quarrels.

See chap. 7, n. 77, below.

5. See Zechariah Chafee, *Freedom of Speech* (Cambridge: Harvard University Press, 1920), pp. 32-34:

> . . . It is sometimes argued that the Constitution gives Congress the power to declare war, raise armies, and support a navy, that one provision of the Constitution cannot be used to break down another provision, and consequently freedom of speech cannot be invoked to break down the war power. I would reply that the First Amendment is just as much a part of the Constitution as the war clauses, and that it is equally accurate to say that the war clauses cannot be invoked to break down freedom of speech. . . . There are those who believe that the Bill of Rights can be set aside in war time at the uncontrolled will of the government. The first ten amendments were drafted by men who had just been through a war. The Third and Fifth Amendments expressly apply in war. . . . If the First Amendment is to mean anything, it must restrict powers which are expressly granted by the Constitution to Congress, since Congress has no other powers. It must apply to those activities of government which are most liable to interfere with free discussion, namely, the postal service and the conduct of war.

6. "Both the general legislature and the State legislature are expressly prohibited making *ex post facto* laws; though there never was nor can be a legislature but must and will make such laws, when necessity and the public safety require them; which will hereafter be a breach of all the constitutions in the Union, and afford precedents for other innovations." George Mason, of Virginia, in Max Farrand, ed., *The Records of the Federal Convention of 1787* (New Haven: Yale University Press, 1937), 2:640. Cf. James Iredell, in Paul Leicester Ford, ed., *Essays on the Constitution of the United States, Published during Its Discussion by the People 1786-1788* (Brooklyn: Historical Printing Club, 1892), p. 368.

See the extraordinary cases of *Medley, Petitioner*, 134 U.S. 160 (1890) and *Savage, Petitioner*, 134 U.S. 176 (1890). See, also, "The True Meaning of the Prohibition of Ex-Post-Facto Clauses: A Chapter of Judicial Statesmanship from the Eighteenth Century," in Crosskey, *Politics and the Constitution*, pp. 324-51; Joseph Story, *Commentaries on the Constitution of the United States*, 2d ed. (Boston: Little, Brown & Co., 1851), chap. 32, sec. 1345.

7. "We the People of the United States, in Order to form a more perfect Union, establish Justice, insure domestic Tranquility, provide for the common defence, promote the general Welfare, and secure the Blessings of Liberty to ourselves and our Posterity, do ordain and establish this Constitution for the United States of America." U.S., *Constitution*, Preamble. See chap. 6, n. 44, below.

8. Perhaps the Second Amendment suggests an appropriate response: *if* the Preamble could be used in this manner, then there would have been no purpose for the phrase therein, "being necessary to the security of a free State." Was this phrase retained because it had been included in an earlier document declaring the right to keep and bear arms? (This indicates one problem of interpreting materials shaped in part by "history.")

Robert Williams, of North Carolina, argued in the course of the debate in the House of Representatives on the Alien and Sedition Acts of 1798,

> If the principle which the gentlemen from Massachusetts [Harrison Gray Otis and Samuel Sewall] have drawn from the preamble of the Constitution, of providing for the common defence and general welfare of the Union, be correct, it appeared to him unnecessary to have any other provision in the Constitution besides the preamble, as it may be inferred from that, that Congress has all power whatever. If such a construction be allowed, what becomes of the powers of the State Governments? This preamble of the Constitution would swallow up the whole. [*Annals*, V, p. 1962]

9. See "Justice Black and First Amendment 'Absolutes': A Public Interview," *N.Y.U. L. Rev.* 37 (1962): 553, 562-63. See, also, Edmond Cahn, *The Great Rights* (New York: Macmillan Co., 1963), p. 45. Cf. chap. 3, n. 25, below; also, Justice Black's discussion in *Illinois v. Allen*, 90 S.Ct. 1057, 1060 (1970) of whether the Sixth Amendment right to be present at one's trial is an "absolute."

Five states, at the time the Bill of Rights was written in the First Congress, had no separate bill of rights in their constitutions. (See the text at chap. 8, n. 89, above.) Virginia had been (in 1776) the first state to insert in its constitution a clause endorsing the liberty of the press: "That the freedom of the press is *one of the great bulwarks of liberty*, and can never be restrained but by despotick governments." (Italics added) We can see from the italicized words where the phrase discussed in the text after chap. 2, n. 8, probably came from. See, on the Virginia Declaration of Rights, Wilmoore Kendall and George W. Carey, *The Basic Symbols of the American Political Tradition* (Baton Rouge: Louisiana State University Press, 1970), p. 61.

10. Italics added. See Blackstone, *Laws of England*, 4:150-53, for one source of the "abuse" qualification with respect to liberty of the press.

The provisions in the present Illinois Constitution (ratified 1870) comparable to the First Amendment read:

> The free exercise and enjoyment of religious profession and worship, without discrimination, shall forever be guaranteed; and no person shall be denied any civil or political right, privilege or capacity, on account of his religious opinions; but the liberty of conscience hereby secured shall not be construed to dispense with oaths or affirmations, excuse acts of licentiousness, or justify practices inconsistent with the peace or safety of the States. No person shall be required to attend or support any ministry or place of worship against his consent, nor shall any preference be given by law to any religious denomination or mode of worship.
>
> Every person may freely speak, write and publish on all subjects, *being responsible for the abuse of that liberty*; and in all trials for libel, both civil and criminal, the truth, when published with good motives and for justifiable ends, shall be a sufficient defense.
>
> The people have the right to assemble in a peaceable manner to consult for the common good, to make known their opinions to their representatives, and to apply for redress of grievances. [Italics added]

(The constitution written by the Illinois Convention in 1970 is substantially the same with respect to these matters.)

Article 11 of the French "Declaration of the Rights of Man and Citizen" (1789) reads,

> The free communication of thoughts and opinions is one of the most precious rights of men: every citizen then can freely speak, write, and print, *subject to responsibility for the abuse of this liberty* in the cases determined by law. [Italics added]

We find in the French Constitution of 1791 that

> The constitution likewise guarantees as natural and civil rights: . . . Liberty to every man to speak, to write, to print and publish his thoughts without having his writings subject to any censorship or inspection *before their publication*, and to follow the religious worship to which he is attached. . . . [Italics added]

See, for the French texts, A. V. Dicey, *Introduction to the Study of the Law of the Constitution* (5th ed.; New York: Macmillan Co., 1897), p. 228.

See chap. 2, n. 2, above, chap. 4, n. 88, below. See, also, chap. 8, nn. 18, 83, below.

11. There is, however, in the provision relating to the right of assembly and petition, language that may seem less emphatic than that relating to freedom of speech and the press:

Congress shall make no law . . . abridging . . . the right of the people peaceably to assemble, and to petition the Government for a redress of grievances.

We need only note at this point that the qualification, "peaceably," does not reach the speaker and what he says or the publisher and what he prints, but rather the dangers inherent in any gathering (political or otherwise) that does not conduct itself properly.

The guarantee of the right of assembly was thought by the Congress to have the merit attributed to it by Page:

> . . . people have also been prevented from assembling together on their lawful occasions, therefore it is well to guard against such stretches of authority, by inserting the privilege in the declaration of rights. If the people could be deprived of the power of assembling under any pretext whatsoever, they might be deprived of every other privilege in the clause [relating to freedom of speech and of the press]. [*Annals*, I, p. 732]

But a decision was made to run the risk in this instance of a prohibition upon Congress which stipulates the condition, "peaceably"—although it should be noted that the prohibition is absolute insofar as it does restrain Congress from interfering in any way with peaceable assembly. Thus, to the extent that there is a qualification, it is expressly regarded as part of the definition of that which is being unequivocally protected against congressional abridgment. See chap. 4, n. 96, chap. 8, n. 108, below. See, also, chap. 7, n. 67, below.

12. Chafee, *Freedom of Speech*, p. 4, n. 2; Chafee, *Free Speech in the United States*, p. 5, n. 2. See chap. 3, n. 24, below; cf. chap. 3, n. 27, below. I believe this is Justice Frankfurter's position in *Dennis* v. *U.S.*, 341 U.S. 494, 517 (1951) (see the text at chap. 3, n. 23, above). See, also, James Kent, *Commentaries on American Law* (New York: O. Halsted, 1826), 2:17, 26; Story, *Commentaries on the Constitution*, chap. 44, sec. 1880 (chap. 5, n. 116, below); *Patterson* v. *Colorado*, 205 U.S. 454, 462 (1907) (chap. 5, n. 5, below); *Gitlow* v. *New York*, 268 U.S. 652, 666 (1925).

Chafee described, at page 18 of his *Freedom of Speech*, the development of the Pennsylvania constitutional provision (quoted in the text at n. 10 of this chapter) without appreciating the "states' rights" significance of the distinction he thereby noticed between the general government and the states:

> In discussing the brief "freedom of speech" clause in the Pennsylvania Constitution of 1776, [Benjamin Franklin] said in 1789, that if by the liberty of the press were to be understood merely the liberty of discussing the propriety of public measures and political opinions, let us have as much of it as you please. On the other hand, if it means liberty to calumniate another there ought to be some limit; but he has been at a loss to imagine any that may not be construed an infringement of the sacred *liberty of the press*. At length, however, he thinks he has found one that instead of diminishing general liberty shall augment it; he means *the liberty of the cudgel*. If, however, it should be thought that this proposal of his may disturb the public peace, he would humbly recommend to our legislators to take up the consideration of both liberties, that of the *press*, and that of the *cudgel*, and by an explicit law mark their extent and limits. [Citing Benjamin Franklin, *The Writings of Benjamin Franklin*, ed. Albert H. Smyth (London: Macmillan & Co., 1907), 10:36 ff.] Thus Franklin construed this clause so widely as even to grant immunity from private libel actions. Next year [1790] the Pennsylvania Constitution was amended to impose responsibility for the abuse of the liberty, but no such exception was thought necessary in the United States Constitution, probably because private libels were not within the purview of the federal law.

See chap. 4, n. 105, chap. 7, n. 26, below. (Franklin seems to recognize here the distinction referred to in chap. 5, n. 33, below, between the citizen as one of the rulers and the citizen as one of the ruled or subjects. See, also, chap. 4, n. 113, below.)

CHAPTER THREE, NOTE 13: PAGE 43

The powers and duties of the state governments, as distinguished from the general government, were noticed by Chafee. I develop in chapters 6 and 7 various implications of this distinction. See chap. 3, n. 26, chap. 8, n. 83, below.
See, on "the liberty of the cudgel," or at least of fisticuffs, Plato, *Laws* 880A.
13. See, e.g., chap. 5, n. 5, below. Chafee's work is, to the extent the terms are distinguishable, legal and political rather than constitutional. (Thus, he preferred to speak of "interest" rather than of "right." *Freedom of Speech,* pp. 367-68. Cf. chap. 4, n. 116, chap. 9, n. 39, below.)
His work is valuable for its descriptions of incidents and developments, for its analyses of technical defects in laws and legal documents, and for its arguments about the wisdom or folly of various governmental measures. See, e.g., ibid., pp. 152-54. Harry Kalven, Jr., has described Chafee as "the most devoted and concerned student of free speech in our history." *The Negro and the First Amendment* (Chicago: University of Chicago Press, 1966), p. 49.
Chafee's useful political approach is suggested by his comments in 1949 (*Harvard L. Rev.* 62:891, 894) on Alexander Meiklejohn's *Free Speech and Its Relation to Self-Government* (New York: Harper & Bros., 1948):

> In endeavoring to oppose suppressive measures, I have found it best to keep on the level of wisdom and policy as much as possible. In the situation which now confronts us, we have to start by recognizing that a considerable number of decent people want more suppression of speech and opinions because they are sincerely afraid of the dangers of Communism within the United States. The best practical hope is to persuade them that this danger is smaller than they think— small enough so that the risks of toleration are negligible in comparison to the losses to the American way of life which would inevitably follow from a systematic legal campaign against "dangerous thoughts." The First Amendment comes into the discussion chiefly as a powerful means of persuasion. If persuasion fails, then the First Amendment will be invoked in the courts, but that is a last resort. Once a measure is enacted, a large amount of suppression always occurs before it reaches a test in the courts, and plenty of harm is done even if the law is eventually declared unconstitutional. So the most important thing is to prevent the enactment of an unwise measure if possible. And that enactment is most likely to be prevented if a majority of the legislature and of active members of the public can be persuaded that it is undesirable.
> It is much more difficult to conduct the argument on a constitutional level when you are appealing to the public or to a legislative committee. What you are really saying then is that they ought not to pass the measure even though they are not persuaded that it is undesirable. . . .
> Herein lies my main objection to Mr. Meiklejohn's book. He places virtually all his argument against current proposals for suppression on a constitutional position which is extremely dubious. Whereas the supporters of these measures are genuinely worried by the dangers of Communism, *he refuses to argue that these dangers are actually small.* Instead, his constitutional position obliges him to argue that these dangers are irrelevant. No matter how terrible and immediate the dangers may be, he keeps saying, the First Amendment will not let Congress *or anybody else in the Government* try to deal with Communists who have not yet committed unlawful acts. It is hopeless to use reasoning like this in order to win votes against the Mundt-Nixon Bill. Such a view may be courageous, but it won't work.
> Since Mr. Meiklejohn as a philosopher is not a pragmatist, he would probably reply that what has just been said does not matter. . . . He is not trying to frame arguments which will win votes, but is seeking for eternal truth. . . .

[Italics added]

The passages I have italicized indicate two of my departures from the position Meiklejohn represents: I argue now, just as I did in 1950-51 (when I first encountered the preposterous fears and ignoble arguments of eminent Chicago lawyers on my bar admission committee), that "the dangers of Communism" in the United States "are actually small"; I recognize now (in chap. 7, below), just as I did in my 1955 application for admission to the bar of the Supreme Court of the United States, that the absolute restrictions upon the general government need not apply fully to the states. See Appendix F, sec. 9, above.

See chap. 2, n. 39, above, chap. 3, n. 28, chap. 4, n. 37, chap. 5, n. 100, chap. 7, n. 72, chap. 8, nn. 83, 181, below.

14. *Schenck* v. *U.S.*, 249 U.S. 47, 52 (1919). See chap. 3, n. 22, below, for a description of the case. Chief Justice Vinson observed in *Dennis* v. *U.S.*, 341 U.S. 494, at 503 (1951), "No important case involving free speech was decided by the Court prior to *Schenck* v. *U.S.* . . ." (An unadorned and more moderate version of Justice Holmes's *Schenck* language, drawing perhaps on his state court experience, may be found in his opinion for the Court in *Debs* v. *U.S.*, 249 U.S. 211, 216 [1919]: "We should add that they could not find the defendant guilty for advocacy of any of his opinions unless the words used had as their natural tendency and reasonably probable effect to obstruct the recruiting service, &c., and unless the defendant had the specific intent to do so in his mind." Even so, the imprisonment by the Wilson administration of Eugene Debs was as if the Truman administration had imprisoned Henry Wallace, or as if the Nixon administration should now imprison George Wallace. See chap. 4, n. 54, chap. 6, n. 38, below.)

I consider in chap. 7, secs. 9-12, above, what may have contributed to the disposition on the part of both public men and scholars to permit qualifications to be read into the First Amendment. I consider in chap. 7, sec. 6, above, "the substantive evils that Congress has a right to prevent." See, on the application of this test to state action, chap. 3, n. 21, below.

The *Schenck* case, I shall argue, has been to litigation respecting "freedom of speech" what *Plessy* v. *Ferguson*, 163 U.S. 537 (1896), was for more than half a century to litigation respecting "the equal protection of the laws." These landmark decisions need not have gone the way they did, but once they did they added the authority of judicial ratification to the strength of the faction that had advocated them. See chap. 4, n. 37, chap. 8, n. 95, below. *Schenck*, like *Plessy* v. *Ferguson*, was questioned from the beginning. It has been eroded over the years. But *Plessy* v. *Ferguson* could not, despite its erosion, be laid to rest until it was directly and explicitly repudiated by the Court in *Brown* v. *Board of Education*, 347 U.S. 483 (1954). Such repudiation, to be effective and decisive, must be on the highest ground, so appealing to the enduring principles of the regime as to engage the respect of all thoughtful citizens. See chap. 2, n. 28, above. It would be fitting if, in a case involving congressional abridgment of freedom of speech, Justice Black could be permitted to cap his career as the modern judicial champion of the First Amendment with an opinion for a unanimous court repudiating *Schenck* and its progeny: *Schenck* has now had *its* half century of mischief. See chap. 7, n. 72, below. See, also, chap. 3, n. 22, chap. 7, n. 69, below.

15. See the chapter, "Clear and Present Danger," in Alexander Meiklejohn, *Political Freedom: The Constitutional Powers of the People* (New York: Harper & Bros., 1960), p. 29; also, Kalven, *Negro and First Amendment*, pp. 12-13.

Is the "clear and present danger" test drawn from the common law notion of "attempt or solicitation"? Is it drawn, that is, from situations where the enterprise is clearly criminal, or at least never privileged? See Chafee, *Freedom of Speech*, pp. 165, 173; Yosal Rogat, "The Judge as Spectator," *U. Chicago L. Rev.* 31 (1964): 213; Martin Shapiro, *Freedom of Speech: The Supreme Court and Judicial Review* (Englewood Cliffs, N.J.: Prentice-Hall, 1966), pp. 55-57; also, chap. 5, n. 121, below.

Cf. Justice Holmes (dissenting), *Hammer* v. *Dagenhart*, 247 U.S. 251, 280 (1918): "But I had thought that the propriety of the exercise of a power admitted to exist in some cases was for the consideration of Congress alone and that this Court always had disavowed the right to intrude its judgment upon questions of policy or morals." See, also, Justice Gibson, *Eakin* v. *Raub*, 12 Sergeant and Rawle (Pa. Sup. Ct.) 330, 352 (1825): "The power is said to be restricted to cases that are free from doubt or difficulty. But the abstract existence of a power cannot depend on the clearness or obscurity of the case in which it is to be exercised. . . ."

CHAPTER THREE, NOTES 16-17: PAGE 45　　　　　　　　　　　　　　　445

Another passage from Justice Holmes (dissenting, *Northern Securities Co. v. U.S.*, 193 U.S. 197, 402-3 [1904]) suggests a different kind of argument against the "clear and present danger" test:

> I assume, for the purposes of discussion, although it would be a great and serious step to take, that in some case that seemed to it to need heroic measures, Congress might regulate not only commerce, but instruments of commerce or contracts the bearing of which upon commerce would be only indirect. But it is clear that the mere fact of an indirect effect upon commerce not shown to be certain and very great, would not justify such a law. . . . Commerce depends upon population, but Congress could not, on that ground, undertake to regulate marriage and divorce. If the act before us is to be carried out according to what seems to me the logic of the argument for the Government, which I do not believe that it will be, I can see no part of the conduct of life with which on similar principles Congress might not interfere.

See Woodrow Wilson, *Political Thought of Woodrow Wilson*, ed. E. D. Cronon (Indianapolis: Bobbs-Merrill, 1965), p. 133.

16. Language reflects and at the same time makes possible the reason of man: grace of language suggests a high level of reasoning. Thus, Hobbes notices, "Eloquence is power, because it is seeming prudence." *Leviathan*, 1:10; see, also, ibid., 1:4 (on *logos*).

The man who writes well gives the impression that he has hold of the truth. But see, in chap. 8, sec. 16, above, Justice Holmes's reservations about truth. (Francis Biddle has referred to Justice Holmes as "a great man whom little men are trying to pull down." *Justice Holmes, Natural Law, and the Supreme Court* [New York: Macmillan Co., 1961], p. 31.)

Chafee warned us, "A rule is not desirable simply because it reads well. It must also work well." *Freedom of Speech*, p. 66. See chap. 4, n. 60, below, on the rhetoric of President Wilson.

Justice Holmes's rhetorical flourish has become a cliché in our language. Thus, e.g., one finds in Title V, sec. 501, of the Armed Services Procurement Authorization Bill (H.R. 17123), enacted September 29, 1970, the following observation (*Congressional Record* 116: H9344 [Sept. 29, 1970]; italics added):

> The Congress views with grave concern the deepening involvement of the United States in the Middle East and the *clear and present danger* to world peace resulting from such involvement which cannot be ignored by the United States.

See, also, the use of Justice Holmes's phrase in the Anti-Riot Act of 1968, chap. 6, n. 75, below.

17. See Herman Melville, *Moby Dick* (New York: Random House, Modern Library, 1926), pp. 411-12:

> . . . Stubb then in a plain, business-like, but still half humorous manner, cursed [the Negro boy] Pip officially [for having jumped out of the whale-boat]; and that done, unofficially gave him much wholesome advice. The substance was, Never jump from a boat, Pip, except—but all the rest was indefinite, as the soundest advice ever is. Now, in general, *Stick to the boat*, is your true motto in whaling; but cases will sometimes happen when *Leap from the boat*, is still better. Moreover, as if perceiving at last that if he should give undiluted conscientious advice to Pip, he would be leaving him too wide a margin to jump in for the future; Stubb suddenly dropped all advice, and concluded with a peremptory command "Stick to the boat, Pip, or by the Lord, I won't pick you up if you jump; mind that. We can't afford to lose whales by the likes of you; a whale would sell for thirty times what you would, Pip, in Alabama."

Cf., ibid., pp. 412-13. See, also, Melville, *Billy Budd* (New York: Holt, Rinehart & Cox, 1950), pp. 356-57, 371.

See chap. 5, n. 75, below.

18. The 1940 Smith Act provisions (54 Stat. 670, 671, ch. 439, 18 U.S.C. [1946 ed.] secs. 10, 11 [see present 18 U.S.C. sec. 2385]) that are referred to in this study (see chap. 7, n. 47, below) are set forth here as found in *Dennis* v. *U.S.*, 341 U.S. 494 (1951):

> Section 2.
> (a) It shall be unlawful for any person—
> (1) to knowingly or willfully advocate, abet, advise, or teach the duty, necessity, desirability, or propriety of overthrowing or destroying any government in the United States by force or violence, or by the assassination of any officer of such government;
> (2) with the intent to cause the overthrow or destruction of any government in the United States, to print, publish, edit, issue, circulate, sell, distribute, or publicly display any written or printed matter advocating, advising, or teaching the duty, necessity, desirability, or propriety of overthrowing or destroying any government in the United States by force or violence;
> (3) to organize or help to organize any society, group, or assembly of persons who teach, advocate, or encourage the overthrow or destruction of any government in the United States by force or violence; or to be or become a member of, or affiliate with, any such society, group or assembly of persons, knowing the purposes thereof.
> (b) For the purposes of this section, the term "government in the United States" means the Government of the United States, the government of any State, Territory, or possession of the United States, the government of the District of Columbia, or the government of any political subdivision of any of them.
> Section 3. It shall be unlawful for any person to attempt to commit, or to conspire to commit, any of the acts prohibited by the provisions of . . . this title.

See chap. 6, n. 75, below, for the Anti-Riot Act of 1968.

19. *U.S.* v. *Dennis*, 183 F.2d 201, 212 (C.A. 2, Aug. 1, 1950). This statement was adopted by Chief Justice Vinson, writing the leading opinion in *Dennis* v. *U.S.*, 341 U.S. 494, 510 (1951).

The resemblance between the "clear and present danger" test and the now more fashionable "balancing" test is evident in the passage quoted from Judge Hand's opinion. Cf. Shapiro, *Freedom of Speech: The Supreme Court and Judicial Review*, pp. 46, 48, 76-77, 79-80, 81, 103, 105 (n. 1), 123. (See, for an apt repudiation of the "balancing" test, note 20 of Chief Justice Warren's Opinion for the Court in *U.S.* v. *Robel*, 389 U.S. 258 [1967].) See Frank R. Strong, "Fifty Years of 'Clear and Present Danger': From *Schenck* to *Brandenburg*—and Beyond," *Supreme Court Review* 1969: 41, 56-57. See, also, pp. 374-75, above, chap. 8, n. 173, below.

It is instructive to recall that Zechariah Chafee dedicated his 1920 book, *Freedom of Speech*, "To LEARNED HAND United States District Judge for the Southern District of New York who during the turmoil of war courageously maintained the tradition of English-speaking freedom and gave it new clearness and strength for the wiser years to come." Even the better men, it would seem, need the reminder and support provided by firm constitutional principles: Judge Hand's retreat is intimately related to Justice Holmes's earlier concession. The tradition had been cut out from under the judge by the justice. Cf. Chafee, p. 93; also, chap. 3, n. 28, below.

Does Judge Hand's use of quotations for "evil" suggest that with respect to that also there are no absolutes?

20. "Language" is vital to this portion of the charge (Transcript, p. 16,056), which is quoted and approved in *Dennis* v. *U.S.*, 341 U.S. 494, 511-12 (1951).

Was not Walter Berns substantially correct when he observed that "the Smith Act declares mere advocacy illegal; in effect, Congress has officially declared a permanent state of clear and present danger"? Walter Berns, *Freedom, Virtue and the First Amendment* (Baton Rouge: Louisiana State University Press, 1957), p. 204.

What Berns's "mere advocacy" refers to can be seen by a study of the instructions of the trial court to the jury in another Smith Act prosecution (reproduced in *Yates* v. *U.S.*, 354 U.S. 298, 313-15 [1957], which was an appeal from conviction under sections 2(a)(1) and (3) of the Smith Act). The trial court had charged the jury:

> As used in the Smith Act and the indictment:
> (1) the word "advocate" means to urge or "to plead in favor of; . . . to support, vindicate, or recommend publicly. . . .";
> (2) the word "teach" means "to instruct . . . show how . . . to guide the studies of; . . ."
>
> The holding of a belief or opinion does not constitute advocacy or teaching. Hence the Smith Act does not prohibit persons who may believe that the violent overthrow and destruction of the Government of the United States is probable or inevitable from expressing that belief. Whether such belief be reasonable or unreasonable is immaterial. Prediction or prophecy is not advocacy.
>
> Any advocacy or teaching which does not include the urging of force and violence as the means of overturning and destroying the Government of the United States is not within the issue of the indictment here and can constitute no basis for any finding against the defendants.
>
> . . . The defendants, in common with other persons living under our Constitution, have the right protected by the First Amendment to criticize our system of Government and the Government itself, even though the speaking or writing of such criticism may undermine confidence in the Government or cause or increase discontent. They have the right also to criticize the foreign policy of the United States and the role being played by this country in international affairs; and to praise the foreign policy of other governments and the role being played by those governments in international affairs.
>
> The right of the defendants to enjoy such freedom of expression is unaffected by whether or not the opinions spoken or published may seem to you to be crudely intemperate, or to contain falsehoods, or to be designed to embarrass the Government. No inference of conspiracy to advocate and teach the necessity and duty of overthrow and destruction of the Government of the United States by force and violence, or of intent to cause or bring about the overthrow and destruction of the Government of the United States by force and violence as speedily as circumstances would permit, may be drawn from such expressions alone.

Thus juries, who were told about (or already knew of?) the unpopular sentiments of Communist defendants, were instructed that they should not permit such sentiments to arouse them against defendants. (I recall from my own bar admission hearings how hazardous it was to remind respectable Chicago lawyers in 1951 and even in 1958 that the principle of rightful rebellion had been endorsed by Americans long before the Communist party had been heard of. It was evident that these men had, despite their experience and intelligence, simply lost control of themselves: they were like children torn between fright and vindictiveness. How can a jury be expected to be any more sensible in such circumstances? See p. 418, above.)

It should be evident, no matter what courts say, that the Smith Act defendants were convicted because they were thought to hold the beliefs and opinions they (as Communists) were supposed to hold. I do not recall learning from the press of a single instance of an acquittal (as a result of the jury's finding) of any Communist defendant since *Dennis*: for some reason, the proportion of convictions secured by the general government (on cases that went to the jury) were, if not the 100 percent one gathered from the press, remarkably higher than that secured in any other class of cases the government prosecutes. ("Criminal trials, no matter how efficient the police are, are not sure bets for the prosecution, nor should they be if the evidence is not forthcoming. Under the present law, the prosecution fails to prove its case in about thirty percent of the criminal cases actually tried in the federal courts." Justice White, dissenting, *Miranda* v. *Arizona*, 384 U.S. 436, 541-42 [1966].) Is not the reason for the vulnerability of the unpopular defendant that anticipated by Albert Gallatin in his comments in the Fifth Congress (chap. 7, n. 64, below) about "political crimes" and the futility of reliance upon "the purity of our courts and juries" in such cases? (Indeed, is not a "political crime" one which has just the features of the Smith Act prosecutions? Do we really want to imprison men who are as easy as this to identify, arrest, prosecute, and convict? That is, should we not suspect that such a crime may not be like all other crimes? This is a question which, I am afraid, will again seem more relevant some day than it may seem now. [I have stressed the press accounts of the rate of conviction of Communist defendants, since those accounts both established and reflected the tone in the country at large in the 1950s. Cf. chap. 7, nn. 72, 76, below. See Appendix D, above.] One reason why I do not foresee an immediate return to the degree of *general* repression [such as it was] of the 1950s is that even those whom one would expect to be most repressive seem to be alert to that danger today. Thus, a congressional candidate from Wisconsin on the American Party ticket can say about "the revolutionary youth movement," "My greatest fear is that due to this seditious movement, the people of the country will become alarmed, and will call for extreme repressive controls by the government, and this could lead to a police state, which in turn becomes a fascist totalitarian government." *Milwaukee Sentinel*, Sept. 2, 1970, pt. 3, p. 6. [Consider, also, the significance of the fact that a "conservative" Republican such as Senator Barry Goldwater could accuse the press and opponents of Judge G. Harrold Carswell of "neo-McCarthyism" because they ignored testimonials to Carswell's fairness as a judge. *Chicago Sun-Times*, Apr. 3, 1970, p. 20.] See, also, chap. 2, n. 22, above; chap. 8, n. 52, below.)

Whether the Supreme Court subsequently confirmed the convictions of Communists seemed to depend primarily on considerations other than the dictates of constitutional law. When a reversal seemed (for whatever reason) to be desired, the Court could find something on which to base its decision: it may even pretend (as Justice Harlan did in *Yates*) that it makes a difference *in such cases as these* precisely what *is* said to the jury (354 U.S., at 313-18, 320):

> After telling the jury that it could not convict the defendants for holding or expressing mere opinions, beliefs, or predictions relating to violent overthrow, the trial court defined the content of the proscribed advocacy or teaching in the following terms, which are crucial here:
>
> "Any advocacy or teaching which does not include the urging of force and violence as the means of overthrowing and destroying the Government of the United States is not within the issue of the indictment here and can constitute no basis for any finding against the defendants.
>
> "The kind of advocacy and teaching which is charged and upon which your verdict must be reached is not merely a desirability but a necessity that the Government of the United States be overthrown and destroyed by force and violence and not merely a propriety but a duty to overthrow and destroy the Government of the United States by force and violence."
>
> There can be no doubt from the record that in so instructing the jury the [trial] court regarded as immaterial, and intended to withdraw from the jury's consideration, any issue as to the character of the advocacy in terms of its capacity to stir listeners to forcible action. Both the petitioners and the Government submitted proposed instructions which would have required the jury to find that the proscribed advocacy was not of a mere abstract doctrine of forcible overthrow, but of action to that end, by the use of language reasonably and ordinarily calculated to incite persons to such action. The trial court rejected these proposed instructions on the ground that any necessity for giving them which may have existed at the time the *Dennis* case was tried was removed by this Court's subsequent decision in that case. The court made it clear in colloquy with counsel that in its view the illegal advocacy was made out simply by showing that what was said dealt with forcible overthrow and that it was uttered with a specific intent to accomplish that purpose, insisting that all such advocacy was punishable "whether it is in language of incitement or not." . . .
>
> We are thus faced with the question whether the Smith Act prohibits advocacy and teaching of forcible overthrow as an abstract principle, divorced from any effort to instigate action to that end, so long as such advocacy or teaching is engaged in with evil intent. We hold that it does not. . . .

CHAPTER THREE, NOTE 20: PAGE 45   449

> The Government's reliance on this Court's decision in *Dennis* is misplaced. The jury instructions which were refused here were given there, and were referred to by this Court [in *Dennis*] as requiring "the jury to find the facts *essential* to establish the substantive crime." . . . It is true that at one point in the late Chief Justice's opinion it is stated that the Smith Act "is directed at advocacy, not discussion," . . . but it is clear that the reference was to advocacy of action, not ideas, for in the very next sentence the opinion emphasizes that the jury was properly instructed that there could be no conviction for "advocacy in the realm of ideas." The two concurring opinions in that case likewise emphasize the distinction with which we are concerned. . . .

The *Dennis* instructions referred to by Justice Harlan are those set forth in the text to which this note is keyed. Justice Clark's dissenting opinion in *Yates* includes these irreverent sentiments (354 U.S., at 349-50):

> . . . I have studied the section of the opinion concerning the instructions and frankly its "artillery of words" leaves me confused as to why the majority concludes that the charge as given was insufficient. . . . Apparently what disturbs the Court now is that the trial judge here did not give the *Dennis* charge although both the prosecution and the defense asked that it be given. Since he refused to grant these requests I suppose the majority feels that there must be some difference between the two charges, else the one that was given in *Dennis* would have been followed here. While there may be some distinction between the charges, as I view them they are without material difference. I find, as the majority intimates, that the distinctions are too "subtle and difficult to grasp."
> However, in view of the fact that the case must be retried, regardless of the disposition made here on the charges, I see no reason to engage in what becomes nothing more than an exercise in semantics with the majority about this phase of the case. Certainly if I had been sitting at the trial I would have given the *Dennis* charge, not because I consider it any more correct, but simply because it had the stamp of approval of this Court. Perhaps this approach is too practical. But I am sure the trial judge realizes now that practicality often pays.

Even more practical, I argue in this book, would be to take such cases away from the jury altogether by treating the Smith Act as unconstitutional. Otherwise we will continue to have constitutional rationalizations which, as the puzzled Justice Clark indicated, cannot make sense to the American people. (See, for further discussion of *Yates*, chap. 7, n. 72, below, and of the relation of trial by jury to freedom of speech, chap. 8, secs. 6, 8, 9. Cf. chap. 6, nn. 30, 31, chap. 7, n. 77, below.)

But, citizens of Justice Clark's turn of mind might ask, how long is the government obliged to wait before it acts against a suspected political conspiracy? (See Transcript of Record, *Dennis* v. *U.S.*, pp. 213-16, 4392, 4394. See, also, Earl Browder's letter, reproduced in chap. 7, n. 46, below.) Should not the government (in so delicate a matter as this) wait until it has evidence of more than such words which, without action, would not be in themselves illegal? It seems to be conceded in opinions upholding the convictions of Communist party leaders that if we could be sure that nothing more were to happen than what had already happened, there would be no reason to prosecute. But, it is said, the Communist *will* do more when he can do so and get away with it. It is conceded that this may be a long time from now. Thus, the language, "as speedily as circumstances would permit," means essentially that evident bad intention or even bad character is penalized. (See Montesquieu, *Spirit of the Laws*, 12:5; chap. 6, n. 33, below.) But even a prosecution for treason requires overt acts. See chap. 5, n. 119, below. See, also, chap. 5, n. 118, below. (In the "Chicago Conspiracy Trial" one important question was whether the defendants were being held accountable, because of their words and "life styles," for the misdeeds in August, 1968, of Chicago officials and police: that is, there was no question that *someone* had misbehaved. See, also, chap. 8, n. 83, below.

See, on the secret desires of most men (which would be acted upon "as speedily as circumstances would permit"), Plato, *Republic* 359B, 360E, 619C-D. See, also, Lincoln on *habeas corpus*, chap. 4, n. 59, below.

See, for a brief discussion of the Communist party and the Smith Act prosecutions, my review of Jaffa, *Equality and Liberty*, in N.Y.U. L. Rev. 41 (1966): 664. See, also, chap. 5, n. 66, chap. 7, sec. 5, chap. 7, n. 124, below. Cf. chap. 9, n. 7, below. A popular polemic offering important (even though qualified) support of the Smith Act prosecutions of the Communist party was Sidney Hook's *Heresy, Yes—Conspiracy, No!* (New York: John Day Co., 1953). A salutary response is found in Edmund Burke's "Speech on Moving His Resolutions for Conciliation with the Colonies": "And I would, sir, recommend to your serious consideration, whether it be prudent to form a rule for punishing people, not on their own acts, but on your conjectures? Surely it is preposterous at the very best. It is not justifying your anger, by their misconduct; but it is converting your ill-will into their delinquency." Edmund Burke, *Works*, World Classics (London: Oxford University Press, 1930), 2:205. See chap. 5, n. 149, chap. 8, n. 105, below.

21. *Whitney* v. *California*, 274 U.S. 357, 376-77 (1927) (concurring opinion) (see chap. 7, n. 69, below). "That the necessity which is essential to a valid restriction does not exist unless speech would produce, or is intended to produce, a clear and imminent danger of some substantive evil which the state may constitutionally seek to prevent has been settled [citing *Schenck*]." *Whitney*, 274 U.S., at 373. What "clear and imminent" meant for him is suggested by the passage, "If there be time to expose through discussion the falsehood and fallacies, to avert the evil by the processes of education, the remedy to be applied is more speech, not enforced silence. Only an emergency can justify repression. . . . It is therefore always open to Americans to challenge a law abridging free speech and assembly by showing that there was no emergency justifying it." Ibid., at 377. See chap. 8, n. 172, below. (See chap. 6, n. 69, below, for the effect on *Whitney* of Brandenburg v. Ohio, 395 U.S. 444 [1969].)

This Brandeis test is implicitly endorsed and applied by Justice Douglas, in his dissent in the *Dennis* case:

> Communism in the world scene is no bogeyman; but Communism as a political faction or party in this country plainly is. Communism has been so thoroughly exposed in this country that it has been crippled as a political force. Free speech has destroyed it as an effective political party. It is inconceivable that those who went up and down this country preaching the doctrine of revolution which petitioners espouse would have any success. [341 U.S., at 588]

It should be noted, however, that even the Brandeis formulation in *Whitney*, insofar as it bears on congressional legislation (as distinguished from state legislation), is without foundation in the First Amendment. (Compare, in Appendix E, p. 327, above, my adaptation of the Brandeis formula to academic circumstances.)

22. Montesquieu, *Spirit of the Laws*, 18:22. The comparison of Christianity and communism does not, of course, originate with me. See, e.g., Judge Hand, *U.S.* v. *Dennis*, 183 F.2d 201, 212 (1950):

> The American Communist Party, of which the defendants are the controlling spirits, is a highly articulated, well contrived, far spread organization, numbering thousands of adherents, rigidly and ruthlessly disciplined, many of whom are infused with a passionate Utopian faith that is to redeem mankind. It has its Founder, its apostles, its sacred texts—perhaps even its martyrs. It seeks converts far and wide by an extensive system of schooling, demanding of all an inflexible doctrinal orthodoxy. The violent capture of all existing governments is one article of the creed of that faith, which abjures the possibility of success by lawful means. . . .

See, also, ibid., at 234 ("the only gospel which will redeem this sad Planet").

What does "capture of all existing governments" mean? I doubt that the Communist party could hold for one week any government in the United States even if its "thousands of adherents" were elevated overnight to high government posts (if, to use an absurd hy-

CHAPTER THREE, NOTE 22: PAGE 46   451

pothesis [since I can see at this time no prospect of peacetime success by the Communist party in this country], the elevation came about because of momentary physical paralysis of all noncommunist Americans, who continued to hold the opinions about communism they now have). See Machiavelli, *The Prince*, chap. 5; also, chap. 3 (". . . Upon the Cardinal of Rouen telling me that the Italians had no understanding of war, I answered that the French had no understanding of politics . . ."). See chap. 7, n. 124, chap. 8, nn. 9, 169, below.

The *Schenck* document, a circular printed on two sides, was published in about fifteen thousand copies and partially distributed in August, 1917. The defendants—the general secretary and recording secretary of the Socialist party of Philadelphia—were convicted after a two-day trial and sentenced, respectively, to six and three months in jail.

The circulars were evidently distributed, for the most part, to members of the armed services or to men about to be inducted. I suspect that if the distribution had been made to these men *and* to many others—that is, to the public at large (e.g., in a full-page advertisement in the *New York Times* [see chap. 8, n. 108, below])—the offense would have been far less obvious. But defendants were running a shoestring operation. Even so, it is difficult to find anything objectionable in the language of the circular: citizens were called upon to assert their rights; a change in the draft law (the constitutionality of which was still in doubt at the time) was demanded. And yet Justice Holmes found here a "clear and present danger." See chap. 8, n. 172, below. Cf. chap. 6, n. 9, below.

My appraisal of that circular (which is reproduced with the *Schenck* indictment, in Appendix B [see chap. 3, n. 28, below]) is substantially confirmed even by Chief Justice Vinson (in the leading opinion upholding the conviction of the Communist leaders in the *Dennis* case), who observed, "This insubstantial gesture toward insubordination in 1917 during war was held to be a clear and present danger of bringing about the evil of military insubordination." 341 U.S. 494, 504 (1951). (See Thomas I. Emerson, "Toward a General Theory of the First Amendment," *Yale L. J.* 72 [1963]: 877, 891, esp. n. 17.)

We need not wait thirty years to dismiss, in a similar manner, the rulings of the courts of the United States which have sent Communists to jail. Unfortunately, however, we have already suffered both at home and abroad the repercussions of this political folly. See chap. 8, n. 169, below. Perhaps we have, at least for awhile, gotten the worst of it "out of our system": the lack of any serious "anti-Red" campaign after the assassination of President Kennedy (evidently by a professed Marxist) makes me hope so. See chap. 8, n. 135, below. Compare the reprisals following upon the assassination of President McKinley, Chafee, *Freedom of Speech*, p. 230. (But it is naïve to believe that certain current exercises of "liberty" will not provoke repressive counterattacks, which will be as "principled" and as immoderate as what provoked them. An editorial in the *Door County Advocate* [Sturgeon Bay, Wis.], Sept. 1, 1970, p. 4, has warned:

> If the rioters and bomb throwers think they are suffering under a repressive police state now they ain't see nuttin' yet if they continue their bloody course. . . . It is going to get harder and harder to stay cool in the face of this small, hard core of deluded but dangerous anarchists. . . . If citizens are alert and will unite for law the criminals will not be able to operate. If they are not, vigilante groups like the Minutemen will take the law into their own hands and a bad situation could become far worse.

One remarkable feature of the "Chicago Conspiracy Trial" [Appendix D, above] is that the defendants were as successful as they were, in court and out. See chap. 3, n. 35, below.) Compare, also, the panicky response in October, 1970, of the Canadian government to the kidnappings of two public officials. See chap. 3, n. 28, chap. 7, n. 73, chap. 9, n. 1, below. Cf. chap. 7, n. 123, below. See, also, *Congressional Record* 116:11057.

The single-mindedness of frightened, or angry, people may be seen in the assessment of a candidate for superintendent of public instruction by the *Chicago Tribune*, Oct. 21, 1970, p. 20: the editorial complains that although the candidate "takes a hard line" toward campus rioters, "he talks about finding 'root causes,' which seems to soften his stand"! See chap. 7, n. 113, below. Among the "root causes" for the alleged breakdown in law and order may be the plausible opinion among significant minorities, on campus and off, that the conventional advocates of law and order are rather partisan about the existing laws they do not insist upon seeing enforced, including laws (among which is the Constitution) relating to the declaration of war, to racial discrimination, to the community effects of the uses of private property, to the duties of landlords, and to the behavior of the police. In a sense, virtually everyone in this country is for "law and order, properly defined." Consider, for example, the following excerpts from the passionate speeches made by Adam Walinsky as a candidate for attorney general of New York (*Chicago Sun-Times*, Oct. 23, 1970, p. 30):

> There is no law in this country for a lot of people. You talk about narcotics, and tough laws against them. To talk about a life sentence for a 12-year-old pusher just isn't in the same universe. I know where law and order starts when we're talking about the drug traffic. The center of the drug traffic is in the corruption in the New York City police department. That's what paralyzes you. . . . Laws are being violated on construction sites all over this state today. Not just laws against discrimination, either. . . . Look at job safety. There were 140 fatal industrial accidents last year, and a report by the state agency responsible found that 58 of them were because of violations of the law. But there were never any prosecutions. . . . Pollution. There's pollution inside factories, dust inhalation, metal dust, all of it in violation of the law. . . . By God, we're going to have one system of law and one system of justice—white and black— or we aren't going to have a system that works for anyone. It's about time for some real law and order in this society, law and order that really means justice.

Consider, on the other hand, the endorsement by the *Chicago Tribune* (Oct. 24, 1970, p. 12) of the conclusion reached in a *New York Times* article by Professor Sidney Hook (chap. 8, n. 105, below),

> that the main root of student violence is not objective social and political conditions, which are always less than perfect, but rather "the mistaken ideas and ideological myths of militant extremists and their faculty allies." . . . We particularly commend Hook's criticism of excusing bomb throwers and arsonists as almost inevitably motivated by revulsion against some of the evils of this world. As he well says, campus terrorists are no more entitled to be excused as socially conditioned than are lynchers and red-necked bigots whose violence does not appeal to the New Left. People are responsible for what they do, Hook rightly contends. . . .

See Sidney Hook, "The Survival of the Free University," *Humanist*, Sept.-Oct. 1970, p. 26. See, also, chap. 7, nn. 42, 67, below. For still another juxtaposition of the voices of passion and reason (of which one can hear echoes on campus), we have the sentiments of an unemployed Montreal painter with respect to the "less than perfect" "social and political conditions" in his city (Tom Fitzpatrick, "Montreal Glum on Eve of Vote," *Chicago Sun-Times*, Oct. 25, 1970, p. 5):

> . . . Because he is French and without an education he is in the same position as a black man in Chicago. . . . [He] has thought about the Front for the Liberation of Quebec. He does not necessarily view its members as terrorists, however. Black people in Chicago are not so vehement about the Black Panthers, either. "I don't believe in kidnaping and murder," this gray-haired man in unpressed clothes says. "But now one man is killed and the whole country is in an uproar. People in our district die all the time because of poor health, poor food, poor housing and no doctors. But what has anyone done about that? They won't spend a cent to keep us from dying." If you go to a place in this rundown area called St. Jacques Clinic on St. Christopher, a volunteer medical agency, you can see a placard that shows how deeply the city's alienated French-speaking people feel. The sign declares, for all to see, that Mayor Jean Drapeau and the

CHAPTER THREE, NOTE 23: PAGE 46   453

Ottawa government allocated millions to subsidize Expo 67 and the Montreal Expos baseball team and the International Olympics. While spending all this money, it is said, not one cent has been made available to the clinic to supply free vaccines for children.

In any event, *Schenck* remains the classic model of how the First Amendment and other constitutional guarantees may be subverted (by the "Right" or by the "Left," by the "reasonable" or by the "passionate") in the name of "law and order," or for the sake of justice, or "under color of law." See chap. 3, n. 14, above. See, also, chap. 2, n. 31, above. The *Schenck* circular should be reassessed from time to time by the American constitutionalist, if only to remind himself of how we *can* go wrong. (What the circular said about the Wilson administration, after the election campaign of 1916, was said by critics about the Johnson administration after the campaign of 1964. Many of the arguments made in the circular against American intervention in the European war had been made by President Wilson himself less than a year before, just as some of President Johnson's public evaluations in 1964 about American intervention in Vietnam were adopted by critics of his subsequent policies. Is it not virtually certain, by the way, that many men *in* the army had far worse things to say about the draft than were said in the *Schenck* circular and that they said these things to prospective soldiers?)

See, for other leaflets assessed by Justice Holmes, chap. 3, n. 28, below. See, also, chap. 8, n. 83, below.

23. 341 U.S. 494, 521 (1951). Three admissions of congressional abridgment of freedom of speech should suffice to indicate how courts regard these matters:

"To the end that war may not result in defeat, freedom of speech may, by act of Congress, be curtailed or denied so that the morale of the people and the spirit of the army may not be broken by seditious utterances; freedom of the press curtailed to preserve our military plans and movements from the knowledge of the enemy. . . ." *U.S.* v. *Macintosh*, 283 U.S. 605, 622-23 (1931). Crosskey, *Politics and the Constitution*, p. 512, quotes this passage with approval, as well as one preceding it, "From its very nature, *the* war power, when necessity calls for its exercise, tolerates no qualifications or limitations, unless found in the Constitution or in applicable principles of international law." But is not the First Amendment one of those "qualifications or limitations" upon "the war power"? (I show elsewhere in this book that what Congress may not do by legislation may still be done, especially if defeat in war is to be avoided, by legitimate constitutional means. If Crosskey had been as interested in the subject of this book as he was in the commerce power of the United States, he would have noticed that the *Macintosh* opinion in effect argued that one part of the Constitution could be disregarded in applying another part. See chap. 5, n. 88, chap. 8, n. 83, below.) Cf. chap. 5, n. 83, above.

What I have said about *Macintosh* may also be said about *Abrams* v. *U.S.*, 250 U.S. 616 (1919); see chap. 3, n. 28, below. Even the dissenting opinion of Justice Holmes exhibits the assumption that the First Amendment may on occasion be disregarded by Congress in its legislative capacity: "Only the emergency that makes it immediately dangerous to leave the correction of evil counsels to time warrants making any exception to the sweeping command, 'Congress shall make no law . . . abridging the freedom of speech.'" 250 U.S., at 630-31. (See chap. 3, n. 21, above.)

I return to Justice Frankfurter for my third illustration, to his description (in *Dennis*, 341 U.S., at 532) of *American Communications Assn.* v. *Douds*, 339 U.S. 382 (1950) as recognizing

> that the exercise of political rights protected by the First Amendment was necessarily discouraged by the requirement of the Taft-Hartley Act that officers of unions employing the services of the National Labor Relations Board sign affidavits that they are not Communists. But we held that the statute was not for this reason presumptively invalid. The problem, we said, was "one of weighing the probable effects of the statute upon the free exercise of the right of speech and assembly against the congressional determination that political strikes are evils of conduct which cause substantial harm to interstate commerce. . . ."

(*Douds* has been identified as "the first major opinion on Cold War-inspired legislation. . . ." Shapiro, *Freedom of Speech: The Supreme Court and Judicial Review*, p. 62. See, also, the dissenting opinion of Chief Justice Stone in *Schneiderman* v. *U.S.*, 320 U.S. 118, 170 [1943]. See chap. 3, n. 34, chap. 7, n. 72, below. See, also, chap. 7, n. 41, chap. 8, n. 126, below.)

24. Cf. Chafee, *Freedom of Speech*, p. 7:

> At the outset, we can reject two extreme views in the controversy. First, there is the view that the Bill of Rights is a peace-time document and consequently freedom of speech may be ignored in war. This view has been officially repudiated. [See chap. 3, n. 5, above.] At the opposite pole is the belief of many agitators that the First Amendment renders unconstitutional any Act of Congress without exception "abridging the freedom of speech, or of the press," that all speech is free, and only action can be restrained and punished. This view is equally untenable. The provisions of the Bill of Rights can not be applied with absolute literalness, but are subject to exceptions.

See the text at chap. 3, n. 12, above.

25. See, for a criticism of the idea of "absolutes" in constitutional law, Erwin N. Griswold, "Absolute Is in the Dark: A Discussion of the Approach of the Supreme Court to Constitutional Questions," *Utah L. Rev.* 8 (1963): 167. (Cf. chap. 3, n. 9, above.) The analysis at p. 177 of Griswold's article is of a situation that resembles one that had on Martin Buber an effect markedly different from that which Griswold supposed. (The Buber reaction is reported in Maurice Friedman, "Christianity and the Contemporary Jew," in *Rediscovering Judaism*, ed. A. J. Wolf [Chicago: Quadrangle Books, 1965], p. 211.) Another scholar has spoken of the "absolute command of the two religious clauses" of the First Amendment. Philip B. Kurland, *Religion and the Law of Church and State and the Supreme Court* (Chicago: Aldine Publishing Co., 1962), p. 105. Still another set of "absolutes" may be found in the "diplomatic privileges and immunities" discussed in John R. Wood and Jean Serres, *Diplomatic Ceremonial and Protocol: Principles, Procedures and Practices* (New York: Columbia University Press, 1970), p. 46.

I add my opinion that it is impossible to talk seriously about any subject if there are no "absolutes" involved somewhere. (See chap. 9, n. 3, below.) Thus, critics of "absolutes" either unknowingly regard constitutional law as not serious or leave their absolutes underground and hence unexamined. (See chap. 2, n. 39, above.) There is touched upon here the problem of truth discussed in chap. 8, sec. 16, below. (Professor Paul A. Freund has been quoted [in Charles S. Desmond *et al.*, *Mr. Justice Jackson* (New York: Columbia University Press, 1969), p. 33], ". . . There are, I am afraid, no absolutes in law or art except intelligence." Is intelligence itself gauged by an "absolute"? If it is, then something in addition to intelligence is or reflects an absolute. If it is not, then intelligence is nothing but mere opinion—or it is an absolute of which we are immediately aware, in and of itself, without reference to anything else. But if we can be thus aware of one absolute, why not of others? Do other absolutes exist of which we are also aware? Freund himself, in the passage quoted from, invokes absolutist-sounding things of which he, at least, seems aware, "a measure of *order*" and "a *proper* tension." [Italics added.] The really interesting question, however, may be not whether there are absolutes but why it is so fashionable to insist there absolutely are none, or at best only *one* and it of a "procedural" character. See chap. 4, n. 43, chap. 8, n. 178, below.) Cf. Kurland, *Religion and the Law*, pp. 9-10.

See chap. 5, n. 116, below. Cf. chap. 2, n. 31, above, chap. 5, n. 37, chap. 6, n. 50, chap. 7, n. 77, chap. 8, nn. 177, 193, below. Cf., also, Aristotle's caution about "delusive geometrical accuracy in moral arguments." Burke, *Works*, 2:226-27.

26. See, for Justice Frankfurter's discussion of the protection in Art. III, sec. 1, of the Constitution, of judicial compensation, *O'Malley* v. *Woodrough*, 307 U.S. 277 (1939) (his second footnote is rather nice).

But what if it should be suggested that the meaning of "freedom of speech" itself changes as circumstances change, just as the meaning of "excessive" in the Eighth Amendment ("excessive bail shall not be required") depends on the circumstances of the case? No doubt, that which is excessive bail for a traffic offender might be trivial for a murder suspect, that which is excessive for a resident of long standing might be trivial for a transient offender. If such an approach should be adopted, an approach which implies as part of the meaning of "freedom of speech" the stipulation that the speech involved creates no "urgent and extreme necessity," the problem would remain that of determining just what (if anything) the First Amendment unqualifiedly protects against *congressional* abridgment. (See chap. 8, n. 83, below, on the "abuse" qualification.)

I anticipate my discussion in chapter 7 when I observe that one of the reasons Justice Frankfurter and those of like mind have been so permissive of abridgments of freedom of speech is that they may not (despite their reputations as champions of states' rights) fully appreciate the role of the states in our constitutional system. See chap. 3, n. 12, above.

27. In *Dennis*, Chafee suggested, the Court "cut down the First Amendment to mean about this: 'Congress shall make no law abridging the freedom of speech and of the press unless Congress does make a law abridging the freedom of speech and of the press.'" *Harvard L. Rev. 65* (1951): 1, 50.

"Congress, we are now told," Meiklejohn wrote, "is forbidden to destroy our freedom except when it finds it advisable to do so." *Political Freedom*, p. 30.

28. Chafee said on several occasions that he regarded Justice Holmes's *Schenck* formulation as a contribution to the cause of civil liberties. (See, e.g., the book review cited in chap. 3, n. 13, above. Cf. Chafee, *Freedom of Speech*, p. 93.) I try to show in this book why this is not so, why the position of the "agitators" referred to in chap. 3, n. 24, above, is both safer for the country and closer to the dictates of the Constitution.

Others suggest that the Supreme Court went too far with Justice Holmes's phrase and that its author eventually had to renounce it. See, e.g., John Paul Frank, *Marble Palace: The Supreme Court in American Life* (New York: Knopf, 1958), p. 186. But such an explanation must make of the *Schenck* case circular much more than I (or Chief Justice Vinson) can make of it (see chap. 3, n. 22, above). Chafee reprinted, at pp. 120-23 of his *Freedom of Speech*, the leaflets distributed by the defendants in *Abrams* v. *U.S.*, 250 U.S. 616 (1919). He approved of Justice Holmes's dissent in *Abrams*; but the *Abrams* leaflets can be regarded as more inflammatory than those in *Schenck* (which Chafee did not reprint but which may be found in Appendix B to this book). I realize that circumstances are distinguishable; but it is understandable why the Court could, on the authority of *Schenck*, uphold the conviction in *Abrams*: the constitutional bars were down—and questions only of "wisdom and policy" remained, questions almost foreclosed to a court by the fact that someone in authority had decided to prosecute. See chap. 3, n. 19, above, chap. 8, n. 45, below. (Consider a report from Ottawa in the *Chicago Tribune*, Oct. 20, 1970, p. 2 [chap. 3, n. 22, above, chap. 7, n. 73, below]:

> Parliament today [Oct. 19] gave resounding support to Prime Minister Pierre Trudeau's use of the all-powerful War Measures Act to put down a state of "apprehended" insurrection by the Quebec Liberation Front.... The government had invited a debate and expression of parliamentary approval of the proclamation of the act [on Oct. 16], altho no submission to Parliament was required. The government promised before the vote today to introduce a bill by the end of this month to replace the War Measures Act. The measure first was enacted in 1914 by Parliament in a move which was later described as "parliamentary suicide." It enables the cabinet to do anything it deems necessary for the security, peace and order of Canada in time of war, invasion or insurrection, real or apprehended. The mere proclamation of the act by the cabinet is declared to be conclusive evidence that the need for the act exists.

Consider, also, from Montreal, Tom Fitzpatrick, "A Police State Inflicts Wounds That Don't Bleed," *Chicago Sun-Times*, Oct. 22, 1970, p. 8 [see chap. 3, n. 22, above]:

> Trudeau believes he is taking the path that must be followed. But he is building

up a reservoir of hate and resentment that may haunt him the rest of his career. Small things are happening every day that show what a horrible thing a police state can be. . . . It's minor incidents like this, multiplied hundreds of times each day, that are building up this rancor against total government control of everyone's life. They are quickly becoming a silent majority. They are silent, however, only because if they speak, they can be put in jail for 21 days, without charge. . . . But how many people can you jail? And how long can you keep them behind bars without a hearing? As of [Oct. 21st], Quebec provincial police admit that 336 persons have been arrested and are being held without bond and without a hearing. The police have carried out more than 1,700 raids without warrants. This figure is not exaggerated, apparently. It's the number released by the police themselves who are quite proud of the energy they have displayed. But they haven't come close yet to capturing the members of the cell who murdered Mr. [Pierre] Laporte. [James R.] Cross is still a hostage.

Thus, it is likely that the measures employed were not only the ones that the Quebec Liberation Front would have had the Government employ, but they were quite inappropriate for dealing with the most immediate police problem. John Diefenbaker, former Conservative prime minister, registered a protest which bears upon the "states' rights" arguments I make in chap. 7 of this book. He told Parliament that the convoking of the War Measures Act

> puts the civil rights of all Canadians in cold storage. Why should we in the province of Saskatchewan have our rights taken away, our fundamental freedoms, when what is intended to be secured is the safety of the state at the request of the government of Quebec and the mayor of Montreal? [*National Observer*, Oct. 19, 1970, p. 1]

See chap. 4, n. 59, below. [There are, it should be noted, a number of sensible observations about federalism, and hence states' rights, in Pierre Trudeau, *Federalism and the French Canadians* (New York: St. Martin's Press, 1968). But his thought would be essentially hollow if he should be correct in his self-appraisal, "The only constant factor to be found in my thinking over the years has been opposition to accepted opinions." Ibid., p. xix. (To be thus determined is, essentially, to be subject to the vagaries of [if only by reacting to] public opinion. See chap. 8, sec. 16, above, chap. 4, n. 117, below.) Less negative, in that it implies a positive goal, is his observation, "My political action, or my theory—insomuch as I can be said to have one—can be expressed very simply: create counterweights." Ibid., p. xxiii. Cf. ibid., p. 206.]

One should, in any event, be skeptical about hailing as freedom-minded those opinions which justify defendants' being bundled off to jail. Even Justice Brandeis's brave words in the *Whitney* case (chap. 3, n. 21, above) conclude (because of a flaw in pleading) with an affirmation of the defendant's conviction. See chap. 4, sec. 6, above, chap. 7, nn. 77, 84, below.

29. Indeed, all that the First Amendment may accomplish, under this interpretation, is actually to give Congress power to control speech that Congress might not otherwise have had! That is, Congress is told that it may not suppress speech that is not dangerous or that is not likely at some time or another to become dangerous—and this implies that Congress is empowered to suppress dangerous speech or potentially dangerous speech. See *Federalist* No. 84; also, chap. 6, sec. 2, above, chap. 3, n. 37, chap. 6, n. 63, below.

See, for an attempt to redeem the "clear and present danger" test, Shapiro, *Freedom of Speech: The Supreme Court and Judicial Review*, pp. 123, 125, 169, 171. Absolute prohibitions seem necessary, on the other hand, to counter the tendency even of judges to regard such "fundamental canons" as "freedom of speech and of the press" "to be no more than admonitions of moderation, as appears from the varying and contradictory interpretations that judges themselves find it necessary to put upon them." See Learned Hand, *The Spirit of Liberty*, ed. Irving Dilliard (New York: Knopf, 1953), p. 278.

See chap. 3, n. 17, above; cf. chap. 9, n. 28, below.

30. See, on the pedagogical usefulness of exaggeration, the man writ large in the form of a city. Plato, *Republic* 368D-369A, 402D. See, for "hypothetical rewordings" of the First Amendment, Irving Brant, *The Bill of Rights: Its Origin and Meaning* (Indianapolis: Bobbs-Merrill, 1965), pp. 73, 175, 212, 259.

> [C]onstitutions are not so necessary to regulate the conduct of good rulers as to restrain that of bad ones. —Wise and good men will exercise power so as to promote the public happiness under any form of government. If we are to take it for granted, that those who administer the government under this system [the Constitution], will always pay proper attention to the rights and interests of the people, nothing more was necessary than to say who should be invested with the powers of government and leave them to exercise it at will and pleasure. Men are apt to be deceived both with respect to their own dispositions and those of others. Though this truth is proved by almost every page of the history of nations, to wit, that power, lodged in the hands of rulers to be used at discretion, is almost always exercised to the oppression of the people, and the aggrandizement of themselves; yet most men think if it was lodged in their hands they would not employ it in this manner. . . . Hazael had no idea that he ever should be guilty of such horrid cruelty [as prophesied by Elisha], and said to the prophet, "Is thy servant a dog that he should do this great thing?" Elisha answered, "The Lord hath shewed me that thou shalt be king of Syria." The event proved, that Hazael only wanted an opportunity to perpetuate these enormities without restraint, and he had a disposition to do them, though he himself knew it not. ["Letters of Brutus No. IV," *New York Journal*, Nov. 29, 1787 (The episode drawn upon is recorded in 2 Kings 8:12-13.)]

See chap. 7, n. 78, chap. 8, n. 160, below.

31. "In December [1776], in an awful fright, the Congress made Washington dictator-general for six months with full power to raise troops, collect supplies, and punish disaffected persons; and a short time after the expiration of this period it renewed the high authority, under closer limitations." Charles A. and Mary R. Beard, *The Rise of American Civilization* (New York: Macmillan Co., 1930), p. 251. See, for Virginia's experience in this respect, Jefferson, *Notes on the State of Virginia*, Query XIII. See, also, Jonathan Elliot, *Debates in the Several State Conventions on the Adoption of the Federal Constitution* (Philadelphia: J. B. Lippincott & Co., 1863), 3:227, 4:298.

Winston Churchill wrote of President Roosevelt in 1934,

> . . . Although the Dictatorship is veiled by constitutional forms, it is none the less effective. Great things have been done, and greater attempted. To compare Roosevelt's effort with that of Hitler is to insult not Roosevelt but civilisation. The petty persecutions and old-world assertions of brutality in which the German idol has indulged only show their smallness and squalor compared to the renaissance of creative effort with which the name of Roosevelt will always be associated. [*Great Contemporaries* (London: Odhams Press, 1937), pp. 295-96]

See chap. 4, n. 59, below. See, also, James M. Burns, *Roosevelt: The Soldier of Freedom* (New York: Harcourt Brace Jovanovich, 1970), p. 67. Cf. chap. 8, n. 96, below.

32. "Subjects extol public tranquillity, citizens individual liberty. . . ." Rousseau, *The Social Contract and Discourses* (New York: E. P. Dutton & Co., Everyman Edition, 1950), book 3, chap. 9.

One of the purposes of the analysis of various rights in chapter 8 is to suggest what our unwritten Constitution may include. See chap. 7, n. 77, below.

33. See Blackstone, *Laws of England*, 1:244-45 (see p. 418, above):

> The supposition of *law* therefore is, that neither the king nor either house of parliament, collectively taken, is capable of doing any wrong; since in such cases the law feels itself incapable of furnishing any adequate remedy. For which reason all oppressions which may happen to spring from any branch of the sovereign power, must necessarily be out of the reach of any *stated rule* or *express legal*

provision; but, if ever they unfortunately happen, the prudence of the times must provide new remedies upon new emergencies.

See chap. 7, n. 3, below; cf. chap. 3, n. 4, above, chap. 7, n. 60, chap. 8, n. 18, below.

34. The First Amendment becomes under this interpretation little more than a souvenir of better days, not a shield with which to protect a vital part of the community. I am reminded of an English jurist's sentimental recollection of Justice Jackson, a recollection which is introduced "as a final personal tribute" to him:

> My last memory of Bob is of lunching in his room at the Supreme Court with Felix Frankfurter during the height of the McCarthy horror. There were the four flags from the Nuremberg Court behind Bob's desk with the Hammer and Sickle of the Soviet flag unashamedly exposed. [Desmond et al., Mr. Justice Jackson, p. 136 (Justice Jackson had been the chief American prosecutor at Nuremberg.)]

It would have been naïve for the narrator to suppose that there was ever the slightest risk run by Justice Jackson in displaying such a Soviet flag in his private office. Nor should it be supposed that much, if any, good was done by this display, except perhaps to permit a false sense of sophistication in those who unashamedly ratified judicially the crude but crippling anticommunist measures of that day. The display that *would* have counted as a check upon "the McCarthy horror"—for I assume that would have been more important for the country than a mere reminder of better times at Nuremberg—would have been for Justices Jackson and Frankfurter to vote with the minority in *Douds* and *Dennis*. (How they "privately" felt about the excesses of the time was of no value to us then and is of little value to us now.) See chap. 3, nn. 20, 23, above, chap. 7, n. 72, below. See, also, chap. 8, nn. 45, 73, 79, below. (I should also note that "horror" is too strong a word here, as is the language used to describe the recent polemical depredations of Vice-President Agnew. See chap. 8, n. 135, below.)

35. The effect of even a "small" war on the character of debate and of political life can be remarkable. (See the text at chap. 7, n. 116, below.) Walter Lippmann could, on July 5, 1965 (*Newsweek*, p. 11), praise President Johnson as "deserv[ing] high marks from the historians for having preserved freedom of discussion in such a critical time. It would have been as easy as it must have been tempting for him to beat the tom-toms and silence his critics by saying that they were giving aid and comfort to the enemy." A few months later Lippmann argued,

> While the student demonstrations are quite evidently self-defeating, they are, it seems to me, a pathetic reminder of what happens in a free country when responsible debate on great matters of life and death is throttled down and discouraged. The unhappy youths who burn their draft cards are no doubt misguided. But we must not forget that they come from a nation which expects to understand what its government is doing, from a nation which is not habituated to obedience and to the idea that it must listen to its superiors and not talk back. . . . It may be said that there has been no suppression of freedom of speech, which is indeed true. But nevertheless the fact is that debate has been shut down to an inadequate minimum in the Senate and it is only in the Senate that some men outside the executive branch have access to all authentic information. It is the shutting down of debate in the Senate which is at the root of our uneasiness. [*Chicago Sun-Times*, Oct. 26, 1965, p. 30. See, also, his column in the *Sun-Times*, Mar. 30, 1967, p. 82.]

Johnson attempted to reassure uneasy citizens by affirming, "We believe, with Macaulay, that men are never so likely to settle a question rightly as when they discuss it freely." *Newsweek*, Mar. 7, 1966, p. 23. This was followed, however, by the President's nervous speech of May 17, 1966, on "nervous Nellies." And Clayton Fritchey could report, on June 24, 1966 (*Chicago Sun-Times*, p. 64),

CHAPTER THREE, NOTE 35: PAGE 48

> The hostility the President has inspired in [the Senate Foreign Relations Committee] is by no means confined to the chairman. . . . Why does the President choose to aggravate this situation, rather than, as his custom, ameliorate it? The only answer seems to be that, where Viet Nam is concerned, he has lost his political touch, and is unable to control his personal feelings toward those who have criticized and opposed his Asian policy.

James Reston observed in his column of March 11, 1969 (*Dallas Morning News*, Mar. 11, 1969, p. 15A):

> In fairness to those in the Johnson inner circle who silenced or muffled their dissent, both privately and publicly, it has to be said that Johnson did not make it easy for his colleagues to differ with him on fundamental issues. Nobody ever talked so much or encouraged so much free speech on themes he liked to hear.

See chap. 8, n. 150, below. Earlier in this column, Reston had said:

> One thing that is fairly clear from the record is that the art of resigning on principle from positions close to the top of the American government has almost disappeared. Nobody quits now, as Anthony Eden and Duff Cooper left Neville Chamberlain's cabinet, with a clear and detailed explanation of why they couldn't be identified with the policy any longer. . . . Most [of Johnson's colleagues] at the critical moment of escalation gave to the President the loyalty they owed to the country.

One of the President's colleagues, Undersecretary of State Nicholas Katzenbach (formerly of the University of Chicago Law School faculty), has admitted (*Chicago Tribune*, July 29, 1970, p. 4):

> Frankly, I think the decision [to commit American combat troops to Viet Nam] was made partly because of the stand Mr. Goldwater was taking in the campaign. I think a great many votes were gotten in the [1964] campaign because of it. Today, I think it was a mistake. I don't see anything evil about it, or immoral. It was meant to accomplish something, and if that could have been accomplished quickly, I might have a different view today.

Was it not obvious after November 1963 that the President would be elected in 1964? *Is it not immoral for a President or his colleagues to sacrifice any lives in order to make an election victory even more impressive than it would otherwise have been?* Perhaps "the art of resigning on principle" requires practice in one's youth or a congenital streak of mule-headness. See Appendix F, above; see, also, Appendixes C and E, above, and chap. 6, n. 1, chap. 7, n. 72 (John L. Lewis), below.

"When the sword is once drawn," *Federalist* No. 16 explains, "the passions of men observe no bounds of moderation." (Cf. the "sword in hand" in the text at chap. 8, n. 50, above.) See, for a remarkable exhibition of what war hysteria can do even to a distinguished legal scholar, John H. Wigmore's "Abrams v. U.S.: Freedom of Speech and Freedom of Thuggery in War-Time and Peace-Time," *Ill. L. Rev.* 14 (1920): 539. A comparable exhibition from the Bench may be seen in the judge's statement upon pronouncing sentence in the *Rosenberg* trial. See chap. 7, n. 75, below. (Chaerephon and Critias, who were to become mortal enemies [as democrat and oligarch] when the Peloponnesian War went badly for Athens, are shown in the early days of that war as civilly coexisting. Plato, *Charmides* 153C. Socrates could be, before passions had become most immoderate, a link between them: is it in these circumstances, with monstrous developments waiting offstage, that a discussion of moderation is most appropriate? Cf. Shakespeare, *Henry IV, Pt.* 2, act 4, sc. 5, lines 213-16, act 5, sc. 5, lines 102-5. Cf., also, on the spirit of Israel today, chap. 8, n. 150, below. But see Anastaplo, "The Daring of Moderation: 'Student Power' and *The Melian Dialogue*," *School Review* 78 [1970]: 451, 471, 481, n. 13. See, also, chap. 4, n. 103, below.)

Richard H. Rovere was moved to warn in his "Letter from Washington," *New Yorker*, Oct. 8, 1966, p. 197,

> The feeling grows that we are moving rapidly into an ugly and dangerous time similar to that which lasted through the first half of the fifties. Many of the circumstances seem dreadfully familiar. Casualties mount in an Asian war. Demagogues are being listened to and favored in elections. Conspiracy theories abound and are more and more being used to account for our internal disorders.

One critical difference should be noticed, however: the assassination of President Kennedy did seem to have the cathartic effect on this country that the deaths of their youngsters had, in Shakespeare's *Romeo and Juliet*, on the Capulets and Montagus. See chap. 8, n. 135, below. See, also, chap. 3, n. 22, above.

36. See chap. 4, sec. 4, above. It should be remembered that the Declaration of Independence invoked the right to rebel only after Great Britain had failed to do what she could legitimately have done to deal with the conditions causing or even justifying rebellion. See pp. 332, 336, 350-53, 368-69, 376-77, above.

37. I return to Walter Berns for another illuminating comment:

> The clear and present danger test actually becomes a rationale for avoiding *the impossible prohibitions* of the First Amendment and for convicting persons for speech that the government has forbidden. Professor Chafee may prefer to look upon the test as "placing a great area of discussion beyond the reach of the government," but it is closer to the facts to regard the test as placing a great area of discussion *within* the reach of the government." [(First italics added.) Berns, *Freedom, Virtue and the First Amendment*, p. 56; also, pp. 70, 94]

See chap. 3, n. 29, above. See, also, chap. 6, n. 63, chap. 8, n. 83, below.

38. Walter Lippmann opened his discussion of freedom of speech in *The Public Philosophy* (New York: New American Library, Mentor Books, 1962), p. 96, with these observations:

> Only within a community which adheres to the public philosophy is there sure and sufficient ground for the freedom to think and to ask questions, to speak and to publish. Nobody can justify in principle, much less in practice, a claim that there exists an unrestricted right of anyone to utter anything he likes at any time he chooses. There can, for example, be no right, as Mr. Justice Holmes said, to cry "Fire" in a crowded theatre. Nor is there a right to tell a customer that the glass beads are diamonds, or a voter that the opposition candidate for President is a Soviet agent.

The three examples Lippmann uses are unfortunate ones for any useful introduction to the problem of freedom of speech, its advantages and limitations. First, Justice Holmes denied the right *falsely* to cry "Fire" in a theater—Lippmann, like others before him, overlooked the qualification. (Even with this qualification, Justice Holmes's example raises no free speech problem. See chap. 8, sec. 3, above.) Second, no one I have ever heard of tries to apply freedom of speech criteria and immunities to commercial transactions—the case of the glass beads is simply irrelevant. Third, as to his denial of a right of a candidate to tell a voter that the opposition candidate for President is a Soviet agent: certainly, he may have that right if the opposition candidate *is* or appears to be such an agent. And should he not be left free to accuse that opponent of advocating projects that seem, in effect, much more in the interest of other countries than of his own? See, for a discussion of Lippmann's *Public Philosophy*, the lecture (appended to my dissertation), "On the Use and Abuse of Old Books."

39. Samuel Johnson believed that "when a man knows he is to be hanged in a fortnight, it concentrates his mind wonderfully." *Oxford Dictionary of Quotations* (London: Oxford University Press, 1959), p. 273. Cf. Plato, *Crito* 46E-47A.

CHAPTER IV

1. Adam Smith, *An Inquiry into the Natural Causes of the Wealth of Nations* (New York: Random House, Modern Library, 1937), p. 881: ". . . But it ought to be remembered, that when the wisest government has exhausted all the proper subjects of taxation, it must, in cases of urgent necessity, have recourse to improper ones." See chap. 3, n. 6, above. See, also, chap. 7, n. 3, below. Cf. chap. 3, n. 4, above.

2. Madison to Jefferson, Oct. 17, 1788. The "engineers" referred to in the text would be either the Congress and states which established such an amendment or the courts which have thus interpreted the Fourteenth Amendment. But see chap. 4, n. 107, chap. 7, nn. 26, 86, 107, below. I provide an extended discussion of this problem in chapter 7. See, also, chap. 8, n. 83, below.

Related to this problem is the warning found in Justice Black's dissenting opinion in *Griswold* v. *Connecticut*, 381 U.S. 479, 509-10 (1965):

> One of the most effective ways of diluting or expanding a constitutionally guaranteed right is to substitute for the crucial word or words of a constitutional guarantee another word or words, more or less flexible and more or less restricted in meaning. . . . I have expressed the view many times that First Amendment freedoms, for example, have suffered from a failure of the courts to stick to the simple language of the First Amendment in construing it, instead of invoking multitudes of words substituted for those the Framers used. See, e.g., *New York Times Co.* v. *Sullivan*, 376 U.S. 254, 293 (concurring opinion) [1964]; cases collected in *City of El Paso* v. *Simmons*, 379 U.S. 497, 517, n. 1 (dissenting opinion) [1965]; Hugo L. Black, "The Bill of Rights," 35 N.Y.U. L. Rev. 865 [1960]. For these reasons I get nowhere in this [Connecticut birth control information] case by talk about a constitutional "right of privacy" as an emanation from one or more constitutional provisions.

3. See William Blackstone, *Commentaries on the Laws of England*, 1:49:

> By the sovereign power . . . is meant the making of laws; for wherever that power resides, all others must conform to and be directed by it, whatever appearance the outward form and administration of the government may put on. For it is at any time in the option of the legislature to alter that form and administration by a new edict or rule, and put the execution of the laws into whatever hands it pleases; by constituting one, or a few, or many executive magistrates: and all the other powers of the state must obey the legislative power in the discharge of their several functions, or else the constitution is at an end.

In the ultimate sense, of course, the American people, as authors of constitutions, are the sovereign legislative authority. See chap. 9, n. 39, below. (White spoke to Madison's argument in the quotation from *Annals*, I, pp. 466-67, found at pp. 161-62, above.)

4. See, e.g., *Annals*, I, pp. 769-70. See, also, the Kentucky Resolution of Nov. 10, 1798.

5. *Senate Journal*, p. 105. This proposal evidently originated with Madison (*Annals*, I, p. 435, but without "freedom of speech"), not with any of the state ratifying conventions. Irving Brant, *James Madison, Father of the Constitution, 1787-1800* (Indianapolis: Bobbs-Merrill, 1950), pp. 265, 273. See chap. 7, n. 2, below.

6. See, e.g., the six amendments proposed in and rejected by the Senate, all of which deal with Congress, four of the six actually mentioning "Congress." *History of Congress*, pp. 163-64.

7. Ibid., pp. 169-70; also, 1 *U.S. Statutes* 97 (1789).

8. Why then is "Congress" used in the First Amendment and not in the remaining articles of the Bill of Rights? This is the first of the amendments incorporating restraints based on the rights of the people—two earlier amendments proposed by Congress, which failed of ratification by the states (and which were clearly related only to the general government), were devoted to the proper composition and compensation of Congress. As

what is now the First Amendment opens a series of amendments protecting the rights of the people, it may have been thought appropriate to indicate the focus of concern by introducing the restraints with a reference to Congress. (See chap. 2, n. 25, above.) The emphasis upon the general government (as distinguished from the states) would have been more readily apparent had the amendments been put where it was first proposed that most of them be put, in Article I, section 9, that part of the Constitution incorporating restraints upon Congress. The restraints there do not apply also to the states. This is emphasized by the fact that certain of the restraints on government found in section 9 are repeated in section 10, that part of the Constitution devoted exclusively to restraints upon the states. See Appendix A, above, esp. p. 291.

Even while the amendments were still being thought of as incorporated in Article I, section 9, a suggestion was made by Livermore that the religious provision be changed to read,

> Congress shall make no laws touching religion, or infringing the rights of conscience [*Annals*, I, p. 731].

This was accepted, replacing the version which had read,

> No religion shall be established by law, nor shall the equal rights of conscience be infringed [*Annals*, I, p. 729].

Thus, the "Congress shall make no law" pattern was first adopted at a stage of the proceedings *when it could not have been intended to distinguish that amendment from the others that followed.* The proposed placement of the bulk of amendments in Article I, section 9, suggests that only Congress or, at most, the general government was being addressed.

The reason why "Congress" was used in Livermore's version, even while the amendment was intended to be placed in Article I, section 9, seems to have been primarily that of emphasis, to reassure those who were suspicious lest power be given the general government to interfere with existing state religious establishments. Those least familiar with, and therefore perhaps for that reason most suspicious of, the Constitution and its effects would be those for whom this form of assurance would be most reassuring. Technically, this reference to Congress was unnecessary—but perhaps no more so than the reference to Congress in the opening provision in Article I, section 9,

> The Migration or Importation of such Persons as any of the States now existing shall think proper to admit, shall not be prohibited by the Congress prior to the Year one thousand eight hundred and eight, but a Tax or duty may be imposed on such Importation, not exceeding ten dollars for each Person.

The context of this slave trade provision, in Article I, section 9, should have been sufficient (especially when compared to the language and evident purpose of section 10) to indicate that all of the limitations contained therein applied only to Congress. (If it should be thought that it was necessary to mention "Congress" in the first provision in Article I, section 9, in order to indicate the tendency of that section, the same consideration would apply to the First Amendment as the first of a list of rights reserved by the people.)

Whatever may be said about the rest of the Bill of Rights, would not clearer language than that of the Fourteenth Amendment be required to justify so great a departure from the previous organization of the Constitution as to have the First Amendment as well applied to the states? See chap. 8, n. 83, below.

9. See chap. 8, sec. 12, above.

10. See H. von Holst, *John C. Calhoun*, American Statesmen (Boston: Houghton Mifflin Co., 1892), p. 64:

> . . . it seems hardly probable that the reason for Calhoun's celebrated de-

cision, which denied the right of the Vice-President to call a Senator to order, was really, as [President John Quincy] Adams believed, only unwillingness to check Randolph's violent abuse of the administration. There was more than enough of the doctrinarian in him to render it likely that he honestly thought this power would be, or at least could lead to, an abridgment of the liberty of speech.

See chap. 8, n. 118, below.

11. See Patrick Devlin, *The Enforcement of Morals* (London: Oxford University Press, 1965), p. 129:

> It is a doctrine firmly embedded in English law that power which is given for one purpose, whether to a minister or to a judge, must not be used for another purpose. That is abuse of power: and its prevention is essential to the existence of a free society.

See, also, chap. 6, n. 66, below.

12. See Zechariah Chafee, *Freedom of Speech* (Cambridge: Harvard University Press, 1920), p. 282:

> ... classification of the objects of any recognized Congressional power must not be used solely for the purpose of accomplishing a result prohibited by the First Amendment. Congress can tax all incomes, but an income tax of 50 per cent on Socialist college professors alone would be a convenient but unconstitutional way to suppress freedom of speech.

See, also, *New York Times Co. v. Sullivan*, 376 U.S. 254, 277 (1964):

> What a State may not constitutionally bring about by means of a criminal statute is likewise beyond the reach of its civil law of libel. The fear of damage awards under a rule such as that invoked by the Alabama courts here may be markedly more inhibiting than the fear of prosecution under a criminal statute. See *City of Chicago v. Tribune Co.*, 307 Ill. 596, 607, 139 N.E. 86, 90 (1923).

What is said of a state here should apply, it seems to me, to the legislative activity of the general government as well. See chap. 7, nn. 66, 81, below.

13. Thus, Chief Justice Marshall observes in *Brown v. Maryland*, 12 Wheat. [U.S.] 419, 444 (1827), "It is impossible to conceal from ourselves that this is varying the form, without varying the substance." See chap. 4, n. 35, below.

> To evade the bondage of system and habit, of family maxims, class opinions, and, in some degree, of national prejudices; to accept tradition only as a means of information, and existing facts only as a lesson to be used in doing otherwise and doing better; to seek the reason of things for oneself, and in oneself alone; to tend to results without being bound to means, and *to strike through the form to the substance*—such are the principal characteristics of what I shall call the philosophical method of the Americans. [Alexis de Tocqueville, *Democracy in America* (New York: Random House, Vintage Books, 1954), 2:3; italics added]

We should be reminded as well of Captain Ahab's defiance of the universe:

> ... All visible objects, man, are but as pasteboard masks. But in each event—in the living act, the undoubted deed—there, some unknown but still reasoning thing puts forth the mouldings of its features from behind the unreasoning mask. If man will strike, *strike through the mask!* How can the prisoner reach outside except by thrusting through the wall? To me, the white whale is that wall, shoved near to me. Sometimes I think there's naught beyond. But 'tis enough. He tasks me; he heaps me; I see in him outrageous strength, with an inscrutable malice sinewing it. That inscrutable thing is chiefly what I hate; and be the white whale agent, or be the white whale principal, I will wreak that hate upon him. Talk

not to me of blasphemy, man. . . . [Herman Melville, *Moby Dick*, chap. 36 (italics added)]

See chap. 2, n. 39, above, on Hamlet striking through the mask; also, chap. 6, n. 74, chap. 9, n. 7, below.

14. Emerson reported that Carlyle

thinks the first thing he would do, if he got into Parliament, would be to turn out the reporters, and stop all manner of mischievous speaking to Buncombe, and wind-bags. "In the Long Parliament," he says, "the only great Parliament, they sat secret and silent, grave as an ecumenical council, and I know not what they would have done to anybody that had got in there and attempted to tell out of doors what they did." [Ralph Waldo Emerson, *Selected Writings* (New York: Random House, Modern Library, 1950), p. 926]

See chap. 4, n. 17, below. See, also, *Annals*, VI, pp. 63, 68-96, 103-4, 105, 109, 111-12, 113-16, 117-19, 121-22, 122-24, 180, 183-84. Cf. *Newsweek*, Aug. 10, 1970, p. 18 (on how publicity emanating from systematic gallery observation was used to force the House of Representatives to announce all the votes of its members).

15. One must take into account here the doctrine with respect to a state's imposing "unconstitutional conditions" upon the granting of a privilege controlled by that state. "The Doctrine of Unconstitutional Conditions," chap. 8 of Gerard C. Henderson, *The Position of Foreign Corporations in American Constitutional Law* (Cambridge: Harvard University Press, 1918); *Wheeling Steel Corp. v. Glander*, 337 U.S. 562 (1949); *Frost Trucking Co. v. R.R. Com.*, 271 U.S. 583 (1926); *Gomillion v. Lightfoot*, 364 U.S. 339 (1960); *Pickering v. Board of Education*, 391 U.S. . . . (1968). See chap. 6, n. 74, below.

The problem here, as elsewhere, is to devise institutions that will bring about (with reliance upon the least amount of supervision and perhaps even of goodwill) what is desired. The classic statement may be that set forth in *Federalist* No. 10. (My federalism argument recognizes just such a use of institutions in our circumstances.) An illustration may be useful, or at least diverting: A cherished prize is to be awarded to the owner whose mounted horse comes in *last* in a race. What is the simplest way of arranging this horserace to make it both interesting to spectators and a fair test of the horses? The "Constitutionalist," especially if he should be of a Roman inclination, should have no trouble with this problem.

16. We (and the Constitution) take a narrower view of the legislative guarantee in Article I, section 6, than does Jackson: if we did not, the public evaluation of a member of Congress as well as meaningful elections would be difficult if not impossible to have. That is, Jackson had not grasped some of the implications, spelled out in this book, of the form of government established by the Constitution of the United States.

17. One is reminded of the memorable Constitutional Convention of 1787, which sat behind closed doors. Thomas Jefferson (in a letter to John Adams, Aug. 30, 1787) observed of this convention,

I am sorry they began their deliberations by so abominable a precedent as that of tying up the tongues of their members. Nothing can justify this example but the innocence of their intentions, & ignorance of the value of public discussions. I have no doubt that all their other measures will be good & wise. It is really an assembly of demigods. [Max Farrand, ed., *The Records of the Federal Convention of 1787* (New Haven: Yale University Press, 1937), 3:76. Cf. ibid., 3:28, 33, 478, 532. (Was "*liberty* of the press" sacrificed on this occasion to "*freedom* of debate"? See chap. 5, sec. 13, above.)]

See chap. 4, n. 113, below, for the constitutional recognition of the occasional need for secrecy in congressional deliberations and business. Does this recognition suggest the natural limits of self-government?

18. One legitimate remedy which Congress has availed itself of in the circumstances considered is to publish its own account of debates. See *Burke's American Speeches*, ed. F. G. Selby (London: 1956), p. 183 (first note). Cf. Henry Street, *Freedom, the Individual and the Law* (London: Penguin Books, 1963), pp. 176-77. See the passage from James Mill, chap. 4, n. 100, below. See, also, chap. 2, n. 6, above.

19. Article I, section 10, of the Constitution provides that "No State shall, without the consent of Congress, . . . enter into any Agreement or Compact with another State, or with a foreign Power. . . ."

The states are left free by the First Amendment to abridge freedom of speech. (The rationale of this arrangement is discussed in chapters 5 and 7. See, e.g., the text at chap. 5, n. 88, above.) Some "speech" problems might require cooperation between states. (See, e.g., chap. 5, n. 137, below.) May Congress, consistent with the prohibitions upon it of the First Amendment, *consent* to a compact two states might try to make "abridging the freedom of speech"? If it could not, the states would not be as effective as they could be. See chap. 8, n. 19, below. Cf. chap. 4, n. 60, below.

See, for a description of an unsuccessful attempt by Congress to act upon "the notion that the federal government was a kind of senior and controlling partner in the interstate compacts to which it consented," Richard H. Leach, "War on the Port Authority," in R. J. Tresolini and R. T. Frost, eds., *Cases in American National Government and Politics* (Englewood Cliffs, N.J.: Prentice-Hall, 1966), p. 10.

20. But see the commonsensical observation by Chief Justice Warren, speaking for the Court in *Watkins* v. *United States*, 354 U.S. 178, 197 (1957):

> . . . Clearly, an investigation [by a congressional committee] is subject to the command that the Congress shall make no law abridging freedom of speech or press or assembly. While it is true that there is no statute to be reviewed, and that an investigation is not a law, nevertheless an investigation is part of law-making. It is justified solely as an adjunct to the legislative process. The First Amendment may be invoked against infringement of the protected freedoms by law or by law-making. [Note: See *United States* v. *Rumely*, 345 U.S. 41, 43-44 (1953); *Barsky* v. *United States*, 167 F.2d 241, 244-50 (1948); *United States* v. *Josephson*, 165 F.2d 82, 90-92 (1948).]

21. If the witness has something else to tell Congress, or any of its committees, he can on his own authority as a citizen exercise the right of petition. See chap. 8, n. 108, below. (See chap. 8, sec. 12, above, for a disastrously provocative use of petitions.)

22. An outstanding exception was the special committee to investigate the national defense program during the Second World War (which was in marked contrast to its Civil War counterpart). The reputation thereby won by its chairman was critical in his elevation to the presidency in 1945, just as (it may be said) the notoriety associated with another congressional investigator helped keep him from the presidency in 1960. See chap. 9, n. 17, below. A decade later that notoriety had been converted into mere familiarity.

23. Bagehot concluded his review of the functions of the House of Commons with the observation,

> Lastly, there is the function of legislation, of which of course it would be preposterous to deny the great importance, and which I only deny to be *as* important as the executive management of the whole state, or the political education given by Parliament to the whole nation. [*The English Constitution*, World Classics (London: Oxford University Press, 1963), p. 119]

Similar sentiments may be found in Woodrow Wilson, *Congressional Government* (Boston: Houghton Mifflin Co., 1913), p. 303.

See chap. 4, n. 102, below.

24. Vice-President Calhoun addressed the House of Representatives (in a letter of Sept. 29, 1826) "in its high character of grand inquest of the nation." (Von Holst,

John C. Calhoun, p. 50.) But this related to its constitutional role as initiator of any impeachment of officers of the general government. See *Federalist* No. 65.

> We start with several basic premises on which there is general agreement. The power of the Congress to conduct investigations is inherent in the legislative process. That process is broad. It encompasses inquiries concerning the administration of existing laws as well as proposed or possibly needed statutes. It includes surveys of defects in our social, economic or political system for the purpose of enabling the Congress to remedy them. It comprehends probes into departments of the Federal Government to expose corruption, inefficiency or waste. But broad as is this power of inquiry, it is not unlimited. There is no general authority to expose the private affairs of individuals without justification in terms of the functions of the Congress. This was freely conceded by the Solicitor General in his argument of this case. [Note: "Now, we don't claim on behalf of the Government that there is any right to expose for the purposes of exposure. And I don't know that Congress has ever claimed any such right. But we do say, in the same breath, that there is a right to inform the public at the same time you inform the Congress."] Nor is the Congress a law enforcement or trial agency. These are functions of the executive and judicial departments of government. No inquiry is an end in itself; it must be related to and in furtherance of a legitimate task of the Congress. Investigations conducted solely for the personal aggrandizement of the investigators or to "punish" those investigated are indefensible. [*Watkins* v. *United States*, 354 U.S. 178, 187 (1957)]

25. See Harry Kalven, Jr., "Mr. Alexander Meiklejohn and the Barenblatt Opinion," *U. Chicago L. Rev.* 17 (1960): 315. See, also, Malcolm P. Sharp, Foreword, Alexander Meiklejohn, *Political Freedom: The Constitutional Powers of the People* (New York: Harper & Bros., 1960), pp. xxii-xxiii. (Even Communist party leaders, it should be remembered, used to appear voluntarily to testify against bills affecting their interests. See Ralph Brown, *Loyalty and Security: Employment Tests in the United States* [New Haven: Yale University Press, 1958], p. 325.)

> There was very little use of the power of compulsory process in early years to enable the Congress to obtain facts pertinent to the enactment of new statutes or the administration of existing laws. The first occasion for such an investigation arose in 1827 when the House of Representatives was considering a revision of the tariff laws. In the Senate, there was no use of a fact-finding investigation in aid of legislation until 1859. In the Legislative Reorganization Act [of 1946], the Committee on Un-American Activities is the only standing committee of the House of Representatives that was given the power to compel disclosures. [Note: 60 Stat. 828-29. All standing committees in the Senate were invested with the power of compulsory process. 60 Stat. 830-31. During the 83rd Congress, two other standing committees in the House of Representatives, the Appropriations and Government Operations Committees, possessed that power. 99 Cong. Rec. 16-19.] [*Watkins* v. *United States*, 354 U.S. 178, 192-93 (1957)]

On congressional investigations generally, see an issue of the *University of Chicago Law Review* devoted entirely to that subject. (Vol. 18, no. 3 [1951].)

See, on "the separation of powers," chap. 4, n. 102, below. See, also, *U.S.* v. *Brown*, 381 U.S. 437 (1965). Cf. Morton Grodzins, *The American System* (Chicago: Rand McNally, 1966), pp. 260-70.

26. A letter dated July 10, 1957, which I had occasion to offer to Chicago newspapers, illustrates the arguments that can be made:

> Americans dedicated to constitutional government and the rule of law should study carefully the McClellan Senate Committee rackets hearings that have been televised to the Chicago area this past week. There is, of course, the obvious problem, familiar to all alert and responsible citizens, of the partial breakdown

of law enforcement in various parts of our country. But the television network would have performed a real public service by providing a running commentary pointing out many serious defects of the hearings, including the unconstitutional usurpation by a legislative committee of judicial functions, the callous disregard of elementary rules of evidence and fair play, the unjust tendency of the Senators to cross-examine only "unfriendly" witnesses, the irresponsible handling of facts, the uncalled for attacks by Committee counsel and members on the characters and careers of certain witnesses, and the unseemly moralizing for the benefit of the television audience.

It is good, as various Senators proclaimed, that citizens should respect their government and support law and order. This rule, however, seems to be difficult for a congressional investigating committee to live up to.

See, for similar comments by Malcolm Sharp on the prosecution and conviction of James Hoffa, *University of Chicago Maroon*, May 15, 1964, p. 8. See, also, the arguments recently developed by eminent Chicago lawyers (such as Albert E. Jenner, Jr.) in support of clients (such as Dr. Jeremiah Stamler) opposed to the House Un-American Activities Committee. Thus, Mr. Jenner could advise Dr. Stamler (in a publicly distributed letter of May 28, 1965),

> You . . . told the Committee that your refusal to answer questions put by Committee counsel was a matter of principle and conscience, and did not result from a desire to hide the facts. Moreover, you expressly rejected reliance on the Fifth Amendment privilege against self-incrimination. My associates and I are in full accord with your belief that the time has come for citizens of stature and reputation to test before an impartial and dispassionate court whether United States citizens, be they good or bad, guilty or innocent, may be subjected to the kind of degrading and unfair tactics used by the House un-American Activities Committee.

It is hard to believe that such a public declaration could come out of the same bar that I found so cowed in 1950. But, then, it may not be the same bar. It may well be, that is, that a few citizens of no "stature and reputation," but with a dedication to constitutional government, left the bar better than they found it. See chap. 4, nn. 84, 116, below, Appendix F, above. See, also, *Stamler* v. *Willis*, 371 F.2d 413 (1966), 287 F.S. 734 (1968), 393 U.S. 407 (1969).

27. Congress does have the power to propose amendments to the Constitution. But if it is indeed considering the possibility of amendments, it should at least be obliged to say so—and conduct itself in a manner respectful of the fact that the power to ratify amendments has been reserved for the states. That is, it cannot proceed as if the proposed amendments were already ratified even before they are submitted to the states or, indeed, written for adoption by two-thirds of both houses. We are entitled, in assessing congressional investigations, to strike through the mask. See chap. 4, n. 13, above, chap. 8, n. 29, below.

See, for a further limitation on Congress's power to investigate, pp. 18-19 of the article on "interstate compacts" cited in chap. 4, n. 19, above.

28. Such legislation includes the provision for punishment, through the courts, of those who unlawfully refuse to testify. It was once generally agreed that it is possible for either house to take direct and immediate action, at the bar of the house, to punish (but only during the life of the Congress) those in contempt of the body. Does the abandonment of this approach reflect a recognition of the distinctively American extent of the doctrine of the separation of powers. See, for a description of this legislation and of the older practice of contempt proceedings at the bar of a house of Congress, *Watkins* v. *U.S.*, 354 U.S. 178, 188-89 (1957). See, also, James Kent, *Commentaries on American Law* (New York: O. Halsted, 1826), pp. 235-36.

29. To illustrate: a defendant would not be acquitted in a trial upon indictment for the shooting of a senator on the floor of the Senate if his sole defense was that the senator

(and the Senate) had been engaged, at the moment of the assault, in the enactment of a constitutionally invalid *ex post facto* criminal statute.

30. It was encouraging to see, in the papers of February 3, 1966, more congressmen than usual voting against contempt of Congress citations of uncooperative witnesses. The "uncooperative" witnesses on that occasion were members of the Ku Klux Klan. See chap. 5, n. 55, below.

It should also be noted that the Fifth Amendment might be brought to bear upon the power of congressional investigatory committees. This is in addition to its self-incriminatory provision, which has been virtually interpreted by the courts to mean, in effect, that anyone who is willing to lie (and claim jeopardy) can safely resist the demands of a committee. (See *Malloy* v. *Hogan*, 378 U.S. 1, 13, n. 9 [1964].) This protection is limited, in the Fifth Amendment, to "criminal cases." See, also, *Annals*, I, p. 753. It may be that the extent of application of this protection has had to be expanded because Congress has usurped judicial functions. (Cf. pp. 195-99, above.)

The requirement of the Fifth Amendment that every person must be afforded "due process of law" before he can be deprived of "life, liberty or property" seems to apply to congressional investigations as well as to other exercises of governmental authority. See *Watkins* v. *U.S.*, 354 U.S. 178, at 196, n. 27 (1957). This protection is seen in such elements of "due process" as the specification of the subject of inquiry and the opportunity (with the aid of counsel) to confront accusers and to present evidence on one's own behalf. But even when such safeguards are respected by a congressional investigatory committee, enough difficulties remain to raise serious doubts that Congress should be permitted to assume the role of the judiciary. It should be remembered that the effective curb on freedom of the press in the colonial period came not from the courts (since American juries would neither indict nor convict for seditious libel) but from the exercise of summary power by legislatures and by royal governors.

31. "The Congress shall have Power . . . To exercise exclusive Legislation in all Cases whatsoever, over such District (not exceeding ten Miles square) as may, by Cession of particular States, and the acceptance of Congress, become the Seat of the Government of the United States . . ." U.S., *Constitution*, Art. I, sec. 8.

"The Congress shall have Power to dispose of and make all needful Rules and Regulations respecting the Territory or other Property belonging to the United States . . ." U.S., *Constitution*, Art. IV, sec. 3.

See chap. 8, n. 14, below.

32. I faced this problem in my own litigation: does one insist upon an accurate formulation of constitutional law or upon a formulation more in accordance with that currently accepted by the Supreme Court? See chap. 7, n. 82, below. See, also, Appendix F, sec. 9, above, and chap. 4, n. 107, below.

The legal realist might say that the only "accurate formulation of constitutional law" is precisely that which is "in accordance with that currently accepted by the Supreme Court." What, then, would he understand competent counsel to be invoking in a "petition for rehearing"? Cf. chap. 6, n. 50, chap. 8, n. 28, below.

33. The extent and effect of the loyalty programs (I use this term to refer to both loyalty and security programs) have been described in considerable detail by Professor Ralph Brown of the Yale Law School in *Loyalty and Security*. Brown presented as "the two dominant conclusions" of his valuable book, "First, that loyalty and security tests have been practiced with too much rigor and too little humanity. Second, that these tests needlessly impair the great freedoms of belief, of speech, and of association enshrined in the First Amendment." (Ibid., p. 485.) See Richard Rovere, *The American Establishment* (New York: Harcourt, Brace & World, 1962), pp. 118, 131-32, 239-41 (on "kept witnesses").

These programs, it seems to me, have had since the Second World War some of the effects that executive deportations of aliens had after the First World War. (See, on those deportations, Chafee, *Freedom of Speech*, p. 229. See, also, chap. 6, n. 75, below.) But there are evidently far fewer aliens to work on now than then, with the result that the desire to persecute (a recurring postwar phenomenon?) finds American citizens being turned upon and, in effect, deported from normal life in their country. See chap. 7, n. 70, below. Cf. chap. 6, n. 75, below. See, also, chap. 8, n. 126, below.

See, on these programs, Anastaplo, "Due Process of Law—An Introduction," *U. Detroit L. J.* 42 (Dec., 1964): 195, 199, 215. The following passage, which bears on the discussion of this study, should have been added to the end of section 3 of the article:

"Thus, the process that is due is, *in part*, that which is traditional and expected—and, in this respect, both the Common Law and the Fourth, Fifth, Sixth and Seventh Amendments to the Constitution include instructive reminders. As we further consider the standards and objectives of due process of law, we are reminded also of three of the guarantees found in Magna Carta:

> No freeman shall be captured or imprisoned or disseised or outlawed or exiled or in any way destroyed, nor will we go against him or send against him, except by the lawful judgment of his peers or by the law of the land.
> To no one will we sell, to no one will we deny or delay right or justice.
> Now all these aforesaid customs and liberties, which we have granted, in so far as concerns us, to be observed in our kingdom toward our men, all men of our kingdom, both clergy and laity, shall, in so far as concerns them, observe toward their men.

We find here the constitutional bedrock upon which the laws of all American jurisdictions rest."

The American is, as citizen—as both ruler and subject—*the* constitutionalist.

34. A letter from William Short in Paris to Gouverneur Morris, Sept. 12, 1790, suggests how Americans in the constitutional period reacted to loyalty inquiries with features that have become distressingly familiar to us since the Second World War:

> . . . there is no danger of talking of you in this manner as you are not here but if you were within the jurisdiction of the committee *des recherches*, I should be afraid of their making you a nocturnal visit.—these visits have lately become fashionable—one of the most remarkable is one which took place lately—a washerman found a letter in the dirty pockets of one of his fair customers, which had the appearance to him as he did not know how to read of a counter-revolution—by means of the district this came to the knowledge of the committee *des recherches*—the lady in question was called before them late at night, underwent an interrogatory of some hours, her papers were examined—nothing found—the committee *des recherches* made their report to the Assembly—informed them, as a proof of their vigilance & zeal, that they had passed the whole night without sleeping—were applauded by the assembly—&c. all this is considered as the sure & certain road to the establishment of a free government, & particularly to the securing of personal liberty. [Gouverneur Morris, *A Diary of the French Revolution*, ed. Beatrix C. Davenport (Boston: Houghton Mifflin Co., 1939), 1:591]

35. The attorney general's list of subversive organizations during this period has had the character of both *ex post facto* laws and bills of attainder. *Cummings* v. *Missouri*, 4 Wall. [U.S.] 277 (1867) and *Ex parte Garland*, 4 Wall. [U.S.] 333 (1867) did not prove as effective barriers against such experiments as some had hoped. The spirit of *Cummings*, 4 Wall., at 325, in its application of the bill of attainder clause, needs to be cherished:

> In all these cases there would be the legislative enactment creating the deprivation without any of the ordinary forms and guards provided for the security of the citizen in the administration of justice by the established tribunals. . . . The purpose of the law maker in the case supposed would be openly avowed; in the case existing it is only disguised. The legal result must be the same, for what cannot be done directly cannot be done indirectly. The Constitution deals

with substance, not shadows. Its inhibition was levelled at the thing, not the name. It intended that the rights of the citizen should be secure against deprivation for past conduct by legislative enactment, under any form, however disguised. If the inhibition can be evaded by the form of the enactment, its insertion in the fundamental law was a vain and futile proceeding.

Cf. *American Communications Assn.* v. *Douds*, 339 U.S. 382 (1950). But see *United States* v. *Brown*, 381 U.S. 437 (1965). See, also, *U.S.* v. *Lovett*, 328 U.S. 303 (1946); chap. 4, n. 13, above.

Justice Jackson wrote in 1955:

> In 1951 the Court cast serious doubt upon the legality of the Attorney General's list of subversive organizations promulgated in 1947. [*Joint Anti-Fascist Refugee Committee* v. *McGrath*, 341 U.S. 123 (1951).] But the list had long been widely circulated and accepted, and despite the Court's views it has never ceased to be used in the press, in the executive department, by and before congressional committees, and even in courts to prejudice individuals in their liberty, position, and good name. [*The Supreme Court in the American System of Government* (New York: Harper & Row, 1965), p. 25]

Thus, responsible officials have conducted themselves not as "men truly bred to the law" but rather as would any petty politician determined to take whatever he can "get away with." Should honorable men have to depend on courts to remind them of their oaths "to support this Constitution"? (See chap. 8, n. 83, below. Cf. chap. 5, n. 17, below.)

Perhaps we have become careless about such developments partly because of our now uncritical acceptance of government regulatory commissions. (These are "in reality miniature independent governments set up to deal with the railroad problem, the banking problem, or the radio problem. They constitute a headless 'fourth branch' of the Government, a haphazard deposit of irresponsible agencies and uncoordinated powers." Quoted by Justice Jackson, ibid., p. 45.) But, we are told, "It is too late in the day to continue the argument as to whether these statutory bodies which defy the constitutional principle of separation of powers are unconstitutional. They have been accepted as a valid part of our legal system [citing *Crowell* v. *Benson*, 285 U.S. 22 (1932)]." Ibid., p. 46. Is it, indeed, "too late in the day"? Cf. ibid., p. 55.

It is well, in any event, to apply to the operations of "big government" the much-documented caution voiced by Justice Brennan in speaking for the Court in *N.A.A.C.P.* v. *Button*, 371 U.S. 415, 433, 438 (1963):

> . . . These [First Amendment] freedoms are delicate and vulnerable, as well as supremely precious in our society. The threat of sanctions may deter their exercise almost as potently as the actual application of sanctions. Cf. *Smith* v. *California*, [361 U.S. 147, at 151-54 (1959)]; *Speiser* v. *Randall*, 357 U.S. 513, 526 [1958]. Because First Amendment freedoms need breathing space to survive, government may regulate in the area only with narrow specificity. *Cantwell* v. *Connecticut*, 310 U.S. 296, 311 [1940]. . . . Broad prophylactic rules in the area of free expression are suspect. See, e.g., *Near* v. *Minnesota*, 283 U.S. 697 [1931]; *Shelton* v. *Tucker*, 364 U.S. 479 [1960]; *Louisiana ex rel. Gremillion* v. *N.A.A.C.P.*, 366 U.S. 293 [1961]. Cf. *Schneider* v. *Irvington*, 308 U.S. 147, 162 [1939]. Precision of regulation must be the touchstone in an area so closely touching our most precious freedoms.

Cf. Herbert J. Storing, "The Problem of Big Government," in R. A. Goldwin, ed., *A Nation of States* (Chicago: Rand McNally, 1963), p. 65.

See, in "Due Process of Law," pp. 195, 203, 215, my suggestion "that a vigorous application of the Hatch Act, first enacted in 1939, which prohibits political activity on the part of a federal employee, would have taken care of most of the legitimate purposes behind the federal loyalty program." I observe that the application of such a prohibition would be "truly general and hence more likely to be restrained and reasonable [than the loyalty programs]." (See, for the still unresolved question of the constitutionality of the Hatch Act itself, *United Public Workers* v. *Mitchell*, 330 U.S. 75 [1947].)

I also observe,

> [T]here seems no reason why government supervisors should not be allowed the discretion of making judicious reassignments of employees in designated sensitive positions without, on the one hand, having to make explanations and, on the other hand, mistreating the employee, ruining his reputation, and convicting him of something that has been aptly called "bargain-counter treason." It is a formal program which resembles a judicial proceeding, with its pretense of due process despite the atmosphere of uncertainty and arbitrariness, that aggravates the problem. (If administrative hearings are desired, they can be limited to the determination of whether the position is in fact one that should be designated as "sensitive." Thus, the "case" for due process does not rest upon the assumption that all governmental action must conform to the historical due process standards; but when the government does presume to act in a certain way, with a certain effect, then it should do so in a certain manner.) . . . This discretion [to transfer personnel, without prejudice to the employee, to other governmental posts of comparable status and perquisites] could be guided not only by confidential reports but even by intangible and perhaps irrational "hunches" and intuition. Of course, the supervisor would have an incentive, if only in the interest of efficiency and morale, to be judicious in his exercise of this power. [Anastaplo, "Due Process of Law," *U. Det. L. J.* 42 (1964): 195, 203-4, 215-16]

Cf. Street, *Freedom, the Individual and the Law*, pp. 222, 226, 229, 230.

See, on the definition of sensitive positions, Brown, *Loyalty and Security*, pp. 248-53.

36. Blackstone, *Laws of England*, 4:431. I am reminded also of the dedication inscribed by William W. Crosskey in his *Politics and the Constitution* (Chicago: University of Chicago Press, 1953), "To the Congress of the United States, in the hope that it may be led to claim and exercise for the common good of the country the powers justly belonging to it under the Constitution." See James B. Reston, *The Artillery of the Press: Its Influence on American Foreign Policy* (New York: Harper & Row, 1967), p. 72.

Have not the covert distributions of funds to private organizations by the CIA been designed primarily to deceive Congress? Even so, it can be argued, "[T]he United States Congress is probably more powerful as a legislative body vis-à-vis the executive than is any other legislative body in the world today." Lewis A. Froman, Jr., *The Congressional Process: Strategies, Rules, and Procedures* (Boston: Little, Brown & Co., 1967), p. 3. See *Federalist*, pp. 327-28, 330, 338-41, 341-42, 454-56, 461-62, 466; chap. 8, n. 38, below.

37. We see in Chafee an insistence upon legislative, rather than judicial, safeguards as primary. "The lesson of United States v. Abrams," he observed, "is that Congress alone can effectively safeguard minority opinion in times of excitement. Once a sedition statute is on the books, bad tendency becomes the test of criminality. Trial judges will be found to adopt a free construction of the act so as to reach objectionable doctrines, and the Supreme Court will probably be unable to afford relief." *Freedom of Speech*, pp. 158-59. See chap. 3, n. 13, above.

This position is supported by Wallace Mendelson's argument:

> . . . Congress has killed thousands of bills reflecting every imaginable form of bigotry, intolerance, and demagogery; the Supreme Court has not yet struck down a national measure on the basis of any provision in the first amendment. . . . My point is that liberals appreciate the political process far too little, and expect far more from judicial review than it has ever been able to deliver. . . . Man after all is a political, not a legal, animal. ["On the Meaning of the First Amendment: Absolutes in the Balance," *Calif. L. Rev.* 50 (1962): 821, 828]

(Mendelson might not consider his point significantly affected by the rulings in *Lamont* v. *Postmaster General of the United States*, 381 U.S. 301 [1965] and in *U.S.* v. *Robel*, 389 U.S. 258 [1967].) But I believe his argument underestimates the influence of the judiciary, not only for educational purposes but even for immediate political purposes (as is evident in the segregation and reapportionment cases). See chap. 3, n. 14, above, chap. 4, n. 116, chap. 7, n. 72, chap. 8, nn. 82, 95, below.

Still, the advice of *Federalist* No. 73 should be recalled:

> It may perhaps be said that the power of preventing bad laws includes that of preventing good ones; and may be used to the one purpose as well as to the other. But this objection will have little weight with those who can properly estimate the mischiefs of that inconstancy and mutability in the laws, which form the greatest blemish in the character and genius of our governments. They will consider every institution calculated to restrain the excess of lawmaking, and to keep things in the same state in which they happen to be at any given period, as much more likely to do good than harm; because it is favorable to greater stability in the system of legislation. The injury which may possibly be done by defeating a few good laws, will be amply compensated by the advantage of preventing a number of bad ones.

See, also, *Federalist* No. 62; Cicero *Laws* 3.18.42; chap. 6, n. 14, chap. 7, n. 40, below.

I find it convenient to put what I say in this book in a form appropriate for the judiciary, but it should be useful as well for the judicious and Constitution-minded legislator or executive officer. Several comments in chap. 8, n. 83, below, are addressed to the legislator mindful of his oath of office. See chap. 8, nn. 52, 93, below.

38. The Fourteenth Amendment does distinguish between "making" and "enforcing" laws, enjoining the states in both capacities. This reminds us of the failure of the First Amendment to address itself explicitly to "enforcing." Cf. *South Carolina* v. *Katzenbach*, 383 U.S. 301, 324-27 (1966).

39. But should not the evident purposes of the First Amendment guide the President in the exercise both of his power to pardon and of whatever discretion he may have in ordering prosecutions? See, on President Jefferson's use of the pardoning power, chap. 8, n. 14, below.

40. One result of Madison's original intention of having the proposed Bill of Rights amendments inserted into the original Constitution would have been the addition of an eighth article to the instrument. There is in the extant records of debates no indication of a concern that such a change might disturb the numbering patterns in the Constitution. Thus, it seems likely that primacy in the context was understood by the framers of the Constitution not in terms of centrality (which the addition of amendatory articles in the instrument itself would have altered), but rather in terms of sequential priority.

The argument of this study, however, recognizes the provisions in Article IV as critical, if not central, to our constitutional system.

See chap. 6, n. 43, below.

41. See, on the power of Congress to canvass and count electoral votes, Lincoln, *Complete Works*, ed. John G. Nicolay and John Hay (New York: Century Co., 1902), 2:639.

The Constitution seems to regard the legislative as the most important branch of state governments as well. When one branch of these governments is singled out, it is likely to be the legislative. For example, the senators, who represent the states, were chosen by the state legislatures. See Anastaplo, "Notes on the First Amendment" (Ph.D. diss., University of Chicago, 1964), p. 535.

42. Whether the President is obliged to enforce only laws made by Congress is also a general constitutional problem, not one raised especially by the First Amendment. See Crosskey, *Politics and the Constitution*, pp. 433-34. Cf. *Dallemagne* v. *Moisan*, 197 U.S. 169, 174 (1905). Crosskey argued, "[S]tate laws are among the laws which the President has sworn faithfully to enforce. There is no doubt about this, for in early drafts of the Constitution the presidential duty of law enforcement was limited to the laws of the United States; but late in the Federal Convention sessions, when the ensurance of domestic tranquillity was added as one of the objects of the new government, this limitation was removed and the President's duty thus broadened to its present form in which it covers

all the laws, whether state or national in character." "The Constitutionality of the President's Seizure of the Steel Industry," *University of Chicago Roundtable*, No. 738, May 18, 1952, p. 2.

The executive branch of the general government must be reminded from time to time that the decisive legislative restraint upon it remains, as once upon the British monarch, that of the purse:

> One circumstance constantly irritated [Secretary of State John Foster Dulles], at times causing him to speak explosively. "I spend at least a fourth of my time testifying before the congressional committees," he would say, "and the galling thing is that much of my time there is wasted at the very moment I have so many other things I must do." Among the time-consuming appearances before congressional committees were those dealing with State Department appropriations. One year Foster determined to change the routine: Instead of sitting through weeks of detailed hearings, he would make a broad opening statement on the work and needs of the Department and then turn over to the Under Secretary the task of following and coordinating the testimony of Assistant Secretaries and Bureau Chiefs. When the Secretary failed to put in an appearance at the Appropriations subcommittee the day following his opening testimony, the chairman of the subcommittee phoned him and snapped, "Mr. Secretary, my subcommittee has just reduced the budget for your immediate office by 50 per cent; if you wish to restore the original figure I'd suggest you come back here and stay throughout our hearings." Angry but realistic, Foster went back. [Dwight D. Eisenhower, *Waging Peace, 1956-1961* (Garden City, N.Y.: Doubleday & Co., 1965), pp. 371-72]

See chap. 2, n. 34, above, chap. 4, n. 60, chap. 8, n. 38, below.

43. Related to this observation is Madison's belief that the greatest danger to liberty lies "in the body of people, operating by the majority against the minority." *Annals*, I, p. 437. See chap. 8, sec. 10, above, for more from Madison on this point.

The President has become more and more powerful since the early days of the Republic, evidently because (1) foreign affairs (and hence military activities) have continually grown in both importance and dramatic interest, (2) the regime has steadily become more democratic (with the President alone elected by "all the people"), and (3) the states have diminished in stature. Modern technology and industry have influenced these developments. Americans do not generally appreciate the extent to which mere size restricts the alternatives available to them. Gouverneur Morris could speak of "the executive Authority" as "the Key Stone in the great Arch of Empire." *Diary*, 1:380. See Tocqueville, *Democracy in America*, 1:130-31; Jackson, *Supreme Court in American System*, pp. 64-65. See, also, chap. 7, nn. 35, 102, 114, 116, below. Cf. chap. 9, n. 1, below.

"The key departments in modern times," Walter Lippmann has written, "are State, Defense, Treasury, and Central Intelligence." *Chicago Sun-Times*, Nov. 28, 1961, p. 29. See chap. 7, n. 116, below. This concentration of power is reflected in the fact that the Senate has become, more than governorships, the source of presidential candidates. "This is not because of the superior quality of [the Senate's] men," Richard H. Rovere has explained, "but because national and international issues have become the crucial ones to most voters, and also because the mediums of publicity have taken on an increasingly national character." *New Yorker*, Jan. 30, 1960, p. 82. See Reston, *Artillery of the Press*, pp. 46, 59, 76, 103. See chap. 3, n. 35, above.

"Modern times" may really have begun for Americans with the Civil War. Alexander H. Stephens, the vice-president of the Confederacy, said of Lincoln that "the Union with him in sentiment rose to the sublimity of a religious mysticism." Edmund Wilson, *Patriotic Gore* (New York: Oxford University Press, 1966), pp. 96-97. Lincoln, says Roy F. Nichols, in his deceptively modest *Blueprint for Leviathan: American Style* (New York: Atheneum, 1963), p. 209, "held an almost mystic concept of himself as tribune of the people . . . " (See chap. 7, n. 95, below.) (These developments, I suspect, are intimately related to the rise of universal suffrage.) See chap. 4, n. 61, below.

"If the war left a lasting trauma, and resulted in, not an apocalypse, but, on the one hand, a rather gross period of industrial and commercial development and, on the other, a severe disillusionment for the idealists who had been hoping for something better, these are matters about which we in the North have rarely thought and even less often spoken." Wilson, *Patriotic Gore*, p. 125. See, also, ibid., pp. 159-60, where the Northern victory is seen as resulting in the "unleashing of the money-grubbing interests." (But, it should be noticed, Wilson tends [perhaps this is one effect upon him of the trauma he speaks of?] to be skeptical of any invocation of either nobility or justice, especially wherever the influence of religious fervor is suspected by him. [Is not the suspicion of absolutes (see, e.g., chap. 3, n. 25, above) partly a legacy of the secularism of the Enlightenment?]). See, e.g., ibid., pp. 171, 184 (on Grant's insistence to Bismarck, "In the beginning, yes [the Union was the dominant sentiment], but as soon as slavery fired upon the flag it was felt, we all felt, even those who did not object to slaves, that slavery must be destroyed. We felt that it was a stain to the Union that men should be bought and sold, like cattle."). Cf. U. S. Grant, *Personal Memoirs* (New York: Charles L. Webster & Co., 1894), pp. 629-30; chap. 4, n. 48, chap. 8, n. 2, below. See chap. 4, n. 60, below.

44. Madison developed this argument later on:

> [An objection is] that the Legislature itself has no right to expound the Constitution; that wherever its meaning is doubtful, you must leave it to take its course, until the Judiciary is called upon to declare its meaning. I acknowledge, in the ordinary course of Government, that the exposition of the laws and Constitution devolves upon the Judiciary. But I beg to know, upon what principle it can be contended, that any one department draws from the Constitution greater powers than another, in marking out the limits of the powers of the several departments? The Constitution is the charter of the people to the Government; it specifies certain great powers as absolutely granted, and marks out the departments to exercise them. If the Constitutional boundary of either be brought into question, I do not see that any one of these independent departments has more right than another to declare their sentiments on that point.
> . . . There is not one Government on the face of the earth, so far as I recollect, there is not one in the United States, in which provision is made for a particular authority to determine the limits of the Constitutional division of power between the branches of the Government. In all systems there are points which must be adjusted by the departments themselves, to which no one of them is competent. If it cannot be determined in this way, there is no resource left but the will of the community, to be collected in some mode to be provided by the Constitution, or one dictated by the necessity of the case. [*Annals, I*, pp. 500-501.]

See chap. 2, n. 28, above, and the text at chap. 8, n. 87, above.

45. This independence is recognized in the rejection of one of the amendments that Tucker suggested in the House of Representatives, that the President not be considered simply as "commander-in-chief" but rather should have power to direct, "agreeably to law," the operations of the armed forces. *Annals, I*, p. 762. The Constitution acknowledges Locke's observation that war, "which admits not of plurality of governors, *naturally* devolves the command into the king's sole authority." *Second Treatise of Government*, sec. 108. (Italics added.)

I attempt in my constitutional interpretation to take due account both of what is natural and of what is considered natural. The natural is reflected in references to "the necessity of the case" (as in the preceding note) and is incorporated in the unwritten Constitution discussed in chapter 8 of this book. See chap. 7, n. 77, chap. 9, n. 20, below.

46. It should be evident that not all our privileges have explicit constitutional protection. See chap. 2, n. 30, above.

Much of chapters 8 and 9, it should be added, serves to remind us that the preservation of our rights depends on the proper respect for our duties.

47. Thus, it was reported, in *U.S. v. Clark*, 31 Fed. 710, 716 (1887),

CHAPTER FOUR, NOTES 48-49: PAGE 68

> . . . The first duty of a soldier is obedience, and without this there can be neither discipline nor efficiency in the army. If every subordinate officer and soldier were at liberty to question the legality of the orders of the commander, and obey them or not as he may consider them valid or invalid, the camp would be turned into a debating school, where the precious moment for action would be wasted in wordy conflicts between the advocates of conflicting opinions.

The court also said, 31 Fed., at 717, " . . . an order given by an officer to his private which does not expressly and clearly show on its face, or the body thereof, its own illegality, the soldier would be bound to obey, and such order would be a protection to him."
    Compare, however, *Axtell's Case* (All the Judges of England, 1660. Reported J. Kel. 13),

> Memorandum, That upon the tryal of one Axtell, a soldier, who commanded the guards at the king's tryal and at his murder; he justified that all he did was as a soldier, by the command of his superior Officer, whom he must obey or die. It was resolved that was no excuse, for his Superiour was a Traiter, and all that joyned with him in that Act were Traytors, and did by that approve the Treason; and where the command is Traiterous, there the Obedience to that Command is also Traiterous.

Consider, also, the instructions given by a military judge to a court-martial which then found a marine private guilty of the premeditated murder of a dozen Vietnamese women and children: ". . . A marine is a reasoning agent, who is under a duty to exercise judgment in obeying orders to the extent that where such orders are manifestly beyond the scope of the authority of the one giving the order and are palpably illegal upon their face, then the act of obedience to such orders will not justify acts pursuant to such illegal orders." *Chicago Sun-Times*, June 22, 1970, p. 2.
    48. "The Nation may raise armies and compel citizens to give military service. *Selective Draft Cases*, 245 U.S. 366 [1918]. It follows, of course, that those subject to military discipline are under many duties and may not claim many freedoms we hold inviolable as to those in civilian life." Justice Jackson, *West Virginia Board of Education* v. *Barnette*, 319 U.S. 624, 642, n. 19 (1943). (See ibid., at 634, n. 14, on the controversial use of "Nation" [as distinguished from "federation"]; cf. his use there of "Republic" [as distinguished from "democracy"].)
    See Lincoln, *Complete Works*, 2:241-42 (on the 1862 dismissal from military service of an officer for expressing the sentiment, "The object is that neither army shall get much advantage of the other, that both shall be kept in the field till they are exhausted, when we will make a compromise and save slavery."). See, also, ibid., 2:254; cf., ibid., 2:291, 464, 480-81, 491.
    See Plutarch, *The Lives of the Noble Grecians and Romans* (New York: Modern Library, n.d.), p. 876.
    49. See chap. 5, n. 142, below.
    This analysis is complicated, however, by the problem raised upon consideration of the situation when a military man is the only one equipped to inform the public of developments crucial to political decisions. President Truman released military personnel to argue against his armed forces unification policy. James Forrestal, *The Forrestal Diaries* (New York: Viking Press, 1951), pp. 118-19. Cf. ibid., pp. 149, 151-53, 159-63, 169, 228-29. (I discuss this problem in chap. 8, secs. 13-14, where I consider the effectiveness of freedom of speech today.) See Curtis E. LeMay, *America Is in Danger* (New York: Funk & Wagnalls, 1968), pp. viii, xi, 1-4, 7, 9, 12, 16-19, 35, 269, 293-94. See, for this dedicated officer's dubious political judgment, ibid., pp. 313-28. Cf. S. L. A. Marshall's informed review of this book, which included the observation, "LeMay's spelling out in depth of how and why [Secretary of Defense Robert S.] McNamara went wrong is done in such detail that the book becomes an education in the complexities of national defense in this tormented age. The surprises are frequent, the revelations breathtaking." *Book Week*, June 9, 1968, p. 7. See chap. 5, n. 29, chap. 8, n. 179, below. See, also, a letter to

the editor (on the inadequacies of the information program provided by the army for its enlisted men) which contributed to the court-martial of its soldier-author (who was also an experienced radio news broadcaster), *New Republic*, June 18, 1951, p. 4. Not too long afterward Americans were shocked to learn of the inadequate preparation of our soldiers in Korea for withstanding the pressures brought to bear by the Chinese upon prisoners of war. See George Anastaplo, "Closing Argument," *Lawyers Guild Rev.* 19 (1959): 143, 161-63; *Transcript of Record*, U.S. Supreme Court, *In re Anastaplo* (Appendix F, above), pp. 357-62.

See the Aug. 10, 1961, press conference of President Kennedy on the advantages, to both the public and the military, when the military is kept out of and protected from politics. This has been illustrated in Greece since April, 1967, where the army has been seriously damaged by a handful of junior officers who consider themselves entitled to dismantle the army in their efforts to retain power. (I discuss this development in the articles cited in chap. 6, n. 1, below. See, also, chap. 7, n. 67, chap. 8, n. 149, chap. 9, n. 38, below.)

Walter Lippmann recalled, upon "President [Johnson's] bringing Gen. William C. Westmoreland home in order to explain the war," an incident of the Second World War:

> [Senator Warren Austin] said in effect "I know you are seeing the prime minister this afternoon and I wish you would ask him to tell his chiefs of staff to come to Congress and testify in favor of our strategical policy." Quite innocently I said I would do this, and when Churchill received me that afternoon I began by saying that I had a message from Sen. Austin. "Would the prime minister instruct his chiefs of staff to go to the Senate Foreign Relations Committee . . ." I never finished the message. For the old lion let out a roar demanding to know why I was so ignorant of the British way of doing things that I could dare to suggest that a British general should address a parliamentary body. As I remember it, what he said was "I am the minister of defense and I, not the generals, will state the policy of his majesty's government." No one who ever aroused the wrath of Churchill is likely to forget it. I certainly have not forgotten it. I learned an indelible lesson about one of the elementary principles of democratic government. And therefore, I take a very sour view of a field commander being brought home by the President to educate the Congress and the American people. ["Intervention of the General," *Chicago Sun-Times*, Apr. 27, 1967, p. 94]

(Lippmann concluded his reminiscence, "The President is indeed playing with fire. If there are any plain-spoken men to whom he still listens, they should speak before it is too late.")

Cf. James M. Burns, *Roosevelt: The Soldier of Freedom* (New York: Harcourt Brace Jovanovich, 1970), p. 223: "The day Wake Island fell [American Secretary of the Navy Frank] Knox complained to Churchill at the White House that the fleet had been ordered to fight the Japanese and after a few hours of steaming had turned back. 'What would you do with your Admiral in a case like this?' Churchill replied mildly that it was 'dangerous to meddle with Admirals when they say they can't do things. They have always got the weather or fuel or something to argue about.' One thing Roosevelt and Knox could do was to reshuffle the shaken Navy command. . . ."

50. Is this judgment made on the basis of the Constitution generally or on the basis of what I understand by "freedom of speech"? See chap. 2, n. 34, above. How does this judgment apply to the regulation of federal employees and to such developments as loyalty programs?

Cf. Francis Biddle, *Justice Holmes, Natural Law and the Supreme Court* (New York: Macmillan Co., 1961), pp. 66-67; Sidney Hook, *Heresy, Yes—Conspiracy, No!* (New York: John Day Co., 1953), p. 49.

51. It should be noted, however, that there are on the President no special prohibitions against executing other laws, such as *ex post facto* laws, which are prohibited to both the states and the general government. The general prohibition of certain kinds of enactments, if respected by legislatures, would effectively bind him as well.

52. "Nothing justifies the suspending of the civil by the military authority, but mili-

CHAPTER FOUR, NOTES 53-55: PAGES 69-70   477

tary necessity, and of the existence of that necessity, the military commander, and not a popular vote, is to decide." Lincoln, *Complete Works*, 2:620-21.

Congress can impeach *the* military commander—i.e., the commander in chief. Can it do anything less than that to control executive action, such as reversing the suspension of the civil by the military authority or again making available the writ of *habeas corpus*?

See for an assessment of Lincoln's view, and its dependence on a doctrine of national common law, Lord Charnwood, *Abraham Lincoln* (Garden City, N.Y.: Garden City Pub. Co., 1917), pp. 377-80. See, also, *Ex Parte Milligan*, 4 Wall. [U.S.] 2 (1866) (and Chafee, *Freedom of Speech*, p. 33, n. 71). Cf. Alan Bullock, *Hitler: A Study in Tyranny* (New York: Harper & Row, 1964), p. 675. See chap. 3, n. 31, above.

53. I have already pointed out that the cession of the "ten miles square" that later became the District of Columbia was made in conformity with an act of Congress which stipulated that the laws of the ceding state would continue in force until Congress acted to change or eliminate them. Among these laws could be some abridging freedom of speech. May it not be in the interest of the inhabitants of the "ten miles square," and of the country at large, that such laws should be available and on occasion executed?

This is related to other questions already mentioned. See, e.g., chap. 2, n. 34, above. Is Congress, to the extent that it acts as the "state legislature" for the District of Columbia (and for the territories), vested with inherent and broad powers that the states of the Union have with respect to their respective inhabitants? Or are these state governments themselves merely the recipients of powers given to them by their respective peoples, usually through local constitutions, and hence not possessors of inherent powers? See chap. 8, nn. 25, 71, below.

54. That is, the suspension of the writ does not seem to add to Congress's legislative powers or put the President in Congress's place. Lincoln denied that the President "may make permanent rules of property by proclamation" or that he may "expressly or impliedly seize and exercise the permanent legislative functions of the government." The President, he argued, should in such circumstances leave "all questions which are not of vital military importance to the more deliberate action of the legislature." *Complete Works*, 2:81, 103. See, also, ibid., 2:347-48, 361. Cf. Edward Crankshaw, *Gestapo* (London: Pantheon Books, 1960), pp. 54, 68.

> . . . But Lincoln's policy, apart from all questions of its legality, was very different from most of the Espionage Act prosecutions and sentences [at the end of the First World War]. He was proceeding against men who were so far within the test of direct and dangerous interference with the war that they were actually causing desertions, and even then he acted to prevent and not to punish. Vallandigham was sent through into the Confederate lines, and left unmolested on his return. Lincoln would not have allowed an old man [Eugene V. Debs], a Presidential opponent and the choice of nine hundred thousand American citizens, to lie in prison for sincere and harmless, even though misguided, words, over a year after the last gun was fired. [Chafee, *Freedom of Speech*, p. 117]

Cf. Appendix B, chap. 3, n. 14, above.

It is appropriate, before ordinary statesmen presume to imitate Lincoln's experimentation, to recall C. S. Lewis's observation:

> In other words, there are rules behind the rules, and a unity which is deeper than uniformity. A supreme workman will never break by one note or one syllable or one stroke of the brush the living and inward law of the work he is producing. But he will break without scruple any number of those superficial regularities and orthodoxies which little, unimaginative critics mistake for its laws. *Miracles: A Preliminary Study* (New York: Macmillan Co., 1947), p. 99.

See Plato, *Republic* 330D-331E.

55. See chap. 4, n. 59, below. The suspension of the writ legitimates the power "to arrest, and detain, without resort to the ordinary processes and forms of law, such indi-

viduals as [the commanding general] might deem dangerous to the public safety." Lincoln, *Complete Works*, 2:59. See James G. Randall, *Constitutional Problems under Lincoln* (Urbana: University of Illinois Press, 1951), p. 153.

It should be noticed that after Lincoln asked his famous rhetorical question, whether "all the laws but one [should] go unexecuted, and the government itself go to pieces lest that one be violated," he went on to argue that there had in fact been no violation of any law, that the provision permitting the suspension of the writ of *habeas corpus* had made it possible to avoid this choice. Lincoln, *Complete Works*, 2:60. See chap. 7, n. 62, below.

56. See, for a useful discussion of Lincoln's justification for his suspension of the writ of *habeas corpus*, Harry V. Jaffa, *Equality and Liberty* (New York: Oxford University Press, 1965), p. 171. The question Lincoln considered was whether the President as well as Congress was empowered to suspend the writ. (See Joseph Story, *Commentaries on the Constitution of the United States*, 2d ed. [Boston: Little, Brown & Co., 1851], chap. 32, secs. 1338-1342; Lincoln, *Complete Works*, 2:60, 360.) See chap. 2, n. 35, above, chap. 8, n. 60, below. See, also, chap. 3, n. 28, above.

In the course of his discussion, Jaffa observed that "since the Constitution . . . provides that the privilege of the writ of habeas corpus may be suspended 'when in cases of rebellion or invasion the public safety may require it,' the Constitution must contemplate the lawful abridgment under certain circumstances of the freedoms of the First Amendment." Ibid., p. 171. This is certainly true. But it does not follow, as Jaffa seems to suggest, that the *habeas corpus* provision and the First Amendment are in conflict, even "in direct contradiction," with each other: "As we have seen, the command of the First Amendment that 'Congress shall make no law . . . abridging the freedom of speech,' is in a certain sense incompatible with the proposition that Congress may, in time of rebellion or invasion, suspend the writ of habeas corpus." Ibid., p. 172.

There are (in the situation here considered) two principal constitutional alternatives: either the writ of *habeas corpus* can be suspended (thereby permitting the detention by the President of civilians, outside [as well as within] zones of military operations, who may exercise freedom of speech in a manner likely to obstruct the war effort) or there can be no lawful action taken by the general government abridging the freedom of speech of such civilians. By defining with care the exceptions that it does permit, the Constitution emphasizes for us the absoluteness of such restraints as those found in the First Amendment. (Francis Dana assured the 1788 Massachusetts Ratifying Convention, "The safest and best restriction [on the power of Congress to suspend the writ of *habeas corpus*] arises from the nature of the cases in which Congress are authorized to exercise the power at all, namely, in those of rebellion or invasion. These are clear and certain terms, facts of public notoriety, and whenever these shall cease to exist, the suspension of the writ must necessarily cease also." Jonathan Elliot, *Debates in the Several State Conventions on the Adoption of the Federal Constitution* [Philadelphia: J. B. Lippincott & Co., 1863], 2:108)

It is salutary to emphasize today the extent to which the Constitution provides for almost every contingency that may confront the country. Otherwise one is likely to give aid and comfort to those (here and abroad) who regard constitutional government and the rule of law as something that is likely to stand in the way of securing the common good. The remarkable feature of Lincoln's administration, in this respect, was the effort he made to stay within constitutional limitations, even in circumstances when it must have seemed to other reasonable men that the Constitution no longer really existed. The careful formulation of the Emancipation Proclamation is instructive as to his respect for constitutional government, as is his insistence upon regular wartime elections. (Cf. chap. 6, n. 39, below.) Even the sporadically severe abridgments of freedom of speech during the Civil War were, arguably, within the precise terms of the First Amendment as defined in this book. (Most such restrictions were imposed under martial law.)

Indeed, it can be said that the essentially Lincolnian position on civil liberties and the rule of law is reflected in the opinion for the Supreme Court by Justice Davis (an old

CHAPTER FOUR, NOTES 57-58: PAGE 70

friend whom Lincoln had appointed to the Court), in *Ex parte Milligan*, 4 Wall. 2 (1866). Justice Davis argued, at p. 125 of his opinion,

> This nation, as experience has proved, cannot always remain at peace, and has no right to expect that it will always have wise and humane rulers, sincerely attached to the principles of the Constitution. Wicked men, ambitious of power, with hatred of liberty and contempt of law, may fill the place once occupied by Washington and Lincoln; and if this right is conceded, and the calamities of war again befall us, the dangers to human liberty are frightful to contemplate. If our fathers had failed to provide for just such a contingency, they would have been false to the trust reposed in them. . . . Not one of [the safeguards they incorporated in a written Constitution] can the President, or Congress, or the Judiciary disturb, except the one concerning the writ of *habeas corpus*.

(Cf. Arthur E. Sutherland, *Constitutionalism in America: Origin and Evolution of Its Fundamental Ideas* [New York: Blaisdell Pub. Co., 1965], pp. 416-21.)

One notices, upon turning to Jaffa's excellent study of the Lincoln-Douglas Debates, that he used as an epigraph these lines from *Measure for Measure* (act 2, sc. 2):

> O, it is excellent
> To have a giant's strength; but it is tyrannous
> To use it like a giant.

The companion epigraph that he employs is from *Macbeth*, that play which so intrigued Lincoln, a man fascinated with the temptations, glories, and pitfalls of usurpation. Harry V. Jaffa, *Crisis of the House Divided* (Garden City, N.Y.: Doubleday & Co., 1959), p. 15. We, like Lincoln, must be alert against the tyrant's plea of necessity, even when it is invoked in the name of "works of evident utility to the public, 'the supreme reason above all reasons, which is the salvation of the king's lands and people.'" Blackstone, *Laws of England*, 3:vi, 74; cf. 1:vii, 245, 250-51. See chap. 5, n. 115, below. (Would not Macbeth and Banquo, properly combined, make the complete ruler? See p. 271, above.)

The Constitution can be said to recognize (as does Shakespeare) that it is rare, however excellent, to have a giant's strength and not to use it like a giant. Lincoln, in the First Inaugural Address, put this sentiment in these words:

> By the frame of government under which we live, this same people have wisely given their public servants but little power for mischief; and have, with equal wisdom, provided for the return of that little to their own hands at very short intervals. While the people retain their virtue and vigilance, no administration, by any extreme of wickedness or folly, can very seriously injure the government in the short space of four years. [*Complete Works*, 2:7]

57. Additional constitutional alternatives to the clear and present danger test are discussed in chapter 7. See, for an indication of how one may assess better and worse alternatives, the final footnote in my article, "Due Process of Law."

See chap. 3, nn. 4, 33, chap. 4, n. 1, above.

58. The states retain primary authority with respect to traffic regulation even though traffic accidents have killed almost three times as many Americans as have wars, and even though it is known that such accidents still constitute a far greater and far more immediate menace to life and property than any of the talk that has thus far been prosecuted by the general government in sedition cases.

> . . . Some 1,365 American military men lost their lives in Viet Nam in 1965 and 6,110 were wounded. The war's cost is running around $10.5 billion a year. The toll on the highways in 1965 was 50,000 dead and about 350,000 injured. The cost of these accidents is estimated at about $8 billion for the year. [Charles Bartlett, *Chicago Sun-Times*, Jan. 30, 1966]

It has been reported, "States not implementing a federally approved safety program [including mandatory auto inspection each year and reexamination of drivers at least every four years] by the end of 1968 face the loss of their highway safety funds and 10 per cent of their federal highway construction money." *Chicago Sun-Times*, Dec. 6, 1966, p. 16. See Grodzins, *American System*, p. 323.

59. Every Utopia must deal with this problem, usually by isolating itself. See the lecture, "Utopia or Tyranny: The Universal Declaration of Human Rights," appended to my dissertation, "Notes on the First Amendment."

I do little more in this book than touch upon what could be in some circumstances the central freedom of speech problem, the problem that we are reminded of here of the effect on foreign relations of the exercise by Americans (in the United States) of their right to freedom of speech. Thus, there are here considerations of national security, as is evident in a private letter of Lincoln (Sept. 22, 1861), "I do not say this in the public letter, because it is a subject I prefer not to discuss in the hearing of our enemies." *Complete Works*, 2:82. (See chap. 8, n. 139, below; also, President Kennedy's speech of Apr. 27, 1961, before the American Newspaper Publishers' Association; cf. Arthur M. Schlesinger, Jr., *A Thousand Days* [Boston: Houghton Mifflin Co., 1965], p. 296.) There are here considerations of how distinguished visitors and current negotiations should be treated in the press. (See, e.g., chap. 7, nn. 43, 44, below.) And there are here considerations as well of how peoples, and even leaders, abroad will react to what is said in the American press, especially in those countries where local experience is such as to make it difficult for them to imagine a press that is not a mere organ of the government.

> Khrushchev was obviously much concerned [at the beginning of his 1959 tour of the United States] about the extent of the newspaper and television coverage that would be given to his speeches while he was in the United States. He alleged that our publicity media had not covered his side of things adequately in the Moscow debates. To this I replied that our press, radio, and television companies were free to report what they regarded as news, or to decline to disseminate any story that had, in their opinion, little news value. I said that his utterances would be reported according to this kind of editorial judgment, not mine. Despite my insistence, he refused to believe that we have in this country a free press, without governmental censorship. He said, "Of course, the American government gets printed what it wants printed and is able to suppress what it does not want printed." [Eisenhower, *Waging Peace*, pp. 436-37. Cf. ibid., p. 445]

An article in the [Calcutta, India] *Statesman–Overseas Weekly*, Dec. 9, 1961, p. 6, suggests the problem of democratic regimes in a nondemocratic world:

> The Prime Minister [Jawaharlal Nehru] is by nature so frank and truthful that he now and then unwittingly offers the Chinese argument for use against India. His statement that Ladakh was a barren country where not a blade of grass grew was used by the Chinese in their propaganda to show India's lack of interest and, by inference, possession in the areas in dispute. Even during the talks between the official teams of India and China, the Chinese quoted on numerous occasions from Mr. Nehru's speeches. . . . The Prime Minister has a unique gift of detachment and a transparent honesty of approach difficult to match; but in the Chinese, India has an adversary which does not understand the democratic method of functioning nor the nuances of parliamentary debate. They would rather take full advantage of any given situation and distort or tear out of context whatever is said in India on these controversial matters.

Cf. chap. 8, n. 139, below.

One finds in the *Federalist* several indications that the truth should be veiled when matters affecting foreign relations are discussed. See, e.g., *Federalist* No. 4, No. 11 ("would involve topics not proper for a newspaper discussion"), No. 43 ("The time has been when

CHAPTER FOUR, NOTE 60: PAGE 71

it was incumbent on us all to veil the ideas which this paragraph exhibits"), No. 64. (See, also, *Federalist*, pp. 328-29.)

> The marked difference between foreign affairs and domestic affairs . . . is recognized by both houses of Congress in the very form of their requisitions for information from the executive departments. In the case of every department except the Department of State, the resolution *directs* the official to furnish the information. In the case of the State Department, dealing with foreign affairs, the President is *requested* to furnish the information "if not incompatible with the public interest." A statement that to furnish the information is not compatible with the public interest rarely, if ever, is questioned. [*U.S. v. Curtiss-Wright Export Corp.*, 299 U.S. 304, 321 (1936)]

See chap. 4, n. 113, below.

In ordinary times a republic must depend on its citizens' sense of duty and of restraint in discussing foreign relations. But in the most serious circumstances—when the existence or independence of the community is threatened by war, foreign or domestic—emergency measures may have to be considered (to limit in an extraordinary way what citizens say or do). Such a measure was the carefully prescribed institution of the dictatorship in the Roman republic. Rousseau's chapter on this institution in *The Social Contract* (book 4, chap. 6) is instructive, as is Montesquieu, *The Spirit of the Laws*, 2:3; 11:16; 12:19. (The bill of attainder, like the ostracism of Athens, may have served in England somewhat the same function as the dictatorship in Rome. See, on ostracism, Plutarch, *The Lives of the Noble Grecians and Romans* [New York: Random House, Modern Library, n.d.], p. 148; Machiavelli, *Discourses on Livy*, I, xxviii; see, on the usefulness of attainders, Leonard W. Levy, *Jefferson and Civil Liberties: The Darker Side* [Cambridge: Harvard University Press, 1963], pp. 39-41 [for Jefferson's opinion]; Farrand, ed., *Records*, 2:550.) See chap. 3, n. 31, above. See, also, Sallust, *Catiline*, sec. 29; Thomas Jefferson, *Notes on the State of Virginia* (New York: Harper & Row, Harper Torchbooks, 1964), pp. 121-24; *Federalist*, p. 454; Henry Hallem, *Constitutional History of England* (New York: A. C. Armstrong & Son, 1882), 2:342-43.

Is not the suspension of the writ of *habeas corpus* the Anglo-American substitute for the Roman dictatorship? (But see chap. 4, n. 54, above.) The extraordinary character of the circumstances when the privilege of *habeas corpus* may be suspended is defined by Lincoln in a letter of June 12, 1863:

> [T]he *habeas corpus* provision plainly attests the understanding of those who made the Constitution that ordinary courts of justice are inadequate to "cases of rebellion"—attests their purpose that in such cases, men may be held in custody whom the courts, acting on ordinary rules, would discharge. *Habeas corpus* does not discharge men who are proved to be guilty of defined crime; and its suspension is allowed by the Constitution on purpose that men may be arrested and held who cannot be proved to be guilty of defined crime, "when, in cases of rebellion or invasion, the public safety may require it." . . . Indeed, arrests by process of courts and arrests in cases of rebellion do not proceed altogether upon the same basis. The former is directed at the small percentage of ordinary and continuous perpetration of crime, while the latter is directed at sudden and extensive uprisings against the government, which, at most, will succeed or fail in no great length of time. In the latter case arrests are made not so much for what has been done, as for what probably would be done. The latter is more for the preventive and less for the vindictive than the former. In such cases the purposes of men are much more easily understood than in cases of ordinary crime. . . . [*Complete Works*, 2:347-48]

See chap. 3, nn. 4, 28, above, chap. 7, nn. 66, 67, below. Cf. chap. 5, n. 11, below.

60. Justice Holmes pointed out, in the leading case on the domestic effect of a treaty (*Missouri v. Holland*, 252 U.S. 416, 433 [1920]), "The [migratory bird] treaty in question does not contravene any prohibitory words to be found in the Constitution." He does not

say how he would have voted if the treaty provisions had contravened prohibitory words. Justice Black did say, in Reid v. Covert, 354 U.S. 1, 16-17 (1957),

> [N]o agreement with a foreign nation can confer power on the Congress, or on any other branch of Government, which is free from the restraints of the Constitution. Article VI, the Supremacy Clause of the Constitution, declares: "This Constitution, and the Laws of the United States which shall be made in Pursuance thereof; and all Treaties made, or which shall be made, under the Authority of the United States, shall be the supreme Law of the Land; . . ." There is nothing in this language which intimates that treaties and laws enacted pursuant to them do not have to comply with the provisions of the Constitution. . . . The prohibitions of the Constitution were designed to apply to all branches of the National Government and they cannot be nullified by the Executive or by the Executive and the Senate combined. There is nothing new or unique about what we say here. This Court has regularly and uniformly recognized the supremacy of the Constitution over a treaty. . . .

Cf. chap. 4, n. 19, above.

See, on the difficulty of getting any treaty ratified by the Senate (a requirement that is referred to as "the original mistake of the Constitution"), Henry Adams, *The Education of Henry Adams* (Boston: Houghton Mifflin Co., 1918), p. 374.

> The Secretary of State has always stood as much alone as the historian. Required to look far ahead and round him, he measures forces unknown to party managers, and has found Congress more or less hostile ever since Congress first sat. The Secretary of State exists only to recognize the existence of a world which Congress would rather ignore; of obligations which Congress repudiates whenever it can; of bargains which Congress distrusts and tries to turn to its advantage or to reject. Since the first day the Senate existed, it has always intrigued against the Secretary of State whenever the Secretary has been obliged to extend his functions beyond the appointment of Consuls in Senators' service. [Ibid., p. 422]

"Both Guicciardini and Machiavelli," an English student of diplomacy wrote,

> express horror at the action of Ferdinand and Isabella in refusing to ratify a treaty negotiated and signed with France by Spanish ambassadors bearing full powers. Such repudiation, they rightly suggested, would, if it became a habit, render impossible all sound negotiation between States. It would have seemed inconceivable to them, for instance, that in the year 1919 the United States legislature should have repudiated a treaty negotiated and signed by the President in person. They would have found it difficult to understand the mysteries of the American Constitution. [Harold Nicolson, *The Evolution of Diplomacy* (New York: Macmillan Co., Collier Books, 1962), pp. 58-59]

> President Wilson was an idealist and, what was perhaps more dangerous, a consummate master of English prose. . . . He possessed, moreover, the gift of giving to commonplace ideas the resonance and authority of biblical sentences, and, like all phraseologists, he became mesmerised by the strength and neatness of the phrases that he devised. During the long months of the Paris Peace Conference, I observed him with interest, admiration and anxiety, and became convinced that he regarded himself, not as a world statesman, but as a prophet designated to bring light to a dark world. It may have been for this reason that he forgot all about the American Constitution and Senator Lodge. [Ibid., p. 114]

See chap. 3, n. 16, above, chap. 8, n. 135, below.

Was not the repudiation of President Wilson by the Senate one of the great moments of American constitutionalism, with the same consequences for good as well as ill as the execution of Charles I? See *Youngstown Sheet & Tube Co. v. Sawyer*, 343 U.S. 579 (1952); chap. 4, n. 42, above, chap. 8, n. 38, below.

See chap. 4, n. 43, above.

61. Gouverneur Morris advised President-elect Washington in a letter from Paris:

> Will you excuse me, my dear Sir, . . . for making one Remark on the Subject of Economy and Example taken into joint Consideration. I think it of very great Importance to fix the Taste of our Country properly, and I think your Example will go very far in that Respect. It is therefore my Wish that every Thing about you should be substantially good and majestically plain; made to endure. Nothing is so extravagant in the Event as those Buildings and Carriages and Furniture and Dresses and Ornaments which want continual Renovation. Where a Taste of this Kind prevails, each Generation has to provide for itself. Whereas in the other there is a vast Accumulation of real Wealth in the Space of half a Century. [Morris, *Diary*, 1:380]

See Herodotus, *History*, 1:155-57; Plato, *Republic* 401A-B, 424B-425B; Aristotle, *Politics* 5.8-9; Tacitus, *Agricola* 21; Hobbes, *Leviathan*, I, x (on the uses of honor). Machiavelli describes the papacy as an elective monarchy framed so as to receive the pope as if he were its hereditary lord. *The Prince,* chap. 19. Can this be said of the American President today? Should we try to restore to the presidency "the modest simplicity of republican government" (*Federalist* No. 34)? Or was Montesquieu correct to insist that only monarchy could govern properly an extensive empire? Cf. *Federalist* No. 14. See chap. 4, n. 43, above.

62. The placement of the treason provision in Article III, rather than in Article II, suggests that over this crime at least—and perhaps over other common law crimes as well—the Judiciary was intended to have or was thought (or feared) to have some power independent of and perhaps even prior to an enactment by Congress.

63. Crosskey is useful on this point. See, e.g., chap. 4, n. 65, below. See, also, chap. 4, n. 44, above.

64. The unsentimental character of eighteenth-century political thought is suggested by the reference here to "loss of life or member" (or, in the Fifth Amendment, to "life or limb"). See chap. 8, n. 185, below.

65. It has also been argued, e.g., Crosskey, *Politics and the Constitution*, pp. 557-62, that Congress, as the legislative body coordinate with the United States Judiciary, has a general rule-making power with respect to the courts. See Edmund Burke, *Works* (London: World Classics, 1930), 3:365 (chap. 6, n. 5, below). See, also, chap. 8, n. 88, below.

66. Livermore makes the same point, adding that the state courts would be more convenient and less oppressive to citizens. *Annals, I,* p. 784.

67. The same speaker (Smith), in countering the proposal that the state courts handle all the trial work that federal district courts would conduct, was led to make an argument on behalf of "states' rights" to which I will return in chapter 7:

> If the State courts are to take cognizance of those causes which, by the Constitution, are declared to belong to the judicial courts of the United States, an appeal must lie in every case to the latter, otherwise the judicial authority of the Union might be altogether eluded. To deny such an appeal would be to frustrate the most important objects of the Federal Government, and would obstruct its operations. The necessity of uniformity in the decision of the Federal courts is obvious; to assimilate the principles of national decisions, and collect them, as it were, into one focus, appeals from all the State courts to the Supreme Court would be indispensable. It is, however, much to be apprehended that this constant control of the Supreme Federal Court over the adjudication of the State courts, would dissatisfy the people, and weaken the importance and authority of the State judges. Nay, more, it would lessen their respectability in the eyes of the people, even in causes which properly appertain to the State jurisdictions; because the people, being accustomed to see their decrees overhauled and annulled by a superior tribunal, would soon learn to form an irreverent opinion of their importance and abilities. . . . [*Annals, I,* p. 798]

Jackson was not concerned about the danger that Smith predicted:

> He was clearly of opinion that the people would much rather have but one appeal, which, he conceived, would answer every purpose; he meant from the State courts immediately to the Supreme Court of the continent. An Admiralty court of jurisdiction he would grant might be necessary for the trial of maritime affairs, and matters relative to the revenue, to which object he would cheerfully enlarge it. . . . [*Annals*, I, p. 803]

68. Whether the Judiciary, and particularly the Supreme Court, properly exercises the power of judicial review—i.e., a determination of the constitutionality of *congressional* legislation—is another question that may not be peculiar to a study of the First Amendment. See chap. 8, sec. 10, above, especially chap. 8, n. 85.

69. See, on a national common law of crimes, chap. 6, secs. 3-6, above. See, also, chap. 7, n. 77, below.

70. This was most obvious with respect to land tenures and ecclesiastical matters. See, e.g., Crosskey, *Politics and the Constitution*, p. 419.

One scholar has argued:

> When Madison proposed an amendment in Congress guaranteeing freedom of the press, he did not employ the emphatic language of the Virginia ratifying convention's recommendation that the press cannot be abridged "by any authority of the United States." [Citing Elliot's *Debates*, 3:656] The amendment, in the form in which Madison introduced it, omitted the important clause "by any authority of the United States," which would have covered the executive and the judiciary as well as Congress. The omitted clauses would have prohibited the federal courts from exercising any common-law jurisdiction over criminal libels. As ratified, the First Amendment declared only that Congress should make no law abridging the freedom of speech or press. [Leonard W. Levy, "Liberty and the First Amendment: 1790-1800," *American Historical Review* 68 (Oct. 1962): 22, 27]

See, also, ibid., pp. 29, 30-31.

I believe it is to misconceive the nature of the common law (with its recognition of the supremacy of the legislature over the judiciary) to assume (as Levy seems to do here) that the federal judiciary might be able as common law courts to develop general rules (e.g., abridging freedom of speech) that Congress could not undo or could not itself develop. I understand the common law to recognize, instead, that the legislature may do some things that the judges cannot undo or cannot themselves do. See chap. 6, n. 5, below.

71. See, for the proposed amendment (*Annals*, I, p. 729), chap. 2, n. 38, above.

72. See the text at chap. 2, n. 38, above.

Madison had stated (as we have seen) that he apprehended "the meaning of the words to be, that Congress should not establish a religion, and enforce the legal observation of it by law, nor compel men to worship God in any manner contrary to their conscience." *Annals*, I, p. 730.

73. It is left open, in this exchange, whether "establishment" *could* be read to include the practices which had prevailed in Rhode Island. Huntington was concerned to make certain that "religious establishment" was not "construed" to include such practices.

See, on the relations of church and state before 1800, Sutherland, *Constitutionalism in America*, pp. 264-301. See, also, chap. 2, n. 38, above.

74. Such cases could arise under the diversity jurisdiction of the federal courts. Is this how the hypothetical case described by Huntington, *Annals*, I, p. 730, would get into a federal court?

Suppose, for instance, that a citizen of one state sues in a federal court a citizen of another for failure to abide by a contract to rent quarters to him in defendant's state (and that the amount of damages sought is above the minimum required to establish jurisdiction). Suppose, further, that plaintiff had had plans to use these quarters for purposes illegal under the sedition law of defendant's state, a law that provides for forfeiture to the state of premises used for illegal purposes. (Such forfeiture [e.g., of automobiles] is occasionally provided for today with respect to certain crimes. The licensing act against which Milton wrote provided for forfeiture of printing presses in specified situations.) Defendant, having learned of this intended use (after making the lease), refuses to allow the plaintiff to occupy the premises contracted for. The federal court trying this matter must take into account the state criminal law, even if it should be a law clearly abridging freedom of speech, and must be able to give it full weight. (Let us assume, in order not to complicate this matter unnecessarily, that this law is consistent with the *state* constitution.)

75. But perhaps all this is forced: for Congress also, it could be argued, might find itself exercising the powers of the state legislatures (either in circumstances where the state legislature is not acting or where no state government has yet been formed); and yet, I have assumed that Congress may do so (and abridge freedom of speech when it acts in that capacity), even though Congress is clearly governed by the First Amendment. Perhaps, then, the emphasis should again be placed on the fact that a restraint upon Congress is, for most purposes, a restraint upon the other two branches of the general government.

I proceed thus with tentative explorations throughout this study in order to exhibit and examine the articulation between the parts of the Constitution and to suggest the ramifications both of the problems posed by the First Amendment and of the questions raised by a practical constitutionalism. (See, on how lawyers "reason," Appendix F, above. See, also, chap. 4, n. 42, above, chap. 8, n. 83, below.

76. Compare, on the one hand, the control by the Executive of speech or writing by military personnel that interferes with effective direction of the military and, on the other hand, the control by the branches of Congress of speech or writing that interferes immediately and directly with the conduct of their legislative affairs. Cf. chap. 2, n. 12, above.

77. This anticipates what will be said in chapter 5 about the essentially political character of this freedom, the functions freedom of speech and of the press have and do not have in our constitutional system.

See Justice Black's dissenting opinion in *Cox v. Louisiana*, 379 U.S. 559 (1965).

78. A recent British formulation of the contempt power may be found in E. C. S. Wade and G. G. Phillips, *Constitutional Law*, 4th ed. (London: Longmans, Green & Co., 1951), pp. 365-66:

> ... Criminal contempt of court takes two forms: (a) *conduct by strangers or parties to a suit which scandalizes the court.* A court of record may fine or commit to prison for contempt any person who uses threatening words or abuses any judge of the court. It is, of course, permissible to discuss the merits of a judgment or sentence, but the court has power to punish any criticism which it regards as mere invective or as tending to bring into ridicule and contempt the administration of justice; (b) *conduct which is calculated to prejudice a pending proceeding.* The offence is not confined to criminal proceedings, but committal for this form of contempt of court is mainly used to prevent comments which might influence a jury about to try a criminal offence. The applicant must show that something has been published which is intended or calculated to prejudice a pending trial.

The first of these two forms of contempt reflects the standards and attitudes of the eighteenth-century crime of seditious libel: it would probably be governed by the First Amendment. Indeed, it is reminiscent of the Sedition Act of 1798, reflecting the continuing differences between American and British practices and standards. See chap. 6, n. 17, below, and chap. 6, sec. 6, above.

79. See chap. 8, secs. 4, 6, above.

80. Citizens are left free to make suggestions about changes in the contempt power

or the jurisdiction of courts, to advocate changes in the law being applied, and even to recommend impeachment of judges. We are reminded of the "Impeach Earl Warren" billboards which distinguished the career of the chief justice. See chap. 8, n. 96, below.

It has been held that without the safeguard of a jury trial, summary punishment imposed by a court for criminal contempt must be limited to that appropriate for a petty offense. Consider the disturbing implications of the statement of the U.S. Attorney in Chicago in securing the dismissal of the charges against Bobby G. Seale which had associated him with "the Chicago Conspiracy Trial" (Appendix D, above): "The court will recall that . . . all of the other seven defendants were acquitted by the jury on the conspiracy count. Accordingly, it is thought that it would be inappropriate to try Seale alone on a conspiracy charge. *Moreover, he stands convicted of direct contempt of the court, and a sentence aggregating 48 months has been imposed against him.* Hence, in the government's view, it is proper to dismiss the indictment as to the substantive count." *New York Times*, Oct. 20, 1970, p. 32 (italics added). See chap. 8, n. 52, below. (The imposition of the 48-month sentence was without benefit of either trial or jury, to say nothing of representation by counsel of one's choice at this stage of the proceedings.)

81. These objects are suggested in chapter 8 as well as in my article, "The Declaration of Independence," *St. Louis U. L. J.* 9 (1965): 390.

"A fair trial in a fair tribunal is a basic requirement of due process." Justice Black (in the Opinion of the Court), *In re Murchison*, 349 U.S. 133, 136 (1955); reaffirmed in *Holt* v. *Virginia*, 381 U.S. 131, 136 (1965).

See chap. 4, n. 33, above.

82. Nothing is said about repugnancy to the Constitution. That is, there is no recognition *here* of any right in the courts to second-guess Congress in its determination of what is valid law.

The federal courts are limited by what Congress states to be the rules. Some of these rules are given in the Judiciary Act of 1789, rules relating to *habeas corpus*, to taking parties from one district to another, and to the extent of jurisdiction to be exercised. This suggests why the courts are not given that which both houses of Congress are given, an unfettered power to make their own rules of procedure. Congress is to have the critical "last word" in this, to be able to make corrections and adjustments. And, as is seen here, Congress may permit the courts considerable discretion about what they can provide on their own.

83. Does the right of appeal have constitutional support, irrespective of what either the Congress or the courts provide for? Madison speaks of giving any person "who conceived himself aggrieved" (because of an action by the comptroller in the Treasury Department) "a right to petition the Supreme Court for redress." *Annals*, I, p. 612. This language suggests the possibility that the right of appeal may fall within the right "to petition the Government for redress of grievances" guaranteed in the First Amendment. Stone thought it unnecessary to consider the comptroller as a judge, as Madison had to some extent, "and give, by an express clause in the bill, a right to the complainant to appeal from his decision. He considered this as the right of every man, upon the principles of common law, therefore securing it by the statute would be a work of supererogation." *Annals*, I, p. 613. Does the First Amendment's "right . . . to petition" protect "the right of every man [to appeal], upon the principles of common law"?

84. See, on the distinctive contribution to American republicanism of a judiciary served by a competent bar, Appendix F, chap. 2, nn. 1, 17, above, chap. 4, n. 116, chap. 8, nn. 22, 174, 190, chap. 9, n. 39, below. See, also, Burke, *American Speeches*, pp. 29, 30-31, 83, 93, 97, 141, 208; Tocqueville, *Democracy in America*, 1:284, 286, 288, 298, 304-6.

> But why should we pick on the Generals? Why assume in them a special responsibility towards the German people? The answer is that they claimed such responsibility. The officer caste regarded itself, and was so regarded by large sections of the population, as the repository of German honour. It was also powerful. Hitler could do nothing without its assent and connivance. It tolerated Hit-

ler, whom it despised, because Hitler promised it a return to its vanished glory. For this it was prepared to put up with Himmler and Heydrich too, and the methods of this precious pair. It was the only organised body which could have stopped Hitler in time. . . . And in the end, of course, they found they could not hold up their heads after all. [Crankshaw, *Gestapo*, p. 80; see, also, ibid., pp. 182-83. (Were the German officers abandoned, if not actually misled, by their intellectual betters? See chap. 2, n. 7, above, chap. 8, n. 140, below. If lawyers are to our community what officers were to the German, what should be said about the American teachers of lawyers in the 1950s?)]

85. I consider in chapter 7 the rationale and wisdom of the arrangement whereby the states were left free, under the Bill of Rights, to do what the general government could not do (that is, abridge freedom of speech or of the press), as well as the wisdom of attempts to extend against the states, through the Fourteenth Amendment or otherwise, all the restrictions placed upon Congress. See chap. 7, n. 107, chap. 8, n. 83, below.

86. References to the Fourteenth Amendment here are to the attempt to apply against the states the prohibitions of the First Amendment against the general government. Whatever the basis for this attempt, there is no doubt that the states are bound (at least under the Fourteenth Amendment, and perhaps on other grounds as well, such as the "Republican Form of Government" guarantee) to extend due process in the course of any state proceeding which threatens to deprive any person of life, liberty, or property. This may insure, as I indicate in chapter 5, that the states are at the least bound to respect that aspect of "freedom of the press" which is seen primarily in terms of "no previous restraint." See chap. 8, n. 83, below.

It is curious that Lincoln seems to assume (without challenge from Douglas) that the due process provision of the Fifth Amendment applies to the states as well as to the general government. See Lincoln, *Complete Works*, 1:416-17, 454-55, 459-60, 553-54. See the discussion by Crosskey (as indicated in his Index, *Politics and the Constitution*) of *Barron v. Baltimore*, 7 Pet. [U.S.] 243 (1833).

87. Cf. Willmoore Kendall, "The Bill of Rights and American Freedom," in Frank S. Meyer, ed., *What Is Conservatism?* (New York: Holt, Rinehart & Winston, 1964), pp. 62-63. Crosskey argued that this result was intended, that there should be state power (and state power alone?) over speech, press, and assembly, "subject to a negative control in Congress to prevent abuses by the states." See the text at chap. 5, n. 88, above. See, also, chap. 7, nn. 18, 86, chap. 8, n. 83, below.

Another scholar has argued:

> . . . It now appears that the prohibition on Congress was motivated far less by a desire to give immunity to political expression than by a solicitude for states' rights and the federal principle. The primary purpose of the First Amendment was to reserve to the states an exclusive legislative authority in the field of speech and press.
>
> This is clear enough from the countless states' rights arguments advanced by the Antifederalists during the ratification controversy, and it is explicit in the Republican arguments during the controversy over the Sedition Act. In the House debates on the bill, Albert Gallatin, Edward Livingston, John Nicholas, and Nathaniel Macon all agreed—to quote Macon on the subject of liberty of the press: "The States have complete power on the subject. . . ." [citing *Annals of Congress*, 5th Cong., 2d sess., July 10, 1798, p. 2152; ibid., Gallatin at 2163, Nicholas at 2142, and Livingston at 2153]. Jefferson's Kentucky Resolutions of 1798 expressed the same proposition [citing Elliot's *Debates*, 4:540-41], as did Madison's "Address of the General Assembly to the People of the Commonwealth of Virginia" in 1799 [citing *The Writings of James Madison*, ed. G. Hunt (New York: G. P. Putnam's Sons, 1900-10), 6:333-34]. [Levy, "Liberty and the First Amendment," *Am. Hist. Rev.* 68 (1962): 30]

I would, however (as will be evident in chapters 5 and 8, below), shift the emphasis in the first two sentences I quote here from Levy. See chap. 4, n. 100, chap. 5, n. 34, below.

It should be noted that the states are governed by the provision in Article I, section 6, of the Constitution assuring members of Congress that "for any speech or debate in either House they shall not be questioned in any other place." I believe that this provision (in conjunction with the Necessary and Proper Clause) empowers Congress to protect members of Congress from anything the states might do that would be in effect a penalty or harassment for what has been said in Congress. That is, the legislative masks need not be taken at face value. (See chap. 4, n. 61, above.) Should not Congress (in order to function properly) also be able to protect from state harassment anyone who is permitted to testify before a congressional committee or who submits a report called for by Congress or a committee? I believe Congress may even have the duty, as well as the power, to protect from state harassment any citizen who exercises the First Amendment "right of the people peaceably to assemble and to petition the Government for a redress of grievances." It should be evident, that is, how an imaginative respect for certain apparently narrow provisions of the Constitution can be employed to insure that local tyranny may be exposed, examined, and to some extent curbed in Congress. See chap. 5, n. 37, below.

88. It should again be noticed that almost all of these state constitutional limitations are less absolute than those found in the First Amendment. That is, more than forty of them have an explicit reference to "abuse" (such as is seen in the state constitutional provisions reproduced in the text at chap. 3, n. 10, above): freedom (or, usually, "liberty") of the press is subject to responsibility for the abuse thereof; others imply the notion (e.g., by making provision for criminal libel); Louisiana, Massachusetts, and New Hampshire seem to be as unqualified as the First Amendment but the latter two refer only to "liberty of the press." The 1959 Hawaii Constitution has, as did the recently proposed constitution for New York, a speech and press provision based on the First Amendment text. Both the 1956 Alaska Constitution and the 1964 Michigan Constitution (chap. 5, n. 128, below) retain the "abuse" qualification, as did the recently proposed constitution for Maryland and as does the new constitution proposed for Illinois. See, for Vermont's provisions, chap. 5, n. 104, below. See, also, chap. 4, n. 53, above, chap. 8, nn. 25, 71, 83 (on the significance of the "abuse" qualification), below.

Article I, section 1.01 of the *Model State Constitution* (National Municipal League [New York, 1963]) suggests, on the other hand, "No law shall be enacted respecting an establishment of religion, or prohibiting the free exercise thereof, or abridging the freedom of speech or of the press, or the right of the people peaceably to assemble and to petition the government for a redress of grievances." (Article IV, section 4.10, suggests, "For any speech or debate in the legislature, the members shall not be questioned in any other place.") See Albert L. Sturm, "Bills of Rights in New State Constitutions," in Carl Beck, ed., *Law and Justice: Essays in Honor of Robert S. Rankin* (Durham: Duke University Press, 1970), p. 160.

See chap. 5, n. 105, below, on the effect with respect to freedom of speech of a bicameral legislature.

89. Is "respecting" a little broader in its scope than "touching"?

Another simple form of construction is seen in an imprecise index summary of the First Amendment in the Connecticut Code of 1808: "1. The freedom of religion, of speech, and of the press, and right to assemble and petition the government, secured." *The Public Statute Laws of Connecticut*, Book 1 (Hartford: Hudson & Goodwin, 1808).

90. See chap. 7, n. 18, below.

The possibility of a minor form of encouragement of freedom of the press was recognized early in the First Congress. A committee was established in the Senate to confer with a House committee and report "what newspapers the members of Congress shall be furnished with at the public expense." The Senate later disagreed with a report from the House which suggested supplying at the public expense one paper of his choice to each member. There is no reason to believe, however, that the disagreement was based on reservations about the propriety of the House's conclusion that "the publication of newspapers [was] highly beneficial in disseminating useful knowledge throughout the United States, and deserving of public encouragement. . . ." *Annals*, I, pp. 35, 43.

CHAPTER FOUR, NOTES 91-97: PAGES 83-84   489

The Inter-American Press Association adopted at its annual convention, Oct. 8, 1959, at San Francisco, this declaration of principle: "It is contrary to the existence of a free and independent press and to the principles of the I.A.P.A. for newspapers to accept subsidies or any other form of economic help from governments." *Chicago Tribune*, Oct. 9, 1959, pt. 2, p. 2. See Alexander Meiklejohn, *Political Freedom*, pp. 19-20, on how Congress may enlarge and enrich freedom of speech. See, also, *Book Week*, Feb. 5, 1967, pp. 1-2. Cf. *Chicago Tribune*, editorial, Aug. 15, 1970, p. 8.

91. Cf. the passage from *Federalist* No. 84 reproduced in the text at chap. 6, n. 2, below. See Crosskey, *Politics and the Constitution*, pp. 486-87, on "necessary negative implication"; *Federalist*, p. 196, on "negative pregnant." (Consider the implications required by the assumption of Chief Justice Marshall in *Osborne* v. *Bank of the United States*, 9 Wheat. [U.S.], at 849-50: "The Eleventh Amendment is the limitation of a power supposed to be granted in the original instrument; and to understand accurately the extent of the limitation, it seems proper to define the power that is limited.") See, also, chap. 2, n. 30, above.

92. An example of this is the power to suspend the writ of *habeas corpus* in specified circumstances. Lincoln argued, "The provision of the Constitution that 'The privilege of the writ of *habeas corpus* shall not be suspended, unless when, in cases of rebellion or invasion, the public safety may require it,' is equivalent to a provision—is a provision—that such privilege may be suspended when, in cases of rebellion, or invasion, the public safety does require it." *Complete Works*, 2:60.

93. See, on how a limited negative may be interpreted, *Federalist* Nos. 32 (at pp. 195-96), 83 (at p. 539), 84 (at p. 559).

It was argued in the Fifth Congress that the provision in Article I, section 9, "The Migration or Importation of such Persons as any of the States now existing shall think proper to admit, shall not be prohibited by the Congress prior to [1808]," suspended the operation of power already in Congress. *Annals*, V, p. 1958. Did this argument assume that Congress had, as part of its commerce power, authority to regulate the slave trade (both international and "interstate")? See pp. 149-50, 175-76, 240-53, above. Cf. Elliot, *Debates*, 2:452. See Story, *Commentaries on the Constitution*, chap. 32, sec. 1337. See, also, Walter Berns, *Yale L. Rev.* 78 (1968): 98.

94. Or, to take another driving illustration, does not a lone sign, "No left turn," imply that it is permissible to turn right or to go straight ahead at the intersection? But it would not imply that wings may be extended for an ascent: that is, the sign must be interpreted in its intended context. Even a U-turn may be questionable, since that maneuver is known to be sometimes governed by special considerations.

95. I anticipate here the consideration, in chapter 6, of what source of congressional power there would have been to abridge freedom of speech, or of the press, if the First Amendment had not been added to the Constitution.

96. See, for the application of this power to a 1956 state sedition case, chap. 7, n. 86, below.

Does the right-of-assembly provision imply or, at least, preserve a power in Congress to act to suppress assemblies that are not peaceable? Would this be a critical power to be employed in the suppression of rebellions within a state?

See chap. 3, n. 11, above, chap. 8, n. 108, below.

97. I again mention in passing the problem of whether there is a national common law of crimes or a general power in Congress to deal with crime. (A national common law would imply, if the Judiciary is not to be supreme, an accompanying overriding power in Congress.) If there is such a common law or a general power, then Congress might well have had (prior to the First Amendment) plenary power over the subjects of speech, press, and religion: it would retain the power to expand the freedoms of speech, press, and religion or to regulate the states in this respect after the First Amendment limits what Congress might do. These are matters I discuss at length in chapter 6. I restrict myself at this point to what are generally understood to be the powers of Congress under the original Constitution.

98. In addition, should a house of Congress—pursuant to its authority as "the Judge of the Elections, Returns and Qualifications of its own Members" (Article I, section 5)—refuse to seat members "elected" from constituencies where freedom of speech has been severely curtailed?

The use and abuse of this authority are reported by Edward S. Corwin and Jack W. Peltason, *Understanding the Constitution* (New York: Henry Holt & Co., 1958), p. 54:

> Thus in 1900 the House refused to admit Brigham H. Roberts from Utah because he was a polygamist and, in the opinion of the majority, morally unfit. A more extreme case is that of Victor L. Berger who was twice elected by his constituents in Wisconsin but twice excluded from the House because of his purported "un-American" beliefs. . . . Such precedents, which spring in the first instance from the practice of the British Parliament and the early state legislatures, open the way for a majority in either house to deprive the people of a congressional district or of a state of representation on purely partisan or doctrinal grounds.

Chafee provided, at pages 321-48, 353 of his *Freedom of Speech*, detailed descriptions of such actions. The reader should be familiar with the Adam Clayton Powell controversy of 1967. See *Powell* v. *McCormack*, 395 U.S. 468 (1969).

The discussion that follows in this section recognizes the concern about state action abridging freedom of speech which is indicated in Justice Robert's opinion (in which Justice Black concurred) in *Hague* v. *Committee for Industrial Organization*, 307 U.S. 496, 513 (1939): "Citizenship of the United States would be little better than a name if it did not carry with it the right to discuss national legislation and the benefits, advantages, and opportunities to accrue to citizens therefrom." (The authority of *U.S.* v. *Cruikshank*, 92 U.S. 542, 552-53 [1875] is invoked.) See chap. 7, n. 86, chap. 8, n. 83, below.

99. Burke's proposed amendment is reproduced in the text at chap. 3, n. 3, above.

It was recognized in an opinion for the Court by Justice Miller in *Ex parte Yarbrough*, 110 U.S. 651, 662 (1884), that it is the duty of the general government

> to see that [a voter] may exercise this right freely, and to protect him from violence, while so doing, or on account of so doing. This duty does not arise solely from the interest of the party concerned, but from the necessity of the government itself, that its service shall be free from the adverse influence of force and fraud practised on its agents, and that the votes by which its members of Congress and its President are elected shall be the *free* votes of the electors, and the officers thus chosen the free and uncorrupted choice of those who have the right to take part in that choice. [Italics his]

100. The relation between freedom of the press and genuine elections was pointed up in the Fifth Congress (July, 1798) by opponents in the House of Representatives of the Sedition Act enacted that session (which is set forth in the text at chap. 6, n. 9, below). Albert Gallatin (of Pennsylvania) argued,

> This bill and its supporters suppose, in fact, that whoever dislikes the measures of Administration and of a temporary majority in Congress, and shall, either by speaking or writing, express his disapprobation and his want of confidence in the men now in power, is seditious, is an enemy, not of Administration, but of the Constitution, and is liable to punishment. That principle . . . was subversive of the principles of the Constitution itself. If you put the press under any restraint in respect to the measures of members of Government; if you thus deprive the people of the means of obtaining information of their conduct, you in fact render their right of electing nugatory; and this bill must be considered only as a weapon used by a party now in power, in order to perpetuate their authority and preserve their present place. [*Annals*, V, p. 2110]

John Nicholas (of Virginia) developed further Gallatin's argument:

> He desired them to reflect on the nature of our Government; that all its officers

CHAPTER FOUR, NOTE 101: PAGE 86   491

are elective, and that the people have no other means of examining their conduct but by means of the press, and an unrestrained investigation through them of the conduct of the Government. Indeed, the heart and life of a free Government, is a free press; take away this, and you take away its main support. You might as well say to the people, we, your Representatives, are faithful servants, you need not look into our conduct; we will keep our seats for a little longer time than that for which you have given them to us. To restrict the press, would be to destroy the elective principle, by taking away the information necessary to election, and there would be no difference between it and a total denial of the right of election, but in the degree of usurpation. [*Annals*, V, p. 2144; also, pp. 2103-4]

See, also, Kent, *Commentaries on American Law*, 2:17. Cf. chap. 4, n. 87, above.

James Mill argued, at pp. 19-20 of his article, "Liberty of the Press" (in his *Essays on Government, Jurisprudence, Liberty of the Press, and Law of Nations* [New York: Augustus M. Kelley, 1967]) (cf. chap. 2, n. 6, chap. 4, n. 18, above):

It is perfectly clear, that all chance of advantage to the people, from having the choice of their rulers, depends upon their making a good choice. . . . We may then ask, if there are any possible means by which the people can make a good choice, besides the *liberty of the press*? The very foundation of a good choice is knowledge. The fuller and more perfect the knowledge, the better the chance, where all sinister interest is absent, of a good choice. How can the people receive the most perfect knowledge relative to the characters of those who present themselves to their choice, but by information conveyed freely, and without reserve, from one to another? There is another use of the freedom of the press, no less deserving the most profound attention, that of making known the conduct of the individuals who have been chosen. This latter service is of so much importance, that upon it the whole value of the former depends. . . . Without the knowledge, then, of what is done by their representatives, in the use of the powers entrusted to them, the people cannot profit by the power of choosing them, and the advantages of good government are unattainable. It will not surely cost many words to satisfy all classes of readers that, without the free and unrestrained use of the press, the requisite knowledge cannot be obtained. That an accurate report of what is done by each of the representatives, a transcript of his speeches, and a statement of his propositions and votes, is necessary to be laid before the people, to enable them to judge of his conduct, nobody, we presume, will deny. This requires the use of the cheapest means of communication, and, we add, the free use of those means. Unless every man has the liberty of publishing the proceedings of the Legislative Assembly, the people can have no security that they are fairly published. If it is in the power of their rulers to permit one person, and forbid another, the people may be sure that a false report, —a report calculated to make them believe that they are well governed, when they are ill governed, will be often presented to them.

We find in the English text, Wade and Phillips, *Constitutional Law*, p. 361, a summary of these sentiments (see chap. 4, n. 108, chap. 9, n. 34, below):

Without free elections the people cannot make a choice of policies. Without freedom of speech the appeal to reason which is the basis of democracy cannot be made. Without freedom of association electors and elected representatives cannot band themselves into parties for the formulation of common policies and the attainment of common ends.

101. Does not the guarantee of protection against invasion and domestic violence relieve state governments of the necessity of maintaining substantial armed forces and thereby make even more likely the success of republican government in each state (and hence in the United States)? Is not this arrangement equivalent to the "deep Ditch" that Gouverneur Morris saw as essential to the development and preservation of freedom in England? Thus, he records in his *Diary* (2:72) a Paris conversation with Lafayette:

> . . . I reiterate to him the Necessity of restoring the Nobility, at which of Course he flinches and says that he should like two Chambers as in America. I tell him that an American Constitution will not do for this Country & that two such Chambers would not answer where there is an hereditary Executive. That every Country must have a Constitution suited to its Circumstances, and the State of France requires a higher toned [stronger] Government than that of England. He starts at this with Astonishment. I pray him to remark that England is surrounded by a deep Ditch and being only assailable by Sea can permit many Things at Home which would not be safe in different Situations. . . .

See, also, Aristotle, *Politics* 2.10 (on Crete); Montesquieu, *Spirit of the Laws*, 18:5; Tocqueville, *Democracy in America*, 1:169; *Federalist*, pp. 23 (chap. 7, n. 34, below), 45-47, 79, 97-98, 153-54, 263, 266 (parallel to atomic weapons?); Farrand, *Records*, 1:464-65; chap. 7, nn. 35, 117, below. Cf. chap. 7, n. 95, chap. 9, n. 1, below.

My argument on the relation of federalism and freedom, which is developed further in chapter 7, below, was dismissed by Lenin as a "prejudice which is very widespread, particularly among petty-bourgeois democrats." *Essential Works of Marxism*, ed. A. P. Mendel (New York: Bantam Books, 1961), p. 159.

It is evident in Morris's *Diary* that the English reliance upon the "deep Ditch" required an adequate navy, which in turn required the use of press gangs. Thus, press gangs and English freedom can be said to have gone hand in hand. Is the critical cost of American federalism that provincialism (affecting both education and administrative efficiency) which induces some to dismiss "states' rights" as "the first refuge of a reactionary"? Paul Samuelson, *Newsweek*, Feb. 13, 1967, p. 88.

See, also, Michael Harrington's rather partisan column of Aug. 17, 1969 (*Chicago Sun-Times*, sec. 2, p. 13):

> [President Nixon] claims to be fighting federal bureaucracy, yet the major single problem he identified [with respect to welfare programs] is the result of too much state's rights and he proposes to solve it by more state's rights. . . . The problem with welfare, the President told us, is that "a third of a century of centralizing power and responsibility in Washington has produced a bureaucratic monstrosity, cumbersome, unresponsive, ineffective." Hardly were these words uttered than Mr. Nixon contradicted them. There must be a minimum guarantee for families, he said, precisely because Mississippi pays only $39 a month to a mother and three children while the New Jersey benefits are $263 (he mentioned the exact amounts but delicately forgot to identify the states.) This evil is not a function of federal power but of the inhumane use of state's rights.

Cf. chap. 7, n. 31, below.

I have elsewhere argued, in effect, that the North Atlantic Treaty Organization can be for Greece what the "deep Ditch" has been for England and what federalism is for us:

> The political man knows that he must take into account the prejudices of his people. He takes account of prejudices both by changing them when he can and by conforming to them when he cannot change them. The [Greek] Army's, and to a lesser extent the [Greek] people's, fear about the present Communist threat to Greece has to be moderated. This, at least, can be altered, even though the memory and hence the effects of the fierce Communist atrocities of the Civil War (prepared for by the harshness of Metaxas and by the bestialities of the Germans and their collaborators) cannot be erased for generations. The Greek politician who seeks to contain politically the Greeks' blinding anti-Communism should exploit domestically the NATO assurances. That is, politicians of the Left should consider the advantages for them of the fact of such protection for Greece: properly explained, the NATO arrangement can be used to persuade Greeks that they are free to take domestic reconstruction far more seriously than any threat, foreign or domestic, from Communism. ["Retreat from Politics: Greece, 1967," *Massachusetts Review*, 9 (1968): 83, 110-11 (reprinted with corrections in the *Congressional Record*, Apr. 2, 1969, 115: E2632.)]

CHAPTER FOUR, NOTE 102: PAGE 87 493

See chap. 6, n. 1, below. The critical cost to Greece of such assurance may be the prospect of further naïve American "participation" in the volatile maneuvers of Greek parliamentarians.

The limits of a "deep Ditch" (Maginot Line?) mentality were anticipated in a speech by Cromwell to Parliament in 1658:

> He pointed to the uneasy posture of affairs abroad. He warned them that the royalists were projecting an invasion and had honeycombed the land with their plots. England stood alone, *and could only save herself by unity, boldness, and a constant vigilance.* "You have accounted yourselves happy in being environed with a great ditch from all over the world beside. Truly you will not be able to keep your ditch, nor your shipping, unless you turn your ships and shipping into troops of horse and companies of foot, and fight to defend yourselves on terra firma." Domestic concord was a prime need. . . . [John Buchan, *Oliver Cromwell* (London: Holder & Stoughton, 1934), p. 482; italics added]

The royalists did, despite the "great ditch," return to power. The decisive threat, however, was not from abroad but from within the English soul: ". . . The bow must relax [on the death of Cromwell], for it had been strung too tight. The satiety with high endeavour which led to the Restoration was now manifest." Ibid., pp. 539-40.

102. The Supreme Court has held that it is for Congress (not the Court) to determine whether a state has a republican form of government. See chap. 7, nn. 84, 86, below, for my critique of this holding. See, also, chap. 7, n. 107, below. (Citations to discussions of this question may be found in William B. Lockhart, Yale Kamisar, and Jesse H. Choper, *Constitutional Law* [St. Paul: West Publishing Co., 1964], pp. 138-39. See, also, Crosskey, *Politics and the Constitution*, pp. 390, 522, 531, 535.)

Should not "the separation of powers" be considered to be implied by the American standard, "a Republican Form of Government"? But compare the observations by Chief Justice Warren in *Sweezy v. New Hampshire*, 354 U.S. 234, 255 (1957):

> The conclusion that we have reached in this case [reversing the conviction for contempt of a witness who had refused to answer questions about lectures he had delivered at the state university and about his knowledge of the Progressive party and its adherents] is not grounded upon the doctrine of separation of powers. In the Federal Government, it is clear that the Constitution has conferred the powers of government upon three major branches: the Executive, the Legislative, and the Judicial. *No contention has been made by petitioner that the New Hampshire legislature, by this investigation, arrogated to itself executive or judicial powers.* We accept the finding of the State Supreme Court that the employment of the Attorney General as the investigating committee does not alter the legislative nature of the proceedings. Moreover, this Court has held that the concept of separation of powers embodied in the United States Constitution is not mandatory in state governments. *Dreyer v. Illinois*, 187 U.S. 71 [1902]; but cf. *Tenney v. Brandhove*, 341 U.S. 367, 378 [1951]. [Italics added]

See *Federalist*, pp. 229, 238-39, 312-20, 321-26, 327-41, 429-30.

See, for an instructive manifestation of the "separation of powers" debate in the financial world, "The One-Bank Holding Company," *Business Conditions* (Federal Reserve Bank of Chicago), July 1970, p. 2: "The fundamental reason for concern has been the tendency of one-bank holding companies to acquire non-banking businesses. To some, this development poses a serious threat to the traditional separation of banking from commerce. It raises the spectre of an American economy dominated by multi-industry combines similar to the Japanese *Zaibatsu* or German *Kartellen*. To others, the same development holds promise of greatly improved efficiency in meeting modern demands for financial services." See Appendix C, chap. 4, n. 25, above, chap. 8, n. 36, below.

See chap. 5, n. 105, below, on the freedom of speech implications of parliamentary government and even of a bicameral legislature. The absolute privilege of parliamentary immunity reflects the necessary dependence of parliaments on *parler*. Cf. *Hamlet*, act 1, sc. 1, l. 74 ("an angry parle").

103. See, for passages bearing on the meaning of "republican form of government," *Federalist*, pp. 59-60, 80-81, 84-85, 119, 120, 134, 137-38, 140-41, 227, 243-46, 282-85, 322-23, 327-28, 330, 338-41, 341-42, 365, 370, 373-74, 376, 403, 442, 454-56, 461-62, 464-65, 502, 557-58. See, also, Kant, *Perpetual Peace*, sec. 2; Bagehot, *English Constitution*, p. 250.

John Adams could, in 1789, refer to England as "a monarchical republic." *The Political Writings of John Adams*, American Heritage (Indianapolis: Bobbs-Merrill, 1954), p. 166. "For 'tis the Republican and not the Monarchical part of the Constitution of England which Englishmen glory in, viz. the liberty of choosing an House of Commons from out of their own body. . . ." Thomas Paine, *Common Sense* (New York: Random House, Modern Library, 1945), pp. 17-18. See Hume, *Political Essays* (Indianapolis: Bobbs-Merrill, 1953), pp. 3, 5; Joseph Cropsey, in *Ancients and Moderns: Essays on the Tradition of Political Philosophy, in Honor of Leo Strauss* (New York, 1964), pp. 65-66 (on Adam Smith); cf. *Federalist*, p. 243.

One finds in Rousseau (*Social Contract*, II, vi) an understanding of republican government that practically equates it with the rule of law. Thus, even a monarchy (in which the monarch is the minister of the general will) is a republic. Indeed, he can call Machiavelli's *Prince* "the book of republicans" (III, vi). Hobbes, too, regarded as essentially republican "the books of Policy, and Histories of the antient Greeks, and Romans," especially writers such as Aristotle and Cicero. *Leviathan*, pt. 2, chaps. 21, 29. See, also, Montesquieu, 6:3. It is this deeper meaning of republicanism, and the relevance of classical thought for us, that I have alluded to in litigation (see chap. 4, n. 107, below). "Republican Form of Government" is *our* way of indicating (in a democratic age) our concern that the political affairs of men should be subject to reason and a sense of decency. The protection we give to freedom of speech reflects this concern. ("It may now be affirmed of civilized monarchies what was formerly said in praise of republics alone, *that they are a government of laws, not of men*." Hume, *Political Essays*, p. 106. [One of his essays is entitled, "Whether the British Government Inclines More to Absolute Monarchy, or to a Republic."]) Emerson complained in his essay, "Politics,"

> Republics abound in young civilians who believe that the laws make the city, that grave modifications of the policy and modes of living and employments of the population, that commerce, education and religion may be voted in or out; and that any measure though it were absurd, may be imposed on a people if only you can get sufficient voices to make it a law.

See, also, Leo Strauss, "Liberal Education and Responsibility," in his *Liberalism Ancient and Modern* (New York: Basic Books, 1968), p. 24:

> . . . But perhaps one can say that their [Marx's and Nietzsche's] grandiose failures make it easier for us who have experienced those failures to understand again the old saying that wisdom cannot be separated from moderation and hence to understand that wisdom requires unhesitating loyalty to a decent constitution and even to the cause of constitutionalism. Moderation will protect us against the twin dangers of visionary expectations from politics and unmanly contempt for politics. . . .

See chap. 6, n. 1, chap. 8, nn. 22, 140, chap. 9, nn. 33, 38, below; also, Martin Diamond, Winston Fisk, and Herbert Garfinkel, *The Democratic Republic* (Chicago: Rand McNally, 1966), p. 73. See chap. 2, n. 20, chap. 3, n. 35, chap. 4, n. 40, above.

104. This latter assumption is reflected in the response in the House of Representatives (First Congress) to the suggestion of a title for the President. First, we have Page declaring himself

> a good deal hurt, that gentlemen on this floor, after having refused their per-

CHAPTER FOUR, NOTES 105-6: PAGE 87 495

> mission to the Clerk to enter any more than their plain names on the journal, should be standing up and addressing one another by the title of "the honorable gentleman." He wished the practice could be got over, because it added neither to the honor nor dignity of the House. [*Annals*, I, p. 318]

Tucker asked,

> Shall we [by considering the possibility of titles for officers] not justify the fears of those who were opposed to the Constitution, because they considered it as insidious and hostile to the liberties of the people? . . . Does this look like a democracy, when one of the first acts of . . . the Legislature is to confer titles? . . . Does the dignity of a nation consist in the distance between the first magistrate and his citizens? [*Annals*, I, p. 319]

Madison testified that he was against titles, "because they are not very reconcilable with the nature of our Government or the genius of the people." *Annals*, I, p. 321. (We are reminded of the fact that both the United States and the states are forbidden by the Constitution [Article I, sections 9 and 10] to "grant any Title of Nobility.") Finally, we have Parker's wish

> to have done with the subject, because while it remained a question in the House, the people's minds would be much agitated; it was impossible that a true republican spirit could remain unconcerned when a principle was under consideration, so repugnant to the principles of equal liberty. [*Annals*, I, p. 322]

No doubt this suspicion of titles is an accommodation to the idea of natural equality at the heart of American thought.

105. Blackstone concedes, "The liberty of the press is indeed essential to the nature of a free state. . . ." (See the passage from *Laws of England*, 4:151-53, reproduced in the text at chap. 5, n. 3, above.)

See chap. 5, n. 57, n. 71, n. 79, below. Benjamin Franklin's editorial in the *Pennsylvania Gazette*, Nov. 10-17, 1737, made this comment on the *Zenger* case: "Freedom of Speech is a *principal Pillar* in a free Government: when the Support is taken away, the Constitution is dissolved, and Tyranny is erected on its ruins. Republicks and limited Monarchies derive their strength and vigour from a *Popular Examination* into the Actions of the Magistrates. This Privilege in all Ages has been and always will be abused." (See chap. 3, n. 12, above.) Lincoln's plea for reliance on "time, discussion, and the ballot-box" also acknowledges discussion as an essential feature of republican government. *Complete Works*, 2:56. The Supreme Court has long recognized the relevance of certain First Amendment rights to republican government: "The very idea of a government, republican in form, implies a right on the part of its citizens to meet peaceably for consultation in respect to public affairs and to petition for a redress of grievances." *U.S. v. Cruikshank*, 92 U.S. 542, 552 (1875), reaffirmed by a unanimous Court in *DeJonge v. Oregon*, 299 U.S. 353, 364 (1937). (See, on the *Zenger* case, pp. 142, 144, above, chap. 5, nn. 57, 71, 79, below.)

See the passage from *Federalist* No. 71 quoted in chap. 6, sec. 1, above; also, *Federalist*, p. 134 ("the fundamental maxim of republican government, which requires that the sense of the majority should prevail"); Tocqueville, *Democracy in America*, 1:433-34; Pius XII, "On Democracy and Lasting Peace" (Dec. 24, 1944).

106. We find in Thomas Erskine's speech on behalf of Thomas Paine this observation:

> Gentlemen, I will yet refer you to another author, whose opinion you may think more in point [than John Milton's], as having lived in our own times, and as holding the highest monarchical principles of government. I speak of Mr. Hume, who, nevertheless, considers, that this liberty of the press extends not only to abstract speculations, but to keep the public on their guard against all the acts of their government.

After showing the advantages of a monarchy to public freedom, provided it is duly controlled and watched by the popular part of the constitution, he says, "These principles account for the great liberty of the press in these kingdoms, beyond what is indulged in any other government. It is apprehended, that arbitrary power would steal in upon us, were we not careful to prevent its progress, and were there not an easy method of conveying the alarm from one end of the kingdom to the other. The spirit of the people must frequently be roused, in order to curb the ambition of the Court; and the dread of rousing this spirit must be employed to prevent that ambition. Nothing is so effectual to this purpose as the liberty of THE PRESS, by which all the learning, wit, and genius of the nation, may be employed on the side of freedom; and every one be animated to its defence. As long, therefore, as the republican part of our government can maintain itself against the monarchical, it will naturally be careful to keep the press open, as of importance to its own preservation." [*The Speeches of Thomas Erskine on Subjects Connected with the Liberty of the Press and Against Constructive Treasons* (London: James Ridgway, 1813), 2:147-48 (italics omitted)]

107. One can find in my bar-admission arguments prepared for the Supreme Court of the United States not only the conventional approach to the Fourteenth Amendment but an indication as well of considerations based on the "Republican Form of Goverment" guarantee. In fact, the passages from my arguments that Justice Black quoted in his dissenting opinion refer several times to "republican government." *In re Anastaplo*, 366 U.S., at 104 and 110 (1961). See, also, Justice Black's opinion in *South Carolina* v. *Katzenbach*, 383 U.S. 301 (1966).

In my bar admission case, many of the arguments I made with respect to freedom of speech (which was the formulation the Court could be expected to accept) would apply as well to the "Republican Form of Government" standard. See chap. 4, n. 32, above, and chap. 4, n. 111, below. See, also, chap. 7, n. 84, below, Appendix F, sec. 9, above. (Justice Black's dissenting opinion in my case may be found in sec. 6 of Appendix F.)

108. See Justice Jackson's dissenting opinion in *Beauharnais* v. *United States*, 343 U.S. 250, 298-99 (1952), for similar sentiments with respect to the application against the states of "the concept of ordered liberty." See, also, chap. 8, n. 13, below.

Congress, on the other hand, is denied any option of abridging freedom of speech for any reason. I return in chapter 7 to this critical distinction between congressional and state legislative power with respect to freedom of speech or of the press.

Do not the electoral provisions in Article I which I have discussed, as well as the "Republican Form of Government" guarantee in Article IV, section 4, also imply some congressional power (prior to the First Amendment) to abridge freedom of speech and of the press, since (in some circumstances) the exercise of these rights could affect, and affect adversely, the manner of holding elections? That is, the exercise of freedom of speech can be so abused as to make a fair, or deliberate, election difficult. This suggests that the First Amendment deals with more than shadows or imaginings: there is the possibility (if this argument is accepted) of a power in the Constitution to abridge freedom of speech which is indeed negated by that amendment. A choice can be said to have been made between the possibility that citizens may abuse freedom of speech and the possibility that Congress may abuse its power of regulating elections.

109. My inquiry in this section has been directed to whether there is power in the general government to police state government restraints upon freedom of speech and of the press. Before we leave this subject, let us consider still another possible constitutional restraint upon the states. Article IV, section 2, provides that

> The Citizens of each State shall be entitled to all Privileges and Immunities of Citizens in the several States.

Should we number among the privileges and immunities of citizens all those guaranteed to citizens (whether against the general government or against the states) anywhere in the Constitution? These would include, upon ratification of the Bill of Rights, the right

CHAPTER FOUR, NOTES 110-11: PAGE 88   497

to freedom of speech and of the press. (See Crosskey, *Politics and the Constitution,* pp. 1083-96, 1119-34.)

This suggestion raises several problems. The simplest meaning of the provision that suggests itself to me is that each state must treat citizens of other states no worse than it does its own citizens; that is, each state must provide citizens of other states the same privileges and immunities (the same rights) that it provides *all* its citizens. For example, a citizen of another state should expect a jury trial for the same kind of crime that a citizen of the state would. This kind of provision would tend to eliminate harmful action against noncitizens, inasmuch as the state's own citizens would be exposed to the same burden. (Is there any other provision of the Constitution which insures this kind of equal treatment? It is unlikely that such a provision, which would seem to be necessary for ease of movement and for cordial relations between states and the citizens thereof, would not be found somewhere. An exception seems implied for aliens: they may be discriminated against.) Thus, the language of this provision seems to mean, in effect, "The Citizen of each State shall be entitled, in whatever State he may go, to the Privileges and Immunities of the Citizens in that State." This, then, would have nothing to do with rights guaranteed under the Constitution that a state would be obliged to respect for all its inhabitants (whether citizens of that state or of another in the Union). See chap. 8, n. 27, below.

One would otherwise be hard put to explain why both the state and general governments are precluded from exercising any power to pass *ex post facto* laws or bills of attainder. If these guarantees are privileges and immunities of citizens, why should they have been mentioned with respect to the states (in Article I, section 10) if once secured (in Article I, section 9) against the general government (and, by virtue of the Privileges and Immunities Clause, against the states as well)? (See Chief Justice Marshall's argument to this effect in *Barron* v. *Baltimore,* 7 Peters [U.S.] 243 [1833].) Similarly, there would have been no need for a special provision, such as that suggested by Madison, securing the rights of trial by jury, to freedom of speech, of the press, and of conscience against state infringement. For Madison to offer such an amendment in these circumstances would mean he had overlooked the Privileges and Immunities Clause. Evidently, the applicability of the clause in this way did not occur either to Madison or to the select committee in the House or, indeed, to the House which approved the amendment restricting the states and sent it to the Senate. It seems much more likely that this clause had the limited meaning that I have attributed to it, and therefore would not affect the power of a state to abridge freedom of speech or of the press, provided the abridgment did not discriminate between citizens of that state and citizens of other states.

See *Hague* v. *C.I.O.,* 307 U.S. 496, 511 (1939); chap. 8, n. 83, below.

110. I have not developed this argument with respect to possible supervision by the general government of state prohibitions of the "free exercise [of religion]." The same considerations would not apply, especially those that depend on the political (e.g., electoral) usefulness of freedom of speech and of the press. Indeed, any supervision by the general government with respect to such matters would probably have to be based primarily on the necessary negative implications of the First Amendment. (But if such implications apply with respect to religion, they would apply with respect to speech and the press as well.) Does modern republicanism depend on the political impotence of religion which tends to result from a multiplicity of sects even while it relies on the moral character promoted by religious sentiment? See Lincoln, *Works,* 1:12. See, also, chap. 2, n. 20, above, chap. 8, n. 135, below.

One should be reminded, also, of the "hands-off" injunction against Congress with respect to religious establishments (as distinguished from the free exercise of religion). See chap. 2, n. 38, above, chap. 8, n. 4, below.

See *Permoli* v. *First Municipality of New Orleans,* 3 Howard [U.S.] 589 (1845).

111. See Leo Strauss, *Spinoza's Critique of Religion* (New York: Schocken, 1965), p. 6:

To realize that the Jewish problem is insoluble means ever to bear in mind the truth proclaimed by Zionism regarding the limitations of liberalism. Liberalism stands or falls by the distinction between state and society, or by the recognition of a private sphere, protected by the law but impervious to the law, with the understanding that, above all, religion as particular religion belongs to the private sphere. Just as certainly as the liberal state will not "discriminate" against its Jewish citizens, so is it constitutionally unable and even unwilling to prevent "discrimination" against Jews by individuals or groups. To recognize a private sphere in the sense indicated means to permit private "discrimination," to protect it and thus in fact to foster it. The liberal state cannot provide a solution to the Jewish problem, for such a solution would require a legal prohibition against every kind of "discrimination," i.e., the abolition of the private sphere, the denial of the difference between state and society, the destruction of the liberal state. . . .

Cf. chap. 4, n. 108, above, chap. 9, nn. 7, 33, below. (Is it relevant to ask whether nonliberal states have done better by the Jews in modern times than have "liberal states"?)

112. Rousseau declares that "there is in the state no fundamental law that cannot be revoked, not excluding the social compact itself; for if all the citizens assembled of one accord to break the compact, it is impossible to doubt that it would be very legitimately broken." *Social Contract*, III, xviii.

Federalist No. 78 (see chap. 8, n. 89, below) puts this sentiment more prudently:

. . . Though I trust the friends of the proposed Constitution will never [question] that fundamental principle of republican government, which admits the right of the people to alter or abolish the established Constitution, whenever they find it inconsistent with their happiness, yet it is not to be inferred from this principle, that the representatives of the people, whenever a momentary inclination happens to lay hold of a majority of their constituents, incompatible with the provisions in the existing Constitution, would, on that account, be justifiable in a violation of those provisions; or that the courts would be under a greater obligation to connive at infractions in this shape, than when they had proceeded wholly from the cabals of the representative body. Until the people have, by some solemn and authoritative act, annulled or changed the established form, it is binding upon themselves collectively, as well as individually; and no presumption, or even knowledge, of their sentiments, can warrant their representatives in a departure from it, prior to such an act. But it is easy to see, that it would require an uncommon portion of fortitude in the judges to do their duty as faithful guardians of the Constitution, where legislative invasions of it had been instigated by the major voice of the community.

113. The First Amendment ratifies the self-governing character of the American people. Hobbes argues that "it is annexed to the Soveraignty, to be Judge of what Opinions and Doctrines are averse, and what conducing to Peace. . . ." *Leviathan*, chap. 18. See, also, ibid., chap. 29. But I believe even he would grant that the sovereign, whatever it may do to prevent the distribution among its subjects of harmful opinions, would not truly be sovereign if opinions were kept from it. (Is this not implied by Franklin's exhortation, "If by liberty of the press were to be understood merely the liberty of discussing the propriety of public measures and political opinions, let us have as much of it as you please"? See chap. 2, n. 12, above.) See, also, chap. 7, n. 3, chap. 8, n. 46, below.

Thus, in Plato's *Republic*, the rulers must know—must not be lied to—if they are to be able to rule properly. (See *Republic* 389B-C; also, chap. 5, n. 112, below.) Would, then, the American people truly be sovereign if they should not have before them all opinions bearing on the decisions they must, as a people, make? See chap. 5, n. 43, chap. 8, n. 24, below.

What should be made, in this respect, of the provision in Article I, section 4, "Each House [of Congress] shall keep a Journal of its Proceedings, and from time to time publish the same, *excepting such Parts as may in their Judgment require Secrecy* . . ."? (Italics added) See chap. 4, nn. 17, 59, above. See, also, chap. 5, nn. 66, 69, 112, 133, below.

114. Lincoln, *Complete Works*, 1:422. See, also, ibid., 1:298, 557, 560, 2:586, 613. Cf. ibid., 1:619: "No policy that does not rest upon *philosophical* public opinion can be permanently maintained." (Italics added) See chap. 9, n. 7, n. 23, n. 29, below.

115. Xenophon, *Hellenica* 1. 7. See Plato, *Epistles* 8. 354D-E. See, also, chap. 2, n. 18, above, and chap. 5, n. 119, below (the italics are Justice Gibson's).

116. See, on the nature of public opinion, Plato, *Crito* 44D; Machiavelli, *The Prince* (on the relation of public opinion to appearance), chaps. 18 and 24; the closing lines of Flaubert's *Madame Bovary*. See, also, chap. 8, n. 70, below.

Cf. Justice Gibson's observation that "it is a *postulate* in the theory of our government, and the very basis of the superstructure, that the people are wise, virtuous, and competent to manage their own affairs. . . ." *Eakin* v. *Raub*, 12 Sergeant and Rawle 330, 355 (Penna., 1825).

Public opinion would be completely worthless as a reflection of the reasonable if the "people" should come to be the "mass." (This is a term evidently taken from modern physics. Is it not assumed that a masslike people is moved only by force [including the force, or impact, of propaganda and of advertising playing upon the feelings] rather than by reason or by the semblance of reason utilized by responsible rhetoric? See chap. 8, n. 45, below. Is this sense of "mass," with its pseudo-scientific, as well as romantic, aura, reflected in the use of numbers in the designation of codefendants, such as "the Hollywood Ten," "the Conspiracy Eight," and "the New York Twenty-one"? The individual human being is lost sight of. See, also, chap. 9, n. 39, below.)

> . . . The people and a shapeless multitude (or, as it is called, "the masses") are two distinct concepts. The people lives and moves by its own life energy; the masses are inert of themselves and can only be moved from outside. The people lives by the fulness of life in the men that compose it, each of whom—at his proper place and in his own way—is a person conscious of his own responsibility and of his own views. The masses, on the contrary, wait for the impulse from outside, an easy plaything in the hands of anyone who exploits their instincts and impressions; ready to follow in turn, today this flag, tomorrow another. [Pius XII, "On Democracy and Lasting Peace"]

(Cf. *Federalist*, e.g., pp. 359, 370, "the mass of the people"; Blackstone, *Laws of England*, 2:2, "the masses of mankind." See chap. 5, n. 136, below.)

> From my own observations, especially in exile, I have come to the conclusion that for the success of his work the political leader, whatever his qualities may be, depends more on the moral atmosphere of his time than on anything else. I do not think that a positive moral climate is created by a purely emotional humanitarianism, sincere though it undoubtedly is on the part of those who are now called "the common men" but in my youth were still called "citizens." Such emotional humanitarianism is, indeed, a danger to farsighted, constructive policy, and it is easily transformed by disappointment into cynicism. [Heinrich Bruning, "The Statesman," in R. B. Heywood, ed., *The Works of the Mind* (Chicago: University of Chicago Press, 1966), p. 117]

Freedom of speech, as I understand it, develops the reasonable element in public opinion and preserves in circumstances such as ours "a positive moral climate." To stress as I do the judicial rather than the legislative forum means that immediate political gains may sometimes be sacrificed to more durable educational advances: it is in the judicial forum that the arguments are made which, whatever the result in particular cases, shape the thought, and hence the legislators, citizens, and public opinion, of the future: for it is in the judicial forum, more than any other, that argument (rather than interest) is still acknowledged to be decisive. (The *New York Times* said editorially of the Supreme Court justices on October 5, 1953, the day that Chief Justice Warren took his seat. "They are, at their best, America thinking, just as the President, a general, a manufacturer, a labor leader, a professional man, may be America acting. . . ." C. Herman

Pritchett, *The American Constitution* [New York: McGraw-Hill, 1968], p. viii.) See chap. 9, n. 39, below. Cf. chap. 3, n. 13, chap. 4, n. 37, above. See, also, chap. 8, nn. 93, 95, below.

117. Lord Charnwood said of Lincoln (see chap. 8, n. 70, below):

> When it was over it seemed to the people that he had all along been thinking their real thoughts for them; but they knew that this was because he had fearlessly thought for himself. . . . Beyond his own country some of us recall his name as the greatest among those associated with the cause of popular government. He would have liked this tribute, and the element of truth in it is plain enough, yet it demands one final consideration. He accepted the institutions to which he was born, and he enjoyed them. His own intense experience of the weakness of democracy did not sour him, nor would any similar experience of later times have been likely to do so. Yet if he reflected much on forms of government it was with a dominant interest in something beyond them. For he was a citizen of that far country where there is neither aristocrat nor democrat. . . . [*Abraham Lincoln*, pp. 454-55]

See, on the people's "real thoughts," the opening sentences of Aristotle's *Nicomachean Ethics* and *Politics*, as well as *Federalist* No. 71. See, on the relation of Pericles to the people and public opinion of Athens, Plutarch, *Lives*, pp. 187, 188, 194-95, 207-8, 211. See, also, Story, *Commentaries on the Constitution*, chap. 45, sec. 1914.

> Down to 1850, and even later, New England society was still directed by the professions. Lawyers, physicians, professors, merchants were classes, and acted not as individuals, but as though they were clergymen and each profession were a church. In politics the system required competent expression; it was the old Ciceronian idea of government by *the best* that produced the long line of New England statesmen. They chose men to represent them because they wanted to be well represented, and they chose the best they had. . . . The little group of men in Mount Vernon Street were an offshoot of this system; they were statesmen, not politicians; they guided public opinion, but were little guided by it. [*Education of Henry Adams*, p. 32]

See chap. 7, n. 16, below. Cf. Burke, *Works*, 2:296-97; chap. 8, n. 119, below.

CHAPTER V

1. My comment on Leonard Levy's *Legacy of Suppression* cited in chap. 2, n. 16, above, considers the limitations and pitfalls of "history." See, also, Jacob Klein, "History and the Liberal Arts," Proceedings of the Colloquium on the Liberal Arts Curriculum (Saint Mary's College, 1965). See, e.g., chap. 5, nn. 34, 141, 143, below.

Cf. Daniel Boorstin, *The Americans: The National Experience* (New York: Random House, 1965), pp. 399-400, 414, 430.

Our reliance upon Anglo-American history reflects the relative recency of "freedom of speech" as a serious problem. Thoughtful political men were once interested more in "the common good" and in "virtue" (especially the virtue of justice) than in "liberty" and in "self-expression." Cf. my review of Harry V. Jaffa, *Equality and Liberty*, N.Y.U. L. Rev. 41 (1966): 664. Indeed, there can be something pedestrian, even mechanical, about an overriding concern for "freedom of speech." See chap. 2, n. 19, above, chap. 9, n. 28, below. Cf. chap. 7, n. 77, chap. 8, nn. 68, 94, below.

2. Thus, the New York editor of an American edition of Blackstone could report in 1832,

> The Commentaries of Blackstone continue to be the text book of the student and of the man of general reading, notwithstanding the alterations in the law since the time of their author. The great principles which they unfold remain the same and are explained in so simple and clear a style, that, however much the details of the law may be changed, they will always be read with interest. It

CHAPTER FIVE, NOTES 3-4: PAGE 94   501

is no small commendation of Blackstone, that many of the modern improvements adopted in England and in the United States were suggested by him: and that the arrangement which he used in treating the different subjects, has been followed in a great degree by the Revisers of the Statutes of New York.

Story described Blackstone as "a man in many respects distinguished for habitual moderation, and a deep sense of justice." *Commentaries on the Constitution of the United States*, 2d ed. (Boston: Little, Brown & Co., 1851), chap. 43, sec. 1847. See, also, chap. 5, n. 41, below.

3. William Blackstone, *Commentaries on the Laws of England*, 4:151-53. This chapter lists thirteen offenses against the public peace. The passage in the text follows in the *Laws of England* upon Blackstone's description of libels. "No previous restraints" and "no prior restraints" are used interchangeably in the literature. I have adopted Blackstone's usage (the former).

What the "publications" are which may not be "previously restrained" and which are entitled to other privileges can itself become a question. See chap. 2, n. 6, above, chap. 5, n. 89, chap. 8, n. 170 (end), below. Consider the analysis in a *Milwaukee Sentinel* editorial, Sept. 2, 1970, p. 12 (see chap. 7, n. 66, below):

> The case of Mark Knops, 27, editor of the Madison Kaleidoscope, jailed for refusing to testify before a state grand jury investigating the [University of Wisconsin] bombing, appears to be a weak one in so far as freedom of the press is concerned. *The first question to be raised is whether the Madison Kaleidoscope is a newspaper. This is a debatable point* to say the least. We do not believe that the underground *press* deserves to be treated as *legitimate* newspapers. Indeed, the underground press itself takes pride in the same view and goes out of its way to disassociate itself from responsible journalism. Nevertheless, *publications* such as the Madison Kaleidoscope are printed on presses, which is all the loose constructionists of the Constitution need to qualify the underground press for the protection afforded by the First Amendment. Assuming for the sake of the argument that the Madison Kaleidoscope is a newspaper, the next question is whether Knops is legally bound to tell the grand jury what he knows, if anything, about the bombing of the UW building. Knops' attorney argued that a newspaperman must have the right to protect his sources or he will be handicapped in his reporting job. This is, to be sure, a most vital right. . . . But. . . . " [Italics added]

All this is what comes of trying to have one's cake and eat it too. (I am reminded of *Federal Baseball Club* v. *National League*, 259 U.S. 200 [1922], *Toolson* v. *New York Yankees*, 346 U.S. 356 [1958], and *Radovich* v. *National Football League*, 352 U.S. 445, 449-52 [1957]. Cf. chap. 7, n. 112, below.) See the useful article by John N. Mitchell, "Free Press and Fair Trial: The Subpoena Controversy," *Ill. Bar J.* 59 (1970): 282. See, on "symbolic speech," chap. 5, n. 135, below.

4. A footnote at this point in Blackstone's text recounts the history of press censorship:

> The art of printing, soon after its introduction, was looked upon (as well in England as in other countries) as merely a matter of state, and subject to the coercion of the crown. It was therefore regulated with us by the king's proclamations, prohibitions, charters of privileges and of license, and finally by the decrees of the court of starchamber; which limited the number of printers, and of presses which each should employ, and prohibited new publications, unless previously approved by proper licensers. On the demolition of this odious jurisdiction in 1641, the long parliament of Charles I after their rupture with that prince, assumed the same powers as the starchamber exercised with respect to the licensing of books; and in 1643, 1647, 1649, and 1652 (Scobell, i. 44. 134. ii. 88. 230.) issued their ordinances for that purpose, founded principally on the starchamber decrees of 1637. In 1662 was passed the statute 13 & 14 Car. II. c. 33, which (with some few alterations) was copied from the parliamentary ordinances. This act expired in 1679, but was revived by statute 1 Jac. II. c. 17, and con-

tinued till 1692. It was then continued for two years longer by statute 4 W. & M. c. 24, but though frequent attempts were made by the government to revive it, in the subsequent part of the reign (Com. Journ. 11 Feb. 1694. 26 Nov. 1695. 22 Oct. 1696. 9 Feb. 1694. 31 Jan. 1698) yet the parliament resisted it so strongly that it finally expired, and the press became properly free, in 1694; and has ever since so continued.

See chap. 5, n. 43, below.

5. Thomas M. Cooley, *A Treatise on the Constitutional Limitations Which Rest Upon the Legislative Powers of the States of the American Union*, 8th ed. (Boston: Little, Brown & Co., 1927), II, xii, 883. The parenthetical reference to the Petition of Rights and the Bill of Rights is a footnote in Cooley's text. The next quotation in the text is from Cooley, p. 885.

Justice Holmes, speaking for the Court in *Patterson* v. *Colorado*, 205 U.S. 454 (1907), at 462, set forth the Blackstonian position (see chap. 6, n. 7, below):

> . . . the main purpose of such constitutional provisions [as are found in the First Amendment] is to "prevent all such *previous restraints* upon publications as had been practiced by other governments," and they do not prevent the subsequent punishment of such as may be deemed contrary to the public welfare. *Commonwealth* v. *Blanding*, 3 Pick. [Mass.] 304, 313, 314 [1826]; *Respublica* v. *Oswald*, 1 Dallas [U.S.] 319, 325 [1788]. The preliminary freedom extends as well to the false as to the true; the subsequent punishment may extend as well to the true as to the false. This was the law of criminal libel apart from statute in most cases, if not all. . . . [Italics his]

See chap. 6, nn. 29, 38, below. Cf. the comment on Justice Holmes's view of the First Amendment in the dissent in *Patterson* by Justice Harlan, part of which comment may be found in chap. 7, n. 107, below; also, *Near* v. *Minnesota*, 283 U.S. 697, 714-15 (1931); *Lovell* v. *Griffin*, 303 U.S. 444, 451 (1938); *Burstyn* v. *Wilson*, 343 U.S. 495, 503 (1952). (It should be noticed that in neither of the cases cited by Justice Holmes [*Blanding* and *Oswald*] had there been involved a "freedom of speech [and] of the press" provision as unequivocal in tone as that in the First Amendment. My impression is that Justice Holmes never really *looked* at the First Amendment! See the text at chap. 3, n. 12, above. See, also, chap. 5, n. 135, chap. 8, n. 83, below.)

6. See Zechariah Chafee, *Freedom of Speech* (Cambridge: Harvard University Press, 1920), p. 11; cf. ibid., p. 69. See chap. 5, nn. 23, 24, below.

7. The licensing statute against which Milton wrote in his *Areopagitica* was that of 1643 referred to in the footnote reproduced from Blackstone in chap. 5, n. 4, above. See, for a preliminary discussion of Milton and due process, my article, "Due Process of Law—An Introduction," *U. Detroit L. J.* 42 (1964): 195. See, also, Chafee, *Freedom of Speech*, p. 108, on "previous restraint" and the exercise of the postal power; chap. 5, n. 50, chap. 8, n. 74, below.

8. A. V. Dicey, *Introduction to the Study of the Law of the Constitution*, 5th ed. (London: Macmillan & Co., 1897), pp. 237-40.

9. Dicey observes in a footnote that the one exception is the licensing of the performance of stage plays by the Lord Chamberlain. See chap. 5, n. 24, below.

See Lincoln's distinction, in a discussion of *habeas corpus*, between "preventive" and "vindictive" measures. See chap. 4, n. 59, above.

10. Thus, there probably cannot be, under a strict interpretation of this view, even any licensing of the press comparable to that of automobile drivers or of taverns; nor can there be any insurance requirements of the kind sometimes laid down for drivers or taverns. It should be noticed, however, that the traditional licensing of the press was essentially different from these, requiring previous approval of each publication by the publisher, not merely a general license to publish. (It would be as if a bartender had to have a government official clear each transaction that took place in his tavern.)

11. The lawyer realizes that the extension to the press of the rule of law affects the

CHAPTER FIVE, NOTES 12-16: PAGES 97-98				503

vital (and often decisive) question of where the burden of proof lies in a legal proceeding. Compare the effects of Plato's *Crito* and Lessing's *Nathan the Wise*: the Athenians are in effect told that only well-behaved laws (e.g., laws which provide for an opportunity for critics to criticize or to leave) need be obeyed; the Germans are in effect told that only Jews as well behaved as Nathan need be tolerated (or so it must seem to many).

An intelligent layman's impatience with such distinctions is reflected in Samuel Johnson's comment in 1779 on Milton's *Areopagitica*:

> The danger of unbounded liberty and the danger of bounding it have produced a problem in the science of Government which human understanding seems hitherto unable to solve. If nothing may be published but what civil authority shall have previously approved, power must always be the standard of truth; if every dreamer of innovations may propagate his projects, there can be no settlement; if every murmurer at government may diffuse discontent, there can be no peace; and if every sceptic in theology may teach his follies, there can be no religion. The remedy against these evils is to punish the authors; for it is yet allowed that every society may punish, though not prevent, the publication of opinions which that society shall think pernicious. But this punishment, though it may crush the author, promotes the book; and it seems not more reasonable to leave the right of printing unrestrained because writers may be afterwards censured, than it would be to sleep with doors unbolted because by our laws we can hang a thief. [Samuel Johnson, *Lives of the British Poets*, ed. William Hazlitt (London: Nathaniel Cooke, 1854), 2:23]

Dr. Johnson's impatience is reflected in *In re Debs*, 158 U.S. 564 (1895). Cf. chap. 4, n. 59, chap. 5, n. 99, chap. 6, nn. 40, 67, chap. 8, n. 18, below.

12. Blackstone footnote, reproduced in chap. 5, n. 4, above. Cf. chap. 5, n. 77, below. See William W. Crosskey, *Politics and the Constitution* (Chicago: University of Chicago Press, 1953), pp. 477-83.

13. Americans, except in the earliest period of colonization, do not seem to have had much experience with the press as anything but another occupation, the government monopoly having long since been given up. (Does our use of "royalties" reflect the original government monopoly of printing?)

14. Ames observed, in the First Congress, "I apprehend it will be as frequently necessary to prevent crimes as to punish them; and it may often happen that the only prevention is by removal [of an officer by impeachment]." *Annals*, I, p. 475.

The question remains, of course, what means may generally be used to *prevent* the commission of crimes: perhaps the most important peacetime means, aside from education, is the assurance that is given, in part by experience, that arrest and punishment follow quickly upon commission. The impeachment provision of the Constitution provides an exception, however, to the usual mode: even so, only removal from office can follow; any further punishment or penalty must come after indictment, trial, etc. We again see that when the usual rule of law is to be set aside, the Constitution provides for it.

See chap. 5, n. 41, below. See, also, p. 327, above, chap. 7, n. 67, below.

15. Dicey regarded this "mere application" as vital. See Thomas I. Emerson, "The Doctrine of Prior Restraints," *Law & Contemp. Prob.* 20 (1955): 648. Martin Shapiro, *Freedom of Speech: The Supreme Court and Judicial Review* (Englewood Cliffs, N.J.: Prentice-Hall, 1966), pp. 151-57.

16. See chap. 4, n. 86, above. See, also, chap. 8, n. 190, below.

> Before Yamashita could be executed, the sentence had to be approved by General MacArthur. The defense hoped that General MacArthur would be moved to grant clemency on the basis of the dissenting opinions [*In re Yamashita*, 327 U.S. 1 (1946)]. But shortly after being notified by radio that the Court had refused to issue a writ of habeas corpus in behalf of Yamashita and before seeing the photostatic copies of the decision, General MacArthur ordered that Yamashita be hanged in disgrace—"stripped of uniform, decoration, and other appurte-

nances signifying membership in the military profession." MacArthur's true sentiments were revealed clearly in the order, for at one point he stated that the proceedings of the military commission "were guided by that primary rationale of all judicial purpose—to ascertain the full truth unshackled by any artificialities of narrow method or technical arbitrariness. The results are beyond challenge." [R. J. Tresolini and R. T. Frost, *Cases in American National Government and Politics* (Englewood Cliffs, N.J.; Prentice-Hall, 1966), pp. 213-14]

See Alpheus T. Mason, *Harlan Fiske Stone* (New York: Viking Press, 1956), pp. 666-71. (Such harshness may be seen as well in the *Rosenberg* case. See chap. 7, n. 74, below.)

17. I have suggested that a regard for due process provides substantial protection against the abuses of congressional investigations.

An article in the *Chicago Tribune*, Mar. 9, 1961, records the admission on behalf of the Justice Department that the constitutional principle of due process was regarded as a substantial check upon the loyalty programs of the general government and that due process was deliberately subverted in the zealous search for subversives:

> Making a "confession of a former attorney general," Supreme Court Justice Tom Clark today admitted to misgivings about one of his actions.
>
> Referring to a list of subversive organizations put out when he headed the justice department, Clark said that "perhaps we should have given the parties an opportunity to be heard before issuing it."
>
> . . . He said that, at the time of the listing, the opinion among other justice department men was that if hearings were granted first, there was a prospect of so much delaying action that the list would never be put out.
>
> He added that such a list had been circulated confidentially in the government during World War II, before he became attorney general. . . .

See a letter to the editor, "He Was Warned," *Nation*, Nov. 28, 1953. See, also, chap. 4, n. 35, above, chap. 8, n. 161, below.

18. To what extent Congress may have power to deal at all with speech or the press was touched upon in chap. 4 and will be discussed in chap. 6.

19. This seems to have long been true in Great Britain as well. We see in the trial of Lord George Gordon the extent to which the rule of law protects even the most imprudent and the most "obviously" guilty. *The Speeches of Thomas Erskine*, 2d ed. (London: James Ridgway, 1813), 1:59.

20. Dicey, *Law of the Constitution*, pp. 229-31.

21. Cf. Sir Alfred Denning, *The Changing Law* (London: Stevens & Son, 1953), pp. 7, 10-11, 18. But see Henry Street, *Freedom, the Individual and the Law* (London: Penguin Books, 1963), pp. 10, 103, 243.

Judge Hand observed, in *U.S. v. Dennis*, 183 F.2d 201, 234 (1950):

> The record discloses a trial fought with a persistence, an ingenuity and—we must add—with a perversity, such as we have rarely, if ever encountered. . . . Once the question is answered whether the Smith Act is valid, and whether there was evidence before the jury from which they might hold it violated, we can find no privilege and no right denied [defendants] which had substance. We know of no country where they would have been allowed any approach to the license here accorded them; and none, except Great Britain, where they would have had so fair a hearing.

But it is only fair to add that the war-weakened and much more vulnerable British managed to survive the "present danger" found by Judge Hand without instituting such prosecutions as these.

Is it indeed "so fair a hearing" when the assessment of the evidence is as fanciful, for American conditions, as it has been in the Smith Act cases? The reader can divert himself with the law student's testimony which Justice Harlan saw fit to reproduce at length in his opinion for the Court in *Scales* v. *U.S.*, 367 U.S. 203, 244-49 (1961). This witness, having previously established contact with the Federal Bureau of Investigation for this purpose, "sent a postcard to petitioner [in 1948], informing him that he was a law student and that he was interested in communism." Petitioner replied by sending him "a large cardboard box filled with Communist literature." It is hard to determine, upon reading about the conversations that the author of this opinion thought important to record, who is silliest: the Communists who may have said what is here recorded, the witnesses who saw fit to elicit and to report such nonsense, the judges who could take seriously any of this stuff and allow men to be sent to prison on such evidence, or the legal scholars who did not immediately laugh all this out of court. (See chap. 7, n. 69, below.)

"Great Britain," indeed! The Great Britain of Lewis Carroll, perhaps.

See, for an even more recent exhibition of official folly, Appendix D, above.

22. By judicious offers of rewards and threats of punishment, the bad action will be substantially restrained and the good encouraged. See chap. 8, n. 184, below. Such education or training is a legitimate form of previous restraint.

See chap. 7, n. 59, below.

23. Walter Berns noted (*Freedom, Virtue & the First Amendment* [Baton Rouge: Louisiana State University Press, 1957], p. 251), "The writer suspects, but cannot yet prove, that the intention of the First Amendment was merely to outlaw previous restraints on the freedom *of speech and* press." (Italics added.) See chap. 5, n. 34, below. Cf. Walter Berns, "Freedom of the Press and the Alien and Sedition Laws: A Reappraisal," *Supreme Court Review* (1970), n. 59. The occasions on which speaking *could* be licensed are relatively few, while it has been possible to regulate prior to publication virtually all printing done in a community. See, on assembly and petition, chap. 8, n. 108, below.

See, also, the passage from Cooley quoted in the text at chap. 5, n. 6, above ("inasmuch as of words to be uttered orally there can be no previous censorship").

24. The licensing of a kind of "speech" is seen in the requirement in England of the Lord Chamberlain's approval of a stage production (but even here, it is a written script that is reviewed). Cf. the reference to Lear's "all-licens'd fool," Shakespeare, *King Lear*, act 1, sc. 4, line 220.

See, for the most primitive form of "the liberty to speak" (i.e., with one's tongue), Jonathan Swift, *Gulliver's Travels* (New York: Rinehart & Co., 1948), p. 178; also, *Annals*, V, p. 2160. "So when we *speak freely* it is not the liberty of voice or pronunciation but of the man, whom no law has obliged to speak otherwise than he did." Hobbes, *Leviathan*, II, xxi. See, for another primitive form of "the liberty to speak," Jonathan Swift, *The Drapier's Letters*, in *Jonathan Swift: Selected Prose and Poetry*, ed. Edward Rosenheim, Jr. (New York: Holt, Rinehart & Winston, 1963), p. 281: "For those who have used Power to cramp Liberty, have gone so far as to resent even the Liberty of Complaining; although a Man upon the Rack was never known to be refused the Liberty of roaring as loud as he thought fit." (But care may be taken, as in Athens in recent years, to drown out the "roaring" of the tortured by other noises. See chap. 6, n. 1, below.)

> The apparent Reasons for this Toleration of so great an Evil [as the Mischief of the Art of Printing], in the most arbitrary Countries, are, 1. The Benefits of the Press, which outweigh the Mischiefs of it; and, 2. The extreme Difficulty of totally depriving Men of a Liberty, *derived from the natural Right and Faculty of Speech.* Thus the Liberty of the Press is connected with Natural Liberty. ["An Essay on the Liberty of the Press Chiefly As It Respects Personal Slander" (London, 1755), p. 5 (included among *Tracts on the Law of Libel*, The Library of the Law Society, London). (Anonymous; italics added)]

See chap. 7, n. 77, below.

"The United States may give up the Post Office when it sees fit, but while it carries it on the use of the mails is almost as much a part of free speech as the right to use our tongues. . . ." Justice Holmes, dissenting, *Milwaukee Pub. Co.* v. *Burleson*, 255 U.S. 407, 437 (1921). (See chap. 4, n. 15, above.)

25. Bernard Shaw, in a New York address of April 11, 1933, put it in his own perverse way: "When you came to examine the American Constitution, you found that it was not really a constitution, but a Charter of Anarchism. It was not an instrument of government: it was a guarantee to the whole American nation that it never should be governed at all. And this is exactly what the Americans wanted." (See, on Shaw himself, the quotation in the text at chap. 8, n. 167, above.) One is reminded of Samuel Johnson's *Taxation No Tyranny* and its attribution to Americans and their supporters of "the delirious dream of republican fanaticism." See Boorstin, *The Americans*, pp. 81-82 (and epigraph to the book); *Autobiography of Bertrand Russell* (Boston: Little, Brown & Co., 1967), 1:104, 196.

Cf. Street, *Freedom, the Individual and the Law*, pp. 220-21:

> A British student of government will often learn more from a short period in Washington about the American administrative process than he can learn about his own from a lifetime in England. . . . And American visiting scholars, accustomed to a more liberal order, to whom it never occurs to seek permission, are not popular with the British Treasury and other departments when they inform the British public for the first time of the processes by which they are governed.

See chap. 2, n. 12, above, chap. 8, n. 74, below.

American circumstances and attitudes are different enough from the British to make one question the emphasis upon history and "our English ancestors" found in Justice Frankfurter's concurring opinion in *Dennis*, 341 U.S. 494, 523-24 (1951):

> The language of the First Amendment is to be read not as barren words found in a dictionary but as symbols of historic experience illumined by the presuppositions of those who employed them. Not what words did Madison and Hamilton use, but what was it in their minds which they conveyed? . . . "The law is perfectly well settled," this Court said over fifty years ago, "that the first ten amendments to the Constitution . . . were not intended to lay down any novel principles of government, but simply to embody certain guaranties and immunities which we had inherited from our English ancestors, and which had from time immemorial been subject to certain well-recognized exceptions arising from the necessities of the case. In incorporating these principles into the fundamental law there was no intention of disregarding the exceptions, which continued to be recognized as if they had been formally expressed." *Robertson* v. *Baldwin*, 165 U.S. 275, 281 [1897]. . . .

(The passage Justice Frankfurter quoted from *Robertson* in *Dennis* continues immediately with an enumeration of exceptions regarding the First Amendment language which seems to me *not* to provide for the *Dennis* exception: "Thus, the freedom of speech and of the press (art. 1) does not permit the publication of libels, blasphemous or indecent articles, or other publications injurious to public morals or private reputation. . . ." Furthermore, *did* Justice Frankfurter accept as a "well-recognized exception" a prohibition upon "the publication of . . . blasphemous . . . articles"? If not, why not? It may have been rhetorically effective for him to stop when he did in his quotation from and reliance upon that dubious precedent. Cf. Justice Harlan's dissent in *Robertson*, 165 U.S. 281, at 293, 296-97. See the opinion of Judge Frank in *U.S.* v. *Roth*, 237 F.2d 796, 804 (1956), where he recognizes that what was said in *Robertson* about the First Amendment was "in passing." It is on such foundations that the subversion of the First Amendment in *Dennis* and other cases rests!)

Much of what follows in this chapter is designed to show why Justice Frankfurter's emphasis upon the historic cannot suffice. (See, e.g., chap. 5, nn. 35, 143, below.) The reader who thinks more of history than I do might be tempted to make more than I do

CHAPTER FIVE, NOTES 26-28: PAGE 101   507

of the fact that Hamilton is not known, despite Justice Frankfurter's suggestion, to have had anything to do with the writing of the First Amendment. (See, also, Justice Holmes's opinion for the Court in *Frohwerk v. U.S.*, 249 U.S. 204 [1919].)

26. Is not this a kind of military federalism? See Machiavelli, *The Prince*, chap. 4. ("To understand what is happening, it is necessary to get a feel for the way Washington runs the war [in Viet Nam]. In the air, civilian control is nearly absolute. No bomber goes out without advance approval of targets at high civilian levels. But in the ground war, Washington has stuck by the old-fashioned doctrine of according maximum discretion to the military commander on the spot. . . ." Joseph Kraft, *Chicago Daily News*, Dec. 15, 1967, p. 16.)

27. Compare Prime Minister Churchill's remarks of July 2, 1942, in the House of Commons:

[The generals who are conducting the battle] have to fight the enemy. Although we have always asked that they should keep us informed as much as possible, our policy has been not to worry them but to leave them alone to do their job. Now and then I send messages of encouragement and sometimes a query or a suggestion, but it is absolutely impossible to fight battles from Westminster or Whitehall. The less one interferes the better, and certainly I do not want generals in close battle—and these desert battles are close, prolonged and often peculiarly indeterminate—to burden themselves by writing full stories on matters upon which, in the nature of things, the home Government are not called upon to give any decision. After all, there is nothing we can do about it here while it is going on, or only at very rare intervals. [Winston Churchill, *The End of the Beginning* (Boston: Little, Brown & Co., 1943), pp. 165-66]

See chap. 4, n. 49, above.

28. Wilmot, *The Struggle for Europe* (London: Collins, 1952), pp. 463-64. This account reminds one of the importance, for the American immigrant of the early twentieth century, of being in business for himself.

Wilmot added (at p. 465),

The American attitude to Montgomery cannot be accounted for on grounds of national prejudice alone, although this was a contributing factor. His manner and methods would have been equally distasteful in an American. General Douglas MacArthur, who also exercised his authority with an autocratic hand, as though it were his by more than mortal dispensation, was heartily detested by many Americans, even by those who recognized his greatness in the field of strategy. . . .

Burke warned his colleagues in Parliament in 1775,

In this character of the Americans, a love of freedom is the predominating feature which marks and distinguishes the whole: and as an ardent is always a jealous affection, your colonies become suspicious, restive, and untractable, whenever they see the least attempt to wrest from them by force, or shuffle from them by chicane, what they think the only advantage worth living for. This fierce spirit of liberty is stronger in the English colonies probably than in any other people of the earth; and this from a great variety of powerful causes. . . . In other countries, the people, more simple, and of a less mercurial cast, judge of an ill principle in government only by an actual grievance; here they anticipate the evil, and judge of the pressure of the grievance by the badness of the principle. They augur misgovernment at a distance; and snuff the approach of tyranny in every tainted breeze. [Burke, *Works*, 2:185, 189-90]

("If there be one fact in the world perfectly clear, it is this: 'That the disposition of the people of America is wholly averse to any other than a free government;' and this is indication enough to any honest statesman how he ought to adapt whatever power he finds in his hands to their case. If any ask me what a free government is, I answer, that, for any practical purpose, it is what the people think so; and that they, and not I, are the natural, lawful, and competent judges of this matter. . . ." Ibid., 2:273.)

Among the "great variety of powerful causes" responsible for the "fierce spirit of liberty" among Americans is that described by Arthur M. Schlesinger, *New Viewpoints in American History* (New York: Macmillan Co., 1922), p. 109:

> As Professor Van Tyne has pointed out in a notable passage, the tendency of colonization was to stock the American colonies with radicals and dissenters and to leave behind in England the conservatives and conformists, thereby rendering inevitable sharp contrasts in temperament and outlook between the colonists and the mother country. This process has repeated itself with endless variations in the later history of our country. The incoming tides of foreign immigration have deposited upon our shores many of the restless and rebellious spirits of the Old World Civilization. . . .

Thus, *Federalist* No. 12 can report:

> In most parts of [America], excises must be confined within a narrow compass. The genius of the people will ill brook the inquisitive and peremptory spirit of excise laws. . . . In France, there is an army of patrols (as they are called) constantly employed to secure their fiscal regulations against the inroads of the dealers in contraband trade. . . . The arbitrary and vexatious powers with which the patrols are necessarily armed, would be intolerable in a free country.

This recognition of the American character, it should be noticed, is found in a work which is, in spirit, the American Blackstone. Cf. chap. 8, n. 36, below (on the income tax).

See chap. 3, n. 35, above. See, also, chap. 4, n. 117, above, chap. 7, n. 77, chap. 9, nn. 19, 38, below.

29. The remarkable freedom of the American military has continued to amaze foreign observers. A reviewer in the *Times Literary Supplement* (London), Sept. 9, 1960, observed (at p. 579), "General Maxwell D. Taylor is one of the most distinguished American soldiers of recent times. His last appointment was that of Chief of Staff of the Army, and it is with this phase of his career, ending just over a year ago, that he is concerned [in his book, *The Uncertain Trumpet* (New York: Harper & Bros., 1960)]. It is an astonishing book to British eyes; we may feel that had a similar work been produced by Field-Marshall Sir Gerald Templer—supposing the incredible—he would now be in grave trouble, if not in the Tower." See chap. 4, n. 49, above.

30. My remarks about the American military apply to the common soldier as well. Lincoln remarked, in a letter to Count Gasparin, "With us every soldier is a man of character, and must be treated with more consideration than is customary in Europe." Lincoln, *Complete Works*, ed. John G. Nicolay and John Hay (New York: Century Co., 1902), 2:218. See, also, the opening and closing paragraphs of Emerson's "History," in *Essays: First Series*.

31. I have noticed the effect of American freedom on the military. A similarly significant effect may be found in another well-disciplined organization, the clergy of the Roman Catholic Church in the United States. The Jesuit theologian John Courtney Murray wrote in *America* of "the many efforts [in the Vatican Council] to block discussion" of a proposed pronouncement on religious liberty. Thus, Xavier Rynne reported,

> The issue of religious liberty is of the highest interest to me both as a theologian and as an American. It is, as it were, *the* American issue at the Council. . . . Through Cardinal Spellman, the American bishops made a strong intervention, demanding that the issue be presented to the conciliar Fathers. . . . First, the text asserts that every man by right of nature (*jure naturae*) has the right to the free exercise of religion in society according to the dictates of his personal

conscience. This right belongs essentially to the dignity of the human person as such. Secondly, the juridical consequences of this right are asserted—namely, that an obligation falls on other men in society, and upon the state in particular to acknowledge this personal right, to respect it in practice, and to promote its free exercise. This is . . . the heart of the matter. [*New Yorker*, Jan. 18, 1964, p. 94; also, pp. 97, 100]

See Alexis de Tocqueville, *Democracy in America* (New York: Random House, Vintage Books, 1954), 1:311-12, 2:28. Cf. Blackstone, *Laws of England*, 4:54-55; Joseph Story, *Commentaries on the Constitution of the United States* (2d ed.; Boston: Little, Brown & Co., 1851), chap. 43, secs. 1847-49. See chap. 2, n. 38, above.

Should we not recognize a similar Americanization of the Communist party of the United States, whatever may be said of the behavior of Communists elsewhere (see, e.g., George Kennan, *Russia and the West under Lenin and Stalin* [Boston: Little, Brown & Co., 1961], pp. 274-75)? See chap. 3, n. 20, above, chap. 7, nn. 46, 124, below. See, also, chap. 6, n. 1, below.

32. Those dedicated to the patriot cause "simply contended that liberty belonged solely to those who spoke the speech of liberty." Arthur M. Schlesinger, *Prelude to Independence: The Newspaper War on Britain, 1764-1776* (New York: Knopf, 1938), p. 189.

33. Leonard W. Levy, *Legacy of Suppression: Freedom of Speech and Press in Early American History* (Cambridge: Harvard University Press, 1960). See chap. 5, n. 1, above.

34. My comments, at *N.Y.U. L. Rev.* 39 (1964): 735, which include some general remarks about the nature of historical revisionism, provide the outline of a systematic review of the Levy book. See chap. 2, n. 16, above, chap. 5, n. 143, below. Some of my readers prefer that discussion of Levy's thesis to this one.

Herbert J. Storing, in his review of Levy's book (*American Political Science Review* 55 [1961]: 385), reported:

> . . . He raises the question whether it was the intention of the Framers to reject common law notions of free speech and press, which acknowledged "the power of government to punish words that do not directly incite to acts in violation of law." . . . Levy's answer, based on thorough research among masses of original materials, is an emphatic no. Neither in the Anglo-American liberal tradition nor in American thought and action after the Revolution does Levy find any substantial denial of "the notion that the state might be criminally assaulted merely by words, even by words which had no consequence other than producing disesteem or contempt in the minds of the people." As for the First Amendment itself, no one can say for sure what the Framers meant—perhaps they did not know themselves—but the evidence tends to support the proposition that the freedom of *speech-and*-press clause "substantially embodied the Blackstonian definition [freedom from previous restraint] and left the law of seditious libel in force. . . ." [Italics added]

See chap. 3, n. 12, chap. 5, n. 23, above, chap. 5, n. 52, below.

Levy's thesis, about the generally understood meaning of the First Amendment language at the time of its adoption, is implicitly, and perhaps decisively, challenged by what Crosskey (a defender of the Sedition Act of 1798 [see chap. 7, n. 6, below]) says in the passage reproduced in the text at chap. 5, n. 88, above. Cf. chap. 4, n. 87, above. There is one critical difference between Crosskey and Levy that should be noticed here: it does not really matter to Levy what the intended or original meaning of a constitutional provision is. ("Professor Levy himself does not find his 'revisionist' history of the First Amendment binding or distressing, because the Constitution, at least in the area of civil liberties, need not, on his view, 'be anchored in the past' [citing Levy, *Legacy of Suppression*, p. 4]." Harry Kalven, Jr., *The Negro and the First Amendment* [Chicago: University of Chicago Press, 1966], p. 220, n. 102.) I should also mention that I believe Levy's article, "Liberty and the First Amendment," *American Historical Review* 68 (Oct. 1962): 22, makes the principal points (but in a more moderate, and hence more valuable, manner) of both his *Legacy of Suppression* and his *Jefferson and Civil Liberties* (Cambridge: Harvard University Press, 1963). See chap. 6, n. 37, below.

The limitations of *any* historical study, on the other hand, are suggested in what Milton has to say about the essentially arbitrary, and even accidental, character of the materials upon which the student must rely (the Dead Sea Scrolls come to mind):

> Whatsoever time, or the heedless hand of blind chance, hath drawn down from of old to this present, in her huge dragnet, whether fish or seaweed, shells, or shrubs, unpicked, unchosen, those are the fathers. . . . [I]t came into my thoughts to persuade myself, setting all distances and nice respects aside, that I could do religion and my country no better service for the time, than doing my utmost endeavour to recall the people of God from this vain foraging after straw, and to reduce them to their firm stations under the standard of the gospel; by making appear to them, first the insufficiency, next the inconveniency, and lastly, the impiety of these gay testimonies, that their great doctors would bring them to dote on. And in performing this, I shall not strive to be more exact in method, than as their citations lead me. [Milton, *The Prose Works of John Milton* (London: J. Johnson, 1806), 1:61]

See Aristotle, *Poetics* 1451b5. Cf. Aristotle, *Nicomachaean Ethics*, 1094b25-27, 1102a25. See, also, chap. 3, n. 16, chap. 5, n. 1, above, chap. 5, n. 141, below.

See, on the dependence of discovery upon chance, Marcel Proust, *Remembrance of Things Past* (New York: Random House, 1934), 1:33-36, 2:991-1007; chap. 8, n. 88, chap. 9, n. 23, below. Cf. Plato, *Gorgias* 448C.

Consider, also, how one publication by an author may change retroactively the significance of everything he had published or done before.

35. See chap. 6, nn. 29, 30, below. See, on "sedition," chap. 5, n. 142, below.

Central to the first half of Francis Bacon's *Essays or Counsels Civil and Moral* (which is the more public, or civil, half, culminating in Number 29, "Of the True Greatness of Kingdoms and Estates") is Number 15, "Of Seditions and Troubles." Thus, seditions and troubles are to the well-being of states what deformity (Number 44, which is central to the second half of the *Essays*) is to the health of the body (Number 30, with which the second half opens).

> Seditious libel is the doctrine that flourished in England during and after the ascendancy of the Star Chamber. In brief, it is the doctrine that criticism of government officials and policy may be viewed as defamation of government and may be punished as a serious crime. . . . The treatment of such speech as criminal is based on an accurate perception of the dangers in it; it is likely to undermine confidence in government policy and in the official incumbents. But it is a profound tenet of democracy that no government official has the legal power to silence such commentary about itself. . . . On my view, the absence of seditious libel as a crime is the true pragmatic test of freedom of speech. This I would argue is what freedom of speech is about. Any society in which seditious libel is a crime is, no matter what its other features, not a free society. A society can, for example, treat obscenity as a crime or not treat it as a crime without thereby altering its basic nature as a society. It seems to me it cannot do so with seditious libel. Here the response to this crime defines the society. [Kalven, *Negro and First Amendment*, pp. 15-16]

(Kalven's position on obscenity is indicated in his article, "The Metaphysics of the Law of Obscenity," *Supreme Court Review* [1960]: 1.) See chap. 5, nn. 130, 143, below. What is said here by Kalven about control of obscenity applies as well to the control of guns. See chap. 7, n. 67, below. See, also, Burke, *Works*, 2:242-43; p. 383, above.

There is an older sense of "libels" (as is evident in Adam Smith, *Wealth of Nations*, at p. 814) which is equivalent to the modern "pamphlets."

36. Levy, *Legacy of Suppression*, skirted this problem at pp. 6, 7, 50-51, 107, 149, 245-46, 251-52, 259, 268, 274-75, 283, 293, 295-96.

Levy, in his attempt (in interpreting the First Amendment) to deduce principle from

CHAPTER FIVE, NOTE 36: PAGE 103

what may have been practice, used the equivalent of the argument of Senator Stephen A. Douglas in the Galesburg Debate (Oct. 7, 1858):

> . . . I tell you that this Chicago doctrine of Lincoln's—declaring that the negro and the white man are made equal by the Declaration of Independence and by Divine Providence—is a monstrous heresy. The signers of the Declaration of Independence never dreamed of the negro when they were writing that document. They referred to white men, to men of European birth and European descent, when they declared the equality of all men. I see a gentleman there in the crowd shaking his head. *Let me remind him* that when Thomas Jefferson wrote that document he was the owner, and so continued until his death, of a large number of slaves. Did he intend to say in that Declaration that his negro slaves, which he held and treated as property, were created his equals by divine law, and that he was violating the law of God every day of his life by holding them as slaves? *It must be borne in mind* that when that Declaration was put forth, every one of the thirteen colonies were slave-holding colonies, and every man who signed that instrument represented a slaveholding constituency. *Recollect*, also, that no one of them emancipated his slaves, much less put them on an equality with himself, after he signed the Declaration. On the contrary, they all continued to hold their negroes as slaves during the Revolutionary War. Now, do you believe—are you willing to have it said—that every man who signed the Declaration of Independence declared the negro his equal, and then was hypocrite enough to continue to hold him as a slave, in violation of what he believed to be the divine law? And yet when you say that the Declaration of Independence includes the negro, you charge the signers of it with hypocrisy. [Lincoln, *Complete Works*, 1:434. See, ibid., 1:343-44. (I have italicized the phrases which call to mind the analysis in section 119 of Kant's *Logic* of "questions being directed either to the understanding or merely to the memory.")]

See Anastaplo, "Law and Morality," *Wis. L. Rev.* (1967): 231, 245-51.

Lincoln had made, the year before, the decisive argument in opposition to Douglas's:

> I think the authors of that notable instrument [the Declaration of Independence] intended to include all men, but they did not intend to declare all men equal in all respects. They did not mean to say all were equal in color, size, intellect, moral developments, or social capacity. They defined with tolerable distinctness in what respects they did consider all men created equal—equal with "certain inalienable rights, among which are life, liberty and the pursuit of happiness." This they said, and this they meant. They did not mean to assert the obvious untruth that all were then actually enjoying that equality, nor yet that they were about to confer it immediately upon them. In fact, they had no power to confer such a boon. They meant simply to declare the right, so that enforcement of it might follow as fast as circumstances should permit. They meant to set up *a standard maxim for free society, which should be familiar to all, and revered by all; constantly looked to*, constantly labored for, and even though never perfectly attained, constantly approximated, and thereby constantly spreading and deepening its influence and augmenting the happiness and value of life to all people of all colors everywhere. The assertion that "all men are created equal" was of no practical use in effecting our separation from Great Britain; and it was placed in the Declaration not for that, but for future use. Its authors meant it to be—as, thank God, it is now proving itself—a stumbling-block to all those who in after times might seek to turn a free people into the hateful paths of despotism. They knew the proneness of prosperity to breed tyrants, and they meant when such should reappear in this fair land and commence their vocation, they should find left for them at least one hard nut to crack. [Lincoln, *Complete Works*, 1:232. (The words I have italicized could be applied as well to the First Amendment, serving as it does as a stumbling-block to all those who, perhaps even in the name of equality, would suppress in public forums the expression of dissenting opinions.)]

See, ibid., 1:437, 448, 500-501. See, also, pp. 417-18, above.

I argue, as did Lincoln, from the principles implicit in our regime. See chap. 5, n. 43, below. See, also, chap. 9, n. 36, below.

37. Levy, *Legacy of Suppression*, pp. 5-6, 16, 44, 48-49, 108-9, 113, 271-72, 295-96. Even lawyers who are skeptical about "absolutes" (see, e.g., chap. 3, n. 25, above) speak otherwise with respect to parliamentary "freedom of speech." Thus, Justice Harlan wrote, in an opinion joined by Justices Frankfurter, Clark, and Whittaker, "[T]he Constitution itself gives an absolute privilege to members of both Houses of Congress in respect to any speech, debate, vote, report, or action done in session. [Footnote: U.S. Constitution, Art. I, sec. 6. See *Kilbourn* v. *Thompson*, 103 U.S. 168 (1881).]" *Barr* v. *Matteo*, 360 U.S. 564, 569 (1959). (Justice Harlan, in *U.S.* v. *Johnson*, 383 U.S. 169, at 177 [1966], argued that the current constitutional language is essentially the same as the "freedom of speech and debate in Congress" language in the Articles of Confederation.) See, also, Justice Frankfurter's opinion in *Tenney* v. *Brandhove*, 341 U.S. 367 (1951).

The extent to which congressional immunity *may* be carried is suggested by the ruling of a federal judge dismissing

bribery charges against Sen. Daniel B. Brewster (D.—Md.) on grounds that as a member of Congress he was immune from prosecution. . . . The judge said the case related to bribes allegedly made while Brewster was performing his duties as a member of Congress. He said members of Congress are protected from prosecution by the speech and debate clause of the Constitution during performance of their duties in committees or on the floor of Congress. . . . The judge said that if he was to hold Brewster could be prosecuted, he would, in a sense, be opening congressmen to pressures from anyone who disagreed with actions they might take in performing their duties. [*Chicago Sun-Times*, Oct. 10, 1970, p. 10]

I think the ruling dubious but nevertheless revealing. See chap. 2, n. 6, chap. 3, n. 25, chap. 4, nn. 87, 102, above, chap. 5, nn. 101, 104, 106, below.

38. Levy, *Legacy of Suppression*, p. 261; also, pp. 173-74. (See the text at chap. 5, n. 6, above; also, chap. 5, nn. 23, 34, above.) Levy does record (ibid., p. 5, n. 9) that "freedom of speech" was a term rarely used before 1776. I, on the other hand, consider significant its emergence, and general application, in America. See chap. 5, n. 36, above, chap. 5, n. 43, below.

39. Ibid., p. 15. See chap. 5, n. 143, below.

40. Ibid., pp. 19-21, 82. See chap. 6, sec. 6, above.

41. Even so, the many publications of the *Junius* papers suggest that the law of seditious libel was losing its effect in England as well. Ibid., pp. 159, 161. If opinion had been as solidly Blackstonian as Levy describes it, the adoption of Fox's Libel Law in 1792 should have been more strenuously resisted than it was. See chap. 6, n. 30, below. (The first publication of the *Junius* papers was in 1769.)

"The common law known to the literate people [in America in 1789] was the common law of Blackstone, who 'described rather its theory than its practice,' and its theory was many years behind its practice.' " Robert Jackson, *The Supreme Court in the American System of Government* (New York: Harper & Row, 1963), p. 29 (quoting James Bryce, *American Commonwealth* [New York: Macmillan & Co., 1893], 1:29).

Consider, for the difference (as reported a century later) between what the law provided and what the people (and hence juries) believed, James F. Stephens, *A History of the Criminal Law of England* (London: Macmillan & Co., 1883), 2:349:

I do not know that any one ever attempted to distinguish between liberty and license; but the expression liberty of the press had a definite legal meaning and also a definite popular meaning. Lord Mansfield before [Fox's] Libel Act [of 1792] [chap. 6, sec. 6, above] and Lord Kenyon after it gave correct and clear definitions of its legal meaning. It consisted, according to Lord Mansfield, in the power of publishing without a license, subject to the law of libel. It consisted, according to Lord Kenyon (after the Libel Act, which, however, in his opinion made no change in the law), in the power of publishing without a license, *subject to the chance* that a jury might think the publisher deserving of punishment. Each definition was in a legal point of view complete and accurate, *but what the public at large understood by the expression was something altogether different,*—namely, the right of unrestricted discussion of public affairs, carrying with it the right of finding fault with public personages of whose conduct the writer might disapprove. [Italics added]

See chap. 5, n. 52, below. I, on the other hand, find it useful in this book to recognize "liberty of the press" in the "definite legal meaning" and "freedom of the press" in the "definite popular meaning." The latter, it should be noted, reduces the role of chance and emphasizes the role of rational discourse in political affairs. See chap. 8, secs. 6, 9, 13-14, above. See, also, p. 97, above, chap. 5, n. 144, below.

42. See, e.g., ibid., pp. 67-69, 141-42. Some of these expressions are given in my article, "Freedom of Speech and the First Amendment," *U. Detroit L. J.* 42 (1964): p. 55. Many of them, I suspect, were oral, reflecting general public opinion. Levy dismissed as simply uninformed or incompetent the statements by men who do not venerate as much as he believes they should the common law rule. The credentials of Hume (cf. chap. 4, n. 106, above), Montesquieu, Furneaux, and Bentham are questioned by him. Ibid., pp. 139, 156, 169, 170-75. Again and again, he dismisses statements telling against his conclusions with the epithet of "rhetorical." See ibid., pp. 76, 80-81, 87, 105-6, 108-9, 116-17, 120-21, 135, 174-75, 177-78, 188, 215, 227; see, also, pp. 44-45, 46-49, 63-64, 193-97. See chap. 5, n. 94, below, for my suggestion of how Blackstone himself would interpret American experience.

43. My interpretation here anticipated Justice Brennan's observation for the Court (in *New York Times* v. *Sullivan*, 376 U.S. 254, 273 [1964]) about "the great controversy over the Sedition Act of 1798 [having] first crystallized a national awareness of the central meaning of the First Amendment." The opinion refers at this point to "Levy, *Legacy of Suppression* (1960), at 258 *et seq.*; Smith, *Freedom's Fetters* (1956), at 426, 431, and *passim*." (See chap. 5, nn. 142, 143, below.)

But a distinction should be noticed. Levy wrote, "Under the pressure of the Sedition Act, which ironically was passed by the Senate on July 4, writers of the Jeffersonian party were driven to originate so broad a theory of freedom of expression that the concept of seditious libel was, at last, repudiated." *Legacy of Suppression*, pp. 259-60. Thus, where Justice Brennan said "crystallized," Levy had said "originate." ("Crystallize" means "to become settled and definite in form" rather than to make something new.)

There is, I believe, a significant difference between these two expressions: ultimately, the difference is between living under a constitution and pretending to do so. Cf. Edward H. Levi, "An Introduction to Legal Reasoning," *U. Chicago L. Rev.* 15 (1948): 501. See chap. 6, n. 50, chap. 7, nn. 71, 124, chap. 8, n. 28, below. (Story distinguished between "the argument of an able advocate" and "the reasoning of a constitutional statesman." *Commentaries*, 2:656, sec. 1863. See chap. 4, n. 117, above.) See, also, chap. 8, n. 122, below.

Kalven (*Negro and First Amendment*, p. 67) has noticed the similar development with respect to "the effort to make the United States Supreme Court confront the Negro's constitutional claims and grievances and give the Negro his constitutional due": "I am old-fashioned enough to read the development, not as a political pressure on the Court which then as a political institution responded, but rather as a strategy to trap democracy in its own decencies. *The Negro rights in an important sense were always there.* What was needed was a strategy for bringing them to light." (Italics added.) I believe this reading is even more "old-fashioned" than lawyers now suspect: it draws, that is, upon the approach to the common law by the student of natural right. Compare, in Plutarch's *Lives*, p. 839, the ways of Callisthenes and Anaxarchus.

Cf., in Berns, "Freedom of the Press and the Alien and Sedition Laws," the significance of Alexander Hamilton's efforts in *People* v. *Croswell*, 3 Johns 336 (N.Y., 1804). But is it not likely that the determined opposition to the Sedition Act of 1798 on repub-

lican principles (as well as on "states' rights" grounds) prepared the way of Hamilton's argument and for Judge Kent'sopinion in *Croswell*?
See chap. 4, n. 113, chap. 5, n. 36, above, chap. 7, nn. 77, 81, below. See, also, chap. 5, n. 4, above ("the press became properly free, in 1694"); *Federalist*, p. 160 ("English liberty was completely triumphant" in 1688). Cf. chap. 5, n. 1, above, chap. 6, n. 37, below.

44. The difficulty and unreliability of a dependence upon what is found in the statute books (or even in what the opinions of judges say) in order to determine the general understanding of terms such as "freedom of speech" are illustrated by a comment by White about the state of Virginia law during colonial days:

> About the year 1670 an insurrection was raised in Virginia. After its suppression, the Assembly, to manifest their loyalty, passed an act giving the same privilege to the Governor and Council, with respect to scandalous words spoken of them, as the statute *De Scandalis Magnatum* gives to the Peers of Great Britain. The Assembly were soon after impressed with an opinion that these privileges were incautiously transferred, and endeavored to recover them. It was a uniform practice of the House of Representatives to send up a bill for that purpose every session; but although the Council always proved themselves the friends of liberty, and joined the Assembly, both in their legislative and individual capacities, in a warm and spirited opposition to British tyranny, yet they would never consent to repeal that act to the very last moment of their existence. [*Annals*, I, pp. 360-61]

Anyone studying the laws of Virginia for an indication of what was understood by "freedom of speech" would find the limitation therein that White refers to. But his evaluation of the evidence would be mistaken if he did not realize that the Assembly had tried to change the law many times: the general notion of what "freedom of speech" meant would not include this law as part of it. (E.g., "scandalous words" *could* be spoken of the governor and Council, it seems to have been thought; and if the Assembly reflected popular opinion, such words would not result in a conviction by a jury, whatever the statute said.) Even the disparaging remarks one reads about bills of rights (as in *Federalist* No. 84 [see text at chap. 6, n. 2, above] and in Gouverneur Morris, *A Diary of the French Revolution*, ed. Beatrix C. Davenport [Boston: Houghton Mifflin Co., 1939], 1:220) serve as a warning that the effective law may not be that found on paper. (See, on Virginia, *Annals*, VI, pp. 968-70.)

45. See chap. 6, n. 30, below, for the suggestion that in England as well the dominant opinion on the question of seditious libel by 1791 was not simply that found in the collections of statutes and judicial opinions.

The notorious John Wilkes should not be forgotten. See Levy, *Legacy of Suppression*, pp. 145-49, for an account of his controversies. (Has anyone attempted to trace in the career of John Wilkes Booth the influence of the strong-minded libertarian for whom he was evidently named? The two careers may not be unrelated.)

46. Levy, *Legacy of Suppression*, pp. 63-64, 87, 123.

47. Alexander Meiklejohn, *Political Freedom: The Constitutional Power of the People* (New York: Harper & Bros., 1960), p. 20:

> The men who adopted the Bill of Rights were not ignorant of the necessities of war or of national danger. It would, in fact, be nearer to the truth to say that it was exactly those necessities which they had in mind as they planned to defend freedom of discussion against them. Out of their own bitter experience they knew how terror and hatred, how war and strife, can drive men into acts of unreasoning suppression. They planned, therefore, both for the peace which they desired and for the wars which they feared. And in both cases they established an absolute, unqualified prohibition of the abridgment of the freedom of speech.

See chap. 3, n. 5, above. Cf. chap. 3, n. 21, above, chap. 5, n. 71, below.

48. Levy, *Legacy of Suppression*, conceded this lack of power in the general govern-

ment at pp. 181-82, 188, 201-4, 225, 261, 263-64. I discuss this in chap. 6 (see chap. 6, n. 37, below).

49. *The Works of James Wilson*, ed. James DeW. Andrews (Chicago: Callaghan & Co., 1896), 1:14-15.

Cf. Blackstone, *Laws of England*, 1:161-64, 212-13, 245. See, also, George Bernard Shaw, *Man and Superman*, "Preface to the Revolutionist's Handbook":

> The constitution of England is revolutionary. To a Russian or Anglo-Indian bureaucrat, a general election is as much a revolution as a referendum or plebiscite in which the people fight instead of voting. The French Revolution overthrew one set of rulers and substituted another with different interests and different views. That is what a general election enables the people to do in England every seven years if they choose. Revolution is therefore a national institution in England; and its advocacy by an Englishman needs no apology.

Cf. chap. 2, n. 10, above, chap. 8, n. 57, below. See pp. 417-18, above.

50. Milton, *Prose Works*, I, 237. See chap. 8, sec. 13, above.

It is the freewheeling tone of Milton, with its exuberant sense of liberty, that seems to have influenced modern opinion about free discussion. This tone has been more important in this respect than the precise terms, and qualifications, of his arguments. (See chap. 2, n. 29, above, chap. 8, nn. 155, 195, chap. 9, n. 9, below. Cf. chap. 5, n. 128, chap. 8, nn. 170, 171, below.) Thus, one should not be surprised to find him moderating in his private correspondence (e.g., 1:xiv, xviii) the "rather harsh expressions" against Roman Catholicism in his public utterances.

"[F]or the letter killeth, but the spirit giveth life." 2 Cor. 3:6. See, also, Rom. 2:29; 7:6.

51. Preamble for the Virginia Statute of Religious Freedom of 1786. But see Harry V. Jaffa, *Equality and Liberty* (New York: Oxford University Press, 1965), p. 186, for the argument that the distinction for Jefferson between religious opinion and other opinions was fundamental. See Lincoln, *Complete Works*, 2:291, 464.

Cf. chap. 8, n. 14, below. See chap. 5, n. 92, below. See, also, chap. 2, n. 38, above.

52. See Chafee, *Freedom of Speech*, p. 20:

> It is obvious that [according to Blackstone] liberty of the press was nothing more than absence of the censorship . . . All through the eighteenth century, however, there existed beside this definite legal meaning of liberty of the press, a definite popular meaning: the right of unrestricted discussion of public affairs. There can be no doubt that this was in a general way what freedom of speech meant to the framers of the Constitution.

Cf. chap. 5, n. 100, below. (See Kalven, "Upon Rereading Mr. Justice Black on the First Amendment," *U.C.L.A. L. Rev.* 14 [1967]: 428, 432, 440, 441, 447.)

Storing concluded his review of *Legacy of Suppression* (see chap. 5, n. 34, above),

> Levy expresses some concern that he may be condemned as an apostate from libertarianism, "or what is even worse, . . . hailed as a convert to the 'new conservatism' . . . ." On the contrary, he deserves praise, in the style of his praise of the Framers, for doing much more than he intended. He has reminded us of the full resources of authentic liberalism, which its strident and over-simplifying contemporary exponents have tended to obscure.

Praise has come as well from Paul A. Freund et al., *Constitutional Law: Cases and Other Problems* (2d ed.; Boston: Little, Brown & Co., 1961), p. 1545, who described Levy's *Legacy of Suppression* as "a radical and learned reinterpretation of English and American backgrounds of the First Amendment. . . ." Cf. Walter Berns, "Freedom of the Press and the Alien and Sedition Laws." See chap. 5, n. 41, above.

On the other hand, the argument I develop here and in chapters 6 and 7, below, was anticipated in the Fifth Congress by opponents to the Sedition Act of 1798. Thus, Edward Livingston of New York argued in the House of Representatives,

> The Constitution declares that "no law shall be passed to abridge the liberty of speech or of the press." Let us inquire . . . what was the liberty enjoyed at the time this declaration was agreed to, and see whether citizens will enjoy the same liberty after this law passes that they then enjoyed. Will gentlemen say that the same liberty of writing and speaking did not exist then that now exists? If they will not say this, must they not allow that the Constitution is positive in prohibiting any change in this respect? Gentlemen may call this liberty an evil, if they please; if it be an evil (which he was far from believing) it is an evil perpetrated by the Constitution. . . . This privilege is connected with another dear and valuable privilege—the liberty of conscience. What is liberty of conscience? Gentlemen may tomorrow establish a national religion agreeably to the opinion of a majority of this House, *on the ground of a uniformity of worship being more consistent with public happiness than a diversity of worship. The doing of this is not less forbidden than the act which the House are about to do.* But, it is said, will you suffer a printer to abuse his fellow-citizens with impunity, ascribing his conduct to the very worst of motives? . . . There is a remedy for offences of this kind in the laws of every State in the Union. Every man's character is protected by law, and every man who shall publish a libel on any part of the Government, is liable to punishment. Not . . . by laws which we ourselves have made, but by laws passed by the several States. . . . The States are as much interested in the preservation of the General Government as we are. . . . [*Annals*, V, pp. 2153-54; italics added]

Cf. chap. 6, n. 23, below. See chap. 8, n. 83, below.

53. The extent of the colonial newspaper press, as distinguished from pamphlets, should not be exaggerated. "My brother had, in 1720 or 1721, begun to print a newspaper. It was the second that appeared in America . . . At this time (1771) there are not less than five-and-twenty." Benjamin Franklin, *Autobiography* (New York: Simon & Schuster, Pocket Books, 1940), p. 22. Cf. chap. 2, n. 6, above.

It should be noted, however, that "our people, having no publick amusements to divert their attention from study, became better acquainted with books, and in a few years were observ'd by strangers to be better instructed and more intelligent than people of the same rank generally are in other countries." Ibid., p. 90.

54. The patriots would have said, for instance, that their attacks on the crown should have been protected even in an English court in England, not only in America. See chap. 5, n. 25, above, chap. 5, nn. 63, 69, 70, below.

55. "The most practical and the shortest method of distinguishing between good and bad measures, is to think what you yourself would or would not like under another emperor." Thus the Emperor Galba advised his intended (but ill-fated) successor. Tacitus, *History* 1. 16.

One is reminded not only of the Golden Rule, but also of Kant's maxim, in the *Metaphysical Foundations of Morals*, "I am never to act in any way other than so I could want my maxim also to become a general law." Locke, in his *Letter Concerning Toleration*, gave the maxim this application:

> It may be said, what if a church is idolatrous, is that also to be tolerated by the magistrate? I answer, what power can be given to the magistrate for the suppression of an idolatrous church which may not in time and place be made use of to the ruin of an orthodox one? For it must be remembered that the civil power is the same everywhere, and the religion of every prince is orthodox to himself. If, therefore, such a power be granted unto the civil magistrate in spirituals, as that at Geneva, for example, he may extirpate, by violence and blood, the religion which is there reputed idolatrous; by the same rule another magistrate, in some neighboring country, may oppress the reformed religion, and, in India, the Christian.

Rousseau, however, advised in his *Discourse on the Origin of Inequality* what he considered a more realistic approach than that of the Golden Rule:

> [It is compassion] which, instead of inculcating that sublime maxim of rational justice, *Do to others as you would have them do unto you*, inspires all men with that other maxim of natural goodness, much less perfect indeed, but perhaps more useful; *Do good to yourself with as little evil as possible to others*. In a word, it is rather in this natural feeling [of compassion] than in any subtle arguments that we must look for the cause of that repugnance, which every man would experience in doing evil, even independently of the maxims of education. Although it might belong to Socrates and other minds of the like craft to acquire virtue by reason, the human race would long since have ceased to be, had its preservation depended only on the reasonings of the individuals composing it.

56. See, for example, the passages quoted in my article, "Freedom of Speech and the First Amendment." (The sentiments of Franklin, quoted in chap. 2, n. 12, above, and commented on in chap. 4, n. 113, above, seem to recognize an unlimited "liberty of discussing the propriety of public measures and political opponents.") See, also, chap. 5, n. 78, below, on the significance in this respect of Shays's Rebellion.

The attitude of the patriots is reflected in the response Samuel Johnson was moved to make in *Taxation No Tyranny* to their arguments:

> When they tell us of laws made expressly for their punishment, we answer that tumults and sedition were always punishable and that the new law prescribes only the mode of execution. . . . If their assemblies have been suddenly dissolved, what was the reason? Their deliberations were indecent, and their intentions seditious. The power of dissolution is granted and reserved for such times of turbulence. . . .

57. The celebrated New York case (1735) of the printer John Peter Zenger, in its vindication of the legal and moral right (as well as the acknowledged power) of the jury to acquit whomever they wished in a trial for seditious libel, can be said to have established in North America the principle that the people could, consistent with their solemn oaths as jurymen, protect from governmental sanctions the most radical critic of the authorities. (The judge, on the other hand, had insisted on what was then, and was long thereafter to continue to be, the English rule, that only the fact of publication of the alleged libel, not its criminality, was to be determined by the jury. Its criminality was a matter of law and to be left solely to the judge to decide.)

The First Amendment can be understood (in my view) as assuring "acquittal" in all such confrontations, even when "juries" (i.e., the people) are disposed to side with the authorities against the alleged offender. Otherwise, as I have argued earlier in this section, there would be no practical distinction between "the right of trial by jury" and "freedom of speech." See, also, pp. 224-29, above.

See, for a contemporary account of the Zenger case, James Alexander, *A Brief Narrative of the Case and Trial of John Peter Zenger, Printer of the New York Weekly Journal* (Cambridge: Harvard University Press, 1963). See, also, Arthur E. Sutherland, *Constitutionalism in America: Origin and Evolution of Its Fundamental Ideas* (New York: Blaisdell Publishing Co., 1965), pp. 119-23; chap. 4, n. 80, n. 105, above, chap. 5, n. 79, chap. 6, n. 30, below.

58. This is not simply comparable to the criminal pleading for a more tolerant view of his activities when he is caught, for the calculating criminal would recognize that certain activities cannot be generally permitted if the community is to survive and if he is to enjoy his ill-gotten gains. Nor is it a matter of renegades asking that certain rights be granted them which they would be willing to concede to all others, rights that no decent man would exercise and that no community could tolerate. See Plato, *Republic* 351C-D; Aristotle, *Nicomachean Ethics* 1167b6-16. See, also, chap. 7, n. 77, below.

59. But, on the other hand, may the common good be harmed if passion and self-interest are not given their head, if artificial barriers are placed in the way of venting passion on such deserving targets as unpopular dissenters? The duty of the good man is to oppose, or at least not acquiesce in, unjust public opinion: the need is not for mere suppression, but (in our circumstances) for education. See chap. 4, n. 111, above, chap. 7, n. 107 (on Lincoln and the reenslavement of emancipated men), chap. 8, n. 135, below.

60. See Shakespeare, *King Lear*, act 3, sc. 4, lines 35-44. See, also, Lincoln, *Complete Works*, 1:202; chap. 9, n. 20, below.

61. But certainly risks *are* run by unvarying recourse to any institution, including freedom of speech and of the press. Levy suggested that, "Had Cushing written that a good government or an honest administrator could not be injured by error of opinion or even by malicious falsehood, he would have evinced a libertarian understanding that was incompatible with the concept of seditious libel." (Levy, *Legacy of Suppression*, p. 199) It is folly, however, to claim that "error of opinion," to say nothing of "malicious falsehood," cannot injure at all a good government or honest administrators. If this claim is critical to Levy's view of what it means to be "Brandeisians," then the "Blackstonians" have clearly the better of the argument (ibid., p. 309). See James B. Reston, *The Artillery of the Press: Its Influence on American Foreign Policy* (New York: Harper & Row, 1967), p. 58; chap. 6, n. 7, below. Cf. chap. 5, n. 35, chap. 6, nn. 23, 66, below. See, also, chap. 7, n. 67, below.

Is not Levy's position essentially that of John Stuart Mill's *On Liberty*, "the basic assumption of [which is] the complete compatibility of truth and its pursuit [on the one hand] and political good [on the other]"? Walter Berns, "Freedom of the Press and the Alien and Sedition Laws," n. 111. See chap. 9, n. 28, below.

62. See chap. 5, n. 65, below. See, also, chap. 4, n. 59, chap. 5, n. 14, above, and chap. 7, n. 59, below.

63. Thus, in the Constitutional Convention, Pinckney observed, "Much has been said of the Constitution of G. Britain. I will confess that I believe it to be the best constitution in existence; but at the same time I am confident it is one that will not or can not be introduced into this country, for many centuries." Max Farrand, *The Records of the Federal Convention of 1787* (New Haven: Yale University Press, 1937), 1:398.

Even James Otis could say (in 1764), "[The British constitution] is the most free one, and by far the best, now existing on earth: that by this constitution, every man in the dominions is a free man. . . ." Samuel Eliot Morison, *Sources and Documents Illustrating the American Revolution, 1764-1788, and the Formation of the Federal Constitution* (London: Oxford University Press, 1962), p. 8.

64. Senator Daniel Webster conceded, in 1834, partly for immediate rhetorical purposes, that the rebels' grievances had been, in a sense, trifling.

The entire passage from Webster reveals as well the attitude of one of our great constitutional lawyers to the problems I have examined in chapters 3 and 4:

> . . . The question is, therefore, whether, upon the true principles of the Constitution, this exercise of power by the President can be justified. Whether the consequences be prejudicial or not, if there be an illegal exercise of power, it is to be resisted in the proper manner. Even if no harm or inconvenience result from transgressing the boundary, the intrusion is not to be suffered to pass unnoticed. Every encroachment, great or small, is important enough to awaken the attention of those who are intrusted with the preservation of a constitutional government. We are not to wait till great public mischiefs come, till the government is overthrown, or liberty itself put into extreme jeopardy. We should not be worthy sons of our fathers were we so to regard great questions affecting the general freedom. Those fathers accomplished the Revolution on a strict question of principle. The Parliament of Great Britain asserted a right to tax the Colonies in all cases whatever; and it was precisely on this question that they made the Revolution turn. The amount of taxation was trifling, but the claim itself was inconsistent with liberty; and that was, in their eyes, enough. It was against the recital of an act of Parliament, rather than against any suffering under

its enactments, that they took up arms. They went to war against a preamble. They fought seven years against a declaration. They poured out their treasures and their blood like water, in a contest against an assertion which those less sagacious and not so well schooled in the principles of civil liberty would have regarded as barren phraseology, or mere parade of words. . . .

The necessity of holding strictly to the principle upon which free governments are constructed, and to those precise lines which fix the partitions of power between different branches, is as plain, if not as cogent, as that of resisting, as our fathers did, the strides of the parent country against the rights of the Colonies; because, whether the power which exceeds its just limits be foreign or domestic, whether it be the encroachment of all branches on the rights of the people, or that of one branch on the rights of others, in either case, the balanced and well-adjusted machinery of free government is disturbed, and, if the derangement go on, the whole system must fall. [*The Works of Daniel Webster* (Boston: Little, Brown & Co., 1869), 4:109-10]

F. A. Hayek has noted:

On the great influence of legal thought on American politics during the period [of James Wilson, John Marshall, Joseph Story, James Kent, and Daniel Webster] see particularly Tocqueville, *Democracy*, I, chap. xvi, 272-80. Few facts are more indicative of the change of atmosphere than the decline of the reputation of men like Daniel Webster, whose effective statements of constitutional theory were once considered classic but are now largely forgotten. [*The Constitution of Liberty* (Chicago: University of Chicago Press, 1960), p. 476, n. 50]

We should be reminded as well of Burke's 1774 "Speech on American Taxation":

No man ever doubted that the commodity of tea could bear an imposition of three-pence. But no commodity will bear three-pence, or will bear a penny, when the general feelings of men are irritated, and two millions of people are resolved not to pay. The feelings of the colonies were formerly the feelings of Great Britain. Theirs were formerly the feelings of Mr. Hampden when called upon for the payment of twenty shillings. Would twenty shillings have ruined Mr. Hampden's fortune? No! but the payment of half twenty shillings, on the principle it was demanded, would have made him a slave. . . . [Burke, *Works* (London: World Classics, 1930), 2:101; see, also, ibid., 2:242]

Compare the attitude of the Justice Department as reflected in the confession of Justice Clark, chap. 5, n. 17, above. (Cf. chap. 4, n. 34, above.) See, also, the discussion of John Quincy Adams in chap. 8, sec. 12, above, chap. 8, n. 169, below.

65. Is this not one of the everyday political implications of that right of revolution sanctified by the Declaration of Independence? It is to be hoped that the critical citizen acts in good faith, that the government is strong enough to withstand (and even to profit from) such attack, and that citizens distinguishing legitimate from illegitimate criticism will take in hand the mistaken dissenter.

Locke addressed himself to this problem, in his *Letter Concerning Toleration*, when he argued,

For if men enter into seditious conspiracies, it is not religion inspires them to it in their meetings, but their sufferings and oppressions that make them willing to ease themselves. Just and moderate governments are everywhere quiet, everywhere safe; but oppression raises ferments and makes men struggle to cast off an uneasy and tyrannical yoke. I know that seditions are very frequently raised upon pretense of religion, but it is as true that for religion subjects are frequently ill treated and live miserably. Believe me, the stirs that are made proceed not from any peculiar temper of this or that church or religious society, but from the common disposition of all mankind, who when they groan under any heavy burden endeavor naturally to shake off the yoke that galls their necks. . . . But there is only one thing which gathers people into seditious commotions, and that is oppression.

I return to this problem in chapter 6 (where the powers of the general government, especially with respect to treason, are discussed) and in chapter 8. The relation of freedom of speech both to the Declaration of Independence and to the English doctrine of treason is suggested by the following passage from William Wirt's *Life of Patrick Henry* (Philadelphia, 1818), p. 65 (describing the debate in the Virginia Assembly, May 30, 1765, on the Stamp Act):

> It was in the midst of this magnificent debate, while he [Patrick Henry] was descanting on the tyranny of the obnoxious Act, that he exclaimed, in a voice of thunder, and with the look of a god, "Caesar had his Brutus—Charles the first, his Cromwell—and George the third—('Treason,' cried the Speaker—'treason, treason,' echoed from every part of the House.—It was one of those trying moments which is decisive of character.—Henry faltered not an instant; but rising to a loftier attitude, and fixing on the Speaker an eye of the most determined fire, he finished his sentence with the firmest emphasis) *may profit by their example*. If *this* be treason, make the most of it."

Has not this kind of "treason" been repudiated for Americans both by precept (i.e., the Constitution) and by example (e.g., Patrick Henry's declaration and the respect with which it has been regarded)?

That the Speaker may have been correct in denouncing Henry's sentiments as treason (according to the law of England) is suggested by the circumspection of a private letter from Virginia, of June 21, 1765, "Mr. ———— has lately blazed out in the Assembly, where he compared ———— to a Tarquin, a Caesar, a Charles the First, threatening him with a Brutus, or an Oliver Cromwell; yet Mr. ———— was not sent to the Tower: but having prevailed to get some ridiculous Resolves passed, rode off in triumph." Morison, *Sources and Documents*, p. 16. (I am not concerned about what may actually have been said by Henry on that occasion [cf. ibid., pp. 14-15, 16-17] but rather with what Americans have thought he said and how they have responded to what they have thought he said.)

A statement such as Patrick Henry's, it should also be noted, would be (considering the circumstances and intentions of the speaker and his audience) subject to the Smith Act provision that "it shall be unlawful for any person—(1) to knowingly or willfully advocate, abet, advise, or teach the duty, necessity, desirability, or propriety of overthrowing or destroying any government in the United States by force or violence, or by the assassination of any officer of such government." (See the text in chap. 3, n. 18, above.) Indeed, should we not say of the Smith Act what Madison said in response to the Sedition Act of 1798 (in his *Report of 1799*, for the Virginia Assembly)?

> Had "sedition acts," forbidding every publication that might bring the constituted agents into contempt or disrepute, or that might excite the hatred of the people against the authors of unjust or pernicious measures, been uniformly enforced against the press; might not the United States have been languishing at this day, under the infirmities of a sickly confederation? Might they not possibly be miserable colonies, groaning under a foreign yoke?

It should be remembered that vigorous (and sometimes unfair) attacks upon the British constitution were followed by vigorous (and also sometimes unfair) attacks upon the subsequent constitution (i.e., the Articles of Confederation).

66. I am speaking here of political discussion, not of every use of words or language, nor (in Justice Douglas's formulation, with which Justice Black concurred) of expression that is (and to the extent that it is) "so closely brigaded with illegal action as to be an inseparable part of it." Dissenting in *Roth* v. *United States*, 354 U.S. 476, 514 (1957) (citing Justice Black's opinion for the Court, *Giboney* v. *Empire Storage Co.*, 336 U.S.

490, 498 [1949]; *Labor Board* v. *Virginia Power Co.*, 314 U.S. 469, 477-78 [1941]). (Justice Douglas, again with Justice Black concurring, reaffirmed this formulation in *Garrison* v. *Louisiana*, 379 U.S. 64, 82 [1964]. What this means for Justice Black is suggested by his dissenting opinion in *Griswold* v. *Conn.*, 381 U.S. 479, 507 [1965].)

Words and deeds can be distinguished for this purpose. (See chap. 8, n. 1, below.) Thus Lincoln argued, in his Cooper Institute speech,

> . . . Invasions and insurrections are the rage now. Will it satisfy [the Southern people] if, in the future, we have nothing to do with invasions and insurrections? We know it will not. We so know, because we know we never had anything to do with invasions and insurrections; and yet this total abstaining does not exempt us from the charge and the denunciation. . . . Most of them would probably say to us, "Let us alone, *do* nothing to us, and *say* what you please about slavery." But we do let them alone,—have never disturbed them,—so that, after all, it is what we say, which dissatisfies them. They will continue to accuse us of doing, until we cease saying. [*Complete Works*, 1:611-12; italics added]

Meiklejohn, in a 1955 statement to the Hennings Senate Subcommittee on Constitutional Rights, offered this counsel:

> [T]he most troublesome issue which now confronts our courts and our people is that of the speech and writing and assembling of people who find, or think they find, radical defects in our form of government, and who devise and advocate plans by means of which another form might be substituted for it. And the practical question is, "How far, and in what respects, are such revolutionary planning and advocacy protected by the First Amendment?" It is, of course, understood that if such persons or groups proceed to forceful or violent action, or even to overt preparation for such action, against the government, the First Amendment offers them, in that respect, no protection. Its interest is limited to the freedom of judgment-making—of inquiry and belief and conference and persuasion and planning and advocacy. It is concerned only with those political activities by which, under the Constitution, free men govern themselves. . . . An incitement, I take it, is an utterance so related to a specific overt act that it may be regarded and treated as a part of the doing of the act itself, if the act is done. Its control, therefore, falls within the jurisdiction of the legislature. An advocacy, on the other hand, even up to the limit of arguing and planning for the violent overthrow of the existing form of government, is one of those opinion-forming, judgment-making expressions which free men need to utter and to hear as citizens responsible for the governing of the nation. If men are not free to ask and to answer the question, "Shall the present form of our government be maintained or changed?"; if, when that question is asked, the two sides of the issue are not equally open for consideration, for advocacy, and for adoption, then it is impossible to speak of our government as established by the free choice of a self-governing people. [*Political Freedom*, pp. 122-23; cf. ibid., pp. xx-xxi, 39-43, 46]

See chap. 8, n. 181, below. See, in James Mill's article, "Liberty of the Press," the section, "In Matters of Government, Undeserved Praise Is As Mischievous As Undeserved Blame." See, also, chap. 4, n. 113, above. "It is my downfall if I note too carefully how you praise me and disregard how you live. . . ." Augustine, *Sermons*, 334, sec. 1. Cf. chap. 9, n. 27, below.

The "clear and present danger" test, on the other hand, was designed and has been employed to get at political expression that is not "closely brigaded with illegal deeds": the deeds invoked by the government are essentially prospective and even conjectural. See chap. 3, n. 20, above. Notice, on the other hand, the concluding words (which I italicize) in Justice Holmes's sentence (in *Schenck*): "The most stringent protection of free speech would not protect a man in falsely shouting fire in a theater, *and causing a panic*." Thus, not even Justice Holmes, in his most famous illustration, dealt with "mere words" alone: in the incident he used to illuminate his doctrine, the words were "so closely brigaded with illegal action [i.e., causing a panic] as to be an inseparable part of it." But in the cases prosecuted by the general government since the Second World War—to say nothing of *Schenck* itself—no one pretends that the illegal action about which Americans might legitimately be concerned is likely in the foreseeable future to follow upon the words which conveniently identify the potential culprits. See, also, Montesquieu, *The Spirit of the Laws* XII, 11, 12; Erskine, *Speeches*, 2:152-53; O. John Rogge, *The First and Fifth* (New York: Thomas Nelson & Sons, 1960), pp. 10-11, 22; Street, *Freedom, the Individual and the Law*, p. 200; Leslie Stephen, *An Agnostic's Apology* (London: Smith, Elder & Co., 1893), pp. 281-82.

 67. See Charles A. and Mary R. Beard, *The Rise of American Civilization* (New York: Macmillan Co., 1930), pp. 160-65, on the history of religious toleration and persecution in Maryland. See, also, James Kent, *Commentaries on American Law* (New York: O. Halsted, 1826), 2:35-36; Sutherland, *Constitutionalism in America*, pp. 286-87; Thomas Jefferson, *Notes on the State of Virginia* (New York: Harper & Row, Harper Torchbooks, 1964), pp. 148-49.

 Even the pure in heart, Gibbon would have us understand, cannot always be relied upon to return good for good, toleration for toleration:

> The first fifteen bishops of Jerusalem were all circumcised Jews; and the congregation over which they presided united the law of Moses with the doctrine of Christ. It was natural that the primitive tradition of a church which was founded only forty days after the death of Christ, and was governed almost as many years under the immediate inspection of his apostle, should be received as the standard of orthodoxy. The distant churches very frequently appealed to the authority of their venerable Parent [the church of Jerusalem], and relieved her distresses by a liberal contribution of alms. But when numerous and opulent societies were established in the great cities of the empire, in Antioch, Alexandria, Ephesus, Corinth, and Rome, the reverence which Jerusalem had inspired to all the Christian colonies insensibly diminished. The Jewish converts, or, as they were afterwards called, the Nazarenes, who had laid the foundations of the church, soon found themselves overwhelmed by the increasing multitudes that from all the various religions of polytheism enlisted under the banner of Christ: and the Gentiles, who, with the approbation of their peculiar apostle [Paul], had rejected the intolerable weight of Mosaic ceremonies, at length refused to their more scrupulous brethren [the Nazarenes] the same toleration which at first they had humbly solicited for their own practice. [*The Decline and Fall of the Roman Empire* (New York: Random House, Modern Library, n.d.), 1:389]

Martin Luther argued in 1523:

> If the Apostles, who also were Jews, had dealt with us Gentiles as we Gentiles deal with the Jews, there would have been no Christians among the Gentiles. But seeing that they have acted in such a brotherly way towards us, we in turn should act in a brotherly way towards the Jews in case we might convert some. For we ourselves are still not yet fully their equals, much less their superiors. . . . But now we use force against them . . . what good will we do them with that? Similarly, how will we benefit them by forbidding them to live and work and have other human fellowship with us, thus driving them to practise usury? ["The Aryan Clauses," in Dietrich Bonhoeffer, *No Rusty Swords* (New York: Harper & Row, 1965), pp. 221-22]

 68. John Adams, *A Defense of the Constitutions of Government of the United States of America* (London: C. Dilly, 1787-88), 1:129. See, also, Malcolm Sharp, "The Classical American Doctrine of 'The Separation of Powers,'" *U. Chicago L. Rev.* 2 (April 1935): 385, 400; Hayek, *Constitution of Liberty*, p. 449, n. 4. Cf. Aristotle, *Nicomachean Ethics* 1130a1 ("Office will show a man").

 69. Locke, in his *Letter Concerning Toleration*, suggests that

> those [have no right to be tolerated by the magistrate] that will not own and

CHAPTER FIVE, NOTE 69: PAGE 109

teach the duty of tolerating all men in matters of mere religion. For what do all these and the like doctrines signify but that they may and are ready upon any occasion to seize the government and possess themselves of the estates and fortunes of their fellow subjects; and that they only ask leave to be tolerated by the magistrate so long until they find themselves strong enough to effect it?

See, also, the uncharacteristically bitter article on Leon Trotsky in Churchill's *Great Contemporaries* (London: Odhams Press, 1949), especially pp. 152-54. (Such bitterness may have distorted Churchill's policy in Greece as the Second World War drew to an end, a distortion which is reflected in "the Greek anomaly" to this day: collaborators with the Germans were enlisted in the battle against communism. See chap. 6, n. 1, below.)

The argument for freedom of speech, unlike the argument for toleration in religion, does not rest ultimately upon considerations of self-defense and of justice (in the sense of reciprocity), but rather upon considerations of what is needed to make a people truly self-governing and hence both informed and free. Meiklejohn spoke in this fashion to the question posed by Locke:

> Shall we, then, as practitioners of freedom, listen to ideas which, being opposed to our own, might destroy confidence in our form of government? Shall we give a hearing to those who hate and despise freedom, to those who, if they had the power, would destroy our institutions? Certainly, yes! Our action must be guided, not by their principles, but by ours. We listen, not because they desire to speak, but because we need to hear. If there are arguments against our theory of government, our policies in war or in peace, we the citizens, the rulers, must hear and consider them for ourselves. That is the way of public safety. It is the program of self-government. [*Political Freedom*, p. 57]

Locke, on the other hand, had insisted in his *Letter* that "no opinions contrary to human society, or to those moral rules which are necessary to the preservation of civil society, are to be tolerated by the magistrate." But, presumably, the magistrate—the sovereign authority?—is permitted to hear and weigh such opinions: if so, we face the problem about true self-government touched upon at chap. 4, n. 113, above.

See my lecture, "Principle and Passion: The American Nazi Speaker on the University Campus," appended to my dissertation, "Notes on the First Amendment," which closes with this argument:

> We have still another lesson to learn from Mr. Rockwell's visit. [Rockwell was national commander of the American Nazi party.] It is sometimes argued that the rights of free speech should not be extended to those whose aim is to destroy freedom. There seems, on its face, a certain justice to this proposition (assuming that the aim, the destruction of freedom, is accurately discovered). [But] so long as those whose aim is to destroy freedom are significant in our community, we are entitled, we are obliged, to learn what they are saying so that we might better judge the validity or the tendency of their claims and, if need be, prepare ourselves to confront them. No doubt, the motives of the speaker are not necessarily benevolent: but we should not be concerned only with the question of his good will but much more with what he has to say and with what there is to it. If, in political matters, we limit our students to secondhand reports and settle for passionate denunciations, we substitute gratification for education and thereby disarm ourselves.

"[Congressional] investigators estimate that the [American Nazi party] has never had more than 100 members and that usually it has been less than 50. Rockwell's income was said to have been no more than $10,000 a year. However, he was able to get additional funds from time to time from anti-Semites and other radical sources." *Dallas Morning News*, Dec. 10, 1967, p. 42A. See, for a position opposed to mine with respect to the Rockwell visit (to the University of Chicago campus in 1963), the strong letter reprinted in my dissertation (at p. 748), signed by Leonard Binder, Robert A. Goldwin, David

Grene, Zvi Grilliches, Bert F. Hoselitz, Arcadius Kahan, Ralph Lerner, Marvin Meyers, J. Coert Rylaarsdam, Herbert J. Storing and Leo Strauss. Cf. pp. 311, 409, above.

"Continued distribution of *Sputnik* [a new Russian magazine, printed in English] in the U. S., [the State Department] said, will hinge on Russian willingness to grant American publications . . . equal opportunity to earn rubles in the Soviet Union." *Newsweek*, Jan. 23, 1967, p. 47. Insofar as the State Department position is based on an insistence upon "cultural exchange," aside from what is said about rubles, it seems to me improper: indeed, no matter what the Russians are willing to do about permitting American magazines to circulate in Russia, it is in our interest to have available a popular magazine designed to show us "articles culled [by the Russians themselves] from the Soviet press." See Eisenhower, *Waging Peace*, pp. 410-11; chap. 8, n. 160 (end), below.

See, also, Laszek Kolakowski, "The Conspiracy of Ivory Tower Intellectuals," in Arthur P. Mendel, ed., *Essential Works of Marxism* (New York: Bantam Books, 1961), pp. 351-52.

70. It should be noticed that even the most intolerant are tolerant of some, if only of those like themselves. The same may be said of the tolerant who act according to Locke's suggestion: that is, both the tolerant and the intolerant would be tolerant in some cases (with respect to those like themselves) and intolerant in other cases (with respect to those unlike themselves). But see, in Plato, *Republic* 349C-350D, the decisive lack of discrimination exhibited by Thrasymachus's unjust man.

There is something refreshing in the exchange reported by Arthur Garfield Hays (*Wilson Bulletin*, June, 1935, p. 529):

> Some years ago the American Civil Liberties Union wrote a letter to a communist group in New York protesting against their interference with Menshevik and socialist meetings and pointed out that it seemed rather presumptuous for them to ask the assistance of the American Civil Liberties Union where their rights were attacked, while they were suppressing the meetings of others. The reply was pertinent, if not impertinent: "You fellows defend us because you believe in free speech; we break up the meetings of others because we don't." I do not assume that this group spoke for the Communist party, but the logic was sound. Are we to justify acts of repression in the United States on the ground that the communists or fascists would indulge in more repression? Are we to adopt the principles or logic of the communists or fascists in order to save democracy? . . .
> [J. E. Johnsen, ed., *The Reference Shelf* (New York, 1936), 10:117]

Cf. Kolakowski, "Conspiracy of Intellectuals," in Mendel, *Essential Works of Marxism*, pp. 351-52 (the Intellectual says to the Revolutionary, "Over and over again, you din into my ears Saint-Just's motto: 'There is no freedom for the enemies of freedom.' To some extent I am willing to recognize that. But I must know who determines the division of men into enemies and defenders of freedom. . . .").

See chap. 7, n. 124, below. See, also, chap. 8, n. 127, below.

71. Washington recognized that Americans ruled their slaves as arbitrarily as Great Britain wanted to rule Americans. *Basic Writings of George Washington*, ed. S. Commins (New York: Random House, 1948), p. 103.

> The opinion-making role of the newspapers inescapably involved them in the issue of freedom of the press. As long as the Crown wielded effective control, the Whig journalists endlessly extolled the virtues of unfettered discussion, calling in witness such notables of the past and present as the authors of *Cato's Letters*, John Wilkes and Zenger's attorney, Andrew Hamilton. And though the common-law doctrine of seditious libel ran squarely to the contrary, the patriots actually succeeded by hook or crook in preventing a single editor or contributor from suffering the judicial consequences of defaming the government. As the crisis deepened, however, and the Whigs gradually gained the upper hand, they unblushingly invoked for their own purposes the murky distinction between liberty and license of the press which, when it was advanced by their adversaries, they had earlier so passionately rejected. . . . The great and honorable

CHAPTER FIVE, NOTES 72-75: PAGES 109-10

exception to this reign of intolerance, though affording no relief to Tories, was the free and open debate within the Whig party itself during the first half of 1776 over the question of Independence. [Schlesinger, *Prelude to Independence*, pp. 297-98]

In a sense, the entire American people today is "within the Whig party" and is entitled, as in 1776 and during the ratification campaign of 1787-89, to free and open debate of the issues before the country. See chap. 6, n. 17, below.
See chap. 4, n. 113, chap. 5, nn. 47, 66, 69, above, chap. 8, n. 29, below.

72. Such attempts suggest it was recognized that the wartime suppression and confiscation may not have been just. See, e.g., Morison, *Sources and Documents*, pp. 191-92, 212-13.

The restoration of Loyalist (Tory) property, under the exercise of the treaty power of the United States, may be considered an instance of action on the part of the general government removing and correcting state abridgments of freedom of speech.

73. A typical denunciation is found in a Tory diary entry of 1774: "The New Englanders, by their canting, whining, insinuating tricks have persuaded the rest of the colonies that the Government is going to make absolute slaves of them. This I believe never was intended, but the Presbyterian rascals have had address sufficient to make the other colonies come into their scheme." Beard and Beard, *Rise of American Civilization*, p. 229. See, for a Tory opinion of John Adams, the text at chap. 6, n. 24, above, as well as the note.

The Beards calculated that,

> In the stormy year of 1765 when Boston was shaken from center to circumference over the Stamp Act, an election was held for the colonial assembly, with Sam Adams stirring up furor as a candidate; four hundred and forty-eight votes were cast—two hundred and sixty-five for Adams, awarding victory to him. In other words, the firebrand of revolution elected on that occasion spoke for less than 10 per cent of the eligible voters of Boston. [Ibid., p. 256]

I am reminded of what educators say today about the very small minority of troublemakers on campuses. (But not all troublemakers are tolerated by the majority?)

74. The opponents of the Sedition Bill, Samuel W. Dana charged in the Fifth Congress, argued for the liberty of lying. *Annals*, V, p. 2112. Cf. *Annals*, V, pp. 2140-41. When, as is permitted by an effective freedom of speech, the characters and intentions of the leading citizens of the community are examined and, if need be, exposed, it is inevitable that passions should be aroused. See Montesquieu, *Spirit of the Laws*, xxix, 16; Hume, *Political Essays* (Indianapolis: Bobbs-Merrill, 1953), p. 7; William W. Crosskey, *Politics and the Constitution* (Chicago: University of Chicago Press, 1953), pp. 676, 678.

75. "That the power, and consequently the security of the monarchy, may not be weakened by division, it must descend entire to one of the children. To which of them so important a preference shall be given, must be determined by some general rule, founded not upon the doubtful distinctions of personal merit, but upon some plain and evident difference which can admit of no dispute." Adam Smith, *An Inquiry into the Natural Causes of the Wealth of Nations* (New York: Random House, Modern Library, 1937), p. 362. One need not, in conceding the merits of this argument, accept as a general proposition Smith's observation (relating to information dependent on the quality of various cloths "during the course of the present century"), "Quality, however, is so very disputable a matter, that I look upon all information of this kind as somewhat uncertain." Ibid., p. 244.

The recourse to quantifiable objectivity, as is reflected in Adam Smith's observation, is prompted by the fact that it *is* the kind of world in which someone of judgment can say, "There certainly was some great mismanagement in the education of those two young men. One has got all the goodness, and the other all the appearance of it." *The Complete Novels of Jane Austen* (New York: Random House, Modern Library, n.d.), p. 366. Even so, the reality of *goodness* is asserted even as the difficulty of its discernment is recognized. See Plato, *Republic*, Book 2. Cf. George Frederic Handel, *Solomon* (act 2):

> From morn to eve I could enraptur'd sing
> The various virtues of our happy king;
> In whom, with wonder, we behold combin'd,
> The grace of feature with the worth of mind.

See Aristotle, *Nicomachean Ethics*, 1123a34 ff., 1145a23 ff. See, also, chap. 5, n. 94, chap. 7, n. 77, chap. 9, n. 22, below.

76. J. V. Cheney, ed., *Memorable American Speeches* (Chicago: Lakeside Press, 1907), 1:289-90. Cf. Hiller B. Zobel, *The Boston Massacre* (New York: W. W. Norton & Co., 1970), pp. 302-3.

The writ of assistance was a general search warrant and was employed in the colonies by the British government to curb illicit trade. (The Virginia Bill of Rights, June 12, 1776, declared in Article 10, "That general warrants, whereby an officer or messenger may be commanded to search suspected places without evidence of a fact committed, or to seize any person or persons not named, or whose offence is not particularly described and supported by evidence, are grievous and oppressive, and ought not to be granted.") See the discussion in the text at chap. 6, n. 73, above.

See, also, Jacob W. Landynski, *Search and Seizure and the Supreme Court* (Baltimore: Johns Hopkins Press, 1966), p. 32n. "The fight for freedom of the press waged in England for nearly three centuries was thus connected with the issue of the scope of the search power. [Note: The restrictions on freedom of the press in England during this period and the utilization of the search power as an instrument of suppression are thoroughly and expertly discussed in Frederich Seaton Siebert, *Freedom of the Press in England: 1476-1776* (Urbana, Ill.: University of Illinois Press, 1952).]" Ibid., p. 21. See, for the Fourth Amendment, chap. 6, n. 73, below. See, also, Story, *Commentaries on the Constitution*, chap. 44, sec. 1902.

Cf. chap. 8, n. 29, below.

77. Adams, *The Political Writings of John Adams*, American Heritage (Indianapolis: Bobbs-Merrill, 1954), p. 191n.

78. "Xenophon as good as shows us this battle by eyesight, not as past event, but as a present action, and by his vivid account makes his hearers feel all the passions and join in all the dangers of it. . . ." Plutarch, *The Lives of the Noble Grecians and Romans* (New York: Modern Library, n.d.), p. 1255.

Compare Adams's characterization of Otis as "a flame of fire" with Justice Holmes's dictum about falsely shouting fire in a theater. See, also, Justice Holmes, in *Frohwerk* v. *U.S.*, 249 U.S. 204, 209 (1919): "the circulation of the paper was in quarters where a little breath would be enough to kindle a flame." (Franklin, at his death, was reproached in "some pretty unowned verses" as one who had come as "a spark from Lucifer" and "first kindled the blaze of sedition." Hester Lynch Piozzi, *British Synonymy; or, An Attempt at Regulating the Choice of Words in Familiar Conversation* [London: G. G. and J. Robinson, 1794], 2:319-20.) The eulogy of Otis is most revealing of the American spirit in that it comes from so sturdy and respectable a character as Adams. It is easy to forget that the founders did make a revolution before they took to fathering.

Nor should it be forgotten that revolutionary zeal did not die out with independence. Madison reported on Shays's Rebellion (chap. 6, n. 28, below), in a letter of Mar. 18, 1787, to General Washington:

> By our latest and most authentic information from Massachusetts, it would seem that a calm has been restored by the expedition of General Lincoln. The precautions taken by the State, however, betray a great distrust of its continuance. Besides their act disqualifying the malcontents from voting in the election of members for the Legislature, &c., another has been passed for raising a corps of 1,000 or 1,500 men, and appropriating the choicest revenues of the country to its support. It is said that at least half of the insurgents decline accepting

CHAPTER FIVE, NOTE 79: PAGE 111 527

> the terms annexed to the amnesty, and that this defiance of the law against Treason is countenanced not only by the impunity with which they shew themselves on public occasions, even with insolent badges of their character, but by marks of popular favor conferred on them in various instances in the election to local offices. [*Letters and Other Writings of James Madison* (Philadelphia: J. B. Lippincott & Co., 1865), 1: 282]

One can imagine how people who elect to office men whom Madison considered traitors would understand the "freedom of speech" provision they later asked to be added to the Constitution. (See, for the effect on sober men of Shays's Rebellion, *The Federalist* [New York: Random House, Modern Library, n.d.], pp. 29, 33, 126-27, 157, 171, 283, 483.)

79. A prosecutor in the *Zenger* case (chap. 5, n. 57, above) argued,

> The case before the Court is whether Mr. Zenger is guilty of libeling His Excellency the Governor of New York, and indeed the whole administration of the government? Mr. Hamilton [Zenger's attorney] has confessed the printing and publishing, and I think nothing is plainer than that the words in the information are scandalous, and tend to sedition, and to disquiet the minds of the people of this Province. *And if such papers are not libels, I think it may be said there can be no such thing as a libel.* [Alexander, *Brief Narrative*, p. 68; italics added]

Is it not, indeed, the distinctively American attitude that "there can be no such thing as a [seditious] libel"? (See the quotation in the text at chap. 5, n. 141, above.) This attitude is suggested as well in a letter of 1780 from John Adams in Paris:

> There is not in any nation of the world so unlimited a freedom of the press as is now established in every State of America, both by law and practice. Every man in Europe who reads their newspapers must see it. There is nothing that the people dislike that they do not attack. They attack officers of every rank in the militia and in the army; they attack judges, governors, and magistrates of every denomination; they attack assemblies and councils, members of congress, and congress itself, whenever they dislike their conduct. . . . [Adams, *Works of John Adams*, ed. Charles F. Adams (Boston: Little, Brown & Co., 1850-56), 7:182]

See, for a useful comparison, John Moore, *A View of Society and Manners in France, Switzerland, and Germany*, 4th ed. (London: Strahan & Cadell, 1781), 2:187-89.

I discuss at length in chapter 8 both the advantages and the abuses of freedom of speech. That discussion may be appropriately anticipated here, partly because of a use of "inflammatory" which reminds of both Adams on Otis and Holmes on Schenck, by observing that there is in *Federalist* No. 84 a recognition (in successive paragraphs) of both the good and the evil that can be expected from freedom of the press:

> It ought also to be remembered that the citizens who inhabit the country at and near the seat of government will, in all questions that affect the general liberty and prosperity, have the same interest with those who are at a distance, and that they will stand ready to sound the alarm when necessary, and to point out the actors in any pernicious project. The public papers will be expeditious messengers of intelligence to the most remote inhabitants of the Union.
>
> Among the many curious objections which have appeared against the proposed Constitution, the most extraordinary and the least colorable is derived from the want of some provision respecting the debts due to the United States. This has been represented as a tacit relinquishment of those debts, and as a wicked contrivance to screen public defaulters. The newspapers have teemed with the most inflammatory railings on this head; yet there is nothing clearer than that the suggestion is entirely void of foundation, the offspring of extreme ignorance or extreme dishonesty.

Nothing worse was ever said even of Thersites. But there is no suggestion by Publius that the offending newspapers should be chastised. (See chap. 5, n. 88, below.) Americans engaged in public debate should not be punished, it seems to be assumed, even when their "inflammatory railings" are "the offspring of extreme ignorance or extreme dishonesty."

Cf. *Scales* v. *U.S.*, 367 U.S. 203 (1961). See chap. 5, n. 21, above, chap. 7, n. 69, below.

80. See, e.g., *Annals*, V, pp. 2153-54. The common law is reconsidered from another perspective when I discuss in chapter 6 the Sedition Act of 1798.

81. *History of Congress*, p. 161. Since, as I have noted, the Senate debates in the First Congress are not available, we do not have the arguments made in that body.

82. Thus, divergencies made it difficult for the First Congress to define the right of trial by jury. See, e.g., *Annals*, I, p. 2193. See, also, *Federalist* No. 83.

83. My concern in this book is primarily with the constitutional limitations on the general government. But the attitude I have described toward freedom of speech would affect the practice of state governments as well, even though the "distinctively American attitude" (chap. 5, n. 79, above) is (in my view) more likely to be expressed in the Constitution of the United States rather than in a state constitution. See chap. 7, n. 107, chap. 8, n. 83, below.

84. Malcolm Sharp has touched upon this philological problem several times in his writings: in his foreword to Meiklejohn, *Political Freedom*, pp. xvii-xviii; in the long footnote at pp. 536-37 of his article, "The Old Constitution," *U. Chicago L. Rev.* 20 (1953): 529; and in a letter of May 9, 1957, printed in U.S., Congress, Senate, Committee on the Judiciary Subcommittee on Constitutional Rights, *The Right to Travel and United States Passports*, 85th Cong., 2d sess., 1958, Sen. Doc. 126, p. 281. See *Federalist*, p. 355 ("it is admitted, that if the laws were to restore the rights which have been taken away, the negroes could no longer be refused an equal share of representation with the other inhabitants"). See, also, chap. 7, n. 86, below.

85. See, e.g., the text at chap. 5, n. 108, above. A letter of May 28, 1789, from Senator Richard Henry Lee (of Virginia) to Patrick Henry suggests (in a passage which bears on the writing of the Bill of Rights) that "abridge" and "enlarge" are antonyms:

> . . . Mr. Madison has given notice that, on Monday S'n-night he will call for the attention of the house to the subject of amendments. I apprehend that his ideas, and those of our convention [the Virginia ratifying convention], on the subject, are not similar. We shall carefully attend to this, and when the plan comes to the senate, we shall prepare to abridge, or enlarge, so as to effect if possible, the wishes of our legislature. I think, from what I hear and see, that many of our amendments will not succeed, but my hopes are strong that such as may effectually secure civil liberty will not be refused. . . . [*Letters of Richard Henry Lee*, ed. James C. Ballagh (New York: Macmillan Co., 1914), 2:487]

See, also, on "abridge" and "enlarge," Chief Justice Marshall in *Osborne* v. *Bank of the United States*, 9 Wheat. [U.S.] 738, 827 (1824); *Eakin* v. *Raub*, 12 Sergeant and Rawle 330, 346 (Pa., 1825).

86. See Blackstone, *Laws of England*, 1:54:

> Those rights then which God and nature have established, and are therefore called natural rights, such as are life and liberty, need not the aid of human laws to be more effectually invested in every man than they are; neither do they receive any additional strength when declared by the municipal laws to be inviolable. On the contrary, no human legislature has power to *abridge* or destroy them, unless the owner shall himself commit some act that amounts to a forfeiture.

> But when these invaders themselves were converted to Christianity, and settled into regular and potent governments, this retreat of the ancient Britons grew every day narrower; they were overrun by little and little, gradually driven from one fastness to another, and by repeated losses *abridged* of their wild independence. [Ibid., 1:93]

CHAPTER FIVE, NOTE 87: PAGE 112

And these may be reduced to three principal or primary articles; the right of personal security, the right of personal liberty, and the right of private property: because, as there is no other known method of compulsion, or of *abridging* man's natural free will, but by an infringement or diminution of one or other of these important rights, the preservation of these, inviolate, may justly be said to include the preservation of our civil immunities in their largest and most extensive sense. [Ibid., 1:129]

In a former part of these commentaries we expatiated at large on the personal liberty of the subject. This was shown to be a natural inherent right, which could not be surrendered or forfeited unless by the commission of some great and atrocious crime, and which ought not to be *abridged* in any case without the special permission of law. [Ibid., 3:133. Italics have been added throughout this note.]

There is in appendix 3 of my dissertation, "Notes on the First Amendment," a First Amendment "glossary" drawn from Blackstone's *Laws of England*. See, for uses of "abridging," as well as "infringing," "confining," "diminishing," and "restraining": Blackstone, *Laws of England*, 1:28, 40, 53, 54, 86-87, 93, 94, 118, 128, 129, 130, 134, 135, 138, 143, 144, 154, 164, 186, 192-93, 235, 243, 261, 336, 337, 362, 376, 422, 427, 445, 478, 482; 2:117-18, 130-31, 147, 230-31, 323, 335, 344-45, 361, 400-401, 403, 411-12; 3:36, 53, 78-79, 140, 217, 240-41, 360-61, 367, 435, 451; 4:85, 150-53, 333, 399-400, 431, 432.

"Abridge" is employed much less frequently by nonlegal writers. It is rarely used, for instance, by Benjamin Franklin. I have noticed no uses at all of "abridge" in *Gulliver's Travels*, although "diminish" is used several times. Additional eighteenth-century uses of "abridge" may be found in quotations in this book in the text at chap. 6, n. 69, at chap. 8, n. 11, above; and in the following notes: chap. 5, n. 85, above, chap. 5, nn. 87, 108, chap. 6, n. 14, below. See, also, chap. 5, n. 128, chap. 6, n. 49, chap. 7, n. 106, below.

87. "Abridge" and "nature" are joined in the following passages:

It was civil and national laws that brought in these words, and differences, of civis and exterus, alien and native. And therefore because they tend to *abridge* the law of nature, the law favoureth not them, but takes them strictly: even as our law hath an excellent rule, that customs of towns and boroughs shall be taken and construed strictly and precisely, because they do *abridge* and derogate from the law of the land. So by the same reason, all national laws whatsoever are to be taken strictly and hardly in any point wherein they *abridge* and derogate from the law of nature. [*The Works of Francis Bacon*, ed. J. Spedding and R. Ellis (New York: Hurd & Houghton, 1864), 15:226; see also 15:225]

But the Right of Nature, that is, the naturall Liberty of man, may by the Civill Law be *abridged*, and restrained: nay, the end of making Lawes, is no other, but such Restraint; without the which there cannot possibly be any Peace. And Law was brought into the world for nothing else, but to limit the naturall liberty of particular men, in such manner, as they might not hurt, but assist one another, and joyn together against a common Enemy. [Thomas Hobbes, *Leviathan*, II, xxvi]

Why *abridge* our native freedom . . . ? It is evident, that, if governments were totally useless, it never could have place, and that the sole foundation of the duty of allegiance is the advantage, which it procures to society, by preserving peace and order among mankind. [David Hume, *An Enquiry concerning the Principles of Morals*, sec. 4 (opening paragraph)]

Why should we then affect a rigour contrary to the manner of God and of nature, by *abridging or scanting* those means, which books, freely permitted, are, both to the trial of virtue and the exercise of truth? [Milton, *Areopagitica*, in *Prose Works of John Milton*, ed. Charles Symmons (London: Johnson, Nichols & Son, 1806), 1:306]

The Author of nature directs all his operations to the production of the greatest good, and has made human virtue to consist in a disposition and conduct which tends to the common felicity of his creatures. An *abridgment* of the natural freedom of man, by the institution of political societies, is vindicable only on this foot. [Attributed to Samuel Adams in Philadelphia, Aug. 1, 1776, William V. Wells, *The Life and Public Service of Samuel Adams* (Boston: Little, Brown & Co., 1866), 3:412]

All disputes between the different States and all continental concerns, are to be managed by a Congress of representatives from each. What a security for liberty, for union, for every species of political happiness! Small States are weak and incapable of offence; large ones are unwieldly, greatly *abridge* natural liberty; and their general laws, from a variety of clashing interests, must frequently bear hard on many individuals; but our confederation will give us the strength and protection of a power equal to that of the greatest, at the same time that, in all our internal concerns, we have the freedom of small independent commonwealths. [David Ramsay in Charleston, S.C. (July 4, 1778), Cheney, ed., *Memorable American Speeches*, 1:119. Cf. *Federalist*, No. 10; chap. 4, n. 101, above, chap. 7, n. 35, below.]

"The natural liberty of man is to be free from any superior power on earth, and not to be under the will or legislative authority of man, but only to have the law of nature for his rule." This is the liberty of independent states; this is the liberty of every man out of society, and who has a mind to live so; which liberty is only *abridged* in certain instances, not lost to those who are born in or voluntarily enter into society; this gift of God cannot be annihilated. [James Otis, "The Rights of the Colonies," in Morison, *Sources and Documents*, p. 5. Italics have been added throughout this note.]

The reader will find uses of "abridge" at the pages indicated (among other places) in the following collections: Farrand, *Records*, 1:169, 295, 375, 380; 2:202, 203, 215, 286, 372; 3:79, 127, 134, 239, 429; 4:28; *Federalist* (Modern Library ed.), pp. 51, 93, 105, 154, 178, 194, 195, 223, 279, 342, 535, 537, 540, 554, 558, 560 (only one of these is in an article attributed to Madison [p. 279]; another [p. 342] is in an article whose author is uncertain); Jonathan Elliot, *Debates in the Several State Conventions on the Adoption of the Constitution* (Philadelphia: J. B. Lippincott & Co., 1863), 2:91, 256, 293 ("abridge their natural right"), 295, 326; 3:82, 87, 103, 567, 608; 4:56, 68, 113-14, 148. See, also, chap. 6, n. 49, below. ("Abridge" is rarely used today, except with respect to the condensation of books or in discussions of constitutional questions. Cf. Arthur Krock, *Memoirs* [New York: Funk & Wagnalls, 1968], p. 281 [where it seems to be used as if it meant "alter".] See the *Congressional Record*, 116: H6186 [June 29, 1970]: "Ninety million Americans drink—and they just don't like the privilege abridged.")

Adam Smith can, with respect to trade, speak of "perfect liberty," "perfectly free," and "the most perfect freedom": see *Wealth of Nations*, pp. 56, 62, 99, 114, 118, 437, 508, 547, 572, 637, 785.

88. Crosskey, *Politics and the Constitution*, pp. 1060-61. See chap. 7, n. 18, below; see, also, ibid., pp. 1057, 1070-72. (A description of Shays's Rebellion may be found in chap. 6, n. 28, below.)

I do not believe Crosskey appreciated, in his discussion of the Sedition Act of 1798 (see, e.g., the passage in the text at chap. 6, n. 6, above), the significance of what he himself implied here about the First Amendment language having "blot[ted] out all [national] governmental power, respecting the subjects of 'free speech,' 'free press,' and 'free assembly,' . . . subject to a negative control in Congress to prevent abuses by the states. . . ." See chap. 3, n. 23, above, chap. 8, n. 83, below.

See, in my article, "Freedom of Speech and the First Amendment," a discussion of the implications of John Adams's reference to freedom of speech "that was far advanced and well established." *U. Detroit L. J.* 42 (1964): 55, 66. I notice there that that which Adams called "freedom of speech" in the demagogic Thersites (Homer, *Iliad* 2), Alexander Pope, in a footnote to his translation of the *Iliad*, called "sedition." Adams, *Defence*

CHAPTER FIVE, NOTES 89-90: PAGE 113   531

of Constitutions, 1:246. Homer, *Iliad* (trans. Alexander Pope, 2d ed., 1720) 1:92 (in the 1796 edition, 1:127). This difference in characterizations suggests the difference between the American and the English (or traditional common law) approaches to these matters. See chap. 5, n. 35, above, chap. 5, n. 142, below.

89. It is evident that not every use of words (or sounds) is included. Thus St. Augustine had to direct the commandment, "Thou shalt not kill," to its proper object:

> And so some attempt to extend this command even to beasts and cattle, as if it forbade us to take life from any creature. But if so, why not extend it also to the plants, and all that is rooted in and nourished by the earth? For though this class of creatures have no sensation, yet they also are said to live, and consequently they can die; and therefore, if violence be done them, can be killed. So, too, the apostle, when speaking of the seeds of such things as these, says, "That which thou sowest is not quickened except it die"; and in the Psalm it is said, "He killed their vines with hail." Must we therefore reckon it a breaking of this commandment, "Thou shalt not kill," to pull a flower? Are we thus insanely to countenance the foolish error of the Manichaeans? Putting aside, then, these ravings, if, when we say, Thou shalt not kill, we do not understand this of the plants, since they have no sensation, nor of the irrational animals that fly, swim, walk, or creep, since they are dissociated from us by their want of reason, and are therefore by the just appointment of the Creator subjected to us to kill or keep alive for our own uses; if so, then it remains that we understand that commandment simply of man. The commandment is, "Thou shalt not kill man"; therefore neither another nor yourself, for he who kills himself still kills nothing else than man. [*The City of God* (New York: Random House, Modern Library, 1950), p. 26]

Cf. ibid., pp. 27-34; chap. 7, n. 21, below. See chap. 5, n. 3, above.

The most primitive form of "liberty to speak" is recorded in chap. 5, n. 24, above.

90. We notice here the distinction made a half century later by Blackstone (ratifying a tradition that goes back at least to Hobbes), that it is not the holding of opinions that should be subject to criminal sanctions, but rather their expression. This distinction tends to ignore a fact of human nature and of society, that opinions that are not expressed or expressible are likely to be forgotten and become extinct: a people that is obliged to conceal opinions is often thereby led to abandon them in favor of the "legitimate" opinions of the community. Plato, *Republic* 415C-D; *Laws* 838C-D; Leo Strauss, *Persecution and the Art of Writing* (Glencoe, Ill.: Free Press, 1952), pp. 22-37; Harry Kalven and Hans Zeisel, *The American Jury* (Boston: Little, Brown & Co., 1966), pp. 462-63. Cf. Edward Crankshaw, *Khrushchev's Russia* (London: Penguin Books, 1959), pp. 103, 139. See chap. 8, nn. 18, 100, 101, below.

Hobbes (in chapter 37 of his *Leviathan*) would have us believe:

> A private man has alwaies the liberty, (*because thought is free,*) to beleeve, or not beleeve in his heart, those acts that have been given out for Miracles, according as he shall see, what benefit can accrew by means of belief, to those that pretend, or countenance them, and thereby conjecture, whether they be Miracles, or Lies. But when it comes to confession of that faith, the Private Reason must submit to the Publique. . . . [Italics added]

He seems to assume here and elsewhere (because of his Christian-like faith in the sovereignty of the human will?) that men can somehow manage to work their way to the truth in the face of massive (and publicly unchallengeable) propaganda. Must he assume this if he is to be able to argue for both unquestioning public obedience and unimpaired private pursuit of the truth? That is, does Hobbes thus avoid the serious question of the underlying conflict between the political and the philosophical of which the "seditious" ancients were always aware? He seems to reconcile the political and the philosophical by disregarding the conditions for the philosophical. (Cf. the Socratic reconciliation in the "philosopher-king.") Of course, a sensible Hobbesian sovereign would permit the philosophically-minded to teach one another "in private." But if that should be forbidden by law, and publicly disparaged, would the overriding right of self-preservation (which legitimates resistance to laws which threaten one's very existence) extend to the preservation of oneself as an inquiring or thinking "self"? (It should be noted, however, that the more serious threat to philosophy in Hobbesian circumstances would be likely to come not from outright suppression but from the deadening effect of the success of a pervasive selfish materialism. All we moderns have to do to confirm this is to look at the prospects around us all over the world, on both sides of the "Iron Curtain." See chap. 8, nn. 193, 195, chap. 9, n. 7, below. Still, is not truth "a necessity of the soul" of truly human beings? See chap. 5, n. 128, below. See, also, chap. 5, n. 126, chap. 8, n. 140, chap. 9, n. 39, below. This "necessity" is reflected in the movement in Alfarabi's *Philosophy of Plato and Aristotle* from "happiness" *to* "the perfection of man.")

91. "A Voyage to Brobdingnag," chap. 6 of *Gulliver's Travels*. See Allan Bloom, "An Outline of *Gulliver's Travels*," in Joseph Cropsey, ed., *Ancients and Moderns: Essays on the Tradition of Political Philosophy, in Honor of Leo Strauss* (New York: Basic Books, 1964), p. 245.

The strictures we find here in Swift remind us of the shift from the common law of England to American constitutional law on what should be done by government about "poisonous opinions." Blackstone endorses what seems to be Swift's attitude against the vending of "poisons." These writers draw on a heritage that may perhaps be best seen in Hobbes, whose position has been summed up by one scholar thus:

> . . . [It] is a breach of his duty for the sovereign to lay aside any of his rights. Furthermore, it is a breach of his duty to allow the people to be misinformed or ignorant of the grounds of his rights. The first task in this regard is to purge the commonwealth of "the poisons of seditious doctrines." [See *Leviathan*, 2:xix.] The first group of seditious doctrines proceed mainly from the words of unlearned divines, who, misconstruing Scripture, induce men to think that sanctity and natural reason cannot stand together. They teach that every private man is the judge of good and evil action. This is true in the state of nature, but in civil society the civil law and the sovereign are the measure and the judge of good and evil. [Laurence Berns, "Thomas Hobbes," in Leo Strauss and Joseph Cropsey, eds., *History of Political Philosophy* (Chicago: Rand McNally, 1963), p. 372]

(See also ibid., p. 376.) Cf. chap. 4, n. 113, above.

Swift himself had been obliged shortly before the publication of *Gulliver's Travels* to publish anonymously in his *Drapier's Letters* opinions regarded by the Lord Lieutenant of Ireland as "prejudicial to the public." *Jonathan Swift: Selected Prose and Poetry*, ed. Edward Rosenheim, Jr. (New York: Holt, Rinehart & Winston, 1963), pp. 268-87. A quarter century earlier Swift had cautiously "vend[ed] about for cordials" in his *Discourse concerning the Mechanical Operation of the Spirit*, a document which can be discerned to be "founded upon a single lewd conceit." *Swift: Prose and Poetry*, p. 185. ("No writer, except of the most broken reputation, would venture at this day on the malignant calumnies of Swift." Henry Hallem, *Constitutional History of England* [New York: A. C. Armstrong & Son, 1882], 2:377.)

U.S. v. *Ballard*, 322 U.S. 78 (1944), indicates how reluctant we are today to permit any official action against any "words of unlearned divines," even when there is strong suspicion of fraud and exploitation involved. (See chap. 5, n. 148, below.) But it is not only with respect to religious doctrines, and not only recently, that we (as a people) have come to think that "every private man is the judge of good and evil action." In *Federalist* No. 14, for instance, "the People of the State of New York" are urged to reject doctrines which condemn the proposed Constitution as rash, utterly novel, and "impossible to accomplish": "No, my countrymen, shut your ears against this unhallowed language. Shut your hearts against the poison which it conveys. . . ." Thus, the people (who are now the sovereign) have to be relied upon to protect themselves against the poisons available: public servants are not relied upon to purge the commonwealth as formerly. (Cf. *Fed-*

eralist No. 49, p. 329. But see "Poisonous Opinions," in Stephen, *An Agnostic's Apology*, p. 242; also, chap. 5, n. 79, above.) This does not mean, however, that purgation is not needed: but it is evidently to be done primarily by the Philopoemens among us, if not by the states, rather than by the general government. (See chap. 9, n. 18, below.)

How much official suppression (direct and indirect) there in fact is among us of opinions thought to be poisonous is, of course, another matter. The reader is referred, for instance, to Appendixes D, E, and F, above.

It should also be noted, as indicative of what is currently being "endured [even though] men fight," that one is able to purchase openly at a Chicago newsstand near the Civic Center the *Vietnam Courier*, published weekly in Hanoi as the "Information Weekly" of North Vietnam. The only official restriction seems to be the notice stamped on each copy, complying with a requirement for all publications distributed in this country by foreign governments, which reads (in this case):

> A copy of this material has been filed with the Foreign Agents Registration Section, Department of Justice, Washington, D.C. where the registration statement of China Books & Periodicals, 2929 - 24th St., San Francisco, Calif. 94110 as an agent of Xunhasaba of Hanoi, Democratic Republic of Viet-Nam, is available for inspection. The fact of registration does not indicate approval of this material by the Government of the United States.

92. "Civil and religious liberty are so commonly associated in people's mouths, and are so rare in fact, that their definition is evidently as little understood as the principle of their connection. The point at which they unite, the common root from which they derive sustenance, is the right of self-government. . . ." Lord Acton, *Essays on Freedom and Power* (London: Thames & Hudson, 1956), p. 114. See Blackstone, *Laws of England*, 2:455; also, Leo Strauss, *Spinoza's Critique of Religion* (New York: Schocken, 1965), p. 3. See chap. 8, n. 193, chap. 9, n. 9, below. Cf. chap. 5, n. 51, above.

Justice Brennan, speaking for the Court in *Malloy v. Hogan*, 378 U.S. 1, 5 (1964), referred to "the freedoms of speech, press, religion, assembly, association, and petition for redress of grievances" as "the cherished rights of mind and spirit." The relation among these was indicated in a speech of Wendell Phillips (Dec. 8, 1837), in which he recalled that "freedom to preach was first gained, dragging in its train freedom to print." Alexander K. McClure, ed., *Famous American Statesmen and Orators* (New York: F. F. Lovell Publishing Co., 1902), 5:168.

Of the three pairs of rights protected by the First Amendment, "freedom of speech, or of the press" is central. The first and third pairs can be seen as similar in that each recognizes the right of the people to assemble freely in order to direct supplications to "the Government" (in the first pair, the government of the universe, in the third pair, the government of the United States). May we say that the central part of the First Amendment reflects the rights of Americans as a self-governing people, the other parts reflect the needs of Americans as subjects? See chap. 5, n. 133, chap. 8, n. 108, below.

93. Does "learning" refer to what we have come to know as "academic freedom," that on which (at least for us) free government and free religion depend? Does not due process effectively promote academic freedom to the extent that educational institutions are allowed to conduct their affairs according to the rules the community has permitted them to lay down for themselves? Cf. chap. 8, n. 19, below.

> The essence of the matter, I think, is that under modern conditions, the area of a University's free choices must be smaller than it was. . . . I think it vital that the Universities should each retain full responsibility for its own appointments: that it alone, subject to the ordinary law of the land, should choose its teachers, should settle the conditions of tenure, and should, if need be, dismiss them. That is the primary condition of University freedom, and the only ground of assurance that its members may speak and teach in whatever way they are responsibly led to do. I do not need here to emphasize the obligation which correspondingly is laid on them. And the corollary is that the University must

retain full responsibility for the organization of its courses, and for the character and standards of the instruction given within its walls. [Sir Hector Hetherington, *Times* (London), Aug. 10, 1966, p. 9]

State governments are likely to be restrained in what they do to their schools if the national academic community maintains appropriate standards for accreditation. See, e.g., a *New York Times* article of Oct. 31, 1965:

It appears likely that the North Carolina General Assembly will be called into special session next month in an effort to remove a threat to the accreditation of the consolidated University of North Carolina and other state-supported institutions of higher learning. A law, adopted in the closing hours of the 1963 legislative session, forbids known Communists or persons who have pleaded the Fifth Amendment's protection against self-incrimination in connection with subversive activities from speaking on campuses of state universities and colleges. The state has been informed that this represents political interference with administration of the schools and that accreditation has been jeopardized.

See *Dartmouth College* v. *Woodward*, 4 Wheat. [U.S.] 518 (1819); Bacon, *The Advancement of Learning*, in *Selected Writings of Francis Bacon*, ed. H. G. Dick (New York: Random House, Modern Library, 1955), p. 288 (on "a fraternity in learning and illumination"); Mason, *Harlan Fiske Stone*, p. 543.

See, also, Anastaplo, "The Daring of Moderation: 'Student Power' and *The Melian Dialogue*," *School Review*, 78:451 (1970); *Legal and Economic Aspects of Pollution* (Chicago: Center for Policy Study, University of Chicago, 1970), pp. 18-21, 26-29, 31; Appendix E, above; chap. 2, n. 7, above, chap. 5, n. 124, chap. 7, n. 113, chap. 8, n. 122, below.

94. See chap. 6, n. 37, below. See also Street, *Freedom, the Individual and the Law*, p. 187.

But what is good for one country may be bad or simply unavailable for another. This sentiment is reflected in a comment by Laszek Kolakowski, a Marxist:

The observation that English democracy is practically attainable only after one has had more than ten decades of English history is unquestionably right, but it is an equally unquestionable fact that it is virtually impossible to persuade public opinion of that truth. To convince the masses that it is impossible to transfer Poland to the British Isles is an undertaking almost as difficult as actually transferring Poland to the British Isles. [Mendel, *Essential Works of Marxism*, p. 367]

See, also, Meiklejohn, *Political Freedom*, p. xvi.

Rousseau agrees with the classics by explicitly agreeing with the "principle established by Montesquieu" that "liberty not being a fruit of all climates, is not within the reach of all peoples" (*Contrat social*, III, 8). Acceptance of this principle explains the moderate character of most of Rousseau's proposals which were meant for immediate application. [Strauss, *Natural Right and History* (Chicago: University of Chicago Press, 1953), p. 277, n. 44]

See, e.g., Bacon, *Advancement of Learning*, p. 175; Plato, *Laws* 625D-626B, 636A-C (this is critical for assessing the apparent conclusion of Plato's *Meno* that virtue comes by divine dispensation, not by training: the informed trainer of horsemen knows that not everyone is equipped to become a good horseman; he knows, that is, that it would be no more reasonable to try to make a horseman out of everybody than it would be to try to raise horses everywhere). Cf., on Weimar Germany, Kennan, *Russia and the West*, pp. 274-75; Jaffa, *Equality and Liberty*, p. 183. See, also, Anastaplo, "Notes on the First Amendment," pp. 552-69 (Gouverneur Morris on the French Revolution and the character of the French people); Anastaplo, book review: Shri D. Gopalakrishna Sastri, *The Law of Sedition in India* (Bombay: N. M. Tripathi Private, 1964), in *Law Library Journal*, 58 (1965): 197. See chap. 7, n. 112, chap. 9, n. 22, below.

Sun Yat-sen said, a year before he died, that if one spoke of freedom to the man in the street, "he would certainly not understand. The reason why the Chinese do not in fact attach the slightest importance to freedom is that the very word which designates it was only recently imported into China." André Malraux, *Anti-Memoirs* (New York: Holt, Rinehart & Winston, 1968), p. 352. Modern Greek, it should be noted, uses the same word (*democratia*) for both "republic" and "democracy," a usage which is reflected in volatile Greek politics. (See chap. 6, n. 1, below.) Cf. chap. 5, n. 151, below. (One hears apologists in Greece for the colonel's regime insisting there is indeed "liberty" in that country: "If you do what you are told, no one bothers you." This is a variation of "liberty" as "doing what one ought" [see pp. 12-13, above], with the law providing *the* measure of oughtness. But then, is not one obliged to assess the legitimacy of the regime responsible for the "law"? See pp. 417-18, above, chap. 8, n. 142, below.)

95. The order of June 14, 1643, against which Milton directed his *Areopagitica*, opens (chap. 5, nn. 4, 7, above):

> Whereas divers good Orders have bin lately made by both Houses of Parliament, for suppressing the great late abuses and frequent disorders in Printing many, false forged, scandalous, seditious, libellous, and unlicensed Papers, Pamphlets, and Books *to the great defamation of Religion and government*. . . . [Italics added.]

96. See the text at chap. 5, n. 20, above. Milton writes of the counselors of Queen Elizabeth having persuaded her "that the altering of ecclesiastical policy would move sedition." *Prose Works*, 1:10. An act against seditious prophecies was debated in Queen Elizabeth's first parliament (1559) and passed in her second (1563). Shakespeare, *King Lear*, ed. G. L. Kittredge (Boston: Ginn & Co., 1940), pp. vii-viii. (The continuance in Great Britain of a critical role for religion in public life is reflected in how the offense of "sacrilege" can be regarded even in a "detective story." See, e.g., J. J. Maric, *Gideon's Wrath* [New York: Harper & Row, 1967], pp. 3-4, 13-14, 22-25, 37, 74-75, 77-79, 81-82, 97-101, 104-8, 125-26, 136-37, 139-56, 161-66, 168-71, 182-200, 204-5. In this country, on the other hand, a reverential attitude [toward which man in society has a natural inclination?] is much more apt to be found today in a concert hall or "rock-fest" audience than in conventional religious gatherings. See chap. 7, n. 75 [end], below.)

97. If all forms of expression had been protected by this amendment, there may not have been any necessity to include "free exercise [of religion]" in the same provision with "freedom of speech or of the press" and "the right . . . peaceably to assemble"— since these two together should take care of religious freedom (i.e., expression and assembly). How does the presence of an established church bear on this? See the passage quoted at pp. 117-18, above.)

Cf. Hallem, *Constitutional History of England*, 2:379: "Civil, indeed, and religious liberty had appeared, not as twin sisters and co-heirs, but rather in jealous and selfish rivalry. . . ." This rivalry, as the work of Machiavelli indicates, can be deadly. Must not the statesman take seriously such self-centered disparagement of temporal matters for the generality of mankind as is found in this exchange (see Matt. 10:21):

> Prudence: Do you not think sometimes of the country from whence you came?
>
> Christian: Yes, but with much shame and detestation: truly, if I had been mindful of that country from whence I came out, I might have had opportunity to have returned; but now I desire a better country, that is, a heavenly one (Heb. xi. 15, 16.).

John Bunyan, *The Pilgrim's Progress* (London: Thomas Nelson & Sons, n.d.), p. 53. See, ibid., pp. 60-61, 98. "Is not general incivility the very essence of love?" *The Complete Novels of Jane Austen* (New York: Random House, Modern Library, n.d.), p. 316.

Cf. Hobbes, *Leviathan*, chaps. 12, 32-47, *Federalist* No. 10, Lincoln, *Complete Works*,

1:12. (See Eva Brann, "A Reading of the Gettysburg Address," *The College* [St. John's College], April, 1969, p. 6. Cf., also, *Federalist* No. 51; chap. 5, n. 126, below. See chap. 7, nn. 21, 34, 59, 124, chap. 9, n. 9, below. Gertrude speaks [*Hamlet*, act 1, sc. 2, l. 77] of "passing through nature to eternity.")

98. See the opening pages of chapter 2, above. Two statements, two centuries apart, suggest the continuity in America on this subject (see, also, the Mayflower Compact):

> A democracy is then erected when a number of free persons do assemble together in order to enter into a covenant for uniting themselves in a body, and such a preparative assembly hath some appearance already of a democracy. It is a democracy in embryo properly in this respect, that every man hath the privilege freely to deliver his opinion concerning the common affairs. [John Wise, in the Staff, Social Science I, College of University of Chicago, eds., *The People Shall Judge* (Chicago: University of Chicago Press, 1949), 1:36]

> While our Court has held that some kinds of speech and writings, such as "obscenity," *Roth* v. *U.S.*, 354 U.S. 476 [1957], and "fighting words," *Chaplinsky* v. *New Hampshire*, 315 U.S. 568 [1942], are not expression within the protection of the First Amendment, freedom to discuss public affairs and public officials is unquestionably, as the Court today holds, the kind of speech the First Amendment was primarily designed to keep within the area of free discussion. [Justice Black, concurring, *New York Times Co.* v. *Sullivan*, 376 U.S. 255, 296-97 (1964)]

(Justice Black indicates, by citations to *Smith* v. *California*, 361 U.S. 147, 155 [1959] and *Roth* v. *U.S.*, 554 U.S. 476, 508 [1957], his personal reservations about the first half of this sentence.) See, also, the Franklin sentiments cited in chap. 5, n. 56, above.

99. Such passages are found in this book at chap. 4, n. 105, above, chap. 5, n. 104, below. Cf. chap. 4, n. 106, above.

"Previous restraint" of expression by licensing was supplemented by punishment—imprisonment and execution—for seditious libel, which, as it persisted in England until after our Revolution, consisted in any publication intentionally finding fault, directly or indirectly, with the sovereign, truth being no defense. In 1791 free speech meant to the Framers the unrestricted right to discuss public affairs [citing Giles J. Patterson, *Free Speech and a Free Press* (Boston: Little, Brown, 1939), pp. 123-29]. [Henry S. Drinker, *Some Observations on the Four Freedoms of the First Amendment* (Boston: Boston University Press, 1957), p. 4]

> "Once the Lord Chamberlain has been abolished," wrote Mr. John Mortimer in a recent number of the magazine "Censorship," "the really interesting problems of censorship will have to be faced." . . . Assuming that society decides it needs a censor, in the sense of persons *distinct from the law of the land* and the Government of the day who are entrusted with the control of at least some genres of public cultural expression, should they operate from hunch, departmental case-law, or from continuous appeal to shifting public opinion through something like a jury system? [*Manchester Guardian Weekly*, Feb. 24, 1966, p. 7 (italics added). (See, on the same page, Victor Zorza, "Paradox of Moscow Trial.")]

See "After the Chamberlain . . . ," *Observer* (London), June 25, 1967, p. 11; *Times* (London), June 22, 1967, pp. 2, 11 (cf. chap. 8, nn. 18, 74, below):

> . . . Quite apart from the Obscene Publications Acts, which would have to be amended to take in stage performances, the law has a battery of guns trained on obscenity, indecency, public disorder, and matters injurious to public morals. The battery has been masked by the existence of the Lord Chamberlain's power of censorship, but with that out of the way there is no knowing what might be discharged from it.

See chap. 8, nn. 18, 74, below. See, for "insurance" as a form of licensing or previous restraint, App. E, above.

CHAPTER FIVE, NOTE 100: PAGE 115

100. Chafee, in his review of Alexander Meiklejohn's *Free Speech and Its Relation to Self-Government* (New York: Harper & Bros., 1948), questioned Meiklejohn's emphasis on the "political" character of the speech and press provisions of the First Amendment (cf. chap. 5, n. 52, above, chap. 7, n. 71, below):

> Is there any historical evidence that the framers of the First Amendment . . . intended the Amendment to apply only to discussions of matters connected with the process of self-government? Surely they did not link the Amendment with "universal suffrage" as the author [Meiklejohn] insists, because the much-restricted state franchises of 1791 were left completely untouched by the Constitution. . . . No doubt, the Zenger trial and the controversy over Wilkes and Junius in England did associate the struggle for freedom of speech to some extent with popular discussion of political questions, but the struggle was also related to the abolition of the censorship of books of any sort. Milton's *Areopagitica* advocated freedom for much else besides political tracts. The First Amendment brackets freedom of speech with freedom of the press, which Mr. Meiklejohn never mentions. If "speech" is limited as he proposes, so is "press." Yet that is impossible in view of the address of the Continental Congress in 1774 to the people of Quebec, in which freedom of the press, in addition to its political values, is said to be important for "the advancement of truth, science, morality and arts in general." Jefferson's vigorous support of the Philadelphia bookseller, Dufief, when Dufief was arrested for selling a French book on the creation of the world, shows how closely Jefferson connected freedom of the press with freedom of religion and of all thinking. . . . [Chafee, *Harvard L. Rev.* 62 (Mar. 1949): 891, 896-97. Cf. chap. 5, n. 51, above.]

The argument I am making does not depend on "universal suffrage." (In any event, "We the People" is not restricted to citizens eligible to vote.) As for the Milton precedent, it should be noticed that the principal argument there is against previous restraint, which *would* apply to the publication of *all* kinds of books—and our constitutional standard of freedom of the press (I have argued) begins with that as a minimum (as the liberty, or liberating, of the press). (Cf. the passage from Milton in the text at chap. 5, n. 50, above.) Cannot Jefferson's attitude with respect to Dufief be understood in terms of "the free exercise [of religion]," aside from arguments he may have made on general policy as distinguished from precise constitutional grounds? Even the Quebec Letter (of Oct. 26, 1774), referred to by Chafee, puts the emphasis on the "political":

> The last right we shall mention, regards the freedom of the press. The importance of this consists, besides the advancement of truth, science, morality, and arts in general, in its diffusion of liberal sentiments on the administration of Government, its ready communication of thoughts between subjects, and its consequential promotion of union among them, whereby oppressive officers are shamed or intimidated, into more honourable and just modes of conducting affairs. [*Journals of the Continental Congress, 1774-1789* (Washington: Government Printing Office, 1904), 1:105, 108]

Are "truth, science, morality, and arts in general" advanced partly because of the general political freedom, partly because of the lack of previous restraints for any publication? I suggest in the remainder of this section why Meiklejohn's emphasis on "freedom of speech" is particularly appropriate for the American regime. (It should be noticed that Chafee's celebrated books on this subject reveal a similar emphasis in their titles, *Freedom of Speech* and *Free Speech in the United States* [Cambridge: Harvard University Press, 1941]).

The reader can assess for himself the concern for the political (and for self-government) of "freedom of speech [and] of the press" by considering, in addition to the quotations in this section, the quotations elsewhere in this book which also tend to point to the conclusion I suggest here. (See chap. 5, n. 99, above.) The political context of the First Amendment protection is suggested, for example, by Dicey's argument that what there is of "liberty of the press" in English law is to be found in the law of libel. (See chap. 5, n. 20, above.) The question there was how far the citizen may go in criticizing his government and his political leaders (and, perhaps because of the connection between religion and politics under the Establishment, his religious leaders as well).

101. Meiklejohn, on the other hand, described as "derivative" what I think it more useful to regard as the prototype (see chap. 4, n. 102 [end], above):

> . . . In the last resort, it is not our representatives who govern us. We govern ourselves, using them. And we do so in such ways as our own free judgment may decide. And, that being true, it is essential that when we speak in the open forum, we "shall not be questioned in any other place." . . . The freedom which we grant to our representatives is merely a derivative of the prior freedom which belongs to us as voters. . . . [*Political Freedom*, pp. 35-36]

(Thus, Congresswoman Patsy T. Mink invoked on the floor of the House of Representatives, in voicing opposition to development of the ABM program, the right of freedom of speech guaranteed to every citizen to express his opinion in open debate. *Congressional Record*, 115: H3447 [May 7, 1969].)

A similar derivation is seen by Madison (toward the end of his *Report of 1799*, for the General Assembly of Virginia) on behalf of the states (rather than of individual representatives):

> What is allowable for one, must be allowable for all; and a free communication among the States, where the Constitution imposes no restraint, is as allowable among the State governments, as among other public bodies, or private citizens. This consideration derives a weight, that cannot be denied to it, from the relation of the State legislatures, to the federal legislature, as the immediate constituents of one of its branches.

See, on parliamentary immunity today, Street, *Freedom, the Individual and the Law*, p. 151. See, also, Anastaplo, book review of Levy, *Legacy of Suppression*, in *N.Y.U. L. Rev.*, 39 (1964): 735, 737-39; Anastaplo, "Freedom of Speech," pp. 55, 67-69.

102. One of the earliest as well as one of the best arguments for freedom of speech for the House of Commons was made in 1521 by Thomas More, as speaker of the house, in remarks addressed to Henry VIII:

> . . . Myne other humble requeste, most excellent prince, is this: Forasmuche as there be of the Commons here by your high commandment assembled for your Parliament, a greate number which are, after the accustomed manner, appoynted in the Common House to treate and advise of the common affayres amongst themselves aparte; and albeit, most deere leige lord, that accordinge to your prudente advise, by your honorable writtes everye where declared, there hath beene as due dilligence used in sendinge up to your highnes courte of parliament the most discreete persons out of everye quarter that menne could esteeme meete thereto; whereby yt is not to be doubted but that ther is a substanciall assemblye of right wise, and politicke persons; yet, moste victorious prince, sithe amonge soe many wise menne, neither is every man wise alike, nor among soe many men like well witted is every man like well spoken, and it often happenethe that likewise as muche follye is uttered with paynted polished speeche, soe many, boysterious and rude in language, see deepe indeede, and give righte substanciall councell; and sithe also in matters of great importance, the mynde is often soe occupied in this matter, that a man rather studiethe what to saye, then howe; by reason whereof the wisest man and best spoken in a whole countrye fortunethe, while his mynde is fervent in the matter, somewhat to speake in such wise as he would afterwardes wishe to have beene uttered otherwise, and yet noe worse will had when he spoke it, then he hathe when he would soe gladly change it. Therfore, most gratious Soveraygne, consideringe that in your high courte of Parliament is nothing intreated but matter of weyghte and importance concerning your Realme and your owne Royall Estate, yt could not faile to lett and put to silence from the givinge of their advise and councell many of your discreete Commons, to the greate hinderance of the common

affayres, excepte that everye one of your Commons were utterly dischardged of all doubtes and feare howe any thinge that it should happen them to speake, should happen of your highnes to be taken. . . . Yt may therfore like your most aboundante grace, our most benigne and godly Kinge, to give all your Commons here assembled your most gratious lycence and pardon, freely witheout doubte of your dredfull displeasure, everye man to dischardge his conscience, and boldly in every thinge incidente amongst us, to declare his advise; and what soever happen any man to say, that yt maye like your majestie of your inestimable goodnes to take all in good parte, interpreting everye mans wordes, howe unconningly [unlearnedly, ignorantly] soever they be couched, to proceede yet of good zeals towards the profit of your realme, and honor of your Royall personne, the prosperous estate and preservacion whereof, most excellent sovereygne, is the thing which we all, your most humble loving subjects, accordinge to the most bounden dewtye of our naturall allegeance, moste highly desire and praye for. [*The Lyfe of Sir Thomas More Knighte, Sometyme Chauncellor of Englande, Written by his Sonne-in-Lawe, William Roper*, George Sampson, ed., in *The Utopia of Sir Thomas More* (London: G. Bell & Sons, 1910), pp. 211-13 (notice the discreet uses of "happen," especially the second)]

See Xenophon, *Hiero*; Leo Strauss, *On Tyranny* (New York: Free Press of Glencoe, 1963); Robert Lowell, "Sir Thomas More," *Notebook 1967-68* (New York: Farrar, Straus and Giroux, 1969), p. 41. See, also, chap. 4, n. 102 (end), above.

103. See, also, Blackstone, *Laws of England*, 3:29, on the encouragement in lawyers of "due freedom of speech in the lawful defence of their clients. . . ."

The perils of limiting parliamentary discussion were alluded to by Ambassador Adlai E. Stevenson in connection with the censure in the United Nations of South Africa because it repeatedly stated its racial position "while knowing that it was offensive to nations represented in the General Assembly":

I think the freedom of speech, the opportunity to express one's position without let or hindrance, without limitation, is inherent in any parliamentary system, and that if you say that a fellow cannot say the same thing three times because he is getting tiresome and we are going to be able to spank him you have started a process the limits of which are very hard to foresee. [*Chicago Sun-Times*, Oct. 16, 1961, p. 2]

104. The juxtaposition of two sections of the Vermont Constitution of 1787 (I, 15, 16) illustrates this extension:

That the people have a right to freedom of speech, and of writing and publishing their sentiments, concerning the transactions of government: —and therefore the freedom of the press ought not to be restrained.

The freedom of deliberation, speech and debate, in the Legislature, is so essential to the rights of the people, that it cannot be the foundation of any accusation of prosecution, action or complaint, in any other court or place whatsoever.

The Constitution of the United States provides in Article 1, section 6, ". . . and for any Speech or Debate in either House, they shall not be questioned in any other Place." (If "freedom of speech" had been used here, would this have limited congressional immunity to the discussion of political matters, thereby inviting such inconveniences as the harassment of legislators with respect to borderline cases? See, on penalizing citizens who adopt and promulgate provocative language used in Congress, the leaflet, briefs, and opinion in *Schenck* v. *U.S.*, 249 U.S. 47 [1919] [Appendix B, above].) See *Federalist*, p. 435. See, also, chap. 2, n. 6, chap. 4, n. 102, chap. 5, n. 37, above.

105. See chap. 8, secs. 8-12, above.

The parliamentary regime lives by discussion; how shall it forbid discussion? Every interest, every social institution is here transformed into general ideas, debated as ideas; how shall any interest, any institution sustain itself above thought and impose itself as an article of faith? The struggle of the orators on the platform evokes the struggle of the scribblers of the press; the debating club in Parliament is necessarily supplemented by debating clubs in the salons and the pothouses; the representatives, who constantly appeal to public opinion, give public opinion the right to speak its real mind in petitions. . . . [Karl Marx, "The Eighteenth Brumaire of Louis Bonaparte," *Marx and Engels: Basic Writings on Politics and Philosophy*, L. S. Feuer, ed. (Garden City, N.Y.: Doubleday & Co., Anchor Books, 1959), pp. 332-33]

See Woodrow Wilson, *The Political Thought of Woodrow Wilson*, ed. E. David Cronon (Indianapolis: Bobbs-Merrill, 1965), pp. 31-32.

Does not the institution of a bicameral legislature, with the consent of each house essential for the enactment of laws, itself imply freedom of speech? This is comparable to the effect of the requirement of unanimity in a jury decision. See chap. 9, n. 34, below.

106. John Moore, in *View of Society*, 1:46-47, observed:

> When [the French] hear of the freedom of debate in [the British] parliament, of the liberties taken in writing or speaking of the conduct of the king, or measures of government, and the forms to be observed, before those who venture on the most daring abuse of either can be brought to punishment, they seem filled with indignation, and say with an air of triumph, C'est bien autrement chez nous: Si le Roi de France avoit affaire à ces Messieurs là, il leur apprendroit à vivre. And then they would proceed to inform you, that, parbleu! their minister would give himself no trouble about forms or proofs; that suspicion was sufficient for him, and without more ado he would shut up such impertinent people in the Bastille for many years. . . .

See chap. 8, n. 18, below.

107. G. W. Prothero, *Select Statutes and Other Constitutional Documents Illustrative of the Reigns of Elizabeth and James I* (4th ed.; Oxford: Oxford University Press, 1949), p. 310. The observation by James I that "men's particulars" "have their due motion in our ordinary courts of justice" anticipates the intimate relation in our constitutional system between "separation of powers" and "due process of law." See chap. 4, nn. 25, 102, above, chap. 6, n. 5, chap. 7, n. 67, chap. 8, n. 88, below.

108. This must be one of the earliest, if not the earliest, use in an official declaration of "abridge" in conjunction with "freedom of speech." It would be appropriate if the authors of the First Amendment, even in the choice of the words seen in the combination of "abridging" and "freedom of speech," drew on this great tradition and thereby implicitly acknowledged the transformation of the American people into the sovereign deliberative body that Parliament had become in Great Britain.

The more immediate source of "abridging" in the First Amendment is suggested by the reminder toward the end of the Virginia Resolutions of 1798,

> That this State [had] by its Convention, which ratified the Federal Constitution, expressly declared, that among other essential rights, "the Liberty of Conscience and of the Press cannot be cancelled, abridged, restrained, or modified by any authority of the United States," and from its extreme anxiety to guard these rights from every possible attack of sophistry or ambition, [had] with other States, recommended an amendment for that purpose, which amendment was, in due time, annexed to the Constitution. . . .

109. Prothero, *Select Statutes*, pp. 311-12.

110. Ibid., pp. 312-13. In another letter, dated December 16, read in the House on December 17, the king said, "The plain truth is, that we cannot with patience endure our subjects to use such antimonarchical words to us concerning their liberties, except they had subjoined that they were granted unto them by the grace and favour of our predecessors." Ibid., p. 313. See the following footnote on this point.

The "dearest son" referred to by the king in these letters became Charles I, who was beheaded in 1649. It should also be noted that James I is said to have won from Henry IV of France the title, "the wisest fool in Christendom."

111. Ibid., pp. 313-14. The Great Protestation (which I quote at greater length in "Freedom of Speech," p. 68) included the insistence that "the liberties, franchises, privileges and jurisdictions of parliament are the ancient and undoubted birthright and inheritance of the subjects of England. . . ."

112. Hobbes states, in *Leviathan*, II, xxix:

> The people of Athens bound themselves but from one onely Action; which was, that no man on pain of death should propound the renewing of the warre for the Islands of Salamis; And yet thereby, if Solon had not caused to be given out he was mad, and afterwards in gesture and habit of a mad-man, and in verse, propounded it to the People that flocked about him, they had had an enemy perpetually in readinesse, even at the gates of their Citie; such dammage, or shifts, are all Commonwealths forced to, that have their Power never so little limited.

Cf. Sallust, *The War against Catiline*, chap. 51, sec. 43 (the proposal made by Julius Caesar, about the disposition of the conspirators, which Cicero probably would have done well to support. See p. 635, below; also, chap. 8, n. 78, below.)

Thus, as I anticipated in chap. 4, n. 113, above, even the evidently antidemocratical Hobbes would grant that a sovereign people should deny itself no discussion bearing on public matters if it is to be able to act sensibly. Cf. chap. 7, n. 3, below. It is to be hoped, for instance, that there are responsible people in the Kremlin who have access to all information necessary for realistic appraisals of the world beyond the confines of Russia. See chap. 8, n. 147, below. Cf. Edmund Wilson, on Svetlana Alliluyeva's description of Stalin's Russia:

> . . . But she says that in her father's last years she found it very hard to get to see him [Stalin] and that when she visited him at his dacha she found it extremely painful because it was so difficult to talk to him. She does not see how he could have taken seriously the apotheosis that became official. She thinks that it was all "the system, in which he himself was held prisoner, in which he himself was stifling, from lack of companionship, from loneliness, from emptiness."
> [*New Yorker*, Dec. 9, 1967, p. 236]

Cf., also, chap. 8, n. 146, below: "That's not what I read in the papers!" (Hitler's disability, it seems, was even more crippling: "In retrospect I sometimes ask myself whether this intangibility, this insubstantiality, had not characterized [Hitler] from early youth up to the moment of his suicide. It sometimes seems to me that his seizures of violence could come upon him all the more strongly because there were no human emotions in him to oppose them. He simply could not let anyone approach his inner being because that core was lifeless, empty." Albert Speer, *Inside the Third Reich* [New York: Macmillan Co., 1970], p. 471. See chap. 9, n. 1, below.)

113. See, for a more extensive discussion of these benefits, chap. 8, secs. 9, 13, 14, above.

114. See, on decisions made in a single day, Plato, *Apology* 37A-B.

115. See, in Lincoln's speech, "The Perpetuation of Our Political Institutions," his recourse to "reason—cold, calculating, unimpassioned reason." *Complete Works*, 1:15.

116. I find it useful, just as in chapters 3 and 4, to indicate what I do mean by suggesting some of the things I do not mean. See Meiklejohn, *Political Freedom*, p. 21; also, Hobbes, *Leviathan*, I, iv; *Chaplinsky* v. *New Hampshire*, 315 U.S. 568, 571-72 (1942). Consider Aristotle, *Nicomachean Ethics* 1105b18-1106a13.

I collect here references to the passages in Blackstone, *Laws of England*, where a limitation is indicated upon some form of expression: 1:16, 128, 134, 143, 144-45, 160, 162, 163, 166, 179, 180, 181, 182, 183, 208, 217, 218, 229, 230, 230-31, 237, 247, 312-13, 318-19, 366-67, 402, 416, 451-52; 2:257, 405-7, 410, 437-38, 481; 3:29, 93,

101-2, 104, 123-27, 131-38, 158, 166, 216, 322-23, 356, 369-70, 373-74, 375, 381-82, 383, 394, 429; 4:3-5, 15, 15-16, 41-43, 43-65, 78-81, 81-82, 83, 87-89, 91-92, 103-17, 120, 123-24, 126, 133-34, 137-38, 140, 143, 144, 146, 146-47, 149, 150-53, 159, 163, 167-68, 247, 254-57, 267, 285-86, 286-88, 291, 294, 400.

A summary recapitulation of this section is provided in chap. 5, n. 139, below. See Story, *Commentaries on the Constitution*, chap. 44, sec. 1880: "That [the First Amendment] was intended to secure to every citizen an absolute right to speak, or write, or print, whatever he might please, without any responsibility, public or private therefor, is a supposition too wild to be indulged by any rational man." Cf. chap. 3, n. 12, above.

117. Some of the activities considered in this section, including perhaps those of the press and political speeches, are not within the power of Congress to regulate even under the original Constitution (i.e., before the Bill of Rights was added). (See chapter 6, below.) Since, however, the powers Congress does have may affect some forms of expression, this further indication of what is meant by political expression is relevant. (James Mill observed, in the opening paragraphs of his article, "Liberty of the Press," "There is scarcely a right, for the violation of which, scarcely an operation of government, for the disturbance of which the press may not be employed as an instrument. The offences capable of being committed by the press are indeed nearly co-extensive with the whole field of delinquency.") See chap. 6, n. 50, below.

The catalog of this section may be most useful for those who consider the full guarantee of "freedom of speech [and] of the press" to be now extended by the Fourteenth Amendment against the states (which would otherwise have extensive power to regulate speech and the press). Cf. Kalven, *Negro and First Amendment*, pp. 31-34, for a discussion of the suggestion "that freedom of speech is different under the First Amendment measuring *federal* power than it is under the Fourteenth Amendment measuring state power." See *Beauharnais v. Illinois*, 343 U.S. 250, 299 (1952). See, also, chap. 7, n. 107, below. Cf. also chap. 5, n. 153, chap. 8, n. 83, below.

118. The controlling provision reads (Article III, section 3) (see chap. 6, n. 16, below):

> Treason against the United States, shall consist only in levying War against them, or in adhering to their Enemies, giving them Aid and Comfort. No Person shall be convicted of Treason unless on the Testimony of two Witnesses to the same overt Act, or on Confession in open Court. The Congress shall have power to declare the Punishment of treason, but no Attainder of Treason shall work Corruption of Blood, or Forfeiture except during the Life of the Person attainted.

See chap. 3, n. 35, chap. 4, nn. 102, 103, 107, chap. 5, nn. 65, 78, above, chap. 5, nn. 119, 120, 142, chap. 6, nn. 25, 61, chap. 7, nn. 78, 84, 85, 86, 120, chap. 8, nn. 13, 22, 23, 29, below. See, also, Story, *Commentaries on the Constitution*, chap. 2, sec. 1797. Cf. David Lawrence, "A need to define insurrection," *Chicago Sun-Times*, July 20, 1969, sec. 2, p. 16. Treason is referred to in *Federalist* No. 74 as "a crime levelled at the immediate being of the society." But see the cautions with respect to prosecutions for treason found in *Federalist*, pp. 280-81; Hallem, *Constitutional History of England*, 2:360-75. We have seen in our own time (in the *Rosenberg* case, chap. 7, nn. 74, 75, below) how useful and humane it would be if the courts were bound to respect, in all proceedings dealing with crimes resembling treason, the constitutional safeguards with respect to treason prosecutions.

119. I know of no serious suggestion that the First Amendment modified the carefully drawn treason provision in the Constitution, nor of any indication that the good-faith application of that provision was ever regarded as a threat to freedom of speech (once "treason" had been restricted to the narrow limits prescribed in the Constitution). Words can be part of the required "overt acts," if such words not only give "aid and comfort" to an enemy (i.e., in time of war) but are uttered primarily for that purpose. But words alone, we are often told, cannot constitute the required overt acts. Precisely what this means would require an extensive examination. See Montesquieu, *Spirit of the*

Laws, 12:7, 8, 10, 11, 12; Elliot, *Debates*, 3:102-3; Chafee, *Freedom of Speech*, pp. 148 n., 322, 326. Cf. Kent, *Commentaries on American Law*, 2:26, n. a: "Words may constitute an imprisonment, if they impose a restraint upon the person, and he be accordingly restrained and submits."

120. We are reminded of the suggestion of "high treason" that James I made in response to certain discussions in the Commons. (See the passage quoted in the text at chap. 5, n. 110, above.)

I reserve for consideration in chapter 6 whether the careful definition of "treason" in the Constitution forbids by implication any congressional establishment of the crime of "sedition" (which may have once been considered by some to be one branch of treason). See chap. 6, n. 61, below. See, also, chap. 5, nn. 142, 143, below.

121. I see here no special problem with acts of "incitement." If one intends and does something illegal, it should not make any difference whether words were deliberately employed in doing so (if the deed, absent any such words, would be punishable). See the formulation, quoted in chap. 5, n. 66, above, as well as the comment in chap. 3, n. 20, above. See, also, Chafee, *Freedom of Speech*, pp. 25-26; Irving Dilliard, *One Man's Stand for Freedom: Mr. Justice Black and the Bill of Rights* (New York: Knopf, 1963), pp. 477-78; chap. 5, n. 150, below.

Consider, for the meaning of "incitement," William James's dedication in 1896 for *The Will to Believe and Other Essays in Popular Philosophy* (New York: Dover, 1956): "To My Old Friend, Charles Sanders Peirce, to whose philosophic comradeship in old times and to whose writings in more recent years I owe more incitement and help than I can express or repay." See chap. 7, n. 69, below.

122. Some of them, however, may raise due process problems, especially when war, class, or other passions lead to a disregard of the usual standards with respect to evidence, procedure, and the general conduct of trials. See chap. 8, n. 19, below.

Procedural requirements can be particularly important (and restrictive of government) with respect to such proceedings as obscenity prosecutions (to which I turn next). See, e.g., *Smith v. California*, 361 U.S. 147 (1959). Cf. Street, *Freedom, the Individual and the Law*, pp. 161-62.

The dissenting opinion of Justice Black in *Ginzburg v. U.S.*, 383 U.S. 463, at 476, 480-81 (1966), points up the due process problems that obscenity prosecutions should be obliged to cope with:

> Only one stark fact emerges with clarity out of the confusing welter of opinions . . . in this and two other cases today. That fact is that Ginzburg, petitioner here, is now finally and authoritatively condemned to serve five years in prison for distributing printed matter about sex which neither Ginzburg nor anyone else could possibly have known to be criminal. . . .
>
> My conclusion is that certainly after the fourteen separate opinions handed down in these three cases today no person, not even the most learned judge much less a layman, is capable of knowing in advance of an ultimate decision in his particular case by this Court whether certain material comes within the area of "obscenity" as that term is confused by the Court today. For this reason even if . . . this country is far along the way to a censorship of the subjects about which the people can talk or write, we need not commit further constitutional transgression by leaving people in the dark as to what literature or what words or what symbols if distributed through the mails make a man a criminal. As bad and obnoxious as I believe governmental censorship is in a Nation that has accepted the First Amendment as its basic ideal for freedom, I am compelled to say that censorship that would stamp certain books and literature as illegal in advance of publication or conviction would in some ways be preferable to the unpredictable book-by-book censorship into which we have now drifted.

I do not understand Justice Black to be asking here for "previous restraint," but rather for generally ascertainable standards of criminality. (Justice Brennan, in his Opinion for the Court in *Ginzburg*, 383 U.S. at 470, noted that petitioner unconditionally guaranteed, in advertisements of his wares, "full refund of the price of *The Housewife's Handbook on Selective Promiscuity* if the book fails to reach you because of U.S. Post Office censorship interference.")

See, on the relation of the Anti-Riot Act of 1968 to the commerce power of Congress, chap. 6, n. 75, below.

123. Senator Gale McGee is quoted as promising, "I'm going to introduce a resolution to have the Postmaster General stop reading dirty books and deliver the mail." J. B. Simpson, ed., *Contemporary Quotations* (New York: Thomas Y. Crowell, 1964), p. 277. See, also, the *New York Times* editorial, "Why Not Just Carry the Mail?" Feb. 14, 1961.

The most practical restraint upon the distribution of obscene materials, I venture to suggest, would be trespass suits (or their equivalent) by parents whose children had been (without parental consent) exposed to and damaged by such materials. (I suspect, as well, that a few substantial damage awards to victims of cigarette smoking will do much more than legislation to induce cigarette producers to redirect their efforts to healthier enterprises.) I set great store, that is, by the ingenuity of lawyers in the presence of available money. See Joseph L. Sax and Fred J. Hiestand, "Slumlordism as a Tort," *Michigan L. Rev.* 65 (1967): 869. Cf. Walter J. Blum and Allison Dunham, "Slumlordism as a Tort—A Dissenting View," *Michigan L. Rev.* 66 (1968): 451.

See, also, Congressman Abner J. Mikva's discussion of H.R. 15693, which would "restrict, and impose criminal sanctions on, the use of the mails or interstate commerce to circulate unsolicited salacious advertising." *Congressional Record*, 116: E7318 (Aug. 4, 1970).

124. A critical problem, that reflected in publicly disseminated photographs and stories prying into and revealing the most private anguish of the human soul (often after an unexpected death in the family), is rarely confronted either by the law or by those who study "obscenity." Instead, prizes are given for such exhibitions. See chap. 8, sec. 15, above.

Richard M. Weaver observed, "This failure of the concept of obscenity has been concurrent with the rise of the institution of publicity which, ever seeking to widen its field in accordance with the canon of progress, makes a virtue of desecration." *Ideas Have Consequences* (Chicago: University of Chicago Press, 1948), p. 28. Such desecration may be seen in the callous exploitation by the "mass media" of private misfortunes, in the daily display before all of the essentially intimate, and in the parading before us of the monumentally vulgar. How can it be good for a people to be exposed as we are to such images day after day, whether in the press or on television? How can it help having a coarsening and corrupting effect on our souls? What does it mean that we get "used" to these assaults upon our sensibilities? Only rarely can such publication be justified by the public's need to know in order for it to be able to exercise intelligently its political judgment. (The political usefulness of a "prying press" may be seen in Vassilis Vassilikos's *Z* [New York: Farrar, Straus & Giroux, 1968]. See, also, Helen Vlachos, *House Arrest* [Boston: Gambit, 1970].)

It does not encourage communal self-restraint in these matters when influential people, who should know and do better, lead photographers and editors astray by their appetite for publicity. See, e.g., *Life*, Oct. 29, 1965, pp. 104-5. There may be, furthermore, a connection between the shocking displays found in *Time*, May 28, 1965, pp. 22, 28, and those found in *Evergreen*, Apr., 1970, pp. 33-39: "anything goes" seems to be the order (or, rather, the lack of order) of the day, to which we can expect eventually an equally undiscriminating reaction. See chap. 5, nn. 131, 155, 156, chap. 7, n. 59, below.

A breakdown in civility may be observed as well in the language used by "radicals" in attacks upon "the Establishment" (e.g., "pigs") and by the Vice President of the United States (who *has* been something of a safety-valve) in its defense:

> In his partisan and often ungenerous critiques, which neglect long-run political consequences, Professor Papandreou is curiously akin to Vice-President Agnew. One may detect in both men a volatile combination of intelligence, ambition, forensic energy and political inexperience. Both of these attractive men, it should

CHAPTER FIVE, NOTE 125: PAGE 121
545

be added, can and should be better than they mistakenly believe it expedient to appear in public: their countries need them at their best. [Anastaplo, book review: Andreas Papandreou, *Democracy at Gunpoint: The Greek Front* (New York: Doubleday & Co., 1970), *Book World*, May 24, 1970, p. 5]

See chap. 6, n. 1, below. See Alexander M. Bickel's useful article, "The Tolerance of Violence on the Campus," *Congressional Record*, 116: E5959 (June 26, 1970); chap. 5, n. 93, above.

Jane Austen provides a useful antidote all around, as does Xenophon. See Leo Strauss, *What Is Political Philosophy?* (Glencoe, Ill.: Free Press, 1959), p. 104.

125. In D. H. Lawrence, *Lady Chatterley's Lover* (New York: Grove Press, 1959), p. 146, we find:

> But the novel, like gossip, can also excite spurious sympathies and recoils, mechanical and deadening to the psyche. The novel can glorify the most corrupt feelings, so long as they are *conventionally* "pure." Then the novel, like gossip, becomes at last vicious, and like gossip, all the more vicious because it is always ostensibly on the side of the angels. Mrs. Bolton's gossip was always on the side of the angels. "And he was such a *bad* fellow, and she was such a *nice* woman." Whereas, as Connie could see even from Mrs. Bolton's gossip, the woman had been merely a mealy-mouthed sort, and the man angrily honest. But angry honesty made a "bad man" of him, and mealy-mouthedness made a "nice woman" of her, in the vicious, conventional channeling of sympathy by Mrs. Bolton.
>
> For this reason, the gossip was humiliating. And for the same reason, most novels, especially popular ones, are humiliating too. The public responds now only to an appeal to its vices.

See the *Times* (London), July 7, 1966, p. 7, for a discussion in the House of Commons of a "flood of pornography." The attorney general (Sir Elwyn Jones [see chap. 6, n. 66, below]) reported "180,808 books and 1,076,139 magazines" had been "seized by the police and customs authorities in 1965." Upon being asked "what size of staff was employed to arrive at the conclusion that such huge quantities of imported literature should be designated pornographic and obscene," the attorney general replied, "It does not need a great staff. This stuff is filthy trash which no one has any difficulty in identifying." One member suggested that "the precursor of this flood of pornography was the legitimizing of the distribution of *Lady Chatterley's Lover*."

Louis MacNeice remarked, under the heading "Dark God,"

> As D. H. Lawrence was well slapped down in the 'twenties by Mr. Wyndham Lewis there is no need now to take another slap at one who, in spite of his unfortunate effect on adolescents, was a great writer and a godsend. . . . Lawrence had imagination without commonsense—and got away with it—but in most people this divorce will degrade imagination itself. [Quoted in *The Penguin Book of Contemporary Verse* (London: Penguin Books, 1956), p. 64]

What Lawrence tried to do may be seen in Emerson's "The Poet":

> Thought makes everything fit for use. The vocabulary of an omniscient man would embrace words and images excluded from polite conversation. What would be base, or even obscene, to the obscene, becomes illustrious, spoken in a new connection of thought. The piety of the Hebrew prophets purges their grossness. The circumcision is an example of the power of poetry to raise the low and offensive. Small and mean things serve as well as great symbols. . . .

Cf. Katherine Anne Porter's "A Wreath for the Gamekeeper," *Encounter*, Feb. 1960, p. 69. (See her letter, *Encounter*, May 1960, p. 85.) See Alistair Cooke, "Focus on the Arts," in *1965 Year Book, World Book Encyclopedia* (Chicago: Field Enterprises Educational Corporation, 1965), pp. 50, 51-52.

We should, in considering the proper attitude toward artists such as D. H. Lawrence and Lenny Bruce, keep in mind the advice given in 1960 by C. S. Lewis respecting the question of publishing Pepys's *Diary* in its unexpurgated entirety:

> The moral problem comes down to the question "Is it probable that the inclusion of these passages will lead anyone to commit an immoral act which he would not have committed if we had suppressed them?" Now of course this question is strictly unanswerable. No one can foresee the odd results that any words may have on this or that individual. We ourselves, in youth, have been both corrupted and edified by books in which our elders could have foreseen neither edification nor corruption. But to suggest that in a society where the most potent aphrodisiacs are daily put forward by the advertisers, the newspapers, and the films, any perceptible increment of lechery will be caused by printing a few obscure and widely separated passages in a very long and expensive book, seems to me ridiculous, or even hypocritical. [*Letters of C. S. Lewis*, ed. W. H. Lewis (New York: Harcourt, Brace & World, 1966), p. 294]

In any event, the healthy reader or the serious writer should not require more eroticism than what Homer says of Odysseus and Calypso: "The sun fell and twilight deepened as he spoke. They rose and went far into the smooth-walled cave—to its very end: and there by themselves they took their joy of one another in the way of love, all night," or what Circe says to Odysseus, "I pray you sheathe that sword and let us go lie together, that we may mingle our bodies and learn to trust one another by proofs of love and intercourse." *Odyssey* V, 225-27, X, 333-35. Cf. ibid., XXIII, 300-309, 321-25, 333-37. See, also, ibid., VIII, 266-369 (the Hephaestus-Aphrodite-Ares episode). Cf. Plato, *Republic* 457 A-B.

126. See, for a useful introduction to the problem of obscenity, Weaver, *Ideas Have Consequences*, pp. 28-30. Weaver regarded as "obscene" "that which should be enacted off-stage because it is unfit for public exhibition." (Cf. Aristotle, *Nicomachean Ethics* 1128a23.) See Plato, *Phaedo* 116A-B.

It should be added that that which should be enacted offstage is sometimes too precious and delicate to submit to public view, that to keep it private is truly to preserve and to cherish it. Mark Twain observed, in the Preface to his *Autobiography*, "The frankest and freest and privatest product of the human mind and heart is a love letter; the writer gets his limitless freedom of statement and expression from his sense that no stranger is going to see what he is writing." (Does modern psychoanalysis, despite its sympathy for love, or at least for the powers of love, make love [by the therapist's perhaps necessary intrusion into the most private things] difficult if not impossible to maintain?)

When one writes to one's beloved, no matter what the subject, something may be found of the love letter (with its celebration of the very existence of the beloved, of that which is central to the lover's life, and hence of the truth about eternal things), including the lover's instinctive desire to share everything with the beloved, to become one with the beloved, and to exclude the profane from this communion. (There is even something philosophical about this regard for existence, this turning away from the unpredictable movement one usually has to contend with in dealing with others. See Plato, *Crito* 44D-E, Maimonides, *Guide of the Perplexed*, p. 440. [Whether the beloved is truly worthy of the single-minded attention described here can become curiously irrelevant. Dante's Beatrice comes to mind.] Compare the opening lines and the tone of the *Iliad* with the tone of the *Odyssey* [as reflected in the quotations in chap. 5, n. 125, above]: the corrosiveness of anger yields to the balm of love. See Aristotle, *Nicomachean Ethics* 1139b18-25.) Consider Burke, *Works*, 1:194-95, 86-87, 179-80.

Does not Aristophanes' union of lovers (Plato, *Banquet* 192D-E) suppose not only that two become one but also that they exclude from their union everything, including third-party observation, which might mar the completeness of the union? That is, "completeness" means that nothing is absent which should be present, nothing is present which is superfluous. (That there is something delusory about this frantic striving for perfect union is suggested even by Aristophanes' recognition that men were striving against the

CHAPTER FIVE, NOTE 126: PAGE 121

gods—that is, that men were aware of their imperfection—even before the ancient partition that lovers now try to repair. *Banquet* 190B-C. [Love necessarily directs itself, in its yearning for wholeness, to possession of that "infinite variety" which promises to satisfy the many ever-changing desires with which we have always to contend. See Shakespeare, *Antony and Cleopatra*, II, ii, 241.] Thus, one who is aware of all this might better move toward the completion sought, the perfection, by directing his attention not to the union of love but to that which even united lovers would again contend [i.e., aspire] for, to be godlike. But, the poet might reply, it is possible for mankind to make that move toward perfection only through the body, not by circumventing it—only by making much of the universals implicit in particulars properly conceived, not by neglecting the demands and lessons of the body. [See Aristotle, *Poetics* 1451b5.] The limits imposed by the body, on the other hand, are playfully alluded to in the hiccoughs Plato ascribes to Aristophanes [*Banquet* 185C-E]; a more serious critique of the Aristophanic position may be found, of course, in Socrates' contribution to the occasion. [Does not Socrates stand for the proposition that only the knowing man fully is? Is not he alone among mortal men, if only temporarily, in full communion with eternal *nous*? Only he who knows what it is to be can fully be: for to lack such knowledge would mean that one is not being something he could be, a knowing being. But may not the same be said of one who does not rule or of one who does not indulge himself in the most intense physical pleasures—that he is not something he could be? Still, can one truly rule if one does not know? Can one, without knowing, select what is worth ruling? And what, indeed, are the most intense pleasures—those of the body or those of the knowing mind? Who is best able to decide even this? After all, have not the most intense physical pleasures been experienced by all? Neither wealth nor skill is required: everyone, for instance, knows what it is to relieve a great thirst on a hot day by drinking cool water. See Plato, *Phaedo* 60B-C. See, also, Aristotle, *Nicomachean Ethics* 1170a25-b19, *Politics* 1278b25-30.]) It should also be noted that in order to have a full account of love, the shamefully intimate must be dealt with as well: lovers, when properly left to themselves, redeem the shameful by converting the *many* of the public into the apparent *one* of the love union. Alcibiades, in order to speak openly of such matters, must be intoxicated: that is, he must be unable or uninclined to distinguish between the public and the private. *Banquet* 214E, 217E, 222C. Cf. *Banquet* 176C, 214A-B, 223C-D, *Phaedo* 118A-B. (See chap. 9, nn. 16, 21, below.)

Does not the community—most of whose members have had their most (if not their only) elevated moments as lovers (and thereafter as parents)—sense all this and try to protect such intimacy from the public view that would cheapen and corrupt it for everyone? ("When Siminov, the popular author of *Days and Nights*, published a volume of moderately passionate love poems a few years ago, Stalin was said to have remarked that only two copies should have been printed—one for the writer and the other for the lady." John Fischer, *Why They Behave like Russians* [New York: Harper & Bros., 1948], p. 28. See, also, Milovan Djilas, *Conversations with Stalin* [New York: Harcourt, Brace & World, 1962], p. 158.) See Graham Greene, *Essays* (New York: Viking Press, 1969), pp. 366-68. The Supreme Court (in *Kingsley Corp.* v. *Regents*, 360 U.S. 684, 688-89 [1959]) held void the ban on the motion picture, "Lady Chatterley's Lover," on the ground that the "basic guarantee of freedom" by the First Amendment "is not confined to the expression of ideas that are conventional or shared by a majority. It protects advocacy of the opinion that adultery may sometimes be proper, no less than advocacy of socialism or the single tax." To argue that "adultery may sometimes be proper" is one thing—indeed, I am prepared to believe there may be unusual circumstances in which that which should be central to marriage and gives that institution ostensible priority is naturally found elsewhere (see Machiavelli, *Mandragola*; cf. Aristotle, *Nicomachean Ethics* 1107a15)—but to portray in print or on film certain activities of lovers (whether married or not) is quite different from advocacy of adultery. (It is only realistic to add that such transcendence of marriage as I have justified here is all too rare: what is much more likely is a shabby affair based on and debased by deception which is maintained by simulated intimacy with the partners prescribed by law. [See, on the relation of adultery to law, Euripides, *Heracles* 1316, 1341, 1345.] "Disbelief in the virtue of chastity is not confined to those who from the purest motives would like to help spinsters lead a fuller life. . . ." Patrick Devlin, *The Enforcement of Morals* [London: Oxford University Press, 1965], p. 114. See chap. 7, n. 23, below. Still, it is nice to recall "the sweet sin of lechery—a man and woman in a garden on a May morning," of which Sir Thomas More said, "If God would not forgive it, I would." "Weeeknd Review," *Observer* [London], July 3, 1966, p. 24. [What should constitute marriage, and hence adultery, is a political subject touching on the fundamental character of the regime. See Aristotle, *Politics* 1306a38-1306b4, 1335b39-1336a2, 1334b29-1335b38. (Indeed, one may even question whether it is possible for someone *as citizen* to commit adultery in a country other than his own.) See, also, Seth Benardete, *Herodotean Inquiries* (The Hague: Martinus Nijhoff, 1969), pp. 11-13.])

127. Yuli Daniel and Andrey Sinyavsky were convicted in a Russian court in 1966 on charges which included "disseminating slander [of the regime] dressed up as literature." (They were sentenced to five and seven years hard labor, respectively.) Yuli Daniel, *This Is Moscow Speaking* (New York: E. P. Dutton & Co., 1969), p. 9.

> . . . There is no doubt that Sinyavsky's interest in political and social questions or in the recent history of Russia is secondary, and he could claim without hypocrisy at his trial that he had no political intention in his literary works. Daniel, on the other hand, is an explicitly "political" writer and he has not tried to hide from the consequences of this. He said at his trial: "my writings [published abroad under a pseudonymn] have a political tinge and they would have been rejected [by Soviet publishers] on political grounds," and again in his final plea: "I do not wish to deny the political content of my works." . . . Daniel's dialogue with his Prosecutor and Judge was about the question: Was his work fair comment or slander on the Soviet system and people? [Ibid. (Foreword by Max Hayward), p. 12]

Is not literature much more apt to be "political" under those regimes where ordinary political expression is strictly controlled. Or, put another way, would not anyone seriously interested in political things usually prefer to discuss them directly rather than through the use of fiction? Is, under a free political regime, literature much more likely to be devoted to private things, to the cultivation of "individuality," not to public things? (Is it also more likely to be shallow?) See chap. 8, nn. 135, 193, below.

> William Bradford Huie, a native and present resident of Alabama, has written . . . a powerful and shocking novel of the Ku Klux Klan as it operates in Alabama today. . . . He says he probably will write no more nonfiction, since he believes it is possible to give a more accurate picture of an event or a movement if you present the truth in fictional, and therefore legally unassailable form. He added that he was tired of lawsuits, even the ones he won. [*Chicago Tribune*, Sept. 25, 1967, p. 19]

Consider, also, Margaret L. Hartley, "Is Science Fiction Subversive?" *Southwest Review* 38 (1953): 244, 249: "All the fields in which science fiction is expressing thoughts that would be promptly condemned if they were to appear in more earthly forms of writing have one thing in common: they contemplate change."

When a novel, such as *Uncle Tom's Cabin*, is politically important, it should enjoy the protection of political expression extended by "freedom of the press." If a government proceeds against a novel for political offenses (such as the seditious libel apparently alleged in the Yuli Daniel trial), the novel would be (or would then become) to that extent "political" and hence would be eligible for whatever protection political expression is entitled to. But what if a government alleges and prosecutes for obscenity in order to suppress seditious sentiments? It is to be hoped that courts and juries, to say nothing of public opinion, would put a stop to such subterfuges: such a subterfuge would be of the same effect, however different in intention or in wording, as the "clear and present danger" test. That is, no guarantee will be of much effect if prosecutors, courts, juries, and public opinion conspire to ignore it. (See chap. 7, n. 66, below.)

CHAPTER FIVE, NOTE 128: PAGE 121   549

The first exposure of the white slave traffic was in a magazine article: "the English law did absolutely nothing to the profiteers in vice, but put [the author of the article] in prison for a year for writing about an indecent subject." Chafee, *Freedom of Speech*, p. 171. This should remind us, whatever may have been the truth in the matter Chafee referred to, that subterfuges can go either way: that is, some may try to give a veneer of the political to material otherwise criminal (as, for instance, to obscene or fraudulent publications). See Kalven, *Negro and First Amendment*, p. 195; cf. ibid., p. 219, n. 82. See chap. 5, n. 148, below.

We should be reminded as well of the problem implicit in the political career of Jacques René Hébert (the French revolutionist who organized the "worship of Reason" in opposition to the theistic cult inaugurated by Robespierre): "Hébert's influence was mainly due to his articles in his journal *Le Père Duchesne*, which appeared from 1790 to 1794. These articles, while not lacking in a certain cleverness, were violent and abusive, and *purposely couched in foul language in order to appeal to the mob*." *Encyclopedia Britannica*, 11th ed., 13:167 (italics added). See, for a more recent instance of the alliance in France of the political and the obscene, Louis Ducloux, *From Blackmail to Treason: Political Crime and Corruption in France, 1920-1940* (London: A. Deutsch, 1958), e.g., pp. 50-51, 65.

Much more complicated is the career of Lenny Bruce, which is recapitulated in a sympathetic obituary in the *Times* (London), Aug. 5, 1966, p. 12:

> Lenny Bruce could, when he cared to do so, command all the techniques by means of which a comedian can succeed. Against these, as against the society in which he lived, he was an inveterate rebel whose rebellion was not merely political; he opposed a world which, in his view, was given cohesion only by the repressions it endured from authority. His act, an unprepared improvisation on his experience and his state of mind, sought to deal with the tensions of which he felt his audience to be as keenly aware as he was himself, and if the discussion of sex and sexual experience was an obvious way to ventilate this, it was also the most powerfully disturbing, and Bruce sought to disturb rather than to amuse. Paradoxically, he was a moralist attempting to find some sort of lasting truth from his experience of life. . . .

Another sympathetic account of Lenny Bruce may be found in Sydney J. Harris, "Changing Standards of Humor," *Chicago Daily News*, Oct. 29, 1969, p. 12. See Leo Strauss, *Socrates and Aristophanes* (New York: Basic Books, 1966), p. 198; chap. 8, n. 171, below.

John Adams observed, in an article published Jan. 23, 1775, "There may be occasion to say very severe things before I shall have finished what I propose in opposition to this writer, but there ought to be no reviling. *Rem ipsam dic, mitte male loqui,* which may be justly translated, 'speak out the whole truth boldly, but use no bad language.' " *The Political Writings of John Adams*, American Heritage Series (Indianapolis: Bobbs-Merrill, 1954), p. 29.

128. See Gotthold E. Lessing, *Laocoon* (New York: Noonday Press, 1963), p. 10:

> We laugh when we read that the very arts among the ancients were subject to the control of civil law; but we have no right to laugh. Laws should unquestionably usurp no sway over science, for the object of science is truth. Truth is a necessity of the soul, and to put any restraint upon the gratification of this essential want is tyranny. The object of art, on the contrary, is pleasure, and pleasure is not indispensable. What kind and what degree of pleasure shall be permitted may justly depend on the law-giver.

(See chap. 4, n. 113, above, on the sovereign's need to know the truth if he is to know what he is doing. See, also, Plato, *Republic* 607A, *Laws* 658E-659A.)

Compare the formulation of an English judge in R. v. *Burdett*, 4 B. & Ald. 95, 131 (1820):

> In forming their opinion on the question of [seditious] libel, I told the jury that

they were to consider whether the paper contained a sober address to the reason of mankind, or whether it was an appeal to their passions, calculated to incite them to acts of violence and outrage. If it was of the former description, it was not a libel; if of the latter description, it was.

Cf. chap. 5, nn. 66, 121, above. (The language of the indictment in this case is instructive as to how libels were regarded: it was charged that the defendant "unlawfully and maliciously did compose, write, and publish . . . a certain scandalous, malicious, and seditious libel of and concerning the government of the regime. . . ." 4 B. & Ald. 95, 116. The offending text, which is about as inoffensive as that in *Schenck* v. *U.S.* [see Appendix B, above], is included in the indictment and published in the court's opinion at pp. 116-17.)

The distinction between pleasure (or passions) and truth (or reason) may be discerned in the distinction between sections 13 and 14 of chapter 8, above. See, also, chap. 8, n. 170, below, for a reflection of this distinction in Milton's evident assumption that the previous restraint he argued against in the *Areopagitica* (with respect to the press) need not be objectionable with respect to "publick sports and festival pastimes."

It should be noticed that the word, "sentiments," often found in eighteenth-century "liberty of the press" formulations, referred somewhat to one's opinions or ideas rather than, as is much more likely today, almost exclusively to one's feelings. (See the opening pages of Martin Heidegger's *What Is Philosophy?* [New Haven: College and University Press, 1956]. Cf. Tocqueville, *Democracy in America*, 1:253 ff.; William James, "The Sentiment of Rationality," in *The Will to Believe*, p. 63 [*sentiment* seems to mean *feeling*, as at pp. 76-78].) Passages using "sentiment" are reproduced in this volume in the text at chap. 4, n. 85, at chap. 4, n. 114, at chap. 5, n. 3, at chap. 5, n. 98, above; at chap. 5, n. 141, at chap. 8, n. 105, at chap. 8, n. 106, at chap. 8, n. 115, at chap. 8, n. 187, above; and in the following notes: chap. 5, nn. 100, 104, above, chap. 6, nn. 38, 66, chap. 8, n. 16, chap. 9, n. 13, below. See, for the use of "sentiment" by Publius, *Federalist*, pp. 5, 8, 9, 49, 55, 87, 104, 160, 168, 178, 180, 206, 235, 256, 291, 305, 309, 349, 372, 373, 388, 437, 509, 570. (Compare its frequent use in Jane Austen.)

The 1908 Michigan Constitution had provided, Article 2, section 4, "Every person may freely speak, write and publish his sentiments on all subjects, being responsible for the abuse of such a right; and no law shall be passed to restrain or abridge the liberty of speech or of the press." (See chap. 3, n. 10, chap. 4, n. 88, above.) The 1964 Constitution provides, Article 1, section 5, "Every person may freely speak, write, express and publish his views on all subjects, being responsible for the abuse of such right; and no law shall be enacted to restrain or abridge the liberty of speech or of the press." The convention comment on this provision was,

> This is a revision of Sec. 4, Art. II, of the present [1908] constitution preserving these traditional guarantees. It broadens them by including the word "express" and substituting the word "views" for "sentiments." Addition of the word "express" is intended to recognize development of new means of communication in recent years. The word "views" seems to have a sharper and more specific meaning than the former word "sentiments." [*Michigan Statutes Annotated* (1965), 1:331]

The use by eighteenth-century writers of the passion-tinged "sentiments" (rather than "opinions" or "ideas") may have reflected their awareness of the practical limits of political discourse (even while they recognized the potentiality of private discourse). Thus, Jefferson can say of someone that "we find him always substituting sentiment for demonstration." *Notes on the State of Virginia* (New York: Harper & Row, 1964), p. 135. (A century later Robert Louis Stevenson said, in *The Master of Ballantrae*, "It is one of the worst things of sentiment, that the voice grows to be more important than the words, and the speaker than that which is spoken." Stevenson, *Two Major Novels* [New York: Bantam Books, 1960], p. 83.) It was recognized in *Federalist* No. 85 that it is rare when "a political truth can be brought to the test of a mathematical demonstration." Or, as was said in *Federalist* No. 21, "in political arithmetic, two and two do not always make four." See Aristotle, *Nicomachean Ethics* 1094b25-27. Thus, the responsible statesman (in office or out) must both study and display the power of rhetoric.

129. But, it should be remembered,

> The licensing of plays was imposed not to protect the morals of the British public but to safeguard the reputation of politicians. This happened in 1737 when the Prime Minister, Sir Robert Walpole, infuriated by the stage lampoons of Henry Fielding and others, determined to silence these much enjoyed exposures of his alleged corruption and incompetence. [Ivor Brown, "British Censor Relents," *New York Times*, Jan. 1, 1961]

See Street, *Freedom, the Individual and the Law*, p. 54. Cf. Crankshaw, *Khrushchev's Russia*, pp. 119-20.

130. See, e.g., D. H. Lawrence, *A Propos of Lady Chatterley's Lover* (London: Penguin Books, 1961), which was first published in Great Britain in 1929, a generation before the complete novel whose suppression is therein discussed.

> . . . More fundamentally, the delay argument seems artificial in the context of this case and in the area of obscenity generally. Both the incentive for officials to promote delay and the adverse consequences of delay are considerably less in this area than in the field of political and social expression. If controversial political writings attack those in power, government officials may benefit from suppression although society may suffer. In the area of obscenity, there is less chance that decision-makers will have interests which may affect their estimate of what is constitutionally protected and what is not. It is vital to the operation of democratic government that the citizens have facts and ideas on important issues before them. A delay of even a day or two may be of crucial importance in some instances. On the other hand, the subject of sex is of constant but rarely particularly topical interest. Distribution of *Ulysses* may be thought by some to be more important for society than distribution of the daily newspaper, but a one- or two-month delay in circulation of the former would be of small significance whereas such a delay might be effective suppression of the latter. [Justice Harlan, dissenting, *A Quantity of Copies of Books* v. *Kansas*, 378 U.S. 205, 224-25 (1964)]

See chap. 5, n. 35, above, chap. 7, n. 107, below.

". . . In an assault on free speech, [the Securities and Exchange Commission] has issued cease-and-desist orders against shareholders of A T & T for running ads protesting highhanded rulings of the FCC." *Barron's*, Jan. 23, 1967, p. 1. See chap. 6, n. 75, below.

Perhaps the only sober observation in Professor Wigmore's wild comment on the *Abrams* case (see chap. 3, n. 35, above), is that found at *Ill. L. Rev.* 14:557:

> Let A., however, if he pleases, argue with his friends that [a particular legal] restriction is excessive, and let him persuade them to appeal to the legislature for a repeal of the statute. But, so long as it remains law, let him not be licensed to undermine its operation on the pretext of freedom of speech. The pretext is needless, for he is still at liberty to discuss the wisdom of the law and to seek to change it by the usual methods of changing the public opinion to sounder judgment. And that is all that the right of freedom of speech exists for, in the last analysis.

(I note in passing that the exhortation found in the *Schenck* case circular reprinted in Appendix B, below, should be studied carefully with this observation in mind.)

"A riot, Martin Luther King tells us [in *Where Do We Go from Here? Chaos or Community* (New York: Harper & Row, 1967)], is the language of the unheard." *Catholic Worker*, Sept. 1967, p. 6. (But the "unheard" are not all "of one mind.")

131. Does this suggest that American individuality and nonconformity—the resentment of authority Wilmot referred to—will find *some* form of expression, that if it is not permitted in the public sphere it will in the process of attempted restoration erupt

in the private sphere? (Has this, in fact, happened in America since the First World War, perhaps because of the loss of confidence in our communal sense of morality that political suppression among us both represents and encourages?)

> "I observe to the honorable Mrs. Damer that the French, having no Liberty in their Government, have compensated to themselves that Misfortune by bestowing a great Deal upon Society. . . ." Morris, *Diary*, 1:187-88. (One danger of such a development, especially in a country as moralistic at its roots as is ours, is that the inevitable, almost natural, popular reaction against private license may bring public freedom down as well. If, however, private license is prudently restrained initially [see chap. 9, nn. 1-39, below], serious political freedom can be safely enlarged or at least more easily defended.)

What, on the other hand, should be said of the Russian character?

> The general attitude to sex may be pointed by a significant personal anecdote. A few days ago, perhaps as a small tease, I lent a young Soviet diplomat a copy of *Lady Chatterley*. He returned it the next day. His only comment was: "No, *really!*" When I pressed him for a more articulate opinion, he said: "You know Russia well enough. Don't you know that, to us, such a book is just inconceivable!" [Alexander Werth, "Love among the Russians," *New Statesman*, Jan. 6, 1961, p. 12]

(Russian pedestrian traffic, on the other hand, exhibits the problem of preserving order among them, especially where they can easily remain anonymous.

> The organization imposed on Russia by Peter was external; the chaos remained, immemorial and unchangeable; and the order became merely a part of it, the most schematized and irrelevant part, put there, God knew how, or simply because a man of tremendous character had happened to exist. Peter, like Lenin, was Western in training and aspiration. . . . [Edwin Muir, *Latitudes* (New York: B. W. Huebsch, 1924), p. 126])

132. I return to the problem of the relation of literature (i.e., education) to politics in section 15 of chapter 8. See, e.g., chap. 8, nn. 170, 171, below.

That I have been speaking of the "political" in a narrow sense should be evident to anyone who notices the many literary references in this work and who appreciates Shelley's observation (at the very end of his *Defence of Poetry*) that "poets are the unacknowledged legislators of the world." See Plato, *Republic* 377, 379A, 397E-398A, 607A-D, *Laws* 660E, 661E-663A, 663D-664B, 665C-E; Aristotle, *Politics* 1336a29; Plutarch, *Lives*, p. 51 (the poet Thales and Sparta), pp. 192-93 (the passage among the epigraphs at the head of this book) (we should notice that these works of art are identified by Plutarch as Pericles', not as the artists'; see, also, ibid., p. 233). See Shaftesbury, *Characteristics of Men, Manners, Opinions, Times* (Indianapolis: Bobbs-Merrill, 1964), 1:6-8, 14, 23, 44-45, 50-51, 104, 296-97, 2:296-99; Handel, *Solomon*, act 3; Allan Bloom, *Shakespeare's Politics* (New York: Basic Books, 1964). See, also, chap. 9, n. 20, below, as well as the animated controversy between Allan Bloom and Sigurd Burckhardt in *American Political Science Review* 54 (1960).

"'A great writer,' [A. I. Solzhenitsyn] writes in *The First Circle*, 'is, so to speak, something like a second government. That is why no regime, anywhere, has ever loved its great writers, only its minor ones.'" *Newsweek*, Oct. 19, 1970, p. 67. See, on the authoritative effect on painting of Renoir, Proust, *Remembrance of Things Past*, 1:950.

Among the glass mosaics that have been discovered recently in underwater excavations (directed by Robert L. Scranton, of the University of Chicago) at Kenchreai (near Corinth, Greece) is one "of a large life-size mosaic portrait of a figure labelled 'Homer' in Greek, with some of the characteristics we associate with the figure of the Christ in later Byzantine art." *University of Chicago Magazine*, Jan. 1967, p. 3. I have suggested that this figure (from the third or fourth century A.D.), which anticipates Christian representations of prophets and holy writers, reflects wonderfully the Platonic understanding of the role of the poet as the source of man's information about the activities (as

CHAPTER FIVE, NOTE 133: PAGE 122 553

distinguished from the nature) of the named gods. See, e.g., Plato, *Ion, Republic* 365E, *Gorgias* 523A-524A, 525D-E. That is, Homer was to the Greeks what revelation has been to the Hebrews and the Christians. (I have learned, since making this suggestion, that a figure of Plato himself has been found immediately facing Homer.) Cf. the opening paragraphs of Bacon's essays, "Of Unity of Religion," and "Of Superstition."

See, with respect to these matters, the analysis of Aristotle's *Poetics* by Laurence Berns in the collection of essays, Cropsey, *Ancients and Moderns*. See, also, chap. 9, n. 21, below.

For an account of the place of the poet in a primitive community—of how song may bring meaning and hence reassurance to life—see chapter 4, "The Song of the Forest," and chapter 8, "*Molimo*: the Dance of Death," in Colin M. Turnbull, *The Forest People: A Study of the Pygmies of the Congo* (New York: Doubleday & Co., Anchor Books, 1961). Consider, also, for the kind of threats to the community's integrity which citizens must be aware of even when the law cannot (or, because of its impreciseness, should not) interfere with, these lines from one of Judah Halevi's songs:

> Thou comest to meet me with sweet speeches,
> But within them lie men in wait bearing swords—
> Words wherein stinging bees lurk,
> A honeycomb prickling with thorns.

Three Jewish Philosophers (New York: Harper & Row, 1965), pt. 3, p. 135. See chap. 8, n. 171, below. See Pitt in chap. 7, n. 38, below.

It is salutary to be reminded, as we conclude our discussion here of obscenity, of the sentiments that indignation can voice (cf. Lear's "Touch me with noble anger"):

> One thing, however, isn't said often enough. It is that to grant liberty to the smut peddlers may be justified, on libertarian or even on sociological grounds. But the creation of that kind of smut, even if it is legal, ought to at least remain a shameful profession, and the very interesting question is why the Kenneth Tynans of this world aren't treated to the contempt they deserve, alongside the Danish pornographers. [William F. Buckley, Jr., *Chicago Daily News*, Mar. 10, 1970, p. 16]

(It may be, by the way, that the Danish experiment of virtually unlimited traffic in pornography is, for various peoples, the best available policy in their circumstances. But this does not mean that the suppliers [or steady customers] in such circumstances are not somewhat depraved by transactions of this character. [We should consult Lincoln's comments upon the status of the slave-dealer and the slave-breeder even in a community where slavery is legal. *Complete Works*, 1:194, 218.]) Kenneth Tynan is the once-respectable producer of "Oh! Calcutta!," of which Brendan Gill said in opening and closing his *New Yorker* review (June 28, 1969, pp. 72, 75), "With all my heart, I recommend staying away from [this] slick and repulsive come-on. . . . An audience that sits and listens to such a message is abased and defiled." See chap. 5, n. 147, chap. 8, n. 74, below. (Much the same should be said about narcotics peddlers.)

In any event, to defend either obscenity or censorship today can be embarrassing. Still, it should be recognized that although censorship is not likely to work at this time, our potential censors are usually better people than those who profit from obscenity. Is there not in the deliberate (even gratuitous) affront of obscenity an assault upon the sense of honor of a concerned community? (See chap. 7, n. 59, chap. 8, n. 169, below.)

133. Implicit throughout this section, as well as in the rest of this book, is the distinction (noted elsewhere) between the citizen as one of the rulers (who thereby shares an unabridgeable freedom of speech) and the citizen as one of the ruled or subjects (whose activities are governed by the laws that citizens-as-rulers make). See chap. 4, n. 113, chap. 5, n. 92, above, chap. 8, n. 108, below. Both aspects of the citizen seem to be indicated in the Franklin sentiments quoted in chap. 2, n. 12, above, and commented on in chap. 4, n. 113, chap. 5, n. 56, below. (May not "liberty of the press"

concern itself more than does "freedom of the press" with the right of expression of the subject-aspect of the citizen?)

". . . And thus morality and good government go together. There is no real love of virtue, without the knowledge of public good. And where absolute power is, there is no public." Shaftesbury, *Characteristics*, 1:72. See, also, ibid., 1:75-76, 2:83, 349-51. "The doctrines of Tocqueville's contemporaries are especially pernicious, since they serve to reinforce the feeling of helplessness that characterizes modern man." Marvin Zetterbaum, *Tocqueville and the Problem of Democracy* (Stanford: Stanford University Press, 1967), p. 14. (Perhaps "the feeling of helplessness" is most acutely felt by most men today, on a day-to-day basis, in their dealings with those soulless, computerized monopolies known as "public utilities": it should not be beyond the means of our technology to arrange things so as to restore at least some semblance of competition to these activities and thereby provide modern man somewhat more "choice," and hence apparent "control of his affairs," than he can now believe himself to have in these most "essential" of dealings. See chap. 8, n. 36, below.)

134. Could Congress, pursuant to power it may have under the First Amendment to extend freedom of speech and of the press, prohibit libel or slander suits or make them more difficult to prosecute? Would this in fact protect freedom of speech and of the press? See *New York Times* v. *Sullivan*, 376 U.S. 254 (1964) (chap. 7, n. 81, below); Dilliard, *One Man's Stand for Freedom*, pp. 476-77. (May not Congress even legislate the "clear and present danger" test for the *states* to apply if the states' standard would otherwise be more restrictive of freedom of speech? See chap. 7, n. 82, chap. 8, n. 83, below.)

A bill for a "First Amendment Freedoms Act" was introduced in the Senate on June 16, 1970, "to make it unlawful to interfere in any way with any person's exercise of his constitutional rights of religion, speech, press, assembly, or petition." *Congressional Record*, 116: S9150-S9153 (July 16, 1970). It has received respectable endorsement. See, e.g., ibid., 116: S9850-S9851 (June 25, 1970). But may it not be entrusting the chickens to the tender mercies of the chicken-hawk (otherwise known as the attorney general)? See Joseph Alsop, "Dismal Sign of the Times," *Chicago Sun-Times*, June 19, 1970, p. 76; Plato, *Republic* 343B. Cf. chap. 5, n. 3 (end), above.

See, for their bearing on "group libel" or "race libel" criminal prosecutions, two of the lectures appended to my Ph.D. dissertation, "Notes on the First Amendment": "Principle and Passion: The American Nazi Speaker on the University Campus" and "Neither Black nor White: The Negro in America." See Kalven, *Negro and First Amendment*, p. 7 ff., on the eclipse of *Beauharnais* v. *Illinois*, 343 U.S. 250 (1952). See, also, Street, *Freedom, the Individual and the Law*, p. 150.

135. I merely mention here the regulation of sound trucks and the supervision of the use of parks and streets for speeches or for the distribution of handbills. There is not likely to be any "free speech" problem if the primary concern of the regulation or supervision is with something other than the content of expressions (such as the volume of the sound or the comfort of other citizens). This would apply as well to the regulation of demonstrations in the streets. Other things will no doubt suggest themselves to the reader—such as the granting and protection of copyrights—since I have attempted only to suggest the criteria of "inclusion and exclusion," not to provide an exhaustive catalog. We should notice that one of the criteria is *not* that the government should not "take sides," although there may be a presumption against its doing so in any particular contest or controversy, since government most emphatically does and should "take sides" in what it prescribes for the education of the citizen. I return to this problem in chapters 8 and 9, as well as in chapter 7 (where the role of the states is discussed).

It is appropriate to notice here Kalven's observation ("Upon Rereading Mr. Justice Black on the First Amendment," *U.C.L.A. L. Rev.* 14:428, at 447-48):

> This survey of Justice Black's life work on the Court on behalf of freedom of speech is brought to a poignant conclusion by consideration of one further group of cases, those involving symbolic speech in public or semi-public places. . . . Even though several of his colleagues on the Court are moved to protect it as

CHAPTER FIVE, NOTE 136: PAGE 123   555

speech, the 'speech' in question falls beyond the pale of his generous view of
the reach of the [First Amendment]. In brief, at the close of his great career
it is Justice Black's fate to be confronted with a kind of speech he cannot feel
the first amendment protects. . . . The problem has thus far involved two somewhat different situations best dealt with separately: public issue picketing arising
out of the civil rights movement [*Cox* v. *Louisiana*, 379 U.S. 536 (1965)],
and protest gestures like the sit-in [*Garner* v. *Louisiana*, 368 U.S. 157 (1961);
Brown v. *Louisiana*, 383 U.S. 131 (1966)].

It seems to me, however, that one difficulty with Kalven's "symbolic speech" argument, turning as it does deeds into speech, is that the same approach has been used (as in *Dennis*) and may again be used by apologists for repression to turn speech into deeds. The approach is reflected in Nikolai Lenin's 1920 speech in Moscow,

Why should freedom of speech and freedom of press be allowed? Why should
a government which is doing what it believes to be right allow itself to be criticized? It would not allow opposition by lethal weapons. Ideas are much more
fatal things than guns. Why should any man be allowed to buy a printing press
and disseminate pernicious opinions calculated to embarrass the government?
[Reston, *Artillery of the Press*, p. 1]

It is convenient to notice here still another reservation I have about Kalven's generous salute to Justice Black's "thirty years of noble service." Kalven said, at page 429 of
his article, "In both the popular and the professional eye, Justice Black has inherited
the mantle of Holmes and Brandeis. The [first] amendment now bears his personal trade-
mark as it once did theirs." I believe, however, that Justice Black is in the tradition not
of Justice Holmes but rather of the original Justice Harlan. See, e.g., *Patterson* v. *Colorado*, 205 U.S. 454 (1907). Cf. 366 U.S. 82-97 (1961); Shakespeare, *Julius Caesar*,
act 1, sc. 2, lines 164-67 ("There was a Brutus once . . . ").

136. The most serious problems with television, however, may not be those mentioned here in the text but rather those that are imposed by commercial and technological
considerations. (See *Manchester Guardian Weekly*, Oct. 8, 1959, p. 3: "Fifteen minutes
is such a long lonely stand for anybody [making a political talk on television].")

The studio preparations for a routine television broadcast are fantastically complicated; they have to be seen to be believed. But the following schedule for one *fifteen-
minute* network Sunday evening news program I watched "backstage" in the summer
of 1964 does suggest the complexity (to say nothing of the ultimate lack of seriousness)
of an operation in which the exposure of ideas and politics is measured down to the
second. (My only change in this fifteen-minute schedule is to substitute "Commentator"
for the name listed [a national television "personality"]. I believe the reference to "SCR"
in items 3 and 4 is to Governor William W. Scranton of Pennsylvania, and the reference
to "SF" in item 13 is to the Republican National Convention in San Francisco. Items
1, 7, 15, and 20 are commercials. "VTR" means "Video Tape Recording.")

1. OPEN/BB/FRENCHETTE		:40	:40
2. [Commentator]	live	:20	1:00
3. SCR/LODGE	VTR	:50	1:50
4. [Commentator]	live	:15	2:05
5. SCR/LODGE RALLY		1:15	3:20
6. [Commentator]	live	:20	3:40
7. ARRID		1:00	4:40
8. [Commentator]	live	:20	5:00
9. GOLDWATER		1:15	6:15
10. [Commentator]	live	:25	6:40
11. RHODES	VTR	1:05	7:45
12. [Commentator]	live	:15	8:00
13. SF SITUATIONER		1:15	9:15
14. [Commentator] (Taylor, Malaysia, Cyprus, and Mexico)	live	:45	10:00

15. ANACIN		1:00	11:00
16. [Commentator]	live	:15	11:15
17. MISSISSIPPI	VTR	1:15	12:30
18. [Commentator] (baseball)	live	:30	13:00
19. [Commentator] (think)	live	:30	13:30
20. CARTER'S		:30	14:00
21. CLOSE/CREDITS		:15	14:15

We are told that one half of our people now get all their news from television. Should they be permitted to believe that they are equipped as citizens to judge public affairs on the basis of the information they get in this fashion? The people who thus supply them their information rely on much more than television for their own news: that is, they know better than they do. Should not television itself stress regularly the desirability of supplementing television fare with extensive reading? This would at least have the advantage of impressing upon nonreaders that they should willingly defer to their betters. (See p. 277, above. See, on "access," chap. 8, n. 37, below.)

An appropriate comment on all this is found in the concluding paragraphs of Willa Muir's sensitive study, *Living with Ballads* (London: Hogarth Press, 1965) (dedicated, as is also appropriate, to the memory of her husband, Edwin Muir, one of the best poets of the twentieth century):

> The appearance of a public who pay to be entertained was bound sooner or later to put an end to Ballads, which are made to be sung for love in an intimate circle familiar with the traditional background from which Ballads spring. That background happens to be rural, the old prevailing background of agriculture and gentry which lasted for hundreds of years, and which is now out of date. It cannot be reconstituted, nor can the Ballads which grew out of it. Yet the human need which shaped the Ballads remains, and, likely enough, will shape another culture to express itself in. . . . The Ballad culture is not like a mass-culture, for that term seems to me an abstraction connoting a mass of humanity which is merely recipient and submits to purposive manipulation by various agencies. . . . The kind of culture presented by the cinema or by television, the latter of which especially is closely related to clock-time and the focused eye of consciousness, is also unlike the Ballad culture. Whether mankind will again shape a popular culture that provides as much deep satisfaction as Ballads have done I cannot tell; I can only hope so.

See, also, Edwin Muir, "A Note on the Scottish Ballads," in *Latitudes*, p. 12, as well as his poem, "Complaint of the Dying Peasantry," with its opening stanzas:

> Our old songs are lost,
> Our sons are newspapermen
> At the singers' cost.
> There were no papers when
>
> Sir Patrick Spens put out to sea
> In all the country cottages
> With music and ceremony
> For five centuries.

Edwin Muir, *Collected Poems* (London: Faber & Faber, 1960), p. 262. See, on what may lie ahead for mankind, one of Muir's finest poems, "The Horses," ibid., p. 246. Cf. his "The Animals," ibid., p. 207. See, also, chap. 4, n. 116, above, chap. 8, n. 165, below.

137. That is, the general government would be bound by the First Amendment, the states by the facts of technology. To the extent that federalism makes freedom of speech and of the press feasible (see chapter 7), to that extent television and radio would be in a kind of "no-man's land." The technological facts of life have led, of course, to control by the general government of such facilities (as instruments of commerce), the role of the states having been pretty much set aside. (Would compacts between states be useful here? See chap. 4, n. 19, above.)

The problem here is illustrated by the effect Radio Luxembourg has had in shaping the tastes and thus, to some extent, the morals of the youth of countries such as Norway and Great Britain. (A large-circulation newspaper in London may regularly publish the programs of the commercial Radio Luxembourg station but not those of the much more elevated B.B.C. Third Programme.) What should the authorities responsible for the education of Norwegian youth do—make their own radio programs more attractive to the youth? But it is often impossible to make the salutary appear attractive, or at least more attractive than its irresponsible competitors, in such circumstances. The authorities, it can be presumed, are moved, at least in part, by considerations of what is good for their fellow citizens; the broadcaster, on the other hand, is much more likely to be looking out only for himself (especially when his audience is in another country, thereby liberating him from some of the influences that tend to transform "ought" into "wish"). (It should be conceded that most of American commercial radio broadcasting is worse than Radio Luxembourg.) See Great Britain's "Marine etc. Broadcasting (Offences) Act," which came into force August 15, 1967. Cf. Plato, *Apology* 25C-E, *Republic* 343A-C, 345B-E.

See Hugh C. Greene, "The Future of Broadcasting," *Listener*, Nov. 17, 1960, p. 875; also, Meiklejohn, *Political Freedom*, pp. 86-88.

138. As for the specialness of radio, motion pictures, and television, compare the concurring opinion of Justice Douglas in *Freedman* v. *Maryland*, 380 U.S. 51, 61 (1965), with that of Chief Justice Warren (joined by Justice Douglas) in *Estes* v. *Texas*, 381 U.S. 532, 552 (1965). See Lockhart, Kamisar, and Choper, *Constitutional Law* (Saint Paul: West Publishing Co., 1964), pp. 1128-30. C. L. Sulzberger, in a column on the distorting effects of television both in international relations and domestic politics, quoted from the London *Economist* (*Dallas Morning News*, May 1, 1970, p. 23):

> The United States is the first free country that has ever tried to fight a televised war under the rules of democracy—free reporting, opinion polls, the lot—and if the result has been the unsurprising discovery that people loathe war, that is something that all democracies will have to chew over in the future. . . . One wonders whether in the future a democracy which has uncensored television in every home will ever be able to fight a war, however just.

It is also argued that television, by featuring "Czechoslovakia's brief surge toward liberalism," probably "helped create a situation which led in turn to a major act of international policy, the Russian invasion." (I should add, however, that my own opposition, from the very beginning, to our Indochinese, as distinguished from our Korean, intervention [see chap. 8, n. 150, below], has had nothing to do with television, inasmuch as I rarely watch it. Nor is television likely to affect our recognition that the Israelis, with all their faults, are much more worthy of admiration and support than the governments we have pretended to regard as allies in Saigon.)

Related to these problems is the concern for special protection for children (see Street, *Freedom, the Individual and the Law*, pp. 78, 94; Elmer Gertz, *A Handful of Clients* [Chicago: Follett, 1965], pp. 260, 271), and for the effect of paperback editions of certain books (see Tresolini and Frost, *Cases in American National Government*, p. 178). See chap. 5, n. 125, above.

As for the significance of "limited air rights," it should be noted that, strictly speaking, all resources are limited: there are, for instance, limited supplies of newsprint for presses as well. See Milton Friedman, "How to Free TV," *Newsweek*, Dec. 1, 1969, p. 82. Cf. *Legal and Economic Aspects of Pollution*, pp. 5-6, 16-17, 20, 23-24.

139. The seven categories I have collected in this section, of uses of words that are not included within my understanding of "political matters," touch upon (i) treason, espionage, sabotage, assassination, criminal fraud; (ii) obscenity; (iii) defamation; (iv) contempt of court; (v) offenses affecting military discipline; (vi) contempt of Congress; (vii) problems of radio, motion pictures, and television.

These seven merely illustrate four broader groupings of the uses of language which the student of freedom of speech must fit into his account: (I) Activities that threaten the community as a whole and that would generally be regarded as crimes, including enticements to breaches of the peace. (See pp. 196, 204, below.) Incitements appear here as inducements to do something recognized as criminal. (See chap. 5, n. 66, above.) (II) Activities that are harmful to individual members of the community (such as category ii), and that may be harmful to the community as well (such as category iii). Certain frauds can be included here, as well as various activities subject to the law of torts and contract. (III) Activities that are thought to interfere with the effective operation of the various branches of government (categories iv, v, vi). (IV) Activities that raise special problems because of the means of propagation employed (category vii). The control of sound trucks and of the distribution of literature would be included here as would be the special problems relating to copyrights.

I should stress that this categorization, implicit elsewhere in this book, is set forth here as suggestive. Is "freedom of speech" like "rebellion," "as easily known in fact as it is difficult to define in words"? Burke, *Works*, 2:247.

140. Winston Churchill observed:

> [John Morley's] literary output was very large. He earned his living by his pen. His celebrated essay on "Compromise" was for many years a guide to Liberal youth, and its insistence on the duty of independent individual judgment in every sphere of life and in respect of every creed and institution, is a healthy tonic in these days of totalitarian heresy. [Winston S. Churchill, *Great Contemporaries* (London: Odhams Press, 1949), p. 73 (first published in 1937)]

See chap. 9, n. 33, below, chap. 4, n. 113, above.

It should be evident throughout this book, and is made explicit in chapter 9, below, that there is for man discussion much more important than political discussion. See, e.g., chap. 5, nn. 90, 126, above.

141. William S. Holdsworth, *A History of English Law* (4th ed.; Boston: Little, Brown & Co., 1926), 8:337-38 (citing Stephen, *Hist. Crim. Law*, 2:299-300). The epigraph used for this work is from Roger North: "To say truth, although it is not necessary for counsel to know what the history of a point is, but to know how it stands resolved, yet it is a wonderful accomplishment, and, without it, a lawyer cannot be accounted learned in the law." Cf. C. S. Lewis, *Letters*, p. 125:

> Indeed it is the curse and the fascination of literary history that there are no real beginnings. Take what point you will for the start of some new chapter in the mind and imaginations of man, and you will invariably find that it has always begun a bit earlier; or rather, it branches so imperceptibly out of something else that you are forced to go back to the something else. The only satisfactory opening for any study is the first chapter of Genesis. . . .

Cf., also, *Federalist*, pp. 343 ("Let us consult experience, the guide that ought always to be followed wherever it can be found."), 457 ("the dim light of historical research" is distinguished from "the dictates of reason and good sense"); chap. 2, n. 16, above. See chap. 2, n. 39, chap. 5, n. 36, above.

142. Meiklejohn, *Political Freedom*, p. 21, conceded:

> No one can doubt that, in any well-governed society, the legislature has both the right and the duty to prohibit certain forms of speech. Libellous assertions may be, and must be, forbidden and punished. So too must slander. Words which incite men to crime are themselves criminal and must be dealt with as such. Sedition and treason may be expressed by speech or writing. And, in these cases, decisive repressive action by the government is imperative for the sake of the general welfare. All these necessities that speech be limited are recognized and provided for under the Constitution. They were not unknown to the writers of the First Amendment. . .

CHAPTER FIVE, NOTES 143-45: PAGE 125

Meiklejohn added in 1960, to the text originally published in 1948, the following note:

> I shall be grateful if the reader will eliminate from the sentence, "Sedition and treason may be expressed by speech or writing," the words "Sedition and." "Treason" is a genuine word, with an honest and carefully defined procedural meaning. But "sedition," as applied to belief or communication, is, for the most part, a tricky and misleading word. It is used chiefly to suggest that a "treasonable" crime has been committed in an area in which, under the Constitution, no such crime can exist.

See chap. 5, n. 79, above, chap. 6, n. 61, below. See, also, chap. 5, nn. 119, 120, above.

Is it still true—for it is certainly fitting—that "in the acts of Congress the word 'sedition' appears to occur only in the army and navy articles"? *Encyclopedia Britannica*, 11th ed., s.v. "sedition." (The current edition does not mention this point.) See the discussion in the text at chap. 4, n. 49, above. See, also, chap. 5, nn. 35, 88, above. Cf. U.S. Code, Title 10, sec. 894, Title 18, sec. 3486.

A seaman was charged and tried by the Navy in April, 1970, on the charge of having committed "sedition" by publishing (while stationed at the Pentagon!) an antiwar servicemen's newspaper. *Chicago Tribune*, Apr. 15, 1970, p. 14. He was acquitted of the sedition charge but convicted of others. *Chicago Sun-Times*, Apr. 24, 1970, p. 12.

See Shaftesbury, *Characteristics*, p. 76.

143. Holdsworth, *History of English Law*, 8:338.

Thus, Tunis Wortman, "a New York lawyer prominent in Tammany politics," observed in his *Treatise Concerning Political Enquiry, and the Liberty of the Press* (New York: G. Forman, 1800), p. 262, that the crime of seditious libel could "never be reconciled to the genius and constitution of a Representative Commonwealth." Levy, "Liberty and First Amendment," p. 33, n. 51; p. 35. But whereas Levy and perhaps many other professional historians see this observation as something essentially new in 1798-1800, I consider it as implicit in the regime established for the United States under the Constitution (however many years, decades, or even centuries it may take fully to recognize and to realize the meaning and significance of the regime established pursuant to the Declaration of Independence).

This difference in interpretation (see chap. 5, n. 34, above) may rest ultimately on radically different opinions about the nature of an idea and about what it means to know something. The historian would tend to dismiss my account as, at best, poetic. But I am reminded of Aristotle's observation that poetry is more philosophical than history. *Poetics* 1451b5 (poetry "speaks more of universals, while history speaks more of particulars"). (See, for what may be *the* poet's comment on history, chap. 2, n. 16, above.) Or, to put this in terms more familiar to the lawyer: the common-law judge (despite Justice Holmes's mischievous dictum that the common law "is not a brooding omnipresence in the sky, but the articulate voice of some sovereign or quasi-sovereign that can be identified" [*Southern Pacific Co.* v. *Jensen*, 244 U.S. 205, 222 (1917)]) finds rather than makes the law; he discovers and declares it. See Hobbes, *Leviathan*, I, iv, I, vi, III, xxxxvi; Francis Biddle, *Justice Holmes, Natural Law, and the Supreme Court* (New York: Macmillan Co., 1966), pp. 16-17. Cf. Moses Maimonides, *The Guide of the Perplexed* (Chicago: University of Chicago Press, 1963), p. 507.

See chap. 5, nn. 35, 43, above, chap. 6, n. 50, chap. 8, n. 193, chap. 9, n. 4, below.

144. Holdsworth reports that this view was "gathering strength" during the latter part of the eighteenth century. I have argued in this chapter why it should have gathered strength faster in America than in England. It should be noted, furthermore, that if Holdsworth is correct in his appraisal of this as "the accepted view" when he wrote, then Dicey is mistaken in his discussion of the state of English law at the end of the nineteenth century. See chap. 5, n. 41, above.

145. Freedom of speech and freedom of the press were conceived of as covering different activities. I do not recall an instance of the two being regarded by anyone in the First Congress as speech and assembly were by Sedgwick: ". . . shall we secure the

freedom of speech, and think it necessary, at the same time, to allow the right of assembling? If people freely converse together, they must assemble for that purpose. . . ." (*Annals*, I, p. 731.) He seems, however, to have overlooked the riot acts which were directed specially against assembling and which had given a separate status to this activity (this legislative history is reflected in the use of "peaceably"). Cf. chap. 4, n. 105, above. See, on numbers and "riot," chap. 6, n. 61, below, p. 595, below.

We are now able to use "freedom of speech" to refer to both speech and press because the broad parliamentary privilege of "freedom of speech" has prevailed over the narrower common law notion of "liberty of the press." No distinction in the standards to be applied is indicated by the First Amendment between speech and press, despite the adage recorded by Blackstone, *Laws of England*, 4:80, *Scribere est agere*. (See, also, ibid., 1:217, 2:123-27; Judah Halevi, *The Kuzari* [New York: Schocken, 1964], pp. 126, 229.) Franklin wrote of the famous Reverend Mr. Whitefield,

> His writing and printing from time to time gave great advantage to his enemies; unguarded expressions, and even erroneous opinions, delivered in preaching, might have been afterwards explain'd or qualifi'd by supposing others that might have accompani'd them, or they might have been deny'd; but *litera scripta manet*. [*Autobiography*, p. 124]

(Does Franklin suggest that the preacher would have resorted to equivocation if he could have?)

James Boswell quotes with approval, in the last footnote in his *Life of Samuel Johnson*, Pierre Bayle's distinction "between what a man speaks without preparation, and that which he prepares for the press."

See, also, Burke, *Works*, 3:367-68; Montesquieu, *Spirit of the Laws*, 12:13; Kent, *Commentaries on American Law*, 2:16. See chap. 8, n. 102, below.

146. See the Connecticut statute of 1728 reproduced in chap. 6, sec. 1, above.

147. Justice Holmes did say "*falsely* shouting fire in a theatre." (Italics added.) (See Meiklejohn, *Political Freedom*, p. 39, n. 4; chap. 3, n. 38, above.) See, also, Dilliard, *One Man's Stand for Freedom*, pp. 477-78; chap. 8, n. 177, below. Cf. Tom Stoppard, *Rosencrantz and Guildenstern Are Dead* (beginning of act 2).

May it not be even worse, in some circumstances, to shout fire when there is indeed a fire? See chap. 6, n. 7, chap. 9, n. 27, below.

On the other hand, New York City in 1969 had 72,000 false fire alarms, "five times as many as ten years earlier. Last year, one of every three alarms was false. This year, the number of false alarms is running fifteen percent ahead of last year. Even worse, their frequency is highest in neighborhoods with the greatest need for quick response to firemen." Mervin Block, "Playing with Fire," WNBC-TV editorial, June 19, 1970. (Does not a television statement become "real" only when it is distributed thereafter on the printed page [as is done by WNBC-TV]? Or does such a question merely reveal a "generation gap"? See chap. 5, n. 136, above, chap. 9, n. 17, below.)

I see no "freedom of speech" problem in curtailing the "free expression" of false alarms, just as there is no problem in the regulation of commercial advertisements or in the establishment of "truth-in-lending" requirements for credit operations. The June 19, 1970, WNBC-TV editorial concluded (in an attempt to shape the most immediately relevant public opinion for the misconduct to which it had addressed itself) with an observation that needs wide application if there is to be a revitalization of moral training and of a sense of community in our disturbed cities:

> The Fire Department—with the Board of Education and Police Department—has been trying to teach people, mostly teenagers, not to turn in false alarms. But the most important group of all must be reached to dampen the mischievous spark that burns in many children, a group that has to assume most of the responsibility for the children: parents. They're the people whose help we need.

The editorial had opened with the report that seven children had died in a fire in Brooklyn while the two nearest fire companies were answering a false alarm elsewhere. Thus, an important consideration in justifying restrictions upon how we conduct our business—whether it is that of entertaining ourselves (false alarms) or that of making money (by selling or lending)—is the efficient use of our resources. This is summed up by Hans Zeisel and Paul Boschan, "The Simple Truth-in-Lending," *U. Pa. L. Rev.*, 116 (1968): 799, 829:

> Thus, what on the surface may look like only a plan to protect the unwary borrower is in fact more. The larger function of proper disclosure laws is to bring the decisions of all potential borrowers to an optimum for the economy as a whole. Some will borrow at the offered rate; some will go to another credit source; some will prefer to draw on their cash savings; and some will save before they buy. But the relative proportion of persons making each decision will be closer to the proportions that are optimal for the economy as a whole. Thus, the ultimate function of proper disclosure is to restore the fungible character of credit which it was allowed to lose in the jungle of a hundred individual labels.

Perhaps this is really the "penultimate function": perhaps, that is, we should recognize as the "ultimate function" of our laws the encouragement among us of the virtues (in the case of consumer credit disclosure laws, the virtues of temperance and justice on the part of both borrowers and lenders). See Aristotle, *Nicomachean Ethics* 1179b31-1181b25. See, also, chap. 8, nn. 171, 181, below.

148. Similarly, the effects of fraudulent representations in religious matters (e.g., contributions to the "minister" of a sect) cannot be corrected easily, even while certain kinds of actions (e.g., polygamy), though flowing from sincere beliefs, can be easily controlled. See *Reynolds v. U.S.*, 98 U.S. 145 (1878); *U.S. v. Ballard*, 322 U.S. 78 (1944). (See chap. 5, n. 91, above.) Cf. Hobbes, *Leviathan*, II, 27 (end), III, 36 (end), 39 (end), 42 (beginning), 43 (beginning); Sir James Fitzjames Stephen, *Liberty, Equality, Fraternity* (New York: Holt & Williams, 1873), pp. 59-60 (for a sensible critique of the *Ballard* principle); also, Bernard Taper, "Annals of Crime," *New Yorker*, Jan. 17, 1959, p. 33 ff., esp. p. 58. See, also, Lincoln, *Complete Works*, 2:254, 291, 464, 480-81, 491; Stephen, *An Agnostic's Apology*, pp. 280-81, 283; *Documents of Vatican II*, pp. 681, 683, 698-99. (Hobbes can conveniently distinguish between "religion" and "superstition" [*Leviathan*, chap. 6]: "*Feare* of power invisible, feigned by the mind, or imagined from tales publiquely allowed, RELIGION; not allowed, SUPERSTITION. And when the power imagined, is truly such as we imagine, TRUE RELIGION." One can begin to study this provocative formulation, and hence Hobbes's private opinion on this subject, by considering what could possibly be the status of that "fear of power invisible" which "is truly such as we imagine" but which is not based on tales which are "publiquely allowed." See Aristotle, *Politics* 1328b12-13, 1329a28-34, 1331a24-31, 1335b12-17, 1342b33-35. See, also, chap. 2, n. 38, above.)

149. The distinction between "political" and "nonpolitical" is, in everyday terms, fairly easy to make. We use it, for instance, with respect to employees of the general government regulated by the Hatch Act and with respect to income tax exemptions and deductions. The British with respect to what royalty may comment upon publicly. The observations of Lord Cockburn, reproduced above at p. 383, are instructive: "To see no difference between political and other offenses is the sure mark of an excited or of a stupid head." (See with respect to the content of television advertising, Street, *Freedom, the Individual and the Law*, p. 93.) See chap. 5, n. 127, above.

This is a distinction that is seen even in President Lincoln's instruction to General Grant that he was not to "decide, discuss, or confer upon any political questions" with General Lee. *Complete Works*, 2:656. (See, also, ibid., 2:503-4.) See J. G. Randall, *Constitutional Problems under Lincoln* (Urbana: University of Illinois Press, 1951), p. 184, n. 20, on Vallandigham's case being considered "military" rather than "political." Even the members of my bar admission committee "caught on" to the distinction I was drawing between "political" and "nonpolitical" questions: they realized, that is, the kind of question I would not answer (i.e., about possible political affiliations), perversely devoting themselves to the elaboration of such and leaving the other kind alone. See Appendix F, sec. 3, above. See, also, chap. 2, n. 12, chap. 5, n. 56, above, chap. 6, n. 59, chap. 7, n. 71, chap. 8, nn. 68, 138, 179, below.

A passage from Khrushchev's speech, *Make Fuller Use of Potentialities for Further Progress in Agriculture*, Dec. 25, 1959 (Moscow: Foreign Languages Publishing House, 1960), pp. 26-27, reminds us of the Russians' appreciation of the distinction between "political" and "nonpolitical":

> It should be borne in mind that the farther we advance, and the more impressive our achievements are, the more exacting and irreconcilable will be the attitude of the working people toward shortcomings. Why? Because if there are successes in economic development, the people want to feel them in the shops and in their shopping bags. Our Party gives free play to the initiative of the working people, gives them every opportunity for greater activity so that life in the country may become fuller and better. In our country one can say openly and directly what he thinks, say it to anyone he likes, and everyone to whom questions are addressed must reply to them.

I suspect that Khrushchev believed what he said in the last sentence: he might even have admitted that the fundamental political questions and the plans emanating therefrom were *not* open for discussion but have insisted that all other important questions (particularly with respect to the administration and implementation of the plans accepted) were open. Thus, the ordinary Russian citizen (if anyone can properly be called a "citizen" of a tyranny) would indicate his awareness of the distinction by carefully abstaining in public from any serious political discussion. (The Khrushchev distinction is not a recent one for Russian Communists. Thus Stalin pointed out in 1928, in the course of an attack upon the "kind of 'self-criticism' that the Trotsky opposition was urging upon us recently,"

> A strict distinction must be drawn between this "self-criticism," which is alien to us, destructive and anti-Bolshevik, and our, Bolshevik self-criticism, the object of which is to promote the Party spirit, to consolidate the Soviet regime, to improve our constructive work, to strengthen our economic cadres, to arm the working class. [J. Stalin, *Against Vulgarizing the Slogan of Self-Criticism* (Moscow: Foreign Languages Publishing House, n.d.), pp. 13-14]

One is reminded by the orthodox view of self-criticism of the "suggestion box" of an American business organization. See chap. 8, n. 36, below. Cf. chap. 5, nn. 66, 69, above.)

See Burke, *Works*, 3:370; Richard Henry Lee, *Letters*, p. 458; Bonhoeffer, *No Rusty Swords*, pp. 230, 240-42, 248-49; Kalven, *Negro and First Amendment*, p. 177, n. 82; Sutherland, *Constitutionalism in America*, pp. 116-17.

150. See, e.g., the quotation in the text at chap. 3, n. 23, above. See Rogge, *First and Fifth*, pp. 110-14, for a review of the cases since the Second World War. Rogge, a former assistant United States attorney general in charge of the Criminal Division of the Department of Justice, described at pp. 92-93 his prosecution of the American Nazi sedition case during the Second World War.

It is encouraging to see both the reservations Rogge had at that time about the prosecution of the Nazis and the conclusions he has since reached (on several First Amendment problems) which are similar to those of this book. Thus, he observed at p. 93,

> As a result of his experiences in the [Nazi] sedition case and his reflections on the First Amendment since then, the writer tends to the conclusion that even a conspiracy to cause a violation of the law, if the means to be employed consist of advocacy, should go unpunished. Legislatively, the proscription of such a conspiracy is both unwise and ineffective; and constitutionally, at least so far as the Congress is concerned, it violates the First Amendment. From a federal standpoint, only those conspiracies should be punished where the defendants intend to effectuate them either with acts or with acts as well as advocacy.

See chap. 5, nn. 66, 121, above.

151. Does any other modern language have the alternative provided in English? German has, I believe, only *die Pressefreiheit* for "freedom [or liberty] of the press"; French, only *liberté de la presse*. The alternatives in English draw on two divergent sources and may therefore provide us a richer idea both to think about and to work with.

Eric Partridge's *Origins (A Short Etymological Dictionary of Modern English)* (New York: Macmillan Co., 1939), is suggestive. "Freedom" has in its heritage the connotations of "love," "peace," and perhaps "independence"; "liberty" may have in its heritage the connotations of "people," "not-slave," and perhaps "growth" (and is akin to the Greek *eleutheros*). (See Montesquieu, *Spirit of the Laws*, 30:20 [on *fredum*]; Hayek, *Constitution of Liberty*, p. 422, n. 5. *Eleutheros* connotes "free" in the sense of "not in bondage." Richard Cunliffe, *A Lexicon of the Homeric Dialect* [Norman: University of Oklahoma Press, 1963].) Are not these differences reflected in the distinction drawn in the quotation at the end of this section? (" . . . [T]he central issue between Roosevelt and Hitler by mid-1943 was the meaning and application of the old Jeffersonian issue of liberty, or, in the more modern and positive connotation, *freedom*." Burns, *Roosevelt: The Soldier of Freedom*, p. 387)

See, on *parresia*, page 275, above.

Cf. chap. 5, n. 94, above (on ancient Chinese and modern Greek).

152. A speech of September 10, 1959, by President Eisenhower, for example, used "freedom" a dozen times to one use of "liberty."

153. But what of "life, liberty, or property" in the Fifth and Fourteenth Amendments? (One curious feature of constitutional law today is the strikingly different meanings of "liberty" in the two amendments. See Justice Holmes, dissenting, *Gitlow* v. *New York*, 268 U.S. 652, 672 [1925]; Justice Jackson, dissenting, *Beauharnais* v. *Illinois*, 343 U.S. 250, 291 [1952]. See chap. 5, n. 117, above, chap. 7, n. 3, chap. 8, n. 83, below.)

154. But in H. von Holst's *John C. Calhoun*, American Statesmen (Boston: Houghton Mifflin Co.) published in 1892, "liberty" is used almost exclusively both by Holst and in the quotations from Calhoun. This may be because it is often presented there in opposition to "slavery." See Plato, *Republic* 557B-C.

155. See chap. 2, sec. 1, above.

Cf. Hayek, *Constitution of Liberty*, p. 421, n. 1:

> There does not seem to exist any accepted distinction in meaning between the words "freedom" and "liberty," and we shall use them interchangeably. Though I have a personal preference for the former, it seems that "liberty" lends itself less to abuse. It could hardly have been used for that "noble pun" (Joan Robinson, *Private Enterprise or Public Control* [London, 1943]) of Franklin D. Roosevelt's when he included "freedom from want" in his conception of liberty.

(See chap. 8, n. 31, below.)

The need to restrain "liberty" seems to be acknowledged by the use in Jefferson's *Notes on the State of Virginia* of "temperate liberty" and in *Federalist* No. 53 of "rational liberty." (Cf. Blackstone, *Laws of England*, 3:29, the lawyers' "due freedom of speech in the lawful defence of their clients.") Patrick Henry observed in the Virginia Ratifying Convention that the friends of the proposed Constitution stressed "union" and "justice," the foes, "liberty." Elliot, *Debates*, 3:313. Rousseau believes "the essence of the body politic to lie in the reconciliation of obedience and liberty." *Social Contract*, I, xiii. See Plato, *Republic* 564A: "Probably, then, tyranny develops out of no other constitution than democracy—from the height of liberty, I take it, the fiercest extreme of servitude." See chap. 5, nn. 94, 124, above, chap. 7, n. 59, below.

See chap. 9, n. 39, below.

156. English "liberty" (as well as "freedom"), we should notice, can include the dimension seen in the passage from Cicero (in the text at chap. 2, n. 11, above). Thus, John Buchan could say of Oliver Cromwell:

> . . . Liberty was his ultimate goal, the liberty of God's people where all were free because all were servants of the same high purpose, and Milton was not

wrongly inspired when he hailed him as *patriae liberator, libertatis creator, custosque idem et conservator*. But liberty to him meant not a mechanic thing measured out in statutory doses, still less a disordered license, but the joyous collaboration of those whom the truth had made free, "a partnership," in Burke's great words, "in every virtue and in all perfection." [*Oliver Cromwell* (London: Holder & Staughton, 1934), p. 523]

The "two writers" quoted in the text are Robert Graves and Alan Hodge, *The Reader over Your Shoulder: A Handbook for Writers of English Prose* (New York: Macmillan Co., 1961), p. 413. Cf. chap. 5, n. 94, above ("do what you are told").

Ralph Barton Perry distinguished between "freedom" as rightness of choice and "liberty" as absence of restraining circumstances. Richard P. McKeon, *Freedom and History* (New York: Noonday Press, 1952), p. 54. See John D. Godsey, ed., *Karl Barth's Table Talk* (Richmond, Va.: John Knox Press, 1963), p. 77: "The State must protect the *freedom* (not 'liberty,' which is a strange Latin word) of man, which means also responsibility. Freedom and responsibility are not opposed, but go together." Also pp. 13, 37. See, for still another distinction between "freedom" and "liberty," Meiklejohn, *Political Freedom*, pp. xv-xvi, 36-37, 38, 52. Cf. chap. 8, n. 3, below.

See, also, Shakespeare, *Julius Caesar*, act 3, sc. 1, lines 103-19; chap. 9, n. 9, below (Milton's "honest liberty of free speech"); Bloom, *Shakespeare's Politics*, pp. 92-105.

CHAPTER VI

1. Other circumstances may call for other principles. I have attempted, since the colonels' coup which imposed a tyranny upon Greece in April, 1967, to apply to the affairs of that country what I have learned in my own. (See chap. 4, n. 101, above.) See, for an indication of what can and cannot be exported of "American freedom," my discussions of Greek affairs which have been reprinted in Volume 115 of the *Congressional Record* at pages E1875 (Mar. 11, 1969), E2631 (Apr. 2, 1969), E2632 (Apr. 2, 1969), E5156 (June 23, 1969), E5978 (July 15, 1969), E6294 (July 28, 1969) and E10873 (Dec. 20, 1969), and in Volume 116 of the *Record* at pages E935 (Feb. 16, 1970), E1818 (Mar. 10, 1970), and S7535 (May 20, 1970). See, also, chap. 4, n. 49, chap. 5, nn. 24, 69, 94, 124, above, chap. 7, nn. 27, 67, 78, 81, chap. 8, nn. 18, 46, 57, 161, 165, 179, chap. 9, nn. 1, 34, below.

Thus, I have had occasion to observe, in my "Guide to Contemporary Greece," *Congressional Record* 115: E6294 (July 28, 1969),

> . . . The most serious indictment one might make of pre-1967 Greece is that such people as [the colonels now ruling the country] were permitted to remain in the Army, that they were given an opportunity to seize power, that they could try to seize power and that they could get away with it. It is to be hoped that the Greeks, especially the legitimate political and military leaders of that country, have learned the appropriate lessons from that experience. One lesson is that decent Greeks of all parties and allegiances have much more in common than any of them have in common with the kind of men who are apt to seize power if decent men are not moderate in their political differences. It is also to be hoped that the United States will be moved by this experience to reflect on whether its policies and attitudes in Greece helped prepare the ground upon which the colonels were able to execute their conspiracy.

See the quotation from Strauss, chap. 4, n. 103, above.

Meiklejohn addressed himself, at page xvi of the 1960 Foreword to his *Political Freedom: The Constitutional Powers of the People* (New York: Harper & Bros., 1960), to a question put him by Malcolm Sharp (in the Foreword prepared by Sharp):

> You say that teachers and others in Germany under occupation after the Second World War had no moral claim to the kind of freedom of speech protected by our Constitution, since they were not part of a self-governing community. Does this observation indicate a significant general principle? What other cases of the sort might be considered or imagined?

CHAPTER SIX, NOTE 1: PAGE 134

This is a question I had urged upon Sharp, since I had found that some readers of the 1948 edition of Meiklejohn's book had overlooked this qualification. See, ibid., pp. 84-85. The New England town meeting can serve as Meiklejohn's model.

A question often urged upon me is whether Americans should "support" the present Greek government by visiting that country as tourists, especially since it has been long established that that regime deliberately uses torture to secure its power. Thus, a sensitive art historian (but not a Jew) who had conducted himself honorably in Germany during the 1930s has written me these observations (on the eve of his own visit to Greece):

> I wonder whether the poor people are happy or resentful with foreigners coming to Greece these days. In Nazi Germany we resented tourists happily coming to, say, Bayreuth to enjoy Wagner, with Hitler thrown in. How can one make clear that one visits Greece, the people, art, country, and not the colonels?

There *is* a problem here since the colonels do parade the growth of tourism as proof of their success in making the country attractive to foreigners seeking a place where they can safely enjoy themselves.

I have visited Greece annually for almost a decade. I have never discouraged visitors since the colonels' coup (except members of my own family: I do not intend to offer the Greek tyrants, who have been rather displeased by my publications about them, an opportunity to seize hostages [on trumped-up charges] in order to coerce my "good behavior" either during my next visit there or upon my return home). But I have urged visitors to Greece not to go merely as self-centered or uninformed tourists: they should be prepared to make prudent but persistent efforts to talk to Greeks about the regime, to offer what information and comfort they can to that suppressed people (including lawful materials about Greece published abroad), and to publicize when they return home what they manage to learn about that country (especially since the support of our government has been essential to the continuation of the colonels' regime). That is, I have urged prospective visitors to Greece to do for that people what we would want done for ourselves in like circumstances: we can also learn thereby what to be vigilant about in our own community.

The position I have taken about visitors to Greece is essentially that indicated in a letter of mine published in the *Observer* (London), Aug. 14, 1960, during a six-month family camping tour of Europe in the spring and summer of 1960:

> I should like, as a recent visitor to the Soviet Union, to take issue with Mr. John Wain's suggestion that Western tourists provide that country with "unpaid propaganda work when they get home."
>
> Almost invariably the fellow tourists with whom my wife, children and I exchanged impressions at the end of each day shared our serious reservations about the dreary, uncomfortable, restricted and monumentally tasteless life the Russian people seem to have had imposed upon them. The tourists with whom we came in contact most were young people using the camping facilities we lived in outside Minsk, Smolensk and Moscow.
>
> Visits by tourists provide a valuable source of information for both the West and the Russians. The eagerness of Soviet citizens to talk to and question visitors reflects their interest in the outside world.
>
> I should like to urge increased contacts of the kind that only tourists can make. I say this despite the fact I was expelled from the Soviet Union last month, midpoint in a two-week visit, for having presumed first, to photograph and then to attempt to counsel three American and English students detained (and subsequently expelled) for allegedly distributing copies of the United States State Department exchange magazine, *Amerika*, on a Moscow street.

I was declared guilty during my trial (the afternoon of July 28, 1960) of having "subverted public order." (I myself had neither previously known the detained students nor attempted to distribute any of the magazines they did have: I got "involved" upon trying to suggest a prudent course of action for them to follow after the authorities pounced. Their rashness got us all in trouble—and gave me a valuable opportunity to confirm what I had heard about Russian police practices and judicial "procedures.") See, for more information about this episode, Anastaplo, "Notes on the First Amendment," pp. 838-43, an appendix which is prefaced by an observation of Lord Cockburn's in 1853: "In a country like Russia where no one is safe in saying anything against the Government, or like America where every one seems to be safe in saying anything he pleases, obedience to the law is easy." (See, also, Malcolm P. Sharp, "The Conservative Fellow Traveller," *U. Chicago L. Rev.*, 30 [1963]: 704, 718-19.)

The Greece of the colonels is much more like Russia (of the Czars, both extinct and contemporary) than it is like America. The Greek tyrants, however, are more dependent upon and hence more responsive to American public opinion than are their Russian counterparts. See, e.g., my comparison of the effectiveness in Athens of American diplomats with the effectiveness there of foreign correspondents, which is found in a memorandum of October 12, 1970 (*Congressional Record* 116: E10520), "American Aid and Greek Tyranny." This memorandum was prepared as a result of my most recent adventures in Greece. (One does acquire a sense of some obligation toward a country which one visits often or from which one has otherwise gotten much. Cf. chap. 8, n. 100, below.) These adventures saw me deported from Greece to Rome in September, 1970 (for what I had written theretofore) and then invited by the Greek government to return after my fellow foreign correspondents in Athens had intervened on my behalf.

I should note that the efforts I have made to explain the Greek tyranny to Americans (who *are* partly responsible for the state of affairs there) have been endorsed by virtually every pre-1967 Greek leader, whether liberal or conservative, whether royalist or antiroyalist. (That is, the legitimate leaders of that country, unlike the colonels, do not regard my efforts as illegitimate "foreign interference in Greek domestic affairs.") I should also note that I did not concern myself with Greek political affairs before 1967 (see chap. 7, n. 100, below) and do not expect to be obliged to continue to do so upon the reestablishment of genuine parliamentary government in Greece. I am afraid, however, that the colonels' regime (which is actively supported by most influential Greek-Americans) is likely to remain in power a long time: things have settled down to a dreary sameness, with little to report from year to year. Tyrannies *can* be tiresome.

2. *Federalist* No. 84. The possibility that a prohibition implies the existence otherwise of a power in Congress to deal with such matters is addressed in the statement prefixed to the set of amendments sent to the states for ratification in 1789, which includes the description of the proposed amendments as "declaratory and restrictive clauses."

See p. 292, above. See, also, chap. 3, n. 29, above, chap. 6, n. 63, below.

3. See chap. 6, n. 37, below. The complications of preparing and adopting amendments prior to ratification would have proved dangerous to the success of the ratification campaign. See Joseph Story, *Commentaries on the Constitution of the United States* (2d ed.; Boston: Little, Brown & Co., 1851), chap. 44, secs. 1858-68. See, also, Woodrow Wilson, *The Political Thought of Woodrow Wilson*, ed. E. David Cronon (Indianapolis: Bobbs-Merrill, 1965), pp. 508, 536.

It was observed in *The Letters of Brutus*, no. 14 (*New York Journal*, Feb. 28, 1788): "It has been the fate of [any clause of the proposed Constitution] against which unanswerable objections have been offered, to be explained different ways, by the advocates and opponents to the constitution."

See, for the opponents' alarmist interpretations of the extent of powers implicitly given the general government by the Preamble and by the Necessary and Proper Clause, *Letters of Brutus*, no. 5 (*New York Journal*, Dec. 13, 1787), no. 6 (Dec. 27, 1787), and no. 12 (Feb. 7, 1788). See, also, chap. 2, n. 37, above, chap. 8, nn. 83, 89, below.

4. Indeed, insofar as this chapter is concerned with the discussion of the power of Congress (independent of the First Amendment) to abridge freedom of speech, Publius's argument would suggest that we could proceed as directly to the point as the eighteenth-century guide to Iceland which has in the chapter, "Concerning Owls in Iceland," one sentence only: "There are no Owls in Iceland." *Manchester Guardian Weekly*, June 26, 1958, p. 5. Cf. H. L. Mencken, *A New Dictionary of Quotations* (New York: Knopf, 1942), p. 566 (s.v. Iceland).

May not much of not only this chapter, but even of the book as a whole, be considered similarly superfluous by the citizen who simply considers himself entitled to hear all possible arguments before he exercises his sovereign judgment? See chap. 4, n. 113, above, chap. 6, n. 78, below.

Much of the argument of this chapter is summed up in chap. 6, n. 70, below.

See, for a systematic introduction to the Constitution, my lecture, "The American Constitution of 1787: Form and Matter," in "Notes on the First Amendment" (Ph.D. diss., University of Chicago, 1961), p. 531.

5. Edmund Burke, *Works*, World Classics (London: Oxford University Press, 1930), 3:364, explained:

> I have always understood, that a superintendence over the doctrines as well as the proceedings of the courts of justice, was a principal object of the constitution of this House; that you [the House of Commons] were to watch at once over the lawyer and the law; that there should be an orthodox faith as well as proper works: and I have always looked with a degree of reverence and admiration on this mode of superintendence. For being totally disengaged from the detail of juridical practice, we come something perhaps the better qualified, and certainly much the better disposed, to assert the genuine principles of the laws; in which we can, as a body, have no other than an enlarged and a public interest. . . . So that with our minds perfectly disengaged from the exercise, we may superintend the execution of the national justice. . . .

See chap. 5, n. 107, above, chap. 8, n. 88, below.

See, on whether the common law is one of "the Laws of the United States," *U.S. v. Hudson and Goodwin*, 7 Cranch [U.S.] 32 (1812). See, on the development of the common law in America, Daniel J. Boorstin, *The Americans: The National Experience* (New York: Random House, 1965), pp. 35-42. See, also, chap. 4, n. 52, above.

6. William W. Crosskey, *Politics and the Constitution in the History of the United States* (Chicago: University of Chicago Press, 1953), pp. 767-68. The omitted footnote is discussed in chap. 6, n. 11, below. More detail on the calumnies referred to by Crosskey is provided in chap. 6, n. 23, below. (The next quotation in the text is from ibid., p. 770.) See chap. 6, n. 33, below, for another defender of the Sedition Act.

I use Crosskey's discussion as my point of departure. I can only indicate difficulties in Crosskey's views, at least as they bear on freedom of the press; I cannot demontrate the contrary. Still, Crosskey is deservedly the best-known exponent today of the view that there are, under the Constitution, national common-law crimes. See Crosskey, "Mr. Chief Justice Marshall," in Allison Dunham and Philip B. Kurland, eds., *Mr. Justice* (Chicago: University of Chicago Press, 1964), pp. 8-11, 28 (n. 12).

Robert L. Stern (who was then first assistant to the solicitor general) opened his review of Crosskey's work,

> When I had finished this two-volume work, I did not know whether *Politics and the Constitution* was (1) a magnificent feat of legal and historical scholarship, the greatest contribution to constitutional law since the Constitution itself, or (2) a tremendous but untrustworthy job of research and analysis in support of a particular theory as to what the Constitution ought to mean or must have been intended to mean. The work is devoted to proving that ever since about 1800 the most important portions of the Constitution having to do with the distribution of power between state and nation have either been completely misunderstood or intentionally misconstrued. [*Northwestern U. L. Rev.* 49 (Mar.-Apr. 1954): 107]

John P. Frank opened his review of the work with the observation that Crosskey's "basic technique is acute intellectual analysis of the Constitution and its language; his greatest single contribution as a theorist may be that he has actually read the document under analysis and thought about *it*, rather than about the gloss put on it." Ibid., p. 132. See, also, the reviews by Charles E. Clark and others, *U. Chicago L. Rev.* 12 (1953): 1; by Malcolm P. Sharp, *Columbia L. Rev.* 54 (1954): 439. Cf. chap. 3, n. 23, above.

One student of the Alien and Sedition Acts of 1798, on the other hand, considered Crosskey's materials bearing on seditious libel as the "least reliable" of those he had considered, attributing to him a "devil theory of constitutional development. . . ." James Morton Smith, *Freedom's Fetters: The Alien and Sedition Laws and American Civil Liberties* (Ithaca: Cornell University Press, 1956), p. 445. I, on the other hand, am much more disposed to say of Crosskey's entire work what Walter Berns said of the Crosskey "argument that the privileges and immunities referred to [in Article IV, section 2, of the Constitution include] the first eight amendments to the Constitution," that it "is sufficiently persuasive to merit close study" (Walter Berns, *Freedom, Virtue and the First Amendment* [Baton Rouge: Louisiana State University Press, 1957], p. 102. Cf. Boorstin, *The Americans*, p. 493. See chap. 4, n. 109, above.) My own interpretation may be considered more of an "angel theory of constitutional development." See chap. 7, n. 59, below. Cf. chap. 2, n. 1, above.

I should add that I know from experience how thorough Crosskey was: whenever I have tracked down an obscure publication on constitutional law or history in the University of Chicago Library, the most recent and often the only name on the card (many years before) has usually been Crosskey's. Cf. chap. 2, n. 16, above. See chap. 6, n. 50, below. See, also, chap. 5, n. 88, above, chap. 8, n. 83, below.

7. It had been recognized at common law that truth could be harmful to the stability of government. It may be true, for example, that the king is dishonest: this assertion could be more harmful to his authority with the people than would such a statement about an honest king, since in the former case the assertion might be particularly difficult to counteract.

> . . . The old maxim, "the greater the truth the greater the libel," has a true side to it, and when it applies it is obvious that an opinion is silenced without any assumption of infallibility. The opinion that a respectable man of mature years led an immoral life in his youth may be perfectly true, and yet the expression of that opinion may be a crime, if it is not for the public good that it should be expressed. [James Fitzjames Stephen, *Liberty, Equality, Fraternity* (New York: Holt & Williams, 1873), p. 38]

See William Blackstone, *Commentaries on the Laws of England*, 4:123-24; James Kent, *Commentaries on American Law* (New York: O. Halsted, 1826), 2:18-19; Story, *Commentaries on the Constitution*, chap. 44, sec. 1890; chap. 5, n. 61, above. Cf. Plato, *Republic* 414D-E; chap. 9, n. 27, below. See, also, chap. 5, n. 5, above.

8. Crosskey, in his analysis and defense of the Sedition Act of 1798, did not consider the First Amendment as having drastically modified the common law of seditious libel. But consider how extensively he considered "freedom of speech, or of the press" to reach, so far as to call into question "governmental control" over such agitation as had led to Shays's Rebellion. Crosskey, *Politics and the Constitution*, pp. 1060-61 (reproduced in the text at chap. 5, n. 88, above). Cf. chap. 6, n. 28, below. See, also, chap. 7, n. 99, chap. 8, n. 83, below.

Crosskey's position on freedom of speech under the Constitution is discussed in Malcolm Sharp, "The Old Constitution," *U. Chicago L. Rev.* 20 (1953): 529, 531.

9. U.S., *Statutes at Large* (Boston: Little & Brown, 1845), 1:596-97. (Italics added) This version of the text reads, in section 3, "And be it further enacted and declared. . . ." The Alien Act is at U.S., *Statutes at Large*, 1:570-71. I have copied the text of the Sedition Act from *Annals*, V, pp. 3776-77 (published in 1857). (The Sedition Act was enacted July 14, 1798. The Alien Act, which may be found at *Annals*, V, pp. 3745-46, was enacted June 25, 1798.) Kalven has said of the Sedition Act of 1798 that it is "a perfect expression of the doctrine of seditious libel." Harry Kalven, Jr., *The Negro and the First Amendment* (Chicago: University of Chicago Press, 1966), p. 18. See Kent, *Commentaries on American Law*, 2:24; Arthur E. Sutherland, *Constitutionalism in America: Origin and Evaluation of Its Fundamental Ideas* (New York: Blaisdell Publishing Co., 1965), pp. 253-60.

CHAPTER SIX, NOTES 10-14: PAGE 139   569

The Smith Act (enacted in 1940) may be found in chap. 3, n. 18, above. (See, on a controversy about Alexander Hamilton's "real views" on the Alien and Sedition Acts of 1798, Frederick B. Tolles's letter, *New York Times Book Review*, Oct. 21, 1956. See, also, chap. 5, n. 43, above.)

Three of the four sections of the Sedition Act of 1798 have been reproduced in the text. Section 1, which was not a matter of contention in the controversy, read:

> Be it enacted, &c., That if any persons shall unlawfully combine or conspire together, with intent to oppose any measure or measures of the Government of the United States, which are or shall be directed by proper authority, or to impede the operation of any law of the United States, or to intimidate or prevent any person holding a place or office in or under the Government of the United States, from undertaking, performing, or executing, his trust or duty; and if any person or persons, with intent as aforesaid, shall counsel, advise, or attempt to procure, any insurrection, riot, unlawful assembly or combination, whether such conspiracy, threatening, counsel, advice, or attempt, shall have the proposed effect or not, he or they shall be deemed guilty of a high misdemeanor, and on conviction, before any court of the United States having jurisdiction thereof, shall be punished by a fine not exceeding five thousand dollars, and by imprisonment during a term not less than six months, nor exceeding five years; and, further, at the discretion of the court, may be holden to find sureties for his good behaviour in such sum, and for such time, as the said court may direct. [*Annals*, V, p. 3775]

It should be noticed that the fine and term of imprisonment permitted under section 1 are more than double that under the controversial section 2. See, with respect to "counsel, advise, or attempt to procure," chap. 5, n. 66, above, chap. 6, n. 38, below.

10. There is, in the 1808 *Compiled Laws*, a 1756 provision respecting defamation—but defamation only of courts, it seems, not of other officers of the government. It is unlikely that libel was limited to this (and the word *libel* is not mentioned). "Libellers" are mentioned in another act, not to establish the crime, but (it seems) to make special provisions against disturbance of the peace by libelers.

11. Crosskey, in the footnote I omitted (at p. 136 of the text, above) from p. 767 of his book, argued that Congress may have done as much as it did because of doubt expressed on circuit by Justice Chase (of the Supreme Court of the United States) as to the existence of a national common law. *U.S. v. Worrall*, 2 Dall. [U.S.] 384 (1798). (Cf. *Annals*, VI, p. 416.) Is this to read the Sedition Act as in effect ratifying Justice Chase's doubt?

See chap. 5, n. 94, above, chap. 6, nn. 15, 60, below.

12. *Annals*, V, 1st sess., pp. 3687, 3689, 3693; 2d sess., pp. 3704, 3711, 3717, 3721, 3744, 3777; 3rd sess., pp. 3798, 3933, 3939, 3995.

13. *Annals*, V, p. 3795. Unauthorized communication with foreign states was regarded by the Sedition Act Congress as interference with the conduct of foreign relations, not as an essential part of the self-government in which citizens may of right participate. See chap. 4, n. 59, above.

The Sedition Act of 1798 was entitled, "An Act, in addition to the act, entitled, 'An act for the punishment of certain crimes against the United States.'" The original act thereby added to was enacted in the First Congress. *Annals*, I, p. 2215.

14. See the discussion in chap. 5, n. 44, about the difficulty of repealing the *De Scandalis Magnatum* statute in Virginia. In any event, certain legislation deals with subjects over which the Congress should retain control. Thus, Tucker observed,

> If the House passed a perpetual revenue law, which had not an immutable object, they would abridge their own power, and destroy one of the great privileges of the people. Every bill of this nature, more or less, narrows the powers of this House, and throws it into the hands of the Executive and a minority of the Senate.... [*Annals*, I, p. 361]

Thus, today, it is much more difficult to repeal the Smith Act than it would be to block the extension of such an act upon its expiration. See, for an account of the successful effort to prevent congressional nullification of the decision in *Pennsylvania* v. *Nelson*, 350 U.S. 497 (1956) (see chap. 7, n. 76, below), Donald H. Riddle, "How to Stop a Bill," in R. J. Tresolini and R. T. Frost, *Cases in American National Government and Politics* (Englewood Cliffs, N.J.: Prentice-Hall, 1966), p. 114.

15. See chap. 6, n. 34, below. Did the expiration of this act implicitly nullify any preexisting common-law crime of sedition? Even if the act was phrased as it was partly because of the doubts Justice Chase had expressed, the failure of those who disagreed with Justice Chase to preserve the liberalizing provisions in section 3 upon the extinction of the act suggests there should be no further concern about seditious libel in the federal courts. See chap. 6, n. 37, below.

16. The opening sections of "An Act for the punishment of certain crimes against the United States" (of Apr. 30, 1790; *Annals*, I, p. 2215) provided,

> Be it enacted, &c., That if any person or persons, owing allegiance to the United States of America shall levy war against them, or shall adhere to their enemies, giving them aid and comfort within the United States or elsewhere, and shall be thereof convicted, on confession in open court, or on the testimony of two witnesses to the same overt act of the treason whereof he or they shall stand indicted, such person or persons shall be adjudged guilty of treason against the United States, and shall suffer death.
>
> Sec. 2. And be it further enacted, That if any person or persons, having knowledge of the commission of any of the treasons aforesaid, shall conceal, and not as soon as may be, disclose and make known to the President of the United States, or some one of the judges thereof, or to the President or Governor of a particular State, or some one of the judges or justices thereof, such person or persons, on conviction, shall be adjudged guilty of misprision of treason, and shall be imprisoned not exceeding seven years, and fined not exceeding one thousand dollars.

Cf. chap. 7, n. 52, below. See chap. 5, n. 118, above, chap. 6, nn. 30, 34, below.

17. The Judiciary is not mentioned in the Sedition Act of 1798, only the government in general, the President, and Congress (or the houses thereof). Was there sufficient power inherent in the courts for them to protect themselves? Was it necessary to define and establish the crime (with respect to the legislature and executive) because of the shift from royalist to republican institutions? But why had not this shift eliminated this crime in Connecticut as well? Perhaps because the crime continued there was primarily against the state government, whereas in the country at large it would have had to continue against the government which had come to reform the central monarchical government? The Connecticut government was so little changed by the Revolution that the royal charter was not replaced by a new constitution until 1818.

The general government was, in effect, more revolutionary than the state governments: it is, after all, *the* government resulting from and decisively dependent upon discussion. See Tocqueville, *Democracy in America* (New York: Random House, Vintage Books, 1954), 1:117-18; cf. ibid., 1:42, 58, 60. (The states, it seems to have been understood, would continue to have, but for the Constitution, all the typical powers of government. The concern of Congress in the 1790s would not have been, therefore, to provide the states means of defending themselves but rather to curtail the powers of the states so as to assure not only that the general government could function but also that the states would conform to standards and practices appropriate to republican government. See chap. 6, n. 27, below. Cf. chap. 4, n. 53, above.)

18. See Editor's Note, 1821 Connecticut Code, p. 8. The tendency had been by then to put all crimes in statutory form and make them more certain. But some remained uncodified.

19. Crosskey, *Politics and the Constitution*, pp. 1356-57. I do not presume to determine here whether there was intended a *general* national common law. My concern has

been, instead, to examine the evidence that has been advanced in support of the proposition that the Sedition Act of 1798 implied a national common-law crime of seditious libel. The common law did provide the "substratum" of national laws, at least in the sense that terms, models, and forms were drawn from the common law in devising those laws. See, e.g., *Annals*, VI, pp. 417-18, 420-22, 948-49. (Was the question of a "national common law" implied in the removal power controversy in the First Congress? See chap. 2, n. 34, above.)

See, on Marshall and the Alien and Sedition Laws, Robert K. Faulkner, *The Jurisprudence of John Marshall* (Princeton: Princeton University Press, 1968), pp. 15-17, 87-88, 171-73. See, also, the discussion in his text at note 94 by Walter Berns, "Freedom of the Press and the Alien and Sedition Laws: A Reappraisal," *Supreme Court Review* (1970); chap. 6, n. 63, below.

20. Whether there was a national common law, there would still be (as we have seen) the vulnerability of the common-law crime of sedition, at least as known in England, to the demands and spirit of republican government. See the discussion in the text at chap. 4, n. 70, above.

21. See chap. 5, nn. 57, 79, above. See, also, chap. 6, n. 30, below.

22. The Sedition Act of 1798 dealt with the press, not with speech, thereby reflecting the common-law approach to these matters. (*Utter* in section 2 of the act means *distribute* or *circulate*, not *speak*. See *Annals*, I, p. 2218 [sec. 14].)

Did the common law remain unchanged with respect to speech? Or was there any "liberty of speech" in the common-law sense? See chap. 5, nn. 23, 28, 43, above.

23. See chap. 6, n. 3, above.

If the Sedition Act is seen as evidence of the meaning of the First Amendment, in that it reflects popular understanding of "freedom of the press," its early and unlamented end is even more telling evidence of the general popular understanding. The act had been enacted by a small margin (44-41) in the House of Representatives. (The margin in the Senate was much larger, 17-5. *Annals*, V, p. 609. Does not the House vote, reflecting more than the Senate the sentiments of the populous states, anticipate the support Jefferson would have two years later [1800] in the Electoral College [where the population of states makes itself felt]?) Would it have passed the House if an early expiration date had not been provided for?

The abuses of freedom of the press which defenders of the Sedition Act declared themselves concerned about are suggested in remarks by Harrison G. Otis (of Massachusetts) in the House of Representatives in January, 1801 (see, also, pp. 136-37, above):

> Mr. Chairman, I pity the blindness of that man who does not perceive that the press is the engine which is probably destined to overturn the Government of this country. It has been instrumental, indeed, of the greatest benefits to mankind, by the destruction of systems founded in civil and religious tyranny, but it may be rendered not less formidable to governments which have the freedom and happiness of man for their basis. In no country was a more systematical and inveterate design to destroy a government by means of the press manifested than it is in ours. There is nothing sacred in virtue, nor fair in character, nor endeared by services, which does not fall a prey to the insatiable fury of certain printers and their abettors. The immortal WASHINGTON has been charged with murder, and with speculating in the funds with the public money; the President of the United States has been accused of designs to change the Constitution, to establish monarchy, and to maintain himself in place by an army; the late Secretary of State has been represented as a peculator; the late Secretary of the Treasury, a man who is an ornament to his country, has been stigmatized as the felonious burner of public offices and records. No mercy has been observed in the violation of truth and decency; no character has escaped, unless protected by its own congenial infamy and baseness. Yet, sir, these are offences which we have no power to punish! These are merely the feverish symptoms of liberty, which truth alone is sufficient to allay! [*Annals*, VI, 955-56]

See, also, chap. 2, n. 6, above, chap. 6, n. 66, chap. 8, nn. 172, 173, below. Cf. *Annals*,

VI, pp. 973-75: a defense of himself by one of the victims of the Sedition Act of 1798.

24. Arthur M. Schlesinger, *Prelude to Independence: The Newspaper War on Britain, 1764-1776* (New York: Knopf, 1938), p. 92. See the text at chap. 5, n. 73, above.

Governor Hutchinson could call Sam Adams "that Matchiavil of Chaos." Schlesinger, *New Viewpoints in American History* (New York: Macmillan Co., 1922), pp. 173-74. Adams, in turn, could write in 1776 of "that Fiend Hutchinson & his Confederates." *The Writings of Samuel Adams*, ed. H. A. Cushing (New York: G. P. Putnam's Sons, 1907), 3:288.

25. The theme of such of John Adams's works as his *Defence of the Constitutions of the United States* is that "power is always abused when unlimited and unbalanced." Adams, *The Political Writings of John Adams*, American Heritage Series (Indianapolis: Bobbs-Merrill, 1954), p. 106.

See, for President Adams's commendably "strict views of treason," Leonard W. Levy, *Jefferson and Civil Liberties: The Darker Side* (Cambridge: Harvard University Press, 1963), p. 210, n. 25 (citing *Works*, 9:58; 10:154). See, also, chap. 8, n. 190, below.

26. Of the 44 members of the House of Representatives who voted for the Sedition Act of 1798, at least 28 were lawyers; of the 41 who voted against it, only 12. See chap. 6, n. 23, above. The bar had not yet awakened to the significance of the Declaration of Independence. See, also, pp. 209-13, above, chap. 8, n. 98, below.

"Numbers of Republicans quit their seats in Congress and hastened home, and the Federalists thus left in control, passed the Alien Enemy Act, the Alien Friends Act, the Naturalization Act, and the Sedition Bill. . . ." John Bach McMaster, *The Political Depravity of the Founding Fathers* (New York: Noonday Press, 1964), p. 189. It seems to me unlikely that the Sedition Act could have been enacted if Madison had been in Congress rather than in Virginia at that time.

Connecticut had, in its Constitution of 1817, a free press provision with the "responsible for the abuse of that liberty" qualification. This is more Blackstonian in tenor than the unqualified version seen in the First Amendment. (In fact, as I have indicated, the abuse qualification may be essentially the "no previous restraint" rule.)

27. The Vermont Constitution of 1793 provided in its "Declaration of the Rights of the Inhabitants of the State of Vermont," "That the people of this state by their legal representatives, have the sole, inherent, and exclusive right of governing and regulating the internal police of the same." Vermont was admitted to the Union in 1791. Similar provisions had been included in the Vermont Constitutions of 1777 and 1786. A comparable provision in the Pennsylvania Constitution of 1776, on the other hand, seems to have been excluded from the Pennsylvania Constitution of 1790. Had the intervening Constitution of the United States restricted in some particulars that "sole, inherent and exclusive right" of the states respecting "internal police"? See chap. 6, n. 17, above, chap. 6, n. 50, below.

28. See chap. 7, nn. 47, 48, 49, below.

See, on Shays's Rebellion, chap. 5, nn. 78, 88, and chap. 6, n. 8, above. Cf. Max Farrand, *The Fathers of the Constitution* (New Haven: Yale University Press, 1921), p. 95:

> Shays' Rebellion [in Massachusetts, 1786-87] was fairly easily suppressed, even though it required the shedding of some blood. But it was the possibility of further outbreaks that destroyed men's peace of mind. There were similar disturbances in other States; and there the Massachusetts insurgents found sympathy, support, and finally a refuge. When the worst was over, and Governor Bowdoin [of Massachusetts] applied to the neighboring States for help in capturing the last of the refugees, Rhode Island and Vermont failed to respond to the extent that might have been expected of them. The danger, therefore, of the insurrection spreading was a cause of deep concern. This feeling was increased by the impotence of Congress. The [general] Government had sufficient excuse for intervention after the attack upon the national arsenal in Springfield. Congress, indeed, began to raise troops but did not dare to admit its purpose and offered as a pretext an expedition against the Northwestern Indians. The rebellion

was over before any assistance could be given. The inefficiency of Congress and its lack of influence were evident. . . .

See, in the text at chap. 7, n. 63, above, Livermore's suggestion about the kind of causes that led to Shays's Rebellion. See, for Washington's advice on how to deal with the rebellion, Samuel Eliot Morison, *Sources and Documents Illustrating the American Revolution, 1764-1788, and the Formation of the Federal Constitution* (London: Oxford University Press, 1962), p. 218. The disturbance did contribute to the establishment of a stronger central government better equipped to deal with the conditions and difficulties which led to the rebellion. See chap. 7, n. 71, below.

29. See Harry Kalven, "The Law of Defamation and the First Amendment," in *Law School Conference on the Arts: Publishing and the Law* (Chicago: University of Chicago Law School, 1952), p. 9:

> . . . the most exciting free speech question of our day is oddly enough whether the Sedition Act of 1798 was and would be constitutional. For it is on this issue that the real stakes in free speech turn. Not the least of the fascinations of the question is the contrast in reputation between the Sedition Act and Fox's Libel Act, although the Sedition Act provided all the safeguards of Fox's Libel Act and in addition explicitly made truth a defense. It is easy to line up authorities on either side. Certainly Hall, Corwin and Carroll, all writing after the batch of prosecutions for speech crimes during World War I, regard the Sedition Act as constitutional and this seems also to have been the view of Story [chap. 27, secs. 1293-94; chap. 44, secs. 1891-92]. On the other hand, Cooley would appear to dissent, and it is to Chafee that we owe the most explicit argument against the view that we adopted the English law of seditious libel. The Supreme Court never had the opportunity of passing on the Act, and it is Holmes' dictum in his dissent in [*Abrams* v. *U.S.*, 250 U.S. 616, 630 (1919)] that has perhaps been his greatest contribution to free speech. He said: "I wholly disagree with the argument of the Government that the First Amendment left the common law as to seditious libel in force. History seems to me against the notion."

(See Kalven, *Negro and First Amendment*, pp. 17-20.) Justice Holmes continued, in the passage quoted by Kalven,

> I had conceived that the United States through many years had shown its repentance for the Sedition Act of 1798, by repaying fines that it imposed. Only the emergency that makes it immediately dangerous to leave the correction of evil counsels to time warrants making any exception to *the sweeping command*, "Congress shall make no law . . . abridging the freedom of speech." Of course I am speaking only of exhortations, which were all that were uttered here. . . .
> [Italics added]

More important than "history [being] against the notion" is the fact that our regime is in principle hostile to the law of sedition. See, e.g., chap. 5, nn. 1, 36, above. Cf. chap. 5, n. 5, above, chap. 6, n. 38, below. See, on what has been said since 1798 about the Sedition Act, Justice Brennan's opinion for the Court, *New York Times* v. *Sullivan*, 376 U.S. 254, 276 (1964).

See, on the relation between history and the common law, chap. 5, n. 37, above, chap. 6, n. 37, below.

30. 32 Geo. 3, c. 60 (1792). Edmund Burke had spoken, in 1771, in support of a motion "to bring in a Bill for explaining the Powers of Juries in Prosecutions for Libels." Burke, *Works*, 3:364. The text of this rejected bill, as set forth and explained in Burke's *Works* (3:365-81, 382), indicates that for at least a generation there had been serious efforts in England to change the common law of seditious libel. In England, too, I suggest, the dominant opinion on this question may not have been by 1791 simply that found in collections of statutes and judicial opinions. Cf. Leonard Levy, *The Legacy of*

Suppression: Freedom of Speech and Press in Early American History (Cambridge: Harvard University Press, 1960), p. 161. The Libel Bill proposed in 1771, which should be compared to Fox's Libel Act of 1792, read:

> Whereas doubts and controversies have arisen at various times concerning the right of jurors to try the whole matter laid in indictments and informations for seditious and other libels: and whereas trial by juries would be of none or imperfect effect, if the jurors were not held to be competent to try the whole matter aforesaid; for settling and clearing such doubts and controversies, and for securing to the subject the effectual and complete benefit of trial by juries in such indictments and informations; BE it enacted, &c. That jurors duly empannelled and sworn to try the issue between the king and defendant upon any indictment or information for a seditious libel, or a libel under any other denomination or description, shall be held and reputed competent to all intents and purposes, in law and in right, to try every part of the matter laid or charged in said indictment or information, comprehending the criminal intention of the defendant, and the evil tendency of the libel charged, as well as the mere fact of the publication thereof, and the application by innuendo of blanks, initial letters, pictures, and other devices; any opinion, question, ambiguity, or doubt to the contrary notwithstanding.

See chap. 5, n. 41, above.

Albert Gallatin (of Pennsylvania) (an opponent both of the Sedition Act of 1798 and of the common law of seditious libel) said in the House of Representatives in January, 1801:

> In a cause of this kind [seditious libel] in England, a judge gave it in charge to the jury that they were only to inquire whether a certain paper was printed and published by the accused. As well might he in a case of murder tell them they were only to inquire whether the accused had killed the man, without any attention to the criminality of his intention. [*Annals*, VI, p. 951]

It had been said in the House the day before by Jonas Platt (of New York), the chairman of a committee which had brought in a report proposing that the Sedition Act be continued (on the eve of Thomas Jefferson's inauguration) beyond its March, 1801, expiration date (it was not):

> To those who believed [as Platt did] the rules of common law of force and effect in the United States, [the Sedition Act of 1798] must be truly gratifying. By the common law two practices were established, which this law most effectually removed by its ameliorating provisions. First, the common law rejected the evidence of truth in cases of libel. Secondly, the court had unlimited authority to ascertain the penalty. By this law the truth must be given in evidence, and the penalty is ascertained. [*Annals*, VI, p. 917]

I had occasion during a brief recess toward the end of the "Chicago Conspiracy Trial" (Appendix D, above) to observe to one of the counsel that this was the kind of case in which the defense could properly (on the authority of the *Zenger* case of 1735 [chap. 5, n. 57, above]) appeal past the judge to the jury on the constitutionality of the statute itself (the Anti-Riot Act of 1968 [chap. 6, n. 75, below]). I, in turn, was reminded that counsel had been cited for contempt in *Zenger* for trying to do just that. It was apparent during the "Conspiracy Trial" that both the trial judge and the U.S. attorney were quite concerned that defense counsel might try to make such an appeal to the jury in their closing arguments. Stern warnings were given defense counsel that they should not do so, that the "question of law" was up to the judge alone. It was also apparent by the time of our conversation, however, that defense counsel were going to be cited for contempt anyway. I myself would have much preferred being cited for reviving one of the great arguments of the American legal tradition than for failing to conceal my exasperation in the face of a very bad judge or for some of the other reasons for which contempt citations were eventually handed down in Chicago. (Interviews of jurors reported in the press after the trial suggest that a hung jury might well have resulted—it almost did anyway—if the defendants had been allowed to tell the jury that it had the right to consider not only the "facts" but also the propriety of the Anti-Riot Act. See chap. 3, n. 20, above, chap. 6, n. 31, below. See, also, chap. 8, n. 85, below.)

31. "The form which, in the eighteenth century, the demand for an increased liberty of the press took in England, was a demand for an extension of the powers of juries in proceedings for libel [citing Stephen]; and in 1792 the demand was conceded in this form by Fox's Libel Act." William S. Holdsworth, *Some Lessons from Our Legal History* (New York: Macmillan Co., 1928), p. 91.

In Fox's Libel Act, it is provided that "on every such trial the jury sworn to try the issue may give a general verdict of guilty or not guilty upon the whole matter put in issue upon such indictment or information." In the Sedition Act of 1798, it is provided that "the jury, who shall try the cause, shall have a right to determine the law and the fact, under the direction of the court, as in other cases." But in *Dennis*, 341 U.S. 494 (1951), the trial court was upheld in its ruling that the question of "clear and present danger" was a question of law, not an issue in the case to be presented to the jury. (See Justice Douglas's dissenting opinion, 341 U.S., at 581.) Was not this a usurpation of the role of the jury and, consequently, an avoidance of the showing that should be made on this issue before submitting it to a jury? See chap. 6, n. 30, above. Cf. chap. 3, n. 20, above.

32. *Halsbury's Statutes of England*, 2d ed. (London: Butterworth & Co., 1949), 13:1130. The bitter controversy in England regarding the extension of suffrage pointed up the resistance encountered well into the nineteenth century to the principle of popular self-government. One would expect American laws respecting speech and the press to be much more liberal, insofar as those institutions bear on the activities of self-governors.

See chap. 8, sec. 11, above. See, also, chap. 2, n. 20, above.

33. Smith, *Freedom's Fetters*, p. 424, concluded:

> To summarise, then, the clause on truth [in the Sedition Act of 1798] was nullified by the courts; the right of the jury to decide the criminality of the writing was usurped by the presiding judges: and the test of intent was reduced to the seventeenth-century common law test of bad tendency. Without these procedural safeguards, the Sedition Law was almost a duplicate of the English common law of seditious libel. Since intent was presumed from tendency, the test of criminality became the same: the tendency of the words to bring rulers into disrepute.
>
> The evidence is conclusive that the Sedition Law, as enforced, reduced the limits of speech and press in the United States to those set by the English common law in the days before the American Revolution. This was the standard advocated by the Federalists who enacted the law, and it was the standard applied by the Federalist judges who interpreted the law.

Compare the observations in Mathew Carey's *The Olive Branch, or Faults on Both Sides Federal and Democratic: A Serious Appeal on the Necessity of Mutual Forgiveness & Harmony to Save Our Common Country from Ruin* (Philadelphia: M. Carey, 1814), pp. 30-31, 33, 34, 35, 55-56:

> The factious clamour excited against the sedition and alien laws, and against the eight per cent loan—which clamour was the principal means of changing the administration, and taking it from the hands of the federalists, to place it in those of the democrats—may be justly reckoned among the errors, to use no harsher term, of the latter party. A candid review of the so-stiled sedition law, at the present hour, when the public ferment to which it gave rise, has wholly subsided, will satisfy any reasonable man, that so far from being the monstrous, outrageous infringement of liberty that it was supposed, it was a measure not merely defensible—but absolutely necessary and indispensable towards the support of government. [Footnote: It is but justice to avow that the writer

of this pamphlet was as ardent in his opposition to, and as much alarmed at the probable consequences of, the alien and sedition laws, as any man in the community. As it requires an extraordinary degree of corporeal sanity to resist the effects of an violent epidemical disorder: so it requires great strength of mind to keep out of the vortex of factious contagion, when prevalent with those whose opinions are generally congenial with our own. Of this strength of mind the writer was destitute in common with a large portion of his fellow citizens.] . . . The alien and sedition laws were made the subject of an elegant, but violent and inflammatory report, agreed to by the legislature of Virginia; allowed at the time to be as respectable and enlightened a deliberative body, as any in the United States. But they were bitten by the mad dog of faction in common with so large a portion of their fellow citizens, and were seized with the prevalent disorder, the gag-law phobia. They regarded the two obnoxious laws, as inroads upon public liberty, that required to be repelled with the utmost firmness. It would be uncandid not to state, that the trials under this act, for libels against the president, and, as far as my recollection serves me, against some of the other public functionaries, were managed with very considerable rigour; and, from the abuse of the law, tended to give an appearance of propriety and justice to the clamour against it. . . . But the fault rests not in the law. It lay at the door of the juries. I have little to say respecting the alien law. It was liable to strong objections. It invested the president with powers that might be much abused. But it certainly never warranted the awful outcry that was raised against it. . . . The eight per cent loan remains. That was united with, and increased the clamour against, the alien and sedition laws; and the trio completed, as I have already observed, the downfall of the federalists. Yet we have since found that their successors, the democrats, have themselves given a greater interest than eight per cent. . . . The alien law was not, as far as I can ascertain, ever carried into effect. It was hung up in terrorem over the heads of several foreigners, who, in the language of the day, were rank jacobins, and of course enemies to God and man. . . .

See chap. 3, n. 20, above.

34. If Congress had been interested primarily in liberalizing the common law of sedition, it could have had the expiration section apply to all of the act but section 3. The expiration clauses in certain of the other acts listed in chap. 6, n. 12, above, designate the parts of the act to be affected. Would the Jeffersonian Congress have repealed section 3 in 1801 if that section alone had been left on the statute book? Cf. *Annals,* V, p. 609.

An attempt was made in January, 1800 (evidently as a way of getting section 2 of the Sedition Act repealed before its March, 1801, expiration date [see page 138, above]) to have the following resolution approved by Congress:

Resolved, That the second section of the act, passed the fourteenth of July, one thousand seven hundred and ninety-eight, . . . ought to be repealed; and the offences therein specified shall remain punishable as at common law. Provided, that, upon any prosecution, it shall be lawful for the defendant to give in evidence, in his defence, the truth of the matter charged as a libel. [*Annals,* VI, p. 404]

Joseph Eggleston (of Virginia) warned other opponents of the Sedition Act that

by voting against the resolution, the present law expires in March, 1801, but if the common law was *adopted* it was a sore which would never wear away, and a sore much worse in its nature than the law now in force, hateful as it was. [*Annals,* VI, p. 425; italics added]

If the January, 1800, resolution had become law, the national debate would then have turned to the question of what *was* "punishable . . . at common law." But the resolution was rejected 87-11. See *Annals,* VI, pp. 404-25. See, also, chap. 6, n. 30, above.

A Connecticut Federalist introduced a resolution in the House of Representatives in 1807 in an unsuccessful attempt to make truth a defense in common-law trials for criminal libels in the federal courts. The resolution, which would have had an unwilling Congress recognize the existence of a national common law, asked

> that a committee be appointed to inquire whether prosecutions at common law should be sustained in the courts of the United States, for libellous publications, or defamatory words, touching persons holding offices or places of trust under the United States, and whether it would not be proper, if the same be sustained, to allow the parties prosecuted the liberty of giving the truth in evidence, and that the committee report by bill or otherwise. [*Annals*, IX, p. 248]

35. The significance of the Virginia and Kentucky Resolutions (written, respectively, by Madison and Jefferson) is heightened by the fact that much of the original impetus for the Bill of Rights in the First Congress came from Madison, who was speaking for his Virginia constituency. (See chap. 4, n. 70, above, chap. 7, n. 2, below.) It was appropriate that Virginia's approval of the proposed amendments on December 15, 1791, should have happened to complete their ratification. Cf. *Annals*, VI, pp. 968-70. See chap. 5, n. 44, above. See, also, chap. 8, n. 118, below.

36. Charles Francis Adams (John Adams's grandson), writing in 1856, passed this judgment on the Sedition Act:

> Indeed, it must be now conceded that the greatest and most fatal error of the federal party is to be found in the enactment of this law . . . [I]t cannot be denied that the attempt to punish individuals for *mere expressions of opinion of public measures and public men*, to subject them perhaps to fine and imprisonment, and certainly to heavy and burdensome charges in their defence, for exercising a latitude of speech, however extreme, in the heat and excitement attending the political conflicts of a free country, verged too closely upon an abridgment of the liberty of speech and of the press to be quite reconcilable to the theory of free institutions. [*Works of John Adams*, ed. Charles F. Adams (Boston: Little, Brown & Co., 1850-56), 1:560-61 (italics added)]

I record my impression that the opponents of the Sedition Act in the Fifth Congress have the better of the debate. See, for the best consistent statement I know in defense of the Alien and Sedition Acts, *Annals*, V, pp. 2985-93. See, also, chap. 7, n. 2, chap. 8, n. 190, below. Cf. Walter Berns, "Freedom of the Press and the Alien and Sedition Laws: A Reappraisal," *Supreme Court Review* (1970).

37. The common law, Blackstone wrote, is "nothing else but custom arising from the universal agreement of the whole community"; "the only method of proving that this or that maxim is a rule of the common law, is that it hath always been the custom to observe it." Blackstone, *Laws of England*, 1:472, 68. See, also, Thomas M. Cooley, *A Treatise on the Constitutional Limitations Which Rest upon the Legislative Powers of the States of the American Union*, 8th ed. (Boston: Little, Brown & Co., 1927), p. 77; Crosskey, *Politics and the Constitution*, pp. 546, 594, 598.

Whatever the intentions of the framers of the Constitution may have been, has not the insistence of judges for more than a century that there is no national common law repudiated that "universal agreement" and long-standing custom of which Blackstone spoke and put another agreement and custom in its place? See chap. 2, n. 28, above. See, also, chap. 7, nn. 72, 82, below.

My discussion in the remainder of this chapter, which is summed up at chap. 6, n. 70, below, is anticipated by the following passage from Leonard W. Levy's "Liberty and the First Amendment," *American Historical Review* 68:28 (I believe Levy's documentary impressions and conclusions here are correct, but not all the preceding arguments by which he reaches these sound conclusions: he seems to read "abridging the freedom of speech or of the press" as if it read "respecting speech or the press"; he does not seem to recognize that Congress may indeed have power to regulate speech or the press but not that speaking or publishing which falls within "freedom of speech or of the press"):

... The [First Amendment] was intended and understood to prohibit any congressional regulation of the press, whether by means of a licensing law, a tax, or a sedition act. The framers meant Congress to be totally without power to enact legislation respecting the press. They intended a federal system in which the central government could exercise only such powers as were specifically enumerated or were necessary and proper to carry out the enumerated ones. Thus James Wilson declared that, because the national government had "no power whatsoever" concerning the press, "no law . . . can possibly be enacted" against it. [Citing John B. McMaster and Frederick D. Stone, eds., *Pennsylvania and the Federal Constitution, 1787-1788* (Philadelphia: Historical Society of Pennsylvania, 1888), p. 308] Thus Hamilton, referring to the demands for a free press guarantee, asked, "Why declare that things shall not be done which there is no power to do?" [Citing *Federalist* No. 84; see chap. 6, n. 2, above.] *The illustrations may be multiplied fiftyfold.* [Italics added] In other words, no matter what was meant or understood by freedom of speech and press, the national government, *even in the absence of the First Amendment*, could not make speech or press a legitimate subject of restrictive legislation. [Levy's italics] The amendment itself was superfluous. To quiet public apprehension, it offered an added assurance that Congress would be limited to the exercise of its delegated powers. The phrasing was intended to prohibit the possibility that those powers might be used to abridge speech and press. From this viewpoint, the Sedition Act of 1798 was unconstitutional.

See chap. 4, n. 87, chap. 5, nn. 34, 58, above. See, also, chap. 4, n. 70, chap. 5, n. 43, above.

38. See, e.g., *Annals*, I, p. 469 (Boudinot). See, also, the emphasis on "Safety and Happiness" in the Declaration of Independence.

Defenders of Justice Holmes's opinion in *Schenck* may regard the *salus populi* as the object of his argument: thus, he may be seen as having permitted government to do no more than curb efforts to obstruct the exercise of its lawful powers (in this instance, the power to raise armies). (See *The Holmes-Pollock Letters: The Correspondence of Mr. Justice Holmes and Sir Frederick Pollock, 1874-1932*, ed. Mark DeW. Howe [Cambridge: Harvard University Press, 1946], 2:7; *Frohwerk* v. *U.S.*, 249 U.S. 204, 206 [1919]. Cf. Sidney Hook, *Heresy, Yes—Conspiracy, No!* [New York: John Day Co., 1953], pp. 103-4.) One is reminded of the "counsel, advise, or attempt to procure" language in section 1 of the Sedition Act of 1798. (See chap. 6, n. 9, above. Cf. chap. 6, n. 29, above, chap. 8, n. 172, below. See, also, chap. 4, nn. 5, 52, above.)

But should any criticism among Americans of statutes and government policies be treated as criminal efforts to obstruct or oppose "any measure or measures of the Government of the United States, which are or shall be directed by proper authority, or to impede the operation of any law of the United States"? (See chap. 5, n. 88, above, on John Adams, Thersites and "the freedom of speech [that] was far advanced and well established.") Indeed, is not any criticism of a policy or statute likely to obstruct the exercise by government of lawful powers? (See, on incitement, chap. 5, nn. 35, 121, above.)

After undergoing two days of preinduction mental and physical tests in New York City, Mr. [Stokely] Carmichael, 25, had publicly vowed he would refuse to serve in the U.S. armed forces if drafted. "I'd rather go to Leavenworth first," he said. The next day, before a crowd of 14,000 students at the University of California in Berkeley, Mr. Carmichael had said: "The only way we have to stop the war in Vietnam is to reject the draft. No one has the right to take a man for two years and train him as a killer. . . . I am saying, 'To hell with the draft.' "

The Justice Department received so many inquiries about the Carmichael statements that it drafted a form reply letter. The letter notes that the Universal Military Training and Service Act provides that whoever "knowingly counsels, aids, or abets another to refuse or evade registration or service in the armed forces" shall be guilty of a felony punishable by a maximum penalty of five years' imprisonment or a $10,000 fine or both.

CHAPTER SIX, NOTE 39: PAGE 149   579

But, the letter continues, "We know of no [court] decisions indicating that counseling evasion contemplates expressions of views and opinions made to a general audience."

Nonetheless, Justice initiated an investigation of Mr. Carmichael's statements. [*National Observer*, Nov. 7, 1966, p. 10]

Would the *Schenck* case pamphlets be regarded today as suitable for prosecution? (The audience to which those pamphlets were directed was probably not as apt to respond sympathetically to them as the audience to which the Carmichael statements were addressed.) But although the *Schenck* evidence might not be sufficient today, the principle conjured up on that occasion by Justice Holmes remains available for invocation by the general government (especially, today, with respect to government employment and to the decisive allocations of government funds). See chap. 8, n. 126, below.

Less influential than *Schenck* but more ominous is *Eugene V. Debs* v. *U.S.*, 249 U.S. 211 [1919], ratifying the conviction and imprisonment of a nationally known and widely respected political leader for the expression of "views and opinions made to a general audience." If a Debs can be imprisoned, to the tune of an opinion from Justice Holmes, "the great dissenter," then no serious political critic of our government can be safe. But there are opinions and opinions—and it was in *Schenck*, not in the largely forgotten *Debs*, that Justice Holmes brought forth the language that has made the difference. (See chap. 3, n. 14, above.) Or, to put it otherwise, in the beginning is the word—which reflects the fact that we, as reasoning beings, are more impressed ultimately by ideas than by deeds, a fact that has made the First Amendment as vital as it is to our way of life. See p. 208, above. Cf. Faust, who is certain that "In the beginning was the deed": he would "get to the roots of those secret powers which hold together this world of ours . . . and dabble in words no more"; "To rule, to own, that is my thought. The deed is all, the fame is nought." Johann W. von Goethe, *Faust* (London: Everyman's Library, 1954), pp. 40, 14, 355. Do not contemporary radicals agree with Faust, especially those who argue that they must even refashion our language to suit their purposes? They, like Faust and Caliban, will not be confined (i.e., disciplined). See chap. 4, nn. 14, 54, 116, above, chap. 7, n. 124, chap. 8, n. 193, below. See, also, chap. 7, n. 2 (end), below.

See Lincoln, *Complete Works*, ed. John G. Nicolay and John Hay (New York: Century Co., 1902), 2:239, 346, 349, 361-62, 403, 407, 416, 471-72, 523, 551, 590-91, 620-21, 656. See, also, Tocqueville, *The Old Regime and the French Revolution* (New York: Doubleday & Co., 1955), p. 3:

> Meanwhile the Revolution followed its destined course. And the attitude of the outside world towards it gradually changed, the more it revealed its aspect as a grim, terrific force of nature, a newfangled monster, red of tooth and claw; when, after destroying political institutions, it abolished civil institutions; when, after changing laws, it tampered with age-old customs and even the French language; when, not content with wrecking the whole structure of the government of France, it proceeded to undermine the social order and seemed even to aim at dethroning God himself; when, worse still, it began to operate beyond the frontiers of its place of origin, employing methods hitherto unknown, new tactics, murderous slogans—"opinions in arms," as Pitt described them. . . .

O. John Rogge, *The First and Fifth* (New York: Thomas Nelson & Sons, 1960), p. 30: Bentham spoke of "the security [under free government] with which malcontents may communicate their sentiments, concert their plans, and practise every mode of opposition short of actual revolt, before the executive power can be legally justified in disturbing them." See Halevi in chap. 5, n. 132, above.

39. Not much, General Grant seems to have thought:

> [Secretary of War] Stanton was an able constitutional lawyer and jurist; but the Constitution was not an impediment to him while the war lasted. In this latter particular I entirely agree with the view he evidently held. The Constitu-

tion was not framed with a view to any such rebellion as that of 1861-5. While it did not authorize rebellion it made no provision against it. Yet the right to resist or suppress rebellion is as inherent as the right of self-defence, and as natural as the right of an individual to preserve his life when in jeopardy. The Constitution was therefore in abeyance for the time being, so far as it in any way affected the progress and termination of the war. Those in rebellion against the government of the United States were not restricted by constitutional provisions. . . . [U. S. Grant, *Personal Memoirs* (New York: Charles L. Webster & Co., 1894), pp. 639-40]

See Lord Charnwood, *Abraham Lincoln* (Garden City, N.Y.: Garden City Publishing Co., 1917), p. 188: "[President] Buchanan, instead of acting on or declaring his intention [in the face of threatened secession], entertained Congress, which met early in December [1860], with a Message, laying down very clearly the illegality of secession, but discussing at large [the] abstract question of the precise powers of the Executive in resisting secession."
See, also, Walter Bagehot, *The English Constitution*, World Classics (London: Oxford University Press, 1928), pp. 198-201; chap. 3, n. 33, chap. 4, n. 56, chap. 5, n. 21, above.

40. Does, for example, Congress have the power under the Constitution to deter or to suppress rebellion by legislating a President into a hereditary monarch? See chap. 9, n. 12, below.

Edward S. Corwin and Jack W. Peltason reported (*Understanding the Constitution* [New York: Henry Holt & Co., 1958], pp. 77-78, 105):

From an early date the President has been authorized by Congress to employ not only the state militias, but also the armed forces of the United States against "combinations of persons too powerful to be dealt with" by the ordinary judicial processes. Although in 1957 Congress repealed an 1866 statute specifically authorizing the President to use armed forces to enforce civil rights legislation, it left in effect older statutes that empower the President to use troops to enforce all federal laws and federal court orders when ordinary processes are inadequate. . . . In the exercise of these powers the President may in case of "necessity" declare "martial law." Of this there are various degrees and kinds, the most extreme being that in which military courts temporarily take over the government of a region. . . . Congress has delegated to the President the authority to send troops into a state to protect it from "domestic violence," on the request of the appropriate state authority. . . . The President may also send troops into a state without the consent of state officials, even against their protests, if he finds it necessary in order to enforce federal laws or to preserve the property or "the peace of the United States" [citing *In re Debs*, 158 U.S. 564 (1895)].

See Jonathan Elliot, *Debates in the Several State Conventions on the Adoption of the Federal Constitution* (Philadelphia: J. B. Lippincott & Co., 1863), 2:521.
I would question, however, any action based on "the peace of the United States" if republican government should still exist in such states. (See chap. 7, n. 85, below.) I do not believe, that is, "peace of the United States" should be substituted for the Constitutional standard of "Republican Form of Government." See chap. 7, n. 84, below. See, also, chap. 2, n. 20, chap. 4, n. 52, above, chap. 6, n. 60, below.

41. See *The Federalist* (New York: Random House, Modern Library, n.d.), pp. 82-83, 98-99, 101-3, 114-15, 142-46, 153-54, 169-70, 261-97, 303-4.

42. See, in Harry V. Jaffa, *Equality and Liberty* (New York: Oxford University Press, 1965), at p. 140, the discussion of the Emanicipation Proclamation.
I have adopted "compound republic" from the *Federalist* (e.g., p. 339 ["the compound republic of America"], p. 401 ["a compound republic, partaking both of the national and federal character"]). (Other descriptions used by the *Federalist* include "the extended republic of the United States" [pp. 340-41] and "a confederated republic" [p. 410]; but we seem to be warned against "an improper consolidation of the States into one simple republic" [p. 402].) See, on "coordinated electorates," chap. 7, n. 35, below.

43. And, Jackson went on to argue, even if this [removal] power is "incident to the Executive branch of Government, it does not follow that it vests in the President alone, because he alone does not possess all Executive powers. . . ." See, on the removal power discussion, chap. 2, sec. 6, above.

I have already indicated (e.g., chap. 4, sec. 4, above) the critical role today of the Executive with respect to effective freedom of speech. The "woof and the warp" of this study (see Plato's *Statesman* 309-B) may be traced in the line between chap. 2, n. 20, chap. 4, n. 59, chap. 6, nn. 39, 40, above, and chap. 8, n. 98, below, and in the line between chap. 3, n. 20, chap. 5, nn. 78, 79, above, chap. 7, nn. 62, 63, and chap. 9, n. 20, below. Cf. p. 614 (beginning), below.

Critical to a study of this character should be the objective of a Maimonides: "For it is a great wall that I have built around the Law, a wall that surrounds it warding off the stones of all those who project missiles against it." *The Guide of the Perplexed* (Chicago: University of Chicago Press, 1963), p. 298. Perhaps we can begin to work our way out of our labyrinth by inquiring what "the Law" and its protection can mean for us. A dialogue, which has come to hand by courtesy of Isaac Bickerstaff (see chap. 4, n. 15, above, chap. 6, n. 51, below) may illuminate, or at least enliven, our inquiries:

Agricola: What kind of community are you really advocating?
Graveson: A community in which thoughtful men have significant influence.
A: What do you mean by "thoughtful men"?
G: Men who, because they are grounded in the most serious thought that reaches across millennia, have an awareness of what the best is and hence are equipped to adapt traditional principles to changing circumstances.
A: But can such men really do anything?
G: Doesn't that depend on the circumstances? Anyone who is aware of the best is aware also of the inevitable shortcomings of the political institutions he happens to encounter. Even so, he does not, in his efforts to reconstitute them, overestimate the intelligence or underestimate the good will of the people who are likely to man the institutions he manages to shape.
A: How does one insure, or at least make it more likely, that thoughtful men will indeed have significant influence in their community?
G: There is in mankind a certain * * * * * * * * * * * * * * * * [*Ingens hiatus hic in* MS.] * * * * * * * * * * * * * * * * * * * happen among us without freedom of speech. And this I take to be a clear solution of the matter. [Citing Plato, *Republic* 480B-483E, 541C-542E, 417C-418E]
A: You don't say! Seven-hundred and eighty-seven? Don't you mean sev-en*teen*-hundred and eighty-seven?
G: Take your pick. What's a millennium among friends? In any event, we have made our way to the vital center of what I have to say, which is also our point of departure. And, now * * * * * * * * * * * * * * * * * [*Desunt cætera.*]

See Seth Benardete, "The Right, the True, and the Beautiful," *Glotta* 41 (1963): 54. Cf., on "irrational aspiration," Diskin Clay, Note, *Glotta* 46 (1968): 15, 17.

See, also, chap. 8, n. 135, chap. 9, n. 12, below.

44. See chap. 6, n. 56, below; see, also, Elliot, *Debates*, 1:305.

What is the significance of a preamble? Sumter, in considering amendments to the Constitution, wished the Congress would pass over the Preamble "until they had gone through all the amendments, and then, if alterations [in the Preamble] were necessary, they could be accommodated to what had taken place in the body of the Constitution," *Annals*, I, p. 718; Page responded that he "thought the preamble no part of the Constitution. . . ." *Annals*, I, p. 718.

It should be noted that in the writing of the Constitution itself, the Preamble was prepared in the closing days of the Convention, evidently after decisions had already been reached in the document as to the distribution and extent of the most important powers of the government. Cf. Crosskey, *Politics and the Constitution*, 1:363-79; Crosskey, "Mr.

Chief Justice Marshall," pp. 12-14. See chap. 6, n. 65, below. (It is now standard practice, *Robert's Rules of Order* tells us, that "if there is a preamble it is considered last." [Glenview, Ill.: Scott, Foresman & Co., 1951, p. 214] Was that the practice in the eighteenth century as well? See, also, on preambles, Plato, *Laws* 719E, 870D-C, 887A, Hobbes, *Leviathan*, chap. 30.)

45. A question was raised in the First Congress whether this power, or the power to declare war, could be so used as to permit the House of Representatives to have an indirect voice in the making of treaties. *Annals*, I, pp. 690, 693. See chap. 4, n. 12, above.

46. See, e.g., *Annals*, I, pp. 117-18, 141. Cf. John Dickinson's explanation, in 1768: "To the word 'tax,' I annex that meaning which the Constitution and history of England require to be annexed to it; that is—that it is an imposition on the subject, for the sole purpose of levying money." Morison, *Sources and Documents*, p. 46. See, also, Chief Justice Taft's opinion for the Court in *Bailey v. Drexel Furniture Co. (The Child Labor Tax Case)*, 259 U.S. 20 (1922).

47. See, also, *Annals*, I, p. 111. Cf. *Federalist* No. 10. Would Madison make the same qualification in his theory of "freedom of the press" that he was obliged to make here with respect to "free commerce"? But there is no constitutional prohibition of abridgments of free commerce. See chap. 6, n. 70, below.

48. See, for a position later recanted by Calhoun, H. von Holst, *John C. Calhoun*, American Statesmen (Boston: Houghton Mifflin Co., 1892), pp. 36-37.

The comparable passages in the Constitution of the United States read simply:

> Section 8. The Congress shall have Power to lay and collect Taxes, Duties, Imposts and Excises, to pay the Debts and provide for the common Defence and general Welfare of the United States; but all Duties, Imposts and Excises shall be uniform throughout the United States;
> To borrow Money on the credit of the United States;
> To regulate Commerce with foreign Nations, and among the several States and with the Indian Tribes.

49. Crosskey's interpretation of the Constitution depended in great part on the intended meaning of "Commerce" in that instrument: this was for him critical in determining the extent of powers of the general government. (His work consists, in large part, of an alternative explanation of enumerated powers to that offered by *Federalist* No. 41 [esp. pp. 268-69]. See, also, *Federalist*, p. 453.)

The student of the Constitution might find it useful to consider some uses of *commerce* in context by a Scottish writer, himself a great student of commerce, Adam Smith, *An Inquiry into the Natural Causes of the Wealth of Nations* (New York: Random House, Modern Library, 1937), pp. 19, 21, 22, 25, 28, 32, 115, 125, 192, 203, 273, 276, 296, 305, 356, 360, 372, 385, 388, 389, 392, 393, 394, 395, 397, 407, 462, 477, 602, 628, 644, 681, 682, 690, 691, 712, 713, 755, 773, 845, 851, 862, 881, 882. (The uses of *abridge* I found in Smith were not helpful. See pp. 7, 9, 190, 260, 265, 266, 326, 592, 648.) See, for the use of *commerce* by Publius, *Federalist*, pp. 14, 25, 28, 30, 31, 32, 37, 44, 62-65, 66-67, 68, 70, 71, 72, 73, 75, 78, 79, 88, 101-2, 121, 128, 131-32, 137, 142, 144, 152, 184, 205, 213, 222, 266-68, 271, 272, 274-75, 277-78, 303, 350, 366, 392-93, 406, 417, 453.

See, on the relation of commerce to modern republicanism, Montesquieu, *Spirit of the Laws*, chap. 20-21; David Lowenthal, "Montesquieu," in Leo Strauss and Joseph Cropsey, eds., *The History of Political Philosophy* (Chicago: Rand McNally, 1963), pp. 485-88.

50. Tocqueville can refer to the right of levying imposts as "in a way contain[ing] within itself [but only in France?] all other powers." *Old Regime*, p. 36.

The rulings of the Supreme Court with respect to the question of the proper use of the revenue power were reported in this manner by Corwin and Peltason, *Understanding the Constitution*, at page 67 of their 1958 edition:

> If Congress can spend for regulatory purposes can it also tax for such purposes? Although the Supreme Court has in past struck down ostensible tax laws

CHAPTER SIX, NOTE 50: PAGE 155

because they regulated subjects reserved to the states, today if the measure is a tax on its face, it is unlikely that the courts will interfere. Congress may not tax in such a way as to deprive persons of rights secured by the Constitution, or to interfere seriously with a state's power to govern, but it is otherwise free to tax whatever it wishes and judges are not likely to inquire into congressional motives. Taxes which produce practically no revenues but which authorize considerable federal control have been sustained on sawed-off shotguns, white phosphorous matches, narcotics, and gamblers. The regulation of gambling has given gamblers the option of complying with federal license and tax requirements and thereby alerting local officials to their illegal activities (illegal except in Nevada) or not complying and thereby running the risk of federal prosecution. Obviously these tax measures were passed not to raise revenue but to authorize federal regulation of subjects that the national government cannot regulate directly.

But in the 1970 edition, Peltason reported considerable movement in Supreme Court adjudication with respect to these matters. Thus, the passage I have quoted has had to be revised to read (at p. 54 of J. W. Peltason, *Corwin and Peltason's Understanding the Constitution* [New York: Holt, Rinehart & Winston, 1970]):

If Congress can spend for regulatory purposes, can it also tax for such purposes? Although the Supreme Court in the past has struck down ostensible tax laws because they regulated subjects reserved to the states, today, if the measure is a tax on its face, judges are not likely to inquire into congressional motives or to set aside the tax because it is actually an attempt to regulate subjects reserved to the states. However, in recent years, the Supreme Court has carefully scrutinized congressional tax measures that conflict with specific rights secured by the Constitution. For example, Congress has attempted to regulate narcotics, gamblers, and dangerous weapons under the guise of elaborate tax laws. But, in order to comply with the federal tax laws, gamblers, narcotics peddlers, and sellers of dangerous weapons had to, in effect, produce evidence that they were engaging in illegal activity. Under these circumstances, the Court has ruled that the tax measures violated the guarantees against compelling persons to testify against themselves and cannot be applied against persons who plead the Fifth Amendment. [Citing *Marchetti* v. *United States*, 390 U.S. 39 (1968); *Haynes* v. *United States*, 390 U.S. 85 (1968); *Leary* v. *United States*, 395 U.S. 6 (1969). See, also, *Grosso* v. *United States*, 390 U.S. 62 (1968).] Of course Congress can heavily tax activities—for example dangerous white phosphorous matches; the fact that the impact of the tax might make the activity uneconomic raises no constitutional problem.

The authors go on to say (in both, and in intervening, editions) essentially what is said at p. 54 of the 1970 edition:

Thus the power to tax and to spend has become one of the two major sources— the other is the power to regulate commerce—of the so-called national police power. What is meant by "police power" is the power to regulate persons and property for the safety, health, and welfare of society. Congress has no general grant of police power, but it may use its delegated powers for police-power purposes.

"A former Cook County [Illinois] state's attorney has said: '. . . Federal laws are essentially based on revenue laws. Our state laws are criminal laws. The result is that in some fields it is easier to get convictions under the federal law than under the state law. . . .'" Morton Grodzins, *The American System* (Chicago: Rand McNally, 1966), p. 114. See chap. 7, n. 50, below.

Cf. chap. 4, n. 11, above, chap. 6, n. 62, chap. 8, n. 36, below.

The passages I have quoted from Corwin and Peltason are useful as well for reminding us of a fundamental problem in constitutional law. (See chap. 2, sec. 6, above.) Peltason prefaced *Corwin and Peltason's Understanding the Constitution*, at p. vi, with a tribute to his late colleague:

I think it may be said without exaggeration that [Professor Edward S. Corwin] knew more about the Constitution of the United States than any man who ever lived. At least those of us who had the privilege of studying under him know that Chief Justice Hughes was in error when he said that the Constitution is what the Supreme Court says it is—we know that the Constitution is what Corwin says it is.

But were not both Chief Justice Hughes and Professor Peltason wrong? That is, must we not wonder—for wonder *is* elicited when we realize that things appear first one way and then another—*when* was the Supreme Court (or, for that matter, any scholar) correct about how Congress may use its tax power, in 1958 or in 1970? It is not enough to say that the Constitution "is" whatever this or that authority says it is: on what basis does the authority choose one alternative over another? or, on what basis do we choose our authority? Peltason observed (at p. v of the 1970 edition), just as Corwin and he had done in earlier editions of their useful text, "The author is well aware that there is no such thing as 'the interpretation' of the Constitution; the reader is warned that others would find different meaning in the words of the Constitution and in the opinions of the judges who interpret it." But if it should be correct that there is no correct interpretation—however difficult it may be either to find the correct interpretation or to demonstrate it to others when it is found—, then it is also correct that it would be empty praise to say of anyone that he "knew more about the Constitution . . . than any man who ever lived." The most that could be said is that one knows best the history of what has been said about the Constitution (but even to speak of history as something which can be known raises difficulties [see, e.g., chap. 5, n. 1, above]). One can see here the significance of constitutional scholars as far apart as Justice Black and Professor Crosskey: they do agree, despite their differences, upon one principle which separates them from most of their colleagues, that there *is* a correct interpretation of the Constitution, if we can but discover it. Only if they are right about this is there any sense in trying to study the Constitution in order to learn and hence know something about it. Otherwise, one is left only with white phosphorous matches and no true light on the subject. See chap. 3, n. 25, above. See, also, chap. 8, n. 181, below.

Is not the desire to *know* about political things intimately related to the "natural" disposition to regard one's regime as perpetual? That which is eternal really *is*—and hence is truly knowable. See chap. 5, nn. 126, 143, above, chap. 8, n. 178, chap. 9, n. 30, below. See, also, chap. 5, n. 90, above, chap. 8, nn. 177, 186, chap. 9, nn. 3, 38, 39, below.

51. It was left to Ames (whom Albert J. Beveridge, *The Life of John Marshall* [Boston: Houghton, Mifflin & Co., 1916], 3:53, called "that delightful reactionary") to observe that smuggling (which would be encouraged by high duties) is also bad for the morals of the people. *Annals*, I, p. 136.

It is appropriate to record here, and not only because Ames would have approved, the best solution I know to the problem put in chap. 4, n. 15, above: No owner rides his own horse. (Is not this answer in the spirit of Sancho Panza, the spiritual godfather of *Federalist* No. 10? See, e.g., Cervantes, *Don Quixote* [New York: Viking Press, 1949], pp. 798-803, 858-60, 847-49; also, ibid., pp. 842-43. Cf., e.g., Acts 5:1-11, 10:26, 12:18-19; also, 1 Pet. 4:18.) See chap. 9, n. 12, below.

52. Earlier, Ames (of Massachusetts) protested against a heavy duty on molasses for the harm it would do to New England trade. Ames conceded that he would "concur in any [gradual] measure calculated to exterminate the poison [rum], covered under the form of ardent spirits, from our country. . . ." *Annals*, I, p. 134. The six-cent tax on molasses eventually adopted did not secure his vote. *Annals*, I, p. 229.

53. Jackson expressed the sentiment that "gentlemen ought to let their neighbors [of South Carolina and Georgia] get supplied [with slaves], before they imposed such a burden upon the importation." *Annals*, I, p. 336. Jackson expressed also the hope that the motion, if it ever came forward again, "would comprehend the white slaves as well as black, who were imported from all the jails in Europe; wretches, convicted of the most flagrant crimes. . . ." *Annals*, I, p. 337.

I do not mean to suggest that Jackson and Tucker are correct in their view of the Constitution here or elsewhere, but they do voice the sentiments of a significant minority.

54. Since only a few of the duties listed in the 1789 revenue act affected morality, a reference to morality would have been less relevant than the reference to "domestic manufactures." (See chap. 7, nn. 59, 117, below.)

The way that powers are acknowledged by the Constitution to be distributed between the general government and the state governments reflects the opinion that it is the states which are best equipped to encourage among us the virtues. (See chap. 5, n. 147, above.) But as the powers of the general government indicate, and as the Preamble to the Constitution instructs us, the general government also has duties in this respect: thus, it is empowered and obliged to promote the virtues of justice and courage, not only for their own sake but also because these virtues are essential if the general government is to be able to do its duty in maintaining in the states (and safe from foreign dangers, as well) that form of local government which we have decided is most likely in our circumstances to develop and preserve our well-being both as citizens and as human beings. It is by making too much of self-defense, however, that we have made more of the general government than we should (see *Federalist*, pp. 206-7): it is all too often easier to be moved by dangers to be avoided than by goals to be achieved. See, e.g., the Hobbesian attitude of even the Christian pilgrim: "Had even Obstinate himself but felt what I have felt of the powers and terrors of what is yet unseen, he would not thus lightly have given us [his] back." John Bunyan, *Pilgrim's Progress* (London: Thomas Nelson & Sons, n.d.), p. 17. Or, as Machiavelli argues, it is natural for men to be more likely to be moved (and hence controlled) by fear than by love. *Prince*, chap. 17. But this is not true of the best men or of the best in men. See, e.g., Plato, *Apology* 37C; chap. 9, n. 37, below. (See note 51 of my *Apology* article [chap. 2, n. 1, above].) It is elevating, that is, to be reminded from time to time of the sergeant's challenge at Belleau Woods, "Come on, you. . . . Do you want to live forever?"

See chap. 6, n. 71, below. Cf. chap. 7, nn. 67, 92, below. See, also, chap. 6, n. 27, above, chap. 8, nn. 10, 186, below.

55. Jaffa commented as follows on President Washington's proposal in his last annual message to Congress that a national university be established:

> Choosing select youth from the whole country, and bringing them to the national capital, to a national university, to be instructed in the science of government, as the future guardians of the liberties of the Republic! Alas, that Washington's platonic wisdom was turned aside by his countrymen. But let us be clear at least on one point: There is no principle of constitutional construction which could justify Washington's proposal for a national university, and which would forbid any other national legislation in the field of education. [Harry V. Jaffa, "The Case for a Stronger National Government," in Robert A. Goldwin, ed., *A Nation of States* (Chicago: Rand McNally, 1963), p. 120]

One tendency of such development of "the future guardians of the liberties of the Republic" would be to concentrate power even more in Washington and to make the national bureaucracy (and perhaps elected officials as well) even less dependent on and responsive to local circumstances than they are. In any event, there *is* a principle of constitutional construction which could justify the proposal for a national university without permitting "other national legislation in the field of education": such a university could be established by the exercise of the special power Congress has to govern the District of Columbia. Thus, there is recorded in Madison's notes (in the Convention) for September 14, 1787:

> Mr. Madison and Mr. Pinkney then moved to insert in the list of powers vested in Congress a power—"to establish an University, in which no preferences or distinctions should be allowed on account of religion."
> Mr. Wilson supported the motion.
> Mr. Govr Morris. It is not necessary. The exclusive power at the Seat of Government, will reach the object. [Farrand, *Records*, 2:616]

The proposal was voted down. (See, on *Schenck* and government funds, chap. 6, n. 38, above.) See chap. 7, nn. 5, 30, eblow. See, also, chap. 9, n. 1, below.

The ultimate dependence of virtually all our elected officials upon local elections can be exploited in self-defense by legislators who are threatened by concentrated power (whether political or economic) from Washington, thereby helping us to preserve the integrity of local communities. Thus, Senator Albert Gore found it rhetorically useful to be able to say, upon being made "Target No. 1" of the Nixon Administration (and of its Vice-President) in the 1970 elections: "I am grateful for Agnew's promised service. There is nothing the voters of Tennessee appreciate more than having distinguished outsiders come in and instruct them on how to vote." *Chicago Sun-Times*, July 25, 1970, p. 14. Senator Russell Long replied, upon being warned that he would be subjected in his home state to the same abuse by drug companies as had plagued Senator Estes Kefauver if he undertook to expose their practices, "A Kefauver in Tennessee ain't the same as a Long in Louisiana." *Chicago Sun-Times*, Feb. 9, 1969, p. 42. See chap. 7, n. 1, below. Cf. chap. 7, n. 119, below. See, also, chap. 7, n. 35, below, chap. 3, n. 34, above.

56. See the text at chap. 6, n. 44, above.

> . . . [W]e find [among the enumerated powers of the general government] the great powers to lay and collect taxes; to borrow money; to regulate commerce; to declare and conduct a war; and to raise and support armies and navies. The sword and the purse, all the external relations, and no inconsiderable portion of the industry of the nation, are entrusted to its government. . . . [*McCulloch* v. *Maryland*, 4 Wheat. 316, 407 (1819)]

See, also, *Federalist* Nos. 14, 41-44; Tocqueville, *Democracy in America* (New York: Random House, Vintage Books, 1954), 1:60, 107n., 118-19, 120, 148-49, 152, 398-99; Woodrow Wilson, *Political Thought*, pp. 132-33; Crosskey, *Politics and the Constitution*, p. 212 (on Jefferson's original suggestions about the powers of the general government); chap. 3, n. 5, chap. 4, n. 12, above.

57. An advocate for the Constitution, James Iredell of North Carolina, described in this manner the limited criminal jurisdiction of Congress:

> As to the constituting of new crimes, and inflicting unusual and severe punishment, certainly the cases enumerated wherein the Congress are empowered either to define offences, or prescribe punishments, are such as are proper for the exercise of such authority in the general Legislature of the Union. They only relate to "counterfeiting the securities and current coin of the United States," to "piracies and felonies committed on the high seas, and offences against the laws of nations," and to "treason against the United States." These are offences immediately affecting the security, the honor or the interest of the United States at large, and of course must come within the sphere of the Legislative authority which is intrusted with their protection. Beyond these authorities, Congress can exercise no other power of this kind, except in the enacting of penalties to enforce their acts of legislation in the cases where express authority is delegated to them, and if they could not enforce such acts by the enacting of penalties those powers would be altogether useless, since a legislative regulation without some sanction would be an absurd thing indeed. [Paul Leicester Ford, ed., *Essays on the Constitution of the United States, Published during Its Discussion by the People 1786-1788* (Brooklyn: Historical Printing Club, 1892), p. 359]

See ibid., p. 374.

An opponent of the Constitution, reputedly Richard Henry Lee, observed, "The trial by jury is secured [by the Constitution] only in those few criminal cases, to which the federal laws will extend—as crimes committed on the seas, against the laws of nations, treason and counterfeiting the federal securities and coin." Ibid., p. 307. Cf. Crosskey, *Politics and the Constitution*, pp. 469-71.

We find in Albert Gallatin's 1798 description of Congress's criminal jurisdiction an elaboration of what Iredell and Lee had said a decade earlier:

. . . the Constitution had actually specified the cases in which Congress should have power either to define or to provide for the punishment of offences; and they were the following: piracies, felonies on the high seas, and offences against the law of nations, which they had a right to define and punish; counterfeiting the coin or public securities of the United States; treason, which they had a right to punish, but not to define, it being expressly defined by the Constitution itself; all offences that might be committed within the ten miles square, forts, arsenals, &c., over which the United States might, with the consent of a State, acquire exclusive jurisdiction; and, finally, opposition or offences against the laws or exercise of the Constitutional authority of any department—which offences Congress had a right to define and punish, by virtue of the clause of the Constitution which empowered them to pass all laws necessary and proper for carrying into execution any power vested by the Constitution in them, or in any department. . . . It was in that manner that the authority of Congress had heretofore been exercised; they had passed no penal laws, except such as arose from the necessity of carrying into effect some of the specific powers vested in them. Thus, as they had the exclusive power to establish post roads, they had made it penal to rob the mail; and as they were authorized to lay taxes, they had passed laws to punish frauds of revenue officers, or evasions of the revenue laws. . . . [*Annals*, V, pp. 2158-59]

Cf., e.g., *Annals*, V, p. 1969.

58. The powers of the branches of the general government with respect to legislative and judicial contempt and with respect to military discipline help insure that those branches will be able to do what they are supposed to do. See chap. 5, n. 139, above.

59. See the discussion in the text at chap. 6, n. 28, above. See, also, chap. 7, nn. 47, 49, below; cf. chap. 7, n. 48, below.

. . . I cannot say that our country could have no central police without becoming totalitarian, but I can say with great conviction that it cannot become totalitarian without a centralized national police. At his trial Hermann Goering, with great candor, related the steps by which the Nazi party obtained complete domination of Germany, and one of the first was the establishment of the supremacy of the national over the local police authorities. So it was in Russia, and so it has been in every totalitarian state. . . . All that is necessary is to have a national police competent to investigate all manner of offenses, and then, in the parlance of the street, it will have enough on enough people, even if it does not elect to prosecute them, so that it will find no opposition to its policies. Even those who are supposed to supervise it are likely to fear it. [See chap. 8, n. 18, below.] I believe that the safeguard of our liberty lies in limiting any national policing or investigative organization, first of all to a small number of strictly federal offenses, and *secondly to nonpolitical ones*. The fact that we may have confidence in the administration of a federal investigative agency under its existing heads does not mean that it may not revert again to the days when the Department of Justice was headed by men to whom the investigatory power was a weapon to be used for their own purposes. [Robert H. Jackson, *The Supreme Court in the American System of Government* (New York: Harper & Row, 1963), pp. 70-71 (italics added)]

See the text at chap. 7, n. 51, above. It is too bad that Justice Jackson did not see fit to apply, in his *Dennis* case opinion, the First Amendment criteria implied in the words I have italicized. See Justice Jackson, dissenting, *Beauharnais* v. *Illinois*, 343 U.S. 250, 299 (1952). See, also, chap. 5, n. 149, above, chap. 7, n. 5, below.

60. Edmund Pendleton, president of the Virginia Convention that ratified the Constitution, interpreted Article 4, section 4, thus:

This is a restraint on the general government not to interpose. The state is in full possession of the power of using its own militia to protect itself against domestic violence; and the power in the general government cannot be exercised, or interposed, without the application of the state itself. This appears to me to be the obvious and fair construction. [Elliot, *Debates*, 3:441]

See *Federalist*, pp. 100, 167-72.

It may not be amiss further to observe, (in the language of another commentator), that every pretext for intermeddling with the domestic concerns of any state, under color of protecting it against domestic violence, is taken away by that part of the provision, which renders an application from the legislature, or executive authority of the state endangered necessary to be made to the general government, before its interference can be at all proper. On the other hand, this article becomes an immense acquisition of strength, and additional force to the aid of any state government, in case of internal rebellion, or insurrection against lawful authority. . . . [Story, *Commentaries on the Constitution*, chap. 41, sec. 1825]

The third decade of our history under the Constitution covers the war of 1812. A week before the war was formally declared General Dearborn, by order of the President, issued a call on the States for militia. In most of the States the call was promptly obeyed. But in Massachusetts, Connecticut, and Rhode Island the troops were flatly refused. There were, in the opinions of the Governors, but three purposes for which the militia of a State could be called out by a President, and these three were: to repel invasion, to execute the laws, to suppress insurrections. But the laws were everywhere executed. There were no insurrections to put down. No enemy had invaded the soil. The call was therefore unconstitutional. This interpretation was approved in Massachusetts by the judges, in Rhode Island by the Council, and in Connecticut by the Assembly. . . . [McMaster, *Political Depravity*, p. 197]

See Schlesinger, *New Viewpoints*, p. 240. Cf. Crosskey, *Politics and the Constitution*, p. 424n. See, also, chap. 4, n. 101, above.

See chap. 6, n. 40, above, chap. 7, n. 55, below.

61. I provide an extensive discussion of this arrangement, and its rationale, in chapter 7.

An additional limitation upon whatever power Congress may have to deal with sedition may be implied by the limitation placed in the Constitution upon the treason power (chap. 5, n. 117, above). It has been asked,

If certain conduct is not within the scope of the constitutional definition, either because it is not treason under any historic definition, or because it is one of the historic branches of the crime which the framers omitted from their delimitation, does this mean simply that the actor may not be indicted for treason as such, though his conduct may subject him to another charge; or does it mean that he may not be charged with an offense, the gravamen of which is the allegedly subversive character of that conduct? Does the treason clause merely define a particular crime, or does it express a policy exempting certain types of activity from the risk of criminal prosecution? [Willard Hurst, "Treason in the United States," *Harvard L. Rev.* 58 (1945): 417]

The fact that some of the "historic branches of the crime [of treason]" were explicitly mentioned in the Constitution as within the criminal jurisdiction of Congress (such as the crime of counterfeiting) suggests that those branches not mentioned may be exempt "from the risk of criminal prosecution [by the general government]." (See Montesquieu, *Spirit of the Laws*, 12:7, 8; cf. Crosskey, *Politics and the Constitution*, p. 472.) Was sedition ever regarded as one of the historic branches of the crime of treason? See, for materials bearing on this problem, *The Speeches of Thomas Erskine on Subjects Connected with the Liberty of the Press and against Constructive Treasons* (London: James Ridgway, 1813), 1:236, 253; 2:52-53; Elliot, *Debates*, 4:205, 209, 219; *Federalist* No. 74 (at p. 483). Consider, in this connection, Blackstone's account,

... between the reign of Henry the fourth and queen Mary, and particularly in the bloody reign of Henry the eighth, the spirit of inventing new and strange treasons was revived; among which we may reckon the offences of clipping money; . . . counterfeiting foreign coin; . . . *execrations against the king, calling him opprobrious names by public writing;* . . . refusing to abjure the pope; . . . *judging or believing (manifested by any overt act) the king to have been lawfully married to Ann of Cleve, derogating from the king's royal style and title; impugning his supremacy;* and assembling riotously to the number of twelve, and not dispersing upon proclamation: all which new-fangled treasons were totally abrogated by the statute 1 Mar. c. 1. which once more reduced all treasons to the standard of the statute 25 Edw. III. Since which time, though the legislature has been more cautious in creating new offences of this kind, yet the number is very considerably increased, as we shall find upon a short review. [Blackstone, *Laws of England,* 4:86-87; also, ibid., 4:91-92 (italics added)]

See Malcolm P. Sharp, *Was Justice Done? The Rosenberg-Sobell Case* (New York: Monthly Review Press, 1956), pp. 5, 109; James Alexander, *A Brief Narrative of the Case and Trial of John Peter Zenger, Printer of the New York Weekly Journal* (Cambridge: Harvard University Press, 1963), pp. 66 (on the relation, for the Star Chamber, between treason and sedition), 220. See, also, chap. 2, n. 10 (Soame Jenyns's observation), chap. 5, n. 142, above, chap. 6, n. 74, below.

See, on the bad name that "treason" can give to salutary laws, Tacitus, *History* 1. 77. See, also, chap. 6, n. 25, above.

62. See the text at chap. 6, n. 74, above. Consider the use of income tax evasion prosecutions not only to uphold the revenue laws but also to harass and imprison gangsters who may be otherwise immune from congressional control. See chap. 4, n. 11, chap. 6, n. 50, above, chap. 6, n. 74, chap. 8, n. 36, below.

63. The reader is reminded of the question I discussed earlier, whether the First Amendment somehow implies, if only retroactively, the existence in the Constitution of a power to deal with speech and the press. It should be noticed that Publius did not say that such an amendment would implicitly give such power to Congress; rather, he warned that "it would furnish, to men disposed to usurp, a plausible pretence for claiming that power." Cf. *John Marshall: Major Opinions and Other Writings,* ed. John P. Roche (Indianapolis: Bobbs-Merrill Co., 1967), pp. 45-46 (which includes the observation, "[The First Amendment] which declares that Congress shall make no law abridging the property of the press, is a general construction made by all America on the original instrument, admitting its application to the subject: it would have been certainly unnecessary thus to have modified the legislative powers of Congress concerning the press, if the power itself does not exist."). Do we not see in Marshall's observation what Publius anticipated as a "plausible pretence"? Cf. pp. 141-42, above, chap. 2, n. 31, above.

Willmoore Kendall restated Publius's argument effectively (but without making clear the reservation I have emphasized):

> As Hamilton puts it, in effect, in No. 84 [see the text at chap. 6, n. 2, above], to tell the new Federal government that it must not impair freedom of the press is to create a presumption, not present in the Constitution as it came from Philadelphia, that its power somehow does extend to such matters; erect the dam, so to speak, and the water of Federal power will flow right up to it, where otherwise it would remain right back where the fifty-five at Philadelphia had left it. [Willmoore Kendall, "The Bill of Rights and American Freedom," in Frank S. Meyer, ed., *What Is Conservatism?* (New York: Holt, Rinehart & Winston, 1964), p. 47]

See chap. 3, n. 29, above. See, also, chap. 4, n. 93, above, chap. 8, n. 83, below.

64. The amendments proposed by the states, which are scattered through Elliot's *Debates,* are collected conveniently in Edward Dumbauld, *The Bill of Rights* (Norman: University of Oklahoma Press, 1957). See Appendix A, above.

65. Hobbes, *Leviathan,* I, xiv, points out,

> He that transferreth any Right, transferreth the Means of enjoying it, as farre as lyeth in his power. As he that selleth Land, is understood to transferre the Herbage, and whatsoever growes upon it; Nor can he that sells a Mill turn away the Stream that drives it. And they that give to a man the Right of government in Soveraignty, are understood to give him the right of levying mony to maintain Souldiers; and of appointing Magistrats for the administration of Justice.

See *Federalist* No. 44 (at p. 294). See, also, *P. Anastaplo v. N. Radford*, 14 Ill. 2d 526, 153 N.E. 2d 37 (1958).

The ease with which both the "necessary and proper" clause and the Preamble to the Constitution were accepted by the Convention suggests that no significant change was made by either of them in the powers otherwise granted by the Constitution. See chap. 6, n. 44, above. Cf. *John Marshall: Major Opinions*, pp. 43-44.

66. See, e.g., *Federalist*, pp. 292-95. James A. Bayard, of Delaware, indicated (in defending in January, 1800, the Sedition Act of 1798) how the "necessary and proper" clause could be used to empower Congress to regulate speech and the press:

> This clause expressly delegates a general power of self-preservation. The right given to the Government to make laws proper for carrying into execution the powers delegated, necessarily carries with it the right to make laws proper to preserve and maintain the powers delegated, because the powers cannot be executed unless they are preserved. To preserve its powers the Government must certainly defend the foundation on which they rest. The Government of the United States is immediately bottomed on public opinion. It originates with the people and depends on their will for its existence, and on their arms for its protection. Poison the fountain of its being and the whole frame is palsied, and must sink into lethargy or die in convulsions. The Government is bound not to deceive the people, and it is equally bound not to suffer them to be deceived. Delusion leads to insurrection and rebellion, which it is the duty of the Government to prevent. This they cannot prevent unless they have a power to punish those who with wicked designs attempt to mislead the people. . . .
> The gentleman from North Carolina [Nathaniel Macon], however, has said the truth needed not the aid of a law; that in the end it would always prevail against falsehood. This was a fine moral sentiment, but our limited knowledge of events did not verify it. There was scarcely a period of the world, at which the empire of falsehood was not as extensive as that of truth. . . . [*Annals*, VI, pp. 408-9]

See chap. 6, n. 23, above, chap. 8, nn. 172, 173, below. See, also, chap. 2, n. 30, above.

Chief Justice Marshall writes, "Let the end be legitimate, let it be within the scope of the constitution, and all means which are appropriate, which are plainly adapted to that end, which are not prohibited, but consistent with the letter and spirit of the constitution, are constitutional." *McCulloch v. Maryland*, 4 Wheat. 316, 421 (1819). (See, also, *Osborne v. Bank of the U.S.*, 9 Wheat. [U.S.] 738, 762 [1824].) I am concerned in this book to set forth both what is prohibited by the First Amendment and what can be said to be "the letter and spirit of the Constitution." I am reminded of Lincoln's "proposition, so long and well established, that what you cannot do directly, you cannot do indirectly." Lincoln, *Complete Works*, 1:482. See ibid., 1:482, 553, 567; cf. ibid., 1:548, 2:65. (See *John Marshall: Major Opinions*, pp. xxiv, 27, 29, 31 ff., 43-46.)

A recent attempt to apply this proposition is indicated in an excerpt from a news article about the handling of the pathetic *Soblen* case in England:

> Mr. Elwyn Jones [counsel for Dr. Robert Soblen—see chap. 5, n. 125, above] [submitted this argument] to support his plea for a writ of habeas corpus:
> The court could go behind the deportation order and declare it invalid if it was being used for a collateral purpose.
> "My submission is that deportation which is simply a machinery to say 'Get out and stay out' is a machinery being sought to be used here for the purposes of extradition."

CHAPTER SIX, NOTES 67-70: PAGES 160-63   591

Mr. Elwyn Jones described this as "the abuse of power argument" and in citing previous cases quoted the remark of a judge in one of them who had said: "You can never beat into the heads of people exercising bureaucratic authority that they must exercise their power singly and not for collateral objects."

The deportation order, he submitted covered up something illegal, the extradition of an alien to a foreign Power [the United States] in circumstances where he had committed no extraditable offence. [*London Daily Worker*, Aug. 23, 1962]

See, also, chap. 4, n. 11, above, chap. 7, n. 71, below. (See, on the *Soblen* case, Henry Street, *Freedom, the Individual and the Law* [London: Penguin Books, 1963], pp. 265-68.)

Coke observes that "when any thing is prohibited, every thing is prohibited which necessarily leads to it." Francis S. Sullivan, *Lectures on the Constitution and Laws of England* (Portland: Thomas B. Wait & Co., 1805), 2:274.

67. That this question could have been pressed, despite the explicit constitutional provision requiring that every state official "shall be bound by Oath or Affirmation to support this Constitution," indicates the care with which a possible extension of the powers of Congress was regarded. See Elliot, *Debates*, 3:204.

Compare Chief Justice Marshall's argument in *McCulloch* v. *Maryland*, 4 Wheat. 316, 417, 420-21 (1819) about the significance of the "necessary and proper" clause:

> . . . This power ["to establish post-offices and post-roads"] is executed by the single act of making the establishment. But, from this has been inferred the power and duty of carrying the mail along the post-road, from one post office to another. And, from this implied power, has again been inferred the right to punish those who steal letters from the post office, or rob the mail. It may be said, with some plausibility, that the right to carry the mail, and to punish those who rob it, is not indispensably necessary to the establishment of a post office and post road. This right is indeed essential to the beneficial exercise of the power, but not indispensably necessary to its existence. . . . If no other motive for [insertion in the Constitution of the "necessary and proper" clause] can be suggested, a sufficient one is found in the desire to remove all doubts respecting the right to legislate on that vast mass of incidental powers which must be involved in the constitution, if that instrument be not a splendid bauble.

See chap. 4, n. 13, chap. 6, n. 57, above. See, also, chap. 2, nn. 30, 31, above.

68. This is the first bill Congress passed, prescribing an oath of office for officers of both the general and state governments. *Annals*, I, pp. 2127-28. See Story, *Commentaries on the Constitution*, chap. 43, sec. 1845.

69. *Annals*, I, pp. 914-15. See the text at chap. 4, n. 19, above. See, on what "strict construction" and "broad construction" mean, a letter by Arthur Schlesinger, Jr., *Time*, May 4, 1970, p. 2; Richard Rovere, *New Yorker*, Apr. 18, 1970, p. 141.

70. James Wilson saw fit, during the ratification campaign, to speak in the following manner of the powers delegated by the Constitution (see chap. 6, n. 47, above):

> When the people established the powers of legislation under their separate governments, they invested their representatives with every right and authority which they did not in explicit terms reserve: and therefore upon every question, respecting the jurisdiction of the house of assembly, if the frame of government is silent, the jurisdiction is efficient and complete. But in delegating foederal powers, another criterion was necessarily introduced: and the congressional authority is to be collected, not from tacit implication, but from the positive grant, expressed in the instrument of union. . . . For instance, the liberty of the press, which has been a copious subject of declamation and opposition: what controul can proceed from the foederal government, to shackle or destroy that sacred palladium of national freedom? If, indeed, a power similar to that which has been granted for the regulation of commerce, had been granted to regulate literary publications, it would have been as necessary to stipulate that the liberty of the press should be preserved inviolate, as that the impost should be general in its operation. [Ford, *Essays*, p. 156]

The concluding sentence in the Wilson quotation sums up much of the argument in this chapter of my book. See chap. 6, n. 37, above. True, it comes from one of the leading authors of the Constitution, from a supporter of the Constitution who wanted to expose as groundless the arguments of those who urged that ratification should await the addition to that instrument of a bill of rights. But it is evident from an examination of the collections of both Elliot and Ford that the *opponents* of the Constitution were very hard put to find therein any plausible grounds for arguing that Congress may have been given power to abridge the freedom of speech or of the press. (See Elliot, *Debates*, 2:449-50; 3:203, 217-18, 466; also, chap. 6, n. 57, above.) Rather, I find Nathaniel Macon (of North Carolina) to be on solid ground, in the course of the debate on the Sedition Act of 1798:

> Mr. Macon then proceeded to quote the opinions of the leading members in several of the State conventions, in order to show, from the opinions of the friends of the Constitution, that it was never understood that prosecutions for libels could take place under the General Government; but that they must be carried on in the State courts, as the Constitution gave no power to Congress to pass laws on this subject. Not a single member in any of the conventions gave an opinion to the contrary. . . .
> Mr. Macon also quoted the opinions of members of Congress at the time the amendments to the Constitution were adopted, to prove the same thing. And he inquired how it was come to pass, notwithstanding all the positive opinions which he had quoted to the contrary, that Congress should now conceive that they have power to pass laws on this subject? He could himself find no ground to justify the change. [*Annals*, V, pp. 2151-52; cf. *Annals*, V, pp. 1959, 1969, 1986, 2146]

71. Gouverneur Morris, *A Diary of the French Revolution*, ed. Beatrix C. Davenport (Boston: Houghton Mifflin Co., 1939), 1:496.

> This relative matter of national power and State rights, as a principle, is no other than the principle of generality and locality. Whatever concerns the whole should be confided to the whole—to the General Government; while whatever concerns only the State should be left exclusively to the State. This is all there is of original principle about it. Whether the National Constitution in defining boundaries between the two has applied the principle with exact accuracy, is not to be questioned. *We are all bound by that defining, without question.* [Lincoln, *Complete Works*, 2:62-63 (italics added)]

This insistence upon respecting the boundaries that have been defined is particularly persuasive in a constitutional system which provides for amendments and which has, in fact, been amended more than a score of times. See chap. 7, n. 65, below. (Compare the attitudes North and South to still another constitutional bargain, that relating to slavery, its status in the country, and its representation in Congress. See Staughton Lynd, *Class Conflict, Slavery, and the United States Constitution* [Indianapolis: Bobbs-Merrill, 1967], chaps. 7, 8. How Lincoln kept to this bargain is indicated in chap. 7, n. 14, below.) See, also, chap. 2, n. 34, chap. 4, n. 12, above.

Is it not salutary for a democratic people to regard itself bound by its constitutional bargains (including its bargain with respect to amendment of the Constitution)? Such a disposition is useful discipline which can accustom a people to restrain bursts of passion, especially since passion is all too apt to serve selfish interests even when it invokes the name of justice. (Similar salutary discipline may be seen in the meter and form to which even an inspired poet submits, or in the outline and numbers by which a careful writer works. It may be seen as well in economic analysis:

> At the Planning Board [in New Delhi], I used the occasion to express the importance I attach to exports—it enforces cost discipline, shows foreign leaders that India will have foreign exchange to repay loans, and encourages attention to the naturally efficient industries, some of which, like tea and textiles, seem rather

old-fashioned and hence are easily neglected. [John Kenneth Galbraith, *Ambassador's Journal* (Boston: Houghton Mifflin Co., 1969), p. 85])

See *Federalist*, p. 509; *Annals*, I, p. 283-84, 739; chap. 7, nn. 59, 124, chap. 8, n. 96, below. See, also, Justice Black, 346 U.S. 946 (1954); chap. 9, n. 12, below.

72. Thus, under the First Amendment, Congress is left free to make laws to revive or enlarge freedom of speech in a state in order to assure genuine elections and republican government there; but Congress cannot abridge freedom of speech in order to attain these ends. See chap. 4, n. 108, above.

73. The Fourth Amendment reads (see chap. 5, n. 76, above):

The right of the people to be secure in their persons, houses, papers, and effects, against unreasonable searches and seizures, shall not be violated, and no Warrants shall issue, but upon probable cause, supported by Oath or affirmation, and particularly describing the place to be searched, and the persons or things to be seized.

74. See chap. 4, n. 11, chap. 6, nn. 50, 62, above, and chap. 8, n. 36, below. The history of the English press is instructive here:

... a further attempt to renew the [Licensing Act] in 1695 was negatived by the commons, and thenceforth the censorship of the Press has ceased to form part of the law of England. The Press was now theoretically free; but in practice it was still subject to several methods of restraint. ... The way in which the summary jurisdiction of Parliament was employed to check the publication of debates has already been referred to, with reference to the privileges of the House of Commons; and the government also made use of two other means of controlling the Press: (1) the stamp duty on newspapers, and (2) the law of libel. ... [Theodore F. T. Plucknett, *Taswell-Langmead's English Constitutional History*, 11th ed. (London: Sweet & Maxwell, 1960), pp. 663-64]

Consider, also, the long footnote in *Federalist* No. 84. See the text at chap. 4, n. 16, and at chap. 6, n. 62, above. See, also, Ford, *Essays*, pp. 113-14; the Staff, Social Science I, the College of the University of Chicago, eds., *The People Shall Judge* (Chicago: University of Chicago Press, 1949), p. 340; Morison, *Sources and Documents*, p. 47; Charles A. Beard and Mary R. Beard, *The Rise of American Civilization* (New York: Macmillan Co., 1930), p. 209; Street, *Freedom, the Individual and the Law*, p. 97; W. M. Clyde, *The Struggle for the Freedom of the Press from Caxton to Cromwell* (New York: Burt Franklin, 1970); chap. 4, n. 13, above, chap. 8, n. 175 (concluding paragraph), below.

75. See, e.g., the Licensing Act of 1643 and Milton's concluding remarks in the *Areopagitica*. See, also, Crosskey, *Politics and the Constitution*, pp. 477-86.

"Looking at the [proposed Constitution] in detail, [Robert Whitehill, in the 1787 Pennsylvania Ratifying Convention] saw many difficulties and dangers. He warned that the provision giving Congress the right to secure to authors the rights to their own writings could be twisted into authority to license the press and thus suppress it." Robert G. Crist, *Robert Whitehill and the Struggle for Civil Rights* (Lemoyne, Pa.: Lemoyne Trust Co., 1958), p. 33.

Another recognized power of the general government that can be so used as to discourage the exercise of freedom of speech is that with respect to naturalization and deportation. See, e.g., *Harisiades* v. *Shaughnessy*, 342 U.S. 580, 581, 592 (1952), with its invocation by Justice Jackson of *Dennis* v. *U.S.* (see chap. 7, n. 22, below) in support of his affirmative answer to the "ultimate question ... whether the United States constitutionally may deport a legally resident alien because of membership in the Communist Party which terminated before enactment of the Alien Registration Act of 1940." (See, also, *Flemming* v. *Nestor*, 363 U.S. 603 [1960].) I do not believe it would be difficult to show how ostensibly lawful assaults upon the opinions and associations of one group among us (even aliens) affect what even respectable citizens (and not only those who have alien relatives whom they may want to protect) are likely to say. After all, what does the ordinary citizen think—or dare not to think—upon hearing that someone is deported (after more than thirty years among us) because he is or was a Communist? I believe that the popular teaching of *Schneiderman* v. *U.S.*, 320 U.S. 118 (1945) is much healthier for Americans. See Zechariah Chafee, *Freedom of Speech* (Cambridge: Harvard University Press, 1920), pp. 109, 229 ff.; Kalven, "Upon Rereading Mr. Justice Black on the First Amendment," *U.C.L.A. L. Rev.* 14 (1967): 431-32.

In the United States, restrictive legislation of various sorts has been adopted from time to time. Some of the most radical provisions of this kind were included in the Alien Registration Act (1940) [the Smith Act]. At the time, because of its title, most people believed that it was a statute concerned with the fingerprinting of foreigners and similar matters. Zechariah Chafee, Jr., wrote a little later: "Not until months later did I for one realize that this statute contains the most drastic restrictions on freedom of speech ever enacted in the United States during peace. . . . The act gives us a sedition act for everybody, especially citizens of the United States." [Carl J. Friedrich, *Constitutional Government and Democracy*, 4th ed. (Waltham, Mass.: Blaisdell Publishing Co., 1968), p. 161]

In addition, as I have already noted, two of the great powers of Congress have been used in this century to justify serious legislative encroachments upon freedom of speech and of the press. The war power was exploited, for example, in *Schenck* v. *U.S.*, 249 U.S. 47 (1919) (Appendix B, above), the case upon which all subsequent judicially sanctioned repression of the twentieth century by the general government can be said to have been grounded. The commerce power was exploited in *American Communications Assn.* v. *Douds*, 339 U.S. 382 (1950). Cf. *U.S.* v. *Brown*, 381 U.S. 437 (1966). (Consider the comment by *Barron's* on the Security and Exchange Commission, chap. 5, n. 130, above.) See chap. 3, n. 24, above.

The most recent major illustration of such exploitation may be seen in the Anti-Riot Act of 1968, the act under which the misconceived "Chicago Conspiracy Trial" of 1969-70 (Appendix D, above) was brought. The statute is instructive for displaying not only how an acknowledged power of Congress (in this case, the commerce power) can be used to permit Congress to move into areas where it does not belong, but also how Congress *has* been affected by Supreme Court decisions (with respect to "clear and present danger" [chap. 3, sec. 5, above], with respect to the jurisdiction of the states [chap. 7, sec. 7, above], and with respect to constitutional limits upon legislation which may seem to interfere with "advocacy of ideas" or "expression of belief" [chap. 8, sec. 10, above]). Thus, we can see support here for the much-challenged proposition that Congress does consider itself obliged to conform to (or, at least, to work its way around) judicial restrictions upon legislative activity.

The principal provisions, for our purposes, of the Anti-Riot Act of 1968 (18 U.S.C., chap. 102) follow:

Section 2101.

(a)(1) Whoever travels in interstate commerce or foreign commerce or uses any facility of interstate or foreign commerce, including, but not limited to, the mail, telegraph, telephone, radio, or television, with intent—

(A) to incite a riot; or

(B) to organize, promote, encourage, participate in, or carry on a riot; or

(C) to commit any act of violence in furtherance of a riot; or

(D) to aid or abet any person in inciting or participating in or carrying on a riot or committing any act of violence in furtherance of a riot; and who either during the course of any such travel or use or thereafter performs or attempts to perform any other overt act for any purpose specified in subparagraph (A), (B), (C), or (D) of this paragraph—

CHAPTER SIX, NOTE 76: PAGE 166

Shall be fined not more than $10,000, or imprisoned not more than five years, or both. . . .

(c) A judgment of conviction or acquittal on the merits under the laws of any State shall be a bar to any prosecution hereunder for the same act or acts. . . .

(e) Nothing in this section shall be construed to make it unlawful for any person to travel in, or use any facility of, interstate or foreign commerce for the purpose of pursuing the legitimate objectives of organized labor, through orderly and lawful means.

(f) Nothing in this section shall be construed as indicating an intent on the part of Congress to prevent any State, any possession or Commonwealth of the United States, or the District of Columbia, from exercising jurisdiction over any offense over which it would have jurisdiction in the absence of this section; nor shall anything in this section be construed as depriving State and local law enforcement authorities of responsibility for prosecuting acts that may be violations of this section and that are violations of State and local laws.

Section 2102.

(a) As used in this chapter, the term "riot" means a public disturbance involving (1) an act or acts of violence by one or more persons part of an assemblage of three or more persons, which act or acts shall constitute a clear and present danger of, or shall result in, damage or injury to the property of any other person or to the person of any other individual or (2) a threat or threats of the commission of an act or acts of violence by one or more persons part of an assemblage of three or more persons having, individually or collectively, the ability of immediate execution of such threat or threats, where the performance of the threatened act or acts of violence would constitute a clear and present danger of, or would result in, damage or injury to the property of any other person or to the person of any other individual.

(b) As used in this chapter, the term "to incite a riot," or "to organize, promote, encourage, participate in, or carry on a riot," includes, but is not limited to, urging or instigating other persons to riot, but shall not be deemed to mean the mere oral or written (1) advocacy of ideas or (2) expression of belief, not involving advocacy of any act or acts of violence or assertion of the rightness of, or the right to commit, any such act or acts.

The passage "damage or injury to the property of any other person or to the person of any other individual" should remind us of the far-reaching constitutional consequences of courts' having included a century ago within the "person" of the Fourteenth Amendment entities other than human beings. A "person" (including a corporation), we are implicitly told by Congress in this act, may have property, but only an individual may have a person! That is, is it not difficult to avoid the conclusion that at the very core of the "person" is the human being? Indeed, it may be difficult as well (even for the most "scientific" legal scholars) to ignore in any serious inquiry into the "person," just as it should be for a psychologist to ignore in any serious inquiry into dreams or into those ghost stories which manage to move us, an awareness of the human soul (in the classical, not the Christian, sense). And it is the proper shaping of the soul which can be seen to be the "ultimate function" of politics (and hence of constitutions and laws). See chap. 5, n. 147, above, chap. 9, n. 20, below. (See, on "soul," *Osborne v. Bank of the United States*, 9 Wheat. [U.S.] 738, 861-2 [1924], and on the nature and care of the human soul, Kurt Riezler, *Man: Mutable and Immutable* [Chicago: Henry Regnery Co., 1950]. See, also, chap. 9, n. 17, below.) See, on the ultimate function of politics, the conclusion of Aristotle's *Nicomachean Ethics*.

Where, by the way, does the Anti-Riot Act of 1968 leave a sober public defense (after having crossed state lines, and all that) of the "right of revolution"? See Appendix F, above, esp. pp. 417-18. See, also, chap. 7, nn. 76, 78, below.

76. See pp. 160-61, above. The amendment can also be taken, I have argued, as limiting or eliminating whatever national common-law control over speech or the press existed upon the establishment of the Constitution. See chap. 6, nn. 34, 37, above.

77. We can appreciate this degree of inquietude by imagining the dismay there would be in some quarters today if the First Amendment should be removed from the Constitution. Thus, James Reston observed (*New York Times*, Apr. 19, 1970), after noting a nation-wide poll which concluded "that the majority of American adults now seem willing to restrict some of the basic freedoms constitutionally guaranteed by the Bill of Rights":

> Well, save my old habeas corpus, what goes on here? Are we to fight a war for the liberties of the Vietnamese people and lose our own in the process? Let the Government take us into an obscene war by stealth at the cost of over 40,000 dead and not be free to criticize its stupidities or even report its blunders?

Cf. chap. 8, n. 135, below. Cf., also, chap. 5, n. 73, above.

78. Also available to the citizen-teacher are critical provisions of the state constitutions as well as of the original Constitution of 1787.

The First Amendment is particularly useful for the simple reason that, in its absence, a citizen would be obliged—in order to challenge Congress or to alert his less sophisticated fellow citizens against harmful legislation abridging freedom of speech—to make a long and necessarily difficult argument, such as I have made in this chapter, whereas now one need only cite the amendment (if its evident meaning has not been undermined by executive usurpation or by judicial and legislative misconstruction). The longer argument (about, for instance, the powers of Congress or the likely effects of the legislation in question) may be sound, but it requires greater attention and information than many citizens can be expected to have.

The argument from the First Amendment itself, on the other hand, is both sound and short: indeed, it can make this chapter superfluous for the citizen as distinguished from the student. See Locke, *Reasonableness of Christianity*, in *Works of John Locke* (London: Rivington, Egerton et al., 1824), 6:145-47. See, also, chap. 2, n. 39, chap. 3, n. 13, above ("The First Amendment comes into the discussion chiefly as a powerful means of persuasion." Chafee, book review, *Harvard L. Rev.* 62 [1949]: 891, 894).

See chap. 7, n. 107, below. See, also, chap. 8, n. 181, below.

CHAPTER VII

1. Various comments by Richard M. Weaver, among others, anticipate the argument of this chapter: "Acton believed that the preservation of liberty depended on the maintenance of different centers of power, authority, and influence." And to this is added the note, "This is the real meaning of [Acton's] otherwise puzzling reference to 'the securities of medieval freedom.' The medieval world was organized into various corporate bodies with sharply defined and recognized areas of liberties." Richard M. Weaver, "Lord Acton: The Historian as Thinker," *Modern Age*, Winter 1960-61, p. 20. See chap. 2, n. 3, chap. 6, n. 55, above, chap. 8, n. 83, below. See, also, chap. 9, n. 28, below.

The reference Weaver made is found in Acton, *Essays on Freedom and Power* (London: Thames & Hudson, 1956), p. 198. Related to this is another observation by Acton in the same essay ("Political Causes of the American Revolution"): "The dispute between absolute and limited power, between centralisation and self-government, has been, like that between privilege and prerogative in England, the substance of the constitutional history of the United States [between 1787 and 1861]." Ibid., p. 173. Cf. chap. 7, n. 16, below. See Marvin Zetterbaum, *Tocqueville and the Problem of Democracy* (Stanford: Stanford University Press, 1967), pp. 49, 59.

Also important for the argument of this chapter is the observation by Crosskey about "state power [over speech, press, and assembly being] subject to a negative control in Congress to prevent abuses by the states," which is reproduced in the text at chap. 5, n. 88, above. Such an approach is reflected in the testimonial by Justice Harlan:

> The more I see of these obscenity cases the more convinced I become that in permitting the States wide, but not federally unrestricted, scope in this field, while holding the Federal Government with a tight rein, lies the best promise for

CHAPTER SEVEN, NOTE 2: PAGE 172

achieving a sensible accommodation between the public interest sought to be served by obscenity laws . . . and protection of genuine rights of free expression. [*Jacobellis* v. *Ohio* (dissenting), 378 U.S. 184, 204-5 (1964)]

Compare the rebuke of such arguments as I develop in this chapter found in the opinion for the Court of Justice Clark in *School District of Abington* v. *Schempp*, 374 U.S. 203, 215-17 (1963):

[T]his Court has decisively settled that the First Amendment's mandate that "Congress shall make no law respecting an establishment of religion, or prohibiting the free exercise thereof" has been made wholly applicable to the States by the Fourteenth Amendment. . . . Second, this Court has rejected unequivocally the contention that the Establishment Clause forbids only governmental preference of one religion over another. . . . While none of the parties to either of these cases has questioned these basic conclusions of the Court, both of which have been long established, recognized and consistently reaffirmed, others continue to question their history, logic and efficacy. *Such contentions, in the light of the consistent interpretation in cases of this Court, seem entirely untenable and of value only as academic exercises.* [Italics added]

The character of this book may be revealed by the fact that the first of the two arguments Justice Clark dismissed as virtually worthless still seems to me worthy of serious reconsideration, if only as a way of inducing us to *think* about the underlying problems. See chap. 2, n. 39, chap. 5, n. 1, above, chap. 7, n. 35, chap. 9, n. 1, below.

2. My argument in this chapter *on this point* is not that of the Madison of the First Congress. I am closer, instead, to the Madison of the Virginia Resolutions and the Report of 1799. (See chap. 4, n. 5, above.)

In the famous Virginia and Kentucky resolutions of 1798 [wrote the great grandson of John Adams!], Mr. Madison and Mr. Jefferson set forth [their] ideas with a care and an authority which gave the two papers a character hardly less decisive than that of the Constitution itself. The hand which drafted the Declaration of Independence drafted the Kentucky Resolutions; the hand which had most share in framing the Constitution of the United States framed that gloss upon it which is known as the Virginia Resolutions of 1798. [Henry Adams, *John Randolph*, American Statesmen (Boston: Houghton Mifflin Co., 1890), p. 34]

See chap. 6, n. 36, above. (My critical departure from the Virginia Resolutions is with respect to judicial review. See chap. 8, n. 85, below. See, also, James Morton Smith, "The Grass Roots Origins of the Kentucky Resolutions," *William and Mary Q*. 27 [1970]: 221, 245: "A close examination of Kentucky public opinion at the level of county rallies, newspaper and pamphlet commentaries, and the legislature's resolutions makes it reasonably clear that no matter how ambiguous the political theory of the Kentucky Resolutions might appear to be, the immediate practical issue which concerned Kentucky was repression, not secession." Cf. chap. 5, nn. 23, 52, above, chap. 8, nn. 68, 118, below.)

A different view of the Virginia and Kentucky Resolutions is presented by William Graham Sumner (*Andrew Jackson*, American Statesmen [Boston: Houghton Mifflin Co., 1897], pp. 212-13):

Those resolutions now came to have [in 1827] for a certain party in the South the character and authority of an addendum to the Constitution. They were, in truth, only the manifesto of a rancorous opposition, and they belong, in the history of the country, in the same box of curious products of political passion with the resolutions of the Hartford convention. Yet, at that time, to call a man a "federalist" would have been a graver insult throughout the South than it would be now [1882], in the North, to call a man a secessionist.

"[A] convention, called by invitation of the Massachusetts legislature [in opposition to the War of 1812, 'Mr. Madison's war'] assembled in secret session at Hartford, Conn. [in October, 1814], and was attended by Federalist delegates from Conn., R.I., Mass., N.H., and Vt. . . . The report issued [in January, 1815] included a statement (echoing the states'-rights doctrines of the Kentucky and Virginia resolutions) that 'in cases of deliberate, dangerous and palpable infractions of the Constitution, affecting the sovereignty of a State and liberties of the people; it is not only the right but the duty of such a State to interpose its authority for their protection. . . . News of Jackson's victory at New Orleans and the signing of the Treaty of Ghent . . . made the Hartford Convention the butt of popular ridicule." Richard B. Morris, ed., *Encyclopedia of American History* (New York: Harper & Row, 1961), pp. 141, 153. See chap. 7, n. 83, below.

Sumner had said (*Andrew Jackson*, p. 28), "Jefferson has remained a popular idol, and has never been held to the responsibility which belonged to him for his measures. The alien and sedition laws were not nearly so unjust and tyrannical as the laws for enforcing the embargo, and they did not touch one man where the embargo laws touched hundreds." A footnote refers to the work by Mathew Carey quoted in chap. 6, n. 33, above, "for the opinion of a democrat on [the alien and sedition laws] after party spirit had cooled down."

But perhaps it is an important distinction that the Sedition Act touched the mind, and the Embargo Acts merely the pocketbook. The same distinction suggests itself when one considers the status of the Bantu in the Republic of South Africa today. Cf. chap. 8, sec. 5, above. See chap. 6, nn. 38, 50, above, chap. 7, n. 115, chap. 9, nn. 38, 39, below.

3. " . . . No ingenuity could reason out of the Constitution the power of Congress over slavery in the District [of Columbia]; *for somewhere the power had to be lodged*, and the legislative power of Congress over the District was expressly declared to be 'exclusive in all cases whatsoever.' " H. von Holst, *John C. Calhoun*, American Statesmen (Boston: Houghton Mifflin Co., 1892), p. 127. (Italics added.) See *The Federalist* (New York: Random House, Modern Library, n.d.), pp. 279-80.

"There ought to be in every Constitution an available authority somewhere. The sovereign power must be *come-at-able*." Walter Bagehot, *The English Constitution*, World Classics (London: Oxford University Press, 1928), p. 87. "Hobbes told us long ago, and everybody now understands that there must be a supreme authority, somewhere. The idea of government involves it—when that idea is properly understood." Ibid., p. 195. See Hobbes, *Leviathan*, II, xxix. See, also, William Blackstone, *Commentaries on the Laws of England*, 1:160; George Anastaplo, "Notes on the First Amendment" (Ph.D. diss., University of Chicago, 1964), pp. 545-46; chap. 7, n. 96 (end), below.

These sentiments are evident in *Federalist* No. 36 (in a discussion of the tax power):

> . . . There are certain emergencies of nations, in which expedients, that in the ordinary state of things ought to be forborne, become essential to the public weal. And the government, from the possibility of such emergencies, ought ever to have the option of making use of them. . . . And as I know nothing to exempt this portion of the globe from the common calamities that have befallen other parts of it, I acknowledge my aversion to every project that is calculated to disarm the government of a single weapon, which in any possible contingency might be usefully employed for the general defense and security.

See *Federalist* (New York: Modern Library, n.d.), pp. 142-46, 150-52, 156, 190; cf. ibid., pp. 101, 165, 285. (See chap. 4, n. 1, above.) Chief Justice Marshall could thereafter speak of the Constitution as "intended to endure for ages to come, and consequently to be adapted to the various crises of human affairs." *McCulloch* v. *Maryland*, 4 Wheat. [U.S.] 316, 415 (1919). Cf. chap. 9, nn. 3, 30, below.

Are not the requirements of due process, and the prohibition of *ex post facto* legislation, both of which are generally recognized as applying to both the state and general governments, significantly different from the prohibition altogether in the United States of any government control over freedom of speech, press, and religion? Cf. chap. 4, n. 113, chap. 5, n. 112, above.

See chap. 8, n. 83, below. (C. Herman Pritchett, *The American Constitution* [New

CHAPTER SEVEN, NOTES 4-5: PAGE 173   599

York: McGraw-Hill, 1968], p. 593, characterized as "a more pedantic argument" that made by Justice Matthews in *Hurtado* v. *California*, 110 U.S. 516 [1884], a case in which a petitioner under sentence of death challenged on the basis of the due process clause of the Fourteenth Amendment his conviction for murder in a state court trial initiated by an information [chap. 8, n. 54, below] rather than by a grand jury indictment. The opinion in *Hurtado* [from which only Justice Harlan dissented] is discussed by Pritchett in these terms:

> Since the Fifth Amendment [Justice Matthews argued] contains both the guarantee of due process and of indictment by grand jury, and since it must be assumed that no part of the Constitution is superfluous, it follows that due process as used in the Fifth Amendment does not include indictment by grand jury. When the same phrase is repeated in the Fourteenth Amendment, it must be given the same meaning. Thus [Justice] Matthews emerged with the remarkable conclusion, directly opposed to that of [Justice] Curtis [in *Murray's Lessee* v. *Hoboken Land and Improvement Co.*, 18 How. (U.S.) 272 (1856)], that the due process clause in both the Fifth and Fourteenth Amendments must be interpreted to *exclude* any rights specified elsewhere in the Constitution.

See chap. 2, sec. 6, above, chap. 8, nn. 13, 15, below. See, also, chap. 7, n. 107, below.)

4. There were similar extensions of freedom of speech and of the press in other countries during the nineteenth century, extensions that might well be traced back to the influence of the Enlightenment. This would not account, however, for the peculiarly American experience, an experience which was successful, permanent, and widely known and upon which subsequent experiments elsewhere were based. The history of American immigration reflects the reputation, as well as the attraction, of the United States as a sanctuary from European political despotism—as well as from the despotism of poverty.

See chap. 8, n. 44, below.

5. This condition, which requires vigorous local government, is to be found in that other great modern country in which freedom of speech and of the press have been permanently established. Thus, it can be said even today of the police in Great Britain

> that they are still very largely a local service, to an extent which surprises many people. There are in fact one hundred and twenty-six separate police forces in England and Wales. . . . The Metropolitan Police are the one exception to the rule that forces are free from any Government control in their management. For they are under the direct control of the Home Secretary. . . . The justification for this arrangement lies in the great importance which any Government must attach to the preservation of order in the Capital, and in the fact that the Metropolitan Police are employed in the protection of the person of the Sovereign and of the Houses of Parliament, and for various other purposes of a national as opposed to a merely local character. [Gwilym Lloyd-George, "The Arm of the Law," in *Liberty in the Modern State* (London: Conservative Political Centre, 1957), pp. 19-20]

See chap. 7, n. 51, below.

More than a century earlier Hegel wrote:

> The Constitution of England is a complex of mere *particular Rights* and particular privileges: the Government is essentially administrative—that is, conservative of the interests of all particular orders and classes; and each particular Church, parochial district, county, society, takes care of itself, so that the Government, strictly speaking, has nowhere less to do than in England. This is the leading feature of what Englishmen call their Liberty, and is the very antithesis of such a centralized administration as exists in France, where down to the least village the Maire is named by the Ministry or their agents. . . . In England, on the contrary, every parish, every subordinate division and association has a part of its own to perform. . . . [*The Philosophy of History* (New York: Wiley Book Co., 1956), p. 454]

See Tocqueville, *The Old Regime and the French Revolution* (New York: Doubleday & Co., Anchor Books, 1955), pp. 41-43, 45, 48, 49, 51, 60, 61, 74; Stendhal, *The Red and the Black*, trans. M. R. B. Shaw (Baltimore: Penguin Books, 1953), p. 27. See, also, chap. 8, sec. 9, chap. 2, n. 7, chap. 6, n. 55, above.

6. But see, on Shays's Rebellion and the wording of the First Amendment, the text at chap. 5, n. 88, above; cf. chap. 6, n. 28, above. See, also, *Federalist*, pp. 29, 33, 100, 126-27; Arthur E. Sutherland, *Constitutionalism in America: Origin and Evolution of Its Fundamental Ideas* (New York: Blaisdell Publishing Co., 1965), pp. 165-67.

7. "The best way to learn the nature and effects of different systems of government, is not from theoretical dissertations, but from experience—from what has actually taken place among mankind." Governor Huntington, Connecticut Ratifying Convention, 1788, Jonathan Elliot, ed., *Debates in the Several State Conventions on the Adoption of the Federal Constitution* (Philadelphia: J. B. Lippincott & Co., 1863), 2:198.

See, for a useful set of "observations on particular parts of the constitution," the letter from Roger Sherman and Oliver Ellsworth (of Connecticut) transmitting to Governor Huntington a copy of the instrument. Max Farrand, ed., *The Records of the Federal Convention of 1787* (New Haven: Yale University Press, 1937), 3:99-100.

8. See, for a suggestion of how Blackstone may be reconciled with the American standard of freedom of the press, the text at chap. 5, n. 94, above. See, also, chap. 6, nn. 23, 30, 34, 66, above.

9. It remains to be seen whether an essentially blind process can be relied upon in this manner. We do speak of *enlightened* self-interest. But is not the ultimate emphasis and dependence on the self-interest (which is, unless one is interested only in the best, fundamentally ignorant)? At what point must understanding intervene to take advantage of chance developments and to curb self-interest? See chap. 9, n. 38, below.

The role of chance is suggested by Lord Charnwood's observation:

> The American Constitution owes its peculiarities partly to the form which the State Governments had naturally taken, and partly to sheer misunderstanding of the British Constitution, but much more to the want at the time of any strong sense of national unity and to the existence of a good deal of dislike to all government whatsoever. [*Abraham Lincoln* (Garden City, N.Y.: Garden City Publishing Co., 1917), pp. 22-23]

See chap. 5, nn. 25, 28, above, chap. 7, n. 94, below. See, also, chap. 8, sec. 5, above.

10. In such matters, the right beginning may be essential to success. One is reminded of the game of "Fox and Geese": there is a move that one can make at the outset of the match that can assure success or, if not made and if the opposition is alert, means certain failure.

See, for august ways of putting this sentiment, Plato, *Republic* 540E-541B; Aristotle, *Nicomachean Ethics* 1104b12, *Politics* 1302a1; Heidegger, *An Introduction to Metaphysics* (Garden City, N.Y.: Doubleday & Co., Anchor Books, 1961), p. 13. Cf. chap. 2, n. 7, above. See, also, chap. 9, n. 12, below.

11. The earliest important adjustment of the controversy is reflected in the constitutional provision for the numbering of slaves for electoral and taxation purposes. Three-fifths of such persons were to be counted for both purposes. It seems that the slave-holding states got the better of this bargain, since it was decided in the First Congress (and adhered to thereafter) that direct taxation (toward which the slaves counted, to the detriment of slave-holding states) would not be resorted to "until it is found that sufficient funds cannot be obtained in any other way." *Annals*, I, p. 302. See *Federalist* No. 54; Harry V. Jaffa, *Crisis of the House Divided* (Garden City, N.Y.: Doubleday & Co., 1959), p. 433; Sutherland, *Constitutionalism in America*, pp. 237-38; Staughton Lynd, *Class Conflict, Slavery, and the United States Constitution* (Indianapolis: Bobbs-Merrill, 1967), pp. 160-67. See chap. 6, n. 71, above, chap. 7, n. 14, below.

12. See Bagehot, *English Constitution*, pp. 195-96; Charnwood, *Abraham Lincoln*, pp. 126-27; Jaffa, *Crisis of the House Divided*, p. 98.

CHAPTER SEVEN, NOTES 13-14: PAGE 175   601

13. One of the earliest questions raised in the First Congress about the extent of the power of the general government was with respect to slavery. This discussion followed the proposal that a ten-dollar duty be levied on the importation of each slave from abroad. *Annals*, I, pp. 336-37.

"The new Congress abolished the slave trade on the first day on which the Constitution allowed it to do so, that is, on January 1, 1808. The mother country abolished it just about the same time. But already all but three of the States had for themselves abolished the slave trade in their own borders." Charnwood, *Abraham Lincoln*, p. 38. See Joseph Story, *Commentaries on the Constitution of the United States*, 2d ed. (Boston: Little, Brown & Co., 1851), chap. 32, secs. 1332-36; Lincoln, *Complete Works*, ed. John G. Nicolay and John Hay (New York: Century Co., 1902), 1:202-3.

Lincoln argued (ibid., 1:623-24), on the status of slavery in the Constitution:

> When men are framing a supreme law and chart of government to secure blessings and prosperity to untold generations yet to come, they use language as short and direct and plain as can be found to express their meaning. In all matters but this of slavery the framers of the Constitution used the very clearest, shortest, and most direct language. But the Constitution alludes to slavery three times without mentioning it once! The language used becomes ambiguous, roundabout, and mystical. They speak of the "immigration of persons," and mean the importation of slaves, but do not say so. In establishing a basis of representation they say "all other persons," when they mean to say slaves. Why did they not use the shortest phrase? In providing for the return of fugitives they say "persons held to service or labor." If they had said "slaves," it would have been plainer and less liable to misconstruction. Why didn't they do it? We cannot doubt that it was done on purpose. Only one reason is possible, and that is supplied us by one of the framers of the Constitution—and it is not possible for man to conceive of any other. They expected and desired that the system would come to an end, and meant that when it did the Constitution should not show that there ever had been a slave in this good free country of ours.

It is understandable that Lincoln argued thus. But we must notice that the words *slavery*, *slave*, and *previous condition of servitude* may now be found in the Constitution (in the Thirteenth, Fourteenth, and Fifteenth Amendments, respectively). That is, we can, now that we have corrected that blemish in our institutions, plainly acknowledge it. I am reminded of Themistocles' guidance for the people of Athens:

> After the triumphs of Salamis and Plataea, the Athenians returned to their beloved home, which was now unimaginably devastated, but they were now bolder and more optimistic than ever before. It seems that Themistocles' first thought was to fortify the city. The ancient Mycenaean wall of the Acropolis must have suffered greatly for them to think of fortifying it with a new wall. It was built straighter than the old wall, of hewn stone, without towers or bastions. On its outside north side great architectural fragments of temples destroyed by the Persians were incorporated in an orderly fashion. It is said that Themistocles wished this to be done so that the forgetful Athenians might see them from the Agora and be reminded of the past. [Yannis Miliadhis, "The Acropolis—Its Historical Site," *Greek Heritage* 2, no. 5 (1965): 22]

The column drums, which remain visible from the city below, bear to this day the marks of Persian fire. The Athenians, reminded thus of what the barbarian had done to the temples of their gods, were thereby urged to remain vigilant. The marks of slavery in our Constitution should likewise promote vigilance among us, not so much against foreign enemies as against the self-righteousness of which a prosperous self-governing people is peculiarly capable and from which few of us are completely free. See, e.g., chap. 7, nn. 21, 74, below.

Cf. Lynd, *Class Conflict*, pp. 159-62. See *Federalist* No. 54 (ibid., p. 358: "a little strained"). See, also, chap. 8, n. 181, below.

14. J. G. Randall, *Constitutional Problems under Lincoln* (Urbana: University of Illinois Press, 1951), pp. 350-51, remarked:

It is of interest to notice that the war did not swerve President Lincoln from the view that he had previously expressed (in the debate with Douglas and elsewhere) that Congress had no constitutional power to overthrow slavery in the States. [Footnote: In conversation with Senator Browning of Illinois, Lincoln expressed his conviction that Congress had no power over slavery in the States (Diary of Orville H. Browning, July 1, 1862).] In his public pronouncement concerning the Wade-Davis bill of 1864, of which he disapproved because of its drastic process of "reconstruction," Lincoln said: "I am . . . unprepared . . . to declare a constitutional competency in Congress to abolish slavery in [the] States." He added that he hoped the object would be achieved by constitutional amendment.

See chap. 6, n. 71, above.

But what of the slave trade between the states, which may have been vital not only for the spread but perhaps even for the perpetuation of slavery where it already was? Did the Commerce Clause "declare a constitutional competency in Congress" to regulate or abolish such trade? Consider Lincoln's response:

In regard to the fifth interrogatory, I must say here that as to the question of the abolition of the slave-trade between the different States, I can truly answer, as I have, that I am pledged to do nothing about it. It is a subject to which I have not given that mature consideration that would make me feel authorized to state a position so as to hold myself entirely bound by it. In other words, that question has never been prominently enough before me to induce me to investigate whether we really have the constitutional power to do it. I could investigate it if I had sufficient time to bring myself to a conclusion upon that subject, but I have not done so, and I say so frankly to you and to Judge Douglas. I must say, however, that if I should be of opinion that Congress does possess the constitutional power to abolish the slave-trade among the different States, I should still not be in favor of the exercise of that power unless upon some conservative principle as I conceive it, akin to what I have said in relation to the abolition of slavery in the District of Columbia. [Lincoln, *Complete Works*, 1:308 (Aug. 27, 1858)]

Cf. ibid., 1:352.

Lincoln's "conservative principle"—which reflects his respect for both the advantages and limitations of the rule of law under a constitution—may be seen in the care with which the Emancipation Proclamation was drafted. The limited interference with slavery in that instrument was "sincerely believed to be an act of justice, warranted by the Constitution upon military necessity. . . . " Ibid., 2:288. See, also, chap. 4, n. 56, above; chap. 7, nn. 54, 55, 95, below.

See Walter Berns, "The Constitution and the Migration of Slaves," *Yale L. Rev.* 78 (1968): 198.

15. It was argued by Calhoun and others in 1836 that "discriminating, in reference to character, what publication shall not be transmitted by the mail" would be an abridgment of "the liberty of the press." The First Amendment limitation on Congress in this respect was said to be decisive. The slave states were reduced to controlling that which they *could* control on the local level, the possession by and circulation among slaves of inflammatory literature. (The deliberate efforts to keep slaves illiterate served the same purpose.)

However, Calhoun did prepare a bill (defeated in the Senate, 25-19) in which he attempted to secure the respect and support of the general government *for local regulations* —a bill which would have made it unlawful

for any deputy postmaster, in any State, Territory, or District of the United States, knowingly to deliver to any person whatever, any pamphlet, newspaper, handbill, or other printed matter or pictorial representation touching the subject of slavery, where, by the laws of the said State, Territory, or District, their circulation is prohibited; and any deputy postmaster who shall be guilty thereof shall be forthwith removed from office.

See, for the quotations employed in this note and for useful discussions of this matter, Holst, *John C. Calhoun*, pp. 134-39; O. John Rogge, *The First and Fifth* (New York: Thomas Nelson & Sons, 1960), pp. 26-27, 91, 309; Sumner, *Andrew Jackson*, pp. 350-51. See, also, p. 245, above.

16. Cf. Bagehot, *English Constitution*, p. 202:

> The Americans now extol their institutions, and so defraud themselves of their due praise. But if they had not a genius for politics; if they had not a moderation in action singularly curious where superficial speech is so violent; *if they had not a regard for law, such as no great people have yet evinced, and infinitely surpassing ours*,—the multiplicity of authorities in the American Constitution would long ago have brought it to a bad end. Sensible shareholders, I have heard a shrewd attorney say, can work *any* deed of settlement; and so the men of Massachusetts could, I believe, work *any* Constitution. [Initial italics added]

(Cf. chap. 7, n. 1, above.) Bagehot added in a footnote, at this point, "Of course, I am not speaking here of the South and South-East, as they now are. How any free government is to exist in societies where so many bad elements are so much perturbed, I cannot imagine." See, also, ibid., pp. 232-33. Cf. Adam Smith, *An Inquiry into the Natural Causes of the Wealth of Nations* (New York: Random House, Modern Library, 1937), pp. 203, 537-38.

See chap. 4, n. 117, above. Cf. chap. 8, n. 27, below.

17. See Tocqueville, *Democracy in America* (New York: Random House, Vintage Books, 1954), 1:161, 175, 401. One factor in this depreciation of local government seems to be the publicity given in the press to misconduct of city and state government officials. It is easy to conclude, as a result of the evidence of corruption in local government that is brought to the public attention, that only the servants of the general government are worthy of trust. But this difference in "public image" depends, in part, on the much more intimate contact on the part of most newspapers with local government institutions and personnel (as well as the kinds of activities such local institutions and personnel are responsible for). Besides, does not a newspaper justify its political existence much more easily by exploiting local grievances, about which it can expose something of interest, than by retailing information about what goes on in Washington?

One must account for the fact that the thoughtful man is often persuaded, upon working closely with state, county, and city employees, that the level of dedication and performance is higher than he had anticipated. (A staff member of a business management study of operations of the state of Illinois—a study financed and staffed by private industry—"commented that as a result of the study of the whole scope of operations, he had this impression of it: 'One thing I was particularly impressed with was that the state is producing its product, and doing a damn fine job of it.' " *Chicago Sun-Times*, Feb. 24, 1967, p. 19.) But that this will continue after another generation of press depreciation—of an irresponsible use of freedom of the press, it should be noted—is hard to believe. Many of the problems with state governments could be easily handled by a people determined to do so—by a people that appreciates that unless the states fashion their constitutions in response to the problems of today, more and more power will inevitably go to Washington.

Illinois, for instance, could do much better with a constitution one-fifth the size of the treatise we now have. See "Short Constitution Needed," *New York Times*, Feb. 6, 1967, p. 26. See, also, "Let's Stick to Essentials," *Chicago Tribune*, Aug. 10, 1970, p. 20. (The constitution for Illinois written in 1970 is about as long as its predecessor.) No sooner is an American state constitution ratified than it is in need of radical amendment. Obsolescence is built into it partly because its draftsmen act as if they were a legislative body, not a constitutional convention. The necessity of restricting themselves to a draft of only a few pages would help them to recognize what is needed in such a document, especially after they have had an apprenticeship of several months of effort along the usual lines. (Cf. chap. 5, n. 83, above, chap. 7, nn. 81, 82, below.) One thing needed is an effort to return to the constitutional attitude recorded in *Federalist* No. 31: "The State governments, by their original constitutions, are invested with complete sovereignty. In what does our security consist against usurpation from that quarter? Doubtless in the manner of their formation, and in a due dependence of those who are to administer them upon the people." (See, also, *Federalist* No. 32.)

Thus, the government of a state could be defined (in a state constitution kept to bare essentials) as possessing all powers not delegated exclusively to the federal government by the Constitution of the United States and not prohibited therein to state governments, subject to such limitations (including, perhaps, with respect to taxation) as may be spelled out in a state bill of rights. Provision would also be made in such a state constitution for the selection, functions, privileges, and regulation of the officers of the various branches of the state government, for the powers within the state of designated local governments, and for subsequent amendment of the new constitution. All this could be best provided for in less than a dozen pages, with most details of implementation left for periodic adaptation to changing circumstances by the branches of the state government established pursuant to the constitution. See my call "to the People of the State of Illinois," published as a letter to the editor in (among other papers) the *Chicago Tribune*, July 2, 1970, and in the *Chicago Daily News*, July 6, 1970.

But even more important than the length of a constitution, and a condition for significant reform, is that the people be properly instructed about the role of the states in our constitutional system. The massive state legislative reapportionment we have been seeing may help citizens take seriously again governments more representative, and hence more responsive to public opinion, than their predecessors. See chap. 7, n. 84, below. Even so, public opinion is such that it can indicate, in response to the Gallup Poll question, "Which do you think spends the taxpayer's dollar more wisely—the state government or the federal government?" "State government, 49%; Federal government, 18%; Neither, 17%; No opinion, 16%." *Chicago Sun-Times*, Jan. 1, 1967, p. 15. See "The States," *Time*, Aug. 4, 1967, p. 21.

See Edward Crankshaw, *Khrushchev's Russia* (London: Penguin Books, 1959), pp. 94-98.

18. Bagehot, *English Constitution*, p. 203 (on how the British constitution permits the discharge of "a dangerous accumulation of inhibited power").

Even a scholar so hostile to the "states' rights" doctrine as Crosskey recognized the special role of the states, as distinguished from the general government, with respect to the regulation of speech and the press. This is evident in the passage in the text at chap. 5, n. 88, above. It is also evident in this passage:

> . . . [T]he great "States' Rights" Chief Justice [Roger Brooke Taney] claimed for the states, in *The License Cases* [5 How. (U.S.) 503, 574, and 582 (1847)], a police power that was, in fact, a power of complete and very largely inviolable intrastate sovereignty. The tremendous change from the ideas of 1787 which this claim involved may be seen from these considerations: . . . (3) that, under the original Constitution, there were, in fact, no paramount "States' Rights" of any kind, except in reference to the election of Presidential electors and, in a very technical and limited sense, in reference to certain matters relating to the militia; and (4) that, by the initial amendments of 1791, no such "rights" were intended to be created, except in the limited areas covered by the First Amendment, and even in these, the states were left subject to Congressional control in favor of "Liberty," save in the case of "religious establishments." [William W. Crosskey, *Politics and the Constitution* (Chicago: University of Chicago Press, 1953), p. 1164]

See chap. 7, n. 95, below.

19. See chap. 8, sec. 12, above, chap. 6, n. 7, above.

20. Sumner, in *Andrew Jackson*, pp. 97, 99, explained:

CHAPTER SEVEN, NOTE 21: PAGE 177   605

The elected President is the person who gets a majority of the votes constitutionally described and cast, and the power and right of the House of Representatives in the contingency which the Constitution provides for is just as complete as that of the electoral college in all other cases. But the electoral college by no means necessarily produces the selection which accords with the majority of the popular vote. The issue raised by [Thomas H.] Benton and his friends [in 1825] was therefore nothing less than constitutional government *versus* democracy. . . . The Constitution provides only specified ways for ascertaining "the will of the people," and that will does not rule unless it is constitutionally expressed. That is why we are, fortunately, under a constitutional system, and not under an unlimited and ever-changing democracy. . . . The "*demos krateo* principle," to use Benton's jargon, belongs in the same category with Louis Fourteenth's saying: *L'état c'est moi.* One is as far removed from constitutional liberty as the other.

See chap. 6, n. 71; pp. 14-15, above.

21. *Federalist* No. 25. The illustration used by Publius for this teaching is drawn from a failure in constitutionalism among the ancients:

It was a fundamental maxim of the Lacedaemonian [i.e., Spartan] commonwealth, that the post of admiral should not be conferred twice on the same person. The Peloponnesian confederates, having suffered a severe defeat at sea from the Athenians, demanded Lysander, who had before served with success in that capacity, to command the combined fleets. The Lacedaemonians, to gratify their allies, and yet preserve the semblance of an adherence to their ancient institutions, had recourse to the flimsy subterfuge of investing Lysander with the real power of admiral, under the nominal title of vice-admiral. This instance is selected from among a multitude that might be cited to confirm the truth already advanced and illustrated by domestic examples; which is, that nations pay little regard to rules and maxims calculated in their very nature to run counter to the necessities of society. Wise politicians will be cautious about fettering the government with restrictions that cannot be observed, because they know that every breach of the fundamental laws, though dictated by necessity, impairs the sacred reverence which ought to be maintained in the breast of rulers towards the constitution of a country, and forms a precedent for other breaches where the same plea of necessity does not exist at all, or is less urgent and palpable.

See, also, *Federalist*, pp. 159-60, 163, 223, 241-42, 256-59, 262, 271; chap. 6, n. 71, above.

Indeed, it was "sacred reverence" (successfully circumvented on this occasion) upon which the Spartan constitution rested. See, for the significance of traditional piety (and of its deterioration) among the Spartans, Xenophon, *Hellenica*, especially 2.2.19-20; 3.2.21-26; 3.3.1-11; 4.3.13-14; 4.4.12; 4.7.2-7; 4.8.36-39; 5.1.29-30; 5.3.27-4.1; 7.1.29-32; 7.4.32. See, also, Thucydides, *History of the Peloponnesian War*, 2.72.2; 3.89.1; 5.54.2; 53.3, 116. (Sparta and Rome are compared by Bacon in his essay "On the True Greatness of Kingdoms and Estates.") See, on the Athenian Miltiades as a pious "constitutionalist," Herodotus, *History* 6.110. Cf. Plutarch, *The Lives of the Noble Grecians and Romans* (New York: Random House, Modern Library, n.d.), p. 136.

What should be made, on the other hand, of that pious "constitutionalism" which binds Hindu regimes to prohibit the slaughter of cows (and which discourages the elimination even of the multitudinous rats which consume food grains equal to what India has to import)? It is said that the prophet Zoroaster (in the tenth century B.C.), "protested against a new teaching with extravagant emphasis upon sacrifice and the slaughter of cattle which he felt was undermining the ancient lore and endangering the material and social values of the agricultural, cattle-raising community." *Encyclopedia of Religion* (Patterson, N.J.: Littlefield, Adams & Co.), p. 842. Is the orthodox Hindu teaching based on such considerations? Is a new prophet needed to prepare Indians for a world in which the mortality rate has been radically affected by science and technology (just as a new prophecy may be needed to prepare Mormons to come to terms with the emancipated and politically significant Negro)? See chap. 7, nn. 34, 55, 124, below. Did Mohandas Gandhi pass up the last opportunity to make the necessary change in this respect within Hinduism, thereby leaving the problem for irreverent Marxism to resolve? Or would this have meant the corruption of, or at least a vital change in, the Hindu soul? Cf. chap. 5, n. 89, above. Even more vital was the change Gandhi did make serious efforts to effect, a change with respect to Indian opinions about caste. See André Malraux, *Anti-Memoirs* (New York: Holt, Rinehart & Winston, 1968), pp. 128-29, 135-36. See, also, ibid., pp. 225-26, 238, 245; John F. Muehl, *Interview with India* (New York: John Day Co., 1950), pp. 58-59, 124-28, 181-95, 195 ff., 251-57, 261-62, 301-2. (How difficult it is to appreciate the hold upon other peoples of irrational opinions should become apparent to Americans who try to justify to others the hold that our infatuation for automobiles and guns has upon us. Thus, for example, Mervin Block observed on WNBC-TV [May 18, 1970], in terms which remind us of what Americans have said about the voraciousness of India's quarter of a billion cows, "A third of all land in New York City is given over to streets, roads, highways and parking places." It is said that there is one cow for every two Indians. It is also said that there is one gun for every two Americans. See *Newsweek*, Aug. 17, 1970, p. 15; chap. 7, n. 67, below. Perhaps we could do with a prophet or two ourselves.) See, for an introduction to the Mormons, Bernard A. Weisberger, "The Moses of Mormonism [Brigham Young]," *Book World*, Nov. 16, 1969, p. 14.

See Plato, *Republic* 415C-D; Thomas More, *Utopia*; Francis Bacon, *New Atlantis*; Jean Jacques Rousseau, *The Social Contract and Discourses* (Everyman Edition; New York: E. P. Dutton & Co., 1950), II, vii.

22. Acton quoted with approval Publius's proposition,

> A large and well-organised republic can scarcely lose its liberty from any other cause than that of anarchy, to which a contempt of the laws is the high-road. . . . A sacred respect for the constitutional law is the vital principle, the sustaining energy of a free government. . . . The instruments by which it must act are either the authority of the laws, or force. If the first be destroyed, the last must be substituted; and where this becomes the ordinary instrument of government, there is an end to liberty. [Acton, *Essays on Freedom and Power*, p. 185]

One factor making for law-abidingness in the United States is the insistence that discussion is available on all subjects, that peaceable redress is thus available. This not only assures those who labor under grievances but also arms with a useful righteousness those who are content and law-abiding.

> Our Constitution sought to leave no excuse for violent attack on the status quo by providing a legal alternative—attack by ballot. To arm all men for orderly change, the Constitution put in their hands a right to influence the electorate by press, speech and assembly. This means freedom to advocate or promote Communism by means of the ballot box, but it does not include the practice or incitement of violence [citing *Dennis* v. *U.S.*]. [Justice Jackson (in the Opinion of the Court), *Harisiades* v. *Shaughnessy*, 342 U.S. 580, 592 (1952)]

(Cf. chap. 6, n. 75, above.) What is the significance in this respect of the refusal (as in Illinois) to permit members of the Communist party to appear on the ballot?
See chap. 8, sec. 13, above, chap. 7, nn. 45, 124, below.

23. *Federalist* No. 25. Consider, on the other hand,

> . . . [The philosophers] recommend good and dissuade from evil in the most admirable manner. And in order to resemble the Creator who arranged everything so perfectly, they have contrived laws, or rather regulations without binding force, and which may be overridden in times of need. The religious law [of Judaism], however, is not so except in its social parts, and the law itself sets down those which permit exceptions and those which do not. [Judah Halevi, *The Kuzari* (New York: Schocken Books, 1964), p. 225]

See, ibid., pp. 166-68. See, also, chap. 8, n. 14, chap. 9, n. 21, below. Cf. chap. 7, n. 3, above.

Federalist No. 41 warns against "plant[ing] in the Constitution itself necessary usurpations of power, every precedent of which is a germ of unnecessary and multiplied repetitions." Indeed, constitutionalism may be somewhat like marriage in that much will be put up with out of habit: but when something happens again and again to accustom the parties to the idea of seriously considering alternative arrangements, that which had seemed so secure can be suddenly (and perhaps even irretrievably) undermined. That is, practical affairs (and the institutions serving such affairs) may require a certain amount of unexamined illusion if one is to care. Perhaps, indeed, many men may encounter in their spouses and in the institutions of their country both evident love and latent anger: the problem is in each instance whether the hostility is ameliorated by love or the love vitiated by hostility. In the best regime, whether domestic or political, the evident and the central (the surface and the core) unite or at least peacefully coexist. See chap. 4, n. 40, chap. 5, nn. 126, 132, above. See, also, chap. 7, nn. 35, 59, 115, below.

24. Much of what has been said about the need to provide for the abuses and dangers of freedom of speech and of the press applies as well to the people's concern for supposed abuses. Such concern, which is often reflected in the complaint that "the government ought to do something," cannot be safely ignored. People, perhaps mistakenly, demand action, and they must be assured that some responsible government is empowered to take action. (See the text at chap. 5, n. 88, above.) Otherwise, just as in the case of real abuses, there is a strain on the better interpretation of the controlling constitutional provision with the result that distorting rationalizations (if not simple disrespect for the Constitution) follow. The wise politician so arranges matters that his people learn to distinguish the abuses from the supposed abuses or, at least, instills respect in them for the institutions and constitutional arrangements that do so distinguish. See chap. 6, nn. 71, 78, above. See, on the use and abuse of safety valves, chap. 5, n. 124, above.

See chap. 5, n. 147, above, for various "activities of speech and press" of a primarily local character which the states are left free to deal with. False alarms, whether in theaters or out, are included. See, also, chap. 5, sec. 10, above.

But, on the other hand, *is* it good for the prestige of the states that they be permitted the more repressive power I recognize the Constitution to leave with them? Is it good for the states that the general government is seen as more liberal, as more concerned for civil liberties, than the states, especially at a time when the legitimacy of many of the powers of government is being challenged? How the states would come to be regarded would depend on how this state power is supervised and hence moderated by the general government and on how those of us who discuss such matters explain the role of the states. See, for a discussion of "necessary" evils, *Federalist* No. 54. See, also, chap. 7, n. 107, below. (This is one reason why it would be desirable for the states to have the dominant role in such popular enterprises as pollution control.) See chap. 8, n. 135, below.

25. The second sentence in this paragraph was eliminated from the Bill of Rights in the West Virginia Constitution of 1872. Does that mean that such attempts ("to justify and uphold," etc.) are now immune from prosecution in that state? (Cf. the last paragraph of the Anti-Riot Act of 1968 reproduced in chap. 6, n. 75, above.)

26. It seems to have been feared that (unless qualifications were added) the known impotence of the general government with respect to these matters might be attributed to West Virginia, especially since the First Amendment formulation was used. (This impotence of the general government, I have argued, resulted both from the meaning of "freedom of speech, or of the press" and from the limited powers of the general government.) See chap. 3, n. 12, above.

Is it likely that the Fourteenth Amendment was intended to impose extensive restraints on the states with respect to speech and the press so soon after such qualifications as those in the West Virginia Constitution had been put into a "northern" state constitution? On the other hand, Sharp (chap. 2, n. 13, above) has argued (cf. chap. 8, n. 83, below) that the illustrations of freedom-of-speech interests among abolitionists, collected by Crosskey in the debate found at *U. Chicago L. Rev.* 22 (Autumn 1954): 1, support the proposition that the Fourteenth Amendment was indeed intended to extend against the states the guarantees of the First Amendment. See chap. 7, nn. 84, 86, 107, chap. 8, n. 13, below.

27. The victims are spared the rigors of exile; and the community is spared the peculiarly distorted attacks from abroad of embittered exiles.

Thomas B. Macaulay, in his *History of England*, described the plight of politicians who had fled the England of James II (see chap. 7, nn. 70, 71, below):

> These refugees were in general men of fiery temper and weak judgement. They were also under the influence of that peculiar illusion which seems to belong to their situation. A politician driven into banishment by a hostile faction generally sees the society which he has quitted through a false medium. Every object is distorted and discoloured by his regrets, his longings and his resentments. Every little discontent seems to him to portend a revolution. Every riot is a rebellion. He cannot be convinced that his country does not pine for him as much as he pines for his country. [Robert Graves and Alan Hodge, *The Reader over Your Shoulder: A Handbook for Writers of English Prose* (New York: Macmillan Co., 1961), p. 108]

Cf. *Annals*, V, p. 1990. The sad plight of exiles may be seen among those who have fled Greece. (See chap. 6, n. 1, above.) Some of the best fled early and have been left stranded. It is not enough to flee *from* something; one needs to flee *to* something.

28. This argument does presuppose a presumption (discussed in chapter 8) for freedom of speech and against its curtailment.

My general argument presupposes as well the political desirability (whatever the constitutional limits may be) of restricting the criminal jurisdiction of the general government (in Justice Jackson's words) "first of all to a small number of strictly federal offenses, and secondly to nonpolitical ones." (Chap. 6, n. 59, above.)

> ... My hold of the colonies is in the close affection which grows from common names, from kindred blood, from similar privileges, and equal protection.... Let the colonies always keep the idea of their civil rights associated with your government;—they will cling and grapple to you; and no force under heaven would be of power to tear them from their allegiance. But let it be once understood, that your government may be one thing, and their privileges another ... and everything hastens to decay and dissolution. As long as you have *the wisdom to keep the sovereign authority of this country as the sanctuary of liberty*, the sacred temple consecrated to our common faith, wherever the chosen race and sons of England worship freedom, they will turn their faces towards you.... Deny them this participation of freedom, and you break that sole bond, which originally made, and must still preserve, the unity of the empire. ["Speech ... on Conciliation with the Colonies," Burke, *Works*, World Classics (London: Oxford University Press, 1930), 2:234-35 (italics added)]

29. For good or ill, however, the residents of southern states *are* somewhat influenced by the attitude not only in the northern states, but also abroad, in the measures they may take to preserve segregation. See Farrand, *Records*, 2:124.

Did not the August, 1969, storm which has been called "the most savage hurricane ever known to have hit North America" (*Chicago Sun-Times*, Aug. 23, 1969, p. 18) help cause the remarkably pleasant weather enjoyed in Chicago that month even as it devastated the Gulf Coast? The same sort of thing happened in early August, 1970.

See chap. 6, n. 55, above, for one beneficent effect of Huey Long's legacy in Louisiana. See, also, chap. 6, n. 40, above.

30. Walter Kaufmann, ed., *The Portable Nietzsche* (New York: Viking Press, 1954), p. 91. (A world apart from Nietzsche's, despite its seeming similarity, is Voltaire's sentiment, "Killing a man is murder unless you do it to the sound of trumpets." Frank Harvey, *Air War—Vietnam* [New York: Bantam Books, 1967], p. 86. Is not Nietzsche more profound, whereas Voltaire is more modern?)

The following passage illustrates the lengths to which a concern for national security may drive the citizen (cf., on *Schenck* and government funds, chap. 6, n. 38, above):

CHAPTER SEVEN, NOTES 31-32: PAGE 180

> It is conceded by all informed observers that the contest for the world in which we are now engaged, and shall in all likelihood be engaged during the lifetime of everyone now living, peculiarly requires the mobilization of the intellectual resources of the nation. If a Negro child in Mississippi, who has within himself the gifts of a Nobel Laureate, is denied the educational opportunities which might enable those talents to flower, the country will lose what it cannot, in a sense never before so compelling, afford to lose. Whatever may once have been true, a citizen of New York and a citizen of Mississippi now have the same long-run interests in the educational opportunities of the children of their own and of each other's State. Mississippi should be expected to support the educational establishment of the United States as much as it should be expected to support the defense establishment, and the reason is plain: *they are fundamentally one and the same.* . . . As Mississippi has the same obligation *to the nation* to educate its children as has New York, so does New York have the same obligation *to the nation* to be taxed, if need be, to help pay for the children of Mississippi's children. . . . [Jaffa, "The Case for a Stronger National Government," in R. A. Goldwin, ed., *A Nation of States* (Chicago: Rand McNally, 1963), p. 107 (initial italics added)]

I have made several references to the work of Jaffa since he is a particularly thoughtful and articulate representative of one of the schools of thought to which the argument of this book is addressed. (See Shakespeare, *Coriolanus*, act 1, sc. 1, lines 221-28. See, also, nn. 26, 39, and 52 of my article on Plato's *Apology* cited in chap. 2, n. 1, above.) Another essayist argued,

> Nevertheless, the educational centralizer protests, we need to spend more money on schooling, or at least to distribute the money equally over the states. But, in fact, *our educational problems really are not those of finance.* We already spend far more on education, per head of population, than has any other nation in history. Even the state of Mississippi spends more per capita than do most of the highly civilized countries of western Europe. [Russell Kirk, "The Prospects for Territorial Democracy in America," in Goldwin, *A Nation of States*, p. 57]

(I believe the observation by Kirk which I have italicized may well be true. See Anastaplo, "The Daring of Moderation: Student Power and *The Melian Dialogue*," *School Review* 78:451, 480, n. 6 [1970]; chap. 8, n. 122, below.) See, also, chap. 7, n. 113, below.

31. Senator Wallace Bennett of Utah reported to the Senate that whereas in January, 1961, only 1,000 North Carolina residents were on the free food rolls, the number had "skyrocketed" to 147,000 by June after the Kennedy administration had greatly expanded the program; from July, 1960, to July, 1961, the number in Utah had increased from 11,378 to 21,098; nationally, the number of persons receiving free food was 3.3 million in June, 1960 (with the country in recession), with the number increased to 6.2 million a year later (when the recession was said to have ended). The senator observed, "By failing to keep this program within reasonable bounds, the administration is aiding and abetting a process which erodes character, destroys self-respect, and breeds contempt for the American tradition of working for a living." *Chicago Tribune*, Sept. 16, 1961, pt. 3, p. 14. We need not concern ourselves here with the justification for such disbursements (cf. chap. 4, n. 101, above), but merely note the grandiose scale on which the general government is financially equipped to act even with respect to nonmilitary matters.

32. See Ralph S. Brown, *Loyalty and Security: Employment Tests in the United States* (New Haven: Yale University Press, 1958), p. 195. The *Chicago Daily News* observed, in an editorial of April 23, 1970 (p. 12):

> Somewhere in Washington—unless they've gone fishing—there are five men who get $36,000 a year each for doing absolutely nothing. They are the members of the Subversive Activities Control Board, whose official functions, never definite or demanding, have now been eliminated by the Supreme Court.
> The court ruled this week, in effect, that the board could not declare individuals to be members of the Communist Party. So now this control board

controls nothing at all, and its sole remaining function is unofficial. This in fact has been its major function all along—to provide opportunities for political bargaining and nesting places for political pets who otherwise might have been unemployed. This exploitation has been sweetly bipartisan. . . . There remains no possible reason for the board to continue as merely a source of pensions for political hacks, or for its $180,000-a-year cost to be longer diverted from useful purpose.

(See Pritchett, *The American Constitution*, pp. 334-36, 545; U.S. v. *Robel*, 389 U.S. 258 [1967]; chap. 7, n. 45, below.) This is to be contrasted to the inability in 1959 of even so prosperous a state as Michigan to pay its officers and teachers. Compare, however, the observation by Mervin Block about government expenditures in New York City:

Every year, 25,000 [part-time] inspectors are hired to register voters. There used to be a need for many inspectors because voters had to register once a year, but since 1957 there has been permanent registration. . . . The new president of the Board of Elections wants to trim 16,000 inspectors from this force, keeping 9,000 for registration and election day duties. He estimates that taxpayers would save a million dollars a year by adoption of this long overdue reform. [WNBC-TV editorial, July 24, 1970]

According to a standard text, state and local government expenditures (which are a useful rough measure [of what is now done]) have been moving quite steadily upward. In 1957 they stood at about 11 per cent of Gross National Product; in 1948 the figure was about 7.9 per cent, and in 1929 about 7.3 per cent. The rate of increase has been considerably higher than that of domestic program expenditures of the federal government; federal expenditures on such programs (i.e., exclusive of national security and military and foreign aid programs) increased about 50 per cent and state and local ones about 60 per cent in the 1948-1957 period. And, surprisingly in view of the often-expressed feeling that the federal bureaucracy is overwhelming, state and local expenditures on such programs are consistently over five times as large as the federal. [Citing Charles R. Adrian, *State and Local Governments* (New York: McGraw-Hill, 1960), chap. 5] [Martin Diamond, Winston Fisk, and Herbert Garfinkel, *The Democratic Republic* (Chicago: Rand McNally, 1966), p. 120, n. 28]

But the federal expenditures, especially in matters of national security, are in larger "chunks": I am reminded of Secretary of the Treasury George M. Humphrey's lament, "It's a terribly hard job to spend a billion dollars and get your money's worth." *Look*, Feb. 23, 1954, p. 26. See *Newsweek*, Aug. 10, 1970, pp. 53-54. Cf. chap. 7, n. 17, above.

Should the states rely on the more efficient tax apparatus of the general government to collect money for them? Would this lower the states even more in the eyes of citizens, making the states appear to be clients of the general government? Compare a state income tax using the taxpayer's federal income tax return as the base. But see Raymond Moley, "Taxation as Discipline," *Newsweek*, Jan. 2, 1966, p. 68; chap. 6, n. 71, above.

See, also, *Federalist*, pp. 89-95, 183 ff., 204-5, 219-20; *Business in Brief* (Chase Manhattan Bank), Apr. 1967, pp. 5-7; "'Tax Sharing' Is Already Here," *Christian Science Monitor*, May 2, 1967, sec. 2, p. 9. (Does sharing encourage irresponsible reporting?)

33. See chap. 5, nn. 93, 99, above, on due process in educational matters; also, chap. 7, n. 1, above ("the securities of medieval freedom"). Cf. chap. 2, n. 7, above.

See chap. 6, n. 54, above, chap. 7, n. 67, below. See, also, Appendix E, above.

34. Did not the position of those who challenged the verdict in the Tennessee evolution trial of John Scopes ignore the demands and difficulties of civilization and the community? (See, with respect to an antievolution law in Arkansas, *Epperson* v. *Arkansas*, 393 U.S. 97 [1968]. Consider, in Justice Black's concurring opinion, his suggestions with respect to mootness and to states' rights.) See, also, chap. 9, n. 38, below.

The "liberal" position may not appreciate that ideas do have consequences: young men can be carried away by "modern liberal ideas" and are moved to overlook moral considerations which are critical (especially when the generally accepted underpinnings of

CHAPTER SEVEN, NOTE 34: PAGE 180

conventional morality are subverted before they can be properly replaced). One must ask, for example, whether popular Darwinism or modern astronomy is good for morality.

> The old wounds inflicted during my adolescence when my teacher divulged the two great secrets to me, that the earth is not the center of the universe and that man is not a privileged creature issuing directly from the divine hand, these old wounds, which had been closed for a number of years, opened once again on the Holy Mountain [Mount Athos]—the two metaphysical torments: where do we come from and where are we going. . . . [Nikos Kazantzakis, *Report to Greco* (New York: Simon & Schuster, 1965), p. 235]

See Blackstone, *Laws of England*, 1:41, 2:15, 4:45, 63. See, also, the lecture, "Church and States: The Beginnings of an Argument," appended to my dissertation, "Notes on the First Amendment"; chap. 8, n. 178, below.

Sir James Fitzjames Stephen, *Liberty, Equality, Fraternity* (New York: Holt & Williams, 1873), p. 40, argued that, "The notorious result of unlimited freedom of thought and discussion is to produce general scepticism on many subjects in the vast majority of minds." He went on to say, p. 307:

> We cannot judge of the effects of Atheism from the conduct of persons who have been educated as believers in God and in the midst of a nation which believes in God. If we should ever see a generation of men, especially a generation of Englishmen, to whom the word God had no meaning at all, we should get a light upon the subject which might be lurid enough. Great force of character, restrained and directed by a direct sense of duty, is the noblest of noble things. Take off the restraint which a sense of duty imposes, and the strong man is apt to become a mere tyrant and oppressor. Bishop Berkeley remarked on his countrymen in the early part of the last century, "Whatever may be the effect of pure theory upon certain select spirits of a peculiar make or in other parts of the world, I do verily think that in this country of ours reason, religion, law are all together little enough to subdue the outward to the inward man; and that it must argue a wrong head and weak understanding to suppose that without them men will be enamoured of the golden mean, to which my countrymen are perhaps less inclined than others, there being in the make of a English mind a certain gloom and eagerness which carries to the sad extreme." The remark is as true now as it was then.

See, for an adaptation of Bishop Berkeley's sentiments to American circumstances, President Washington's Farewell Address of 1796. See, also, Farrand, *Records*, 3:471-72, 478; Story, *Commentaries on the Constitution*, chap. 43, sec. 1856. (Perhaps, in many cases [considering the diversity of the opinions which have been vital to various peoples], it is not the content of new "great secrets" which has been so devastating so much as it is that the teachings *are* new and hence different from those which had been long established and around which the previously healthy community had been organized by its authoritative teacher-founder: the authoritative may be thus called into question "across the board," cutting a people loose from its moorings. See chap. 2, n. 38, above, chap. 7, n. 108, chap. 8, nn. 135, 169, chap. 9, nn. 28, 35, below. See, also, pp. 641-43, below.)

> When the Bolsheviks seized power in October 1917, the Church of Russia found itself in a position for which there was no exact precedent in Orthodox history. The Roman Empire, although it persecuted Christians, was not an atheist state, opposed to all religion as such. The Turks, while non-Christians, were still worshippers of One God and, as we have seen, allowed the Church a large measure of toleration. But communism is committed by its fundamental principles to an aggressive and militant atheism. . . . [Timothy Ware, *The Orthodox Church* (London: Penguin Books, 1960), p. 152]

Leo Strauss observes that "it is almost shocking to be suddenly confronted by the more than Machiavellian bluntness" with which bold intellectuals today can speak "of such terrible things as atheism and tyranny and take them for granted." *On Tyranny* (New York: Free Press of Glencoe, 1963), p. 198. Even the bold Bacon recognized an obligation, in his essay "Of Unity in Religion," to speak of religion as "the chief band of human society."

> In the light of the original conception of modern republicanism, our present predicament appears to be caused by the decay of religious education of the people and by the decay of liberal education of the representatives of the people. By the decay of religious education I mean more than the fact that a very large part of the people no longer receive any religious education. . . . Is our present concern with liberal education of adults, our present expectation from such liberal education, not due to the void created by the decay of religious education? Is such liberal education meant to perform the function formerly performed by religious education? Can liberal education perform that function? [Leo Strauss, "Liberal Education and Responsibility," in his *Liberalism Ancient and Modern* (New York: Basic Books, 1968), pp. 18-19]

See, also, Leo Strauss and Joseph Cropsey, *History of Political Philosophy* (Chicago: Rand McNally, 1963), pp. 481-82; chap. 8, n. 122, below. In his second and third Catilinarian speeches, which were made to the people (as distinguished from his first and fourth speeches, which were made to the Senate), Cicero seems to me not only more boastful about himself but also much more emphatic about the gods and about the dreadful crimes and character of the conspirators. See chap. 8, n. 181, chap. 9, n. 27, below.

See, on the usefulness of religion for the commonwealth, Homer, *Odyssey* 24.351-2; Herodotus, *History* 1.89, 90-91; Plato, *Republic* 427B-C, 540B-C, *Laws* 948C-D; Aristotle, *Politics* 7.12, 16; Cicero, *Laws* 2.7.15-16; Plutarch, *Lives*, pp. 78, 80, 139, 142, 145-46, 285, 354, 821, 853; Machiavelli, *Discourses on Livy*, V, xi; Hobbes, *Leviathan*, chaps. 12, 40-43; Milton, *The Prose Works of John Milton* (London: J. Johnson, 1806), 1:82; *Federalist*, pp. 9, 84, 86, 231 (cf. ibid., pp. 23, 88 [on relation of nature and national boundaries]); Gouverneur Morris, *A Diary of the French Revolution*, ed. Beatrix C. Davenport (Boston: Houghton Mifflin Co., 1939), 2:452; Tocqueville, *Democracy in America*, 1:314; Leo Strauss, *Persecution and the Art of Writing* (Glencoe, Ill.: Free Press, 1952), p. 130 ("To deny that religion is essential to society, is difficult . . . for anyone who puts any trust in the accumulated experience of the human race."). See, also, chap. 4, n. 110, chap. 5, n. 96, above.

Cf. Edward Gibbon, *The Decline and Fall of the Roman Empire* (New York: Random House, Modern Library, n.d.), 1:20 ("On that celebrated ground the first consuls deserved triumphs; their successors adorned villas, and *their* posterity have erected convents."); Twain, *Autobiography* (New York: Harper & Bros., 1924), 1:131 (this could well serve to illustrate the nineteenth-century American iconoclastic movement:

> The shooting down of poor old Smarr in the main street at noonday supplied me with some more dreams; and in them I always saw again the grotesque closing picture—the great family Bible spread open on the profane old man's breast by some thoughtful idiot, and rising and sinking to the labored breathings, and adding the torture of its leaden weight to the dying struggles. . . . In my nightmares I gasped and struggled for breath under the crush of that vast book for many a night.)

Cf., also, *The Early Writings of Karl Marx*, ed. T. B. Bottomore (New York: McGraw-Hill, 1969), pp. 9-10. See chap. 4, n. 43, chap. 5, n. 97, chap. 7, n. 21, above, chap. 7, nn. 59, 124, chap. 8, n. 177, chap. 9, n. 9, below.

35. "No modern thinker has understood better than Rousseau the philosophic conception of the *polis*: the *polis* is that complete association which corresponds to the natural range of man's power of knowing and loving." Leo Strauss, *Natural Right and History* (Chicago: University of Chicago Press, 1953), p. 254, n. 2. (See, e.g., Rousseau, *Social Contract*, II, ix-x; III, i; Allan Bloom, "Jean-Jacques Rousseau," in Strauss and

CHAPTER SEVEN, NOTE 35: PAGE 180 613

Cropsey, *History of Political Philosophy*, p. 516 [cf. Richard Kennington, "Rene Descartes," in ibid., p. 390].) Cf. Morton Grodzins, "Centralization and Decentralization in the American Federal System," in Goldwin, *A Nation of States*, p. 1. See chap. 8, nn. 40, 71, below. See, with respect to the *polis* and to the relevance today of various of its features, Aristotle, *Politics* 1325b33-1326b26; Moses Maimonides, *The Guide of the Perplexed* (Chicago: University of Chicago Press, 1963), pp. 601-2 ("For fraternal sentiments and mutual love and mutual help can be found in their perfect form only among those who are related by their ancestor. Accordingly a single tribe that is united through a common ancestor—even if he is remote—because of this, love one another, help one another, and have pity on one another; and the attainment of these things is the greatest purpose of the Law"; cf. ibid., p. 342); *Federalist*, pp. 14-15, 53-62, 80-85, 101-3, 107-8, 112, 185, 262-63, 305, 341, 410; Leo Strauss, *The City and Man* (Chicago: Rand McNally, 1957), p. 30 (cf. Jaffa, "Aristotle," Strauss and Cropsey, *History of Political Philosophy*, pp. 65-67); Zetterbaum, *Tocqueville and the Problem of Democracy* (on the separation of justice and excellence, with modernity moved by claims for the priority of justice), pp. 46-47, 54, 70, 76-77, 78-79, 80-81, 84, 86-87, 88, 129, 146, 153, 156, 157; Thomas S. Schrock, "The Liberal Court, the Conservative Court, and Constitutional Jurisprudence," in *Left, Right and Center*, ed. Robert A. Goldwin (Chicago: Rand McNally, 1965), pp. 87, 94-96; Gerald Stourzh, *Alexander Hamilton and the Idea of Republican Government* (Stanford: Stanford University Press, 1970), pp. 153-70, 256, n. 98. (I attempt in this book to salvage and adapt to our circumstances as much of the *polis*—its spirit and its standards—as it might be sensible for decent men to try to make use of today. Echoes of that spirit may be heard in the prayerful sentiment of President deGaulle: "We want our country to be itself, internally and externally." *New York Times*, Aug. 11, 1967, p. 13. Is the United States, on the other hand, small enough or unified enough "to be itself"? See David Ramsay in chap. 5, n. 87, above.) See, on the "*polis* dream," chap. 8, n. 181, below. See, also, chap. 2, n. 1, chap. 4, n. 116, above.

An attempt is made by an architect interested in the urban canals of England to appeal, in the context of a modern industrial society, to our natural inclination toward things of human scale (that inclination which makes academic communities such as St. John's Annapolis and Chicago's Hyde Park [unless ruined by an airport in Lake Michigan] attractive, as well as countries such as Ireland, Finland, and Scotland):

> Now that the commercial traffic has shifted [from canals] to the roads, the canals offer a secluded environment protected from the noise, fumes and danger of road traffic, with the towpaths as a unique segregated circulation system for pedestrians and cyclists. The BCN canals vary from the rural at the edge (the Wyrley and Essington and Rushall) to those at the centres of Walsall, Warley and Wolverhampton, thoroughly urban in character. In all, the towpaths offer long distance routes away from roads and irate farmers, but canalside buildings give the urban stretches the additional asset of being a hidden private world within the fabric of the town; and here it would be a mistake, as sometimes advocated, to "open up" the canals visually, though this does not mean access should be restricted or further use discouraged.
>
> The canal area has also considerable architectural attractions as a living museum of early industrial England; the cast-iron footbridges, timber lockgates, bollards and precise brickwork have a natural feeling for form and materials, as do the best canalside buildings whose merits are just beginning to be appreciated. Travelling along an urban canal with limited but rapidly changing vistas one has an exciting impression of movement, while every object has a pleasant human scale. So even if parts of the canal area are at present undoubtedly dirty and scruffy, a canalside walk is interesting, secluded and within a human scale—true of few other walks in today's towns. [Lewis Braithwaite, "The Future of the Black Country Canals," *The Blackcountryman*, Spring 1970, pp. 29, 30-32]

The *Federalist* was addressed to "The People of the State of New York"; a comparable book today would be addressed not to one's state, but either to one's family or to the country at large (the former reflects the intimacy, the latter the political character, of the *polis*). (An author can get some idea of "the natural range of man's power of knowing and loving" by reflecting on the difficulty of organizing a book with the care and control sometimes evident in an article or lecture.) Walter Lippmann has observed, "The fact of the matter is that the country is too big to be managed and administered from Washington, and the local authorities are as yet backward and inefficient and unable to do their necessary part." *Chicago Sun-Times*, Jan. 12, 1967, p. 80. See Richard Rovere, "Letter from Washington," *New Yorker*, July 18, 1970, p. 72 (on our need to decentralize and the difficulty of doing so). (See Jerry F. Hough, *The Soviet Prefects*: *The Local Party Organs in Industrial Decision-making* [Cambridge: Harvard University Press, 1969], pp. 1-6, 8-11, 97-113, 124-25, 199-205, 212-13, 256-88.) See, also, Burke, *Works*, 4:217-18; chap. 8, n. 192, chap. 9, n. 1, below.

Storing, on the other hand, would have "our modern advocates of localism" understand:

> The state governments may be closer to the Chamber of Commerce, but today it is the national government that in all fundamental respects is closer to the people. Indeed the national government, including the Senate and the Supreme Court, seems to have been infused with the popular spirit. And although the President is still obliged to reconcile popular wants and national needs, he has to do so today as a great popular leader rather than as one chosen by a small group of judicious men. ["The Problem of Big Government," in Robert A. Goldwin, *A Nation of States* (Chicago: Rand McNally, 1963), pp. 85-86]

See Morton Grodzins, *The American System* (Chicago: Rand McNally, 1968), pp. 198-211; cf. ibid., p. 383.

Compare James Jackson Kilpatrick, "The Case for 'States' Rights,' " in Goldwin, *A Nation of States*, pp. 101-2 (see chap. 6, nn. 38, 41, above):

> . . . One of the reasons for the success [of the Republic as a whole] is that the States and the localities must always be closer to the people than the central government. . . . The government that [has] counted most, because we felt the greatest sense of community with it, was the government at the courthouse, and the government at the State Capitol. A part of this feeling rests in the belief that local government can be controlled in a way that the central government cannot be controlled. Restraints can be applied close at hand, through the devices of referendum and recall, that cannot be applied far away. The county commissioner dwells low on Olympus, and the local alderman is accessible in ways that United States Senators and Cabinet Secretaries are not accessible. When a citizen of Virginia travels to the Capitol at Richmond, he travels with a sure sense of participation and of community; he speaks to the committees of the General Assembly, supporting or opposing particular legislation, as a fellow-citizen in the community of four million that is Virginia. When he travels to the Capitol at Washington, by contrast, he feels insecurity gnawing at his vitals. He finds the palace ringed by the glassy castles of potent baronies—the Machinists, the Mineworkers, the Educationists—and the marbled catacombs of the Senate Office Building are filled with total strangers. In this distant opulence, he stands subdued. It is out of this sense of helplessness that the citizen draws his prudent fear of "Federal control." He sees Federal control as an inescapable corollary of "Federal aid." He knows that it cannot possibly be otherwise. Nor is he the least impressed by the remonstrances of political doctors who assure him that the history of numerous grant-in-aid programs fails to support his apprehensions.

It should be noticed in judging this debate that in both the general and state governments (under the Constitution of 1787), ultimate control is left in the hands of the people. The people's control of government is regulated and moderated, but it is nevertheless there—and ultimately it can be as decisive as the people choose to make it. This control is further assured since the people supply the officers of the country: it is a rankless society, one which is more likely to be kept so by the inability of either the states or the

CHAPTER SEVEN, NOTE 35: PAGE 180 615

United States to grant titles of nobility. The advantages of both union and popular control are assured, or at least made more likely to be enjoyed, by an arrangement whereby those best equipped to select the men to fill each post under the Constitution are given the power to make such selections.

Those best equipped are presumed to be those who are most likely to know the candidates best: the original Constitution provides, that is, for the coordination of the decisions of relatively small "electorates." Thus, the state legislatures (made up of members chosen in small legislative districts in each state) select the senators; the members of the House of Representatives are chosen, in effect, by electoral districts within the states (even when the voting is at large rather than, as is now common, by congressional districts); the President is chosen by a body of electors (whom we call the Electoral College: they are chosen as the state legislatures prescribe); the other officers of the general government, including the judges, are nominated by the President and consented to by the Senate or are selected by the President alone or by one of his lieutenants. The largest "electorate" under the Constitution of 1787—the largest body of men who have to pass on the qualifications of "candidates" for any office in the general government—is likely to be that of the congressional district. The "candidate" can be known, and known well, by those who must select him: one is never obliged to choose among complete strangers. The people retain ultimate control—but they are a people so organized as to bring out the best in them. (Thus, it could be said in the Sixth Congress that federal judges are "nominated by the President of the United States, and chosen by the Senate agreeably to the Constitution." *Annals*, VI, p. 923. See *Federalist*, pp. 494-95. See, also, chap. 4, n. 117, above. Cf. chap. 7, n. 118, below.)

Bearing upon the role of the people and the decisions they must make by means of this system of what I choose to call "coordinated electorates" is the provision made throughout the Constitution for reliance upon discussion. Somehow, reason—or, at least, that deliberation which informs the members of the "electorates"—is to play a part. Free debate is guaranteed in Congress, subject only to the power of either house to discipline a member; the President, when he vetoes a bill, must return it to that house of Congress in which the bill originated, returning it "with his Objections," which objections shall be entered on the journal of each house as it proceeds to reconsider the bill. Furthermore, the very selections in the states on which the presidency and Congress, directly or indirectly, depend—these elections imply, if republican institutions are to be effective, a meaningful discussion of issues and men by the relevant electorate. (See, as bearing on coordinated electorates, *Federalist*, pp. 301, 338-39, 417, 441-44. There is some indication that the election of presidential electors by districts was intended by the Constitutional Convention. See *Congressional Record* 115: E3665 [May 6, 1969].)

It should also be noticed that the states today, even the largest, are roughly of the order of magnitude and perhaps of complexity that the United States was when our institutions were established (and hence probably diverse enough, according to the argument of *Federalist* No. 10, to moderate serious faction within their respective borders). Census figures for the entire country (not including Indians) were 3,929,214 in 1790 and 5,308,483 in 1800. (Sumner could write by 1882, "There are features of American democracy which are inexplicable unless one understands this frontier society. Some of our greatest political abuses have come from transferring to our now large and crowded cities maxims and usages which were convenient and harmless in backwoods county towns." *Andrew Jackson*, p. 7. See Stewart Alsop, "Dr. John Calhoun's Horrible Mousery," *Newsweek*, Aug. 17, 1970, p. 96 [reporting experiments upon the crowding of mice].)

See Aristotle, *Nicomachean Ethics* 1139b18-25, 1170b30-1171a9. "It has been pointed out how when absent from Monticello [Thomas Jefferson] wrote his neighbours, eagerly begging for the news, 'the small news,' of the neighborhood." Paul Wilstach, *Jefferson and Monticello* (Garden City, N.Y.: Doubleday, Doran & Co., 1930), p. 153. See, also, chap. 7, n. 23, above, chap. 7, nn. 59, 115, chap. 8, n. 195, below.

What should we make of—should we, perhaps, even be comforted by—the testimony of the transportation administrator of New York City:

> In 1907 it was found that the average speed of horse-drawn vehicles through the city's streets was 11.5 miles per hour. In 1966 the average speed of motor vehicles through the central business district was 8.5 miles per hour—and during the mid-day crushes slower still. [*New York Times*, Nov. 17, 1967, p. 45]

See Pete Hamill, "Split the City," *New York Post*, Sept. 22, 1969:

> The 51st state won't happen because Congress would never allow another Northern state without a matching Southern state, and Albany cannot give up our tax revenue. The idea of making neighborhoods function with true political power inside a larger city unit can only happen if the size of [New York City] is reduced. . . . Even with five cities, instead of one, the political units might be too large. But [this] would be a beginning, and if joined with the growing block association movement, we might actually begin to cut down on the sense of personal futility that infects so many of us in this town.

Finally, it should be said, electronic communications and computers do not radically increase "the natural range of man's power of knowing and loving," but only encourage the illusion of such increase. One does hear talk of "a global village": but such an association is no more than a city of cities, not a city (or community) of human beings. See chap. 9, nn. 7, 32, below. See, on Israel as perhaps a genuine community, chap. 8, n. 150, chap. 9, n. 10, below. Cf. chap. 4, n. 111, above.

36. The glaring exception has been with respect to the problem of race relations, the legacy of the problem of slavery: the conflict here between, for example, the demands of liberty and those of property (or between two different kinds of liberty) had to be resolved by the amendments explicitly curtailing the power of the states (but not of the general government) to discriminate according to color. See chap. 7, n. 96, below.

37. This has been seen in Illinois state legislative investigations of the University of Chicago and Roosevelt University. Such investigations die out after the respectable figures behind these institutions begin to make their influence felt with their local legislators. The influence of Chancellor Robert M. Hutchins upon the state legislature, in defense of the University of Chicago, was always much more effective than the efforts either of President Hutchins's Fund for the Republic or of the university itself before congressional committees.

38. Perhaps Senator McCarthy even knew from personal observation that there really was nothing to worry about at the University of Wisconsin. Nathan M. Pusey, president of Harvard University, confirmed recently my impressions of the senator's behavior in Wisconsin:

> "My first months as president of Harvard were made unnecessarily difficult by the ostensible campaign of hate [Senator McCarthy] was then conducting against universities in general and Harvard in particular," [Pusey said].
> Pusey was president of Lawrence College, in Appleton, Wis., McCarthy's home state, at the time McCarthy was first elected to the Senate.
> "As long as I remained in Appleton he had taken no public notice of me," Pusey said. "But when I came into the light of the Harvard presidency I was quickly numbered among his targets."
> While at Lawrence, Pusey said, he participated in an effort to prevent McCarthy's reelection, but the senator won by a large plurality. . . . [*Chicago Sun-Times*, June 10, 1970, p. 10]

See, for a critique of the demagogue as evil, Walter Berns, *Freedom, Virtue and the First Amendment* (Baton Rouge: Louisiana State University Press, 1957), pp. 123-25. As for Senator McCarthy himself: I record my impression of that period that he was, despite his misdeeds and even thoughtless or at least desperate cruelty, curiously casual, perhaps even bored with the role he had stumbled into. He would have been more dangerous if he had known and *cared* more about what he was doing. See Sam Houston Johnson, *My Brother Lyndon* (New York: Cowles Book Co., 1970), p. 90. See, also, chap. 3, n. 34, above. The serious problem is not men such as Senator McCarthy but rather those respectable men who permit such opportunists to exploit the fears and ignorance and concerns of their fellow citizens. The supineness of law school deans and faculties during the bar admission controversies of the 1950s is a case in point. See, e.g., Appendix F, above.

39. A Senate committee led by Senator William E. Jenner investigated the University of Chicago in 1953. The senator from Indiana became properly respectful of the faculty witness (the witness himself told me) who had occasion to remind the senator that he, too, came from Indiana where dozens of his Mennonite relatives remained as members of the electorate. See Kermit Eby, "How to Get a Federal Subpoena," *University of Chicago Magazine*, Oct. 1953, p. 10.

40. If there exists the power to do good, there necessarily accompanies it the power to do evil. Consider the warning of a Bahrain pearl merchant, upon learning of a proposed school for girls: "If girls learn to read and write, what is to prevent them from getting letters from men, without their parents' knowledge?" *Oxford* [England] *Mail*, Sept. 1, 1960.

41. The regulation by the general government of speech and the press can be indirect but nevertheless pervasive, thereby stifling discussion of vital public issues and discouraging (if not even penalizing) criticism of government measures. Thus, for example, the growth of the general government as an employer has increased tremendously the power of government over public opinion (especially, as in the 1940s and the 1950s, when well-established government employees still bore the scars of the economic insecurity of the 1930s): those loyalty proceedings meant (until Americans finally learned to "live with them") that millions of government employees, and their relatives, were moved to be most guarded in what they said about controversial issues and in their choice of associates. This caution was to be seen as well in defense industries and, to a lesser extent (depending, in part, on the source of one's funds), in the universities of the country. The significance of the 1948 indictment and 1950 conviction of Alger Hiss was not lost on many timid souls: if someone as exalted as he could be, in effect, condemned for what he may have done a generation before, then no one was safe. One could not, of course, change the past—but one could try to become so inconspicuous as not to have a present which would lead to inquiries about one's past. (And, on the other side of the fence, if someone as respectable as Hiss was guilty of espionage, then no one's loyalty should be above suspicion.) My own impression is, for what it is worth, that Hiss was probably guilty of perjury before a congressional committee, particularly with respect to whether he had ever known Whittaker Chambers intimately. I suspect, that is, that he figured that what was long past, and perhaps in some sense atoned for or at least superseded by events, should not be permitted to interfere with a useful and ever more promising career. A confession of youthful indiscretion probably could have salvaged a good deal for him (especially if it could have headed off, as it might well have, charges of espionage); but a little bluffing must have seemed to him to offer even more than such confession or than reliance upon the Fifth Amendment. In this he was essentially like President Lyndon Johnson of whom I say in chap. 8, n. 150: "He tried, that is, to exercise even more control over the situation than he could have had easily for the taking." And, like the President, Hiss miscalculated, destroying himself, compromising his friends, helping to discredit American liberalism for almost a decade, and "legitimating" the expansion of the power of government to search the lives and to judge the opinions of all citizens. See chap. 8, nn. 126, 135, below.

My impression with respect to whether Hiss was guilty of perjury rests in part on considerations which he himself recognized the significance of. Before being sentenced in 1950 to five years' imprisonment, Hiss said merely this:

> I would like to thank your Honor for this opportunity again to deny the charges that have been made against me. I want only to add that I am confident that in the future the full facts of how Whittaker Chambers was able to carry out forgery by typewriter will be disclosed. [Alger Hiss, *In the Court of Public Opinion* (New York: Knopf, 1957), p. 323]

Much of the remainder of his book is devoted to an attempt to show how "forgery by typewriter" was committed. But his attempt is not, for me, persuasive, if only because the very defense counsel whom Hiss regarded as intelligent and conscientious was obliged to admit in 1952:

> After all my investigations, I still do not know exactly what Chambers did, or how he did it, or exactly what motivated him to frame Alger Hiss. Some signs point to the conclusion that, though his personal interest may have been largely to protect himself in the libel suit [Hiss had brought against Chambers], the availability to him of the means for such self-protection may have been part of a much larger scheme, involving other people, and far larger objectives than the mere framing of Alger Hiss. This, however, is speculation. [Ibid., pp. 413-14]

(Here as in other cases, recourse to a "conspiracy" explanation makes me suspicious.) The expertise and expense required to duplicate a typewriter for the defense, in order to suggest how the alleged forgery was committed, must have made the trial judge even more dubious than he had been about the probability of such activity many years before when it would have been either pointless or incredibly demonic of Chambers to have fabricated a typewriter with a view to perhaps destroying Hiss someday. (See, for a description of the duplication, ibid., pp. 369-73. See, also, Martin K. Tytell, "The $7500 Typewriter I Built for Alger Hiss," reprinted from *True* magazine, 1952, in Kurt Singer, ed., *The World's Best Spy Stories* [New York: Wilfred Funk, 1954].) Even so, it probably would have been better for the country at large if Hiss could have been acquitted, if only to discourage the notion (which our youthful "radicals" have adopted from crusading anticommunist conservatives) that men of reputation and accomplishments can be unseated by the disinherited. Is it not true, that is, that conservatives should prefer the justice of stability to the justice of truth-seeking? Certainly, that community is healthier in which it is known that not everything is permitted in the passionate pursuit of either truth *or* justice. See chap. 5, n. 61, above, chap. 7, n. 45, chap. 8, nn. 76, 124, below. It might have helped settle partisan passions (left over from the depression and the war) had a Republican been President in 1948-52, the period which proved so decisive for a generation.

One side effect of the expansion of power on the part of the general government has been the extension of its influence at the expense of the state governments. This power, once well established, is very likely to be directed toward educational institutions, thereby depreciating the role of the states in managing these activities. When one of our governments assumes power, it almost always is taken from another government or from the people. Cf. chap. 7, n. 35, above, chap. 7, nn. 79, 114, below.

42. Vigorous opposition was expressed by the most patriotic "hard hats," and even by the President of the United States who exercised his legislative veto, to the labor injunction provision of the Taft-Hartley Act. Yet, it is far more certain that some national strikes are much more dangerous or pervasive in the community than practically any indictable abuse of freedom of speech or of the press in our time. That is, we have lost our sense of proportion in measuring the effect of the words as well as the deeds of dissenting elements in this country. The public disturbances and riots we have endured in recent years have been much more the effects of unduly repressive or unimaginative government (see, e.g., Appendix D, above) than of either the talents or the malice of "agitators." Indeed, there is rarely serious malice on either side in these "confrontations." See chap. 7, n. 67, below. Cf. chap. 3, n. 22, above. But see chap. 8, n. 80, below.

43. The *Chicago Sun-Times*, Sept. 18, 1959, reported:

> [President Eisenhower] added what seemed to be his own prescription for the way Americans should greet Khrushchev during his other stops in the country: "I do not believe extreme convictions should be expressed one way or the other."
>
> But he disagreed vigorously with a reporter's suggestion that perhaps Khrushchev in his nationwide television-radio performance from the National Press Club here Wednesday might have insidiously sold some of the Communist line to the American people.

CHAPTER SEVEN, NOTES 44-45: PAGES 182-83   619

"I think the American public is strong enough to see and hear this man, or any other man, and be capable of making its own decision," he said.

"I do not believe a master debater or a great appearance of sincerity or anything else is going to fool the American public long."

See chap. 9, n. 17, below.

It should be noticed that President Eisenhower could give this advice even though he knew that the Khrushchev visit to the United States resulted from a State Department misunderstanding of his instructions. Dwight D. Eisenhower, *Waging Peace* (Garden City, N.Y.: Doubleday & Co., 1965), pp. 407-8. Thus, the visit cannot be understood as a "calculated risk" undertaken by the administration. (Cities all over the country, including Abilene, Kansas, vied with each other to get Khrushchev to visit—in order to be considered important enough to be subverted by him?)

[General de Gaulle] has travelled through Russia with open arms; he has put down the red carpet for Mr. Kosygin; he has welcomed trade agreements and shared cultures; he stresses continually the need for an opening to the East. It is impossible to equate all this with the idea of the Communists as a race of ogres. [Nesta Roberts, "The General Helps Communists to Become Respectable," *Manchester Guardian Weekly*, Mar. 16, 1967]

See chap. 8, n. 105, below.

44. The *Chicago Tribune*, Oct. 1, 1959, pointed out:

Washington, Sept. 30.—The American taxpayer will foot the bill for the visit of Russian Premier Nikita Khrushchev but won't be told what it is.

The 13 day visit of the Red leader cost a minimum of $130,000 and it's a safe guess that the final bill will be around $1,000,000.

But the state department won't give the figures on the cost of the tour.

The *Tribune* reporter described various expenditures, no doubt savoring such items as this, "Members of [Mr. Khrushchev's] party, which totaled 71 persons, ate well and enjoyed good quarters. They soon learned how to sign checks on the American taxpayer." I can add, on the basis of a conversation in Moscow the following summer with a friend of a member of Khrushchev's party, that the Russian visitors had been quite impressed by what they had seen in America (especially in California). See chap. 6, n. 1, above.

45. See chap. 3, n. 20, above. Justice Black, dissenting, *Communist Party* v. *Subversive Activities Control Board*, 367 U.S. 1, 142 (1961), observed, "The [Subversive Activities Control Act of 1950] thus makes it extremely difficult for a member of the Communist Party to live in this country and, at the same time, makes it a crime for him to try to get a passport to get out." Cf. Plato, Crito 51D. See Universal Declaration of Human Rights, Article 13/2; International Convention on the Elimination of All Forms of Racial Discrimination, Part I, art. 5, par. 1; *Redemption: Jewish Freedom Letters from Russia*, ed. Moshe Decter (New York: American Jewish Conference on Soviet Jewry, 1970). See, also, chap. 5, n. 130 (end), chap. 7, nn. 22, 32, above. Cf. *Aptheker* v. *Secretary of State*, 378 U.S. 500 (1964).

The gravity of the offenses with which [Governor Ross R.] Barnett and [Lieutenant-Governor Paul B.] Johnson [of Mississippi] could have been charged under federal law can hardly be overstated. They employed the physical power of a state to defy the authority of the federal government—a more genuine effort at violent overthrow of that government than has ever been attempted by the Communist Party—and yet even the effort to penalize them for contempt of court proved unavailing. No attempt was made to collect the fines that the Court of Appeals set as the penalty for civil contempt, but that court, on November 15, 1962, instructed the Department of Justice to institute criminal contempt proceedings against the two men. . . . On May 5, 1965, however, the Court of Appeals, by a vote of 4-3, dismissed the criminal contempt charges.

Although . . . the two members of the panel that had initially ordered [James H.] Meredith's admission to the university argued that, because of the enormity of the charges, the court had the responsibility to the nation of bringing Barnett to trial, the majority ruled that the "lapse of time" and the "changed circumstances and conditions" since 1962 had made it unnecessary and inadvisable to press prosecution to its conclusion. [Dean Alfange, Jr., "James H. Meredith, Transfer Student," in R. J. Tresolini and R. T. Frost, *Cases in American National Government and Politics* (Englewood Cliffs, N.J.: Prentice-Hall, 1966), p. 249]

See, also, Brown, *Loyalty and Security*, p. 355 (on southern lawyers having expressed since 1954 greater defiance of the Constitution, as interpreted by the Supreme Court, than all Communist lawyers since 1917). Compare the furor aroused among lawyers and laymen alike by the behavior of counsel in the "Chicago Conspiracy Trial," but not by the indefensible behavior (for many years) of the judge who was largely responsible for the spectacle. See Appendix D and chap. 6, n. 30, above, chap. 8, n. 141, below. See, also, pp. 404, 409, above. (Should not "lapse of time" and "changed circumstances" have been considered critical as well in the *Hiss* case [chap. 7, n. 41, above] and in the *Rosenberg* case [chap. 7, nn. 74, 75, below]?)

46. Justice Black said, in his dissenting opinion in *Dennis* v. *U.S.*, 341 U.S. 494, 579 (1951):

At the outset I want to emphasize what the crime involved in this case is, and what it is not. These petitioners were not charged with an attempt to overthrow the Government. They were not charged with overt acts of any kind designed to overthrow the Government. They were not even charged with saying anything or writing anything designed to overthrow the Government. The charge was that they agreed to assemble and to talk and publish certain ideas at a later date: The indictment is that they conspired to organize the Communist Party and to use speech or newspapers and other publications in the future to teach and advocate the forcible overthrow of the Government. . . .

"I repeat that we deal here with speech alone, not with speech *plus* acts of sabotage or unlawful conduct. Not a single seditious act is charged in the indictment." Justice Douglas (dissenting opinion), ibid., at 584. Justice Jackson admitted, in his concurring opinion, "There is no charge of actual violence or attempt at overthrow." Ibid., at 561. See chap. 3, n. 20, above, chap. 7, n. 72, below.

Earl Browder, in a letter to the editor published in the *New York Times*, Jan. 8, 1954, wrote:

> Your reporter . . . has been the victim of misinformation in his story in The Times of Jan. 4 when he indicates that perhaps I am the "high former Red" who is expected to expose subversion before the Jenner committee.
>
> *I have already given sworn testimony* before a Senate committee on April 27, 1950, that the Communist party under my leadership from 1930 to 1945 was not a conspiracy for the overthrow of the existing Government of the United States, that it did not engage in espionage for Russia, that it did not accept orders from Moscow, and did not wish to subordinate America to Russia. *That is the truth and any and all testimony in contradiction to it is perjured.* To the extent that any member of the Communist party engaged in such activities or held such views, they were in violent contradiction to their own party. After 1945 I have no responsibility for or knowledge of the Communist party activities.
>
> The idea suggested in your correspondent's story that years of persecution from both the Communist party and the United States Government have "softened" me up so that today I would give a different kind of testimony displays a profound ignorance of the facts. I have survived a lifetime of persecution without being "softened" into becoming anybody's agent, whether it be the McCarthys of Moscow or of Washington.
>
> I am rather old and tired, and my wife has been made an invalid by the special persecution against her and we wish nothing more than to be left in peace for our remaining years. [Italics added]

See chap. 5, n. 31, above, chap. 7, n. 124, below.

47. *Pennsylvania* v. *Nelson*, 377 Pa. 58, 104 A.2d 133 (1954); 350 U.S. 497 (1956). A sentence of twenty years was imposed in 1952 upon the convicted defendant (a leader of the Communist party) after trial in a state court for violation of a Pennsylvania statute. (In addition, a fine of $10,000 and the costs of prosecution of $13,000 were assessed.) The ruling in this case is described and discussed at pp. 188-91, above, and in chap. 7, n. 76, below.

Congress's Smith Act (see chap. 3, n. 18, above) was "patterned after" a New York statute of 1902. California had had a similar statute since 1919. The Smith Act, on the other hand, was not enacted until 1940. *Yates* v. *U.S.*, 354 U.S. 298, 309 (1957). See, also, *Dennis* v. *U.S.*, 341 U.S. 494, 562, n. 2 (1951); Zechariah Chafee, *Freedom of Speech* (Cambridge: Harvard University Press, 1920), pp. 44-45.

In 1939, Pennsylvania passed a drastic act requiring the registration of all aliens in the state. In 1940, Congress passed a milder Alien Registration Act [the Smith Act]. In *Hines* v. *Davidowitz*, 312 U.S. 52 (1941), the Court held that the federal statute supplanted the state statute. It said: "the regulation of aliens is so intimately blended and intertwined with responsibilities of the national government that where it acts, and the state also acts on the same subject, the act of Congress . . . is supreme; and the law of the state . . . must yield to it." [Robert E. Cushman, *Leading Constitutional Decisions* (New York: Appleton-Century-Crofts, 1966), p. 25]

48. See the passage from Stone (*Annals*, I, p. 825) in the text at chap. 6, n. 58, above.
The Supreme Court of Pennsylvania stated (in a passage quoted by the opinion of the majority in the Supreme Court of the United States):

And, while the Pennsylvania statute proscribes sedition against either the Government of the United States or the Government of Pennsylvania, it is only alleged sedition against the United States with which the [*Nelson*] case is concerned. Out of all the voluminous testimony, we have not found, nor has anyone pointed to, a single word indicating a seditious act or even utterance directed against the Government of Pennsylvania. [*Pennsylvania* v. *Nelson*, 350 U.S. 497 (1956), at 499, quoting from *Commonwealth* v. *Nelson*, 377 Pa., at 69, 104 A.2d at 139 (1954)]

See chap. 7, n. 76, below.
See Story, *Commentaries on the Constitution*, chap. 2, sec. 1301.

49. Thus, although there is no recognized legal compulsion upon a state to give up a fugitive from justice upon the demand of another state for extradition, this is usually done without question. An appreciation of the occasions when a question about extradition is raised reinforces one of the arguments of this chapter: that is, extradition is sometimes denied when a "political" question is involved or when there is doubt in the extraditing state about the justice of the reception awaiting the fugitive upon return to the demanding state. See chap. 7, n. 71, below. See, also, chap. 6, n. 66, above.

50. Another comparison reflects the relation of state and general governments: there were 2,604,400 serious crimes (including larceny over fifty dollars) reported in the United States in 1964; in the same year, there were only 14,973 federal prisoners received from the courts. *World Almanac* (1966), p. 307; *Information Please* (1966), p. 319. There are about half a million state and local law enforcement officers in the United States, but only about 20,000 federal officers. See chap. 6, n. 50, above, chap. 7, n. 68, below. Cf. *Federalist*, pp. 93-94, 144-45, 153-54, 307-8. But see, ibid., pp. 308-9; chap. 5, n. 52, above.

51. *Chicago Tribune*, Oct. 4, 1960. J. Edgar Hoover's address was to the 67th Annual Conference of the International Association of Chiefs of Police. Cf. Grodzins, *The American System*, pp. 117-18, 122-23. See chap. 6, n. 59, chap. 7, n. 5, above.

52. The Continental Congress enacted on June 24, 1776, a resolution that provided:

That it be recommended to the legislatures of the several United Colonies, to pass laws for punishing in such manner as to them shall seem fit, such persons before described, as shall be proveably attainted of open deed, by people of their condition, of any of the treasons before described. [*Journals of the Continental Congress* (Washington: Government Printing Office, 1906), 5:475]

The state laws recommended by Congress are illustrated by a Connecticut statute of 1776, entitled, "An Act for the Punishment of High Treason and other atrocious Crimes against the State":

> Be it enacted . . . that if any Person . . . belonging to, or residing within this State, and under the Protection of its Laws, shall levy War against the State or Government thereof, or knowingly and willingly shall aid or assist any Enemy at open War against this State, or the United States of America, by joining their Armies, or by Inlisting or procuring or perswading others to inlist for that Purpose, or by furnishing such Enemies with Arms or Ammunition, Provision, or any other Articles for their Aid or Comfort, or by carrying on a treacherous Correspondence with them, or shall form or be any Way concerned in Forming any Combination, Plot, or Conspiracy for betraying this State, or of the United States into the Hands or Power of any foreign Enemy, or shall give or attempt to give or send any Intelligence to the Enemies of this State for that Purpose, every Person so offending, and being thereof convicted, shall suffer Death.
>
> And be it further Enacted . . . That if any Person . . . shall endeavour to join the Enemies of this State, or of the United States, or use their Influence to perswade or induce any Person . . . to join, aid, comfort, or assist them in any Way or Manner whatsoever, or shall have Knowledge of any Person or Persons endeavoring or using their Influence aforesaid, and shall conceal the same, shall be punished by Fine, according to the Nature of his Offence, and shall be imprisoned at the Judgment of the Superior Court, in any of the Gaols in this State, not exceeding Ten years.

A current instance of reliance upon state officials to serve federal functions is implied in Title 18, section 2382, of the United States Code:

> Whoever, owing allegiance to the United States, and having knowledge of the commission of any treason against them, conceals and does not, as soon as may be, disclose and make known the same to the President of the United States, or to the governor or to some judge or justice of a particular State, is guilty of misprision of treason, and shall be fined not more than $1,000 or imprisoned not more than seven years, or both.

See, also, *Federalist*, pp. 279, 302; Pritchett, *The American Constitution*, p. 152. Cf. chap. 6, n. 16, above.

53. It should be noticed that Article IV, section 2, of the Constitution recognizes that a person "may be charged in [a] State with treason." Treason against a state is not defined by the Constitution as is treason against the United States (Art. III, sec. 3). Cannot, however, the general government moderate state treason laws (if, for example, such laws abridge freedom of speech)? But "moderation" (and even complete negation) should be distinguished from the "supersession" (or "preemption") described and discussed at pp. 188-91, above, and in chap. 7, n. 76, below.

54. I reconsider and develop here, in a different context, some points made in chapters 4 and 6, above. Two instances, a century apart, of deference by the general government to state prerogatives with respect to the treatment of nonwhites are recorded in the two passages that follow:

> Fellow-citizens of the Senate and House of Representatives: I recommend the adoption of a joint resolution by your honorable bodies, which shall be substantially as follows: "Resolved, That the United States ought to cooperate with any State which may adopt gradual abolishment of slavery, giving to such State pecuniary aid to be used by such State, in its discretion, to compensate for the

inconveniences, public and private, produced by such change of system." [Lincoln, *Complete Works*, 2:129 (Mar. 6, 1862)]

"Your state is getting an undeserved reputation for backwardness because the law in Maryland permits discrimination in places of public accommodations," the State Department's assistant chief of protocol . . . told the legislative council of Maryland's general assembly. In an unprecedented federal appeal for a new state antidiscrimination law, he continued, "Four African ambassadors were humiliated by private restaurant owners in Maryland. . . . How can we persuade these Africans and these Asians that we believe in human dignity when we deny our own citizens the right to basic dignity on the basis of color?" [*Life*, Sept. 22, 1961, p. 44]

But whereas Lincoln thought that Congress had no power to interfere with a state's internal police with respect to slavery (see chap. 7, n. 14), the Fourteenth Amendment gives Congress power "to enforce, by appropriate legislation, the provisions of [that Amendment]." The amendment provides, among other things, that no state shall "deprive any person of life, liberty, or property without due process of law; nor deny to any person within its jurisdiction the equal protection of the laws." See chap. 7, n. 96, below. See, also, chap. 8, n. 83, below.

55. Abraham Baldwin, a Federalist member of the House of Representatives from Georgia (having been raised in Connecticut), said during the debate about the Alien Act of 1798:

that if this bill passed into a law, Congress would again be appealed to by the advocates for an abolition of slavery, with requests that the President may be authorized to send these persons out of the country, and strong arguments will be used in favor of the measure. He recollected it was asked, on a former occasion, "Suppose a cargo of leprous persons were to be landed in the country, would not Congress have the power to send them out of the country? Slavery, said they, is an incurable leprosy; you surely, then, will eradicate it?" This reasoning, however, did not prevail. There are other mischiefs which might be done, against which the Federal Constitution makes no provision. Persons might burn our towns and slay our inhabitants. But our Constitution goes upon an idea that there are State Governments who divide the powers of Government with the Federal Government. . . . [*Annals*, V, p. 1969]

Cf. *Annals*, V, p. 2146; *Federalist*, pp. 171-72.
See chap. 6, n. 60, above.

56. Members of Congress and the President, as citizens, can use their influence to have the legislatures of their respective states enact appropriate laws respecting sedition or murder or theft.

The language in the text is Justice Holmes's. (See the text at chap. 3, n. 14, above.) Does Justice Holmes speak of Congress's having a "right" rather than the "power" in order to counter one right (that to freedom of speech or of the press) by another?

57. These steps have been discussed in chapters 4 and 6. See, also, *The Works of Francis Bacon*, ed. J. Spedding and R. Ellis (New York: Hurd & Houghton, 1864), 12:123-31, 379-82.

The powers of Congress have been examined at length in chapter 6. Can even an overt act of ordinary domestic violence within a state be moved against by the general government without a request from the state involved? See chap. 6, nn. 40, 60, above.

Several of the considerations reviewed here apply also to Congress's power with respect to treason.

58. I have noted the care with which Lincoln defined and justified his Emancipation Proclamation. See chap. 7, n. 14, above.

Compare Jackson's observation:

. . . The United States are to protect each other against invasion. If an invasion was only apprehended, the General Government are bound to exert themselves to ward off the blow, but we call not for those exertions on mere surmise. Georgia has been invaded [by Creek Indians]; the fact is absolute and notorious. [*Annals*, I, p. 695]

59. See Aeschylus, *The Eumenides* 696-703 (Athena advises Athenians "not to cast fear utterly from your city. What man who fears nothing at all is ever righteous?"); Sophocles, *Electra* 1503; cf. Euripides, *Electra* 1051, 1244. See, also, Plato, *Republic* 359D-367E, *Gorgias* 523A-524A; Blackstone, *Laws of England*, 1:56 ("the dread of evil is a much more forcible principle of human actions than the prospect of good," citing Locke, *On Human Understanding*, 2:21); chap. 6, n. 54, above. It has been observed (Leo Strauss, *Jerusalem and Athens: Some Preliminary Reflections* [New York: City College, 1967], p. 21):

> ... Plato's explicit theology is presented within the context of the first discussion of education in the *Republic*, within the context of what one may call the discussion of elementary education; in the second and final discussion of education—the discussion of the education of the philosophers—theology is replaced by the doctrine of ideas. As for the thematic discussion of providence in the *Laws*, it may suffice here to say that it occurs within the context of the discussion of penal law.

Consider Halevi, *The Kuzari*, pp. 44, 116, 199-200, 227, 273-78; Maimonides, *Guide of the Perplexed*, pp. 496-502, 625-26. See chap. 7, nn. 21, 34, above, chap. 7, n. 124, below. See, also, Victor Gourevitch, "Philosophy and Politics," *Review of Metaphysics*, 22 (1968): 281, 294-99; chap. 2, n. 38, above, chap. 9, n. 38, below.

One student of my argument (in its dissertation form) observed,

> The crucial problem is whether the people are capable of behaving with the dignity and freedom you would afford them. Treating them *as if* they were so capable helps them to become such. But if they become corrupt or unaccustomed to thinking and acting independently (by the mass media, technological interdependence, crowding, etc.), then "discipline" becomes the order of the day. So the crucial question may be whether we can maintain a society where people are law-abiding on their own, because they think it right to be so, rather than only because of the fear of punishment. If it looks like the doctrines promoting independent, free, dignified law-abidingness will not be able to win out in the "market place of ideas," could it not be prudent as a temporary emergency power to curb seditious opinions? This may be a qualification you may not think it prudent to elaborate upon.

See chap. 6, n. 6, above (on an "angel theory of constitutional development").

Chap. 7, nn. 60, 71, and 107, below, bear on this, as does chap. 7, n. 72, below. Does not liberty depend, to some extent, on intermittent inefficiency, just as community depends on some residual puritanism? It is this puritanism—the *caring* by the community about certain more or less primitive things even when sophistication would teach it otherwise—upon which the current literary permissiveness is likely to founder. (See chap. 5, nn. 131, 132, above.) Indeed, "community" can be understood as that association which "cares" about such things. (See chap. 8, n. 171, below.) Here, too, is the obstacle which the current attempt to legitimate homosexuality will not be able to overcome (except in the hidden recesses of our larger cities). Cf. *New Yorker*, July 11, 1970, p. 19. Mere sexual gratification is, among us, too much the proclaimed purpose of homosexual relations: that is, such relations do not have that obvious purpose in nature (related to the family) which heterosexual relations have and which the community (even in its most puritanical frenzy) cannot help respecting. The prudent statesman should make the best of the "confrontation" by counseling one side to be discreet, the other side to be compassionate. (The community's awareness of what is natural—an awareness which can be expected to survive the efforts of modern social science—will also set limits upon "women's liberation" movements. It is this awareness of nature, of its mysteries and its "intentions," which is reflected in the solemnity in the autopsy room of normally irreverent medical students, in the effect upon even experienced doctors of an untimely death, and in the sense of purposelessness which is evoked in the adult by the permanently retarded child. The autopsy-room experience [which is accented for survivors by the puzzling trauma of a recent passing from life to death] is further illuminated if we should notice the parts of the body which have, in the course of dissection, a sobering effect even in the typically boisterous anatomy room: the face, the hand, and the genitalia—perhaps because they remind us of what is intimately ours, the distinctively human [that is, of man as both social and rational], and hence, of ourselves. I suspect that the principal reason why dissection of the hand affects the anatomist in this way is that he sees before him a hand being worked upon by a hand, thereby bringing home to him both the humanity of the object being worked upon and the mortality of the workman.) See chap. 5, n. 126, above, chap. 8, nn. 133, chap. 7, n. 77, below.

See *Federalist*, pp. 167-68; cf. ibid., pp. 170-71.
60. See chap. 4, n. 59, above.

[Halevi] has spoken on [his] subject with a remarkable restraint: not being a fanatic, he did not wish to supply the unscrupulous and the fanatic with weapons which they certainly would have misused. But this restraint cannot deceive the reader about the singleness of his primary and ultimate purpose. [Strauss, *Persecution and the Art of Writing*, p. 141]

See chap. 9, n. 27, below.
61. Related to this may be the declaration of martial law in specified areas of military activity. See chap. 8, nn. 161, 162, below. See, also, chap. 8, n. 17, below.
62. Robin Hood's legendary vindication by Richard I comes to mind. (Cf. Edwin Muir, *Latitudes* [New York: B. W. Huebsch, 1924], pp. 25-27.)

If the people have been careful about whom they entrust with the power of the presidency, they may be fortunate to have in a great crisis a Lincoln who can observe to a cabinet officer, "I don't intend precisely to throw the Constitution overboard, but I will stick it in a hole if I can." On another occasion Lincoln instructed a messenger to the secretary of the treasury, "Tell him not to bother himself with the Constitution. Say that I have that sacred instrument here at the White House, and I am guarding it with great care." Carl Sandburg, "Abraham Lincoln: An Appreciation," *Chicago Sunday Tribune Magazine*, Feb. 8, 1959. (See chap. 3, n. 33, above.)

See, on the people themselves, the following note.
63. Aristotle counsels us, "The true friend of the people should see that they be not too poor, for extreme poverty lowers the character of a democracy." *Politics* 1320a34. Cf. ibid., 1331b39, 1332a19, 1329b37, 1330a2. See Burke, *Works*, 2:158-59, 7-8.

Cf. chap. 9, n. 36, below.
64. Albert Gallatin said of the crime defined by the Sedition Act of 1798,

It is a political crime, and will always be determined according to the situation of the parties at the time. For . . . we may say as much as we please about the purity of our courts and juries, and of our own purity; decisions upon political questions, will always be influenced by party spirit. It is we . . . that have introduced this spirit into the courts; and having given them political questions to decide, it need not be expected that courts will be free from party prejudice any more than others. Therefore, the falsehood or maliciousness of a publication will be determined by the political opinion of the jury. [*Annals*, V, p. 2972]

See chap. 3, n. 20, above. See, also, *Annals*, VI, pp. 951-52.
65. It has been an experience subject to, and hence ratified by, the power in the people to amend the Constitution.

It may be said that it is difficult to amend the Constitution. To some extent that is true. Obviously the Founders wanted to guard against hasty and ill-considered changes in the basic charter of government. But if the necessity for alteration becomes pressing, or if the public demand becomes strong enough, the Constitution can and has been promptly amended. The Eleventh Amendment was ratified within less than two years after the decision in *Chisholm* v. *Georgia*, 2 Dall. [U.S.] 419 [1793]. And more recently the Twenty-First Amendment, repealing nationwide prohibition, became part of the Constitution within ten months after congressional action. On the average it has taken the States less than two years to ratify each of the twenty-two amendments which have been made to the Constitution. [Justice Black, in *Reid* v. *Covert*, 354 U.S. 1, 14, n. 27 (1957)]

Only five amendments have been proposed by Congress which have failed of ratification. Two of these came from the First Congress [chap. 2, n. 25, above]. The most recent was the child labor amendment, proposed in 1924 to give Congress authority to regulate or prohibit child labor, which had been denied by Supreme Court decisions in 1918 and 1922 [but which was recognized by the Court in 1941]. [Pritchett, *The American Constitution*, pp. 35, 262]

See chap. 6, n. 71, above, chap. 8, n. 84, below.

66. See chap. 3, n. 29, chap. 4, nn. 59, 111, chap. 5, n. 107, above.

My "under law" qualification reminds one of such exceptions as the suspension of the writ of *habeas corpus*. Protective custody of the young and of the insane is, however, no exception: the government may be legitimately empowered to act on behalf of anyone whose judgment is deficient or whose will is crippled and thereby to do for such people what a reasonable man would want to have done for himself should this happen to him. (Of course, such exceptions can be abused by recourse to definitions which are designed to permit plausible suppression of dissenters. Consider the Russian use of incarceration in mental hospitals. See chap. 8, n. 46, below. Consider, also, the sophisms reproduced in chap. 5, n. 3, above, about the "underground press" in this country. Thus, when suggested exceptions are assessed, one must take into account how the terms invoked are usually employed by the parties involved. See, e.g., the use by Swann and Odette of "do a cattleya," Marcel Proust, *Remembrance of Things Past* [New York: Random House, 1934], 1:178-79, 209, 285-86. See, also, chap. 7, nn. 107 [on Kant], 109, below.)

67. What may be done to "develop the community" (with respect to education, defense preparations, health measures, etc.) should be distinguished from what may be done to restrain a particular citizen. See chap. 5, n. 107, chap. 6, n. 54, above. I do not deny that a citizen may be penalized for acts of commission (or omission) in defiance of a restraint or duty imposed upon him as a part of the community being developed.

Nor do I suggest that the government (and we are talking, for the most part, of local authorities in such matters) must sit by until a situation deteriorates to the point where only massive force can work. See Lincoln, *Complete Works*, 2:361-63; cf. ibid., 2:38. The Chicago police has been praised, for example, for its restraint during the July 27, 1970, "rock fest" rioting in Grant Park (the scene, two summers earlier, of some of the Democratic National Convention week police violence [Appendix D, above]). But far too much that officials do in this country is in immediate reaction to a crisis, not because of scruples they may have against "preventive measures" or against "previous restraints" but because of a lack of foresight or of disciplined imagination. Of course, when a situation deteriorates, force may have to be used. But why not anticipate what may happen and head it off firmly (but not harshly) even before signs of trouble develop? It seems, however, that officials are too often crippled because they have come to rely too much upon force or because they are too much concerned that they not be blamed for anything.

In appraising the July 1970 "rock fest" rioting in Chicago, careful consideration should be given to the following account in the *Chicago Tribune* of July 29, 1970, at page 2 (in the same issue which had a front-page editorial condemning the rioting "hoodlums" in Grant Park):

CHAPTER SEVEN, NOTE 67: PAGE 187 627

Despite the mayor's and [park board chairman's] opinions, police of the Subversive and Gang Intelligence Units said they believed the riot was spontaneous, touched off by beer and wine drinking, the hot weather [in the 90s], the size of the crowd [between 30,000 and 75,000 youngsters], and the reports that [the announced principal musicians] would not perform as scheduled.

Baseball bats, which were among the weapons used to attack police, are not uncommon in parks and not uncommon at rock concerts, detectives said.

The rioting began about five o'clock. But, it was evident to me upon talking with youngsters I know well who were present at one o'clock for a program announced for four o'clock, that serious "cooling off" action should have been started by officials by two o'clock, if not even before noon. (The "rock fest" on this occasion was sponsored by the city.) In any event, so large a crowd should not be permitted to gather in such circumstances without detailed advance preparation for self-policing and for how police will be used in various contingencies. See Appendix E, above. (Certainly, one should not be surprised to learn that there are in any assembly of this size troublemakers and disturbed people disposed to exploit the situation. See, also, chap. 5, n. 14, above.

The problem is, in short, not really a police problem but essentially a political problem: in 1968, the political leaders used the police too soon and too harshly; in 1970, the political leaders did not use the police soon enough and with finesse. In all such cases, the police are most effective when they are subordinate to the overriding policy and guidance of the community. See Cyril D. Robinson, "Police and Prosecutor Practices and Attitudes Relating to Interrogation as Revealed by Pre- and Post-*Miranda* Questionnaires: A Construct of Police Capacity to Comply," *Duke L. J.*, 1968, pp. 425, 500-506.

The same fundamental issues may be seen in the relation between political and military policies. Thus, I observed in my article, "Swan Song of an Eagle: America in Greece," *Southwest Review*, 55 (1970): 105, 124-25 (*Cong. Rec.* 116: S7538 [May 20, 1970]):

> Even more serious for America than the deterioration of a valuable alliance between the United States and Greece is what our behavior with respect to Greece may reveal about how we conduct our affairs all over the world.
> If our political leaders, including our State Department experts, had a better idea of what they were doing, and were to insist upon their professional and constitutional prerogatives, our military people would be more likely to do their jobs properly. To some extent, the usurpation of political functions and judgments by military men may represent a sincere attempt on their part to take up the slack left by the incompetence, diffidence, or negligence of civilians. But our military are ill-equipped to make political judgments: in this they share the disabilities of the Greek colonels, who can seize and hold power but who do not really know what to do with it. Our military (if permitted to behave elsewhere as they have behaved, or as they *seem* to have behaved, in Greece) can succeed only in undermining our traditional respect for them, that public trust and accompanying honor which most fittingly reward and sustain men who devote their lives to the defense of their country.
> Thus, we cannot be fair either to our military or to ourselves if we permit or require them to assume duties and make judgments for which they are not equipped. We are not realistic about the enduring sources of our influence and self-confidence as a republican people if we "pragmatically" exclude from our calculations in our relations abroad considerations of either political integrity or human dignity.

See chap. 4, n. 49, chap. 5, nn. 29, 30, chap. 6, n. 1, above, chap. 7, n. 72, chap. 8, nn. 37, 149, below. (It should be added, however, that our civilian leaders are ultimately to blame in Greece, as in Vietnam, for our failures.)

No discussion today of American rioting—whether segregationist or integrationist, whether on campus or off, whether pro-war or anti-war—or of "crime in the streets" should be concluded without observing that our current fears are rather exaggerated, reflecting perhaps both our pampered existence and our ignorance of what has happened before in this country and what is happening in other countries at this very time. Indeed, we as a community seem far more moved by the tens and hundreds who may be killed in our city streets than we are by the death of 50,000 of our own youth and several hundreds of thousands of the Vietnamese because of our folly in Indochina, to say nothing of what we permit to happen on our highways and to the life expectancy of our poor. One is even tempted to add that a people which is as paralyzed as ours has been by "crime in the streets," so much so that many city sidewalks are abandoned at night to a handful of ruffians, deserves the slavery it thereby exchanges for security. See chap. 8, n. 142. (Perhaps it would help [and be healthier as well] if we were all obliged to rely on public transportation for movement within our cities. In addition, it would help if we reduced the number of guns held in this country by private citizens and by the police. See chap. 7, n. 21, above. [The "states' right," not personal, guarantee in the Second Amendment of "the right of the people to bear Arms" has nothing to do with this problem. See chap. 8, n. 4, below. Does the large-scale private possession of arms make usurpation less likely? Or does the fear resulting from the misuse of such arms make usurpation *more* likely?] The principal problem is neither that of who among us should be permitted to possess guns nor that of whether weapons should be registered, but rather whether guns [and the ammunition for them] should be permitted to exist among us in large quantities. It is virtually impossible to determine in advance who will use a gun improperly, particularly since so many are used in domestic quarrels or in accidents. It is also virtually impossible to determine how guns can be kept out of the hands of people we may not want to have them, if there are large numbers of them available in homes and shops. What it is possible to determine is that the quantity of guns we do have among us makes us all too casual about their presence and use, which means that they will be frequently misused.) See chap. 8, n. 4, below.

68. The reliance of the general government upon the states is seen in such diverse matters as the trial of presidential assassins (which hitherto has usually been under the jurisdiction of a state) and the development of the militia which "may be employed in the service of the United States" (with the states having reserved to them, under Article I, section 8, "the appointment of the officers, and the authority of training the militia according to the discipline prescribed by Congress"). See Chafee, *Freedom of Speech*, pp. 165-66.

Cf. *Annals*, V, pp. 1990, 2146. See *Federalist* No. 16. See, also, chap. 7, n. 47, above.

See, on the opposition of the Department of Justice to legislation making it a federal crime to kill any postal employee, *New York Times*, June 27, 1968, p. 17. A spokesman for the department explained that expanding the coverage of the present law—which does make it a federal crime to kill a postal inspector—"would create an inordinate investigative load on the Federal Bureau of Investigation to the possible detriment of the performance of its functions in major areas."

It should be noted that each state even has jurisdiction over the holidays it will observe. The President and Congress designate holidays only for the District of Columbia and for federal employees. (Is this a legacy of the original power of states with respect to religious establishments?) See *U.S.C.A.*, Title 5, sec. 6103.

69. Ammon Hennacy observed, in the course of a discussion of the despotic manner in which Communists exercised authority during the Spanish Civil War, that "Steve Nelson was the one Communist of whom I have not heard criticism in that respect." *Catholic Worker*, Dec. 1958, p. 4.

> The appellant, Anita Whitney [*Whitney* v. *California*, 274 U.S. 357 (1927); see chap. 3, n. 21, above.], was charged and convicted of violating California's Criminal Syndicalism Act (1919) by organizing, and being a member of a group advocating unlawful force as a political weapon, contrary to the statute. . . . Specifically, Miss Whitney was charged with participating in a convention of the Communist Labor Party of California, which was affiliated with the Communist International of Moscow. Evidence showed that she had personally proposed a strictly political role for the Party, which the convention had rejected in favor of a national program advocating various revolutionary measures including national strikes. Appellant remained until the end of the convention,

and did not withdraw from the party. [Alpheus T. Mason and William M. Beaney, *American Constitutional Law*, 3rd ed. (Englewood Cliffs, N.J.: Prentice-Hall, 1964), pp. 498-99]

(*Whitney* has been said by a unanimous court in *Brandenburg* v. *Ohio*, 395 U.S. 444 [1969] to have been overruled. What makes this most curious is that *Dennis* v. *U.S.*, 341 U.S. 494 [1951] is relied upon by the Court in announcing that criminal syndicalism statutes of the California and Ohio variety are unconstitutional—and, in effect, had been considered so by the Court for almost twenty years! It will probably take some time for the Court to sort out what it did in *Brandenburg*, and why. It is difficult for me to believe that the Court knew what it was doing or that *all* of the justices meant to say what they did say: if *Dennis* can be used in this manner against *Whitney*, it can be used as well not only against *Schenck* but even against *Dennis* itself. See Frank R. Strong, "Fifty Years of 'Clear and Present Danger': From *Schenck* to *Brandenburg*—and Beyond," *Supreme Court Review* 1969, p. 41.)

> Junius Scales [was] the only person to serve a prison sentence for membership in the Communist Party. [*Scales* v. *U.S.*, 367 U.S. 203 (1961); see chap. 5, n. 21, above.] . . . The extravagance of the situation was aggravated by the fact that while Scales was a Communist at the time of his first trial in 1955, in the following year he was shocked out of his faith by Khrushchev's revelations of Stalin's crimes and also by the brutal Soviet repression of the Hungarian uprising. He publicly left the party in 1957. Later that year the Supreme Court set aside his conviction on technical grounds . . . ; but the Department of Justice had him retried in 1958. His trial was for his membership within the three-year period from 1951 to 1954. Technically it was all correct; but if the law supposed that that was enough, Mr. Bumble had warrant for saying that "the law is a ass—a idiot." A petition signed by 550 prominent citizens . . . asked President Kennedy to bring the unbecoming spectacle to a merciful end. . . . The sentence was commuted on the day before Christmas, 1962, after Scales had served about fifteen months of his six-year term. [Milton R. Konvitz, *Expanding Liberties: Freedom's Gains in Postwar America* (New York: Viking Press, 1966), p. 129]

See Appendix F, above; chap. 7, n. 27, above. See, also, chap. 7, n. 45, above.

70. Cf. Chafee, at p. 68 of an *amicus* brief filed in the *Summers* bar admission case (325 U.S. 561 [1945]),

> Let us hope there will still be a few liberal havens [among the states] which will admit such men to pursue their profession, but religious freedom in the United States should surely mean more than the existence of some Holland or Geneva here and there among the forty-eight States. The possibility of exile is a poor remedy for persecution.

(This litigation grew out of the refusal of the Illinois Supreme Court to admit to the bar an applicant who had been a conscientious objector during the Second World War. See Irving Dilliard, "Tradition of Bigotry in the Illinois Bar," *Focus/Midwest*, Jan. 1963, p. 6.) See chap. 7, n. 27, above. See, also, chap. 8, n. 83, below.

71. See chap. 7, n. 49, above. The reader is no doubt reminded of the fugitive slave problem. Compare the following passage with chap. 5, n. 28, above.

> [T]he Illinois [sedition] law has been enforced by wholesale arrests in Chicago. Furthermore, the governors of other states are already granting the extradition of accused persons to Illinois. Under this policy, a state with a drastic sedition law like Montana will be able to hunt a man down in the most liberal part of the nation, and there will be practically no chance for a review by the United States Supreme Court. The United States has always refused to allow the extradition of persons charged by other countries with political crimes, even if the charge (as often happened with Russians) involved the advocacy of violence and revolution. [Note: See the state papers in *Moore's Digest of International*

Law, 4:322 ff. The possible exception of anarchists who actually cause explosions (ibid., p. 354) may be disregarded, since we are dealing at most with unsuccessful incitement to anarchy, and in general with the expression of revolutionary views and membership in revolutionary organizations, which would clearly be political crimes and unextraditable.] Since state governors under the Constitution cannot be compelled to permit extradition [citing *Kentucky* v. *Dennison*, 24 How. (U.S.) 66 (1860)], it is to be hoped that in future they will follow the wise policy of the national government. [Chafee, *Freedom of Speech* (1920), p. 191]

See chap. 6, n. 66, above. (Cf., on the use of "political," chap. 5, n. 100, above.)
See chap. 7, n. 76, below (on the extent of state sedition legislation).

72. Many of these activities, by both the states and the general government, would have been discouraged had the Supreme Court ruled for the petitioners on First Amendment grounds in *American Communications Assn.* v. *Douds*, 339 U.S. 382 (1950) and in *Dennis* v. *U.S.*, 341 U.S. 494 (1951), and thereby educated the public as it subsequently did in the politically sensitive segregation cases and the reapportionment cases. The Justice Department did not proceed with Smith Act prosecutions against "second-string" Communists until after the decision in *Dennis*: this was the signal for further action by officials throughout the country. (Even my bar admission committee held off for five months announcing its first decision excluding me from the bar, until the day after *Dennis* was announced on June 4, 1951, Appendix F, above.) See chap. 3, n. 34, above. Cf. chap. 4, n. 37, above. (A useful survey of the Smith Act prosecutions may be found in Pritchett, *The American Constitution*, pp. 526-33. He described the government's case in *Dennis* as "a most peculiar one":

> The evidence presented at the trial was primarily concerned with what was in the basic texts of Marxism-Leninism extending all the way back to 1848, as distributed by the Communist Party and discussed at their meetings. The guilt of the Communist leaders was established by connecting them with the organization of the Party and the teaching of these texts. [Ibid., p. 529]

See chap. 7, n. 46, above. Pritchett also noted that the government was almost uniformly successful in the prosecutions of lesser Communist party leaders after the 1951 decision in *Dennis*, "in none of which did the Supreme Court grant certiorari, until October, 1955," when it agreed to review the California convictions which led to the decision in *Yates* v. *United States*, 354 U.S. 298 [1957]. Ibid., p. 530. By that time a decade of damage had been done [the *Dennis* prosecution began in 1948], damage which was anticipated by Justice Black's 1950 protest in *American Communications Assn.* v. *Douds*: "Never before has this Court held that the Government could for any reason *attaint* persons for their political beliefs or affiliations. It does so today." 339 U.S., at 449; italics added. See chap. 7, n. 78, below. Throughout this period, apologists for the government explained that patriotic citizens remained free to speak their minds—but to be free in such circumstances depends in great part on believing oneself free, something that too many people simply could not do. [See chap. 7, n. 41, above.] One man who did conduct himself as a free man during that period was John L. Lewis, president of the United Mine Workers, whose obituary included these observations:

> In 1942, Mr. Lewis took his mine workers out of the CIO, and in 1946 he took the UMW back into the AFL. But two years later, in a quarrel arising from his refusal to sign a non-Communist affidavit, Mr. Lewis excoriated the AFL leaders as "intellectually fat and stately asses" because they decided to comply with the Taft-Hartley Act requiring union officers to swear they were not Communists. [It was this statutory requirement of an affidavit which was ruled constitutional in *American Communications Assn.* v. *Douds*.] Lewis was not a Communist, needless to say, but he detested the Taft-Hartley Law, describing it as "damnable, vicious, unwholesome and a slave statute."

CHAPTER SEVEN, NOTE 73: PAGE 188   631

> . . . In 1964, Mr. Lewis was awarded the presidential Medal of Freedom at a ceremony in the White House. [*Chicago Sun-Times*, June 12, 1969, p. 50]

See chap. 8, n. 126, below. Cf., on liberty as doing what one is told, chap. 5, n. 94, above.) Those of us involved in the controversies of the late 1940s and the 1950s very much needed and wanted an authoritative statement in support of freedom of speech from the Court with which to counter the authorities (some of them judicial) advanced by the advocates of suppression. We got instead opinions which reinforced such advocates—opinions and arguments which exploited for all they were worth the "clear and present danger" test and its "balancing" substitute. By the time the Court began to move in the late 1950s, it was not so much leading as following men of good will. Cf. pp. 236-37, above. Even such decisions as *Yates* v. *U.S.* do not suffice: the Court did reverse in *Yates* the convictions of fourteen Communist party leaders, ordering the acquittal of some and new trials for others; but the decision rested upon the conclusion that the convictions had relied upon improper statutory construction, insufficient evidence, and an improper charge to the jury (rather than the charge that had been used and approved in *Dennis*).

The opinion for the Court in *Yates* should be compared with Justice Black's opinion, which opens,

> I would reverse every one of these convictions and direct that all the defendants be acquitted. In my judgment the statutory provisions [the Smith Act] on which these prosecutions are based abridge freedom of speech, press and assembly in violation of the First Amendment to the United States Constitution. [354 U.S., at 339]

See, on *Yates*, chap. 3, n. 20, above. See, on *Scales* v. *U.S.*, 367 U.S. 203 (1961), chap. 5, n. 21, chap. 7, n. 69, above.

It was the First Amendment which was subverted in *Douds* and *Dennis*—a subversion which has its roots in *Schenck*—and it is the First Amendment which must be revived if we are to have a clear standard by which an excited or frightened public can be directed to take its bearings. See chap. 3, n. 14, above. Konvitz has argued, "For whatever comfort it may be, the Smith Act is constitutional and is part of the United States criminal code; but it is an almost wholly useless relic, and one's interest in it in the future can be only historical and clinical." *Expanding Liberties*, p. 134. Indeed, one *can* counter *Douds* with *U.S.* v. *Brown*, 381 U.S. 437 (1965); *Dennis* with *Baggett* v. *Bullitt*, 377 U.S. 360 (1964) (see Justice Clark's dissent, 377 U.S., at 383-84); and *Scales* with *Noto* v. *U.S.*, 367 U.S. 290 (1961). (See, also, chap. 7, n. 69, above, on *Brandenburg* v. *Ohio*, 395 U.S. 444 [1969].) But I am not concerned for the immediate future but rather for the next serious crisis during which the doctrines of such cases as *Dennis* will be resurrected, as have been in our time the "plausible pretexts" (chap. 6, n. 63, above) of the doctrines of *Schenck*, to justify suppression that may be even more dangerous than anything we have yet seen. (See chap. 8, n. 169, below.) Americans may not be so fortunate the next time as to have available a popular and good-natured general to help clear the air. See chap. 7, n. 60, above, chap. 8, n. 148, below. Or, if they do, he may be a Caesar, not an Eisenhower dedicated to constitutional government. (The existence of military files on civilians, although not an immediate threat, does not bode well for the third century of the Republic. Cf. the sensibleness in political life of such officers as William Anderson of Tennessee. *Congressional Record* 116: E10819 [1970]. See Burke, *Works* 4:234.)

Aside from all this, the suppressions of the late 1940s and of the 1950s probably contributed to that state of the public mind which permitted (if it did not encourage) our incredible folly in Vietnam. This is indeed a high price to pay for prejudice, ignorance, and demagoguery—but it *is* the price to be expected when a people's constitutional principles are openly repudiated. See chap. 8, n. 169, chap. 9, nn. 10, 37, below. See, on the cosmic rendering of accounts, Shakespeare, *King Lear*, act 5, sc. 3, ll. 206-9 ("The gods are just . . ."). See, on "contempt" and the Vietnam war, p. 320, above.

73. See Chafee's account of *Abrams* v. *U.S.*, 250 U.S. 616 (1919):

Rosansky was given three years in prison, Molly Steimer fifteen years and $500 fine, Lipman, Lachowsky, and Abrams twenty years (the maximum), and $1,000 on each count. If they had actually conspired to tie up every munition plant in the country and succeeded the punishment could not have been more. "I did not expect anything better," said Lipman. "And may I add," replied the judge, "that you do not deserve anything better." [*Freedom of Speech*, p. 148]

The patriotic spirit which has moved our courts in many of the "sedition" and "conspiracy" prosecutions in this century was made explicit by the Supreme Court of Illinois in *People* v. *Walters Chapter D.A.R.*, 311 Ill. 304, at 310 (1924) (which was called to my attention by J. William Hayton [on whom I draw as well in chap. 7, n. 86, below, to confirm my suggestions about the interpretation of wills]):

> The organization of the [D.A.R.] chapter and the uses to which its property was devoted were not only for the establishment and maintenance of a community rest room and improvement of social conditions, which were applied religion, but also to impress upon the people the value of our inheritance of freedom and reverence for those who achieved it, to maintain and perpetuate our established system of government which has fulfilled the purposes and expectations of its founders, and to discourage and prevent opposition to the government and its institutions by discontented venders of political nostrums for the cure of government or due to thwarted personal ambitions.

Consider, also, the excessive response of the Canadian government in October, 1970, to a state of "apprehended insurrection" in Quebec Province. "The government was accused in [the parliamentary debate in Ottawa] of waiting too long to stamp out revolutionary activities in Quebec before it finally responded with 'too much too late.'" *Chicago Tribune*, Oct. 20, 1970, p. 2. See Herbert Marx, "The Emergency Power and Civil Liberties in Canada," *McGill Law J.* 16 (1970): 39. See, also, chap. 3, nn. 22, 28, above. See, for Pollock's response to the *Abrams* sentences, chap. 7, n. 77, below. I found during an early November, 1970, visit to Montreal, however, that the bark of the Canadian government had been worse than its bite. See chap. 9, n. 1, below. Even so, a government can only arrest *once* "for the first time" the hundreds arrested in October, 1970: they have now been "blooded," not deterred, for the next encounter. See, for Emerson's advice in such matters, chap. 8, n. 80, below.

74. Malcolm P. Sharp, *Was Justice Done? The Rosenberg-Sobell Case* (New York: Monthly Review Press, 1956). Sharp's publications on this and other subjects are cited in the bibliography included in the issue of the *University of Chicago Law Review* dedicated to him, at *U. Chicago L. Rev.* 33 (1966): 221. See, also, his favorable review, in the Jan. 1966 *Progressive*, of Walter and Miriam Schneir, *Invitation to an Inquest* (Garden City, N.Y.: Doubleday & Co., 1965).

We will know that we have indeed recovered from the loss of confidence of the 1950s when we do what we can to correct the excesses of which there remain legacies. (See chap. 8, n. 14, below.) Thus, the American press never recognized its duty during the 1960s to call for the immediate release from prison of Morton Sobell. (His thirty-year sentence [the maximum permitted by law], even if he should have been guilty of the offense charged [which was *not*, in his case, that of atomic espionage], was most vindictive, made even worse by his improper confinement in Alcatraz for five years. [I prepared in 1954, at the request of one of Sobell's attorneys, a memorandum on the administrative order consigning a well-behaved, nonviolent prisoner to Alcatraz. There was, I discovered from my legal research, little to appeal to in any attempt to secure a reversal of the Alcatraz order but the good faith and the sense of honor of the Department of Justice and of the Bureau of Prisons. Cf. Justice Jackson's observation, in chap. 8, n. 79, below, "In Great Britain, to observe civil liberties is good politics and to transgress the rights of the individual or the minority is bad politics."] Sobell was released from Lewisburg Federal Penitentiary in 1969, several years after he had first become eligible for parole. He served a total of seventeen years and nine months. *New York Times*, Jan. 15, 1969, p. 1.)

CHAPTER SEVEN, NOTE 74: PAGE 188   633

The shortcomings of the press, which have been partly responsible for the difficulties we have had, are alluded to in a letter of June 30, 1953, about the Rosenberg executions which I offered to the *New York Times* and other newspapers. (The bracketed material, as distinguished from the parenthetical remarks, is added by me at this time.)

I would like to note for the record a lapse in the accuracy and alertness of the general American press as illustrated by The New York *Times*. This is in connection with the Rosenberg case.

Much was made of the fact that the convicted couple would not be and were not executed during the Jewish Sabbath. [The execution, of Mr. Rosenberg and thereafter his wife, took place on Friday, June 19, 1953.] The New York *Times* reported, June 20, 1953, page 6, column 8, that defense counsel had argued before Judge Kaufman that it would be "an outrageous insult to world Jewry to permit the execution to go forward" after the Sabbath had begun. No doubt, the desire of counsel was to secure a postponement of the execution from Friday to Saturday night, or perhaps even to a later date. Instead, as we now know, the concern of counsel unexpectedly contributed to hastening the time of execution, with the press and radio stressing that this was done to keep the Sabbath undefiled.

Even if one were not already somewhat disturbed about the haste with which the Supreme Court and the Executive moved in the closing days of this case, the statements and actions relating to the Jewish Sabbath should give one cause to wonder. No one, it seems, has bothered to question in print [and this, so far as I know, is still true] whether the executions were in fact completed before the commencement of the Sabbath.

In the article already referred to, The New York *Times* reported that defense counsel had pointed out to the District Court "that there was some doubt as to when the Jewish Sabbath actually began." The *Times*, however, was able to explain in an adjoining column (June 20, 1953, page 6, column 7) why "the Jewish Sabbath began last night at 8:13 o'clock, exactly eighteen minutes before official sundown." In the lead article on the front page of the same issue, however, The *Times* asserts that the Jewish Sabbath began at 8:31 o'clock (i.e., the time of sundown indicated on page 6) the night of the execution (which is the "last night" referred to in the article on page 6, column 7). The significance of this discrepancy becomes apparent when it is noticed that the executions were not completed until 8:16 o'clock (Mrs. Rosenberg "entered the chamber at 8:11 P.M. and was pronounced dead five minutes later," The *Times* and other newspapers reported).

Thus, according to the Sabbath-commencement data given by The *Times* at page 6, the Sabbath was three minutes old before Mrs. Rosenberg was pronounced dead; but, according to the data given in the front page story, where the execution time and the Sabbath-commencement time were brought together for the reader, the Sabbath was still 15 minutes off. (Most newspapers, I should add, gave 8:31 as the time of the commencement of the Sabbath and 8:16 as the time of the completion of the executions. One Chicago newspaper, however, The Chicago Daily *News*, gave 8:13 as the time that "the religious holiday began officially" and reported that Mrs. Rosenberg "was electrocuted at 8:11 1/2 p.m.," compressing into one-half minute the act that lasted four or five minutes for the other newspapers.)

One should be most cautious in drawing conclusions from circumstances such as these. It is possible, even likely, that honest slips were made by editors or that assumptions were inadvertently left unverified. Still, there is a suggestion, in all this, that there was carelessness and perhaps even repression, conscious or unconscious, of facts by both the press and the government with respect to this relatively minor aspect of the Rosenberg affair. It is to be hoped, of course, that the factors which led to these errors did not influence the press's coverage and the government's handling of the more important aspects of the case as well.

Walter and Miriam Schneir reported that sunset was at 8:31 that day, that the executions had been scheduled for 8:00, and that they were completed by 8:16. *Invitation to an Inquest*, pp. 249-53. The "eighteen minutes before official sundown" calculation I quote in my letter to the *New York Times* reflects the centuries-old differences of opinion among Jewish rabbis as to when observance of the Sabbath should begin. Some insist it should begin, to be on the safe side, one hour before sunset; many more settle for one half hour before sunset. (The more cautious approach is described in the *Jewish Encyclopedia* [New York: Funk & Wagnalls Co., 1905], 10:594: "With a view to more thoroughly safeguarding the Sabbath against profanation an hour of the previous day . . . was added to it. This was called 'adding from the profane to the holy.' . . .") But far more important than the precise time for the Sabbath is that our government was permitted (by Jews and Gentiles alike) to treat this entire episode in so cavalier a manner. (I have long believed that a Pulitzer Prize awaits the respectable newspaperman who investigates this case properly and, perhaps even more difficult, succeeds in getting his reports published in the daily press. The press was considerably better in reporting the "Chicago Conspiracy Trial" [Appendix D, above], perhaps in part because of the talent for public relations of several of the defendants. Cf. chap. 8, n. 79, below.)

Particularly distressing is the realization of the kinds of arguments that were made to President Eisenhower by those urging that the executions be carried out. These are reflected in a letter from Eisenhower to his son, then serving in Korea,

> about one aspect of the case: "To address myself more specifically to the Rosenberg case for a minute, I must say that it goes against the grain to avoid interfering in the case where a woman is to receive capital punishment. Over against this, however, must be placed one or two facts that have great significance. The first of these is that in this instance it is the woman who is the strong and recalcitrant character, the man is the weak one. She has obviously been the leader in everything they did in the spy ring. The second thing is that if there would be any commuting of the woman's sentence without the man's then from here on *the Soviets would simply recruit their spies from among women.*" [Dwight D. Eisenhower, *Mandate for Change* (New York: New American Library, Signet Books, 1965), p. 281; italics added]

Eisenhower's evident naïveté with respect to this matter (would Klaus Fuchs, for instance, have been told that his role was reserved for a woman?) should be compared with the common sense displayed in the deliberations that led to his selection of Governor Earl Warren later that same year as chief justice of the United States. Ibid., pp. 282-86. (One encountered in this case the "if you only knew what I know" argument all too often used to hint at a justification for government action for which there does not seem to be any other justification.

> Emmett Hughes wrote in his memoirs of the Eisenhower administration that the Rosenberg case was discussed by the Cabinet while it was pending before the Supreme Court. Hughes states that Attorney General Brownell told President Eisenhower: "I've always wanted you to look at evidence that wasn't usable in court showing the Rosenbergs were the head and center of an espionage ring here in direct contact with the Russians—the prime espionage ring in the country." Hughes, however, reports nothing further concerning this discussion.
>
> We know little more about another official attempt to allay doubts concerning the Rosenbergs' guilt. In 1956, Attorney General Brownell ordered a full report on the case to be prepared by the Department of Justice, apparently with a view toward publication of a "white paper." A department attorney was reportedly given complete access to the FBI files and to all of the evidence in the department's possession, and he interviewed various witnesses, members of the prosecutor's staff, and [Morton] Sobell and [David] Greenglass. Unfortunately, the report was never made public. [Abe Krash, "Malcolm Sharp and the *Rosenberg* Case: Remembrance of Things Past," *U. Chicago L. Rev.* 33 (1966): 202, 206 (citations to references omitted)]

The patriot must hope that the attorney general was correct in 1953, that the government did have overwhelming evidence about not only wartime espionage but also extensive espionage continued by the Rosenbergs long after the war: that is, one must hope that

CHAPTER SEVEN, NOTE 74: PAGE 188   635

one's country did not behave quite as badly on that occasion as it then seemed to be doing. "When former Attorney General Brownell was apprised of [the] statement attributed to him by Hughes, his secretary replied: 'Mr. Brownell advised me that he has no recollection of the alleged incident, nor does he have any such evidence as referred to therein. . . .' " Schneir and Schneir, *Invitation to an Inquest*, p. 245n. Cf. ibid., pp. 296-97, 302-3, 349, 360-61. A press really vigilant about such matters would, in any event, have insisted that the report supposedly prepared by the Department of Justice more than a decade ago be released, if only to provide us guidance and encourage self-restraint hereafter. See chap. 8, n. 79, below. Cf. E. H. Cookridge, "The Strangest Trade in the World: Bartering Spies," *London Telegraph Magazine*, Oct. 10, 1969, pp. 26, 28.)

"Magnanimity in politics is not seldom the truest wisdom," Edmund Burke counsels, "and a great empire and little minds go ill together." Burke, *Works*, 2:236. "Whilst *manners* remain entire, they will correct the vices of law, and soften it at length to their own temper. But we have to lament, that in most of the late proceedings we see very few traces of that generosity, humanity, and dignity of mind, which formerly characterized this nation. War suspends the rules of moral obligation, and what is long suspended is in danger of being totally abrogated." Ibid., 2:252. Cf. Randall, *Constitutional Problems under Lincoln*, p. 91: "It is a striking fact that no life was forfeited and no sentence of fine and imprisonment carried out in any judicial prosecution for treason arising out of the 'rebellion' [the American Civil War]." See Sallust, *The War with Catiline*, chap. 51, sec. 8, where Julius Caesar suggests, "If a punishment commensurate with [the conspirators'] crimes can be found, I favour a departure from precedent; but if the enormity of their guilt surpasses all men's imagination, I should advise limiting ourselves to such penalties as the law has established." See, also, Deut. 4:6; chap. 8, nn. 18, 78, below.

The lack of "generosity, humanity, and dignity of mind" was seen as well in the lack of support by the bar of the Rosenbergs' counsel, Emmanuel Bloch.

> Mr. Bloch's heart attack and death on January 30, 1954, may well have been the result of his long labors on behalf of his friends, the Rosenbergs, and their sons. During the last two and a half weeks of the case, working with Miss [Gloria] Agrin and Mr. Emmanuel Bloch, I came to think of them, with Mr. Justice Black and Mr. Justice Douglas, as symbols of justice in a time of difficulty. [Sharp, *Was Justice Done?* pp. xxxv-xxxvi. See, also, ibid., p. 172.]

I have been told by several lawyers who knew Bloch that he felt "terribly isolated" from the bar during most of the time he had this case: he knew his limitations as a criminal trial lawyer and realized he was making mistakes which prejudiced the case for his clients, but he could not get competent lawyers to advise him or, as an experienced and successful Chicago trial lawyer recently told me, "even to talk to him."

The Smith Act defendants also had trouble securing respectable counsel in the 1950s. New York and California attorneys for the National Lawyers Guild (David Scribner, Leonard B. Boudin, Ben Margolis, and William B. Murrish), at page 17 of the 1960 *amicus curiae* brief filed by the Guild in the Supreme Court of the United States on behalf of both Raphael Konigsberg and me, endorsed the following 1954 appraisal by Henry Commager that

> . . . persons charged with subversive activities are finding it almost impossible to obtain counsel. In the Baltimore case . . . , defendants appealed in vain to more than 30 lawyers to take their case. In the [*Nelson* case, in Pennsylvania], the defendant was forced to represent himself in the trial for sedition, after having appealed in vain to 700 lawyers in Pittsburgh and other eastern cities. In the [New York case, after *Dennis*], defendants submitted to the U.S. Circuit Court of Appeals an affidavit stating that "they have written to more than 28 law firms throughout the country requesting an interview to discuss the retainer of said firms on the appeal therein. Of this number 12 did not reply at all to appellants' request; all 16 who did reply refused to grant the requested interview on the grounds that they either could not or would not accept a retainer therein."

Lawyers whom I have heard try to justify their reluctance to take on such cases talk as if they are never obliged to deal with clients who have outrageous opinions about what their rights are and about what the law should be. I now believe that a very unpopular party, which is prosecuted for noncapital political crimes and which cannot secure first-class counsel, should explain the situation to the court and thereafter proffer no defense until such counsel should be made available. If the court, the bar, and the public cannot by such action be shamed into providing adequate counsel, a second-rate defense will not help and may even make matters worse. Cf. Appendix D, above. (See, for Nelson's account of his efforts to find himself a lawyer, Steve Nelson, *The Thirteenth Juror* [Leipzig: Panther Book, 1956], pp. 145-54. See, also, chap. 8, n. 20, below.)

We should recall—or rather the bar should—the famous advice of Thomas Erskine in 1792 about the duty of the lawyer to take difficult or unpopular cases:

> I will for ever, at all hazards, assert the dignity, independence, and integrity of the English bar; without which, impartial justice, the most valuable part of the English constitution, can have no existence. From the moment that any advocate can be permitted to say that he will or will not stand between the Crown and the subject arraigned in the court where he sits daily to practice, from that moment the liberties of England are at an end. If the advocate refuses to defend from what he may think of the charge or of the defence, he assumes the character of the judge; nay, he assumes it before the hour of judgment, and in proportion to his rank and reputation, puts the heavy influence of perhaps a mistaken opinion into the scale against the accused, in whose favour the benevolent principle of English law makes all presumptions, and which commands the very judge to be his counsel. [T. B. Howell, ed., *A Complete Collection of State Trials and Proceedings for High Treason and Other Crimes and Misdemeanors* (London: Longman, Hurst, et al., 1817), 22:411; italics omitted]

(A courtroom exchange in 1784 illustrates nicely that great lawyer's attitude:

> Mr. Justice Buller: Sit down, Sir; remember your duty, or I shall be obliged to proceed in another manner.
> Mr. Erskine: Your Lordship may proceed in what manner you think fit; I know my duty as well as your Lordship knows yours. I shall not alter my conduct.

Erskine, *The Speeches of Thomas Erskine*, 2d ed. [London: James Ridgway, 1813], 1:228-29.) The difference respectable counsel can make is indicated in a recollection by Justice Frankfurter:

> ... I paid no attention to [the *Sacco-Vanzetti* case], but one day I saw that William G. Thompson had become counsel for Sacco and Vanzetti and that interested me. William G. Thompson was one of the most conspicuous lawyers in Boston and particularly conspicuous as a trial lawyer and an appellate lawyer. ... When I saw this notice I said, "Hello!" Up to that time Sacco and Vanzetti had some class conscious lawyers and a blatherskite from the west called Fred Moore, but William Thompson was something else. He was as good a lawyer and as esteemed a lawyer as there was at the Boston bar. [*Felix Frankfurter Reminisces*, ed. Harlan B. Phillips (New York: Reynal & Co., 1960), pp. 210-11]

See, for a compassionate account of the Rosenbergs' execution, Dorothy Day's article in the *Catholic Worker*, June 1950, pp. 2, 6. See, also, chap. 8, n. 190, below, for John Adams's concern about death sentences which "would have been as foul a Stain upon this Country as the Executions of the Quakers or Witches, anciently."

75. The classic commentary upon this kind of case, growing (in this instance) out of alleged wartime atomic bomb espionage on behalf of what was then an important ally, is found among Francis Bacon's "Maxims of the Law":

> The law construeth neither penal laws nor penal facts, but considereth the offence

CHAPTER SEVEN, NOTE 75: PAGE 188   637

in degree as it standeth at the time when it is committed; so as if any circumstance or matter be subsequent, which laid together with the beginning should seem to draw it to a higher nature, yet the law doth not extend or amplify the offence. [*Works*, 14:221]

(See, also, the Bacon quotation in chap. 5, n. 87, above.) The spirit of this sentiment is seen in Edmund Burke's argument:

> If, on the other hand, we admit, that they who are actually exchanged are pardoned, but contend that you may justly reserve for vengeance those who remain unexchanged; then *this unpleasant and unhandsome consequence* will follow; that you judge of the delinquency of men merely by the time [at which they are captured and judged guilty], and not by the heinousness of it; and you make fortune and accidents, and not the moral qualities of human action, the rule of your justice. [Burke, *Works*, 2:246-47; italics added]

(That is to say, it is disturbing to realize that the Rosenbergs would have been treated far more humanely had they been caught *in flagrante delicto*. See chap. 7, nn. 91, 115, chap. 8, n. 2, below. See, also, ibid., 2:242.)

A commentary similar to Bacon's is implied in an article in the *Chicago Tribune* of Sept. 2, 1953:

> Paris, Sept. 1. Marshal Alphonse Juin, commander in chief of all North Atlantic treaty forces in the central Europe sector, today called upon the United States to share atomic bomb secrets with him and other French and British generals.
> "European military leaders want to know the damage America's new atomic weapons can do if they are going to be made available to us, so America has got to agree to modify its atomic secrets law," the marshal told a correspondents' luncheon here.
> Many of the reporters present recalled that Juin ordered his French troops to fire on American infantry men landing in North Africa on Nov. 8, 1942. Later, Juin switched sides and fought the Germans.
> Juin implied that his American colleagues at supreme headquarters had already leaked information to him about the United States' secret atomic weapons by saying: "There is not much hidden from me personally, but there are certain things which America could divulge to certain important persons."

What should our attitude be, now that General deGaulle has so dramatically altered military relations between the United States and France, toward the American officers who supplied Marshal Juin with the information referred to here? It should be noticed that, according to the Atomic Energy Act of 1946, "intent to harm the United States" must be shown if the death penalty is to be imposed for atomic espionage. (See Sharp, *Was Justice Done?*, pp. 165-67, on the refusal of the Supreme Court to extend this safeguard of the Atomic Energy Act to the Rosenbergs [whose espionage activities were alleged to have begun before the passage of this act, but which, it also seems to have been alleged, continued after the effective date of the act]. See chap. 7, n. 86, below.)

David E. Lilienthal, *The Journals* (New York: Harper & Row, 1966), entry of June 19, 1953 (3:404), reflects several of the difficulties I have touched upon:

> The country has had a most unedifying spectacle, with its tremendous climax tonight, in the execution of the Rosenbergs, convicted of securing and passing on information about the atomic bomb. The whole case has been badly handled. They have certainly been given the fullest kind of legal protection, and there is every evidence they knew what they were doing.

Much more than this needs to be said about the matter. It should be noticed, for instance, that the Rosenbergs were sentenced to death April 5, 1951, and executed June 19,

1953. Justice Black opened his dissenting opinion in *Rosenberg* v. *U.S.*, 346 U.S. 273 (1953), at 296, with the observation,

> It is argued that the Court is not asked to "act with unseemly haste to avoid postponement of a scheduled execution." I do not agree. I do not believe that Government counsel or this Court has had time or an adequate opportunity to investigate and decide the very serious question raised. . . . Certainly the time has been too short for me to give this question the study it deserves.

A similar complaint was registered by Justice Frankfurter, 346 U.S., at 289. The "unseemly haste" with which these legal proceedings were concluded is indicated by the fact that the Opinion of the Court and the dissenting opinion of Justice Frankfurter were not filed until after the executions had taken place. (Cf. Walter A. Lunden, "Time Lapse between Sentence and Execution: The United States and Canada Compared," *A.B.A.J.* 48 [1962]: 1043.)

Justice Douglas had gallantly granted a stay of execution the morning of June 17, just one day before the scheduled executions, "until the question of the applicability of the penal provisions of [the] Atomic Energy Act to this case can be determined by the District Court and the Court of Appeals. . . ." Thus, the Rosenbergs seemed to have gained at least a summer's grace. But the attorney general prevailed upon Chief Justice Vinson to reconvene the Court even though it had already dispersed for its summer recess, saying: "It is important in the interests of the administration of criminal justice and in the national interests that this case be brought to a final determination as expeditiously as possible." Since a decision in the Rosenbergs' favor would not have meant an expeditious "final determination," the attorney general's language could only mean that he was determined to get a decision which would permit the couple to be executed immediately. The Court met at noon on the eighteenth to hear arguments and at noon on the nineteenth to set aside Justice Douglas's stay of execution (with Justices Black, Frankfurter, and Douglas dissenting). Less than nine hours later the Rosenbergs were dead. See Schneir and Schneir, *Invitation to an Inquest*, pp. 243-46. See, also, Plato, *Gorgias*, 469B-C, 474C-476A, 481B-C, 489A-C, 508D-510A, 521B-D, 523A-527E. A Georgia congressman introduced on that occasion resolutions in the House of Representatives calling for Justice Douglas's impeachment for "high crimes and misdemeanors" in office, which only goes to show that the silly business with respect to him in the current Congress is not without precedent.

Justice Clark argued in his opinion (346 U.S., at 296): "Over two years ago the Rosenbergs were found guilty by a jury of a grave offense in time of war. Unlike other litigants they have had the attention of this Court seven times; each time the pleas have been denied." Justice Black pointed out, however (346 U.S., at 301), "that this Court has never reviewed this record and has never affirmed the fairness of the trial below." The question of the "fairness of the trial" included the necessity of evaluating the state of mind of a trial judge who could say, in imposing death sentences on the Rosenbergs,

> I believe your conduct in putting into the hands of the Russians the A-bomb years before our best scientists predicted Russia would perfect the bomb has already caused, in my opinion, the Communist aggression in Korea, with the resultant casualties exceeding 50,000 and who knows but that millions more of innocent people may pay the price of *your treason*. Indeed, by your betrayal you undoubtedly have altered the course of history to the disadvantage of your country. [346 U.S., at 312. Italics added]

The words I have italicized suggest that the Rosenbergs may have been, without due regard for constitutional limitations, sent to their deaths for "treason," an offense which was neither alleged nor *provable* by the government. (The Russians, it should be remembered, were not our enemies in the sense of Article 3, section 3, of the Constitution at the time of the actions alleged. See chap. 5, n. 118, above. See, also, chap. 3, n. 35, above.) In effect, the judge may have condemned the Rosenbergs either for a mistaken prediction by "our best scientists" or for a mistaken judgment by Secretary of State Ache-

CHAPTER SEVEN, NOTE 76: PAGE 189   639

son (in discounting publicly, before the North Koreans' move south in 1950, the value to the United States of the Korean Peninsula). See chap. 7, n. 45, above.

The Rosenberg-Sobell case remains a sad and shameful episode for the American bench and bar. Although I have read all of the lengthy record in their trial, I do not know whether or not the Rosenbergs were guilty of what they were charged with. But I do know that the United States was guilty on that occasion of offenses far more dangerous for the security of this country, and for decency and the rule of law everywhere, than even atomic espionage can be. One of the significant advantages we have over our equally fearful competitors in Moscow, it should be added, is that we do remain free to expose and examine our government's misdeeds, and, if need be, to repudiate and correct them. We should make such a comparison, however, not to lull ourselves into self-esteem but to spur us to preserve the vital difference that exists between our traditional way of life and that which allows alleged enemies of the regime to be summarily dispatched. See, e.g., chap. 8, n. 18, below. Squeezing in two executions, with (at most) fifteen minutes to spare, is an unseemly halfway house between what we aspire to be and what we dare not degenerate into. (The most sobering critique of communism may be found in such unintentional self-revelation as may be seen in the description of the execution of Barembayev [a soldier] in Alexander Beck's novel, *On the Forward Fringe* [reprinted as "Judge Me," in Joshua Kunitz, ed., *Russian Literature since the Revolution* (New York: Boni & Gaer, 1948), p. 811]. See, also, chap. 8, nn. 36, 140, below. Cf., on Russia's great contributions and sacrifices in the Second World War, James M. Burns, *Roosevelt: Soldier of Freedom* [Harcourt Brace Jovanovich, 1970]; Senator Stephen Young, *Congressional Record*, 116: S21490 [1970]. Cf., also, the almost liturgical devotion exhibited by the Russians in their recent filming of Tolstoy's *War and Peace*.

76. The ruling in *Pennsylvania* v. *Nelson*, 350 U.S. 497 (1956), has been described and discussed in this manner:

> In applying the supremacy clause [in Article VI of the Constitution] to subjects which have been regulated by Congress, the primary task of the [Supreme] Court is to ascertain whether a challenged State law is compatible with the policy expressed in the federal statute. When Congress condemns an act as unlawful, the extent and nature of the legal consequences of the condemnation are federal questions, the answers to which are to be derived from the statute and the policy which it has adopted. To the federal statute and policy, conflicting State law and policy must yield. But Congress in enacting legislation within its constitutional authority will not be deemed to have intended to strike down a State statute to protect the health and safety of the public unless its purpose to do so is clearly manifested.
>
> As might be anticipated, the Court's conclusions that Congress, in adopting specific legislation, intended to preempt an entire area of regulation with consequential suspension of State enactments touching thereupon have not infrequently been criticized as faulty; and perhaps few rulings of the Court in recent years have generated as much controversy and extended consideration of corrective legislation as its holding in *Pennsylvania* v. *Nelson*. There the Court sustained the conclusion of the Pennsylvania Supreme Court that Congress, in adopting the Smith Act proscribing the knowing advocacy of the forcible overthrow of the Federal Government, had occupied this entire field of regulation to the end that the Pennsylvania Sedition Act, insofar as it prohibited sedition against the National Government as distinguished from the Government of Pennsylvania, was superseded. Evidence that if the States were permitted to exercise a concurrent jurisdiction in this area, a peculiar danger of interference with the federal program would arise, coupled with the fact that the National Government had urged local authorities not to intervene in such matters was deemed sufficient to support the conclusion that the scheme of regulation embodied in the Smith Act was so pervasive as to permit no inference that Congress had left room for the States to supplement it.
>
> The dissenting Justices (Reed, Burton, and Minton) were of the belief that preemption ought not to rest on inference of probable conflict in administration, but upon congressional enactment specifically barring the exercise of State

power. In *Uphaus* v. *Wyman*, 360 U.S. 72, 76-77 (1959), the Court reiterated that "the *Nelson* decision did not strip the States of the right to protect themselves. States legitimately can conduct investigations and prosecutions for sedition against the State itself." In the *Nelson* case, however, the Court emphatically asserted that "the Smith Act . . . [proscribed] advocacy of the overthrow of any government—federal, state or local—by force. . . ." 350 U.S. at 502. [Edward S. Corwin, Norman J. Small, and Lester S. Jayson, *The Constitution of the United States: Analysis and Interpretation* (Washington: Government Printing Office, 1964), pp. 808-9]

See chap. 7, n. 48, above. Cf. Anti-Riot Act of 1968, chap. 6, n. 75, above. (See, for Nelson's understanding of the *Nelson* ruling, *The Thirteenth Juror*, p. 312.)

Although the decision in *Pennsylvania* v. *Nelson* protected Nelson from liability under the Pennsylvania sedition law, it left him liable for prosecution in federal court for similar offenses (where the maximum penalty has been since 1956 imprisonment for twenty years or a fine of $20,000, or both). That is, the Court did not decide the state case on "freedom of speech" principles which, whatever their relevance in the states, should certainly govern congressional legislation. (See, for Nelson's experiences in federal courts, *U.S.* v. *Mesarosh* [*alias Nelson*], 115 F.S. 332 [1953], 116 F.S. 345 [1953], 223 F.2d 449 [1954]; *Mesarosh* v. *U.S.*, 352 U.S. 1 [1956].)

> In all there were fourteen [Smith Act] conspiracy trials, resulting in one hundred and four convictions. There were ten acquittals, and a hung-jury verdict for one. . . . Most of the defendants were sentenced to five years' imprisonment; the lightest sentence was for a two-year term. But only twenty-nine of the Communists convicted on conspiracy charges actually served their sentences. [Konvitz, *Expanding Liberties*, pp. 123-24]

See, also, Lucius J. Barker and Twiley W. Barker, Jr., *Freedoms, Courts, Politics: Studies in Civil Liberties* (Englewood Cliffs, N.J.: Prentice-Hall, 1965), pp. 93-95. Cf. chap. 3, n. 20, above. Had the sentences been anywhere near as severe in *Schenck* (Appendix B, above) as they were in *Abrams*, Justice Holmes probably could not have "gone along"— and the First Amendment litigation and discussion of the subsequent half century would not have had to get around his rhetorical excesses in support of suppression. (In the "Chicago Conspiracy Trial" [Appendix D, above], on the other hand, two of seven defendants were acquitted by the jury on all charges and all defendants were acquitted on the conspiracy charges. The hostility and severity of the trial judge on that occasion may prove *his* undoing: he could have made a plausible case for contempt sentences of three or even six months. His hostile attitude toward the defendants is reflected as well in the question which has been raised on appeal about whether the judge and his marshals behaved themselves as they should have during the jury deliberations at the end of the "Conspiracy Trial." It would indeed be poetic justice to have the convictions reversed on this ground. The public saw, in any event, what *can* happen in our courts.)

77. This is not to suggest that the attorneys for Nelson should not have pressed the arguments which proved successful. An attorney must work within the constitutional framework accepted by the courts. The humanitarian spirit which moved the Supreme Court in the *Nelson* case would have found another, and probably legitimate, form of expression within what I consider a preferable constitutional framework. I am reminded that Chief Justice Waite once observed that his associate, Justice Davis, "used frequently to say that when he was sure justice required a decision in a particular way, he could always find *a good reason* for doing so." John Paul Frank, *Marble Palace: The Supreme Court in American Life* (New York: Knopf, 1958), p. 149; italics added. (See chap. 7, n. 74, above, chap. 7, n. 86, below.) Such a case was *West Virginia State Board of Education* v. *Barnette*, 319 U.S. 624 (1943). Cf. *Minersville School Dist.* v. *Gobitis*, 310 U.S. 586 (1940). See Alpheus T. Mason, *Harlan Fiske Stone* (New York: Viking Press, 1956), pp. 525-35, 598-601. Sir Frederick Pollock observed, in a letter to Justice Holmes, that the monstrously excessive sentence in the *Abrams* case (chap. 7, n. 73, above) was enough

to make one astute in favor of the defense. *The Holmes-Pollock Letters: The Correspondence of Mr. Justice Holmes and Sir Frederick Pollock, 1874-1932*, ed. Mark deW. Howe (Cambridge: Harvard University Press, 1946), 2:31. See chap. 3, n. 20, above. I suggest that the duty of the true constitutionalist is to find a legitimate way—that is, a way consistent with the Constitution—to do justice and to advance the common good. See, also, Appendix F, sec. 9, above.

In such circumstances as are referred to in this note it is well to recall the maxim, "That which is not just, is not Law; and that which is not Law, ought not to be obeyed." Algernon Sidney, *Discourses concerning Government*, chap. 3, sec. 11. Even the lawyer can grant, "the doctrine of the law then is this: that precedents and rules must be followed, unless flatly absurd or unjust. . . ." Blackstone, *Laws of England*, 1:70. And Coke had said in *Dr. Bonham's Case*, 8 Rep. 118a (1610): "It appeareth in our books, that in many cases the common law will controul Acts of Parliament and adjudge them to be utterly void; for where an Act of Parliament is against common right and reason or repugnant or impossible to be performed, the common law will controul it and adjudge it to be void." See James Kent, *Commentaries on American Law* (New York: O. Halsted, 1826), 1:16-17. See, also, chap. 8, n. 86, below.

In opposition to this understanding of the law is that tradition, also seen in Justice Holmes, which can be traced back to Hobbes and even to the classical world (e.g., Thrasymachus, in Plato's *Republic*), the tradition which would define law in terms of will, not reason. (See Hobbes, *Leviathan*, II, xxvi; Laurence Berns, "Thomas Hobbes," in Strauss and Cropsey, *History of Political Philosophy*, p. 370; chap. 8, n. 193, below.) James Otis, on the other hand, stated in 1764 what should still be the public position of the thoughtful American (see pp. 417-18, above):

> To say the Parliament is absolute and arbitrary is a contradiction. The Parliament cannot make 2 and 2, 5: Omnipotency cannot do it. The supreme power in a state is *ius dicere* only: —*ius dare*, strictly speaking, belongs alone to God. Parliaments are in all cases to declare what is for the good of the whole; but it is not the declaration of Parliament that makes it so: There must be in every instance a higher authority, viz. God. Should an Act of Parliament be against any of His natural laws, which are immutably true, their declaration would be contrary to eternal truth, equity, and justice, and consequently void: and so it would be adjudged by the Parliament itself, when convinced of their mistake. Upon this great principle, Parliaments repeal such Acts, as soon as they find they have been mistaken, in having declared them to be for the public good, when in fact they were not so. . . . [Samuel Eliot Morison, *Sources and Documents Illustrating the American Revolution, 1764-88, and the Formation of the Federal Constitution* (London: Oxford University Press, 1963), p. 7]

Supporting Otis's argument—for it is an argument in which God and Nature may be seen as interchangeable—is an observation by Francis Bacon in his essay "Of the True Greatness of Kingdoms and Estates": "For there is that justice imprinted in the nature of men, that they enter not upon wars (whereof so many calamities do ensue) but upon some, at the least specious, grounds and quarrels." Consider, also, the significance of the reluctance of even the Nazis to commit to paper explicit orders for the extermination of the Jews. Edward Crankshaw, *Gestapo* (London: Pantheon Books, 1960), pp. 147, 186. Do we not see in "that justice imprinted in the nature of men" some support for the proposition that virtue comes with wisdom or that vice is the result of ignorance? See Halevi, *The Kuzari*, pp. 224-25. We say more than we realize when we observe of someone who misbehaves that "he does not know better." But what of those who do not *want* to "know better"—or does this, again, make too much of the will? See chap. 8, n. 193, below.

I may not seem in this study to make much of freedom of speech as a "natural right." (Cf. chap. 5, n. 24, above.) Natural rights, as I understand them, are to be thought about, not merely invoked like an incantation: for their proper use, a careful study of institutions, circumstances, and the nature of man is needed. To the extent that freedom of speech *is* a natural right, it can be invoked (independent of constitutional provisions) against either a state or the general government. See the conclusion of sec. 3 of chap. 5, above. See, also, chap. 6, n. 37, above.

> We suggest, without intending to decide, that there may be a distinction between certain natural rights, enforced in the Constitution by prohibitions against interference with them, and what may be termed artificial or remedial rights, which are peculiar to our own system of jurisprudence. *Of the former class* are the rights to one's own religious opinion and to a public expression of them, or, as sometimes said, to worship God according to the dictates of one's own conscience; the right to personal liberty and individual property; to freedom of speech and of the press; to free access to courts of justice, to due process of law and to an equal protection of the laws; to immunities from unreasonable searches and seizures, as well as cruel and unusual punishments; and to such other immunities as are indispensable to a free government. *Of the latter class* are the rights to citizenship, to suffrage, . . . and to the particular methods of procedure pointed out in the Constitution, which are peculiar to Anglo-Saxon jurisprudence. . . . [*Downes* v. *Bidwell*, 182 U.S. 244, 282-83 (1901); italics added]

See Burke, *Works*, 2:242-43. See, also, chap. 5, n. 1, above, chap. 8, nn. 13, 14, below.

I suspect it was a lingering sympathy for natural right that occasionally manifested itself in Justice Frankfurter's opinions. (See, e.g., *Rochin* v. *California*, 342 U.S. 165 [1952]; chap. 8, n. 13, below. Cf. Justice Black's concurring opinion in *Rochin*, 342 U.S., at 174; also, dissenting, in *Griswold* v. *Connecticut*, 381 U.S. 479, 522 [1965]; dissenting, in *Harper* v. *Virginia State Board of Elections*, 383 U.S. 663, 675 [1966].) Both Justice Black and he rebelled against what I think is a distortion of the traditional natural-right teaching. (But that is another story: see Anastaplo, "Natural Right and the American Lawyer," *Wis. L. Rev.* 1965: 322, 336-41. One can begin to think about natural right by observing how troublesome it is to find parents ruled by their children. One can see that thinking *is* required when one observes how different in temperament even brothers raised in the same household can be. But notice how much alike Sophocles' Laius and Oedipus are, although living apart from one another. See chap. 9, n. 32, below.

Justice Cardozo spoke "of some principle of justice so rooted in the traditions and conscience of our people as to be ranked as fundamental." *Snyder* v. *Massachusetts*, 291 U.S. 97, 105 (1934). The natural-right teaching, whatever it may have said in particular circumstances, would have thought not of "the traditions and conscience of our people" but rather of "the nature of man" as that in which "some principle of justice" is rooted. See, for a detailed and sensitive account of an East African legal system, Lloyd A. Fallers, *Law without Precedent: Legal Ideas in Action in the Courts of Colonial Busoga* (Chicago: University of Chicago Press, 1969). A 1941 Uganda Native Courts Ordinance (ibid., p. 39) is instructive to keep in mind while reflecting upon the material presented in Professor Fallers's book (see p. 611, above, chap. 8, n. 30, below):

> A native court shall administer and enforce . . . native law and custom in the area of the jurisdiction of the court, so far as it is applicable and is not repugnant to natural justice and morality.

Fallers observed (ibid., p. 332):

> These legal systems, in both their precolonial and colonial manifestations, are surely among Africa's greatest cultural achievements. Without written records, they produced regimes of law, tempered by justice, whose centrality to African life, and whose success in ordering the affairs of millions of people, is perhaps difficult for persons not closely familiar with African communities to appreciate.

He indicated (ibid., pp. 36-37) that the anthropologist all too often does not know what he should have been inquiring into until after he has returned home and reflected on the data he did gather. It would be instructive, for social scientists and students of "natural

CHAPTER SEVEN, NOTE 78: PAGE 189   643

justice" alike, if anthropologists in the field would make a point of addressing themselves explicitly and in detail to the question of whether the bulk of the decisions rendered according to "native law and custom" are indeed fair and (if they are) why this should be so. This judgment should take into account, of course, the expectations, the experiences, and the likely future of the people involved. I believe such an inquiry would be both revealing and reassuring. See, e.g., ibid., pp. 19, 63, 66, 156-57, 190, 316-20. Cf. ibid., pp. 214-29. I am struck by how fair-minded the doctrines and institutions worked out over many years in their circumstances by a healthy community tend to be. See, e.g., ibid., pp. 101 (epigraph), 112. (This is not to deny, however, that some communities are better than others: there are, for example, circumstances which are better suited than others for the development of that which is distinctively, or most fully, human. [See, e.g., chap. 8, nn. 16, 177, chap. 9, n. 39, below.] But fundamental to the human ability to form communities, and hence [when all goes well] the best community, may be "that justice imprinted in the nature of men" which Bacon noticed. Thus, the critical shortcomings of a people may be in the realm of judgment, not in the realm of desire. See the opening lines of both the *Nicomachean Ethics* and the *Politics* of Aristotle.) In assessing the institutions of another people one should take care neither to overestimate one's own sense of justice nor to underestimate another's subtlety. See, e.g., the test provided (in Num. 5:11-31) when "the spirit of jealousy" comes upon a husband with respect to his wife. Is it not likely that this test is, in the circumstances in which it was devised and administered, of immeasurable value to the woman, despite its outward appearance as an early instance of "male chauvinism"? See pp. 610-11, chap. 7, n. 59, above.

See Halevi, *The Kuzari*, pp. 55, 236, 257; Jacob Klein, "On the Nature of Nature," Feb. 28, 1964, mimeographed (Annapolis, Md.: St. John's College Bookstore); Joseph Cropsey, "Political Life and a Natural Order," *Journal of Politics* 23 (Feb. 1961): 46; Jason Aronson, "Shaftesbury on Locke," *American Political Science Review* 53 (1959): 1101, 1103-4; Aristotle, *Nicomachean Ethics* 1138a4-14 (for the dependence of one's humanity and hence natural rights on community).

See, also, chap. 8, sec. 16, chap. 2, n. 31, chap. 3, nn. 3, 4, chap. 4, n. 45, above, chap. 9, nn. 3, 20, 22, 38, 39, below. Consider, for intimations of natural right, the *conclusion* of the remarks by Nikita Khrushchev quoted in chap. 8, n. 18, below; the basis of the worldwide appeal of and to the Nuremberg Judgments since the end of the Second World War; the restrictions, noted in chap. 8, n. 124, below, on the emancipation of slaves. Consider, also, Burke, *Works*, 2:242 ("the natural distinctions of things").

78. This is reflected in the prohibition of *ex post facto* legislation and bills of attainder. I suspect that many state sedition acts (chap. 7, nn. 47, 69, above) are vulnerable as effective bills of attainder; some of them are probably *ex post facto* legislation as well. (See, for Justice Black's use of *attaint*, chap. 7, n. 72, above.)

The same may be said of such congressional legislation as the Smith Act and the McCarran Act (enacted Sept. 23, 1950, three months after the beginning of the Korean War).

> Supporters of the [Smith Act] in Congress made it clear in their discussions that they knew that Congress could not ban any organization *by name* without violating the constitutional prohibition on bills of attainder; but they wished Congress to go as far as it could constitutionally to outlaw Nazi, Fascist, and Communist organizations [citing *Congressional Record* 86:9032 ff. (1940)]. [Konvitz, *Expanding Liberties*, pp. 110-11]

But should not such legislation be seen (despite its mask) for what it is? See chap. 4, n. 13, above. Cf. Justice Frankfurter's labyrinthine opinion (summarized at Konvitz, *Expanding Liberties*, pp. 144-46) in *Communist Party* v. *Subversive Activities Control Board*, 367 U.S. 1-115 (1961); Harold W. Chase, "The Libertarian Case for Making It a Crime to Be a Communist," *Temple L. Q.* 29 (1956): 121. But see *Communist Party* v. *U.S.*, 331 F.2d 807 (1963); *Aptheker* v. *Secretary of State*, 378 U.S. 500, 518 (1964); *Albertson* v. *S.A.C.B.*, 382 U.S. 70 (1965).

Fortunately for the cause of freedom, the men who are today most intent upon instituting repressive measures are also most likely to be negligent in the procedures they employ: that is, they are men who are not likely to be able to restrain and discipline themselves. (See chap. 3, n. 30, above.) See, e.g., *Baggett* v. *Bullitt*, 377 U.S. 360 (1964).

The significance of an adherence by well-trained courts to traditional procedural standards is suggested by the remarkable delaying action that the South African judiciary was able to carry on for years against the full implementation of tyrannical legislation. See Lionel Forman and E. S. Sachs, *The South African Treason Trial* (London: J. Calder, 1967), pp. 41, 101, 109, 170, 211. (Consider the newspaper accounts, in early October, 1970, of the recourse by the South African government to "the serving of [house arrest orders and public-gathering bans] on 19 Africans acquitted for the second time in Pretoria on Sept. 14." *Guardian* [London], Oct. 5, 1970, p. 4.) See chap. 8, n. 96, below.

In any event, it is somewhat reassuring that there does seem to be in the world of practical affairs *some* connection between vice and ignorance (or incompetence):

> The Report [on Torture in Greece issued in November 1969 by the European Human Rights Commission in Strasbourg] is a historic step in international human rights law, as it is perhaps the first time that an international body carried out such a thorough investigation of a police state. The horror of the situation emerges vividly from the Report, despite its legal and technical style. Another aspect that emerges is the extraordinary ineptitude of the Greek authorities in handling this case. Especially when the sub-Commission heard evidence in Greece, the confusion of the authorities is manifest. They let the jurists see some witnesses and places and then refused them others. Documents such as police ledgers and medical reports were patently falsified. The Greek government witnesses and lawyers seemed to believe that the argument, "It is a communist lie" was a sufficient and effective rebuttal to the mass of evidence produced by the Scandinavians. It is clear that the Greek authorities, unaccustomed to the rule of law in their own country, were totally unprepared for the rigors of a proper hearing. [James Becket, *Barbarism in Greece* (New York: Walker & Co., 1970), pp. 107-8]

See chap. 6, n. 1, above. I suspect the Russian authorities would be equally inept—but they, unlike the Greek government, are not dependent on Western support and can therefore ignore altogether such proceedings. See Anastaplo, "American Aid and Greek Tyranny," *Congressional Record* 116: E10520 (1970).

79. The addition of "or to the people" (*Annals, I*, p. 761) (chap. 2, n. 33, above) to the Tenth Amendment seems to have had the effect of making certain that restraints on the state governments incorporated in the state constitutions would not be implicitly removed or negatived by the amendment. It also recognized, in effect, that the people, not the states, are the ultimate source of the powers distributed by the Constitution.

80. State officials are no longer compelled to think seriously about these issues. I would not be surprised to learn that free-speech discussion in state court opinions has steadily deteriorated since it was decided that the freedom of speech and of the press guarantees of the First Amendment are applicable against the states as well and that the states are therefore subject to correction by the federal judiciary. See chap. 7, nn. 88, 118, below.

Cf. Grodzins, *American System*, p. 115, n. 53; Russell M. Ross and Kenneth F. Millsap, *State and Local Government and Administration* (New York: Ronald Press, 1966), p. 319:

> The federal courts have only declared slightly more than eighty acts passed by Congress and administrative orders unconstitutional in the more than one hundred and sixty years the power has been exercised by the United States Supreme Court. The federal courts have been equally prudent since less than nine hundred state statutes have been nullified by judicial actions. State courts have struck down a much larger proportion of state laws on the grounds of conflict with the state constitution. *Hardly a year passes* without judicial nullification being used to strike down *nearly a hundred state laws*. No complete count of the exact number has ever been compiled. [Italics added]

CHAPTER SEVEN, NOTE 81: PAGE 189

81. Cf. *New York Times* v. *Sullivan*, 376 U.S. 254 (1964). See Harry Kalven, "The New York Times Case: A Note on the Central Meaning of the First Amendment," *Supreme Court Review*, 1964, p. 191. Kalven (*The Negro and the First Amendment* [Chicago: University of Chicago Press, 1966], p. 57) said of Justice Brennan's majority opinion in this case, "It reads as though we are starting all over again to build a freespeech doctrine afresh. There is not a word of clear and present danger or of balancing." (But see the Anti-Riot Act of 1968 [chap. 6, n. 75, above] for an awkward congressional revival of "clear and present danger.")

Do we have in *New York Times* v. *Sullivan* a freedom of the press problem, or is it fundamentally a race relations problem in which the press happens to be involved? (See chap. 7, n. 84, below.) To what extent should the Fourteenth and Fifteenth Amendments affect with respect to racial matters the constitutional arrangement left upon the ratification of the First Amendment? See chap. 4, n. 13, chap. 7, n. 54, above, chap. 7, n. 96, below.

It seems to me that the *New York Times* case is more critically one bearing on problems of the rule of law (or of due process of law) than on problems of freedom of the press. (See, e.g., chap. 8, n. 15, below.) Why should a state court be permitted to retain jurisdiction over a libel suit against a newspaper printed elsewhere when only 394 copies containing the alleged libel out of an edition of 650,000 are circulated in the state (and only 35 of them in the county where the suit arose)? (I put aside the question of whether the defendant waived jurisdictional objections by entering a general appearance.) My arguments on behalf of states' rights do not require us to concede to a state the power, in effect, to legislate with respect to the national press. (A local newspaper, because it does have local readers, and hence a local "constituency," is better equipped than is an out-of-state newspaper to protect itself politically against efforts to repress it in state courts.) Thus, states' rights cannot mean that Alabama may, because of its concern about what is barely happening in Alabama, control in vital respects what does happen in New York: to permit this would be to permit one state to usurp the rights of another. (One is reminded here as well of the spirit of *Gibbons* v. *Ogden*, 9 Wheat. [U.S.] 1 [1824]. See, also, chap. 8, nn. 83, 85, below.)

The Supreme Court in the *New York Times* case did what Congress could do, if it should become aware of its power to protect and extend freedom of the press in the states. The Court could also have had recourse to the "Republican Form of Government" guarantee to protect criticism of public officers. Did the constitution of Alabama protect the *New York Times* in what it did? See chap. 7, n. 82, below. In any event, due process means that the evidence adduced and the penalties levied are not unreasonably related to what the parties have done or suffered. *Farces will not be permitted*. See chap. 4, n. 12, above.

Kalven (*Negro and First Amendment*, pp. 63-64) has observed,

> ... The great civil liberties issues of the postwar decade centered on the national efforts to curb the domestic communist conspiracy. It is not entirely poetry to say that the NAACP is from the standpoint of the beleaguered South a second domestic conspiracy aiming at a revolution. And the Southern states have responded to the challenge by seeking to adapt the legal methods used to fight communism. Thus far the tactic has been highly unsuccessful. There is, therefore, little suspense in the story we are about to tell; the outcome is wholly predictable. The Court will protect the NAACP.

Has the preoccupation since the Second World War with the Communist menace enlisted all of the available respectable American talent for suppression? (See the quotation from Hobbes in chap. 2, n. 7, above, and from Tocqueville in chap. 2, n. 3, above.) Or is it that we have been reminded since the war of what is wrong with "the legal methods used to fight communism" and therefore do not dare permit them to be extended? (See, e.g., chap. 8, n. 169, below.) Or is it that we are now obliged to show the world that the black man finds in the United States a worthy ally? (See Anastaplo, book review,

N.Y.U. L. Rev. 41 [1966]: 664.) We can say, in any event, that the times have been such as to permit the success of the strategy of bringing to light "the Negro rights [which were] in an important sense . . . always there." See chap. 5, n. 43, above.

It is curious, by the way, that racial discrimination (in such countries as South Africa and Rhodesia) can be made so much of in the United Nations while severe curtailments of everyone's political rights and liberty (in such countries as Russia and Greece) are ignored. Thus, it is more fashionable these days to "stand up" for racial justice than for political freedom (or constitutionalism). I, on the other hand, regard the latter as much more important for the community. So did Lincoln, the Great Emancipator.

An experienced attorney could observe to me in 1960, while I was in Washington for the oral arguments in my bar admission case (and in the case of Raphael Konigsberg, who unsuccessfully sought admission to the California bar [Appendix F, above]), "If Konigsberg and you were Negroes, you would have been admitted long ago!" But, it should also be added, we would have been (had we been Negroes) far less able than we have been to absorb the unexpected loss of our careers at the bar. (Konigsberg has become, I have been told, a prosperous real estate dealer in Los Angeles. See p. 404, above.)

82. See the passage from Madison quoted in the text at chap. 7, n. 2, above. May state constitutional provisions protecting freedom of speech be successfully invoked in a federal court? Is it a denial of the rule of law—of due process in the procedural sense—if the state government does not apply such provisions properly? Should this failure on the part of the state supply the basis for any action in a federal court?

It is generally said that federal courts are bound by the decision of a state court ruling that a state statute has been enacted in accordance with the state constitution. (See *Luther* v. *Borden*, 7 How. [U.S.] 1 [1849]; *Patterson* v. *Colorado*, 205 U.S. 454, 459 [1907]; *Bulchalter* v. *New York*, 319 U.S. 427, 429 [1943]; *Bizup* v. *Tinsley*, 316 F.2d 284, 285 [1963]; Robert Jackson, *The Supreme Court in the American System of Government* [New York: Harper & Row, 1963], pp. 36-37.) Why should this be? Should not a federal court be able to interpret and respect state constitutional provisions and state statutes as well as a state court? Would not a federal court be at least as apt to give such provisions their due as would be a state court? See William W. Crosskey, "Mr. Chief Justice Marshall," in Allison Dunham and Philip B. Kurland, *Mr. Justice* (Chicago: University of Chicago Press, 1964), pp. 20-24.

Could Congress, by exercising its power to protect freedom of speech in the states, provide that federal courts apply to state laws their own (not the state courts') interpretation of state constitutional provisions? (Congress could certainly make a law, under my interpretation of the First Amendment, requiring federal courts to enforce against the states the safeguards of freedom of speech and of the press that are enforced against the general government.) Is not this the view of First Amendment rights in which Congress and the states have acquiesced since the *Gitlow* decision in 1925? See Section 9 of Appendix F for my attempt to apply in my 1960 *Brief on the Merits* (pp. 82-84, 88-94) the following argument to a review of bar admission proceedings:

> Although petitioner has serious reservations about the policy of the Fourteenth Amendment as interpreted in the *Gitlow* case, he recognizes that some such limitation upon the States must be insisted upon so long as Congress does not acknowledge and exercise the power that seems to have been given it under the First Amendment to ameliorate or remove state abridgments of the freedom of speech.

See chap. 5, n. 134, above, chap. 8, n. 83, below.

I have gotten the impression that federal courts are apt to search carefully for due process or other irregularities in state criminal proceedings upon being shown that a state court has willfully and obviously disregarded a state constitutional provision. See, e.g., *Baker* v. *Carr*, 369 U.S. 186, 258, where Justice Clark (in his concurring opinion) reported, "Like the [U.S.] District Court, I conclude that appellants have met the burden of showing 'Tennessee is guilty of a clear violation of the state constitution and of the [federal] rights of the plaintiffs.'" (The second bracketed insertion is Justice Clark's.)

See chap. 4, n. 107, above.

83. Were not the Virginia and Kentucky Resolutions just such resistance by state legislatures to usurpation by the general government? See chap. 7, n. 2, above, chap. 8, n. 85, below. See, also, *Federalist*, pp. 99-100, 140-41, 309; Pritchett, *The American Constitution*, p. 75.

The governor of Massachusetts signed on April 2, 1970, a law passed by the legislature of that state which purports to authorize Massachusetts servicemen to refuse to be sent to a combat zone in an undeclared war. This law has in it familiar echoes (especially in the italicized phrases) of the Hartford Convention, the Virginia and Kentucky Resolutions, and (more sobering) the Civil War (chap. 7, n. 2, above, chap. 9, n. 28, below):

> Section 1. No inhabitant of the commonwealth inducted or serving in the military forces of the United States shall be required to serve outside the territorial limits of the United States in the conduct of armed hostilities *not an emergency and not otherwise authorized in the powers granted to the President of the United States in Article 2, Section 2, of the Constitution of the United States* designating the President as the Commander in Chief, unless such hostilities were initially authorized or subsequently ratified by a congressional declaration of war according to the constitutionally established procedures in Article 1, Section 8, of the Constitution of the United States.
>
> Section 2. *The attorney general* [of Massachusetts] *shall, in the name and on behalf of the commonwealth* and on behalf of any inhabitants thereof who are required to serve in the armed forces of the United States in violation of section one of this act, bring an appropriate action in the Supreme Court of the United States [or in an appropriate inferior federal court] to defend and enforce *the rights* of such inhabitants and *of the commonwealth* under section one. . . .
> [*Massachusetts Acts* 1970, ch. 174; italics added.]

See James J. Kilpatrick, "Massachusetts Law, [Governor Claude R.] Kirk's Act Just 'Curiosities,'" *Chicago Daily News*, Apr. 10, 1970, p. 14. See, also, *Federalist*, pp. 295, 309, 362-63, 389-90, 398, 416; chap. 8, n. 71, below.

84. The Supreme Court (I have noted) has argued that it is for Congress (not the Court) to determine whether a state has a republican form of government. (See chap. 4, n. 102, above, chap. 7, n. 107, below.) Justice Frankfurter described in his opinion in *Colegrove* v. *Green*, 328 U.S. 549, 556 (1946) (an Illinois congressional districting case) this and similar situations:

> To sustain this action would cut very deep into the very being of Congress. Courts ought not to enter this political thicket. The remedy for unfairness in districting is to secure State legislatures that will apportion properly, or to invoke the ample powers of Congress. The Constitution has many commands that are not enforceable by courts because they clearly fall outside the conditions and purposes that circumscribe judicial action. Thus, "on Demand of the executive Authority," Art. 4, §2, of a State it is the duty of a sister State to deliver up a fugitive from justice. But the fulfillment of this duty cannot be judicially enforced. *Kentucky* v. *Dennison*, 24 How. [U.S.] 66 [1860]. The duty to see to it that the laws are faithfully executed cannot be brought under legal compulsion, *Mississippi* v. *Johnson*, 4 Wall. [U.S.] 475 [1866]. Violation of the great guaranty of a republican form of government in States cannot be challenged in the courts. *Pacific Telephone Co.* v. *Oregon*, 223 U.S. 118 [1912]. The Constitution has left the performance of many duties in our governmental scheme to depend on the fidelity of the executive and legislative action and, ultimately, on the vigilance of the people in exercising their political rights.

See, also, Jackson, *Supreme Court in American System*, pp. 54-55.

It is remarkable how quickly and how relatively painlessly this particular thicket has been thinned out, and how salutary this has already been. (See chap. 7, n. 17, above). The turning point can be considered to have been a reapportionment case exhibiting such obvious discrimination with respect to race as to induce Justice Frankfurter himself to lead an expedition into the thicket. *Gomillion* v. *Lightfoot*, 364 U.S. 339 (1960). (See chap. 7, n. 81, above, for a parallel in libel litigation.) The Court did reaffirm, in the critical reapportionment case (*Baker* v. *Carr*, 369 U.S. 186, 218 [1962]), the doctrine that claims based on the Republican Form of Government Clause "involve those elements which define a 'political question,' and for that reason and no other, they are nonjusticiable." But the reconsideration by the Court of the justiciability of electoral districting controversies suggests that a similar reconsideration might be appropriate for claims based on the Republican Form of Government Clause, particularly since the latter *is* addressed to "The United States" (not, as is seen in the electoral provisions in Article I, to Congress alone). (The republican form of government provision, it should also be noticed, does not have the explicit reference to congressional legislative power that the Civil War amendments have. See chap. 7, n. 96, below.)

Why should not the Court, as a branch of the general government, pass on the republican form of government issue except in such instances where Congress has explicitly declared itself? The justices are groping toward something which they speak of as "the peace of the United States" (chap. 6, n. 40, above) or as "the concept of ordered liberty" (chap. 8, n. 13, below): but the Founding Fathers anticipated them with the guarantee to each state of "a Republican Form of Government." See chap. 2, n. 20, above.

See chap. 4, nn. 107, 108, above. See, also, on "the separation of powers" and republicanism, chap. 4, n. 102, above. See, for a scholarly review of what "Republican Form of Government" might have meant for eighteenth-century Americans, Gerald Stourzh, *Alexander Hamilton and the Idea of Republican Government* (Stanford: Stanford University Press, 1970), pp. 38-75. This review includes many useful references in the notes to other discussions of the subject. (It is encouraging to encounter an author with sufficient awareness of and confidence in what he has said elsewhere to permit himself repeated citations of his other publications.) Professor Stourzh observed, "Remote indeed from his ['monarchical'] arguments in the [Constitutional] Convention is Hamilton's stress in *The Federalist* on the sovereignty of the 'people' as the ultimate creator of government." Ibid., p. 52. Does not this suggest that the popular notion of "Republican Form of Government" —that notion which would be held by the general reader of the *Federalist*—was more "democratic" than that of Hamilton and many of his colleagues? And is not the more popular notion that which was understood by the people who ratified the Constitution? See, also, David Lowenthal, "Montesquieu and the Classics: Republican Government in *The Spirit of the Laws*," *Ancients and Moderns: Essays on the Tradition of Political Philosophy, in Honor of Leo Strauss*, ed. Joseph Cropsey (New York: Basic Books, 1964), p. 258; Robert K. Faulkner, *The Jurisprudence of John Marshall* (Princeton: Princeton University Press, 1968), p. 114.

See chap. 8, n. 83, below.

85. Lincoln, *Complete Works*, 2:65, 333, 389, 408, 454, 545. President Lincoln's arguments were anticipated by Chief Justice Taney in *Luther* v. *Borden*, 7 How. [U.S.] 1 (1849). See, also, Story, *Commentaries on the Constitution*, chap. 41, secs. 1814-17.

86. I say "presumptive invalidity" since the republican form of government guarantee takes account of consequences (i.e., whether republican government *would* be secured). See chap. 4, n. 107, above, for Justice Black's openness to an argument based on the nature of republican institutions. (See, also, his opinion in *South Carolina* v. *Katzenbach*, 383 U.S. 301, 359 [1966].)

I would begin a critique of my federalism argument in this book by considering the significance of the fact that someone of Justice Black's origins, political experience, and legal skill should think it desirable to extend fully against the states the absolute prohibitions (i.e., regardless of immediate consequences) of the First Amendment. See the dissenting opinion of Justice John Marshall Harlan in *Twining* v. *New Jersey*, 211 U.S. 78, 114 (1908); the dissenting opinion of Justice Black in *Adamson* v. *California*, 332 U.S. 46, 68 (1947); chap. 4, n. 98, above. See, also, chap. 7, n. 26, above, chap. 7, n. 107, chap. 8, n. 83, below.

Another argument in support of the effect of *Nelson*—for I do believe that Nelson did not belong in jail, that it would have been good neither for the people of Pennsyl-

CHAPTER SEVEN, NOTE 86: PAGE 191   649

vania nor for the United States nor for him to spend the rest of his life in prison—would exploit another part of my discussion in chapter 4, section 6 (see the text at chap. 4, n. 96, above): whatever Congress may have intended to do when it "occupied" the field of sedition, and whatever validity Congress's own legislation may have under the First Amendment, the effect of Congress's legislation may be regarded as essentially an exercise of congressional power to police-state abridgments of freedom of speech. Even if current congressional legislation should be unconstitutional under the First Amendment, in that it abridges freedom of speech, it would still be valid as an inadvertent, but providential, exercise of Congress's implied power under the First Amendment to enlarge freedom of speech by negating state abridgments. See chap. 7, n. 78, above.

The lawyer is familiar with this kind of situation: thus, for example, a testator who revokes a will, explicitly or perhaps even only implicitly, succeeds in such revocation (provided the later document is in form correct) even if the later will should, because of the character of its provisions, be in other respects void. It might be argued that this result was not "intended" by him, that he would want the earlier will to be revived if, for instance, the more generous provision in the later will should be void. But how can we be certain of this if he did not say so? All that we can safely assume is that he intended each will to be read as such things have been read among us. Similarly, the Founding Fathers knew that the Constitution would be interpreted in circumstances where men would be moved to develop from the available materials subtle arguments respecting the minutest details: that is, they could expect the kind of documentary interpretation to be applied to the Constitution that they had seen applied for generations to both public and private legal instruments. (See chap. 2, n. 31, above.) An example of subtle interpretation may be seen in *Federalist* No. 32 (pp. 195-97). See Somerset Maugham, "A Point of Law," in John Welcome, ed., *Best Legal Stories 2* (London: Faber & Faber, 1970), p. 31. (See, for the extent to which the law can go [not without good reasons] in replacing natural inferences by a "conclusive presumption," *Hess* v. *Whitsitt*, 257 Cal.App.2d. 552, 65 Cal. Rptr. 45 [1967]; *Louis* v. *Louis*, 86 Cal. Rptr. 834 [1970]. See, also, Jonathan M. Purver, "Race or Color of Child as Admissible in Evidence on Issue of Legitimacy or Paternity, or as Basis of Rebuttal or Exception to Presumption of Legitimacy," A.L.R. 3d 32:1303 [1970]; chap. 8, n. 64, below.)

It should be noticed, in support of the plausibility of my testamentary illustration, that invalid congressional acts have been held to have sufficient effect to be evidence of an intention to occupy a part of the regulatory field in interstate commerce, thereby ousting the states from the field. Oliver P. Field, *The Effect of an Unconstitutional Statute* (Minneapolis: University of Minnesota Press, 1935), pp. 5, 284-85; cf. ibid., pp. 286-87. See *Chicago, J. & L. Ry* v. *Hackett*, 227 U.S. 559 (1912); see, also, *Bentley* v. *Board*, 152 Ga. 836, 111 S.E. 379 (1921).

See chap. 5, n. 84, above, for an instance of an application to constitutional interpretation (in this case, the significance of "abridging" in the First Amendment) of the skills of an eminent student of the law of contracts.

Perhaps still another argument in support of the effect of *Nelson* could be a variation upon one advanced without success in *Scales* v. *U.S.*, 367 U.S. 203, 206-7 (1961), "that Sec. 4(f) of the Internal Security Act of 1950 [the McCarran Act], 64 Stat. 987, 50 U.S.C. § 781 et seq., constitutes a pro tanto repeal of the membership clause of the Smith Act by excluding from the reach of that clause membership in any Communist organization." Section 4(f) provides, "Neither the holding of office nor membership in any Communist organization by any person shall constitute per se a violation of subsection (a) or subsection (c) of this section *or of any other statute*." May not the words I have italicized be interpreted as an exercise by Congress of its power to enlarge freedom of speech in the states? That is, "any other statute" would include state statutes, certainly those of Indiana, Massachusetts, Pennsylvania, and Texas, which Konvitz has described as "expressly, explicitly, and by name outlawing the Communist Party." *Expanding Liberties*, p. 141. (See *Medley, Petitioner*, 134 U.S. 160 [1890].) Was not Nelson condemned to prison in Pennsylvania primarily for "holding of office . . . in [a] Communist organization"? See chap. 4, n. 13, chap. 7, nn. 72, 75, above.

And thus arguments can be developed. Nelson, I repeat, did not belong in jail—in school, perhaps (with many of his fellow citizens), but not in jail. There *is* a difference. With this difference in view, the Constitutionalist has an inducement (in addition to that of duty) to find means of achieving a humane result: he, like Francis Bacon, can endorse Caesar's sentiment: *Hoc quemadmodum fieri possit, nonnulla mihi in mentem veniunt, et multa reperiri possunt* [How this may be done, some things occur to me and more may be thought of]. *The Advancement of Learning*, 2. See, on Justice Davis, chap. 7, n. 77, above.

87. The rule of law, by which both the states and the general government are bound, requires that judges respect the record made in a case. It means that a reasonable effort should be made to apply the law of the case to the evidence before the tribunal. This reflects the distinctive obligation and skills of the lawyer. See Appendix F, above, esp. sec. 9.

88. *Commonwealth* v. *Nelson*, 377 Pa. 58, 104 A.2d 133 (1954). See chap. 7, nn. 47, 76, above.

Would it not have been more prudent for the United States Supreme Court not to have taken this case, thereby simply allowing the ruling of the state supreme court to stand? This not only would have spared the federal court considerable criticism but might also have encouraged other state courts to regard themselves as guardians of their citizens' liberties. See chap. 7, n. 80, above.

Did the Supreme Court of the United States avoid the question of the constitutionality of the state statute, restricting itself instead to the question of whether the statute had been superseded by congressional legislation, because it was not prepared to invoke criteria which would bear on the Smith Act as well? Cf. chap. 7, n. 69, above.

89. The effect of argument on the Supreme Court of Illinois in my bar admission case is significant. See Appendix F, above. The first decision was against me, 7-0 (3 Ill. 2d 471, 121 N.E. 2d 826 [1954]); the second decision was also against me, but only 4-3 (18 Ill. 2d 186, 163 N.E. 2d 431 [1959]).

I have been told, on the highest authority, that during the course of long conferences by the Illinois court on the case, the 4-3 vote was sometimes in my favor and that every justice who read the record voted for me in 1959. See chap. 8, n. 96 (end), below.

I believe it is a serious mistake to ignore the role the states can play in protecting American freedom. The Supreme Court of the United States, with the best will in the world, cannot police everything that is done. The states are not likely to do better until better is generally expected of them. See chap. 7, n. 80, above.

90. Thus, it is not unusual today to see the governor of a state surrender his office in order to take a place in the cabinet of a President. Is there a corresponding shift in the control of political parties from state governors to members of Congress as well as to mayors of cities? (Richardson Dilworth, former mayor of Philadelphia, has said, "The mayor of any city with a population of more than one million certainly has greater responsibilities and problems than the governors of three quarters of our states, but he has greater opportunities, too." *Newsweek*, Mar. 13, 1967, p. 22.)

Of Lincoln's original cabinet (seven members), three of them came from the Senate (two of these three had once been governors of their states); all had been active in political life and had run for public office. Of the Kennedy cabinet a century later (ten members), only four of them had ever sought public office (three of the four going to the cabinet directly from service as governors of their states, one of them going from the House of Representatives) (additional governors and ex-governors were appointed to high posts in the government or tried to secure such posts: see Arthur M. Schlesinger, Jr., *A Thousand Days* [Boston: Houghton Mifflin Co., 1965] p. 143).

> The men who came together [in 1787] to devise a new plan of government for the United States were an extraordinary assemblage. Fifty-five delegates attended at least some of the Convention sessions. Thirty-four were lawyers or had at any rate studied law. Forty-six had been members of colonial or State legislatures. . . . They were not really what Jefferson called them—"an assembly of demi-gods"; but they were highly able men, most of them well experienced in public affairs. . . . [Sutherland, *Constitutionalism in America*, p. 169]

91. Traces of this attitude (which represents a preference for the ties of blood and tradition to those of reason and an idea) seem to survive among us today only in the South. Thus, James F. Byrnes of South Carolina returned to service as a state governor after severing relations with the general government in which he had held high posts. Cf. chap. 7, n. 109, chap. 9, n. 10, below. See chap. 4, n. 43, above.

> ... The great Southerner [Robert E. Lee] appears [at Appomattox] with his jewelled sword, presented by some ladies in England; his handsomely spurred new boots, stitched at the top with red silk; his new uniform, buttoned to the throat; his silver-gray hair and beard and his long gray buckskin gauntlets; while [Ulysses S.] Grant, not expecting to meet him so soon, has arrived in an unbuttoned blue flannel blouse, swordless and spattered with mud and with nothing but his lieutenant-general's shoulder-straps to show that he is not a private. ... [T]his ideal of the powerful leader, with no glamor and no pretensions, who is equally accessible to everybody and who almost disclaims his official rank ... is an ideal that he shared with Lincoln, and that was perhaps something new in the world. It was to reappear in Russia with Lenin, and in the Red Army in its Leninist phase, before the restoration of epaulettes. ... [Edmund Wilson, *Patriotic Gore* (New York: Oxford University Press, 1966), p. 148]

See, for a useful assessment of the southern gentleman, Richard M. Weaver, "Scholars or Gentlemen?" *College English* 7 (1945): 72. See, also, in the *Partisan Review* (Mar.-Apr. 1954), Robert Warshow's "The Westerner" (is *Butch Cassidy and the Sundance Kid* the engaging, even fitting, end of a noble line?):

> The Westerner is the last gentleman, and the movies which over and over again tell his story are probably the last art form in which the concept of honor retains its strength. ... Honor is more than [virtue and justice and courage]: it is a style, *concerned with harmonious appearances as much as with desirable consequences*, and tending therefore toward the denial of life in favor of art. [Italics added]

One is reminded of Sophocles' Antigone: she is prepared to sacrifice life, and even justice, to the noble. (See chap. 9, n. 32, below.) See, also, Wilmot, *The Struggle for Europe* (London: Collins, 1952), pp. 465-66; Roger Ebert, *Chicago Sun-Times*, Oct. 22, 1970, p. 98 ("In a sense, the motorcycle movie is a Western that's lost the sense of decency"); William Faulkner, *Intruder in the Dust* (New York: Signet Books, New American Library, 1949), p. 148 ("For every Southern boy fourteen years old, not once but whenever he wants it, there is the instant when it's still not yet two o'clock on that July afternoon [at Gettysburg] in 1863 ...").

See, on the confrontation of the noble and the useful, chap. 8, n. 2, below. (Still another community in which "the concept of honor retains its strength" is that of the "Mafia," as described by Mario Puzo in his best-selling novel, *The Godfather* [New York: G. P. Putnam's Sons, 1969]. However, the sporadic concern of the author with sexual adventures—his evident willingness to exploit the public's appetites—suggests that he is neither restrained enough to be accurate in his representation of the warriors he portrays nor subtle enough to appreciate the refinements of nobility. The result is a curious mixture of high adventure and self-indulgent sentimentality. The book could easily have been much better and hence worthy of much more than a transient popularity. It is, nevertheless, very informative and, in its way, even reassuring: even the "Mafia," we are told, is becoming "Americanized" [see chap. 7, n. 124, below].)

Alexander Hamilton, it was said by Gouverneur Morris, "was of that kind of men, who may most safely be trusted, for he was more covetous of glory than of wealth or power." Stourzh, *Alexander Hamilton*, p. 202. See, also, ibid., p. 240, n. 94, p. 267, n. 110. Cf. Burke, *Works*, 2:141, 152; also, Hamlet's dying requests to Horatio.

92. But, one must wonder, can any government long remain important and attractive which does not deal with foreign affairs, with the exhilarating questions of peace, war, and

survival? The answer to this question must depend on, first, the nature of the times (e.g., are foreign relations critical to the life of the country?), and, second, the instincts and virtues of a people (reinforced by reminders of the importance of local government).

A nation that is to a large degree self-sufficient and is more in the position of leadership than in that of being led can still expect its domestic political life to be taken seriously by serious men, if only as a means to participation in world affairs. If America should be regarded abroad as a model of how to accomplish the ends of modern social legislation without that concentration of political power which undermines local and individual initiative, foreign relations could even help revive (rather than suppress) general interest in the importance of our political institutions. Cf. chap. 4, n. 43, chap. 6, n. 54, above. See chap. 8, n. 150, below.

93. The *Chicago Tribune*, Feb. 12, 1960, editorialized:

> The idea that this country and its people formed a Union which could not be broken grew and spread as Lincoln, out of the shattered fragments of war, re-formed the fabric of a nation which had been split asunder. That idea reached down into the minds of the simplest soldier, so that, on the morning of Shiloh [April 6, 1862], it was first in the thoughts of an Illinois rifleman.
>
> When the first "pum!" of the Confederate cannon sounded, the colonel of the 61st Illinois infantry came galloping down the line to form his ranks. "Gentlemen," he cried, "remember your state, and do your duty today like brave men."
>
> To Leander Stillwell, in the ranks, this seemed a little like Confederate talk. "A year later in the War," Stillwell reflected, "the old man doubtless would have addressed us as 'soldiers' and not as 'gentlemen,' and he would have omitted his allusion to the 'state,' which smacked a little of Confederate notions."

Was there not a corresponding change during the year from "the colonel" to "the old man"? And what has happened since 1862 to "duty"?

94. Crosskey argued:

> Thus, in the case of the Commerce Clause, if the power of Congress thereunder had been actively used in the early days, as originally was expected, the question of the true scope of the power would repeatedly have come up; the original view of it would, in many different ways, undoubtedly have been recorded; and a later misconception of the power, based upon changed meanings of certain of the words in which it is given, would not, it seems certain, have been possible. . . . The long inactivity of Congress before the Civil War was thus absolutely essential as a predisposing cause to the particular misinterpretation of this power which has occurred. . . . [Crosskey, *Politics and the Constitution*, p. 1162]

See chap. 7, n. 9, above.

> The truth is that the theory of mutually exclusive state and national powers, which runs all through the opinion of the Court in *Gibbons* v. *Ogden* [9 Wheat. (U.S.) 1 (1824)], was one of the devices, by the date of that case, of the Jeffersonian antinationalist party. For the states, as a practical fact, had done most of the governing, up to 1824; and if the theory of mutually exclusive powers could once be established, the powers of the nation would, on the basis of practical construction, be crowded into narrow quarters, indeed. Nearly every assertion of national power would then have to meet the objection that the states had exercised such power from the beginning of the Government, and that the nation, therefore, could not be deemed to possess it. [Crosskey, *Politics and the Constitution*, p. 695]

Cf. my discussion in chapter 6, above.

95. See, for Lincoln's disparagement in 1861 of the "magical omnipotence of 'State Rights,'" *Complete Works*, 2:62. Cf. ibid., 1:285, 308, 352-53, 370, 507. Henry Adams

CHAPTER SEVEN, NOTE 96: PAGE 193   653

could write in 1905 of the "antiquated . . . rebel doctrine of State rights." *The Education of Henry Adams* (Boston: Houghton Mifflin Co., 1918), p. 344. See, also, Henry Adams, *John Randolph*, pp. 38, 61, 272-74, 275-77, 278, 290-91. Cf. chap. 4, n. 101, chap. 7, nn. 18, 54, above.

Alexander Stephens, on the other hand, wrote (in his *Constitutional View of the Late War between the States* [Philadelphia: National Publishing Co., 1868-70]) of

> a conflict fierce and bitter . . . for seventy years . . . between those who were for maintaining the Federal character of the Government, and those who were for centralizing all power in the Federal Head. . . . It was a conflict between the true supporters of the Federal Union of States established by the Constitution, and those whose object was to overthrow the Union of States established by the Constitution, and by usurpation to erect a National Consolidation in its stead. [Edmund Wilson, *Patriotic Gore*, p. 405]

See Lynd, *Class Conflict, Slavery, and the United States Constitution*, pp. 153-83; chap. 8, sec. 12, above. Would not the abolitionists have agreed with Stephens? William Lloyd Garrison, "when faced with the argument that the Constitution did guarantee property in slaves and provided no way of freeing them, . . . denounced it, in the language of Isaiah, as 'a covenant with death and an agreement with hell.'" Wilson, *Patriotic Gore*, p. 91. See chap. 8, n. 118, chap. 9, n. 28, below.

See, also, chap. 4, n. 43, above; Roy F. Nichols, *Blueprint for Leviathan: American Style* (New York: Atheneum, 1963), pp. 133, 179-80, 181, 196-97, 201, 220, 233, 239.

96. Does the stipulation at the end of each of the three postwar amendments, that Congress shall have power to enforce the articles "by appropriate legislation," empower Congress to abridge (*would* that be "appropriate"?) or enlarge freedom of speech or of the press when necessary for the implementation of the objectives of these amendments? See chap. 7, nn. 54, 81, above. Cf. chap. 4, n. 8, above, chap. 8, n. 83, below.

It does not seem to be generally noticed that these amendments leave some power in the general government to discriminate according to race. Thus, we see here (with respect to race) just the reverse of the arrangement left by the First Amendment (with respect to freedom of speech and of the press). But the Supreme Court has argued,

> In view of our decision that the Constitution prohibits the states from maintaining racially segregated public schools, it would be unthinkable that the same Constitution would impose a lesser duty on the Federal Government. We hold that racial segregation in the public schools of the District of Columbia is a denial of the due process of law guaranteed by the Fifth Amendment to the Constitution. [*Bolling* v. *Sharpe*, 347 U.S. 497, 500 (1954)]

See Sutherland, *Constitutionalism in America*, p. 537.

Does it follow, however, that just because the states are prohibited from doing something, the general government should be also? (If all discriminatory arrangements are to be regarded as denials of due process, why was the Equal Protection Clause included [in addition to a due process provision] in the Fourteenth Amendment?) Did not the Court reveal how unrealistic its position was—the position taken in the *Bolling* opinion, "Segregation in public education is not reasonably related to any proper governmental objective. . . ."—when it failed to order all segregation immediately abolished? Obviously, a continuance of segregation was thought by the Court "reasonably related to" a proper governmental objective (reflecting a desire on the part of the Court to avoid chaos and civil strife, to permit feelings to change, to permit changes to be made in school facilities, perhaps to permit implementation of a program of desegregation which begins at certain levels of the schools and works up or down). Has the Court, by its orders permitting delay and thus continued segregation, denied segregated Negroes due process of law? That is what the Court's injudicious language might lead some to believe. Is it not more prudent and closer to the language of the Constitution to recognize both that there may be occasions when racial discrimination is appropriate and that the general government is entrusted with power for those occasions? See Burke, *Works*, 4:101-2, 156 ("A certain *quantum* of power must always exist in the community, in some hands, and under some appellation."); chap. 7, n. 3, above. See, also, Appendix C, sec. 3, above.

97. *Gitlow* v. *N.Y.*, 268 U.S. 652 (1925). The reader who questions whether state governments can be entrusted with a concern for national interests with respect to sedition and subversion (see section 5 of this chapter) should remember that the New York statute enforced in the 1925 *Gitlow* case was the model for the Smith Act enacted in 1940 by Congress. See chap. 3, n. 18, chap. 7, n. 47, above.

98. Chafee said that the "greatest victory for freedom of speech in my lifetime was won in 1925 . . . in the *Gitlow* case." Zechariah Chafee, *Freedom of Speech and Press* ("Freedom Agenda" series; New York: Carrie Chapman Catt Memorial Fund, 1955), p. 54.

99. I do not attempt in this book to determine the correctness of that interpretation of the Fourteenth Amendment which incorporates in it various of the rights protected by the Bill of Rights. There remains the question, for instance, whether such incorporation is accomplished by the "due process" or by the "privileges and immunities" clause of the Fourteenth Amendment. There is the problem also of determining just which rights are incorporated. The materials collected by Crosskey contribute to the correct interpretation of the Fourteenth Amendment. See chap. 7, nn. 26, 84, above, chap. 8, n. 83, below. See, also, p. 415, above.

I am concerned in this chapter to suggest, rather than an interpretation of the Fourteenth Amendment, the effects upon constitutional law, and particularly upon the official view of the First Amendment, of the current orthodox interpretation of the Fourteenth Amendment. See Sutherland, *Constitutionalism in America*, pp. 462, 540. See, also, Charles Fairman, "Does the Fourteenth Amendment Incorporate the Bill of Rights?" *Stanford L. Rev.* 2 (1949): 5; Crosskey, "Charles Fairman, 'Legislative History,' and the Constitutional Limitations on State Authority," *U. Chicago L. Rev.* 22 (1954): 1; Alexander M. Bickel, *The Least Dangerous Branch: The Supreme Court at the Bar of Politics* (Indianapolis: Bobbs-Merrill, 1962), pp. 99-102. See chap. 7, n. 107, below.

100. As I have indicated, this implicit rationale may be developed extensively for the first time in this volume. It is not original with me, however. See, e.g., the text at chap. 5, n. 88, above; also, chap. 6, n. 28, above, chap. 7, nn. 107, 108, below. Much of what I have developed in my studies of the Constitution I have later found suggested elsewhere. This can reassure the citizen-student that he is working with and talking about the same Constitution as his predecessors: perhaps, indeed, too much originality in these matters should be suspect, since it is an old and much-studied Constitution we are expounding. See chap. 2, n. 13, above. All this can reassure one as well that others can be depended upon to do much of what one might otherwise consider oneself obliged to do in expounding the Constitution. Thus, the serious man can, without injustice, devote most of his time to even more important things. See chap. 9, sec. 4, above. See, also, chap. 6, n. 1, above, chap. 7, n. 124, below (on the life dedicated to communal endeavor).

Cf. chap. 4, n. 16, above.

101. The exceptions to reliance on state power, which were limited to difficult local situations for the most part, were not effected by congressional enactment, but depended upon the exercise of the power of the commander-in-chief of the military forces and upon the application of martial law. There was also the suspension of the writ of *habeas corpus*, the significance of which I discuss elsewhere in this book. See U. S. Grant, *Personal Memoirs* (New York: Charles L. Webster & Co., 1894), pp. 636-40; Chafee, *Freedom of Speech*, p. 116; cf. Jaffa, *Crisis of the House Divided*, pp. 67, 200-203. See, on the treatment of Clement Vallandigham during the Civil War, Sutherland, *Constitutionalism in America*, pp. 413-14. See chap. 4, nn. 52, 54, above, chap. 7, n. 108, below.

102. To the extent that the Fourteenth Amendment contributed to this tendency, to that extent the Senate (in assenting to that amendment) retreated from the position taken by the Senate in the First Congress which rejected the amendment restraining the states proposed by the House of Representatives. No doubt, the Senate upon the conclusion of the Civil War saw itself less as the guardian of the interests and powers of the

states and much more (than its predecessor in the First Congress) as the instrument by which party and sectional interests might be advanced. (The Civil War amendments, even though they increased the powers of the Congress at the expense of the states, contributed eventually [because of the increasing role played in our affairs by the general government] to the domination of the Congress by the President. Is it not true that the more powerful and extensive the country, the more important the executive is likely to be? See chap. 4, n. 61, above, for Montesquieu's observation on this point. Cf. chap. 4, n. 36, above. The President as symbol of the United States is reflected in the fact that he is much more often the target of assassins than either other United States officials or state officials. See *Congressional Record* 116: S17514 [Oct. 8, 1970]. See, on the "many lunatic attempts" on Victoria's life, Elizabeth Longford, *Queen Victoria* [New York: Harper & Row, 1964], pp. 151-52, 390-91.)

The change to direct popular election of senators was still another indication of a departure from the original role of the Senate. See Tocqueville, *Democracy in America*, 1:211-12.

> Until the unfortunate adoption of the Seventeenth Amendment in 1913, Senators were chosen by State legislatures and served in effect as State ambassadors. And thinking rapidly over half a century of Senate history, I am inclined to believe the great Senators since 1913 most likely would have been named by their State legislatures if the Seventeenth Amendment never had been adopted; the senatorial mediocrities, for the most part, have been second-raters who owed their election to a gift for gab and never would have made it without the process of popular election. [James Jackson Kilpatrick, "The Case for 'States' Rights,'" in Goldwin, *A Nation of States*, p. 93]

(It may have been that the threat to use the Constitutional Convention method for amending the Constitution was influential in inducing the Senate to accept the amendment for the popular election of senators. See *Congressional Record*, 115: S9013, S9014 [Aug. 4, 1969]. Cf. chap. 4, n. 14, above.)

Richard H. Rovere, on the other hand, reported that the Senate today "boasts more first-rate intellectual equipment than it has had at any other time in this century." (But, it seems, many of the best men devote themselves primarily to running for President.) *New Yorker*, Jan. 30, 1960, p. 82. See chap. 4, n. 43, above.

Jaffa suggested that "by making the choice of United States senator an issue in the general election [which led to the Lincoln-Douglas debates], the Illinois Republicans initiated the first long step toward the Seventeenth Amendment." *Crisis of the House Divided*, p. 431. Does not this contribute to the establishment of the pervasive authority of the people anticipated in the last line of the Gettysburg Address?

103. Walter Bagehot wrote in 1872,

> It is too soon as yet to attempt to estimate the effect of the Reform Act of 1867. The people enfranchised under it do not yet know their own power: a single election, so far from teaching us how they will use that power, has not been even enough to explain to them that they have such power. The Reform Act of 1832 did not for many years disclose its real consequences; a writer in 1836, whether he approved or disapproved of them, whether he thought too little of or whether he exaggerated them, would have been sure to be mistaken in them. A new Constitution does not produce its full effect as long as all its subjects were reared under an old Constitution, as long as its statesmen were trained by that old Constitution. It is not really tested till it comes to be worked by statesmen and among a people neither of whom are guided by a different experience. [Bagehot, *The English Constitution*, pp. 260-61]

See chap. 7, n. 119, chap. 8, n. 98, below. See, also, chap. 8, n. 2, below.

This passage bears as well on my discussion in chapter 5 of Levy's *Legacy of Suppression*. Cf. Burke, *Works*, 4:95-96; Lincoln, *Works*, 2:13; chap. 7, n. 107 (end), below.

104. Eighty years ago a scholar could report:

> Professor Jameson, in his "Introduction to the Constitution and Political History of the Individual States" (Johns Hopkins University Studies in Historical and Political Science, 1886), illustrates the extensiveness of the power of the States by reference to recent important legislation of the British Parliament. Ten out of the twelve great subjects of legislation in England during this century, which has caused this period to be called the epoch of reform, viz., Catholic emancipation, parliamentary reform, the amendment of the poor-laws, the reform of municipal corporations, the admission of the Jews to Parliament, the disestablishment of the Irish Church, the alteration of the Irish land laws, the establishment of national education, the introduction of the ballot, and the reform of the criminal law, would, if passed in this country, have been enacted by State legislatures. [William F. Willoughby, "State Activities and Politics," in *Papers of the American Historical Association* (New York: G. P. Putnam's Sons, 1891), 5:117]

But of the ten subjects of legislation considered in 1891 to be state business, eight are now regarded as (to some extent) within the jurisdiction of the general government.

105. Of course, practically all our ideas (and, in another sense, none) are "foreign," but some have been naturalized. Cf. Justice Frankfurter's opinion for the Court in *Communist Party* v. *S.A.C.B.*, 367 U.S. 1, 35-55 (1961). See, also, Woodrow Wilson, *The Political Thought of Woodrow Wilson*, ed. E. David Cronon (Indianapolis: Bobbs-Merrill, 1965), p. 515. (One can see here how much the White House may have been responsible for the repressive bigotry in this country during the First World War, of which the doctrines of *Schenck* v. *U.S.* [Appendix B, above] are troublesome legacies. President Wilson sometimes exhibited himself as a curiously petty man. See, e.g., ibid., pp. 99-100, 231, 232, 394, 395.)

106. The final form of this aspect of the development I am describing is the "supersession" doctrine of *Nelson*. See, e.g., chap. 7, n. 76, above.

The extent to which the states are assumed to be subject to at least the restraints which are imposed upon the general government is reflected in one scholar's offhand comment on the First Amendment:

> Note the language: "Congress shall make no law . . . abridging the freedom of speech. . . ." This is not a guaranty of freedom from private interference. It is a guaranty that the government may not interfere with freedom of speech. *No government in this country*, federal, state or local, may abridge the freedom of speech. The word "abridge" means to shorten, to limit, or to reduce in size. The freedom of speech may not be reduced by governmental action. . . . [Roger Fisher, "The Constitutional Right of Freedom of Speech," in Harold J. Berman, ed., *Talks on American Law* (New York: Random House, Vintage Books, 1961), pp. 85, 86; italics added]

Justice Black, concurring in *Smith* v. *California*, 361 U.S. 147 (1959), gives at 157-59 a more precise comment on these matters (a comment which fits in better than does Professor Fisher's with my analysis in chapters 3 and 4, above):

> Certainly the First Amendment's language leaves no room for inference that abridgments of speech and press can be made just because they are slight. That Amendment provides, in simple words, that "Congress shall make no law . . . abridging the freedom of speech, or of the press." I read "no law . . . abridging" to mean *no law abridging*. The First Amendment, which is the supreme law of the land, has thus fixed its own value on freedom of speech and press by putting these freedoms wholly "beyond the reach" of *federal* power to abridge.
>
> No other provision of the Constitution purports to dilute the scope of these unequivocal commands of the First Amendment. Consequently, I do not believe that any federal agencies, including Congress and this Court, have the power or authority to subordinate speech and press to what they think are "more important interests." The contrary notion is, in my judgment, court-made, not Constitution-made.

CHAPTER SEVEN, NOTE 107: PAGE 196   657

> State intrusion into or abridgment of freedom of speech and press raises a different question, since the First Amendment by its terms refers only to laws passed by Congress. But I adhere to our prior decisions holding that the Fourteenth Amendment made the First applicable to the States. . . .

Cf. chap. 8, n. 83, below.

107. A respected student of the Supreme Court wrote in 1926:

> No one who read [Justice] Sanford's opinion [in the 1925 *Gitlow* case] would imagine that, for over fifty years, counsel had, time and again, attempted to get the Court to hold that rights similar to the right of freedom of speech were protected by the Fourteenth Amendment against infringement by State legislation, and that in every instance the Court had declined so to hold. Yet, in this *Gitlow* case, without even mentioning these previous cases, the Court assumes, without argument, that this right of free speech is so protected by the Fourteenth Amendment. [Charles Warren, "The New 'Liberty' under the Fourteenth Amendment," *Harvard L. Rev.* 39 (Feb. 1926): 432-33]

See *Malloy v. Hogan*, 378 U.S. 1 (1964); Crosskey, *Politics and the Constitution*, p. 1375.

Justice Holmes said for the Court, in *Patterson v. Colorado*, 205 U.S. 454, 462 (1907), " . . . We leave undecided the question whether there is to be found in the Fourteenth Amendment a prohibition similar to the First. . . . " The doctrine of the *Gitlow* case was anticipated by Justice Harlan, who wrote in his dissenting opinion in *Patterson*, 205 U.S. 454, 465 (cf. chap. 8, n. 83, below):

> I cannot assent to that view [as seen in the passage from Justice Holmes in chap. 5, n. 5, above], if it be meant that the legislature may impair or abridge the rights of a free press and of free speech whenever it thinks that the public welfare requires that to be done. The public welfare cannot override constitutional privileges, and if the rights of free speech and a free press are, in their essence, attributes of national citizenship, as I think they are, then neither Congress nor any State since the adoption of the Fourteenth Amendment, can, by legislative enactments or by judicial action, impair or abridge them.

For many practical purposes, my view of the Republican Form of Government guarantee (e.g., chap. 7, n. 84, above) would have the effect of Justice Harlan's doctrine, insofar as that doctrine protects political discussion in the states. The Constitution does leave to the states, with the understanding that the general government should be aware of its supervisory duties, the power to regulate discussion (even political discussion) that threatens the stability or is vital to the education of the community. This is not to suggest, however, that citizens should never resist the exercise of such power by the states (or by any other government). (See, e.g., Lincoln, *Complete Works*, 2:615:

> . . . I repeat the declaration made a year ago, that "while I remain in my present position I shall not attempt to retract or modify the Emancipation Proclamation, nor shall I return to slavery any person who is free by the terms of that proclamation, or by any of the acts of Congress." If the people should, by whatever mode or means, make it an executive duty to reenslave such persons, another, and not I, must be their instrument to perform it.

See, also, ibid., 2:380, 455, 379: "Those who shall have tasted actual freedom I believe can never be slaves or quasi-slaves again"; Aristotle, *Nicomachean Ethics* 1130b29: "For it would seem that to be a good man is not in every case the same thing as to be a good citizen." See Aristotle, *Politics* 1276b15-1277b34. See, also, in Appendix F, above, my discussion of the Declaration of Independence: does not the right of revolution recognize both that being a good citizen may be at times incompatible with being a good man and that most men very much need to be citizens? See pp. 417-18, above, chap. 9, n. 30, below.)

If *a choice must be made* between an absolute prohibition with respect to abridgments of freedom of speech upon both the general government and the state governments, on the one hand, and a qualified prohibition upon both the general government and the state governments, on the other hand (which is now the orthodox opinion), I would argue that the former alternative poses the lesser danger to this country. But I do think it even more salutary for me to argue that only the general government should be subjected under the Constitution of the United States to an absolute prohibition with respect to these matters. Only if the power of the general government is properly understood and restrained can the power of the states be dealt with intelligently.

See Matt. 3:3; Matt. 5:5; Matt. 7:29. See, also, B. H. Liddell Hart, *Strategy* (New York: Frederick A. Praeger, 1967), p. 274 (on "the Japanese [and German] tide of conquest [having] spread too far for permanence"); chap. 5, n. 130, chap. 7, nn. 60, 86, 100, above, chap. 9, nn. 27, 28, below.

But there is one choice we do not have, a choice which would permit us to solve once and for all every problem confronting us. To believe we have such a choice—to be, that is, unaware of the essential mortality and hence decay which affect community and individual alike—is to be unaware of the nature of the human being and hence to deprive ourselves of what can be attained here and now (including that satisfaction which comes from the realization [for which there is now and then some justification] that although things could be somewhat better, they could also be far worse). See chap. 5, n. 97, chap. 7, n. 24, above, chap. 8, nn. 71, 74, 181, chap. 9, nn. 2, 3, 4, below.

It is man's judicious and encouraging satisfaction with what *is* attainable that such critiques as Kant's *Perpetual Peace* undermine. (Does not Kant depend on an immoderate faith in inevitable progress? This unrealistic dependence is even seen in the way *he* interprets [in a kind of self-deception?] the motto, *Fiat iustitia, pereat mundus*: "Let justice reign even if *all the rascals* in the world should perish." *Perpetual Peace*, Appendix 1. This is indeed to have one's cake [i.e., of unvarying moral commands] and to eat it, too [i.e., not having to take consequences into account in "doing the right thing"].) Compare Laurence Berns's Jeffersonian (pp. 14-15, above) counsel of moderation, "Reasonable Politics and Technology," *The College* (St. John's College), Sept. 1970, p. 1:

> Because opinions are essentially disputable, and because political disputes, by the passions they arouse, can often be more harmful to society than the original difficulties prompting them, it is frequently more important for political practice to maintain reasonable procedures for settling and dispensing with problems than it is to be certain that the solutions are correct solutions. Imperfect solutions are not necessarily unreasonable solutions in a free society: what is most to be avoided is action that could destroy those procedures and institutions for compromise and debate which, by the discussion attendant upon them, open up the way for reason to make the limited but saving contribution that it might make to free political life.

Such counsel is vital to a viable constitutionalism. See chap. 6, n. 78, above, chap. 9, nn. 7, 9, below. (I have italicized in Kant's translation of the motto the words he had to add. Does not his use of "reign" for *fiat* try to avoid bad consequences by definition?)

108. I do not know of anyone in the first third of the twentieth century who planned or even saw this development this way. But all observers recognize that the general government *legislated* on sedition during the First World War for the first time since the Sedition Act of 1798. The fact of a great war may have simply exposed the need to look to *the* government for action and may have revealed developments that had been long underway. My analysis is intended, in part, to explain the facts reported generally by students of the period. (We again see how critical *Schenck* v. *U.S.* [Appendix B, above] was in at least crystallizing and thus ratifying this development. See chap. 3, n. 22, above.)

See Rogge, *The First and Fifth*, p. 100.

109. At the national convention of the Republican party in 1880, Roscoe Conkling placed Ulysses S. Grant in nomination (for President) with a speech which opened,

> If asked which state he hails from
> Our sole reply shall be

> He hails from Appomattox
> And its famous apple tree!

New York Herald-Tribune (Paris edition), Apr. 8, 1960. See Charnwood, *Abraham Lincoln*, p. 172. Cf. chap. 7, n. 91, above.

To expect too much of "freedom of speech" is to make it likely that it will fail to do what it *can* do. Consider Charmides' and Critias' immoderate claims for temperance (or moderation) in Plato's *Charmides*, which permitted them (as potential tyrants) to avoid serious consideration of the practical restraints upon the appetite by temperance. Cf. Aristotle, *Politics* 1267a10; Shakespeare, *Hamlet*, act 4, sc. 1 ("His liberty is full of threats to all"); Burke, *Works*, 4:7-9, 137, 272-73; chap. 8, sec. 12, above.

110. Aristotle remarks (*Politics* 1303a20):

> Another occasion [of constitutional change] is the neglect of trifling changes. A great change of the whole system of institutions may come about unperceived if small changes are overlooked. In Ambracia, for example, the property qualification for office—small to begin with—was finally allowed to disappear, under the idea that there was little or no difference between having a small qualification and having none at all.

Also, ibid., 1306b5, 1307b1, 1308b5. See Montesquieu, *The Spirit of the Laws* (New York: Hafner Publishing Co., 1949), 8:14; Tocqueville, *Democracy in America*, 1:59.

> With regard to devises in general, experience soon shewed how difficult and hazardous a thing it is, even in matters of public utility, to depart from the rules of the common law; which are so nicely constructed and so artificially connected together, that the least breach in any one of them disorders for a time the texture of the whole. [Blackstone, *Laws of England*, 2:376]

111. Federal relations may have been changed most decisively since 1787 by the Louisiana Purchase:

> No one doubted, and Randolph least of all, that it completely changed the conditions of the constitutional compact; rendering the nation, independent of the States, master of an empire immensely greater than the States themselves; pledging the nation in effect to the admission of indefinite new States; insuring an ultimate transfer of power from the old original parties in the compact to the new States, thus forced on their society; and foreboding the destruction of states' rights by securing a majority of States, without traditions, history, or character, the mere creatures of the general government, thousands of miles from the old Union. . . . [Henry Adams, *John Randolph*, p. 89]

See, on the frontier, Farrand, *Records*, 1:571, 578, 583; Tocqueville, *Democracy in America*, 1:54, 301; chap. 8, n. 188, chap. 9, n. 2, below. See, also, Grant, *Personal Memoirs*, p. 130; Sumner, *Andrew Jackson*, p. 10; Charnwood, *Abraham Lincoln*, p. 175. Our constitutional hope is that, with a little luck, the original thirteen states will be manifest in each new state, even if we should have as many as sixty. (See chap. 9, n. 1. Do we display thereby faith in a kind of political transubstantiation? See Lincoln, *Complete Works*, I, 12. Thus, it can be said in Congress, upon assessment of the career of a senator defeated for reelection, "The people give and the people take away; blessed be the name of the people." *Congressional Record* 116: S2146 [1970]. See, also, chap. 9, n. 9, below.)

"One of the compelling reasons for the division of the United States [leading to the Civil War] had been the inability of one legislative body to meet the problems arising from the growth of a society in a wilderness." Nichols, *Blueprint for Leviathan*, p. 200. See, also, ibid., pp. 94-95.

See, on the effect of the size of political bodies, Aristotle, *Politics* 1265a11, 1276a20; Montesquieu, *Spirit of the Laws*, 5:7, 8:16, 19, 20, 9:1, 2; *Federalist*, pp. 322-23 (cf. *Federalist* No. 10); Tocqueville, *Democracy in America*, 1:167-68, 171; Daniel J. Boorstin, *The Americans: The National Experience* (New York: Random House, 1965), p. 418 (quoting Jefferson). See, also, chap. 4, n. 43, chap. 7, n. 35, above.

112. Inadequate institutions must simply be substituted for if the community is not to suffer. In this, as in many other respects, baseball is *the* distinctively American game:

> [Baseball] is the only game in which the individual always is on his own. No teammate can help a batter or a pitcher or a shortstop or a right fielder when the play of the moment comes his way. Baseball also is the only game in which it is impossible to "hide" a player. The moment of truth inevitably will reveal his inadequacy. A football guard can be mediocre but his weaknesses will be camouflaged by the excellence of teammates at center and tackle. A basketball team, on the high school and college level, can win with two or three below-average players in the lineup. But when a ground ball is hit to a third baseman, the only help he can be given is vocal. He can't wait for another man to make the play. [Bill Gleason's Column, *Chicago Sun-Times*, Apr. 13, 1969, p. 136]

Indeed, to the spectator who knows what is going on, baseball must surely be the most interesting team sport with popular appeal played in this country, and not only because it reflects so many of our political institutions. For one thing, people who are ordinary with respect to weight and height can nevertheless excel in it: intelligence and perseverance make a difference, along with some natural ability. See chap. 5, n. 94, above, chap. 8, n. 23, chap. 9, nn. 20, 22, below. The increased popularity of professional football—with its evident and commercial emphasis on regimented violence—is a disturbing symptom of the 1960s. Cf. the more refreshing, and even good-natured, mayhem of an amateur rugby match.

See Adam Smith, *Wealth of Nations*, pp. 435-36. See, also, Jackson, *Supreme Court in American System*, pp. 71-72.

113. Do large business corporations serve the interests of property as the states (i.e., the senators in Congress) had been thought by some to do? (Cf. *Federalist*, p. 357.) What relation is there between the rise in importance of corporations and the decline of the states?

> Of the 117 member countries in the United Nations, 113 have a lower gross national product income than General Motors. In 1964 General Motors did a gross business of approximately $17 billion. Only four UN member nations—the U.S., U.S.S.R., Great Britain, and France—did more than that. [*Parade*, Feb. 6, 1966, p. 14]

One massive fact should be kept in mind, however: "At an educated guess, there are some 102,000 tax-levying governments in the country." Grodzins, "Centralization and Decentralization," in Goldwin, *A Nation of States*, p. 1. "Illinois has more local governments than any other state. There are some 6,400 counties, townships, municipalities and special districts, and the number is growing each year." Frank X. Yackley, "Amid a Thicket of Governments: Regional Planning in Northeast Illinois," *Ill. Bar J.* 57 (1969): 348.

The universities, too, it has been said, serve among us the interests of property. But this "charge" either confuses the university with certain administrators thereof or depends on a meaning of "property" which includes all attainments of mankind. (See p. 213, above.) There is a sense, however, in which education is in this country a separate interest or nation, a federation of somewhat autonomous communities (with somewhat common standards and traditions) organized in the following manner:

> 1. There are now more than five and a half million students in institutions of higher education in the United States—more than the populations of nations like Denmark and Ireland, more than the populations of over half the sovereign members of the United Nations. It is estimated that by 1980 this number will reach eleven million students.

2. Giant universities tend to dominate American higher education quantitatively. As of 1963, ninety-three institutions, only 5 per cent of the institutions of higher learning, had enrollments of ten thousand students or more, but their combined enrollments constituted almost 40 per cent of the national enrollment.

3. Even so, a quite small number of institutions continue to dominate the American educational scene qualitatively. Of all the universities that grant doctorates, about 5 per cent—twelve in all—award about 40 per cent of all the earned doctorates granted in the United States. [*Higher Education and Modern Democracy: The Crises of the Few and the Many*, ed. Robert A. Goldwin (Chicago: Rand McNally, 1967), p. v]

It is in these communities—on these reservations—that self-government should be most effective and should provide guidance for the rest of the country both by precept and by example. But it is in higher education itself that one can detect today a critical loss of confidence, of which student protests (whether against "Vietnam" or "racism" or "poverty" or "pollution") are merely the current symptoms. The underlying problem is that educators themselves no longer have a sense of what cultivation of the human mind is and what it requires. But they still have sense enough to realize that much of what they do and say is simply not serious—and so they carry on with bad consciences (or allow themselves to be guided by the all-too-active consciences of their more determined students). See chap. 7, n. 30, above, chap. 8, nn. 122, 168, below. See, also, the editorial report, "Politics and the College," *The College* (St. John's College), July, 1970, pp. 19-21.

(The loss of confidence I refer to is diagnosed by Professor Allan Bloom as "a sickness which is corrupting our understanding of old writers and depriving a generation of their liberating influence." Letter, *New York Review of Books*, Apr. 9, 1970, p. 46.)

114. It has been argued:

> In sum, strong as well as weak states turn "demands for political action to Washington." More important, the ability of the central government to meet citizen needs that cannot be met by either strong or weak states, whatever those adjectives mean, also accounts for the expansion (as well as for the very existence) of the federal government. Strengthening states, in the sense of building more effective parties and of providing legislatures and executives who have a readiness and capacity for action, may indeed prevent an occasional program from being taken up by the federal government. The total possible effect can only be insignificant. The only way to produce a significant decline in federal programs, new and old, would be to induce citizens to demand fewer activities from all governments. (The cry, "Strengthen the states," in many cases only means, "Decrease all governmental activity.") This is an unlikely development in an age of universal literacy, quick communications, and heightened sensitivities to material factors in the good life, as well as to the political appeals of an alternative political system. One can conclude that strengthening the states so that they can perform independent functions and thereby prevent federal expansion is a project that cannot succeed. [Grodzins, "Centralization and Decentralization," *A Nation of States*, p. 20]

Cf. George C. S. Benson, "Values of Decentralized Government—1961," in *Essays in Federalism* (Claremont, Calif.: Institute for Studies in Federalism, 1961), pp. 3-4, 7, 15; Martin Diamond, "The Federalist's View of Federalism," ibid., pp. 53-62; Felix Morley, *Freedom and Federalism* (Chicago: Henry Regnery Co., 1959). Alfred de Grazia, "Federalism," in Melvin R. Laird, ed., *The Conservative Papers* (Garden City, N.Y.: Doubleday & Co., Anchor Books, 1964), p. 228.

115. I return to this development in section 17 of chapter 8 and in chapter 9. See, on the perils of money-making, Plutarch's "Lycurgus" and "Numa."

Federalist No. 35 endorses merchants "as the natural representatives" of the artisan and manufacturing classes in the community. (See chap. 7, n. 117, below.) I prefer to make more of lawyers in this capacity. This divergence may reflect ultimately a difference of opinion as to what is fundamental to human action, ideas (especially that of justice, which alone makes the lawyer's life meaningful), or the material and its motions (espe-

cially money) (see, e.g., the quotation from *Federalist* No. 79 in chap. 8, n. 36, below).
I would, for instance, make more of the Declaration of Independence in American life
than does the *Federalist*. See chap. 7, n. 120, chap. 8, n. 44, below. (The Declaration is
echoed at several points in the *Federalist*. I have noticed only one passage [it is in *Federalist*
No. 40] which is put in quotation marks and attributed by Publius to the Declaration—
and *it* is inaccurately quoted. [See *Federalist*, p. 257. Cf. *Federalist*, pp. 85, 249, 287,
311, 407-8, 508 (chap. 4, n. 112, above), 569.] Are men most careful about the things
they really care for? Some men, for instance, cannot trouble themselves enough about
money to make much of it. See Aristotle, *Nicomachean Ethics* 1120b15, 1163b6-15. Is a
man who has cared enough about money to make a fortune in business unlikely to be
both serious and competent about political things? Averell Harriman said of businessmen
that "people have to be given big jobs when they are young, or else their minds become
permanently closed. The men who work their way step by step to the top in business
are no good for anything big in government. They have acquired too many bad habits
along the way." Schlesinger, *A Thousand Days*, pp. 149-50. See Montesquieu, *Persian
Letters*, No. 48. See, also, chap. 8, n. 159, below. Tocqueville describes the Ohioan, whom
he distinguishes from the Kentuckian, as one whose "avidity in the pursuit of gain amounts
to a species of heroism." *Democracy in America*, 1:378. See chap. 8, sec. 5, above.)

The difference of opinion to which I have referred (as to what may be fundamental
in human action) is often reflected in how nobility and beauty are interpreted. The partnership between Pericles and Phidias is thought by Plutarch worthy of celebration (as is
evident in the epigraphs with which this study opens). In *Federalist* No. 6, on the other
hand, the same enterprise is explained in the most selfishly petty terms. See, also, *Federalist*
No. 18. Does anyone who emphasizes the material and the role of interest in the affairs
of men find it difficult to recognize properly the noble and the beautiful? (See Sallust,
The War with Catiline, chap. x-xiv; chap. 7, n. 91, above, chap. 9, n. 31, below.)

I do not believe, that is, that the Founding Fathers (with the possible exception of
Jefferson) addressed themselves properly to the problem of education. (Jefferson directed
that his tombstone bear "the following inscription, and not a word more,"

> Here was buried Thomas Jefferson
> Author of the Declaration of American Independence
> of the Statute of Virginia for religious freedom
> and Father of the University of Virginia.

[*The Complete Jefferson*, ed. Saul K. Padover (New York: Duell, Sloan & Pearce,
1943), p. 1300])

See Willmoore Kendall, "How to Read Richard Weaver: Philosopher of 'We the (Virtuous)
People,'" *Intercollegiate Review* 2 (1965): 77, 85.

116. In fact, the more defensible the war, the more power it would permit to be
acquired by Washington: an unjust war discourages the general government from calling
for the sacrifices (and the power) which might induce people to look too carefully at
what is happening. (This, by the way, is one reason why a mercenary [i.e., "all-volun-
teer"] army should be avoided by a republic: a self-governing people needs to be prompted
to consider whether military action in faraway places *is* worth the price of its sons' blood,
thereby making it less likely that bureaucratic or military miscalculations can be seen as
merely matters of dollars-and-cents. We need the strongest inducements to examine the
justice of dubious causes. Besides, when men are conscripted rather than bought for battle,
we are much more apt to assess the conflict in which they participate as a political, not
merely as an economic or a logistic, problem. There are already too many inducements
among us to put personal considerations before those of the community: consider, for instance, how casually we accept the announcement we hear from time to time that an adviser to the President of the United States is resigning his post in order to be able to return
to his university [usually Harvard, it seems] in time to save the tenured appointment from
which he had taken a leave of absence. If job security is that important to a man, how
can he be depended upon to put the national interest before his own in exercising the

great powers of the President's office?) In any event, *Federalist* No. 8 pointed out, "It is of the nature of war to increase the executive at the expense of the legislative authority." See chap. 4, n. 43, above. See, also, chap. 3, n. 35, above.

See Woodrow Wilson, *Congressional Government* (Cleveland: World Publishing Co., Meridian Books, 1956), p. 42. Cf. Tocqueville, *Democracy in America*, p. 283; Zetterbaum, *Tocqueville and the Problem of Democracy*, p. 136.

To what extent has the "white backlash" in recent years been provoked, or at least been reinforced, by resentment, or at least uneasiness, about Vietnam? The stature of the country's leaders has been affected by the war, perhaps so much so as to permit thoughtless citizens to question what leaders advocate with respect to racial matters. Such questioning is, in addition, a "patriotic" way ("a good old American way") of expressing the resentment there might be about the war itself.

It is sometimes said that dissent at home (even if in an effort to examine the justness of our wars) encourages our enemies abroad and discourages our soldiers. (But it would not be urged by these critics of our freedom of speech that we should be careful not to be prosperous lest it encourage greedy conquerors from abroad.) Compare, however, the comment by General Eisenhower at a twenty-fifth anniversary dinner of the military newspaper, *Stars and Stripes*:

> One reason I think the morale of the army in Viet Nam today is so high—it's a rather odd conclusion—is that because of the tremendous fight here at home, with the doves and the hawks fighting each other, he, the soldier, knows darn well no one has forgotten him. [*Chicago Tribune*, Nov. 5, 1967, p. 18]

See Burke, *Works*, 2:90. See, also, p. 320, above, chap. 8, n. 150, below.

117. Sparta maintained for centuries a regime fitted primarily for war—but the citizen body was shaped, and limited, accordingly. (But more can be said for that constitution than does commerce-minded *Federalist* No. 6: "Sparta was little better than a well-regulated camp. . . ." That is, it was a regime with a continual concern for citizen virtue, something which is not an explicit concern of the American Constitution. See chap. 7, n. 115, above. Cf. Plato, *Laws* 666D-E; Aristotle, *Politics* 1338b11-39; chap. 6, n. 54, above.)

General Eisenhower revealed in his memoirs that the use of atomic weapons was seriously considered in the Korean War: "My feeling was then, and still remains, that it would be impossible for the United States to maintain the military commitments which it now sustains around the world (without turning into a garrison state) did we not possess atomic weapons and the will to use them when necessary." *Mandate for Change*, p. 180. See Woodrow Wilson, *Political Thought*, pp. 342-52. See, on the "Deep Ditch" for which atomic weapons may seem a substitute (since such weapons, like a navy, cannot be easily used to police one's own country), chap. 4, n. 101, above. But is it not almost inevitable that such weapons will be used on a large scale if they should remain available for use? Not only are accidents possible, but also unpredictable madness in men who hold responsible positions and over whom there can be no effective supervision. Then, of course, there is the gamble, the bluff, or the act of desperation by the "sane." ("The announcement by General Eisenhower that he had been prepared to drop atomic bombs to induce the Chinese to make a treaty over Korea has shocked more people in Europe than perhaps the General realizes." Denis W. Brogan, "Naiveté versus Reality in Vietnam," *Atlantic*, July 1967, p. 53.) Cf. Herman Kahn, *Thinking about the Unthinkable* (New York: Avon Books, 1962), pp. 27-30, 153-56, 267 ff. See Woodrow Wilson, *Political Thought*, p. 513. (Does General Eisenhower's "feeling" require us, before it is too late, to reconsider "the military commitments . . . around the world" which make recourse to atomic weapons plausible? Cf. chap. 8, n. 150, below.)

118. In an address delivered before the annual conference of state supreme court justices, we find:

> In conclusion, I want to say this in support of my plea that you undertake to study the federal judicial code and make suggestions to Congress for the proper

distribution of judicial power. The centralization of governmental power in this country has come about primarily for three reasons. The first is the necessity for central power resulting from the increased interdependence of the people within this nation and within the world community. The second is the unwarranted usurpation of power by the federal authorities in many areas. The third is the unwillingness of the states to shoulder the responsibilities which are properly theirs. If the existing distribution of judicial power is unfortunate in many respects, it is due in part to the failure of the state judiciaries to make their voices heard on the subject of the allocation. The responsibility is yours and I hope that you will exercise it. [Philip B. Kurland, "The Distribution of Judicial Power between National and State Courts," *Journal of the Amercian Judicature Society* 42 (Feb. 1959): 164]

It should be added that one reason the federal judiciary *has* tended to expand its powers is that state courts have not been as competent and fair-minded as they should be. (See, e.g., the actions of the state courts in *In re Summers*, 325 U.S. 561 [1945] and *West Virginia Board of Education* v. *Barnette*, 319 U.S. 624 [1943]. See, also, chap. 7, nn. 70, 77, above.) The popular election of judges has all too often led to just the kind of judges one can expect to be chosen by men who cannot know what they are doing. See chap. 7, n. 35 (on coordinated electorates), nn. 80, 82, above, chap. 8, n. 179, below.

It should be recognized as well that a thoughtless condemnation of the exercise of the powers of the general government is of no value, especially when Washington is nevertheless looked to for financial aid. The editorial page of the *Carterville* (Ill.) *Herald* of Mar. 26, 1959, illustrates the typical attitude: a cartoon (evidently distributed by a newspaper service) shows the "tidal wave" of "Federal Government" about to engulf a man clinging to a tree on the island, "States' Rights"; just beneath the cartoon is an editorial celebrating the receipt of the "good news" that the community had been tentatively allocated federal funds for a low-rent housing project.

119. There might then be a serious effort made to work out, perhaps even along the lines of the argument in this book, the role of the states in these matters. It would also be well to maintain those institutions which tend to preserve the states as political entities, such as the practice of having each state's votes cast as a unit in presidential elections. The inhibition this arrangement provides upon nationwide demagoguery as well as upon election fraud has never been adequately appreciated. (See chap. 7, n. 110, above.) In economic matters, on the other hand, more use could be made of regional alliances among the states and of partnerships between the general government and the states (such as the Tennessee Valley Authority).

I am disposed to take issue, however, with the radical implications in the paragraph with which Jaffa opened the provocative essay I have several times referred to:

> The case for a stronger national government rests upon one simple proposition: the problems which face the American people, to an extent unprecedented, are national problems and can be dealt with effectively only by the common direction and close coordination of the efforts of all Americans. The only agency which can marshal all the resources of the nation, and order all its efforts to the overriding purposes which all share, is the government of the United States. This does not mean that State and local governments are superfluous: in many instances the efficient centralization of government not only permits but requires the decentralization of administration. If the States did not now exist, we would have to invent them, although we could certainly invent regional subdivisions of the United States that would be far more rational in relation to the requirements of administration. [Jaffa, "The Case for a Stronger National Government," in Goldwin, *A Nation of States*, p. 106]

See Farrand, *Records*, 1:177, 180. See, also, Burke, *Works*, 4:191-93, 202, 218.

Another student of American politics, who is far to the left of Jaffa, said in the course of his campaign for President as the candidate of the Socialist Labor Party, "We will dissolve state boundaries, because political boundaries are obsolete." *Chicago Sun-Times*,

CHAPTER SEVEN, NOTE 120: PAGE 200   665

Sept. 29, 1960, p. 18. (Tom Paine wrote, in No. 15 of the *Crisis Papers*, "The division of the empire into states is for our own convenience, but abroad this distinction ceases.") It has been predicted by an Illinois senator that we will see the time "when the only people interested in state boundaries will be Rand McNally." *Newsweek*, Aug. 16, 1965, p. 17. See *Federalist* No. 14 (pp. 82-83). See, also, p. 273, above, chap. 6, n. 55, above.

I prefer on this matter the observation of an English student of American political institutions,

> A federal Senate, a second House, which represents State Unity, has this advantage; it embodies a feeling at the root of society—a feeling which is older than complicated politics, which is stronger a thousand times over than common political feelings—the *local* feeling. "My shirt," said the Swiss state-right patriot, "is dearer to me than my coat." . . . [Bagehot, *English Constitution*, p. 99]

See *Federalist*, pp. 154, 168-70, 192-93, 305-6, 385. See, also, chap. 9, n. 32, below.

The caution with which proposed changes to our institutions should be studied is exhibited in an observation by Senator John F. Kennedy with respect to suggested alterations in the manner of allocating electoral college votes: "The proposed system could change the whole political habits of the country, with results which are hard to predict now." James MacGregor Burns, *The Deadlock of Democracy* (Englewood Cliffs, N.J.: Prentice-Hall, 1963), p. 305. See Laurence Berns's letter to the editor, *Washington Post*, Aug. 25, 1968, p. 36; Pritchett, *The American Constitution*, pp. 312-20; *Time*, May 4, 1970, p. 27. See, also, chap. 7, n. 107, above.

120. Indeed, I venture to suggest that the task confronting us (or our children) may be greater than that which rested upon either Washington or Lincoln, partly because what has been done by our predecessors restricts us to fewer alternatives than they had to choose among. I even venture to suggest that we need to read more carefully than they did the great students of republican institutions. Montesquieu is a case in point: he was widely read, much quoted, but little understood by Blackstone and the Founding Fathers. It is my impression that Montesquieu cannot be understood without recourse to his unacknowledged teacher (and a republican, at that), the notorious Machiavelli. (See chap. 8, n. 18, below.) See David Lowenthal, Introduction, Montesquieu, *Considerations on the Causes of the Greatness of the Romans and Their Decline* (Ithaca, N.Y.: Cornell University Press, 1968), pp. 6-10, 19-20. See, also, Stourzh, *Alexander Hamilton*, pp. 34-36, 43, 228, n. 91. (Cf. Burke, *Works*, 4:99: "Man is by his constitution a religious animal.")

Montesquieu concludes the preface to *The Spirit of the Laws*,

> When I have seen what so many great men, in France, in England and in Germany, have written before me, I have been lost in admiration, but I have not lost courage. "And I also am a painter," I have said with Correggio.

The deliberate, and even conspicuous, omission among the countries of the modern world whose writers he acknowledges is Italy. He alerts us to this omission not only by quoting twice within a few pages thereafter a contemporary Italian poet and jurist but even by concluding the passage I have quoted (and hence the preface) with the name of an Italian painter. Just as Machiavelli "legitimates" the teachings of the *Prince* with the concluding chapter, which displays him as no more than an Italian patriot, so Montesquieu in the incongruous concluding section of his great book presents a history of the French legal institutions which presumably shaped his thought. (In each case, the closing line of the book quotes an "Italian" poet, Petrarch in the case of Machiavelli and Virgil in the case of Montesquieu.) It is not on the basis of such indications alone, however, that I form my impression of the relation of Montesquieu to Machiavelli: these indications do no more than almost playfully hint at the influence of Machiavelli which seems to me evident in *The Spirit of the Laws* (e.g., IV, iv; XII, 26; XIII, 16). (See, on literary playfulness, Alexandre Kojève, "The Emperor Julian and His Art of Writing," in Joseph Cropsey, ed., *Ancients and Moderns*, p. 95. See, also, chap. 6, n. 43, above, chap. 9, n. 12, below.)

One further impression of mine may be worth recording here, that Tocqueville's *Democracy in America* rests upon Montesquieu's work. I consider it worthy of investigation that Tocqueville (who refers to the *Federalist* many times) should have written his study of democracy in the United States without a single explicit reference to the Declaration of Independence as the authoritative statement of the American creed. See chap. 7, n. 115, above, chap. 8, n. 44, below. See, on Tocqueville and the challenge of democracy, Zetterbaum, *Tocqueville and the Problem of Democracy*.

For a serious study of Machiavelli, Leo Strauss, *Thoughts on Machiavelli* (Glencoe, Ill.: Free Press, 1958), is indispensable. This should be supplemented by Leo Strauss, "Machiavelli and Classical Literature," *Review of National Literatures* 1 (1970): 7. See Willmoore Kendall, review of Leo Strauss, *Thoughts on Machiavelli*, *Philosophical Review* 75 (Apr. 1966): 247. Cf. Richard C. Clark, "Machiavelli: Bibliographical Spectrum," *Review of National Literatures* 1 (1970): 93, 116-18. (Professor Clark perceived "veneration" in Warren Winiarski's useful essay on Machiavelli in Strauss and Cropsey, *History of Political Philosophy*, p. 247.) (Rousseau, as I have noted, says even of Machiavelli's *Prince* that it is "the book of republicans." *Social Contract*, III, vi. Insofar as republicanism is the rule of reason, with advancement along prescribed paths open to anyone with ambition, energy, and merit, the distinctively modern political thinkers have been "republicans." See Stendhal's *Red and the Black*, for the effects of suppressed republicanism.) See chap. 8, n. 22, below.

121. Lincoln, *Complete Works*, 1:9 (speech of 1837).

122. To what extent does "a new birth of freedom" depend on the "Discoveries, Inventions and Improvements" about which Lincoln lectured in 1859 and 1860? *Complete Works*, 1:522. See the text at chap. 9, n. 2, above. Cf. Aristotle, *Politics* 1268b23-1269a29; chap. 7, n. 110, above. See the concluding chapter on the "conquest of nature" in Laurence Berns, "An Introduction to the Political Philosophy of Francis Bacon" (Ph.D. diss., University of Chicago, 1957). See, also, his article, "Reasonable Politics and Technology," *The College* (St. John's College), Sept. 1970, p. 1 (chap. 7, n. 107, above).

Strauss says of Alexandre Kojève, "He regards unlimited technological progress and universal enlightenment as essential for the genuine satisfaction of what is human in man." *On Tyranny*, p. 199. Kojève's position, which seems to be in this respect that of Francis Bacon (but without the evident insistence on the curbs to be placed on innovation seen in Bacon's *New Atlantis*), is indicated in his article, "Tyranny and Wisdom," published in the 1963 edition of Strauss, *On Tyranny*, p. 143. See Enrico Fermi, *Collected Papers* (Chicago: University of Chicago Press, 1965), 2:411, 997-98; cf. ibid., pp. 226-27.

See Howard B. White, "Francis Bacon," in Strauss and Cropsey, *History of Political Philosophy*, p. 324; cf. Richard Kennington, "Rene Descartes," ibid., pp. 391-92. See, also, Strauss, *What Is Political Philosophy?* (Glencoe, Ill.: Free Press, 1959), p. 311.

See, on Strauss's *On Tyranny* and on other of his works, Victor Gourevitch's meticulous essay, "Philosophy and Politics," *Review of Metaphysics*, 12 (1968): 58, 281. See, also, Pierre Hassner, review of Leo Strauss, *Thoughts on Machiavelli*, and *What Is Political Philosophy?*, *Revue Française de Science Politique*, 10 (1960): 945. (There is available from the Rosary College bookstore an index to proper names in the works of Leo Strauss which I have compiled from work done by students at Rosary College and the University of Dallas.)

123. Cf. Henry Bergson, *Creative Evolution* (New York: Random House, Modern Library, 1944), p. 146:

> So the heavy hoplite was supplanted by the legionary; the knight, clad in armor, had to give place to the light free-moving infantryman; and in a general way, in the evolution of life, just as in the evolution of human societies and of individual destinies, the greatest successes have been for those who have accepted the heaviest risks.

Kalven has written, in summarizing Justice Black's opinions, "It is a sign of weakness to control speech; only democracies can afford the gallant gamble on utter freedom of

CHAPTER SEVEN, NOTE 124: PAGE 201 667

speech—it is too dangerous for tyranny." "Upon Rereading Mr. Justice Black on the First Amendment," *U.C.L.A. L. Rev.* 14 (1967): 428, 432.

We should not, however, exaggerate the risks of freedom of speech: "But so long as the minority seeks to advance its beliefs through lawful forms of expression and political agitation, cannot the majority confine itself to similar weapons?" Brown, *Loyalty and Security*, p. 483. Johnny Unitas, the Baltimore Colts quarterback, was asked, after a celebrated overtime playoff game against the New York Giants, about the risk he had taken in passing in the "sudden death" overtime period. He responded, "Nothing's dangerous if you know what you are doing." Robert Markus, "Sports Trail," *Chicago Tribune*, July 29, 1968, sec. 3, p. 3. See Winston S. Churchill, *My Early Life: A Roving Commission* (New York: Charles Scribner's Sons, n.d.), pp. 272-73.

124. Respect for the Constitution is for us, I have argued, a form of self-discipline (as well as of self-respect). See, e.g., chap. 6, n. 71, above. A dim, if sometimes distorted, reflection of this may be seen even in the conduct of court proceedings. Thus, one of the defendants in the "Chicago Conspiracy Trial" (Appendix D, above) has observed,

> None of us [defendants] had ever been required to appear on time every morning for six months anywhere—much less at a trial where we were worked over for seven hours a day. The trial necessitated discipline—we had to produce our witnesses, our motions and our bodies—or else. . . . When the other defendants asked me to "coordinate" this work I had no idea it would be the worst organizational ordeal of my life. Working within that structure of trial discipline made me into a high-pressure machine. It seemed necessary to push aside anyone who could not work efficiently and compatibly, and it was impossible to tolerate hang-ups, identity problems, or even demands for a full discussion of what we were doing. My personal relationships shriveled to nothing in Chicago. . . . [Tom Hayden, "The Trial," *Ramparts*, July 1970, p. 44]

A revolution, Hayden added, "requires periods of discipline and painful work." Ibid., p. 44. But he challenged the discipline of language when he said:

> The language of the establishment is mutilated by hypocrisy. When "love" is used in advertising, "peace" in foreign policy, "freedom" in private enterprise, then these words have been stolen from their humanist origins, and new words become vital for the identity of people seeking to remake themselves and society. Negroes become "blacks," blacks become "Panthers," the oppressors become "pigs." . . . Clearly, some rhetoric of the Left is wooden, inflated, irrelevant; crippling to the mind and an obstacle to communication. If we were interested in mild improvements to the system, perhaps we would use the prevailing language of the system. But one of the first tasks of those creating a new society is that of creating a new and distinct identity. This identity cannot be fully conscious at first, but as a movement grows, through years or generations, it contains its own body of experience, its styles and habits, and a common language becomes part of the new identity. The old language is depleted. In order to dream, to invoke anger or love, new language becomes necessary. Music and dance are forms of communication partly because they are directly expressive of feelings for which there is as yet no language. [Ibid., pp. 23-24]

See Sallust, *The War with Catiline*, chap. 52, sec. 10, on how the same issue Hayden spoke to was seen by the Roman "establishment." Cato is recorded as complaining to the Senate (see Burke, *Works*, 4:156):

> Now, however, the question before us is not whether our morals are good or bad, nor how great or glorious the empire of the Roman people is, but whether all that we have, however we regard it, is to be ours, or with ourselves is to belong to the enemy. At this point someone hints at gentleness and long-suffering! But in very truth we have long since lost the true names for things. It is precisely because squandering the goods of others is called generosity, and recklessness in wrong doing is called courage, that the republic is reduced to extremities.

A fundamental critique of Hayden's position (and that of contemporary radicalism) could well begin by noticing the uses to which it is assumed that language is to be put: "to dream," "to invoke anger or love," to be "expressive of feelings," to contribute to "creating a new and distinct identity." The "communication" which is aspired to is emphatically directed to action and to self-expression, not to the reason and understanding: that is to say, contemporary radicalism must ultimately be challenged for having turned its back (even though, like its Christian forebears, in the cause of social justice and personal redemption) on the life of the mind as something worthy of the most serious effort for its own sake. See Exod. 3:6, 33:17-23; Deut. 34:4-6. (A highminded statement of the popular preference for the life of communal endeavour to that of contemplation may be found in the convocation prayer by Michael S. Littleton published in *The College* [St. John's College], July 1970, p. 17: "Keep alive in us that freshness which lies deep down in things, yet ever close at hand, and with it the patience to forge for ourselves tools of understanding, sturdy and precise, which shall enable us to continue on the path of knowledge in pursuit of the common good." Cf. chap. 6, n. 43, above, chap. 9, n. 39, below. See, also, the comparison of the prophet with the philosopher in Martin Buber, *On the Bible* [New York: Schocken Books, 1968], p. 159.) See for a useful introduction to contemporary radicalism, as seen by "one old conservative," Joseph Cropsey, "Radicalism and Its Roots," *Public Policy*, 18 (1970): 301. See, also, Burke, *Works*, 4:3 ff.; chap. 7, n. 107, above, chap. 8, nn. 10, 28, 57, 171, 181, 193, 195, below.

That facet of modern radicalism which has been most extensively worked out is, of course, Marxism, of which the American Communist party is one manifestation. I have not tried, in this study, to deal with the American Communist party systematically. But I have dealt with it as much as I have, to illustrate problems about the meaning and application of the First Amendment, because the American citizen since the Second World War has regarded the Communist (just as the Englishman did in Milton's day the Roman Catholic) the practical "test case" on the limits of "freedom of speech, or of the press," especially since the Communist party is or is thought by some to be (as was the Roman Catholic church) the domestic agent of a threatening foreign power. Thus, I adapt to my purposes "Euclid's method [which] is to give one case only, for choice the most difficult, leaving the reader to supply the rest for himself." *The Thirteen Books of Euclid's Elements*, ed. Thomas L. Heath (New York: Dover Publications, 1956), 1:246. (This is called "the really classical manner." I myself believe, by the way, that there is expression far more harmful among us than that of the Communist party, but expression which most of my fellow citizens would not only condone but even support and applaud.)

The defender of freedom of speech for Communists is apt to be reminded, "The Communist Party realistically is a state within a state, an authoritarian dictatorship within a republic." Justice Jackson, *Dennis* v. *U.S.*, 341 U.S. 494, 477 (1951). (But what can this mean in the United States, with the Communist party's high rate of turnover in membership and with the inducements we offer for apostasy from Communism? [See Brown, *Loyalty and Security*, p. 315; cf. Sidney Hook, *Heresy, Yes—Conspiracy, No!* (New York: John Day Co., 1953), pp. 28-29, 103.]) I believe Justice Jackson's sentiment is no more realistic than that of the Federal Bureau of Investigation, which has seen ten close sympathizers of the Communist party for each member. [This has been called "one of the shakiest statistics in American politics." Brown, *Loyalty and Security*, p. 313] One is also reminded that "the war of Marxism against the ruling principles of Western constitutionalism [including inalienable, irreducible rights] must never be mistaken for a mere skirmish." Joseph Cropsey, "Karl Marx," in Strauss and Cropsey, *History of Political Philosophy*, p. 702. (See, also, Cropsey's letter to the editor, *New York Times*, Feb. 20, 1961.) One confronts as well the lulling assurance that the speech for which Communists have been prosecuted "ranks low" "on any scale of values which we have hitherto recognized." Justice Frankfurter, in *Dennis* v. *U.S.*, 341 U.S. 494, 545 (1951).

It is only prudent to treat the Communist party of the United States in a friendly or at least fair way if only to help shape it to American conditions (as the Roman Catholic church has been—see chap. 5, n. 31, above): Communists are going to be around a long time, partly because of what is wrong with them and partly because of what is

CHAPTER SEVEN, NOTE 124: PAGE 201   669

wrong with the modern world (including the United States). (See, for Leslie Stephen's objection to the "quack remedies" of persecution and suppression, *An Agnostic's Apology* [London: Smith, Elder & Co., 1893], pp. 264-65, 273.) Should a Communist party member, with his sincere concern to improve the life of mankind, be treated like a common criminal? (See Burke, *Works*, 2:243; Dorothy Day, *Catholic Worker*, Mar. 1957, pp. 3, 6; Bobby Seale, *Seize the Time* [New York: Random House, 1970], pp. 289-314, 350-52. It is encouraging to notice, by the way, that Chief Justice Burger seems to have made it his business to have the treatment of common criminals improved in our prisons.) I discuss the Communist party more systematically (if only in outline) in a book review in *N.Y.U. L. Rev.* 41 (1966): 664, a review for which one reader has suggested the title, "On Greatness of Soul": it is the self-respecting American soul we must protect against the well-meaning but stifling embraces of a petty and frightened Americanism. (Unlike either the Communist party or the Roman Catholic church, the Black Panther party does not need to be shaped to American conditions; it does not neeed to be "Americanized." Indeed, the Black Panther party may well be the most *American* unpopular minority among us since the Ku Klux Klan. Certainly, its self-destructive recourse to guns is, as someone has said, "as American as cherry pie." See Anastaplo, "Neither Black nor White: The Negro in America," "Notes on the First Amendment," pp. 767-68.)

It is also prudent to note, for its implications about the usefulness among us of certain unpopular organizations (such as the John Birch Society, the Communist party, Ku Klux Klan, Black Panther party, and the Black Muslims), that the probable assassin of President Kennedy was evidently a professed Marxist in a state where Communist party membership has long been so serious an offense that the local organization of that party may well be destroyed. (See Texas Civil Statutes, Title 120A, Articles 6889-3, 6889-3A; Texas Penal Code, Title 4, Articles 153, 155.) Would the assassination have been less likely to occur if this seriously disturbed man had been subject to "party discipline"? See, e.g., chap. 7, n. 46, above. See, also, chap. 6, n. 71, above. ("The Communist Party, U.S.A. says that its leaders 'reject today the organizing of armed uprisings in black communities,' and that they believe the country's 22 million Negroes still have opportunities for 'democratic change.'" *New York Times*, Nov. 12, 1967, p. 52.)

That is, must we not rely to a large extent, in a society as impersonal and as "open" as ours, upon voluntary organizations to supply the guidance and discipline provided elsewhere by customs, by intimacy, and by civic institutions? Religious institutions come first to mind. (See Shaftesbury, *Characteristics*, 1:237 ff., 264-65, 266-67, 270, 271-72, 275-80, 287, 291; 2:45, 49-50, 55, 352; Rousseau, *Social Contract*, IV, viii; Zetterbaum, *Tocqueville and the Problem of Democracy*, pp. 22n, 47, 109-10, 112, 114, 115-16, 117, 120n, 123, 151n. See, also, chap. 7, nn. 21, 34, 59, above. Cf. *Federalist*, pp. 339-40; chap. 5, n. 97, above. Cf., also, Burke, *Works*, 4:50: "the little platoon we belong to.")

Indeed, may there not be disturbed peoples in the world for whom only communism, in its capacity as the religion of technological righteousness, is apt to be able today to provide the discipline, illusions (or aspirations), and organization necessary to subdue their barbarity and *start* them on the path to civilization? (Cf. chap. 8, nn. 46, 140, below.) Contemporary liberal democrats, it can be argued, are more apt as colonialists to corrupt themselves than to elevate others. (We will certainly have an unhealthy, even dangerous, attitude toward the use as a people of our tremendous power if we should agree with Secretary of State Rusk, "While we are sleeping, two-thirds of the world is plotting to do us in." *Chicago Tribune*, July 2, 1970, p. 22. See chap. 8, n. 150, below.)

Consider, also, the American campus:

> Old-line communist organizations oriented to both Moscow and Peking are gaining increasing influence and control over the nation's new left youth movement, J. Edgar Hoover . . . warned today. . . . Old left groups are working hard to capture at least a part of the movement, Hoover said, because they recognize that "the antidiscipline, free-wheeling, individualistic, anarchistic mood of the new left must be controlled and molded into a strong, centralized, Marxist-Leninist revolutionary force." [*Chicago Tribune*, May 31, 1969, sec. 1A, p. 18]

See *Congressional Record* 116: E5921 (June 24, 1970). Academic administrators could no doubt be found who would suggest that this prospect of "old-line communist" discipline is not something to be "warned" against but perhaps even to be "prayed for." See Art Buchwald, "The Reds Are Dead," *International Herald Tribune* (Paris), Sept. 29, 1970, p. 16. See, also, chap. 8, n. 105, below.

In any event, it is well to remind ourselves of Brown's observation that if we silence the Communist, "we have actually abrogated freedom of speech, whereas he has merely talked about doing it." *Loyalty and Security*, p. 342. See chap. 5, n. 70, above, chap. 8, n. 46, below. See, also, chap. 8, n. 150 (end), below.

It seems useful to close this chapter, with its unfashionable suggestions about the virtues of local government and "states' rights," by recording the following incident from the Second World War: General George Patton was in England, having taken leave temporarily of his battlefield command, at a time when the V-2 rockets were bombarding London. These rockets were silent and were capable of destroying an entire city block. A V-2 hit near him. "Come on," he told his chief of staff, "let's get the devil out of here. This is too impersonal." *Dallas Morning News*, Aug. 31, 1969, sec. C, p. 1.

The general had the security of the battlefield to which he could return. But where are we to go? What is *our* natural habitat? See chap. 2, nn. 31, 38, chap. 7, n. 35, above, chap. 8, nn. 16, 135, below. See, also, Burke, *Works*, 5:100-102.

CHAPTER VIII

1. Even in official publications, a distinction is recognized between the *debates* of Congress and the *acts* of Congress. What legislators say on the floor of Congress may not be penalized elsewhere, although what they do (in the form of legislation, a special kind of "saying") may be challenged elsewhere for its constitutionality.

Milton distinguishes, in the passage reproduced in the text at chap. 5, n. 50, above, between being "pursued with bad words" and being "persecuted . . . with bad deeds."

2. William Graham Sumner, *Andrew Jackson*, American Statesmen (Boston: Houghton Mifflin Co., 1897), pp. 24-25. See, also, ibid., pp. 33-34, 68-69, 72, 279-80.

> This young lawyer [Andrew Jackson], like most of those who had seen and felt what liberty had cost, was a very warm lover of his country. . . . He could scarcely place other citizens upon the same level as the soldiers of the Revolution; whom he regarded as a kind of republican aristocracy, entitled above all others, to honor and office. . . . In these respects, he was the most American of Americans—an embodied Declaration-of-Independence—the Fourth-of-July incarnate! [James Parton, *Life of Andrew Jackson* (Boston: Houghton Mifflin Co., 1887), 1:113]

(Cf. chap. 8, n. 42, below.) I believe that Sumner failed to see, because of Jackson's "barbarian" appearance, that this folk hero (a frontier Saint George) was closer to the well-born Lee than to Lincoln or even to Grant. (See chap. 7, n. 91, above.) Donald Davidson's poem, "Andrew Jackson," goes deeper than Sumner's description of this man (see chap. 2, n. 39, above):

> What makes men live but honor? . . .
> . . . . What was it then but honor
> That blazed too hot for British regulars
> At New Orleans? Then all the people knew
> That I was of their breed and trusted me.
> Cowards and lies and little men will pass,
> But honor, by the Eternal, will endure.

[E. W. Parks, ed., *Southern Poets* (New York: American Book Co., 1936), p. 287]

One is reminded of Plutarch's description *(The Lives of the Noble Grecians and Romans* [New York: Random House, Modern Library, n.d.]) of Coriolanus (despite that Roman's lack of popular regard), esp. pp. 263, 272. Cf. chap. 9, n. 31, below. (See, on Jackson, Tocqueville, *Democracy in America* [New York: Random House, Vintage Books, 1954], 1:299, 431; Emerson, *The Complete Works of Ralph Waldo Emerson*, ed. E. W. Emerson [Boston: Houghton Mifflin Co., 1911], 11:521. A visit to the Hermitage is also instructive.)

It was of Lincoln, on the other hand, that James Russell Lowell sang, in his *Ode* of 1865:

> One whose meek flock the people joyed to be,
> Not lured by any cheat of birth,
> But by his clear-granted human worth,
> And brave old wisdom of sincerity!
>
> Nothing of Europe here,
> Or, then, of Europe fronting mornward still,
> Ere any names of Serf and Peer
> Could Nature's equal scheme deface
> And thwart her genial will:
> Here was a type of the true elder race,
> And one of Plutarch's men talked with us face to face.
> . . . .
> Our children shall behold his fame,
> The kindly-earnest, brave, foreseeing man,
> Sagacious, patient, dreading praise, not blame,
> New birth of our new soil, the first American.

When one wonders which of "Plutarch's men" is referred to, the description of Aristides comes to mind. Plutarch, *Lives*, esp. pp. 146, 392-94.

Should we not discern in the confrontation between Jackson and Lincoln, or between Coriolanus and Aristides, or between Lee and Grant, the fundamental confrontation in political life between the noble and the useful (or the just)? This confrontation may be evident as well in the distinction I develop in this study between the self-expression aspect and the public-participation aspect of "freedom of speech." (See, e.g., the movement from section 3 to section 4 of chapter 5, above, and from section 13 to section 14 of chapter 8, above. See, also, chap. 8, n. 193, below.)

It is one of my principal arguments, especially in this chapter, that it can be said to be the genius of freedom of speech among us—and perhaps, indeed, the genius of America itself—to ennoble the common and to make the noble useful. Section 9 of this chapter is indeed central to the argument. See, also, chap. 4, n. 43, chap. 7, n. 91, above, chap. 8, n. 56, chap. 9, n. 32, below. See, on the proper relation between "judgment" and "feeling," chap. 8, n. 45, below. Cf. chap. 8, n. 187, below. See Edmund Burke, *Works*, World Classics (London: Oxford University Press, 1906), 2:146-47, on "order and beauty" as the ends of sound government. See, also, ibid., 5:129-34.

3. Blackstone endorses Montesquieu's observation that "political or civil liberty is the direct end of [the British] constitution." William Blackstone, *Commentaries on the Laws of England*, 1:145. See ibid., 2:94. ("We began already to converse together in some sort; and the first words I learnt were to express my desire that he would please to give me my liberty, which I every day repeated on my knees." Jonathan Swift, *Gulliver's Travels*, pt. 2, chap. 2.) William W. Crosskey identified "the Security of the general Liberty" as the "peculiar 'object' of the American Revolution." *Politics and the Constitution* (Chicago: University of Chicago Press, 1953), p. 374. See chap. 2, n. 8, above.

It was said many times during the ratification campaign that the best safeguard for American liberty was the Constitution itself, that it was all the Bill of Rights that Americans needed. (*Federalist* No. 84 argues, "The truth is, after all the declamations we have heard, that the Constitution is itself, in every rational sense, and to every useful purpose, A BILL OF RIGHTS." It had been said in the preceding number, "The truth is that the general GENIUS of a government is all that can be substantially relied upon for permanent effects. Particular provisions, although not altogether useless, have far less virtue and efficacy than are commonly ascribed to them. . . ." Compare "the adage that the parliament [of Great Britain] was the palladium of liberty." Max Farrand, ed., *The Records of the Federal Convention of 1787* [New Haven: Yale University Press, 1937], 2:301.)

Lincoln referred to the Constitution as "the great charter of liberty" (and to the Declaration of Independence as "this charter of freedom"). *Complete Works*, ed. John G. Nicolay and John Hay (New York: Century Co., 1902), 1:504, 619. (I believe it would have been better to interchange "liberty" and "freedom" in these two phrases. See chap. 5, sec. 8, above. Lincoln's more mature usage of "liberty" and of "freedom" in the Gettysburg Address supports my suggestion.)

See, on the relation of liberty to equality, my review in *N.Y.U. L. Rev.* 41 (1966): 664, of Jaffa, *Equality and Liberty*. Cf. the first passage from Rousseau quoted in chap. 8, n. 192, below. The tension between liberty and equality (i.e., between two aspects of justice) may even be seen at the root of the issues raised by the current abortion controversy. (The case for virtually unrestricted abortion, even in the early months of pregnancy, is not as strong as most intellectuals believe today: it is a case that makes too much of the adult self and not enough of nature, community, and perhaps the incipient self. See Anastaplo, "Natural Right and the American Lawyer," *Wisc. L. Rev.* 1965: 322, 337-38, esp. n. 41. See, also, chap. 5, n. 126, above, chap. 8, n. 193, chap. 9, n. 28, below.)

4. Much of my discussion of freedom of speech and of the press, especially in section 13 of this chapter, would apply as well to the rights of religious conscience. Religious freedom, which some would (not without justice) nominate as the best safeguard for liberty, can be understood (for present purposes) as derivative from (if not similar to or even productive of) freedom of speech and the right of property. See the passage from Madison cited in chap. 8, n. 34, below. (Thomas Paine called, in *Common Sense*, for "a Continental Charter, or Charter of the United Colonies [answering what is called the Magna Charta of England]," in which there would be secured "freedom and property to all men, and above all things, the free exercise of religion, according to the dictates of conscience. . . ." Paine, *Writings* [New York: G. P. Putnam's Sons, 1894], 1:98.)

The right to privacy may be regarded as an aspect of the right to property. See chap. 8, n. 36, below. (An exaggerated regard for these rights means that community is sacrificed to "individuality" and a childish "self-expression." [This may be seen in the recourse today to drugs and in the careless use of tobacco and alcohol, to say nothing of the assumption that homosexuality is merely "a private affair."] Thus, a limitation upon privacy and property, in the name of such virtues as temperance, may be seen in a community's right to inspect, to superintend, and thereby to shape the souls of its citizens. See chap. 7, n. 59, above. To insist that everyone can and should be left "free" to "choose" what he will do and even what he will be assumes that we somehow are what we are independent of a significant role by and for the community. See chap. 5, n. 90, above. But which is, or should be, the decisive community? Consider, e.g., the Jews in Russia today. See chap. 7, n. 45, above.) See, also, chap. 2, n. 38, above.

I have suggested that the right of revolution may be said to be transformed, in ordinary times, into freedom of speech. See, also, section 11 of this chapter. Justice Story (*Commentaries on the Constitution*, chap. 44, sec. 1897) domesticates less than I do the right of revolution:

> The importance of [the Second Amendment] will scarcely be doubted by any persons who have duly reflected upon the subject. The militia is the natural defence of a free country against sudden foreign invasions, domestic insurrections, and domestic usurpations of power by rulers. It is against sound policy for a free people to keep up large military establishments and standing armies in time of peace, both from the enormous expenses with which they are attended, and the facile means which they afford to ambitious and unprincipled rulers to subvert the government, or trample upon the rights of the people. The right of the citizens to keep and bear arms, has justly been considered as the palladium of the liberties of a republic; since it offers a strong moral check against the usurpation and arbitrary power of rulers; and will generally, even if these are successful in the first instance, enable the people to resist and triumph over them. . . .

See chap. 7, n. 67, n. 77 (for another list of principal rights), above. Cf. Burke, *Works*, 4:68: "Men have no right to what is not reasonable, and to what is not for their benefit."
   5. "A free people is indeed mostly fair, liberty practises men in a give-and-take, which is the rough essence of justice." Walter Bagehot, *The English Constitution*, World Classics (London: Oxford University Press, 1963), p. 118. See chap. 8, n. 194, below.
   The current movement on behalf of the civil rights of Negroes may be seen as an effort to secure for all citizens the full enjoyment of these and other rights. "The more I advanced in the study of American society, the more I perceived that this equality of condition is the fundamental fact from which all others seem to be derived and the central point at which all my observations constantly terminated." Tocqueville, *Democracy in America*, 1:3.

> I almost always feel inclined, when I happen to say anything to soldiers, to impress upon them, in a few brief remarks, the importance of success in this contest. It is not merely for today, but for all time to come, that we should perpetuate for our children's children that great and free government which we have enjoyed all our lives. I beg you to remember this, not merely for my sake, but for yours. I happen, temporarily, to occupy this White House. I am a living witness that any one of your children may look to come here as my father's child has. It is in order that each one of you may have, through this free government which we have enjoyed, an open field and a fair chance for your industry, enterprise, and intelligence; that you may all have equal privileges in the race of life, with all its desirable human aspirations. It is for this the struggle should be maintained, that we may not lose our birthright—not only for one, but for two or three years. The nation is worth fighting for, to secure such an inestimable jewel. [Lincoln, *Complete Works*, 2:567 (address of Aug. 22, 1864, to the 166th Ohio Regiment)]

See, also, ibid., 2:570; Leo Strauss, *Socrates and Aristophanes* (New York: Basic Books, 1966), pp. 106-8, 110.
   6. Blackstone, *Laws of England*, 3:350; also, 3:379-81. Cooley, in *A Treatise on the Constitutional Limitations Which Rest upon the Legislative Powers of the States of the American Union*, 8th ed. (Boston: Little, Brown & Co., 1927), pp. 637 and 639, described trial by jury as "perhaps the most important of the protections to personal liberty."

> The friends and adversaries of the plan of the convention [i.e., the Constitution], if they agree in nothing else, concur at least in the value they set upon the trial by jury; or if there is any difference between them it consists in this: the former regard it as a valuable safeguard to liberty; the latter represent it as the very palladium of free government. [*Federalist* (Random House, Modern Library, n.d.), pp. 542-43]

(This passage is continued in chap. 8, n. 55, below.) See, also, Story, *Commentaries on the Constitution*, chap. 38, sec. 1780.
   That a jury was not thought by all Englishmen to be infallible is indicated by Bunyan's description of the one in the town of Vanity which condemned Faithful to death (see, also, Paine, *Writings*, 2:398-99):

> Then went the jury out, whose names were Mr. Blindman, Mr. No-good, Mr. Malice, Mr. Love-lust, Mr. Live-loose, Mr. Heady, Mr. High-mind, Mr. Enmity, Mr. Liar, Mr. Cruelty, Mr. Hate-light, and Mr. Implacable; who every one gave in his private verdict against him among themselves, and afterwards unanimously concluded to bring him in guilty before the judge [Lord Hate-good]. And first among themselves, Mr. Blindman, the foreman, said, I see clearly that this man is a heretic. . . . [*Pilgrim's Progress* (London: Thomas Nelson & Sons, n.d.), p. 99]

   7. *Federalist* No. 83 and No. 84. The right there given the longest separate treatment is trial by jury; next is liberty of the press (*habeas corpus* is linked to trial by jury).

Nevertheless, the right of suffrage is assumed to be basic, reflecting the emphasis in the Declaration of Independence upon "the consent of the governed." Authority over the regulation of suffrage is called by Ames "the supreme authority." *Annals*, I, p. 770. See the text at chap. 4, n. 100, above.

See, on "parchment guarantees," *Federalist*, pp. 158, 177, 321, 326, 331, 476. Cf. ibid., p. 291; chap. 8, n. 78, below.

8. "The foundation of English liberty and of all free government is a right in the people to participate in their legislative council." Declaration of Colonial Rights, Resolutions of the First Continental Congress, Oct. 14, 1774.

9. The *Chicago Sun-Times*, June 12, 1966, p. 6, col. 2, reported:

> In Natchez, Miss., Charles Evers, state director for the National Assn. for the Advancement of Colored People, said he felt the long march to Jackson wouldn't do much good. "I don't really criticize the march," he said. "What I feel is that instead of spending all that money on airplane tickets and camp-outs, we should spend it on registration—what James Meredith was shot for. The only time we can stop the shootings and beatings will be when we get at least 300,000 registered—and then we can change governors, mayors, sheriffs and county supervisors. I am a Mississippian and I have a right to say what I think about things here. I don't care what people say in New York and California and we don't let people use us for publicity stunts or anything else."

It should be noticed, however, that registration is now possible in Mississippi because of legislation that followed upon nationwide publicity and discussion. (Since passage of the Voting Rights Act of 1965, "nearly a million Southern Negroes have been registered as voters. Supporters of the act have called it the most effective civil rights legislation in the nation's history." *Dallas Morning News*, Mar. 14, 1970, p. 1. See Congressman Abner J. Mikva's useful assessment of the effects of the act, *Hyde Park Herald*, Chicago, Illinois, May 20, 1970, p. 4.) To what extent did that legislation reflect the power in northern cities of registered Negroes? Years of discussion, which led to the desegregation decisions of the 1940s and 1950s, should not be lost sight of, nor the influence of Joe Louis and Jackie Robinson and the effect both of the Second World War and of related developments in Africa. (Cf. William F. Russell, "Success Is a Journey," *Sports Illustrated*, June 8, 1970, pp. 80, 81, 83.) But are we not obliged, in order to understand what has been happening and what is likely to happen, to go back ultimately to the Declaration of Independence and its authoritative teaching for Americans that "all men are created equal"? See chap. 9, n. 39, below. Cf. p. 241, above ("but if they are once raised to the level of freemen, they will soon revolt at being deprived of almost all their civil rights").

It does seem to me uncharitable, if not simply callous (as well as impolitic), for the educated and prosperous sons and grandsons of penniless immigrants to counsel ambitious Negroes to "go slow." It seems to me, on the other hand, irresponsibly romantic, and hence callous in a different way, for anyone today to urge people in this country with serious grievances to arm themselves and "take to the streets." I had occasion to observe, in a talk of April 7, 1968, entitled, "Martin Luther King and the Soul of America" (which was published in *The Organon* [Chicago: Basic Program, University of Chicago], June 1968, p. 5):

> Mr. King preached a doctrine of dedicated nonviolence—a doctrine supported in his speeches by arguments both principled and pragmatic. There is one further argument, however, which should also be noticed by everyone who cares for his Negro friends and for the soul of America, and that is the dreadful vulnerability of our Negro fellow-citizens (an easily identifiable minority) if the confrontation between black and white should really be taken to the streets. I have long doubted that provocative marches through the streets of our cities, in the name of freedom of speech, constitute a right that any community is obliged to permit to be exercised, especially when other means of communication (culminating in the ballot-box) are available. In any event, anyone of stature who is at the center of bitter controversy has the duty—for the good of his people and

CHAPTER EIGHT, NOTE 10: PAGE 208

of his potential murderers, if not of himself or of his family—to take reasonable precautions for his physical safety.

See, in my doctoral dissertation, "Notes on the First Amendment" (University of Chicago, 1964), the lecture, "Neither Black nor White: The Negro in America." See, also, chap. 7, n. 67, above, chap. 8, nn. 27, 135, 141, below.

Need one add that also irresponsible are those among us who allow serious grievances either to pile up or to be exploited by would-be revolutionaries? Do not the teachings of the Declaration of Independence remain among us the best check upon both bad government and mindless rebellion? In any event, the rebel would have to deal tomorrow, even if he should happen to succeed today, with essentially the same attitudes, limitations, and hence problems which confronted and baffled his predecessors—and his task would not be made easier by the repressive measures he would "have" to take (far more severe than anything we have ever seen) to maintain himself in power. See chap. 5, n. 94, above, chap. 8, n. 56, below. Neither childish rebelliousness nor romantic posturing is a substitute for understanding and prudence. We have been told, "Political power grows out of the barrel of a gun." *Quotations from Chairman Mao Tse-Tung* (Peking: Foreign Languages Press, 1966), p. 61. (Cf., ibid., pp. 102, 139, 140.) But it is well to remind ourselves that "a man is not free if he cannot see where he is going, even if he has a gun to help him get there." (Attributed to A. J. Liebling in Marshall McLuhan, *Understanding Media: The Extensions of Man* [New York: New American Library, Signet Books, 1964], p. 34)

10. "For where your treasure is, there will your heart be also." Matt. 6:21. See Joseph Cropsey, "On the Relation of Political Science and Economics," *American Political Science Review* 54 (1960): 3; George Grant, *Lament for a Nation* (Princeton: Van Nostrand, 1965), pp. 17-18, 43, 47, 69-70. It can be said of the rights I am surveying here that each of them would tend to contribute to the self-preservation of its claimant. But property may be especially regarded as "self-preservation which has taken on flesh." Leo Strauss, *Thoughts on Machiavelli* (Glencoe, Ill.: Free Press, 1958), p. 249. See Job 1:9-11; Aristotle, *Nicomachean Ethics* 1120a1-3.

I refer here to the self-preservation of the human being, for which there is obviously a basis in nature, not to the self-preservation of states which some make so much of today. According to authorities as diverse as the Declaration of Independence and Thomas Aquinas, the right of self-preservation of a government is far from being foremost. A tyrannical or unjust regime has no moral or natural right to preserve itself. If anything, it has only the right to change (i.e., improve) or perish. The moral right of governments to exist is directly dependent upon and proportionate to their justice. The major cause of the contemporary error may be a misunderstanding of Hobbes's doctrine of sovereignty. It is one thing to trace all the rights of government to rights of the sovereign and to conceive of the sovereign as a legal or fictional person; it is quite another to confuse the passions of men (e.g., the fear of violent death) and the rights supposedly deduced from them (e.g., the right of self-preservation) with the passions and rights of artificial or legal persons (i.e., states). (Dependent upon such confusion may be the emergence as well of the mischievous doctrine of the "self-determination of peoples." See Harold Nicolson, *The Evolution of Diplomacy* [New York: Collier Books, 1962], p. 117.)

> . . . And it is further Rousseau's argument that the modern state based on self-preservation constitutes a way of life precisely contrary to that which would make men happy. The life of the big nations is characterized by commerce and, consequently, by the distinction between rich and poor. Each man can pursue his gain within the framework laid down by the state. Money is the standard of human worth, and virtue is forgotten. . . . The result of the oversimplified and onesided concentration on preservation is the destruction of the good life which is the only purpose of preservation. [Allan Bloom, "Jean-Jacques Rousseau," in Leo Strauss and Joseph Cropsey, *History of Political Philosophy* (Chicago: Rand McNally, 1963), p. 515]

See chap. 8, n. 16, below. (Cf. Hobbes, *Leviathan*, chap. 30 [middle]; *Federalist*, pp. 261-62, 287, 298-99, 384; Justice Harlan, *Barenblatt* v. *U.S.*, 360 U.S. 109, 128 [1959] ["the right of self-preservation, 'the ultimate value of any society'"].) See chap. 6, n. 54, above. Cf. chap. 6, n. 66, above. "The formation of society, and the alteration of its constituent rules, are admitted by our policy to be rights exclusively lodged in the people, in which rights the governments they establish have no share." John Taylor, *An Inquiry into the Principles and Policy of the Government of the United States* (Fredericksburg, Va.: Green & Cady, 1814), p. 394. Is this not what the Declaration of Independence is all about? See Paine, *Writings*, 2:276-81, 303-5, 317, 359, 435.

11. Justice Cardozo, in *Palko* v. *Connecticut*, 302 U.S. 319, 326 (1937). I have been told (by Philip Hablutzel) that German courts rarely quote from American judicial opinions (as distinguished from the Constitution itself). It is fitting that this praise by Justice Cardozo of freedom of speech should be one of the rare exceptions: "*Es ist in gewissem Sinn die Grundlage jeder Freiheit überhaupt*, 'the matrix, the indispensable condition of nearly every other form of freedom' (Cardozo)," German Constitutional Court, Decision of Jan. 15, 1958, 7 BVerfGE 198, 208 (First Senate). (Justice Story [*Commentaries on the Constitution*, chap. 44, sec. 1885] quoted *Junius* [1769-72], "The liberty of the press is the palladium of all the civil, political, and religious rights of an Englishman, and the right of juries to return a general verdict in all cases whatsoever, is an essential part of our constitution." See chap. 5, n. 57, chap. 6, n. 30, above.)

12. Property rights are protected in various provisions of the original Constitution (e.g., in the stipulation in Article I, section 8, that "Imposts and Excises shall be uniform throughout the United States") as well as in the Fifth Amendment. See chap. 8, n. 32, below. See, also, Richard McKeon, "The Concept of Property," *Ethics* 48 (1938): 297.

13. See, for a chronological account of the evolution of the "preferred position" doctrine, Justice Frankfurter's concurring opinion in *Kovacs* v. *Cooper*, 336 U.S. 77, 89 (1949). (See, also, Walter Berns, *Freedom, Virtue and the First Amendment* [Baton Rouge: Louisiana State University Press, 1957], pp. 73-128; Alpheus T. Mason and William M. Beaney, *American Constitutional Law*, 3rd ed. [Englewood Cliffs, N.J.: Prentice-Hall, 1964], pp. 487-90; Mason, *Harlan Fiske Stone* [New York: Viking Press, 1956], pp. 513-17, 601.) Justice Frankfurter wrote,

> My brother Reed speaks of "the preferred position of freedom of speech," though, to be sure, he finds that the Trenton ordinance does not disregard it. This is a phrase that has uncritically crept into some recent opinions of this Court. I deem it a mischievous phrase, if it carries the thought, which it may subtly imply, that any law touching communication is infected with presumptive invalidity. . . . I say the phrase is misleading because it radiates a constitutional doctrine without avowing it. [336 U.S., at 90]

Justice Frankfurter insisted, instead, on other preferred phrases, as is evident in this passage from his opinion in *Wolf* v. *Colorado*, 338 U.S. 25, 27 (1949) (see, also, chap. 8, n. 34, below):

> Due process of law thus conveys neither formal nor fixed nor narrow requirements. It is the compendious expression for all those rights which the courts must enforce because they are basic to our free society. . . . It is of the very nature of a free society to advance in its standards of what is deemed reasonable and right. Representing as it does a living principle, due process is not confined within a permanent catalogue of what may at a given time be deemed the limits or the essentials of fundamental rights. . . . The security of one's privacy against arbitrary intrusion by the police—which is at the core of the Fourth Amendment—is basic to a free society. It is therefore implicit in "the concept of ordered liberty" and as such enforceable against the States through the Due Process Clause.

The "ordered liberty" phrase may be traced back to Justice Cardozo's opinion in *Palko* v. *Connecticut*, 302 U.S. 319, 324-25 (1937) (omitting citations):

[T]he due process clause of the Fourteenth Amendment may make it unlawful for a state to abridge by its statutes the freedom of speech which the First Amendment safeguards against encroachment by the Congress, or the like freedom of the press, or the free exercise of religion, or the right of peaceable assembly, without which speech would be unduly trammeled, or the right of one accused of crime to the benefit of counsel. In these and other situations immunities that are valid as against the federal government by force of the specific pledges of particular amendments [the First and the Sixth] have been found to be implicit in the concept of ordered liberty, and thus, through the Fourteenth Amendment, become valid as against the states.

See, in Justice Harlan's concurring opinion in *Pointer* v. *Texas*, 380 U.S. 400, 408 (1965), his preference for "ordered liberty" over "incorporation." See chap. 7, n. 3, above.

I have indicated (e.g., chap. 7, n. 84, above) my own preference for the phrase supplied by the Constitution itself, "Republican Form of Government," a phrase which reminds us of the very foundations of our institutions. Cf. chap. 2, nn. 20, 39, above.

See chap. 7, nn. 26, 86, 107, above. See, also, chap. 8, n. 83, below.

14. See chap. 2, n. 25, above.

In the 1798 debates with respect to the Sedition Act (e.g., in the Virginia House of Delegates), the First Amendment was sometimes identified as "the third article of the amendments to the Constitution." *Resolutions of Virginia and Kentucky* (Richmond: R. I. Smith, 1835), p. 77. See, also, *Annals*, VI, p. 968 (1801). The assent of one more state would have ratified one of these two discarded amendments. (See chap. 2, n. 25, above.) Action was often taken by one state without knowledge of what other states had already done or would be likely to do. It is also the result of chance, therefore, that there are ten articles (a magisterial, even divine, number for commandments) in the Bill of Rights.

A great sage of the Talmud maintained that of all the 613 commandments in the Torah, only two were spoken by God, as it were, while the other 611 commandments were articulated by Moses. These two commandments, which constitute the divine core of revelation, are the first and the second of the Ten Commandments—"I am the Lord Thy God who has taken thee out from the land of Egypt, from the house of bondage" and "Thou shalt have no other gods beside Me." This seminal observation is, as Maimonides noted, an excellent introduction to the meaning of revelation in Judaism. [Jacob B. Agus, "The State of Jewish Belief," *Commentary*, Aug. 1966, p. 73]

See Ralph Lerner and Muhsin Mahdi, *Medieval Political Philosophy* (New York: Free Press, 1965), pp. 223-24, 229. See, also, chap. 9, n. 3, below. Cf. chap. 7, n. 23, above.

Is the First Amendment, with its distinctive express limitation by Congress upon itself, the "seminal observation" for an introduction to the meaning of American republicanism? See Paine, *Writings*, 2:396-99.

Jefferson, as President, pardoned those who had been convicted and sentenced under the [Sedition Act of 1798] and remitted their fines, stating: "I discharged every person under punishment or prosecution under the sedition law because I considered, and now consider, that law to be a nullity, as absolute and palpable as if Congress had ordered us to fall down and worship a golden image." Letter to Mrs. [John] Adams, July 22, 1804, Jefferson, *The Writings of Thomas Jefferson*, ed. H. A. Washington (New York: H. W. Derby, 1861), 4:555, 556. [*New York Times Co.* v. *Sullivan*, 376 U.S. 254, 276 (1964)]

(Cf. chap. 5, n. 51, above.) Indeed, is not sedition legislation for Americans what the golden calf was for the people of Israel, an act of desperate folly by a people wandering in the desert and forgetful of what distinguishes it from all other peoples? See chap. 7, n. 72, above. See, also, Grant, *Lament for a Nation*, pp. 5-6, 21-22, 37-38, 53-67, 70-71, 75-76, 88-97.

Edward S. Corwin and Jack W. Peltason, *Understanding the Constitution* (New

York: Henry Holt & Co., 1958), p. 122, record a distinction developed by the Supreme Court between "fundamental and formal parts of the Constitution," a distinction which may be considered a precursor of both the "preferred position" and the "ordered liberty" doctrines:

> When Puerto Rico, the Philippines, and Hawaii were annexed, the question arose whether or not "the Constitution followed the flag." The chief difficulty sprang from the fact that the new territories had not been molded in the political and legal traditions of the Constitution, and that in certain areas their inhabitants were only semicivilized. . . . [T]he Supreme Court met the problem by distinguishing between fundamental and formal parts of the Constitution and by holding that in "unincorporated territories" [those that Congress has not explicitly or impliedly made an integral part of the Union] only the fundamental provisions of the Constitution, those that guarantee fair trials, freedom of speech, and so on, applied, unless and until Congress provided otherwise [citing *Hawaii v. Mankichi*, 190 U.S. 197 (1903); *Balzac v. Porto Rico*, 258 U.S. 298 (1922)].

See, also, chap. 7, n. 77, above. Cf. *Reid v. Covert*, 354 U.S. 1 (1957). See the discussion in the text at chap. 4, n. 31, above.

15. We can see that the First Amendment rights are the only ones among the first eight amendments explicitly addressed to the general government. I have argued that the other amendments also govern the general government alone, not the states. See chap. 4, n. 8, chap. 7, n. 3, above, chap. 8, n. 83, below.

We have seen that an effort was made in the First Congress to extend the rights of freedom of speech, freedom of the press, freedom of religion, and trial by jury in criminal cases by an explicit amendment binding the states also. No attempt was made by Madison to include in this proposed amendment (which was rejected by the Senate) the right to the writ of *habeas corpus*. Yet this right of *habeas corpus* had been considered important enough to include in the original constitution. Perhaps it was thought that any detention or imprisonment in the United States, by whatever authority, could be called into question by a *habeas corpus* proceeding in a *federal* court. Thus, no further provision may have been thought necessary. (This would suggest that the rule of law was required of all governments in the country, even before the Fourteenth Amendment. See, e.g., *Federalist*, p. 291; chap. 4, n. 33, above.) Cf. *Bizup v. Tinsely*, 316 F.2d 284, 285 (1963).

Since trial by jury in criminal cases in federal courts was already provided for in the Constitution, no simple amendment to that effect was needed in the Bill of Rights, but rather elaborations of the jury trial guarantee in criminal cases as well as provision for it in civil cases. (If the jury trial amendments apply to the states as well as to the general government, there would have been no need for Madison to include a simple jury trial guarantee in the proposed amendment explicitly addressed to the states.)

See chap. 8, n. 50, below.

16. Graham Greene has reported:

> I went to a cinema [in Laredo, Texas] and saw William Powell and Annabella in *The Baroness and the Butler*—it wasn't any good; then I went to Pete's bar and had a brandy and Coca-Cola highball. Pete was a Greek and had been in America for thirty-seven years, but he couldn't speak enough English for you to notice it. Germany was a fine country, he said; America was no good at all; Greece wasn't so bad—his opinions puzzled me till I realised that he judged every country by its drink laws—I suppose, if you are in the business, that's as good a way as any other. We writers are apt to judge a country by freedom of the Press, and politicians by freedom of speech—it's the same, really. [Graham Greene, *The Lawless Roads* (London: W. Heinemann, 1955), p. 28]

Is it the same? Is what a man drinks and eats as vital to him as what he says and thinks? May not "we writers" happen to reflect the essential human being? See, e.g., chap. 7, n. 77, above.

CHAPTER EIGHT, NOTE 17: PAGE 209

[The virtuous man] needs, therefore, to be conscious of the existence of his friend as well, and this will be realized in their living together and sharing in discussion and thought; for this is what living together would seem to mean in the case of man, and not, as in the case of cattle, feeding in the same place. [Aristotle, *Nicomachean Ethics* 1170b10]

See Judah Halevi, *The Kuzari* (New York: Schocken Books, 1964), p. 243 ("If a nation perishes it is first the higher classes which disappear, and literature with them"). See, also, chap. 8, n. 10, above, chap. 8, n. 184, below.

Are "politicians [apt to judge a country] by freedom of speech" because they recognize the public role of reason, deliberation, and hence speech, if justice is to be secured by the community? (See sections 13 and 14 of this chapter.) Even a "band of robbers" must, if it is to survive, show some respect for justice (just as a healthy army purges its murderers). Plato, *Republic* 351C-D; Aristotle, *Nicomachean Ethics* 1167b5-15.

"Do we carve 'em up, Pinkie?" Dallow said. Spicer stood at the window watching the storm. He said nothing, staring out at the flames and chasms of the sky.
"Ask Spicer," [Pinkie] said. *"He's been doing a lot of thinking lately."* They all turned and watched Spicer. Spicer said: "Maybe we ought to lay off a while. You know a lot of the boys cleared out when Kite got killed."
"Go on," [Pinkie] said. "Listen to him. *He's what they call a philosopher."*
"Well," Spicer said angrily, *"there's free speech in this mob, ain't there?* . . . I was always against murder," Spicer said. "I don't care who knows it. What good's revenge? It's sentiment."
"Sour and milky," [Pinkie] said.
Spicer came into the middle of the room. "Listen, Pinkie," he said, *"Be reasonable."* He appealed to them all: *"Be reasonable."* [Graham Greene, *Brighton Rock* (New York: Viking Press, 1956), pp. 72-73; italics added]

Pinkie does use reason, in scheming how to protect himself, in working out ways of eliminating those whom he does not trust. (See chap. 8, n. 45, below.) But reason is not permitted full scope, that scope necessary to counter and control the passions which drive him to the destruction of himself and his associates. (Nor is reason given its due in Greene's work, in his reflections on [as distinguished from the execution of] his calling: that is, he is aware of more than he realizes.)

Is Greene's assignment of "freedom of speech" to politicians a legacy of the traditional parliamentary privilege? In any event, "Pete the Greek" sounds suspiciously like a George Bernard Shaw who has taken to drink. See chap. 2, n. 10, above.

17. Consider the English anticipation by almost a century of our Thirteenth Amendment:

. . . as the history of the writ of *Habeas Corpus* shows, Parliament and the common lawyers were careful to guard the principle of the thirty-ninth clause of the Great Charter, that a man could not be imprisoned except by due process of law. That in effect meant that any restraint of liberty must be proved to be legally justified, and that all restraints which could not be thus justified, were illegal. That this principle so stated, and safeguarded by the writ of *Habeas Corpus*, was a better protection to liberty than any number of abstract declarations of right, can be seen by the famous *Sommersett's Case* [(1771) 20 S.T. 1.], in which the idea that the status of slavery was recognized by English law was finally given its quietus. . . . Lord Mansfield, following a decision of Holt C. J. [*Smith* v. *Brown* (1707) 2 Salk. 666.], decided that [it] was not law [that a master could bring his slaves to England without losing his rights over them]; and that Harrison, in Elizabeth's reign, had correctly stated the law when he said that "if any [slaves] come hither from other realms, so soon as they set foot on land they become as free in condition as their masters." . . . I think the decision was largely due to maintenance of the view, that *any interference with liberty must be justified by law*. There was legal warrant for recognizing the status of a villein: there was none for recognizing the status of a slave. [William S. Holdsworth, *Some Lessons from Our Legal History* (New York: Macmillan Co., 1928), pp. 71-72; final italics added]

See Henry Street, *Freedom, the Individual and the Law* (London: Penguin Books, 1963), pp. 32-33. See, also, chap. 4, n. 33, above.

Burke considered "the common law, and the statute *Habeas Corpus*" "the sole securities either for liberty or justice." Edmund Burke, *Works*, World Classics (London: Oxford University Press, 1930), 2:248. See, on the suspension of the privilege of the writ of *habeas corpus*, ibid., 136, 142-43, 287; chap. 4, n. 59, above. See, also, Eugene V. Rostow, "The Robe That Fit like a Glove," *Book Week*, Feb. 6, 1966, p. 2; Lincoln, *Complete Works*, 2:39, 45, 54; Crosskey, *Politics and the Constitution*, p. 1129.

See, on due process of law in everyday affairs, Appendix C, above, and in academic affairs, Appendix E, above.

18. The censor can suppress on the basis of suspicion alone, to say nothing of whim. But the prosecutor of allegedly criminal writing must rely, if due process of law is at all respected, on more than mere suspicion to sustain his burden of proof. See Leo Strauss, *Persecution and the Art of Writing* (Glencoe, Ill.: Free Press, 1952), pp. 24-26. One finds in Strauss's discussion the usually unarticulated premises of the principal argument against "previous restraints." See chap. 5, nn. 90, 106, above. See, also, chap. 5, n. 10, chap. 6, n. 26, above.

I had occasion, during a visit in the summer of 1967 in Athens with Helen Vlachou (the Greek publisher who had refused to publish her newspapers under the colonels' censorship) to prepare at her request the following memorandum:

> Anyone familiar with the Anglo-American tradition of "liberty of the press" appreciates the importance for friends of liberty of an insistence upon "no previous restraints." That is, the effort in the 18th and 19th Centuries to establish and secure the liberty of the press was, in large part, an effort to protect the right of anyone to publish whatever he chose without any prior control by government of the contents of such publication. It was accepted that there could be, when something was published contrary to the law of the time or disliked by the government of the day, prosecution of the offending publisher. But it was nevertheless thought that such prosecution was not as destructive of the common good or as offensive to personal dignity as a prior review by the government of the contents of publication. Indeed, some publishers have always preferred the safety of censorship to the risk of undertaking the obligation of deciding in each case what could be responsibly and safely published.
>
> What is or should be prosecuted after publication depends on particular circumstances, both social and personal. It should be remembered that the censor's prior restraint may be completely arbitrary and without any challenge, while the punishment for publication has at least the safeguard (except in the most oppressive regimes) of some judicial process in open court. It should be remembered as well that self-regulation recognizes the dignity and sense of responsibility of the publisher.
>
> In the best of all worlds, there would be neither censorship (previous restraint) nor any punishment for honest publication. But it is certainly important that there at least be no censorship, leaving the publisher free to run the risks of honest publication.

It is significant that these observations, drawing on the centuries-old Atlantic tradition, made sense to Mrs. Vlachou, who had been obliged to work out similar arguments that summer on the shores of the Mediterranean. See chap. 8, n. 51, below, for a similar argument alluded to by Justice Frankfurter. Mrs. Vlachou was arrested shortly after our meeting. Her account of her adventures is recorded in *House Arrest* (Boston: Gambit, 1970), which I reviewed for the *Chicago Sun-Times*, June 24, 1970, p. 47. See chap. 6, n. 1, above. I included in my review the following observations which, with appropriate adjustments to our circumstances, should be taken to heart as well by American conservatives and liberals alike:

CHAPTER EIGHT, NOTE 18: PAGE 209

[Mrs. Vlachou] has, among other things, a gift for the apt image, as is indicated by her observation that the colonels have "hijacked the country," a seizure made possible by "the arms NATO had confided to them to protect Greece from real danger." This hijacking, it must be added, was also made possible by the imprudent feuding from 1963 to 1967 of the politicians, press and Palace of Greece. What makes Greece both exciting and vulnerable is the existence there of a sense of self-importance: each Greek is prepared to lead his country to glory; few are prepared to submerge themselves (except in the face of foreign invasion) to a common purpose. Liberals conveniently detected such an invasion in the maneuverings in Athens of the American C.I.A. Conservatives were more effective in conjuring up foreign threats, partly because of the distorting legacy in Greece of a cruel civil war a generation ago: they could, Mrs. Vlachou admits, publish "whipped-up warnings of 'Communist danger'—always a useful pre-election vote winner for the parties of the right, in which we [her newspapers] had also indulged." That is, she seems to recognize now the irresponsibility of such thoughtlessly partisan tactics. She has yet to recognize in print the extent to which Greek liberals feared and resented (with some justification) the oppressiveness of the police, particularly outside Athens, an oppressiveness which Vassilis Vassilikos portrays so well in his novel, Z. But there were at least available in the world of Z unfettered journalists and jurists—unlike conditions in Greece today. Traditional political rivals in Greece do concede these days that they have much more in common with one another than any of them has with the colonels. However responsible Mrs. Vlachou may have been in contributing to the political paranoia and the self-righteousness of the colonels (they were among her most devoted readers), she was perceptive enough to see that such upstart extremists could not be the saviours of Greece—and she was courageous enough, while others preferred to see in the colonels a useful solution to a disruptive constitutional crisis, immediately to declare herself in opposition to them. . . .

(See chap. 5, n. 124, above, for my review of a book by one of Mrs. Vlachou's political rivals, Andreas Papandreou.)

What may be done to suppress suspect doctrines when legal procedure need not be relied upon and when the authorities have access to sanctions that touch the souls of men is suggested by the pronouncement in 1276 of the bishop of Paris:

> We have received frequent reports . . . to the effect that some students of the arts in Paris are exceeding the boundaries of their own faculty and are presuming to treat and discuss, as if they were debatable in the schools, certain obvious and loathsome errors. . . . These students are not hearkening to the admonition of Gregory, "Let him who would speak wisely exercise great care, lest by his speech he disrupt the unity of his listeners," particularly when in support of the aforesaid errors they adduce pagan writings that—shame on their ignorance—they assert to be so convincing that they do not know how to answer them. . . . We excommunicate all those who shall have taught the said errors or any one of them, or shall have dared in any way to defend or uphold them, or even to listen to them, unless they choose to reveal themselves to us or to the chancery of Paris within seven days; in addition to which we shall proceed against them by inflicting such other penalties as the law requires according to the nature of the offense. [Lerner and Mahdi, *Medieval Political Philosophy*, p. 337]

See chap. 7, n. 120, above, chap. 9, n. 7, below.

Consider, also, the explanation of the death in 1953 of Lavrenti Beria, as Nikita Khrushchev is said to have given it to a French socialist:

> Very soon after the death of Stalin we in the Presidium began to get reports of some double game which Beria was playing. We began to have him followed and in a few weeks we established the fact that our suspicions were justified. He was clearly preparing a conspiracy against the Presidium. After waiting for a favorable moment, we designated a special session of the Presidium, to which, of course, Beria was invited, too. He appeared, apparently not suspecting

that we knew anything. And right there we began to cross question him, to adduce facts, data, to put questions to him, in other words, we put him through a cross examination which lasted four hours.

For all of us it was clear that he was really guilty, and that this man could be dangerous to the party and the country.

We left him alone in the room, in this very room in which we are now conversing, with him sitting on the very chair on which you are sitting now. And we went into another room and there had a discussion of what should be done with him.

Our inner conviction of his guilt was unshakable. *But at that time we did not have at our disposal a sufficient amount of juridical evidence of his guilt.* And we found ourselves in a difficult position. *Evidence for his consignment to a court we still did not have,* yet to leave him at liberty was impossible.

We came to the unanimous decision that the only correct measure for the defense of the Revolution was to shoot him immediately. This decision was adopted by us, and carried out on the spot.

But we felt much easier when, some time after his condemnation we received sufficient and irrefutable evidence of his guilt. [Bertram D. Wolfe, *Khrushchev and Stalin's Ghost* (New York: Frederick A. Praeger, 1957), pp. 316-17; italics added]

See *Newsweek*, Jan. 19, 1970, p. 45. Cf. chap. 7, nn. 74, 75, above.

See Leslie Stephen, *An Agnostic's Apology* (London: Smith, Elder & Co., 1893), pp. 269-70. See, also, *Federalist*, p. 288; chap. 3, n. 33, chap. 6, n. 59, above.

19. See, also, Henry Adams, *John Randolph*, American Statesmen (Boston: Houghton Mifflin Co., 1890), pp. 140-43; chap. 5, n. 93, above. Compare Justice Harlan's opinion in *Cohen* v. *Hurley*, 366 U.S. 117 (1961), endorsing the shocking unlawyerlike decision by a bar grievance committee deliberately to circumvent established disbarment procedures. (This case was argued and decided the same days as my bar admission case.) Cf. *Malloy* v. *Hogan*, 378 U.S. 1 (1964); *Spevack* v. *Klein*, 385 U.S. 511 (1967); *Uniformed Sanitation Men Ass'n* v. *Commissioner of Sanitation*, 392 U.S. 280 (1968); *Gardner* v. *Broderick*, 392 U.S. 273 (1968) (which includes, at page 277 of Justice Fortas's opinion for the Court, a description of the *Spevack* case as holding that "a lawyer could not be disbarred solely because he refused to testify at a disciplinary proceeding on the ground that his testimony would tend to incriminate him"). Burke, in the course of a valuable discussion of the dangers of a partial suspension of *habeas corpus* (*Works* 2:248-49), calls the common law and the *Habeas Corpus* Act "the sole securities either for liberty or justice." *Habeas corpus*, it can be said, guarantees that everyone arrested will be either tried or released; the common law prescribes what may be done at one's trial. (See, for the guarantees of the Fourteenth Amendment in this respect, chap. 8, n. 83, below.)

See chap. 2, n. 18, above.

20. Dissenting in *Frank* v. *Mangum*, 237 U.S. 309, 347 (1915). Critical to our conception of "due process" and of "a fair trial" is the understanding implicit in our rules of evidence about the nature of the world, about how the truth may be learned about it, and about how men's limitations and interests are likely to affect our efforts as a community to learn for practical purposes what happened in particular circumstances. See chap. 8, n. 51, below.

Perhaps there should be included here, if only to make meaningful the "opportunity to be heard," that privilege which has been regarded as "perhaps the privilege most important to the person accused of crime, connected with his trial, [which] is that to be defended by counsel." Cooley, *Constitutional Limitations*, p. 696.

See, for Erskine's insistence upon this privilege, chap. 7, n. 74, above. Judicial implementation of it may be found in *Gideon* v. *Wainwright*, 372 U.S. 335 (1963). See Anthony Lewis, *Gideon's Trumpet* (New York: Random House, 1964). (It should be noted that Cooley considered *habeas corpus* "one of the principal safeguards to personal liberty" (p. 709), even though he devoted far less space to it than to other rights. On the other hand, the basic principle of *habeas corpus*, the rule of law, is reflected in the very constitutions to which his voluminous work is devoted.) The right against self-incrimination, which has attracted so much interest in recent years, may be fitted in here as still another incident of a fair trial and, hence, of that rule of law which requires the government to make its case independent of what the defendant may be compelled to say. Holdsworth (*Some Lessons from Our Legal History*, p. 60) considered it as "probable that the words 'by the law of the land' mean, as Coke said, 'by due process of law.' . . . "

21. See, e.g., chap. 4, n. 33, above. Cf. Thomas S. Schrock, "The Liberal Court, the Conservative Court, and Constitutional Jurisprudence," in Robert A. Goldwin, ed., *Left, Right and Center: Essays on Liberalism and Conservatism in the United States* (Chicago: Rand McNally, 1965), p. 87.

> . . . One legal aspect of Nuremberg, hardly touched on by the jurists who have commented on the jurisprudence of Nuremberg, nearly wrecked the satisfactory outcome of the trial. The British, in their overweening sense of the exclusive fairness of the English criminal trial system, wanted to impose upon the International Military Tribunal the English rules of evidence. Had that been done all hearsay evidence and a mass of documentary evidence would have been inadmissible at the trial, thus almost certainly leading to the acquittal of the accused—a result that could hardly have been more disastrous once a trial had been embarked upon.
> The legal advisers at the Home Office and the Foreign Office fought this battle with Lord Wright, chairman of the United Nations War Crimes Commission, who, though a Law Lord, favoured jettisoning the English rules in favour of the Continental system which makes all relevant evidence admissible. Ultimately, the Lord Chancellor . . . came down heavily on Lord Wright's side, and the possibility of a nonsensical trial was obviated. And so Nuremberg became added to the short list of those portions of English law where the strict laws of evidence are disregarded, as they are in bankruptcy and matters of Exchange Control. . . . [John Foster, Q.C., M.P., "In Defence of Nuremberg," *London Observer*, July 8, 1962]

See, for the procedures and rules of evidence of British commissions under the Tribunals Act, Stanley W. Baron, *The Contact Man* (London: Secker & Warburg, 1966).

22. See Emil Brunner, *Revelation and Reason* (Philadelphia: Westminster Press, 1946), pp. 330-31:

> [I]t lies in the very nature of that which is according to law, that it is sure of itself only so long as it can "walk by law." Legalism and rationality are inseparable. That which transcends law also transcends reason. . . . Love is the suprarational element which leaps over all barriers, which goes forth to the "other" for his own sake, which will sacrifice himself for the "thou," but not for an ideal. In the last resort, therefore, rational morality can create only people who are governed by "duty," but not those who are controlled by love. . . .

See Montesquieu, *The Persian Letters*, No. 14. See, also, chap. 7, n. 120, above.

The city characterized by the rule of reason (in Plato's *Republic*) is distinguished by the suppression of the manifestations of love as commonly understood (e.g., the possession of one's own spouse and children; see chap. 8, n. 30, below). Cf. Plato, *Banquet*. See chap. 5, n. 126, above. See, also, Pierre Vallières, *Negres Blancs d'Amerique* (Montreal: Editions Parti Pris, 1969), pp. 223-24 (chap. 3, sec. 9).

23. Is this an attempt, which must ultimately fail, to make reason and society completely compatible? See chap. 9, sec. 4, above. Does not the Anglo-American detective story represent a popular celebration of just such an attempt? (Does the attraction of espionage stories reflect the contemporary problem of divided political allegiances? See, on John Buchan's *Thirty-nine Steps*, chap. 8, n. 150, below. The popularity of sports can be seen as a reflection of the common man's alienation, in an impersonally industrialized world, from serious politics *and* drama. See chap. 7, n. 112, above.) See chap. 8, nn. 96, 135, below.

See chap. 4, n. 15, chap. 6, n. 51, above.

24. I have referred (chap. 4, n. 103, above) to eighteenth-century passages in which the British government was regarded as a monarchical republic. See Burke, *Works*, 4:138; cf. Paine, *Writings*, 1:72, 83; 2:387-88, 421-22.

A true monarchy can be thought of as that form of government in which one man rules, not always by the use of law but always (and in this way he is distinguished from the tyrant) in the interest of the community. See, e.g., Plato, *Republic* 345B-347A. Ames "contemplated [the American] Government as a Government of laws, and not of men. The makers of them could command nothing as to themselves; the Executive, with the Judges, were those who exercised the authority of the law. . . ." *Annals*, I, p. 909. See Hobbes, *Leviathan*, chap. 21; F. A. Hayek, *The Constitution of Liberty* (Chicago: University of Chicago Press, 1960), p. 462, n. 37.

See, on the submission of royal power to wisdom and justice, Shakespeare, *Henry IV, Part 2*, act 5, sc. 2, ll. 65-121. Cf. ibid., act 4, sc. 2. See, also, ibid., act 5, sc. 5, ll. 46, 50 ("I know thee not, old man. . . . But being awak'd, I do despise my dream").

25. One might even see in this historical sequence some of the considerations that went into the making (and acceptance) of the "clear and present danger" test. For although this test is unconstitutional, it does recognize and attempt to deal with problems that no people can long ignore. The troubles we have had, I have argued, arise in part from the failure of our constitutional authorities to maintain for the states their proper place in our constitutional order. See chap. 8, n. 83, below.

Many of the state constitutions, it should be noted, have their bill of rights provisions at the front of the instrument. There is, it seems, no need to establish first that the local community exists. See, e.g., chap. 8, n. 71, below. See, also, chap. 4, n. 53, above.

See, on the origin of the "clear and present danger" test, Appendix B, above.

26. Daniel Webster, *The Works of Daniel Webster* (Boston: Little, Brown & Co., 1869), 2:393. See Burke, *Works*, 4:3-14, 36-37, 102-3, 147, 272; 5:34-40, 132.

Charles I, in his refusal of January 21, 1649, to recognize the court established to try him, argued:

> . . . For how can any free-born subject of England call life or anything he possesseth his own, if power without right daily make new and abrogate the old fundamental laws of the land—which I now take to be the present case? . . . There is no proceeding just against any man but what is warranted either by God's laws or the municipal laws of the country where he lives. Now I am most confident this day's proceeding cannot be warranted by God's laws; for, on the contrary, the authority of obedience unto kings is clearly warranted and strictly commanded in both the Old and New Testament. . . . Then for the law of this land, I am no less confident that no learned lawyer will affirm that an impeachment can lie against the king, they all going in his name. And one of their maxims is that the king can do no wrong. . . . Thus you see that I speak not for my own right alone . . . , but also for the true liberty of all my subjects— which consists, not in the power of government, but in living under such laws, such a government, as may give themselves the best assurance of their lives and property of their goods. . . . [C. Stephenson and F. G. Marcham, eds., *Sources of English Constitutional History* (New York: Harper & Row, 1937), p. 517]

The right of revolution, it should be noted, may be warranted by something other than either "God's law or the municipal laws of [a] country." See pp. 331-32, chap. 7, n. 77, above. See, also, pp. 417-18, above. Cf. Burke, *Works*, 2:226-27.

27. The *habeas corpus* discussion referred to is at Blackstone, *Laws of England*, 3:379-83.

Respect for the law is said to be more deeply ingrained in the British than in the American character. An English police officer reported a conversation, before the Second World War, with several policemen in New York:

> But when I told them that killings in broad daylight on the streets of London

CHAPTER EIGHT, NOTE 28: PAGE 212   685

would be unthinkable and they asked me why, I said that from all I could gather, in New York especially, if a killing took place where others could see, the others all fled the scene. In London they'd chase a culprit till they chased him down, many outraged women joining in the pursuit. This seemed to amuse the police officers a great deal. [Walter Henry Thompson, *Assignment: Churchill* (New York: Popular Library, 1961), p. 112]

See, also, ibid., p. 114. Cf. chap. 7, n. 16, above, chap. 9, n. 10, below.

See "Father Killed in Bank Raid," *London Times*, June 30, 1967, p. 1. "Mr. Jenkins, Home Secretary, agreed . . . that the shooting did raise difficult questions about when it was right to 'have a go.' " *London Times*, July 1, 1967, p. 1. Cf. *Time*, Aug. 18, 1967, p. 60 ("Non-involvement, British Style").

The salutary effect of having the law of the land applicable in all cases is pointed up in Mike Royko's column of June 11, 1969, in the *Chicago Daily News* (the summer before the "Chicago Conspiracy Trial" opened in federal court [Appendix D, below]):

> The city administration [of Chicago] has found itself in a delightfully foolish position. Namely: Boy Scouts cannot camp overnight in a city park. For years the scouts have been doing it, with the approval of the Park District. Every June, hundreds of them gathered for a big weekend in Marquette Park, on the Southwest Side, pitching their tents, cooking their food, sleeping outdoors at night. That's the best part of scouting. . . . But this year for the first time, they were told they had to be out of the park by 11 o'clock at night. They could do their thing during the day, but at night they would have to leave. So on Friday and Saturday nights, hundreds of scouts got in their parents' cars and drove home. In the mornings, they got back in the cars and were driven to the campsite. That is not exactly in keeping with the spirit of scouting. It made little sense to some of the kids and their parents. After all, what is a park for, if not to be used by the people? And what better use could there be than letting hundreds of kids camp on the grass, 'neath the whispering leaves, awakening to the sounds of birds and the crackling of bacon? And why, a few asked, were they ordered out this year, but not past years?
>
> Everybody knows the answer to that—or they should. It is against the law to be in a city park after 11 o'clock. Of course, the law was not rigidly enforced in past years because it is an impractical law. There can be many excellent reasons—such as the scout camp—for people to be in the parks after 11 p.m. But it had to be enforced this year because the mayor could have been embarrassed by those scouts. Remember, last August? Some people wanted to camp overnight in Lincoln Park. Just like the scouts, they wanted to sleep in the great outdoors, sing songs, talk, and all that. But these were antiwar demonstrators so the city dug out an obscure law and decided to enforce it. The administration was inflexible. When the people didn't get out after 11 o'clock, they were gassed, beaten and chased through nearby streets. After that internationally acclaimed bit of statesmanship by the mayor, he couldn't turn around in less than a year and decide the same law didn't apply to Boy Scouts. That would have been an admission his motives were more complex than just enforcing a pointless curfew. . . .
>
> Many of the scouts and their parents were disappointed, irritated and angry. Some said it is possible they won't hold the camp in the park next year. But they shouldn't feel that way. After all, most of them live on the far Southwest Side. And that part of town gave the mayor strong and affectionate support last August when he routed decent people from Lincoln Park. That's the one democratic aspect of injustice. If enough people support it, then everybody finally gets it.

28. Is not this essentially the position of Thrasymachus in the first book of Plato's *Republic*? The modern Thrasymachus is the lawyer attracted to the power promised by the rhetorical devices of legal realism. See, e.g., Edward H. Levi, "An Introduction to Legal Reasoning," *U. Chicago L. Rev.* 15 (Spring 1948): 501. Cf. Anastaplo, "Natural Right and the American Lawyer," *Wis. L. Rev.*, 1965, p. 322, nn. 3, 35. See chap. 5,

n. 43, above. See, also, chap. 2, n. 31, chap. 4, n. 32, above, chap. 8, nn. 122, 181, chap. 9, n. 13, below.

See *Alfarabi's Philosophy of Plato and Aristotle*, ed. Muhsin Mahdi (New York: Free Press of Glencoe, 1962), pp. 44-47, 56-57, 66-67, 88-92. Cf. ibid., pp. 48-49, p. 130 ("Therefore philosophy must necessarily come into being in every man in the way possible for him"). See, also, chap. 8, n. 135, below.

29. Tocqueville, *Democracy in America*, 1:285. Consider the proviso noted by Pritchett in *The American Constitution* (New York: McGraw-Hill, 1968), p. 534, in his discussion of the Internal Security Act of 1950 (also known as the McCarran Act):

> Section 4 provides: "It shall be unlawful for any person knowingly to combine, conspire, or agree with any other person to perform any act which would substantially contribute to the establishment within the United States of a totalitarian dictatorship." There is a proviso that this language does not apply "to the proposal of a Constitutional amendment." . . . But such a loose definition of sedition is rather clearly unconstitutional, and the Department of Justice has brought no prosecutions under section 4.

See chap. 4, n. 27, above.

Does not the British insistence on search warrants reflect the emphasis on the rule of law as seen by Tocqueville? Little is said about the standards to be applied by the magistrate in issuing the warrant; rather, the critical point usually is that the warrant must be obtained, that the officer must proceed according to form.

> The first eight months of the Protectorate were a quiet season in England, but to an observer there were ugly movements in the air. An ordinance early in the year [1654] had made it treason to conspire against, or to speak evil of [Cromwell's] person and government, and the law was strictly enforced. Men went to gaol for its breach, and, since a trial would have meant their condemnation and death, [Cromwell] kept them untried in confinement—a piece of humanity which did him no good with the people: he would have consulted his own interests better if he had permitted batches of Fifth Monarchists and Levellers to be hanged. England loved neither group, but she loved still less arbitrary imprisonment. . . . [John Buchan, *Oliver Cromwell* (London: Holder & Stoughton, 1934), p. 445]

See Jacob Klein, "The Problem of Freedom," *The College* (St. John's College), Dec. 1969, pp. 4, 6-7. See, also, Paine, *Wrtngs*, 1:204, 253; 2:296, 334.

30. Rousseau, *The Social Contract and Discourses* (Everyman Edition; New York: E. P. Dutton & Co., 1950), pp. 311-12; cf. pp. 251-52; Tocqueville, *The Old Regime and the French Revolution* (New York: Doubleday & Co., Anchor Books, 1955), pp. 112-13; Herbert Hoover, "The Fifth Freedom," *The Rotarian* (Apr. 1943) (reprinted in Alpheus T. Mason, *Free Government in the Making* [New York: Oxford University Press, 1965], p. 819). See chap. 9, n. 33, below ("the typical mistake of the conservative").

The pervasiveness (as well as the potential pettiness) of possessiveness is reflected in two sayings quoted by Sancho Panza: "And to whatever the governor may say there's no answer to be made, any more than there is to 'Get out of my house' or 'What do you want with my wife?'" Cervantes, *Don Quixote* (New York: Viking Press, 1949), p. 787. But one begins to unravel the assumptions by which the notion of private property is held together if one wonders what should happen when it is the governor himself who is in "my house" or who "wants my wife." That is, what, other than the law (and hence the governor) legitimates the "my" or permits (and assists) me to retain "my house" and "my wife" against all comers? Cf. chap. 2, n. 17, above. See chap. 8, n. 193, below.

See chap. 5, n. 126, chap. 7, n. 115, chap. 8, n. 10, above. See, also, chap. 7, nn. 9, 36, 63, 77, 113, 116, above. Consider the difficulties in Burke's assurance (*Works*, 4:36), "[The idea of inheritance] leaves acquisition free, but it secures what it acquires."

31. Milton, *The Prose Works of John Milton* (London: J. Johnson, 1806), 1:42. See, for its reflection in Magna Carta, Bagehot, *English Constitution*, p. 249.

The importance of "goods and purses" is recognized in the call today for "freedom from want." (See chap. 5, n. 155, above.) Cf. Plutarch, *Lives*, pp. 235-36 (with respect to Alcibiades); Plato, *Laws* 679B-C. See Appendix C, above.

32. One of Virginia's Stamp Act resolves read:

> *Resolved*, That the taxation of the people by themselves, or by persons chosen by themselves to represent them, who can only know what taxes the people are able to bear, or the easiest method of raising them, and must themselves be affected by every tax laid on the people, is the only security against a burdensome taxation, and the distinguishing characteristick of British freedom, without which the ancient constitution cannot exist. ["The Virginia Resolves on the Stamp Act (May 30, 1765)," in Samuel Eliot Morison, *Sources and Documents Illustrating the American Revolution, 1764-1788, and the Formation of the Federal Constitution* (London: Oxford University Press, 1962), p. 17]

(See *Federalist*, pp. 215, 373, 422. See the *Chicago Tribune*, Sept. 16, 1961, p. 4, on prominent politicians who have evaded paying the taxes they helped to lay. See, also, chap. 5, n. 55, above.)

> Let these truths be indelibly impressed on our minds—that we cannot be happy without being free—that we cannot be free without being secure in our property—that we cannot be secure in our property if without our consent others may as by right take it away—that taxes imposed on us by Parliament do thus take it away.... [John Dickinson (1768), in Morison, *Sources*, p. 53]

See, also, ibid., p. 91; Burke, *Works* 2:185-86, 204-5, 225-26.

See Cooley, *Constitutional Limitations*, p. 76, citing Francis Bacon's essay, "The True Greatness of Kingdoms and Estates." See, also, Tocqueville, *Old Regime*, pp. 98-99, 105.

George Mason observed in the Constitutional Convention that he "considered the caution observed in Great Britain [in requiring periodical enactment of revenue acts] as the paladium of the public liberty." Farrand, *Records*, 2:327.

Consider, also, "the formulation [by Alexander Hamilton] in *The Continentalist* of 1782, concerning tax laws: 'The genius of liberty reprobates everything arbitrary or discretionary in taxation. It exacts that every man by a definite and general rule should know what proportion of his property the state demands.'" Gerald Stourzh, *Alexander Hamilton and the Idea of Republican Government* (Stanford: Stanford University Press, 1970), p. 227, n. 83.

33. I say "respectable," since the less judicious Hobbes had already expressed essentially the opinions that Locke domesticated. See chap. 8, n. 135, below.

34. See John Locke, *Second Treatise of Government*, secs. 3, 6, 12, 123, 124, 222; also, secs. 149, 228, 229. See, also, the passage from Madison's *Essay on Property* reproduced in Mason and Beaney, *American Constitutional Law*, p. 290, and the passage from John Marshall reproduced in chap. 6, n. 63, above ("the *property* of the press").

The seriousness, and hence reliability, that has come to be associated with property (as we now know it) is suggested by that curious phrase, "a good-faith pocketbook action" (see, e.g., Justice Jackson's opinion for the Court, Doremus v. *Board of Education*, 342 U.S. 429, 434 [1952]). Justice Frankfurter's dissenting opinion, in Adler v. *Board of Education*, 342 U.S. 485, 501, 503 (1952), stands upon the solid "pocketbook action" phrase and attempts to reinforce it with such expressions as "earthy stuff" and "the immediacy and solidity of interest necessary to support jurisdiction." See chap. 8, n. 13, above.

Is not Hamlet moved to attempt, in the passage discussed at chap. 2, n. 39, above, to reduce human life to the material substratum of things? See chap. 9, n. 39, below.

35. Consider the implications of these illustrations (which the context does moderate somewhat):

> ... the preservation of the army, and in it of the whole commonwealth, re-

> quires an absolute obedience to the command of every superior officer, and it is justly death to disobey or dispute the most dangerous or unreasonable of them; but yet we see that neither the sergeant, that could command a soldier to march up to the mouth of a cannon or stand in a breach where he is almost sure to perish, can command that soldier to give him one penny of his money; nor the general, that can condemn him to death for deserting his post or for not obeying the most desperate orders, can yet, with all his absolute power of life and death, dispose of one farthing of that soldier's estate or seize one jot of his goods, whom yet he can command anything and hang for the least disobedience. Because such a blind obedience is necessary to that end for which the commander has his power, viz., the preservation of the rest; but the disposing of his goods has nothing to do with it. [Locke, *Second Treatise of Government*, sec. 139]

See, also, Blackstone, *Laws of England*, 4:402-3; Burke, *Works*, 4:55-56, 115 ff., 167-73, 321-22; 5:98-99; chap. 7, n. 66, chap. 8, n. 16, above, chap. 8, n. 179, below.

See Robert Goldwin, "John Locke," in Strauss and Cropsey, *History of Political Philosophy*, pp. 433, 465-66.

See, for John Quincy Adams's version of the combined influence of Machiavelli-Locke and St. Paul, p. 244, above.

36. Leon Trotsky, *The Revolution Betrayed* (Garden City, N.Y.: Doubleday, Doran & Co., 1937), p. 76. See, also, Milton Friedman, *Capitalism and Freedom* (Chicago: University of Chicago Press, 1962), p. 7; Hayek, *Constitution of Liberty*, pp. 125-30, 447, n. 7. *Federalist* No. 79 anticipated such sentiments with the observation, "In the general course of human nature, a power over a man's subsistence amounts to a power over his will." Cf. chap. 7, n. 115, above.

"It seems an inescapable conclusion that the New Deal's practice of making special investigations of the income-tax payments of individuals and groups which opposed it is an instance of a trend toward economic excommunication." Richard M. Weaver, *Ideas Have Consequences* (Chicago: University of Chicago Press, 1948), p. 135. See Clayton Fritchey, "[Internal Revenue Service] Feathering Hawks' Nest?" *Chicago Sun-Times*, Mar. 5, 1966, p. 20. See, also, chap. 4, n. 11, chap. 6, nn. 50, 62, above.

> One of the more extraordinary invasions of individual privacy is the modern income tax. I am aware that this example will appear ludicrous to some, yet I am convinced that it has a very serious side. If we take a detached view and realize the extent to which it places everybody under surveillance, we are amazed at what it assumes. I am familiar with the arguments for it on political and humanitarian grounds. What I am pointing out is that this tax makes the individual's entire economic and financial life subject to annual government audit. It is just as if we were all criminals out on parole, required once a year to file an affidavit of our doings before a public official. The fact to be pondered is that arguments against the income tax based on the right to privacy would be dismissed as trivial or irrelevant. The claim to privacy would simply not supply any leverage. The decline of privacy is traceable, to the best of my perception, to a belief that man is or should be one-dimensional. There should be no depths, no recesses, no area of being that cannot be unfolded simply. . . . [Richard M. Weaver, "Individuality and Modernity," in Felix Morley, ed., *Essays on Individuality* (Philadelphia: University of Pennsylvania Press, 1958), p. 73]

(Are not the decline of privacy and the decline of serious religious sentiment related to one another? Cf. chap. 8, n. 18, above.) See chap. 8, n. 4, above. Cf. chap. 5, n. 28, above.

I was glad, in 1955, to be able to take refuge, at a time when employment possibilities had been severely curtailed by my bar admission difficulties, in the private pursuit of driving a taxicab. (See Appendix F, section 2, above.) Refuges seemed to be available as well at that time in certain kinds of farming and in ordinary moneymaking (i.e., business) as well as on the fringes of academic life. It would have been quite useful, of course, to have had a private fortune or, better still (see chap. 8, n. 37, below), friends with fortunes. See, on the limits of privacy, chap. 8, n. 193, chap. 9, n. 3, below.

See Appendix C, above. Cf. chap. 2, n. 3, above.

37. But this (Plato would have us notice) is said (in bk. 1 of the *Republic*) to a man (Socrates) notorious for his poverty and, according to some, for his eminent virtue.

It should also be noticed, however, that Socrates had something better than wealth—that is, friends with wealth, which meant that he did not have to care for the wealth that he benefited from. (After all, is it not better in a large city to have friends with automobiles than to have one oneself? And, in return, may not one's friends benefit from what one can learn or do because one is not encumbered by material possessions? See Xenophon, *Memorabilia* 2.9; Aristotle, *Nicomachean Ethics* 1120b17-19; chap. 7, n. 115, above.)

To have (or at least to make) money is regarded by many among us as a sign of virtue. Thus, for example, the simplest means available to us today of reforming our urban police departments may be immediately to double police salaries: we would need fewer police as a consequence, since they would become full-time public servants, better trained and better regarded (both by themselves and by others). It is likely that we would make better use of them, thereafter, if only because one is much more apt to use carefully what is expensive. That is, many of the police abuses we now see are due to the fact that police manpower is cheap: it can be misused and wasted. Either we should pay the police much more or (if police work could be transformed into a sacred vocation) much less than we do now: the former is, in our circumstances, much more practical. Cf. Colin MacInnes, *Mr. Love and Justice* (New York: Ballentine Books, 1970.)

It is sometimes alleged that the wealthy or the managers of wealth (e.g., corporation executives) are the real rulers of the United States, that they are the ones who control the decisive public opinion. But it is my impression, from the "rich and powerful" I have known, that they, too, have their opinions shaped for them by others: indeed, they seem as much moved by the things that move the public as "the man in the street." How, then, *is* public opinion shaped in this country, by chance or by those who know? Only in the latter case may one properly speak of "real rulers." See Plato, *Crito* 443; *Republic* 489B-C. (And if we are ruled by those who know, are they our contemporaries or our predecessors or have they always been? See chap. 7, n. 77, above.)

This bears as well on the problem, considered by some to be vital, of who should own the means of publication. (Cf. chap. 8, n. 18, above.) Are not the antitrust laws and a required diversity of ownership of newspapers and radio and television stations (in a locality) a safer assurance of an open forum than any government intervention which would tend to be based on partisan judgments about the quality of the ideas being promulgated? See Herbert Wechsler, "Toward Neutral Principles of Constitutional Law," *Harvard L. Rev.* 73 (1959): 1. See, also, chap. 5, n. 134, above.

The current insistence upon the government's assuring "access" for all to the means of publication is based not only upon a kind of economic determinism but also upon a striving for equality and for the justice equality represents or contributes to. But liberty (and the justice *it* makes possible) may suffer in the process: is there not always likely to be a serious enough difference between those in power and those out of power (poor and rich alike, of whatever color or creed they may be) to warrant continuing to put the emphasis (as does the First Amendment) upon *restraining* the government? Has a naïve materialism (as well as a long and fortunate experience) obscured for some of us the brute fact of tyranny? See chap. 6, n. 1, above, chap. 9, n. 26, below.

See, also, the passage from Cicero in the text at chap. 2, n. 11, above; chap. 8, nn. 70, 79, below.

38. Noah Webster, "An Examination into the Leading Principles of the Federal Constitution" (Philadelphia, 1787) in Paul Leicester Ford, *Pamphlets on the Constitution of the United States, Published during Its Discussion by the People 1787-1789* (New York: DaCapa, 1968), p. 57. All italics in the quotations from Webster are his.

It is reassuring to see Congress retain its power over the purse, even as exhibited in the necessity of congressional authorization for reimbursement or compensation of relatively small amounts not already provided for by law. (See, e.g., *Congressional Record*, 116: S12579-S12593 [Aug. 3, 1970], with respect to payments of such sums as $3,628.22, $751.50, $1,506.49, $1,500, $1,034.50, $76.32, $2,135.28.) See chap. 4, n. 42, above, for the legislative equivalent of the casual assumption by the feeble but wealthy Cephalus in Book I of the *Republic,* that if *he* cannot travel to town, neither can (i.e., may) the sons dependent upon him.

39. This and the three long quotations that follow from Noah Webster may be found at pages 58-61 of Ford's collection.

See John Taylor, *An Inquiry into the Principles and Policy of the Government of the United States* (Fredericksburg, Va.: Green & Cady, 1814), pp. 51-52, 244, 274-75, 325-32, 395-97, 655-56.

40. The requirements, and effects, of efficient technology are such as to require not only very large communities but also extensive commerce (and hence contact) among communities. See, e.g., Adam Smith, *An Inquiry into the Natural Causes of the Wealth of Nations* (New York: Random House, Modern Library, 1937), pp. 17-18, 70-71. Cf. Tocqueville, *Democracy in America,* 1:442-43; chap. 7, n. 122, above. See, also, chap. 7, n. 35, above.

41. A candidate promises that he will, if elected governor, go about the country inducing large corporations to build new plants in his state. He proposes, in effect, to improve the economic condition in one state at the expense of other states. Insofar as all governors should be equally adept in such salesmanship, the distribution of plants would remain unchanged. The success of any governor would likely mean that something other than the relevant economic considerations had affected the distribution: thus, chance rather than the rationalization of industry would tend to govern and considerable unpredictable fluctuation would likely result, to the detriment of the economy of the national community. (Cf. Huey P. Long, *Every Man a King* [Chicago: Quadrangle Books, 1964], p. 334: "[E]xcept for being a part of the United States, [Louisiana] would never have known a depression.")

42. I say *"certain"* passions" because of the implications of this passage from Adam Smith (*Wealth of Nations,* p. 12):

> Compared, indeed, with the more extravagant luxury of the great, [the European workman's] accommodation must no doubt appear extremely simple and easy; and yet it may be true, perhaps, that the accommodation of an European prince does not always so much exceed that of an industrious and frugal peasant, as the accommodation of the latter exceeds that of many an African king, the absolute master of the lives and liberties of ten thousand naked savages.

Thus, the political passions are subordinated to those associated with ministering to the physical desires of the body? Is the condition of a prosperous American working thirty hours a week to be preferred to that of an Agamemnon or an Achilles, to say nothing of Odysseus? Such leaders, with the men *they* rule, it may be pointed out, are quite unlike Smith's African king. But see *The Wealth of Nations,* pp. 898-900 (disparaging, as an accountant would, the "splendid and showy equipage of empire"). Cf., on Mr. Hampden, chap. 5, n. 64, above; on Alexander the Great, chap. 9, n. 31, below. Cf., also, chap. 8, n. 186, below.

James Parton observed of George Washington that he learned "how to govern himself and his country in the school in which genuine statesmanship is learned—the management of a private estate." *Andrew Jackson,* I, 46-47. Consider, also, the value of practice in ruling and being ruled in turn during the decades one is in school.

43. Joseph Cropsey, *Polity and Economy: An Interpretation of the Principles of Adam Smith* (The Hague: M. Nijhoff, 1957), p. 86. See, on the relation of one's own to the good, chap. 2, n. 3, above, chap. 9, n. 15, below.

> A small proprietor, however, who knows every part of his little territory, who views it all with the affection which property, especially small property, naturally inspires, and who upon that account takes pleasure not only in cultivating but in adorning it, is generally of all improvers the most industrious, the most intelligent, and the most successful. [Adam Smith, *Wealth of Nations,* p. 392]

("Commerce and manufactures, in short, can seldom flourish in any state in which there is not a certain degree of confidence in the justice of government." Ibid., pp. 863-64. Is not this a critical step toward understanding the problem posed by Shakespeare's *Merchant of Venice*?)

"Although only three per cent of all Soviet farmland was under private cultivation, in 1964 it produced 34 per cent of the gross farm output. This included 75 per cent of the eggs, 55 per cent of the fruits and vegetables, 48 per cent of the potatoes, and 43 per cent of the meat eaten by Russians that year." *Athens News*, July 7, 1966, p. 7. Similar statistics were published in the *Chicago Tribune*, Nov. 7, 1964, p. 2. If these figures are accurate, they provide a startling confirmation of Adam Smith's thesis.

See Edward Crankshaw, *Khrushchev's Russia* (London: Penguin Books, 1959), pp. 86-87; Liz Carpenter, *Ruffles and Flourishes* (New York: Doubleday, 1970), p. 189.

44. There is, for example, surprisingly little in Benjamin Franklin's *Information to Those Who Would Remove to America* (a short pamphlet published in 1784) about the political aspect of life in the United States. (See chap. 7, nn. 115, 120, above.)

See, on the meaning of America abroad, Emerson, *Works*, XI:515-16. See, also, a conversation with a Greek banker, which concludes with his assurance to me, "You see, it is like America in this country. . . . A smart man can make money and become very rich." Anastaplo, "Notes on the First Amendment," pp. 625-26; Anastaplo, "Retreat from Politics: Greece, 1967," *Massachusetts Review* 9 (1968): 83, 108-9 (*Congressional Record* 115: E2632 [Apr. 2, 1969]). See, also, chap. 7, n. 115, chap. 8, n. 16, above.

45. Hobbes, *Leviathan*, pt. 1, chap. 8: "For the Thoughts, are to the Desires, as Scouts, and Spies, to range abroad, and find the way to the things Desired. . . ." See chap. 8, n. 193, below.

Cf. Aristotle, *Nicomachean Ethics* 1.4-8; also, chap. 8, n. 16, above.

The proper relation of the reason to passion is suggested by a lawyer's comment on Justice Frankfurter's concurring opinion in *Louisiana ex rel. Francis* v. *Resweber*, 329 U.S. 459 (1947), affirming the power of the state to proceed to a second attempt at execution after the failure of the first attempt ("The executioner threw the switch but, presumably because of some mechanical difficulty, death did not result" [329 U.S., at 460]—another age might have been inclined to leave more room for the possiblity of a miracle than the justices' use of "presumably" seems to do):

> Mr. Justice Frankfurter's opinion, joined in by no other justice and yet decisive in the [5-4] result, must have been torn from the soul. For Frankfurter is an avowed opponent of capital punishment. He opposes it not only on intellectual grounds but on grounds of conscience, morality, and personal revulsion. He abhors the sensationalism accompanying a death case, the subjection of human beings to the agonies involved in preparing for death, and the taking of life itself. *And so his opinion stands as a personal monument to judgment over feeling.* [Barrett Prettyman, Jr., "Cruel and Unusual Punishment: The Electric-Chair Case," in C. Herman Pritchett and Alan F. Westin, ed., *The Third Branch of Government* (New York: Harcourt, Brace & World, 1963), p. 111; italics added]

One sees here something which his admirers have to justify all too often in Justice Frankfurter's opinions (e.g., as in *West Virginia State Board of Education* v. *Barnette*, 319 U.S. 624 [1943]), the conflict within him of "judgment" and "feeling." (Cf., for one of Justice Frankfurter's finer hours, chap. 7, nn. 74, 75, above.) Does not the prevalence of such a conflict reflect that view of virtue which rests upon a suspicion of any moral decision which gives pleasure or, at least, is not unpleasant? But if one repeatedly finds one's "judgment" in conflict with one's "feeling," should one not reexamine one's judgment or reshape one's feeling? (The independent status of the "feeling" may depend upon the notion of the "self" discussed in chap. 8, n. 193, below.)

One passage in Justice Frankfurter's opinion in the *Francis* case is useful as well in considering the nature of due process of law:

> One must be on guard against finding in personal disapproval a reflection of more or less prevailing condemnation. Strongly drawn as I am to some of the senti-

ments expressed [in the dissenting opinion of Justice Burton], I cannot rid myself of the conviction that were I to hold that Louisiana would transgress the Due Process Clause if the State were allowed, in the precise circumstances before us, to carry out the death sentence, I would be enforcing my private view rather than that consensus of society's opinion which, for purposes of due process, is the standard enjoined by the Constitution. [329 U.S., at 471]

I doubt that the "consensus of society's opinion" *is* the standard enjoined by the Constitution for due process. But, however that may be, it does not seem to me likely that "society," in "the precise circumstances" of this case, wanted to have this teenaged murderer subjected to a second full-scale attempt at electrocution. My comments, I should add, do not depend on an opinion that capital punishment is unjustified, but rather on the "feeling" that for a civilized community "one whack is enough" and on the "judgment" that the repeated obligation to restrain itself is what helps keep a community civilized. (If one assumes that "society's opinion" is authoritatively indicated by what the Louisiana officials publicly proposed to do, then one must assume as well that there can never be any open violations by government officers of "due process" standards. Or, as Justice Black said at 366 U.S. 111, "this so-called 'balancing test' . . . as applied to the First Amendment means that the freedoms of speech, press, assembly, religion and petition can be repressed whenever there is a sufficient governmental interest in doing so.")

Justice Frankfurter virtually confessed to a strong "personal feeling of revulsion against a State's insistence on its pound of flesh" on this occasion. (329 U.S., at 471) Thus, a Portia—"a Daniel come to judgment"—was needed. But Chief Justice Vinson and Justices Black, Frankfurter, Jackson, and Reed could not supply what was needed to keep Louisiana from trying again. (Would not strict construction of the relevant Louisiana capital punishment statute have sufficed for a case conceded by all [329 U.S., at 473] to be "unique in judicial history"? See 329 U.S., at 475.) See, for the much more sensible approach of Justice Davis to such matters, chap. 7, n. 77, and Appendix F, sec. 9, above: a sensible approach is one which permits harmony (in matters upon which one, in a decent society, is obliged to act and over which one has some control) between "judgment" and "feeling." But then, is that not what moral education is all about? See Aristotle, *Nicomachean Ethics* 1104b4-13:

> An indication of our states of character is afforded by the pleasure or pain that accompanies our actions. . . . In fact, pleasures and pains are the things with which moral virtue is concerned. For pleasure causes us to do base actions and pain causes us to abstain from doing noble actions. Hence the importance, as Plato points out, of having been definitely trained from childhood to like and dislike the proper things. This is what good education means.

See, also, ibid., 1099a15-21; Plato, *Republic* 401E-402A; *Laws* 653A-654D; pp. 205-6, above; chap. 8, n. 73, below.

46. *Chicago Tribune*, Dec. 4, 1961, pt. 3, p. 21. See chap. 5, n. 149, above. "By freedom is meant, under the present bourgeois conditions of production, free trade, free selling and buying." "Manifesto of the Communist Party," in L. S. Feuer, ed., *Marx and Engels: Basic Writings on Politics and Philosophy* (Garden City, N.Y.: Doubleday & Co., Anchor Books, 1959), p. 22.

> The materialist conception of history starts from the proposition that the production of the means to support human life—and, next to production, the exchange of things produced—is the basis of all social structure; that in every society that has appeared in history, the manner in which wealth is distributed and society divided into classes or orders is dependent upon what is produced, how it is produced, and how the products are exchanged. From this point of view, the final causes of all social changes and political revolutions are to be sought not in men's brains, not in man's better insight into eternal truth and justice, but in changes in the modes of production and exchange. They are to be sought not in the *philosophy*, but in the *economics* of each particular epoch.

CHAPTER EIGHT, NOTE 46: PAGE 217

[Friedrich Engels, "Socialism: Utopian and Scientific," in Feuer, *Marx and Engels*, p. 90]

(See David Shub, *Lenin*, p. 145, where Lenin is recorded as asking, "Can't we bridle those scoundrels? Tell me, what kind of a dictatorship do you call this?" See, also, Wolfe, *Khrushchev and Stalin's Ghost*, pp. 290-92.)

> Free speech [said Lenin in 1920] is a bourgeois prejudice, a soothing plaster for social ills. In the Workers' Republic economic well-being talks louder than speech. . . . [The dictatorship of the proletariat] faces very grave difficulties, the greatest of them the opposition of the peasants. They need nails, salt, textiles, tractors, electrification. When we can give them these, they will be with us. . . . In the present state of Russia all prattle of freedom is merely food for the reaction trying to down Russia. Only bandits are guilty of that, and they must be kept under lock and key. [Louis Fischer, *The Life of Lenin* (New York: Harper & Row, 1964), p. 410]

See chap. 8, n. 175, below.

Compare the Romanian Constitution of 1965, which is described in the [London] *Observer*, July 4, 1965, p. 1, as

> more liberal than that of any other country in the Communist world. It promises civil liberties, such as the equivalent of *habeas corpus*, unknown in Rumania before. . . . The main points of the new Constitution are: 1. Freedom of speech for Press, assembly, meetings and demonstrations, with the exception of those of a Fascist and anti-democratic nature. 2. Nobody can be detained or arrested unless there is evidence, or a clear indication, that he has committed a punishable offence. Detention must not exceed 24 hours. Arrests will be made only on warrants issued by court or public prosecutor. 3. No one may enter the home of a person without his consent except in cases specifically provided by law.

See Robert Conquest, *Common Sense about Russia* (London: Victor Gollancz, 1960), pp. 15-16, 105 (on Rosa Luxembourg).

> [T]he Soviet magazine *Yunost* carried [in 1967] an interview with Professor Kapitsa, the grand old man of Soviet physics, who once worked with Rutherford in Cambridge. . . . The interviewer put the old, old Soviet question: "It is said that of two debaters, one is always wrong. May I ask whether a platform for disputes would not become a source for the dissemination of incorrect views?" Kapitsa exploded. "Rubbish!", he exclaimed. "First, out of two debaters both may be wrong, or both may be right. Secondly, one cannot know the truth in advance, and one can only reach it and test it as a result of the struggle of opposites. Thirdly, mistakes always retreat under pressure from the truth, despite all obstacles; at worst, it is a question of time and of the number of victims, as the history of mankind, beginning with the fires of the Inquisition and even earlier, has shown. And fourthly, I should like to speak of the right of a man to make his own mistakes." [Edward Crankshaw, "Russians Who Think like Svetlana," *Observer*, Apr. 30, 1967, p. 13]

See, for "Madison versus Marx," Martin Diamond, Winston Fisk, and Herbert Garfinkel, *The Democratic Republic* (Chicago: Rand McNally, 1966), pp. 76-77; also, Cropsey, "Adam Smith," "Karl Marx," in Strauss and Cropsey, *History of Political Philosophy*, pp. 549, 697. Communism invokes Christian sensibilities when it rebels against the view of capitalism examined by George Fitzhugh in his *Sociology for the South: Or the Failure of Free Society* (Richmond: A. Morris, 1854):

> [Adam Smith] saw only that prosperous and progressive portion of society whom liberty or free competition benefited and mistook its effects on them for its effects on the world. He had probably never heard the old English adage, "Every man for himself, and Devil take the hindmost." This saying comprehends the

whole philosophy, moral and economical, of the *Wealth of Nations.* . . . Adam Smith's philosophy is simple and comprehensive (*teres et rotundus*). Its leading and almost its only doctrine is that individual well-being and social and national wealth and prosperity will be best promoted by each man's eagerly pursuing his own selfish welfare unfettered and unrestricted by legal regulations, or governmental prohibitions, further than such regulations may be necessary to prevent positive crime. That some qualifications of this doctrine will not be found in his book we shall not deny; but this is his system. . . . [Staff, Social Science I, the College of the University of Chicago, eds., *The People Shall Judge* (Chicago: University of Chicago Press, 1949), 1:699]

The reader interested in considering further the Marxist attitude toward freedom of speech and toward the related subjects discussed in this study should consult Feuer, *Marx and Engels*, especially pp. 1, 22-23, 27, 57, 60, 65-66, 91, 128, 276, 332-33, 360-61, 443, 458, 461, and 473; as well as A. P. Mendel, ed., *Essential Works of Marxism* (New York: Grosset & Dunlap, Bantam Books, 1961), especially pp. 110, 114-15, 130, 136-37, 138, 156-57, 160, 169-70, 177, 220, 241-42, 280, 295, 327, 341-43, 351-52, 357, 367, 368, 543-44, and 553-54. See, also, Paine, *Writings*, 4:475-76.

It should be noticed that Nietzsche would question the underlying seriousness of the confrontation between Madison (or Mill), on the one hand, and Marx, on the other. He would, that is, emphasize similarities which he would regard as distinctively modern and as dependent upon and promoting a mediocrity moved ultimately by bodily pleasures. See chap. 8, n. 140, below. Cf. chap. 9, n. 33, below.

But it should also be noticed that on the level of everyday affairs there can be a world of difference between the regimes available today. (See chap. 6, n. 1, above, chap. 9, n. 7, below.) A *Chicago Tribune* editorial (Aug. 22, 1970, p. 8) makes the point:

> Brian Flanagan, that fiery young member of the Weathermen, walked out of a Chicago courtroom free Thursday after being acquitted by a jury of all four charges growing out of a street riot last fall in which [a city prosecutor] was knocked unconscious and paralyzed.
> . . . While Brian Flanagan was obscenely denouncing as a "farce" the Chicago court which had just (and rather generously) set him free, and rejoicing that he could stop "playing games," a very different sort of game was being played in a Moscow court. There, too, the defendant was a young dissenter from the system, a woman named Olga Iofe, and her crime was nothing more serious than the possession of anti-Stalinist leaflets which police found in her room. The court declared her insane and had her locked up in a criminal psychiatric hospital. Miss Iofe is the latest of many dissenters who have suffered this indignity at the hands of Soviet "justice." . . .
> In Moscow, the defendant is afraid to call a farce a farce; while in Chicago, the defendant is not afraid to call the whole judicial system a farce when it is not a farce, and to embellish his charge with an obscene torrent of militant threats and utter absurdities. The supreme irony of it all is that the foreign guerrilla groups which Flanagan and his fellow Weathermen seem to worship are, for the most part, protagonists of the system which would produce the sort of justice dispensed in Moscow—or, more likely even worse, the sort dispensed in Peking, which people rarely hear about at all.
> If there is any satisfaction to be derived from Flanagan's outburst, therefore, it is in knowing that under our system he is free to make a fool of himself if he wants. This is the freedom from which Flanagan apparently wants to liberate us.

Ours is also a system under which even those newspapers which have supported enthusiastically various campaigns of domestic repression mounted among us since the Second World War are free to compare us favorably with regimes where repression is more pervasive than we have ever permitted it to become here. See chap. 9, n. 35, below. What would become of such newspapers if repression should become well established among our people—if, that is, our people should be moved more by its fears than by its aspirations?

CHAPTER EIGHT, NOTES 47-49: PAGES 217-18　　　　　　　　　　　　695

See chap. 8, n. 18, below. See, e.g., Lisa Peattie, "Cuba Notes," *Massachusetts Review* 10 (1969): 652, 671-72, for a description of the Cuban press today. Her account included the observation, "The newspaper is supposed to contain items which will do you good; it is not for entertainment or the satisfaction of curiosity." And, she added, "A special newspaper is distributed to Party members." Presumably, this is the one necessary for those who govern the country: *they* have to have some idea of what is really going on. See chap. 4, n. 113, above. I have the impression that the colonels who "govern" Greece still talk rather frankly among themselves. (See Myron Rush, *The Rise of Khrushchev* [Washington: Public Affairs Press, 1958] on how Russian leaders "talk" openly in the press to Party members without the rest of the country's "listening in.")

47. Cooley regarded various incidents appurtenant to the trial by jury as part of this right, including the rules relating to double jeopardy, the unanimity of the jury, and the privilege against self-incrimination. See chap. 8, n. 20, above. See, also, p. 320, above.

See, for a detailed study of the criminal trial jury, Harry Kalven, Jr., and Hans Zeisel, *The American Jury* (Boston: Little, Brown & Co., 1966). This text provides as well (in effect) a useful, readable introduction to American criminal law.

48. Oliver Wendell Holmes, *Collected Legal Papers* (New York: Harcourt, Brace & Howe, 1920), p. 237. Cf. Mark DeW. Howe, ed., *The Holmes-Pollock Letters: The Correspondence of Mr. Justice Holmes and Sir Frederick Pollock, 1874-1932* (Cambridge: Harvard University Press, 1946), p. 13 (the jury and *fronisos*); Kalven and Zeisel, *American Jury*, pp. 125, 126, 128, 132-33, 144, 389-90.

On the other hand, an experienced Chicago judge (who is quite impressed by Bacon's essay, *On Judicature*) has told me that of four hundred jury trials in civil suits that he has conducted, he recalls only one jury verdict with which he seriously differed. See Kalven and Zeisel, *American Jury*, pp. 521-23.

See, also, Thomas Erskine, *The Speeches of Thomas Erskine on Subjects Connected with the Liberty of the Press, and against Constructive Treasons* (London: James Ridgway, 1813), 1:200; Patrick Devlin, *The Enforcement of Morals* (London: Oxford University Press, 1965), pp. 21, 99; Appendix D, above, chap. 6, n. 31, above.

49. See Holdsworth, *Some Lessons from Our Legal History*, pp. 75, 92-93; Blackstone, *Laws of England*, 4:238. The common law, too, "produces a law which is eminently adaptable to the needs of a changing society." Holdsworth, *Some Lessons from Our Legal History*, p. 19. See ibid., pp. 90-91, on "the use of the jury as helping to give a political education to the citizen. . . ."

> The trial by jury is very important in another point of view. It is essential in every free country, that common people should have a part and share of influence, in the judicial as well as in the legislative department. To hold open to them the offices of senators, judges, and offices to fill which an expensive education is required, cannot answer any valuable purposes for them; they are not in a situation to be brought forward and to fill those offices; these, and most other offices of any considerable importance, will be occupied by the few. The few, the well-born, &c., as Mr. Adams calls them, in judicial decisions as well as in legislation, are generally disposed, and very naturally too, to favour those of their own description.
>
> The trial by jury in the judicial department, and the collection of the people by their representatives in the legislature, are those fortunate inventions which have procured for them, in this country, their true proportion of influence, and the wisest and most fit means of protecting themselves in the community. Their situation, as jurors and representatives, enables them to acquire information and knowledge in the affairs and government of the society; and to come forward, in turn, as the sentinels and guardians of each other. . . . [Richard Henry Lee, "Letters from the Federal Farmer to the Republican" (1787), in Paul Leicester Ford, ed., *Pamphlets on the Constitution of the United States* (Brooklyn, N.Y., 1888), pp. 315-16]

Is there any good reason why the opportunity is lost in our cities to permit prospective jurors to "acquire information and knowledge in the affairs and government of the society"? Much (perhaps even most) of a citizen's jury-duty time is spent in the "bull-pens" awaiting an occasional call rather than in court (as a spectator) watching trials in progress. There is nothing in the tradition of trial by jury which requires prospective jurors either to remain ignorant of what happens in courts or to become bored and even angry because of the way their time is spent while waiting for jury service. What should make the simple reform I am here advocating even more attractive to everyone is that it is difficult for the typical citizen in a large city to attend court regularly.

50. *Federalist*, p. 558. Cf. chap. 3, n. 35, above.

In addition to the guarantee in the original Constitution of trial by jury in criminal cases, there is an elaboration of this guarantee in the Bill of Rights as well as the confirmation therein of the same right in civil cases. Trial by jury in common-law suits was called by Madison "one of the best securities to the rights of the people." Such a right not only protects the property of the people but also prevents or mitigates the injustice of government favorites who sue for the property either of those held in disfavor by the government or of those who are simply powerless. See chap. 4, n. 33, above.

51. See chap. 7, n. 18, above (on the practical effects of "no previous restraints").

Justice Frankfurter observed, in his concurring opinion in *Niemotko* v. *Maryland*, 340 U.S. 268 (1951), at 282, "a sanction applied after the event [unlike a licensing arrangement which permits officials to censor before publication] assures consideration of the particular circumstances of a situation." See, also, Paine, *Writings*, 4:475.

52. A contemporary parallel is seen in the difficulty encountered in the South by the general government, even in federal courts, when an effort is made to convict white men who have deprived Negroes of civil rights.

The following comment by Senator James O. Eastland of Mississippi, *Reporter*, June 27, 1957, p. 13, bears on the propriety of the four-year sentences handed down by the judge for contempt of court in the "Chicago Conspiracy Trial" (Appendix D, above):

> Senator Eastland has said that "there can be, under our Constitution, no right or privilege which is more sacred and more fundamental to the preservation of liberty than that of trial by jury in all cases where the victims can be confined for long prison sentences." But Senator Paul Douglas of Illinois calls the measure's supporters "overnight champions of jury trials," concluding that "Opponents of civil rights are not fighting for jury trials, but for the right to violate the law. Their entire argument is based on the expectation that civil-rights decrees of the Federal court will be violated and disregarded. They are fighting for the right of defiance to the law of the land without fear of punishment or restraint."

See chap. 4, n. 80, chap. 7, n. 6, above.

Cf. William Raspberry's column in the *Chicago Sun-Times*, Aug. 10, 1970, p. 30 (which indicates, among other things, the duty the Supreme Court *is* thought by members of Congress to have with respect to judicial review):

> While several Senate liberals were either actively working for, quietly supporting or saying nothing about that repressive piece of legislation known as the District of Columbia crime bill, a couple of Southern conservatives were standing up for the Constitution. It was one of the conservatives, Sen. Sam J. Ervin (D–N.C.) who was principally responsible for calling attention to the worst features of the legislation [such as " 'preventive detention,' its provision for jailing people for crimes they might possibly commit at some future time"] and working tirelessly, if unsuccessfully, for its defeat. [See *Congressional Record* 115: S13237 (Oct. 27, 1969).]
>
> ... Listen to Mississippi's arch-conservative, [Senator John Stennis (D–Miss.)]: "I, too, would like to support a sound (anti-crime) bill. I am not indifferent to conditions in the District of Columbia. ... A member of my family has been a victim of some of the lawlessness here. ... (But) I think we are planting seeds of great disappointment in this bill. In the first place, almost everyone has doubts about its constitutionality." Then, referring to those of his

colleagues who had taken the position that they would do their political thing and pass the bill, leaving it to the Supreme Court to handle the constitutional question, Stennis said: "When those who doubt the constitutionality of statutes rely on the courts to overturn them, that does more to undermine our Constitution than anything else I know of. . . ." None of this suggests that Stennis has suddenly become a liberal or champion of the people of the District of Columbia. All it suggests is that the man took a stand for common sense and the Constitution without even the remotest possibility of a political payoff. . . .

It also suggests to me that there must be in virtually every American—certainly in every American who devotes himself to politics and the law—*something* of the Constitutionalist. It is this dedication to constitutionalism, with its roots in the Declaration of Independence, to which statesmen (and the advisers of statesmen) can appeal in their efforts to moderate the inevitable differences among us. Cf. chap. 6, n. 1, chap. 8, n. 18, above, chap. 8, n. 105, below. See chap. 3, n. 20, above, chap. 8, n. 190, below.

53. Violations of the Stamp Act of 1765 were to be triable in admiralty court without recourse to a jury trial. Arthur M. Schlesinger, *Prelude to Independence: The Newspaper War on Britain, 1764-1776* (New York: Knopf, 1938), p. 68.

See Burke, *Works*, 2:223; Crosskey, *Politics and the Constitution*, p. 142.

54. An information was an "indictment"—i.e., an accusation of misconduct upon which a trial could be based—that could be entered by the Executive independent of a grand jury. See Joseph Story, *Commentaries on the Constitution of the United States*, 2d ed. (Boston: Little, Brown & Co., 1851), chap. 38, sec. 1786. See, also, chap. 7, n. 3, above, chap. 8, n. 112, below.

"[T]he abuses of the Star Chamber had rendered the process of information odious." *Respublica* v. *Oswald*, 1 Dallas [U.S.] 319, 323-24 (1788).

55. Instances of this are to be found in Schlesinger, *Prelude to Independence*, pp. 63, 64-65, 68, 81. Cf. Paine, *Writings*, 2:396-98.

See chap. 4, n. 20, above, on the treatment by juries of defendants who are identified with unpopular sentiments. Cf. Appendix D, above.

> For my own part [following upon the sentence quoted in chap. 8, n. 6, above], the more the operation of the institution [of trial by jury] has fallen under my observation, the more reason I have discovered for holding it in high estimation; and it would be altogether superfluous to examine as to what extent it deserves to be esteemed useful or essential in a representative republic or how much more merit it may be entitled to, as a defence against the oppressions of an hereditary monarch, than as a barrier to the tyranny of popular magistrates in a popular government. Discussions of this kind would be more curious than beneficial, as all are satisfied of the utility of the institution, and of its friendly aspect to liberty. [*Federalist* No. 83]

56. Mark Twain, *Collected Writings* (Author's National Edition, New York: Harper & Bros., 1903), 2:86. Supporting comments are found at pp. 73-74, 76, and 350 of the same volume. There is also found, at pp. 87-95, his account of a sea-captain who was determined to see justice done despite the efforts of others to persuade him to let the law take its dilatory and uncertain course. See, for additional uses of *palladium*, ibid., 20:345, 346. Passages using *palladium* may be found in chap. 6, n. 70, chap. 8, nn. 3, 4, 6 (see, also, *Federalist*, pp. 286, 327), nn. 11, 32, above, chap. 8, nn. 63, 68, below.

Today, Pallas Athena is lost sight of: *palladium* is used among us to refer either to "a silver-white ductile malleable metallic element of the platinum group that is used especially as a catalyst and in alloys" or to entertainment "palaces." We are, indeed, an irreverent age, and Mark Twain is our prophet. (Cf. Justice Black, speaking for the Court in *Illinois* v. *Allen*, 90 S.Ct. 1057, 1062 [1970]: "But our courts, palladiums of liberty as they are, cannot be treated disrespectfully with impunity." Paine speaks of the *union* of the states as the "great palladium of our liberty and safety." *Writings*, 1:375.)

57. The effective duration of this act of the people has been discussed. "The people of England regards itself as free: but it is grossly mistaken: it is free only during the

election of members of parliament. As soon as they are elected, slavery overtakes it, and it is nothing. . . ." Rousseau, *Social Contract*, book 3, chap. 15. Cf. chap. 5, n. 49, above. (The Deputy Prime Minister of Greece, Stylianos Pattakos, advised me in September, 1970, that I had no right as an American citizen to advise the American government about its policy toward Greece. [See chap. 6, n. 1, above.] He berated me in the most violent terms when I challenged his insistence that all I was entitled to do in America was to vote for officials who would then do what they deemed necessary, without any "interference" from citizens. [Cf. chap. 8, n. 97, below.] Indeed, our exchanges in the course of this semipublic debate were such [especially after I indicated I needed no lessons in citizenship from an army officer who had, in order to advance himself, substituted tanks for ballots] that it seemed for awhile I would be expelled from Greece for the second time that month. See Anastaplo, "American Aid and Greek Tyranny," *Congressional Record* 116: E10520 [1970]. See, also, Paine, *Writings*, 3:120.)

See Bagehot, *English Constitution*, pp. 18-19:

> Whether the government will go out or remain is determined by the debate, and by the division in the parliament. And the opinion out of doors, the secret pervading disposition of society, has a great influence on that division. The nation feels that its judgement is important, and it strives to judge. It succeeds in deciding because the debates and the discussions give it the facts and the arguments. But under a presidential government a nation has, except at the electing moment, no influence; it has not the ballot-box before it; its virtue is gone, and it must wait till its instant of despotism again returns. It is not incited to form an opinion like a nation under a cabinet government; nor is it instructed like such a nation.

Cf. chap. 9, n. 12, below. Are not both the President and Congress more responsive to "opinion out of doors" than is Parliament today with its rigidly disciplined parties?

58. The 1961 municipal elections in East Germany resulted in the successful election of every one of the 209,000 candidates of the "All-Party National Front," by a record 99.86 percent favorable vote, which is better than Hitler ever did. *Manchester Guardian Weekly*, Sept. 21, 1961, p. 2. See Milovan Djilas, *The New Class* (New York: Frederick A. Praeger, 1957), p. 93; Tocqueville, *Democracy in America*, 1:204, 265. See chap. 9, n. 34, below.

59. See Shakespeare, *King Lear*, act 1, sc. 1. Cf. Harry V. Jaffa, "The Limits of Politics: *King Lear*, Act I, Scene i," in Allan Bloom, *Shakespeare's Politics* (New York: Basic Books, 1964), p. 113. See chap. 9, n. 20, below.

The relation between radical equality and Christianity is suggested by Augustine's being able to say of Moses, "that great man," "we all come from the same lump, and what is man, saving that Thou art mindful of him?" *Confessions* (New York: Pocket Library, 1957), pp. 266, 261. Cf. Leo Strauss, *The City and Man* (Chicago: Rand McNally, 1957), pp. 38-41. Is the story of Er needed, in bk. 10 of the *Republic*, to "justify" (i.e., to give a plausible explanation of) the apparent injustices which undermine the case for the possibility of the rule of reason and of justice among men (i.e., the apparent injustices derived from chance and the distribution of natural endowments)? See Plato, *Timaeus* 42D; Lerner and Mahdi, *Medieval Political Philosophy*, p. 233.

See, further, on Augustine's sentiment, Matt. 11:11. Cf. Matt. 13:10-11.

60. Consider the implications of the difference between the United States and Great Britain during great national crises: the British are much more likely than we are to suspend regular elections.

> It has long been a grave question whether any government not too strong for the liberties of its people, can be strong enough to maintain its existence in great emergencies. On this point the present rebellion brought our republic to a severe test, and a presidential election occurring in regular course during the rebellion, added not a little to the strain. . . . But the election was a necessity. We cannot have free government without elections; and if the rebellion could force us to

forego or postpone a national election, it might fairly claim to have already conquered and ruined us. [Lincoln, *Complete Works*, 2:595 (a speech of Nov. 10, 1864)]

Cf. Lincoln's willingness to suspend temporarily, "by means of military arrests," "the liberty of speech and press, the law of evidence, trial by jury, and *habeas corpus*." *Works*, 2:350 (June 12, 1863). See Lord Charnwood, *Abraham Lincoln* (Garden City, N.Y.: Garden City Publishing Co., 1917), pp. 425-27. See, also, chap. 4, n. 56, above.

Careful study of the operation of these matters of democratic behavior in both the Confederacy and the Union give a reassuring picture of the vitality of the American system. Despite the terrible strain and uncertainty of domestic warfare, all elections were held as scheduled in both sections, and the results were tabulated and accepted. There was no sign, even in the dread days of 1864, that there was any thought of postponing or omitting the presidential election. [Roy F. Nichols, *Blueprint for Leviathan: American Style* (New York: Atheneum, 1963), pp. 241-42]

Democracy based upon universal suffrage and free Parliamentary institutions expresses itself most effectively through party organisations. In time of peace these may correct and balance each other and promote a healthy and lively public opinion. In a war like this they must all march together, for only in this way will the shortest and surest road be found out of our many troubles and dangers. [Winston S. Churchill, *The End of the Beginning* (Boston: Little, Brown & Co., 1943), p. 142 (letter of May 31, 1942)]

Cf. ibid., pp. 160-62, 185 (on full and free debate [even in wartime] relating to a vote of confidence in the House of Commons). See chap. 3, n. 31, chap. 4, nn. 55, 56, 59, above, chap. 8, n. 139, below. Cf., for Pollock's opinion, chap. 8, n. 67, below.

61. Consider the suggestion of a "conservative" Supreme Court justice:

. . . Does "indigence" as defined by the application of the California statute constitute a basis for restricting the freedom of a citizen, as crime or contagion warrants its restriction? We should say now, and in no uncertain terms, that a man's mere property status, without more, cannot be used by a state to test, qualify or limit his rights as a citizen of the United States. "Indigence" in itself is neither a source of rights nor a basis for denying them. The mere state of being without funds is a neutral fact—constitutionally an irrelevance, like race, creed, or color. [Justice Jackson (concurring), *Edwards* v. *California*, 314 U.S. 160, 184-85 (1941)]

See *Harper* v. *Virginia Board of Elections*, 383 U.S. 663 (1966).

62. See, also, *Annals*, I, pp. 737, 741.

63. I have already referred to Ames's observation that the control over elections is "the supreme authority" under the Constitution. *Annals*, I, p. 770. See Montesquieu, *Spirit of the Laws*, II, 2. Thus, we speak of the *people* "having *their* say" on election day.

A writer in the *New Haven* (Conn.) *Gazette*, Aug. 25, 1785, urged his readers to "maintain that fundamental part of our constitution—that great palladium of civil liberty, Annual Elections." Crosskey, *Politics and the Constitution*, p. 1207.

64. See note 8 of my review of Jaffa's *Equality and Liberty*, in *N.Y.U. L. Rev.* 41 (1966): 664. See, also, Arthur E. Sutherland, *Constitutionalism in America: Origin and Evolution of Its Fundamental Ideas* (New York: Blaisdell Publishing Co., 1965), p. 261; chap. 7, n. 119, above.

Madison observed, at *Annals*, I, p. 708, "Form is always of less importance than substance—but on this occasion form is of some consequence." See, also, *Federalist*, p. 257. See, on the effect questions of form (even the shape of a conference table) can have on questions of substance, Francis Bacon's essay, *Of Counsel*. (Churchill explained, in concerning himself with the size and arrangements of the House of Commons, "We shape our buildings, and afterwards our buildings shape us." *Fortune*, Feb. 1970, pp. 99-100.

Consider, e.g., the effect in a community of streets of houses with front porches on which leisurely sitting is possible.)

See pp. 14-15, above, for Jefferson's observations on the usefulness of forms, even when they are not "the most rational." The speaker of the House of Commons there quoted from seems to have been Arthur Onslow (who served from 1728 to 1761 in that capacity), of whom it was said by Horace Walpole, "[T]hough he was so minutely attached to forms that it often made him troublesome in affairs of higher moment, it will be difficult to find a subject whom gravity will so well become, whose knowledge will be so useful and so accurate, and whose fidelity to his trust will prove so unshaken." *Dictionary of National Biography* s.v. Onslow, Arthur. See chap. 5, n. 16 (on the *Yamashita* case) and chap. 7, n. 75 (on the *Rosenberg* case) for displays of singlemindedness, and even ruthlessness, on the part of officials who obviously regarded forms as unduly "troublesome in affairs of higher moment." See, also, pp. 237-38, chap. 4, nn. 13, 35, chap. 8, n. 18, above. Cf. Mickey Spillane, *I, the Jury* (New York: E. P. Dutton, 1947).

See, on forms, technicalities, and their usefulness, Henry Cecil, *A Child Divided* (New York: Harper & Row, 1966), pp. 17, 28, 46, 54-56, 173, 208, 215. See, also, chap. 7, nn. 86, 107, above. Cf. Paine, *Writings*, 3:216.

65. A vigorous exponent of this position is Polemarchus (not a citizen himself of Athens), in bk. 1 of Plato's *Republic*.

Lincoln, in his last public address, observes,

> The amount of constituency, so to speak, on which the new Louisiana government rests, would be more satisfactory to all if it contained 50,000, or 30,000, or even 20,000, instead of only about 12,000, as it does. It is also unsatisfactory to some that the elective franchise is not given to the colored man. I would myself prefer that it were now conferred on the very intelligent, and on those who serve our cause as soldiers. [*Complete Works*, 2:675]

66. "Ye shall do no injustice in rendering a judicial decision. Thou shalt not show partiality to the poor nor have undue consideration for the powerful, but justly shalt thou judge thy neighbor." Lev. 19:15. See, also, 2 Sam. 12:1.

See, on the two cities which are erroneously called one, Plato, *Republic* 422E-423A, 551D. See, also, Burke, *Writings*, 4:195-97.

67. *West Virginia State Board of Education* v. *Barnette*, 319 U.S. 624, 638 (1943). (Justice Jackson, perhaps because of his experience at the Nuremberg trials, became more "European," less "American," than he displayed himself in this opinion. See, for example, his concurring opinion in *Dennis* v. *U.S.*, 341 U.S. 494, 561 [1951]. Was it something he learned over there, or something he forgot? Chief Justice Stone was provoked to protest in a private letter, "Jackson is away conducting his high-grade lynching party in Nuremberg." Mason, *Harlan Fiske Stone*, p. 716. Cf. chap. 6, n. 58, chap. 7, n. 77, above.)

The British attitude toward a constitution is indicated in the observation, "We draw no legal distinction between constitutional laws and other laws. We can change a fundamental law just as easily as a transient law. But in point of practice we do not do so. We may modify our laws to meet changing needs, but we keep the fundamental principles intact." Sir Alfred Denning, *The Changing Law* (London: Stevens & Son, 1953), p. 17. (It was Sir Frederick Pollock's "private opinion . . . that there is no liberty of the subject in time of war within the realm." Howe, *Holmes-Pollock Letters*, 1:245.)

> Parliamentary sovereignty in Britain ensures that Parliament can change any law, however fundamental, by the same process as, say, a law which increases the amount which a local authority may charge for dustbins. Even more important is the power given to Courts like the Supreme Court of the United States to intervene if laws inconsistent with the Constitution are passed. Judicial review of administrative interference with civil liberties is much more frequent and effective there than in Britain. . . . Because English lawyers have comparatively few chances to participate in cases affecting civil liberties, there is little interest in the subject professionally—there is no money in it for lawyers—and the dearth

of case law makes the universities also inactive in research. This explains, but does not excuse, the fact that this is the first book ever to attempt a detailed survey of the content of British civil liberties, whereas in the United States there are dozens of such books, ranging from the highly specialized monograph to the survey for the general reader. [Street, *Freedom, the Individual and the Law*, p. 285]

See chap. 2, n. 18, chap. 5, n. 123, above. Cf. chap. 7, n. 103, above, chap. 8, n. 79, below.

68. Cf., in Milton's *Areopagitica*, "Give me the liberty to know, to utter, and to argue freely according to conscience, above all liberties." Patrick Henry argued, in the Virginia Ratifying Convention,

With respect to the freedom of the press, I need to say nothing; for it is hoped that the gentlemen who shall compose Congress will take care to infringe as little as possible the rights of human nature. This will result from their integrity. They should, from prudence, abstain from violating the rights of their constituents. They are not, however, expressly restrained. But whether they will intermeddle with that palladium of our liberties or not, I leave you to determine. [Jonathan Elliot, *Debates in the Several State Conventions on the Adoption of the Federal Constitution* (Philadelphia: J. B. Lippincott & Co., 1863), 3:449]

"The first born of American rights," a Virginia legislator argued in 1798, "was the free examination of public servants." *Resolutions of Virginia and Kentucky*, p. 80. (A generation later, John Taylor of Caroline observed:

[We have] submitted to the consideration of the reader a few general arguments to prove, that for the preservation of civil liberty, sound policy dictates an unlimited freedom of discussion, concerning magistrates and their measures; and that if the magistracy can restrain discussion, human reason, instead of being a check, will be made an accomplice of usurpation.... [*Inquiry into the Principles and Policy of the Government of the United States*, p. 282]

Instructive are his observations on sedition acts [ibid., pp. 479-89, 494-96] and on the Kentucky Resolutions [ibid., p. 648 ff.]. Thus, he argues [ibid., p. 649]:

The best restraint upon legislative acts tending to the destruction of a true republican government consists of the mutual right of the general and state governments to examine and controvert before the publick each others proceedings.

See chap. 8, n. 118, below [for Senator Webster on the Virginia Resolutions]; chap. 4, n. 113, above. See, also, chap. 2, n. 13, above.)

See, at chap. 5, n. 5, above, Judge Cooley's report "that liberty of the press, as now understood and enjoyed, is of very recent origin." Erskine's explanation of this development supports the argument of this study:

It is because the liberty of the press resolves itself into this great issue, that it has been, in every country, the last liberty which subjects have been able to wrest from power. Other liberties are held under governments, but the liberty of opinion keeps Governments themselves in due subjection to their duties. [Erskine, *Speeches*, 2:139-40]

See chap. 5, n. 1, above.

69. I suggest in section 6 of chapter 4 that the power to protect or revive freedom of speech in the states may be implied in Congress's power to supervise the state conduct of congressional and presidential elections.

70. Unreflecting public opinion—is a reflecting public opinion impossible, or at least highly unlikely?—is displayed through the well-intentioned Crito. (See, for an introduction to the *Crito*, Anastaplo, "On Civil Disobedience: Thoreau and Socrates," *Southwest Review* 54 [1969]: 203. See, for the sentiments of a contemporary apostle of Thoreau,

Milton Mayer, *On Liberty: Man v. The State* [Santa Barbara: Center for the Study of Democratic Institutions, 1969]. The title of his book is particularly revealing of his understanding of political things. Cf. Aristotle, *Politics* 1253a19-30.) Do not Glaucon and Adeimantus, in the second book of the *Republic*, conjure up and confront Socrates with a world in which the opinions of the public (whether the public be men or gods) are either misinformed or count for nothing? See chap. 8, n. 37, above, chap. 8, n. 184, below.

See, also, chap. 4, nn. 114, 116, above. (Is not the romantic, even anarchical, character of Mayer's thought reflected in the dedication of his *On Liberty*, "To the memory of Scott Buchanan, who taught me that the questions that can be answered are not worth asking"? See Paine, *Writings*, 1:69-70. Cf. chap. 2, n. 4, above, chap. 8, n. 181, below.)

Plato's *Crito* shows us that for most people most of the time what is "proper and right" (p. 89, above) or just is very much dependent on what the law prescribes. See, also, the first book of Plato's *Republic*; chap. 4, n. 117, above, chap. 8, n. 135, below. Cf. pp. 417-18, above. (It is noted in *Alfarabi's Philosophy*, at p. 63, that the *Crito* "is also called the *Apology of Socrates*," with another of Plato's works, which must be what we call the *Apology of Socrates*, referred to as "the *Protest of Socrates Against the Athenians*." There *is* something to this nomenclature: the *Crito* is *the* defense by Socrates which will eventually move the Athenians, whereas the other statement may be intended primarily to instruct potential philosophers and friends of philosophers about the relation of philosophy to the city. See chap. 2, n. 1, above, chap. 8, n. 195, below. See, also, *Alfarabi's Philosophy*, pp. 143-44 [sec. 1, n. 1]. Thus, Socrates instructs the many by speaking in private [that is, in prison] to one man; he instructs the few by speaking in public to the many. See chap. 8, n. 28, above, chap. 9, nn. 11, 13, below.)

71. I have tried to make sense, that is, of the critical difference in wording of the free speech and press provisions in the constitutions of the states and the Constitution of the United States. Cf. chap. 3, n. 12, above. I have, in chap. 7, above (e.g., notes 107 and 119), indicated why it is better to leave with the states rather than with the general government some power to regulate speech and the press. The general government, it should be remembered, retains supervisory power with respect to the states in this respect. The concluding sentences of *Federalist* No. 10 suggest why it made sense to leave with the states, rather than with the general government, power to deal with abuses of freedom of speech or of the press:

> The influence of factious leaders may kindle a flame within their particular States, but will be unable to spread a general conflagration through the other States. A religious sect may degenerate into a political faction in a part of the Confederacy; but the variety of sects dispersed over the entire face of it must secure the national councils against any danger from that source. A rage for paper money, for an abolition of debts, for an equal division of property, or for any other improper or wicked project, will be less apt to pervade the whole body of the Union than a particular member of it; in the same proportion as such a malady is more likely to taint a particular county or district, than an entire State. In the extent and proper structure of the Union, therefore, we behold a republican remedy for the diseases most incident to republican government. And according to the degree of pleasure and pride we feel in being republicans, ought to be our zeal in cherishing the spirit and supporting the character of Federalists.

It should be remembered as well that local governments had "proved" themselves as champions of freedom not only by having insisted upon the Bill of Rights but also by having once sounded the alarm against the usurpations of the central government (i.e., the king and Parliament). Is a national freedom of speech important because there are not, in the nation at large, those intimate relations with one another and that immediate knowledge of the origins and effects of government policies which it is possible to have in a smaller community? Freedom of speech can be said to provide a substitute for such intimacy and immediacy. Indeed, the general government is distinctively the child of discussion (in the Constitutional Convention and in the state ratifying conventions) by the people of the Declaration of Independence; the state governments, on the other hand, are more the prerevolutionary products of unreflecting nature and less a deliberative act (and require supervision by the authoritatively republican general government). See Daniel J. Boorstin, *The Americans: The National Experience* (New York: Random House, 1965), pp. 408, 409; chap. 8, n. 25, above. Cf. Lincoln, *Complete Works*, 2:62.

See, also, chap. 6, n. 50, chap. 7, nn. 35, 83, above, chap. 8, n. 83, below.

72. In many instances, the minority protected by certain rights is made up of those who are most apt to come into conflict with the lawmaking and hence law-abiding majority—that is, suspected lawbreakers.

Besides, majorities are not necessarily constant—and the majority of citizens may learn, at some time or another, what it is like to be in the minority. Has not the United States been a country with no permanent majority? See chap. 7, n. 103, chap. 8, n. 37, above.

It should be noticed that liberty of the press (old-style) still serves a purpose in conjunction with (if not even incorporated in) freedom of speech and of the press (new-style), for "liberty of the press" inhibits the government from acting independently of juries—i.e., it prevents previous restraint (or censorship) (which prevention, I have argued, may be implied by "due process of law" as well).

73. One is reminded of Socrates as representative of the rule of reason: he acts independently of that which happens to be prescribed by law (section 4), by men of property (section 5), by the company in which he finds himself (section 6), by the community of comrades (section 7), or by public opinion (section 8). He is, essentially, the man who rises above the city, even though he might respect the law, depend on the property of others, conduct discussions by finding common ground with his interlocutors, recognize the demands of fellow feeling in the city, and take due account of public opinion in what he does. See Plato, *Gorgias* 447A, 475E-476A.

Cf. Dean Acheson's attempt (in a eulogy) to justify, at 382 U.S. xxx (1965), Justice Frankfurter's votes in the *Dennis* and *Flag Salute Cases*: "Popular rule he saw as a moral and practical imperative. . . ." But see chap. 4, n. 117, above. (I suppose it is a good sign that such things do *have* to be explained away by one's friends, just as it is a good sign that we expose our own misdeeds [including massacres] abroad as well as at home. It is a good sign as well that Justice Frankfurter's behavior in the *Rosenberg* case does *not* have to be explained away today. See chap. 7, nn. 74, 75, above. Cf. chap. 8, n. 45, above.)

74. We find in Isocrates' *Areopagiticus* a call for a return to "the old way," a call for the restoration to its old powers of the Areopagus (the high court of Athens). (See, also, the *Eumenides* in Aeschylus' *Oresteia*.) Such a reform would have represented a moderation (not the abolition) of the democracy. The Areopagus, which had been the supreme tribunal of censorship over public decorum and morality, came to be regarded by "democrats" such as Pericles as dangerous to the progress of democracy. See Plutarch, *Lives*, pp. 187-89. To call for its restoration and elevation was therefore recognized as calling for a greater role for the aristocratic element in the community. (See, e.g., the characterization of Demosthenes' recourse to the Areopagus as "aristocratical." Ibid., p. 1030.) See Burke, *Works*, 4:229.

What, then, are we to make (if only briefly, on this occasion) of Milton's appropriation of *Areopagitica* for his "Speech for the Liberty of Unlicensed Printing"? I have noticed Milton's antipathy to custom. (See chap. 2, n. 29, above.) But I also notice his concern for the preservation and development of what is best in the old. (See chap. 8, nn. 170, 171, below.) No serious author, aware of the complexity of the world, is without complexities in his thought, however absolute (and even "simpleminded") prudence may require his call for action to be in particular circumstances. Thus, Milton can (as circumstances require) appeal from contemporary arbitrariness, deterioration, and even ignorance both to the liberated human intelligence and to the "elegance and purity" of disciplined morality and language. (See chap. 5, n. 50, above. See, also, chap. 7, n. 107, above, chap. 9, n. 11, below.)

It is this tension in his thought between the aristocratic and the popular (if not the democratic) which may be reflected in what is said here (section 9 of this chapter) about the aristocratic character of "freedom of speech" among us. See, also, chap. 2, n. 1, above, chap. 9, n. 39, below. Seymour Martin Lipset, in his article, "Democracy and the Social System," *Internal War* (New York: Free Press of Glencoe, 1964), p. 275, quotes from Edward Shils's *Torment of Secrecy* (New York: Free Press of Glencoe, 1956), of which he says that it "deserves recognition as a minor classic of sociological analysis of a social problem, yet curiously it is not well known":

> The United States has been committed to the principle of publicity since its origin. The atmosphere of distrust of aristocracy and of pretensions to aristocracy in which the American Republic spent its formative years has persisted in many forms. Repugnance for governmental secretiveness was an offspring of the distrust of aristocracy. In the United States, the political elite could never claim the immunities and privileges of the rulers of an aristocratic society. . . . American culture is a populistic culture. As such, it seeks publicity as a good in itself. Extremely suspicious of anything which smacks of "holding back," it appreciates publicity, not merely as a curb on the arrogance of rulers but as a condition in which the members of society are brought into a maximum of contact with each other. . . .
> Although democratic and pluralistic, British society is not populist. Great Britain is a hierarchical country. Even when it is distrusted, the Government, instead of being looked down upon, as it often is in the United States, is, as such, the object of deference because the Government is still diffused with the symbolism of a monarchical and aristocratic society. The British Government, of course, is no longer aristocratic . . . [but it] enjoys the deference which is aroused in the breast of Englishmen by the symbols of hierarchy which find their highest expression in the Monarchy. . . . The acceptance of hierarchy in British society permits the Government to retain its secrets, with little challenge or resentment. . . .

Cf. Jefferson's letter to John Adams, Oct. 28, 1813, on "a natural aristocracy" of "virtue and talents"; James B. Reston, *The Artillery of the Press: Its Influence on American Foreign Policy* (New York: Harper & Row, 1967), pp. 101-8, on the "saving remnant." See chap. 5, nn. 25, 79, chap. 8, nn. 2, 97, above. The continuing difference between the American and British settings is reflected in the London reception in July, 1970, of *Oh! Calcutta!* (see chap. 5, n. 132, above), which "was roundly panned by the critics":

> The opening night performance was a decided letdown after tremendous advance publicity. Only 2 of the 14 skits drew more than polite applause. One young woman at intermission said she had seen the show in New York and "liked it better there. Here it seems sort of lewd." [*Chicago Tribune*, July 29, 1970, sec. 2, p. 6]

The use of "lewd" should remind us that it *is* useful to call things by their right names. See Burke, *Works*, 2:247. See, also, Lincoln, *Complete Works*, 2:61:

> It might seem, at first thought, to be of little difference whether the present movement at the South be called "secession" or "rebellion." The movers, however, well understand the difference. At the beginning they knew they could never raise their treason to any respectable magnitude by any name which implies violation of law. They knew their people possessed as much of moral sense, as much of devotion to law and order, and as much pride in and reverence for the history and government of their common country as any other civilized and patriotic people. They knew they could make no advancement directly in the teeth of these strong and noble sentiments. Accordingly, they commenced by an insidious debauching of the public mind. They invented an ingenious sophism. . . . With rebellion thus sugar-coated they have been drugging the public mind of their section. . . .

See, also, Shakespeare, *Henry IV, Part II*, act 1, sc. 1, ll. 199-201 ("This word 'rebellion' it had froze them up, as fish are in a pond. But now the Bishop turns insurrection to a religion"). Thus, in Chicago, it has been necessary for informed citizens (but not yet the *Chicago Tribune*) to recognize as anything but "justifiable homicide" the deaths resulting from the Dec. 4, 1969, police raid against a Black Panther apartment. But the standards invoked in condemnation of the police action on that occasion also require us to see the gunning down of police from ambush for what it is, not "political assassination" or "revolution" but rather "cowardly murder" or "criminal insanity." See chap. 8, n. 135, below, on the duty of intellectuals. See, also, chap. 5, n. 131, above. Cf. chap. 8, n. 141, below.

See, for a provocative introduction to Milton's classic, Willmoore Kendall, "How to Read Milton's *Areopagitica*," *Journal of Politics* 22 (1960): 439 (which includes the observation, at p. 473, that Milton is "on the crucial issues . . . the soul of intolerance"). For a provocative introduction by him to still another classic, see "The People Versus Socrates Revisited," *Modern Age*, Winter 1958-1959, p. 98. Compare his review of the article on the *Apology* in *Ancients and Moderns*, ed. Joseph Cropsey, in *American Political Science Review* 61 (1967): 783. See Burke, *Works*, 4:166.

See, on the differences between American and British public information practices, Harry Howe Ransome, *The Intelligence Establishment* (Cambridge: Harvard University Press, 1970), pp. 180-207. Cf. ibid., 251-52, 264-66. Cf., also, chap. 5, nn. 25, 29, chap. 8, n. 17, above.

75. One would expect that liberty of the press in England would be more likely than in this country to permit the worst elements in the community to express themselves freely. (The aristocrat, or the legitimate successor to the aristocrat, would tend to speak freely under that regime, regardless of what the press law permits or provides.) (See Montesquieu, *The Spirit of the Laws* [New York: Hafner Publishing Co., 1949], 4:2.) This expectation is realized in the caliber of the more popular English press. But, Churchill explained, "In England, it is not what is said but who says it that matters." Charles G. L. DuCann, *Miscarriages of Justice* (London: F. Muller, 1960), p. 101.

76. It has been argued,

> . . . we would take cognizance of the notorious preference of Hamilton for some of the aristocratic institutions of English Whiggery to stabilize the democratic passions. The difference between Lincoln and Hamilton—his greatest intellectual predecessor in the Federalist-Whig-Republican tradition—was that Lincoln grasped the necessity of evolving aristocratic restraints upon democracy, not by borrowing contra-democratic devices from a non-democratic past, but by evolving them from within the democratic ethos as perfections of that ethos. [Harry V. Jaffa, *Crisis of the House Divided* (Garden City, N.Y.: Doubleday & Co., 1959), p. 417]

To what extent did Lincoln rely upon careful speeches by the best men to supply "aristocratic restraints upon democracy"? See the lecture, "The Gettysburg Address: America's Political Religion," appended to my dissertation. See, also, chap. 8, n. 82, and chap. 9, n. 39, below; Burke, *Works*, 5:100-101. Cf. Paine, *Writings*, 2:323, 347.

"Liberal education is the necessary endeavor to found an aristocracy within democratic mass society." Leo Strauss, *Liberalism Ancient and Modern* (New York: Basic Books, 1968), p. 5. Henrik Ibsen observed in 1895, "The absolutely imperative task of democracy is to make itself aristocratic." *Ibsen: Letters and Speeches*, ed. Evert Sprinchorn (New York: Hill & Wang, 1964), p. 320. And, Professor Cropsey (or at least Thomas Hobbes) has reminded us, "Aristotle indeed had a republican, libertarian, perhaps even democratic inclination, and at the same time taught that men are by nature unequal in their qualification to bear rule so that only the wise or the best deserve to govern." Joseph Cropsey, "Hobbes and the Transition to Modernity," in *Ancients and Moderns: Essays on the Tradition of Political Philosophy, in Honor of Leo Strauss*, ed. Joseph Cropsey (New York: Basic Books, 1964), p. 215.

It has not been generally appreciated that the criteria invoked by opponents of both G. Harrold Carswell and Clement Haynsworth, when these judges were nominated to the

Supreme Court of the United States, concede a great deal to the political principles of thoughtful conservatives. Cf. chap. 7, n. 41 (end), above, chap. 8, n. 179 (beginning), below.

77. See chap. 7, n. 83, above, chap. 8, n. 85, below. See, also, Leonard W. Levy, *Jefferson and Civil Liberties: The Darker Side* (Cambridge: Harvard University Press, 1963), p. 211, n. 43.

See, on the limited safeguards of a jury trial of defendants with unpopular ideas, chap. 3, n. 20, above. "In England the liberty of the impassioned many guarantees the liberty of the thoughtful few." David Lowenthal, "Montesquieu," in Strauss and Cropsey, *History of Political Philosophy*, p. 481.

It was said of Athens, "One man calls it democracy, another man, according to his fancy, gives it some other name; but it is in truth an aristocracy backed by popular approval." Plato, *Menexenus* 238C-D. (See Thucydides, *Peloponnesian War*, bk. 2, chap. 65, secs. 9-10; Pierre Bayle, *The Dictionary Historical and Critical* [London: D. Midwinter et al., 1737], s.v. Pericles.) *Aristocracy* means either "the influence . . . of great names and great wealth" or "the natural aristocracy of knowledge and virtue." Tocqueville, *Democracy in America*, 1:54. It is the former, more than the latter, that Americans had in mind when they warned against aristocratic tendencies in the Constitution. (How much the latter depends, for its development and influence, upon the former remains an open question.) The government under the Constitution commenced as a "moderate aristocracy." Farrand, *Records*, 2:640. There was in the America of 1787 "little separation between power and merit." Diamond, Fisk, and Garfinkel, *Democratic Republic*, p. 35.

Tocqueville observed, "On my arrival in the United States [in 1831] I was surprised to find so much distinguished talent among the citizens and so little among the heads of the government." *Democracy in America*, 1:207. ("[T]he American statesmen of the present day are very inferior to those who stood at the head of affairs fifty years ago." Ibid., 1:210.) And, he reported, "If I were asked where I place the American aristocracy, I should reply, without hesitation that it is not among the rich, who are united by no common tie, but that it occupies the judicial bench and bar." Ibid., 1:288. (This may still be true, if amended to include the faculties of academic institutions, some of the press, and certain business [especially financial] institutions. Nor must the ministry and a self-respecting, and therefore self-policing, military be forgotten.)

My argument is that *the* aristocratic right—"freedom of speech [and] of the press" —was turned against, and providentially replaced, the aristocratic party which would have eventually been left behind by the democratic revolution already in progress: the First Amendment acknowledges the role of "knowledge and virtue" in good government; the Fourteenth Amendment recognizes the radical equality to which American democrats aspire (Thomas Erskine May argued in *The Constitutional History of England since the Accession of George the Third, 1760-1860* [New York: A. C. Armstrong & Son, 1899], 1:310-11:

> Having viewed the imperfections of the representative system, and the various forms of corruption by which the constitution was formerly disfigured, we pause to inquire how popular principles, statesmanship, and public virtue were kept alive, amid such adverse influences? . . . Two other causes, which exercised a wholesome restraint upon Parliament and the governing class, are to be found in the divisions of party,—finely called by Sir Bulwer Lytton "the sinews of freedom,"—and the growing influence of the press. However prone the ruling party may sometimes have been to repress liberty, the party in opposition were forced to rely upon popular principles; and pledged to maintain them, at least for a time, when they succeeded to power. . . .)

See the Epistle Dedicatory to Bernard Shaw, *Man and Superman*.

78. The execution by Cicero of the Catilinian conspirators without the forms of law is generally acknowledged to have been a serious blunder. (See, e.g., Rousseau, *Social Contract*, book 4, chap. 6. See, also, chap. 5, n. 112, above.) Cicero probably violated the constitution in executing the conspirators. Certainly he laid himself open to the

CHAPTER EIGHT, NOTE 78: PAGE 230

attacks of his enemies. His strength had rested theretofore, in large part, on his adherence to the constitution. A vital constitutionalism, with its support in both the ancestral and the legal, is the good man's hold on the respect and even affections of the people. This is implicit in Plato's *Crito*. See chap. 8, n. 96, below.

An article in the *New York Times*, Apr. 19, 1961, suggests the public education needed today:

> Warwick, R.I. Police chief James F. Lynch has a system for keeping known racketeers out of the city. He said at a Boy Scout dinner meeting that when a known gangster moved into the city, the police placed a round-the-clock tail on his activities. Then the police go to his home in unmarked cars. "If he is a real racketeer," Chief Lynch said, "he won't let us into his home without a search warrant."

Cf. chap. 5, nn. 76, 78, above.

As for "public education," what effect have the "comic strips" had on the effort among us to impress upon people Madison's "some degree of respect" for constitutional barriers? It depends, I suppose, on the strip. "Dick Tracy," for instance, could always be depended upon (even before the "Warren Court") to deride restraints upon law enforcement: there was, for example, the character named "Fifth," with his "Mouthpiece" named "Flyface":

> F. I need Flyface!
> A. Fifth, are you losing your marbles? What's he ever done for you?
> F. He taught me to say, "I Refuse To Answer!" The most important words us guilty criminals ever used. [*Chicago Tribune*, Dec. 8, 1959]

Ten years later "Dick Tracy" was still at it. The detective is about to be murdered by criminals who announce, "Final proof that we are winning our constitutional rights over the law." *Chicago Tribune*, Dec. 1, 1968. Two weeks later we see another unattractive criminal lawyer who bears the name, "Habe Corpussle." *Chicago Tribune*, Dec. 16, 1968.

"Little Orphan Annie" has also made its contributions to popular respect for law and order. Typical were such exchanges as this (before the strip changed markedly upon the death of its talented creator):

> Daddy Warbucks: . . . He'll tell us all about it, up at the castle!
> A. Bah! I tell nothing!
> Punjab: Oh, but you will, little pig! Here are no soft judges, shyster lawyers, or sniveling bleeding hearts to turn killers free! Here a hoodlum talks, loud and clear! To the castle! Move! [*Chicago Tribune*, Jan. 7, 1962]

Or, a few years earlier, Punjab assures Annie that wiretapping is used efficiently where they are: "The President of this republic and his judges do not sympathize much for the health or safety of traitors." *Chicago Tribune*, May 8, 1958. Ten years later, "Little Orphan Annie," too, was still at it:

> C. Oh, the police have known for weeks who hired that gang to try to kill Pete, the price, the whole plan!
> A. Then why aren't they all in jail, captain?
> C. Ah, we're living in a new era! *Now* even admitted violent crime doesn't count! The *legal* question is, *how* the dickens did the cops find out?
> A. But that's crazy!
> C. Some of us, in *my* business think so, but it's the *law*, lady! We also know the men in that group of hired killers! They got back to their home city yesterday, but by a recent judicial decision it's illegal for a cop even to ask a suspect his name!

A. Why, that's incredible!
C. Nope; invasion of the suspect's constitutional right to privacy, said the learned judge!
P. Whose side are the courts on, anyway?
C. A very good question! I imagine any criminal attorney would be delighted to answer it for a suitable fee!
P. But, interstate kidnaping! That's a capital crime!
C. So I've heard! But how long since *you've* heard of any kidnaper being *executed*?
A. Poor, poor little Annie! What will happen to her?
C. Oh, you'll soon get a call demanding a huge ransom! When you do, *tell me at once*, folks, and I *guarantee* we'll do a *lot better*!
A. Oh, Peter! Isn't there any protection for *decent* people?

The author had prefaced this exchange with two worthy quotations:

"If the law supposes that," said Mr. Bumble, "the law is a' ass."—Dickens.
"A state with defective laws will have defective morals."—Seneca.

And he concluded the exchange, before introducing the bestial kidnapper, with a self-parodying comment:

Shucks! Killers! Kidnapers! They're *people*, aren't they? They've got rights! What's the Constitution for? [*Chicago Tribune*, Apr. 16, 1967]

Somewhat more sophisticated are strips such as "Apartment 3-G" (with its mixed feelings about "Women's Lib") and "Mary Worth" (who has certainly risen in the world since her Depression days as "Apple Mary"). Consider, for example, the treatment in "Mary Worth" of the crusading young radical who (it turns out) *has* something to be said for him. *Chicago Sun-Times*, Apr.-May, 1967. Even more interesting, in that it ratifies a shift of American attitudes toward the Cold War, is the not unsympathetic presentation in "Terry" of a Russian officer, Colonel Karsov (who is shown using his skills as "the best gunner in the Soviet Army" against the common enemy of Terry Lee and himself, the Chinese Communists). *Chicago Tribune*, May 18, 1970.

See Plato, *Republic* 376E ff., 401B ff., *Laws* 659E ff.

79. Compare the Sedition Act of 1798, which was used against partisans of the more popular party. See Albert J. Beveridge, *The Life of John Marshall* (Boston: Houghton Mifflin Co., 1916), 2:383, n. 2; Paine, *Writings*, 3:414 ("[the Adams administration] entrenched itself within a magic circle of terror, and called it a SEDITION LAW").

I am a fairly consistent reader of British newspapers. I have been repeatedly impressed with the speed and certainty with which the slightest invasion of British individual freedom or minority rights by officials of the government is picked up in Parliament, not merely by the opposition but by the party in power, and made the subject of persistent questioning, criticism, and sometimes rebuke. There is no waiting on the theory that the judges will take care of it. In this country, on the contrary, we rarely have a political issue made of any kind of invasion of civil liberty. . . . In Great Britain, to observe civil liberties is good politics and to transgress the rights of the individual or the minority is bad politics. In the United States, I cannot say that this is so. Whether the political conscience is relieved because the responsibility here is made largely a legal one, I cannot say, but of this I am sure: any court which undertakes by its legal processes to enforce civil liberties needs the support of an enlightened and vigorous public opinion. . . . [Robert H. Jackson, *The Supreme Court in the American System of Government* (New York: Harper & Row, 1963), pp. 81-82]

See, e.g., "Who Breaks a Butterfly on a Wheel?" *London Times*, July 1, 1967, p. 11.

80. Adolf Hitler was able to say on February 15, 1933:

CHAPTER EIGHT, NOTES 81-82: PAGE 231   709

Herr Bolz says that he must condemn the gagging of liberty by the present Government. . . . For almost fourteen years our Movement, which sought only Germany's resurrection and liberation, has experienced nothing but oppression and persecution. Today, as Chancellor, I did not need to do anything else in opposition to the enemies of the nationalist cause in Germany than to use all the means which you formerly employed against the friends of the nation. I only needed to issue a law for the protection of the national State such as that which you formerly made against us for the protection of the Republic. All that the present Government had to do was to repeat word for word the measures against the Press which for fourteen years were used against our Press; they had only to copy out these regulations and turn them against their authors. [Norman H. Baynes, ed., *Speeches of Adolf Hitler, 1922-1939* (London: Oxford University Press, 1942), 1:498]

A republic that undertakes a program of political suppression of evil men should remember the ancient counsel of which Emerson was reminded upon reading a youthful essay critical of Plato: "Holmes, when you strike at a king, you must kill him." *Felix Frankfurter Reminisces*, ed. Harlan B. Phillips (New York: Reynal & Co., 1960), p. 59. (Justice Holmes, however, did not "kill" what he struck at when he brought forth the "clear and present danger" test.) I find it prudential, in a country with established free institutions, to pursue the course suggested by an article in the *London Telegraph* of Sept. 19, 1962 (entitled, "Mosley Claims 'Victory' "):

After speaking almost uninterruptedly for three-quarters of an hour in Southam Street, North Kensington, last night, Sir Oswald Mosley, leader of the Union Movement, said: "This is a decisive victory. The Red opposition has thrown in its hand."
Police stood in double ranks behind and in front of a van from which Sir Oswald spoke. The only interruptions from the crowd of 300 were cheers by his supporters and one or two boos.

See *Terminiello* v. *Chicago*, 337 U.S. 1 (1949); cf. *Kunz* v. *New York*, 340 U.S. 290 (1951).

See, also, Prime Minister Churchill's remarks in the House of Commons, July 15, 1952, about proposed action against Dr. Hewlett Johnson, "the Red Dean of Canterbury." "We must keep a sense of proportion," he counseled, "and not add to the harm that has already been done."

. . . Anyone who has listened to the explosive utterances of orators at Hyde Park Corner and watched their orderly audiences realizes the value of such safety valves. The story of the London bobby listening to a particularly inflammatory speech and finally drawling, "All those who are going to burn down Buckingham Palace make a line on this side," is not untypical. . . . [Gwendolen M. Carter and John H. Herz, *Major Foreign Powers* (New York: Harcourt, Brace & World, 1967), p. 53]

See chap. 5, n. 135, chap. 7, n. 42, above.

81. *Missouri, Kansas and Texas Railway Co.* v. *May*, 194 U.S. 267, 270 (1904). See, "on the place of the Supreme Court in our political structure," Thomas I. Emerson, "Toward a General Theory of the First Amendment," *Yale L. J.* 72 (1963): 877, 905, n. 24.

See, for a detailed technical analysis of Supreme Court cases bearing on the First Amendment, Thomas I. Emerson, *The System of Freedom of Expression* (New York: Random House, 1970). See, for collections of materials on this subject, Thomas I. Emerson, David Haber, and Norman Dorsen, *Political and Civil Rights in the United States*, 3d ed. (Boston: Little, Brown & Co., 1963); Edward DeGrazia, *Censorship Landmarks* (New York: R. R. Bowker Co., 1969). See, also, chap. 2, n. 27, above.

82. The rule of law, especially as embodied in *habeas corpus*, presupposes an independent *and* competent judiciary. See Djilas, *The New Class*, p. 88.

It may be affirmed without extravagance that the free institutions we enjoy have developed the powers and improved the condition of our whole people beyond any example in the world. Of this we now have a striking and an impressive illustration. So large an army as the government has now on foot was never before known, without a soldier in it but who has taken his place there of his own free choice. But more than this, there are many single regiments whose members, one and another, possess full practical knowledge of all the arts, sciences, professions, and whatever else, whether useful or elegant, is known in the world; and there is scarcely one from which there could not be selected a President, a cabinet, a congress, and perhaps a court, abundantly competent to administer the government itself. [Lincoln, *Complete Works*, 2:64 (speech of July 4, 1861)]

Lincoln's qualification with respect to personnel for a court should be noticed: popular government may not produce judges as readily (i.e., without special training) as it does "a President, a cabinet, a congress." See chap. 7, n. 118, chap. 8, n. 76, above.

The courts are most effective in the "short-run" and in the very long run: their prestige and sanctions are of effect in the former, their educational powers are of effect in the latter. It is in the intermediate stage, which can be quite a long period, that they may be vulnerable to the resistance of public opinion or to the attacks of other parts of the government. Cf. p. 236, above. See Burke, *Works*, 4:85.

See Ralph Lerner, "The Supreme Court as Republican Schoolmaster," *Supreme Court Rev.* (1967), p. 127. See, also, Appendix F, chap. 4, nn. 37, 116, above.

83. Another orthodox opinion discussed throughout this book (and which I find it salutary to question) is the belief that the provisions of the Bill of Rights are extended against the states by virtue of "incorporation" through the Fourteenth Amendment. (See, e.g., *Malloy* v. *Hogan*, 378 U.S. 1 [1964] and the cases cited therein.) Whatever may be true of most of the provisions of the Bill of Rights, I believe that so great a departure from the relations between governments reflected in the First Amendment would require clearer language for this purpose (if the courts are to be bound by it) than that found in the Fourteenth Amendment (whatever may have been said in the 1860s about the amendment). Clarity is not served, moreover, when advocates of such "incorporation" have recourse to readings of the "privileges and immunities" and "due process of law" language of the Fourteenth Amendment markedly different from readings of the same language elsewhere in the Constitution. (Why, for example, is the "due process" clause of the Fourteenth Amendment needed if the Fifth Amendment, with *its* "due process" clause, is now extended by Fourteenth Amendment incorporation to apply to the states as well? If, however, it is by virtue of the due process clause of the Fourteenth Amendment that incorporation of the Bill of Rights is effected, are *all* the other provisions of Sec. 1 of the Fourteenth Amendment needed? See Crosskey, *Politics and the Constitution*, pp. 1101-2, 1109-10, 1116-17, 1154-58. See, also, pp. 28-30, above.)

The courts' use of the Fourteenth Amendment has always been remarkable. Even though my primary constitutional inquiry in this book must be directed to a careful reading of the First Amendment text, it is useful to develop further at this point in my discussion of the judiciary my necessarily tentative opinions about the Fourteenth Amendment. See Malcolm P. Sharp, "The Master," *Univ. Chicago L. Rev.* 35 (1968): 239-40 ("Anyone working in the law must of course operate with alternative, mutually inconsistent systems of thought." Cf. chap. 6, n. 50, above).

Sec. 1 of the Fourteenth Amendment opens with the stipulation that "All persons born or naturalized in the United States, and subject to the jurisdiction thereof, are citizens of the United States and of the State wherein they reside." The most immediate and obvious beneficiaries of this stipulation in 1868 were the recently liberated slaves. The remainder of Sec. 1, it seems to me, is devoted to an attempt to anticipate state attempts to evade the full application of the opening stipulation: such evasions may (if not prevented) come about by a state's "abridg[ing] the privileges or immunities of citizens of the United States," or by a state's "depriv[ing] person[s] of life, liberty, or property, without due process of law" or by a state's "deny[ing] person[s] within its jurisdiction

CHAPTER EIGHT, NOTE 83: PAGE 231

the equal protection of the laws." That is, it was anticipated that the rights of American citizenship might be blatantly taken away, or that life, liberty, and property might be discreetly taken away through proceedings which pretend to due process, or that persons might be accorded genuine due process of law but only in the application to them of laws which are not the same as the laws applied to others in like circumstances. Thus, three possible alternative attempts by states to refuse to respect fully the citizenship of all its residents are foreclosed.

What *are* the "privileges and immunities of citizens of the United States"? Perhaps section 2 of the Fourteenth Amendment is our most reliable guide to what the framers of the amendment may have had in mind. The evident concern in section 2 is to protect "the right to vote at any election for the choice of electors for President and Vice-President of the United States, Representatives in Congress, the Executive and Judicial officers of a State, or the members of the Legislature thereof," a right which belongs (subject to specified limitations) "to any of the male inhabitants of such State, being twenty-one years of age, and citizens of the United States." Citizenship seems the distinctive feature here in qualifying a male resident for the vote. (It may be worth noting, as further suggesting a connection between section 2 and the "privileges and immunities" provision of sec. 1, that "abridge" is used in both places.) Protection of the right to vote is reinforced by providing for the reduction of the number of representatives of a state in Congress in proportion to the number of male citizens resident therein who have had their right to vote improperly taken away. (This right to vote, it should be noted, extends to the selection of state officers, thereby reinforcing the "Republican Form of Government" guarantee in Article IV, section 4, of the Constitution.) Section 3 of the Fourteenth Amendment suggests, by implication, that the right to be a candidate and to hold office in the general government or in a state government (again subject to specified limitations) may also be one of the "privileges and immunities" of citizenship. (Still another may be, if one *is* to enjoy due process and equal protection, the standing to sue in the courts of the general government and of the states. Cf. *Dred Scott* v. *Sandford*, 19 How. [U.S.] 393 [1857]. See *Corfield* v. *Coryell*, 4 Wash. C. C. 371 [U.S. Cir. Ct., E.D. Pa., 1825]; *Slaughter-House Cases*, 16 Wall. [U.S.] 36 [1873]. See, also, Crosskey, *Politics and the Constitution*, chaps. 31-32.) See, on national citizenship, Paine, *Writings*, 1:375.

To what extent is the First Amendment's "freedom of speech [and] of the press" protected against state abridgment in order that "the right to vote" might be assured? Section 5 of the Fourteenth Amendment can be understood as making explicit what I have argued is an implication of the First Amendment, that "Congress shall have power to enforce, by appropriate legislation, the provisions of [the Fourteenth Amendment]"— that is, that Congress may supervise and moderate state abridgments of freedom of speech and of the press, especially when such abridgments threaten the effective exercise of the right of suffrage. (A technical problem with the "incorporation" argument should be noticed here. Since the national "privileges and immunities" of citizens with respect to speech and the press prior to the Fourteenth Amendment provided that *Congress* could not abridge "freedom of speech or of the press," what could the states have done, or do, to abridge *that* right? Since, that is, the states could not authorize or empower Congress to abridge "freedom of speech or of the press," an extension against the states of that precise immunity from Congressional abridgment would be meaningless. Cf. Crosskey, *Politics and the Constitution*, pp. 1092-95. The language of the other articles of the Bill of Rights [except the Seventh] does make the "incorporation" argument more plausible with respect to them, but perhaps only at first glance.)

We should be cautious in our use of the "due process" clause of the Fourteenth Amendment in applying against the states the freedom of speech and press provisions of the First Amendment. Certainly, one cannot be deprived by the states of *any* liberty, including the liberty of speaking and of publishing, without due process of law. The liberty of publishing is reflected in the traditional prohibition of "previous restraints" (or censorship) with respect to publications. But in extending against the states in this manner (through the Fourteenth Amendment or through such provisions of the original constitution which imply the rule of law as the *ex post facto* clauses or the "Republican

Form of Government" guarantee) a substantial part of the First Amendment protection, we should take care that we do not permit Congress to be empowered to regulate speech to the extent the states are empowered to do so consistent with "due process of law." That is, we should insist that Congress may not, even if it should respect due process of law in doing so, abridge freedom of speech or of the press. (Thus, I am saying here, in a different way, what I have suggested in chapter 7 about the emergence of the "clear and present danger" test. One effect of confining the states' power with respect to speech and the press has been to enlarge the power of the general government, an enlargement reflected in the Chicago mayor's use of the federal courts [through his protégé in the U.S. Attorney's office] to prosecute his grievances against those who had protested so vigorously in 1968 his self-defeating management of the Democratic National Convention. See Appendix D, above. Cf. chap. 9, n. 32 [end], below. See, also, *Federalist*, p. 559.)

However this may be, it is prudent to observe that if the framers of the Fourteenth Amendment had intended to extend First Amendment (or, for that matter, Sixth Amendment) rights against the states, they could have imitated the language directed against the states in the provision sent by the House of Representatives in August, 1789, to the Senate for inclusion in the Bill of Rights: "No State shall infringe the right of trial by Jury in criminal cases, nor the rights of conscience, nor the freedom of speech, or of the press." See Appendix A, above. The fact remains, moreover, that the uses of speech which *are* immediately dangerous for us (and not necessarily because of any bad intention on the part of the speaker) tend to be local in origin and effect. What the states did, and do, want from the general government in *our* constitutional system is an assurance of help (but only upon request) should matters get out of hand locally (whether because of inappropriate speech or because of other causes). U.S., *Constitution*, Art. 4, sec. 4. What citizens and the country at large require is power in the general government (which is itself dedicated to and dependent upon freedom of speech) to supervise and correct state regulation of speech in the event that the states should become harmful in exercising the regulatory powers left with them.

The great national controversies (such, for example, as the question of the good sense of an incredibly foolish war which lies at the root of the 1917-19 *Schenck* controversy) are essentially political, not something to be dealt with by penal statutes and in the courts, at least not if our "Form of Government" is to be preserved. If such controversy does threaten to get out of hand—if, that is, neither moderating arguments nor the exercise of state power nor the prospect of federal prosecution directed at the actions resulting from speech nor actual federal prosecution of these resulting actions can "contain" such threatening controversy—then the general government does have recourse to its emergency powers. See, e.g., the discussions in this book of the suspension of the writ of *habeas corpus*. (Cf. the premature use in Canada of the War Measures Act.)

But in the ordinary course of events, Congress neither has nor should have any power to deal with the occasional abuses of freedom of speech and of the press among us. On this both the "federalists" and the "anti-federalists" (or states'-rightists) in the First Congress seem to have been agreed. Thus, Madison could suggest that the proposed 1789 restriction upon the states with respect to speech and press would have been "the most valuable amendment in the whole list." *Annals*, I, p. 755. Livermore, on the other hand, could protest that the proposed Bill of Rights (directed against the general government) did not really deal with anything substantial: his constituents, he said, "would not value [the amendments now found in the Bill of Rights] more than a pinch of snuff; they went to secure rights never in danger." *Annals*, I, pp. 774-75. That is, Madison recognized that the states, not Congress, had substantial power to abridge freedom of speech and of the press; consequently, he attempted to have the states restricted in this respect. Others (such as Livermore and Tucker) recognized that the substantial powers Congress did have were not with respect to speech and the press but rather with respect to *taxation and commerce*; consequently, they attempted to have Congress restricted in these matters. (Even in the Ratification Campaign of 1787-89, imaginative "anti-federalists" were hard put to find in the original constitution any powers of Congress which could be plausibly exhibited as posing a danger to freedom of speech and of the press.

Cf. *John Marshall: Major Opinions and Other Writings*, ed. John P. Roche [Indianapolis: Bobbs-Merrill Co., 1967], pp. 34-48, esp. pp. 43-44. But see *ibid.*, pp. xxiv, 27-32; Burke, *Works*, 2:94, 103, 115, 118-19, 121, 130-33, 137, 142-43, 145-46, 147-48, 149-50, 184-85, 191-93, 213-14, 223, 227, 268-78.)

It should be noticed, in assuring those who want to see the states held in check, that state constitutions do have provisions (although usually with an "abuse" qualification) protecting freedom of speech and of the press. (The presence of such "abuse" qualifications reminds us that "freedom of speech [and] of the press" cannot be defined to encompass only that speaking and publishing which is not "abused." There *are* risks to be run for the sake of a useful liberty.) State officers, as well as officers of the general government, should not only be reminded of their oaths of office but also instructed about the meaning, purposes, and value of the constitutional provisions which they are sworn to uphold. It should also be noticed that many, if not most, of the arguments for freedom of speech on the national level would of course apply to some extent on the local level as well, especially since those "levels" are often difficult to distinguish in practice.

See, for further discussion of various of the points gathered together in this note, pp. 6, 21, 22-23, 43, 54, 69-70, 79, 80-88, 98, 120-22, 134-35, 159, 161-66, 171-74, 176-77, 185-86, 189-97, 208, 210, 306-11, 415-16, chap. 2, nn. 13, 37, chap. 3, nn. 2, 13, 23, chap. 4, nn. 2, 5, 8, 86, 88, 98, 107, 109, chap. 5, nn. 117, 153, chap. 6, nn. 8, 70, 75, chap. 7, nn. 1, 3, 26, 35, 54, 81, 82, 84, 96, 97, 98, 99, 106, 107, chap. 8, nn. 13, 15, 18, 26, 77, above, chap. 8, nn. 85, 95, 96, 181, chap. 9, nn. 1, 11, below.

We can now turn, having reviewed one facet of the federalist argument of this book, to a consideration of the current orthodox opinion about judicial review, particularly since judicial review may be for us a prudent form of a perhaps inevitable states'-rightist tendency to intervene in the affairs of the general government. See, for the minimum extent of judicial review, Crosskey, *Politics and the Constitution*, pp. 1107-8, 1155.

84. There does not seem to be any question that the Supreme Court can pass on the conformity of state acts with the Constitution of the United States. Thus, Justice Holmes once observed:

> I do not think the United States would come to an end if we lost our power to declare an Act of Congress void. I do think the Union would be imperiled if we could not make that declaration as to the laws of the several States. For one in my place sees how often a local policy prevails with those who are not trained to national views and how often action is taken that embodies what the Commerce Clause was meant to end. [Holmes, *Collected Legal Papers*, pp. 295-96]

See chap. 7, nn. 65, 81, above.

Hobbes's *Dialogue between a Philosopher and a Student of the Common Laws of England* (reprinted in 1971, with a most valuable introduction by Joseph Cropsey, by the University of Chicago Press) discusses in the most serious way the underlying problems of judicial review. See, also, Hobbes, *Leviathan*, chap. 26. Thus, one must assess with Hobbes the traditional opinion that law is informed by reason and cannot be law if it conflicts with reason. Cf. pp. 331-32, 417-18, above.

85. *Marbury* v. *Madison*, 1 Cranch [U.S.] 137 (1803). See, also, *McCulloch* v. *Maryland*, 4 Wheat. [U.S.] 316, 423 (1819). Cf. Beveridge, *John Marshall*, 3:177-78. See Tocqueville, *Democracy in America*, 1:107, 289; Sutherland, *Constitutionalism in America*, pp. 318-41.

Can Congress provide by statute for judicial review of (as distinguished from advisory opinions about) acts of Congress? (See Pritchett, *The American Constitution*, pp. 158 ff.) Have the people and Congress acquiesced in, and hence implicitly granted, the jurisdiction exercised by the Supreme Court with respect to such matters? (See *Norris* v. *Clymer*, 2 Pa. St. 277, 281 [1845].) Indeed, has not Congress ratified, if not invested, such power in the Court by sometimes providing for what is to happen to the remainder of a statute if one part should be declared unconstitutional? See chap. 8, n. 91, below. See, also, chap. 5, n. 134, above, chap. 8, n. 96, below.

I can do little more than mention here a suggestion to be developed on another occasion, that the recognition of judicial review in *Marbury* v. *Madison* is the Federalist substitute for the remedy against unconstitutional legislation that had been promoted in 1798 by the Virginia and Kentucky Resolutions. See Sutherland, *Constitutionalism in America*, pp. 253-61. (Judicial review, with its aristocratic connotations, has always been regarded with suspicion by democrats. See chap. 8, n. 77, above. See, also, Taylor, *Inquiry into the Principles of the Government*, pp. 204 ff., 222 ff.) The Federalists had said, both in the Fifth Congress (e.g., *Annals*, V, p. 2016) and in the state legislatures responding to the Resolutions (e.g., Rhode Island, Massachusetts, New Hampshire, Vermont), that the proper remedy against unconstitutional legislation by Congress was not state interposition or nullification but judicial review.

> So stood the formal record; but, since it had been written, the Jeffersonian propaganda had drawn scores of thousands of voters into the Republican ranks. . . . Nothing was plainer than that, if the Kentucky and Virginia Resolutions had been submitted to the Legislatures of the various States in 1801-1803, most of them would have enthusiastically endorsed them. Thus the one subject most discussed, from the campaign of 1800 to the time when Marshall delivered his opinion in Marbury *vs*. Madison, was the all-important question as to what power, if any, could annul acts of Congress. During these years popular opinion became ever stronger that the Judiciary could not do so, that Congress had a free hand so far as courts were concerned, and that the individual States might ignore National laws whenever those States deemed them to be infractions of the Constitution. . . . Should this conclusion go unchallenged? If so, it would have the sanction of acquiescence and soon acquire the strength of custom. What then would become the condition of the country? . . . At the very least it would provoke a relapse into the chaos of the Confederation and more probably a civil war. . . . The fundamental question as to what power could definitely pass upon the validity of legislation must be answered without delay. . . . Only second in importance to these reasons for Marshall's determination to meet the issue [in *Marbury* v. *Madison*] was the absolute necessity of asserting that there was one department of the Government that could not be influenced by temporary public opinion. The value to a democracy of a steadying force was not then so well understood as it is at present, but the Chief Justice fully appreciated it and determined at all hazards to make the National Judiciary the stabilizing power that it has since become. [Beveridge, *John Marshall*, 3:107-9]

(Chief Justice Marshall's most famous statement of limitations upon *state* power may be that of *McCulloch* v. *Maryland*, 4 Wheat. [U.S.] 316, 436 [1819]: "[T]he States have no power, by taxation or otherwise, to retard, impede, burden, or in any manner control the operations of the constitutional laws enacted by Congress to carry into execution the powers vested in the general government." The limits of judicial review, even when invoked by a state, are indicated, on the other hand, in *Frothingham* v. *Mellon*, 262 U.S. 447 [1923]. Cf. *Flast* v. *Cohen*, 392 U.S. 83 [1968].)

Thus, if judicial review is justified, it should be particularly appropriate with respect to First Amendment controversies. (See, for John Marshall's opinions about the Sedition Act, Beveridge, *John Marshall*, 2:388-89, 404-5, 451-52; 3:106-7. Cf. ibid., 2:389 ff.) Should it be said as well that there is (short of revolution) no effective way, aside from judicial review, of immediately removing legislative restrictions upon freedom of speech? Thus, for instance, the ballot could become, for practical purposes, useless if opposition cannot be openly expressed to what the government is doing. See Erskine's observation in chap. 8, n. 68, above. See, also, chap. 9, n. 34, below.

Even without judicial review, the First Amendment would mean that courts should reach for that interpretation of a statute which avoids an abridgment of freedom of speech and of the press. That is, courts should proceed whenever possible on the assumption that Congress could not have intended to abridge freedom of speech. See, e.g., *Federalist*, pp. 523-24. (See Zechariah Chafee, *Freedom of Speech* [Cambridge: Harvard University Press, 1920], pp. 91, 118, on what the Department of Justice, the Post Office, and the judges did with "the moderate language of the Espionage Act of 1917.") See Herodotus, *History* 1.137. See, also, chap. 4, n. 52, chap. 6, n. 50, chap. 7, n. 83, above.

86. Crosskey, *Politics and the Constitution*, pp. 1031-32. Crosskey considered the authority of Coke's "ill-founded ideas" on this subject (see chap. 7, n. 77, above) discredited by "the glorious Revolution" of 1688, which established the supremacy of Parliament. Ibid., p. 941. But Congress is not supreme in the sense Parliament is said to be. See, e.g., chap. 8, n. 97, below. It cannot, for instance, extend the terms of office of its members. See chap. 8, n. 60, above.

See, for the challenge of Coke's authority by Hobbes (with the support of Bacon), the *Dialogue* by Hobbes and the introduction by Cropsey cited in chap. 8, n. 84, above.

87. This thought is implicit in another statement by Madison (*Annals, I*, pp. 500-501) quoted in chap. 4, n. 44, above.

88. Cf. Madison in chap. 4, n. 44, above. The context of the Benson quotation may be found at the end of chap. 3, sec. 3, above.

One way of posing the problem of this section is to ask who has the "rights," and hence who may invoke the remedies, provided by the First Amendment, individual citizens or the people as a whole? Does the reference in the First Amendment to "*the right of the people* to assemble, and to petition . . . " imply that "freedom of speech [and] of the press" are not rights of the people? (Or is the "right of the people" wording merely traditional phrasing?) That is, just whose freedom or right is guarded from abridgment? (Are "freedom" and "right" synonymous to the degree that "right" and "liberty" may be?)

"The very essence of civil liberty," Chief Justice Marshall said, "certainly consists in the right of every individual to claim the protection of the laws, whenever he receives an injury." *Marbury* v. *Madison*, 1 Cranch 137, 163 (1803). The chief justice's pronouncement would have even more force if the applicant involved in this case had indeed been given the protection he had sought. See Beveridge, *John Marshall*, 3:126-43; chap. 8, n. 135, below.

One difficulty with judicial review is that it is, or can be, less systematic than the exercise of legislative judgment. That is, what the courts decide may depend on such factors as the cases that *happen* to be presented for review and even the order of their presentation:

> It is one of the ironies of the flow of constitutional litigation that two [bar admission] cases come to the [Supreme Court of the United States] at the same time and that the court chooses first to dispose of the issue in *Konigsberg*, and then to apply it as a precedent to *Anastaplo*. [See Appendix F, above.] The issues might have been joined with greater clarity, and maybe, with different outcome, had the sequence been the other way around. [Harry Kalven, Jr., and Roscoe T. Steffen, "The Bar Admission Cases: An Unfinished Debate between Justice Harlan and Justice Black," *Law in Transition* 21 (1961): 155, 187]

I suspect, also, that things would have turned out differently for both Konigsberg and me if the Court had taken my case when I first took it up in 1955: Justice Harlan might not have become "locked into" the hostile attitude aroused in him by the record in the first *Konigsberg* case, an attitude which dominated his judgment thereafter in our bar admission cases. See chap. 4, nn. 44, 65, 82, 116, chap. 6, n. 5, above. Cf. Count Rumford, *Complete Works* (Boston: American Academy of Arts and Sciences, 1870), 1:392 (italics have been added by me to point up the role of chance even in scientific inquiry):

> I cannot finish this Essay ["Of the Propagation of Heat in Fluids"] without giving my reader an account of one more experiment, the result of which was not only *quite unexpected*, but uncommonly interesting.
>
> *Happening accidentally* to place in a window the little instrument I had contrived for rendering visible the internal motions which are occasioned in water when Heat is propagated in that fluid, as it was winter, and the room was warmed by a German stove, that side of the instrument which *happened* to be

nearest the window being exposed to a current of cold air, while the instrument received Heat continually on the other side from the warmer air of the room, the liquid in the instrument was thrown into motions which never ceased, and afforded a very interesting sight.

With a view merely to amuse myself, and the friends who should happen to call in to visit me, and without the smallest expectation of making any new discoveries, I contrived. . . .

See chap. 5, n. 34, above. See, also, James D. Watson, *The Double Helix: A Personal Account of the Discovery of the Structure of DNA* (New York: Atheneum, 1968); Burke, *Works*, 4:174 ("wisdom cannot create materials"), chap. 9, n. 39, below.

See chap. 7, n. 83, above, for a duty imposed upon the Attorney General of Massachusetts on behalf of that Commonwealth.

89. Lincoln elaborated upon this with the statement that "It is a maxim held by the courts, that there is no wrong without a remedy; and the courts have a remedy for whatever is acknowledged and treated as a wrong." *Complete Works*, 1:358. Blackstone, on the other hand, had said (*Laws of England*, 1:91), that "[if] the judges are at liberty to reject [a statute of parliament,] that were to set the judicial power above that of the legislature, which would be subversive of all government." But what if the rejection by the judges should be in the name of the "statute" of an even higher "legislature"—that is, in the name of the Constitution ordained and established by the people? Cf. Blackstone, *Laws of England*, 3:23, 109.

The extent to which Blackstone's teaching was modified in America (see the text at chap. 4, n. 70, above; see, also, chap. 6, nn. 20, 29, 37, above) is suggested by a passage from *Federalist* No. 78:

> The complete independence of the courts of justice is peculiarly essential in a limited Constitution. By a limited Constitution, I understand one which contains certain specified exceptions to the legislative authority; such, for instance, as that it shall pass no bills of attainder, no *ex-post-facto* laws, and the like. Limitations of this kind can be preserved in practice no other way than through the medium of courts of justice, whose duty it must be to declare all acts contrary to the manifest tenor of the Constitution void. Without this, all the reservations of particular rights or privileges would amount to nothing.
>
> . . . If it be said that the legislative body are themselves the constitutional judges of their own powers, and that the construction they put upon them is conclusive upon the other departments, *it may be answered*, that this cannot be the natural presumption, where it is not to be collected from any particular provisions in the Constitution. . . . A constitution is, in fact, and must be regarded by the judges, as a fundamental law. It therefore belongs to them to ascertain its meaning, as well as the meaning of any particular act proceeding from the legislative body. If there should happen to be an irreconcilable variance between the two, that which has the superior obligation and validity ought, of course, to be preferred; or, in other words, the Constitution ought to be preferred to the statute, the intention of the people to the intention of their agents.
>
> Nor does this conclusion by any means suppose a superiority of the judicial to the legislative power. It only supposes that the power of the people is superior to both. . . .

I have italicized four words which raise for me the question whether the author (this article is attributed to Hamilton) meant this statement to represent his own sentiments or merely those convenient in these circumstances. Crosskey, at pp. 1026-28, did not notice the italicized words in his attempt to establish that what Hamilton says in *Federalist* No. 33 (against judicial review) "accords much better with what is known to have been his true conviction as to what was desirable" than what he says in *Federalist* No. 78. (In the passage from *Federalist* No. 33 [to which Crosskey referred] the author recognizes, "But it may be again asked." In his reply there may be found not "it may be answered" but rather [at two points] "I answer." It may be that a careful check of the *Federalist* would permit one to separate Publius's "true conviction" from what was said for the occasion. See chap. 8, n. 181, below; cf. chap. 2, n. 37, above.) See *Federalist*, pp. 295, 327-32, 332-35, 335-41, 346, 425-26, 523-24, 526.

I should add that I am not satisfied by Crosskey's disposition of *Federalist* No. 78. It is good to be reminded, in Crosskey's words at p. 1026, "that advocates for the Constitution, in the ratification campaign, were apt to say about it, not what they actually thought, but what they thought would help it to be adopted." (See chap. 6, n. 3, above.) But what, then, was the understanding of the people who ratified the instrument? One must, in such circumstances, look at the cogency and effect of the arguments themselves rather than at what the authors' "true convictions" might otherwise be determined to be. And, it may be said, the argument I have quoted from *Federalist* No. 78 seems a particularly salutary one in our circumstances.

Also salutary is that our people be reassured, as in the words of Article I, section 19, Constitution of Illinois, "Every person ought to find a certain remedy in the laws for all injuries and wrongs which he may receive in his person, property or reputation. . . ." (See, on "person," chap. 6, n. 75, above.)

90. *Annals*, I, p. 248. Cf. *Annals*, I, pp. 31-32. Whether these rights were really threatened is another matter. Washington had advanced as one reason for a bill of rights that it would help settle "the degree of inquietude" aroused by its absence; he argued that "a regard for the public harmony" should be taken into account. *Annals*, I, pp. 28-29.

91. I overstate the case a bit: it is obvious (as I have already noted) that Congress does suppress many bad bills that are introduced. See chap. 4, n. 37, above; chap. 8, n. 151, below. See, also, Milton R. Konvitz, *Expanding Liberties: Freedom's Gains in Postwar America* (New York: Viking Press, 1966), pp. 142, 162; *Federalist*, pp. 402-3; Daniel Webster, at p. 212, above.

92. The quotation from Madison may be found in the text at chap. 7, n. 83, above.

To some degree, this function of the states does not depend on an understanding among state government men of this role. Reservations were expressed from the beginning about the quality of state governments. Thus, Jackson observed that in Rhode Island "liberty is changed to licentiousness." *Annals*, I, p. 442.

Is not the shift in the House of Representatives from guarding the rights of the people to implementing the will of the people a shift from one view of "liberty" to another? See chap. 2, n. 10, above.

See Jacob Klein, "The Problem of Freedom," *The College* (St. John's College), Dec. 1969, p. 4. See, in Strauss and Cropsey, *History of Political Philosophy*, the following articles as they bear on the problem of freedom: Muhsin Mahdi, "Alfarabi," pp. 178-80; Duncan B. Forrester, "Luther and Calvin," pp. 292-97, 300-302; Herbert J. Storing, "William Blackstone," pp. 539, 542, 545-46; Warren Winiarski, "Niccolo Machiavelli," p. 275, n. 13; Francis Canavan, "Edmund Burke," p. 612; Werner Dannhauser, "Friedrich Nietzsche," p. 742; and Pierre Hassner, "Georg W. F. Hegel," pp. 635-37. Cf. Robert Horwitz, "Scientific Propaganda: Harold D. Lasswell," in Herbert J. Storing, ed., *Essays on the Scientific Study of Politics* (New York: Holt, Rinehart & Winston, 1962), p. 293, n. 119.

93. Sumner reported, in *Andrew Jackson*, pp. 361-62:

> The proceedings of the Supreme Court are almost always overlooked in ordinary narrations of history, but he who looks for real construction or growth in the institutions of the country should look to those proceedings first of all. Especially in the midst of a surging democracy, exposed to the chicane of political mountebanks and the devices of interested cliques, the firmness and correctness with which the court has held its course on behalf of constitutional liberty and order had been of inestimable value to the nation.

See, also, Henry Adams, *The Education of Henry Adams* (Boston: Houghton Mifflin Co., 1918), p. 277.

Much of what I say here begins from the perspective of the lawyer—that is, from the perspective of the Supreme Court. Every American writer on constitutional law today sits, in effect, with the judiciary. The nine justices of the Supreme Court are, for Americans, recognized custodians of that "knowledge and virtue" to which the appeals of responsible free men are made. "In this case, final recourse is had to the high trusteeship vested in this Court by the people of the United States over the constitutional process by which their own lives may be taken." Justice Burton (dissenting), *Louisiana ex rel. Francis v. Resweber*, 329 U.S. 459, at 477 (1947). (Cf. chap. 8, n. 45, above, chap. 9, n. 39, below.) See chap. 4, nn. 37, 116, above.

94. See Aristotle, *Nicomachean Ethics* 1095a25-26. Walter Berns has expressed the hope that many entertain:

> The practice of judicial review, possible under a system of separated powers, can to a limited extent overcome the bigotry of legislators and censors and citizens; judicial review, used wisely and courageously, can make up some deficiency of virtue in the community. . . . The First and Fourteenth Amendments permit, but do not guarantee, a further opportunity for wisdom and prudence to be introduced into the American Constitution, that is, into the American way of life. [Berns, *Freedom, Virtue and the First Amendment*, p. 254]

(Willmoore Kendall observed, citing Berns's book, "Freedom, we have lately been reminded, is a 'problem.' " He then added, "Professor Berns sometimes seems to forget that virtue also is 'a problem.' " "How to Read Milton's *Areopagitica*," *Journal of Politics* 22 [1960]: 439.) Cahn observed that

> Year by year, save only its mottled performance in the field of national security, the Court seems to bring deeper understanding, wider sympathy, and more intelligent analysis to the moral aspects of legal problems. . . . Often the Court demonstrates that one or another provision of the Bill of Rights is not only binding law, it is also good and true and morally right. [Edmond Cahn, *The Great Rights* (New York: Macmillan Co., 1963), pp. 9-10]

See John Paul Frank, *Marble Palace: The Supreme Court in American Life* (New York: Knopf, 1958), p. 284.

Meiklejohn, on the other hand, insisted in 1948 that "the Supreme Court of the last forty years, more than any other agency or person in our society, must be held responsible for the destruction of those Constitutional principles which that court is commissioned to interpret and to defend." Alexander Meiklejohn, *Political Freedom: The Constitutional Powers of the People* (New York: Harper & Bros., 1960), p. 106. See chap. 2, n. 15, above. Does judicial review moderate our politics by seeming to settle more than it can (and by providing for some a convenient scapegoat) when change is critical?

95. Perhaps it is not what the Court does but what it is feared it might do that restrains Congress. But, Sharp (chap. 2, n. 14, above) has argued, it would be better if the Court did nothing rather than, as has almost uniformly been its practice when congressional legislation has been subjected by it to the test of the First Amendment, tell the Congress that nothing is wrong. See chap. 8, n. 83, above. (Biddle reported that, as attorney general, he prosecuted certain Trotskyists under the Smith Act during the Second World War with the hope and expectation that the Supreme Court would invalidate the act. The Supreme Court did not review the case. Francis B. Biddle, *In Brief Authority* [Garden City, N.Y.: Doubleday & Co., 1962), pp. 151-52. See *Dunne v. U.S.*, 138 F.2d 137 [1943], cert. den., 320 U.S. 790 [1943].) I would prefer, however, to notice what Federalist No. 78 says about the judiciary, that it has "neither FORCE nor WILL, but merely judgment. . . . "

Is it not the judgment of man that the First Amendment should be said to serve as well? See Burke, *Works*, 4:102-3.

See chap. 2, n. 28, chap. 3, n. 14, chap. 4, n. 37, chap. 7, n. 72, above, chap. 9, n. 39, below. The effect on Congress and the President of Supreme Court decisions, or of the anticipation of decisions, may be seen (among other places) in chap. 6, nn. 38, 75,

CHAPTER EIGHT, NOTE 96: PAGE 237   719

chap. 8, nn. 29, 52, above. Consider the significance of the question to which newspaper articles have recently been addressed (e.g., *Chicago Sun-Times*, June 28, 1970, p. 5), "Will the Supreme Court go along with vote at 18?"

96. See *Progressive*, Sept. 1957, p. 6. Cf. chap. 7, n. 72, above. See *New Yorker*, May 30, 1970, pp. 23-24.

See Hayek, *Constitution of Liberty*, pp. 190-91, on the public and congressional response to President Roosevelt's "Court Packing Bill." Hayek quoted from the report of the Senate Judiciary Committee,

> If the Court of last resort is to be made to respond to a prevalent sentiment of a current hour, politically imposed, that Court must ultimately become subservient to the pressure of public opinion of the hour, which might at the moment embrace mob passion abhorrent to a more calm, lasting, consideration. . . . No finer or more durable philosophy of free government is to be found in all the writings and practices of great statesmen than may be found in the decisions of the Supreme Court when dealing with great problems of free government touching human rights. [Hayek then commented,] No greater tribute has ever been paid by a legislature to the very Court which limited its powers. And nobody in the United States who remembers this event can doubt that it expressed the feelings of the great majority of the population. [Note: I shall not easily forget how this feeling was expressed by the taxi driver in Philadelphia in whose cab we heard the radio announcement of President Roosevelt's sudden death. I believe he spoke for the great majority of the people when he concluded a deeply felt eulogy of the President with the words: "But he ought not to have tampered with the Supreme Court, he should never have done *that*!" The shock had evidently gone very deep.]

The Senate Report quoted from is "Reorganization of the Federal Judiciary: Adverse Report from the [Senate] Committee on the Judiciary Submitted to Accompany S. 1392" (75th Cong., 1st sess., Senate Rept. No. 711, June 7, 1937). See Mason, *Harlan Fiske Stone*, pp. 437 ff. See, also, chap. 8, n. 78, above.

"The people have seemed to feel that the Supreme Court, whatever its defects, is still the most detached, dispassionate, and trustworthy custodian that our system affords for the translation of abstract into concrete constitutional commands." Jackson, *Supreme Court in American System*, p. 23. See pp. 27-28, above.

(Allen W. Dulles suggested, in a statement prepared for Congress when it was considering the National Security Act of 1947, "The duties the Chief [of Central Intelligence] will have to perform will call for the judicial temperament in high degree." Ransom, *The Intelligence Establishment*, p. 259. Indeed, the terms and tone of this memorandum reinforce my general impression that there is much more uniting Americans than dividing them. It is the duty of prudent men—and especially men of judicial temperament—to "contain" our differences by ratifying and implementing the fundamental principles to which virtually all Americans may be said to be dedicated. The serious heretic or would-be usurper is still rare among us. See chap. 8, n. 135, below.)

Perhaps the relation between the American people and its judges is best illustrated by the story told to the Phaecians about Odysseus and the Sirens (in bk. 12 of Homer's *Odyssey*). The sovereign Odysseus instructs his shipmates:

> Our prime duty will be to turn a deaf ear to [the Sirens'] singing. Only I may listen, after you have so fastened me with tight-drawn cords that I stand immovably secured against the tabernacle of the mast, with further short lashings dependent upon the mast itself: and if I beg you or bid you let me loose, then must you redoubly fasten me into place with yet more bonds.

Odysseus then filled with wax the ears of all his party before permitting himself to be tied to the mast. He concludes thus his story about their encounter with the Sirens:

> Such words [the Sirens] sang in lovely cadences. My heart ached to hear them

out. To make the fellows loose me I frowned upon them with my brows. They bent to it ever the more stoutly while Perimedes and Eurylochus rose to tighten my former bonds and wreathed me about and about with new ones: and so it was till we were wholly past them and could no more hear the Sirens' words nor their tune: then the faithful fellows took out the wax with which I had filled their ears, and delivered me from bondage.

Similarly, the sovereign American people has been able to insure constitutional bonds upon even itself, foreseeing in a time of calm and reflection the passions that can move it. Public servants have been empowered, no matter how much they are frowned upon, to stand by the trust vested in them. Reason is reinforced in this manner by institutions: Odysseus identifies Circe as the source of warnings concerning the Sirens; but the prudential arrangement, which permits Odysseus to have the best of both worlds, must really be the inspiration of Pallas Athena, the wise goddess who guides him in the best of what he says and does (including what he chooses to say to the Phaecians). (See, on the relation of Athena and Poseidon, and on the extent to which practical life can be reasonably expected to rely upon reason, Anastaplo, *Brief on the Merits,* Supreme Court of the United States [Appendix F, above], July 4, 1960, p. 78, n. 56.) It is appropriate to notice that it is Pallas Athena who may be regarded as the founder among men of judicial institutions (with the right assured each party to state fully its case). See Aeschylus, *The Eumenides.* Cf. Exod. 18:13-27.

I conclude this judicial toast with an American illustration. Laurence Berns wrote in an account of my oral argument in 1961 before the Supreme Court, which is reproduced in sec. 5 of Appendix F, above:

> I was impressed by the great dignity of the court. The manly bearing of Chief Justice [Warren] contributed to this impression. His large size, handsomeness and apparent strength, combined with his kindly, pleasant and almost gentle manners, in addition to his quite plain diction, would seem to have the effect of putting those facing the bench at their ease and at the same time impressing them with the dignity of the court. I thought him a kind of living argument for democracy.

It is true that "the great dignity of the court" notwithstanding, I did not secure on that occasion the bar admission decision I was entitled to. But I know as well that I would not at that time have secured in any legislative body or administrative agency or public opinion poll in this country the amount of support indicated by the 5-4 vote in the Supreme Court of the United States, the 4-3 vote in the Supreme Court of Illinois, or even the 11-6 vote among the lawyers of the Committee on Character and Fitness. Nor would there have been the legacy of records, briefs, and opinions for others to examine, to think about, and to use. Cf. chap. 7, n. 89, chap. 8, n. 18, above.

See chap. 9, n. 39, below.

97. The tendency of Britons to regard the national legislature rather than the people as "sovereign"—or more so than do Americans—is reflected in the rule which bars speakers on the BBC from discussing subjects due for parliamentary debate within fourteen days. Prime Minister Churchill defended this rule with the statement:

> I have always attached the greatest importance to Parliament and the House of Commons. I am sure the bringing on of exciting debates in this vast new robot organization of TV and broadcasting, timed to take place before a debate in this House, may have deleterious effects on our interests. [*Chicago Tribune,* Feb. 24, 1955]

See, also, Street, *Freedom, the Individual and the Law,* pp. 85-86.

It is recorded that the prime minister

> did once hold a press conference in the Queen Mary on his return from a visit to President Truman. It was a momentous occasion. He thanked the press for

CHAPTER EIGHT, NOTE 98: PAGE 237   721

their courtesy in coming down from London to see him, and added: "Of course, gentlemen, it was made plain to you before you left London that I would answer no questions about policy. I must leave that for the House of Commons." [*Manchester Guardian Weekly*, May 9, 1963]

It is, moreover, unconstitutional—when Parliament is sitting—for policy statements to be made to the press before they are made in Parliament, and I am surprised that the House of Commons has not made an issue of privilege of some of the statements which have been made at London Airport. For instance, after the Nassau meeting, Mr. Macmillan gave a full report to the nation as soon as he landed, and his subsequent report to the House added nothing of substance to what he had already said. Unless and until we become explicitly a Presidential democracy, Parliament ought not to allow itself to be so insulted. [John Grigg, "Too Busy by Half," *Manchester Guardian Weekly*, July 28, 1966, p. 6]

See, on the "sovereignty" of Parliament, *Federalist*, p. 348; Taylor, *Inquiry into the Principles of the Government*, pp. 212, 484, 487. Also revealing is an article in the *London Observer*, Oct. 12, 1969, p. 1:

Mrs. Margaret McKay, 58-year-old Labour MP for Clapham, may be dropped by her constituency executive as a candidate at the General Election because it disapproves of some of her recent public statements in support of the Arab cause in the Middle East. . . . The committee asked Mrs. McKay if she would meet them to discuss the matter. Mrs. McKay declined. The committee issued a statement disassociating the local party. A few days later Mrs. McKay . . . said: "It is just a little handful of Jewish and ardent Zionist members who have persuaded the rest of the committee. It is a matter of complete unimportance. They are local people who don't even know it isn't their business to interfere with their MP on foreign affairs, especially when she's an expert and they are not."
. . . Unlike previous conflicts between MPs and their constituents, Mrs. McKay's parliamentary activities are not in question. The committee recognizes her right to argue the Arab case in the Commons and vote according to her conscience. What angers it is what its members regard as the immoderate character of her extra-Parliamentary statements. The constitutional question is: tasteless or not, is this any of their business?

See Shils's observations in chap. 8, n. 74, above. See, on the use in Great Britain of the "D-Notice," Ransom, *The Intelligence Establishment*, pp. 197-207.

See Edmund Burke's 1780 speech to his constituents at Bristol, *Works*, 3:1. (Much of what I suggest about constitutionalism is anticipated in that speech, which has been called "the finest piece of oratory in our language." Ibid., p. viii. At the core of his argument is the observation, "I could hardly serve you *as I have done*, and court you too." Ibid., p. 6; italics his.) Cf. chap. 6, n. 57, above. ,

98. I have argued in this book and elsewhere that freedom of speech is the everyday equivalent for Americans of that right and duty of revolution insisted upon by the Declaration of Independence. The tentative interpretation which follows of the votes in the House of Representatives of the Fifth Congress on the Sedition Act of 1798 may reinforce this suggestion.

Of the 44 who voted for that act, we know the ages of 43; of the 41 who voted against it, we know the ages of 38. The known ages range from 23 through 68. I arrange them, for my purposes, in the age groups, 23-37, 38-54, 55-68 (which are of approximately equal spread in years: the "young," the "middle-aged," and the "old" members of the House of Representatives). Of the 43 known yeas, approximately 37% (16) were young, 47% (20) were middle-aged, and 16% (7) were old. Of the 38 known nays, 21% (8) were young, 71% (27) were middle-aged, and 8% (3) were old. It can be said of this difference in age distribution among the yeas and the nays that, statistically, one would expect, in only one of five chances, to find a random distribution of yeas and nays to show such a deviation or greater between the observed voting behavior and the voter's year of birth. (I am indebted for this formulation of the preceding sentence to Jeremiah J. German, my former colleague in the Industrial Relations Center of the University of Chicago. Adjustments can be made in the age groupings, which would affect somewhat the proportions, but would still leave significant disparities between yeas and nays.)

The difference in distribution, which shows the middle-aged, and only the middle-aged, significantly more disposed to vote nay than yea, may be explained in these terms: the middle-aged of 1798 were, at the beginning of the Revolution (twenty-two years before), between the ages of 16 and 32; the old of 1798 were already formed politically by the time of the Revolution; the young of 1798 were formed politically by events subsequent to the Revolution. My conclusion independent of these statistics has been that men shaped by the Declaration of Independence are more likely than others to be opposed to the Sedition Act of 1798 and to be sympathetic to freedom of speech as defined in this book. Are not the middle-aged among the age groups in the House of 1798 the very ones most likely to have been formed by the Revolution and its Declaration? (Cf. chap. 7, n. 103, above.) (The distribution of the voting of lawyers on the Sedition Act was noticed at chap. 6, n. 26, above. If one observes that the voting on the Sedition Act was along regional lines, and that the age distribution may be related to the regions of the members' origins, then one should consider what this reveals about how various regions of the country may have been shaped by the Declaration of Independence.)

I set forth these speculations here in order to invite suggestions and interpretations from others. See, e.g., chap. 9, n. 39, below. (Ages have been calculated from the information provided by the *Biographical Dictionary of the American Congress, 1774-1961* [Washington: Government Printing Office, 1961]. The year of birth recorded there is subtracted from 1798.)

See Jefferson's letter to Madison, Mar. 15, 1789 (*The Writings of Thomas Jefferson*, 14:659-61); Richard Henry Lee's letter to Samuel Adams, Aug. 8, 1789 (*The Letters of Richard Henry Lee*, ed. James C. Ballagh [New York: Macmillan Co., 1914], 2:496); Charles Warren, *The Making of the Constitution* (Boston: Little, Brown & Co., 1937), p. 759, n. 1; Crankshaw, *Khrushchev's Russia*, pp. 90-91, 136.

See, on rightful rebellion, pp. 417-18, above, p. 736 (Burke), below.

99. Even the *Federalist* speaks primarily of the press. See, e.g., the text at chap. 6, n. 2, above.

100. Should the freedom of speech of the people at large ever be suppressed by the general government, there would still remain, as a last peaceable resort for the expression and examination of differences, the immunities enjoyed by members of Congress and, perhaps, by members of the legislatures of the states. See *Annals*, V, pp. 2149-50. See, also, *Tenney v. Brandhove*, 341 U.S. 367 (1951). Cf. *Bond v. Floyd*, 385 U.S. 116 (1966). Consider Lincoln, *Complete Works*, 2:38; Paine, *Writings*, 2:330.

There would also remain, as a peaceful but extraconstitutional resort, the protest dissenters can make use of by dealing with foreign correspondents (who may have an immunity, up to a point, denied to citizens, an immunity which borrows from that enjoyed by diplomats). I have seen this in effect in Greece (where I have taken the precaution, ever since the colonels came, of having myself accredited as a foreign correspondent for American journals). See chap. 6, n. 1, above. Anatole Shub reported from Moscow activities similar to those I have observed in Greece (*A New Russian Tragedy* [New York: W. W. Norton & Co., 1969], pp. 65-66):

> The uninterrupted flow of *samizdat* manuscripts to the West (and thereby back to Russia by foreign radio) is a history in itself. Some of the pages of that history are perfectly straightforward, as when Russian democrats pass their protest petitions to Western newsmen outside courthouses.

See *Congressional Record* 116: E10520 (1970).

101. "Freedom of speech," which was rarely used before 1776, may be taken (as separate from "freedom of the press") to include all forms of political expression other

CHAPTER EIGHT, NOTES 102-3: PAGE 237

than those requiring the more formal processes of the press. Should this include, for instance, the writing of letters, even of the kind exchanged by the Committees of Correspondence in pre-Revolution days? Should "press" refer, that is, only to such publications as would once have been or now could be subject to censorship and "previous restraint"? See chap. 5, n. 3, above.

See chap. 5, n. 145, above. Both cost and detection are avoided in Communist countries by the use of wall posters and the *samizdat* (the manuscripts which are both copied and circulated by hand).

> As one China-watcher put it: "It takes more than a one-man effort to put out a newspaper. Some teen-ager can slap up a poster in the dead of night and never be seen again. But if someone publishes a newspaper, he has to stand up and defend what he has printed. And since he becomes more vulnerable to attack, he's going to make more of an effort to ensure that what he prints has been approved and is correct." [*Newsweek*, July 17, 1967, p. 29]

See, also, *London Sunday Times*, Aug. 29, 1967, p. 1:

> A year ago foreigners in Peking were allowed to read the wall posters—as proof that freedom of expression and democracy really existed in China. But the posters began to reveal too much, and now foreigners who pause to read them, or who buy Red Guard newspapers or other revolutionary material, risk being mobbed.

102. See, on the superiority of speech to writing, Plato, *Phaedrus* 274D-275E; Plato, *Epistles* 314B-C, 344C-D; Papias: "For I did not consider that I got so much profit from the contents of books as from the utterances of a living and abiding voice." Henry Bettenson, ed., *Documents of the Christian Church* (New York: Oxford University Press, 1947), p. 38. Cf. Milton: "Christ urged it as wherewith to justify himself, that he preached in public; yet writing is more public than preaching; and more easy of refutation, if need be . . . ," *Areopagitica*; Hume:

> We need not dread from this liberty [of the press] any such ill consequences as followed from the harangues of the popular demagogues of Athens and tribunes of Rome. A man reads a book or pamphlet alone and coolly. There is none present from whom he can catch the passion by contagion. He is not hurried away by the force and energy of action. And should he be wrought up to never so seditious a humour, there is no violent resolution presented to him by which he can immediately vent his passion. The liberty of the press, therefore, however abused, can scarce ever excite popular tumults or rebellion. ["Of the Liberty of the Press," in *David Hume's Political Essays*, ed. Charles W. Hendel (Indianapolis: Bobbs-Merrill, 1953), p. 6]

Cf., also, U.S., *Constitution*, Art. II, sec. 1: "[The President] may require the Opinion in writing, of the principal Officer in each of the executive Departments, upon any subject relating to the Duties of their respective Offices"; Lincoln, *Complete Works*, 1:528. But see Blackstone, *Laws of England*, 4:80 (discussed in chap. 5, n. 145, above). See, also, Hobbes, *Leviathan*, part 1, chap. 4; Street, *Freedom, the Individual and the Law*, p. 150; Crankshaw, *Khrushchev's Russia*, pp. 52, 57-58, 64-65, 113-14; Crankshaw, *Gestapo* (London: Random House, Pantheon Books, 1960), pp. 147, 186.

Is not speech made even better than it would otherwise be when there are writings to refer to and to discuss? And the better the writings (chap. 8, n. 122, below), the better the speech thereupon is likely to be? See Xenophon, *Memorabilia* I.vi.14.

103. This is so, in any event, as to political matters. The citizen does not have the immunity to libel and slander others that the legislator has, except perhaps in the context of political discussion.

See *Washington Post Co. v. Keogh*, 365 F.2d 965 (1966).

See chap. 5, section 9, above.

104. But, as a practical matter, it was conceded by a supporter of the Sedition Act of 1798 that a member of Congress could utter as much treason as he pleased on the floor. Members, he said, have to regulate themselves by their own sense of "propriety and decorum." *Annals*, V, p. 2102.

105. See chap. 5, n. 101, above. Although there are no legal sanctions with respect to these matters, American politicians (as well as citizens generally) have been most reluctant to advocate desegregation in the South or segregation in the North or admission of the mainland Chinese government to the United Nations in the North or South, regardless of what they really think. See Sidney Hook, "The 'Flawed' Fulbright," *St. Louis Globe-Democrat*, Sept. 2-3, 1967, p. 2F; cf. J. William Fulbright, "The Legislator," in Robert B. Heywood, *The Works of the Mind* (Chicago: University of Chicago Press, 1966), pp. 128-30. A more understanding, and hence political, approach to the southern legislator "flawed" by racism than that of Professor Hook may be found in the *New York Times* editorial upon Senator Lister Hill of Alabama:

> Now that he has announced his forthcoming retirement after 45 years of service in both houses of Congress, he leaves a dwindling band of Southern white liberals of his generation on Capitol Hill. These were men trapped by the racial history of their region and who dared to be progressive on every issue except civil rights. Despite this handicap, Lister Hill has served his state and nation well. [Jan. 27, 1968, p. 28]

Professor Hook, too, as is evident in his polemical writings about radicalism in America since the Second World War, has been "trapped" and even "flawed" by the bitter intellectual battles on the East Coast of his generation, battles which go back to the 1930s if not even to the 1920s. Professor Henry David Aiken (*New York Review of Books*, Feb. 12, 1970, p. 11) considered him one of those "ex-radical conservatives [who are] so full of bile and so full of animus against anyone who dares to tip the boat of our all-too-national society." I would observe that Professor Hook means well, that his immoderate indignation seems to be the indignation of a Callicles at the very thought of the good being destroyed with impunity by the wicked. Plato, *Gorgias* 511B. Thus, although it is probably too late to change Professor Hook, it is not too late to understand him as well as the well-meaning prisoners in the South. See pp. 252-53, above, chap. 8, n. 135, below. See, also, chap. 3, n. 20, above. (Is it significant in Hook's book that it is the negation of conspiracy, not the affirmation of heresy, which is emphasized by an exclamation point?)

"Office-seeking," Richard H. Rovere has observed, "is a great leveler." *The American Establishment* (New York: Harcourt, Brace & World, 1962), p. 82.

> There is every indication that George C. Wallace, as he approaches the culminating days of his bid for the highest office in the land, is moving nearer the political center. He has not yet become any sort of symbol of moderation, but at least he is showing signs that he wants to be in the mainstream of the American system, if and when he becomes president. This was fully reflected this week when he delivered his first dissertation on foreign affairs before the National Press Club. . . . Wallace's speech before the press club undoubtedly reflects the briefings he has been receiving from the administration from time to time on international affairs. He has acquired an understanding of the complex nature of the problems confronting this country abroad, and he obviously has no desire to advocate strange and unrealistic schemes to unravel them. Wallace, who evidently believes that he just might be elected president, appears to be a man who is now willing to modify his demagoguery and assume a mantle of respectability and high purpose. [Robert E. Baskin, "Wallace Moves Nearer Center," *Dallas Morning News*, Oct. 10, 1968, p. 5A]

> . . . Throughout the [1967 French electoral] campaign the desire of the Communists for acceptance and respectability had been striking. They are tired of the wilderness. They are eager for office and ready to assume the responsibilities that go with it, besides making the sacrifices that might lead to it. . . . [Nesta

CHAPTER EIGHT, NOTES 106-8: PAGE 240

Roberts, "The General Helps Communists to Become Respectable," *Manchester Guardian Weekly*, Mar. 16, 1967]

See chap. 7, n. 43, above. (The French Communists lost to the party of President de Gaulle in the June, 1968, parliamentary elections what they had gained in March, 1967:

> The Gaullist tactic was simple—blame the Communist Party for provoking and exploiting last month's [May 1968] upheaval and warn that a victory for the combined Communist and Socialist left would lead to a totalitarian dictatorship. . . . Caught flat-footed by the upheaval in May, the Communists were forced to take the lead in the strike movement to prevent being outflanked on the left. They applied the brakes to the movement in the name of order. Nevertheless, the charges by Prime Minister Georges Pompidou and other Gaullist leaders that the Communists were a step away from revolution apparently convinced and alarmed many Frenchmen. [Stephens Broening, "Gaullists Appear Certain to Control French Assembly," *Chicago Sun-Times*, June 25, 1968, p. 7]

See, with respect to the Communists "appl[ying] the brakes," the discussion in chap. 7, n. 124, above, of the usefulness of "party discipline.")

106. In this instance, the previous question was, "Shall the main question be now put?" This was negatived, thus shutting off further discussion of the Rhode Island proposal. See Sutherland, *Constitutionalism in America*, p. 444.

See chap. 8, n. 116, below.

107. Lincoln, *Complete Works*, 2:274. Lincoln's care in the use of language is exhibited by the shift in prepositions in his phrase, "through time and in eternity." Cf., at p. 200, above, the younger Lincoln. (Does not Hamlet, on the other hand, consider time to continue "through" eternity? See pp. 30-31, above. Would the lack of change "in" eternity make the notion of "eternal punishment" [say, of Claudius] unrealistic?) See chap. 9, n. 30, below. See, also, Paine, *Writings*, 2:277-79, 4:211.

108. Frank, *Marble Palace*, p. 183. It would not be thought today that the refusal of the House to refer certain petitions to committees would be inconsistent with the constitutional injunction against abridging "the right of the people . . . to petition the Government for a redress of grievances." Congress is prohibited, however, from imposing limitations on the right of petition (such as prescribing criminal liability for petitioners), whatever either House may do in disposing of the petitions submitted to it.

Precisely what is included in the traditional "right of the people to assemble and to petition the government for a redress of grievances," which is not included in "freedom of speech, or of the press," is hard to say. But to have left this traditional formulation out of the constitutional enumeration might have suggested that there is guaranteed something less than there could have been. (Cf. chap. 3, n. 11, above.)

The right of petition had been vital to the colonists in their dealings with Great Britain. ("In every stage of these Oppressions We have Petitioned for Redress in the most humble terms. Our repeated Petitions have been answered only by repeated injury." U.S., *Declaration of Independence*.) Petitions had had, in English law, a privileged character, at least compared with ordinary publications. (Cf. chap. 5, n. 145, above.) They have become less important in a regime which is as dependent as ours is on freedom of speech and of the press. (Cf. chap. 4, n. 105, above.) Are petitions more apt to be employed today by citizens acting in their capacity as subjects rather than in their capacity as rulers? (See chap. 5, nn. 92, 133, above. "The extraordinary tact and sure instinct of the Negro protest has made it primarily a massive petition for the redress of grievances, a form of political action, in the courts and in the streets." Harry Kalven, Jr., *The Negro and the First Amendment* [Chicago: University of Chicago Press, 1966], p. viii. This was said in September, 1964.)

Congress, in any event, cannot interfere with the access the people have to the Executive and to the Judiciary. (See, e.g., chap. 4, n. 83, above. See, also, chap. 4, nn. 87, 96, above.) No redress is guaranteed, but one has at least the satisfaction of having had one's say, of having been heard:

> *Katherina*: Why, sir, I trust I may have leave to speak:
> And speak I will; I am no child, no babe:
> Your betters have endured me say my mind,
> And if you cannot, best you stop your ears.
> My tongue will tell the anger of my heart,
> Or else my heart concealing it will break;
> And rather than it shall, I will be free
> Even to the uttermost, as I please, in words.

Shakespeare, *Taming of the Shrew*, act 4, sc. 3. (See chap. 8, n. 127, below.)
   See Story, *Commentaries on the Constitution*, 2:secs. 1893-96. See, also, Carl J. Friedrich, *Constitutional Government and Democracy: Theory and Practice in Europe and America* (Waltham, Mass.: Blaisdell Publishing Co., 1950), p. 159, on "assembly" having been broadened to include "association." (The right of petition and freedom of the press seem to have been blended in a recent development noted in *Parade*, June 1, 1969, p. 5:

> Petitions are a traditional democratic means of voicing dissent. But buying newspaper space at $5,000 and $10,000 a throw in The New York *Times* for that purpose is not. In a recent issue of *Science* magazine Everett Carll Ladd Jr., director of the political data center at the University of Connecticut, gives some facts about this new procedure. In 1953, a year with its fair share of political controversy, not one issue of the Sunday New York *Times* contained a petition. Last year the Sunday editions were jammed with paid petitions. Ladd reveals that for the last four years the war in Viet Nam has been the major subject of advertised protest, and that virtually all the mass-signature petitions have opposed government policy. . . .

Are not such advertisements a means of expressing *dissent* rather than of voicing grievances? See chap. 3, n. 22, chap. 5, n. 24, above.)
   109. This was said of Adams and of Rufus Choate by Justice Holmes. Howe, *Holmes-Pollock Letters*, p. 95. Choate himself had said, "John Quincy Adams had an instinct for the jugular and the carotid artery, as unerring as that of any carnivorous animal." Gilbert J. Clark, ed., *Great Sayings by Great Lawyers* (Kansas City, Mo.: Vernon Law Book Co., 1926), p. 12. One problem with "going for the jugular" is that men become desperate and even irresponsible in defending the jugular. (See chap. 8, n. 118, below.)
   One should not go for the jugular unless one is fairly sure it can be reached. (See chap. 8, n. 80, above.)

> [D]issenters frequently force the majority to take positions more extreme than was originally intended. The classic example is the *Dred Scott Case* [19 How. (U.S.) 393 (1856)], in which Chief Justice Taney's extreme statements were absent in his original draft and were inserted only after Mr. Justice McLean, then a more than passive candidate for the presidency, raised the issue in dissent. [Jackson, *Supreme Court in American System*, p. 19]

See chap. 2, n. 28, above.
   Emerson spoke of Adams as "a man of an audacious independence that always kept the public curiosity alive in regard to what he might do. None could predict his word, and a whole congress could not gainsay it when it was spoken." *Works*, 11:521.
   110. Tocqueville, *Democracy in America*, 1:394. See, also, ibid., 1:418-19. See, on whether slavery was indeed prejudicial to the economic interests of the southern planter, Harry V. Jaffa, *Crisis of the House Divided* (Garden City, N.Y.: Doubleday & Co., 1959), p. 396:

> The thesis that slavery would not have gone into the territories, whether it was prohibited by law or not, is the fundamental thesis of revisionism in dealing with the political causes of the Civil War. But this thesis is itself a subordinate manifestation of an apology for the South which has received a classic formula-

tion in the work of [Charles W.] Ramsdell [in "The Natural Limits of Slavery Expansion," published in the *Mississippi Valley Historical Review*, Oct. 1929]. The main thesis of this apology . . . is that slavery as an economic institution had reached its peak in 1860 and was about to decline. Gradual emancipation was "just around the corner," if only the Republicans had not placed the South on the defensive. This contention has recently received its most detailed and circumstantial refutation in a monograph written under the auspices of the National Bureau of Economic Research by two Harvard economists, Professors Alfred H. Conrad and John Meyer. "The Economics of Slavery in the Ante-Bellum South," published in *The Journal of Political Economy*, April 1958, is the most enlightening piece of original research we have encountered on the slavery question.

111. The references to *Diary* in this section are to *The Diary of John Quincy Adams, 1794-1845*, ed. Allan Nevins (New York: Charles Scribner's Sons, 1951). Adams was President for one term, 1825-29.

112. The House of Representatives brings the "indictment" (the impeachment) before the Senate, where the "trial" is held. See *Federalist*, p. 424: "a method of national inquest into the conduct of men." See, also, chap. 7, n. 3, chap. 8, n. 54, above.

113. The more politically minded Lincoln, on the other hand, spoke of Jefferson in this manner (in 1854):

> Mr. Jefferson, the author of the Declaration of Independence, and otherwise a chief actor in the Revolution; then a delegate in Congress; afterward, twice President; who was, is, and perhaps will continue to be, the most distinguished politician of our history; a Virginian by birth and continued residence, and withal a slaveholder—conceived the idea of taking that occasion to prevent slavery from going into the Northwestern Territory. He prevailed on the Virginia legislature to adopt his views, and to cede the Territory, making the prohibition of slavery therein a condition of the deed. Congress accepted the cession with the condition; and the first ordinance (which the acts of Congress were then called) for the government of the Territory provided that slavery should never be permitted therein. This is the famed "Ordinance of '87," so often spoken of. Thenceforward for sixty-one years, and until, in 1848, the last scrap of this Territory came into the Union as the State of Wisconsin, all parties acted in quiet obedience to this ordinance. It is now what Jefferson foresaw and intended —the happy home of teeming millions of free, white, prosperous people, and no slave among them. [*Complete Works*, 1:181-82]

Lincoln later corrected the statement that the prohibition was "a condition of the deed"—but his general appraisal of Jefferson's attitude and effort with respect to slavery remains and invites comparison with Adams's. See Lincoln, *Complete Works*, 1:570-72.

114. This geographical sequence for "calling" the states is evident in the Declaration of Independence and the Constitution, and was used for many years thereafter until the admission of many new states to the Union led (as it did in many other respects) to an abandonment (after the Civil War) of the old way of doing things.

115. "They were anti-slavery by birth, as their name was Adams and their home was Quincy." Adams, *Education of Henry Adams*, p. 25.

116. The effect of tabling such petitions was to shut off all debate respecting them. See chap. 8, n. 106, above. See, for a southerner's assessment of the seventy-year conflict of which this gag-rule controversy was an episode, chap. 7, n. 95, above.

Robert Waln (of Pennsylvania) presented in the House of Representatives on Jan. 2, 1800:

> a petition of Absalom Jones and others, free men of color, of the city and county of Philadelphia, praying for a revision of the laws of the United States relative to fugitives from justice; and for the adoption of such measures as shall in due course emancipate the whole of their brethren from their present situation; which he moved to have referred to the committee appointed to inquire whether

any and what alterations ought to be made in the existing law prohibiting the slave trade from the United States to any foreign place or country. [*Annals, VI*, p. 229]

The House voted, 85-1 (the one being George Thatcher of *Massachusetts*), that

the parts of the said petition which invite Congress to legislate upon subjects from which the General Government is precluded by the Constitution, have a tendency to create disquiet and jealousy, and ought therefore to receive no encouragement or countenance from this House. [*Annals, VI*, p. 244]

See, also, Webster, *Works*, 3:279-82; Lincoln, *Works*, 1:565; chap. 7, n. 14, above.

117. The editor notes that from this date on the diary entries become increasingly scattered and feeble. Adams continued to serve in the House until February 21, 1848, when he was fatally stricken there. He died on February 23 at the age of eighty.

118. A comparable struggle in the Senate is reported in H. von Holst's *John C. Calhoun*, American Statesmen (Boston: Houghton Mifflin Co., 1892), at pp. 122-34. "[Calhoun] shares with the abolitionists the merit of having always probed the wound to the bottom, without heeding in the least the protesting shrieks of the patient." Ibid., p. 309. See chap. 8, n. 109, above; see, also, chap. 7, n. 95, above.

The two [hospitalized Civil War soldiers] were chatting of one thing and another. The fever soldier spoke of John C. Calhoun's monument, which he had seen, and was describing it. The veteran said: "I have seen Calhoun's monument. That you saw is not the real monument. But I have seen it. It is the desolated, ruined south; nearly the whole generation of young men between seventeen and thirty destroyed or maim'd; all the old families used up . . . all that is Calhoun's real monument." [*The Portable Walt Whitman* (New York: Viking Press, 1945), p. 580]

See chap. 4, n. 10, above. Cf. Paine, *Writings*, 1:177.

. . . As early as the 1820's the South Carolinian [Calhoun] had been increasingly conscious of a change taking place in the equilibrium of the power structure of the republic, a change harmful to the South. He sensed that some ingenuity was called for to maintain the balance. He was a man of ingenious mind, and he built upon the work of the Virginia dynasty. In the spirit of the Virginia and Kentucky resolutions of 1798 he could advocate nullification. . . . [Nichols, *Blueprint for Leviathan*, p. 133]

Daniel Webster, in his second reply to Senator Hayne of South Carolina, January 26, 1830, interpreted in this way the resolutions written by Madison for the Virginia legislature:

I cannot undertake to say how these resolutions were understood by those who passed them. Their language is not a little indefinite. In the case of the exercise by Congress of a dangerous power not granted to them, the resolutions assert the right, on the part of the State, to interfere and arrest the progress of the evil. This is susceptible of more than one interpretation. It may mean no more than that the States may interfere by complaint and remonstrance, or by proposing to the people an alteration of the Federal Constitution. This would all be quite unobjectionable. Or it may be that no more is meant than to assert the general right of revolution, as against all governments, in cases of intolerable oppression. This no one doubts, and this, in my opinion, is all that he who framed the resolutions could have meant by it; for I shall not readily believe that he was ever of opinion that a State, under the Constitution and in conformity with it, could, upon the ground of her own opinion of its unconstitutionality, however clear and palpable she might think the case, annul a law of Congress, so far as it should operate on herself, by her own legislative power. [*Works*, 3:332]

(See, for the opinion of John Taylor of Caroline, chap. 8, n. 68, above. See, also, chap. 7, n. 2, above.)

119. John Quincy Adams, *Diary*, pp. xv-xvi. Nevins's evaluation of Adams's career seems to be that of most contemporary students. A reviewer of Samuel F. Bemis, *John Quincy Adams and the Union* (New York: Knopf, 1956), wrote:

> John Quincy Adams was an anomaly in American public life. A scholarly, truculent, suspicious, little man, he despised the ways of politics yet let the politicians make him President. At a time when sectionalism was dominant, he thought in terms of a national interest that transcended internal differences. In an age of compromise, he remained inflexible. He came to the Presidency better equipped by training and experience than any man before or since his time but allowed his idealistic program to collapse because he would not deal with political realities. Then, at the age of sixty-three, Adams entered the House of Representatives, where he achieved the true greatness that was in him. . . .
>
> Bemis is at his best in the chapters dealing with the anti-slavery crusade, with the long battle for the right of petition . . . but it was here that Adams himself was at his best. . . . In the House of Representatives, he acknowledged responsibility to no party or clique but only to his conscience. There his deep moral fervor, his "compulsive genius for political contention," his vast learning, the constantly whetted keenness of his mind, and the undiluted vitriol of his tongue made him one of the most feared debaters in congressional history—a fierce, unyielding champion of human freedom who could not be frightened, or coerced, or silenced. . . . [Charles M. Wiltse, *American Historical Review* 61 (1955-56): 981-82]

Ralph Waldo Emerson said, in a talk at Concord in 1844 (*Works*, 11:133-34):

> Gentlemen, I am loath to say harsh things, and perhaps I know too little of politics for the smallest weight to attach to any censure of mine,—but I am at a loss how to characterize the tameness and silence of the two senators and the ten representatives of the State at Washington. To what purpose have we clothed each of those representatives with the power of seventy thousand persons, and each senator with near half a million, if they are to sit dumb at their desks and see their constituents captured and sold;—perhaps to gentlemen sitting by them in the hall? . . . I may as well say, what all men feel, that whilst our very amiable and very innocent representatives and senators at Washington are accomplished lawyers and merchants, and very eloquent at dinners and at caucuses, there is a disastrous want of *men* from New England. I would gladly make exceptions, and you will not suffer me to forget one eloquent old man, in whose veins the blood of Massachusetts rolls, and who singly has defended the freedom of speech, and the rights of the free, against the usurpation of the slave-holder. [Editorial note: John Quincy Adams, who, though disapproving, as untimely, the legislation urged on Congress by the abolitionists, yet fought strongly and persistently against the rules framed to check their importunity, as inconsistent with the right of petition itself.] But the reader of Congressional debates, in New England, is perplexed to see with what admirable sweetness and patience the majority of the free States are schooled and ridden by the minority of slaveholders.

Cf. Strauss, *What Is Political Philosophy?*, p. 147; chap. 4, n. 117, above.

120. "But I must make it clear that I accept no fetters on my liberty of debate [in Parliament] except those imposed by the rules of Order or by the public interest." Churchill, *End of the Beginning*, p. 167. See chap. 5, n. 124, above.

See Plato, *Republic* 536C.

121. *The Works of Francis Bacon*, ed. J. Spedding and R. Ellis (New York: Hurd & Houghton, 1864), 13:83-84. (Plutarch writes of Cato the younger, *Lives*, pp. 896-97 [in the translation of John Dryden]:

> His manners were little agreeable or acceptable to the people, and he received

very slender marks of their favour; witness his repulse when he sued for the consulship, which he lost, as Cicero says, for acting rather like a citizen in Plato's commonwealth, than among the dregs of Romulus's posterity, the same thing happening to him, in my opinion, as we observe in fruits ripe before their season, which we rather take pleasure in looking at and admiring than actually use; so much was his old-fashioned virtue out of the present mode, among the depraved customs which time and luxury had introduced, that it appeared, indeed, remarkable and wonderful, but was too great and too good to suit the present exigencies, being so out of all proportion to the times.

See Burke, *Works*, 4:189. Cf. Appendix F, above.)

Bacon's fable is found in his *Wisdom of the Ancients*, with the full title, "Cassandra; or Plainness of Speech." (In the Latin original, the title is *Cassandra, sive Parrhesia*. See, on *parresia*, chap. 9, n. 9, below.)

It is impossible to imagine the scenes described by John Quincy Adams as taking place either in the Constitutional Convention of 1787 or in the First Congress. Compare, in Gouverneur Morris (*A Diary of the French Revolution*, ed. Beatrix C. Davenport [Boston: Houghton Mifflin Co., 1939], 1:232, 382), his disapproving description of the proceedings in the French Assembly during the Revolution. See, for a selection of extended comments by Morris, pt. 2 of the lecture on the Constitution appended to my dissertation. See, on Morris, Paine, *Writings*, 3:152 ff., 180 ff., 232.

See, also, chap. 9, n. 7, below.

122. Lincoln, *Complete Works*, 1:15. See, also, Jaffa, *Crisis of the House Divided*, pp. 197-98, 200-203; Lord Acton, *Essays on Freedom and Power* (London: Thames & Hudson, 1956), pp. 213-14, 217. (See, on the "intrinsic evil [for Lincoln] of the repeal [in 1854] of the Missouri Compromise," Jaffa, *Crisis of the House Divided*, pp. 302-7.)

> Lincoln was ready to give the slave States any possible guarantee that the Constitution should not be altered so as to take away their existing right of self-government in the matter of slavery. He had remained in the past coldly aloof from the Abolitionist propaganda when Herndon and other friends tried to interest him in it, feeling, it seems, that agitation in the free States against laws which existed constitutionally in the slave States was not only futile but improper. . . . This side of Lincoln's doctrine is apt to jar upon us. We feel with a great American historian that the North would have been depraved indeed if it had not bred Abolitionists, and it requires an effort to sympathise with Lincoln's rigidly correct feeling—sometimes harshly expressed and sometimes apparently cold. It is not possible to us, as it was to him a little later, to look on John Brown's adventure merely as a crime. . . . [Charnwood, *Abraham Lincoln*, p. 126]

Cf. Nichols, *Blueprint for Leviathan*, pp. 128-32. (Would we not be a depraved people today if some of our youth did not feel strongly enough about the war in Vietnam and about racial discrimination to express illegal opposition to them? See, on Callicles and immoderate indignation, chap. 8, n. 105, above. See, also, the discussion in my article, "On Civil Disobedience: Thoreau and Socrates," *Southwest Review* 54 [1969]: 203, of abolitionist passion and of Lincoln's use of that passion. It is prudent to remember that the likely alternative to such illegal opposition [among a people such as ours] is not cool, legal opposition but rather passive acquiescence and apathy. See chap. 7, n. 72, above.)

The following comments in Emerson's journals on the Fugitive Slave Law should be compared to those of Lincoln (*Complete Works*, 1:359, 574):

> We shall never feel well again until that detestable law is nullified in Massachusetts and until the Government is assured that once for all it cannot and shall not be executed here. . . . This is not meddling with other people's affairs: this is hindering other people from meddling with us. This is not going crusading into Virginia and Georgia after slaves, who, it is alleged, are very comfortable where they are:—that amiable argument falls to the ground: but this is befriending in our own State on our own farms, a man who has taken the

risk of being shot, or burned alive, or cast into the sea, or starved to death, or suffocated in a wooden box, to get away from his driver: and this man who has run the gauntlet of a thousand miles for his freedom, the statute says, you men of Massachusetts shall hunt, and catch, and send back again to the dog-hutch he fled from. And this filthy enactment was made in the nineteenth century, by people who could read and write. I will not obey it, by God. . . . Very little reliance must be put on the common stories that circulate of Mr. [Daniel] Webster's or Mr. [Rufus] Choate's learning their Greek or their varied literature. That ice won't bear. Reading!—do you mean that this senator or this lawyer, who stood by and allowed the passage of infamous laws, was a reader of Greek books? That is not the question; but to what purpose did they read? [*Selections from Ralph Waldo Emerson*, ed. S. E. Whicher (Boston: Houghton Mifflin Co., 1957), pp. 354, 355, 358]

(What "Greek books" meant can be seen by a study of the 1835 and the 1868 curricula of St. John's College, in that college's current catalog. [See, for Jefferson on the lawyer's education, Padover, ed., *The Complete Jefferson* (New York: Duell, Sloan & Pearce, 1943), p. 1043.] The present St. John's program is probably closer in intention to the education of the late eighteenth and early nineteenth centuries than anything else available in America today. Indeed, the state of American education is reflected in the fact that St. John's College is by far the easiest of the better undergraduate schools to which the serious student can secure admission. There is no frantic competition to get into St. John's, a competition which is fueled elsewhere by conventional opinions about what one gets out of education rather than by an awareness of what it should do to one. See Plato, *Republic* 620C-D [the choice of Odysseus]; chap. 9, n. 23, below. See, also, chap. 7, nn. 30, 34, above, as well as chap. 8, nn. 168, 171, below. The truly great books offer us a plateau to and from which we can aspire to ascend. See chap. 8, n. 102, above.)

123. See, for a discussion of the "presumption in favour of liberty," A. L. Goodhart, "Lessons from America," in *Liberty in the Modern State* (London: Conservative Political Centre, 1957), pp. 22-23. See, also, Hayek, *Constitution of Liberty*, pt. 1, "The Value of Freedom."

"The values sought by society in protecting the right to freedom of expression" have been usefully grouped by one legal scholar in "four broad categories":

> Maintenance of a system of free expression is necessary (1) as assuring individual self-fulfillment, (2) as a means of attaining the truth, (3) as a method of securing participation by the members of the society in social, including political, decision-making, and (4) as maintaining the balance between stability and change in the society. [Emerson, "Toward a Theory of the First Amendment," pp. 878-79]

It is sad that American conservatives—who can be thought of as the proper guardians of valuable things—should sometimes seem to have lost sight of all freedom except that of property. The Republican statesman who declares such legislation as the Smith Act unconstitutional and such adventures as the Vietnam intervention unjustified, should touch bedrock in the American soul. See Malcolm Sharp, "The Conservative Fellow-Traveler," *U. Chicago L. Rev.* 30 (1963): 705. See, also, chap. 8, n. 80, above, chap. 9, n. 35, below, as well as Appendix F, above.

124. Sidney, *Discourses concerning Government* (London, 1698), II, xi. (See chap. 9, nn. 13, 37, below.)

That liberty is not desirable in all circumstances, however, is recognized in a Connecticut statute of 1792:

> . . . if any Master or Owner of any Slave, shall be disposed to emancipate and make free such Slave, and shall apply to any of the Civil Authority . . . of the Town, to which he belongs, it shall be the duty of said Authority . . . to enquire into the health and age of such Slave, and if they find upon examina-

tion, that such Slave is in good health, and is not of greater age than forty-five years, or less age than twenty-five years, said Authority . . . shall give to the Owner or Master of said Slave, a certificate thereof, under their hands. Provided, that previous to giving such certificate, the persons giving the same shall be convinced by actual examination, of the Slave to be made free by such certificate, that he or she is desirous thereof.

One can see here a fundamental limitation upon any argument for "freedom of speech [and] of the press": justice is more important than liberty (even though liberty is often critical to a just regime). See chap. 7, n. 77, above. See, on justice, chap. 8, n. 150 (end), below. See, also, Burke, *Works*, 4:6.

125. A politician more devious than John Quincy Adams could be suspected of having deliberately provoked southerners into taking positions that would be condemned as unconstitutional, thereby undercutting the moral stature of the South in the Union. See Charnwood, *Abraham Lincoln*, p. 51.

126. "I have found that men who have not even been suspected of disloyalty are very averse to taking an oath of any sort as a condition to exercising an ordinary right of citizenship." Lincoln, *Complete Works*, 2:507 (Apr. 4, 1864); also, 2:478. See Justice Black, dissenting, *American Communications Ass'n v. Douds*, 339 U.S. 382, 447 (1950); Zechariah Chafee, Foreword, Alan Barth, *The Loyalty of Free Men* (New York: Simon & Schuster, Pocket Books, 1951).

The Sedition Act of 1798 aroused a "gag-law phobia." Chap. 6, n. 33, above. So did, but only for a while, the "loyalty oath" prescribed in California (which is reproduced at p. 332, above). Justice Douglas observed, in his concurring opinion in *Brandenburg v. Ohio*, 395 U.S. 444, at 456 (1969):

> I think that all matters of belief are beyond the reach of subpoenas or the probings of investigators. That is why the invasions of privacy made by investigating committees were notoriously unconstitutional. That is the deep-seated fault in the infamous loyalty-security hearings which, since 1947, when President Truman launched them, have processed 20,000,000 men and women. Those hearings were primarily concerned with one's thoughts, ideas, beliefs, and convictions. They were the most blatant violations of the First Amendment we have ever known.

See chap. 4, nn. 33, 35, chap. 7, n. 72, above. (It should be noticed that the inauguration of such programs by executive decree is not attended by the public debate that proposed legislation can evoke and be affected by. Rather, it is like the dropping of the atomic bomb, a *fait accompli*. See chap. 5, n. 17, above, chap. 8, nn. 160, 161, below.)

See, also, Sophocles, *Antigone* 30-34, 38-39; Shakespeare, *King Lear*, act 1, sc. 1. Cf. Hobbes, *Leviathan*, chap. 37 (end), chap. 43 (end). But see chap. 5, n. 90, above.

127. Winston Churchill, *The New World: A History of the English Speaking Peoples* (New York: Grosset & Dunlap, Bantam Books, 1963), p. 162.

"It is not the diversity of opinions (which cannot be avoided), but the refusal of toleration to those that are of different opinions (which might have been granted), that has produced all the bustles and wars that have been in the Christian world upon account of religion." Locke, *A Letter concerning Toleration*. "The Manifesto was published as the platform of the Communist League, a workingmen's association, first exclusively German, later on international, and, under the political conditions of the Continent before 1848, unavoidably a secret society." Friedrich Engels, *Preface to the English Edition of 1888, Manifesto of the Communist Party*. See, also, Chafee, *Freedom of Speech*, p. 219, n. 82.

A shepherd notices, in the fourteenth-century *Second Shepherds' Play*,

> It does me good, as I walk thus alone,
> Of this world for to talk and make here my moan.

Edwin Muir wrote, in 1921:

You become aware of the vitality of the republican idea in Prague as soon as you enter it. Whether you walk the streets or sit in the *cafés* you hear politics being discussed; it seems as if the whole people, old and young, after being denied all their life any voice in their political fate, had resolved to enjoy an orgy of self-government. They argue about politics, interests, grievances, new acts, with measureless gusto: they enjoy their very difficulties because of the freedom with which they can discuss them. . . . [*An Autobiography* (London: Hogarth Press, 1954), p. 186]

Cf. ibid., pp. 194 (" . . . what once appeared innocent—a harmless excess of liberty, perhaps, a naive trustfulness—may have been the stuff which a Hitler or a Stalin would later on manipulate for his ends. . . ."), 199-200 ("We felt free without practising freedom; we merely talked; and to talk freely gives an illusion of freedom hardly to be distinguished, except by an intellectual effort, from the reality."), 201-2, 228-29. ("It was now in the middle of the 'twenties, and the cult of untrammelled freedom had become an established fashion among some of the intellectuals and artists. With the removal of restraint nothing, not even enjoyment, seemed to matter to them any longer, and life, under its assumed carelessness, was joyless and without flavour. . . . There was something ambiguous in that life, for its freedom was not real freedom, but merely the rejection of choice.") Does not understanding presuppose moral judgment?

Certainly, one has to take care lest "toleration" become mere thoughtlessness. Cf. Robert P. Wolff, Barrington Moore, Jr., and Herbert Marcuse, *A Critique of Pure Tolerance* (Boston: Beacon Press, 1965), esp. pp. 109-17; chap. 2, n. 7, above. See chap. 5, n. 70, above. See, on "privacy," chap. 9, n. 3, below.

128. Milton, *Prose Works*, 1:158. This passage continues:

. . . Whereas *now this permission of free writing*, were there no good else in it, yet at some times thus licensed, is such an unripping, such an anatomy of the shyest and tenderest particular truths, as makes not only the whole nation in many points the wiser, but also presents and carries home to princes, men most remote from vulgar concourse, such a full insight of every lurking evil, or restrained good among the commons, as that they [princes] shall not need hereafter, in old cloaks and false beards, to stand to the courtesy of a night-walking cudgeller for eaves-dropping, nor to accept quietly as a perfume, the overhead emptying of some salt lotion. *Who could be angry, therefore, but those that are guilty, with these free-spoken and plain-hearted men that are the eyes of their country, and the prospective glasses of their prince?* But these are the nettlers, these are the blabbing books that tell, though not half your fellows feats. You love toothless satires; let me inform you, a toothless satire is as improper as a toothed sleek-stone, and as bullish. [Italics added]

The expression in the text, "which way the wind is blowing," recalls another, "blowing off steam." Milton speaks (against the authority of Machiavelli) at *Prose Works*, 1:237 (in the passage reproduced in the text at chap. 5, n. 50, above) of "anger thus freely vented spend[ing] itself ere it break out into action. . . ." See, also, Milton, *Prose Works*, 1:157. Cf. Shakespeare, *Comedy of Errors*, act 3, sc. 1, lines 75-76 ("words are but wind").

See chap. 8, nn. 142, 143, below.

129. The humanity of one's fellows is thus acknowledged. Numa granted "even to actual slaves a licence to sit at meat with their masters at the feast of Saturn, that they also might have some taste and relish of the sweets of liberty." Plutarch, *Lives*, p. 93. Consider the license allowed toward one's betters during the Christmas feast-days in Elizabethan times and on the eve of St. Nicholas's day in European universities today.

130. Thomas R. Fitzgeralds, "Limitations on Freedom of Speech in the Athenian Assembly" (Ph.D. diss., University of Chicago, 1957), p. 63. The poet was Nicostratus.

"The most tyrannical governments are those which make crimes of opinions, for everyone has an inalienable right over his thoughts—nay, such a state of things leads to the rule of popular passion." Benedict de Spinoza, *Tractatus Theologico-Politicus* (London: George Routledge & Sons, n.d.), p. 241. See chap. 2, n. 3, above, chap. 8, n. 140, below.

131. Aristotle, *Athenian Constitution* 22.4; Thucydides, 3.47; Plutarch, *Lives*, p. 350; Machiavelli, *The Prince*, chap. 9; John Adams, *The Works of John Adams*, ed. Charles F. Adams (Boston: Little, Brown & Co., 1850-56), 4:17.

Kermit Eby and I discovered, upon exchanging impressions during the worst days with Senator Joseph R. McCarthy, that the groups of midwestern small-town businessmen which we had been meeting with were far less excited about the senator's "revelations" than were newspapermen, lawyers, and university faculties.

> The people has made itself master of everything, and administers everything by decrees and by jury-courts in which the people is the ruling power, for even the cases tried by the Council have come to the people. And they seem to act rightly in doing this, for a few are more easily corrupted by gain and by influence than the many. [Aristotle, *Athenian Constitution* 41.2]

(Plutarch refers to the Athenians' "natural hereditary inclination to be kind." *Lives*, p. 350. See Thucydides, *History of the Peloponnesian War*, 3.49; cf. ibid., 5.85-116, 7.29. See, also, Anastaplo, "The Daring of Moderation: Student Power and *The Melian Dialogue*," *School Rev.* 78 [1970]: 451, 477.)

132. *Annals*, V, p. 2105. This sentiment, expressed in the course of the debate on the Sedition Act of 1798, can serve as part of the epitaph of the Federalist Party. See Paine, *Writings*, 3:414, n. 1 (on Hamilton). Cf. chap. 8, n. 190, below.

> The policy of repression has been finally discarded [in Great Britain]; and rulers have at length recognized in practice the truth and wisdom of Lord Bacon's maxim that the "punishing of wits enhances their authority; and a forbidden writing is thought to be a certain spark of truth, that flies up in the faces of them that seek to tread it out." [Theodore F. T. Plucknett, ed., *Taswell-Langmead: English Constitutional History*, 11th ed. (London: Sweet & Maxwell, 1960), p. 668]

133. Leo Strauss, *Natural Right and History* (Chicago: University of Chicago Press, 1953), p. 294. Freedom would include, in this view, religious liberty as well.

Coriolanus' problem was that the people could be easily persuaded that he did not respect them, that he could not be trusted to treat them with consideration. See chap. 9, n. 16, below. See, also, chap. 4, n. 103, above.

To speak of "an ultimate sanctity of the individual as individual" is to remind ourselves of that respect for humanity which distinguishes a civilized people. This respect was spoken of with feeling by Thomas McDonald, in a funeral address of Dec. 6, 1961:

> Nothing, perhaps, better may express all that Jason Aronson sought to live and die by, than a little story to which he continually recurred in his affliction, especially before his earlier operation, which he was told had perhaps one chance in twenty of being successful, and again in the last few weeks when he knew for certain what he must face. "Nine days before his death Immanuel Kant was visited by his physician. Old, ill, and nearly blind, he rose from his chair and stood trembling with weakness and muttering unintelligible words. Finally his faithful companion realized that he would not sit down again until the visitor had taken a seat. This he did, and Kant then permitted himself to be helped to his chair and, after having regained some of his strength, said, 'Das Gefühl für Humanität hat mich noch nicht verlassen.'—The feeling for, the sense of humanity has not yet left me." [Thomas McDonald, Leo Strauss, and George Anastaplo, *Jason Marvin Aronson: Three Funeral Addresses* (Chicago: University College, University of Chicago, 1961), pp. 9-10]

See chap. 8, n. 186, below.

134. Even Sumner conceded "that no modern free state can exist without wide popular rights." *Andrew Jackson*, p. 279. See Anastaplo, "Dissent in Athens," *Notes on World*

CHAPTER EIGHT, NOTE 135: PAGE 255

Events (Chicago: Council on Foreign Relations), May 1969, p. 1 (chap. 9, n. 34, below).

"The periodical assemblies of which I have already spoken are designed to prevent or postpone [usurpation], above all when they need no formal summoning; for in that case, the prince cannot stop them without openly declaring himself a law-breaker and an enemy of the State." Rousseau, *The Social Contract*, book 3, chap. 18. See chap. 8, n. 192, below.

To take from Plato's *Republic* only the institution of censorship, it should be noted, is to mistake one ingredient for the entire prescription. That is, I believe it salutary to say with Milton (in his *Areopagitica*), "But that Plato meant this law [of censorship] peculiarly to that commonwealth which he had imagined, and to no other, is evident." *Prose Works*, 1:303. See chap. 9, n. 35, below.

135. Sidney, chap. 2, sec. 28. Similar comments may be found in Pericles' Funeral Address (Thucydides 2.60), in Aristotle's *Politics* (4.4), and in the Constitutional Convention of 1787 (Farrand, *Records*, 1:112).

It does seem, sometimes, that freedom of speech is maintained in this country by the relatively few who take it seriously—and that their efforts are by and large successful because most of their fellow citizens do not care enough to bother. (This may be the reason public opinion polls on this, as well as other subjects, are deceptive and should not be taken too seriously. See chap. 6, n. 77, above.) "Perhaps never does a community contain more than 5 per cent of active and informed citizenry. The average is closer to 3 per cent, or three out of one hundred adults." Alfred DeGrazia, "Federalism," in Melvin Laird, ed., *The Conservative Papers* (New York: Doubleday & Co., Anchor Books, 1964), pp. 240-41. (See chap. 5, n. 73, above. Cf. chap. 8, n. 136, below.)

An English political commentator has observed, upon assessing some of the sensational publications about the assassination of President Kennedy, "It is my judgment that the American people today are in a remarkably unhysterical frame of mind, even in the middle of a difficult and controversial war. Certainly, they are showing every sign of resisting the temptation to further witch hunts. It would be a tragedy if articulate makers of opinion led them into another." Henry Fairlie, "No Conspiracy, But—Two Assassins, Perhaps?" *New York Times Magazine*, Sept. 11, 1966, p. 159 (concluding paragraph). See chap. 3, n. 35, chap. 7, n. 107 (end), above.

Cf. Professor Morton A. Kaplan's imaginative letter to the editor, entitled in publication, "International Dimensions of the Assassination," *Chicago Tribune*, Nov. 30, 1963 (see, also, his speculations, admittedly without "hard evidence," on the sinking by the Russians of two foreign submarines in the Mediterranean, *Chicago Sun-Times*, Jan. 31, 1968, p. 8); Barbara Garson's *MacBird* (aptly described by Robert Pollak, *Hyde Park Herald*, Chicago, Illinois, Mar. 15, 1967, p. 16, as "an adventure in witless scurrility which implies that the President of the United States plotted the assassination of John F. Kennedy"; see *New York Times*, Apr. 1, 1967, and *Newsweek*, Apr. 10, 1967, p. 61, for J. Edgar Hoover on this play [a play which displays what "freedom of the press" *can* mean for us: chap. 2, n. 6, chap. 5, n. 127, above]); Charles Bartlett, *Chicago Sun-Times*, Mar. 4, 1967, p. 26 (quoting a memorandum by Arthur Schlesinger, Jr., on William Manchester's imaginative *The Death of a President*). It would no doubt be healthier if we did not have certain of these sentiments in the souls of our people, but once there . . .

I myself see no reason to believe, from the dozen works on the assassination I have examined, that there was (or that "the government" believes there was) more than one assassin of President Kennedy. I do know from conversations with a student of mine who was on the fringes of the inquiry how thorough the investigation by the government was on this occasion. I have seen no plausible explanation of why the dead President's brother should have, either while attorney general or thereafter, concealed the truth about this matter and thereby have allowed guilty men to go unpunished. Intellectuals who dabble in politics (including those who write for a general audience) should respect what may be for them the first rule of politics, and that is to leave well enough alone— at least in public. They should also respect the limits of demonstration in practical affairs, remembering that there are (in the words of *Federalist* No. 83; chap. 8, n. 55, above) public discussions "more curious than beneficial." They can, if they should feel deprived, console themselves in their self-restraint with the gracious expression the French employ when suppressing a certain kind of movie or book, that it is "too advanced for the state of our morals." In any event, they should remember that the Federalists, who were more talented and more adept than we are, were nevertheless impolitic enough to destroy themselves—and there is no reason to believe that this fate is reserved only for "conservatives." See Willmoore Kendall, "The 'Open Society' and Its Fallacies," *American Political Science Review* 54 (1960): 972, 977; Strauss, *City and Man*, p. 51, nn. 1, 2, p. 54, n. 5. See, also, chap. 2, n. 39, chap. 4, n. 60, chap. 5, nn. 5, 59, 61, 128, 137, chap. 7, nn. 74, 75, chap. 8, nn. 71, 74, 127, above, chap. 8, nn. 140, 178, 195, chap. 9, nn. 24, 39, below.

In short, the Constitutionalist is a moderate man, reserving his daring (except in emergencies) for speculative matters, and even then only in the carefully guarded recesses of his writings. (These observations should remind us that intellectuals, whether "conservative" or "liberal," have much more in common among themselves than they have with the general public, that very public which they are tempted to cater to in order to "lead." Who is an intellectual today? Someone who reads footnotes. [The reader should consider how many of *his* friends are among the 52 percent of American citizens who never travel more than two hundred miles from home. *Chicago Tribune*, Feb. 13, 1967, p. 1.]) See chap. 9, n. 7, below. See, also, Paine, *Writings*, 2:281.

See Burke, *Works*, 2:147-48; 4:427-28, 331-35, 347 ("The little catechism of the Rights of Men is soon learned; and the inferences are in the passions"), 357 ("Boldness formerly was not the character of Atheists as such"), 360-61, 363, 375; 2:226-27 ("Man acts from adequate motives relative to his interest, and not on metaphysical speculations. Aristotle, the great master of reasoning, cautions us, and with great weight and propriety, against this species of delusive geometrical accuracy in moral arguments, as the most fallacious of all sophistry"). See, also, chap. 8, n. 70, above. Cf. pp. 417-18, above.

Something is to be said on other grounds as well for intellectuals' being compelled to restrain their public expression. Such restraint *can* promote discipline and seriousness in one's thought: it recognizes the limits of human reason in a community; it reflects better than does the casualness of an aimless liberty the character of the moral universe; it encourages a salutary piety; it promotes careful writing and hence reading; it discourages shallowness and deepens human experience, adding dignity and perceptiveness to one's activity; it mirrors and reinforces the more serious discipline of the life of inquiry and of life itself; it reminds the thoughtful of the natural differences among men. Thoughtful men should not need to be reminded of the fundamental political vulnerability of the most profound exercise of human reason, a vulnerability which neither Enlightenment nor Constitution can eliminate. See Disraeli, *Quarrels of Authors*, 2:94, n. 1; chap. 5, n. 90, above. See, also, Strauss, *Persecution and the Art of Writing*, p. 21:

> [Alfarabi] ascribed to Plato the view that in the Greek city the philosopher was in grave danger. In making this statement, he merely repeated what Plato himself had said. To a considerable extent, the danger was averted by the art of Plato, as [Alfarabi] likewise noted. But the success of Plato must not blind us to the existence of a danger which, however much its forms may vary, is coeval with philosophy. The understanding of this danger and of the various forms which it has taken, and which it may take, is the foremost task, and indeed the sole task, of the sociology of philosophy.

See *Alfarabi's Philosophy of Plato and Aristotle*, pp. 49, 62-65, 66-67.

136. Adams, *Works*, 4:19, italics added (borrowing from Benjamin Franklin, *Complete Works of Benjamin Franklin*, ed. John Bigelow [New York: G. P. Putnam, 1887], 2:376). See Tocqueville, *Democracy in America*, 1:252-53, 261-63. (Adlai Stevenson III observed while still treasurer of the state of Illinois, "I think we are beginning to recognize that there may be one thing better than good government—and that is government in which everyone has a part." *Chicago Tribune*, May 28, 1969, p. 2. This is the cautiously advanced thesis, with echoes of John C. Calhoun, of H. A. Fagan's *Coexistence in South Africa* [Cape Town: Juta & Co., 1963]. See chap. 8, n. 143, below.)

CHAPTER EIGHT, NOTES 137-38: PAGE 255   737

See, also, *Federalist*, pp. 457-58. See, on Americans' political activity, John M. Redding, *Inside the Democratic Party* (Indianapolis: Bobbs-Merrill, 1958), pp. 26-27:

> In a congressional election year, upwards of 750,000 elective jobs, at all political levels short of the Presidency itself, are in contention. Assuming conservatively that every office to be filled will be sought by at least the incumbent and one contender, this means approximately 1,500,000 candidates. In addition, most candidates will have a campaign manager, a treasurer and several workers. Thus the total number of people directly affected by such an election will number conservatively from six to eight million people. . . . In 1954 the total who went to the polls was, in round numbers, 42,000,000. In 1956 the total was almost 60,000,000. In 1958, the total vote should be some three to four million higher than 1954. . . .

137. Aristotle, *Nicomachean Ethics* 5.2. The proscription of certain political opinions means that some are denied what others are permitted to enjoy, the satisfaction of displaying one's own opinions. See chap. 8, n. 16, above. See, also, chap. 2, n. 21, above.

138. A less exalted view of what I am talking about here is seen in other writers. Adam Smith writes:

> In great empires the people who live in the capital, and in the provinces remote from the scene of action, feel, many of them, scarce any inconveniency from the war; but enjoy, at their ease, the amusement of reading in the newspapers the exploits of their own fleets and armies. To them this amusement compensates the small difference between the taxes which they pay on account of the war, and those which they had been accustomed to pay in time of peace. They are commonly dissatisfied with the return of peace, which puts an end to their amusement, and to a thousand visionary hopes of conquest and national glory, from a longer continuance of the war. [Adam Smith, *Wealth of Nations*, p. 872]

Another eighteenth-century English writer records his impression that

> the satisfactions which the people in free governments derive from the knowledge and agitation of political subjects . . . excite just enough of interest and emotion, to afford a moderate engagement to the thoughts, without rising to any painful degree of anxiety, or ever leaving a fixed oppression upon the spirits. . . . For my part, (and I believe it to be the case with most men, who are arrived at the middle age, and occupy the middle classes of life) had I all the money, which I pay in taxes to government, at liberty to lay out upon amusement and diversion, I know not whether I could make choice of any, in which I could find greater pleasure, than what I receive from expecting, hearing, and relating public news; reading parliamentary debates and proceedings; canvassing the political arguments, projects, predictions, and intelligence, which are conveyed, by various channels, to every corner of the kingdom. These topics supply [to almost every man] a substitute for drinking, gaming, scandal, and obscenity. Now, the secresy, the jealousy, the solitude and precipitation of despotic governments exclude all this. But the loss, you say, is trifling. I know that it is possible to render even the mention of it ridiculous, by representing it as the idle employment of the most insignificant part of the nation, the folly of village-statesmen, and coffee-house politicians: but I allow nothing to be a trifle, which ministers to the harmless gratification of multitudes. . . . [William Paley, *The Principles of Moral and Political Philosophy* (5th ed.; Boston: John West, 1806), pp. 347-48]

Is there not implicit in this passage from Paley the distinction made in chapter 5 between freedom of speech (as political discussion) and other forms of expression (such as are found, for example, in obscenity cases)? ("And what, pray, does [modern?] civilization soften in us? All civilization does is to develop in man the many-sidedness of his sensations, and nothing, absolutely nothing more. And through the development of his many-sidedness man, for all we know, may reach the stage when he will find pleasure in bloodshed. This has already happened to him." Fyodor Dostoevsky, *Notes from the Underground*, in *The Best Short Stories of Dostoevsky* [New York: Modern Library, n.d.], p. 126. See chap. 9, n. 12, below.)

Cf. Nietzsche, "On Reading and Writing," in *Thus Spake Zarathustra*, pt. 1 ("That everyone may learn to read, in the long run corrupts not only writing but also thinking. Once the spirit was God, then he became man, and now he even becomes rabble."). See chap. 5, n. 53, above.

139. Tocqueville, *Old Regime*, p. 45.

> . . . Prime Minister [Churchill] remained the servant of the House of Commons. In this role he never scamped his duties, showing always a jealous regard for the rights and the susceptibilities of Parliament; and there can be no doubt that this firm adherence to the established order of things, though on the short view it involved a certain waste of time and (since the Germans could read full reports of all debates not held in secret session) a certain risk to security, was a main foundation of the nation's unity and of the Prime Minister's authority. [Peter Fleming, *Operation Sea Lion* (New York: Simon & Schuster, 1957), pp. 138-39]

See chap. 4, n. 59, above. See, on moral authority, chap. 7, n. 22, chap. 8, n. 125, above. Cf. chap. 9, n. 14, below. See, also, chap. 8, n. 97, above.

140. Tocqueville, *Old Regime*, pp. xii-xiv.

> For political freedom, though it has the admirable effect of effecting reciprocal ties and a feeling of solidarity between all the members of a nation, does not necessarily make them resemble each other. It is only government by a single man that in the long run irons out diversities and makes each member of a nation indifferent to his neighbor's lot. [Ibid., p. 81]

Martin Heidegger evidently regards the Marxist interpretation of history as superior to all others today because of what he considers its greater awareness of the alienation and homelessness of modern man. See his *Letter on Humanism* (1949). See chap. 7, n. 124, above. (See, also, his *What Is Philosophy?* [New Haven: College & University Press, 1956], p. 91: ". . . What we come across [in contemporary thinking] is only this— various tunings of thinking. Doubt and despair, on the one hand, blind obsession by untested principles, on the other, conflict with one another. Fear and anxiety are mixed with hope and confidence.") Indeed, Heidegger continues (in his provincial stubbornness) to see as "the inner truth and greatness" of the Nazi movement that it confronted "the encounter between global technology and modern man." *An Introduction to Metaphysics* (New York: Doubleday & Co., Anchor Books, 1961), p. 166. (But what if one form of alienation is replaced by another: "A western friend still living in China frequently received the free confidences of certain Chinese friends over whom he had some influence. One day one of them said, after talking quite openly to him: 'You understand; these are things that I do not say even to my wife.'" Edgar Faure, *The Serpent and the Tortoise: Problems of the New China* [London: Macmillan & Co., 1958], p. 48. See, also, Crankshaw, *Gestapo*, pp. 71-72.)

See, for a penetrating criticism of the racism at the core of nazism, Montesquieu, *Spirit of the Laws*, book 15, chap. 5; and of the hedonism at the core of communism, Nietzsche, "Zarathustra's Prologue," sec. 5 of *Thus Spake Zarathustra* (on "the last man"). See, also, chap. 4, n. 103, chap. 7, n. 75, above.

See, on Heidegger himself, Jacob Klein and Leo Strauss, "A Giving of Accounts," *The College* (St. John's College), Apr. 1970, p. 1; Stanley Rosen, *Nihilism: A Philosophical Essay* (New Haven: Yale University Press, 1969), pp. 119 ff. (which includes a useful collection of citations to discussions of Heidegger's Nazi adventure); Anastaplo, book review, *N.Y.U. L. Rev.* 41 (1966): 664, nn. 12, 13, 22, 26. See, also, chap. 2, n. 7, above, chap. 8, n. 193, below. The troublesome character of Heidegger's experiment with Nazism is in part due to the fact that it can be seriously said of him that "he is the greatest thinker of our century, and the greatest sophist who ever lived, greater even than Protagoras." How did he go wrong, and why? He seems to me to be to philosophy what Macbeth is to tragedy. (And, like Macbeth, he is "obsessed" with and consequently led astray by excessive concern for "his own": in the one case, the royalty of "his" posterity; in the other case, the historic and hence philosophic mission of "his" country.) Heidegger seems to have moved from the pre-Socratics to the post-Socratics without having been touched as Plato and Aristotle were by the *life* (including the death) of Socrates, a life which testifies to the realization that there are certain things that the truly human being does not do. Even so, he also had at hand a more than respectable German model which he ignored, one sanctified by the language in which he discerns special powers: *Das Gefühl für Humanität hat mich noch nicht verlassen.* (See chap. 8, n. 133, above.) Obviously, much more needs to be said about why certain things were and were not left unsaid by him. (See chap. 8, nn. 181, 186, chap. 9, n. 19, below.) But it should also again be said:

> This castle hath a pleasant seat. The air
> Nimbly and sweetly recommends itself
> Unto our gentle senses.

Shakespeare, *Macbeth*, act 1, sc. 6, ll. 1-3. (Compare, however, "the view" from within as well as without after the murder of Duncan, ibid., act 2, sc. 3, ll. 1-19.)

See, on the significance of Socrates' life and death for Plato, *Alfarabi's Philosophy of Plato and Aristotle*, pp. 62-65, 49, 66-67; on Protagoras, ibid., pp. 54-55.

141. Harry V. Jaffa, *Equality and Liberty* (New York: Oxford University Press, 1965), p. 189. One can support Professor Jaffa's observation by noting the salutary effect upon minority opinion of the evident intention of the community to deal intelligently and humanely with the problems confronting it. Indignation and repression do not suffice:

> A preliminary report defining rules for dealing with disruptive courtroom tactics was submitted to the American Bar Association while several panelists warned that more basic issues were being ignored.
> "It's extraordinary—the amount of attention that's being focused on disruption," said A. Leon Higginbotham, Jr., a U. S. District Court judge from Philadelphia who was among those discussing the subject at the 93rd annual meeting of the ABA [in St. Louis].
> "I think it indicates we're sort of lost in our society. If we got down to the more important issues—poverty, racism, injustice—it would do more to limit disruptions in the courtroom."
> Higginbotham, an imposing black man with a powerful voice, Tuesday told an overflow crowd of 300 persons listening to the panel that it was the duty of lawyers to eradicate "the villany of poverty, the villany of racism, the villany of injustice just as much as it is to have an orderly courtroom."
> Several panelists who agreed with him mentioned the tumultuous Chicago 7 conspiracy trial as the prime cause of the concern about disruptive courtroom tactics. [James W. Singer, "ABA Gets Rules to Handle Courtroom Disruptions," *Chicago Sun-Times*, Aug. 13, 1970, p. 32]

See, on the "Chicago Conspiracy Trial," Appendix D, above.

142. Tacitus, *History* 1.1. See Machiavelli, *Discourses*, book 1, chap. 10; cf. Strauss, *Thoughts on Machiavelli*, pp. 33-34.

There is recorded, in Voltaire's *Philosophical Dictionary* (New York: Basic Books, 1962), at p. 356, this exchange:

> *Boldmind.* . . . The tyrants of the mind have caused part of the misfortunes in the world. We have been happy in England only since everyone has freely enjoyed the right of speaking his mind.
> *Medroso.* In Lisbon, where nobody can speak his, we're very tranquil too.
> *Boldmind.* You are tranquil, but you're not happy; it is the tranquility of galley slaves who row in cadence and in silence.

Medroso. Do you believe, then, that my soul is in the galleys?
Boldmind. Yes; and I would deliver it.
Medroso. But if I'm content in the galleys?
Boldmind. In that case you deserve to be there.

See chap. 5, n. 94, above.

143. Erskine, *Speeches*, 2:141. The italics are Erskine's. Consider the difficulty an American politician has of determining which Negro leaders are in touch with the opinions of their people. See "Terror in Johannesburg," *National Review*, Aug. 25, 1964, p. 728; Anthony Sampson, "Behind the Black Curtain," *London Observer*, Apr. 19, 1970, p. 25; Fagan, *Co-existence in South Africa*, pp. 38-39, 47, 50 (". . . We shall be closing the mouths of many Bantu by closing that of their spokesman [Chief Luthuli]. Can we risk doing that—for our sakes as well as for theirs? For we shall not be stopping their thoughts; we shall only be cutting off our knowledge of what they think."), 67, 80-81, 83 ("We cannot govern well unless we keep ourselves informed of the needs, the grievances, the feelings, the wishes, ambitions and aspirations of those whom we govern."), 92, 98 ("Channels of communication between the various race groups . . . are so few and are hemmed in by so many restrictions and inhibitions that we, the Whites, must to a considerable degree be strangers to the non-Whites, and certainly, to an even greater degree, they are strangers to us."), 124-25 ("[It is evident] that there is still sufficient restiveness to allow considerable elements among the Bantu to be roused to sabotage and even murder by movements aiming at the overthrow of the existing order. We may blame Communist agitators, but agitators can only put a match to already inflammable material." See Appendix D, above.).

See, also, "Letter from Israel," *New Yorker*, Dec. 30, 1967, p. 42.

144. Lincoln, *Complete Works*, 1:113.

145. See Winston S. Churchill, *Great Contemporaries* (London: Odhams Press, 1949), p. 40; Lincoln, *Complete Works*, 1:527.

146. See, for the deference paid to "informed men" before we were subjected to (and corrupted by?) our Vietnam adventure:

> When he testified before the Senate Foreign Relations Committee, [George] Kennan refused to appear as the expert who could solve the major problems now before the world. Again and again in his testimony he emphasized that there was much information that could be known only to the men who had to make the final decisions. [*Manchester Guardian Weekly*, May 21, 1959]

> This is, as I understand it, the position taken by President Kennedy. He will resume testing in the open air if and as it is necessary to the maintenance of our "relative position." . . . This means that the decisions will have to be made by the President, that they cannot be made by public debate. It is not only because the President has the final responsibility. It is also because he is the only man with complete access to all the knowable facts. Whether, when and how to test is not something that can be decided by the governor of New York or by members of Congress or by editors and columnists, or by the man in the smoking car. None of them knows enough. None of them can know enough. [Walter Lippmann, *Chicago Sun-Times*, Nov. 9, 1961]

> At a press conference . . . Eisenhower told a questioner he would have nothing to say about the Berlin crisis. He said the President was conducting relations in this area. "Only he can have the complete information on the methods we must use to get some workable agreement with these people," Eisenhower said. "For somebody like myself to try to outline a formula, it would be futile, it would be unwise." [*Chicago Tribune*, Oct. 18, 1961]

> Although General Eisenhower won't go into details where military spending could be cut—he no longer has access to the information on which the requests are based—it is known he believes the Army ground forces are too large. [*New York Herald-Tribune*, Paris ed., June 30, 1962]

CHAPTER EIGHT, NOTE 147: PAGE 256   741

Adm. Arleigh Burke, who retired Tuesday as chief of naval operations, said . . . "I know, after three days out of uniform, that I don't know what the hell's going on." [*Chicago Tribune*, Aug. 4, 1961]

[President Kennedy said,] "This is no time for rash and irresponsible talk which strengthens the claims of our adversaries. This is no time for confused and intemperate remarks on the part of those who have neither the facts nor the responsibility to determine this nation's course." [*Chicago Sun-Times*, Oct. 14, 1962]

Cf. Lippmann's column, *Newsweek*, July 5, 1965, p. 11, as well as his London speech of May 27, 1965 (on the value of press coverage of events in the Dominican Republic):

. . . From a sheaf of papers, [President Johnson] will recite encouraging tidings from his military advisers, a favorable report from Ambassador Ellsworth Bunker on the South Vietnamese election campaign, a note from Jack Valenti assuring him of his popularity. Mrs. Johnson dropped in during one such [presidential] discourse recently. "That's not what I read in the papers!" she exclaimed. [*Time*, Aug. 25, 1967, p. 7]

See, for my assessment of how badly informed the United States has been about its interests in Greece, "Greece Today and the Limits of American Power," *Southwest Review*, 54 (1968): 1. (See chap. 6, n. 1, above.) See, also, chap. 5, n. 112, above, chap. 8, n. 159, below. (The *Souhwest Review* article is also available in the *Congressional Record* 115: E1875 [Mar. 11, 1969].)

The decade which opened with considerable deference paid the superior judgment of the informed men "who had to make the final decisions" closed with such irreverent observations as those of Art Buchwald (see Proust, *Remembrance of Things Past*, 1:888-89):

One of the strongest proponents of the ABM is a friend who has been assigned by the Pentagon to convince skeptics like myself that we really need it. "I don't think I could make a stronger argument for the ABM," he said, "than the fact that Secretary Laird has revealed the Soviets will have a first-strike nuclear capability by 1975." "That's pretty strong," I admitted. "But how come Secretary Laird found out about this first-strike Soviet capability and Secretaries McNamara and Clifford knew nothing about it?" "Laird reads more." [*Chicago Sun-Times*, May 18, 1969, sec. 2, p. 8]

147. The *New York Times* reported:

Mr. Salinger [President Kennedy's press secretary] said that as a test, a committee recently had been assigned the task of developing estimates of the nation's military strength, policy and capability, using only materials available to the public. "Their estimate was almost totally accurate," Mr. Salinger said. "And I believe this indicates we have been going too far in discussing matters affecting the national security." [Jan. 26, 1961]

See *Memoirs of Harry S Truman* (New York: Signet Books, New American Library, 1965), 2:333-35; Richard C. Snyder and Glenn D. Paige, "The United States Decision to Resist Aggression in Korea," *Administrative Science Q.* 3 (1958): 342, n. 8. See, also, *Congressional Record*, 116: S7898-9 (May 27, 1970); Ransom, *The Intelligence Establishment*, pp. 17-18, 19, 31-32, 151n. Cf. ibid., pp. 20 ff.

There remains the question of how much secrecy is really possible in military developments today, especially when vast technological facilities have to be organized. It may be that an effective control of the press in this respect would mean that only the American people would be kept from information that both the United States government and all foreign governments share. See chap. 4, n. 36, above.

The *war-time* development of the atomic bomb, however, seems to have been kept remarkably secret. I did not hear even the vaguest rumor about it, although I was a flying officer in a bomber group training for the final assault against Japan. (Nor, for that matter, did the vice-president of the United States. Truman, Memoirs, 1:460-61.) On the other hand, the "missile gap," of which so much was made in the 1960 presidential campaign, seemed to me at the time as dubious as it was later revealed to be: one needed only to have tried to get a copy made of an automobile key in Smolensk and Moscow, as I did in the summer of 1960, to have been somewhat skeptical of what was said during the campaign about overall Russian industrial development and technological know-how by those "with complete access to all the knowable facts." (See *Newsweek*, Mar. 13, 1967, p. 78. Cf. Joseph Alsop, *Chicago Sun-Times*, Apr. 7, 1969, p. 34; Stewart Alsop, *Newsweek*, Aug. 11, 1969, p. 84.) (I suspect that a significant disparity still exists between Russia and the United States, a disparity reflected in what we hear about the Russian space program and about their computer industry, to say nothing of their agriculture. [See, e.g., chap. 8, n. 43, above.] Of course, even a "second-rate" economy can become "first-rate" militarily if there is a concentration in armaments—but is not this only for the short run, since one cost of such concentration is the sacrifice of many divergent developments which may eventually be drawn upon in devising the next generation of armaments?) It would be good for Americans (who, since they are not gratuitous bullies, can usually be relied upon to "deal from strength" responsibly when aware of that strength) to realize what Stalin knew in 1948, that the United States is "the most powerful state in the world." Milovan Djilas, *Conversations with Stalin* (New York: Harcourt, Brace & World, 1962), p. 182. Cf. Victor Zorza, "The Battle inside the Kremlin," *Look*, Mar. 18, 1969, p. 93; "America in Danger," *Chicago Tribune*, July 29, 1970, p. 12 (an editorial which opens, "In what he called 'the most fateful testimony I have ever given,' Vice Adm. Hyman G. Rickover has warned that the Soviet Union could start history's biggest war tomorrow and 'I am frankly not confident the outcome of such a war would be in our favor,'" and which closes, ". . . In these circumstances congressional doves who want to scuttle our defenses and pour money into the bottomless rathole of 'welfare' are out of their minds."). See Eugene Davidson, "Behind the Soviet Show Windows," *Modern Age* 8 (1964): 226; *Time*, May 4, 1970, p. 36.

A hidden danger of an escalated arms race lies in the fact that the world (as well as the United States) has more to gain in the long run from having Communist countries (whose economies are less able to absorb such expenditures than is ours) prosperous and hence prudent. (We must take care, in any event, to ease, if not prevent, the conditions which could produce another "demon-genius sprung from the abyss of poverty, inflamed by defeat, devoured by hatred and revenge, and convulsed by his design to make [his] race masters of Europe or maybe the world." Winston S. Churchill [on Adolf Hitler], *The Gathering Storm* [Boston: Houghton Mifflin Co., 1948], p. 249.) The extent to which our growing abundance saves us from the hard choices other peoples have to make is suggested by a report by the Federal Reserve Bank of Chicago: ". . . The increasing burdens of national defense, while diverting labor and materials from civilian uses, have not prevented a steady rise in income and consumption by the typical family." *Business Conditions*, May 1969, p. 2. Consider as well an intriguing report in *Time*, Apr. 18, 1969, at p. 84: "97% of the world population has yet to fly. But 45% of U.S. adults have done so at least once." Cf. Aristotle, *Politics* 1267a14-16; Lincoln, *Works*, 1:13.

148. If one did not recognize as well General Eisenhower's contribution (a contribution that only he as a popular military leader may have been able to make) to the beginning of the relaxation of tensions between the United States and Russia, one could say of his departure from office what was said of that of Charles I, that nothing became his presidency so much as his leaving it. (See Murray Kempton, "The Underestimation of Dwight D. Eisenhower," *Esquire*, Sept. 1967, p. 108; chap. 8, n. 154, below.)

> The other day we carried a brief story setting forth that units of the Atlantic fleet had put to sea to check on unidentified submarines reported off the Atlantic coast. We cannot recall a year that has gone by in recent times when the navy has not issued a "terse announcement" to this effect. All it signifies to us is that the military budget has been submitted to Congress and the ad-

CHAPTER EIGHT, NOTE 149: PAGE 256   743

mirals have found it advisable to toss a little scare into Congress and the public. ["Sighted Budget, Summoned Subs," *Chicago Tribune* editorial, Mar. 9, 1958]

Compare the *Tribune* editorial in chap. 8, n. 147, above. See Ransom, *The Intelligence Establishment*, pp. 215-18.

149. See my contribution to a symposium on pollution in which I suggest that one important effect of the current concern about pollution is to induce us to make explicit the awareness we have always had about "the nature of man and of society." Milton Friedman *et al.*, *Legal and Economic Aspects of Pollution* (Chicago: University of Chicago Center for Policy Study, 1970).

Government officials can be expected to have a better grasp of day-to-day developments, especially with respect to military activities abroad, than the typical citizen. Consider, however, the following exchange during one of President Johnson's press conferences recorded in the *New York Times*, Apr. 1, 1966, p. 18:

> Q.: I wonder, sir, if you can give us your views and comments of the current domestic trouble in South Vietnam, and specifically if there should be a change in government? What effect this might have on the war?
>
> A.: I would answer all your question in one sentence, that there is not any information that I could give you that would add to what you have read in the papers. I think that there is very adequate free flow of information out there, and everything that is reported to this Government in that field is pretty well known to you either simultaneously, by the time I get it, or maybe sometimes a little ahead of me.

Former Ambassador John K. Galbraith quoted Secretary of State Rusk as saying, "I have found that the objectives of American foreign policy are widely understood, respected and supported." Galbraith then commented, "I quote these words very precisely. They are to be read in light of the fact that the Secretary sits at the very center of what is one of the greatest information-gathering organizations in the world. How could a man in his position be so terribly misinformed?" *New York Times*, June 12, 1966, p. 6. See, also, on Rusk, chap. 7, n. 124, above.

See Churchill, *End of the Beginning*, pp. 165-66, explaining to the House of Commons why "the Government are more accurately, but less speedily, less fully and less colourfully informed [about the course of battles] than the newspapers." (This is the context of the passage quoted at chap. 5, n. 27, above.)

Consider also the disclosure, of June 1, 1966, by a *New York Times* editor, that President Kennedy had told a *Times* executive that if the paper had printed all it knew about the impending Bay of Pigs invasion of Cuba, the United States would have been saved from a "colossal mistake."

> The best way to turn off the speculation [about the Bay of Pigs debacle], [the President] said, was to tell the truth: that all the senior officials involved had backed the operation but that the final responsibility was his own. Then he added, with unusual emphasis, "There is only one person in the clear—that's Bill Fulbright. And he probably would have been converted if he had attended more of the meetings. If he had received the same treatment we received—discontent in Cuba, morale of the free Cubans, rainy season, Russian MIGs and destroyers, impregnable beachhead, easy escape into the Escambray, what else to do with these people—it might have moved him down the road too." . . .
> Afterward Kennedy would sometimes recur incredulously to the Bay of Pigs, wondering how a rational and responsible government could ever have become involved in so ill-starred an adventure. . . . He would say at times, "My God, the bunch of advisers we inherited. . . . Can you imagine being President and leaving behind someone like all those people there?" My impression is that, among these advisers, the Joint Chiefs had disappointed him most for their cursory review of the military plans. . . . The director of the Central Intelligence Agency advocated the adventure; the Joint Chiefs of Staff and the Secre-

tary of Defense approved its military aspects. They all spoke with the sacerdotal prerogative of men vested with a unique understanding of arcane matters. "If someone comes in to tell me this or that about the minimum wage bill," Kennedy said to me later, "I have no hesitation in overruling them. But you always assume that the military and intelligence people have some secret skill not available to ordinary mortals." . . . Had one senior adviser opposed the adventure, I believe that Kennedy would have canceled it. Not one spoke against it. One further factor no doubt influenced him: the enormous confidence in his own luck. . . . [Arthur M. Schlesinger, Jr., *A Thousand Days* (Boston: Houghton Mifflin Co., 1965), pp. 289, 292, 295, 258-59]

See Reston, *Artillery of the Press*, pp. 20-21, 30-31, 55-56; Clayton Fritchey, "LBJ Infallible? Not Necessarily," *Chicago Sun-Times*, Nov. 25, 1967, p. 30; *New Republic*, June 28, 1969, pp. 31-32.

"Even the best Presidents are suckers for the CIA, for it is so seductive to know more—or think you know more—than the general public." Clayton Fritchey, "The CIA under Fire," *Harper's*, Oct. 1966, p. 46. See Bruning, "The Statesman," in Heywood, *Works of the Mind*, p. 116 ("I think that the greatest hindrance to constructive political action in the last thirty years has been the influence on final decisions of experts, especially of experts obsessed with the belief that their own generation has gained a vantage point unprecedented in human history."); C. P. Snow, *Science and Government* (New York: Mentor Books, New American Library, 1962), pp. 116-19. Cf. Plato, *Republic* 473C-E, 540D-E. See, also, Burke, *Works*, 4:95-96, 121 ff.

See chap. 4, n. 49, above, chap. 8, n. 160, chap. 9, n. 38, below.

150. President Johnson's press secretary once insisted that there was "no information in this government [about the war in Vietnam] that is not available to members of Congress in both parties." *Chicago Sun-Times*, June 10, 1966, p. 9. (See Reston, *Artillery of the Press*, pp. 72, 103.) I believe this is true as well of the citizen who wants to be informed about Vietnam. (See Herman Kahn, *Stepladder to Extinction*, p. 40.) Thus, it is (in a sense) reassuring to confirm, upon reading such "inside accounts" of an administration in Washington as Townsend Hoopes, *The Limits of Intervention* (New York: David McKay Co., 1969), that the discussions and memoranda relied upon within the State Department and Pentagon depended upon the facts and arguments that had been available at the same time to the alert citizen. See, also, *Newsweek*, Aug. 24, 1970, p. 68. (The sense in which this is not reassuring is, of course, that one does hope "they must know something we don't know" if so much damage is to be done to others and to ourselves by what "they" do in our name. See chap. 7, n. 74, above. But see chap. 8, n. 161, below, for what the Dutch grandmother knew.)

I addressed myself, in a lecture at the University of Chicago of April 29, 1966, "Viet Nam and the First Amendment: The Presumption of Citizenship," to the problem of what the citizen can be expected to know and do about public affairs. The lecture includes the observation:

> One difficulty with the moral sense of many public men—and the President is, to say the least, typical in this respect—is that it may be blunted by their craving for success, for public approval, for honor. The very desire for honor reflects a need for reassurance of one's virtue, a reassurance that is vital for one who will not rely on his own standards for self-appraisal. Men with such appetites are apt to make the sacrifices they regard as useful to secure public approval. The President is, indeed, a case in point. (I can say this with a certain proprietary interest, since I may be the only one in this hall tonight who is recorded to have thought before 1960 that Lyndon Johnson could make a good president. I still think so.) His concern with public opinion polls; his lack of inhibitions where publicity is available; his inability to allow others a share of the limelight, except where it serves his purposes; his temper tantrums (which make one wonder about the calibre of the men who can stay close to him)—all this reveals a childishness that is a serious flaw in a man of great talents. I suspect this may have been the flaw that induced him to gamble away the

CHAPTER EIGHT, NOTE 150: PAGE 257   745

opportunity to settle the Viet Nam war without further intervention, the opportunity provided him by the overwhelming election mandate for which he had asked in 1964. He tried, that is, to exercise even more control over the situation than he could have had easily for the taking. He tried, in an effort to win more public approval ("consensus") than circumstances permitted, to satisfy doves and hawks alike—the hawks by a sudden display of force; the doves by securing peace—with the result that he has gotten into trouble with both flocks and has lost the fleeting opportunity with which he had been entrusted by the electorate. I am reminded of an old lady in my home town: she would not "go to Hell for a dime," but she would fish around the edge for it until she fell in. It is about such matters and such men that moral judgments *can* be made, and which we the people *are* equipped to judge. We may not have that special inhibition of public men, that pride of self, which prevents a man from seeing the truth if it should contradict the public stand in which he may be trapped. The typical public man needs our guidance and restraint to protect from his miscalculations both his country and himself, as well as any other people unfortunate enough to be involved in his misadventures.

Cf. Anastaplo, "Natural Right and the American Lawyer," *Wis. L. Rev.* 1967:340, n. 46. See James Reston's remarkably bitter column, "Should More Lives Be Lost in War?" *Dallas Morning News*, Sept. 1, 1969, p. 19A:

[President Nixon] has been worried about the revolt of the voters against the war, and even about a revolt of the generals if he humiliates them by pulling out too fast, but now he also has to consider the possibility of a revolt of the men if he risks their lives in a war he has decided to bring to a close. This is a devilish problem for everybody concerned, but particularly for men who find themselves . . . [asked] to fight for time to negotiate a settlement with Hanoi that will save [the President's] face but may very well lose their lives. . . .

See chap. 6, n. 66, above, for still another bitter comment by Reston on the war. The following exchange in *Parade*, Aug. 23, 1970, p. 2, may suffice to sum up our understanding of "how Vietnam could happen":

Q.: Does anyone know why Lyndon Johnson sent the amazing total of 540,000 American boys to fight in Vietnam?
A.: Johnson was advised by the military in 1965 that he could win the war in Vietnam on the cheap. He was gradually suckered into further troop escalations as military victory eluded him. He alone was not at fault. His civilian advisers—McNamara, Rostow, Rusk, Bundy—they all went along with the military year by year, promise by promise. The above is the opinion of Jack Valenti, a White House aide under Johnson and now president of the Motion Picture Association of America.

Why President Johnson was "suckered in" while, say, President Eisenhower was not is another problem. A not unimportant consideration is that the Democratic party may well be (for good reasons as well as bad) our twentieth-century "war party." (I do not rely merely on history to support this suggestion. See, e.g., the review I have prepared for the Jan. 1971 *Critic* of James MacGregor Burns, *Roosevelt: The Soldier of Freedom* [New York: Harcourt Brace Jovanovich, 1970].) Nor, I should add, need it be improper to be the "war party" when war is truly in the national interest. See, for Eugene Rostow's defense of the proposition that our intervention in Vietnam has been in the national interest, *New Yorker*, July 4, 1970, p. 30. (It should be said as well that this war does display, even though in a misguided form, the altruistic side of the American character. Cf. chap. 7, n. 72, above. It should also be said that the war has seemed to me, since 1968, essentially over for us.)

The peculiar character of the Vietnam war has been such that a President could be urged to "Win with Air Power" (*Chicago Tribune*, Oct. 4, 1966, p. 14) even though the "bomb tonnage now being dropped on Viet Nam each week is larger than that dropped on Germany at the peak of World War II" (*New York Times*, int. ed., Aug. 22, 1966, p. 4). The *Tribune* editorial endorsed the advice that we should "go for the economic jugular vein of the enemy . . . even at the 'outside risk' that Red China would come into the war." (Cf. chap. 8, n. 109, above.) A curious effect of our efforts in Vietnam, one justification of which was to make our deterrent "credible," is to reveal that a small country can (if not heavily industrialized) absorb a surprising amount of punishment from the most powerful country in the world. To use our power as we have has caused us to lose much of its effectiveness as a deterrent. I do not doubt that we could, by "go[ing] for the economic jugular vein of the enemy" and thereafter (if need be) by attacking much more than we have already the civilian population of North Vietnam, induce the Viet Cong to suspend operations (at least until we got out of the country). I assume, however, that Americans do not want to regard themselves, or to be regarded by the civilized nations of the world, as no better than the Russians in Hungary or the Germans in Holland. (What would China do in response to such developments or perhaps force the Soviet Union to do? Even the most sanguine advocates of radical escalation concede an "outside risk." My own impression is that no one really knows what he is doing in the conduct of this war. "Dean Rusk recently told a close colleague: "If anybody had told me three years ago that we could do all the things we are doing in Vietnam and manage not to get involved with the Russians or the Chinese, I would have laughed at him.'" *Newsweek*, May 8, 1967, p. 35. Why we are doing "all the things we are doing" is anything but a laughing matter. Chinese expansionism was once the target—but supporters of escalation of the war have argued, "Even those who profess fear of Red China's intervention concede that the North Vietnamese, like the South Vietnamese, hate the Chinese and that Ho Chi Minh would be extremely reluctant to call for help on a scale that would make his country a dependency of Red China." Editorial interview, *Chicago Tribune*, May 15, 1967, p. 24.) (See chap. 5, n. 138, above, for a comparison of Israel and South Vietnam. It is, at most, the "body" of the United States which is threatened by the possible falling of "dominoes" in Indochina, while in Israel the very soul of our country is at stake: That is, is it not obvious to most Americans that what Israel stands for, both good and bad, is in large part what we stand for? But we have so compromised our power in Vietnam that "a key [American] admiral" must admit that it would be the "hardest naval job in the world" for the United States to go to Israel's aid from the sea. "We'd have to go through the Russian fleet," he observed, "and if challenged, we'd be forced to fire the first shot. And you know how difficult that would be in the present political climate in the United States." Thomas B. Ross, "U. S. Fleet Is Told to Stay at Least 25 Mi. off Egypt," *Chicago Sun-Times*, July 26, 1970, p. 1. What has happened to all that "credibility" we have been manufacturing and stockpiling in Vietnam since 1965?)

At what point does "the stone [start] rolling" out of control? See the text at chap. 9, n. 11, below.

> All ultimate planning by both defense staffs [in Moscow and Washington] is founded upon the theory that each is aware of the consecutive moves the other may be expected to make in a worsening crisis. Our generation substitutes Herman Kahn's *Stepladder to Extinction* for John Buchan's *39 Steps*. The assumption of U.S. strategy, flexible response, is based on the thought that crises can be controlled and wars limited—because nothing else makes sense. [C. L. Sulzberger, *New York Times*, June 21, 1967, p. 41]

The significance of world opinion was assessed by Walter Lippmann in his column of Jan. 3, 1967 (*Chicago Sun-Times*, p. 28). See, also, his column in *Newsweek*, Jan. 16, 1967, p. 16:

> If, on the other hand, the President goes beyond limited war, and follows Chairman Rivers of the House Armed Services Committee who wants to "flatten Hanoi if necessary and let world opinion go fly a kite," there is every reason for thinking that, having adopted genocide as a national policy, the country will find itself isolated in an increasingly angry and hostile world. That would mean

CHAPTER EIGHT, NOTE 150: PAGE 257

> more than watching world opinion fly a kite. It would mean that we would be suspected and hated not only in the Communist and neutral world but in very large sections of the nations with which we are most closely allied. We would come to be regarded as the most dangerous nation in the world, and the great powers of the world would align themselves accordingly to contain us.

See *The Political Thought of Woodrow Wilson*, ed. E. David Cronon (Indianapolis: Bobbs-Merrill, 1965), p. 535. Cf. chap. 9, n. 1, below.

Perhaps our difficulties in this matter can be traced back to the self-centered assumption that there is a "contest for the world in which we are now engaged, and shall in all likelihood be engaged during the lifetime of everyone now living. . . ." Jaffa, "The Case for a Stronger National Government," in Robert A. Goldwin, *A Nation of States* (Chicago: Rand McNally, 1963), p. 107. (See, on what the rest of the world is up to while we sleep, chap. 7, n. 124, above.) In any event, Vietnam serves to instruct us, as it can be hoped the Cuban missile episode did the Russians (but at far less cost), with respect to the limits of even a superpower's power. It should instruct us as well in the risks a people even as humane as ours runs when it "blow[s] out the moral lights." Lincoln, *Complete Works*, 1:448, 557.

Further light may be thrown on our circumstances by returning to those of Israel. See, e.g., Morton Kondracke, "Israel—The Frontier America Once Was," *Chicago Sun-Times*, Oct. 18, 1970, sec. 2, pp. 1, 2:

> To be sure, the Israelis did not decimate the Palestinian Arab population as the white man did the Indian [in America], but the end result was the same—a resident population was substantially moved off land it had occupied for generations. A sizable portion was pushed into reservations—in Israel's case, into refugee camps.

Are we not obliged to consider, with a compassion which is nevertheless aware of realities, whether long possession (in the ordinary sense) or prior occupancy is ever a sufficient basis for "property"? See chap. 8, n. 30, above, chap. 9, n. 35, below [on the "conservative"]. The use to which the resources of the earth are likely to be put by contending claimants is not an irrelevant consideration in determining their just allocation. (Does not Arab passion today recall the greatness reflected in Alfarabi?) In any event, a Jerusalem newsletter of Oct. 23, 1969, from Rabbi Richard W. Winograd (of the University of Wisconsin), is instructive about how the American way of life today may be assessed:

> Israel does not seem to be suffering from the malaise and disintegration which has afflicted the West for the past twenty years. There does not seem to be a significant generation gap. The youth have a sense of hope and trust in the future. . . . The mood here among the young reminds me of the best days of the civil rights movement [in the United States]. They believe in the past, too, and unlike many of America's young people who tend to view historical persons and events with cynicism and disdain, the youth believe and trust in the founders of the nation. . . .

Consider, also, the observation by Professor Melvyn Hill of York University after visiting Israel (in a letter of Aug. 21, 1970, from which I have been permitted to quote):

> I discovered the uncomfortable distinction between myself as a Diaspora Jew and Israeli Jews: uncomfortable because in certain ways they come off better. Certainly, theirs is a more sober society, and many of them have a nobler sense of the public life, in particular in terms of excellence in the service of one's country, that borders on the heroic. [But] my roots *are* in the West. Besides, I have a strong suspicion that in the last analysis one would have to become a *kibbutznik* to become a true Israeli.

See chap. 7, n. 35, above, especially the quotation from Maimonides. (Cf. Howard Brotz, *The Black Jews of Harlem: Negro Nationalism and the Dilemmas of Negro Leadership*

[New York: The Free Press of Glencoe, 1964].) The question remains whether the Israelis will be able to protect their aspirations (which *are* rooted, despite their secularism, in the Bible) from the corrosive effects of the Cold War, even while they secure from us the support they seem to require. See chap. 8, n. 11, below.

Are not the constitutional principles of the Declaration of Independence our *kibbutz*? See chap. 7, nn. 72, 124 (end), above, chap. 9, n. 10, below. Cf. chap. 3, n. 35, above.

151. In the first session of the 89th Congress (1965), more than 16,000 bills and resolutions were introduced, of which 349 were enacted into law. *Chicago Sun-Times*, Dec. 25, 1965, p. 14.

152. "Those who govern, having much business on their hands, do not generally like to take the trouble of considering and carrying into execution new projects. The best public measures are therefore seldom adopted from previous wisdom, but forc'd by the occasion." Franklin, *Autobiography*, p. 151. (See Kahn, *Thinking about the Unthinkable* (New York: Avon Books, 1962), pp. 35-40, 278-80. "One of the great problems of the world is that all crises are almost certainly managed by tired men." John Kenneth Galbraith, *Ambassador's Journal* [Boston: Houghton Mifflin, 1969], p. 392.)

The reader of memoirs and diaries of public men finds ample confirmation of Franklin's observations. See, e.g., James Forrestal, *The Forrestal Diaries* (New York: Viking Press, 1951), pp. 127-28, 134-38, 143: the daily detail of high officials is overwhelming; there is no time for serious thought; even the highest officers of government have difficulty seeing the President for half an hour. See chap. 8, n. 136, above, and n. 159, below. An assistant secretary of defense has reported,

> Out at the Pentagon, we start work at eight o'clock in the morning and we don't stop till midnight. . . . When I go to New York for the weekend, people ask me, because I've been in the Pentagon, "What's going on?," "What about Korea?," "What's the war situation?" I find I don't know as much as they do from reading the papers. I've been too busy. [John Hersey, "Mr. President," *New Yorker*, Apr. 21, 1951, p. 38]

Lloyd George once said of Prime Minister Ramsay MacDonald, "That man is too busy to do his job." *Manchester Guardian Weekly*, July 28, 1966, p. 6; Reston, *Artillery of the Press*, pp. 31-32. Cf. Winston Churchill, *Triumph and Tragedy* (Boston: Houghton Mifflin Co., 1953), p. 479: "There is no comparison between reading about events afterwards and living through them from hour to hour." See, also, chap. 9, n. 15, below.

153. Aristotle's *Politics* 1281a11-1282b14, remains the classic statement of the advantages to be hoped for from public discussion. See, also, Aristotle, *Metaphysics* 2.1; Hobbes, *Leviathan*, 1.13; Descartes, *Discourse on Method* (beginning of pt. 1); Churchill, *Great Contemporaries*, p. 4; Yves R. Simon, *Philosophy of Democratic Government* (Chicago: University of Chicago Press, 1951), p. 86. (Besides, Lincoln reminds us, "As the proverb goes, no man knows so well where the shoe pinches as he who wears it." *Complete Works*, 2:539.)

Cf. Aristotle, *Politics* 1318b9-16, *Rhetoric* 1354a32-1354b13, *Politics* 1322b13-15, 1299b32-34, 1281b39-1282a14, *Nicomachean Ethics* 1181a13-24, *Politics* 1264a20-23, *Rhetoric* 1355a15-28.

Freud wrote of the value of colloquial speech as "the deposit . . . of ancient knowledge. . . ." *A General Introduction to Psychoanalysis* (New York: Pocket Books, Washington Square Press, 1960), p. 102. And in Timothy Ware's *Orthodox Church* (London: Penguin Books, 1963), at pp. 248-49, we find, "The mystery of the Church consists in the very fact that *together* sinners become *something different* from what they are as individuals; this 'something different' is the Body of Christ."

> There is a "feeling of the House," a "sense" of the House, and no one who knows anything of it can despise it. A very shrewd man of the world went so far as to say that "the House of Commons has more sense than any one in it." But there is no such "sense" in the House of Lords, because there is no life. The Lower Chamber is a chamber of eager politicians; the Upper (to say the least) of *not* eager ones. [Bagehot, *The English Constitution*, p. 101]

154. Churchill, *Great Contemporaries*, pp. 74-75, 79; cf. ibid., pp. 132, 142. See, also, Churchill, *Thoughts and Adventures* (London: Odhams Press, 1949), p. 212.

Walter Lippmann's assessment of the men who have risen to the top in American politics included these perceptive observations (in response to a request that he "rate some of the Presidents [he had] known, starting with Teddy Roosevelt"):

> I think the one who's done the most damage to the United States in the past 100 years is Lyndon Johnson. I think Theodore Roosevelt was very good. He foresaw the role the United States was bound to play in the Twentieth Century and the nature of the problems. I think Franklin Roosevelt was a man who had real problems forced upon him but rose to the occasion and carried out a revolution in American society which on the whole has been very successful. This will surprise you: I think Eisenhower in his first term saw what a mistake it would be to go into Vietnam and had the military ability to end the Korean War. For that I rate him high.
>
> Truman? Oh, yes. Truman was a man who shot from the hip and he made some awfully good decisions and also some bad ones. I don't think history will rate him as high as the English historians rate him, or as low as his enemies do. It's a very mixed record. . . .
>
> There is going to be a whole library of books about Kennedy in the next generation and they are not all going to be Camelot. There is no doubt of his attractiveness and no doubt of his mistakes. Sometimes I think it goes back to his election being very close and not even certain. He was a very insecure President. He made this ghastly mistake of the Bay of Pigs and tried to make up for it the rest of his term. That's why he was in such a hurry with Khrushchev, why he made a mistake about the Berlin Wall, and got us into Vietnam. If you reread his inaugural address, it gives the whole philosophy of being the world policeman and it isn't as good as it seemed. I have very mixed feelings about Kennedy. But, had he lived he would probably have been re-elected. [Mary Blume, "Lippmann, at 80, Looks at the World," *Des Moines Sunday Register*, June 7, 1970, p. 8-T]

155. This recalls the discussion in section 9 of this chapter of the aristocratic character of freedom of speech in our circumstances.

Two editorial comments in the *Chicago Daily News*, dealing with matters foreign and domestic, suggest the usefulness *to public servants* of general discussion:

> But the opportunity must be grasped to build a better, safer, more attractive McCormick Place [Convention Hall] than the last one [which had burned down]—and one essential for accomplishing this is to make all plans out in the open so that the public may know and discuss what's going on. A singularly poor start was made yesterday when the Exposition Authority held its first postfire meeting at the Chicago Club and banned reporters on the ground that it was "just a get-together." We remind the authority that the history of the tragedy-dogged hall is replete with just this kind of cozy secrecy with the public held off at arm's length. We remind the authority that this same history is replete with errors of judgment, many of which might have been avoided if the public had been kept informed of what was being done and planned with its money. To shed light on some of these errors is now the duty of public officials, and the investigating job cannot logically be confined to any close-knit group of politically oriented persons. [*Chicago Daily News*, Jan. 18, 1967, p. 16]

> Americans should be warned that United States support of the British position [in Rhodesia] is fraught with great peril. . . . If Rhodesia is not crushed economically and brought to her knees, the cry will then be heard that military force must be employed. This is how wars are made. Seldom from a single overt act but through a series of gradual involvements. That is the tragedy of Viet Nam—from a few hundred "advisers" in 1954 to nearly a half-million men locked in mortal combat and no end in sight. . . . Many of our readers seem to feel that individual protests go unheeded by the senators and representatives to whom they are addressed. Not so, I assure you, on the issue of war or peace.

> We drifted into the Viet Nam war because so few voices of protest were heard. People were generally oblivious to the threat. . . . [John S. Knight, *Chicago Daily News*, Dec. 10, 1966, p. 16]

156. Zechariah Chafee, *Free Speech in the United States* (Cambridge: Harvard University Press, 1941), p. xi. See, also, Meiklejohn, *Political Freedom*, pp. 58-60, 72.
157. Chafee, *Free Speech in the United States*, pp. viii-ix. See chap. 9, n. 11, below.
158. Karl von Clausewitz, *On War* (New York: Random House, Modern Library, 1943), p. 51. See, also, Tacitus, *History* 3.54. Cf. Hobbes, *Leviathan*, chap. 11 ("Of the Difference of Manners").
159. Truman, *Memoirs*, 1:579.

> I believe that one of the problems of top military leaders is that too many of them come to rely on "briefing." They get most of their facts and their opinions from their staffs, in condensed form. Now any top official must operate that way; the President of the United States has to depend on briefing. But there is one important difference: The President has as his staff people of many different ideas, people who move in and out of his official family; they each have skills and professions of their own; their futures do not depend on their efficiency reports. In the military, however, and especially among the professionals, strong convictions and a critical mind may spell the end of a career. . . . [I know] that a President has to work to keep himself from being encircled by yes-men, while a military leader has far less reason to make that effort. But if he does not, his picture of the situation can gradually become more and more slanted. Because of the practice of rotation of assignments this does not usually happen, but MacArthur had not followed this practice: He had been surrounded by virtually the same group of friends and ardent admirers for years. . . . [Ibid., 2:472]

See chap. 4, n. 49, chap. 7, n. 115, chap. 8, n. 146, above; cf. chap. 9, n. 16, below.
160. Volume 1, chapter 26, of Truman's *Memoirs* is devoted to a report on the development and use of the atomic bomb.

> The final decision of where and when to use the atomic bomb was up to me. Let there be no mistake about it. I regarded the bomb as a military weapon and never had any doubt that it should be used. The top military advisers to the President recommended its use, and when I talked to Churchill he unhesitatingly told me he favored the use of the atomic bomb if it might aid to end the war. [Ibid., 1:462]

(Cf., for a later conversation between Truman and Churchill on this subject, Dean Acheson, *Present at the Creation: My Years in the State Department* [New York: W. W. Norton, 1969], pp. 715-16.)

It may be significant that Truman *recorded* no advice against dropping the bombs on cities. It is certainly significant that the President himself "never had any doubt that it should be used"—which means that the great political and moral problems accompanying its use impressed him no more than they did most of us for whom such ideas as "the rules of war" had long since ceased to mean anything. (See F. J. P. Veale, *Advance to Barbarism: How the Reversion to Barbarism in Warfare and War-trials Menaces Our Future* [Appleton, Wis.: C. C. Nelson Publishing Co., 1953].) But perhaps most significant is Truman's failure to mention any discussion among American leaders, during the three-day interval between the two bombings, about whether the second bomb should be dropped (even though it was known to them [ibid., 1:469] that both the Japanese and the Russians then knew "that the Pacific war would not be of long duration"). See Churchill, *Triumph and Tragedy*, pp. 637-46, 668-70; Enrico Fermi, *Collected Papers* (University of Chicago Press, 1965), I, xxxix; Rovere, *American Establishment*, p. 265; Lilienthal, *Journals* (New York: Harper & Row, 1966), 3:122.

Truman concluded the chapter, "This second demonstration of the power of the

CHAPTER EIGHT, NOTE 160: PAGE 259   751

atomic bomb apparently threw Tokyo into a panic, for the next morning brought *the first indication* that the Japanese Empire was ready to surrender." Ibid., 1:470 (italics added). There seems to be serious doubt whether this was indeed "the first indication." Was he allowed to believe that things were as simple as he now recalls them to have been? In any event, he told an American Legion convention in 1961 that he had no regrets about dropping atomic bombs on Hiroshima and Nagasaki. *Time*, Sept. 22, 1961, p. 20.

Truman's subsequent remarks at the American Legion convention are illuminating:

> These tearjerkers, these fellows who are always saying what oughta been done and they weren't there and they don't know a damn thing about it. . . . They keep crying their eyes out about those people who were killed by those bombs. I haven't heard any of them crying about those boys who were in those upside-down battleships in Pearl Harbor. [*Time*, Sept. 22, 1961, p. 20]

Truman did not seem to appreciate that Americans often expect more from themselves than from other peoples. Cf. chap. 8, n. 18, above. See Churchill, *Triumph and Tragedy*, pp. 641-42. (When Truman makes the criticism of his critics that "they weren't there," one must observe that our development *and his use* of the atomic bombs have placed us all "there." It would be useful as well for an apologist for Truman to suggest what he knew or knows that his critics "don't know." Among his critics, in any event, are men who were moved by Pearl Harbor to enlist in their country's service as soon as they could. I had occasion to observe, in a talk on December 8, 1963:

> That shattering attack [on Pearl Harbor] on just such a Sunday morning as this twenty-two years ago unleashed the passions of war among a people largely indifferent to the affairs of the world. And once such a war begins, it is difficult if not impossible to keep within bounds: from the callous persecution of minorities in Europe, and the surprise bombardment of Pearl Harbor, in time of peace, to the casual destruction of Dresden and of Hiroshima, in time of war, is an almost inevitable "progress." It is folly to expect that once full-scale war begins, anything but full-scale weapons will be used. [Anastaplo, "Notes on the First Amendment," p. 798])

Arthur M. Schlesinger, Jr. (*Book Week*, June 5, 1966, p. 5) has likened President Truman to President Polk who,

> vastly underrated during his Presidency, has won the respect of posterity for his mastery of the instrumentalities of Presidential power as well as for the remarkable accomplishments of his Administration. Like Polk, Truman did great things. But, like Polk, Truman, though endowed with the will to carry out great decisions, lacked the eloquence to rouse the nation to a sense of their historic magnitude and necessity. Like Polk, Truman too had a certain absence of moral imagination—one on slavery, the other on the atomic bomb.

Fletcher Knebel and Charles W. Bailey have provided, in *No High Ground* (New York: Harper & Bros., 1960), an account of preparations and discussions leading up to the atom bombing. (A useful bibliography is appended.) It seems, in any event, that the most serious discussions of the use of the atomic bombs did not take place in the President's office:

> Eisenhower frankly told the War Secretary [Henry L. Stimson] that he hoped the bomb would not have to be used against Japan because he hated to see the United States be the first to employ a weapon with such incredible potential for death and destruction. Thus, in the many weeks in which the decision evolved, no less than six U.S. war leaders had expressed reservations about use of the bomb: Admiral [William D.] Leahy, Generals [Henry H.] Arnold and Eisenhower, Rear Admiral [Lewis L.] Strauss, Assistant Secretary of War [John L.] McCloy and Under Secretary of the Navy [Ralph A.] Bard. Of these, however,

only Bard flatly and formally opposed the use of the bomb without an advance demonstration and warning. On the other side, a score of influential White House advisers supported use of the bomb, including Stimson, [George C.] Marshall, [Leslie R.] Groves, seven of the eight members of the Interim Committee and all of its scientific advisers, plus many other top scientists. [Ibid., p. 94]

> "Listen, Tom," [General Carl Spaatz] said, "if I am going to kill 100,000 people, I'm not going to do it on verbal orders. I want a piece of paper."
> . . . The less in writing, the less chance of breaking security. Spaatz conceded this but stood firm. Anything could happen with a weapon of such strange immensity. "I guess I agree, Tooey," said [the acting Chief of Staff of the U.S. Army] at last, "If a fellow thinks he might blow up the whole end of Japan, he ought to have a piece of paper." [Ibid., pp. 73-74]

Cf. Herbert Feis, *The Atomic Bomb and the End of World War II* (Princeton: Princeton University Press, 1966), pp. 200-201:

> In summary it can be concluded that the decision to drop the bombs upon Hiroshima and Nagasaki ought not to be censured. The reasons were—under the circumstances of the time—weighty and valid enough. But a cluster of worrisome queries remain which the passage of time has coated with greater political, ethical and historical interest. . . . [W]hat if the American government had fully revealed the results of the New Mexico test to the Japanese (and the whole world)? Could that have induced quick surrender? . . .

(Perhaps the increasingly destructive raids in the war against Germany prepared American leaders to order the use of atom bombs:

> Twenty-two years ago on Monday in 68 minutes of bombing, 135,000 people died in an Anglo-American raid on Dresden, the capital of Saxony. It was probably the biggest and quickest single massacre in history. It certainly killed more people than any other air-raid. The Hiroshima atom bomb killed only 71,000. [*Manchester Guardian Weekly*, Feb. 16, 1967, p. 14]

Churchill could counsel early in the war, "[N]eedless bloodshed must never be sought." *Gathering Storm*, p. 524. Cf., e.g., Andrew Wilson, "Dresden—the Anatomy of a Holocaust," *Chicago Sun-Times*, Feb. 22, 1970, p. 91.) See Edward Edelson, "Shaping the Future," *Book Week*, Apr. 9, 1967, p. 4.

I believe the most sobering comment on the atomic bombings, however, is suggested by the account in Bernard Asbell's *When F. D. R. Died* (New York: Holt, Rinehart & Winston, 1961), p. 94, of the Japanese response to the news of President Roosevelt's death:

> [Short-wave radio] carried the flash into the heart of Tokyo. An announcer for Radio Tokyo repeated the bulletin to his people and said, to the puzzlement of *American monitors*: "We now introduce a few minutes of special music in honor of the passing of this great man." But the music did not last long. Japan's new Premier, Kantaro Suzuki, who had heard the news, rushed to the radio station and went on the air himself. Befuddling American eavesdroppers even more, he said: "I must admit that Roosevelt's leadership has been very effective and has been responsible for the Americans' position today. For that reason I can easily understand the great loss his passing means to the American people and my profound sympathy goes to them." [Italics added]

(This response [a few months before the atomic bombs were used] should be compared to the jubilation at the same time among leaders in Hitler's Germany. Ibid., pp. 98-99. Cf., on the German commanding general who refused to do to Paris what had been done to Hamburg and what would be later done to Dresden, Larry Collins and Dominique Lapierre, *Is Paris Burning?* [New York: Simon & Schuster, Pocket Books, 1966], pp.

CHAPTER EIGHT, NOTE 161: PAGE 259   753

23-24, 33-34, 78-80, 87-89, 142-44, 176-77, 182-83, 196-97, 219-20, 239-40, 276-77, 316, 357-58, 369. See Klaus Epstein, book review of David Irving, *The Destruction of Dresden* [New York: Holt, Rinehart & Winston, 1964], *Modern Age*, Summer 1964, p. 311.) See Churchill, *Triumph and Tragedy*, p. 472; James MacGregor Burns, *Roosevelt: The Soldier of Freedom* (New York: Harcourt Brace Jovanovich, 1970), p. 601. See, also, ibid., pp. 138-39. The sense of humanity, or at least of chivalry, displayed by the Japanese in this account should astonish anyone whose impressions of that people were decisively shaped by the attack on Pearl Harbor. Americans should keep such incongruities in mind when confronting Communist leaders abroad (as well as when confronting intimidating youth movements in this country). (See Shakespeare, *Coriolanus*, act 5, sc. 6, ll. 131-55.)

Perhaps the best advice in such confrontations is that implied in the observation by George F. Kennan about differences among Russian leaders:

> . . . Not until the personality of Khrushchev replaced that of Stalin at the pinnacle of authority in the Soviet regime did it again become possible, as it had been in Lenin's time, to have at least a clear-cut dialogue about the differences that divided the Russian Communist world from its non-Communist environment. To many, this distinction will not seem important. "An enemy," they will say, "is an enemy. An antagonism is an antagonism. What difference does it make if one can discuss it?" This is the absolutist view. But it is not the only view one can take. One can remember that *some degree* of conflict and antagonism is present in every international relationship; *some* measure of compromise is necessary everywhere, if political societies are to live together on the same planet. Those who bear this in mind will be inclined to doubt whether there is such a thing as total antagonism, any more than there is such a thing as total identity of interests. Whoever sees it this way will realize that the illusion of total antagonism can be created only by a complete absence of effective communication; and for this reason he will be inclined to doubt, as I myself must confess to doing, whether an enemy with whom one can communicate is really entirely an enemy, after all. [*Russia and the West under Lenin and Stalin* (Boston: Little, Brown & Co., 1961), p. 245]

See chap. 8, n. 169, below. See, also, chap. 3, nn. 30, 35, chap. 8, nn. 149, 150, above. Cf. chap. 9, n. 16, below. It is to our advantage (even as may be our refusal to establish import tariffs just because the countries we trade with harm their economy by so doing) not only that Americans expect more from themselves than from others but also that other peoples expect more from us. That is, we have the benefit of their information and judgment as well in assessing what we should do. Consider John Kenneth Galbraith, *Ambassador's Journal*, p. 169 (see chap. 5, n. 69 [end], above):

> . . . On Berlin and the arms buildup, it is more fun and also more fruitful to criticize the Americans than the Soviets. We listen. There is no similar indication the Soviets do. So it is natural we are lectured [by other countries and peoples]. We cannot be sorry that we are regarded as open to suggestion—not incorrigible.

Is there not hope for any people which recognizes *itself* as "stiffnecked"?

161. It is both sobering and instructive to read the account, by the conscientious attorney general of the day, of how the decision was made to remove everyone of Japanese descent (including native-born American citizens) from the West Coast. Biddle, *In Brief Authority*, pp. 213, 219, 225-26.

It is evident that there was not a showing on that occasion even of military necessity. Ibid., p. 221. The position acted upon by the government of the United States was virtually that of Westbrook Pegler, "The Japanese should be under guard to the last man and woman—and to hell with habeas corpus." Ibid., p. 218. See, also, Mason, *Harlan Fiske Stone*, pp. 672-82; Morton Grodzins, *Americans Betrayed: Politics and the Japanese Evacuation* (Chicago: University of Chicago Press, 1949), pp. 202, 243, 263-64, 267, 269-73, 325-26, 347, 361-74; Burns, *Roosevelt: Soldier of Freedom*, pp. 214-17, 266-68;

Book Week, Apr. 2, 1967, p. 4. Robert Sherrill observed in the *Chicago Sun-Times*, July 5, 1970, sec. 3, p. 10 (in the course of a review of J. A. Donovan, *Militarism* [New York: Charles Scribner's Sons, 1970]):

> To oversimplify Donovan's account: FDR enjoyed playing mastermind strategist with the admirals and generals so much that by the time he died, Adm. Leahy could accurately say, "The Joint Chiefs of Staff at present are under no civilian control whatever." Congress, imbued only with the spirit of victory at any price, had surrendered its controls over the military; it also had made no contingency plans for de-militarizing the nation at the end of the war.

Misplaced confidence in the military is good for neither military officers themselves nor the country they wish to serve. See chap. 7, n. 67, above, chap. 8, n. 179, below. Cf. Grodzins, *Americans Betrayed*, pp. 242-43 (see chap. 5, n. 17, above):

> With the first announcement of prohibited areas, Attorney-General Biddle appointed Thomas C. Clark [who succeeded Biddle as Attorney-General in 1945 and thereafter was appointed to the Supreme Court of the United States] as co-ordinator of the Alien Enemy Control program for the Western Defense Command.... In [one] respect, Mr. Clark disappointed his colleagues in Washington. They hoped that the promulgation of prohibited and restricted areas would quiet the rising clamor for mass evacuation; one of Mr. Clark's first jobs, they thought, would be to reassure the population that the new program provided adequate protection and that sterner measures were unnecessary. Mr. Clark's method of carrying out this part of his mission was one of reassuring the people that the *military* authorities were taking, and would take, all necessary measures.... Mr. Clark's attitude was expressed most graphically after Army authorities had been given full authority but before evacuation policy had been set: "If the military authorities, in whom I have the utmost confidence, tell me it is necessary to remove from any area the citizens as well as the aliens of a certain nationality or of all nationalities I would say the best thing to do would be to follow the advice of the doctor. Whenever you go to a doctor if he tells you take aspirin you take aspirin. If he tells you to cut off your leg so you can save your body you cut off your leg. So I think it is up to the military authorities...."

I had occasion in September, 1968, at a dinner in Athens sponsored by the Greek government, to comment on a similar argument ("Dissent in Athens," *Notes on World Events* [Chicago Council on Foreign Relations], May 1969, pp. 1, 4 [reprinted in *Congressional Record* 115: E5156 (June 23, 1969)]) (see chap. 6, n. 1, above, chap. 9, n. 34, below):

> We have been told several times this evening [by government spokesmen] that Greek affairs of recent years required drastic medicine, that a doctor must sometimes prescribe harsh measures in order to save the life of the patient. But do we not all believe that an adult is entitled to select his own doctor, and to discharge him when he chooses? By what authority does the presiding doctor prescribe what is necessary for Greece? How can the Greeks be said to have selected him, when they did not even know who he was? What diploma does he have as a doctor? What proof of his qualifications is there aside from his self-serving testimony about himself? Certainly, we cannot accept as indicative of public approval of his regimen the fact that an unarmed people does not resist a determined government which is heavily armed.

I am persuaded (as I reflect on such events as those discussed in chap. 3, n. 35, chap. 8, nn. 118, 149, 150, 160, above, chap. 9, n. 11, below) that there is merit to the Dutch grandmother's prediction, "You will be surprised to learn, my boy, with how little wisdom the world is governed." (A similar remark is said to have been made by the Swedish chancellor, Oxenstein, to his son: *Quam parvâ sapientiâ mundus regitur.* H. P. Jones, ed., *Dictionary of Foreign Phrases and Classical Quotations* [Edinburgh: John Grant, 1963], p. 97. Still another version may be found in T. H. White's *The Master*

CHAPTER EIGHT, NOTE 162: PAGE 259   755

[New York: G. P. Putnam's Sons, 1957], p. 105: *Nescis, mi fili, quantillâ prudentiâ mundus regatur*. I believe it appropriate, in this context, to observe that White's book is, in some respects, an adaptation of Shakespeare's *Tempest*, with, however, the "Caliban" [or brutish] element accidentally tripping up "Prospero" [for, in this case, the "brutish" is Romantically allied with the humane]. See chap. 9, n. 16, below.) Indeed, there are times when "freedom of speech" and "self-government" look like delusions (if not even suicidal) and Plato's "best city," or at least Aristotle's adaptation, looks like the most practical constitution in this world! See chap. 9, nn. 28, 30, below. Cf. chap. 2, n. 39, chap. 8, n. 2, above.

James Fitzjames Stephen, *Liberty, Equality, Fraternity* (New York: Holt & Williams, 1873), pp. 245-46, would have us see, "[T]he work of governing a great nation, if it is to be done really well, requires an immense amount of special knowledge and the steady, restrained, and calm exertion of a great variety of the very best talents which are to be found in it." This is especially true, he indicated, with respect to foreign affairs. Ibid., pp. 251-53. See, on the contribution a competent aristocracy can make to the conduct of foreign policy, Henry A. Kissinger, *American Foreign Policy: Three Essays* (New York: W. W. Norton, 1969), pp. 27-28. Consider, also, an exchange at a public lecture between Leo Durocher (of "Nice guys finish last!" fame), manager of the Chicago Cubs, and a member of the audience (David Condon, "In the Wake of the News," *Chicago Tribune*, Sec. 3, p. 1):

> D. I play to win. As long as I'm on the field, I'll try anything because once that locker room door closes behind you the game's over and there's no second chance. Only the second guess.
> Q. Why haven't the Cubs made a trade for Tony Gonzalez of San Diego?
> D. I'd like Gonzalez, but San Diego wanted four of our men. [He named them.] Would you give those four to get Gonzalez?
> Q. Yes.
> D. That's why you're sitting out there and I'm up here.

See *Science* 169 (1970): 927: "The President's problem in Southeast Asia is highly technical and complex. It requires courage, also an expertise not found in baby doctors, college youths, chaplains, politicians, Nobel laureates, . . . however sincere in their protest or competent in their own fields." (Cf. "Does the President Really Know More?" *Time*, May 25, 1970, p. 18. Consider, also, an article in the *Chicago Tribune*, Jan. 2, 1970, sec. 2, p. 20, which recorded, "The Japanese captured Singapore [from the British in 1942] by a land offensive with a force smaller than that of the garrison. Churchill admitted later: 'I ought to have known. My advisors ought to have known, and I ought to have asked. The possibility of Singapore having no landward defenses no more entered my mind than that of a battleship being launched without a bottom.' ") See, for another argument on behalf of deference to experts: "It is strange how so many people claim the right to utter opinions about that supreme and mysterious name of God, just as if they knew the real meaning of the words they use. . . . Would we dare speak about some science without having studied it, or without having at least obtained the aid of a competent person?" Pope Paul VI, *L'Osservatore Romano* (Weekly Edition), Sept. 10, 1970, p. 1. Cf. chap. 9, n. 9, below, esp. Samuel Adams.

162. Thus, one could ask several years ago, for instance, what had become of the detention camps said to have been long prepared for Communists and Communist sympathizers in the event of an emergency; what did Justice Department investigators do during the Kennedy administration in their attempt to intimidate company executives who dared to raise steel prices; how many federal judges make a practice (as some do in Chicago) of conferring privately with the United States attorney prosecuting the cases being tried in their courtrooms; what did our government do to witnesses, counsel, and jurors in its efforts to imprison James Hoffa; what are our chemical and bacteriological weapons (which may be worse even than nuclear weapons) capable of and what *do* we intend to do with them? (See, on the limits of war, Burke, *Works*, 3:320, 5:370.) See chap. 4, n. 26, above. See, also, Congressman Mikva's comments on introducing the Emergency De-

tention Act repealer (not yet enacted). *Congressional Record* 115: H2914 (April 22, 1969).

"[The League of Nations] assembly is the talking body. The assembly was created in order that anybody that purposed anything wrong should be subjected to the awkward circumstance that everybody would talk about it. . . ." Woodrow Wilson, *Political Thought*, p. 520. See, ibid., pp. 420, 518-19. See, also, *Federalist* No. 63.

163. Lincoln, *Complete Works*, 2:423.

164. A newspaper reporter with many years of experience covering local news in a large city responded in this way to an inquiry I made of him several years ago:

> In your letter of 12/9, you asked whether a good reporter could list the honest judges [in a community] within a few weeks. A lot depends on what you mean by "honest." I know a few "honest" judges who wouldn't take dough but would protect or help someone who is dishonest. . . . I think a veteran reporter could compile a good list—including a small number who couldn't be classified—in a few days. It's a sad, sad story. I [enclose] a copy of a story I did a while back. . . . Political pressure kept this story off page one, where it belonged. Not pressure from anyone mentioned, but fear by editors of the No. 2 executive, who was a delegate to the Dem. National Convention, etc.

The 1969 revelations about Illinois Supreme Court members exposed only the very tip of the iceberg of grave improprieties among the bench and bar of Illinois that sophisticated lawyers have long ago charted but have been too "prudent" to reveal. (These financial improprieties, as well as those of a late senator, have been as well known among the bar and as little discussed publicly by lawyers as the longstanding judicial misconduct I describe in Appendix D, above. In short, who are the real "subversives" among us? Who is really for "law and order"? See, e.g., p. 452, above.)

165. "The reporter, quite rightly, said, in effect, 'I am a newsman and until you give me the names of the dead there are none.' . . ." This, and the following comment, were in response to rumors of numerous hushed-up deaths among the rioters in Paris in May, 1968: "For the kind of complicity this [secrecy about the dead] requires among police, doctors, and even parents you would need a truly Fascist state that has been in power a long, long time." *New Yorker*, Sept. 14, 1968, p. 70. Cf. Christopher Wren, "Greece: Government by Torture," *Look*, May 27, 1969, on the use of torture since 1967. (See chap. 6, n. 1, above. See, especially, on torture in Greece, my article on Greece cited in chap. 8, n. 146, above; also, chap. 7, n. 78, above. The character of the Mexican regime is indicated by the fact that dozens, if not hundreds, of students could be deliberately killed in the summer of 1968 with hardly any publicity. See, also, Robert Conquest, *The Great Terror: Stalin's Purges of the Thirties* [New York: Macmillan Co., 1968]. Edward Crankshaw concluded his review of this book in the *Chicago Sun-Times*, Oct. 9, 1968, p. 56, with this observation:

> Now the modernized Soviet Union depends absolutely on [the sort of men Stalin had once been able to do without]. A return to the terror of the 1930's would wreck the Soviet economy. This is not to say that there are not plenty of ape-men in the higher reaches of the Communist Party who, given the chance, are stupid enough to try. The Czechoslovak affair shows how strong these still are, the revived persecution of Soviet intellectuals shows how vicious. One has only to read this book to see why.)

It should be expected that any community that depends on the "mass media" to keep it informed of its own activities, if not of its very being, will tend to be subjected to overly dramatic glimpses of reality which are readily supplanted after a few days, sometimes even after only a few hours, by still more of the same. The curious "subjectivity" that governs the "objective" mass media is reflected in the markedly different handling of two remarkably similar stories in the Apr. 10, 1968, issue of the *Chicago Tribune*: Headlines and the entire left-hand column on the front page were devoted to a report from Wellington, New Zealand, which began, "A ferry carrying 744 persons hit

CHAPTER EIGHT, NOTES 166-68: PAGES 260-61   757

a reef and sank in 125 mile-per-hour hurricane winds today. Police reported heavy loss of life and said at least 65 bodies had been washed ashore. . . ." At page ten of the same issue was a report from Kuwait, to which two inches (and no headlines) were devoted, "More than 90 persons drowned when a ship carrying 400 Pakistanis home from a pilgrimage to Mecca struck a sandbar and sank Friday near Dubai, in the Persian gulf, reports reaching Kuwait today said. Two hundred were believed missing. More than 70 of the dead were women and children."

Cf. Theodore H. White, *The Making of the President 1968* (New York: Atheneum, 1969), pp. 330, n. 6, 341-42, 353, 362; chap. 5, n. 136, above. See chap. 4, n. 116, above, chap. 9, n. 4, below.

166. *Chicago Tribune*, Jan. 27, 1959.

> The *Tribune*'s Washington bureau now consists of ten men, all of them trained in Chicago, and it is one of the largest in the capital. Why do we maintain such a large staff? Why not depend on the news services, which pour out a flood of Washington news daily? The answer is that we believe Chicago and the middle west need press representatives in Washington as much as they need regularly elected representatives in Congress. The federal government has become so vast and complicated that a member of Congress can become well acquainted with only a few of the problems. A Congressman representing hundreds of thousands of constituents cannot reach them to explain how he is voting. Yet without a well informed electorate our form of government would not work; the bureaucrats and pressure groups, not the President and Congress, would make our laws and set our policies. [*Chicago Tribune*, Dec. 6, 1959]

See the articles, in the *Manchester Guardian Weekly* of July 10, 1958, about the contributions to constitutional government of Harry Boardman, parliamentary correspondent of that newspaper. Cf. Magnus Turnstile, "The Dying Art?" *New Statesman*, Sept. 2, 1966, p. 310. Louis Harris, the public opinion pollster, reported,

> I've found people far shrewder than they're credited with being. It fascinates me to compare my own impressions of political figures I know very well with the intuitions of men we poll in their homes. I've discovered people can go wrong on issues but they're rarely wrong in assessing what a man is like. [*Life*, May 11, 1962, p. 89]

167. Churchill, *Great Contemporaries*, pp. 40-41. See Aristotle, *Politics* 1338b2.
168. See Leo Strauss, "What Is Liberal Education?", in his *Liberalism Ancient and Modern*, p. 3.

> True liberals today have no more pressing duty than to counteract the perverted liberalism which contends that "just to live, securely and happily, and protected but otherwise unregulated, is man's simple but supreme goal," and which forgets quality, excellence, or virtue. [Leo Strauss, "The Liberalism of Classical Political Philosophy," in ibid., p. 64]

See Aristotle, *Politics* 3.9, 7.1. See, also, Paine, *Writings*, 2.452-53.

William Rainey Harper made in 1903, as president of the University of Chicago, this address to the entering class:

> Young gentlemen, you have come here in the hope of furthering your education. . . . An educated man is a man who by the time he is twenty-five years old has a clear theory, formed in the light of human experience down the ages of what constitutes a satisfying life, a significant life, and who by the age of thirty has a moral philosophy consonant with human experience. If a man reaches these ages without having arrived at such a theory, such a philosophy, then no matter how many facts he has learned or how many processes he has mastered, that man is an ignoramus and a fool, unhappy, and probably dangerous. That is all. Good afternoon. [*Vital Speeches of the Day* 23 (1956-57): 637]

CHAPTER EIGHT, NOTE 169: PAGE 262

The observation in the text by Gibbon may be found in chapter 26 of his *Decline and Fall of the Roman Empire*. It is there said of the blind general Belisarius, "His imperfections flowed from the contagion of the time; his virtues were his own, the free gift of nature or reflection. . . ." See, also, Buchan, *Oliver Cromwell*, p. 454: ". . . To adopt Cicero's words of Caesar, England was a slave to [Cromwell], and he himself was a slave to the times. . . ."; Cicero, *De Officiis*, bk. 3, chap. 31. See chap. 7, n. 113, chap. 8, n. 122, above.

169. I need not suggest that our corrupters be jailed, but neither should they be treated like decent people. See, e.g., chap. 5, nn. 122, 123, 124, 132, 147, chap. 8, nn. 74, 135, above. The power of government is not irrelevant here, but it should be brought to bear primarily in education, if only because prosecutions today are apt to be self-defeating. See chap. 7, n. 59, above.

On the other hand, I suggest, in my review of Jaffa's *Equality and Liberty*, N.Y.U. L. Rev. 41 (1966): 664, what of importance has been lost in our public discussion by the suppression of the Communist party in this country. The State Department, I should add, still has not recovered from the attacks of Senator Joseph McCarthy. (See Acheson, *Present at the Creation*, pp. 245-46, 369-70, 718-20.) Nor, it should be said, has our ability to think properly about China, although we do seem to be improving somewhat.

> Bureaucratization was only part of the explanation for State's malaise when Kennedy came to office [in 1961]. The other part was the shock of McCarthy—*or rather the shock of the readiness of Dulles, as Secretary of State, to yield up Foreign Service officers to McCarthyism*. The Dulles period was a time of distress and humiliation for the professionals. . . . Circumspection had always eased the path to advancement in the Service; now it became a requirement for survival. The McCarthy era, by demonstrating the peril of dangerous thoughts, elevated conformism into a conditioned reflex. Career men stopped telling Washington what they really thought and consecrated themselves to the clichés of the cold war. . . . [Schlesinger, *A Thousand Days*, p. 411; italics added]

(Cf. ibid., pp. 11-14, on Senator John F. Kennedy's unbecoming silence about Senator Joseph McCarthy's depredations. Was this not akin to Senator Robert F. Kennedy's refusal in 1968 to support Senator Eugene McCarthy's gallant [and remarkably productive] challenge of President Johnson? Why should that which is disparaged as "opportunism" or "ruthlessness" in Richard Nixon be justified as "practical politics" or "healthy ambition" in the Kennedys?)

> Stalin's approach to international affairs was distinguished by a certain crassness; but the West matched his crassness with its silliness. How can we ever have allowed ourselves to be persuaded, even for a moment, that the pretensions of the Moscow Government, whether Moscow itself believed in them or not, had any basis in reality? Why, instead of panicking, did no Western statesmen sit down and work out the fantastic implications of a world run from the Kremlin and show that the very idea was absurd? There may be revolutions still. There may be revolutions all over the place. America herself may go Communist—to continue using this almost meaningless word. But a Communist America will not be run from Moscow. [Crankshaw, *Khrushchev's Russia*, p. 145]

See George F. Kennan, *From Prague after Munich* (Princeton: Princeton University Press, 1968), pp. vii-viii. See, also, chap. 3, n. 22, chap. 7, n. 46, chap. 8, n. 150, above.

See, on China, Faure, *Serpent and Tortoise*. (My impression is that in the East-West confrontation, the French are best equipped by temperament, experience, and style to talk with the Chinese, the Americans with the Russians, and the English perhaps with the eastern Europeans. Cf. chap. 9, n. 37, below.) One cannot understand the Chinese Revolution of Mao Tse-Tung and the recent commotions among the Chinese without reflecting upon Mao's nostalgic recollection: "Once I composed poems, it is true. That was when I lived in the saddle. On horseback, one has the time. One can search out rhymes and rhythms; one can reflect. It was good, that life on horseback. Sometimes, these days, I look back on it with regret." Ibid., p. 32. See chap. 8, n. 160, above; cf. chap. 8, n. 140, above. See, also, Joseph R. Levenson, *Confucian China and Its Modern Fate: A Trilogy* (Berkeley: University of California Press, 1968), 1:134-37, 139-40; 2:13-21; 3:55, 47-56, 76-82, 113-15.

See, for discussion of the proposition that a practical choice has to be made "between tolerating error and suppressing all intellectual activity," Stephen, *Agnostic's Apology*, pp. 256, 265, 274, 298. Ultimately, it cannot be said too often, the concern about suppression in this country (even if it should be suppression "only" of the "radical" or "subversive" opinion of the left or of the right) touches upon what vitally affects even the most respectable among us. Thus, Edmund Burke observed in 1775 (*Works*, 2:193):

> Our late experience has taught us that many of those fundamental principles, formerly believed infallible, are either not of the importance they were imagined to be; or that we have not at all adverted to some other far more powerful principles, which entirely overrule those we had considered omnipotent. I am much against any further experiments which tend to put to the proof any more of these allowed opinions, which contribute so much to the public tranquillity. In effect, we suffer as much at home by this loosening of all ties, and this concussion of all established opinions, as we do abroad. For, in order to prove that the Americans have no right to their liberties, we are every day endeavouring to subvert the maxims which preserve our own. To prove that the Americans ought not to be free, we are obliged to depreciate the value of freedom itself; and we never seem to gain a paltry advantage over them in debate, without attacking some of those principles, or deriding some of those feelings, for which our ancestors have shed their blood.

170. See, for Jefferson's program of required study with respect to "the principles of government" at the University of Virginia, Padover, *Complete Jefferson*, p. 1112. Education means both discipline and liberation: thus, Jefferson could both praise Paris as his second home and regard travel for Americans as corrupting; Lycurgus (Plutarch tells us) discouraged travel for Spartans, although he had learned much on his travels which he used in reforming his city. See Aristotle, *Politics* 7.6; Montesquieu, *Persian Letters*, nos. 23, 24, 34; also, chap. 8, n. 135 (end), above, chap. 9, nn. 4, 39, below.

> There can be no patriotism without liberty, no liberty without virtue, no virtue without citizens; create citizens, and you have everything you need; without them, you will have nothing but debased slaves, from the rulers of the State downwards. To form citizens is not the work of a day; and in order to have men it is necessary to educate them when they are children. [Rousseau, *A Discourse on Political Economy*]

The proper formation of citizens, as a duty of magistrates, is addressed by Milton in these words:

> . . . But because the spirit of man cannot demean itself lively in this body, without some recreating intermission of labour and serious things, it were happy for the commonwealth, if our magistrates, as in those famous governments of old, would take into their care, not only the deciding of our contentious law cases and brawls, but the managing of our publick sports and festival pastimes, that they might be, not such as were authorised a while since, the provocations of drunkenness and lust, but such as may inure and harden our bodies by martial exercises to all warlike skill and performance; and may civilize, adorn, and make discreet our minds by the learned and affable meeting of frequent academies, and *the procurement of wise and artful recitations, sweetened with eloquence and graceful inticements* to the love and practice of justice, temperance, and fortitude, instructing and bettering the nation at all opportunities, that the call of wisdom and virtue may be heard every where. . . . Whether

this may not be, not only in pulpits, but after another persuasive method, at set and solemn paneguries, in theatres, porches, or what other place or way, may win most upon the people to receive at once both recreation and instruction; let them in authority consult. . . . [Milton, *Prose Works*, 1:121-22; italics added]

(It should be noticed that Milton indicates no concern *here* (*The Reason of Church Government Urged against Prelaty*) about previous restraints. See chap. 5, nn. 3, 128, above.) Consider chap. 8, n. 181, below. Consider, also, Paine, *Writings*, 2:462.

171. William Wordsworth proclaimed:

> We must be free or die, who speak the tongue
> That Shakespeare spake; the faith and morals hold
> Which Milton held.

The "tongue that Shakespeare spake" (which includes an appreciation of the things Shakespeare spoke about) requires the vigilance called for by Milton:

> I hold him to deserve the highest praise who fixes the principles, and forms the manners of a state, and makes the wisdom of his administration conspicuous both at home and abroad. But I assign the second place to him, who endeavours by precepts and by rules to perpetuate that style and idiom of speech and composition which have flourished in the purest periods of the language, and who, as it were, throws up such a trench around it that people may be prevented from going beyond the boundary almost by the terrors of a Romulean prohibition. . . . It is the opinion of Plato, that changes in the dress and habits of the citizens portend great commotions and changes in the state; and I am inclined to believe, that when the language in common use in any country becomes irregular and depraved, it is followed by their ruin or their degradation. For what do terms used without skill or meaning, which are at once corrupt and misapplied, denote but a people listless, supine, and ripe for servitude? On the contrary, we have never heard of any people or state which has not flourished in some degree of prosperity as long as their language has retained its elegance and its purity. [Milton, *Prose Works*, 1:xi-xii]

There is suggested here one of the critical issues implied by the *Lenny Bruce* case in Chicago (and elsewhere in the country). *Illinois* v. *Bruce*, 31 Ill.2d 459, 202 NE2d 497 (1964). (See chap. 5, n. 127, above.) Is there not something both healthier and more sophisticated in the diffidence displayed heretofore? See, e.g., Aristotle, *Rhetoric* 1405b7-17; Blackstone, *Laws of England*, 4:215; Moses Maimonides, *The Guide of the Perplexed* (Chicago: University of Chicago Press, 1963), pp. 149, 434-35, 604. See, also, chap. 7, n. 59, above. Should not a people have both the interest and the authority to keep public language from being debased? James Wilson observed in the Constitutional Convention (on July 13, 1787) that "he could not agree that [the protection of] property was the sole or primary object of Governt. & society. The cultivation & improvement of the human mind was the most noble object." U.S., Congress, House, *Documents Illustrative of the Formation of the Union of the American States*, 69th Cong., 1st sess., H. Doc. 398, p. 373. See chap. 5, n. 147, chap. 6, n. 75, chap. 7, n. 77, above, chap. 9, n. 20, below.

See Weaver, "Individuality and Modernity," in Morley, *Essays on Individuality*, pp. 75-78. See, in Kurt Riezler, *Man—Mutable and Immutable* (Chicago: Henry Regnery Co., 1950), the chapter, "Language," which concludes (at p. 108):

> Here and there human speech reaches perfection. Then man delights in his language. It is as if language itself enjoyed its triumph—English in Shakespeare's verses, German in Goethe's lyrics, Greek in Sappho's songs. . . . Then when in perfect speech the thing begins to shine, it throws a gleam of light on the vault of a sky which, if only for a moment, seems to span a world. . . . [The] criteria of perfect speech are not man-made. They do not depend upon the whim of society. A particular society may forget but it cannot alter them. . . .

CHAPTER EIGHT, NOTES 172-73: PAGE 263   761

Thus, Leonard Bernstein said recently of Beethoven's *Ninth Symphony* (cf. chap. 8, n. 193, below): "He has the power to make us feel at the finish that something is right in the world, that there is something we can trust that will never let us down." See chap. 5, nn. 126, 132, chap. 7, n. 124, above, chap. 9, nn. 20, 30, below.

See, also, Burke, *Works*, 2:196; Gibbon, *The Decline and Fall of the Roman Empire* (New York: Random House, Modern Library, n.d.), 1:10; Weaver, *Ideas Have Consequences*, p. 108. (Does it not, considering the centuries-old struggle in our language between the forces of light and those of darkness, impose a great burden upon Americans of African descent to call them "black"? One may be obliged to acquiesce in such usage even while one discourages it. See Burke, *Writings*, 1:69-70, 188 ff.)

172. *Abrams* v. *U.S.*, 250 U.S. 616, 630 (1919). (I do not believe that either "logical" or "naturally" is used correctly by Justice Holmes here.) Justice Holmes continued with a version of his "clear and present danger" test which is less liable to abuse than his more famous language:

> While that experiment is part of our system I think we should be eternally vigilant against attempts to check the expression of opinions that we loathe and believe to be fraught with death, unless they so imminently threaten interference with the lawful and pressing purposes of the law that *an immediate check is required to save the country*. [Italics added]

(See, also, chap. 3, n. 21, above.) Of course, we saw in chapter 6, the problem remains of what *law* he is referring to. It is difficult to conjure up any expression by anyone, other than an eminent officer of the general government, of which it can be said that "an immediate check is required to save the country": other immediately dangerous speech is apt to be of the kind that is local in effect and appropriate for local government to deal with. ("[Liberals] hailed the 'clear and present danger' test, but often did not understand it, imagining that it meant danger to the United States, instead of danger that the substantive act would occur that was forbidden by the particular statute." Francis Biddle, *Justice Holmes, Natural Law, and the Supreme Court* [New York: Macmillan Co., 1961], p. 68. But consider the "save the country" language in *Abrams*. See p. 378, n. 8, above.)

See, for other comments on this opinion (particularly of the portion reproduced in the text), Chafee, *Freedom of Speech*, pp. 155-56; Meiklejohn, *Political Freedom*, pp. 71-75; Sidney Hook, *Heresy, Yes—Conspiracy, No!* (New York: John Day Co., 1953), pp. 19-21, 74 (cf. Berns, *Freedom, Virtue and the First Amendment*, pp. 209-14); Francis Biddle, "Oliver Wendell Holmes," in Allison Dunham and Philip B. Kurland, *Mr. Justice* (Chicago: University of Chicago Press, 1964), p. 137 (Biddle, in this eulogy of Justice Holmes, ignored altogether the *Schenck* opinion: it would be hard to argue that silencing *that* "expression of opinions" was "required to save the country"); Jaffa, *Equality and Liberty*, pp. 184-89. See, also, chap. 6, n. 38, above.

At the opposite pole from Justice Holmes's "market" test of truth is that of the Orthodox Church, "Truth can have no external criterion, for it is manifest of itself and made inwardly plain." Ware, *Orthodox Church*, p. 257. See chap. 3, n. 25, chap. 8, nn. 46, 153, above. Are not both tests equally questionable? See *Alfarabi's Philosophy*, pp. 25-26, 136 (sec. 21, n. 1, sec. 22, n. 1), 140 (sec. 57, n. 3).

173. See, e.g., *Federalist* No. 3:

> It is not a new observation that the people of any country (if, like the Americans, intelligent and well-informed) *seldom* adopt and steadily persevere for many years in an *erroneous* opinion respecting their interests. That consideration naturally tends to create great respect for the high opinion which the people of America have so long and uniformly entertained of the importance of their continuing firmly united under one federal government, vested with sufficient powers for all general and national purposes. [Italics added]

See, also, Aristotle, *Nicomachean Ethics* 1143b12; Bacon, *Novum Organum*, book 1, aph. 27, 43, 54-55; Gibbon, *Decline and Fall*, 1:383; James Anthony Froude, *Short Studies in*

Great Subjects (New York: Charles Scribner & Co., 1868), pp. 155-56; Leo Strauss, *On Tyranny* (New York: Free Press of Glencoe, 1963), p. 162 (Alexandre Kojève [on the perils of the "'isolated' thinker"]; cf. ibid., p. 208).

Consider, however, the observation of Freud:

> I will take this opportunity of assuring you that in these lectures I shall make few controversial references, least of all to individuals. I have never been able to convince myself of the truth of the saying that "strife is the father of all things." I think the source of it was the philosophy of the Greek sophists and that it errs, as does the latter, through the overestimation of dialectics. It seems to me, on the contrary, that scientific controversy, so-called, is on the whole quite unfruitful, apart from the fact that it is almost always conducted in a highly personal manner. . . . [*General Introduction to Psychoanalysis*, p. 257]

Cf. Plutarch, *Lives*, p. 714; Burke, *Works*, 4:187; Paine, *Writings*, 4:195.

Consider, as well, the testimony of a political realist, and not a democrat (in the loosest sense), Winston Churchill: "Over the years I have found that in the long run the politician and the party that wins the most support is the one that sets out to do what it believes to be right, not what it fancies will be immediately popular." *Manchester Guardian Weekly*, Jan. 8, 1959, p. 3. That is, it is integrity (rather than truth) that is likely to win out in the marketplace? If so, it may be because of "that justice imprinted in the nature of men" discerned by Bacon. Chap. 7, n. 77, above.

174. Justice Holmes was of the opinion that

> the greatest works of intellect soon lose all but their historic significance. The science of one generation is refuted or outgeneralized by the science of the next; the philosophy of one century is taken up or transcended by the philosophy of a later one; and so Plato, St. Augustine, and Descartes, and we almost may say Kant and Hegel, are not much more read than Hippocrates or Cuvier or Bichat. [Max Lerner, ed., *The Mind and Faith of Justice Holmes* (Boston: Little, Brown & Co., 1943), p. 374]

See Howe, ed., *Holmes-Pollock Letters*, 1:42, 109; 2:227, 290.

To what extent were Justice Holmes's opinions, both about the "competition of the market" and the temporary relevance of the "greatest works of intellect," influenced by his life in the courts where intellectual efforts are mounted for passing encounters before trained judges and where the participants are subject to cross-examination, rebuttals, and the discipline of forms? See Blackstone, *Laws of England*, 3:373-75.

Cf. Fred Rodell, "Holmes and His Hecklers," *The Progressive*, Apr., 1951, p. 9. See chap. 3, n. 16, above. See, also, chap. 8, n. 122, above.

175. *Dennis v. U.S.*, 341 U.S. 494, 508 (1951). Compare the prudent observation of Chief Justice Warren:

> The essentiality of freedom in the community of American universities is almost self-evident. No one should underestimate the vital role in a democracy that is played by those who guide and train our youth. To impose any strait jacket upon the intellectual leaders in our colleges and universities would imperil the future of our Nation. No field of education is so thoroughly comprehended by man that new discoveries cannot yet be made. *Particularly is that true in the social sciences, where few, if any, principles are accepted as absolutes.* [*Sweezy v. New Hampshire*, 354 U.S. 234, 250 (1957); italics added]

See, on the *Sweezy* case, chap. 4, n. 102, above.

In support of the principles of *Dennis v. U.S.*, however, are such sentiments as these:

> Among individual people, one can hear talk of some kind of absolute personal freedom. I do not know what they have in mind here, but in my opinion there will never be absolute personal freedom, not even under full communism. "We

do not believe in 'absolutes,'" V. I. Lenin once replied to the advocates of "absolute freedom." Even under communism the will of an individual must be subordinated to the will of the collective. If this does not occur, then anarchical self-will will usher disarray and disorganization into the life of society. . . . [Nikita S. Khrushchev, *Problems of Communism*, 12 (Mar.-Apr. 1963): 104]

It should be noticed that the true intellectual offspring of Justice Holmes is not Chief Justice Vinson but rather Justice Frankfurter. (Cf. chap. 7, n. 77, above.) Indeed, one finds in the opinion of Justice Frankfurter in *New York v. U.S.*, 326 U.S. 572, 576 (1946) an urbane anticipation of the *Dennis* pronouncement:

> What [Chief Justice Marshall said, in *McCulloch v. Maryland*, 4 Wheat. (U.S.) 316, 431 (1819), that "the power to tax involves the power to destroy,"] may not have been irrelevant in its setting. But Chief Justice Marshall spoke at a time when social complexities did not so clearly reveal as now the practical limitations of a rhetorical absolute. See Holmes, J., in *Long v. Rockwood*, 277 U.S. 142, 148 [1928], and in *Panhandle Oil Co. v. Mississippi*, 277 U.S. 218, 223 [1928].

See, for the immediate ancestor of such progeny, chap. 8, n. 178, below. Cf. Friedrich Nietzsche, *Thus Spake Zarathustra*, First Part, "On the Flies of the Market Place."

176. It is assumed, by the way, that only virtue, not wisdom, must be preserved once rulers are in office. It is also implied that wisdom must be acquired other than "on the job." Is it further assumed that the choice of rulers will be made from among properly educated men? (Is the virtue referred to that of justice? See chap. 8, n. 124, above.)

177. It was said in 1859 about the theory of evolution (chap. 9, n. 38, below),

> Although I am fully convinced of the truth of the views given in this volume under the form of an abstract, I by no means expect to convince experienced naturalists whose minds are stocked with a multitude of facts all viewed, during a long course of years, from a point of view directly opposite to mine. It is so easy to hide our ignorance under such expressions as the "plan of creation," "unity of design," &c., and to think that we give an explanation when we only re-state a fact. Any one whose disposition leads him to attach more weight to unexplained difficulties than to the explanation of a certain number of facts will certainly reject the theory. A few naturalists, endowed with much flexibility of mind, and who have already begun to doubt the immutability of species, may be influenced by this volume; but I look with confidence to the future,—to young and rising naturalists, who will be able to view both sides of the question with impartiality. Whoever is led to believe that species are mutable will do good service by conscientiously expressing his conviction, for thus only can the load of prejudice by which this subject is overwhelmed be removed. [Charles Darwin, *The Origin of Species and the Descent of Man* (New York: Modern Library, n.d.), p. 368.

"As in intellectual error, so in evil of any other form, its essence is impermanence." Tagore put in this form (quoted by John James, *Why Evil?* [London: Penguin Books, 1960], p. 40) a sentiment familiar to us not only from Plato but also from Milton's *Areopagitica*: "Let her and falsehood grapple; who ever knew truth put to the worse, in a free and open encounter?" Milton, *Works*, 1:326. The problem remains, however, in what "market" (or forum) is such an encounter likely to be truly "free and open." Indeed, there may even be men (and peoples as well) who happen to be so formed as to be as receptive to error as to the truth. Cf. chap. 7, n. 77, above.

Justice Holmes should have recognized this, in any event, in what he implied in *Scheck* about one "*falsely* shouting fire in a theater, and causing a panic." (Italics added) He recognized, that is, that in such a situation it is precisely because the truth is not likely to "get itself accepted in the competition of the market" that the liar merits punishment. (See chap. 5, n. 147, above.) But, someone might respond, the truth will out, if enough time is permitted for examination of contending positions. How much is "enough time"? No doubt the circumstances, and the nature of the "debate," will affect our determination of "enough." Even so, there is the problem of determining how one is to know the truth when it does "get itself accepted." Is the truth accepted in any way different from the way error is accepted? And does it stay accepted longer—that is, what should be made of the fact that an accepted truth can be abandoned and error can "get itself accepted" in its place? (See, on "the true spirit of toleration," Burke, Works, 4:166.)

Before one can speak truly about the power of truth in the market, one must have a clearer idea of what truth is than Justice Holmes seems to have had. He had no basis, that is, for distinguishing between truth and a strongly felt (but erroneous) opinion:

> When I say that a thing is true, I mean that I cannot help believe it. I am stating an experience as to which there is no choice. But as there are many things which I cannot help doing that the universe can, I do not venture to assume that my inabilities in the way of thought are inabilities of the universe. I therefore define the truth as the system of my limitations, and leave absolute truth for those who are better equipped. With absolute truth I leave absolute ideals of conduct equally on one side. [Lerner, Mind and Faith of Holmes, p. 392, from Ill. L. Rev. 10 (1915)]

But how can one legitimately speak of "limitations" if one does not have, independent of such limitations, some awareness of what the truth is and even of what it would be to be absolutely without limitations? Cf. ibid., pp. 395-96. See chap. 6, n. 50, above, chap. 9, n. 3, below. (Consider, for theories of relativity, the significance of the constancy [or absoluteness] of the speed of light.) See, also, Burke, Works, 1:65-66.

I should add that I do not think that Justice Holmes's position can be salvaged by anyone who insists on a distinction between "facts" and the "opinions" or "values" implicit in "fighting faiths," since he himself granted that such faiths may be true or false. Did not Justice Holmes speak most skeptically of truth in those judicial opinions in opposition to the majority of the Court and in nonjudicial writings (rather than in opinions which he wrote for the court)? This, too, reflects an awareness about the different characters of various markets. Compare the two statements reproduced in Appendix E, above, one written for adoption by an assembly, the other a personal statement.

See, for a sounder political approach than Justice Holmes's to these questions, the opening pages of *Federalist* No. 31. See, for an endorsement of Justice Holmes's "competition of the market" words (with a misleading omission of "best" from "the best test of truth"), Hook, *Heresy, Yes—Conspiracy, No!*, p. 19 (which includes a curious identification of Socrates with liberalism [cf. chap. 2, n. 1, above, chap. 8, n. 181, chap. 9, n. 28, below]). Consider, as perhaps bearing on these questions, Plato, *Gorgias* 505D-506B, *Republic* 413A-415E, *Laws* 663E-664C, *Meno* 80D-81E; Aristotle, *Metaphysics* 993a30 ff., *Nicomachean Ethics* 1145b2 ff.; Anselm of Canterbury, *Truth, Freedom and Evil: Three Philosophical Dialogues* (New York: Harper & Row, 1967), pp. 91-92; Thomas Aquinas, *Truth* (Chicago: Henry Regnery Co., 1952), 1:20-34, 42-51; 2:367-74; 3:177-83; Hobbes, *Leviathan* (concluding paragraph); Shaftesbury, *Characteristics of Men, Manners, Opinions, Times* (Indianapolis: Bobbs-Merrill, 1964), 1:15, 73, 264-65, 276, 296-97; 2:30, 209-12, 342, 345-46, 349-50; *Federalist*, pp. 124, 160, 265, 270, 409-10. See, also, chap. 6, nn. 23, 66, above.

Justice Holmes's privileged truth about the nature of "fighting faiths" reminds of those who speak of an "absolute moment": they now know something revolutionary about the nature of knowing never known before, something which is itself not subject to the limitations upon knowing just proclaimed by them. So what else is new? one might ask. See chap. 9, n. 38, below. (Curiously enough, it is precisely such enlightened souls who are apt to proclaim as well that there is no rational basis for preferring one "culture" over another. But, one must wonder, are not some "cultures" superior in that they are better than others in discovering standards or, at least, in concluding that it is difficult to judge objectively among "cultures"? That is, are not some "cultures" better able than most [as are some people] to "step back" and examine themselves as well as others? Are not such "cultures" rare? Yet they are the only ones in which one hears it said [by people who cannot be aware of the implications of what they say] that there is no right or basis to judge whether one "culture" or community is better than another for the human being. See chap. 8, n. 135, above.)

178. It is the nature of the passions, Nietzsche seems to say, that sometimes makes the truth deadly. See, e.g., *Beyond Good and Evil*, chap. 1, aph. 4. (See chap. 7, n. 34, above.) *He* realizes, that is, the implications of radical relativism. Cf. chap. 8, nn. 135, 175, above, chap. 9, nn. 3, 4, below.

Compare, with respect to this perennial question, the sentiments of two venerable contemporaries: E. M. Forster is quoted by W. H. Auden (*Book World*, Dec. 24, 1967, p. 8) as having said, "The people I respect most behave as if they were immortal and as if Society were eternal. Both assumptions are false. Both must be accepted as true if we are to go on working and eating and loving, and are able to keep open a few breathing-holes for the human spirit." Bertrand Russell is quoted by John Hospers (*An Introduction to Philosophical Analysis* [Englewood Cliffs, N.J.: Prentice-Hall, 1967], p. 449) as having said, "I can respect the men who argue that religion is true and therefore ought to be believed, but I can feel only profound reprobation for those who say that religion ought to be believed because it is useful, and that to ask whether it is true is a waste of time." (What would Russell feel for those who would alter the last clause of his statement to read, "and that to ask whether it is true is not something to be done in public"?) Cf. Maimonides, *Guide of the Perplexed*, pp. 6-7, 12, 66, 298, 320, 321-22, 328, 349-50, 359, 383-84, 510, 513-14, 521, 524, 527, 528 ("a gracious ruse"), 619. See, also, chap. 3, n. 25, chap. 6, n. 50, above, chap. 9, n. 30, below.

179. The Athenian democracy went so far as to choose all officers by lot, except those who were to conduct military operations. See Ernest Barker, *The Politics of Aristotle* (New York: Oxford University Press, 1962), pp. 193-94 (on the safeguards in that system). "War, like most other things, is a science to be acquired and perfected by diligence, by perseverance, by time, and by practice." *Federalist* No. 25. See chap. 8, n. 82, above. (Has not the college ROTC tended to moderate our officer corps?)

> . . . In its sudden transformation from isolation to leader of a world-wide coalition of nations, America is still a nation of amateurs. Even today, almost everybody in a position of power or influence in Washington is surprised to find himself where he is. This may not be true of the members of the Joint Chiefs of Staff and some ambassadors in major embassies, who came out of professional military academies and the Foreign Service, but it is true of every member of the President's cabinet. . . . [Reston, *Artillery of the Press*, p. 8]

Are there not thoughtful men associated with the Joint Chiefs of Staff who realize that whatever expertise the military have, it does not equip them to make political judgments, perhaps not even general strategic judgments (for these are often vitally dependent on political judgments)? See chap. 4, nn. 47, 49, chap. 7, n. 67, chap. 8, nn. 35, 161, above, chap. 9, n. 38, below. The military man as such may have the disability—and, indeed, may be good at his job partly because he has the disability—that President Kennedy thought particularly striking in Admiral Halsey: "Bull Halsey is the perfect man to send on a military operation. But he must never participate in the decision on whether or not to go." *Life*, July 10, 1970, p. 22A. Illustrative of improper, and eventually self-defeating, military influence with respect to political judgments by our government is the insistent and decisive role played by the Pentagon in determining our relations with Greece since the colonels took over in 1967. (See chap. 6, n. 1, above.) Thus, Senator Strom Thurmond introduced in Senate debate "an impressive document from the Department of Defense which clearly presents the vital need to maintain our aid to Greece." *Congressional Record* 116: S10131 (June 29, 1970). It is a remarkably shallow document, however influential it may have been in the Senate proceedings, a document which takes at face value practically everything the present Greek government claims. Even the people in our State Department now know better than that. (They know, for instance, that that government is regarded by many patriotic Greeks as "quisling," ibid., p. S13873 [Aug. 20,

1970].) Far healthier for the Republic are the spirit and standards reflected in the telegram sent by President Lincoln's secretary of war to an eminently successful General Grant (Lincoln, *Complete Works*, 2:656):

> The President directs me to say that he wishes you to have no conference with General Lee unless it be for capitulation of General Lee's army, or on some minor or purely military matter. He instructs me to say that you are not to decide, discuss, or confer upon any political questions. Such questions the President holds in his own hands, and will submit them to no military conferences or conventions. Meanwhile you are to press to the utmost your military advantages.

Cf. *Congressional Record* 116: S9643 (June 24, 1970). See ibid., p. E10520.

180. "And do not think, sir," said Don Quixote, "that I apply that term 'mob' solely to plebeians and those of low estate; for anyone who is ignorant, whether he be lord or prince, may, and should, be included in the vulgar herd." Cervantes, *Don Quixote* (New York: Viking Press, 1949), p. 609. See a letter of October 30, 1787, from Gouverneur Morris to Washington (Morison, *Sources and Documents*, p. 306); cf. Philip B. Kurland, *Religion and the Law* (Chicago: Aldine Publishing Co., 1962), pp. 9-10. See, also, Maimonides, *Guide of the Perplexed*, pp. 6-7, 9-10, 43, 495. Cf. Hobbes, *Leviathan*, chap. 13 (beginning). But see Proust, *Remembrance of Things Past*, 1:1012-14.

181. Rhetoric reflects an appreciation of the fact that the simple truth does not suffice in all circumstances, that men sometimes have to be led to virtue or right action by discourse that is (in Milton's words) "sweetened with eloquence and graceful inticements." Chap. 8, n. 170, above. Consider the "demonstration" at the end of *Federalist* No. 39 and the unwarranted claims of impartiality in *Federalist* No. 1 as well as the presentation in *Federalist* No. 54 of the slavery issue in such a way as to seem to endorse the relevant constitutional provision without really doing so. (See chap. 8, n. 89, above. Publius warns his readers, at *Federalist* [New York: Random House, Modern Library, n.d.], pp. 86, 145, 148, 149, 150, 177, 179-80, 198, 310, 440-41, 568-69, 579, against the sophistries and the inflammatory declamations of the opponents to the proposed constitution.) This conforms to what we are told in *Federalist* No. 15: "Why has government been instituted at all? Because the passions of men will not conform to the dictates of reason and justice, without constraint." (See *Federalist*, pp. 27, 70-71, 77, 86, 92-93, 206, 274, 331, 365, 471, 495. See, also, Malcolm Sharp, "The Classical American Doctrine of the Separation of Powers," *U. Chicago L. Rev.* 2 [1935]: 385; Sharp, "Aggression: A Study of Values and Law," *Ethics* 57 [1947]: 1; Sharp, "The Limits of Law," *Ethics* 61 [1951]: 270.) See, on the relation between rhetoric and medicine, Plato, *Gorgias* 456A-C, 459A-E, 464B-465E. See, also, the following articles by Dr. Arthur K. Shapiro, "A Contribution to a History of the Placebo Effect," *Behavioral Science* 5 (1960): 109; "The Curative Waters and Warm Poultices of Psychotherapy," *Psychosomatics* 7 (1966): 21; "Semantics of the Placebo," *Psychiatric Quarterly* 42 (1968): 653. (See, on *placebo*, the concluding lines of Bacon's essay, *Of Counsel*.) Is the *placebo* effect evident also in Elizabeth Kubler-Ross, *On Death and Dying* (New York: Macmillan Co., 1969)? See chap. 8, n. 186, below.

Stephen A. Douglas said with good reason that Lincoln "has a fertile genius in devising language to conceal his thoughts." Lincoln, *Complete Works*, 1:468. Cf. ibid., 1:459, 461. Lincoln himself observed that "I am very little inclined on any occasion to say anything unless I hope to produce some good by it." Ibid., 2:219. See chap. 9, n. 3, below. See, also, chap. 2, n. 1, chap. 7, nn. 13, 95, above, chap. 9, n. 28, below. Notice, in chap. 9, n. 27, below, the requirement of the common law that no legal fiction "shall extend to work an injury."

I have questioned the disposition on Alexander Meiklejohn's part to apply to both the state and the general governments the full restraint of the First Amendment. It is when one turns to traditional political philosophy that other divergencies by me from his thesis become more apparent. Consider, for instance, the language of his observation that the

> First Amendment was not written primarily for the protection of those intellectual aristocrats who pursue knowledge solely for the fun of the game, whose search for truth expresses nothing more than a private intellectual curiosity or an equally private delight and pride in mental achievement. It was written to clear the way for thinking which serves the general welfare. [*Political Freedom*, p. 42]

It is, indeed, the general welfare that the First Amendment can be said to serve; but should the contemplative life, which may be regarded as the peak of human activity, be disparaged and dismissed as Meiklejohn seems to do? A critique should proceed with a consideration of his apolitical requirement "by every consideration of honesty and self respect . . . that we practice what we preach, that we preach what we practice" (ibid., p. 7), of the use he makes of the *Apology* and the *Crito* of Plato (ibid., pp. 21-24), and of his questionable assumption that "the freedom which is guarded by the First Amendment [is] the cause for which the followers of Socrates have fought and died through the ages" (ibid., p. 41). I should immediately add that I have had occasion to record this tribute:

> Mr. Meiklejohn, although profoundly moved by the life of Socrates and the doctrines of Kant, was not a philosopher nor, at heart, a scholar. Rather, he was the very image of the sovereign American citizen, a title he would have been proudest to claim. He was, consequently, a good man. ["On Citizenship: Alexander Meiklejohn (1872-1964)," *The Organon* (Chicago: Basic Program, University of Chicago), Dec. 1965, pp. 1-2]

Cf. chap. 8, n. 140 (on Heidegger and Socrates), chap. 7, nn. 107, 109, above.

The extent to which citizenship, the general welfare, and hence the influence of the community can go is suggested by the reports from the Middle Ages of communal dreams, of the sharing by the community of something which we consider as much "one's own" as a toothache or a thought. Thus, Rabbi Moses ben Jacob of Coucy recorded in the thirteenth century "that the 'polis dream,' a dream experienced by a large group of people on the same night, was an experience of both Jewish and Christian contemporaries." Monford Harris, "Dreams in *Sefer Hasidim*," *American Academy for Jewish Research* 31 (1963): 51, 52. (Rabbi Harris noted at this point in his article, "I am intentionally substituting 'polis dream' for 'political dream,' the usual way of referring to this unusual phenomenon, since the term 'political' has too many other connotations.")

See chap. 7, nn. 35, 124, above, chap. 9, n. 39, below. See, also, chap. 8, nn. 70, 135, above.

182. Exception must be made for the man regarded as divinely inspired. See Plato's *Meno*; also, in chapters 6 and 26 of *The Prince*, Machiavelli's understanding of Moses. See, also, chap. 5, n. 94, above, chap. 9, n. 22, below.

183. Thus, Lincoln could write of a judge that he "was trying to help [secessionists] a little by giving the protection of law to those who were endeavoring to overthrow the supreme law—trying if he could find a safe place for certain men to stand on the Constitution, whilst they should stab it in another place." *Complete Works*, 2:188-89. See ibid., 2:347. See, also, Leo Strauss, *City and Man*, p. 191.

184. See, on the fraternal support needed for the encouragement of virtue, in Anastaplo, "Notes on the First Amendment," p. 433: "The Lamentation of Richard III" (a commentary on Josephine Tey's revisionist novel, *The Daughter of Time*, by Sara Prince Anastaplo). One is reminded in her concluding lines, "Heaven damns weakness, not murder/ And smiles while lies brace a new throne," of the moral fervor (but not the orientation) of Machiavelli. See, also, Anghelos Sikelianos, "Unwritten," in Edmund Keeley and Philip Sherrard, eds., *Six Poets of Modern Greece* (New York: Knopf, 1961), p. 96.

See, also, Thomas Aquinas, *Summa Theologica* (*Treatise on Law*), Q. 90, A. 3, Rep.

Obj. 2; Q. 91, Art. 4 (answer); Q. 95, A. 1 (answer). Cf. chap. 8, nn. 28, 70, above.

185. Such notions as these should not be confused with sentimentality, however. They are addressed to an audience that heard without protest observations such as Livermore's: ". . . it is sometimes necessary to hang a man, villains often deserve whipping, and perhaps having their ears cut off. . . ." *Annals*, I, p. 754. See, also, *Annals*, I, p. 2216 (sec. 14); Morris, *Diary*, 2:316; C. S. Forester, *Mr. Midshipman Hornblower* (Boston: Little, Brown & Co., 1950), pp. 124-28; chap. 4, n. 64, above.

186. Thus, Thomas Jefferson wrote to John Adams in 1813:

> I have thus stated my opinion on a point on which we differ, not with a view to controversy, for we are both too old to change opinions which are the result of a long life of inquiry and reflection; but on the suggestion of a former letter of yours, that we ought not to die before we have explained ourselves to each other. . . . [Padover, ed., *Complete Jefferson*, p. 286]

The relation between death, dying, and the nature of man is considered in remarks I have prepared for a symposium, "Problems in the Meaning of Death," to be presented at the December, 1970, meetings of the American Association for the Advancement of Science. These remarks, which echo those of Jefferson and Adams, include a commentary upon the modern attitude toward death:

> A distinction should be drawn between what a thoughtful man may know about death and dying and what is likely to be felt by most people about dying and death. No serious discussion of anything human is possible without making such a distinction. I believe it fair to say that the prospect of death is for the thoughtful man *not* a matter for "anxiety" or "terror"—it may not even be for him, upon contemplating his own death, a matter for awe. At most, it is for him an occasion for curiosity. . . .
>
> How one responds to death is (aside from physiological changes, in a natural death, which may have psychological effects difficult to counter) probably the result of how one responds to other things. That is, it is primarily the result of the kind of human being one has been taught and habituated to become. . . . It is taken for granted [in most current discussions of dying and death] that all men are being talked about, when in fact *only* most men are. Thus, it is observed that men evade death because they recognize in the event an immensity which towers above their resources for handling it. What is, on the other hand, the effect of holding up a standard of how the best, of how *the* man, acts? Does not this provide a guide for *all* men, something to moderate their desires and to hold in check their fears? We should take care, in any event, not to legitimate cowardice. . . .
>
> Much of what one reads about how many, perhaps most, men die—how they have to be persuaded to accept the imminence of death—suggests that something is seriously wrong with the way most men live. It is this which should be our most vital concern. Life is really too short for the most thoughtful man to waste on anything but the most important concerns, including the concern about how one should live—and, particularly, about how one is to understand the universe in which man is so fortunate as to find himself, even if only temporarily.

See chap. 8, nn. 133, 140, 178, 180, above, chap. 9, nn. 20, 30, 36, 39, below. Cf. Xenophon and Northumberland, chap. 8, n. 193, chap. 9, n. 31, below.

187. This assessment is found in the reply by the House of Representatives to the President's address. *Annals*, I, p. 247.

Care must be taken lest we deserve another assessment such as that of a century ago:

> The success of equality in America is due, I think, mainly to the circumstance that a large number of people, who were substantially equal in all the more important matters, recognized that fact and did not set up unfounded distinctions. How far they actually are equal now, and how long they will continue to be equal when the population becomes dense, is quite another question. It is

also a question, which I cannot do more than glance at in two words in this place, whether the enormous development of equality in America, the rapid production of an immense multitude of commonplace, self-satisfied, and essentially slight people is an exploit which the whole world need fall down and worship. [James Fitzjames Stephen, *Liberty, Equality, Fraternity*, p. 245]

See chap. 8, n. 2, above.

188. Scott, in the First Congress, anticipated the influence of the frontier:

> The forming settlements in a wilderness upon the frontiers, between the savages and the least populated of the civilized parts of the United States, requires men of enterprising, violent, nay, discontented and turbulent spirits. Such always are our first settlers in the ruthless and savage wild; they serve as pioneers to clear the way for the more laborious and careful farmer. These characters are already in the country by thousands. . . . [*Annals*, I, pp. 624-25]

Vining's observation matched Scott's: "I declare that I look on the Western Territory in an awful and striking point of view. To that region the unpolished sons of earth are flowing from all quarters. Men, to whom the protection of the law, and the controlling force of the Government, are equally necessary. . . ." *Annals*, I, p. 848.

There was, in addition, much in the dominant political doctrines of even the more sophisticated residents of the peaceful states on the Atlantic to justify and confirm the frontier distrust of government. Jackson, for example, warned his colleagues,

> All Governments incline to despotism, as naturally as rivers run into the sea. Despotism makes its way gradually, by slow and imperceptible steps; despotic power is never established all at once; we shall, ere we are aware, get beyond the gulf, and then we shall be astonished how we reached there. [*Annals*, I, p. 657]

189. See Aristotle, *Politics* 6.2. When President Roosevelt's wife once asked his advice about her newspaper column, he replied, "Lady, this is a free country." *Time*, Nov. 16, 1962, p. 29. (See p. 741, above [Mrs. Johnson's observation].)

190. " . . . With [the Federalist Party's] early disappearance, there ceased for ever to be in America any party whatsoever which in any sense represented aristocratic principles or leanings." Charnwood, *Abraham Lincoln*, p. 30.

> It is indeed deplorable that instead of being forced to bow to the rule of law, the French nobility was uprooted and laid low, since thereby the nation was deprived of a vital part of its substance, and a wound that time will never heal was inflicted on our national freedom. . . . When such an element of the body politic is forcibly excised, even those most hostile to it suffer a diminution of strength. Nothing can ever replace it completely, it can never come to life again; a deposed ruling class may recover its titles and possessions but nevermore the spirit of its forebears. [Tocqueville, *Old Regime*, p. 111]

Sumner had a different explanation from that in the text for the disappearance of the Federalist party: "[President] Adams was driven to the verge of war with France by his party, but succeeded in averting war, although his party was destroyed by the reaction." *Andrew Jackson*, p. 27. Cf. Tocqueville, *Democracy in America*, 1:183-84. See *Annals*, VI, p. 939; chap. 6, n. 33, above. See, also, Attorney General John H. Mitchell's appraisal of the Sedition Act of 1798: "Designed by the Federalists to perpetuate their power, it contributed to their downfall and left a lasting impression on both Congress and the executive." *Ill. B. J.* 59 (1970): 289.

We should not take leave of John Adams in this book without recognizing a contribution he made to freedom of speech that may have more than made up for his unfortunate association with the Sedition Act of 1798. (Jefferson called the act "that libel on legislation." Adams's response in 1813 was that Vice-President Jefferson was partly responsible, since he had signed the bill as president of the Senate! Robert Harris, book review: *The Adams-Jefferson Letters,* in *American Political Science Review* 54 [1960]: 510-11.)

Adams's contribution was the unpopular duty he undertook as defense counsel in the murder trial of the British soldiers who had participated in the "Boston Massacre":

> Popular feeling [in 1770] very clearly did not rejoice in that triumph of justice over prejudice which later Bostonians have seen in the acquittals. Adams himself always considered his participation in the defense "one of the most gallant, generous, manly and disinterested Actions of my whole life, and one of the best Pieces of Service I ever rendered my Country." The death sentence, he wrote in 1773, "would have been as foul a Stain upon this Country as the Executions of the Quakers or Witches, anciently. As the Evidence was, the Verdict of the Jury was exactly right." Some of his townsmen violently disagreed. They heaped "abuse" on Adams and [Josiah] Quincy. The lawyers heard their names "execrated in the most opprobrious terms whenever [they] appeared in the streets of Boston." "To this hour," Adams complained in 1815, "my conduct in it is remembered, and is alleged against me to prove I am an enemy to my country, and always have been." [Hiller B. Zobel, *The Boston Massacre* (New York: W. W. Norton & Co., 1970), p. 302]

See, also, chap. 6, n. 25, above. Cf. chap. 7, nn. 74, 75, above. His insistence on that occasion upon due process and the rule of law remains a significant example for the bar, and indeed for all of us, of that respect for legal and constitutional principles upon which an effective freedom of speech depends. See the discussion in the text at chap. 5, n. 16, above. See, also, chap. 5, nn. 78, 79, above.

191. See Beveridge, *John Marshall,* 2:407. See chap. 8, n. 135, above.

192. See chap. 8, n. 187, above.

> If we ask in what precisely consists the greatest good of all, which should be the end of every system of legislation, we shall find it reduce itself to two main objects, liberty and equality—liberty, because all particular dependence means so much force taken from the body of the state, and equality, because liberty cannot exist without it. [Rousseau, *Social Contract,* book 2, chap. 11]

> The better the constitution of a state is, the more do public affairs encroach on private in the minds of the citizens. . . . In a well-ordered city every man flies to the assemblies: under a bad government no one cares to stir a step to get to them, because no one is interested in what happens there, because it is foreseen that the general will will not prevail, and lastly because domestic cares are all-absorbing. [Ibid., book 3, chap. 15]

See Montesquieu, *Spirit of the Laws,* 4:5; 5:3; 6, 7; 7:2, 4, 8, 14. See, also, chap. 9, n. 36, below. Cf. p. 777 (top), below.

Whether Rousseau really considered Geneva itself "a well-ordered city" must remain, not only because of the life he chose to lead, questionable. See his *Letter to M. d'Alembert on the Theatre,* published as *Politics and the Arts,* trans. Allan Bloom (Glencoe, Ill.: Free Press, 1960). See, also, Bloom, "Jean-Jacques Rousseau," in Strauss and Cropsey, *History of Political Philosophy,* p. 515. Indeed, Rousseau might have found himself in sympathy with Milovan Djilas who, in describing "contemporary Communism [as in many ways] reminiscent of the exclusiveness of religious sects of the Middle Ages," was reminded of Calvin's accomplishment: "Of the people of Geneva, Calvin made paralytics forever incapable of any joy." *New Class,* pp. 130-31. See chap. 7, n. 35, above.

The typical democratic city, on the other hand, is anything but well-ordered: even the animals in such a city move about "with the utmost freedom and dignity, bumping into everyone who meets them and who does not step aside." Plato, *Republic* 563C. (See, also, ibid., 561A, 561D-E, 563D and, on birds in India, Galbraith, *Ambassador's Journal,* p. 72.) Animals tend to reflect, that is, the discipline (or lack of it) of the community in which they find themselves. I would be surprised to learn, for instance, that falconry has ever flourished in a democratic state: it requires much more discipline and perseverance in the falconer than the typical democratic man is capable of. See, for an engaging (even though, in some ways, intimidating) account of this once-popular sport, T. H. White, *The Goshawk* (London: Penguin Books, 1951). Also quite informative is Robin S. Oggins, "The English Kings and their Hawks: Falconry in Medieval England to the Time of Edward I" (Ph.D. diss., University of Chicago, 1967).

193. Should "self-expression" become our dominant concern, public repression would probably remain available to resist any threatened interference with authorized private pleasure or to attempt to restrain the anarchical tendencies of excessive individuality. "Civic virtue" would thus be transformed into mere "legitimate violence." See, on "the proneness of prosperity to breed tyrants," Lincoln, *Complete Works*, 1:434 (chap. 5, n. 36, above). See, also, p. 245, above: "We are in a state of profound peace and over-pampered with prosperity; yet the elements of exterminating war seem to be in vehement fermentation. . . ." Consider Sallust, *The War with Catiline*, chap. 52, sec. 20-23, chap. 53, sec. 2-6, chap. 54, sec. 1-6. Consider, also, chap. 7, n. 63, chap. 8, n. 147, above.

Does not the common law of England look more kindly on the self-expression aspect of freedom of speech (this is like the use of one's limbs or property sanctioned by the common law and is closer to "the state of nature"?) than on the public-participation aspect (this presupposes self-government and assumes civil society to be natural to man?)? See Blackstone, *Laws of England*, 3:118-43; see, also, the American movement (indicated in James Kent, *Commentaries on American Law* [New York: O. Halsted, 1826], 2:23) from sec. 3 to sec. 4, in chap. 5, above; and the movement from sec. 13 to sec. 14, in chap. 8, above. Consider, as well, chap. 5, nn. 1, 41, chap. 8, nn. 2, 4, above.

One form of this self-expression is seen in the modern creative artist. (See chap. 2, n. 12, above [Robert Frost], chap. 8, n. 195, below [John Milton].) Thus, Stephen Daedalus is moved to proclaim his *credo*: "I will not serve that in which I no longer believe, whether it call itself my home, my fatherland, or my church; and I will try to express myself in some mode of life or art as freely as I can and as wholly as I can, using for my defence the only arms I allow myself to use—silence, exile, and cunning." James Joyce, *A Portrait of the Artist as a Young Man* (New York: Viking Press, 1956), p. 247. He thereby implicitly identifies himself with Lucifer, whose sin "was the sin of pride, the sinful thought conceived in an instant: *non serviam: I will not serve*." Ibid., p. 117. See Anselm of Canterbury, *Truth, Freedom, and Evil*, pp. 155-57 ("How Satan sinned and willed to be like God."); G. F. Yates, ed., *Papal Thought on the State* (New York: Appleton-Century-Crofts, 1958), p. 38 (Leo XIII: "But many there are who follow in the footsteps of Lucifer, and adopt as their own his rebellious cry, 'I will not serve'; and consequently substitute for true liberty what is sheer and most foolish license."). (It is again useful to ask, What are the "I" and "my" independent of and liberated from home, fatherland, and church? See, e.g., chap. 5, n. 90, chap. 8, n. 30, above. See, also, chap. 6, n. 75, above.)

Satan, we are told by Milton, "wouldst seem the Patron of liberty"; "the Fiend," reports Blake, "is party to every work of art." See Gen. 4:17-26 (cf. Maimonides, *Guide of the Perplexed*, pp. 32-33, 357); chap. 9, nn. 9, 16, below. See, also, Churchill on Shaw, in sec. 14 of chap. 8, above. "One of the Fathers [either St. Jerome or St. Augustine], in great severity, called poesy *vinum daemonum* [devil's-wine], because it filleth the imagination. . . ." Bacon, "Of Truth." See chap. 9, n. 16, below.

Aaron Copland asked (cf. chap. 8, n. 171, above):

> What, after all, do we listen for when we listen to a composer? He need not tell us a story like the novelist; he need not "copy" nature like the sculptor; his work need have no immediate practical function like the architect's drawing. What is it that he gives us, then? Only one answer seems possible to me: He gives us himself. Every artist's work is, of course, an expression of himself, but none so direct as that of the creative musician. He gives us, without relation to exterior "events," the quintessential part of himself—that part which embodies the fullest and deepest expression of himself as a man and of his experience as

a fellow being. [*What to Listen for in Music* (New York: New American Library, Mentor Books, 1963), p. 158]

The question remains, of course, whether any particular "self" (i.e., soul) is worth expressing publicly. Certainly not, unless there should be greatness of soul. In any event, such an account of self-expression, with its repudiation of "exterior 'events'" reminds of the Kantian emphasis upon science as a construction rather than a discovery. (See chap. 5, n. 143, above, for a parallel in legal thought.) We should be reminded as well of Rousseau and the essential solitariness of the artist. (See Leo Strauss, *Natural Right and History*, p. 294.) A kind of self-expression may be seen also in Polonius's advice (Shakespeare, *Hamlet*, act 1, sc. 3, ll. 82-84) to Laertes:

> This above all: to thine own self be true,
> And it must follow, as the night the day,
> Thou canst not then be false to any man.

To take one's self as the standard is, in most cases, to impair one's vision: Shakespeare has the night following the day, not the enlightenment of day following night. Is not the self-centered man likely to end up groping in the dark, "liberated" from the light (but not from the limitations) emanating from nature?

The liberated artist should take to heart Emerson's observation, in his essay, "Shakespeare; or, the Poet" (cf. the movement from Burke's aristocrat to Proust's Charlus):

> Sculpture in Egypt and in Greece grew up in subordination to architecture. It was the ornament of the temple wall: at first a rude relief carved on pediments, then the relief became bolder and a head or arm was projected from the wall; the groups being still arranged with reference to the building, which serves also as a frame to hold the figures; and when at last the greatest freedom of style and treatment was reached, the prevailing genius of architecture still enforced a certain calmness and continence in the statue. As soon as the statue was begun for itself, and with no reference to the temple or palace, the art began to decline: freak, extravagance and exhibition took the place of the old temperance. [*Works*, 4:194]

It seems to be difficult to abandon the public for the private and "one's own" without, at the same time, moving from the natural and the noble to the bizarre or at least the petty. (Thus, when the "self" and hence the will become critical, one hears more of such phenomena as "the will to power" and the *acte gratuite*. See, for the latter as an attempt to be fully free, to be moved by neither desire nor reason, but by will alone [which is regarded as distinctively one's own], André Gide, *The Vatican Cellars* [London: Cassell & Co., 1952], pp. 192, 196-97, 199, 203-5, 229, 247. But nature, it seems, must reassert herself: the dominant motive of the criminal who chooses to believe he has committed a motiveless crime immediately becomes that of avoiding detection [otherwise, his deed is merely suicidal]; he becomes as well a prisoner of an effort to conceal even from himself what he has done [it is not a "murder" but rather an "adventure"]. I am reminded, by this self-defeating effort to "liberate" the will, of a story told me on very good authority [i.e., by one of my children] about an incantation which permits one to turn whatever one chooses into gold, *so long as one does not while invoking it think of elephants*. The "will to power," on the other hand, may be the other side of the coin of self-expression: the *acte gratuite* represents an effort to escape completely "outside" limitations that may be placed upon oneself; the "will to power" represents an effort to control completely all that is around one, including "history" itself [which one masters as both essentially repetitive and one's personal construction]. [Are we not obliged to assert *our* selves by refusing our assent to such "theories"?] One finds the "will to power" even in one who is drawn to another primarily because "he needs me." Modern medicine may be unduly influenced both by such a consideration and by the desperate desire to conquer death [and hence be truly free of nature, a view of nature which is dominated by the bodily]. See, for a healthier approach, Dr. Leon R. Kass, "A Caveat on Transplants," *Washington Post,* Jan. 14, 1968, p. B-1. See, also, Aristotle, *Nicomachean Ethics* 1170a25-b19, *Politics* 1278b25-30. Cf. the outburst of Northumberland upon learning of the death of his son: "Now let not Nature's hand keep the wild flood confin'd! Let order die!" Shakespeare, *Henry IV, Pt. II,* act 1, sc. 1, ll. 153-54. Cf. Diogenes Laertius, *Lives and Opinions of Eminent Philosophers,* 2:55: "Some say that [Xenophon] did not even shed tears [upon learning of his son's death in battle], but exclaimed, 'I knew my son was mortal.'" See chap. 8, n. 186, above, chap. 9, n. 31, below.)

Still another form of "self-expression" (but with the "self" transcended) may be seen in the philosopher addressed in chapter 9, below. Compare Dean Acheson's sentiments: ". . . We cannot gird ourselves for the war against poverty or in Vietnam until we exorcise image worship. The Greeks have given us the prescription; psychiatry, the method. 'Know thyself,' said Socrates. Today we say the same thing a little differently, 'Be yourself.' . . ." "The American Image Will Take Care of Itself," *New York Times Magazine,* Feb. 28, 1965, pp. 24-25, 95. But there is a world of difference between the ways of life implied by these two precepts: the disciplined ancient emphasis is on *know;* the fashionably modern, on *self.* The roots of modern self-regarding may be seen in the materialistic realism of a Hobbes (see chap. 8, n. 45, above); its culmination, in the willful patriotism of a Heidegger (see chap. 2, n. 7, chap. 8, n. 140, above). In both stages, the *being* of "one's own" is decisive. See chap. 9, n. 3, below. Cf. chap. 9, n. 19, below.

See Maimonides, *Guide of the Perplexed,* pp. 442, 621.

194. See chap. 9, n. 3, below. "You have only one defect: you do not feel the inherent power and glory of the principle of liberty," John Morley (chap. 5, n. 140, above) said of Walter Bagehot, *Manchester Guardian Weekly,* Mar. 5, 1959. See chap. 4, n. 103, above. Cf. Plato, *Republic* 557C-D (where the democratic constitution is likened to "a garment of many colours, embroidered with all kinds of hues, so this, decked and diversified with every kind of character, would appear the most beautiful"). See Herodotus, *History* 7:135. See, also, chap. 8, n. 2, above. Cf. chap. 8, n. 124, above.

195. "Nothing" may be too absolute a term here. Cf. Milton, *Prose Works,* 1:121-22 (reproduced in chap. 8, n. 170, above).

"Being asked what was the most beautiful thing in the world, Diogenes replied, 'Freedom of speech' [*parresia*]." Diogenes Laertius, *Lives of Eminent Philosophers,* 6:68. (See chap. 9, n. 8, below.) Cf. Emma Bovary (to be) laughingly drinking her curaçao.

Is it not "liberty of speaking" which helps make friendship so pleasurable and which is reflected in Thomas Jefferson's successful effort to have his friends build themselves houses around Monticello? Thus, he wrote James Monroe,

> I wish to heaven, you may continue in the disposition to fix [your house] in Albemarle. Short will establish himself there, and perhaps Madison may be tempted to do so. This will be society enough and in it will be a great sweetener of our lives. Without society, and a society to our taste, men are never contented. [Paul Wilstach, *Jefferson and Monticello* (Garden City, N.Y.: Doubleday, Doran & Co., 1930), pp. 152-53]

See chap. 7, n. 35, above. See, also, chap. 5, n. 126, above (on the love letter as "the frankest and freest and privatest product of the human mind and heart"). Cf. chap. 8, n. 129, above, chap. 9, n. 4, below.

Bacon affirms, in his essay "On Friendship," "that it is a mere and miserable solitude to want true friends; without which the world is but a wilderness. . . ." "Towards comrades and brothers we should use liberty [frankness] of speech [*parresia*], and share all our possessions with them." Aristotle, *Nicomachean Ethics* 1165a30. (This indicates, in another way, why freedom of speech is so important for the democratic regime—in the regime, that is, which is "dedicated to the proposition that all men are created equal.") "Moreover, friendship appears to be the bond of the city; and lawgivers seem to set more store by it than they do by justice, for to promote concord, which seems akin to friendship, is their chief aim, while faction, which is enmity, is what they are most anxious to banish." Ibid., 1155a23-27. Cf. ibid., 1096a14-18: "Perhaps it would seem better, and indeed it would seem to be obligatory, especially for a philosopher, to sacrifice even one's closest personal ties in defence of the truth. Both are dear to us, yet it is pious to prefer the truth." See ibid., 1101a23-b9 (for an "unfriendly," perhaps even antisocial, truth). Cf. Sallust, *The War with Catiline*, chap. 51, sec. 20, chap. 52, secs. 13, 29; Cicero, *Fourth Speech against Catiline*, sec. 4 (end); Plato, *Gorgias* 524-527.

It is the ambivalent relation of philosophy to the city which may be said to be the theme of the next chapter, if not of much of what I have written in this book and elsewhere. See, e.g., the end of chap. 9, n. 9, n. 24, below. Cf. chap. 9, n. 19, below.

See Plato, *Republic* 496C.

CHAPTER IX

1. Some Americans continue to be confronted with the modern version of the Thucydidean question, "Shall we go to Sicily?" Union with Canada sometimes seems inevitable, it can be argued, and after that, union with Mexico is likely. The Canadian union (for which there is already considerable support—especially among those Canadians who see their lives determined more and more by decisions in Washington in which they have no effective voice—and to which the farsighted French-Canadian isolated in an English Protestant setting should be receptive) should bring the United States and Great Britain (with perhaps France) even closer together and should help establish on even firmer ground among us the principle of the rule of law. This sixty-state culmination could (depending on chance [chap. 7, n. 111, above]) provide not only a firmer basis of some kind of union with Mexico—partly because of the incorporation in the United States of Roman Catholic Quebec—but also the time and resources needed to raise the Mexican economy to the level needed to sustain free institutions today. (See chap. 5, n. 94, chap. 7, n. 2, chap. 8, nn. 37, 165, above.) The North American republic would then have both the experience and the moral stature for the gradual establishment both of closer ties with South America and of an Atlantic union. (Is not Cuba's natural tie with the United States, even more so than Puerto Rico's?) It is along such lines that the founder of a federated world republic may direct his efforts. (Cf. the proposals of the demented President in Fletcher Knebel, *Night of Camp David* [New York: Bantam Books, 1966], pp. 78-79, 211, 294-95; Thomas F. Gossett, *Race: The History of an Idea in America* [Dallas: Southern Methodist University Press, 1963] pp. 181-82. Cf., also, chap. 2, n. 3, above, on "so little independence of mind . . . in America." See, for a thoughtful study of the relation of Canada to the United States, George Grant, *Lament for a Nation: The Defeat of Canadian Nationalism* [Princeton: D. Van Nostrand Co., 1965].)

We should not, however, underestimate the value for the United States, and hence for the rest of the world, of the attractive haven provided by Canada for American political and "cultural" dissenters: such a ready and respectable haven may help keep us civilized, by relieving among us the sense of desperation or of depression that closed-off societies can generate today. Thus, refuge has been found there in recent years both by radicals (e.g., from the University of California) and by conservatives (e.g., from Cornell University). Canada can also provide us, in a language and circumstances similar enough to ours to make them plausible, models and attitudes worthy of serious consideration. One can even say that Americans may enjoy in their relations with Canada, as now constituted, many of the advantages (with few, if any, of the disadvantages) of a regime in which "states' rights" flourish. See, e.g., chap. 7, nn. 27, 70, 71, above. (One can also say that panic in Canada, as in October, 1970, need not affect us here. See chap. 3, nn. 22, 28, above. The disturbances, as well as the remedies, were localized. I found during my November 1-4, 1970, visit to Montreal that the Canadian government had acted far more mildly than its language would lead one to believe. It is also evident, however excessive the response of that government, that the resort to extraordinary powers is really temporary, unlike that of the Greek colonels. See chap. 6, n. 1, chap. 7, n. 73, above. See the article on French-Canadian separatism I have prepared as an "Insight" feature for the Nov. 26, 1970, issue of the *Chicago Daily News*. [This article, "Canada and the Dilemmas of Decent Men," may be found in *Congressional Record* 116: E11057.])

CHAPTER NINE, NOTE 1: PAGE 273

Still, the survival of civilization, if not of the human race, inclines thoughtful men to take more seriously than ever before the possibility of world government. But it is only prudent to appreciate the inherent limitations as well as the dangers of such an enterprise. See, e.g., Plutarch, *The Lives of the Noble Grecians and Romans* (New York: Random House, Modern Library, n.d.), p. 199 ("that unblest and inauspicious passion for Sicily"); Leo Strauss, *What Is Political Philosophy?* (Glencoe, Ill.: Free Press, 1959), p. 133 (chap. 9, n. 7, below); George Orwell, *1984* (New York: New American Library, 1961) (with the institutional hostility among Oceania, Eurasia, and Eastasia; Erich Fromm observed in his "Afterword," p. 262: "But anyone who sees in Orwell's description only another denunciation of Stalinism is missing an essential element of Orwell's analysis. He is actually talking about a development which is taking place in the Western industrial countries also, only at a slower pace than it is taking place in Russia and China.").

Far more security for the United States than that provided by our expensive loyalty programs would result from the use of money spent on such programs (chap. 4, n. 33, above) to finance and establish in Washington (perhaps under United Nations auspices) a world university to which students and scholars from all countries would come. (See, in chap. 6, n. 55, above, the constitutional authority for such an enterprise. See, also, Dwight D. Eisenhower, *Waging Peace, 1956-1961* [Garden City, N.Y.: Doubleday & Co., 1965], pp. 410-11.) I proceed on my observation that America seems, to educated men who come to know her, worthy of admiration, respect, and (with appropriate adjustments for circumstances) imitation, just as Rome, Athens, and Britain were at their height.

The unnatural but all too ominous alternative in our industrializing world to a humane constitutionalism is the kind of regime (of the Right or of the Left) described in S. K. Oberbeck's review (in *Newsweek*, Aug. 31, 1970, pp. 74-75) of Albert Speer, *Inside the Third Reich* (New York: Macmillan Co., 1970) (chap. 5, n. 112, above):

> But Speer seems to be emphasizing a greater danger: not the cliché that Hitler was simply a victim of his own delusions, but that he was a victim of technology's seeming power to make the delusions come true. Remarking on the isolation of the technocratic dictator, he says, "All the theaters of war could be directed from Hitler's table in the situation room. The more fearful the situation, the greater was the gulf modern technology created between reality and the fantasies with which [Hitler] operated."

It is well in such a "situation" to remind ourselves of a perspective that is no longer "practical," the perspective of the *polis* with its unavoidable awareness of the human and the natural: "the *polis* is that complete association which corresponds to the natural range of man's power of knowing and loving." (See chap. 7, n. 35, above.) It is well, that is, to assess from the perspective of the *polis* and what it means every proposed change offered us by technology and by the social and biological sciences spawned by technology. Modern man dares not forget what he once abandoned lest he be abandoned to what he would prefer to forget.

Our recollection of the abandonment to the worst in man, which we have seen in the political monstrosities of the twentieth century, should induce us to challenge the assumption of those for whom "most appeals to 'nature' [seem] Fascist in tendency." (See, e.g., Ronald Bryden, [London] *Observer Review*, June 16, 1968, p. 27.) Compare the reaffirmation of the significance for mankind of nature found in the attempt by Leo Paul de Alvarez (in a letter published February 23, 1970, in the *Dallas Morning News*) to explain why the Texas habitat of the golden-cheeked warbler should not be sacrificed to the encroachments of a golf course:

> ... Very few will ever see the warbler or even care about seeing it. If, therefore, the reason for saving the warbler from extinction is said to be that the taxpayers and their children "deserve a continuing look" at this bird, many may say that they do not care if they or their children ever see a golden-cheek warbler. It is of course this indifference that has led to the destruction of so many species and so much of our land.

> I would suggest that the fundamental issue is where we propose to stop in our limitless search for physical gratification. The kind of men who would destroy a species for physical pleasure and profit are ultimately responsible for today's ecological crisis.
> It is in placing limits upon our desires, with regard to small things, that we learn how to save the great things of the world.

(Thus, one form of "placing limits upon our desires" which appeals to me as salutary would be a fairly rigorous insistence upon Sunday closings of most commercial establishments.) See chap. 2, n. 38, chap. 7, n. 59, above, chap. 9, nn. 20, 22, below.

2. Unreflectiveness is consistent with life in a well-ordered community—if someone else has already done the thinking for the community. See Plato, *Republic* 619C-D. See, also, chap. 8, n. 37, above.

> In a real sense, the U.S. road is a proper monument for the U.S., a nation of restless people whose hallmark has always been their willingness to leave behind the familiar and comfortable to discover what is beyond the next hill, sure that the unknown represents opportunity, not danger, and supremely confident that the best is yet ahead. [*Time*, Oct. 6, 1961, p. 71]

This sentiment may have been best anticipated by Hobbes in chapter 11 of the *Leviathan*:

> ... [W]e are to consider that the felicity of this life consists not in the repose of a mind satisfied. For there is no such *finis ultimus*, utmost aim, nor *summum bonum*, greatest good, as is spoken of in the books of the old moral philosophers.... I put for a general inclination of all mankind a perpetual and restless desire of power after power that ceases only in death....

In this sense, Americans may indeed be "*un vrai peuple moderne.*" Walter Bagehot, *The English Constitution*, World Classics (London: Oxford University Press, 1963), p. 253. (See Plato, *Timaeus* 22B: "O Solon, Solon," said an old Egyptian priest, "you Greeks are always children: there is not such a thing as an old Greek.") It may be in his very changeableness that "the typical American of 1900 is on the whole more like his ancestor of 1775 than is the typical Englishman." Lord Charnwood, *Abraham Lincoln* (Garden City, N.Y.: Garden City Publishing Co., 1917), p. 18. (Is not the story of Rip Van Winkle distinctively American? A Spartan, for instance, who slept for twenty years would have awakened to find the world about him essentially unchanged. I do not believe Ithaca is changed, in the sense Rip Van Winkle's world was [or, certainly, as ours would be] upon Odysseus' return after an absence of twenty years. There had been, during Rip's absence, the Revolutionary War: "The very character of the people [in his village] seemed changed. There was a busy, bustling, disputatious tone about it, instead of the accustomed phlegm and drowsy tranquillity [he had known before]." Washington Irving, "Rip Van Winkle," *The Sketch-Book* [New York: G. P. Putnam's Sons, 1864], p. 65. Cf. Henry Adams, *The United States in 1800* [Ithaca: Cornell University Press, Cornell Paperbacks, 1955], pp. 17, 42, 125-26.) See Marvin Zetterbaum, *Tocqueville and the Problem of Democracy* (Stanford: Stanford University Press, 1967), p. 65. Cf. chap. 6, n. 54, above. See, also, chap. 8, n. 193, above.

3. Publius speaks, in *Federalist* No. 57, of "the vigilant and manly spirit which actuates the people of America—a spirit which nourishes freedom, and in return is nourished by it." Lincoln saw as his "larger work," "the restoration of his country to its earliest and noblest tradition, which alone gave permanence or worth to its existence as a nation." Charnwood, *Abraham Lincoln*, p. 15. The connection between nobility and the beautiful (and hence spectacle and appearance) should be traced. See chap. 8, nn. 2, 181, 194, above, chap. 9, nn. 30, 32, below.

"To make us love our country, our country ought to be lovely." Burke, *Works*, 4:85. See chap. 2, n. 3, above. It is Burke, also, who reminds us of "that natural discipline which is the soul of a true republic." Ibid., p. 203. Thus, a legislator should be concerned

CHAPTER NINE, NOTE 3: PAGE 274   777

with the psychic fitness of his people. See, e.g., ibid., 1:180; 4:68 ("Men have no right to what is not reasonable, and to what is not for their benefit. . . ."). Certainly, we should take care lest our "right to privacy" degenerate into merely the right to do things we do not want others to know about, things which are good neither for us nor for the community. See chap. 8, n. 192, above, chap. 9, nn. 9, 19, 29, below.

Americans may be unique, or at least rare among the peoples of the modern world, in that since the later generations have not been the physical descendants of their predecessors, they are free to accept only what is good from the past. That is, the true descendants of the Founding Fathers are identified not by who their parents and grandparents were but by what their understanding of the Declaration of Independence and the Constitution is. (Thus, in this respect, Americans are to most other peoples as Christians are to Jews. Cf. chap. 9, n. 10, below. See Aristotle, *Rhetoric* 1398a20, on who is more akin to the tyrannicides. Cf. Dean Acheson's definition of the national purpose of the United States: "Our purpose is to survive, and perchance to flourish." *Chicago Sun-Times*, Mar. 3, 1969, p. 31. One might then ask, upon considering what the "United States" means—what is it that *is* to survive, "How is this country different from all other countries?" See chap. 8, n. 193, above. See, also, John Morley, *On Compromise* [London: Macmillan & Co., 1886], pp. 6-7.)

The American does not speak, as Samuel Johnson does, of political institutions having been "for the most part formed by chance and settled by custom." The Staff, Social Science I, The College of the University of Chicago, eds., *The People Shall Judge* (Chicago: University of Chicago Press, 1949), 1:170. ("We have made, or rather stumbled on, a constitution. . . ." Bagehot, *The English Constitution*, p. 9. James M. Burns observed, in *Roosevelt: The Soldier of Freedom* [New York: Harcourt Brace Jovanovich, 1970], pp. 180-81:

> The emergent difference [in December 1941] between the [Americans and the British] cast a long shadow on future strategy. . . . The Americans were inclining toward a long build-up and then a massive, concentrated thrust toward the enemy center—Germany. Any other move was a dispersion of effort unless it directly supported this central thrust. The American mind in war planning, as well as in commerce and production, Churchill felt, ran to "broad, sweeping, logical conclusions on the largest scale," while the British allowed more for the role of opportunism and improvisation, trying to adjust to unfolding events rather than to dominate them. To the American military such strategic assumptions led to expediency, dispersion of effort, to that "peripheralism" that had marked so much of Churchill's thinking beginning with the Dardanelles in World War I. To the British, with their limited resources and perhaps more patient view of history, this kind of strategy was more supple, flexible, sophisticated. . . .

See, also, ibid., p. 438; Burke, *Works*, 4:191-205, 218; 5:130-31, 134; chap. 2, n. 18, chap. 7, n. 119, above.)

The typical American today would tend to agree with the Marquis de Condorcet in his expectation that

> nature has set no term to the perfection of human faculties; that the perfectibility of man is truly indefinite; and that the progress of this perfectibility, from now onwards independent of any power that might wish to halt it, has no other limit than the duration of the globe upon which nature has cast us. [*Sketch for a Historical Picture of the Progress of the Human Mind* (New York: Farrar, Straus & Giroux, Noonday Press, 1955), p. 3]

If, as many Americans believe, there is "no term to the perfection of human faculties"—if, that is, there is no state of perfection at which a community should stop if it should be attained (there is no practical limit set on the time available for progress toward such a goal)—then there can be in principle no progress at all: infinite perfectibility means, in effect, no discernible perfectibility, since without an end in view, "however dimly perceived," one cannot know whether any movement is good or bad, forward or back. (Cf. F. A. Hayek, "The Common Sense of Progress," in *The Constitution of Liberty* [Chicago: University of Chicago Press, 1960], p. 38. That chapter bears as an epigraph a quotation from Oliver Cromwell, "Man never mounts higher than when he knows not where he is going.") But see Aristotle, *Metaphysics* 994b12:

> Those who introduce infinity do not realize that they are abolishing the nature of the good (although no one would attempt to do anything if he were not likely to reach some limit); nor would there be any intelligence in the world, because the man who has intelligence always acts for the sake of something. . . .

See, also, Aristotle, *Politics* 1288b25: "The good law giver and the true statesman must therefore have their eyes open not only to what is the absolute best, but also to what is the best in relation to actual conditions." (The pollution symposium cited in chap. 8, n. 149, above, bears on this.) Are not Americans aware of all this, in that they have had from time to time to deliberate upon their Constitution and upon how it can be improved? Thus, their fundamental law is not something merely "given" to them either by "history" or by a godlike lawgiver. The modern argument for progress may be merely an argument for a certain kind of liberty and for the gratification of the hopes and wishes one happens to have. See chap. 2, n. 11, above. See, also, Edwin Muir, *Latitudes* (New York: B. W. Huebsch, 1924), pp. 257-58. (But does not even the chance or the conventional wish depend on something which is independent of chance or convention? Thus, Democritus observes, "Sweet exists by convention, bitter by convention, colour by convention; atoms and Void [alone] exist in reality. . . ." Quoted in Werner Heisenberg, *Philosophic Problems of Nuclear Science* [New York: Fawcett Publications, 1966], p. 110. See chap. 8, nn. 88, 177, below.)

Still, it may be good for the morale of democrats to believe, as one of them did, "It is of the very nature of a free society to advance in its standards of what is deemed reasonable and right." See chap. 8, n. 13, above. See, also, chap. 8, n. 73, above. Cf., e.g., chap. 3, n. 25, chap. 6, n. 50, above. In any event, Publius distinguishes, at *Federalist*, p. 159, between "change after change" and a "material change for the better." It does not seem that the young Lincoln appreciated this fully when he observed, "But the game is caught; and I believe it is true that with the catching end the pleasures of the chase." *Complete Works*, 1:13. Cf. chap. 5, n. 36, above. (Consider, also, the intriguing observation by the chairman of the board of General Motors, "Our future is filled with potential." *Chicago Sun-Times*, May 24, 1969, p. 36. I suppose this is as "value-free" —with every change being inevitably "for the better"—as the Darwinian "survival of the fittest," which seems to me to come down essentially to "survival of the survivors." Here, too, my contribution to the pollution symposium [chap. 8, n. 149, above] is relevant. See chap. 9, n. 38, below.) See Plato, *Timaeus* 28A-B, 29A.

See, for an early adaptation to American conditions of the faith of the Enlightenment, the statement by Thomas Paine in 1792:

> The constitutions of America, and also that of France, have either affixed a period for their revision, or laid down the mode by which improvement shall be made. . . . The best constitution that could now be devised, consistent with the condition of the present moment, may be far short of the excellence which a few years may afford. There is a morning of reason rising upon man on the subject of government, that has not appeared before. As the barbarism of the present old governments expires, the moral conditions of nations with respect to each other will be changed. [*The Writings of Thomas Paine*, ed. M. D. Conway (New York: G. P. Putnam's Sons, 1894), 2:452-53]

See, also, ibid. 2:355; Leon Trotsky, *The Russian Revolution* (Garden City: Doubleday & Co., Anchor Books, 1959), pp. 1, 134-35, 145-47, 482-83. Cf., for an older, and perhaps more salutary, teaching, Edmund Burke's insistence in the course of the trial of Warren Hastings,

> There is one thing, and one thing only, which defies all mutation, — that which existed before the world, and will survive the fabric of the world itself: I mean justice,—that justice which, emanating from the Divinity, has a place in the breast of every one of us, given us for our guide with regard to ourselves and with regard to others, and which will stand, after this globe is burned to ashes, our advocate or our accuser before the great Judge, when He comes to call upon us for the tenor of a well-spent life. [*Selected Writings of Edmund Burke*, ed. W. J. Bate (New York: Modern Library, 1960), p. 338]

See chap. 7, n. 77, above. See, for some practical implications of the idea of progress, Grant, *Lament for a Nation*, pp. 37-38, 53 ff., 88 ff., 94-96.

4. Poetic celebration of variety may be found in Shakespeare, *Antony and Cleopatra*, act 2, sc. 2, l. 241. See chap. 5, n. 126, above. "But change in all things is sweet, as the poet says, owing to some badness in us; since just as a changeable man is bad, so also is a nature that needs change; for it is not simple nor good." Aristotle, *Nicomachean Ethics* 1354b30. The poet is Euripides, the context that in which a fevered man seeks relief (i.e., change) from pain. *Orestes* 234. Cf. Aristotle, *Rhetoric* 1371a26 ("change means an approach to nature" [quoting the same passage from Euripides]). That is, change can be good.

> I truly believe that if [Montaigne] had been alone with his own attendants [his secretary wrote] he would rather have gone to Cracow or toward Greece by land than make the turn toward Italy; but the pleasure he took in visiting unknown countries, which he found so sweet as to make him forget the weakness of his age and of his health, he could not impress on any of his party, and everyone asked only to return home. Whereas he was accustomed to say that after spending a restless night, he would get up with desire and alacrity in the morning when he remembered that he had a new town or region to see. [Montaigne, *Essays and Selected Writings*, ed. D. M. Frame (New York: St. Martin's Press, 1963), p. 471]

Tocqueville observes that "a taste for variety is one of the characteristic passions of democracy." *Democracy in America* (New York: Random House, Vintage Books, 1954), 1:213. (See, also, Tacitus, *History* 3.12.) Is it because the many are distinctively desirous of the good even as they are peculiarly uninformed about it?

> . . . There is in all men a demand for the superlative, so much so that the poor devil who has no other way of reaching it attains it by getting drunk. It seems to me that this demand is at the bottom of the philosopher's effort to prove that truth is absolute and of the jurist's search for criteria of universal validity which he collects under the head of natural law. [Oliver Wendell Holmes, "Natural Law," in *The Holmes Reader*, ed. Julius J. Marke (New York: Oceana Publications, 1955), p. 118]

See chap. 7, n. 77, chap. 8, n. 165, above.

See Plato, *Timaeus* 58A; Aristotle, *Nicomachean Ethics*, 1166a13-30, 1168a5-10, 1170a20-1170b19. Can anything other than the unchanging truly be known? See chap. 5, n. 143, above. See, also, chap. 3, n. 25, chap. 6, n. 50, chap. 8, nn. 193, 177 (on the "absolute moment"), above. (Does not Proust sense that his "method" falls short of the highest? See *Remembrance of Things Past* [New York: Random House, 1934], 1:543-45. Is the elusive image that of Calvary?)

See *Alfarabi's Philosophy of Plato and Aristotle*, ed. Muhsin Mahdi (New York: Free Press of Glencoe, 1962), pp. 15-16, 24-25. See, also, chap. 8, n. 28, above.

5. Revolutionaries, some no doubt hoped, would no longer be either needed or produced once the new regime began to engage men's interests and loyalties. See chap. 8, n. 98, above. See, also, Shakespeare, *Macbeth*, act 1, sc. 4, ll. 7-12.

Lincoln (before he became President) said more than he may have realized when he observed of the question of what was to happen to the importation of slaves after 1808,

"The Constitution is as silent about that as it is silent, personally, about myself." Lincoln, *Complete Works*, ed. John G. Nicolay and John Hays (New York: Century Co., 1902), 1:565. The change in the character of education for the bar bears on the problem of the continued development of civic-minded *and* competent men. See chap. 9, n. 13, below.

6. Educational concerns are addressed in Plato, *Epistles* 11.359A-B:

> ... For they are mistaken if they believe that a constitution could ever be well established by any kind of legislation whatsoever without the existence of some authority in the city which supervises the daily life both of slaves and freemen, to see that it is both temperate and manly. And this condition might be secured if you already possess men who are worthy of such authority. If, however, you require someone to train them, you do not, in my opinion, possess either the trainer or the pupils to be trained; so it only remains for you to pray to the gods. For, in truth, the earlier cities also were most organized in this way; and they came to have a good constitution at a later date, as a result of being confronted with grave troubles, either through war or other difficulties, whenever there arose in their midst at such a crisis a man of noble character in possession of great powers.

See, also, Zetterbaum, *Tocqueville and the Problem of Democracy*, pp. 85-87; chap. 7, n. 10, above.

7. See Plutarch, *Lives*, p. 185:

> But he that saw most of Pericles, and furnished him most especially with a weight and grandeur of sense, superior to all arts of popularity, and in general gave him his elevation and sublimity of purpose and of character, was Anaxagoras of Clazomenae ... the first of the philosophers who did not refer the first ordering of the world to fortune or chance, nor to necessity or compulsion, but to a pure, unadulterated intelligence. ... For this man, Pericles entertained an extraordinary esteem and admiration, and filling himself with this lofty and, as they call it, up-in-the-air sort of thought, derived hence not merely, as was natural, elevation of purpose and dignity of language, raised far above the base and dishonest buffooneries of mob eloquence, but, besides this, a composure of countenance, and a serenity and calmness in all his movements. ...

(Cf. Aristophanes, *Clouds*, for the "up-in-the-air" Socrates and his effect on practical affairs. See, also, on the limited influence of Socrates on Pericles' talented relative Alcibiades, Plutarch, *Lives*, pp. 235 ff.) See, also, on Pericles and Anaxagoras, Pierre Bayle, *Dictionary Historical and Critical* (London: D. Midwinter et al., 1737), 4:565-66; on Cicero and Publius Nigidius, Plutarch, *Lives*, p. 1052; on Alexander and the philosophers, ibid., pp. 805, 839-41. Cf. Plato, *Phaedrus* 269E-270B, *Phaedo* 97B-98C, *Gorgias* 515D-516D.

> Suppose, however, that on hearing this someone were to say: "Plato, as it seems, is claiming to know what is of advantage to democracy; yet when he has had it in his power to speak before the *demos* and to counsel it for the best he has never yet stood up and made a speech"—to this you may reply that "Plato was born late in the history of his country, and he found the *demos* already old and habituated by the previous statesmen to do many things at variance with his own counsel. For he would have given counsel to it, as to his father, with the greatest possible pleasure, had he not supposed that he would be running risks in vain, and would do no good. ...." [Plato, *Epistles* 5.322A-B]

> [T]he Final Tyrant presents himself as a philosopher, as the highest philosophic authority, as the supreme exegete of the only true philosophy, as the executor and hangman authorized by the only true philosophy. He claims therefore that he persecutes not philosophy but false philosophies. The experience is not altogether new for philosophers. If philosophers were confronted with claims of this kind in former ages, philosophy went underground. [See chap. 2, n. 39,

above.] It accommodated itself in its explicit or exotic teaching to the unfounded commands of rulers who believed they knew things which they did not know. [See chap. 9, n. 27, below.] Yet its very esoteric teaching undermined the commands or dogmas of the rulers in such a way as to guide the potential philosophers toward the eternal and unsolved problems. [See chap. 8, n. 76, above.] And since there was no universal state in existence, the philosophers could escape to other countries if life became unbearable in the tyrant's dominions. [See chap. 7, n. 27, above.] From the Universal Tyrant, however, there is no escape. [See chap. 8, n. 18, chap. 9, n. 1, above.] Thanks to the conquest of nature and to the completely unabashed substitution of suspicion and terror for law, the Universal and Final Tyrant has at his disposal practically unlimited means for ferreting out, and for extinguishing, the most modest efforts in the direction of thought. [See chap. 5, n. 90, above.] The coming of the universal and homogeneous state will be the end of philosophy on earth. [Strauss, *What Is Political Philosophy?* pp. 132-33]

See, on persecution and the art of writing, Isaac Disraeli, *Quarrels of Authors: Some Memoirs for Our Literary History, including Specimens of Controversy to the Reign of Elizabeth* (New York: Eastburn, Kirl & Co., 1814), 2:93 ff.; Hans Speier, "Grimmelshausen's Laughter," in Joseph Cropsey, ed., *Ancients and Moderns: Essays on the Tradition of Political Philosophy, in Honor of Leo Strauss* (New York: Basic Books, 1964), pp. 177, 196-200; chap. 5, n. 90, above. See, also, Peter H. von Blanckenhagen, "Two Horses and a Charioteer," in Cropsey, ibid., pp. 88-94. Cf. the implications of the closing lines (with their manipulation of Plato) in Martin Heidegger's 1933 speech on his assumption of a rectorate.

[W]e suggest that the ultimate reason why Aristotle has reservations against even the best kind of democracy is his certainty that the *demos* is by nature opposed to philosophy. [Note: Cf. *Gorgias* 481d3-5 and *Republic* 494a4-7.] Only the gentleman can be open to philosophy, i.e. listen to the philosopher. Modern democracy on the other hand presupposes a fundamental harmony between philosophy and the people, a harmony brought about by universal enlightenment, or by philosophy (science) relieving man's estate through inventions and discoveries recognizable as salutary by all, or by both means. On the basis of the break with Aristotle, one could come to believe in the possibility of the simply rational society, i.e. of a society each member of which would be of necessity perfectly rational so that all would be united by fraternal friendship, and government of men, as distinguished from administration of things, would wither away. . . . [Strauss, *The City and Man* (Chicago: Rand McNally, 1957), pp. 37-38]

See, also, chap. 4, n. 114, chap. 7, n. 122, above, chap. 9, nn. 33, 38, below. Cf. chap. 8, n. 135 above. Cf., also, chap. 2, n. 7, chap. 8, nn. 140, 193, above.

8. Still, one is surprised to learn upon inquiry how many eminent scholars insist that there is *only* the praiseworthy meaning of *parresia* in classical Greek—and this suggests what is wrong with much of classical scholarship today: there is, perhaps because of a misguided liberalism, a fundamental lack of seriousness—and without seriousness there cannot be the care, reflection, and imagination that are needed for a proper interpretation of the greatest works of the mind. See Leo Strauss, "The Liberalism of Classical Political Philosophy," in *Liberalism Ancient and Modern* (New York: Basic Books, 1968), p. 26. See, also, chap. 8, nn. 122, 170, 171, above. Cf. chap. 8, n. 174, above.

The praiseworthy use of *parresia* may be seen in Plato, *Gorgias* 491E (but this is Callicles'), 492D, 521A, *Laws* 694B, 835C, *Epistles* 8.354A (reproduced in chap. 9, n. 38, below); Aristotle, *Nicomachean Ethics* 1124b29, 1165a30 (reproduced in chap. 8, n. 195, above), *Athenian Constitution* 16.6; Diogenes Laertius, *Lives of Eminent Philosophers* 6.68 (reproduced in chap. 8, n. 195, above). But the uses of *parresia* in a derogatory sense are perhaps even more striking, as seen in Plato, *Phaedrus* 240E, *Republic* 357B, *Gorgias* 487D, *Laws* 649B, 671B; Isocrates, *On the Peace* 14, *Areopagiticus* 20; Theophrastus, *Characters* ("Evil Speaking") 28. See, also, Quintilian, *Institutiones Oratoriae* 9.2.27; the passage from Bacon quoted in chap. 8, n. 121, above; Locke, *Reasonableness of Christianity, Works of John Locke* (London: Rivington, Egerton et al., 1824), 6:73. See, for a less ambiguous expression for "free discussion," Plato, *Gorgias* 461E, *Republic* 499A. See, also, Aristotle, *Nicomachean Ethics* 1129b23-24. See, on "plainspokenness," chap. 4, n. 49, above.

Parresia, it should be noticed, is not related to *logos* but to *reo*. The distinction between these two words, which is vital for understanding the relation between philosophy and politics (between free inquiry and free speech), is implied by Laurence Berns in a note to his translation of Aristotle's *Politics* published at St. John's College, Annapolis, Md.:

> *Logos* is often translated reason, argument, ratio, account, speech or word. It comes from the verb *lego*, speak; but it also means pick out, choose, count, hence our cognates select, collect, elect. It means selected, chosen words, hence thoughtful speech. There is another word for word in Greek, *rhema*; it is from the verb *reo*, flow. It is the root of the word "rhetoric."

9. Distinctions are drawn by biblical lexicographers (such as Bauer) between the New Testament *parresia* and the Old Testament covering by Moses of his face in the presence of God. See, e.g., *A Greek-English Lexicon of the New Testament* (a translation and adaptation of Walter Bauer's *Worterbuch*), ed. William F. Arndt and F. Wilbur Gingrich (Chicago: University of Chicago Press, 1957), pp. 635-36.

See Hilda C. Graef, *St. Gregory of Nysea*, Ancient Christian Writers (Westminster, Md.: Newman Press, 1954), p. 183, n. 26. The New Testament attitude is perpetuated in such passages as these by Milton: "But when God commands to take the trumpet, and blow a dolorous or a jarring blast, it lies not in man's will what he shall say, or what he shall conceal." *The Prose Works of John Milton* (London: J. Johnson, 1806), 1:115. "For me, I have determined to lay up as the best treasure and solace of a good old age, if God vouchsafe it me, *the honest liberty of free speech* from my youth, where I shall think it available in so dear a concernment as the church's good." Ibid., 1:116. (Italics added) (Notice how Milton brings together here "liberty" and "free." See chap. 5, sec. 13, above.)

To say everything one thought or believed was regarded by pre-Christian writers as occasionally irresponsible or licentious: that is, social consequences dictated a need for restraint. But Christian writers called for just such saying of everything as the indispensable witness of one's faith: transitory social considerations were not to impede, to the extent that they formerly had, the exercise of such a liberty, indeed of such a duty, so intimately related to the eternal welfare of one's soul. Thus, we see an encouragement of the private, of the individual, of an individuality which turned eventually against organized religion itself. See chap. 8, nn. 193, 195, above. ("Haeresie signifies no more than private opinion. . . ." Hobbes, *Leviathan*, chap. 11.) See, also, the discussion of Kant in chap. 7, n. 107, above.

Francis Bacon observes that the Christian "is one that fears always, yet is as bold as a lion." *The Works of Francis Bacon*, ed. J. Spedding and R. Ellis (New York: Hurd & Houghton, 1864), 14:145. Jesus Christ, said Leo XIII, "restored and exalted the original dignity of man." G. F. Yates, ed., *Papal Thought on the State* (New York: Appleton-Century-Crofts, 1958), p. 31. The exaltation and related boldness of man shaped by Christianity are reflected in Emerson's argument (in his "Politics"), "Democracy is better for us, because the religious sentiment of the present time accords better with it."

The relation between our political and religious institutions has been noticed. See, e.g., Burke, *Works*, 2:187, 196; Tocqueville, *Democracy in America*, 1:436, 2:5; Anastaplo, "The Declaration of Independence," *St. Louis U. L. J.* 9:404-6; chap. 4, n. 110, chap. 5, nn. 51, 92, above. Samuel Adams, in an address of August 1, 1776, attributed to him, "American Independence" (chap. 5, n. 87, above), argued (cf. Paine, *Writings*, 4:4):

CHAPTER NINE, NOTE 9: PAGE 275   783

> Our forefathers threw off the yoke of Popery in religion; for you is reserved the honor of levelling the popery of politics. They opened the Bible to all, and maintained the capacity of every man to judge for himself in religion. . . . This day, I trust, the reign of political protestantism will commence. [We assume] that freedom of thought and dignity of self-direction which [God] bestowed.

(See chap. 2, n. 29, chap. 5, n. 92, above.) See Nietzsche, *Beyond Good and Evil*, Aph. 202, 203; John Morley, *Voltaire* (London: Macmillan & Co., 1888), pp. 218-19. Cf. Rousseau, *Social Contract*, book 4, chap. 8:

> But I am mistaken in speaking of a Christian republic; the terms are mutually exclusive. Christianity preaches only servitude and dependence. Its spirit is so favourable to tyranny that it always profits by such a regime. True Christians are made to be slaves, and they know it and do not much mind: this short life counts for too little in their eyes.

(See chap. 2, n. 29, chap. 5, n. 92, above.) See Nietzsche, *Beyond Good and Evil*, aph. 202, Cf. Burke, *Works*, 4:12; Paine, *Writings*, 4:62, 195, 211; William M. Clyde, *The Struggle for the Freedom of the Press from Caxton to Cromwell* (New York: Burt Franklin, 1970), pp. 10-17, 33-40, 100-103, 224, 249-56, 271-74.

It would be hard, of course, to overestimate the influence of Christianity either upon our instittuions or upon modern man. A doctrine emanating from a Founder who died at thirty-three would be regarded, in ordinary human terms, as not likely to reflect the sobriety and moderation associated with age and experience. When most men raise their sights beyond this world, they tend to forget that prudence is, as Burke says, "the god of this lower world." Burke, *Works*, 2:272. We can see this independence in Tiresias' speech to Oedipus: "If you are tyrant, at least I have the right to speak in my defense. Of that much I am master. I am no slave of yours, but Loxias's [i.e., Apollo's]." Sophocles, *Oedipus* 408. This should remind of the New Testament, but with a vital difference: Tiresias, perhaps alone in his community, was God's slave and was thereby entitled to speak boldly; but with the coming of Christianity (and most evidently in Protestantism), all are today somehow Loxias'. Cf. pp. 252-53, above. ("What if one runs into trouble with a conservative hierarchy? 'A priest has only one boss,' [Archbishop Bernard J.] Sheil answers as he points a finger toward heaven." *Newsweek*, Mar. 20, 1967, p. 16.) The incarnation of God in man has (as Hegel observes) elevated the stature of every man. Seth Benardete has pointed out ("Sophocles' *Oedipus Tyrannus*," in Cropsey, *Ancients and Moderns*, pp. 1, 4):

> . . . Oedipus always speaks for the city as a whole. Tiresias, for example, eight times refers to himself emphatically as *ego*, but never to the city, whereas Oedipus five times in the same scene refers to the city and only once to himself as *ego*: "But it was I, the know-nothing Oedipus, who came and stopped the Sphinx" (396 ff.). Oedipus immediately interprets Tiresias' reluctance to speak as a dishonor to the city and just cause for indignation (339 ff.). Tiresias' silence has nothing lawful (*ennoma*) in it, nor is it an act of kindness to the city that nurtured him (322 ff.). . . .

It is also apparent that Oedipus' lone use in this scene of *ego* refers to the time before he became "citified": he is now one with Thebes; everything (he believes) can now be done and said openly; the distinction between private and public is obliterated in his personal patriotism, an obliteration which follows naturally for a man who has effectively "transcended" still another and related distinction, that between parents and child. Indeed, he is in some respects a "know-nothing." Is this a danger that one runs upon trying to know everything: that one will become unaware of (or, at least, not properly appreciative of) that which "everybody knows" (or, at least, cares for)? See the opening lines of Plato's *Apology of Socrates*. Cf. ibid., 34D. See chap. 9, n. 32, below. See, also, chap. 8, nn. 135, 186, above.

(For the philosopher, too, the "soul is elsewhere." See chap. 4, n. 103, above, chap. 9,

n. 29, below. See, for a discussion of prudence and philosophy, Anastaplo, "Human Being and Citizen: A Beginning to the Study of Plato's *Apology of Socrates*," in Cropsey, *Ancients and Moderns*. See chap. 8, n. 195, above. See, for a prudent comment upon Thomas Paine's *Age of Reason*, Samuel Adams's letter of November 30, 1802, to Paine. Paine, *Writings*, 4:200-208.)

See Paine, *Writings*, 2:431, on the constitution of each American state being (in 1792) "the political bible of the state." "Scarcely a family was without it."

10. I have found students in my University of Chicago adult education classes remarkably insistent on law-abidingness, much more so than one would expect from typical studies of the American attitude. Is this merely because such students are predominantly middle-class? (See chap. 7, n. 16, above. Cf. chap. 8, n. 27, above.) "No doubt our doctrine of constitutional law has had a tendency to drive out questions of justice and right, and to fill the mind of legislators with thoughts of mere legality, of what the constitution allows." James B. Thayer, *Legal Essays* (Boston: Boston Book Co., 1908), pp. 38-39. See Tocqueville, *Democracy in America*, 1:258; cf. Plato, *Republic* 563D. Cf. chap. 7, n. 77, chap. 8, n. 78 (beginning), above.

Indeed, it is difficult to induce such students seriously to consider the possibility of a better life elsewhere or (even more difficult) in an earlier age.

> Jefferson proposed [in 1785] that the seal of the United States should represent the children of Israel led by a pillar of light. . . . In 1801, [he] spoke of the United States as "the world's best hope" and in 1805 he declared in his second inaugural address that "God led our forefathers, as Israel of old." . . . [Thomas F. Gossett, *Race: The History of an Idea in America*, p. 179]

The significance, in this respect, of immigration (as part of the common heritage) cannot be overestimated: whether Americans are "the chosen people" must remain a question; but there can be no doubt that they are "the having-chosen people." Cf. chap. 9, n. 3, above. See, for comparisons of modern Israel and America, chap. 8, n. 150, above.

Even the disillusioned younger students among us see the best as yet to come, if it should appear at all, never as something which has come and gone.

11. See, on this statement by the German chancellor Bethmann-Hollweg, William H. Chamberlin, *Chicago Tribune Magazine of Books*, Jan. 20, 1963, p. 1. This virtually insane loss of control is evident in Barbara Tuchman, *The Guns of August* (New York: Macmillan Co., 1962). See, also, Woodrow Wilson, *The Political Thought of Woodrow Wilson*, ed. E. David Cronon (Indianapolis: Bobbs-Merrill, 1965), pp. 420, 442, 509-10, 513, 520; C. S. Forester, *The General* (New York: American Mercury, 1938); Churchill, "The Ex-Kaiser," in *Great Contemporaries* (London: Odhams Press, 1949).

> The last conservative statesman was the fifth Marquess of Lansdowne; and when he wrote a letter to the *Times*, suggesting that the First World War should be concluded with a compromise, as most of the wars of the eighteenth century had been, the editor of that once conservative journal refused to print it. The nationalistic radicals had their way, with the consequences that we all know—Bolshevism, Fascism, inflation, depression, Hitler, the Second World War, the ruin of Europe and all but universal famine. [Aldous Huxley, Foreword, *Brave New World* (New York: Harper & Bros., 1950), p. xxvi]

Cf. Harold Nicholson, *The Evolution of Diplomacy* (New York: Macmillan Co., Collier Books, 1962), pp. 103, 113-14; George L. Mosse, *New York Times Book Review*, Dec. 24, 1967, p. 3. Were the "half-baked" agitators during the First World War really sensible after all? Cf. pp. 257-58, above. See *Papal Thought on the State*, p. 116. See, also, chap. 8, n. 122, above (Charnwood on the abolitionists).

Churchill lamented in 1956 that Great Britain had "answered all the tests" confronting her in the twentieth century, but that "it was useless." Lord Moran, *Churchill* (Boston: Houghton Mifflin Co., 1966), p. 744. But had she not failed the first great test of the century, and in such a way as to make all later tests merely valiant rearguard actions,

CHAPTER NINE, NOTE 12: PAGE 276   785

by not stopping the First World War before it wrecked Europe spiritually as well as physically?

> When the British ruling class rushed headlong into the holocaust of 1914, they showed their total lack of political wisdom. . . . Whatever the courage of Churchill in 1940, it must be remembered that he was one of those in the Liberal Cabinet of 1914 who pushed their nation into the intemperance of the earlier disaster. . . . [Grant, *Lament for a Nation*, p. 72 (see ibid., p. 34, for a comparison of Churchill and de Gaulle)]

Should we not, in this context, say with Burke that prudence is "the first of all virtues"? Burke, *Works*, 4:68. (Cf., for a depreciation of prudence as "a substitute for principle, and so nearly allied to hypocrisy that it easily slides into it," Paine, *Writings*, 3:236. Paine displayed his "principled" imprudence in his public attacks upon Christianity. See, e.g., ibid., 4:151, 181-82. There is, on the other hand, *something* to be said for his characterization of one zealot as having "persecuted with as much heat as he preached thereafter; the stroke [which had driven him to change sides] had changed his thinking, without altering his constitution." Ibid., 4:177. See chap. 8, n. 74, above.

Vietnam threatened to become for us what the First World War was permitted to become for European civilization, a corrosive crusade undermining the community's aspirations and faith in itself. See p. 320, above. See, also, chap. 8, n. 150, above. (One need not assume, in reaching such a judgment, that the government of North Vietnam is better than that of South Vietnam: rather, there is every reason to believe that the northern regime is significantly more oppressive.) However that may be, the conscientious critic of American involvement in Vietnam should come to grips with the analyses and arguments found in the collection made by Wesley R. Fishel, *Vietnam: Anatomy of a Conflict* (Itasca, Ill.: F. E. Peacock Publishers, 1968). It is Fishel's opinion (ibid., p. viii) that

> the histories of this period . . . will probably show that many of the decisions made [by the United States] have been based not upon the recommendations of scholars or government experts specializing in Vietnamese and Southeast Asian affairs, but upon general political or other expediential considerations.

Still, is not the "explainability" or justifiability of a policy as much a predictable limitation upon government action in a regime such as ours as, for example, the range or effect of military equipment? I suspect, furthermore, that not even the most vigorous advocates of our Vietnam policy would long be comfortable in a regime or with a people which would accept that policy as it has been (or can be?) publicly presented, particularly since *considerable immediate* damage has been inflicted by us upon another people (in both South and North Vietnam) in order to spare ourselves *some possible* damage many years from now. There is, that is, an unconscionable disproportion here between means and ends —and the American people have come to sense this and to be troubled by it. Cf. Harold W. Rood, "Distant Rampart," *United States Naval Institute Proceedings*, Mar. 1967, n. 31. But see chap. 8, n. 192 (end), above. See, also, Burke, *Works*, 2:145:

> If you [the Parliament] do not fall in with this motion [respecting American taxation], then secure something to fight for, consistent in theory and valuable in practice. If you must employ your strength, employ it to uphold you in some honourable right, or some profitable wrong.

12. Cf. chap. 8, n. 148, above. Republican government with fixed terms of office, on the other hand, permits the public servant a better opportunity to resist for awhile the passions of the people. It is in this respect superior to a parliamentary republic. (Cf. Bagehot, *The English Constitution*, pp. 17, 25-26, 29, 117-18, 149-52. But see Don K. Price, "The Parliamentary and Presidential Systems," *Public Administration Review* 3 [Autumn 1943]: 318.) Since a President elected for a fixed term can rearrange his cabinet appointments, flexibility within that term is still possible. In the extreme case,

the elected President and Vice-President could resign, thereby transferring the presidency to the successor designated by law for that contingency. (The Twenty-Fifth Amendment [regulating presidential disability and succession] makes this emergency measure even simpler to effect.)

President Woodrow Wilson seriously considered just such a step in the event of Charles Evans Hughes's election in 1916. He wrote to his secretary of state on November 5, 1916, two days prior to his reelection (at a time when Presidents were still inaugurated on March 4):

> Again and again the question has arisen in my mind, What would it be my duty to do were Mr. Hughes to be elected? Four months would elapse before he could take charge of the affairs of the government, and during those four months I would be without such moral backing from the nation as would be necessary to steady and control our relations with other governments. I would be known to be the rejected, not the accredited, spokesman of the country; and yet the accredited spokesman would be without legal authority to speak for the nation. Such a situation would be fraught with the gravest dangers. The direction of the foreign policy of the government would in effect have been out of my hands and yet its new definition would be impossible until March. I feel that it would be my duty to relieve the country of the perils of such a situation at once. The course I have in mind is dependent upon the consent and cooperation of the Vice President; but if I could gain his consent to the plan, I would ask your permission to invite Mr. Hughes to become Secretary of State and would then join the Vice President in resigning, and thus open to Mr. Hughes the immediate succession to the presidency. [Woodrow Wilson, *Political Thought*, p. 85]

See, also, Lincoln, *Complete Works*, 2:568. Cf. Richard H. Rovere, "Letter from Washington," *New Yorker*, Mar. 23, 1968, p. 139:

> . . . A President who is willing to face personal defeat is a President liberated from all the requirements of political prudence. He can use all the great powers of his office for any ends he chooses. . . . Even if he should be repudiated by his party, he will remain President and Commander-in-Chief until January 20, 1969. It is a thought that heightens anxiety in many quarters here—and creates envy for those parliamentary democracies that can bring such a situation to an end within a matter of hours.

Cf. also Clayton Fritchey, "LBJ Infallible? Not Necessarily," *Chicago Sun-Times*, Nov. 25, 1967, p. 30; chap. 4, n. 56, below. Cf., furthermore, Gene Smith, *When the Cheering Stopped: The Last Years of Woodrow Wilson* (New York: William Morrow & Co., 1964); chap. 9, n. 14, below (the citations to Lord Moran's diary).

The provision for legitimate succession that republican government *can* make is illustrated by the remarkably smooth (even though unexpected) transition from President Kennedy to President Johnson and (even in time of war) from President Roosevelt to the relatively unprepared President Truman.

Does not the seventeenth chapter of Machiavelli's *Prince*, with its concern for the nature of various leaders, discuss this very problem? The seventeen sections of chapter 8 of this study are concerned with what may be considered the natural, as distinct from the historical and the constitutional, aspects of the problem of freedom of speech. See, in *Journal of the History of Philosophy*, 3 (Oct. 1965), at pp. 270-71, the comments on Moses Maimonides, *The Guide of the Perplexed* (Chicago: University of Chicago Press, 1963), p. xxx. See, in the *Guide*, 1:13, 2:13, 3:17, 1:17, 2:17, 3:13, 1:26, 2:26, 3:26. (See, also, ibid., pp. xxx, 272.) Cf. chap. 8, n. 57, above.

See, on Alexandre Kojève and literary playfulness, chap. 7, n. 120, above. There is about such playfulness (and the patterns exploited) a discipline which alerts the reader to the care employed in composition. (Similarly, we naturally esteem our waking life more than our dream life partly because of the greater respect for matter and the resulting discipline evident in our waking life.) See Leo Strauss, *Thoughts on Machiavelli* (Glencoe, Ill.: Free Press, 1958), pp. 52, 312 ff.; Hans Speier, "Grimmelshausen's Laughter," in Cropsey, *Ancients and Moderns*, pp. 198, 210, n. 70; chap. 6, n. 71, above. Cf. chap. 4, n. 40, above. An author, when challenged and disciplined by such considerations, is often led to study and hence know better than he otherwise might the material which he is obliged to mold to his pattern. In addition, he thereby comes to understand better than he might have before, the work of the very best authors, especially when his material will not yield to his efforts (because of its nature or because of the unperceptive interference of others [see the first paragraph of Book 10 of Henry Fielding's *Tom Jones*]). Thus, it has been observed of great poets that "the tyranny of rhyme [may] force them into the discovery of the finest lines." Marcel Proust, *Remembrance of Things Past*, 1:19. See chap. 8, n. 135 (end), above. Cf. chap. 5, n. 90, above.

In this connection, the reader may find helpful the following subdivisions in my article on Plato's *Apology* in *Ancients and Moderns* (chap. 2, n. 1, above): pp. 16, 17, 19, 20, 21, 23 (2), 24, 27, 29, 30, 32, 33. (The major divisions are at pp. 16, 20, 23.)

Consider the Roman "constitutional" relation (even with respect to numerical placement) between chap. 4, n. 15 and chap. 6, n. 51, above. Consider, also, chap. 7, n. 10, above.

13. Robert Filmer's *Patriarcha, or the Natural Power of Kings Asserted* (1680) drew from Algernon Sidney the following comment (*Discourses concerning Government*, chap. 2, sec. 11):

> But I do not more wonder that Filmer should look upon absolute Monarchy to be the Nurse of Vertue, tho we see they did never subsist together, than that he should attribute Order and Stability to it; whereas Order doth principally consist in appointing to every one his right Place, Office, or Work; and this lays the whole weight of the Government upon one Person, who very often does neither deserve, nor is able to bear the least part of it. Plato, Aristotle, Hooker, and (I may say in short) all wise men have held, that Order required that the wisest, best, and most valiant Men, should be placed in the Offices where Wisdom, Vertue and Valour are requisite.

The best of men are needed actually in office only in the most perilous times. In ordinary circumstances, the role of an educated bar is vital for the proper conduct of American republicanism—and makes it possible for the best to do what is necessary in extraordinary times. What I consider useful for the education of the bar should by now be evident to the reader of this book. The law schools should, in any event, take care lest their students deserve the reproach of Jonathan Swift, that lawyers "of all others seem least to understand the Nature of Government in general; like Under-workmen who are expert enough at making a single Wheel in a Clock, but are utterly ignorant how to adjust the several Parts, or regulate the Movement." *The Sentiments of a Church-of-England Man*. See Cicero, *Laws* 1.4.14. See, also, chap. 2, n. 1, above. However this may be, jurisprudence in American law is in a sorry state today, with rhetoric or sociology or anthropology or just plain chicanery mistaken for "legal reasoning." (See, e.g., chap. 8, n. 28, above.) Nor is it appreciated how dangerous an affront this can be to the sense of justice of ordinary men. See chap. 7, n. 77, chap. 8, nn. 84, 135, above.

See, on the relation of Socrates and Thrasymachus, Strauss, *What Is Political Philosophy?* (Glencoe, Ill.: The Free Press, 1959), p. 153; Strauss, *The City and Man* (Chicago: Rand McNally & Co., 1964), pp. 79-85, 123-24. See, also, chap. 8, n. 70, above.

14. Egotism should be distinguished from justified self-confidence. Consider the concluding paragraph in Winston S. Churchill, *The Gathering Storm* (Boston: Houghton Mifflin Co., 1948), p. 667:

> During these last crowded days of the political crisis [relating to the fall of the Chamberlain government], my pulse had not quickened at any moment. I took it all as it came. But I cannot conceal from the reader of this truthful account that as I went to bed at about 3 A.M., I was conscious of a profound sense of relief. At last I had the authority to give directions over the whole scene.

> I felt as if I were walking with Destiny, and that all my past life had been but a preparation for this hour and for this trial. Eleven years in the political wilderness had freed me from ordinary party antagonisms. My warnings over the last six years had been so numerous, so detailed, and were now so terribly vindicated, that no one could gainsay me. I could not be reproached either for making the war or with want of preparation for it. I thought I knew a good deal about it all, and I was sure I should not fail. Therefore, although impatient for the morning, I slept soundly and had no need for cheering dreams. Facts are better than dreams.

Cf. Moran, *Churchill*, pp. ix, xi-xii, 17-18, 452-53, 472-73, 476, 479-81, 487, 488-93, 502-5, 507-9, 665-67, 671-72, 679, 689-90, 768, 774, 837-40. But see ibid., pp. 436, 440, 443, 456, 473, 477, 510-11, 673-74.

15. Even a contemporary partisan of Abraham Lincoln, Carl Schurz, could acknowledge:

> . . . His equipment as a statesman did not embrace a comprehensive knowledge of public affairs. What he had studied he had indeed made his own, with the eager craving and that zealous tenacity characteristic of superior minds learning under difficulties. But his narrow opportunities and the unsteady life he had led during his younger years had not permitted the accumulation of large stores in his mind. It is true, in political campaigns he had occasionally spoken on the ostensible issues between the Whigs and the Democrats, the tariff, internal improvements, banks, and so on, but only in a perfunctory manner. Had he ever given much serious thought and study to those subjects, it is safe to assume that a mind so prolific of original conceits as his would certainly have produced some utterance upon them worth remembering. His soul had evidently never been stirred by such topics. But when his moral nature was aroused, his brain developed an untiring activity until it had mastered all the knowledge within reach. As soon as the repeal of the Missouri Compromise had thrust the slavery question into politics as the paramount issue, Lincoln plunged into an arduous study of all its legal, historical, and moral aspects, and then his mind became a complete arsenal of argument. [Carl Schurz, "Abraham Lincoln," in *Appreciations of Lincoln*, Riverside Literature series (Boston: Houghton Mifflin Co., 1899), pp. 26-27]

See chap. 8, nn. 152, 159, above. See, also, Moran, *Churchill*, pp. 825-26.

Lincoln could plausibly say, as could have Pericles, "[T]he public interest and my private interest have been perfectly parallel." *Complete Works*, 2:576. Cf. ibid., 1:13-14. See Thucydides, *History of the Peloponnesian War*, Book 2, chap. 65, sec. 8-9; Cicero, *Fourth Speech against Catiline*, sections 9-10. See, also, Strauss, *City and Man*, pp. 192-209; chap. 4, n. 117, above.

16. The thoughtful candidate in a democracy would do well to study the character and fate of Coriolanus as presented both in Plutarch and in Shakespeare. Cf. Plutarch, *Lives*, pp. 272, 292. See chap. 8, n. 133, above. See, also, in Churchill's *Great Contemporaries*, the articles on Lord Rosebery ("He would not stoop; he did not conquer." P. 6; cf. p. 294) and on Lawrence of Arabia. ("Part of the secret of this stimulating ascendancy lay of course in his disdain for most of the prizes, the pleasures and comforts of life." P. 127. It is a mistake, however, to regard someone who disdains "the pleasures and comforts of life" as without *eros*: it may simply lie deeper in him and be reserved for the worthiest objects. Such a man may seem cold and hard-hearted even to those who regard themselves as close to him. He merely awaits, whether in affairs of state or of the heart [if not of the mind], the appropriate occasion. He might even seem to make a fool of himself in such circumstances: but he cares too much for what he sees [or believes he sees] and is too sure of himself to care for public opinion. See Aristotle, *Nicomachean Ethics* 1097b32, 1123b1 ff. See, also, chap. 5, n. 126, above.)

Compare the (distinctively American?) assessment of mankind found in chapter 9 of Hawthorne's *Scarlet Letter*:

CHAPTER NINE, NOTE 17: PAGE 277

> When an uninstructed multitude attempts to see with its eyes, it is exceedingly apt to be deceived. When, however, it forms its judgment, as it usually does, on the intuitions of its great and warm heart, the conclusions thus attained are often so profound and so unerring, as to possess the character of truths supernaturally revealed.

This is to be compared to the opinion of the physician, a man intuitively recognized by the multitude as Satanic, who says (in chapter 4 of *The Scarlet Letter*),

> Believe me, Hester, there are few things hidden from the man who devotes himself earnestly and unreservedly to the solution of a mystery. Thou mayest cover up thy secret from the prying multitude. Thou mayest conceal it, too, from the ministers and magistrates. . . . But, as for me, I come to the inquest with other senses than they possess. . . .

(One notices, in chapter 9 of the novel, that devotion to one's art above all else is associated with the Satanic [see chap. 8, n. 193, above]: "But what distinguished the physician's ecstasy [upon making a great discovery] from Satan's was the trait of wonder in it!")

17. Lyndon Johnson, it has been observed many times, simply did not "come across" on television. See, e.g., Eric F. Goldman, *The Tragedy of Lyndon Johnson* (New York: Knopf, 1969), p. 8. On the other hand, it has been said by Mollie Panter-Downes of the July, 1970, general elections in Great Britain (*New Yorker*, July 4, 1970, p. 62):

> There is no doubt in the minds of Conservatives that the upset result of the election was [Edward] Heath's extraordinary personal triumph, won in spite of the polls and in the teeth of the most unflattering press comment possible. He and the public were told encouragingly that he lacked charm and the easy common touch, which Harold Wilson was demonstrating so abundantly in his campaign journeys around the country. He was too serious, too stiff, and even friendly journalists who accompanied his campaign sighed that, in contrast to Mr. Wilson's folksy, wisecracking strolls among the people, his set speeches were frankly boring. Yet what happened, quite clearly, was that large numbers of the British people gazed thoughtfully at Mr. Heath on the telly and voted for honesty when they saw it. *It was a win for character over skillful presentation.* He has no tricks, and Mr. Wilson, who all along had set himself up in confident comparison, knows every trick in the political game. It seems that the brilliant performer misjudged the audience. [Italics added]

The television exposure of the bullying tactics of Senator Joseph McCarthy during the famous Army hearings in 1954 substantially undermined his prestige and appeal.

Consider the editorial comment, in the *Manchester Guardian Weekly*, Nov. 27, 1958:

> The famous television broadcast in 1952, when [Richard M. Nixon] defended himself, his family, and his dog against charges connected with a hitherto undisclosed political fund, would have damned him here even more irrevocably than the allegations themselves.

See, also, Plato, *Republic* 489B; Bagehot, *The English Constitution*, p. 28; chap. 4, n. 22, above.

Compare the comments by Walter Lippmann and Joseph Alsop on the first television debate between two principal candidates for President, *Chicago Sun-Times*, Sept. 29, 1960, p. 40. Cf. chap. 5, n. 136, above. Such a "debate" reminds one that "personality" may be traced back to *persona*, the mask worn by the actors in Greek and Roman drama. See, on *persona*, chap. 6, n. 75, above. Cf. chap. 8, n. 166, above.

> We must either breed political capacity or be ruined by Democracy, which was forced on us by the failure of the older alternatives. Yet if Despotism failed only for want of a capable benevolent despot, what chance has Democracy, which

requires a whole population of capable voters: that is, of political critics who, if they cannot govern in person for lack of spare energy or specific talent for administration, can at least recognize and appreciate capacity and benevolence in others, and so govern through capably benevolent representatives? . . . Yet we must get an electorate of capable critics or collapse as Rome and Egypt collapsed. At this moment the Roman decadent phase of *panem et circenses* is being inaugurated under our eyes. . . . [George Bernard Shaw, "Epistle Dedicatory," *Man and Superman*]

. . . It grows more certain every year that the United States has to choose its President from what it judges to be the character of the man. The country and the world are too complicated for campaign programs and pledges to provide a reliable choice. The character of the man, especially at times of danger and strain, determines the kind of President he will be. [Flora Lewis, *Chicago Sun-Times*, Aug. 5, 1969, p. 28]

Consider the significance of Lawton Chiles's successful effort in 1970 to win election to the Senate from Florida, an effort which featured a walk down the length of his state in lieu of the conventional campaign on television (which he could not finance). (It might be salutary—and to this there need be no serious objection on First Amendment grounds—to limit all use of television for campaign purposes to speeches of at least fifteen minutes' duration. See pp. 122-23, above.)

See, on the discernment of the multitude, Marsilius of Padua, *The Defender of Peace*, Discourse One, chap. 13; Montesquieu, *The Spirit of the Laws* (New York: Hafner Publishing Co., 1949), 2:2. See, also, Walter Berns, "Voting Studies," in Herbert J. Storing, ed., *Essays on the Scientific Study of Politics* (New York: Holt, Rinehart & Winston, 1962), pp. 55-57; Leo Weinstein, "The Group Approach: Arthur F. Bentley," ibid., pp. 220-24.

18. Yet Philopoemen was criticized as unduly obstinate (an insistence upon having one's own way?). See Plutarch, *Lives*, pp. 466-67. Bacon (in bk. 2 of *The Advancement of Learning*) considers Philopoemen's time as that in which "the affairs of Graecia [were] drowned and extinguished in the affairs of Rome." Cf. Burke, *Works*, 2:141-42.

See Plato, *Republic* 592B, *Laws* 875C. See, also, chap. 9, n. 29, below.

19. Ultimately, we must confront the protests of Rousseau (which are distorted in contemporary "radicalism") that beyond the earliest stage of society, progress has been "in appearance so many steps toward the perfection of the individual, and in fact toward the decrepitude of the species." *The First and Second Discourse*, ed. Roger D. Masters (New York: St. Martin's Press, 1964), p. 151. (Should modern philosophy be regarded as the peak of individualism? Was not ancient philosophy aware, that is, that most men could, at best, be either enlightened [not philosophical] *or* civic-minded?) Compare, in Machiavelli's *Mandragola*, the expatriate Callimaco and the homebody (patriotic?) Messer Nicia. See Aristotle, *Politics* 1323b37-1324b5, 1328a18-22. See, also, chap. 8, n. 193, above. Did not Heidegger (chap. 2, n. 7, chap. 8, nn. 140, 193, above) attempt to be radically enlightened *and* radically civic-minded, with disastrous consequences? See the end of chap. 8, n. 195, and the end of chap. 9, n. 9, above. See, also, chap. 8, n. 135, above.

Cf. Lincoln, *Complete Works*, 1:9 ("The Perpetuation of Our Political Institutions"). See Harry V. Jaffa, *Crisis of the House Divided* (Garden City, N.Y.: Doubleday & Co., 1959), p. 183. See, also, chap. 5, n. 19, chap. 6, n. 43, chap. 9, n. 16, above, chap. 9, nn. 30, 38, below.

20. Shakespeare, *King Lear*, act 5, sec. 2, ll. 9-11. See, also, ibid., act 3, sc. 4, ll. 154, 174, 181.

Nature, with its variants, is used four dozen times in *King Lear*. Among the usages is that of nature as the original endowment of an individual in the sense of powers supplied, to be used as their possessor should happen to will; another usage is that of nature as the original endowment of a man, but with the powers guided toward definite ends by an order whose establishment is supported by the divine. The first of these usages is the villainous Edmund's; the second, the prosperous Lear's.

CHAPTER NINE, NOTE 21: PAGE 279

Edmund's life exposes what is wrong with his view of nature: to devote one's natural endowment to the service of base ends, in violation of all that should be respected—common morality, customs, law, age, and even the sources of one's being—leads ultimately to self-destruction. (It is true with Edmund, as with Goneril and Regan, that unnatural cruelty contributes to self-destruction.) But royal Lear, on the other hand, is insufficiently attentive to the difference between nature and the established order, to the limits set by nature on what law can command: this happens partly because he presupposes divine reinforcement of the natural order, ignoring thereby in human affairs the role of chance, the extent of evil, the need for prudence, and the place as well as the limits of law. The story of Lear and Cordelia points to that aspect of nature which is beyond the scope of law and political authority; the stories of the Gloucester family and of Lear's elder daughters point to that aspect of nature which should be subordinate to law and political authority. Thus, the play examines the relation between nature and convention among men. See Plato, *Laws* 875B-D. See, also, Leo Strauss, *Socrates and Aristophanes* (New York: Basic Books, 1966), pp. 211-12.

Lear is moved by his suffering not only to lose his faith in the divine support of the natural and hence of the political order, but even to regard nature as corrupt. Edgar disguised as a mad beggar becomes for Lear, disillusioned as both king and father, the model of natural man: "[T]hou art the thing itself; unaccommodated man is no more but such a poor, bare, forked animal as thou art" (act 3, sc. 4, ll. 111-13). The humbled king preaches patience to the blinded Gloucester, recalling man's beginnings: "[W]e came crying hither . . . the first time that we smell the air we wawl and cry . . ." (act 4, sc. 6, ll. 182-84). Edgar's filial sermon to Gloucester is (as we have seen) more comprehensive: "Men must endure / Their going hence, even as their coming hither; / Ripeness is all" (act 5, sc. 2, ll. 9-11). This sermon considers not only the beginnings, but the end and the middle of life as well: man's chief concern should be not with either the inception of life or its conclusion, but rather with maturation. The much-disguised Edgar is indeed the natural man, but in that full sense of nature which includes completion.

Lear divines more than he knows when he calls Edgar "philosopher" (act 3, sc. 4, l. 181). We are reminded, by the precepts and example of Edgar, of the classical view of nature: nature not only supplies the human powers but also ordains the ends which would most perfect those powers. Thus, nature is the general order of the cosmos, within which the activity of man can be only a part, but an essential part which alone can discern the meaning of the whole. The accomplishment of nature's ends depends partly on chance, partly on what man guided by law chooses to make of the materials and the occasions available to him.

It is characteristic of the self-reliant Edgar that he alone, of the major figures in the play, never uses the word *nature*. He makes use instead in speech of *gods* as well as of *fortune*, neither of which he otherwise relies upon. He may well be, in Shakespeare's world, *the* prudent man. (I have been permitted to draw, for these observations, upon a careful study made by Laurence Berns, which was delivered as a lecture entitled "Piety in *King Lear*," May, 1969, St. John's College, Annapolis, Md.)

I should note that we cannot accept without qualification the unphilosophical Lear's designation of Edgar as the philosopher. Perhaps, indeed, the model for Edgar, a man of action, respectful of his father and remarkably resourceful, is not any philosopher but rather Odysseus. (But see Plato, *Republic* 620C-D.) The model for all-demanding Lear, who, in his majesty, not only assumes divine endorsement of what he wills but even aspires to be as a god, could well be Zeus, that royal Zeus who is so independent of others as to be able by himself to bring forth a daughter.

One may even see in the aspirations and the careers of Lear and Edgar both the attraction and the limitations of political life. See chap. 9, nn. 30, 39, below.

21. Indeed, Achilles as well reverses himself with respect to this very passage in bk. 11 of the *Odyssey*. He says he would prefer life on earth as a serf to the role of ruler over the dead; but he also exults upon learning that his son on earth had distinguished himself in battle, something no serf's son would have had occasion to do. (I disregard for present purposes the question of the reliability of Odysseus as narrator of these tales

from Hades. I do notice, however, the similarity between Odysseus and Socrates. Plato, *Republic*, 390A. Socrates, too, tells a story of men beyond the grave, introducing it with a reminder of Odysseus' story. Ibid., 614B. See, for an even more important point of resemblance, ibid., 620C.) See, on earthly distinctions, Matt. 11:11.

"This ambiguity which could easily have been avoided, is due, as all ambiguities occurring in good books are, not to chance or carelessness, but to deliberate choice, to the author's wish to indicate a grave question." Leo Strauss, *Persecution and the Art of Writing* (Glencoe, Ill.: Free Press, 1952), p. 118. See chap. 8, n. 135 (end), above.

Even the Platonic epistles are not always what they seem (aside from the question of which are genuine, which spurious). See, for example, Plato, *Epistles* 8.363B: "'God' is at the head of the serious letter, but 'gods' [at the head] of the less serious." Cf. *The Works of Plato* (London: William Heinemann, Loeb Classical Library, 1929), 7:611 (see chap. 9, n. 36, below).

Socrates speaks of the ancient quarrel between philosophy and poetry. *Rep.*, 607B. Is Socrates' first attack on the poets (in bks. 2 and 3) from the perspective of the ruler (with the demands of the social order in view) while the second (in bk. 10) from that of the philosopher (who has, "since" bk. 3, been developed in the properly run city and who recognizes the poet as essentially imitative of the philosopher [see chap. 5, n. 126, above])? Socrates, we see, rehabilitates Homer; he even imitates the poets. See, e.g., ibid., 550C, 563C. See, also, Strauss, *Socrates and Aristophanes*, pp. 311, 313-14.

22. *Nature* is also used at Plato, *Republic* 514A, in introducing the story of the cave. See Maimonides, *Guide of the Perplexed*, pp. 271-72, 294-98, 332, 468, 571.

The selective silence of Socrates with respect to nature in his exchanges with Anytus in Plato's *Meno* is critical. See, for an exceptional introduction to that (or any other) Platonic dialogue, Jacob Klein, *A Commentary on Plato's "Meno"* (Chapel Hill: University of North Carolina Press, 1965). (An exceptionally accurate rendering into English of the *Meno* is available in a translation prepared by John Gormly for the introductory close textual reading tutorial of the Basic Program of Liberal Education for Adults, University of Chicago.) See, also, on the *Meno*, Laurence Berns, "Two Old Conservatives Discuss the Anastaplo Case," *Cornell L. Rev.* 54 (1969): 920, 924; Anastaplo, "Law and Morality: On Lord Devlin, Plato's *Meno*, and Jacob Klein," *Wis. L. Rev.*, 1967, p. 231; chap. 5, n. 94, above. See, on nature and natural right, chap. 5, n. 87, chap. 7, n. 77, above. (We do not appreciate the respect for, or dependence upon, different facets of nature exhibited by the *polis* in former times and by farm life today. Consider, also, the opening paragraphs in Alan Monk [an early pen name for Willmoore Kendall], *Baseball: How to Play It and How to Watch It*, Little Blue Book No. 440 [Girard, Kans.: Haldeman-Julius Publications, 1927], p. 5:

> "Baseball," says Manager Miller Huggins of the New York Americans, "is a thing that one cannot pick up—that is, become efficient in, without natural ability. Even constant practice will not make a good player out of a person that hasn't got the stuff in him."
>
> "Therefore," continues Huggins, "the first step in the process of becoming a good baseball player becomes a question of finding out whether one has native talent for the game. The second thing to do is to learn the game: memorize the rules, study the knotty problems given in most rule books, and become a master of the actual theory of baseball. And the third thing to do, and the most important one, is to practice. Although, as I have said, practice won't make a good player out of someone who lacks native baseball ability, it will make a much better player out of anyone."

See Plato, *Meno* [the opening questions]; chap. 7, n. 112, above, chap. 9, n. 32, below.) See, on the relation of "nature," "chance," and the "divine," Aristotle, *Nichomachean Ethics* 1179b22-24.

See *Alfarabi's Philosophy*, pp. 66-67; chap. 8, n. 28, above.

23. Glaucon, like us, listens as Socrates explains to Adeimantus how those naturally suited for philosophy may happen to become philosophers. Plato, *Republic* 496B-C. Or-

dinarily, the man eligible by nature for philosophical pursuits might be saved for philosophy if he should be so "fortunate" as to have been either exiled, born in an insignificant town, born to a lowly craft, or born sickly! Socrates' salvation—his daemonic thing—was rare, he adds. See, also, ibid., 492A, 493A, 578B-C, 592A; *Laws* 875C; *Meno* 99e.

See Plato, *Republic* 496D-E, 516C, 519D, 520A-E, on the self-preserving tactics of the philosopher in the ordinary city. See, also, the twenty-six-line central scene of Lessing's *Nathan the Wise* (act 3, sc. 6).

24. Many indications appear in the dialogue to confirm this suspicion. Thus, at *Republic* 539E, where it is clear that the discussion is about the training of the guardians in the best city, a return to the "cave" is spoken of. Glaucon is later led by Socrates to suggest that the best city may not be found anywhere "on earth." Ibid., 592B. (Cf. ibid., 599C-D.) One alternative is that it is "in heaven" (ibid., 592B); another, that it may be found not "on earth" but "beneath the earth"—that is, in the cave.

It is when we go beneath the ground that we become aware of the foundations of things. (See, on the graveyard scene in *Hamlet*, chap. 2, n. 39, above.) Glaucon, in his story of the ring of Gyges' ancestors—which was taken (stolen?) from a corpse beneath the ground—calls into question man's appetite for justice. Plato, *Republic* 359D-360E. This exposure of the underpinnings of what man says and does is countered by Socrates with an examination of justice and the consequent construction of the best city; but he, too, must go beneath the earth, in the stories which his citizens are to be told (ibid., 414B-E; see chap. 9, n. 27, below), in the story of the cave, and in the story of Er (ibid., 615A; see chap. 9, n. 26, below).

The light of the sun, it should be noticed, does not reach into the cave. Ibid., 516A-B. But then, political life, to the extent that it depends on opinion, is not conducted completely in the light of day. See chap. 8, nn. 135, 169, above. (The *Banquet* of Plato, with its discourses on love, opens with "I opine": consider how much even the "marriage made in heaven" depends on chance and opinion. Former lovers have been known to say of one another, "What did I ever see in her [him]?" See chap. 5, n. 126, above.)

See Judah Halevi, *The Kuzari* (New York: Schocken Books, 1964), pp. 143, 224, 259, 273. (To rise above the city is to rise from the grave?)

25. Opinion is vital with respect to the gods as well. "By Zeus" is the oath that comes from Glaucon at a crucial point, Plato, *Republic* 515B. See, also, Plato, *Epistles* 8.356D. Cf. Anastaplo, "Law and Morality: On Lord Devlin, Plato's *Meno*, and Jacob Klein," p. 249, n. 53.

26. Notice that the mouth of the opening into the earth (another cave?), described in the story of Er in bk. 10 of the *Republic*, is reported as bellowing and otherwise moving as if sensate, 615E. See, on the myth of Er, chap. 8, n. 59, above. (El Greco, in his *Adoration of the Name of Jesus* [ca. 1580], portrays the entrance to Hell as a large fish's mouth into which the condemned are fed.)

Rousseau speaks, in the opening sentence of the first chapter of the *Social Contract*, of man being born free but being "everywhere in chains"; Jefferson (chap. 9, n. 39, below) speaks of "the shackles" which should be "knocked off at the conclusion of this war"; Tocqueville (*Democracy in America*, 2:12-13) speaks of the danger that "after having broken all the bondage once imposed on it by ranks or by men, the human mind would [in a democracy] be closely fettered to the general will of the greatest number." See chap. 2, n. 3, above. Cf. Plato, *Phaedo* 67D. See, also, W. B. Yeats's poem, "To a Wealthy Man Who Promised a Second Subscription to the Dublin Municipal Gallery if It Were Proved the People Wanted Pictures," which concludes:

> Look up in the sun's eye and give
> What the exultant heart calls good
> That some day may breed the best
> Because you gave, not what they would,
> But the right twigs for an eagle's nest!

27. Everyone can see here what the "noble lie" really means: people are to be ruled

by "cheat and . . . illusion." Plato, *Republic* 515D. See ibid., 414B; cf. ibid., 382D. And this, we are told, is required by justice. "Falsehood," Aristotle reminds us, "is in itself base and reprehensible, and truth noble and praiseworthy. . . ." *Nicomachean Ethics* 1127a29. See ibid., 1127b25. See, also, Shakespeare, *Henry IV, Part 2*, act 4, sc. 2. James Mill warned, in his essay, *Liberty of the Press*, "[T]here is no safety to the people in allowing any body to choose opinions for them. . . ."

Blackstone, however, did defend legal fictions,

> these fictions of law [which], though at first they may startle the student, he will find upon further consideration to be highly beneficial and useful; especially as this maxim is ever invariably observed, that no fiction shall extend to work an injury; its proper operation being to prevent a mischief, or remedy an inconvenience, that might result from the general rule of law. [*Commentaries on the Laws of England*, 3:43]

(See ibid., 1:212-13, 2:2, 3:266-68, 350, 390.) See, also, Plato, *Republic* 378A, 381A-382C, 494A, 536D-E, 617E ("the blame is his who chooses") (cf. ibid., 413A); Cicero, *De Officiis* 1.41.148; Plutarch, *Lives*, pp. 805-6, 840-41; Kant, *Critique of Pure Reason* (New York: Cooperative Publication Society, 1900), pp. 420-21; Leo Strauss and Joseph Cropsey, *History of Political Philosophy* (Chicago: Rand McNally, 1963), pp. 341 (Bacon), 718-19 (Kant and Marx). See chap. 2, n. 1, chap. 8, nn. 178, 181, above.

It is said that false carding on defense in bridge is not usually recommended inasmuch as it is apt to fool one's partner as well as the opposition. But it is also said that some men do not "deserve the compliment of rational opposition." Jane Austen, *The Complete Novels* (New York: Modern Library, n.d.), p. 150. Thus, Mike Royko announced, in his *Chicago Daily News* column of Oct. 27, 1970:

> My choice for [United States Senator from Illinois] is Adlai Stevenson III, who has demonstrated that he is a sensible man. He started his campaign by trying to talk sense to the people. He found out that he wasn't getting anywhere that way, so he had the sense to throw in some double-talk and since then things have gone fine.

Or, as Jack Point suggests in Gilbert and Sullivan's *Yeomen of the Guard*,

> When they're offered to the world in merry guise,
> Unpleasant truths are swallowed with a will—
> For he who'd make his fellow-creatures wise
> Should always gild the philosophic pill!

(Does not Kant's transformation of the maxim discussed in chap. 8, n. 107, above, permit him both to seem unequivocal and to *be* sensible?) See Plato, *Charmides* 166D. See, also, Zetterbaum, *Tocqueville and the Problem of Democracy*, pp. 19, 21, 29-30, 89, 108-9, 116, 147, 155, 158, 160. See chap. 8, n. 97, above, for Edmund Burke's salutary reminder, "I could hardly serve you *as I have done*, and court you too." See, also, chap. 8, n. 135, above.

See, for the mandate of Avicenna with respect to these matters, Ralph Lerner and Muhsin Mahdi, *Medieval Political Philosophy* (New York: Free Press, 1965), pp. 100-101. See, also, chap. 6, n. 78, chap. 7, n. 60, above. Cf. Paine, *Writings*, 4:74. But see ibid., p. 202; *Alfarabi's Philosophy*, pp. 36, 41-42; Burke, *Works*, 4:19-20, 100 ("It has been the misfortune [not as these gentlemen think it, the glory] of this age, that everything is to be discussed, as if the constitution of our country were to be always a subject rather of altercation than enjoyment."), 148; 5:96. ("Political problems do not primarily concern truth or falsehood. They relate to good or evil.")

28. Yet, is this not what "freedom of speech, or of the press" looks like to the man who truly knows? See chap. 8, nn. 46, 161, 181, above.

I believe my study may *seem* vulnerable to the criticism that has been directed

CHAPTER NINE, NOTE 29: PAGE 281   795

against John Stuart Mill: "Mill's fundamental difficulty is that he wishes to combine a maximum of duty with a maximum of freedom without granting priority to either." Hilail Gildin, "Mill's *On Liberty*," in Cropsey, *Ancients and Moderns*, p. 301. See, in support of Gildin, Allan Bloom, "Jean-Jacques Rousseau," in Strauss and Cropsey, *History of Political Philosophy*, pp. 514, 532-33; Harry V. Jaffa, *Equality and Liberty* (New York: Oxford University Press, 1965), pp. 42-66. See, also, Willmoore Kendall, "The 'Open Society' and Its Fallacies," *American Political Science Review* 54 (1960): 972; chap. 5, n. 61, above.

    I have tried to reconcile in this book the demands of both duty and liberty, of both the *Apology of Socrates* and the Declaration of Independence. (See chap. 2, n. 1, chap. 6, n. 43, above, chap. 9, n. 39, below.) I realize, however, that an inevitable tension remains, a tension that comes in part from trying to adapt ancient teachings to our modern circumstances. One cannot help moving, in assessing our regime, between "It can't work" and "It works very well." My concern has been—by throwing old light on new problems as well as new light on old problems—to get away from the doctrinaire quarrels that our constitutional issues are often reduced to. See chap. 8, n. 3, above. See, also, chap. 7, n. 60, above.

    I have, in my argument about freedom of speech in the United States, kept in view a prudential rule taught by Tocqueville (*Democracy in America*, 1:172), "A proposition must be plain, to be adopted by the understanding of a people." I dare not, in order to anticipate the abuses of liberty, narrow the meaning of "freedom of speech," but rather indicate which governments need not be bound by that full meaning. See chap. 7, n. 107, above. (Even if I should be thought untimely in my suggestions about the role of the states, the principles of my definitions and of my allocations of power remain available for study and use. See chap. 8, n. 85, above.) I try, furthermore, to preserve the public character of that which is public and to respect the privacy of that which should be private.

    A *somewhat* successful effort to "live with" "inevitable tension" may be seen in the Constitution itself. The original document opens with "We the People" and closes with "the States so ratifying the Same." It opens, that is, with a proclamation of the aspirations of a united people; it closes with a recognition of the reality of disparate states. Both aspiration and reality were needed to make a people one and to make a constitution work. What was the ground upon which aspiration and reality could meet without overtly sacrificing either? It was ground which depended upon the reputations and dedication of the signatories to the document, upon recourse to the seeming unity of a "Unanimous Consent," and upon the common sense of the American people. Otherwise, there would be the bloody ground of civil war from which it would take more than a century to recover.

    29. An obligation of a similar character may be that of children to parents. See Aristotle, *Nicomachean Ethics* 1161b17, 1162a5, 1163b19. Cf. Plato, *Republic* 562E-563B (on the unnatural relation of parents and children in a democracy).

    The philosopher, in the ordinary city, does not throw himself into public affairs, preferring to mind his own business. Plato, *Republic* 500A-C, *Gorgias* 526C. He knows, as Bacon says (in his essay, "Of Great Place"), "Men in great place are thrice servants: servants of the sovereign or state; servants of fame; and servants of business." Cf. Plutarch, *Lives*, pp. 78-79. See chap. 7, n. 100, chap. 6, n. 1, above.

> While philosophy presupposes social life (division of labor), the philosopher has no attachment to society: his soul is elsewhere. Accordingly, the philosopher's rules of social conduct do not go beyond the minimum moral requirements of living together. Besides, from the philosopher's point of view, observation of these rules is not an end in itself, but merely a means toward an end, the ultimate end being contemplation. [Strauss, *Persecution and the Art of Writing*, p. 139]

See, also, Plato, *Republic* 499A; Harry V. Jaffa, *Thomism and Aristotelianism* (Chicago: University of Chicago Press, 1952), p. 199, n. 8, p. 206, n. 40; Jacob Klein and Leo Strauss, "A Giving of Accounts," *The College*, St. John's College (April 1970), pp. 1, 4-5. Cf. chap. 9, n. 9, above.

Strictly speaking, then, the person addressed in this chapter is not the philosopher. See Aristotle, *Nicomachean Ethics* 1095a26, 1162b34-36. See, also, *Alfarabi's Philosophy*, p. 49: "If . . . no use is made of [the true philosopher], the fact that he is of no use to others is not his fault but the fault of those who either do not listen or are not of the opinion that they should listen to him."

30. Naturally, the philosopher (as is the case with any thoughtful man) can present in this manner a much more decisive critique of his argument than anything his much less perceptive critics confront him with. See, e.g., Plato, *Republic* 540E-541B; also, the choice of Odysseus, ibid., 620D; Aristotle, *Politics* 1267a10.

Philosophy serves, in securing the truth, that desire for eternal things that other men seek in the life of pleasure (which culminates in the procreation of children) and in the life of politics (which offers both glory and dedication of oneself to a community that will survive). Aristotle, *Nicomachean Ethics* 1.5, *De Anima* 2.4. (See chap. 5, n. 126, chap. 8, n. 2, above.) The yearning of the political man may be seen in the closing sentence of the Gettysburg Address. See, also, Plutarch, *Lives*, pp. 71-72, 74; Aquinas, *Summa Theologica* (*Treatise on Law*), Q. 96, A. 1 (citing Augustine, *The City of God*, ii, 21, xxii, 6); Max Farrand, ed., *The Records of the Federal Convention of 1787* (New Haven: Yale University Press, 1937), 1:464.

The philosophical reservation with respect to political matters rests, in part, on the sobering (yet liberating) realization that

> thousands upon thousands of cities [have] come into existence, and, on a similar computation, just as many [have] perished. And have they not in each case exhibited all kinds of constitutions over and over again? And have they not changed at one time from small to great, at another from great to small, and changed also from good to bad and from bad to good? [Plato, *Laws* 676B-C]

See, also, Herodotus, *History* 1.5; Plato, *Republic* 497D; Hume, *Political Essays* (concluding paragraph, "Idea of a Perfect Commonwealth": "The world itself probably is not immortal."); Montesquieu, *Spirit of the Laws*, 11:6 ("Have not Rome, Sparta, and Carthage perished?") (cf. Joseph Story, *Commentaries on the Constitution of the United States*, 2d ed. [Boston: Little, Brown & Co.], chap. 38, sec. 1780); Rousseau, *Social Contract*, book 3, chap. 11 ("If Sparta and Rome perished, what state can hope to endure for ever?"); Blackstone, *Laws of England*, 3:325-27; Tocqueville, *Democracy in America*, 1:26. See, for a most revealing clearing among the affairs of the world, Andrew Marvell's wondrously complex poem, "An Horatian Ode upon Cromwell's Return from Ireland."

Americans like to think of the United States as imperishable: after all, they themselves are the government—and if it should perish, so must a vital part of themselves. See the passage from Lincoln in the text at chap. 7, n. 121, above ("through all time"); cf. chap. 7, n. 13, above ("untold generations yet to come"). See, also, chap. 6, n. 50, chap. 8, nn. 178, 186, chap. 5, n. 131, above. Cf. chap. 5, n. 97, chap. 8, n. 107, above.

Consider the tension with respect to these matters in the following remarks by Pericles to the Athenians (cf. chap. 7, n. 107 [end], above):

> . . . Evils that come from heaven you must bear necessarily, and such as proceed from your enemies, valiantly; for so it hath been the custom of this city to do heretofore, which custom let it not be your part to reverse. Knowing that this city hath a great name amongst all people for not yielding to adversity and for the mighty power it yet hath after the expense of so many lives and so much labour in the war, *the memory whereof*, though we should now at length miscarry (*for all things are made with this law, to decay again*), will remain *with posterity forever*. . . . [Italics added]

Thucydides, *History of the Peloponnesian War*, bk. 2, chap. 64. (The translation of Thucydides drawn upon here is, by far, the best one into English, perhaps indeed into any language; that is, Thucydides found in Thomas Hobbes a translator worthy of his Greek. The Hobbes translation is now available in the careful edition prepared by David

CHAPTER NINE, NOTE 31: PAGE 281   797

Grene and published by the University of Michigan Press, 1959.) See, also, Cicero's *Third Speech against Catiline*, sec. 11: but within a decade Caesar's time had come; indeed, it could be said to have come already, even as Cicero was celebrating the salvation of the republic by Cicero. Cf. Churchill in chap. 9, n. 11, above.

Consider, also, the choice of Odysseus in Plato, *Republic* 620C. One easily gets the impression that there is something Socratic about Odysseus and that consequently he knows what he is looking for. Does his choice suggest either that Socrates' "best city" does not, perhaps can not, exist anywhere or that the man who knows would not care to be a philosopher-king (or to live in the regime of the philosopher-king)?

31. Does not the usurper (cf. Banquo's nemesis) who is moved merely by the desire to make a name for himself (a literally childish objective) destroy, if he is successful, the very community by which he wants to be well regarded? That is, it is no longer the country which he knew, the country of his childhood and of his dreams. Such men—who deserve only to be forgotten—should be reminded of the sentiments of Henry Austin Dobson's "Fame and Friendship," "Fame is a food that dead men eat. . . . But Friendship is a nobler thing." See Aristotle, *Nicomachean Ethics* 1095b23-30, 1161b2-10 (chap. 8, n. 195, above); cf. Pascal, *Pensées and the Provincial Letters* (New York: Random House, Modern Library, 1941), sec. 6, 404, sec. 7, 425. See, also, Plato, *Republic* 576A-B, *Menexenus* 235B-C. Cf. Bacon, *The Advancement of Learning*, chap. 2, "acknowledg[ing] that which Cicero saith, borrowing it from Demosthenes, that *bona fama propria possessio defunctorum* . . ." (but see, in his essay, "Of Great Place," "*Illi mors gravis incubat, qui notus nimis omnibus, ignotus moritur sibi* [It is a sad fate for a man to die too well known to everybody else, and still unknown to himself].")); Jaffa, *Crisis of the House Divided*, pp. 210-11 (but see ibid., pp. 216-19, 225, 265). Consider Morris on Hamilton, chap. 7, n. 91, above. Consider, also, the unintentionally self-revealing (and self-disparaging) condemnation by Macbeth of his betters, "Why should I play the Roman fool and die on my own sword?" Shakespeare, *Macbeth*, act 5, sc. 8, ll. 1-2. See chap. 7, n. 115, above. (Consider as well the condemnation by Paine of Homer [*Writings*, 4:119]. Cf. chap. 9, n. 21, above.)

Handel's Solomon (*Solomon*, act 1, sc. 1) dismisses anyone who, "having all the substance lost, attempts to grasp a name." Cf. Pierre Bayle's comment on Alexander the Great (*Dictionary Historical and Critical* [London: J. J. and P. Knapton, D. Midwinter et al., 1734]), 4:4:

> He wept when he heard the Philosopher Anaxarchus say, there were infinite worlds [citing Plutarch, *de Tranquillitate Animi*, page 466]; his tears proceeded from his despair of conquering them all, seeing he had not yet conquered one. . . . The world was to Alexander [paraphrasing Juvenal], what a little island was to malefactors confined in it. If they were straitened in their walks, Alexander for his part looked upon the possession of the whole earth, as the misery of being reduced to a little corner. A Spanish author goes higher than Juvenal; he calls Alexander's heart an archheart, in a corner of which the world sate so easy, that there was room for six more. But does it not seem, that so vast a heart confined its happiness within very narrow bounds, when it proposed only to be praised by the Athenians? . . . Is not this, say some, to be at the same time insatiable, and yet contented with the least thing in the world?

Antonio de Oliveira Salazar was not permitted to learn in the closing months of his life that he had been replaced as premier of Portugal. *New York Times*, July 28, 1970, p. 1.

Consider, also, the despairing speech of Northumberland, Shakespeare, *Henry IV, Part 2*, act 1, sc. 1, ll. 68-81:

> How doth my son and brother?
> Thou tremblest, and the whiteness in thy cheek
> Is apter than thy tongue to tell thy errand.
> . . . This thou wouldst say, "Your son did thus and thus;
> Your brother thus; so fought the noble Douglas"—
> Stopping my greedy ear with their bold deeds;

> But in the end, to stop my ear indeed,
> Thou hast a sigh to blow away this praise,
> Ending with "Brother, son, and all are dead."

See Plutarch, *Lives*, pp. 1044, 1054, 1060, 1064-65; Aristotle, *Nicomachean Ethics* 1094a1-3, 1115a7-1117b21, 1129a3-1133b16, 1144a1-1145a11, 1177b16-26. See, also, chap. 8, nn. 186, 193, above.

32. One may find variations of this problem, seen in the relation between city and family, presented in plays such as Sophocles' *Antigone* and *Oedipus* and Aeschylus' *Oresteia*. (See chap. 7, nn. 35, 91, chap. 8, n. 2, chap. 9, n. 9, above.) Creon, invoking the claim of the city against the family, fails to discern that his authority comes to him through his family; Antigone, invoking the claim of the family against the city, fails to discern that her pride of family has been nurtured by the political role of her family in the city. Agamemnon is greeted on his return home as "king, sacker of Troy's citadel, and issue of Atreus." *Agamemnon* 783-84. But what he had to do to become the sacker of Troy (as well as to remain king?) corrupted his family relations and led to his destruction. (This juxtaposition is seen as well in the conflict in the *Eumenides* between the family-linked old divinities and the city-linked new ones.) Benardete says of the *Oedipus* ("Sophocles' *Oedipus Tyrannus*," pp. 2-3):

> . . . The play therefore moves from the question of who killed Laius to that of who generated Oedipus. It moves from a political to a family crime, which is, paradoxically, from the less comprehensive to the more comprehensive theme (cf. 635 ff.). Oedipus' discovery of his parents *silently discloses his murder of Laius*, but to discover himself as the murderer of Laius would not have disclosed his origins. Sophocles indicates this shift from one theme to the other by the absence of the word *polis* after its twenty-fifth occurrence at 880, the context of which is the denunciation of tyranny. Tyranny links the political and family crime. [Italics added]

Consider the shifting back and forth in the play between "one" and "many" murderers of Laius. See Benardete, ibid., pp. 5, 7, 14, n. 13. It is useful to notice that, although both Oedipus and the audience are convinced he did kill Laius, the evidence is not brought forth to support this conclusion; that inquiry is abandoned when Oedipus gets on the track of who he is. Sophocles leaves this vital question technically (legally?) open. (An identification of Oedipus as the murderer at the crossroads could easily have been brought in to round out the case if the author had so desired.) May not this be because the question remains essentially open? Who *did* kill Laius? One or many? Oedipus, alone, at the crossroads? Or Oedipus as an instrument of the gods, of the "fates," perhaps even of Laius and Jocasta, to say nothing of the city itself? The audience cannot help moving (without perhaps being conscious of it) from one assessment to the other (as does Oedipus himself in *Oedipus at Colonus*?). Does not this contribute to the timeless fascination, and even terror, of the play? One *is* responsible—and yet again one is not?

Consider also Antigone's "distracted" lines at *Antigone* 836-45: these reflect the fact that the family (one's parents and brothers) is for a child something "given," perhaps even natural. One realizes, on the other hand, that one's own husband or child depends upon marriage and hence upon the city. Thus, the lines which scholars dismiss as distracted, perhaps even as spurious, point not (as some say) merely to irrationality on her part but rather to her awareness of both her strength and her vulnerability. But awareness is not the same as understanding: and so she challenges a new convention (Creon's decree) in the name of an older one (which some mistakenly see as either natural or divine in its origin). And yet the city does depend on the very family that it legitimates: it is appropriate that Creon is destroyed through his family. See chap. 8, nn. 135, 169, above.

Consider, in Shakespeare's Roman plays, the parental influence on behalf of the Republic that is brought to bear on Coriolanus and Brutus and the absence of such influence on Julius Caesar. I can suggest the deterioration of the Republic by remarking that what Volumnia was to Coriolanus, Cleopatra was to become to Antony.

CHAPTER NINE, NOTES 33-34: PAGE 282   799

Creon's attitude is reinforced by contemporary anthropology: "Far from being the basis of the good society, the family with its narrow privacy and tawdry secrets is the source of all our discontents," said Edmund Leach, provost of King's College, Cambridge. "The family looks inward upon itself. There is an intensification of emotional stress between husband and wife, and parents and children." *Chicago Sun-Times*, Nov. 27, 1967, p. 5. But the political community would also be vulnerable to the anthropologist's invocation of "the good society," a society which (to the anthropologist) would be in principle worldwide but which is likely in practice to promote "individuality" at the expense of all communities as well as of the family. Cf., in Plato's *Meno*, the first attempt by Meno to say what virtue is (71E-72A): the attempt breaks down, something which Meno himself is perhaps aware of as he limps to his conclusion after a brave (i.e., self-centered) start. Socrates' use in an illustration immediately thereafter (72A-B) of the gregarious bee hints at the crippling lack of respect for the community in Meno's opinion about virtue. (An excessive emphasis upon community may be seen, on the other hand, in the Chorus in *Antigone* immediately after it is discovered that someone has defied Creon [ll. 332-372]: nothing is said, in the comprehensive anthropological history set forth there, about the family! This unnatural state of affairs invites and receives violent correction.) Cf., also, chap. 7, n. 35, chap. 8, n. 193, chap. 9, nn. 3, 21, above.

Cf., on *Oedipus* and *Antigone*, Martin Heidegger, *An Introduction to Metaphysics* (Garden City: Anchor Books, Doubleday & Co., 1961), pp. 90-91, 123-139, 143, 148.

The traditional relation between city and family is revealed by the license plates assigned to the household of Chicago's remarkable mayor, a revelation which reflects the fact that the "real man" is expected to lose himself in political life, while the woman is expected to devote herself to the life of the family. (See Thucydides, *Peloponnesian War* 2.45.) Thus, the license plates on Mrs. Daley's automobile bear the initials of her married name and the number in the street address of the family home; his license plates display the number of votes he secured upon his first election as mayor. They are said to be, as a couple, quite happy. See Plato, *Republic* 433A-E, 453B-D; chap. 7, nn. 59, 77, above. Cf. Plato, *Republic* 454D ff., *Apology* 31D-32A.

33. Perhaps it is sometimes necessary to point out and promote respect for the obvious: it is reported that Churchill, during the Second World War, responded to the complaints of those who said they could not understand what the war was about with the observation, "If Hitler wins, they'll soon find out."

". . . But perhaps Aristotle was even more of a Whig than of a trimmer—a Whig of the type of Locke or Burke. Every analogy has its defects and is no sooner stated than it has to be corrected. But if there is any modern climate which is the climate of Aristotle's *Politics*, it is the climate of 1688." Ernest Barker, *The Politics of Aristotle* (New York: Oxford University Press, 1962), p. xxxi. See Hobbes, *Leviathan*, chap. 21.

See chap. 4, n. 103, chap. 5, n. 140, chap. 8, n. 76, above; cf. chap. 4, n. 111, above; see, also, chap. 9, n. 7, above.

"It would not be difficult to show that the classical argument cannot be disposed of as is now generally thought, and that liberal or constitutional democracy comes closer to what the classics demanded than any alternative that is viable in our age." Strauss, *What Is Political Philosophy?* p. 113. See, also, ibid., pp. 306-7; chap. 4, n. 103, above.

34. I spoke at an Athens dinner in 1968 (see chap. 8, n. 161, above) of the intimate relation between free discussion and a free ballot (see Burke, *Works*, 3:9, 12):

> . . . We know that the most distinguished opponents of your proposed constitution—the politicians who we know have had popular followings for years—have been for some time under house arrest and will not be released before next Monday, and only then in order to be able to vote the following Sunday on the proposed constitution. It has been made clear to them that they are not to speak publicly against the constitution. How can it be said in such circumstances that a genuinely free referendum is being held, irrespective of how the balloting itself is conducted or comes out? . . . Yet, we have been told several times this evening that we are about to witness free balloting, that this is confirmed by the fact that some newspaper criticism of specific articles in

the proposed constitution has been permitted. But we Americans know what a free election is. We know this from our own experience. We know what a free election feels like. We know what it sounds like. We know what it looks like. And we know this is not it.

. . . We Americans do know what to think when we see government resources and government personnel marshalled as they have been here in a massive (and no doubt successful) campaign to produce the desired result. This is no more a free referendum than similar exercises are free either in Spain or in Russia.

And yet our host and his government have tried hard to persuade us that we are witnessing a genuinely free expression of the will of the Greek people. It seems important to them that Americans believe this. We Americans may not be informed enough about or familiar enough with Greek history and Greek affairs to be able to judge other claims of this government. But, as I have said, we do have the experience and the ability and the information to judge whether an election is truly free. And when we can see that this government claim about a free referendum, of which we have heard so much, is simply without foundation, what are we to think of all the other claims that we hear from the same government about what it has done for Greece, about what its motives are, about its innocence of deliberate torture of political prisoners, and about the imminent Communist danger from which it saved Greece by seizing power last year? Are we not entitled to judge what we may not know by what we can and do know?

. . . We have been speaking tonight of liberty. Liberty is what we Americans do know something about. And when an American visitor, who respects both the truth and Greece, is confronted as we have been at such length, not only tonight but ever since our arrival in Athens, by the insistence that liberty is to be found in Greece today, he is obliged to dissent, if he presumes to speak at all.

If what Greek citizens have now is what you mean by "liberty," then we should all reconsider what we mean by "the free world." ["Dissent in Athens," *Notes on World Events* (Chicago Council on Foreign Relations), May 1969, pp. 3-4; *Congressional Record* 115: E5156 (June 23, 1969)]

The vote "for" the colonels' constitution was 92 percent. Cf. chap. 4, n. 100, chap. 8, nn. 58, 85, above. See chap. 6, n. 1, chap. 8, n. 58, above. See, also, *Congressional Record* 116: 10520 (1970).

Consider also the significance of the unanimous vote in juries: every position held by each juror must be given some thought, some argument. See chap. 5, n. 105, above.

35. "Naïve" may be the frustrated politician's way of saying "constitutional." Senator William E. Jenner, who was then chairman of the Senate Internal Security Committee, had occasion to call Senator Robert A. Taft "rather naïve" for having announced (in what turned out to be the last year of Senator Taft's life):

I see no reason why the government should continue to employ people with Communist sympathies. On the other hand, it seems to me doubtful whether anybody ought to be fired from a job in a college or elsewhere if he is not using that job to spread and teach doctrines intended to undermine and overthrow the government of this country in favor of a Communist state.

Senator Taft was, at the time, a member of the board of trustees of Yale University. *Chicago Sun-Times*, Feb. 24, 1953; *Chicago Daily News*, Feb. 21, 1953; Ralph S. Brown, *Loyalty and Security: Employment Tests in the United States* (New Haven: Yale University Press, 1958), p. 15.

This was, I suggest, a resurgence in these matters of Senator Taft's essentially conservative attitude (which had found expression, for instance, in his questioning several years earlier of the Nuremberg Trials and of the Japanese evacuation from the West Coast [Grodzins, *Americans Betrayed*, p. 216]). And this was, one can believe, a repudiation of the desperately radical attitude (moved, in large part, by ambition) that had

CHAPTER NINE, NOTE 36: PAGE 283   801

driven a senator with a reputation for integrity to advise Senator Joseph McCarthy, three years before, to keep on making charges, suggesting to him that "if one case doesn't work [he] bring up others." *New Republic*, Apr. 2, 1951, p. 4. ("If one case doesn't work, try another." *New York Times Book Review*, June 21, 1959, p. 3) See, also, David E. Lilienthal, *The Journals* (New York: Harper & Row, 1966), 3:153, 416-17; *New Republic*, Feb. 4, 1967, p. 6; Acheson, *Present at the Creation*, pp. 364, 370; chap. 8, n. 169, above.

Constitutionalism is, at its core, deeply conservative. But, if it is to endure, it must avoid

> the typical mistake of the conservative, which consists in concealing the fact that the continuous and changing tradition which he cherishes so greatly would never have come into being through conservatism, or without discontinuities, revolutions, and sacrileges committed at the beginning of the cherished tradition and at least silently repeated in its course. [Leo Strauss, *Spinoza's Critique of Religion* (New York: Schocken Books, 1965), p. 27]

See Burke, *Works*, 4:23. ("A state without the means of some change is without the means of its conservation.") See, also, chap. 8, n. 150 (end), above. There is, on the other hand, something deeply radical in any serious examination of the very underpinnings of things, even though it is not done in the full light of day. See chap. 2, n. 39, chap. 8, n. 135, above. The influence of such examinations eventually makes its way to the surface of events. See chap. 8, n. 178, above. See, also, chap. 8, n. 76 (end), above.

Did Edmund Burke's intemperate denunciations of the French Revolution contribute to the "polarization" which led to the execution of Louis XVI, the Reign of Terror, and the subsequent upheavals in Europe? See Paine, *Writings*, 2:260-62 ("While Paine was endeavoring to make the movement in France peaceful, Burke fomented the league of monarchs against France which maddened its people, and brought on the Reign of Terror. . . ."), 3:114-127. The remarkable indignation (or, as Paine called it, ibid., 2:381, "rage") displayed by Burke in his political writings, especially on the French Revolution, may be related to the desperate effort, by a man with genuine philosophical talents, to secure in the world of action the occasional certainty promised by theoretical pursuits. Certainly, his writings on the Revolution need to be balanced by those of Paine, however superior Burke may be to Paine in the final analysis. Or, as Burke himself put it, "I have never yet seen any plan which has not been mended by the observations of those who were much inferior in understanding to the person who took the lead in the business." *Works*, 4:187. (The merit of Paine, despite his naïve and even sometimes irresponsible iconoclasm, is reflected in such sentiments as the following [*Writings*, 4:128]:

> To be happy in old age it is necessary that we accustom ourselves to objects that can accompany the mind all the way through life, and that we take the rest as good in their day. The mere man of pleasure is miserable in old age; and the mere drudge in business is but little better: whereas, natural philosophy, mathematical and mechanical science, are a continual source of tranquil pleasure. . . .

See, also, ibid., 4:178-79; chap. 7, n. 115, above.

See, on the "magical omnipotence of 'State Rights,'" chap. 7, n. 95, above. See, also, chap. 8, n. 10 (end), above.

36. Is not Karl Jaspers correct in saying (*Plato and Augustine* [New York: Harcourt, Brace & World, 1962], p. 53):

> . . . The scene of Plato's political thinking was an Athens which he recognized to be in a disastrous state. . . . He was not an impartial observer, but held himself in readiness. Beneath their cloak of irony, many passages in the dialogues are monuments to Athens.

("What Athens was in miniature America will be in magnitude. The one was the wonder of the ancient world; the other is becoming the admiration of the present." Paine, *Writings*, 2:424.)

R. G. Bury said of the Funeral Address recited by Socrates in Plato's *Menexenus*,

> [It] is obvious that the oration itself is largely intended as an illustration of the most glaring defect of current oratory, its indifference to truth. . . . This being so, we need not wonder at the historical misstatements with which the oration abounds, nor at its exaggerated encomium of Athens and her heroic sons; nor should it even amaze us, in such a connexion, that Aspasia and Socrates are supposed to be cognizant of Greek history down to [387 B.C.], a dozen years after Socrates died! [*Works of Plato*, 7:330-31]

It must be presumed that Plato's readers were as aware of Socrates' historical misstatements as are modern scholars: I suggest that the misstatements were designed both to expose the pretensions of Athens and to indicate what a city truly worthy of praise would look like. I venture to suggest as well that Plato wants us to notice that Socrates is dead: this funeral address (which reminds in some respects of Pericles') is to be understood as distinctively appropriate, for who knows better than a dead man what to say about dying and death? We are not told who the dead are for whom this address is given. Perhaps, indeed, it is Athens which has died, a prosperous Athens which has declined from both the civic-minded exploits of Marathon and the humaneness which had once tolerated a Socrates. See chap. 5, n. 131, chap. 8, nn. 131, 186, above.

The perils of prosperity are anticipated in Plato's *Critias*. (See chap. 5, n. 36, above. Cf. chap. 7, n. 63, above.) The teaching of the *Critias* may be adapted for modern conditions by Rousseau:

> Lands where the surplus of product over labour is only middling are suitable for free peoples; those in which the soil is abundant and fertile and gives a great product for a little labour call for monarchical government, in order that the surplus of superfluities among the subjects may be consumed by the luxury of the prince: for it is better for this excess to be absorbed by the government than dissipated among individuals. I am aware that there are exceptions; but these exceptions themselves confirm the rule, in that sooner or later they produce revolutions which restore things to the natural order. [*Social Contract*, book 3, chap. 8]

Does our space program serve for us in the place of such a monarchy? Cf. Walter Lippmann, *Newsweek*, Feb. 13, 1967, p. 31. But see Anastaplo, "Natural Right and the American Lawyer," *Wis. L. Rev.* 1965: 339, n. 45.

See Montesquieu, *Spirit of the Laws*, 18:1, 2, 3, 4, 17, 20:3; also, chap. 8, n. 192, above.

37. Our recourse to political suppression tends to bring out the worst in both persecutor and victim. (The quotation in the text is from *Federalist*, pp. 570-71, where it is said of the proposed constitution that it "is the best which our political situation, habits, and opinions will admit.")

Algernon Sidney observes (*Discourses concerning Government*, 2:11):

> Machiavel discoursing of these matters, finds Vertue to be so essentially necessary to the establishment and preservation of Liberty, that he thinks it impossible for a corrupted People to set up a good Government, or for a Tyranny to be introduced if they be vertuous; and makes this Conclusion, That where the matter (that is, the body of the People) is not corrupted, Tumults and Disorders do no hurt; and where it is corrupted, good Laws do no good: Which being confirmed by Reason and Experience, I think no wise man has ever contradicted him.

It should be added—and for this the authority of Machiavelli should be evident—fearfulness can prevent a calm approach to foreign affairs and thereby lead to actions that only make matters worse and insure the results most feared. See chap. 7, n. 72, above.

> . . . Russians have learned over the centuries to live happily behind masks. In America, every thought, however banal or insincere, must be fully and open-

CHAPTER NINE, NOTE 38: PAGE 285   803

ly displayed. Those long, relaxed denunciations of the Government's policy in Vietnam which are a commonplace of American television make Russia look light-years behind in political maturity. [Nigel Gosling, *London Observer*, Sept. 17, 1967, p. 17]

See chap. 5, n. 42, chap. 8, n. 169, above. Cf. chap. 2, n. 3, above.

38. No doubt, also, even our regime will eventually confront dangers which it cannot survive, no matter how prudent we may be. (See chap. 9, n. 30, above.) But longevity based on good sense, justice, and self-restraint is not without significance in encouraging others to cherish among men decent regimes, regimes in which the essentially human can be nurtured, reaffirmed, and thereby perpetuated. Thus, we should say in our circumstances what Plato said in his (*Epistles*, viii. 354A):

> If, therefore, any man knows of a remedy that is truer and better than that which I am now about to propose, and puts it openly before us, he shall have the best right to the title, Friend of Greece. The remedy, however, which commends itself to me I shall now endeavor to explain, using the utmost freedom of speech [*parresia*] and a tone of impartial justice.

Does not the possibility of the perpetuation of the essentially human help make our own existence meaningful? That is, may not the human thus continue to be both knowing and knowable? See chap. 8, n. 186, above.

One other thing which should be said in our circumstances is what Nichols has said:

> . . . The statesmen of [1787] had decreed a distribution of power among a variety of units and agencies, with some provision for expansion and periodic redistribution of the power to govern, all done up in a neat system of checks and balances. Such a structure could only have been contrived at the end of the eighteenth century, for only then were men naive enough and brave enough to put their trust in such a rational scheme as adequate to regulate a most confused and irrational society. [Roy F. Nichols, *Blueprint for Leviathan: American Style* (New York: Atheneum, 1963), p. 197]

Cf. chap. 8, n. 74, above.

See, on the distribution of powers among our military, Richard Harwood and Laurence Stern, "Did McNamara Build a Monster at the Pentagon?" *Milwaukee Journal*, June 29, 1969, p. 8 (cf. chap. 8, nn. 16, 77, chap. 9, n. 11 [end], above):

> The Kennedy administration, [some say,] took office with the avowed aim of establishing greater civilian control over the military. Yet the harsh fact is that military considerations today play a greater role in determining American policy than at any time in our national history. In the name of efficiency, we unified the operations of the armed services, introduced the techniques of computer management and encouraged closer interactions between the military and industry. As a result, power once checked by rivalries and inefficiency is now wielded as a single force, defying effective democratic control. . . .
>
> We should be clear on one thing: It is not the uniformed military that has created the present situation, but the civilian leadership and the institutions they have created to centralize and expand the performance of national security functions. The old hawk, Sen. Richard Russell of Georgia, who ran the armed services committee for many years, has come to the same conclusion.

See chap. 4, nn. 47, 49, 84, chap. 5, n. 26, chap. 7, n. 72, chap. 8, nn. 161, 179, above.

Are we still entitled to believe, as did the men of the eighteenth century, in the powers of reason to guide the conduct of human affairs? What, for instance, are the effects of the revolutions represented by the names of Copernicus, Darwin, and Freud? (See Leo Strauss, *Natural Right and History* [Chicago: University of Chicago Press, 1953], p. 12. See, also, chap. 7, n. 34, chap. 9, n. 3, above.) The Copernican revolution is both the most and least troublesome of the three: most, in that it makes it difficult for modern man to locate a steady point by which he may take his bearings; least, in that it is no more than a "confirmation" of a theory intelligent men have always recognized as possible. Men have always recognized as well that the human being progresses from the irrational to the rational (that is, from infancy to maturity): the rational is the culmination and fulfillment. But, the Darwinian may say, whereas it had been assumed that nature "intended" such culmination, "we now know" that nature does not really "care." Still, do not certain criteria with respect to rationality govern when the rational element is (even if only fortuitously) crystallized? Does not evolution theory account merely for the determination and emergence of the material vehicle in which the rational element appears and for the chemical and other causes of the desiring parts (whatever they have happened to become) of the human being? (Cf. chap. 9, n. 3, above.) The claims of Freud must confront at least two challenges (however useful his teaching may be, if only because of the experience and reputation of practitioners, in treating patients). First, is his teaching (and that of his disciples) sensitive to serious moral questions? See, e.g., Freud's heavy-handed analysis of "the case of Dora." Second, is his teaching really equipped to understand the rational human being? Consider two passages, one from the beginning, the other toward the end, of a talk I gave at the National Institutes of Health, Bethesda, Md., October 17, 1969, in a symposium, "Ethical and Social Problems in Neuro- and Psychobiological Research" (with special emphasis on current brain research):

> . . . Is knowledge indeed possible of the transitory things which are the objects of current scientific research? Or, more precisely, is knowledge of these things possible through the use of modern science? This may well be the most serious question we could examine today, the question of whether modern science is capable of knowing anything, of knowing anything significant—but it is a question which transcends the purpose of this symposium. We are not equipped to examine it at this point—but I do venture the suggestion that this may underlie your concerns and our inquiries. (This is related, I further suggest, to the question of the nature of the human soul and of its full development.)
> . . . Perhaps I can put in a much more practical form than I have yet done today my challenge as to the validity of much of contemporary research into how our minds work. Are we, indeed, on the way to learning the truth about this matter? I gather that it seems to be generally believed among the acknowledged specialists that we have today "a better understanding than ever before of how our minds work" (as someone observed this morning). My impression is, however, that this "better understanding" (if it be so) is accompanied by less competence in the *use* of the mind than has been evident for two or three thousand years. For one thing, we are less likely than have been our more thoughtful predecessors to recognize the truly important questions (both theoretical and practical) and to direct our minds to such questions, despite the fact that these questions have been long identified and discussed on the highest levels. That is, we no longer recognize the best working of the human mind; we no longer regard such working with respect; we are no longer moved to emulate it. This lowering in the level of intellectual competence suggests to me that we do not appreciate and hence cannot readily investigate how our minds work. That is, we see minds working less well than they have heretofore, and we do not seem equipped to notice that this is so. . . .

See Kurt Riezler, *Physics and Reality: Lectures of Aristotle on Modern Physics* (New Haven: Yale University Press, 1940); Jacob Klein, *Greek Mathematical Thought and the Origin of Algebra* (Cambridge: M.I.T. Press, 1968); Leo Strauss, *Xenophon's Socratic Discourse: An Interpretation of the Oeconomicus* (Ithaca: Cornell University Press, 1970), p. 209:

> In both the *Oeconomicus* and the *Hiero* [of Xenophon] the wise man is presented partly as a teacher and partly as a pupil of a nonwise man. In the *Hiero* the wise man instructs a tyrant in the ways of beneficent tyranny after the tyrant had instructed him about the shortcomings of the tyrant's life. In the *Oeconomicus* the wise man instructs the son of a gentleman-farmer in both perfect gentlemanship and farming after a gentleman-father had instructed him in both subjects.

CHAPTER NINE, NOTE 39: PAGE 285   805

See, also, Allan Bloom, *The Republic of Plato* (New York: Basic Books, 1968), p. 464, n. 39; Seth Benardete, *Herodotean Inquiries* (The Hague: Martinus Nijhoff, 1969), p. 37, n. 17; Robert D. Sacks, *A Commentary on Genesis* (Annapolis-Santa Fe: St. John's College, n.d.), on Gen. 8:21:

> God's reaction to the sacrifice [by Noah] is mixed. It leads him to promise never to consider total destruction again. But the grounds for that decision is an acceptance of a lower standard. The Torah in general may be viewed as a search for the highest possible standards to which it is reasonable to expect man to attain. In his respect for man God starts at the very highest and from there a Way is found.

The revolution represented by the name of Marx seems to me subordinate to, and less interesting than, the other three I have just touched upon. The nature and practical effects of communist doctrine are considered at the places indicated in the index. The prudent man must wonder whether the Katyn Forest Massacre is the sort of thing one must expect from such doctrines. (Cf. pp. 258-59, 750-53, above.) However that may be, there *is* about twentieth-century communism a shoddiness which has a "chilling effect" upon generosity, rationality, and nobility among men. It is such shoddiness which was all too evident as well in the anticommunist posturings of my bar admission authorities in Chicago, Springfield, and Washington. Are not, that is, the delusions and shallowness of modernity to be found among self-righteous partisans on both sides of the "barricades"?

In any event, the typical partisan needs to learn what the Declaration of Independence teaches, that decent communities are not easy to come by or to preserve, that we should be respectful of what we *do* have. He also needs to learn what it means to learn and to know.

39. See Justice Black, dissenting, *In re George Anastaplo*, 366 U.S., at 116 (concluding sentence) (1961). (His dissenting opinion is reproduced at pages 367-79, above.) Tapes of the 1960 oral arguments in the bar admission cases are now available from the National Archives and Records Service. (See pp. 362-65, above.) The listener to such tapes will find it difficult thereafter to detect in the current bar admission and "conspiracy" cases the sense of desperation evident in the civil liberties (as distinguished from the civil rights) cases of the 1950s. Cf. p. 405, above: "we happy few." (The *current* bar cases even have groups of law students "taking the offensive" [see p. 404, above]; my contemporaries, on the other hand, took pains a generation ago to keep their distance from any possible contamination. See, e.g., pp. 333, 380, above.) However quiescent the bar admission cases of the 1950s may be today, they do remain all too convenient precedents to be exploited "the next time around" by the frightened, the ignorant, and the self-seeking. The same may be said of the dormant, but even more dangerous, precedents of *Dennis* and *Schenck*. (In all such unconstitutional assaults, the respect for evidence within even a decent community is an early casualty. This may be seen in the tapes I have referred to.)

Should we not extend to political matters the advice given in 1781 by Jefferson (*Notes on Virginia*, Query xvii) with respect to Virginia's quiescent tyrannical laws respecting religion? He warned his readers, "From the conclusion of this war we shall be going down hill. . . . [The people] will forget themselves, but in the sole faculty of making money, and will never think of uniting to effect a due respect for their rights. The shackles, therefore, which shall not be knocked off at the conclusion of this war, will remain on us long, will be made heavier and heavier, till our rights shall revive or expire in convulsion." May not the repudiation of the Sedition Act of 1798, if not the enactment of the First Amendment itself, be usefully regarded as just such a deliverance from certain shackles?

Has the country indeed been "going down hill" since the constitutional exploits of 1776-1791 when there was bestowed upon our institutions a "bloom of newness" which nevertheless reminds of the oldest and even of eternal things. (See Plutarch quotation facing title page, above.) It is the new that the liberal, in his ardor for liberty, seeks; it is the old that the conservative, in his respect for order, admires. One cherishes established craftsmanship; the other welcomes daring experiment. The American is the product of repeated attempts to blend these two approaches to political life, approaches which can be said to be represented for us by Jefferson on the one hand and Publius (of the *Federalist*) on the other. (See chap. 2, n. 3, above.)

This common enterprise of liberals and conservatives in pursuit of justice is furthered, and given a special quality, by the role an often divided Supreme Court has long played in our political life. If, as has been said, every political question in America becomes eventually a subject for judicial debate, what happens in front of, and with a view to, the nine justices is vital: we may thus benefit from an informed, refined, and restrained (and hence genuine) freedom of speech exercised before a tribunal which is both aristocratic and popular, a tribunal which is always in need of serious support and even more serious instruction.

This would be reason enough for the education and character of the American bar and bench to remain of critical concern to everyone worthy of the demanding title of "American citizen." But one cannot begin to think seriously about the education of any citizen (an education which should take care not to promote either cynicism or indignation) without considering what education itself means independent of immediate practical consequences and applications. Thus, to begin to understand liberty, chance, and order in human affairs one should have some awareness—either from one's own studies or from those of others—of what change and stability may mean even with respect to inanimate things.

We have been moving, as we have prepared to close (if not throughout this book), from the mundane concerns of the politically-minded Publius to the more enduring concerns and diversions of *the* human being, even to a preliminary examination of that very activity of the reason which may be the most remarkable product as well as the ultimate justification of the community established and preserved by political men. That activity itself, dedicated at its best to understanding for its own sake, *can* be decisively affected by chance—and not only because it seems to depend upon the existence of men and community (which are themselves to some extent subject to chance). Thus, chance may be seen even in the emergence of the problems one happens upon, problems which may in turn point to enduring questions, if not to eternal things. (Chance may be seen as well both in the teachers one discovers or is discovered by and in the capacities one is provided by nature.

Consider, for example, the following challenge (as reported by a mathematician) which one may chance to encounter:

> Collective models of the nucleus [of the atom] have not lacked successes. But many details have eluded them. Take, for example, the seemingly haphazard numbers 2, 8, 20, 28, 50, 82, and 126. Physicists call them magic numbers, a name harking back to the days when the numbers were less well understood than they are now. The magic numbers have special nuclear significance; among the many hundreds of known nuclei, those containing just these numbers of neutrons or protons stand out from the rest because of their greater stability and other tell-tale signs. Clearly they reflect fundamental properties of the possible configurations of nuclear matter. They present a prime challenge to any nuclear theory. [Banesh Hoffmann, *The Strange Story of the Quantum*, 2d ed. (New York: Dover Publications, 1959), p. 239]

The author goes on to explain that "the shell model theory," which "goes back to the earliest days of nuclear quantum theory," "brilliantly met the challenge." However that may be, one can continue to be intrigued by this series of seven numbers and to speculate about it in a manner appropriate (in an age which boasts of its "scientific" political science) for the conclusion of this study, a conclusion which should have the merit and hence run the risk of pointing beyond both this study and the merely political. We can try to move, that is, from that which is occasional to that which is permanent, including the decisive permanent question of what it is to know (whether the knowledge be of Adam or atoms). See the very end of the *Leviathan* for the return of one of my predecessors, at the conclusion of *his* study of political things, to an "interrupted Speculation of Bodies Naturall." (See, also, the opening exchange of his *Dialogue between a Philosopher and a Student of the Common Laws of England*.) Cf., for the perils of such speculation, Isaac Disraeli, "Hobbes's Quarrels with Dr. Wallis, the Mathematician," *Quarrels of Authors* (New York: Eastburn, Kirk & Co., 1814), 2:145-46 ("[Hobbes's] *Amata Mathemata* was a war of idle ambition; it became his pride, his pleasure, and his shame"), 146-47, 148 ("he had always much to say, from not understanding the subject of his inquiries"), 162 ("[Hobbes,] though a most energetic reasoner, [was] so little skilful in these new studies [geometry], that he could never know when he was confuted and refuted"). Cf., also, Plato, *Phaedo* 96A ff. But see Plato, *Republic* 546B-D, 549C ff., *Laws* 737C ff., 771A ff. See, also, Plato, *Phaedo* 96E-97C, *Timaeus* 53A ff., *Epinomis* 976C ff. (Is it certain, by the way, that Hobbes *was* altogether mistaken?)

One obvious feature of the challenging series of numbers which happens to be offered us by the mathematician (2, 8, 20, 28, 50, 82, and 126) is that the seven are all even numbers. Is evenness, one must wonder, a necessary but, of course, not a sufficient cause of the stability reported? Perhaps it would be instructive to consider these nuclei as doubled versions of simpler arrangements. That is, why should we not consider evenness the result of a doubling (or "folding over") effect, thereby "permitting" the object to be less vulnerable (or more cohesive) in that it is "able" to present two similar "sides" "to the world"? (It is not unusual in nature to find unity or strength in pairs, to see a doubling or coupling as a completion. One is reminded of the intuition of Plato's Aristophanes in the *Banquet*. See chap. 5, n. 126, above. See, also, Genesis 2:18. Cf. ibid., 3:12. Nor is it unusual to find in both nature and literature that number is a key to understanding. See, e.g., "The Catalogue of Ships" in Book 2 of the *Iliad*, which has the contingent of the prudent Odysseus central to the array of Achaean ships at Troy, with the contingents of the two great contenders, Agamemnon and Achilles [each with his special claim to preeminence], at an equal distance on either side of the unifying Odysseus. The contingents among the Trojans, we also notice, are one-half those of the much more complicated [and hence much more interesting] Achaeans.)

By halving our seven numbers, then, we can be said to elicit the "simpler arrangements" I have posited. Thus, we are left with this series to conjure with: 1, 4, 10, 14, 25, 41, and 63. Now we have both odds and evens—and perhaps an even more challenging series of numbers, if only in that there has been eliminated one obvious feature (evenness) which had contributed to the unity of the original series. How are *these* seven numbers distinctive? That is, in what are they distinctively alike? Each one is the sum of different squares of whole numbers: that is, each is the sum of squares of whole positive numbers in which sum no square is used more than once. This seemed to me when I first figured it out (it happened to be in Athens in the summer of 1966) rather remarkable, considering the fact that within the range these numbers fall (1-63) there are 40 numbers which are sums of disparate squares, 23 which are not. This still seems to me remarkable. (Even more remarkable may be the explanation which the original seven numbers may merely reflect.)

I note in passing—and what happens to be "in passing" in such matters can turn out to be more interesting than the main line or original purpose of one's inquiry—that I have discovered, upon calculating further, that there are only 31 whole numbers which are *not* sums of squares (in my sense of this designation, since obviously every whole number is the sum of squares if particular squares of whole positive numbers, and especially 1, may be used more than once to make up the number). The 31 numbers which I believe to be thus are 2, 3, 6, 7, 8, 11, 12, 15, 18, 19, 22, 23, 24, 27, 28, 31, 32, 33, 43, 44, 47, 48, 60, 67, 72, 76, 92, 96, 108, 112, and 128. That is, I believe it can be demonstrated that all whole numbers greater than 128 are sums of disparate squares. I have been intrigued and even reassured to discover, in the course of my calculations, that central to this series of 31 special numbers is the number 31 itself. Why all this should be so—and, indeed, what "why" means here—I do not yet know: it is almost as if "number" reasserts itself (here as elsewhere?) by "ruling" in this manner even the "unruly" numbers. See Plato, *Epinomis* 990C; chap. 6, n. 43, chap. 9, n. 12, above. (Nor do I yet know whether others before me have noticed these things: but I do know that the instruction and entertainment one may derive from such inquiry do not depend, ultimately, on that form of "self-expression" which is so self-centered as to emphasize "originality." The existence of such relations among numbers, it should be noticed, does not depend on *will* but rather reflects the nature of things: will and chance may affect their discovery, not their being. [My calculations with respect to the distribution of sums of squares have recently been confirmed for me on an IBM 1130 computer through the courtesy of Hans Neumann and Michael J. Carone of C. F. Murphy Associates. It should also be noticed, in passing, that there are thousands of numbers which are not sums of disparate *cubes*: at the level of 10,000, I find that one-fourth of the numbers still are not sums of cubes.]) Let us return to the point from which we digressed at the end of the preceding paragraph.

Thus, although more than one third of the numbers (between 1 and 63) within which the second series of seven (halved) numbers falls are *not* sums of disparate squares, all seven of these numbers are sums of disparate squares. Why should this be so? It is difficult (as well as uninteresting and unproductive) to dismiss this remarkable uniformity as a mere coincidence. (This uniformity becomes even more striking when one notices that more than one-half of the numbers [between 1 and 25] within which the first five numbers [1, 4, 10, 14, 25] fall are *not* sums of disparate squares.) Perhaps this uniformity has something to do—and on this the "shell model theory" may be, for all I know, useful—with the stability reported in the nuclei from which these numbers are said to be drawn. (The original series of seven numbers, it should be noticed, does not have this uniformity but rather approximates what would be a random distribution: that is, only four of *those* seven numbers are sums of disparate squares. But consider the remarkable uniformity of evenness in that original series.)

A series of questions comes to mind recapitulating and extending what I have said here. These questions, which point to further possible inquiry by both the physicist and the political scientist, suggest perhaps even in their very formulation and arrangement still another "likely story" which can be instructive, salutary, and entertaining (see p. 11 and chap. 2, n. 1, above):

May it be said that the reported material stability of each of the seven nuclei (and perhaps, ultimately, of the universe?) is dependent upon a "simple" (or halved) arrangement which is restricted to a combination of disparate squares—which simple arrangement is itself, because of its reliance on squares, a configuration of elements which "look" the same on all "edges" (as distinguished from the two "sides")?

Thus, does evenness (on the two "sides") insure sameness "front and back" (or, if one prefers to designate the "sides" otherwise, "top and bottom"), while "squareness" (on the "edges") insures sameness "all around"?

May it not even be said, therefore, that "evenness" promotes (or reflects) stability in one dimension and that "squareness" promotes (or reflects) stability in another dimension (*however those "dimensions," as well as "squareness" and "evenness," are understood or defined*)?

Is stability, then, dependent upon the doubling, or "folding over," of elements which are themselves (despite their differences) essentially alike in one critical respect, in that they in turn are made up of disparate "squares"?

Should we not go farther and say (skipping as we do, at least for the moment, the steps which would take us explicitly from the previous questions to this one and to the one following) that there must be an orderly limitation upon variation, upon "liberty," if a complex body is to be relatively stable in the world we know?

Should we not go even farther and say that a free community, if it is to be stable, must rest both upon the "evenness" of such associations as the family (which distinguishes us from members of other families and of other associations) and upon the "squareness" which makes all citizens the same in some essential respect (despite their divergent families, classes, or other associations), with the attractive differences (the liberty we cherish?) being "no more" than surface manifestations but manifestations which are (considering man's nature) nevertheless vital to a good life if not to life itself?

Or is it, in the words of the prudent Horatio, "to consider too curiously, to consider so"?

INDEX

NOTE: Persons discussed primarily as members of judicial tribunals or as parties to litigation may be found in Part II, "Cases and Jurists."

I. SUBJECTS AND NAMES

Abolitionist controversy, follies of, 240-53, 730
"Abridging," significance of, 5, 112, 528-30, 656
Absolute prohibitions, their uses and limitations, 4, 15-17, 22-23, 35-47, 49-51, 53-54, 78, 80-81, 93, 113, 118, 123-24, 126-27, 164, 173-74, 230-31, 237-38, 419-20, 439-41, 444, 454, 461, 475, 488, 512, 657-58, 762-64, 795
Academic freedom, 113-14, 157, 180, 261-62, 311, 324-30, 450, 452, 523, 533-34, 536, 585-86, 609-10, 660-61, 757, 759-60, 775
Acheson, Dean, 638, 703, 777
Achilles, 278, 381, 690, 791, 807
Acton, Lord, 425, 533, 596, 606

Adam, 806
Adams, Charles F., 577
Adams, Henry, 482, 500, 597, 652-53, 659, 727
Adams, John, 106, 109-11, 136-37, 143, 255, 464, 494, 522, 525, 527, 530, 549, 572, 577-78, 597, 636, 695, 704, 708, 768-70
Adams, John Quincy, 240-53, 463, 519, 688, 726-30, 732
Adams, Samuel, 525, 530, 572, 782-84
Adeimantus, 702, 792
Adrian, Charles R., 610
Aeschylus, 624, 703, 720, 798
Agamemnon, 690, 798, 807
Agnew, Spiro T., 433, 458, 544-45, 586
Agrin, Gloria, 635

809

Agus, Jacob B., 677
Ahab, Captain, 424, 437, 463-64
Aiken, Henry D., 724
Alcibiades, 323, 547, 687, 780
Alexander the Great, 31-32, 436, 690, 780, 797
Alfange, Dean, Jr., 620
Alfarabi, 532, 686, 702, 736, 739, 747, 761, 779, 792, 796
Alien and Sedition Acts, 5, 103-4, 136-47, 183, 229, 269, 485, 487, 490, 509, 513, 520, 525, 528, 530, 569-78, 590, 598, 623, 625, 658, 677, 708, 714, 721-22, 732, 769, 805
Alsop, Joseph, 554, 742, 789
Alsop, Stewart, 615, 742
American Bar Association, 236-37, 427
American Civil Liberties Union, 347, 422, 524
Ames, Fisher, 26-27, 29-30, 55, 61, 74-75, 85-86, 101, 118-19, 155-56, 163, 232, 265-66, 430, 503, 584, 674, 684, 699
Anastaplo, George, 331, 419, 787
Anastaplo, John, 475-76
Anaxagoras, 780
Anaxarchus, 513, 797
Anderson, William, 631
Antigone, 651, 798
Anti-Riot Act of 1968, 312-23, 544, 574-75, 607, 645; text of, 594-95
Antony, 798
Apollo, 252-53, 783
Aquinas, Thomas, 347, 351, 427, 675, 764, 767-78, 796
Arabs, 747
Aristides, 671
Aristophanes, 546-47, 780, 807
Aristotle, 255, 347, 361, 393, 419, 422, 424, 435, 454, 483, 492, 494, 500, 510, 517, 522, 526, 541, 546-48, 551-53, 559, 561, 595, 600, 612-13, 615, 625, 642, 653, 659, 662-63, 666-67, 679, 689, 691-92, 702, 705, 718, 735-37, 739, 742, 748, 755, 757, 759, 760-61, 764, 773-74, 777-79, 781, 788, 790, 792, 794-99
Armstrong, Craig, 314
Aronson, Jason M., 643, 734, 739
Asbell, Bernard, 752
Athena, 203, 393, 624, 697, 720
Augustine, Saint, 422, 521, 531, 698, 796
Austen, Jane, 405, 525, 535, 545, 550, 794
Avicenna, 794

Bacon, Francis, 252-53, 323, 426, 439, 510, 529, 534, 553, 605, 606, 612, 623, 636-37, 641, 643, 650, 666, 687, 695, 699, 715, 729-30, 734, 761-62, 766, 771, 773, 782, 790, 795, 797
Bagehot, Walter, 176, 428, 465, 598, 603-4, 655, 665, 673, 686, 698, 748, 773, 776-77
Baker, John E., Jr., 347, 378
Baker, Ray Stannard, 257
"Balancing" test. See "Clear and present danger" test
Baldwin, Abraham, 233, 420, 430, 623
Ballot, significance of, 6, 84-86, 189, 207-8, 219-24, 227-29, 282, 490-91, 495-96, 525, 593, 606, 664, 674, 697-99, 724-25, 798-800
Bane, Charles A., 342-46
Banquo, 271, 479, 797
Bard, Ralph A., 751-52
Barker, Ernest, 765, 799
Barker, Lucius J., 640
Barker, Twiley W., 640
Barth, Karl, 564
Bartlett, Charles, 479, 735
Baskin, Robert E., 724
Bayard, James A., 590
Bayle, Pierre, 560, 706, 780, 797
Beaney, William M., 629
Beard, Charles A., 457, 525
Beard, Mary R., 457, 525
Beck, Alexander, 639
Becket, James, 644
Beethoven, Ludwig van, 761
Belisarius, 261, 758
Benardete, Seth, 548, 581, 783, 798, 805
Bennett, Wallace, 609
Benson, Egbert, 28, 40-41, 55, 234, 430
Bentham, Jeremy, 513, 579
Benton, Thomas H., 605
Berger, Victor L., 490
Bergson, Henri, 666
Beria, Lavrenti, 681-82
Berkeley, George, 611
Berns, Laurence, 347, 362-65, 420, 433, 532, 553, 624, 641, 658, 661, 665-66, 669, 720, 782, 790-92
Berns, Walter, 446-47, 460, 489, 505, 513, 515, 518, 568, 571, 577, 602, 616, 676, 718, 790
Bernstein, Leonard, 761
Berry, Louis, 347
Bethmann-Hollweg, Theobald von, 276
Beveridge, Albert J., 433, 584, 714
Bible, 275, 323, 381, 417, 419, 431, 436, 438, 515, 535, 545, 558, 643, 658, 668, 675, 677, 684, 698, 700, 720, 748, 771, 783, 792, 805-6, 807

INDEX: SUBJECTS AND NAMES   811

Bickel, Alexander M., 545, 654
Bickerstaff, Isaac, 581
Biddle, Francis B., 445, 476, 718, 753-54, 761
Bill of attainder, 39, 98, 209, 469-71, 481, 497, 630, 643
Bill of Rights of 1689, 91, 95
Binder, Leonard, 523
Binder, Lorraine, 347
Black Panthers, 323, 452, 669, 705
Blackstone, William, 5, 20, 66, 94-96, 103-5, 112-14, 125, 144, 187, 207, 209, 212, 237, 424-25, 432-33, 439, 441, 457-58, 461, 471, 479, 495, 499, 500-502, 508-9, 512-13, 515, 518, 528-29, 531-33, 539, 560, 563, 568, 572, 577, 588-89, 598, 600, 611, 624, 641, 659, 665, 671, 673, 684, 688, 695, 716, 723, 760, 762, 794, 796
Blake, William, 771
Blanckenhagen, Peter H. von, 565, 781
Block, Emmanuel, 635
Block, Mervin, 560, 606, 610
Bloom, Allan, 532, 552, 564, 612, 661, 675, 795, 805
Blum, Walter J., 333, 380, 544
Boardman, Harry, 757
Bonhoeffer, Dietrich, 522
Book of Common Prayer, 12
Boorstin, Daniel J., 500, 567
Booth, John Wilkes, 514
Boschan, Paul, 561
Boswell, James, 560
Boudin, Leonard B., 347, 635
Boudinot, Elias, 27, 93, 155, 161, 220, 267, 430, 773
Bovary, Emma, 773
Bradley, Omar N., 101
Braithwaite, Lewis, 613
Brann, Eva, 536
Brant, Irving, 429-30, 457
Broening, Stephens, 725
Brogan, Denis W., 663
Brotz, Howard, 747-48
Browder, Earl, 620
Brown, Ivor, 551
Brown, Ralph S., 364, 398, 410, 466, 468, 471, 609, 620, 667, 670
Brownell, Herbert, Jr., 634-35, 638
Bruce, Lenny, 545, 549, 760
Bruning, Heinrich, 499, 744
Brunner, Emil, 683
Brutus, 520, 555, 798
Bryce, James, 512
Buber, Martin, 454, 668

Buchan, John, 438, 493, 563-64, 683, 686, 746, 758
Buchanan, James, 580
Buchanan, Scott, 702
Buchwald, Art, 670, 741
Buckley, William F., Jr., 553
Bullock, Alan, 477
Bulwer Lytton, Sir, 706
Bundy, McGeorge, 745
Bunyan, John, 535, 585, 673
Burckhardt, Sigurd, 552
Burke, Aedanus, 38, 59, 85-86, 430
Burke, Arleigh, 741
Burke, Edmund, 450, 454, 483, 486, 500, 507, 510, 519, 546, 558, 560, 562, 564, 567, 573, 608, 614, 625, 631, 635, 637, 642, 643, 651, 654-55, 659, 663-65, 667-71, 673, 680, 682, 684, 686-88, 697, 700, 703-5, 710, 713, 716, 718, 721-22, 732, 736, 744, 755, 759, 761-62, 764, 772, 776-79, 782-83, 785, 790, 794, 799, 801
Burns, James M., 457, 476, 563, 777
Butch Cassidy and the Sundance Kid, 651
Byrnes, James F., 651
Byron, Lord, 425

Caesar, Julius, 31, 253, 437, 520, 541, 631, 635, 650, 758, 797-98
Cahn, Edmond, 718
Calhoun, John C., 175, 462-63, 465-66, 563, 582, 602, 728, 736, 755
Callicles, 437, 724, 730
Callisthenes, 513
Calvin, John, 770
Canada, 423, 451, 455-56, 632, 712, 774
Canavan, Frances, 717
Carey, George W., 441
Carey, James P., Jr., 347
Carey, Mathew, 575-76, 598
Carlyle, Thomas, 464
Carmichael, Stokely, 578-79
Carone, Michael J., 808
Carroll, Daniel, 41, 430
Carroll, Lewis, 505
Carter, Gwendolen M., 709
Cassandra, 252-53
Catiline conspiracy, 323, 541, 612, 706
Cato, 252-53, 667-68, 729-30
Cecil, Henry, 700
Central Intelligence Agency, 471
Cephalus, 214, 689-90
Cervantes, Miguel de, 584, 686, 766
Chaerephon, 422, 459
Chafee, Zechariah, 43, 257-58, 378, 429, 440, 442-45, 455, 460, 463, 468, 471,

490, 515, 537, 549, 573, 594, 596, 629-32, 654, 714-15
Chamberlain, Neville, 459
Chambers, Whittaker, 617-18
Charles I, 425, 482, 520, 541, 684, 742
Charmides, 659
Charnwood, Lord, 421, 477, 500, 580, 600-601, 730, 769, 776
Chester, Lewis, 313
Chicago Conspiracy Trial. See U.S. v. Dellinger (Index of Cases and Jurists)
Chiles, Lawton, 790
Choate, Rufus, 726, 731
Choper, Jesse H., 493
Christianity, 46, 275, 431, 450, 522, 531, 535, 552-53, 585, 605-6, 611, 668, 693, 698, 770, 779, 782, 783
Christianson, J. R., 347
Churchill, Winston S., 236-37, 254, 260, 457, 476, 507, 523, 558, 699, 705, 709, 720-21, 729, 738, 742-43, 748, 750-52, 755, 757, 762, 777, 784-85, 787-88, 799
Cicero, 12, 200, 252-53, 323, 426, 472, 494, 541, 563, 612, 689, 706, 730, 758, 774, 780, 787-88, 794, 797
Circe, 546, 720
Clark, Champ, 296
Clark, Ramsey, 322
Claudius, 31-32, 437, 725
Clausewitz, Karl von, 258
Clay, Diskin, 581
Clay, Henry, 421
"Clear and present danger" test, 4, 6, 17, 22, 44-48, 70, 111, 126-27, 148, 161, 166, 187, 197-98, 230-31, 294-305, 324-30, 374-75, 378, 444-46, 450-53, 456, 460, 479, 504, 520-22, 548, 554, 575, 579, 595, 645, 684, 692, 709, 761
Cleopatra, 779, 798
Clor, Harry M., 428
Clyde, William M., 593, 783
Cockburn, Lord, 383, 561, 566
Cohn, Roy M., 311
Commager, Henry, 635
Common law, 5, 15, 20, 75-77, 94-95, 107, 111-12, 114, 135-47, 195, 209-10, 237, 469, 477, 484, 489, 512, 532, 559, 567-71, 573-74, 576-77, 595, 641, 680, 682, 695, 771
Communism, 65, 180, 182, 191, 213-14, 217, 219, 259, 261-62, 311, 323, 332, 348-49, 359-60, 369, 382, 396-97, 405, 431, 443, 447-51, 453, 466, 480, 492, 494, 505, 509, 523-24, 534, 541, 547, 562, 564-66, 606, 611, 614, 618-19, 629, 630, 638-39, 643, 645, 651, 666,

668-70, 675, 681, 691-95, 723-25, 732, 738, 742, 747, 753, 756, 758-59, 763, 775, 778, 803, 805
Condorcet, Marquis de, 777
Congressional investigations, 60-63, 402, 465-68, 488, 504
Conkling, Roscoe, 658
Conquest, Robert, 693, 756
Conrad, Alfred H., 727
Contempt powers, 18, 78-80, 122, 176, 312-23, 467, 485-87, 574-75, 587, 619-20
Cooley, Thomas M., 5, 95-97, 432, 502, 505, 573, 673, 682, 695, 701
Cooper, Duff, 459
"Coordinated electorates," 615
Copernicus, 803-5
Copland, Aaron, 771-72
Coriolanus, 33, 438, 670-71, 734, 788, 798
Corregio, 665
Corwin, Edward S., 431, 490, 573, 580, 582-84, 640, 677-78
Crankshaw, Edward, 487, 641, 693, 756, 758
Creon, 798-99
Crist, Robert C., 593
Critias, 459, 659
Crito, 701
Cromwell, Oliver, 493, 520, 563-64, 686, 758, 778
Cronon, E. David, 432
Cropsey, Joseph, 323, 419, 643, 668, 675, 690, 693, 705, 713, 715
Crosskey, William W., 112-13, 136-42, 147, 173, 231, 421, 429, 434-35, 440, 453, 471-73, 483, 487, 489, 509, 530, 567-69, 582, 584, 586, 596, 604, 607, 652, 654, 671, 710-11, 713, 715, 717
Cushman, Robert E., 621
Cyprian, 431-32

Daedalus, Stephen, 77
Daley, Richard J., 312-23, 685, 712, 799
Dana, Francis, 478
Dana, Samuel W., 525
Daniel, Yuli, 548
Dannhauser, Werner, 717
Dante, 399-400, 546
Darwin, Charles, 610-11, 763, 778, 803-5
Davenport, Beatrix C., 514
Davidson, Donald, 670
Davidson, Jessica, 347
Day, Dorothy, 669
De Alvarez, Leo Paul, 775-76
Death, 30-31, 625, 768, 773, 793, 797-98. See also Love

INDEX: SUBJECTS AND NAMES

Declaration of Independence, 15, 29, 89, 104-5, 108-9, 112, 219-20, 242, 248, 274, 297, 331-32, 350-51, 363-64, 368-70, 379, 382, 384, 396, 399, 403, 411, 417-18, 420, 425, 432-33, 460, 498, 511, 519-20, 526, 559, 572, 578, 597, 657, 662, 666, 670, 672, 674-76, 684, 697, 703, 721-22, 725, 727, 748, 777, 795, 805; text of, 377
De Gaulle, Charles, 613, 619, 637, 725, 785
DeGrazia, Alfred, 661, 735
DeGrazia, Edward, 709
Democritus, 778
Demosthenes, 703
Denning, Alfred, 504, 700
Descartes, Rene, 613, 748
Devlin, Patrick, 428, 463, 548, 695
Diamond, Martin, 494, 610, 661, 693, 706
Dicey, Albert V., 5, 96-99, 109, 114, 189, 209, 227, 441, 502-3, 537, 559
Dickens, Charles, 708
Dickinson, John, 582, 687
"Dick Tracy," 707
Diderot, Denis, 436-37
Diefenbaker, John, 456
Dilliard, Irving, 379-80, 404, 456, 543, 629
Dilsworth, Richardson, 650
Diogenes Laertius, 773
Disraeli, Isaac, 736, 781, 806
Djilas, Milovan, 770
Dorsen, Norman, 709
Dostoevsky, Fyodor, 737-38
Douglas, Paul A., 696
Douglas, Stephen A., 259, 487, 511, 602, 766
Drinker, Henry S., 536
"Due process of law," 14-15, 21, 23, 79, 96-100, 189, 208, 210, 306-11, 324-31, 428, 451-53, 469, 471, 486-87, 502-4, 533, 540, 543, 598-99, 643-46, 649-50, 653-54, 676-77, 680-85, 691-92, 696, 700, 703, 710-13, 770
Dulles, Allen W., 719
Dulles, John F., 473, 758
Dumbauld, Edward, 589
Dunham, Allison, 333, 380, 429, 544
Durocher, Leo, 755

Eastland, James O., 696
Ebert, Roger, 651
Eby, Kermit, 617, 734
Eden, Anthony, 459
Edgar, 278, 437, 791
Eggleston, Joseph, 576

Eidelberg, Paul, 428
Eighteenth Amendment, 455
Eisenhower, Dwight D., 100, 182, 255-56, 395, 473, 480, 563, 618-19, 631, 634, 663, 740, 742, 745, 749, 751-52
Eleventh Amendment, 489, 626
El Greco, 793
Elisha, 457
Elizabeth I, 438, 535
Elliot, Jonathan, 436
Ellsworth, Oliver, 600
Elson, Alex, 407
Emancipation Proclamation, 580, 602, 623, 657
Emerson, Ralph Waldo, 426, 464, 494, 508, 545, 632, 671, 691, 709, 726, 729-31, 772, 782
Emerson, Thomas I., 431, 451, 503, 709, 731
Engels, Friedrich, 692-93, 732
Er, 698, 793
Erskine, Thomas, 255-56, 376, 495-96, 527, 636, 682, 701
Ervin, Sam J., 696
Esau, 330
Espionage Act of 1917, 294-305, 477, 715
Euclid, 422, 668
Euripides, 547, 624, 779
Evers, Charles, 674
"*Ex post facto*" clauses, 39, 98, 209, 440, 469, 476, 497, 598, 636-37, 643, 711, 716

Fagen, H. A., 736-37, 740
Fairlie, Henry, 735
Fairman, Charles, 654
Fallers, Lloyd A., 642
Farrand, Max, 440, 572
Faulconbridge, 437-38
Faulkner, Robert K., 571, 648
Faulkner, William, 651
Faure, Edgar, 579, 738
Federalist, The. See Publius
Feis, Herbert, 752
Fermi, Enrico, 666, 750
Feuer, L. S., 540, 694
Field, Oliver P., 649
Fielding, Henry, 551, 787
Fifteenth Amendment, 601, 645
Fifth Amendment, 440, 469, 563, 583-84, 599, 653, 676, 710
Fillmore, Millard, 283
Finkel, David B., 347
First Amendment: stages in drafting, 289-93; text, 1, 292
Fischer, John, 547

Fischer, Louis, 693
Fishel, Wesley R., 785
Fisher, Roger, 656
Fisk, Winston, 494, 610, 693
Fitzgerald, Thomas R., 733
Fitzhugh, George, 693
Fitzpatrick, Tom, 452-53, 455
Fitzsimmons, Thomas, 155, 430
Flanagan, Brian, 694
Flaubert, Gustave, 499, 773
Fleming, Peter, 738
Foran, Thomas A., 327, 328, 712
Ford, Paul Leicester, 440, 689
Forman, Lionel, 649
Forrester, Duncan B., 717
Forster, E. M., 765
Foster, John, 683
Fourteenth Amendment, 6, 22-23, 54, 190, 193-95, 197-98, 208, 461-62, 472, 487, 496, 542, 563, 595, 599, 601, 607-8, 623, 645-46, 653-54, 657, 677-78, 682, 706, 710-13
Fourth Amendment, 166, 469, 526, 593, 676; text, 37
"Fox and Geese," 600
Fox's Libel Act, 145-47, 512, 573-75; text, 145-46
Frank, John Paul, 455, 567, 640
Franklin, Benjamin, 442, 495, 498, 516-17, 526, 529, 536, 560, 691, 748
Frederick the Great, 254
Freud, Sigmund, 748, 762, 803-5
Freund, Paul A., 404-5, 454, 515
Friedman, Milton, 557, 688, 743
Friedrich, Carl J., 594, 726
Fritchey, Clayton, 458-59, 688, 744
Froman, Lewis A., Jr., 471
Fromm, Erich, 775
Frost, R. T., 426, 504
Frost, Robert, 426
Fuchs, Klaus, 634
Fulbright, J. William, 729, 743

Galba, 516
Galbraith, John K., 592-93, 743, 748, 753
Gallatin, Albert, 447-48, 487, 490, 586-87, 594, 625
Gandhi, Mohandas, 605-6
Garfinkel, Herbert, 494, 610, 693
Garrison, William Lloyd, 653
Garson, Barbara, 735
Gellhorn, Walter, 405-6
German, Jeremiah J., 722
Gerry, Elbridge, 27, 37, 59, 85, 124, 131, 160, 220, 222, 226, 233, 430
Gertz, Elmer, 407, 557

Gettysburg Address, 274, 536, 655, 672, 796
Gibbon, Edward, 261, 522, 612, 758, 761
Gide, André, 772
Gilbert and Sullivan, 794
Gildin, Hilail, 795
Gill, Brendan, 553
Glaucon, 702, 792-93
Gleason, Bill, 660
Goering, Hermann, 587
Goethe, Johann W. von, 579
Goldwater, Barry, 448, 459
Goldwin, Robert A., 523, 585, 613, 660-61, 688
Goodhart, A. L., 731
Gordon, George, 504
Gore, Albert, 586
Gormly, John, 792
Gosling, Nigel, 803
Gossett, Thomas B., 774, 784
Gourevitch, Victor, 624, 666
Grant, George, 675, 677, 774, 785
Grant, Ulysses S., 474, 561, 579-80, 651, 658-59, 670-71, 766
Graves, Robert, 564
Graveson, Agricola, 581
Great Protestation, 117-18, 541
Greece (modern), 425, 564
Greene, Graham, 547, 678-79
Gregory, 681
Grene, David, 523-24, 796-97
Grigg, John, 721
Grilliches, Zvi, 523-24
Griswold, Erwin N., 454
Grodzins, Morton, 466, 583, 660-61, 753-54
Gulliver, 113, 427

Habeas corpus, writ of, 6, 45, 69-70, 98, 186, 207, 209-13, 215, 217, 224, 227, 435, 450, 477-79, 481, 486, 489, 502, 580, 626, 654, 673, 678-80, 682, 684, 693, 698-99, 709, 712, 753; text of constitutional provision on, 36
Haber, David, 709
Hablutzel, Philip, 676
Halevi, Judah, 553, 560, 579, 606, 624-25, 641, 643, 679, 793
Hallam, Henry, 95, 532, 535
Hamill, Pete, 616
Hamilton, Alexander, 436, 506, 513, 569, 578, 589, 648, 651, 687, 705, 716, 734. *See also* Publius
Hamilton, Andrew, 524, 527
Hamlet, King, 31, 438, 494
Hamlet, Prince, 30-32, 436-38, 687, 725

INDEX: SUBJECTS AND NAMES

Hampden, John, 519, 690
Handel, G. F., 526, 797
Hannibal, 436
Harper, William Rainey, 757
Harriman, Averell, 662
Harrington, Michael, 322, 492
Harris, Louis, 757
Harris, Monford, 767
Harris, Sydney J., 549
Hart, B. H. Liddell, 658
Hart, Pearl M., 347
Hartford Convention, 597-98, 647
Hartley, Margaret L., 548
Hartley, Thomas, 37, 59, 152, 163, 222, 266, 430
Harvey, Frank, 608
Hassner, Pierre, 666, 717
Hastings, James E., 347
Hatch Act, 470-71
Hawkins, Gordon, 322
Hawthorne, Nathaniel, 788-89
Hay, John, 421
Hayden, Tom, 322, 667
Hayek, F. A., 425-26, 519, 563, 719, 778
Hays, Arthur Garfield, 524
Hayton, J. William, 632
Hayward, Max, 548
Hazael, 457
Heath, Edward, 789
Hébert, Jacques René, 549
Hegel, G. W. F., 425, 599, 783
Heidegger, Martin, 424, 550, 600, 738-39, 767, 773-74, 781, 790, 799
Henderson, Gerard C., 464
Hennacy, Ammon, 628
Henry IV (of France), 541
Henry VIII, 66, 538, 589
Henry, Patrick, 375, 520, 528, 563, 701
Herodotus, 483, 548, 605, 612, 715, 773, 796
Hersey, John, 748
Herz, John H., 709
Hetherington, Hector, 533-34
Hiestand, Fred K., 544
Hill, Arthur D., 257
Hill, Lester, 724
Hill, Melvyn, 747
Hiss, Alger, 617-18, 620
History and constitutional interpretation, 13, 103, 128, 273, 427, 500, 506-7, 509-11, 513, 558-59, 584, 722
Hitler, Adolf, 351, 486-87, 541, 563, 565, 708-9, 733, 742, 752, 775, 799
Hobbes, Thomas, 323, 423-24, 445, 483, 494, 498, 505, 529, 531-32, 535, 541, 559, 561, 585, 590, 598, 612, 641, 645, 675, 684, 687, 691, 705, 713, 715, 723, 732, 748, 750, 764, 773, 776, 782, 796-97, 807
Hodgson, Godfrey, 313
Hoffa, James, 467, 755
Hoffmann, Banesh, 806
Holdsworth, William S., 124-26, 226, 558-59, 575, 679-80, 683, 695
Holst, H. von, 435, 462-63, 563, 598, 603, 728
Homer, 278-79, 530-31, 546, 552-53, 612, 719-20, 791-92, 797, 807
Hook, Sidney, 450, 452, 476, 578, 668, 724, 761, 764
Hoopes, Townsend, 744
Hoover, Herbert, 686
Hoover, J. Edgar, 184, 621, 669, 735
Horatio, 30-31, 437-38, 651, 808
Horwitz, Robert, 717
Hoselitz, Bert, 523-24
Howe, Mark DeWolfe, 578
Hughes, Emmett, 634-35
Huie, William Bradford, 548
Hume, David, 494-95, 513, 525, 529, 723, 796
Humphrey, George M., 610
Humphrey, Hubert H., 314
Huntington, Benjamin, 76-77, 430, 484, 600
Hurst, Willard, 588
Hutchins, Robert M., 616
Hutchinson, Thomas, 143, 572
Huxley, Aldous, 784

Ibsen, Henrik, 705
Iofe, Olga, 694
Iredell, James, 586
Irving, Washington, 776
Isaiah, 653
Ishmael, 437
Isocrates, 703
Israelis, 557, 616, 746-48. See also Jews

Jackson, Andrew, 205-6, 670-71
Jackson, James, 58-59, 150, 156, 218, 223, 234, 266, 430, 464, 581, 584-85, 598, 623-24, 717, 769
Jacob, 330
Jaffa, Harry V., 255, 435, 450, 478-79, 515, 534, 580, 585, 609, 613, 655, 664, 698, 705, 726-27, 730, 739, 747, 795
James I, 116, 540-41, 543
James II, 608
James, William, 543
Jaspers, Karl, 801
Jay, John, 436

Jayson, L. S., 431
Jefferson, Thomas, 14, 103-4, 106, 136-37, 141, 147, 242-43, 375, 406, 435, 457, 464, 472, 511, 515, 537, 550, 563, 571, 574, 577, 586-87, 597-98, 615, 650, 658, 660, 662, 677, 700, 704, 727, 731, 759, 768-69, 773, 784, 793, 806
Jenner, Albert E., 467
Jenner, William E., 617, 620, 800
Jenyns, Soane, 425
Jesus, 522, 552, 723, 748, 782-83
Jews, 497-98, 503, 522-24, 553, 633, 747, 753, 784
John Birch Society, 402, 669
Johnson, Andrew, 434
Johnson, Hewlett, 709
Johnson, Lyndon B., 453, 458-59, 476, 617, 741, 743-45, 749, 786, 789
Johnson, Mrs. Lyndon B., 741
Johnson, Samuel, 435, 460, 503, 506, 517, 777
Joyce, James, 551, 771
Judicial review, 77, 229-37, 484, 499, 644, 696, 709-20
Judiciary Act of 1789, 78-79, 220-21, 231, 486
Juin, Alphonse, 637
Junius, 512, 537, 676
Jury, trial by, 6, 40, 103, 106-7, 110-11, 146, 207, 212, 215-20, 224-27, 291-92, 447-49, 468, 486, 517, 528, 540, 573-76, 673, 676, 678, 695-97, 699, 703, 706, 800

Kahan, Arcadius, 523-24
Kahn, Herman, 663, 744, 748
Kalven, Harry, Jr., 322, 342, 347, 404, 407-8, 421, 443-44, 466, 509-10, 513, 515, 531, 542, 549, 554-55, 562, 568, 573, 594, 645, 666-67, 695, 715, 725
Kamisar, Yale, 405, 493
Kant, Immanuel, 323, 419, 424, 437, 494, 511, 516, 658, 734, 739, 767, 772, 794
Kapitsa, Peter L., 693
Kaplan, Morton A., 735
Kaplan, Stanley A., 404, 407
Kass, Leon R., 773
Katherina, 726
Katz, Wilber G., 405
Katzenbach, Nicholas, 459
Kazantzakis, Nikos, 611
Kefauver, Estes, 586
Kelly, Kevin, 314
Kempton, Murray, 742
Kendall, Willmoore, 365, 404, 432, 441, 589, 662, 666, 705, 718, 736, 792, 795

Kennan, George F., 509, 534, 740, 753
Kennedy, John F., 451, 460, 476, 480, 609, 629, 650, 665, 669, 735, 740-41, 743-44, 749, 755, 765, 786, 803
Kennedy, Robert F., 323, 758
Kennington, Richard, 613, 666
Kent, James, 434, 513-14, 519, 543
Kentucky Resolutions. See Virginia and Kentucky Resolutions
Khrushchev, Nikita, 182, 480, 562, 618-19, 629, 681-82, 753, 763
Kilpatrick, James J., 322, 614, 647, 655
King, Martin Luther, 323, 423, 551, 674
Kirk, Russell, 609
Kissinger, Henry A., 755
Klein, Jacob, 427, 500, 643, 686, 717, 738-39, 792, 795, 804
Knight, John S., 749-50
Knops, Mark, 501
Knox, Frank, 476
Kojève, Alexandre, 665-66, 762, 786
Kolakowski, Laszek, 524, 534
Konvitz, Milton R., 431, 629, 631, 643, 649
Kraft, Joseph, 507
Krash, Abe, 634
Krock, Arthur, 530
Ku Klux Klan, 369, 382, 390, 396-97, 448, 468, 669
Kunstler, William M., 313, 322, 325-30
Kurland, Philip, 429, 454, 663-64

Lafayette, Marquis de, 491-92
Lafontant, Jewel, 407
Landynski, Jacob W., 526
Laurance, John, 25, 153, 155, 160-61, 232, 430
Lawrence of Arabia, 788
Lawrence, D. H., 121, 545, 551-52
Lawrence, David, 542
Leach, Edmund, 799
Leach, Richard H., 465
Lear, King, 505, 553, 790-91
Lee, Richard Bland, 161, 221, 430
Lee, Richard Henry, 528, 586, 695
Lee, Robert E., 192, 651, 670-71
Leighton, George N., 347
LeMay, Curtis E., 475
Lenin, Vladimir I., 492, 552, 555, 651, 693, 753, 762-63
Leo XIII, 426, 771, 782
Lerner, Ralph, 523-24, 677, 710
Lessing, Gotthold E., 426, 439, 503, 549, 793
Levenson, Joseph R., 759

INDEX: SUBJECTS AND NAMES 817

Levi, Edward H., 333, 380, 401, 433, 513, 685, 787
Levy, Leonard W., 102-4, 427, 484, 487, 500, 509-15, 518, 559, 572, 577-78, 655
Lewis, Anthony, 682
Lewis, C. S., 477, 546
Lewis, Flora, 790
Lewis, John L., 459, 630-31
Lewis, Wyndham, 545
Liebling, A. J., 675
Lilienthal, David E., 637
Lincoln, Abraham, 89, 94, 191, 200, 240-41, 253, 256, 259, 267, 273, 283, 332, 351, 406, 421, 423, 425, 427-28, 431, 435, 439, 449, 472-73, 475, 477-81, 487, 489, 495, 497, 499-500, 502, 508, 511-12, 515, 518, 521, 535, 541, 553, 561, 579-80, 590, 592, 600-602, 625-26, 646, 648, 650-52, 655, 657, 659, 665-66, 670-73, 680, 698-700, 704-5, 716, 722-23, 725, 727-28, 730, 732, 742, 747-48, 756, 765, 767, 771, 776, 778-80, 786, 790, 796
Lippmann, Walter, 458, 460, 473, 476, 614, 740-41, 746-47, 749, 789
Lipset, Seymour M., 704
Literary playfulness, 736, 786-87, 806-7
"Little Orphan Annie," 707-8
Littleton, Michael S., 668
Littleton, Thomas, 438
Livermore, Samuel, 159, 186, 430, 462, 483, 573, 712, 768
Livingston, Edward, 487, 516
Lloyd George, David, 748
Lloyd-George, Gwilym, 599
Locke, John, 213, 431, 474, 516, 519, 522-24, 596, 624, 687, 688, 732, 799
Lockhart, William B., 405, 493
Long, Huey, 179, 608, 690
Long, Russell, 586
Louis XIV, 605
Louis XV, 438
Louis, Joe, 674
Love, 546-48, 607, 667-68, 683, 788, 793, 795. See also Death
Love, Stephen, 347
Lowell, James Russell, 671
Lowell, Robert, 539
Lowenthal, David, 582, 648, 665, 706
Lowi, Theodore J., 420
Lucretius, 438
Lukas, J. Anthony, 322
Lunden, Walter A., 638
Luther, Martin, 522
Lycurgus, 759
Lynch, James F., 707

Lynd, Staunton, 592, 600-601, 653
Lysander, 605

MacArthur, Douglas, 503, 507, 750
Macaulay, Thomas B., 458, 608
Macbeth, 271, 479, 739, 790
McCarran Act (Internal Security Act of 1950), 643, 649, 686
McCarthy, Eugene, 314, 758
McCarthy, Joseph R., 181, 311, 448, 458, 616-17, 734, 758, 789, 801
McDonald, Thomas, 734, 739, 796
Machiavelli, Nicolo, 106, 213, 323, 431, 451, 481-83, 494, 499, 507, 535, 547, 572, 585, 611-12, 665-66, 688, 733-34, 739, 767, 786, 790, 802
MacInnes, Colin, 689
McKeon, Richard P., 564, 576
McLuhan, Marshall, 675
McMaster, John B., 572, 588
McNamara, Robert S., 475, 745, 803
MacNeice, Louis, 545
Macon, Nathaniel, 487, 590, 592
Madison, James, 26, 30, 54-55, 57, 64, 67, 72, 76-77, 80-82, 86-87, 104, 115, 118-19, 126, 144, 149-56, 161-62, 164-67, 171-72, 190, 211, 224, 229-32, 234-35, 237-40, 260, 263, 268, 290, 429, 430, 434-36, 439, 461, 472-74, 484, 486-87, 495, 497, 506, 520, 526-28, 530, 538, 572, 577, 582, 585, 597-98, 646, 678, 687, 694, 696, 699, 707, 712, 715, 728, 773. See also Publius
Magna Carta, 207, 212, 215, 218, 425, 469, 672, 679, 686
Mahdi, Muhsin, 677, 717
Maimonides, Moses, 422, 546, 559, 581, 613, 624, 677, 760, 765-66, 771, 773, 786, 792
Malraux, André, 535
Mao Tse-tung, 675
Marcuse, Herbert, 733
Margolis, Ben, 347, 635
Maric, J. J., 535
Markus, Robert, 667
Marshall, S. L. A., 475
Marsilius of Padua, 790
Martin, William J., 404
Marvell, Andrew, 796
Marx, Herbert, 632
Marx, Karl, 213, 217, 323, 405, 425, 494, 524, 539-40, 606, 668, 694, 805
Mason, Alpheus T., 504, 628-29, 686
Mason, George, 440, 687
Masters, Roger D., 419
May, Thomas Erskine, 706

Mayer, Milton, 702
Mayflower Compact, 536
Meiklejohn, Alexander, 371, 421-22, 443-45, 455, 489, 514, 521, 523, 528, 534, 537-38, 541, 557, 559-60, 564-65, 718, 750, 761, 766-67
Melville, Herman, 9, 423-24, 437, 463-64
Mendel, A. P., 492, 694
Mendelson, Wallace, 471
Meno, 799
Mentschikoff, Soia, 333, 380
Meredith, James H., 619-20, 674
Meyer, Frank S., 432
Meyer, John, 727
Meyers, Marvin, 523-24
Mikva, Abner J., 347, 544, 674, 755-56
Miliadhis, Yannis, 601
Mill, James, 491, 521, 542, 794
Mill, John Stuart, 518, 694, 795
Millsap, Kenneth F., 644
Miltiades, 605
Milton, John, 96, 105, 114, 139, 187, 213, 254, 269, 427, 431-32, 439, 495, 502-3, 510, 515, 529, 535, 537, 550, 563-64, 593, 612, 668, 670, 686, 701, 703, 705, 723, 733, 735, 759-60, 763, 766, 771, 782
Mink, Patsy T., 538
Mitchell, John N., 501, 554, 769
Mitchell, Stephen A., 347, 377-78
Moley, Raymond, 610
Montaigne, Michel E. de, 779
Montesquieu, Baron de, 11, 46, 200, 215, 424-25, 431, 439, 449-50, 481, 483, 492, 494, 513, 522, 525, 534, 542, 560, 563, 582, 588, 655, 659, 662, 665-66, 671, 683, 699, 705, 738, 759, 790, 796, 802
Montgomery, Bernard, 100-101, 507
Moore, Barrington, Jr., 733
Moore, John, 527, 540
Moran, Lord, 784-85, 788
More, Thomas, 538-39, 548, 606
Morison, Samuel Eliot, 426
Morley, Felix, 661
Morley, John, 558, 743, 777
Morris, Gouverneur, 164, 455, 469, 473, 483, 491-92, 514, 534, 552, 585, 651, 730
Morris, Norval, 322
Mortimer, John, 536
Moses, 438, 522, 677, 698, 767, 782
Moses ben Jacob of Coucy, 767
Mosley, Oswald, 709
Muir, Edwin, 424, 552, 556, 733-34
Muir, Willa, 556

Murray, John Courtney, 508
Murrish, William B., 347, 635
Music and the Constitution, 8, 40, 90, 130, 168, 202, 270

Nathan the Wise, 439, 503
Nathanson, Nathaniel L., 407
National Lawyers Guild, 347, 427, 635
Nazism, 180, 219, 259, 424, 523, 562, 565, 587, 641, 643, 738
"Necessary and proper" clause, 5, 22, 148-49, 161, 163, 165-66, 432, 488, 566, 586-87, 590-91; text of, 160
Nehru, Jawaharlal, 480
Neumann, Hans, 808
Nevins, Allan, 252, 727, 729
Newton, Isaac, 433
Nicholas, John, 487, 490-91
Nicolay, John G., 421
Nicols, Roy F., 473, 659, 699, 728, 803
Nicolson, Harold, 482
Nicostratus, 255, 733
Nietzsche, Friedrich, 179, 494, 608, 694, 738, 763, 765, 783
Ninth Amendment, 25, 112, 296, 432; text of, 83
Nixon, Richard M., 314, 444, 492, 586, 745, 758, 789
North, Roger, 559
Numa, 733
Nuremberg Trials, 458, 643, 683, 800

O'Brian, John Lord, 295, 379
Obscenity, 16, 21, 120-22, 127, 261-62, 422, 428, 510, 536, 543-53, 596-97, 624-25, 758-60
Odysseus, 203, 546, 690, 719-20, 731, 776, 791-92, 797, 807
Oedipus, 642, 783, 798
Oggins, Robin S., 771
Olivero, Louis, 314
Onslow, Arthur, 14, 700
Orwell, George, 775
Otis, Harrison G., 571
Otis, James, 110-11, 376, 518, 526-27, 530, 641

Page, Bruce, 313
Page, John, 27, 80, 211-12, 222, 265, 430, 494-95, 581
Paine, Thomas, 255, 494-95, 665, 672-73, 676-77, 684, 686, 696-98, 700, 702, 705, 707-8, 711, 722, 725, 728, 730, 734, 736, 762, 778, 782-85, 794, 797, 801-2
Paley, William, 737

INDEX: SUBJECTS AND NAMES 819

Palmer Raids, 65
Panter-Downes, Mollie, 789
Panza, Sancho, 584, 686
Papandreou, Andreas, 544-45, 681
Papias, 723
Parker, Josiah, 430, 495
Parliamentary immunity, 5, 16, 58, 103, 115-18, 122, 208, 237-38, 247, 423, 488, 494, 512, 538-40, 560, 722
Parresia, 275, 781-82
Parton, James, 670, 690
Pascal, Blaise, 797
Pattakos, Stylianos, 698
Patterson, Bennett B., 430
Patterson, Giles J., 536
Patton, George, 670
Paul, St., 213, 522, 688, 785
Paul VI, 755
Peattie, Lisa, 695
Pegler, Westbrook, 753
Peltason, Jack W., 490, 580, 582-84, 677-78
Pendleton, Edmund, 587
Pericles, 6, 500, 552, 662, 703, 780, 788, 796, 802
Perry, Ralph Barton, 564
Petition, right of, 57, 240-53, 291-93, 300, 441-42, 460, 486, 488-89, 495, 533, 674-75, 725-29
Petrarch, 665
Phidias, 662
Phillips, G. G., 485, 491
Phillips, Wendell, 533
Philopoemen, 277-78, 533, 790
Pierce, William, 420
Pinckney, Charles, 131, 518, 585
Pitt, William, 579
Pius XII, 495, 499
Plato, 217, 223, 253, 278-81, 283, 402, 419-22, 425-26, 437-38, 443, 449-50, 457, 459-60, 477, 483, 498-99, 503, 510, 517, 524, 526, 531, 534, 541, 546-47, 549, 552-54, 557, 563, 568, 581-82, 585, 600, 606, 609, 612, 619, 624, 638, 641, 659, 663, 679, 683-85, 687, 689-90, 692, 698, 700-703, 706-8, 723-24, 729-31, 735-36, 739, 744, 755, 760, 763-64, 766-67, 770, 773-74, 776, 778-84, 789-97, 799, 801-3, 807
Platt, Jonas, 574
Plaut, Max, 424
Plucknett, Theodore F. T., 593, 734
Plutarch, 200, 277-78, 323, 426, 475, 481, 500, 513, 526, 552, 605, 612, 661-62, 670-71, 687, 703, 729-30, 733-34, 759, 762, 775, 780, 788, 790, 794-98, 805

Polemarchus, 700
Polikoff, Alexander L., 347
Polis, 419, 612-16, 659-60, 669, 684, 702-3, 767, 770-71, 773-75, 780-81, 801-2
Polk, James K., 247, 251, 751
Pollak, Robert, 735
Pollock, Frederick, 640-41, 700
Polonius, 772
Pope, Alexander, 530-31
Poseidon, 720
Powell, Adam Clayton, 490
Preamble to the Constitution, 27, 29, 42, 151-52, 157, 566, 581-82, 585, 590; text of, 440
Prettyman, Barrett, Jr., 691
"Previous restraint," 94-100, 103, 228, 304, 324-30, 487, 501-5, 512-13, 515-16, 536-37, 543, 550-51, 572, 593, 626, 680-82, 696, 703, 723, 733, 735, 760
Pritchett, C. Herman, 404, 431, 499-500, 598-99, 626, 630, 686, 691
"Privileges and immunities" clause, 496-97, 568, 654, 710-13
Property rights, 213-17, 660, 662-63, 672, 675, 686-94, 699, 731, 742, 776, 802
Prospero, 437-38, 755
Protagoras, 739
Prothero, G. W., 540
Proust, Marcel, 423, 438, 510, 552, 626, 772, 779, 787
Publius, 3, 4, 51, 66, 134-37, 141-43, 159, 173, 177, 207, 263-64, 423, 431-32, 434-36, 439, 464, 472, 480-81, 489, 495, 498-99, 508, 514, 527-28, 530, 532-33, 535, 542, 550-51, 558, 563, 566, 578, 580, 582, 589, 598, 604-7, 613, 615, 648-49, 659-63, 665-66, 669, 671, 673-75, 678, 682, 687-88, 696-97, 699, 702, 712, 714, 716-18, 721-22, 727, 735-37, 756, 761, 764-66, 776, 778, 802, 806
Pusey, Nathan M., 616
Puzo, Mario, 651

Quilici, George L., 407
Quixote, Don, 766

Ramsay, David, 530
Ramsdell, Charles W., 724
Randall, J. G., 561, 601-2, 635
Randolph, John, 432, 659
Ransom, Harry H., 705
Raspberry, William, 696
Redding, John M., 737
Redlich, Norman, 379

Religion and the law, 19, 26-30, 41-42, 76-77, 81-84, 113-15, 159, 162, 164, 229, 234, 290-93, 297, 369, 378, 414-15, 421, 436-37, 441, 454, 462, 474, 484, 488, 497, 508-9, 515-16, 519-20, 522-24, 532-33, 535, 537-38, 561, 597, 605-6, 610-12, 629, 633, 641-42, 659, 665, 672, 684, 688, 765, 776, 779, 782-83, 785. See also Zeus
Removal power of the President, 28, 30, 67, 161-63, 232-33, 434-35, 581
"Republican Form of Government" guarantee, text of, 86
Republican government, 3-4, 6-7, 14, 16, 23, 48, 86-88, 94, 104-5, 110, 119, 124-26, 128, 133-34, 137, 143, 148, 190-91, 210-11, 215-16, 223, 226, 237, 256, 263-64, 269, 275-78, 281-82, 284-85, 370, 374, 408-9, 421, 428, 475, 483, 486-87, 493-98, 500, 506, 570-71, 580, 582, 593, 606, 612-15, 627, 645, 647-48, 657, 665-66, 677, 702-5, 711-12, 733, 785-86
Reston, James, 459, 518, 555, 596, 704, 745, 765
Rickover, Hyman G., 742
Riddle, Donald H., 570
Riezler, Kurt, 595, 760, 804
Roberts, Nesta, 619, 724-25
Robin Hood, 625
Robinson, Cyril D., 427, 627
Robinson, Jackie, 674
Robinson, Joan, 563
Roche, John P., 589
Rockwell, George, 523
Rodell, Fred, 762
Rogat, Yosal, 444
Rogge, O. John, 522, 562, 579, 603
Rood, Harold W., 785
Roosevelt, Franklin D., 457, 563, 719, 749, 752, 769, 786
Roosevelt, Theodore, 749
Rosebery, Lord, 788
Rosen, Stanley, 738
Rostow, Eugene V., 680, 745
ROTC (Reserve Officers' Training Corps), 765
Rothschild, Edward I., 334, 347
Rousseau, Jean Jacques, 213, 283, 323, 419-20, 457, 481, 494, 498, 517, 534, 563, 606, 612, 666, 669, 672, 675, 686, 698, 706, 735, 759, 770, 783, 790, 793, 796, 802
Rovere, Richard H., 460, 473, 614, 655, 724, 786
Royko, Mike, 685, 795

Rumford, Count, 715-16
Rush, Myron, 695
Rusk, Dean, 669, 743, 745-64
Russell, Bertrand, 506, 765
Russell, William F., 674
Rylaarsdam, J. Coert, 523-24
Rynne, Xavier, 508-9

Sachs, E. S., 644
Sacks, Robert D., 805
Sahid, Joseph R., 313-14
Salazar, Antonio, 797
Sallust, 323, 481, 541, 635, 662, 774
Samuelson, Paul, 492
Sandburg, Carl, 625
Sastri, S. D. G., 534
Sawyier, Calvin P., 334, 407
Sax, Joseph L., 544
Schlesinger, Arthur M., 102, 143, 508, 509, 524-25, 572
Schlesinger, Arthur M., Jr., 591, 650, 662, 735, 744, 751, 758
Schneir, Miriam, 633-35
Schneir, Walter, 633-35
Schrock, Thomas S., 613, 683
Schultz, Richard, 329
Schurz, Carl, 788
Schwamberger, Leo, 314
Scott, Thomas, 41, 119, 152, 430, 769
Scranton, Robert L., 552
Scribner, David, 347, 635
Seale, Bobby G., 322, 486, 669
Second Amendment, 440, 628, 672; text of, 42
Sedgwick, Theodore, 148, 430, 559-60
Sedition, 6, 20, 74, 94, 103-4, 114, 124-25, 136-48, 157-58, 184-85, 188-89, 195, 218, 510, 512, 519-20, 525, 527, 532, 548-50, 558-59, 568-74, 576-77, 588-89, 621, 632, 640, 677, 686
Sedition Act of 1798: text of, 138, 569. See also Alien and Sedition Acts
Seneca, 708
Seventeenth Amendment, 655
Seventh Amendment, 40, 469
Shaftesbury, Earl of, 552, 554, 559, 669, 764
Shakespeare, William, 30-33, 200, 271, 278, 402, 405, 408, 419, 424, 436-38, 459-60, 479, 494, 505, 518, 536, 547, 555, 564, 609, 631, 659, 684, 687, 691, 698, 704-5, 725-26, 732-33, 739, 753, 755, 760, 771, 773, 779, 788, 790-91, 794, 797-98, 808
Shapiro, Arthur K., 766
Shapiro, Martin, 444, 454, 456

INDEX: SUBJECTS AND NAMES   821

Sharp, Malcolm P., 333, 335-37, 365, 371, 402, 404, 421, 427, 466-67, 522, 528, 564-68, 589, 607, 632, 635, 637, 649, 710, 718, 731, 766
Shaw, George Bernard, 260, 679, 789-90
Shays's Rebellion, 113, 173, 186, 517, 526-27, 530, 568, 572-73, 600
Sheil, Bernard J., 783
Shelley, Percy Bysshe, 552
Sherman, Roger, 37, 63, 86, 89, 131, 144, 159, 165, 430, 433, 600
Sherrill, Robert, 754
Shils, Edward, 704
Short, William, 469
Shub, Anatole, 722
Shub, David, 693
Sidney, Algernon, 254-55, 641, 731, 787, 802
Siebert, Frederick Seaton, 526
Sikelianos, Anghelos, 767
Silberstein, Robert J., 347
Simon, Yves R., 371, 427, 740
Singer, James W., 322, 739
Sinyavsky, Andrey, 548
Sirens, 719-20
Sixth Amendment, 40, 441, 469, 677, 712
Small, N. J., 431
Smith Act (Alien Registration Act of 1940), 46, 65, 182-83, 187-88, 447-50, 504, 520, 570, 593-94, 621, 630-31, 635, 640, 643, 649-50, 654, 718, 731; text of, 446
Smith, Adam, 153, 217, 461, 525, 530, 582, 690-91, 693-94, 737
Smith, James Morton, 429, 568, 575, 597
Smith, William, 35, 74, 102, 207, 209-10, 232-34, 430, 434, 483
Soblen, Robert, 590
Socrates, 27, 217, 264, 278-81, 283, 419-20, 422, 437, 459, 517, 531, 547, 689, 702-3, 739, 767, 773, 780, 787, 792-93, 797, 799, 802
Solomon, 319, 410, 797
Solon, 541, 776
Solzhenitsyn, A. I., 552
Sophocles, 624, 642, 651, 657, 732, 783, 798-99
Spaatz, Carl, 752
Speer, Albert, 541, 775
Speier, Hans, 781, 787
Spiegelberg, Herbert, 424
Spinoza, Benedict de, 733
Stalin, 541, 547, 562, 629, 681, 733, 742, 753, 756, 758
Stamp Act, 213, 520, 525, 687
Stanton, Edwin M., 579

States' rights, 6, 23, 154-55, 175-76, 197, 235, 283, 427, 429, 434, 440, 442, 445, 455, 483, 487, 492, 516, 603-4, 607, 610, 623, 645, 652-53, 659, 664, 710-13, 717, 774, 795
Steffen, Roscoe T., 342, 347, 371, 404, 715
Stendhal, 439, 600, 666
Stennis, John C., 696-97
Stephen, James Fitzjames, 124-26, 226, 424, 512-13, 561, 568, 611, 755, 768-69
Stephen, Leslie, 522, 669, 759
Stephens, Alexander H., 473, 653
Stern, Robert L., 567
Stevenson, Adlai E., 539
Stevenson, Adlai E., III, 736, 794
Stevenson, Robert Louis, 550
Stewart, Charles, 347
Stimson, Henry L., 751-52
Stone, Michael Jenifer, 158, 162, 221-22, 234, 267-68, 430, 486
Storing, Herbert J., 470, 509, 515, 523-24, 614, 717
Story, Joseph, 432, 434, 501, 513, 542, 573, 588, 672, 676
Stourzh, Gerald, 613, 648, 651, 687
Strauss, Jefferson, 523-24, 799
Strauss, Leo, 12, 255, 419, 421, 425, 494, 497-98, 524, 531-34, 539, 545, 549, 564-65, 611-13, 624-25, 666, 673, 675, 680, 698, 705, 729, 734, 736, 738-39, 757, 762, 767, 772, 775, 780-81, 786-88, 791-92, 795, 799, 801, 803-5
Street, Henry, 465, 504, 506, 700-701
Strong, Frank R., 446
Sulzberger, C. L., 557, 746
Sumner, William Graham, 205-6, 428, 597-98, 603-5, 615, 717, 734, 769-70
Sumter, Thomas, 37, 430
Sun Yat-sen, 535
Sutherland, Arthur E., 431, 433, 484, 650
Swann, Charles, 423, 626
Swift, Jonathan, 94, 113-14, 427, 505, 529, 532, 581, 671, 787

Tacitus, 200, 255, 483, 516, 589, 739, 750, 779
Taft, Robert A., 800-801
Taft-Hartley Act, 618, 630-31
Talcott, Burt L., 428
Taylor, John, 676, 690, 701
Taylor, Maxwell D., 508
Tefft, Sheldon, 333, 380
Tenth Amendment, 159, 533-34, 644; text of, 438
Thales, 552

Thatcher, George, 728
Thayer, James B., 784
Themistocles, 601
Thersites, 436, 527, 530, 578
Third Amendment, 37, 440
Thirteenth Amendment, 298, 601, 679
Thompson, Walter H., 685
Thoreau, Henry, 323, 701-2
Thrasymachus, 524, 641, 685, 787
Thucydides, 6, 200, 323, 459, 605, 706, 734-35, 774, 788, 796-97, 799
Tiresias, 783
Tocqueville, Alexis de, 212-13, 240-41, 255, 421, 423, 425, 428, 434, 463, 473, 486, 492, 495, 509, 519, 550, 554, 570, 579, 582, 586, 600, 603, 612-13, 645, 655, 659, 662-63, 666, 671, 673, 686, 687, 690, 698, 706, 713, 726, 736, 738, 769, 779, 782, 784, 793, 795, 796
Tolles, Frederick B., 569
Treason, 66, 104, 117, 120, 127, 142, 158, 185, 449, 475, 483, 520, 526-27, 542-43, 557-59, 570, 572, 586-89, 622, 635, 638-39
Tresolini, R. S., 465, 504
Trotsky, Leon, 214, 523, 562, 688, 778
Trudeau, Pierre, 455
Truman, Harry S, 258, 444, 475, 732, 749-50, 786
Tuchman, Barbara, 784
Tucker, Thomas Tudor, 27, 60, 74, 81, 149, 156, 162, 172, 239, 430, 437, 474, 495, 569, 585, 712
Turnbull, Colin M., 553
Twain, Mark, 219, 423, 546, 612, 697
Twenty-first Amendment, 626
Tynan, Kenneth, 553

Valenti, Jack, 741, 745
Vallandigham, Clement, 477, 561, 654
Vallières, Pierre, 683
Van Winkle, Rip, 776
Vassilikos, Vassilis, 544, 681
Veale, F. J. P., 750
Victoria, 655
Vietnam War, 315, 320, 409, 423, 453, 459, 475, 479, 507, 533, 557, 578, 596, 627, 631, 663, 712, 726, 730-31, 740-41, 743-47, 749-50, 784-85
Vining, John, 177, 430, 769
Virgil, 665
Virginia and Kentucky Resolutions, 138, 229, 487, 540, 577, 597-98, 647, 701, 714, 728. *See also* Alien and Sedition Acts
Vlachou, Helen, 544, 680-81

Voltaire, 608, 739

Wade, E. C. S., 484, 491
Walinsky, Adam, 452
Wallace, George, 444, 724
Waln, Robert, 727
Walpole, Horace, 700
Walpole, Robert, 551
Ware, Timothy, 611, 748, 761
Warren, Charles, 426, 656
Warshow, Robert, 651
Washington, George, 48, 94, 105, 136-37, 151, 157, 163, 167, 176, 226, 235, 273, 475, 483, 524, 571, 573, 585, 611, 665, 690, 717
Weaver, Richard M., 336, 544, 546, 596, 651, 688, 760
Webster, Daniel, 212, 299, 351, 518-19, 701, 728, 731
Webster, Noah, 214-16, 688, 690
Wechsler, Herbert, 689
Weinglass, Leonard, 313
Weinstein, Leo, 790
Weisberg, Bernard, 347
Weisberger, Bernard A., 606
Weiss, Jerome S., 346, 361-62, 382-83
Werth, Alexander, 552
Westin, Alan F., 691
Westmoreland, William C., 476
White, Alexander, 54, 144, 150, 161-62, 221, 240, 430, 514
White, Howard B., 425, 437-38, 666
White, T. H., 754-55, 771
Whitehill, Robert, 593
Whitman, Walt, 728
Wigmore, John H., 459, 551
Wilkes, John, 514, 524, 537
Williams, Robert, 440
Willoughby, William F., 656
Wilmot, Chester, 100-101, 507, 551
Wilson, Edmund, 473-74, 541, 651
Wilson, James, 105, 435, 515, 519, 578, 585, 591-92, 706
Wilson, Woodrow, 257-58, 295, 444, 453, 465, 482, 653, 656, 756, 786
Wiltse, Charles M., 729
Winiarski, Warren, 666, 717
Winograd, Richard W., 747
Wirt, William, 519
Wise, John, 426, 536
Wolfe, Bertram D., 682
Wolff, Robert P., 433
Wordsworth, William, 760
Wortman, Tunis, 559
Wren, Christopher, 756
Writs of Assistance, 110-11, 526

Xenophon, 89, 426, 499, 526, 539, 545, 605, 689, 723, 773, 804-5

Yeats, William Butler, 793
Young, Stephen, 639

Zeisel, Hans, 531, 561, 695
Zetterbaum, Marvin, 554, 613, 663, 666, 669
Zeus, 12, 60, 223, 226, 393, 445, 548, 606, 611, 624, 720, 755, 779, 791-93

II. CASES AND JURISTS

Abrams v. U.S. (1919), 262-66, 453, 455, 459, 471, 551, 573, 631-32, 640, 761
Adamson v. California (1947), 357, 648
Adler v. Board of Education (1952), 687
Aikens v. Wisconsin (1904), 304
Albertson v. S.A.C.B. (1965), 643
American Communications Association v. Douds (1950), 453-54, 458, 470, 594, 630-31, 732
Anastaplo, In re (1961), 285, 331, 400-408, 646, 805
Aptheker v. Secretary of State (1964), 403, 619, 643
Axtell's Case (1660), 475

Baggett v. Bullitt (1964), 631, 644
Bailey v. Drexel Furniture Co. (The Child Labor Tax Case) (1922), 582
Baker v. Carr (1962), 646, 648
Balzac v. Porto Rico (1922), 678
Barenblatt v. U.S. (1959), 375, 379, 466, 676
Barnes, John J., 318
Barr v. Matteo (1959), 512
Barron v. Baltimore (1833), 487, 497
Barsky v. Board of Regents (1954), 379
Barsky v. U.S. (1948), 465
Beauharnais v. Illinois (1952), 496, 542, 554, 563, 582
Beilan v. Board of Education (1958), 354, 356-61
Bentley v. Board (1921), 649
Bizup v. Tinsely (1907), 646, 678
Black, Hugo L., 285, 334, 337, 341, 362-64, 367-79, 403, 407, 426, 441, 444, 461, 482, 485-86, 490, 496, 520-21, 536, 543, 554-55, 584, 593, 610, 619-20, 626, 630-31, 635, 638, 642-43, 648, 656, 666-67, 692, 697, 732, 805
Bolling v. Sharpe (1954), 653
Bond v. Floyd (1960), 722
Bonham's Case (1610), 641
Braden v. U.S. (1961), 379
Brandeis, Louis D., 46, 428, 450, 456, 518, 555
Brandenburg v. Ohio (1969), 450, 629, 631, 732

Brennan, William J., Jr., 337, 367, 470, 513, 533, 543-44, 573, 645
Bridges v. California (1941), 426
Bristow, George W., 337, 364, 414-15
Brown v. Board of Education (1954), 431, 444, 646
Brown v. Louisiana (1966), 555
Brown v. Maryland (1827), 463
Bulchalter v. New York (1943), 646
Buller, Francis, 636
Buoscio, Felix M., 319
Burdeau v. McDowell (1921), 428
Burger, Warren E., 669
Burstyn v. Wilson (1952), 502
Burton, Harold H., 639, 692, 718

Cantwell v. Connecticut (1940), 415, 470
Cardozo, Benjamin N., 642, 676
Carswell, G. Harrold, 448, 705-6
Chaplinsky v. New Hampshire (1942), 536, 541
Chase, Samuel, 242, 569-70
Chicago v. Tribune Co. (1923), 463
Chicago Conspiracy Trial. See U.S. v. Dellinger
Chicago, J. & L. Ry. v. Hackett (1919), 649
Chisholm v. Georgia (1793), 626
Clark, Tom C., 362, 380, 449, 504, 512, 519, 597, 631, 638, 640
Cohen v. Hurley (1961), 340-41, 403, 682
Coke, Edward, 432-33, 438, 591, 641, 683, 717
Colegrove v. Green (1946), 647
Commonwealth v. Blanding (1926), 502
Communist Party v. S.A.C.B. (1961), 619, 643, 656
Communist Party v. U.S. (1963), 643
Cooper v. Aaron (1958), 353, 387
Corfield v. Coryell (1825), 711
Cox v. Louisiana (1965), 485, 555
Crowell v. Benson (1932), 470
Cummings v. Missouri (1867), 348, 469
Curtis, Benjamin R., 599

Daily, Joseph E., 338-40, 361
Dallemagne v. Moisan (1905), 472

Dartmouth College v. Woodward (1819), 534
Davis, Charles H., 337
Davis, David, 417, 478-79, 640, 650, 692
Debs, In re (1895), 503, 580
Debs v. U.S. (1919), 444, 477, 579
DeJonge v. Oregon (1937), 495
Dennis v. U.S. (1951), 45-46, 127, 321, 442, 444, 446-51, 455, 458, 504, 506, 555, 575, 587, 593, 606, 620-21, 629-31, 635, 668, 700, 703, 762-63, 805
Doremus v. Board of Education (1952), 687
Douglas, William O., 334, 337, 367, 423, 428, 450, 520-21, 557, 575, 620, 635, 638, 732
Downes v. Bidwell (1901), 642
Dred Scott v. Sanford (1857), 431, 711, 726
Dreyer v. Illinois (1902), 493
Dunne v. U.S. (1943), 718

Eakin v. Raub (1825), 444, 499, 528
Ellenborough, Earl of, 96
El Paso v. Simmons (1965), 461
Epperson v. Arkansas (1968), 610
Estes v. Texas (1965), 557

Federal Baseball Club v. National League (1922), 501
Flast v. Cohen (1968), 714
Flemming v. Nestor (1960), 593
Fortas, Abe, 682
Frank, Jerome, 506
Frank v. Mangum (1915), 682
Frankfurter, Felix, 46, 362, 364, 380, 403, 442, 453-55, 458, 506, 512, 636, 638, 642-43, 647, 656, 668, 676, 680, 687, 691-92, 696, 703, 763
Freedman v. Maryland (1965), 557
Frohwerk v. U.S. (1919), 507, 526, 578
Frost Trucking Co. v. R.R. Comm. (1926), 464
Frothingham v. Mellon (1923), 714

Gardner v. Broderick (1968), 403, 682
Garland, Ex parte (1867), 348, 467
Garner v. Board of Public Works (1951), 356-57
Garner v. Louisiana (1961), 555
Garrison v. Louisiana (1964), 521
Geroulis, James A., 695
Gibbons v. Ogden (1824), 645, 652
Giboney v. Empire Storage Co. (1949), 520
Gibson, John B., 444, 499
Gideon v. Wainwright (1963), 682

Ginzburg v. U.S. (1966), 543-44
Gitlow v. New York (1925), 193-96, 415, 442, 563, 646, 654, 657
Goldman v. U.S. (1918), 305
Gomillion v. Lightfoot (1960), 464, 648
Gompers v. Bucks Stove & Range Co. (1911), 305
Griswold v. Connecticut (1965), 461, 521, 642
Grosso v. U.S. (1968), 583

Hague v. C.I.O. (1939), 490, 497
Hammer v. Dagenhart (1918), 444
Hand, Learned, 45-46, 446, 450, 456, 504
Harisiades v. Shaughnessy (1952), 593, 606
Harlan, John M. (original), 502, 506, 555, 599, 648, 657
Harlan, John M. (current), 341, 356-57, 362, 366-67, 380, 403, 416-17, 448-49, 504-5, 512, 551, 555, 596-97, 676-77, 682, 715, 805
Harper v. Virginia Board of Elections (1966), 642, 699
Harris v. U.S. (1965), 428
Hawaii v. Mankichi (1903), 678
Haynes v. U.S. (1968), 583
Haynsworth, Clement, 705-6
Hess v. Whitsitt (1967), 649
Heydon's Case (1584), 432
Higginbotham, A. Leon, Jr., 739
Hines v. Davidowitz (1941), 621
Hoffman, Julius J., 312-13, 317-21, 636, 640
Holmes, Oliver Wendell, 4, 44-48, 70, 148, 177, 186-87, 210, 217, 231, 262-66, 294, 304-5, 397, 421-22, 435, 444-46, 451, 453, 455, 460, 481-82, 502, 505, 507, 526-27, 555, 559-60, 563, 573, 578-79, 623, 640-41, 657, 695, 709, 713, 761-64, 779
Holt, Lord, 679
Holt v. Virginia (1965), 486
Hughes, Charles E., 376, 379, 584
Humphrey's Executor v. U.S. (1935), 435
Hurtado v. California (1884), 599

Illinois v. Allen (1970), 320, 441, 697
Illinois v. Bruce (1964), 545, 549, 760

Jackson, Robert H., 224, 425, 458, 470, 475, 496, 512, 563, 587, 593, 606, 608, 620, 632, 668, 682, 692, 699, 700, 708, 719, 726
Jacobellis v. Ohio (1964), 596-97
Joint Anti-Fascist Refugee Com. v. McGrath (1951), 470

INDEX: CASES AND JURISTS

Kaufman, Irving, 459, 633, 638
Kentucky v. Dennison (1860), 630, 647
Kenyon, Lord, 512
Kilbourn v. Thompson (1881), 512
Kingsley Corp. v. Regents (1959), 547
Konigsberg v. State Bar of California (1961), 334, 340-41, 349, 352-55, 357-58, 364, 366-67, 378-79, 381, 390, 392, 403-4, 409, 635, 646, 715
Kovacs v. Cooper (1849), 676
Kunz v. New York (1951), 709

Labor Board v. Virginia Power Co. (1941), 521
Lamont v. Postmaster General (1965), 471
Leary v. U.S. (1969), 583
Lerner v. Casey (1958), 354, 356, 358-61
License Cases (1847), 604
Long v. Rockwood (1928), 763
Louis v. Louis (1970), 649
Louisiana ex rel. Francis v. Resweber (1947), 691, 718
Louisiana ex rel. Gremillion v. N.A.A.C.P. (1961), 470
Lovell v. Griffin (1938), 502
Luther v. Borden (1849), 429, 646, 648

McCulloch v. Maryland (1819), 416, 431, 586, 590-91, 598, 713-14, 763
McLean, John, 726
Malloy v. Hogan (1964), 403, 468, 533, 652, 682, 710
Mansfield, Lord, 96, 512, 679
Marbury v. Madison (1803), 231, 713-15
Marchetti v. U.S. (1968), 583
Marshall, John, 58, 141, 147, 431, 433, 463, 489, 497, 519, 528, 571, 589, 590-91, 598, 687, 713-15, 763
Matthews, Stanley, 599
Medina, Harold R., 45, 321
Medley, Petitioner (1890), 440
Miller, Samuel F., 490
Milligan, Ex parte (1866), 477, 479
Milwaukee Pub. Co. v. Burleson (1921), 505
Minersville School District v. Gobitis (1940), 640, 703
Minton, Sherman, 639
Miranda v. Arizona (1966), 447
Mississippi v. Johnson (1966), 642
Missouri v. Holland (1920), 481-82
Missouri, Kansas & Texas R.R. v. May (1908), 709
Murchison, In re (1955), 486

Murray's Lessee v. Hoboken Land and Improvement Co. (1856), 599
Myers v. U.S. (1926), 435

N.A.A.C.P. v. Button (1963), 470
Near v. Minnesota (1931), 470, 502
New York v. U.S. (1946), 763
New York Times v. Sullivan (1964), 461, 463, 513, 536, 554, 573, 645, 677
Niemotko v. Maryland (1951), 696
Norris v. Clymer (1845), 713
Northern Securities Co. v. U.S. (1904), 445
Noto v. U.S. (1961), 631

O'Malley v. Woodrough (1939), 454
Osborne v. Bank of the United States (1824), 489, 528, 590, 595

Pacific Telephone Co. v. Oregon (1912), 647
Palko v. Connecticut (1937), 676
Panhandle Oil Co. v. Mississippi (1928), 763
Patterson v. Colorado (1907), 304, 442, 502, 555, 646, 652
Pennsylvania v. Nelson (1956), 183, 187-89, 191, 198, 570, 621, 628, 635-36, 639-40, 648-50, 656
People v. Croswell (1804), 513-14
People v. Walter's Chapter D.A.R. (1924), 632
Permoli v. First Municipality of New Orleans (1845), 497
Pickering v. Board of Education (1968), 464
Plessy v. Ferguson (1896), 444
Pointer v. Texas (1965), 677
Powell v. McCormack (1969), 490

Quantity of Copies of Books v. Kansas (1964), 551

R. v. Burdett (1820), 549-50
Radovich v. National Football League (1957), 501
Reed, Stanley F., 639, 676, 692
Reid v. Covert (1957), 482, 626, 678
Respublica v. Oswald (1788), 502, 697
Reynolds v. U.S. (1878), 561
Roberts, Owen J., 490
Robertson v. Baldwin (1897), 506
Rochin v. California (1952), 642
Rosenberg v. U.S. (1953), 188, 459, 504, 542, 620, 632-39, 700, 703
Roth v. U.S. (1957), 506, 520, 536

Sacco-Vanzetti Case (1927), 636
Sanford, Edward T., 657
Savage, Petitioner (1890), 440
Scales v. U.S. (1961), 504-5, 528-29, 631, 649
Schaefer, Walter V., 337
Schenck v. U.S. (1919), 44, 46, 127, 148, 177, 294-95, 444, 446, 450-51, 453, 455, 521-22, 527, 550-51, 578-80, 586, 594, 608, 629, 631, 640, 656, 658, 712, 761, 763, 805; circular, 296-300; indictment, 300-304
Schneider v. Irvington (1939), 470
Schneiderman v. U.S. (1943), 454, 594
School District of Abington v. Schempp (1963), 597
Schware v. Board of Bar Examiners of New Mexico (1957), 334, 357, 381, 390, 394, 404, 409
Scopes Trial (1925), 610
Selective Draft Law Cases (1918), 305, 475
Shelton v. Tucker (1960), 470
Slaughter-House Cases (1873), 711
Smith v. Brown (1707), 679
Smith v. California (1959), 470, 536, 543, 656
Snyder v. Massachusetts (1934), 642
Sommersett's Case (1771), 679
South Carolina v. Katzenbach (1966), 472, 496, 648
Southern Pacific Co. v. Jensen (1917), 559
Speiser v. Randall (1958), 378, 470
Spevack v. Klein (1967), 403, 682
Stamler v. Willis (1969), 467
Stewart, Potter, 363, 380
Stone, Harlan F., 454, 700
Summers, In re (1945), 347, 379-80, 629, 664
Sweezy v. New Hampshire (1959), 493, 762

Taft, William Howard, 582
Taney, Roger B., 429, 604, 648, 726
Tenney v. Brandhove (1951), 493, 512, 722
Terminiello v. Chicago (1949), 709
Toolson v. New York Yankees (1958), 501
Tot v. U.S. (1943), 357
Twining v. New Jersey (1908), 648
Uniformed Sanitation Men Assn. v. Comm. (1968), 682
United Public Workers v. Mitchell (1947), 471

Uphaus v. Wyman (1959), 379, 640
U.S. v. Ballard (1944), 532, 561
U.S. v. Brown (1965), 466, 470, 594, 631
U.S. v. Chase (1970), 321
U.S. v. Clark (1887), 474-75
U.S. v. Cruikshank (1875), 490, 495
U.S. v. Curtiss-Wright Export Corp. (1936), 481
U.S. v. Dellinger (The Chicago Conspiracy Trial) (1970), 312-23, 324-30, 449, 451, 486, 499, 574, 594, 620, 634, 640, 667, 685, 696, 712, 739
U.S. v. Hudson and Goodwin (1812), 567
U.S. v. Johnson (1966), 512
U.S. v. Josephson (1948), 465
U.S. v. Lovett (1946), 470
U.S. v. Macintosh (1931), 453
U.S. v. Robel (1967), 446, 471, 610
U.S. v. Rumely (1953), 465
U.S. v. Sobell (1951), 632, 634. See also Rosenberg v. U.S.
U.S. v. Spock (1969), 305
U.S. v. Wiltberger (1820), 433
U.S. v. Worrall (1798), 569

Vinson, Frederick M., 263, 444, 446, 451, 455, 638, 692, 763

Waite, Morrison R., 640
Warren, Earl, 337, 364, 367, 403, 446, 465, 486, 493, 499, 557, 634, 720, 762
Washington Post Co. v. Keogh (1966), 723
Watkins v. U.S. (1957), 465-68
West Virginia Board of Education v. Barnette (1943), 415, 475, 640, 664, 691, 700, 703
Wheeling Steel Corp. v. Glander (1949), 464
White, Byron R., 447
Whitney v. California (1927), 46, 324-30, 450, 456, 628-29
Whittaker, Charles E., 362, 380, 512
Wieman v. Updegraff (1952), 357
Wilkinson v. U.S. (1961), 379
Wolf v. Colorado (1949), 676

Yamashita, In re (1946), 503, 700
Yarbrough, Ex parte (1884), 490
Yates v. U.S. (1957), 349, 352, 447-49, 621, 630-31
Youngstown Sheet and Tube Co. v. Sawyer (1952), 435, 482

Zenger Trial (1735), 142, 144, 495, 517, 524, 527, 537, 574

And Cain knew his wife; and she conceived, and bare Enoch: and he builded [the first] city, and called the name of the city, after the name of his son, Enoch. —MOSES

Undertakings [on the Acropolis], any one of which singly might have required for their completion, several successions and ages of men, were every one of them accomplished in the height and prime of one man's political service. . . . Ease and speed in doing a thing do not give the work lasting solidity or exactness of beauty; the expenditure of time allowed to a man's pains beforehand for the production of a thing is repaid by way of interest with a vital force for the preservation when once produced. For which reason Pericles's works are especially admired, as having been made quickly, to last long. For every particular piece of his work was immediately, even at that time, for its beauty and elegance, antique; and yet in its vigour and freshness looks to this day as if it were just executed. There is a sort of bloom of newness upon those works of his, preserving them from the touch of time, as if they had some perennial spirit and undying vitality mingled in the composition of them. —PLUTARCH

The youth gets together his materials to build a bridge to the moon, or, perchance, a palace or temple on the earth, and, at length the middle-aged man concludes to build a wood-shed with them. —THOREAU

THE CONSTITUTIONALIST

DATE DUE

M.H.C. LIBRARY OCT 1 '77			
DEC 08 '90 Library			
DEC 12 1997			
OCT 05 2000			
		DISCARD	
GAYLORD			PRINTED IN U.S.A.